PUBLIC PAPERS OF THE PRESIDENTS
OF THE
UNITED STATES

PUBLIC PAPERS OF THE PRESIDENTS
OF THE
UNITED STATES

Ronald Reagan

1985

(IN TWO BOOKS)

BOOK II—JUNE 29 TO DECEMBER 31, 1985

UNITED STATES GOVERNMENT PRINTING OFFICE
WASHINGTON: 1988

Published by the
Office of the Federal Register
National Archives and Records Administration

For sale by the
Superintendent of Documents
U.S. Government Printing Office
Washington, DC 20402

Foreword

In the latter half of 1985, the American people continued to enjoy stable economic growth and even lower inflation. Over 2½ million jobs were created in 1985—a record which is the envy of many other industrialized nations. The United States was indeed leading the way, pulling the world economy into better times. This resulted, in the short run, in an increasing trade deficit and pressure for protectionism and trade restrictions. In December, I vetoed a bill that would have severely restricted the import of textiles and shoes. America's prosperity depends upon keeping international trade flowing freely and fairly among the nations, not in restricting it.

In November, the Congress passed an historic piece of legislation which, at long last, addressed the threat of Federal deficit spending. The Gramm-Rudman-Hollings bill mandated a phased-in reduction of the level of deficit spending, establishing a 5-year program to bring about a balanced Federal budget.

Tax reform continued to work its way through the congressional maze, and I continued to speak aggressively on the issue. While there was a general recognition of the counterproductive nature and the inequities of the current tax code, most pundits wrote the issue off, even as I pushed forward.

In August, Congress passed a bill that also has great historical significance. A foreign aid bill explicitly repealed the Clark amendment, which had prevented the United States from assisting the anti-Communist forces of Jonas Savimbi in Angola. In repealing the Clark amendment, Congress reaffirmed that it is both in our national interest and in our tradition as a free people to assist those who are struggling for their liberty and national independence.

The United States must not only be strong and stand with its friends but it also must be willing to reach out to our adversaries in the cause of peace. In November, I met for the first time with General Secretary Gorbachev, the new leader of the Soviet Union. Our summit in Geneva was a good first step and gave us reason for cautious optimism, but optimism nonetheless.

The following pages cover this dramatic period in the final months of 1985.

Ronald Reagan

Preface

This book contains the papers and speeches of the 40th President of the United States that were issued by the Office of the Press Secretary during the period June 29–December 31, 1985. The material has been compiled and published by the Office of the Federal Register, National Archives and Records Administration.

The material is presented in chronological order, and the dates shown in the headings are the dates of the documents or events. In instances when the release date differs from the date of the document itself, that fact is shown in the textnote. Every effort has been made to ensure accuracy: Remarks are checked against a tape recording, and signed documents are checked against the original. Textnotes, footnotes, and cross references have been provided by the editors for purposes of identification or clarity. Speeches were delivered in Washington, DC, unless indicated. The times noted are local times. All materials that are printed full-text in the book have been indexed in the subject and name indexes.

The Public Papers series was begun in 1957 in response to a recommendation of the National Historical Publications Commission. An extensive compilation of messages and papers of the Presidents covering the period 1789 to 1897 was assembled by James D. Richardson and published under congressional authority between 1896 and 1899. Since then, various private compilations have been issued, but there was no uniform publication comparable to the Congressional Record or the United States Supreme Court Reports. Many Presidential papers could be found only in the form of mimeographed White House releases or as reported in the press. The Commission therefore recommended the establishment of an official series in which Presidential writings, addresses, and remarks of a public nature could be made available.

The Commission's recommendation was incorporated in regulations of the Administrative Committee of the Federal Register, issued under section 6 of the Federal Register Act (44 U.S.C. 1506), which may be found in Title I, Part 10, of the Code of Federal Regulations.

A companion publication to the Public Papers series, the Weekly Compilation of Presidential Documents, was begun in 1965 to provide a broader range of Presidential materials on a more timely basis to meet the needs of the contemporary reader. Beginning with the administration of Jimmy Carter, the Public Papers series expanded its coverage to include all material as printed in the Weekly Compilation. That coverage provides a listing of the President's daily schedule and meetings, when announced, and other items of general interest issued by the Office of the Press Secretary. Also included are lists of the President's nominations submitted to the Senate, materials released by the Office of the Press Secretary that are not printed full-text in the book, and acts approved by the President. This information appears in the appendixes at the end of the book.

Volumes covering the administrations of Presidents Hoover, Truman, Eisenhower, Kennedy, Johnson, Nixon, Ford, and Carter are also available.

The Chief Editor of this book was William King Banks.

White House liaison was provided by Marlin Fitzwater, Assistant to the President for Press Relations. The frontispiece and photographs used in the portfolio were supplied by the White House Photo Office.

John E. Byrne
Director of the Federal Register

Don W. Wilson
Archivist of the United States

Contents

Administration of Ronald Reagan

1985

Radio Address to the Nation on Counterintelligence Activities
June 29, 1985

My fellow Americans:

We continue to work for the release of the American hostages held in Lebanon. This terrorism reminds us of the threat posed to open societies and of the great challenges we face in a world where many disdain our values and seek to harm us and our way of life.

One of those challenges is our need to counter the rash of spy activities that threaten our security and interests at home and abroad and to improve our own intelligence-gathering capabilities. The number and sophistication of Soviet bloc and other hostile intelligence service activities have been increasing in recent years.

The Soviet Union is a closed society whose rulers fear the intoxication of freedom, indeed fear it so much they forbid their people to compete freely with us in the great race to create and invent our future for the 21st century. As the West pulled ahead, the Soviets embarked on a major effort to catch up by stealing or buying what they need from classified information on American satellites, reports on future weapon systems, including our combat aircraft bombers, to our most advanced technologies from high-tech areas like Silicon Valley in California.

Besides espionage against our most sensitive secrets, theft of the high technology upon which our defense depends, the Soviets have intensified what they call "active measures"—propaganda and disinformation meant to mislead Western governments and their citizens, subversion, forgeries, and covert action. For example, while American officials and other proponents of freedom are systematically excluded from Soviet radio or TV, hardly a week goes by without a so-called Soviet journalist or scholar on our own airwaves. These men and women should at least be identified for what they are—propagandists whose appearances and statements are totally controlled by the Communist Party.

The Soviets, Communist-bloc nations, and surrogates elsewhere rely on a huge apparatus, including the KGB, to spy on us and influence our public opinion. To equate the KGB with the CIA is an injustice to the CIA and a grave mistake. Far more than an intelligence service, the KGB is a political police operation. As its motto says, "The sword and shield of the Communist Party of the U.S.S.R." The KGB mission to shield the rigid Soviet dictatorship from any internal challenge, to weaken and discredit the United States and the various alliances we've built up, particularly the NATO alliance, and to advance the Soviet quest for power to destroy freedom makes it unique in the world.

What can be done? Well, we can counter this hostile threat and still remain true to our values. We don't need to fight repression by becoming repressive ourselves, by adopting such restrictions as internal passports for our citizens. But we need to put our cleverness and determination to work, and we need to deal severely with those who betray our country. We should begin by recognizing that spying is a fact of life and that all of us need to be better informed about the unchanging realities of the Soviet system. We're in a long twilight struggle with an implacable foe of freedom.

Next, we need to reduce the size of the hostile intelligence threat we're up against in this country. Some 30 to 40 percent of the more than 2,500 Soviet-bloc officials in this country are known or suspected intelligence officers and all can be called upon by the KGB. We need to bring the number of their intelligence officers to a more manageable number. We need a balance between the size of the Soviet diplomatic presence in the United States and the U.S. presence in the Soviet Union. The Soviets currently have a huge advantage. Now, we intend to take steps to accomplish this, and we need to better control foreign intelligence agents working at the U.N., who have utilized that organization as a spy nest.

Another priority is to improve our own counterintelligence during the seventies—well, I should say during the seventies, we began cutting back our manpower and resources and imposed unnecessary restrictions on our security and counterintelligence officials. With help from Congress we've begun to rebuild, but we must persevere. We must work for better coordination between counterintelligence agencies, better analysis of hostile threats, and learn from the mistakes of past restrictions, which unduly hampered us.

There is no quick fix to this problem. Without hysteria or finger pointing, let us move calmly and deliberately together to protect freedom. We've developed a list of things to be accomplished in the counterintelligence and security areas. I'm tasking Cabinet officers to implement the improvements and reforms in every one of these areas on a priority basis.

Until next week, thanks for listening, and God bless you.

Note: The President spoke at 12:06 p.m. from the Oval Office at the White House.

Remarks Announcing the Release of the Hostages From the Trans World Airlines Hijacking Incident
June 30, 1985

Good afternoon. The 39 Americans held hostage for 17 days by terrorists in Lebanon are free, safe, and at this moment, on their way to Frankfurt, Germany. They'll be home again soon. This is a moment of joy for them, for their loved ones, and for our nation. And America opens its heart in a prayer of thanks to Almighty God.

We can be thankful that our faith, courage, and firmness have paid off. But this is no moment for celebration. Let it be clearly understood that the seven Americans still held captive in Lebanon must be released along with other innocent hostages from other countries; that the murderers of Robert Stethem and of our marines and civilians in El Salvador must be held accountable; that those responsible for terrorist acts throughout the world must be taken on by civilized nations; that the international community must ensure that all our airports are safe and that civil air travel is safeguarded; and that the world must unite in taking decisive action against terrorists, against nations that sponsor terrorists, and against nations that give terrorists safe haven.

This drama has reminded us how precious and fragile are the freedoms and standards of decency of civilized societies; how greatly civilized life depends on trust in other human beings; but how those values we hold most dear must also be defended with bravery—a bravery that may lie quiet and deep, but that will rise to answer our call in every time of peril. Freedom, democracy, and peace have enemies; they must also have steadfast friends.

The United States gives terrorists no rewards and no guarantees. We make no concessions; we make no deals. Nations that harbor terrorists undermine their own stability and endanger their own people. Terrorists, be on notice, we will fight back against you, in Lebanon and elsewhere. We will fight back against your cowardly attacks on American citizens and property.

Several countries have been actively involved in efforts to free our fellow citizens. Syria has had a central responsibility. The efforts of the Algerian Government were likewise an example of constructive cooperation against the direct challenge of lawless terrorists. King Hussein spoke out early and forcefully in condemning the hijacking. Saudi Arabia also made an effective contribution. Throughout the past 17 days, we have also been in close touch with Israel and a number of governments in Europe and the Middle East, as well as with international organizations—all of which displayed great concern for the safety and release of the hostages.

We will remember and offer our thanks to all who helped us and who stood with us. And, yes, we'll remember those who did not. We will not rest until justice is done. We will not rest until the world community meets its responsibility. We call upon those who helped secure the release of these TWA passengers to show even greater energy and commitment to secure the release of all others held captive in Lebanon. And we call upon the world community to strengthen its cooperation to stamp out this ugly, vicious evil of terrorism.

I just want to inject a personal note here that, like all of you, Nancy and I have been living with all these 17 days, and like you, we have both been praying for what has now taken place. And like you, we thank God and wait with bated breath their final arrival here on our shores.

Thank you.

Note: The President spoke at 6:01 p.m. from the Oval Office at the White House. His remarks were broadcast live on nationwide radio and television.

Nomination of Anne Graham To Be a Commissioner of the Consumer Product Safety Commission
July 1, 1985

The President today announced his intention to nominate Anne Graham to be a Commissioner of the Consumer Product Safety Commission for a term of 7 years from October 27, 1984. She would succeed Nancy Harvey Steorts.

Since 1981 Ms. Graham has been serving at the Department of Education as Assistant Secretary for Legislation and Public Affairs. During the 1980 Presidential campaign, she was assistant press secretary to the Reagan-Bush Committee. In 1976–1979 she was press secretary to Senator Harrison Schmitt (R-NM). Ms. Graham worked for Secretary of the Treasury Simon in 1974–1975 and served in the White House News Summary Office in 1973. She was special assistant to the deputy director for communications, Republican National Committee, in 1971.

Ms. Graham graduated from Bradford College and attended Columbia University. She was born December 28, 1949, in Annapolis, MD, and now resides in Alexandria, VA.

Executive Order 12524—Amending the Generalized System of Preferences
July 1, 1985

By virtue of the authority vested in me by the Constitution and statutes of the United States of America, including Title V of the Trade Act of 1974 (the Trade Act) (19 U.S.C. 2461 *et seq.*), as amended, section 604 of the Trade Act (19 U.S.C. 2483), and section 503(a)(2)(A) of the Trade Agreements Act of 1979 (93 Stat. 251), and as President of the United States of America, in order to designate, as provided by section 504(c)(6) of the Trade Act (19 U.S.C. 2464(c)(6)), those countries that will be considered to be least-developed beneficiary developing countries not subject to the limitations on preferential treatment of eligible articles for purposes of the Generalized System of Preferences (GSP), after taking into account the considerations in sections

501 and 502(c) of the Trade Act (19 U.S.C. 2461 and 2462(c)); and to modify as provided by sections 504 (a) and (c) of the Trade Act (19 U.S.C. 2464(a) and (c)) the limitations on preferential treatment of eligible articles from countries designated as beneficiary developing countries, it is hereby ordered as follows:

Section 1. In order to designate the countries that will be considered to be least-developed beneficiary developing countries, general headnote 3(c) of the Tariff Schedules of the United States (TSUS) (19 U.S.C. 1202) is modified by adding the following new paragraph 3(c)(iv):

"(iv) The following beneficiary countries are designated as least-developed beneficiary developing countries pursuant to section 504(c)(6) of the Trade Act of 1974:

Bangladesh	Lesotho
Benin	Malawi
Bhutan	Maldives
Botswana	Mali
Burkina Faso	Nepal
Burundi	Niger
Cape Verde	Rwanda
Central African	Sao Tome and Principe
Republic	Sierra Leone
Chad	Somalia
Comoros	Sudan
Djibouti	Tanzania
Equatorial Guinea	Togo
Gambia	Uganda
Guinea	Western Samoa
Guinea-Bissau	Yemen Arab Republic
Haiti	(Sanaa)

Whenever an eligible article is imported into the customs territory of the United States directly from one of the countries designated as a least-developed beneficiary developing country, it shall be entitled to receive the duty-free treatment provided for in subdivision (c)(ii) of this headnote without regard to the limitations on preferential treatment of eligible articles in section 504(c) of the Trade Act, as amended (19 U.S.C. 2464(c))."

Sec. 2. Annex II of Executive Order No. 11888 of November 24, 1975, as amended, listing articles that are eligible for benefits of the GSP when imported from any designated beneficiary developing country, is further amended by inserting in numerical sequence "734.56".

Sec. 3. Annex III of Executive Order No. 11888, as amended, listing articles that are eligible for benefits of the GSP when imported from all designated beneficiary countries except those specified in general headnote 3(c)(iii) of the TSUS, is further amended by striking out "734.56".

Sec. 4. General headnote 3(c)(iii) of the TSUS, listing articles that are eligible for benefits of the GSP except when imported from the beneficiary countries listed opposite those articles, is modified by striking out "734.56 . . . Haiti".

Sec. 5. The amendments made by this Order shall be effective with respect to articles both: (1) imported on or after January 1, 1976, and (2) entered, or withdrawn from warehouse for consumption, on or after July 4, 1985.

RONALD REAGAN

The White House,
July 1, 1985.

[*Filed with the Office of the Federal Register, 11:08 a.m., July 2, 1985*]

Nomination of Michael E. Baroody To Be an Assistant Secretary of Labor
July 2, 1985

The President today announced his intention to nominate Michael E. Baroody to be an Assistant Secretary of Labor (Policy). He would succeed John F. Cogan.

Mr. Baroody is currently serving as Deputy Assistant to the President and Director of Public Affairs at the White House. He joined the White House staff as Deputy Director of Communications in April 1981. Prior to that time, he was executive assistant to the United States Trade Representative, William E. Brock. He was public affairs director, and before that research director, at the Republican National Committee in 1977–1981. Prior to 1977, Mr. Baroody held various political and governmental positions, including service as executive assistant to Senator Bob Dole (R-KS) and legislative assistant to Senator Roman Hruska (R-NE).

Mr. Baroody graduated from Notre Dame University (B.A., 1968). He served in the U.S. Navy in 1968–1970. He is married, has six children, and resides in Alexandria, VA. He was born September 14, 1946, in Washington, DC.

Remarks to the Freed Hostages From the Trans World Airlines Hijacking Incident
July 2, 1985

The President. Mind, my remarks will be brief—if I wait for a second to swallow the lump in my throat. This isn't the time for speeches; this is a time for reunions and families coming together. There is only one thing to say, and I say it from the bottom of my heart and in the name of all the people of our country: Welcome home. We're so happy you are back safe and sound. You know, you may not know this, Nancy's birthday is Saturday. And whether you like it or not, she's already declared that you are the greatest birthday present she's ever gotten.

This has been a trying and a very demanding time for so many people, but for none more than you. I talked to many of your relatives. I met them at various locations throughout the country—and now some of us have met again—while you were being held. And I know you won't be surprised when I tell you how committed they were to winning your freedom and how full of caring and concern they were. I know that they're very proud of you, and I know from personal experience that you should be very proud of them.

All of America was concerned about you; many prayers were said for your safe release. In the days that you were away, our attention was never once distracted from your plight, and we wouldn't rest until you returned to us safe and whole. None of you were held prisoner because of any personal wrong that any of you had done to anyone; you were held simply because you were Americans. In the minds of your captors, you represented us. Well, whatever the presumed grievance or political motive that caused these actions, let there be no confusion—a crime was committed against you. Hijacking is a crime; kidnaping is a crime; murder is a crime; and holding our people prisoner is a crime. When cruelty is inflicted on innocent people, it discredits whatever cause in whose name it is done. And those who commit such deeds are enemies of the peace. Now you're returned to us, and we have a deep felt sigh of relief, but there are promises to be kept.

The day your plane was hijacked, the terrorists focused their brutality on a brave young man who was a member of the Armed Forces of the United States. They beat Robbie Stethem without mercy and shot him to death. Our joy at your return is substantial, but so is our pain at what was done to that son of America. I know you care deeply about Robbie Stethem and what was done to him. We will not forget what was done to him. There will be no forgetting. His murderers must be brought to justice. Nor will we forget the seven Americans who were taken captive before you and who are captive still. They must be released. The homecoming won't be complete until all have come home.

But now we rejoice at your return. Nancy and I prayed for your safety, we prayed for your speedy return, and we weren't alone. Our prayers were only two among millions and millions. We felt a great national concern when you were taken, and it's truly a national joy, as you can see, that greets your return. You are back in the free land of America safe and sound. You withstood your ordeal with extraordinary composure and coolness.

Your family's waiting for you now and your friends—all your loved ones—so, let the rejoicing begin. It's great to have you back where you belong, and thank you—all of you. God bless you all.

Captain Testrake. Mr. President, Mrs. Reagan, dignitaries, ladies and gentlemen of the press, families of the ex-hostages, and the people of America, these words were written by one of our men, one of the hostages. They asked me if I would address them to you, and I wholeheartedly agree with these sentiments.

"Speaking for the 39 ex-hostages, we would like to express our sincere respect and gratitude to President Reagan and the United States Government for their continued efforts which resulted in the safe and peaceful end to our difficult situation. We hope that your efforts will bring back the seven remaining Americans still held very soon.

"Secondly, to the people of America, we are proud and honored knowing how you joined together in our time of crisis to let it be known that our country was behind us a hundred percent. It was your thoughts and

prayers that gave us strength and kept our minds on our main goal: Freedom. We are now free and want to take this opportunity to thank and applaud you."

And just in closing, I'd like to say that many of my fellow hostages share with me the profound conviction that it was our Father, God, that brought us through this ordeal safely. And in the spirit of giving credit where credit is due, I just wonder if you'd join with me in a brief word of thanks to the Lord.

Our Father, we just gather before you in humble adoration and praise and thanks. For we know that it was your strong hands that held us safely through this ordeal, that gave us the courage and the strength to withstand in the darkest times. And, so, Father, we just thank you for this, and we give you all the praise and the glory, through Jesus. Amen.

The President. Thank you very much. Go home! [*Laughter*]

Note: The President spoke at 3:51 p.m. at Andrews Air Force Base, MD. Prior to his remarks, the President went to Arlington National Cemetery to place a wreath at the grave of Petty Officer Robert D. Stethem, the Navy serviceman killed in Beirut during the hijacking incident. Capt. John Testrake was the pilot on the TWA flight.

Appointment of Five Members of the Board of Directors of the Federal National Mortgage Association
July 2, 1985

The President today announced his intention to appoint the following individuals to be members of the Board of Directors of the Federal National Mortgage Association for a term ending on the date of the annual meeting of the stockholders in 1986:

Samuel W. Bartholomew, Jr., will succeed Bert A. Getz. He is an attorney and senior partner in the law firm of Donelson, Stokes & Bartholomew in Nashville, TN. He graduated from West Point Academy (B.A., 1966) and Vanderbilt Law School (J.D., 1973). He was born July 6, 1944, in Columbus, GA, and now resides in

Nashville, TN.

Merrill Butler is a reappointment. He is president of the Butler Group, Inc., a real estate development and construction company, in Irvine, CA. He graduated from the University of Southern California (B.A., 1948). He was born February 18, 1925, in Los Angeles, CA, and now resides in Newport Beach, CA.

Alberto Cardenas will succeed James E. Lyon. He is an attorney at law with the firm of Broad & Cassell in Miami, FL. He graduated from Florida Atlantic University (B.A., 1969) and Seton Hall University (J.D., 1974). He was born January 3, 1948, in Havana, Cuba, and now resides in Miami, FL.

Henry C. Cashen II will succeed James B. Coles. He is an attorney with the firm of Dickstein, Shapiro & Morin in Washington, DC. He graduated from Brown University (B.A., 1961) and the University of Michigan Law School (J.D., 1963). He was born June 25, 1939, in Detroit, MI, and now resides in Washington, DC.

Dianne E. Ingels is a reappointment. She is an independent real estate broker, investor, and consultant with Dianne Ingels and Associates in Denver, CO. She graduated from the University of Colorado (B.S., 1963) and New York University (M.S., 1964). She was born August 8, 1941, in Denver, CO, and now resides in Colorado Springs, CO.

Appointment of Donald A. Schwartz as a Member of the Board of Directors of Federal Prison Industries, Incorporated
July 2, 1985

The President today announced his intention to appoint Donald A. Schwartz to be a member of the Board of Directors, Federal Prison Industries, Incorporated, Department of Justice. He will succeed Monica Herrera Smith.

Mr. Schwartz is president of the Medallic Art Co. in Danbury, CT. Previously he was executive vice president of the Medallic Art

Co. He serves on the development board of Danbury Hospital in Connecticut and is past president of the Rotary Club of New York City.

He graduated from New York University (B.S., 1956) and Stanford University (M.B.A., 1981). He is married, has two children, and resides in Easton, CT. He was born May 19, 1931, in Brooklyn, NY.

Letter to the Speaker of the House and the President of the Senate Transmitting the Annual Report on the Soil and Water Conservation Program
July 3, 1985

Dear Mr. Speaker: (Dear Mr. President:)

Transmitted herewith is the annual report required by Sec. 7(c) of the Soil and Water Resources Conservation Act of 1977 (P.L. 95–192).

The Soil and Water Resources Conservation Act of 1977 (RCA) requires the Secretary of Agriculture to appraise the condition of the soil, water, and related resources on the nonfederal lands of the Nation and to develop a national soil and water conservation program for assisting landowners and land users in their future conservation activities on these lands.

The first appraisal, completed in 1980, was based primarily on the Department of Agriculture's 1977 National Resources Inventory (NRI). The 1977 NRI was the most comprehensive and refined body of such

data that had ever become available. It provided a solid foundation for the appraisal and program.

The first program report, *A National Program for Soil and Water Conservation*, was completed in 1982. It set national conservation objectives and priorities, focused corrective action on areas of the country with the most critical problems, and strengthened the existing partnership among local and State agencies, organizations, and the Federal government for dealing with resource problems.

Guided by this program, the Department of Agriculture has extended more technical and financial assistance than ever before in areas with the most serious problems of soil erosion and dwindling water supplies. It has also begun to evaluate some of its other programs from the standpoint of their impact on soil and water resources.

This accompanying report covers Fiscal Year 1984. It displays soil and water conservation program accomplishments through a number of tables and appendices. The accomplishments are consistent with those reported through the 1986 budget request and the explanatory notes that provide program descriptions and details to support the budget request.

Sincerely,

RONALD REAGAN

Note: Identical letters were sent to Thomas P. O'Neill, Jr., Speaker of the House of Representatives, and George Bush, President of the Senate. The report was entitled "Annual RCA Progress Report, National Program for Soil and Water Conservation, Fiscal Year Ending September 30, 1984" (United States Department of Agriculture).

Message on the Observance of Independence Day, 1985
July 3, 1985

The signing of the Declaration of Independence on July 4, 1776 marked both the beginning of a new nation and the start of a great epoch in the history of political affairs. That day in Philadelphia, a Republic was born based on the idea of liberty for all. The Fourth of July is America's birthday celebration, but it is also a day of importance for anyone who believes in freedom.

The Declaration of Independence opened government to the people as never before. Each individual was acknowledged as possessing certain inalienable rights. And these rights in turn enabled our people to take part in their political system. Here was a true revolution, embodying the idea that government required the consent of those it governed. Overnight, Americans were acknowledged as citizens of a free land where they had once been only colonial subjects of a distant monarch.

To this day, this eloquent document detailing the rights of man and the concept of individual liberty is as moving as it is timely. It continues to hold profound meaning for us. We should remember the words of John Adams when he wrote of its signing to his wife Abigail as, "the most memorable epoch in the history of America. I am apt to believe that it will be celebrated by succeeding generations as the great anniversary festival. It ought to be commemorated as the day of deliverance, by solemn acts of devotion to God Almighty."

This Independence Day, 1985, let us be guided by the wisdom of that great American statesman and of all our Founding Fathers. As we commemorate 209 years of liberty today, let us pray for God's blessing and His help in safeguarding the precious legacy of the Declaration of Independence.

RONALD REAGAN

Appointment of Roger Stanley Johnson as a Member of the President's Committee on Mental Retardation
July 3, 1985

The President today announced his intention to appoint Roger Stanley Johnson to be a member of the President's Committee on Mental Retardation for a term expiring May 11, 1988. He will succeed James L. Kuebelbeck.

Dr. Johnson has been practicing medicine since 1950. He has been a surgeon since 1963. He is a diplomate of the American Board of Surgery, a member of the American Medical Association, and a fellow of the American College of Surgeons.

He graduated from the University of Minnesota (B.A., 1947; B.S., 1948; M.S., 1950; M.D., 1951; master's in surgery, 1963). He is married, has four children, and resides in Irving, TX. He was born April 29, 1924, in St. Paul, MN.

Radio Address to the Nation on the Federal Budget
July 6, 1985

My fellow Americans:

I'd like to take a few minutes out of your Fourth of July weekend, if I might, to talk about business. It's summer in Washington, and as sure as the heat and humidity, we could have predicted another seasonal occurrence: Once again, the budget process has broken down. Even with dangerously large deficits looming over the horizon threatening to destroy the economic progress we've made, it's still business as usual when it comes to the budget. We can only hope that the House will cooperate with us in doing what is right for America.

Unfortunately, as it stands now, the budget proposed by the House is simply not a serious document. At best it could win a prize for creative bookkeeping. Huge so-called savings are simply assumed or invented, funds are juggled back and forth between accounts to show phony deficit reductions, and billions of dollars of expenses are just wished away. Let me give you one example. Right now the Government charges the oil companies for their offshore leases—sort of a yearly rent for the use of Federal property. Well, the House decided that they would take the next 4 years of revenue from certain offshore leases and count it all in 1986. Now, sure, that reduced the 1986 deficit by $4 billion, but it increased our deficits in later years by exactly that same amount.

A full quarter of the so-called deficit reductions in the House budget are gimmicks like this. Most of the rest comes from raiding the national defense. There is nothing proportionate or fair in the House's budgetary assault on defense. They propose making over half their reductions in this one area, which accounts for less than a third of total spending. What the House

Budget Committee calls a defense spending freeze is really a drastic cut requiring a reduction from current plans in research and development, construction, and procurement of 19 percent in 1986, 23 percent in 1987, and 28 percent in 1988. If the House budget were adopted, it would deliver a severe blow to our national security.

The Senate has proposed a budget that is responsible and fair, that holds real defense spending constant and makes the necessary structural changes in domestic spending that will enable us to substantially reduce these deficits. But when the Senate and House budget conferees met, it quickly became clear that the House refused to give up its gimmicks or consider real cuts in domestic spending. If the pattern of past years repeats itself, we can expect the obstructionists to keep the process stymied until the final night before the deadline when they'll go into a budgetary feeding frenzy, loading up huge spending measures with goodies for every special interest group in sight. Well, enough is enough. We refuse to make a choice between a budget that threatens our national security and a spending orgy that undermines our economy.

Of course, as they do every year, some in Congress are using this annual collapse of the budget process as an excuse to call for a tax increase. Well, I've promised before and I will repeat that promise today, I will veto any tax hike that comes across my desk, no matter how it's disguised. And I'm glad to say that I have more than enough votes pledged in the House to sustain that veto. I have some advice for those who talk about tax hikes: Save your breath. I'm going to hold their feet to the fire on this budget until they do the right thing and get government spending under control.

I'm happy to be able to report that the Senate Judiciary Committee will be voting on a bill next week that could put some discipline back in the budget process: the balanced budget amendment. Why shouldn't the U.S. Government be held to even the minimum standards of accountability that we demand of the smallest commercial bank? It's true that amending the Constitution is a lengthy and difficult procedure. Well, that's all the more reason to start right away. More immediate relief would come from a line-item veto that would enable me to veto individual budget items. And that is the way to cut the pork out of the massive appropriations bills that Congress sends me, without vetoing that part of the bill—essentially human needs and our national security. If Congress can't or won't stand up to the special interests, give Presidents the line-item veto. This President would be glad to take them on.

By cutting taxes and stamping out inflation, we've put our economy back on the track of strong and solid growth. America's like a house that we build stronger and prouder every day. But right now, the American economy has termites. It's time to clean them out once and for all. Please tell your Representatives not to waste more time or money, but to come back here ready to put our fiscal house in order and make government live within its means. We must reduce the deficit and make a start on achieving a balanced budget.

Until next week, thanks for listening, and God bless you.

Note: The President spoke at 12:06 p.m. from Camp David, MD.

Letter to Andrey A. Gromyko on His Election as Chairman of the Presidium of the Supreme Soviet of the Soviet Union
July 5, 1985

Dear Mr. Chairman:

Please accept my congratulations upon your election as Chairman of the Presidium of the Supreme Soviet of the Union of Soviet Socialist Republics.

Even though the differences between our nations are many and complex, as I made clear when we met last year, we can and must resolve these differences without threat or use of force, through discussion, patient effort and determination.

I wish you well in the high responsibilities you have now assumed, and I hope that we can cooperate to reduce tensions between our countries.

Sincerely,

/S/ RONALD REAGAN

Note: The original was not available for verification of the content of this letter, which was released by the Office of the Press Secretary on July 8.

Remarks at the Annual Convention of the American Bar Association
July 8, 1985

Thank you, John Shepherd. I want to welcome all of you to the last tax deductible ABA convention. [*Laughter*] Really, I'm delighted you decided to come to the Capital, and believe me, this week Washington belongs to you. I noticed this morning that even Milt Pitts, the White House barber, has a welcome sign up: "Haircutting, $10. Hairsplitting, $100 an hour." [*Laughter*] I was disappointed, though, when the White

House Counsel told me that I couldn't accept an honorarium this morning. Actually, I kind of thought it'd be a first to talk to a group of lawyers and I'd come home with the fee—[*laughter*]—but don't worry, I'm not going to speak very long. I have a lunch scheduled back at the White House with my wife, the Vice President, and my Chief of Staff, or as you would put it—Reagan, Reagan, Regan, and Bush. [*Laughter*]

Seriously, I'm delighted to be able to speak today, not just to the largest voluntary professional association in the world but one whose exclusive concern is the starting point for any free society, a concern that is at the heart of civilized life: the law—our courts and legal system—justice itself.

Now, I want to be very candid with you this morning and tell you I'd been planning to come here today to speak on a number of legal issues: the problems of our courts, our administration's enforcement of antitrust and civil rights laws, as well as our ongoing attack on the drug trade and organized crime in general. But I'm afraid this discussion will now have to wait for another occasion, for it's been overtaken by events of an international nature, events that I feel compelled as President to comment on today. And yet I think these matters will be of interest to you, not only because you're Americans but because, as lawyers, you are also concerned with the rule of law and the danger posed to it by criminals of both a domestic and international variety.

The reason we haven't had time to discuss the issues that I'd originally hoped to address this morning has to do with our hostages and what all of America have been through during recent weeks. Yet my purpose today goes even beyond our concern over the recent outrages in Beirut, El Salvador or the Air India tragedy, the Narita bombing or the Jordanian Airlines hijacking. We must look beyond these events because I feel it is vital not to allow them—as terrible as they are—to obscure an even larger and darker terrorist menace.

There is a temptation to see the terrorist act as simply the erratic work of a small group of fanatics. We make this mistake at great peril, for the attacks on America, her citizens, her allies, and other democratic na-tions in recent years do form a pattern of terrorism that has strategic implications and political goals. And only by moving our focus from the tactical to the strategic perspective, only by identifying the pattern of terror and those behind it, can we hope to put into force a strategy to deal with it.

So, let us go to the facts. Here is what we know: In recent years, there's been a steady and escalating pattern of terrorist acts against the United States and our allies and Third World nations friendly toward our interests. The number of terrorist acts rose from about 500 in 1983 to over 600 in 1984. There were 305 bombings alone last year—that works out to an average of almost one a day. And some of the most vicious attacks were directed at Americans or United States property and installations. And this pattern has continued throughout 1985, and in most cases innocent civilians are the victims of the violence. At the current rate, as many as 1,000 acts of terrorism will occur in 1985. Now, that's what we face unless civilized nations act together to end this assault on humanity.

In recent years, the Mideast has been one principal point of focus for these attacks—attacks directed at the United States, Israel, France, Jordan, and the United Kingdom. Beginning in the summer of 1984 and culminating in January and February of this year, there was also a series of apparently coordinated attacks and assassinations by leftwing terrorist groups in Belgium, West Germany, and France—attacks directed against American and NATO installations or military and industrial officials of those nations.

Now, what do we know about the sources of those attacks and the whole pattern of terrorist assaults in recent years? Well, in 1983 alone, the Central Intelligence Agency either confirmed or found strong evidence of Iranian involvement in 57 terrorist attacks. While most of these attacks occurred in Lebanon, an increase in activity by terrorists sympathetic to Iran was seen throughout Europe. Spain and France have seen such incidents, and in Italy seven pro-Iranian Lebanese students were arrested for plotting an attack on the U.S. Embassy, and this violence continues.

It will not surprise any of you to know that, in addition to Iran, we have identified another nation, Libya, as deeply involved in terrorism. We have evidence which links Libyan agents or surrogates to at least 25 incidents last year. Colonel Qadhafi's outrages against civilized conduct are, of course, as infamous as those of the Ayatollah Khomeini. The gunning down last year—from inside the Libyan Embassy—of a British policewoman is only one of many examples.

Since September 1984, Iranian-backed terrorist groups have been responsible for almost 30 attacks, and most recently, the Egyptian Government aborted a Libyan-backed plot to bomb our Embassy in Cairo. It was this pattern of state-approved assassination and terrorism by Libya that led the United States a few years ago to expel Libyan diplomats and has forced other nations to take similar steps since then. But let us, in acknowledging his commitment to terrorism, at least give Colonel Qadhafi his due. The man is candid. He said recently that Libya was—and I quote—"capable of exporting terrorism to the heart of America. We are also capable of physical liquidation and destruction and arson inside America."

And, by the way, it's important to note here that the recognition of this deep and ongoing involvement of Iran and Libya in international terrorism is hardly confined to our own government. Most police forces in Europe now take this involvement for granted, and this is not even to mention the warnings issued by world leaders. For example, the Jordanian leadership has publicly noted that Libyan actions caused the destruction of the Jordanian Embassy in Tripoli.

Now, three other governments, along with Iran and Libya, are actively supporting a campaign of international terrorism against the United States, her allies, and moderate Third World states.

First, North Korea. The extent and crudity of North Korean violence against the United States and our ally, South Korea, are a matter of record. Our aircraft have been shot down; our servicemen have been murdered in border incidents; and 2 years ago, four members of the South Korean Cabinet were blown up in a bombing in Burma by North Korean terrorists—a failed attempt to assassinate President Chun. This incident was just one more of an unending series of attacks directed against the Republic of Korea by North Korea.

Now, what is not readily known or understood is North Korea's wider links to the international terrorist network. There isn't time today to recount all of North Korea's efforts to foster separatism, violence, and subversion in other lands well beyond its immediate borders. But to cite one example, North Korea's efforts to spread separatism and terrorism in the free and prosperous nation of Sri Lanka are a deep and continuing source of tension in south Asia. And this is not even to mention North Korea's involvement here in our own hemisphere, including a secret arms agreement with the former Communist government in Grenada. I will also have something to say about North Korea's involvement in Central America in a moment.

And then there is Cuba, a nation whose government has, since the 1960's, openly armed, trained, and directed terrorists operating on at least three continents. This has occurred in Latin America. The OAS has repeatedly passed sanctions against Castro for sponsoring terrorism in places and countries too numerous to mention. This has also occurred in Africa. President Carter openly accused the Castro government of supporting and training Katangan terrorists from Angola in their attacks on Zaire. And even in the Middle East, Castro himself has acknowledged that he actively assisted the Sandinistas in the early seventies when they were training in the Middle East with terrorist factions of the PLO.

And finally there is the latest partner of Iran, Libya, North Korea, and Cuba in a campaign of international terror—the Communist regime in Nicaragua. The Sandinistas not only sponsor terror in El Salvador, Costa Rica, and Honduras—terror that led recently to the murder of four United States marines, two civilians, and seven Latin Americans—they provide one of the world's principal refuges for international terrorists.

Members of the Italian Government have openly charged that Nicaragua is harboring some of Italy's worst terrorists. And when we have evidence that in addition to Italy's Red Brigades other elements of the world's most vicious terrorist groups—West Germany's Baader-Meinhoff gang, the Basque ETA, the PLO, the Tupamaros, and the IRA—have found a haven in Nicaragua and support from that country's Communist dictatorship. In fact, the Communist regime in Nicaragua has made itself a focal point for the terrorist network and a case study in the extent of its scope.

Consider for just a moment that in addition to establishing strong international alliances with Cuba and Libya, including the receipt of enormous amounts of arms and ammunition, the Sandinistas are also receiving extensive assistance from North Korea. Nor are they reluctant to acknowledge their debt to the government of North Korea dictator Kim Il-sŏng. Both Daniel and Humberto Ortega have recently paid official and state visits to North Korea to seek additional assistance and more formal relations. So, we see the Nicaraguans tied to Cuba, Libya, and North Korea. And that leaves only Iran. What about ties to Iran? Well, yes, only recently the Prime Minister of Iran visited Nicaragua bearing expressions of solidarity from the Ayatollah for the Sandinista Communists.

Now, I spoke a moment ago about the strategic goals that are motivating these terrorist states. In a minute I will add some comments of my own, but for the moment why don't we let the leaders of these outlaw governments speak for themselves about their objectives. During his state visit to North Korea, Nicaragua's Sandinista leader, Daniel Ortega, heard Kim Il-sŏng say this about the mutual objectives of North Korea and Nicaragua: "If the peoples of the revolutionary countries of the world put pressure on and deal blows at United States imperialism in all places where it stretches its talons of aggression, they will make it powerless and impossible to behave as dominator any longer." And Colonel Qadhafi, who has a formal alliance with North Korea, echoed Kim Il-sŏng's words when he laid out the agenda for the terrorist network: "We must force America to fight on a hundred fronts all over the Earth. We must force it to fight in Lebanon, to fight in Chad, to fight in Sudan, and to fight in El Salvador."

So, there we have it—Iran, Libya, North Korea, Cuba, Nicaragua—continents away, tens of thousands of miles apart, but the same goals and objectives. I submit to you that the growth in terrorism in recent years results from the increasing involvement of these states in terrorism in every region of the world. This is terrorism that is part of a pattern, the work of a confederation of terrorist states. Most of the terrorists who are kidnaping and murdering American citizens and attacking American installations are being trained, financed, and directly or indirectly controlled by a core group of radical and totalitarian governments—a new, international version of Murder, Incorporated. And all of these states are united by one simple criminal phenomenon—their fanatical hatred of the United States, our people, our way of life, our international stature.

And the strategic purpose behind the terrorism sponsored by these outlaw states is clear: to disorient the United States, to disrupt or alter our foreign policy, to sow discord between ourselves and our allies, to frighten friendly Third World nations working with us for peaceful settlements of regional conflicts, and, finally, to remove American influence from those areas of the world where we're working to bring stable and democratic government; in short, to cause us to retreat, retrench, to become Fortress America.

Yes, their real goal is to expel America from the world. And that is the reason these terrorist nations are arming, training, and supporting attacks against this nation. And that is why we can be clear on one point: these terrorist states are now engaged in acts of war against the Government and people of the United States. And under international law, any state which is the victim of acts of war has the right to defend itself.

Now, for the benefit of these outlaw governments who are sponsoring international terrorism against our nation, I'm prepared to offer a brief lesson in American history. A number of times in America's past, foreign tyrants, warlords, and totalitarian dictators have misinterpreted the well-known likeability, patience, and generosity of the American people as signs of weakness or even decadence. Well, it's true; we are an easygoing people, slow to wrath, hesitant to see danger looming over every horizon. But it's also true that when the emotions of the American people are aroused, when their patriotism and their anger are triggered, there are no limits to their national valor nor their consuming passion to protect this nation's cherished tradition of freedom. Teddy Roosevelt once put it this way: "The American people are slow to wrath, but when the wrath is once kindled it burns like a consuming flame." And it was another leader, this time a foreign adversary, Admiral Yamamoto, who warned his own nation after its attack on Pearl Harbor that he feared "we have only awakened a sleeping giant and his reaction will be terrible."

Yes, we Americans have our disagreements, sometimes noisy ones, almost always in public—that's the nature of our open society—but no foreign power should mistake disagreement for disunity. Those who are tempted to do so should reflect on our national character and our history—a history littered with the wreckage of regimes who made the mistake of underestimating the vigor and will of the American people.

So, let me today speak for a united people. Let me say simply: We're Americans. We love this country. We love what she stands for, and we will always defend her. [*Applause*] Thank you very much. Thank you. [*Applause*] God bless you. [*Applause*] Thank you, and God bless you. We live for freedom—our own, our children's—and we will always stand ready to sacrifice for that freedom.

So, the American people are not—I repeat—not going to tolerate intimidation, terror, and outright acts of war against this nation and its people. And we're especially not going to tolerate these attacks from outlaw states run by the strangest collection of misfits, loony tunes, and squalid criminals—[*laughter*]—since the advent of the Third Reich.

Now, I've taken your time today to outline the nature of this network of terrorist states so that we might, as a nation, know who it is we're up against and identify the long-term goals motivating this confedera-

tion of criminal governments. Do not for a moment, however, think that this discussion has been all inclusive. First of all, though their strength does not match that of the groups supported by the terrorist network I've already mentioned, there are some terrorist organizations that are indigenous to certain localities or countries which are not necessarily tied to this international network. And second, the countries I have mentioned today are not necessarily the only ones that support terrorism against the United States and its allies. Those which I've described are simply the ones that can be most directly implicated.

Now, the question of the Soviet Union's close relationship with almost all of the terrorist states that I have mentioned and the implications of these Soviet ties on bilateral relations with the United States and other democratic nations must be recognized. So, too, Secretary of State Shultz in his speech of June 24th of last year openly raised the question of Soviet support for terrorist organizations, as did Secretary Haig before him.

With regard to the Soviet Union, there is one matter that I cannot let go unaddressed today. During the recent hostage crisis in Beirut—39 Americans were brutally kidnaped; an American sailor was viciously beaten; another American sailor stomped and shot to death; the families and loved ones of these hostages undergo indescribable suffering and a sense of distress, anger, and outrage spreading through our nation like a prairie fire—the Soviet Union made some official comments through its government-controlled press. The Soviet Government suggested that the United States was not sincerely concerned about this crisis, but that we were, instead, in the grip of—and I use the Soviets' word here—"hysteria." The Soviet Union also charged that the United States was only looking for a—and, again, I use their word—"pretext" for a military—and, again, I use their word—"invasion." Well now, ladies and gentlemen of the American Bar, there is a non-Soviet word for that kind of talk. [*Laughter*] It's an extremely useful, time-tested original American word, one with deep roots in our rich agricultural and farming tradition. [*Laughter*]

Now, much needs to be done by all of us in the community of civilized nations. We must act against the criminal menace of terrorism with the full weight of the law, both domestic and international. We will act to indict, apprehend, and prosecute those who commit the kind of atrocities the world has witnessed in recent weeks. We can act together as free peoples who wish not to see our citizens kidnaped or shot or blown out of the skies—just as we acted together to rid the seas of piracy at the turn of the last century. And incidentally, those of you who are legal scholars will note the law's description of pirates: "hostis humanis"—the enemies of all mankind. There can be no place on Earth left where it is safe for these monsters to rest or train or practice their cruel and deadly skills. We must act together, or unilaterally if necessary, to ensure that terrorists have no sanctuary anywhere.

Vice President Bush returned from Europe last week after intense consultations with our allies on practical steps to combat terrorism. He'll be heading up a governmentwide task force to review and recommend improvements in our efforts to halt terrorism. For those countries which sponsor such acts or fail to take action against terrorist criminals, the civilized world needs to ensure that their nonfeasance and malfeasance are answered with actions that demonstrate our unified resolve that this kind of activity must cease. For example, I've informed our allies and others that the Beirut International Airport, through which have passed 15 percent of the world's hijackings since 1970, must be made safe. And until that time, the airport should be closed.

Finally, I want you to accept a challenge to become part of the solution to the problem of terrorism. You have a fundamental concern for the law, and it's upon the law that terrorists trample. You need to address this problem in conferences and conventions that will lead us to a better domestic and international legal framework for dealing with terrorism. You must help this government and others to deal legally with lawlessness. Where legislation must be crafted to allow appropriate authorities to act, you should help to craft or change it. In the past lawyers have helped when civilization

was threatened by lawbreakers, and now is the time to do so again.

What I place before you this morning is not pleasant, nor will the solution be easy. The answer to the threat of international terrorism is difficult, but it can be found. It is to be found in a clear understanding of the problem and the expression of our national will to do something about it. It's always been so with any important cause; it's why our Declaration of Independence was more important to our Revolution than any one military maneuver or single battle. And that is why we do not today engage in policy discussions or focus on strategic options but simply state the facts about the nature of international terrorism and affirm America's will to resist it.

But there's another point that needs to be made here, the point I made at the start of this discussion: that in taking a strategic—not just a tactical—view of terrorism, we must understand that the greatest hope the terrorists and their supporters harbor, the very reason for their cruelty and viciousness of their tactics, is to disorient the American people, to cause disunity, to disrupt or alter our foreign policy, to keep us from the steady pursuit of our strategic interests, to distract us from our very real hope that someday the nightmare of totalitarian rule will end and self-government and personal freedom will become the birthright of every people on Earth.

And here, my fellow Americans, is where we find the real motive behind the rabid and increasing anti-Americanism of the international terrorist network. I've been saying for some years now that the cause of totalitarian ideology is on the wane; that all across the world there is an uprising of mind and will, a tidal wave of longing for freedom and self-rule. Well, no one senses this better than those who now stand atop totalitarian states, especially those nations on the outer periphery of the totalitarian world like Iran, Libya, North Korea, Cuba, and Nicaragua. Their rulers are frightened; they know that freedom is on the march and when it triumphs their time in power is over.

You see, it's true that totalitarian governments are very powerful and, over the short term, may be better organized than the democracies. But it's also true—and no one knows this better than totalitarian rulers themselves—that these regimes are weak in a way that no democracy can ever be weak. For the fragility of totalitarian government is the fragility of any regime whose hold on its people is limited to the instruments of police-state repression. That's why the stakes are so high and why we must persevere. Freedom itself is the issue—our own and the entire world's. Yes, America is still a symbol to a few, a symbol that is feared and hated, but to more, many millions more, a symbol that is loved, a country that remains a shining city on a hill.

Teddy Roosevelt—and he is a good President to quote in these circumstances—put it so well: "We, here in America, hold in our hands the hope of the world, the fate of the coming years; and shame and disgrace will be ours if in our eyes the light of high resolve is dimmed, if we trail in the dust the golden hopes of man." And that light of high resolve, those golden hopes, are now ours to preserve and protect and, with God's help, to pass on to generations to come.

I can't close without telling you one little incident here. When I say we are a symbol of hope—I have on my desk at home a letter signed by 10 women in the Soviet Union. They are all in a prison camp in that Union—a labor camp. The letter is no more than 2½ inches wide and just an inch high, and yet, by hand, they wrote a complete letter, signed their 10 names to it, smuggled that and another document just a little bigger—about a 3-inch square of paper— that is the chart of the hunger strikes they have endured. And they smuggled it out to be sent to me because they wanted to tell me and all of you that the United States, where they are, in that prison, still remains their hope that keeps them going—their hope for the world.

So, thank you very much. God bless you all.

Note: The President spoke at 10:32 a.m. at DAR Constitution Hall. He was introduced by John C. Shepherd, president of the association.

Nomination of Joe M. Rodgers To Be United States Ambassador to France
July 9, 1985

The President today announced his intention to nominate Joe M. Rodgers, of Tennessee, to be Ambassador of the United States of America to France. He would succeed Evan Griffith Galbraith.

Mr. Rodgers was chief engineer of A.E. Burgess, Inc., in Birmingham, AL, in 1959–1963. In 1963–1966 he was sales and production manager of Dixie Concrete Pipe Co., Smyrna, TN. He became president and chairman of the board of Joe M. Rodgers & Associates in Nashville, TN, in 1966–1976. Mr. Rodgers then served as chairman of the board, Rodgers Construction International in Nashville, 1976–1979. From 1976 to the present, he has been the proprietor of JMR Investments in Nashville, and from 1979 to the present, he has been chairman and president of American Constructors, Inc., in Nashville. Since 1980 he has also been chairman of the board of CRC Equities, Inc., in Nashville. In 1982 Mr. Rodgers served as U.S. Commissioner General of the U.S. Section at the 1982 World's Fair. In 1984 he became a member of the President's Foreign Intelligence Advisory Board.

Mr. Rodgers was born November 12, 1933, in Bay Minette, AL. He received his B.S. in 1956 from the University of Alabama in civil engineering. In 1956–1958 he was a lieutenant in the U.S. Coast Guard and Geodetic Survey. He is married to the former Helen Martin, and they have two children.

Nomination of Thomas Michael Tolliver Niles To Be United States Ambassador to Canada
July 9, 1985

The President today announced his intention to nominate Thomas Michael Tolliver Niles, of the District of Columbia, a career member of the Senior Foreign Service, Class of Minister-Counselor, as Ambassador of the United States of America to Canada. He would succeed Paul Heron Robinson, Jr.

Mr. Niles entered on duty in the Department of State in 1962. He served at the American Embassy in Belgrade, Yugoslavia, in 1963–1965. In 1965 he became an economic officer in Soviet affairs in the Department, and from there took Russian language training. In 1968 he went to Moscow as an economic officer, where he served until 1971 when he was assigned as a political officer at the U.S. Mission to the North Atlantic Treaty Organization (NATO) in Brussels, Belgium. He returned to Moscow in 1973 as director for commercial affairs, where he served until 1976 when he became a student at the National War College. In 1977–1979 Mr. Niles served in the United Nations Office in the Bureau of International Organization Affairs. He then became Director of Central European Affairs in the Department until 1981, when he was appointed Deputy Assistant Secretary of State for European and Canadian Affairs.

Mr. Niles was born September 22, 1939, in Lexington, KY. He received his B.A. in 1960 from Harvard University and his M.A. in 1962 from the University of Kentucky. His foreign languages are Serbo-Croatian, German, Russian, and French. He is married to the former Carroll Ehringhaus, and they have two children.

Remarks and a Question-and-Answer Session with Regional Editors and Broadcasters
July 9, 1985

The President. Good afternoon, and welcome to the White House. It's always refreshing to speak to representatives of the real America—that vast and wonderful land where a special interest is a hobby like fishing and a lobbyist is somebody who hangs around in hotels. I want you to know how deeply I appreciate this opportunity to speak to you and, through you, to the American people.

I'd like to devote the bulk of our time together to answering your questions. First, however, permit me to say a word about the budget and then about our major new domestic policy initiative—the effort to institute a fair share tax plan. Once again it seems that the budget process has broken down. Growing deficits appear to have made virtually no difference; for too many in this town, it's still business as usual. They're a little like sailors on a ship adrift, painting the gunnels and polishing the brass, but ignoring the broken rudder.

The main problem lies in the House, which has proposed a budget that juggles funds back and forth between accounts, invents savings, and simply wishes away massive costs—a budget that would be laughed at by bookkeepers in any well run shop or business in the country. What the House Budget Committee calls a defense spending freeze, moreover, is really a deep cut. It would require us to scale back our spending on research and development, construction, and procurement by 19 percent next year, 23 percent in 1987, and 28 percent in 1988.

The Senate, by contrast, has to its credit proposed a budget that is responsible and fair, that at least holds real defense spending constant, and that makes the structural changes in domestic spending that will help us to grow out of these deficits. But when representatives of the Senate and House met in conference, it quickly became clear that certain Members of the House still refused to consider real cuts in domestic spending.

My friends, I can promise you that this year things are going to be different. By cutting taxes and forcing down inflation, we've created new growth, new jobs, and hope. And after so much progress, I flatly refuse to be cornered into a choice between a budget that undermines our national security and a spending spree that threatens our prosperity. Together, Republicans and Democrats must make genuine cuts in domestic spending. And to see that this finally happens, I'm willing to go to the American people again and again.

Turning to our tax plan, when the income tax first became law back in 1913, the tax code ran to 15 pages. Today it adds up to 4 volumes and more than 4,000 pages, and one standard interpretation of the code runs to 18 volumes and requires some 6 feet of shelf space and weighs almost 90 pounds. The complexity is staggering, but the injustice it engenders is worse.

Each year, countless Americans pay more in Federal income taxes than the giant corporations they work for. Some wealthy individuals write off ocean cruises as educational; others deduct expenses for sky boxes at sports events. And with our steeply progressive tax code, working men and women struggling on behalf of their families find that the Government lays claim to a bigger chunk of each new dollar they earn. And for them, making economic progress is like climbing a wall with no ladder.

Our tax code has become in a fundamental sense un-American, and I mean that as a serious, moral, and economic assertion. Americans are an expansive and optimistic people. We constantly seek opportunity and work to better our lot. Yet our high marginal tax rates discourage risk-taking, savings, and work and thereby smother growth. Most Americans are straightforward and honest; yet our tax code constitutes one of the most complicated and convoluted legal codes ever devised. Americans look to the future, and yet we're weighed down by a

tax code that is the result of decades of political deals that's become the very embodiment of the dead hand of the past. No wonder the underground economy is so big and thought to be growing. Americans today feel an abiding disappointment, even disgust, with the taxation that represents that most basic transaction between the Government and the people. My friends, this is no way to go about building economic growth.

Maybe it has to do with our early history as a nation of farmers, but when we Americans see a problem, we solve it. If there's a stump in the field, we hitch up the tractor and haul it out. If a new barn needs building, we gather together and raise it. And when we have a mess as big as the tax code that stifles growth and undermines our self-respect as a people, then forgive me, but it's time to clean out the stalls and put down fresh straw.

Our fair share tax plan for America would give families a dramatic benefit by nearly doubling the personal exemption to $2,000. This would mean that an income well into the $25,000 to $30,000 range—a working family with two or three children would pay an effective tax rate of less than 10 percent. Perhaps the central idea in our proposal is this: By curtailing loopholes and eliminating deductions that are only used by a few, we can lower marginal rates sharply, increasing the rewards for savings, investment, and good, hard work. In other words, a fair share tax plan is a progrowth tax plan. Lower tax rates, a near doubling of the personal exemption, and an end to unfair deductions—what it adds up to is simple justice, more jobs and renewed hope for our own future and that of our children.

A great deal has been said about a timetable for passage of our proposal. Well, my own idea is simple: By Thanksgiving Day of 1985, we should cook our turkey of a tax code and get our tax reform passed by both the House and the Senate. Then, by Christmas Day, America's new tax plan should be signed into law and presented to the people as the best gift of the year.

So, thank you. And, now, I know some of you may have some questions and—yes?

Tax Reform

Q. Mr. President, Bill Glass from KPRC–TV in Houston. Thank you for the opportunity to ask you about something that's of great concern to people in Houston, where we are suffering an economic situation because of our oil-based economy. People are wondering how your tax plan is going to impact that industry in Houston and whether it's going to help or hurt our much-looked-for recovery?

The President. We believe it is not going to hurt. There have been some changes. We're phasing out the tax plan now—I can't think of the right word that I want for it—but the depletion allowance. But except for wells that are producing 10 or fewer barrels a day, to keep them in existence, from not shutting down—but we also are keeping the tax breaks that come for exploring and finding—the deduction of the intangibles and so forth. Because we think that is our real problem, is to make sure that we do not make it uneconomic to continue to explore. Half of our trade deficit today is the need for us to buy oil outside our own country. So, the more production we have here, the better off we think we are. We don't believe that it is going to militate against the industry.

Q. Mr. President, Kevin Culp from Chronicle Broadcasting. I am here representing our station in Omaha, Nebraska, and the farmers in Nebraska say that they're concerned about something called farming the tax code or tax farmers; that is to say, people who invest in agriculture for a tax writeoff rather than for the product from the land. And they seem to think that your tax reform proposal doesn't go far enough to stop this kind of thing that they say is driving commodity prices down. Do you think that your tax reform proposal does go far enough, and would you consider any additional ways, and what do you think of the whole idea of tax farming; that is, investing in agriculture for a tax writeoff rather than for the product?

The President. Well, of course, we are pretty strict now, and have been for some several years, about hobby farms as versus real farms. I've had some experience with that; I've had a ranch for years. I can remember when it was deductible, and it isn't anymore.

No, we think that the best thing that we can do for the farm economy—and I grant you, there's going to be some disruption in doing it, and we don't mean to pull the rug out instantly. We think that government itself created the bulk of the farm problems with programs that were well-intentioned, but programs that encouraged people to farm even if there was no market for their product. We would like to feel that we could get farming back into the open market. And we can point to the fact that that part of farming that is and has always been in the open market has never had the problems that the farms—that in the part of agriculture that is government-regulated and with quotas and all that sort of thing—that it seems to be the one that has the most problems. And I think that we are taking some steps that are going to make the tax farmers have to look elsewhere because one of our aims in this tax reform plan is to eliminate some of the so-called tax shelters that have been designed not to raise crops particularly but to give a tax writeoff.

Q. Mr. President, do you think that Governor Mario Cuomo of New York is attempting to turn your fair tax program into a political issue?

The President. Well, I don't know what his motive is. I wouldn't ascribe any motive to him. I'll let him have that. But I know that he's been very vocal, particularly about the nondeductibility anymore of local and State taxes. And at the same time, he couples that with charging us that we're, once again, doing things for the rich. Well, I'd like to point out to him that less than a third of the people in this country itemize, and they are the people with the higher incomes, the so-called rich. They are the ones that benefit from the present tax deduction of State and local taxes. More than two-thirds of our people who don't deduct, who don't itemize on their bills, they get no benefit from that deduction at all. So, we don't see that we're doing any harm in taking it away.

The young lady right there.

Q. Mr. President, Patti Suarez, KWTV,

Oklahoma City. There's a lot of talk about revenue neutrality. Some Congressmen are saying that your plan may fall anywhere from $12 billion to $20 billion short of revenue neutrality. My question is: Intangible drilling costs—might they still be sacrificed to keep it revenue neutral? Are we going to keep intangible drilling cost deductions?

The President. I would object to that because I think it would be counterproductive to an industry that is very important. The exploring for oil is not done by the giant oil companies. The exploration is done by independent people who are out there, the so-called wildcatters, doing this. And we want them to keep on doing it. So, no, I don't feel that we should. And as to that estimate that we're going to fall revenue short, I happen to think that some of those people are the same ones that estimated when we started our economic recovery program in 1981 that it wasn't going to work. Matter of fact, they named it Reaganomics, and it was going to be a failure. Well, it's a success, and they don't call it Reaganomics anymore.

Yes?

American Hostages in Lebanon

Q. Mr. Reagan, Mike Olszewski, WERE Radio in Cleveland. Some families of the seven hostages still in Beirut have expressed interest in meeting with Syria's President in hopes of getting his help in securing the release of their loved ones. I'd like your opinion on that move, also your opinion of Florida Congressman Dan Mica's bill to provide compensation to Federal employees who fall victim to terrorism abroad.

The President. Well, to the first question here, I can't deny them if they feel that they want to try this and it could be of some help. Certainly, we would never interfere with that. But I do want everyone to know that—because there's been some talk here and there, and even some of them out of their frustration and grief have said, out of sight out of mind—that isn't true. There has never been a minute from the first kidnaping on that we've not been doing everything we can. Our great problem is the secrecy, the inability to locate and find. Are they being held by one group all together? Are they separated?

We have reason to believe now, from some of our intelligence gathering, that they are being moved around quite often. And our difficulty with taking some action is the very fact of their lives. And we're continuing, and we meant it when we tried our best to get them included with the 39 that came home. But evidently, they're in the hands of others not having to do with the same hijackers as this last time. We are continuing, we're using every effort we can to bring them back. And yet we do know that there is a threat hanging over them and that we must be very careful and not precipitate that threat being carried out.

You've—all right—[*laughter*]——

Federal Budget

Q. Marlene Schneider, WFSB-TV, Hartford. I'm told that you are going to be having a meeting later this afternoon with the top leaders in the House and Senate on the budget impasse in conference, and I am very curious as to what exactly you are going to say to them.

The President. I'm going to be rather firm. [*Laughter*] And I'm going to say that this is a time to forget the 1986 election and partisan differences, that we've got a job to do, and the job to do is to make this country solvent again and to get the deficit eliminated. And that's what it's all going to be about.

Q. Do you think they're going to be listening?

The President. I'm going to try to get their attention. I've—because I had called on you, yes?

Q. Thank you. I wanted this red suit to work. [*Laughter*]

The President. I heard that there were red suits in the room.

Farm Legislation

Q. Nancy Chandler from KMTV in Omaha, Nebraska. Again, I have a lot of rural people who I speak to, and they are saying this tax code isn't going to expire. The tax laws are going to continue through into 1986 if we don't change the tax code—our farm bill does not. Do we go back and go with the policies of the past, or can we expect the President to step in and also urge the House and the Senate to pass a new farm bill in—[*inaudible*].

The President. Yes, we are working on a farm bill right now. We can't just shove everything aside and say only the budget and the tax plan are all we're talking about. There are a number of legislative matters that are all of vital importance.

Ms. Mathis. One more question.

The President. Oh, always happens to me. [*Laughter*]

American Hostages in Lebanon

Q. Russ Garrett, WICC Radio, Bridgeport, Connecticut. Congressman John Rowland of Connecticut has proposed a rescue mission for the seven hostages if all else fails. How would you react to that, sir?

The President. Well, my reaction—I think I, in a way, answered it in what I said earlier about them. The situation is: How do you rescue someone if you don't know where they are? How do you rescue them if, at the same time, you would have to reveal yourselves to the point that you might be bringing home a body instead of a human being? And this has been our great problem all this time and long before this particular hijacking took place, is, as I say, the trying to learn where, and are they together, are

they one or separate? And unfortunately it just isn't that easy to find out. We've had suspected targets over there, but, again, no knowledge that we could take an action that would not result in their death. And we're going to do everything we can to see that that doesn't happen.

But, as I say, we're continuing our efforts, and we have to feel that the success that we've had this time and part of our problem is—and I think all of you can understand this—part of our problem is we can't answer all your questions on these particular subjects because we can't say what we're going to do next Thursday or there might be someone on the other side that's a little uncomfortable about that. So, we just have to tell you that we're using everything that we know and everything that we have on this entire subject, but we can't talk specifics.

Ms. Mathis. Thank you.

The President. But, again, they've told me that's the last one I can do. I'm sorry. Thank you very much.

Note: The President spoke at 1:10 p.m. at a luncheon in the State Dining Room at the White House. Susan K. Mathis was Deputy Director of Media Relations.

Appointment of Six United States Representatives to the United Nations Program for the Prevention of Crime and the Treatment of Offenders
July 9, 1985

The President today announced his intention to appoint the following individuals to be Representatives of the United States to participate, as National Correspondents, in the United Nations Program for the Prevention of Crime and the Treatment of Offenders for a term of 5 years:

Roy R. Barrera, Jr., is criminal district judge for the 144th district court in San Antonio, TX. He graduated from St. Mary's University (B.A., 1972) and St. Mary's Law School (J.D., 1975). He was born January 25, 1952, in San Antonio, TX, and now resides in Boerne, TX.

Richard A. Boyd is national president of the Fra-

ternal Order of Police in Baltimore, MD. He graduated from the University of Oklahoma (B.S., 1972). He was born January 21, 1943, in Inwood, NY, and now resides in McLoud, OK.

Claire A. D'Agostino is a licensed clinical psychologist in Wilmington, DE. She graduated from Agnes Scott College (B.A., 1967) and Georgia State University (M.A., 1970; Ph.D., 1973). Dr. D'Agostino was born August 15, 1945, in Nashville, GA, and now resides in Wilmington, DE.

Lois Haight Herrington is currently serving at the Department of Justice as Assistant Attorney General, Office of Justice, Research, and Statistics. She graduated from the University of California at Hastings (A.B., 1961; LL.B., 1965). She was born December 6, 1939, in Seattle, WA, and now resides in McLean, VA.

Anthony M. Kennedy is U.S. Circuit Judge for the Court of Appeals for the Ninth Circuit in Sacramento, CA. He graduated from Stanford University (B.A., 1958) and Harvard Law School (LL.B., 1961). He was born July 23, 1936, in Sacramento, CA, and now resides in Sacramento, CA.

Guadalupe Quintanilla is assistant provost at the University of Houston. She graduated from Pan American University (B.S., 1969) and the University of Houston (M.A., 1971; Ed.D., 1976). She was born October 25, 1937, in Ojinaja, Mexico, and now resides in Houston, TX.

Remarks to the United States Delegation to the United Nations Conference on Women
July 10, 1985

Good afternoon, and welcome to the White House. It's an honor for Nancy and me and George and Barbara [Bush] to have all these distinguished members of the Cabinet—all for them to be able to spend this time with all of you before you depart for the United Nations World Conference on Women. You know, I can't tell you why, but somehow this feels like a family affair. [*Laughter*]

Your efforts in Nairobi can help to improve the lot of women around the world—half the population of the globe—and no challenge could be more important. Maureen tells me that the delegation will focus on four issues, each a matter of the greatest importance, each a matter to which the members of your delegation will bring wide knowledge and experience.

First, women's literacy. Millions of the world's women can neither read nor write; some because schools in their countries are scarce, and others because they live in societies that encourage education only for men. Now, I grant you that the men are more in need of it, but—[*laughter*]. But even in our own country—[*laughter*]—too many women have suffered educational neglect that has left them illiterate. In Nairobi your delegation will work to promote education for all.

Your second focus will be upon women in development, the role that women play as a country becomes more modern. Modern society can offer longer, healthier, and more prosperous lives, but the transition from traditional to modern modes of existence can place families and individuals under great stress. Women not only participate in the economic and social developments which lead to modern life but provide an anchor, a source of stability, as their societies undergo these difficult changes. And you will seek to highlight and enhance this unique role.

Third, you will draw attention to domestic violence against women and children. In our own nation we have just begun to understand the extent of this problem and to take the first steps toward solving it. In other societies domestic violence is sometimes taken for granted or ignored. Let us hope that delegates from around the world will work with you to condemn domestic violence in all its forms wherever it occurs.

Finally, your delegation will concentrate upon the plight of refugee women and children. As refugees, women face unique hardships. Many fall victim to rape and physical abuse. With their children, they often suffer discrimination in the distribution of food and medicine. In Nairobi you will seek to fasten the attention of the world upon these innocent women and children, and you will work to increase the number of women workers in refugee camps themselves. These, then, will be the issues that you champion.

And as we look to the Conference in Nairobi, we would do well to consider the United Nations Conference on Women in Mexico City in 1975 and in Copenhagen in 1980. At these conferences legitimate women's concerns, like the four on which you will concentrate, were all but pushed off the agenda. Commenting on the workings of the United Nations, former Ambassador Jeane Kirkpatrick, a member of your delegation, once said that the biggest challenge for the United States is whether we can learn to be effective at the politics played at the U.N. Well, given the way the Conferences went in Mexico City and Copenhagen, we can be certain that will apply in Nairobi as well.

To make certain that you operate effectively, you have divided your delegation into caucus teams, small groups that will work to establish rapport with other delegations. You have planned informal conversation groups, opportunities to get together in relaxed settings with delegates from other countries. And you'll be visiting development projects, including Peace Corps and AID locations near Nairobi, gaining insights into the problems of women in developing countries.

The members of your delegation firmly believe that the business of this Conference is women, not propaganda. Should it prove necessary, you'll be more than willing to fight to keep the Conference on track. Take it from someone who knows Maureen, that's the way it's going to be. [*Laughter*] But, my friends, you represent the diversity and vitality of American women. And when you reach Nairobi, you, as Americans, will have a powerful story to share. For in our land of political and economic freedom, women take part in virtually every aspect of the life of our nation. I know that in Nairobi you'll work tirelessly with other delegations to help women make strides throughout the world. I thank you from my heart for giving of your time and talents to this historic task. God bless you all.

And now I understand that we'll have the chance to greet each of you personally, George and Barbara and Nancy and myself, in the other rooms. And so I will start out of the room here, and we will see you all again in the Red and the Blue Rooms, all right.

Note: The President spoke at 1:29 p.m. at a luncheon in the East Room at the White House. Maureen Reagan was head of the U.S. delegation.

Nomination of Admiral William J. Crowe, Jr., To Be Chairman of the Joint Chiefs of Staff
July 10, 1985

The President today announced his intention to nominate Adm. William J. Crowe, Jr., to serve as the next Chairman of the Joint Chiefs of Staff, Department of Defense. He will succeed Gen. John W. Vessey, Jr., who is retiring on September 30, 1985. General Vessey has served as the Chairman of the Joint Chiefs of Staff since June 1982.

From 1954 to 1955, Admiral Crowe served as assistant to the naval aide to the President. In 1958 he was assigned as aide and assistant to the Deputy Chief of Naval Operations (Plans and Policy), Office of the Chief of Naval Operations. His first command was U.S.S. *Trout* (SS–566), homeported in Charleston, SC. He served as commanding officer from 1960 to 1962. Upon completion of postgraduate education in 1966, he assumed commanding officer duties of submarine division 31, homeported in San Diego, CA. In 1967 he became the head of East Asia and Pacific Branch, Politico-Military Division, Office of the Chief of Naval Operations. This was followed 3 years later by assignment as senior adviser to the Vietnamese Navy Riverine Force, Republic of Vietnam. After this tour, he served as director of the Office for Micronesian Status Negotiations, Department of the Interior, until 1973. In 1973 Admiral Crowe received his promotion to rear admiral and subsequently was assigned as Deputy Director, Strategic Plans, Policy, Nuclear Systems and NSC Affairs Division, Office of the Chief of Naval Operations. In

1975–1976 he served as Director, East Asia and Pacific Region, Office of the Assistant Secretary of Defense (International Security Affairs). On June 30, 1976, he assumed duties as Commander Middle East Force, a post which he held until July 1977 when he returned to Washington, DC, for another tour of duty in the Office of the Chief of Naval Operations, as Deputy Chief of Naval Operations, Plans and Policy. He was assigned as Commander in Chief, Allied Forces, Southern Europe, in 1980–1983. Since July 1983 he has been serving as Commander in Chief, U.S. Pacific Command.

Admiral Crowe graduated from the U.S. Naval Academy (B.A., 1947), Stanford University (M.S., 1956), and Princeton University (M.A., 1964; Ph.D., 1965). He is married and has three children. He was born January 2, 1925, in La Grange, KY.

Appointment of 11 Members of the National Graduate Fellows Program Fellowship Board
July 10, 1985

The President today announced his intention to appoint the following individuals to be members of the National Graduate Fellows Program Fellowship Board for the terms indicated. These are new positions:

For terms of 6 years:

Martis Jones Okpalobi is a consultant for executive development at the Southland Corp. in Dallas, TX. She graduated from Miami University (Ohio) (B.A., 1969), New York State University (M.A., 1972), and Vanderbilt University (Ph.D., 1977). She was born November 6, 1946, in Dayton, OH, and now resides in Dallas, TX.

J. Ronald Thornton is associate director for industrial programs and director of National Southern Technology Applications Center at the University of Florida. He graduated from Berry College (B.S., 1961) and Wake Forest University (M.A., 1964). He was born August 19, 1939, in Fayetteville, TN.

For terms of 4 years:

John Audley Grant, Jr., is a member of the Florida house of representatives. He graduated from the University of South Florida (B.A., 1964), Florida State University (M.A., 1965), and Stetson University (J.D., 1968). He was born July 12, 1943, in Tampa, FL, where he now resides.

Peter R. Greer is superintendent of the Portland public school system in Portland, ME. He graduated from the University of New Hampshire (B.A., 1963; M.A., 1964) and Boston University (Ed.D., 1974). He was born August 14, 1940, in Portsmouth, NH, and now resides in Yarmouth, ME.

Eugene Welch Hickok, Jr., is an assistant professor in the department of political science at Dickinson College. He graduated from Hampden-Sydney College (B.A., 1972) and the University of Virginia (M.A., 1978; Ph.D., 1983). He was born September 6, 1950, in Denver, CO, and now resides in Carlisle, PA.

Anne Paolucci is a professor of English at St. John's University. She graduated from Barnard College (B.A., 1947) and Columbia University (M.A., 1950; Ph.D., 1963). She was born July 31, 1926, in Rome, Italy, and now resides in Beechurst, NY.

James M. Walton is with the Tiber Co. in Pittsburgh, PA. He is former president of Carnegie Institute and Carnegie Library. He graduated from Yale University (B.A., 1953) and Harvard University (M.B.A., 1958). He was born December 18, 1930, in Pittsburgh, PA, where he now resides.

For terms of 2 years:

Reed St. Clair Browning is a professor of history at Kenyon College. He graduated from Dartmouth College (A.B., 1960) and Yale University (Ph.D., 1965). He was born August 26, 1938, in New York City and now resides in Gambier, OH.

William F. Campbell is professor of economics at Louisiana State University. He graduated from DePaul University (B.A., 1960) and the University of Virginia (Ph.D., 1966). He was born February 21, 1939, in Indianapolis, IN, and now resides in Baton Rouge, LA.

James J. Kirschke is associate professor of English at Villanova University. He graduated from LaSalle College (B.A., 1964) and Temple University (M.A., 1970; Ph.D., 1977). He was born August 10, 1941, in Norfolk, VA, and now resides in Bryn Mawr, PA.

Tibor R. Machan is a distinguished visiting professor of philosophy at the University of San Diego. He graduated from Claremont College (B.A., 1965), New York University (M.A., 1966), and the University of California at Santa Barbara (Ph.D., 1971). He was born March 18, 1939, in Budapest, Hungary, and now resides in Spring Valley, CA.

Nomination of Harvey Frans Nelson, Jr., To Be United States Ambassador to Swaziland
July 11, 1985

The President today announced his intention to nominate Harvey Frans Nelson, Jr., a career member of the Senior Foreign Service, Class of Minister-Counselor, to be Ambassador of the United States of America to the Kingdom of Swaziland. He would succeed Robert H. Phinny.

Prior to entering government service, Mr. Nelson was a political science instructor at Bowdoin College in Brunswick, ME, in 1950–1951. Mr. Nelson entered the Foreign Service in 1951. In 1952–1953 he served as consular officer at the U.S. Embassy in Copenhagen, Denmark, to be followed as political officer in 1953–1955. He returned to the Department as a political analyst in the Office of Intelligence Research in 1955–1957 and then took Finnish language training at the Foreign Service Institute. Mr. Nelson studied East European studies at the University of Indiana in 1957–1958. He became desk officer in the Office of Scandinavian Affairs in the Department in 1958–1960. He then went to the U.S. Embassy in Helsinki as political officer, where he served until 1965. This was followed by French language training at the Foreign Service Institute. From there he became political officer at the U.S. Embassy in Kin-

shasa, Zaire. In 1967–1969 he was deputy chief of mission at the U.S. Embassy in Libreville, Gabon. Returning to the Department in 1969, he became deputy chief in the Office of Southern African Affairs. In 1971 he attended the senior seminar in foreign policy at the Foreign Service Institute. In 1972–1975 he was deputy chief of mission at the U.S. Embassy in Lusaka, Zambia. In 1975 he was an adviser on Africa at the United States Mission to the United Nations in New York. In 1976 he served as a legislative management officer in the Office of Congressional Relations. From there, in 1976 he became deputy chief of mission at the U.S. Embassy in Pretoria, South Africa. In 1979–1980 he was a diplomat-in-residence at Arizona State University in Tempe, AZ, and in 1980–1984 he was deputy commandant for international affairs at the U.S. Army War College in Carlisle, PA.

He graduated from Occidental College (B.A., 1947) and the Fletcher School of Law and Diplomacy (M.A., 1950). He served in the U.S. Navy in 1942–1946. His foreign languages are French, Swedish, and Danish. Mr. Nelson has four children. He was born January 6, 1924, in Long Beach, CA.

Nomination of Gary L. Matthews To Be United States Ambassador to Malta
July 11, 1985

The President today announced his intention to nominate Gary L. Matthews, of Virginia, a career member of the Senior Foreign Service, Class of Minister-Counselor, to be Ambassador of the United States of America to the Republic of Malta. He would succeed James Malone Rentschler.

Mr. Matthews was appointed a Foreign Service officer and began his training in 1961. In 1962 he went to Bonn, Germany, as a rotational officer, where he served until 1964 when he returned to the Department as an operations center watch officer. In 1965–1966 he took Polish language training at the Foreign Service Institute. In 1966 he became a consular officer at the U.S. Embassy in Warsaw, Poland, and in 1967–1968 served as political/economic officer at the American Consulate in Poznan, Poland. In 1968 he took Soviet/East European studies at Columbia University in New York. In 1969–1971 he was an international relations officer in the Office of Soviet Union Affairs. From there, in 1971, he became an assistant province adviser in Quang Nam; deputy, then province senior adviser in Thau Thien and the City of Hue in the Republic of Vietnam. In 1973 he became deputy principal officer and political/economic officer at the American Consulate General in Leningrad, U.S.S.R. In 1976 Mr. Matthews went on a detail assignment to the Governor as director of international business development, State government of Missouri, Jefferson City. In 1977–1980 he was officer-in-charge, multilateral political relations in the Office of Soviet Union Affairs, to be followed as special assistant to the special adviser on Soviet affairs in the Department. In 1981–1982 he was Executive Assistant to the Under Secretary of State for Political Affairs and then in 1982 Executive Assistant, to be followed as Executive Assistant to the Deputy Secretary of State. In 1982–1983 he was a member of the executive seminar in national and international affairs at the Department. Since 1983 he has been Senior Deputy Assistant Secretary of State for Human Rights and Humanitarian Affairs.

Mr. Matthews was born January 24, 1938, in Springfield, MO. He graduated from Drury College (B.A., 1960), Oklahoma State University (M.A., 1961), and Columbia University (M.I.A., 1969). He served in the U.S. Army in 1955–1958. Mr. Matthews' foreign languages are Russian, Polish, and German. He is married to the former Virginia Webster, and they have three children.

Nomination of Irvin Hicks To Be United States Ambassador to Seychelles
July 11, 1985

The President today announced his intention to nominate Irvin Hicks, of Maryland, a career member of the Senior Foreign Service, Class of Counselor, as Ambassador to the Republic of Seychelles. He would succeed David Joseph Fischer.

Mr. Hicks began his career in 1961 as a clerk typist at the Department of the Army in Washington, DC. In 1962 he joined the Department of State, where he trained before going to the U.S. Embassy in Libreville, Gabon, as a communications clerk. He then became accounts assistant at our Embassy in Libreville, where he served until 1964 when he returned to the Department for training at the Foreign Service Institute. From 1964 to 1965, Mr. Hicks was accounts assistant at the U.S. Embassy in Bamako, Mali, to be followed as budget and fiscal specialist until 1966. From 1966 to 1967, he was a post management assistant in the Department, and from 1967 to 1968, an administrative support officer. In 1968 he took leave from the Department and served until 1969 as budget director for the Community Development Agency in New York. He returned to the Department in 1969 as an administrative support officer and in 1970 took further training at the Foreign Service Institute. From 1970 to 1973, he went to the American Embassy in Bangui, Central African Republic, as administrative officer. From there, in 1975 he became administrative officer at the U.S. Embassy in

Dar-es-Salaam, Tanzania, where he served until 1977 when he was assigned as administrative officer at the U.S. Mission in Berlin. From 1980 to 1981, Mr. Hicks was deputy chief of mission at the U.S. Embassy, Lome, Togo, and from 1981 to 1982, Chargé d'Affaires. He attended the U.S. Army War College in Carlisle, PA, in 1982–1983. Since 1983 Mr. Hicks has been Deputy Executive Director of the Bureau of African Affairs.

Mr. Hicks was born March 16, 1938, in Baltimore, MD. He received his B.A. in 1983 from the University of Maryland. His foreign language is French. He is married to the former Donita Buffalo, and they have three children.

Nomination of Herbert S. Okun To Be Deputy United States Representative to the United Nations
July 11, 1985

The President today announced his intention to nominate Herbert S. Okun, a career member of the Senior Foreign Service, Class of Minister-Counselor, to be the Deputy Representative of the United States of America to the United Nations with the rank and status of Ambassador. He would succeed Jose S. Sorzano.

Mr. Okun is currently ambassador-in-residence at the Aspen Institute in Washington, DC. Previously he served as United States Ambassador to East Germany. Prior to that assignment, he was deputy head of the U.S. delegation to the Trilateral Negotiations on a Comprehensive Test Ban Treaty and deputy chairman of the U.S. delegation to SALT. Earlier he was deputy chief of mission at the U.S. Embassy in Lisbon. Mr. Okun entered the Foreign Service in 1955 and was assigned to Munich as a consular officer. He then served in Belo Horizonte as consul and in Brasilia as principal officer and then counselor of the U.S. Embassy. After training at the Naval War College, Mr. Okun was Special Assistant to the Secretary of State and then was transferred to the Department's Office of Soviet Affairs. Named political adviser to the commander in chief of U.S. Forces in Southern Europe, he served in Naples until his transfer to Lisbon.

Mr. Okun graduated from Stanford University (B.A., 1951) and Harvard University (M.P.A., 1950). He speaks Portuguese, German, and Russian. He has three children and resides in Washington, DC. He was born November 27, 1930, in New York City.

Nomination of Hugh Montgomery To Be Alternate United States Representative to the United Nations for Special Political Affairs
July 11, 1985

The President today announced his intention to nominate Hugh Montgomery to be the Alternate Representative of the United States of America for Special Political Affairs in the United Nations with the rank of Ambassador. He would succeed Harvey J. Feldman.

He is currently serving as a member of the Senior Review Panel at the Central Intelligence Agency (CIA). He was Director of Intelligence and Research at the Department of State in 1981–1985. In 1953–1981 he was a national intelligence officer for Western Europe with the CIA.

Mr. Montgomery graduated from Harvard University (B.A., 1947; M.A., 1948; Ph.D., 1952). He is married, has three children, and resides in Arlington, VA. He was born November 29, 1923, in Springfield, MA.

Nomination of Patricia M. Byrne To Be Deputy United States Representative to the United Nations Security Council
July 11, 1985

The President today announced his intention to nominate Patricia M. Byrne, a career member of the Senior Foreign Service, Class of Minister-Counselor, to be Deputy Representative of the United States of America in the Security Council of the United Nations with the rank of Ambassador. She would succeed Richard Schifter.

Miss Byrne is currently a foreign affairs fellow at Georgetown University. Previously, she served as Ambassador to Burma, Ambassador to Mali, deputy chief of mission in Colombo, and a political officer in Paris. She also participated in the Geneva conference on Indochina. She entered the Foreign Service in 1949 and was assigned to Athens. After 2 years in Saigon, she was posted to the Laos desk in Washington. An assignment to Izmir was followed by a tour in Ankara. She served in Vientiane as a political officer and then was in charge of dependent areas affairs in the Bureau of International Organization Affairs. After a tour as a personnel officer, she was special assistant in the Central Administrative Office, followed by a training detail at the National War College. She then was political officer in Paris, specializing in Southeast Asia.

Miss Byrne graduated from Vassar College (B.A., 1946) and the Johns Hopkins School of Advanced International Studies (M.A.). She is fluent in French. She was born June 1, 1925, in Cleveland, OH, and now resides in Washington, DC.

Nomination of Joseph Verner Reed To Be United States Representative to the United Nations Economic and Social Council
July 11, 1985

The President today announced his intention to nominate Joseph Verner Reed to be the Representative of the United States of America on the Economic and Social Council of the United Nations with the rank of Ambassador. He would succeed Alan Lee Keyes.

Mr. Reed served as Ambassador to Morocco from 1981 until June 1985. In 1963–1981 he was with Chase Manhattan Bank of North America in New York City, serving as assistant to the director (1963–1968), vice president and executive assistant to chairman David Rockefeller (1969–1981), and vice president and adviser to the chairman (1981). He was an assistant to the President of the International Bank for Reconstruction and Development in 1961–1963.

He graduated from Yale University (B.A., 1961). He is married, has two children, and resides in Greenwich, CT. He was born December 17, 1937, in New York City.

Statement on Signing the Export Administration Amendments Act of 1985
July 12, 1985

I have signed into law S. 883, the "Export Administration Amendments Act of 1985," which amends and reauthorizes the Export Administration Act (EAA) of 1979.

The Congress and the executive branch have worked long and hard to produce the compromise contained in this complex and controversial legislation. Lengthy negotiations nearly produced a bill in the final hours of the 98th Congress. The 99th Congress took up the legislation with renewed determination. The bill I have signed reflects that determination as well as congressional willingness to compromise to resolve difficult problems.

I believe that this new law, which reflects compromise by all concerned parties, strikes an acceptable balance between enhancing our commercial interests and protecting our national security interests.

• To ensure national security, this law provides expanded enforcement authority, takes numerous steps to strengthen COCOM (an informal organization that provides for multilateral controls), and, by establishing new statutory crimes for illegal exports, provides enforcement officials with an effective tool to reduce illegal diversions.

• To make our exporters more competitive, this law decontrols the exports of low-tech items to COCOM members, liberalizes licensing where comparable goods are widely available in the international marketplace, and provides for expanded congressional and private sector roles in the export control program.

During the congressional deliberations on the EAA, I stated that there must be adequate discretionary authority to allow the President to manage the export control program. I regret that in the new law the Congress has prescribed several new administrative arrangements and reporting requirements that make the export control program more difficult to manage. However, I am pleased that the Congress also has acknowledged the administration's efforts to resolve issues administratively. One example of this is my recent instruction to the Commerce and Defense Departments to work together to develop licensing procedures for specific commodities and countries. These procedures are now in place and are being overseen by the National Security Council.

During the EAA debate, the Congress faced numerous controversial issues on which each of the competing sides had compelling arguments for its position. One such contentious issue was whether the contracts of U.S. exporters would be protected if foreign policy controls were imposed. The Congress agreed to compromise language that allows the President to break existing contracts if the strategic interests of the United States are threatened. This provision will allow U.S. exporters to be perceived as more reliable suppliers, while at the same time maintaining adequate presidential authority to respond to those instances where the country's strategic interests are at risk.

Another controversial issue addressed was the administrative arrangements for the enforcement of the act. The new law grants enhanced enforcement powers to the Customs Service and the Department of Commerce by providing both agencies with police powers. In addition, the new law grants primary authority to the Customs Service to conduct investigations overseas and provides that the Commerce Department's overseas activities will relate principally to prelicensing and postshipment investigations. It is clear that the Congress envisions significant roles for both agencies. Thus, I intend to direct both agencies to cooperate to ensure effective and complementary roles in enforcement of our export control laws.

This new law also contains provisions regarding congressional procedures for reviewing nuclear cooperation agreements. It adds a 30-day consultation period to the current 60-day congressional review period. Under these new procedures, the President has the discretion to approve execution of

913

an agreement before transmitting it for either period. If approved for execution before the 30-day period, the agreement would not have to be resubmitted; a single submission would be legally sufficient. I expect that these new procedures for congressional review will apply to the agreement for cooperation with Finland, which I transmitted to the Congress on May 21, 1985.

It is clear that the new EAA involves a delicate balancing of national as well as programmatic objectives. I do want to acknowledge the invaluable role in securing final enactment of this legislation by the bill managers—Senators Jake Garn and John Heinz and Representatives Don Bonker and Toby Roth.

Note: S. 883, approved July 12, was assigned Public Law No. 99-64.

Executive Order 12525—Termination of Emergency Authority for Export Controls
July 12, 1985

By the authority vested in me as President by the Constitution and laws of the United States of America, including section 203 of the International Emergency Economic Powers Act (50 U.S.C. 1702) (hereinafter referred to as "IEEPA"), 22 U.S.C. 287c, and the Export Administration Act of 1979, as amended (50 U.S.C. App. 2401 *et seq.*) (hereinafter referred to as "the Act"), it is hereby ordered as follows:

Section 1. In view of the extension by Public Law 99–64 (July 12, 1985) of the authorities contained in the Act, Executive Order No. 12470 of March 30, 1984, which continued in effect export control regulations under IEEPA, is revoked, and the declaration of economic emergency is rescinded.

Sec. 2. The revocation of Executive Order No. 12470 shall not affect any violation of any rules, regulations, orders, licenses, and other forms of administrative action under that Order that occurred during the period that Order was in effect. All rules and regulations issued or continued in effect under the authority of the IEEPA and that Order, including those published in Title 15, Chapter III, Subchapter C, of the Code of Federal Regulations, Parts 368 to 399 inclusive, and all orders, regulations, licenses, and other forms of administrative action issued, taken or continued in effect pursuant thereto, shall remain in full force and effect, as if issued, taken or continued in effect pursuant to and as authorized by the Act or by other appropriate authority until amended or revoked by the proper authority. Nothing in this Order shall affect the continued applicability of the provision for the administration of the Act and delegations of authority set forth in Executive Order No. 12002 of July 7, 1977, and Executive Order No. 12214 of May 2, 1980.

Sec. 3. All rules, regulations, orders, licenses, and other forms of administrative action issued, taken or continued in effect pursuant to the authority of the IEEPA and Executive Order No. 12470 relating to the administration of Section 38(e) of the Arms Export Control Act (22 U.S.C. 2778(e)) shall remain in full force and effect until amended or revoked under proper authority.

Sec. 4. This Order shall take effect immediately.

RONALD REAGAN

The White House,
July 12, 1985.

[*Filed with the Office of the Federal Register, 2:29 p.m., July 12, 1985*]

Message to the Congress Transmitting a Report on the Termination of Emergency Authority for Export Controls
July 12, 1985

To the Congress of the United States:

This report is submitted pursuant to Section 204 of the International Emergency Economic Powers Act (50 U.S.C. 1703) and Section 401(c) of the National Emergencies Act (50 U.S.C. 1641(c)) to account for government expenditures attributable to the national economic emergency that I declared following the lapse of the Export Administration Act of 1979, as amended (50 U.S.C. App. 2401 *et seq.*) (EAA), on March 30, 1984. On that date, I issued Executive Order No. 12470 to continue in effect the system of controls that had been established under the EAA. In view of the extension by Public Law 99–64 (July 12, 1985) of the authorities contained in the EAA, this emergency authority is no longer needed.

Accordingly, I have today issued Executive Order No. 12525, a copy of which is attached, rescinding the declaration of an economic emergency and revoking Executive Order No. 12470.

The export controls were not significantly expanded during the emergency period, and the administration of the system of controls continued in the normal course. Accordingly, the government spent no funds over and above what would have been spent had the EAA remained in force without interruption.

RONALD REAGAN

The White House,
July 12, 1985.

Nomination of Raymond D. Lett To Be an Assistant Secretary of Agriculture
July 12, 1985

The President today announced his intention to nominate Raymond D. Lett to be an Assistant Secretary of Agriculture (Marketing and Inspection Services). He would succeed C.W. McMillan.

Mr. Lett is currently serving at the Department of Agriculture as Executive Assistant to the Secretary. He was assistant director of the State of Illinois Department of Agriculture in 1977–1981; State executive director of the Agricultural Stabilization and Conservation Service (ASCS) in Illinois in 1971–1977; and district director for northeast Illinois of the ASCS in 1968–1971.

He graduated from Iowa State University (B.A., 1956). He is married, has three children, and resides in Vienna, VA. He was born December 16, 1934, in Sandwich, IL.

Nomination of Vance L. Clark To Be Administrator of the Farmers Home Administration
July 12, 1985

The President today announced his intention to nominate Vance L. Clark to be Administrator of the Farmers Home Administration, Department of Agriculture. He would succeed Charles Wilson Shuman.

Mr. Clark is a member of the board of directors of the Producers Cotton Oil Co. He also serves as a commissioner of the

California Student Aid Commission. He retired from the Bank of America in 1983 after 42 years of service in various positions and locations throughout California. He is past president of the Fresno County and City Chamber of Commerce.

He graduated from Nebraska Business College (1941). He is married, has three children, and resides in Fresno, CA. He was born September 17, 1923, in St. Paul, NE.

Nomination of Joyce A. Doyle To Be a Member of the Federal Mine Safety and Health Review Commission
July 12, 1985

The President today announced his intention to nominate Joyce A. Doyle to be a member of the Federal Mine Safety and Health Review Commission for the remainder of the term expiring August 30, 1986. She would succeed Rosemary M. Collyer.

Ms. Doyle is currently serving as assistant general counsel of Belco Petroleum Corp. in New York City. Previously she was with the New York law firm of Fogarty, McLaughlin and Semel, where she served as an attorney in 1973–1976.

She graduated from Youngstown State University (B.A., 1960), Catholic University (M.A., 1964), and Fordham University School of Law (J.D., 1972). She was born August 13, 1937, in Youngstown, OH, and now resides in New York, NY.

Nomination of Richard S. Nicholson To Be an Assistant Director of the National Science Foundation
July 12, 1985

The President today announced his intention to nominate Richard S. Nicholson to be an Assistant Director of the National Science Foundation (Mathematical and Physical Sciences). He would succeed Edward A. Knapp.

He has been serving as Acting Deputy Director and Staff Director of the National Science Foundation since 1983. He has been at the National Science Foundation since 1970 serving most recently as Deputy Assistant Director for the Mathematical and Physical Sciences in 1980–1982; Director of the Chemistry Division in 1977–1982; Director of the Division of Information Systems in 1979–1980; Senior Planning Officer for the Mathematical and Physical Sciences in 1978–1979; and Special Assistant to the Director in 1976–1977.

He graduated from Iowa State University (B.S., 1960) and the University of Wisconsin (Ph.D., 1964). He is married, has two children, and resides in McLean, VA. He was born April 5, 1938, in Des Moines, IA.

Appointment of Philip B. Elfstrom as a Member of the Advisory Commission on Intergovernmental Relations
July 12, 1985

The President today announced his intention to appoint Philip B. Elfstrom of Kane County, Illinois, to be a member of the Advisory Commission on Intergovernmental

Relations for a term of 2 years. He would succeed William J. Murphy.

Mr. Elfstrom is county commissioner of Kane County in Illinois and also serves as president of the National Association of Counties. He has been a member of the board of directors of the National Association of Counties for 11 years. Since 1982 he has been president of the Kane County Forest Preserve Commission. In 1961–1982 he was owner of Bader Publishing Co. in Batavia, IL.

Mr. Elfstrom graduated from the University of Kentucky (B.S., 1950). He was born July 14, 1928, in Evanston, IL, and now resides in Batavia, IL.

Nomination of George D. Gould To Be Under Secretary of the Treasury
July 12, 1985

The President today announced his intention to nominate George D. Gould to be Under Secretary of the Treasury. He would succeed Norman B. Ture.

Since 1976 he has been serving as chairman and chief executive officer of Madison Resources, Inc. He has also been a general partner in the investment banking firm of Wertheim and Co. since January 1985. Previously he was chairman of the Donaldson, Lufkin & Jenrette Securities Corp. in 1961–1976. He was with Jeremiah Millbank Investments in 1955–1961.

He graduated from Yale University (B.A., 1951) and Harvard Business School (M.B.A., 1955). He is married, has one child, and resides in New York City. He was born May 22, 1927, in Boston, MA.

Appointment of George Deukmejian as a Member of the United States Holocaust Memorial Council
July 12, 1985

The President today announced his intention to appoint George Deukmejian to be a member of the United States Holocaust Memorial Council for the remainder of the term expiring January 15, 1986. He will succeed Mario M. Cuomo.

He was elected Governor of California in 1982 and was inaugurated on January 3, 1983. Previously he was attorney general for the State of California in 1979–1982. He served as a member of the California State Senate in 1967–1979. Prior to that time, he was a member of the California State Assembly (1963–1967).

Governor Deukmejian graduated from Sienna College (B.A., 1949) and St. John's University (J.D., 1952). He is married, has three children, and resides in Sacramento, CA. He was born June 6, 1928, in Albany, NY.

Radio Address to the Nation on the Strategic Defense Initiative
July 13, 1985

My fellow Americans:
In a television address to the Nation on March 23, 1983, I challenged the scientific community to change the course of history

by embarking on a research effort to counter Soviet threats with measures purely defensive—measures to reassure people their security no longer depends alone on threats of mutual nuclear annihilation to deter a Soviet attack, but measures enabling us to intercept and destroy ballistic missiles before they reach our soil or that of our allies. A nonnuclear strategic defense makes good sense. It's better to protect lives than to avenge them. But another reason, equally simple and compelling, persuades us to its merit. As the Book of Luke says: "If a strong man shall keep his court well guarded, he shall live in peace." Well, SDI, our Strategic Defense Initiative, could prove crucial to guarding security and peace for America and her allies.

The strategic challenges we face are far different from those in 1972, when the United States and the Soviet Union signed the SALT I and antiballistic missile treaties. When those treaties were signed, certain assumptions about the Soviets were made that—well, to put it charitably—have not proven justified. For example, it was assumed the treaties would lead to a stable balance and, ultimately, to real reductions in strategic arms. But the Soviet Union has never accepted any meaningful and verifiable reductions in offensive nuclear arms—none. It was assumed the treaties were based on acceptance of parity in offensive weapons systems, but the Soviets have continued to race for superiority. As former Secretary of Defense Harold Brown put it, "When we build, they build. When we stop, they build." It was assumed the Soviets would accept the innocent notion that being mutually vulnerable to attack was in our common interest. They haven't.

The Soviets have repeatedly condemned as provocative our research on defense against their first-strike missiles, while blanketing their own country with the most sophisticated air defense system ever seen to protect against our second-strike bombers. And while we dismantled our lone ABM system 10 years ago, the Soviets have consistently improved the world's only missile defense system deployed around Moscow. They've also developed and deployed the world's only operational killer satellite system and then proceeded to condemn the

United States for daring even to test such a weapon.

It was assumed that an effective defense would not be feasible in 1972. But in that very year, Soviet Marshal Grechko testified to the Supreme Soviet: "The treaty on limiting ABM systems imposes no limitations on the performance of research and experimental work aimed at resolving the problem of defending the country against nuclear missile attack." Thus, the Soviets have devoted a huge share of their military budget to a sophisticated strategic defense program which, in resources already allocated, far exceeds what the United States anticipates spending in the current decade.

Finally, it was assumed that the agreements signed would be complied with, but the Soviets are seriously violating them in both offensive and defensive areas. It is the Soviet Union that has violated the 1972 ABM treaty with its construction of a massive radar facility at Krasnoyarsk. Further, the Soviet Union has tested and deployed sophisticated air defense systems which we judge may have capabilities against ballistic missiles.

Given these facts, is it not preposterous for the Soviets, already researching defense technologies for two decades, to now condemn our embryonic SDI program? And as Paul Nitze, one of my chief arms control advisers, pointed out, Soviet hypocrisy is even more glaring when we realize who's taking advantage of our open society to propagandize against our SDI program. A letter to the New York Times denouncing SDI was signed by the very Soviet scientists who've been developing the Soviet strategic defense program; other Soviet scientists who signed have spent their entire careers developing offensive weapons. I intend to mention this when I meet with Mr. Gorbachev in Geneva this November. I will tell him the United States not only has the right to go forward with research for a strategic missile defense, but in light of the scale of their program we'd be the greatest fools on Earth not to do so.

We're going to put our best scientists to work. We're going to cooperate with our allies. We're going to push forward in full compliance with the ABM treaty on a

918

broad-based research program, whose results to date are immensely encouraging.
And, yes, I hope we will one day develop a
security shield that destroys weapons, not
people.

Until next week, thanks for listening. God
bless you.

*Note: The President's remarks were recorded
at 5 p.m. on July 11 in the Roosevelt Room
at the White House for broadcast at 12:06
p.m. on July 13.*

Letter to the President Pro Tempore of the Senate and the Speaker of the House on the Discharge of the President's Powers and Duties During His Surgery
July 13, 1985

Dear Mr. President: (Dear Mr. Speaker:)

I am about to undergo surgery during
which time I will be briefly and temporarily
incapable of discharging the Constitutional
powers and duties of the Office of the President of the United States.

After consultation with my Counsel and
the Attorney General, I am mindful of the
provisions of Section 3 of the 25th Amendment to the Constitution and of the uncertainties of its application to such brief and
temporary periods of incapacity. I do not
believe that the drafters of this Amendment
intended its application to situations such as
the instant one.

Nevertheless, consistent with my longstanding arrangement with Vice President
George Bush, and not intending to set a
precedent binding anyone privileged to
hold this Office in the future, I have determined and it is my intention and direction
that Vice President George Bush shall discharge those powers and duties in my stead
commencing with the administration of an-
esthesia to me in this instance.

I shall advise you and the Vice President
when I determine that I am able to resume
the discharge of the Constitutional powers
and duties of this Office.

May God bless this Nation and us all.

Sincerely,

RONALD REAGAN

*Note: Identical letters were sent to Strom
Thurmond, President pro tempore of the
Senate, and Thomas P. O'Neill, Jr., Speaker
of the House of Representatives. The Vice
President temporarily assumed the powers
and duties of the Office of the President
from 11:28 a.m. until 7:22 p.m. on July 13.
At 11:28 a.m. the President underwent in-
testinal surgery at Bethesda Naval Hospital
for the removal of a polyp. Subsequent
analysis revealed that it was malignant but
that the cancer had not spread and no further therapy was necessary. The President
recovered more rapidly than anticipated
and was released from the hospital on July
20.*

Letter to the President Pro Tempore of the Senate and the Speaker of the House on the President's Resumption of His Powers and Duties Following Surgery
July 13, 1985

Dear Mr. President: (Dear Mr. Speaker:)

Following up on my letter to you of this
date, please be advised I am able to resume

the discharge of the Constitutional powers
and duties of the Office of the President of
the United States. I have informed the Vice

President of my determination and my resumption of those powers and duties.

Sincerely,

RONALD REAGAN

Note: Identical letters were sent to Strom Thurmond, President pro tempore of the Senate, and Thomas P. O'Neill, Jr., Speaker of the House of Representatives.

Nomination of John Gunther Dean To Be United States Ambassador to India
July 15, 1985

The President today announced his intention to nominate John Gunther Dean, of New York, as Ambassador to India. He would succeed Harry G. Barnes, Jr.

In 1950 Mr. Dean entered government service as economic analyst with the Economic Cooperation Administration in Paris. In 1951–1952 he was an industrial analyst in Brussels. In 1953–1956 he was assistant economic commissioner with the International Cooperation Administration in Saigon, Phnom Penh, and Vientiane. Mr. Dean entered on duty in the Department of State in 1956. In 1956–1958 he served as political officer in Vientiane and in 1959–1960 as consular officer in Lome. In 1960–1961 he was Chargé d'Affaires in Bamako and then became officer in charge of Mali-Togo affairs in the Department in 1961–1963. In 1963 Mr. Dean was adviser to the U.S. delegation to the 18th Session of the United Nations General Assembly, and in 1964–1965 he was an international relations officer in the Department. He went to Paris in 1965 as political officer and served there until 1969. In 1969–1970 he was a fellow at the Harvard Center for International Affairs in Cambridge, MA. He was then detailed to the Agency for International Development and served as Regional Director CORDS in Saigon until 1972. In 1972–1974 he was deputy chief of mission/counselor in Vientiane. In 1974–1975 he was Ambassador to the Khmer Republic; in 1975–1978 he was Ambassador to Denmark; in 1978–1981 he was Ambassador to Lebanon, and since 1981 he has been serving as Ambassador to the Kingdom of Thailand.

Mr. Dean graduated from Harvard University (B.S., 1947; M.A., 1950). He received his doctorate in 1949 from the Institut des Hautes Études (Paris). He served as a lieutenant in the United States Army in 1944–1946. His foreign languages are French, German, and Danish. He is married to the former Martine Duphenieux, and they have three children. He was born February 24, 1926, in Germany (naturalized in 1944).

Nomination of James W. Spain To Be United States Ambassador to Sri Lanka and Maldives
July 15, 1985

The President today announced his intention to nominate James W. Spain, of California, a career member of the Senior Foreign Service, Class of Career Minister, as Ambassador to the Democratic Socialist Republic of Sri Lanka and to the Republic of Maldives. He would succeed John Hathaway Reed.

Mr. Spain began his career as a consultant to the Secretary of the Army in Tokyo, Japan, in 1949–1950. In 1951 he served as a vice consul in Karachi, Pakistan. He taught at Columbia University in 1953–1954 and in 1955 became an analyst, Office of National Estimates at the Central Intelligence Agency until 1963. He served as a member of the policy planning council in the Department in 1963. He then became director, Office of Research and Analysis for the Middle East and South Asia, in 1964–1966. He taught at American University between 1965–1967. In 1966 he was director, Pakistan and Afghanistan affairs, and in 1969 he became Chargé d'Affaires at the U.S. Embassy in Islamabad, Pakistan. From there, in 1970 he went to Istanbul, Turkey, as consul general. In 1972–1974 Mr. Spain was deputy chief of mission in Ankara, Turkey. He went to Florida State University in Tallahassee as diplomat in residence in 1974–1975. In 1975 he became Ambassador to Tanzania. In 1979 he went to New York as Deputy U.S. Representative to the United Nations, returning in 1980 to become Ambassador to Turkey. Since 1982 he has been a foreign affairs fellow, Carnegie Endowment for International Peace and the Rand Corp., in Washington, DC.

Mr. Spain graduated from the University of Chicago (M.A., 1949) and Columbia University (Ph.D., 1959). He served in the United States Army in 1946–1947. His foreign languages are French and Turkish. Mr. Spain has three children and resides in Washington, DC. He was born July 22, 1926, in Chicago, IL.

Nomination of Leo C. McKenna To Be a Member of the Advisory Board of the Saint Lawrence Seaway Development Corporation
July 15, 1985

The President today announced his intention to nominate Leo C. McKenna to be a member of the Advisory Board of the Saint Lawrence Seaway Development Corporation, Department of Transportation. He would succeed Jacob L. Bernheim.

He is a self-employed financial analyst in New York City. He was vice president and member of the board of Dominick & Dominick, Inc., in 1973–1974; president and chief executive officer of Lombard, Nelson & McKenna, Inc., in 1967–1973; and staff assistant to the president of W.R. Grace & Co. in 1961–1967.

Mr. McKenna graduated from Dartmouth College (A.B., 1956) and the Amos Tuck School of Business (M.B.A., 1957). He has four children and resides in New York City. He was born October 9, 1933, in Concord, MA.

Appointment of 14 Members of the President's Blue Ribbon Commission on Defense Management
July 15, 1985

The President today announced his intention to appoint the membership of the President's Blue Ribbon Commission on Defense Management. In addition to David Packard, who was previously announced to serve as Chairman, the President has selected the following individuals to serve as members of the Commission:

Ernest Arbuckle, of California, dean emeritus, graduate school of business, Stanford University;

Gen. Robert H. Barrow, of Louisiana, former Commandant of the U.S. Marine Corps;

Nicholas F. Brady, of New Jersey, chairman, Dillon, Read and Co., Inc.;

Louis Wellington Cabot, of Massachusetts, chairman of the board, Cabot Corp.;

Frank C. Carlucci, of Virginia, chairman and chief executive officer, Sears World Trade, Inc.;

William P. Clark, of California, counsel, Rogers and Wells;

Gen. Paul Francis Gorman, of Virginia, vice president, Burdeshaw and Associates;

Carla Anderson Hills, of Washington, DC, partner, Latham, Watkins and Hills;

Adm. James Holloway, of Maryland, president, Council of American Flagship Operators;

William James Perry, of California, managing director, Hambrecht and Quist;

Charles J. Pilliod, Jr., of Ohio, director and consultant, Goodyear Tire and Rubber Co.;

Gen. Brent Scowcroft, of Maryland, vice chairman, Kissinger Associates, Inc.;

Herbert Stein, of Virginia, senior fellow, American Enterprise Institute; and

Robert James Woolsey, of Maryland, partner, Shea and Gardner.

Appointment of W. Dennis Thomas as Assistant to the President
July 15, 1985

The President announced today his intention to appoint W. Dennis Thomas as Assistant to the President.

Mr. Thomas most recently has been a partner and associate director of the national office of Touche Ross, an international accounting firm. He joined the firm in May 1985. From December 1983 to May 1985, Mr. Thomas worked in the White House as Deputy Assistant to the President for Legislative Affairs, serving as the President's liaison with the House of Representatives. From January 1981 to December 1983, he served as Assistant Secretary for Legislative Affairs, Department of the Treasury. From 1976 to 1981, Mr. Thomas served as administrative assistant to Senator William V. Roth, Jr. (R-DE). From 1974 to 1976, Mr. Thomas was administrative assistant to Senator J. Glenn Beall, Jr. (R-MD). From 1971 to 1974, he served as executive assistant to Senator Beall, and from 1969 to 1970, he served as special assistant to then Congressman Beall. Mr. Thomas was a member of the administrative staff of the Carroll County, MD, board of education from 1967 to 1968.

He graduated from Frostburg State College in Frostburg, MD, in 1965. He received his master's degree from the University of Maryland in 1967. Mr. Thomas is married and has one son. He lives with his family in Bethesda, MD. Mr. Thomas is 41 years old.

Remarks of the First Lady at a White House Reception for the Diplomatic Corps
July 15, 1985

Good evening, and welcome to the White House. My husband is sorry he can't be with you, and I'm sort of a stand-in. But he's asked me to give you his very best wishes and his regrets.

Now, to conductor John Williams and all the members of the Boston Pops, I know I speak for the entire audience when I say thank you for that wonderful performance. Through the years, 19 conductors have presided over the orchestra, including the beloved Arthur Fiedler. John Williams is a noted composer, a brilliant conductor, and, as I think you will all agree, a true showman. So, to one of America's oldest and most enjoyable cultural institutions—thank you, again, and a very happy 100th birthday.

Now, having thanked the performers, I can't resist a remark or two about the audience. A diplomatic manual written long ago by a noted Frenchman comes as close as anything to describing you, the diplomats we here have come to know. "A good diplomat," it states, "must have an observant mind, a spirit of application which refuses to be distracted, a mind so fertile as easily to smooth away the difficulties, an equitable humor, always open, genial, civil, and agreeable." And for your untiring grace and charm, for the dedication which each of you represents your nation, we thank you.

Today we've enjoyed the beauty of music and the pleasures of a summer evening shared with friends. So, we need nothing more to remind us of the fruits of freedom and peace. My husband joins me in wishing and praying that good will may forever reign between the people of our country and those of yours.

Thank you, and God bless you all.

Note: Mrs. Reagan spoke at 5:40 p.m. on the South Lawn of the White House. The President, who was in Bethesda Naval Hospital recovering from surgery, was unable to attend the reception.

Executive Order 12526—President's Blue Ribbon Commission on Defense Management
July 15, 1985

By the authority vested in me as President by the Constitution and the laws of the United States of America, and in order to establish, in accordance with the provisions of the Federal Advisory Committee Act, as amended (5 U.S.C. App. I), a Blue Ribbon Commission on Defense Management, it is hereby ordered as follows:

Section 1. Establishment. (a) There is established the President's Blue Ribbon Commission on Defense Management. The Commission shall be composed of no fewer than ten and no more than seventeen members appointed or designated by the President.

(b) The composition of the Commission shall include persons with extensive experience and national reputations in commerce and industry, as well as persons with broad experience in government and national defense.

(c) The President shall designate a Chairman from among the members of the Commission. The Chairman shall appoint a professional and administrative staff to support the Commission.

Sec. 2. Functions. (a) The Commission shall study the issues surrounding defense management and organization, and report its findings and recommendations to the President and simultaneously submit a copy of its report to the Secretary of Defense.

(b) The primary objective of the Commission shall be to study defense management policies and procedures, including the budget process, the procurement system, legislative oversight, and the organizational and operational arrangements, both formal and informal, among the Office of the Secretary of Defense, the Organization of the Joint Chiefs of Staff, the Unified and Specified Command system, the Military Departments, and the Congress. In particular, the Commission shall:

1. Review the adequacy of the defense acquisition process, including the adequacy of the defense industrial base, current law governing Federal and Department of Defense procurement activities, departmental directives and management procedures, and the execution of acquisition responsibilities within the Military Departments;

2. Review the adequacy of the current authority and control of the Secretary of Defense in the oversight of the Military Departments, and the efficiency of the decisionmaking apparatus of the Office of the Secretary of Defense;

3. Review the responsibilities of the Organization of the Joint Chiefs of Staff in providing for joint military advice and force development within a resource-constrained environment;

4. Review the adequacy of the Unified and Specified Command system in providing for the effective planning for and use of military forces;

5. Consider the value and continued role of intervening layers of command on the direction and control of military forces in

peace and in war;

6. Review the procedures for developing and fielding military systems incorporating new technologies in a timely fashion;

7. Study and make recommendations concerning congressional oversight and investigative procedures relating to the Department of Defense; and

8. Recommend how to improve the effectiveness and stability of resources allocation for defense, including the legislative process.

(c) In formulating its recommendations to the President, the Commission shall consider the appropriate means for implementing its recommendations. The Commission shall first devote its attention to the procedures and activities of the Department of Defense associated with the procurement of military equipment and materiel. It shall report its conclusions and recommendations on the procurement section of this study by December 31, 1985. The final report, encompassing the balance of the issues reviewed by the Commission, shall be submitted not later than June 30, 1986, with an interim report to be submitted not later than March 31, 1986.

(d) The Commission shall be in place and operating as soon as possible. Shortly thereafter, the Commission shall brief the Assistant to the President for National Security Affairs and the Secretary of Defense on the Commission's plan of action.

(e) Where appropriate, implementation of the Commission's recommendations shall be considered in accordance with regular administrative procedures coordinated by the Office of Management and Budget, and involving the National Security Council, the Department of Defense, and other departments or agencies as required.

Sec. 3. Administration. (a) The heads of Executive agencies shall, to the extent permitted by law, provide the Commission such information as it may require for purposes of carrying out its functions.

(b) Members of the Commission shall serve without additional compensation for their work on the Commission. However, members appointed from among private citizens may be allowed travel expenses, including per diem in lieu of subsistence, as authorized by law for persons serving intermittently in the government service (5 U.S.C. 5701–5707), to the extent funds are available.

(c) The Secretary of Defense shall provide the Commission with such administrative services, facilities, staff, and other support services as may be necessary. Any expenses of the Commission shall be paid from such funds as may be available to the Secretary of Defense.

Sec. 4. General. (a) Notwithstanding any other Executive order, the functions of the President under the Federal Advisory Committee Act, as amended, except that of reporting to the Congress, which are applicable to the Commission, shall be performed by the Secretary of Defense, in accordance with guidelines and procedures established by the Administrator of General Services.

(b) The Commission shall terminate 30 days after the submission of its final report.

RONALD REAGAN

The White House,
July 15, 1985.

[Filed with the Office of the Federal Register, 12:43 p.m., July 16, 1985]

Note: The Executive order was released by the Office of the Press Secretary on July 16.

Statement by Principal Deputy Press Secretary Speakes on the Soviet-United States Nuclear and Space Arms Negotiations
July 16, 1985

The United States and the Soviet Union completed today the second round of nuclear and space talks in Geneva. The primary U.S. goal remains significant, equitable, and verifiable reductions in the size of existing nuclear arsenals. The United States entered the second round of the nuclear and space talks with specific, detailed proposals on the table to achieve this goal and was prepared to make progress with the Soviet Union in each of the three negotiating areas.

In the area of strategic nuclear offensive arms, the U.S. delegation has flexibility in pursuing the significant reductions that we seek and is prepared to negotiate a number of specific, alternative paths that could lead to such reductions. With respect to intermediate-range nuclear forces (INF), our ultimate goal remains the elimination of the entire class of nuclear weapons carried on land-based INF missiles. Towards this end, the U.S. delegation also has flexibility and is authorized to pursue an interim agreement resulting in equal U.S. and Soviet global limits at the lowest possible level.

We were equally prepared and remain prepared for detailed exchanges in the area of defense and space. During the second round, regrettably, the Soviet position has remained entrenched, with no movement in their formal positions. The Soviet delegation repeated their moratoria proposals while continuing to precondition progress— or even detailed discussion—of offensive nuclear reductions on acceptance of their demands for unilateral U.S. concessions involving unrealistic and unverifiable constraints on research in the defense and space area.

Late in this round the Soviets surfaced some concepts which could involve possible reductions in existing strategic offensive nuclear arsenals. However, the method of aggregation proposed in these concepts seems designed to favor preservation of the Soviet Union's primary area of advantage; that is, in prompt hard-target kill capability, the most worrisome element in the current strategic equation. Efforts by the U.S. delegation to elicit Soviet answers to our questions about these concepts—with regard to issues such as numbers, ceilings, and rates of possible reduction—have thus far essentially gone unanswered. In this regard, we are disappointed that the Soviet Union has been unable to deal in concrete terms and with hard numbers, even framed as overall negotiating goals. And while the United States immediately probed the Soviet concepts, the Soviets unfortunately have refused to engage in discussion of the U.S. proposals.

In sum, we are about where we had expected to be given that we are ending only the second round of negotiations of such complexity and importance. We hope that the Soviet Union will be more forthcoming during the next round of negotiations.

Appointment of E.V. Hill as a Member of the Commission on the Bicentennial of the United States Constitution
July 16, 1985

The President today announced his intention to appoint E.V. Hill to be a member of the Commission on the Bicentennial of the United States Constitution. This is a new position.

Reverend Hill is pastor of Mount Zion Missionary Baptist Church of Los Angeles, CA. He was a member of the President's Task Force on Private Sector Initiatives in 1982.

He graduated from Prairie View College (B.S., 1955). He was born November 11, 1933, in Columbus, TX, and now resides in Los Angeles, CA.

Appointment of Mary S. Pyle as a Member of the National Council on Vocational Education
July 16, 1985

The President has announced his intention to appoint Mary S. Pyle to be a member of the National Council on Vocational Education for a term expiring January 17, 1987. This is a new position.

Ms. Pyle is supervisor of consumer marketing for the Mississippi Power Co. in Gulfport, MS. She has been with the Missis-sippi Power Co. since 1969 as an energy communications specialist and a home economist.

She graduated from Southwest Junior College (A.A., 1967) and the University of Southern Mississippi (B.S., 1969). She was born March 27, 1948, in Magnolia, MS, and now resides in Gulfport, MS.

Nomination of Douglas H. Ginsburg To Be an Assistant Attorney General
July 17, 1985

The President today announced his intention to nominate Douglas H. Ginsburg to be an Assistant Attorney General (Antitrust Division), Department of Justice. He would succeed J. Paul McGrath.

Since 1984 Mr. Ginsburg has been Administrator for Information and Regulatory Affairs in the Office of Management and Budget. Previously he was Deputy Assistant Attorney General for Regulatory Affairs, Antitrust Division, in 1983–1984. He was at Harvard University as professor of law (1981–1983) and assistant professor of law (1975–1981). He was law clerk at the U.S. Supreme Court (1974–1975) and the U.S. Court of Appeals (1973–1974).

Mr. Ginsburg graduated from Cornell University (B.S., 1970) and the University of Chicago Law School (J.D., 1973). He is married, has two children, and resides in Washington, DC. He was born May 25, 1946, in Chicago, IL.

Nomination of Richard Kennon Willard To Be an Assistant Attorney General
July 17, 1985

The President today announced his intention to nominate Richard Kennon Willard to be an Assistant Attorney General (Civil Division), Department of Justice. He would succeed William F. Baxter.

Since 1983 Mr. Willard has been serving as Acting Assistant Attorney General, Civil Division. Previously he was at the Justice Department as Deputy Assistant Attorney General, Civil Division (1982–1983), and counsel for intelligence policy (1981–1982). He was an attorney with the law firm of Baker & Botts in Houston, TX, in 1977–1981. Prior to that time, he was a law clerk to the Honorable Harry A. Blackmun, Supreme Court of the United States (1976–1977), and to the Honorable Anthony M. Kennedy, U.S. Court of Appeals, Ninth Circuit in Sacramento, CA (1975–1976).

He graduated from Emory University (B.A., 1969) and Harvard Law School (J.D., 1975). He is married, has two children, and resides in Arlington, VA. He was born September 1, 1948, in Houston, TX.

Nomination of Robert Vossler Keeley To Be United States Ambassador to Greece
July 17, 1985

The President today announced his intention to nominate Robert Vossler Keeley, of Florida, a career member of the Senior Foreign Service, Class of Minister-Counselor, to be Ambassador of the United States of America to Greece. He would succeed Monteagle Stearns.

Mr. Keeley began his government career as a personnel clerk with the Department of Agriculture in 1955. In 1956 he joined the Department of State and was assigned to the Executive Secretariat of the International Cooperation Administration. In 1958 he went to the U.S. Embassy in Jordan as political officer and served there until 1961, when he was assigned to Bamako, Mali. In 1963–1965 he was desk officer for Zaire, Congo, Rwanda, and Burundi. Mr. Keeley was then assigned to the U.S. Embassy in Athens, Greece, as political officer and from there in 1971 became deputy chief of mis-

sion in Kampala, Uganda. He returned to the Department in 1974 as Alternate Director of East African Affairs. He then served as deputy chief of mission in 1975–1976 in Phnom Penh, Khmer Republic, Cambodia. He returned to the Department and served as Deputy Director of the Interagency Task Force for Indochina Refugees until 1978, when he became Deputy Assistant Secretary for African Affairs. He was appointed Ambassador to Zimbabwe in 1980. Since 1984 Mr. Keeley has been senior fellow for the study of foreign affairs at the Foreign Service Institute.

Mr. Keeley graduated from Princeton University (A.B., 1951). His foreign languages are French and Greek. He served in the U.S. Coast Guard in 1953–1955. He is married to the former Louise Schoonmaker, and they have two children. He was born September 4, 1929, in Beirut, Lebanon.

Nomination of Francis J. Meehan To Be United States Ambassador to the German Democratic Republic
July 17, 1985

The President today announced his intention to nominate Francis J. Meehan, of Virginia, a career member of the Senior Foreign Service, Class of Career Minister, to be Ambassador of the United States of America to the German Democratic Republic. He would succeed Rozanne L. Ridgway.

Mr. Meehan began his government career as a clerk at the American Consulate General in Bremen, Federal Republic of Germany, in 1947–1948. He then became an administrative assistant with the Economic Cooperation Administration in Washington, DC, in 1948–1951. In 1951 he went to Frankfurt as an information officer with the U.S. High Commission for Germany and served there until 1952, when he was assigned to the American Consulate General

in Hamburg. In 1953 Mr. Meehan served in NATO, Paris, as a political officer. He was there until 1956, when he took Russian language training at the Department of State and Harvard University. He became an intelligence specialist in the Department in 1957 and in 1959 went to the U.S. Embassy in Moscow as political officer. He served there until 1961, when he was assigned to Berlin as political officer. In 1966–1968 Mr. Meehan was watch officer/director of the Department's Operation Center. From there he became deputy chief of mission at the U.S. Embassy in Budapest, Hungary, in 1968–1972. He then went to the U.S. Embassy in Bonn, Federal Republic of Germany, as political counselor in 1972–1975. In 1975 he went to the U.S. Embassy in Austria as deputy chief of mission and served there until 1977, when he returned to Bonn as deputy chief of mission. He served in Bonn until he became Ambassador to Czechoslovakia in 1979–1980. He was then named Ambassador to Poland in 1980 and served there until he became research professor at Georgetown University. He has continued at Georgetown until the present. From October 1984 to April 1985, he was also a senior foreign policy officer in the Office for Management Operations in the Department.

Mr. Meehan graduated from the University of Glasgow (M.A., 1945) and Harvard University (M.P.A., 1957). He served in the United States Army in 1945–1947. His foreign languages are German, French, Russian, Polish, Czech, and Hungarian. He is married to the former Margaret Kearns, and they have four children. He was born February 14, 1924, in East Orange, NJ.

Nomination of John Pierce Ferriter To Be United States Ambassador to Djibouti
July 17, 1985

The President today announced his intention to nominate John Pierce Ferriter, of Florida, a career member of the Senior Foreign Service, Class of Minister-Counselor, as Ambassador of the United States of America to the Republic of Djibouti. He would succeed Alvin P. Adams, Jr.

Mr. Ferriter was a law librarian with Mendes & Mount in New York in 1962–1963. In 1964 he became a junior Foreign Service officer and was assigned to the U.S. Embassy in Brazzaville, Congo, until 1965. He then served at the U.S Embassy in Mauritania. In 1966 he became an economic officer at the U.S. Mission to the Organization for Economic Cooperation and Development in Paris, France. He served there until 1970, when he returned to the Department of State as economic officer. In 1972 Mr. Ferriter became a staff member of the National Security Council, the White House. In 1972–1973 he took university training at Harvard University in Cambridge. In 1973 he went to the U.S. Embassy in Abidjan, Ivory Coast, as economic/commercial counselor until 1975. He then served at Paris, France, as commercial attaché until 1978. He returned to the Department's Economic Bureau first as Division Chief of the Tropical Products Division, then Director of the Office of International Commodities, followed by Director of the Office of Energy Consumer Country Affairs. From 1983 to the present, he has been deputy chief of mission at the U.S. Embassy in Kinshasa, Zaire.

Mr. Ferriter graduated from Queens College at the University of the City of New York (B.A., 1960), Fordham University School of Law (L.L.B., 1963), and Harvard University, J.F.K. School of Government (M.P.A., 1973). He also graduated from the U.S. Army War College in 1983. He served in the United States Marine Corps Reserve in 1955–1961. His foreign languages are French and Italian. Mr. Ferriter is married to the former Daniela Calvino. He was born January 26, 1938, in Boston, MA.

Nomination of Anthony J. Calio To Be Administrator of the National Oceanic and Atmospheric Administration
July 17, 1985

The President today announced his intention to nominate Anthony J. Calio to be Administrator of the National Oceanic and Atmospheric Administration, Department of Commerce. He would succeed John V. Byrne.

Since 1981 Mr. Calio has been serving as Deputy Administrator of the National Oceanic and Atmospheric Administration. Previously, he was Associate Administrator for Space and Terrestrial Applications for the National Aeronautics and Space Administration in 1977–1981; Deputy Associate Administrator for Space Sciences at NASA Headquarters in 1975–1977; Director of Science and Applications at Johnson Space Center in 1968–1975; and at NASA Headquarters as Assistant Director of Planetary Exploration (1967–1968) and Chief of Instrumentation and Systems Integration (1965–1967).

He graduated from the University of Pennsylvania (B.A., 1953). He is married, has four children, and resides in Potomac, MD. He was born October 27, 1929, in Philadelphia, PA.

Nomination of Orson G. Swindle III To Be an Assistant Secretary of Commerce
July 17, 1985

The President today announced his intention to nominate Orson G. Swindle III to be an Assistant Secretary of Commerce (Economic Development Administration). He would succeed J. Bonnie Newman.

Since June 1981 Mr. Swindle has been serving as Georgia State Director of the Farmers Home Administration within the U.S. Department of Agriculture. He was commissioned in the United States Marine Corps in 1959 and became a fighter pilot, flying over 200 missions in Southeast Asia. He was captured in North Vietnam in November 1966, where he was held prisoner for over 6 years. He was repatriated in March 1973. He was a financial manager for the Marine Corps Logistics Base in Albany, GA, in 1975–1979. In 1979 he retired from the Marine Corps with the rank of lieutenant colonel. He has over 20 personal decorations for valor, including two Silver Stars, two Bronze Stars, two Legions of Merit, two Purple Hearts, 13 Air Medals, and the Navy Commendation Medal.

Mr. Swindle graduated from Georgia Institute of Technology (B.S., 1959) and Florida State University (M.B.A., 1975). He is married, has one child, and resides in Camilla, GA. He was born March 8, 1937, in Thomasville, GA.

Message to the Senate Transmitting the United Kingdom-United States Supplementary Extradition Treaty
July 17, 1985

To the Senate of the United States:

With a view to receiving the advice and consent of the Senate to ratification, I transmit herewith the Supplementary Extradition Treaty between the United States of America and the United Kingdom, with annex, signed at Washington on June 25, 1985.

I transmit also, for the information of the Senate, the report of the Department of State with respect to the Supplementary Treaty.

The Supplementary Treaty adds to and amends the Extradition Treaty between United States and the United Kingdom, signed at London on June 8, 1972.

It represents a significant step in improving law enforcement cooperation and combatting terrorism, by excluding from the scope of the political offense exception serious offenses typically committed by terrorists, e.g., aircraft hijacking and sabotage, crimes against diplomats, hostage taking, and other heinous acts such as murder, manslaughter, malicious assault, and certain serious offenses involving firearms, explosives, and damage to property.

The Supplementary Treaty, in addition to narrowing the application of the political offense exception to extradition, will also help improve implementation of the current Extradition Treaty in several other respects. I recommend that the Senate give early and favorable consideration to the Supplementary Treaty and give its advice and consent to ratification.

RONALD REAGAN

The White House,
July 17, 1985.

Appointment of Philip A. Lacovara as a Member of the District of Columbia Judicial Nomination Commission
July 18, 1985

The President today announced his intention to appoint Philip A. Lacovara to be a member of the District of Columbia Judicial Nomination Commission for a term of 5 years. This is a reappointment.

Mr. Lacovara has been a partner in the law firm of Hughes Hubbard & Reed in Washington, DC, since 1974. Previously, he was counsel to the Special Prosecutor, Watergate Special Prosecution Force, in 1973–1974; Deputy Solicitor General of the United States in 1972–1973; special counsel to the police commissioner of the city of New York in 1971–1972; and Special Assistant to the Attorney General of the United States in 1970.

He graduated from Georgetown University (A.B., 1963) and Columbia University School of Law (LL.B., 1966). He is married, has seven children, and resides in Washington, DC. He was born July 11, 1943, in New York City.

Appointment of Anne E. Stanley as United States Representative on the South Pacific Commission
July 18, 1985

The President today announced his intention to appoint Anne E. Stanley to be the Representative of the United States of America on the South Pacific Commission for a term of 2 years. She will succeed William McBride Love.

Ms. Stanley is vice president of Russo-Watts and Associates in Alexandria, VA. She was with the National Republican Congressional Committee in 1979–1983, serving as deputy director of the campaign division; deputy director of the research division; and field director for the Western States. In 1973–1979 she was an account executive with George Young & Associates in Los Angeles, CA.

She graduated from George Washington University (B.A., 1964). She was born October 22, 1942, in Cape Girardeau, MO, and now resides in Alexandria, VA.

Appointment of Two Alternate United States Representatives on the South Pacific Commission
July 18, 1985

The President today announced his intention to appoint the following individuals to be Alternate Representatives of the United States on the South Pacific Commission for terms of 2 years:

John Henry Felix will succeed Frederick William Rohlfing. Mr. Felix is president and chief executive officer of Hawaiian Memorial Services in Honolulu. He has served as chairman of the Honolulu Planning Commission; Honolulu Redevelopment Agency; Honolulu Board of Parks and Recreation; and the Honolulu Civil Service. He is married, has five children, and resides in Honolulu, HI. He was born June 14, 1930, in Honolulu.

Bradford M. Freeman will succeed Frank D. Yturria. Mr. Freeman is a partner in the firm of Riordan, Freeman & Spogli in Los Angeles, CA. In 1966–1983 he was with Dean Witter Reynolds, Inc., serving most recently as managing director and member of the board of directors. Mr. Freeman has one child and resides in Los Angeles, CA. He was born March 11, 1942, in Fargo, ND.

Letter to Senate Majority Leader Dole Endorsing the Line-Item Veto Bill
July 18, 1985

Dear Bob:

As the Senate considers S. 43, I wanted you to know and convey to your colleagues my strong support for this initiative. As you know, I asked the Congress to pass this legislation in my State of the Union Address on February 6th. I am pleased that under your leadership the Senate is acting judiciously on this important matter.

The line-item veto authority would provide a powerful tool for eliminating wasteful and unnecessary spending. I've often made known my willingness to use such a veto authority judiciously—but firmly—to curtail the excesses often embedded in otherwise meritorious legislation. As Governor of the State of California, I had firsthand experience with the line-item veto and found it necessary to keep spending in check and used the line-item veto on over 900 occasions to remove unnecessary spending from the budget. In every instance the legislature agreed with my decision.

Given your strong and courageous efforts to date to reach a budget compromise with the House, I know you share my conviction that bringing Federal spending under control is essential if we are to sustain economic growth. Yet the uncertain outcome of that endeavor underscores the need to move forward on all fronts to hold down government spending.

The American people have a right to expect that all of us in government make every effort to eliminate deficit spending. I hope the Congress can move forward expeditiously on legislation providing line-item veto authority and not get sidetracked on procedural considerations. If the Congress acts responsibly on this issue, I pledge to do my part as well.

Sincerely,

/s/Ron

Note: The original was not available for verification of the content of this letter to Senator Robert Dole.

931

Remarks of the Vice President Announcing the Winner of the Teacher in Space Project
July 19, 1985

The Vice President. We're here today to announce the first private citizen passenger in the history of space flight. The President said last August that this passenger would be one of America's finest—a teacher. Well, since then, as we've heard, NASA, with the help of the heads of our State school systems, has searched the Nation for a teacher with "the right stuff." Really, there are thousands, thousands of teachers with the right stuff. And they're committed to quality in education; to teaching their students the basics—reading, writing, mathematics, science, literature, history—to teaching the foundations of our cultural heritage; to teaching the values that guide us as Americans; and to teaching that important, but difficult to obtain, quality—clarity of thought.

We're honoring all those teachers of merit today, and we're doing something else because the finalists here with me and the more than a hundred semifinalists will all in the months ahead serve, as Jim has said, as a link between NASA and the Nation's school system. These teachers have all received special NASA training to pass on to other teachers and to their students. And together they and NASA will be a part of an exciting partnership for quality in education.

So, let me tell you ow who our teacher in space will be. And let me say I thought I was a world traveler, but this tops anything I've tried. And first, the backup teacher, who will make the flight if the winner can't: Barbara Morgan of the McCall-Donnelly Elementary School in McCall, Idaho. Barbara has been a teacher for 11 years. She first taught on the Flathead Indian Reservation in Montana. She currently teaches second grade. Congratulations. And we have a little thing for you.

And the winner, the teacher who will be going into space: Christa McAuliffe. Where is—is that you? [*Laughter*] Christa teaches in Concord High School in Concord, New Hampshire. She teaches high school social studies. She's been teaching for 12 years. She plans to keep a journal of her experiences in space. She said that—and here's the quote—"Just as the pioneer travelers of the Conestoga wagon days kept personal journies [journals], I as a space traveler would do the same." Well, I'm personally looking forward to reading that journal some day.

And by the way, Christa, while you're in the program, Concord High obviously will need substitute teachers to fill in. And it's only right that we provide—[*laughter*]—one of these substitutes. So, the first class you miss, your substitute will be my dear friend and the President's, Bill Bennett, the Secretary of Education.

So, congratulations to all of you. Good luck, Christa, and God bless all of you. Thank you very much for coming. And you, too, get one of these.

Ms. McAuliffe. It's not often that a teacher is at a loss for words. I know my students wouldn't think so. I've made nine wonderful friends over the last 2 weeks. And when that shuttle goes, there might be one body, but there's going to be 10 souls that I'm taking with me.

Thank you.

Note: The Vice President spoke to the 10 project finalists at 1:18 p.m. in the Roosevelt Room at the White House. He was introduced by James M. Beggs, Administrator of the National Aeronautics and Space Administration. The winner and backup teacher were presented with small statues on behalf of NASA and the Council of Chief State School Officers. The President, who was in Bethesda Naval Hospital recovering from surgery, was unable to attend the event.

Nomination of John Blane To Be United States Ambassador to Chad
July 19, 1985

The President today announced his intention to nominate John Blane, of Illinois, to be Ambassador of the United States of America to the Republic of Chad. He would succeed Jay P. Moffat.

Mr. Blane served in the United States Army in 1953–1955. He entered the Foreign Service in 1956 and was vice consul in Mogadishu (1957), in Asmara (1958–1960), and in Salzburg (1960–1962). He attended Northwestern University in 1962–1963. He was political officer in Yaounde, Cameroon, in 1963–1966. He then returned to the Department as country officer for Togo, Dahomey, Chad, and Gabon (1966–1968) and Acting Director of Research for Northern and Eastern Africa in the Bureau of Intelligence and Research in 1968–1969. Mr. Blane was deputy chief of mission in Ft. Lamy, Chad, in 1969–1972. In 1973–1975 he was Director, Inter-African Affairs, in the Department. He was on detail as Director of Bilateral Programs Division of the Office of International Activities at the Environmental Protection Agency in 1975–1977. He was deputy chief of mission in Nairobi, Kenya, in 1977–1980 and a member of the executive seminar in national and international affairs at the Foreign Service Institute in 1980–1981. In 1981 he was a member of the United States delegation to the 36th Session of the United Nations General Assembly in New York City. Mr. Blane was special Chargé d'Affaires in N'Djamena, Chad, in 1982. He was then appointed Ambassador to the Republic of Rwanda in September of 1982 and has served there until the present time.

He graduated from the University of Tennessee (B.A., 1951; M.A., 1956). In 1952–1953 he attended the University of Vienna. His foreign languages are German and French. He is married to the former Dianne Metzger, and they have two children.

Nomination of Richard Wayne Bogosian To Be United States Ambassador to Niger
July 19, 1985

The President today announced his intention to nominate Richard Wayne Bogosian, of Maryland, a career member of the Senior Foreign Service, Class of Counselor, as Ambassador of the United States of America to the Republic of Niger. He would succeed William Robert Casey.

Mr. Bogosian began his career in the Foreign Service in 1962. He attended the Foreign Service Institute and was then assigned to the Near East and South Asian Affairs Division of the Department of State until 1963, when he went to Baghdad, Iraq. He served there until he returned to study French at the Foreign Service Institute in 1965. In 1966–1968 he served as vice consul in Paris, France, returning to the Department to serve in the Bureau of Intelligence and Research until 1971. In 1972 he studied economics at the Foreign Service Institute and was then assigned as chief of the economic section in Kuwait until 1976. He became deputy chief of mission in Khartoum, Sudan, in 1976, where he served until 1979, when he became chief of the Aviation Negotiations Division in the Department. Since 1982 he has been Director of the East African Affairs Office in the Bureau of African Affairs.

He graduated from Tufts College (A.B., 1959) and the University of Chicago Law School (J.D., 1962). He speaks Arabic and French. He is married to the former Claire Marie Mornane, and they have three children. He was born July 18, 1937, in Boston, MA.

933

Nomination of James C. Miller III To Be Director of the Office of Management and Budget
July 19, 1985

The President today announced his intention to nominate James C. Miller III to be Director of the Office of Management and Budget. He would succeed David A. Stockman.

Since September 1981 Dr. Miller has been serving as member and Chairman of the Federal Trade Commission. Previously, in 1981, he served as Administrator for Information and Regulatory Affairs, Office of Management and Budget. He was also Executive Director of the Presidential Task Force on Regulatory Relief. He was a resident scholar at the American Enterpise Institute and was codirector of AEI's Center for the Study of Government Regulation in 1977–1981. He also served as a member of the board of editors of AEI's journal Regulation and served on the board of editorial advisers of the AEI Economist. In 1974–1975 Dr. Miller served as a senior staff economist with the Council of Economic Advisers, where he specialized in matters relating to transportation, regulation, and antitrust policy. In 1975 he was appointed as the Council on Wage and Price Stability's Assistant Director for Government Operations and Research. He also served as a member of President Ford's Domestic Council Regulatory Review Group, which directed the administration's program in regulatory reform. In 1972–1974 Dr. Miller was an associate professor of economics at Texas A&M University and served as a consultant to the Department of Transportation and the National Bureau of Standards. Previously, in 1972, he was research associate at the Brookings Institution and at AEI. In 1969–1972 he was a senior staff economist at the Department of Transportation.

Dr. Miller graduated from the University of Georgia (B.B.A., 1964) and the University of Virginia (Ph.D., 1969). He is married, has three children, and resides in Washington, DC. He was born June 25, 1942, in Atlanta, GA.

Announcement of a Reward for Information Concerning the Murder of United States Citizens in San Salvador
July 19, 1985

Today the United States Government announced a reward of up to $100,000 for information leading to the effective prosecution and punishment of those responsible for the murders of six U.S. citizens on June 19, 1985, in San Salvador, El Salvador. Those with information in El Salvador should notify the investigating authorities of the Salvadoran Government. Those with information in the United States should notify the Office of Security, Department of State. Those with information in any other country should notify the nearest U.S. Embassy. Information received will be handled on a confidential basis, and the identities of informants will be protected. Officers or employees of any governmental organization who furnish information while in performance of official duties are not eligible for the reward.

Proclamation 5357—Captive Nations Week, 1985
July 19, 1985

By the President of the United States of America

A Proclamation

The unique and historic significance of our Nation has always derived from our role as a model of political freedom, social justice, and personal opportunity. While not a perfect Nation, we have offered to the world a vision of liberty. It is a vision that has motivated all our national endeavors and serves us yet as an anchor of conscience. The humanity and justice of our collective political life and the freedom and limitless opportunity in our personal lives are an inspiration for the peoples of the world, both for those who are free to aspire and for those who are not.

The uniqueness of our vision of liberty comes not only from its historical development, but also from the conviction that the benefits of liberty and justice rightfully belong to all humanity. Hostility to this fundamental principle still haunts the world, but our conviction that political freedom is the just inheritance of all nations and all people is firm. Our dedication to this principle has not been weakened by the sad history of conquest, captivity, and oppression to which so many of the world's nations have been subjected.

We are all aware of those many nations that are the victims of totalitarian ideologies, ruthless regimes, and occupying armies. These are the nations held captive by forces hostile to freedom, independence, and national self-determination. Their captivity and struggle against repression require a special courage and sacrifice. Those nations of Eastern Europe that have known conquest and captivity for decades; those struggling to save themselves from communist expansionism in Latin America; and the people of Afghanistan and Kampuchea struggling against invasion and military occupation by their neighbors: all require our special support. For those who seek freedom, security, and peace, we are the custodians of their dream.

Our Nation will continue to speak out for the freedom of those denied the benefits of liberty. We will continue to call for the speedy release of those who are unjustly persecuted and falsely imprisoned. So long as brave men and women suffer persecution because of their national origin, religious beliefs, and desire for liberty, the United States of America will demand that the signatories of the United Nations Charter and the Helsinki Accords live up to their obligations and respect the principles and spirit of those international agreements and understandings.

Each year we renew our resolve to support the struggle for freedom throughout the world by observing Captive Nations Week. It is a week in which all Americans are asked to remember that the liberties and freedoms which they enjoy as inherent rights are forbidden to many nations. It is a time to affirm publicly our convictions that, as long as the struggle from within these nations continues, and as long as we remain firm in our support, the light of freedom will not be extinguished. Together with the people of these captive nations, we fight against military occupation, political oppression, communist expansion, and totalitarian brutality.

The Congress, by joint resolution approved July 17, 1959 (73 Stat. 212), has authorized and requested the President to designate the third week in July as "Captive Nations Week."

Now, Therefore, I, Ronald Reagan, President of the United States of America, do hereby proclaim the week beginning July 21, 1985, as Captive Nations Week. I invite the people of the United States to observe this week with appropriate ceremonies and activities to reaffirm their dedication to the international principles of justice and freedom, which unite us and inspire others.

In Witness Whereof, I have hereunto set my hand this 19th day of July, in the year of our Lord nineteen hundred and eighty-five, and of the Independence of the United States of America the two hundred and tenth.

RONALD REAGAN

[*Filed with the Office of the Federal Register, 4:33 p.m., July 19, 1985*]

Appointment of Cynthia Grassby Baker as Chairman of the Advisory Council on Historic Preservation
July 19, 1985

The President today announced his intention to appoint Cynthia Grassby Baker to be Chairman of the Advisory Council on Historic Preservation for the term of 4 years expiring June 10, 1989. She will succeed Alexander Aldrich.

Mrs. Baker was Deputy to the Chairman for Private Partnership at the National Endowment for the Arts. In 1979–1982 she was finance director for the Colorado Republican Committee; sales representative for Johns-Manville in 1977–1979; development director for the American Medical Cancer Hospital in Denver, CO, in 1976–1977; and development officer for John Grenzebach and Associates in 1975–1976.

She is on the advisory council for Ford's Theatre and a member of the Symphony Orchestra League and the Denver Center for Performing Arts. She is married and resides in Denver, CO. She was born June 25, 1946, in Denver, CO.

Appointment of Three Members of the Advisory Council on Historic Preservation
July 19, 1985

The President today announced his intention to appoint the following individuals to be members of the Advisory Council on Historic Preservation for terms of 4 years expiring June 10, 1989:

William J. Althaus, mayor of York, PA, will succeed Virginia Workman Bremberg. He was elected to the position of mayor of the city of York in November 1981. Previously he practiced law in the city of York in 1976–1981. He graduated from Johns Hopkins University in Baltimore, MD (B.A., 1969), and Dickinson School of Law (J.D., 1976). He is married, has two children, and resides in York, PA. He was born January 28, 1948, in York.

Gov. Michael Newbold Castle of Delaware will succeed Victor George Atiyeh. He was inaugurated Governor of Delaware in January 1985. Prior to that time, he was lieutenant governor of Delaware. He graduated from Hamilton College (B.A., 1961). He received his law degree in 1964 from Georgetown University. He was born July 2, 1939, in Wilmington, DE, where he now resides.

Jennifer B. Dunn will succeed Calvin W. Carter. She is chairman of the Washington State Republican Party. Previously she was a systems engineer for the Seattle regional office of IBM. She graduated from Stanford University (B.A., 1963). She has two children and resides in Bellevue, WA. She was born July 29, 1941, in Seattle, WA.

Radio Address to the Nation on the President's Recovery From Surgery
July 20, 1985

My fellow Americans:

I'm talking to you today from a little makeshift studio just outside my room in Bethesda Naval Hospital. And at the moment, I'm remembering the little boy who wrote me a letter back in 1981 after I was shot and said, "Mr. President, you'd better get well quick, or you'll have to make your speech to Congress in your pajamas." Well, today I'm in street clothes again so I can go home this afternoon. I'm feeling fine, and there's a lot I want to share with you. So, here goes.

First off, I'm feeling great, but I'm getting a little restless. A lot of you know how it is when you have to endure some enforced bed rest. You get this feeling that life's out there, and it's a big, shiny apple, and you just can't wait to get out and take a bite of it. I'm eager to get back to work. I've been keeping close track of things that are going on, especially the budget process in Congress.

I'll tell you what I think of the House budget proposal so far: I hope it gets well soon. In fact, I told one of the fine surgeons who operated on me that if Congress can't make the spending cuts we need, I'm going to send him up to Capitol Hill to do some real cutting. I know some are saying that we can just keep going with business as usual in the Federal spending department. But, well, forgive me, I don't have as much stomach for that kind of talk as I used to. But that's for another day.

Today I just wanted to say some thank-you's to some very special people. First, the doctors and nurses who helped me and healed me. Now I know why nearly everyone comes to America for a major operation. It's because we have the best doctors and nurses in the world. If you have to be sick, you're better off if you're sick right here in these United States of America.

I want to thank everyone—heads of state, leaders, so many friends and citizens who have written and called and included me in their prayers. There were the balloons and flowers and what seemed like millions of cards. One of the nicest was the one I got from the nurses down the hall who sent me a card from the new babies in Pediatrics. It was signed with their little patients' tiny footprints.

I also want to mention a sort of cautionary note. We all tend to ignore the signs that something may be wrong with us. But may I say, speaking from personal experience, it's important to go and get a checkup if you think something isn't right. So, if you're listening to this right now, and it reminds you of something that you've been putting out of your mind, well, pick up the phone, call your doctor or local hospital, and talk to someone. Just tell them Dr. Reagan sent you.

I'd also like to indulge myself for a moment here. There's something I wanted to say, and I wanted to say it with Nancy at my side, as she is right now, as she always has been. First Ladies aren't elected, and they don't receive a salary. They've mostly been private persons forced to live public lives. And in my book, they've all been heroes. Abigail Adams helped invent America. Dolly Madison helped protect it. Eleanor Roosevelt was F.D.R.'s eyes and ears. And Nancy Reagan is my everything. When I look back on these days, Nancy, I'll remember your radiance and your strength, your support, and for taking part in the business in this nation. I say for myself, but also on behalf of the Nation, thank you, partner, thanks for everything. By the way, are you doing anything this evening?

Just one more thing I wanted to say, and I want to address it to my supporters and opponents, Republicans and Democrats, friends and foes. So many of you have sent gracious notes and messages, and you've made me think of something that I've been pondering the past few days. There are a number of things that keep our country united: a shared reverence for certain ideals, for instance, and certain memories and traditions, but there's something more.

We're a country of 230 million very different souls, and yet here we are—liberals and conservatives, fundamentalists and agnostics, southerners and northerners, recent immigrants and Mayflower descendants— arguing often enough and disagreeing with each other, but at the same time held together, always held together by a tie that can't be seen, yet can't be broken. It is, I think, the great unknowing love of Americans for Americans, the great unknowing love that keeps us together and for which, this day, I'm more thankful than ever.

In the next few minutes, I'll be leaving to go home to get on with the job you gave me. There are no words to express my appreciation for the great honor you've bestowed on me.

Until next week, thank you—all of you— and God bless you.

Note: The President spoke at 12:06 p.m. from Bethesda Naval Hospital in Bethesda, MD.

Informal Exchange With Reporters
July 20, 1985

Q. Mr. President, how are you feeling today?

The President. What?

Q. How do you feel?

The President. Great. A little sad. I was beginning to like it here. [*Laughter*] I know I can't say individual goodbyes, but I just want to thank you from the bottom of my heart. [*Inaudible*] I'm going to—[*inaudible*]. There's another cartoon in the paper this morning. It's the second cartoon I've seen in which a Navy nurse is portrayed. And I'm going to wage a one-man campaign to shape those guys up and get them much closer to the truth about Navy nurses—[*laughter*]—and the way you've been portrayed.

God bless you all, and thank you all.

Audience. Thank you!

The President. Thank you. I'm looking forward to coming back for seconds. [*Laughter*]

Q. Mr. President, how does it feel to be up and around and on your feet, sir?

The President. What?

Q. How does it feel to be up and around and walking around on your feet?

The President. Feels great. Yes?

Q. Mr. President, did you pay for this or did you get free care?

The President. What? I've never asked anyone. If I don't, they'll send a bill.

Note: The exchange began at 12:15 p.m. as the President was leaving Bethesda Naval Hospital in Bethesda, MD. He returned to the White House after greeting and thanking hospital staff members.

Proclamation 5358—Space Exploration Day, 1985
July 20, 1985

By the President of the United States of America

A Proclamation

Sixteen years ago, on July 20, 1969, American astronauts sent a message to Earth: "The Eagle has landed." In a dramatic and compelling moment in history, the first humans had reached solid ground beyond our own planet.

To understand Earth systems we must understand our solar system and the universe beyond. Remotely controlled satellites have been sent on missions to Mars, Saturn, and Jupiter. If all goes well, the outer planets Uranus and Neptune will be studied as the Voyager spacecraft passes by in 1986 and 1989, respectively. Within the next year or so the first comet rendezvous are planned (Giacobini-Zinner and Halley), the powerful Hubble Space Telescope will be placed in orbit, and the Galileo Mission to Jupiter will be launched. Scientists around the world eagerly anticipate the results.

The space shuttle continues to demonstrate and expand its capabilities with each successive flight. Within the past year, satellites have been launched from the shuttle's bay, repaired in space, and retrieved and returned to Earth for repair. We have conducted missions in which a European-designed and -built scientific laboratory—Spacelab—has flown in the shuttle bay's gravity-free environment during which data in a wide range of disciplines have been acquired, materials tested, and chemical reactions monitored.

Under NASA's direction, the next logical step in America's space program—the space station—is being planned, with development scheduled for the latter part of this decade. When it becomes operational in the early to mid-1990s, the space station will be a catalyst for expanding the peaceful uses of space for scientific, industrial, and commercial gain. The station will serve as a laboratory for materials processing and industrial and scientific research; as a permanent observatory for astronomy and Earth observations; as a storage and supply depot; and as a base from which to service other satellites or satellite clusters that will form the world's first space-based industrial park. Japan, Europe, and Canada have joined

with us in partnerships that are designed to serve all our long-term interests.

Space exploration is little more than a quarter century old. In that brief period, more has been learned about the cosmos and our relation to it than in all the preceding centuries combined. The ever-increasing knowledge gained from peaceful space exploration, and the uses to which that knowledge is put, potentially benefit all those aboard Spaceship Earth. The spirit of July 20, 1969, lives on.

In recognition of the achievements and promise of our space exploration program, the Congress, by Senate Joint Resolution 154, has designated July 20, 1985, as "Space Exploration Day" and authorized and requested the President to issue a proclamation to commemorate this event.

Now, Therefore, I, Ronald Reagan, President of the United States of America, do hereby proclaim July 20, 1985, as Space Exploration Day. I call upon the people of the United States to observe the occasion with appropriate ceremonies and activities.

In Witness Whereof, I have hereunto set my hand this twentieth day of July, in the year of our Lord nineteen hundred and eighty-five, and of the Independence of the United States of America the two hundred and tenth.

RONALD REAGAN

[*Filed with the Office of the Federal Register, 11:59 a.m., July 23, 1985*]

Note: The proclamation was released by the Office of the Press Secretary on July 22.

Nomination of Bill D. Colvin To Be Inspector General of the National Aeronautics and Space Administration
July 22, 1985

The President today announced his intention to nominate Bill D. Colvin to be Inspector General, National Aeronautics and Space Administration (NASA). He would succeed June Gibbs Brown.

Mr. Colvin is currently serving as Acting Inspector General and Deputy Inspector

General of NASA. Previously he served as Assistant Inspector General for Technical Services at NASA in 1983–1984. Prior to that time, he was supervisory special agent at the Federal Bureau of Investigation in 1972–1983; head of the data processing department at Western Wyoming College in

1971–1972; and computer systems analyst at Eastern New Mexico College in 1966–1971.

He graduated from Eastern New Mexico University (B.B.A., 1969; M.B.A., 1971). He is married, has two children, and resides in Fredericksburg, VA. He was born June 7, 1940, in Clovis, NM.

Memorandum on Leadership of the Combined Federal Campaign
July 22, 1985

Memorandum for the Heads of Executive Departments and Agencies

Helping people to help themselves through private sector initiatives is a commitment of this Administration, and we are extremely proud of our record in this regard. As leaders in the Federal government, we participate side by side with individuals, groups, voluntary organizations, and corporations to provide opportunities for others less fortunate. We do our part through our leadership of the Combined Federal Campaign in our respective agencies.

It gives me great pleasure to announce that Secretary of Transportation Elizabeth Hanford Dole has agreed to serve as Chairperson of the fall 1985 Combined Federal Campaign of the National Capital Area. I am asking that you support Secretary Dole by personally serving as Chairman of the campaign in your organization and appointing a top official as your Vice Chairman. Please advise Secretary Dole of the person you designate.

Your personal interest, visible support, and active participation are vital to the success of the campaign. Make a special effort to encourage your employees in the Washington area, and in all CFC locations worldwide, to support the Combined Federal Campaign at greater levels than ever before.

RONALD REAGAN

Memorandum Urging Participation in the Combined Federal Campaign
July 22, 1985

Memorandum for All Federal Employees and Military Personnel

Over the past 24 years, Federal employees and members of the Armed Forces have had the opportunity to show their concern for those in need through participation in the Combined Federal Campaign. They have responded to the opportunity during this time by contributing over $1.1 billion to charitable organizations through the CFC.

I ask each of you now to continue that tradition of voluntary sharing.

Through the Combined Federal Campaign, we can assist the less fortunate in our country and extend a nurturing hand to friends around the world. We can help relieve pain and health problems now and support research to eliminate them in the future. We can help our neighbors without making them dependent on government.

You have a record of generosity and concern for others. I am confident that that proud record will continue in the fall 1985 Combined Federal Campaign. While the decision to give is personal and voluntary, I encourage each of you to join me in wholeheartedly supporting this year's CFC.

RONALD REAGAN

Nomination of Winston Lord To Be United States Ambassador to China
July 22, 1985

The President today announced his intention to nominate Winston Lord, of New York, as Ambassador to the People's Republic of China. He would succeed Arthur W. Hummel, Jr.

Mr. Lord worked as a summer intern in the office of Senator Estes Kefauver of Tennessee in 1959. In 1961 he was a volunteer for the New York State Republican Committee, and from 1977 to the present, Mr. Lord has been president of the Council on Foreign Relations in New York City. He entered government service in 1962 as a Foreign Service officer in the Office of Congressional Relations. In 1962–1964 he served in the Office of Political-Military Affairs and then the Office of International Trade. In 1965 he became a member of the negotiating team and special assistant to the Chairman of the United States delegation to the Kennedy round of tariff negotiations in Geneva, Switzerland. In 1967 he was a member of the international security affairs, policy planning staff at the Department of Defense. In 1969–1973 he was a member, planning staff of the National Security Council, and Special Assistant to the President for National Security Affairs. In 1973–1977 he served as director of the policy planning staff and top policy adviser on China in the Department of State. In 1983–1984 he was senior counselor of the National Bipartisan Commission on Central America.

Mr. Lord graduated from Yale University (B.A., 1959) and the Fletcher School of Law and Diplomacy (M.A., 1960). He served in the United States Army in 1961. His foreign language is French. He is married to the former Bette Bao, and they have two children. He was born August 17, 1937, in New York.

Remarks at the Welcoming Ceremony for President Li Xiannian of China
July 23, 1985

President Reagan. It is my pleasure today to welcome you, President Li. This is your first trip to the United States and the first visit by a Chinese head of state to our country. It's a great honor to have you, your wife, and the distinguished delegation who accompanied you as our guests. During my visit to China last year, I had the opportunity to get to know President Li. Under the guidance of President Li and other wise leaders, the Chinese people are enjoying greater productivity and a rising standard of living.

The American people are working with them as friends and partners in enterprise. Trade between us is at a record level and continues to climb. Scientific, technological cooperation is being put to use in a wide range of endeavors, and this too can be expected to increase. Our educational and cultural exchanges—already substantial—are expanding. We're in the initial phases of cooperation in the control of narcotics and antiterrorism. And by our common opposition to aggression, we are not only enhancing our mutual security but bolstering world peace as well.

Both our peoples should be proud that in a few short years a solid foundation of good will has been laid. Ours is an increasingly productive relationship based not on personality or momentary concerns, but on a recognition that our nations share significant common interests and an understanding of the many benefits we've reaped from the good will between us. Now, this doesn't

941

mean that there are no areas of disagreement; however, we will continue to put any differences in perspective. When I met with you, President Li, in the Great Hall of Beijing, I suggested a Chinese principle that can serve as a tool in building an ever-stronger bond between us: *hu jing, hu hui*—mutual respect, mutual benefit. Let us proceed in that spirit—*hu jing, hu hui.* As leaders of great nations, we should expect nothing more and accept nothing less.

President Li, we Americans highly value the ties we have built with the people of China in these last 13 years. We rejoice with you over the economic success your country is enjoying, and I'm pleased to be playing a small part in this modernization effort. We wish for the people of China what we wish for ourselves—to live in peace and to enjoy prosperity. By working together the people of both our countries can achieve this noble goal. We are pleased to have you with us.

On behalf of the people of the United States I say, *huan ying.* Welcome.

President Li. Mr. President and Mrs. Reagan, ladies and gentlemen, at the kind invitation of President Reagan I've come to pay a visit to a great country. On behalf of the Chinese Government and the people, I wish to extend a heartfelt thanks and the best wishes to the American Government and the people. Mr. President, I am very happy to see that you are recovering so fast, and I'm deeply touched by your participation in this welcoming ceremony.

The purpose of my coming to visit is to deepen mutual understanding, enhance our bilateral relations, increase the friendship between our two peoples, and safeguard world peace. I believe this purpose is in conformity with the interests and desires of our two peoples. Both China and the United States are great countries and both

our peoples, great peoples. I am convinced that if China and the United States can establish a long-term and stable relationship of friendship and cooperation on the basis of the five principles of peaceful coexistence, it will greatly benefit our two peoples and world peace.

In the past two centuries or more the Sino-U.S. relations went through a tortuous road, with both exciting moments of joy and the painful periods that provoked thought. It is gratifying to note that since 1972 leaders of the two countries, judging the hour and sizing up the situation, have cooperated to lay down principles guiding bilateral relations and have reached a number of agreements that provide the foundation for the establishment of a long-term and a stable relationship of friendship.

The Sino-U.S. relations have made very big progress. A dozen years ago very few people could foresee the present level of development in our bilateral relations. However, I wish to point out that in our relations there are even today great potentials to be tapped and obstacles and difficulties to be overcome. The new situation demands our fresh efforts and new achievements. I hope that a dozen years hence, when we look back, we shall be able to feel gratified, as we do today, that as we proceed difficulties are increasingly reduced and our steps grow more vigorous.

Thank you.

Note: President Reagan spoke at 10:08 a.m. at the South Portico of the White House, where President Li was accorded a formal welcome with full military honors. President Li spoke in Chinese, and his remarks were translated by an interpreter. Following the ceremony, the two Presidents met in the Residence.

Nomination of Thomas John Josefiak To Be a Member of the Federal Election Commission
July 23, 1985

The President today announced his intention to nominate Thomas John Josefiak to be a member of the Federal Election Commission for a term expiring April 30, 1991.

He would succeed Frank P. Reiche.

Mr. Josefiak is currently serving as special deputy to the Secretary of the Senate for the Federal Election Commission. Previously he was a legal counsel to the National Republican Congressional Committee (NRCC) in 1977–1981. In 1979 he was on leave of absence from NRCC to serve as counsel to the Committee on House Administration.

He graduated from Fairfield University (B.A., 1969) and Georgetown University (J.D., 1974). He was born November 21, 1947, in Adams, MA, and now resides in Alexandria, VA.

Appointment of Ross O. Doyen as a Member of the Advisory Commission on Intergovernmental Relations
July 23, 1985

The President today announced his intention to appoint Ross O. Doyen, a State senator from Kansas, to be a member of the Advisory Commission on Intergovernmental Relations for a term of 2 years. He will succeed Miles Yeoman Ferry.

He was first elected to the Kansas house of representatives in 1958 and served five terms there. He has been a State senator since January 1969 and has served as president of the senate and chairman of several committees, including the Senate Ways and Means Committee. He is president of the National Republican Legislators Association and past president of the National Conference of State Legislatures.

Mr. Doyen graduated from Kansas State University (B.S., 1950). He has two children and resides in Concordia, KS. He was born October 1, 1926, in Rice, KS.

Toast at the State Dinner for President Li Xiannian of China
July 23, 1985

Good evening, and welcome to the White House. Tonight it's my pleasure to return the hospitality that was extended to us by President Li during our visit to China. And I'm grateful to have had the opportunity to develop a personal relationship with him. And it's my honor, President Li, to greet you affectionately as *lao pengyou*. Now, for most of you who don't speak Chinese, that means "old friend." [*Laughter*]

Today when President Li and I renewed our friendship, he expressed his wishes for my full recovery. In fact, he told me that once I was totally back on my feet, a young man like myself could expect to have a long and distinguished career ahead of him. [*Laughter*] President Li comes from a nation whose people are known for their traditional respect for the elders. President Li, I can assure you I'm doing my best to reestablish that tradition in our own country. [*Laughter*]

But I learned about that and many other wonderful aspects of China during our visit last year. Although our stay was brief, I did, as the Chinese say, "look at the flowers while riding horseback"—capturing lasting impressions not only of the magnificence of the culture and the land but also the bold vision of those directing China's future.

The progress we've made is a tribute to individuals with courage and foresight, like President Li, on both sides of the Pacific. The relationship we've built improves the material well-being and increases the security of our countries. Areas of disagreement exist; these should not be ignored, nor should they be permitted to inhibit us from acting together in these many areas of commonality. Historic truths determine our fundamental national interests, and they continue to draw our two peoples together.

After our meeting today, I'm happy to say I remain confident that Chinese-American cooperation will grow and strengthen in the years ahead. Underscoring the momentum of our relationship, I am delighted tonight to announce that the Chinese Government has invited Vice President Bush to China and that he has accepted this most gracious invitation. Such visits as yours, Mr. President, elevate the relationship of the leaders of our two nations, enhance our joint efforts, and open new doors of cooperation.

President Li, by the time you return home you will have seen much of the United States and met many Americans in and out of government. You will have seen our industry, our people, and our land. We Americans came here from almost every nation, including China, to an undeveloped land, a wilderness. We're proud of what we've accomplished. And today we're proud to stand beside the people of China, who are striving to build a better life.

By working together, we can and will create a more prosperous and peaceful world. So, let us drink a toast to that and to President Li and Madame Lin, his wife.

Note: The President spoke at 9:25 p.m. in the State Dining Room at the White House.

Nomination of Frank Shakespeare To Be United States Ambassador to Portugal
July 24, 1985

The President today announced his intention to nominate Frank Shakespeare, of Connecticut, to be Ambassador to the Republic of Portugal. He would succeed Henry Allen Holmes.

Mr. Shakespeare served as president of CBS Television Services, CBS, Inc., in New York in 1950–1969. He was named Director of the United States Information Agency in 1969 and served there until 1973. In 1973–1975 he was executive vice president of Westinghouse in New York. In 1975 he became president/vice chairman, RKO General, Inc., in New York. And from 1981 to the present, he has been Chairman, Board for International Broadcasting.

Mr. Shakespeare graduated from Holy Cross College (B.S., 1946). He has received honorary degrees from the Colorado School of Mines (engineering, 1975), Pace University (commercial science, 1979), Delaware Law School (law, 1980), and Sacred Heart University (law, 1985). He has three children and resides in Greenwich, CT. He was born April 9, 1925, in New York, NY.

Appointment of Three Members of the National Selective Service Appeal Board, and Designation of the Chairman
July 24, 1985

The President today announced his intention to appoint the following individuals to be members of the National Selective Service Appeal Board. The President intends to designate Frank De Balogh as Chairman upon his appointment.

Julius Belso is a partner in the Biro-Belso real estate firm in New Brunswick, NJ. He is also chairman of the board of Magyar Savings and Loan in New Brunswick. He is former commissioner of the New Brunswick Human Rights Commission. He is married and resides in New

Brunswick. He was born August 12, 1918, in Kerkakutas, Hungary.

Frank De Balogh is director of the decision support systems laboratory and assistant professor of systems science for the Institute of Safety and Systems Management at the University of Southern California. He is married, has one child, and resides in South Pasadena, CA. He

was born October 9, 1941, in Budapest, Hungary.

Guadalupe F. Hinckle has been actively involved in community service in Los Angeles for many years. In 1980 she was presented with the Los Angeles Human Relations Commission Certificate of Merit for Outstanding Community Service. She has three children and resides in Los Angeles, CA. She was born April 24, 1916, in Sonora, Mexico.

Message to the Congress Transmitting the Proposed China-United States Nuclear Energy Agreement
July 24, 1985

To the Congress of the United States:

I am pleased to transmit to the Congress, pursuant to sections 123(b) and 123(d) of the Atomic Energy Act of 1954, as amended (42 U.S.C. 2153(b), (d)), the text of the proposed agreement between the United States and the People's Republic of China Concerning Peaceful Uses of Nuclear Energy, with accompanying annexes and agreed minute. The proposed agreement is accompanied by my written determination, approval, and authorization, and the Nuclear Proliferation Assessment Statement by the Director of the United States Arms Control and Disarmament Agency concerning the agreement. The joint memorandum submitted to me by the Secretaries of State and Energy, which includes a summary analysis of the provisions of the agreement, and the views of the Director of the United States Arms Control and Disarmament Agency are also enclosed.

The proposed agreement with the People's Republic of China has been negotiated in accordance with the Nuclear Non-Proliferation Act, which sets forth certain requirements for new agreements for cooperation with other countries.

It is the first peaceful nuclear cooperation agreement with a Communist country and the only such agreement with another nuclear-weapon state (the United Kingdom and France are covered by U.S. agreements with EURATOM).

During the last several years, the People's Republic of China has developed ambitious plans for the installation of a substantial

number of nuclear power stations. The proposed agreement reflects the desire of the Government of the United States and the Government of the People's Republic of China to establish a framework for peaceful nuclear cooperation. During the period of our negotiations and discussions, China took several important steps that clarify its nonproliferation and nuclear export policies. Premier Zhao has made important statements of China's non-proliferation policy that make clear that China will not contribute to proliferation. Those statements have been endorsed by the National People's Congress, thereby giving them official status. Based on our talks with the Chinese, we can expect that China's policy of not assisting a non-nuclear weapon state to acquire nuclear explosives will be implemented in a manner consistent with the basic non-proliferation practices common to the United States and other suppliers. Further, in conjunction with China's membership in the International Atomic Energy Agency, effective January 1, 1984, China has said that it will require IAEA safeguards on its future nuclear export commitments to non-nuclear weapons states.

This agreement will have a significant, positive impact on overall U.S.-China relations. It will provide the United States and its companies an opportunity to participate in another aspect of China's energy programs, with possibly substantial economic benefit. The proposed agreement will, in my view, further the non-proliferation and other foreign policy interests of the United States.

I have considered the views and recommendations of the interested agencies in reviewing the proposed agreement and have determined that its performance will promote, and will not constitute an unreasonable risk to, the common defense and security. Accordingly, I have approved the agreement and authorized its execution.

I have also found that this agreement meets all applicable requirements of the Atomic Energy Act, as amended, for agreements for peaceful nuclear cooperation and therefore I am transmitting it to the Congress without exempting it from any requirement contained in section 123(a) of that Act. This transmission shall constitute a submittal for purposes of both section 123(b) and 123(d) of the Atomic Energy Act. The Administration is prepared to begin immediately the consultations with the Senate Foreign Relations and House Foreign Affairs Committees as provided in section 123(b). Upon completion of the 30 day continuous session period provided in section 123(b), the 60 day continuous session period provided for in section 123(d) shall commence.

RONALD REAGAN

The White House,
July 24, 1985.

Nomination of Donald J. Quigg To Be Commissioner of Patents and Trademarks
July 25, 1985

The President today announced his intention to nominate Donald J. Quigg to be Commissioner of Patents and Trademarks, Department of Commerce. He would succeed Gerald Mossinghoff.

Since 1981 Mr. Quigg has been Deputy Assistant Secretary of Commerce and Deputy Commissioner of Patents and Trademarks. Previously, he was at Phillips Petroleum Co. as patent counsel (1971–1981); associate patent counsel and chief of the legal branch (1954–1971); senior patent attorney, section chief (1950–1954); and staff patent attorney in 1946–1950.

He graduated from the University of Oklahoma (B.S., 1937) and the University of Missouri (J.D., 1940). He is married, has two children, and resides in Falls Church, VA. He was born April 28, 1916, in Kansas City, MO.

Nomination of Larry L. DeVuyst To Be a Member of the Federal Farm Credit Board
July 25, 1985

The President today announced his intention to nominate Larry L. DeVuyst to be a member of the Federal Farm Credit Board, Farm Credit Administration, for a term expiring March 31, 1991. He would succeed Jewell Haaland.

Mr. DeVuyst is a farmer in Ithaca, MI. He serves as director of the Federal Farm Credit Council and as vice president of the Michigan Pork Producers Association. He is past State director of the Michigan Farm Bureau and past director of the Michigan Agricultural Cooperative Marketing Association.

He attended Michigan State University. He is married, has four children, and resides in Ithaca, MI. He was born July 10, 1939, in Ithaca, MI.

Nomination of Three Members of the National Advisory Council on Women's Educational Programs
July 25, 1985

The President today announced his intention to nominate the following individuals to be members of the National Advisory Council on Women's Educational Programs for terms expiring May 8, 1988. These are reappointments:

Betty Ann Gault Cordoba is a teacher in Woodland Hills, CA. She is a member of the board of directors of the Professional Educators of Los Angeles, CA. She graduated from the University of Southern California (B.S., 1949). She is married, has one child, and resides in Woodland Hills, CA. She was born December 23, 1927, in Philadelphia, PA.

Irene Renee Robinson is actively involved in community and charity work. She is a former instructor of Russian at Georgetown University, School of Foreign Service. She graduated from St. Joseph College in Tientsin, China (B.A., 1941). She is married, has one child, and resides in Washington, DC. She was born December 5, 1922, in Harbin, China.

Judy F. Rolfe is vice president of Rolfe & Wood, Inc., an automobile dealership in Bozeman, MT. She attended Montana State University. She is married, has two children, and resides in Bozeman, MT. She was born June 20, 1953, in Analunda, MT.

Appointment of Robert Earl Farris as a Member of the National Council on Public Works Improvement
July 26, 1985

The President today announced his intention to appoint Robert Earl Farris to be a member of the National Council on Public Works Improvement. This is a new position.

Since 1981 Mr. Farris has been serving as a commissioner of the department of transportation for the State of Tennessee. Previously he was the owner of Swimco, Inc. He was assistant sales promotion manager at the Gillette Co. in 1952–1960.

Mr. Farris attended the John F. Kennedy School of Government at Harvard University. He is married, has two children, and resides in Nashville, TN. He was born March 7, 1928, in Etowah, TN.

Appointment of Michael R. Farley as a Member of the National Council on Vocational Education
July 26, 1985

The President today announced his intention to appoint Michael R. Farley to be a member of the National Council on Vocational Education for a term expiring January 17, 1987.

Mr. Farley is currently president of Farley & Associates, a firm specializing in family and business insurance planning, in Tucson, AZ. He is a member of the Southern Arizona Association of Life Underwriters and the National Association of Life Underwriters.

He graduated from the University of Arizona (B.S., 1967) and the American College of Life Underwriters (C.L.U., 1972). He is married, has three children, and resides in Tucson, AZ. He was born March 6, 1944, in Los Angeles, CA.

Radio Address to the Nation on Economic Growth and Minorities
July 27, 1985

My fellow Americans:

Some of the recent economic reports might be seen as spectacular were they not becoming so routine. The Consumer Price Index increased by only two-tenths of 1 percent in June, following an identical two-tenths of 1 percent increase in May. The United States economic expansion is 31 months old. Employment stands near its highest level in history, and yet inflation is below 4 percent.

Not since the 1960's have prices been so well contained for so long a period of economic growth. Most important, the outlook on this summer day for the balance of 1985 and beyond is very good for continued low inflation, renewed economic strength, and rising employment. Productivity growth is strengthening and interest rates have dropped significantly, invigorating housing markets and permitting businesses to better finance investments and machines, technologies, and products for the future. Add to this the increase in business orders, which provides incentives to rebuild inventories, and the pickup of other economics abroad, and we see all the parts falling in place for a new surge of robust expansion.

One of the most hopeful signs for our future is being seen in our black communities. We'll have to wait for the Census Bureau to release the latest poverty figures in August to confirm the new trend, but the evidence of progress seems clear. A record number of blacks—some 10.6 million—now have jobs. Since November 1982 the black unemployment rate has fallen by 6½ percentage points, and nearly one of every five new jobs generated went to a black man, woman, or teenager. Blacks have gained an average of 45,000 new jobs every month for the past 31 months—twice the job gain rate of whites.

Those gains were created by the engines of enterprise, not the horse and buggy system of bureaucratic make-work that broke down long ago. They were created by people getting ahead and breaking free, not because of what society does for them, but what they do for themselves—by people who know complete emancipation must be a spiritual struggle for brotherhood, a political struggle for participation at the ballot box, and an economic struggle for an opportunity society that creates jobs, not welfare; wealth, not poverty; and freedom, not dependency.

We're reaching out to every American who yearns to board the freedom train that can take them to the destination of their dreams. But that train can't keep moving if government keeps blocking the track. We can't rest until everyone who wants to work can find a real job. No American seeking opportunity through an expanding economy can break free if government erodes their take-home pay with new taxes. Minorities and women can't break free if government destroys their earning power with protectionist measures that raise prices and eventually cripple the job market and our economy as well. And workers searching for jobs and advancement can't break free if government upsets the marketplace with harebrained ideas like federally mandated comparable worth, a proposal that would take salary decisions out the hands of employers and employees and give government the power to determine what a fair salary is.

On another front, we'll keep speaking out, pushing as hard as we can, to give all Americans new opportunity to build a better life. That means passage of our tax reform to lower rates, nearly double the personal exemption, raise the standard deduction, and increase the earned-income tax credit. Tax reform is a must, because it would turn private energies away from efforts to save another dollar in taxes toward efforts to earn another dollar. This is how hope and opportunity are created.

We'll keep pushing for passage of enterprise zones as long as areas that could be new sites for economic development remain destitute landmarks of despair. Such neglect is an outrage, and those blocking this legislation should never have the nerve to say a word about compassion again.

Finally, to bring teenage unemployment rates down further, we've asked the Congress for a 3-year test of the youth employment opportunity wage. It enjoys bipartisan support—leading black mayors, 114 historically black colleges, the Fraternal Order of Police, even the National Alliance of Postal Employees. It's time Congress passed this proposal that could create some 400,000 new jobs for our youth. We've got to believe in them if they're to believe in us.

At long last, all Americans are beginning to move forward together. From now on, it's got to be full speed ahead.

Until next week, thanks for listening, and God bless you.

Note: The President spoke at 12:06 p.m. from Camp David, MD.

Excerpts From an Interview With Hugh Sidey of Time Magazine
July 25, 1985

The President's Health

Mr. Sidey. Well, listen, I just—a few questions here to—as you start in again. How do you feel? That's the first one.

The President. Feel fine. Really. Everyday I'm amazed at the improvement. Only a few days ago to bend in the middle, somebody had to help. Now I can get up all by myself.

Mr. Sidey. The sore spot's going away?

The President. Oh, yes.

Mr. Sidey. That sort of thing.

The President. There's an 11-inch line there that——

Mr. Sidey. I see. You don't plan to show your scar like Lyndon Johnson. [*Laughter*] So keep that quiet, huh?

The President. No, no.

Mr. Sidey. On a serious note, you've got another adversary now, cancer. How are you going to deal with that these next 3½ years?

The President. I'm going to do exactly what they've told me to do. The thing is, Hugh, in this—one, the doctor himself was a little concerned because he'd used the term that I "have cancer." He says the proper thing is I "had cancer." And very— to a minor effect—that particular polyp, called adenoma type, is one that, if it is left, it begins to develop cancerous cells. Well, this one had. When they got it out, they found that there were a few of such cells, but it's gone, along with the surrounding tissue. It had not spread; no evidence of anything else. So, I am someone who does not have cancer. But, like everyone else, I'm apparently vulnerable to it. And, therefore, there will be a schedule of checkups for a period to see if it's going to return or if there was a cell that had escaped into the bloodstream or something.

Mr. Sidey. Will the fear of cancer intrude into your life, though?

The President. No. I've never been that way about things of that kind.

Mr. Sidey. Well, I must say, twice you've been brushed by death since you've been in this office, and you seem unfazed. You keep going; you keep your hope up. What is it?

The President. Well, I have a very real and deep faith. Probably, I'm indebted to my mother for that. And I figure that He will make a decision, and I can't doubt that whatever He decides will be the right decision.

Mr. Sidey. That's not going to affect your work?

The President. No.

Mr. Sidey. But, Mr. President, if cancer should show up and you had to undergo treatments, is there the possibility that you would resign, turn the job over to Mr. Bush?

The President. I can't foresee anything of that kind, and that is not just me talking, now. That's on the basis of all that I've been told by the doctors who were all involved in this. I can't see anything of that kind coming. But, as I said once when they were talking about my age before I was elected the first time, if I found myself ever physically incapacitated where I, in my own mind, knew I could not fulfill the requirements, I'd be the first one to say so and step down.

Mr. Sidey. When was the hardest moment in this whole episode for you?

The President. The hardest moment?

Mr. Sidey. Yes.

The President. Golly, that's pretty hard to say. The most difficulty I have is in that period in which time disappears and you're no longer a part of the world—[*laughter*]—under the anesthetic. The most difficult time I had was trying to reorient as to where I was and had I been operated on yet or not. [*Laughter*] And they said, "Oh, yes. It's all over."

Mr. Sidey. I see. Did you suspect you might have cancer before they told you?

The President. No. They've tried to make something of the scheduling of these things. The first polyp had been taken out, the knowledge that I had another one yet to come out, and it was the kind that, as they said, doesn't become cancerous. The schedule was set, and I went in there fully prepared on a Friday afternoon to have that one snipped out. Also, they were going to do this examination then of the intestine to make sure. And I went in with a little handbag, fully convinced that I would be on my way to Camp David the next morning, Saturday. And they came back in after having taken out the polyp and told me that they had found this other type. And they said, about this other type, that we have no evidence whether there are cancer cells, but it is the kind that can be cancerous. And they said, now, you're all prepped, you're here—and that prepping took a lot of imbibing of— [*laughter*]—certain fluids for hours before I went there. They said you can schedule this to come back, or they said, our advice is, you're all ready and you're here and why not now? And I said yes. I didn't want to get back on that fluid again—[*laughter*]—a week or two from now.

Mr. Sidey. I see, I see.

The President. So, I said yes. And then they told me that, yes, there had been a few cancer cells in it, but it had not penetrated the outer wall. It was confined; there was no trace of this going anyplace else.

And, as the doctor said, therefore, all you can say is you had cancer.

Mr. Sidey. Yes.

The President. I've got too many friends—even my brother who—good Lord, he had very severe cancer of the larynx. He was a very heavy smoker, which I have never been. But that was, golly, I guess in the neighborhood of 20 years ago, and he's doing just fine. So, I'll take the checkups that they recommend for them to keep track.

Mr. Sidey. There was some comment when you only spent 5 minutes with the doctors, when they told you that the specimen was cancerous that they took out, you know?

The President. Yes.

Mr. Sidey. But that was all you needed to spend with them?

The President. Yes. They were most reassuring.

Mr. Sidey. You're not unhappy with your medical advice?

The President. Oh, no, not at all.

Mr. Sidey. Why didn't you do it last year, in '84?

The President. Well, I think this is what has been misplayed somewhat. We didn't know about this new polyp. We knew at the time that there were two polyps—one much smaller than the other. And they had gotten one, and then, subsequently, we set a time later when I would go back in.

Mr. Sidey. Have any of your priorities changed because of this illness, as far as being President of the United States goes?

The President. No. If there was any change it was back in 1981, with the indication of mortality after the shooting, that I made up my mind that those things that I believed in doing, for whatever time I might have left.

Mr. Sidey. So, it's full speed ahead?

The President. Yes.

Mr. Sidey. Work is your answer, in a way.

The President. Yes.

Mr. Sidey. One of the things that's been commented on, Mr. President, is Mrs. Reagan, who was, as you said in your speech—she has been remarkable in this. Has she become more of the Presidency in these last couple of weeks, or are we just noticing it?

The President. No, but Nancy is a mother hen. Let something happen to one of the family, and they become the chick. She's very concerned that there be no overdoing. And being a doctor's daughter, a surgeon's daughter, as a matter of fact, she is very insistent that no one's going to overwork me. And that includes me, because she knows that I tend to take such things a little lightly. And I think she reached her high point this morning. You know, she's on her way to Denison University in Ohio for a program on drugs. She'll be back today. But on the table by my side of the bed, there is one of those little cabbage-type dolls in a nurse's uniform. [*Laughter*] And she has named it Nancy and has put it there so that while she's gone, it is to remind me that— [*laughter*]—I'm to do all those things like rest, and so forth.

Mr. Sidey. Well, she's displayed great courage——

The President. Yes, she has.

Mr. Sidey. ——you know, before the world, really, in that time.

The President. And it hasn't been easy because, as she herself admits, she is a worrier. And she has been through a lot, including a most traumatic experience, the death of her father. She was there and with him for a couple of weeks in the hospital, and both knew that he was dying. And then, to have what happened to me—I recovered far more quickly than she did from the shooting. And then, along comes a thing like this. She can't resolve her concern.

White House Staff

Mr. Sidey. There was a little comment, Mr. President, about your staff and whether Mr. Regan assumed too much power and——

The President. No. He was carrying out things that I said. And this whole mixup, Hugh, whether George was shipped away or something—when I found out about the anesthetic, I designated, of course, automatically George Bush. But George had just come back from that very successful, but also very tiring trip. And knowing that this was just for the hours of an operation—and at this time, it was all going to be over on Friday afternoon—I said to Don, I said that I knew that George had gone—as I would have gone to the ranch after that trip—had gone up to Maine. I said, tell George, though, to stay where he is. There's no need—he's as much in contact there as he would be here. I said, "Tell him to stay there and not to break up his weekend simply because I'm going to have this little thing snipped."

So, this was my order. But then when the subsequent thing came along and it was going to be extended hours, it was George's decision to come back. And he just said he just felt that under the circumstances—and he was right—that it just would not look right in the eyes of anyone for me to be there and him to be up there in Maine. And so, he felt that it would be much more reassuring to the people and everything else if he came back. And that was all. I was the one from the very beginning who had said to him, "I don't want you to give up your weekend."

Mr. Sidey. And you think Don Regan's function as the coordinator in that was the way it should be?

The President. Yes, and with all the things here, Don's carrying out the things that I have said. I've witnessed no grabs for power on the part of anyone. Hugh, there seems to be a concerted effort, and has been for the last 4½ years, to try and build feuds within the administration. I think they thrive on—some do—on combat, and there just isn't anything to it.

The White House

Mr. Sidey. You talked of "going home"—I was struck by it—in the hospital. You mentioned it two or three times, how you wanted to go home and get into your bed. I've never heard a President talk of the White House with such affection and warmth. Now, what's the change?

The President. Well, yes. And, Hugh, I think again we go to—Nancy is a nest-builder. If we stop in a hotel for a couple of days, she can't be in a suite for 5 minutes until she's moving the furniture around—[*laughter*]—to make it more homelike. In the hospital there for only those several days, she brought pictures up and some large framed photos that we have of her trying to give

951

the dog a bath and so forth, and hung them on the walls. And at first, I kept saying, "Honey, I'm going to be out of here in a few days. You're going to a lot of trouble." But I have to say, she was right. Suddenly, it was much more pleasant to look around. She had framed photos, family photos that she brought and were around the place. She does that, and the same here with the White House.

Mr. Sidey. So, it has become home despite living over the store and the isolation and all the problems?

The President. Yes, the living quarters there—our own furniture in there. And I just always have had a tendency to settle in.

Mr. Sidey. Maybe you want a third term?

The President. [*Laughter*] I think that's not permitted, but I have to say it is home. And she's done the same with the house at Camp David. That's similar to when we had a house in Los Angeles and the ranch.

The President's Health

Mr. Sidey. One final question, Mr. President, here. What's your favorite joke about your operation?

The President. [*Laughter*] Oh, Lord! Oh, well. Yes, there was a cartoon that came out—[*laughter*]—and somebody brought me a copy of it. I guess it was in the Washington Times. I called him to thank him for it, but also to give him a little warning. It's a cartoon that appeared in the paper. It was of the hospital. Up here in a window was a nurse and a man. The nurse was very angry, and she was pointing down out of sight, below the cartoon. And she was saying, "That crazy clown down there chopping wood, he'll wake the President!" And the man, looking down, says, "That fellow chopping wood is the President!"

Mr. Sidey. I see. [*Laughter*]

The President. And so, I showed it to everyone, but he had quite a cartoon figure for the nurse. And these nurses were all very trim and nice people and all, and they were a little disturbed by the image of a Bethesda nurse. So, when I left the hospital up there, I told all of them—that's what I was saying when I turned my back and was talking to them—I was telling them that I was going to do my utmost to see that the image as portrayed was corrected in the

cartoon industry and that they were not properly portrayed. So, I told him that when I called him.

Administration Goals

Mr. Sidey. Now, I guess one final thing. Your purposes in the Presidency, your priorities, basically have not changed?

The President. No, no, they haven't.

Mr. Sidey. Budget, tax reform——

The President. Peace.

Mr. Sidey. ——strength abroad?

The President. Yes.

Mr. Sidey. You'll go to see Mr. Gorbachev——

The President. Yes.

Mr. Sidey. ——as far as you know?

The President. Yes, yes, all of those things. The view I felt for a long time, that, even if there were no deficit, the Federal Government, out of a number of things and with the best of intentions, embarked on all kinds of programs, some of which are just not the proper function of government, things government shouldn't be doing, and some of which, even if it's doing them, they're not cost-effective at all. Job training programs in which the training was given, but the placement rate of people in jobs was extremely low. And for the cost of training, that was enough to send them to the finest university in the land. Things of that kind, things that we discovered in our own welfare reform.

And part of it—the advantage you see in it, from that State level out there as Governor—the Federal programs mandated on local and State government. And even if you were given some say in the administration of those programs, you were so bound and restricted by regulations and redtape that time after time you found yourself saying we could do this program twice as well and at half the price if we weren't bound by these restrictions. And yet it was the Government saying, you can't change, you've got to do these things this way.

Well, I made up my mind when I came here that we'd done what we could at the State level—our welfare reform in California was tremendously successful, and it didn't throw people out into the snowdrifts or take away from those who had real need at all under some of those programs. We found people that were, say, 2½ times their income—outside income—above the poverty rate, and they were eligible for as many as four Federal aid programs. You said, "We don't think this is what was intended."

I want to see government to where it should be. And a President said it before me. In 1932 Franklin Delano Roosevelt, in campaigning, said one of his purposes would be to restore to the States and local communities, and to the people, authority and autonomy that had been unjustly seized by the Federal Government.

Mr. Sidey. Well now, Mr. Gorbachev—are you up to him?

The President. Yes, looking foward to it.

Mr. Sidey. He's a young fellow and quite vigorous.

The President. Yes, but I'll try not to take advantage of him. [*Laughter*]

Mr. Sidey. Thank you, Mr. President.

Note: The interview began at 11:11 a.m. in the Oval Office at the White House. A tape was not available for verification of the content of this interview, which was released by the Office of the Press Secretary on July 28.

Statement by Principal Deputy Press Secretary Speakes on Limiting Nuclear Weapons Testing
July 29, 1985

President Reagan's central arms control objective, and the objective declared in the U.S.-Soviet joint statement issued in Geneva last January, is to eliminate nuclear weapons altogether. We, therefore, have proposed at the bargaining table in the nuclear and space talks in Geneva radical reductions in the size of existing nuclear arsenals, beginning with the most destabilizing ballistic missiles. We believe such radical reductions, coupled with possible future strategic defenses for both sides, are the most promising avenues to eliminate the danger of nuclear war. We regret that the Soviet Union to date has been unwilling to negotiate in concrete and detailed terms to achieve such reductions in Geneva. In this respect not only have they failed to address our desire for deep reductions and enhanced stability, but they have not been willing to present specific numerical levels supporting their own approach.

While we believe the most direct path is through equitable, verifiable reductions, we also believe that verifiable limitations on nuclear testing can play a useful, though more modest role. For that reason, President Reagan, in his speech to the U.N. General Assembly on September 24, 1984, proposed that the Soviet Union and the U.S.

exchange visits of experts to measure directly at nuclear test sites the yields of nuclear weapons tests. The President views this proposal as a means to increase confidence in verifiable limits on underground testing. To date, the Soviet Union has refused to agree to this practical and fairminded approach.

As a demonstration of our seriousness, the President has extended to the Soviet leadership our invitation for a Soviet team to observe and to measure a nuclear test at our Nevada test site. This offer, which is unconditional, is a unilateral step which clearly demonstrates the U.S. intention to go the extra mile. The Soviet experts are invited to bring any instrumentation devices that the Soviet Union deems necessary to measure the yield of this test. This U.S. initiative demonstrates our commitment to achieving verifiable limitations in nuclear testing.

We would welcome Soviet interest in joining us in developing and putting into place truly verifiable and durable limits on nuclear testing. We believe the President's initiative is the most practical approach to begin addressing this serious problem. We reiterate there are no conditions to this far-reaching offer, and we look forward to a positive and timely Soviet response.

953

Note: Larry M. Speakes read the statement to reporters in the Briefing Room at the White House during his daily press briefing, which began at 9:28 a.m.

Statement by Principal Deputy Press Secretary Speakes on the Fiscal Year 1986 Budget
July 29, 1985

The President a few minutes ago telephoned Senate Majority Leader Bob Dole with the following message:

—A Federal budget for 1986 is essential to maintaining economic recovery. It is up to Congress to act on the budget before they leave for summer vacation.

—The President will not support a tax increase in the form of an oil import fee. He will not support a change in Social Security COLA's nor will he support a change in tax indexing that protects the working American from inflation-generated tax increases.

—He firmly believes there is sufficient ground for a compromise between the Senate and the House that can provide in excess of $50 billion in deficit reductions.

—Deficit reduction is the number one issue in America today. The only way to get true deficit reduction is to cut Federal spending and do so this year.

—He complimented Senator Dole on his and the Senate's efforts to produce a budget and shares his belief that too much is at stake to allow deficit reduction to fall by the wayside. The Senate and House have come a long way toward agreeing on a budget. Reasonable men and women can agree. It's up to the conferees to meet without delay and act with dispatch. They need to put aside their differences, get down to business, and produce a budget.

—This afternoon Chief of Staff Don Regan will meet with Budget Committee Chairmen Pete Domenici and William Gray to express the President's desire to have Congress adopt a budget resolution.

Note: Larry M. Speakes read the statement to reporters in the Briefing Room at the White House during his daily press briefing, which began at 9:28 a.m.

Statement by Principal Deputy Press Secretary Speakes on Trade With Japan
July 30, 1985

The Government of Japan today announced its Action Program for Imports. This program is to be the framework for Japan's market-opening activities over the next 3 years. It fulfills a commitment by Prime Minister Nakasone to provide such a program by the end of July; however, it is difficult to determine from the announcement whether the program will remove the bulk of these barriers in a timely fashion. So, we must reserve judgment until the effect of the program on our exports is realized.

The program focuses on long-term access to the Japanese market. Effective implementation of its initiatives would remove numerous nontariff barriers to trade with Japan. While a long-term effort is welcome, earlier implementation would help resolve the crucial trade problems confronting us today.

The action plan focuses primarily on specific trade barriers, but the removal of such barriers will not result in more imports without an accompanying increase in the willingness of Japanese businessmen and consumers to purchase imported goods. We hope the Prime Minister's countrymen will heed his call to reevaluate and alter their attitudes toward imports. An encouraging note is the recognition of the need for domestic demand expansion, which would result in higher levels of imports. Also announced are steps on the path to capital market liberalization, which we have long encouraged. We are especially aware of the need to improve investment opportunities in Japan.

This program comes at a crucial time in Japan's trading relations with us and with her other trading partners. While United States relations with Japan are amicable and cooperative in nearly all respects, trade issues have been a source of deep and growing concern. U.S. firms believe strongly that they have less access and opportunity to compete in the Japanese market than Japanese firms enjoy here. The administration has made righting this imbalance of market opportunities a number one priority with Japan. We will continue discussions with Japan in an ongoing effort to resolve these troublesome trade frictions. This afternoon the Economic Policy Council will begin a thorough examination and analysis of the plan. We will have more to say upon completion of this review.

Note: Larry M. Speakes read the statement to reporters in the Briefing Room at the White House during his daily press briefing, which began at 9:28 a.m.

Statement on the 10th Anniversary of the Signing of the Final Act of the Conference on Security and Cooperation in Europe
July 30, 1985

Ten years have passed since the United States, Canada, and 33 European governments joined in Helsinki to sign the Final Act of the Conference on Security and Cooperation in Europe (CSCE). Today Secretary [of State] Shultz and the Foreign Ministers of those nations, East and West as well as neutral and nonaligned, are meeting again in the capital of Finland to commemorate this important event.

In 1975 President Ford affirmed the support of the United States for the universal standards of international conduct and the fundamental human freedoms contained in the Helsinki Final Act. Today I reaffirm our commitment to those principles and our equally firm dedication to give them meaning in the daily lives of all citizens whose governments have undertaken the obligations contained in the Helsinki Final Act.

The CSCE process has long been a source of hope that the division of Europe can be overcome and that the human freedoms enjoyed in the West will be honored and respected throughout the continent. The Helsinki process offers the peoples of East and West the way that, by patient and serious dialog, we can improve the lives of our individual citizens and increase security and cooperation among our states.

As Secretary Shultz said in his statement in Helsinki, we had no illusions in 1975, and have none today, that words alone can strengthen security and nurture freedom. When heads of state and government gathered in Helsinki 10 years ago, President Ford stated: "History will judge this conference not by what we say here today, but by what we do tomorrow—not by the promises we make, but by the promises we keep."

Sadly, despite some gains, the Soviet Union and several other signatories of the Helsinki Act have failed to keep their promises. Despite the solemn pledge that citizens have the right "to know and act upon" their rights, brave men and women have suffered for taking this commitment by their governments seriously. Those who have tried to exercise freedoms of religion, thought, conscience, and belief have often paid a tragic price. The Helsinki accords called for freer movement of people and ideas across the European divide, but that flow remains impeded, and in the case of the Soviet Union it is but a trickle.

The Helsinki accords and the Madrid concluding document of 1983 provided standards by which to judge the conduct of the 35 participating states and set down a process which can be used to ensure accountability. The United States will continue to uphold these standards and press for compliance with them. We consider this a commitment on the part of all those who voluntarily subscribed to the Final Act of the Helsinki accords.

As we mark this 10th anniversary and reflect on the hopes initially raised by the CSCE process, it is time to renew our efforts to ensure that those hopes were not totally without foundation. We rededicate ourselves to the code of conduct embodied in the Helsinki Final Act. We call upon all of those who participate with us in CSCE to fulfill their pledges. With commitment and determination, we can make the promise of the Helsinki accords' first 10 years the reality of this second decade of CSCE.

Nomination of J.C. Argetsinger To Be a Commissioner of the Copyright Royalty Tribunal
July 30, 1985

The President today announced his intention to nominate J.C. Argetsinger to be a Commissioner of the Copyright Royalty Tribunal for the term of 7 years from September 27, 1984. He would succeed Douglas Coulter.

Since 1982 Mr. Argetsinger has been serving as General Counsel at ACTION. Previously, he served in various United States Senate staff positions, including chief legislative counsel for Senator Frank Murkowski (1982) and Senator Larry Pressler (1979–1982); professional staff member to the Judiciary Committee (1977–1979); chief minority counsel to the Judiciary Committee in 1975–1977; and counsel to the Criminal Laws and Constitution Subcommittees in 1973–1975. In 1970–1973 he was a trial attorney at the U.S. Department of Justice.

Mr. Argetsinger graduated from Cornell University (B.A., 1963) and Western Reserve University (J.D., 1966). He is married, has three children, and resides in Alexandria, VA. He was born December 24, 1941, in Montour Falls, NY.

Nomination of L. William Seidman To Be a Member of the Board of Directors of the Federal Deposit Insurance Corporation
July 30, 1985

The President today announced his intention to nominate L. William Seidman to be a member of the Board of Directors of the Federal Deposit Insurance Corporation for a term of 6 years. He would succeed William M. Isaac.

Mr. Seidman is dean of the College of Business at Arizona State University. Previously, he was Cochairman of the White House Conference on Productivity in 1983–1984; vice chairman of the Phelps Dodge Corp. in 1976–1982; a member of the Board of Foreign Scholarships at the Department of State in 1977–1980; Assistant to the President for Economic Affairs in 1974–1977; managing partner of Seidman & Seidman, certified public accountants, in New York in 1968–1974; and Chairman (1970) and Director of the Federal Reserve Bank of Chicago, Detroit branch, in 1966–1970.

He graduated from Dartmouth (A.B., 1943), Harvard Law School (LL.B., 1948), and the University of Michigan (M.B.A., 1949). He is married, has six children, and resides in Tempe, AZ. He was born April 3, 1921, in Grand Rapids, MI.

Appointment of W. Jarvis Moody as a Member of the Advisory Committee for Trade Negotiations
July 30, 1985

The President today announced his intention to appoint W. Jarvis Moody to be a member of the Advisory Committee for Trade Negotiations for a term of 2 years. This is a reappointment.

Mr. Moody is a consultant to American Security Bank in Washington, DC. He joined American Security Bank in 1964 as vice president, was elected senior vice president in 1968, executive vice president in 1969, director in 1972, and president in 1973. In 1974 he was elected president and a director of American Security Corp. In 1980 he became chairman and chief executive officer of the bank and corporation. He served as chairman, president, and chief executive officer until January 1985. Prior to joining American Security Bank, he was with Morgan Guaranty Trust Co. of New York for 14 years.

Mr. Moody graduated from Harvard University (B.A., 1950) and New York University (M.B.A., 1957). He is married, has two children, and resides in Washington, DC. He was born April 23, 1928, in Mineola, NY.

Nomination of Charles O. Sethness To Be an Assistant Secretary of the Treasury
July 30, 1985

The President today announced his intention to nominate Charles O. Sethness to be an Assistant Secretary of the Treasury (Domestic Finance). He would succeed Thomas J. Healey.

Since 1981 Mr. Sethness has been associate dean for external relations at Harvard Business School. Previously, he was managing director of Morgan Stanley & Co., Inc., in 1975–1981; U.S. Executive Director of the World Bank Group and special assistant to the Secretary of the Treasury in 1973–1975; and associate and vice president of Morgan Stanley & Co. in 1967–1973.

Mr. Sethness graduated from Princeton University (A.B., 1963) and Harvard University (M.B.A., 1966). He is married, has four children, and resides in Lexington, MA. He was born February 24, 1941, in Evanston, IL.

Nomination of Diana Powers Evans To Be a Member of the National Advisory Council on Women's Educational Programs
July 30, 1985

The President today announced his intention to nominate Diana Powers Evans to be a member of the National Advisory Council on Women's Educational Programs for a term expiring May 8, 1988. She would succeed Gilda Bojorquez Gjurich.

She is actively involved in political, civic, and charitable organizations in Oregon. She is a member of the Oregon Historical Society and a volunteer for the Salem public school system.

She graduated from Stanford University (B.A., 1949). She has three children and resides in Salem, OR. She was born February 28, 1928, in Oakland, CA.

Proclamation 5359—National Disability in Entertainment Week, 1985
July 30, 1985

By the President of the United States of America

A Proclamation

The entertainment industry in America today has an enormous ability to inform and educate at the same time that it entertains. This fact is especially well-known to the thirty-six million Americans with disabilities, because they are aware of the concerted efforts being made by the entertainment industry to dispel the unfair stereotypes that still hinder the progress of disabled people in our society.

One of the most important messages the entertainment industry is delivering to the public is that people with disabilities can live full and rewarding lives. They ask only to be given the same opportunities to compete and achieve as everyone else. To provide them with this opportunity is not only fair, but makes available to society a rich pool of talents and ambitions that would otherwise be lost.

The entertainment industry deserves to be commended for its role in making these worthy developments possible. Because of the industry's continuing efforts, Americans with disabilities can look forward to brighter futures, filled with the wide variety of opportunities they deserve.

The Congress, by Senate Joint Resolution 86, has designated the period from July 25, 1985, through July 31, 1985, as "National Disability in Entertainment Week" and has authorized and requested the President to issue a proclamation in honor of this observance.

Now, Therefore, I, Ronald Reagan, President of the United States of America, do hereby proclaim the week of July 25, 1985, through July 31, 1985, as National Disability in Entertainment Week, and I call upon all Americans to observe this week with appropriate ceremonies.

In Witness Whereof, I have hereunto set my hand this thirtieth day of July, in the year of our Lord nineteen hundred and eighty-five, and of the Independence of the United States of America the two hundred and tenth.

RONALD REAGAN

[*Filed with the Office of the Federal Register, 4:22 p.m., July 30, 1985*]

Message to the Congress Reporting a Budget Deferral
July 30, 1985

To the Congress of the United States:

In accordance with the Impoundment Control Act of 1974, I herewith report one new deferral of budget authority for 1985 totaling $16,004,810. The deferral affects an account in the United States Information Agency.

The details of this deferral are contained

in the attached report.

RONALD REAGAN

The White House,
July 30, 1985.

Note: The attachment detailing the deferral was printed in the Federal Register *of August 5.*

Nomination of Donna R. Fitzpatrick To Be an Assistant Secretary of Energy
July 31, 1985

The President today announced his intention to nominate Donna R. Fitzpatrick to be an Assistant Secretary of Energy (Conservation and Renewable Energy). She would succeed Joseph J. Tribble.

Miss Fitzpatrick is presently serving as Acting Assistant Secretary for Conservation and Renewable Energy at the Department of Energy. Previously she was Principal Deputy Assistant Secretary for Conservation and Renewable Energy in 1984–1985. She was a sole practitioner in the general practice of law and a consultant to the Secretary and Under Secretary of Energy in 1983–1984. She was an associate attorney (1980–1983) and a legal assistant (1976–1980) with the firm of O'Connor & Hannan.

She graduated from the American University (B.S., 1972) and George Washington University (J.D., 1980). She was born May 9, 1948, in Washington, DC, where she now resides.

Nomination of Anthony G. Sousa To Be a Member of the Federal Energy Regulatory Commission
July 31, 1985

The President today announced his intention to nominate Anthony G. Sousa to be a member of the Federal Energy Regulatory Commission, Department of Energy, for a term expiring October 20, 1988. This is a reappointment.

Mr. Sousa has been a member of the Federal Energy Regulatory Commission since 1981. Previously he was vice president and general counsel of the Hawaiian Telephone Co., a subsidiary of General Telephone & Electronics Corp., in 1973–1981. In 1968–1973 he was counsel, later senior counsel, and finally administrative law judge with the California Public Utilities Commission.

Mr. Sousa worked with the U.S. Steel Corp. in 1967. From 1959 to 1967, he worked in the traffic department and was later Western regional distribution manager with Thomas J. Lipton, Inc., of San Francisco, CA. Prior to 1959, he was manager of trade promotion and documentation at the Hong Kong General Chamber of Commerce in Hong Kong.

He graduated from St. Luiz Gonzaga College (B.A., 1945) and the University of San Francisco Law School (J.D., 1966). Mr. Sousa is married, has three children, and resides in Washington, DC. He was born in Hong Kong, China, on August 8, 1927.

Message to the Congress Urging Support of Federal Productivity Improvement and Management Reform Efforts
July 31, 1985

To the Congress of the United States:

We share a common objective—to make government more responsive and sensitive to the needs of the people. Over the past several years, significant progress has been made toward:

- Controlling the growth of government by selectively limiting funding through the budget process and by controlling personnel levels;
- Identifying and preventing waste and fraud in government spending;
- Improving individual agency management, to further reduce costs and make better use of its resources;
- Developing government-wide management systems that can be adapted to the needs of each agency; and
- Improving agency delivery systems to ensure that services are efficiently delivered to the American people.

Throughout this effort, I have sought the advice and counsel of the private sector. The President's Private Sector Survey on Cost Control conducted systematic studies of agencies to determine more effective and efficient approaches to delivering services to the public. Thousands of recommendations were made and a large number have been and are being implemented.

The Congress has also supported our efforts by giving the Executive branch important tools to improve efficiency, including milestone legislation such as the Paperwork Reduction Act, the Congressional Reports Elimination Acts, the Prompt Payment Act, the Debt Collection Act, and the Deficit Reduction Act.

Today, I am requesting your further assistance to build on this foundation of progress through your continued support of our efforts to improve government performance. I am also asking you to pass a joint resolution establishing productivity improvement as a national goal and to enact management legislation that is critical to further improving the government's operations and reducing its costs. Together we can enhance our government's ability to use business-like procedures, providing the public with higher quality and more timely services at a lower cost—an objective shared by the Congress and the Executive branch.

The Productivity Improvement Program

The need for and importance of improving the efficiency with which the Federal government delivers goods and services to the American public cannot be overstated. The Federal government now accounts for 24.6% of the GNP. If we pattern our productivity efforts after those which have proven the most productive in the private sector, it is reasonable to expect that we could match or exceed the private sector's gains, which have recently climbed to about 3% per year.

Therefore, I will shortly establish a government-wide program to improve productivity 20% by 1992. Each agency will be called upon to establish specific priorities for improvement of their services, to examine each of their functions, and to achieve agency-wide productivity goals. They will be asked to focus on results, rather than on process. Agencies will be asked to draw upon the creativity and ingenuity of all employees, to properly reward any achievements in productivity improvement, and to minimize any negative impact productivity increases might have on their employees. This management approach is standard in the private sector and we plan to make it standard in the Federal government.

The President's Management Improvement Program: Reform '88 has provided a solid foundation upon which to base this productivity improvement program, as great strides have been made in establishing effective cash and credit management programs, improving agency management systems, lowering administrative costs, and reducing waste and fraud. Some of our Federal agencies have already demonstrated that they can make real improvements in productivity when they commit their time and talent.

The success of this effort will be reinforced by an early expression of Congressional resolve to make productivity improvement a national goal. Each department and agency will report to me through the Office of Management and Budget on their productivity goals, and on both the progress and the problems in accomplishing them. On the basis of that report, our annual management report to the Congress, which is part of the budget, will also describe our efforts to achieve productivity improvements.

The Administration's Management Legislation Initiatives

The Congress has been most helpful in passing legislation that has made management reform possible. To further assure successful implementation of our Management Improvement Program: Reform '88, I have directed the Office of Management and Budget and agencies to transmit legislative proposals which would make it possible to improve substantially the effectiveness of the Executive branch. These management legislative initiatives cover the important areas of fraud prevention, payment integrity and simplification, procurement, reorganization authority, and reduction in regulatory and paperwork burdens. Some of these proposals have already been sent to the Congress, and others will be transmitted in the days ahead. I want to stress that each of these proposals plays an important role in improving government's management, reducing fraud and waste, or improving productivity. I hope that the Congress can enact them promptly.

Conclusion

Now is the time for us to redouble our efforts to improve the operations of government. The budget deficit, the need to make programs more responsive to their beneficiaries, the complexity of the problems we face, and the very size of government itself all require us to apply the best methods and procedures available to improve productivity. Enactment of the various legislative proposals outlined here will enable us to continue and strengthen our joint effort to improve government management.

Federal managers want to do a good job. Given the necessary tools and support, they can do so. Passage of these proposals will demonstrate our commitment to increased productivity and improved management practices in the Federal government. The American people want and deserve a Federal government that is fair, efficient, effective, and, above all, productive.

RONALD REAGAN

The White House,
July 31, 1985.

Memorandum Directing Improvements in Service Delivery and Agency Productivity
July 31, 1985

Memorandum for the Heads of Executive Departments and Agencies

Four years ago we embarked together upon an ambitious mission to improve management of the Federal government and ensure wiser use of each tax dollar, while simultaneously making government more responsive to the needs of our constituency—the American public. Some observers of government activities have often said it was "mission impossible," but through our progress so far, we have proved them wrong.

In the past, in practice as well as in principle, you have been very supportive of our Management Improvement Program: Reform '88. As a direct result of your efforts, we are instituting vigorous new controls on program growth, trimming administrative costs, reducing waste and fraud, and streamlining the Federal field structure.

These achievements are substantial and

are a necessary first phase in making government work better. Now it is time to focus on the next phase of Reform '88: improving our delivery of goods and services to the public. To facilitate this effort, I have asked the Congress to demonstrate its support for a government-wide program to improve Federal productivity by passing a joint resolution declaring productivity improvement as a national goal. In addition, I am asking the Congress to pass a legislative program to improve government management tools by addressing specific problems relating to fraud prevention, payment integrity and simplification, procurement, reorganization authority, and reductions in regulatory and paperwork burdens.

While Congress works to enact these measures, there is much we can do to lay the groundwork as we enter the beginning stages of the FY '87 budget process. You should begin by identifying specific priorities which will improve service delivery and agency productivity. These initiatives should concentrate on those programs which make a real difference to the American public, as well as on internal administrative processes.

Through demonstrated ability to institute progressive change, we have begun to stem the public's disillusionment with the Federal government's capability to serve them well at a reasonable price. I know you have as one of your highest priorities completion of the next phase of our management improvement journey—improved delivery of public services through higher quality, improved timeliness, and lower cost to the taxpayers.

RONALD REAGAN

Appointment of Calvin M. Whitesell as a Commissioner of the Franklin Delano Roosevelt Memorial Commission
July 31, 1985

The President today announced his intention to appoint Calvin M. Whitesell to be a Commissioner of the Franklin Delano Roosevelt Memorial Commission. He will succeed Anna M. Rosenberg.

Mr. Whitesell is an attorney with the law firm of Whitesell, Morrow and Romine in Montgomery, AL. He is a member of the Alabama Trial Lawyers Association and of the American Bar Association Committee on Governmentally Assisted Housing Programs. He served as a special assistant attorney general of Alabama in 1973–1979.

He graduated from the University of Alabama (J.D., 1951). He is married, has three children, and resides in Montgomery, AL. He was born November 22, 1926, in Bainbridge, GA.

Letter Accepting the Resignation of David A. Stockman as Director of the Office of Management and Budget
July 31, 1985

Dear Dave:

It is with regret and a high regard for your accomplishments that I accept your resignation as Director of the Office of Management and Budget.

Not many people, even here in Washington, could name our Nation's Budget Direc- tors for the past twenty years. But just about everyone knows who has held that post for the past four and a half years. Your analytical intelligence and obvious devotion to the public interest quickly made you one of my most important advisers. The fresh approach you brought to budget issues, and your courage in confronting long-established special interests, earned you the respect even of those who opposed us in specific areas. Most importantly, you have shown that it is possible to reduce Federal spending without sacrificing vital human services.

Sometimes, in dealing with an issue as important and multi-faceted as the preparation of the Federal Budget, it is easy to become discouraged by the sheer magnitude of the task and to wonder if you are really making any progress. But the public tributes coming your way from every quarter are proof that you have indeed made a difference. Future OMB Directors will be measured against the standard of your performance, and they will find it a hard standard to match. I want to thank you personally for a job well done.

Nancy joins me in sending you and Jennifer and your daughter Rachel our best wishes for every future happiness.

Sincerely,

RONALD REAGAN

[The Honorable David A. Stockman, Director, Office of Management and Budget, Washington, D.C. 20503]

Dear Mr. President:

A sad day has arrived for me—the day I leave service in your Administration and embark on a new career and challenge.

I do so with heartfelt gratitude for the opportunity you have given me to participate in an historic and momentous venture. You set out to change the course of American history and to steer the nation back to its true strength, prosperity and greatness. You have succeeded to a remarkable degree and with permanent effect. Even though difficult problems still lie ahead, our nation's direction and goals are clear once again.

I will always be proud of whatever contributions I have made along the way. More importantly, I will always cherish the kindness, consideration and patience you afforded me—sometimes under very trying circumstances. Changing decades' old habits and policies has necessarily given rise to contention and disagreements among all of us entrusted with the responsibilities of governance. But your unfailing grace, spirit and goodwill have made all those debates and battles more pleasant, rewarding and memorable than you can possibly appreciate.

As you know, Jennifer and I are now the parents of a three-month old daughter. Just as Rachel is the pride of our lives, I know that someday the pride of her's will be that her father was privileged to serve President Ronald Reagan. With your leadership America was put on a new path that will mean a bright and hopeful future for her and millions of her fellow citizens. For this, we will always be grateful.

Mr. President, you have my abiding respect as I leave and my best wishes as you continue with the challenges ahead.

With my deepest regard,

DAVID A. STOCKMAN

[The President, The White House, Washington, DC 20500]

Remarks to Members of the Evangelical Press During a White House Briefing on Tax Reform
August 1, 1985

I've kept you waiting long enough. [*Laughter*] I know I'm late, but thank you very much, and welcome to the White House. I know all of you've already heard the wisdom of Vice President Bush and Don Regan and Manley Johnson. Somehow I don't think they had in mind that they were saving the best for last. [*Laughter*]

Seriously, I want to take a moment to first thank so many of you for keeping me in your prayers when I was in the hospital. A number of you sent some very kind words of encouragement, and I'm truly grateful.

May I take a few minutes of your time today to lay out some of the thinking that went into our tax reform proposals, some of the philosophy behind it. When you talk about taxes, you're talking about the movement of money in the United States—what goes to the Government, what stays in the economy and in the pockets of the people. And I want you to know what concerns motivated us as we considered the flow of money. We're concerned about those who would manipulate the system and invest a hundred dollars in a tax shelter to get a thousand dollar writeoff. And it's the system itself that we want to change.

We didn't worry about special interest groups and special interest pleading. We were concerned about the interests of all working Americans, starting with the central entity—an entity that is itself central to the interests of the entire nation. We were concerned about the family, and so, we created a tax reform proposal that puts the family first. Why? Because there's nothing more important to all of us and nothing more important to our society and our nation and our future than the family. The family is where our children learn a moral view; it's where the values of personal responsibility and loyalty and kindness are taught. And it's not saying too much to say as the family goes, so goes the nation. And there are many people who share this view, and it isn't exactly revolutionary. And yet, in spite of that, in spite of our general agreement in this country that the family is important, the public policy of our nation has, in fact, worked against the interests of the family for decades now. You know the facts; you've heard them repeated today.

But I'll just say that for me the biggest proof of how careless we've been in our support of the family is the personal tax exemption for each child and dependent—1948, the amount of that exemption was $600. If we had kept up with inflation, the exemption today would be $2,700. Well, as you know, it hasn't nearly kept up. Administration after administration just hasn't been interested in raising the exemption. They've been more interested in finding new ways to spend each family's earnings.

I'm tired of that kind of behavior, and I'm sick and tired of governments that put the family at the end of the line.

We raised the exemption to $1,000 in 1981 and indexed it to inflation so that today it's $1,040. And now, in our tax reform proposal, we're raising the exemption to $2,000 and, again, indexing it to inflation. Now, I'm proud of this, and there's one thing I want to make clear: Our tax reform plan is not static. We're working with Congress so we can put together a plan that we can all live with. But I'll tell you one thing: The $2,000 exemption is the centerpiece of our program. This is a family-first bill, and that $2,000 is very important to us and, I think, to you. Not only are we going to get the exemption up, we're going to get tax rates down in order to encourage economic growth. And it's economic growth that will give new economic power to the family. We're talking about jobs for your children, a future for your children.

Just parenthetically, by the way, I'm learning about a whole new species of animal as I work on tax reform. I call that animal the "I-like-it-but." [Laughter] I talk to a politician, I ask him how he feels about our plan, he says, "I like it, but . . . ." [Laughter] "Well, I think you should increase capital gains," he says. I talk to another fellow, and he says, "I like it, but you've got to retain deductibility." And it's catching. I listen to them, and I understand why they're saying what they're saying. And they ask if I couldn't just bend on this or that, and I find myself saying, "Well, I like it, but . . . ." [Laughter] But if I give in to everyone who's protecting their little loophole or their little special interest, the good news is we'll get a bill through Congress, and the bad news is it won't be tax reform.

Well, there are many elements of our plan that benefit the family that you're familiar with, such as our attempt to expend full IRA benefits to those who work in the home, as well as those who work outside it. And the point I want to make is that so often in the past we've met and we've discussed issues that are important to you and important to this administration—school prayer and abortion, for instance.

But I want to urge all of you and ask all of you to help us also in the area of the tax reform. It has as much to do with how this nation lives its life as any other proposal or initiative put forth in the past decade. It has as much to do with how the family lives and whether it will flourish as any initiative that's proposed in the past decade. It's nothing less than crucial. And so, I frankly ask for your help and your interest. And if there's any more you need to know or discuss, any questions you have, please contact the members of the staff here, and they'll do whatever they can.

I need your help. I'm not embarrassed to ask for it. And I have faith that you'll come through, because you always have. So, that was the last, I guess, on the agenda here after all the other. I hope I've not been repeating too much of what you might have already heard.

But I thank you all for being here. God bless all of you.

Note: The President spoke at 12:11 p.m. in the East Room at the White House. In his opening remarks, he referred to Donald T. Regan, Assistant to the President and Chief of Staff, and Manley Johnson, Assistant Secretary of the Treasury (Economic Policy).

Nomination of Elizabeth Flores Burkhart To Be a Member of the National Credit Union Administration Board
August 1, 1985

The President today announced his intention to nominate Elizabeth Flores Burkhart to be a member of the National Credit Union Administration Board for the term of 6 years expiring April 10, 1991. This is a reappointment.

Since 1982 Mrs. Burkhart has been a member of the National Credit Union Administration. Previously she was Associate Deputy Administrator for Information Resources Management at the Veterans Administration in 1981–1982. In 1981 she also served at the Veterans Administration as consultant and later as Assistant Deputy Administrator. She was deputy treasurer for the Reagan-Bush Compliance Committee and cost center manager for the Reagan-Bush Committee. In 1979–1980 she was controller of the George Bush for President Committee in Houston, TX. Previously she was assistant vice president of the Texas-Commerce Bank in Houston, having served with that institution in 1968–1979. She served in the United States Marine Corps in 1954–1956.

She graduated from Midwestern University (B.A., 1966) and Houston Baptist University (M.B.A., 1979). She is married and resides in Washington, DC. She was born July 19, 1935, in Waelder, TX.

Nomination of Robert B. Sims To Be an Assistant Secretary of Defense
August 1, 1985

The President today announced his intention to nominate Robert B. Sims to be an Assistant Secretary of Defense (Public Affairs). He would succeed Michael Ira Burch.

Since 1983 Mr. Sims has been at the White House, serving as Special Assistant to the President and Deputy Press Secretary for Foreign Affairs. Previously he was Special Assistant to the President and Senior Director of Public Affairs on the National Security Council in 1982–1983. A former Navy public affairs specialist, Mr. Sims was a senior research fellow at the National Defense University before joining the NSC staff in May 1982. He was Deputy Chief of Information for the Navy Department in 1978–1981 and Special Assistant for Public Affairs to the Secretary of the Navy in 1974–1978. Mr. Sims has worked as a daily newspaper reporter and as a weekly newspaper editor and publisher. His writings include "The Pentagon Reporters," a book published in 1983.

He received a bachelor of arts degree from Union University (1956) and masters degrees in journalism and political science in 1971 from the University of Wisconsin. He was a Rotary Foundation fellow, studying international relations at the University of Sydney, Australia, and is a graduate of the National War College. He is married, has four children, and resides in Washington, DC. He was born November 26, 1934, in Alamo, TN.

Nomination of Four Members of the Board of Directors of the United States Institute of Peace, and Announcement of Three Statutory Members
August 1, 1985

The President today announced his intention to nominate the following individuals to be members of the Board of Directors of the United States Institute of Peace. These are new positions.

For terms of 2 years expiring January 19, 1987:

Sidney Lovett has been the senior minister of the First Church of Christ Congregational in West Hartford, CT, since 1976. He graduated from Yale University (B.A., 1950) and Union Theological Seminary (M.Div., 1953). He was born May 1, 1928, in Boston, MA, and now resides in Hartford, CT.

Richard John Neuhaus is director for the Rockford Institute Center on Religion and Society in New York City. He also serves as editor of the Religion and Society Report and the Lutheran Forum Letter. He graduated from Concordia Seminary in St. Louis, MO (B.A., M.Div.). He was born May 14, 1936, in Ontario, Canada, and now resides in New York City.

W. Bruce Weinrod is director of foreign policy and defense studies for the Heritage Foundation in Washington, DC. He graduated from the American University (B.A., 1969), the University of Pennsylvania (M.A., 1973), and

Georgetown University Law School (M.B.A., 1978). He was born January 7, 1947, in Washington, DC, where he now resides.

For a term of 4 years expiring January 19, 1989:

John Norton Moore is director of the Center for Oceans Law and Policy and a professor of law at the University of Virginia. Previously he was Chairman of the National Security Council Interagency Task Force on the Law of the Sea (1973–1976). He graduated from Drew University (A.B., 1959), Duke University Law School (L.L.B., 1962), and the University of Illinois (L.L.M., 1965). He was born June 12, 1937, in New York City.

In addition, the following will serve as members of the Board of Directors by law:

Kenneth A. Adelman, Director of the United States Arms Control and Disarmament Agency;

Max M. Kampelman, Ambassador of the United States to the United States Office for Arms Reduction Negotiations in Geneva, who will serve as the designee of the Secretary of State;

Richard N. Perle, Assistant Secretary of Defense (International Security Policy), who will serve as the designee of the Secretary of Defense.

966

Message to the Congress Transmitting an Amendment to the France-United States Defense Nuclear Cooperation Agreement
August 1, 1985

To the Congress of the United States:

I am pleased to transmit to the Congress, pursuant to Sections 123 b. and 123 d. of the Atomic Energy Act of 1954, as amended (42 U.S.C. 2153 (b), (d)), the text of an amendment modifying the 1961 defense nuclear cooperation agreement between the United States and France to provide for cooperation on the safety and security of nuclear activities and installations for mutual defense purposes. I am also including a copy of my written approval, authorization, and determination concerning that agreement, as amended. A copy of the joint unclassified letter submitted to me by the Secretaries of Energy and Defense, which provides a summary position on the amendment, is also enclosed. A classified letter and attachments are being transmitted directly to the appropriate congressional committees.

The amendment focuses our cooperation on the safety and security of each nation's nuclear activities and installations. It does not allow transfer of nuclear components or weapons, or special nuclear materials, or source material and, therefore, fully complies with the international agreements in matters of non-proliferation and does not alter other mutual cooperation agreements that exist between the two countries in the field of defense.

I have concluded that the cooperation authorized by the amendment is in the United States' interest and have determined that performance of the amended agreement will promote and not constitute an unreasonable risk to the common defense and security. Accordingly, I have approved the amendment and authorized its execution.

I have also found that the amendment meets all applicable requirements of the Atomic Energy Act, as amended, for agreements for defense nuclear cooperation; and therefore, I am transmitting it to the Congress without exempting it from any requirement contained in Section 123 a. of the Atomic Energy Act. The transmission shall constitute submittal for the purposes of Sections 123 b. and 123 d. of the Atomic Energy Act. The 30-day continuous session period specified in Section 123 b. shall begin immediately. Upon completion of this period, the 60-day continuous session period provided for in Section 123 d. shall commence.

RONALD REAGAN

The White House,
August 1, 1985.

Statement on Congressional Approval of the Federal Budget Resolution
August 1, 1985

Today's budget resolution compromise follows a long and difficult effort by the Senate and House conferees, but it marks only a beginning, not an end. I would have preferred more substantial reductions, such as were in the original Senate version in May, so I will continue to work to reduce spending even further and put budget deficits on a downward path.

In this connection, I plan to examine each and every upcoming appropriations bill line by line; and if it is excessive, out of line, or in any way jeopardizes our national security, I will not hesitate to use my veto pen. I am pleased that the deficit reductions agreed to by the conferees are achieved through spending reductions and not tax increases and are consistent with the budget philosophy we proposed in February. Large budget deficits were not created by the American people paying too little in taxes, but by the Federal Government spending too much of the people's money.

Over the long term, the budget can be brought into balance by a steadily expanding economy and a firm grip on the Federal purse. Therefore, we intend to redouble our efforts in the weeks ahead to secure passage of tax reform, the line-item veto, and a con-stitutional amendment mandating a balanced Federal budget.

With these changes and the prospect of additional budget reductions in the future, there is every reason to expect continued strong economic growth. This should have a positive effect in encouraging lower rates of interest, creating new jobs, and keeping inflation down, which is very good news for every American.

Letter to the Speaker of the House and the President of the Senate Transmitting a Proposed District of Columbia Fiscal Year 1985 Budget Supplemental
August 2, 1985

Dear Mr. Speaker: (Dear Mr. President:)

In accordance with the District of Columbia Self-Government and Governmental Reorganization Act, I am transmitting a fiscal year 1985 budget supplemental of the District of Columbia. This supplemental proposes a net increase of $35 million in the city's General Fund Budget, including $53 million in program increases and $18 million in rescission of budget authority of District agencies.

This increase is in District of Columbia funds and does not affect the Federal Budget.

Sincerely,

RONALD REAGAN

Note: Identical letters were sent to Thomas P. O'Neill, Jr., Speaker of the House of Representatives, and George Bush, President of the Senate.

Appointment of Two Members of the Intergovernmental Advisory Council on Education
August 2, 1985

The President today announced his intention to appoint the following individuals to be members of the Intergovernmental Advisory Council on Education for the remainder of the terms expiring July 27, 1990:

Anne Lindeman will succeed Dalton Sheppard, Jr. She is a member of the State senate in Arizona, where she served as chairman of the Committee on Education in 1979–1984. She is a member of the Education Commission of the States. She served as a member of the State Vocational Education Advisory Commission in 1977. She has three children and resides in Phoenix, AZ. She was born September 10, 1932, in East Orange, NJ.

John K. Andrews, Jr., will succeed Jacqueline E. McGregor. He is vice president for Outreach, Hillsdale College, Michigan, and Shavano Institute for National Leadership in Colorado. Previously he was executive director of Adventure Unlimited, Inc., in Denver, CO. He is married, has three children, and resides in Englewood, CO. He was born May 1, 1944, in Allegan, MI.

Proclamation 5360—Freedom of the Press Day, 1985
August 2, 1985

*By the President of the United States
of America*

A Proclamation

Freedom of the press is one of our most important freedoms and also one of our oldest. In the form of the First Amendment it is permanently embedded in our Constitution, but its roots go back to colonial America and indeed to the traditional laws and customs of England.

Two hundred and fifty years ago, on August 4, 1735, one of the landmark events of American legal history occurred when a court exonerated the newspaper publisher John Peter Zenger, who had been accused of sedition because of his zeal in uncovering official corruption. Since then, his case has become a symbol of our Nation's continuing commitment to maintaining freedom of the press.

Today, our tradition of a free press as a vital part of our democracy is as important as ever. The news media are now using modern techniques to bring our citizens information not only on a daily basis but instantaneously as important events occur. This flow of information helps make possible an informed electorate and so contributes to our national system of self-govern-

ment. Freedom of the Press Day is an appropriate time to remember the contributions a free press has made and is continuing to make to the development of our Nation.

In recognition, the Congress, by House Joint Resolution 164, has designated August 4, 1985, as "Freedom of the Press Day" and authorized and requested the President to issue a proclamation in observance of this event.

Now, Therefore, I, Ronald Reagan, President of the United States of America, do hereby proclaim August 4, 1985, as Freedom of the Press Day. I call upon the people of the United States to observe this occasion with appropriate ceremonies and activities.

In Witness Whereof, I have hereunto set my hand this second day of August, in the year of our Lord nineteen hundred and eighty-five, and of the Independence of the United States of America the two hundred and tenth.

RONALD REAGAN

[*Filed with the Office of the Federal Register, 10:04 a.m., August 5, 1985*]

Note: *The proclamation was released by the Office of the Press Secretary on August 3.*

Radio Address to the Nation on Economic Growth and Tax Reform
August 3, 1985

My fellow Americans:

The month of August marks an important milestone for our country. Four years ago we took our first giant step toward putting this economy back in your hands when I signed our bill to lower and permanently index the tax rates of every working American. After being held back so long, a ringing declaration went forth that the dream of economic freedom was alive and well in America's soul. And you responded, burst-

ing ahead with energy and enthusiasm, ignoring all those who were downright panic-struck that Washington could no longer reach deeper and deeper into the pocketbooks of your families. While they were busy predicting disaster, you began transforming our economy from top to bottom.

From the nightmare of interest rates that, at 21½ percent, had pierced the highest level since the Civil War, double-digit inflation raging like an uncontrollable virus, long gas lines, and the worst tax burden in peacetime history, we awoke to a new dawn of progress—swift, sure, and steady progress that has continued for 4 years and is continuing today. Inflation, which has been as high as 13 percent, has not just eased but has sharply declined to less than 4 percent. The prime interest rate, while still too high, has dropped to its lowest level in almost 7 years. And decontrolling oil prices did not send the price of gas at the pump skyrocketing as some said it would; prices are lower today than 4 years ago.

Progress regained has renewed our confidence. We can see and feel that confidence in the vigorous increases in consumer purchases, in greater incentives to save, and in the advances to record levels in the stock market. All of us are building a new America, a dynamic America that's created nearly 8 million jobs in the last 32 months and almost 500,000 last month alone; an enterprising America with a record 635,000 new business incorporations last year, the auto, housing, and construction industries rejuvenated, and spectacular breakthroughs in new technologies; and, most important, a successful America with one of the most impressive economic expansions in postwar history. Even as we speak, new strength in factory orders, jobs, leading economic indicators, and equity markets show the U.S. economy flexing its muscles for another big push toward greater prosperity.

But this building of a new America is not complete. We still face a great challenge in reducing the deficit, but those who insist that spending cannot be cut any further and that we must increase your taxes to reduce the deficit are flatout wrong.

Last February I submitted a budget calling for large savings, including elimination of 17 costly and wasteful programs. The budget resolution finally agreed to by the Congress this week represents a good-faith beginning to tackle the deficit the right way—by reducing what government can

spend, rather than simply taking more of what you earn so government can keep spending levels high. But when Congress votes on the various spending bills this fall, we will review each one line by line to be sure they don't contain excessive spending levels or might jeopardize our national security.

Let's all recognize that spending has not been cut to the bone and that a tax increase would only reduce our incentives to work, save, and invest and ultimately weaken our economy and make deficits far worse. Sometimes it's difficult to remember that you didn't send us to Washington to feed the alligators; you sent us to drain the swamp. We didn't come to raise your taxes, but to lower them. And what better moment than this anniversary of our first tax cut than to sound the trumpet once more.

This nation is poised to forge ahead, poised to give every citizen the noble chance to break free and taste the thrill of high adventure. Our next great advance must come from a total overhaul of our tax code. And make no mistake, that day is coming. As Congressman Dan Rostenkowski, chairman of the House Ways and Means Committee, indicated this week, "Reports of the death of tax reform are greatly exaggerated." We can pass an historic tax reform to sweep away unjust loopholes favoring the powerful few. We can reduce the top rate of tax to 15 or 25 percent for all but a tiny fraction. We can reach for excellence and make America the most powerful success story for growth and human progress the world has ever known. And, yes, with your help, we can continue the success we began 4 years ago.

Till next week, thanks for listening, and God bless you.

Note: The President spoke at 12:06 p.m. from Camp David, MD.

Remarks and a Question-and-Answer Session With Reporters
August 5, 1985

Administration Goals and Accomplishments

The President. I have a statement here first. I wanted to take this opportunity to look back as well as ahead to our expectations for the fall.

Nineteen eighty-five is shaping up as a year of progress. The economy is in good health; America's at peace and helping to push forward the frontiers of freedom. We can draw confidence from seeing interest rates still trending down, an inflation rate that is still remaining under 4 percent, and nearly 600,000 jobs created this year. And now with the economy's batteries recharged, we're setting forth with new zest. The road ahead looks clear to a strong job market, with no new tax increases to slow us down and no dark clouds of inflation on the horizon.

But there is much we can and must do to make this a better year. We intend to launch a major fall offensive—going to the people and working with Congress to achieve major and much-needed reforms.

We will intensify our efforts for budget reform, for a line-item veto—which 43 State Governors already have—and for a balanced budget amendment, finally mandating Congress may spend no more than it takes in. We cannot reduce chronic overspending by Congress with a mere carrot of friendly appeals to good intentions. We must also be able to bear down with a rod of real discipline. We'll also devote special attention to the areas of farm and trade, which have great impact on the budget and the health of our economy. Come Labor Day, we're going to pull out all the stops for passage of tax reform. We cannot abide the injustices and disincentives in the current code. We must replace it with a new system offering lower marginal tax rates and greater fairness for the American people. For the sake of our future, there is no higher nor more pressing priority.

On the legislative front, we didn't get all the savings we sought, but we held firm on principle, and we did succeed—which I consider crucial—in attacking budget deficits, not by reducing the people's earnings but by reducing government spending. Many appropriations bills will be coming up, and I'm looking forward to examining each one with my veto pen hovering over every line.

In foreign affairs, we've turned the tide of gradual Soviet expansion so evident 5 years ago. Our alliances are stronger, and we have regained our position of leadership, working to resolve the international debt burden, carrying the flag for the spread of democracy, and seeking real gains on key global issues from human rights to nonproliferation. At Geneva we're in the best position in more than a generation to achieve real reductions of nuclear weapons. All we need is a serious approach by the Soviets. I look forward to my meeting with General Secretary Gorbachev in Geneva this November.

Looking elsewhere, we've begun rebuilding our defenses: Our conventional forces are stronger, Congress has supported our strategic modernization program, and our deterrent is stronger. But we must press on and complete that program. We're also going forward with research on our nonnuclear Strategic Defense Initiative, holding forth the great hope that we may one day protect the people of this planet from the threat of nuclear attack.

And we achieved a breakthrough when Congress recognized the importance of Central America to our national security by voting to assist the freedom fighters in Nicaragua. The cause of freedom is the cause of peace, and I commend all those in Congress who voted to support the profreedom movements in Nicaragua, Afghanistan, and Cambodia and to repeal the Clark amendment that banned help for the freedom fighters in Angola.

So, as I said, we've begun well, but we have much more to do.

And now, I suspect there may be some of you that have a question or two.

Federal Budget

Q. Mr. President, some of the Senate Republicans feel you've really pulled the rug out from under them, that you really did not go for a big deficit cut, and that you are going to face a very tough time. Your statement's very rosy, but that isn't the outlook that's coming from the Hill.

The President. Well, there may be some who feel that way. But before they left town, [Senate Majority Leader] Bob Dole came over late in the afternoon, and we had a good meeting up there and were in agreement that, yes, the budget resolution that we got was not as much as we had hoped; a compromise never is. But we think it came very close to the figures that—well, in some instances, were even greater than the figures that I had first proposed in February. And we were in agreement also, and Bob agreed that the Senate and I—the Senate Republicans—we could be working together. And I'm hoping that it'll continue to be a bipartisan effort.

Q. But, Mr. President, the figures that came out of the two Houses—the $56 or $57 billion—are being challenged by the Congressional Budget Office and by some of the legislative leaders who say the first-year savings won't be anywhere close to that. Sir, do you think that next year, a congressional election year, you can do any better in actually eliminating programs as you first proposed?

The President. We're going to try. We're going to try to get—well, in other words, let's say over this 3-year projection we have to make—I have never believed that what we agree to now is the final for the next 3 years and we're frozen in. We're going to continue trying to eliminate programs that have outlived their usefulness and are no longer serving a worthwhile purpose and some things that the Government never should have been doing in the first place. And I think that there will be some pretty sizable support for that because, even though it's an election year, I think most in Congress know that the number one— every poll shows this—the number one concern of the people of the country today is the deficit and the overspending by government. So, I think that they'll be aware of that.

Q. Do you think real deficit reduction is possible without getting into the entitlement area, which you have put off the table with the Speaker?

The President. Well now, let me point something out about the entitlement area. I didn't pull it off. We had a meeting out here in the patio, outside the office one day, with the leadership of both Houses and both parties. And at that meeting, the Democrat leadership made it plain that as far as they were concerned Social Security was off the table—nonnegotiable. Now, at that time, the conference had broken up. There were no longer any conference meetings going on to try and bring a conference resolution.

When the proposal was then made again from the Senate with regard to Social Security COLA's and the tax increase, I immediately called Bob Dole and told him that there was no way that I could support a tax increase; I think this would be counterproductive with regard to spending cuts and all. And I told him also that I thought we all were aware that we couldn't go back into conference if it was based on Social Security COLA's that had been taken off the table.

But let me point out something else about Social Security. Social Security as a part of the deficit is nothing but a bookkeeping gimmick. Social Security runs a surplus. By incorporating it in the budget, you then add to the budget the outgo and the income. But with that surplus, this apparently reduces the size of the deficit. But the Social Security payroll tax goes into a trust fund and cannot be used for anything else; not one penny of it can be used to reduce the deficit in the overall management of government. To continue to say that this could somehow reduce the deficit by reducing Social Security benefits is a snare and a delusion. And that's why I believe that we shouldn't even wait till 1992, when it is slated to be taken out of the budget and made a separate program. It originally was, and it was during the Johnson years that Social Security was incorporated into the budget for the very purpose of making the deficit then look smaller than it was.

Q. You mean L.B.J. would do that?

The President. What? Oh, he had help up on the Hill.

South Africa

Q. Mr. President, a question about South Africa.

The President. All right.

Q. Do you intend to continue your policy of constructive engagement, or do you think the time is quite near when you might have to take some action such as sanctions?

The President. I believe the results that we've had in this constructive engagement with South Africa justifies our continuing on that score. Obviously, and as we've made very plain, we all feel that apartheid is repugnant. Now, this is the actual participation on a more equitable basis of the black citizens of South Africa. But if you look at the gains that have been made so far by our so-called constructive engagement—the increase in complete biracial education; the fact that American businesses there have over the last several years contributed more than $100 million to black education and housing; the fact that the ban on mixed marriages no longer exists; that some, I think, 40-odd business districts have been opened to black-owned businesses; labor union participation by blacks has come into being; and there's been a great desegregation of hotels and restaurants and parks and sport activities and sports centers and so forth.

There are other things—I can't list them all here, but all these have been coming about as they've continued to work toward what is the final answer. And I think just recently, and over the weekend, the words of Buthelezi, who is the leader of the Zulus—and they're a full third or more of the black population of South Africa—he has come out against the idea of hostility, of sanctions, and so forth, and said what we have said, that things of that kind would only hurt the people we're trying to help.

Q. So, you're going to veto the bill?

Q. But, sir, this is the third week of——

Q. Are you going to veto the bill?

The President. I never say what I'm going to do until the——

Q. Sometimes you do.

The President. ——thing gets to my desk.

But I am going to say that in principle I have to say what I've said, that our continuation of our present program, I think, is the best way that we can be of help to the black citizens of South Africa.

Q. But, sir, this is the third week of the state of emergency in South Africa. Your administration has called for it to be lifted, and yet there's been no results on that. What are you going to do to make that point more forcibly to the South African Government?

The President. Well, we're going to continue, as I say, and we think we've had some influence so far, and they have themselves guaranteed that they want to make progress in that direction. You're talking though now about a governmental reaction to some violence that was hurtful to all of the people. We have seen the violence between blacks there, as well as from the law enforcement against riotous behavior. I think we have to recognize sometimes when actions are taken in an effort to curb violence.

Q. Would you veto the bill as it now appears to be going to pass the Senate and has passed the House?

The President. Well, let me wait till I see what comes to my desk. I know that in some of the things that we are talking about in that legislation were things that could be helpful in the very way that I have been talking. I know also, however, that the sanctions would not only be harmful to the black citizens there, they would be harmful to the surrounding black countries whose economies greatly depend on their trade and economic relations with South Africa.

Q. So, would it be fair to say that there'll be no change in U.S. policy, nothing to get tougher?

The President. Well, it depends on what you mean by change. If you mean by turning to the thing of sanctions and so forth, no. But there can be fluctuations in your conversation and your relationship with another government.

Q. Sir, can you give us a brief——

Secretary of State Shultz

Q. What do you think about the conservative attacks upon Secretary Shultz as being insufficiently anti-Communist?

The President. I think that they are without foundation, and they're utterly ridiculous. And I have every confidence in Secretary Shultz and that he is carrying out the policies that I believe in.

The President's Health

Q. Could you give us, sir, in view of your recent medical adventures, a little update from top to bottom, so to speak?

Q. And your nose?

The President. Well, I'm glad that you finally got around to that subject and asked that question.

Q. You didn't think we would?

The President. What? No, I was worrying that—you can see, just like Lyndon, I left my scar exposed here. [*Laughter*] And I know that you've all been losing a lot of sleep over the last several days about my nose.

Q. We worry about you.

The President. Yes. So, if I can, let me give you an update on this. So far, all the statements that have been made—by Larry [Speakes] and by myself, by others—have been the truth as we knew it. And I'm coming to a correction now, but we did not know it at the time.

It is true I had—well, I guess for want of a better word—a pimple on my nose. And the doctors have a word—papule—that sounds nicer than the first one. But I violated all the rules; I picked at it, and I squoze it and so forth and messed myself up a little bit. But it seemed to be getting a little better when I went into the hospital. And then after the operation, when they put that tube in through my nose and down to my innards, they taped on the side of my nose quite heavily to hold that in place. I happen to have an allergy to adhesive tape. I can wear a band-aid maybe overnight or something, but not that kind. And when, finally, they took it off and removed the tube, why, I was quite swollen and inflamed all around here.

And then my little friend that I had played with began to come back. So, after 3 days—well, no, I'm getting 3 days in the wrong place here. Well, when I went over to the doctor for my weekly allergy shot, I called attention to this matter, and it was snipped off. And then, I wore a patch—there's where the 3 days come in—for about 3 days before you all noticed it in the East Room. And I was surprised that no one had paid any attention to it, or maybe you were just being polite.

But I'd heard some talk when they—it only took a couple of minutes—I'd heard some talk about possible—and they wanted to look at it for possible infection because of the irritation around there. But I did not know until this weekend at Camp David—I was informed that it had been examined, and it was indeed a basal cell carcinoma, which is the most common and the least dangerous kind. They come from exposure to the sun. Nancy had one removed above her upper lip some time ago. They're very commonplace, and they do not betoken in any way that you are cancer-prone.

It is a little heartbreaking for me to find out, though, because all my life I've lived with a coat of tan, dating back to my lifeguard days. That's why I didn't have to wear makeup when I was in movies. But now I'm told that I must not expose myself to the sun anymore. And, you know, I don't mind telling you all this because I know that medicine has been waging a great campaign to try and convince people to stop broiling themselves in the sun because of this very ailment. And so, if I can contribute any by saying, here I am a veteran all my life—and it took a long time for it to finally have an effect—but for others to give up their dreams of a good tan, because evidently this is what causes it.

Q. Does this condition require you, sir, to undergo any other examinations?

The President. No. No further examination, no further treatment of any kind. It's gone, and, as I say——

Q. What about your overall health, sir?

The President. Overall health is——

Q. Since the operation.

The President. ——very good. I am amazed myself—when I look at the length of the incision, which I won't show you, and all—that I feel as good as I do.

Q. Sir, we had some trouble getting information about your nose last week. And I wonder to what extent do you think the American people have a right to know about your full condition and your full health and welfare?

The President. No, as I told you, we thought we were giving you all the truth on it, that it was just exactly as I described it. And it wasn't until after I was up at Camp David that the report came to me that it was that mild form, that carcinoma——

Q. But we were told——

The President. ——commonplace thing.

Q. We were told——

Q. Does basal cell carcinoma mean skin cancer, sir?

The President. I think that where life and death or ability to do jobs is concerned, yes, the people have a right to know whether the man sitting at this desk is—or woman sitting at this desk is——

Q. Good catch.

The President. ——capable of performing the tasks. And, on the other hand, I think there can be invasions that go beyond the need to know that. And I think we were trying to tell you as much as we could, what we believed was the truth.

Q. Well, you see, when you put out a statement—the White House put out a statement, they said, "This is it." And we were never told what it was.

The President. Well, that I'd messed around with a pimple and caused some trouble for myself.

Q. But we were not told that there was a biopsy.

The President. What?

Q. We were not told that there was also——

The President. I didn't know.

Q. ——a biopsy.

The President. I didn't know. As I say, all I heard, as I was sitting up and getting ready to walk out of the office, was the doctor mentioned the fact that he needed to check this for possible infection, that it might have become infected from not only my messing around but from the tape and all. And that's all I heard and what it meant, and I didn't know about the other until this weekend at Camp David. And, as a matter of fact, I hope you'll all recognize that at Camp David I decided that when I came back that I would either make that as an opening statement at this mini press conference—*[laughter]*—or let you ask a

question about it. And when it——

Q. It was on the tip of our tongues.

The President. ——well, when it seemed to have disappeared from view, I thought I'd wait for you to ask a question about it.

Q. Sir, does the basic cell carcinoma mean skin cancer, or what's that——

The President. Well, carcinoma, the very word—it is a form of cancer. This is the, as I say, the commonest, the least dangerous. It is not known as becoming or spreading or going someplace else, and it is virtually totally caused by the sun, exposure to the sun.

Q. How soon will you be riding a horse, sir?

The President. I'm hoping to be riding a horse when I get to California next week.

Q. In the shade.

Nuclear Weapons

Q. You know that Gorbachev said that we were barbaric to drop the atomic bomb. What do you think of that?

The President. Well, I always thought it was barbaric of Stalin to kill some 20 million people in his own country, of his own countrymen. But we dropped the bomb in an effort to end what had been the greatest war in man's history. The resistance of the enemy and the island campaigns leading up to an invasion of Japan was such that we knew we would be facing that kind of to-the-death resistance. The casualties were estimated at more than a million if we continued. And I think to second-guess now those who had to make that awesome decision is ridiculous.

I think, horrible as it was, we have to say this, too—that it did give the world a view of the threat of nuclear weapons. And I think that should be an aid in one day, now, ridding ourselves of them. But I think we have to recognize that that and the presence of our nuclear weapons as a deterrent have kept us at peace for the longest stretch we've ever known—40 years of peace.

Q. On a related point, why won't you go along with Gorbachev's suggestion for a joint moratorium on nuclear testing?

Principal Deputy Press Secretary Speakes. Can we make this the last question?

The President. All right. That's the last

question, all right. But I'm delighted to answer that one, too.

The Soviet Union is ahead of us in the development and the modernization of nuclear weapons. They have just finished their tests, or they even have a couple left they might try to sneak in before the 6th, which was their opening date. But they had finished their tests on their 24's and 25's, the 18, which is comparable to our MX. And we have not yet begun the testing and certainly haven't completed it in some of our weapons of that same type to keep pace with them.

So, their suggestion for a mutual—first of all, for a single moratorium for several months—they finished their tests; they don't have any more to do. Their asking us to make it mutual meant that we would then not be able to catch up with them. And we've had an example of that back in the Kennedy era, and this had to do with the testing with regard to ABM's and so forth. And we were begging for a treaty, and the Soviet Union kept refusing. And they'd completed the tests, and then the Congress passed a go-ahead for us. And the Soviets immediately said to President Kennedy, "Oh, yes, we're willing to talk now about a moratorium on testing."

So, this is why we said to them: "Look, we still have our tests to do, same ones that you've been doing. You're welcome to send somebody over and watch all our tests." And I would like to add also that after that limited moratorium, which was supposed to end around December or something, if they want to make that a permanent moratorium or if they want to agree with us and have bilateral inspection of each other's testing, we're willing to do that.

Q. You said watch all our tests?

Q. You would go for a total moratorium, permanent moratorium on all underground tests? All tests?

Q. At the end of the year?

The President. Well, I don't know whether we'd be able to complete ours by that time or not—when we've completed ours and they're not doing any more——

Q. Well, they say we've——

The President. ——yes, that would be fine.

Q. ——completed ours in Nevada.

The President. What?

Q. I understand our tests have been completed.

The President. Oh, no. We're still talking about a Midgetman to match their 24 or 25. And we haven't even come to that stage yet.

Q. When might that be? Within a year or——

The President. I don't know. I don't know. But, in the meantime, let's get back down to real facts. In Geneva is where the decision should be made and not with moratoriums of that kind. Let's get down to the business, once and for all, of reducing the numbers of nuclear weapons, hopefully leading toward a total elimination of them. Then there wouldn't be any need for testing.

Q. Thank you, Mr. President.

The President. All right. Well, it's nice to see you all. Where have you been keeping yourselves?

Q. You should do this more often.

The President. What? [*Laughter*]

Q. You should do this more often.

The President. I always enjoy it.

Baseball Strike

Q. What are you going to do if there's a baseball strike?

The President. Well, I'm not going to go to the ball game. [*Laughter*]

Q. Do you have any views on the baseball strike?

The President. Well, I don't think government should intervene in labor-management affairs of any kind. But I do think that all parties really should sit down there with the fans in their minds and their obligation to the baseball fans.

Q. Thank you, sir.

The President. Bye. [*Laughter*]

Q. We'll be watching you ride the horse.

The President. Yes, I know, from way up on the mountain. [*Laughter*]

Note: The President spoke at 1:01 p.m. in the Oval Office at the White House.

Statement on Signing the Bill Extending the Equal Access to Justice Act
August 5, 1985

I am pleased to be able to approve H.R. 2378, a bill to extend the Equal Access to Justice Act. I support this important program that helps small businesses and individual citizens fight faulty government actions by paying attorneys' fees in court cases or adversarial agency proceedings where the small business or individual citizen has prevailed and where the government action or position in the litigation was not substantially justified. It was with great regret that I vetoed the bill to extend this program that passed at the end of the last session of the Congress. I am pleased that the Congress has corrected the problems I perceived in that bill.

On the important definition of the position of the United States or position of the agency, this bill would allow the court or the agency to look at the agency action that is the basis of the litigation or the agency proceeding, in addition to the position taken by the United States in the court or in the formal agency proceeding, to the extent these differ, in determining whether the position of the United States was substantially justified. I note that the bill strictly limits the court's or the agency's fee inquiry to the agency action that is at issue in the litigation or proceeding and does not permit the examination of any other agency conduct. I note further that the Congress has specifically instructed the courts to base the fee inquiry on the record made in the litigation or agency proceeding for which fees are sought and not to engage in additional discovery or evidentiary proceedings in considering the question of substantial justification. I believe these changes take care of my concerns that the fee proceeding not become another trial and that fee proceedings not involve matters not at issue in the principal litigation. It is with these understandings that I sign this bill.

In addition, it is my understanding in signing this bill that the Congress recognized the important distinction between the substantial justification standard in the fee proceeding and a court's finding on the merits that an agency action was arbitrary and capricious or not supported by substantial evidence. The substantial justification standard is a different standard, and an easier one to meet, than either the arbitrary and capricious or substantial evidence standard. A separate inquiry is required to determine whether, notwithstanding the fact that the Government did not prevail, the Government's position or action was substantially justified. The Equal Access to Justice Act was never intended to create an automatic fee award every time the Government loses a case. The current bill is true to that principle.

Note: H.R. 2378, approved August 5, was assigned Public Law No. 99–80.

Appointment of Two Members of the Board of Directors of the Pennsylvania Avenue Development Corporation
August 6, 1985

The President today announced his intention to appoint the following individuals to be members of the Board of Directors of the Pennsylvania Avenue Development Corporation for terms expiring October 26, 1990:

Lee Atwater will succeed Peter Kelly. He is a partner in the firm of Black, Manafort, Stone and Atwater in Alexandria, VA. Previously he was deputy campaign director and political director for Reagan-Bush '84. He served at the White House in the Office of Political Affairs as

Special Assistant (1981–1982) and Deputy Assistant (1982–1983) to the President. He graduated from Newberry College (B.A., 1973) and the University of South Carolina (M.A., 1975). He is currently studying for his doctorate from the University of South Carolina. He is married and resides in Columbia, SC. He was born February 27, 1951, in Atlanta, GA.

Michael R. Gardner will succeed Julia M. Walsh. Since 1982 he has been a partner with the law firm of Akin, Gump, Strauss, Hauer & Feld in Washington, DC. He also serves as head of the firm's communications division. He serves as chairman of the board of directors of the United States Telecommunications Training Institute. In 1982–1985 he served on the Council of the Administrative Conference of the United States. In 1982 Mr. Gardner was Chairman, with the rank of Ambassador, of the United States delegation to the Plenipotentiary Conference of the International Telecommunications Union in Nairobi, Kenya. He graduated from Georgetown University (1964) and Georgetown Law Center (J.D., 1976). He is married, has two children, and resides in Washington, DC. He was born November 19, 1942, in Philadelphia, PA.

Statement on the 40th Anniversary of the Bombing of Hiroshima
August 6, 1985

This week millions around the world will mark the 40th anniversary of the first and only uses of nuclear weapons—events that brought to an end a long and terrible war. The war over, an unprecedented friendship between the free peoples and democratic governments of the United States and Japan was born. Thus, as we reflect on the meaning of the events of 40 years ago, we and the people of Japan can take pride in having demonstrated that, even between former enemies in warfare, lasting reconciliation is possible.

We must never forget what nuclear weapons wrought upon Hiroshima and Nagasaki, yet we must also remain mindful that our maintenance of a strong nuclear deterrent has for four decades ensured the security of the United States and the freedom of our allies in Asia and Europe. In Europe, these years represent the longest period of peace since the early 19th century. Peace has not made us complacent, for we are continually seeking ways to reduce still further the risks of war. As I have often stated, "A nuclear war cannot be won and must never be fought." This anniversary is, therefore, a time not only for reflection but for action.

The United States will take every reasonable step to build a more peaceful world. Just last week I extended to the Soviet leadership an invitation to send a team of Soviet experts to our Nevada test site to observe and measure the yield of an American nuclear test. My offer involved no preconditions; the Soviet experts were invited to bring with them any instrumentation devices that they deemed necessary to measure the yield of the test. Our objective was straightforward: to set in train a process that, regarding limitations on nuclear testing, could markedly increase confidence and cooperation between our nations.

It is my hope that the Soviet leadership will accept this invitation in the spirit of good will in which it has been tendered. I would also urge the leadership of the Soviet Union to work with us to achieve deep, verifiable, and equitable reductions in nuclear arsenals; to resolve questions relating to compliance with existing arms control agreements; and to establish a constructive dialog on ways to reduce the risk of accidental war.

We must also be vigilant in our efforts to prevent nuclear proliferation—and here all nations must share the burden. Those who would profit from the transfer of sensitive nuclear technology to trouble parts of the globe pose a threat to world peace. Action must be taken, and we encourage all nations to join us in requiring comprehensive safeguards as a condition of nuclear export. We look forward to the third review session of the nonproliferation treaty, which will begin this month. The United States, the

Soviet Union, and all the nations of the world must work to ensure that the atom is never again used as a weapon of war, but as an instrument of peace.

Appointment of Two Members of the Federal Council on the Aging, and Designation of the Chairperson
August 6, 1985

The President today announced his intention to appoint the following individuals to be members of the Federal Council on the Aging for terms of 3 years. The President intends to designate Ingrid Azvedo as Chairperson upon her appointment.

Ingrid Azvedo will succeed Syd Captain. She is active in community and political organizations in Sacramento, CA. She was a delegate to the White House Conference on Aging in 1981 and was also elected to the executive committee of region four, White House Conference on Aging. She is married, has two children, and resides in Elk Grove, CA. She was born February 28, 1934, in Germany.

Albert Lee Smith, Jr., will succeed Josephine K. Oblinger. He is a special representative for Jefferson Standard Life Insurance Co. in Birmingham, AL. He was a member of the United States House of Representatives in 1980–1982. He is married, has three children, and resides in Birmingham, AL. He was born August 31, 1931, in Birmingham, AL.

Message to Hugh Desmond Hoyte on the Death of President Linden Forbes Sampson Burnham of Guyana
August 7, 1985

Dear Mr. President:

It was with sadness that I learned of the unexpected death of President Linden Forbes Sampson Burnham. Please convey my sincere condolences to President Burnham's family and to the people of Guyana at this time of grief.

Sincerely,

/S/ RONALD REAGAN

Note: First Vice President Hoyte succeeded to the Presidency on the death of President Burnham.

Executive Order 12527—Repealing Provisions Establishing an Administrative Position in the Food-for-Peace Program
August 7, 1985

By the authority vested in me as President by the Constitution and laws of the United States of America, including section 301 of title 3 of the United States Code, it is hereby ordered that Executive Order No. 11252, as amended, is further amended by repealing Sections 2 and 3, and by redesignating the current Section 4 as Section 2.

RONALD REAGAN

The White House,
August 7, 1985.

[*Filed with the Office of the Federal Register, 4:29 p.m., August 7, 1985*]

Message to the Congress on the Publication of the Regulatory Program of the United States Government
August 8, 1985

To the Congress of the United States:

The publication of *The Regulatory Program of the United States Government* marks a major milestone in our continuing effort to make government more accountable to the American people and more responsive to their needs. This document presents, for the first time, a comprehensive program of regulatory policy to be carried out over the coming year.

Regulations are a feature of almost every government program. Though many regulations accomplish worthwhile ends, we should not forget the huge hidden costs they entail. The Federal government mandates tens of billions of dollars of expenditures every year—dollars paid for by the people but not included in any of the Federal budget accounts, not appropriated by the Congress, and not constrained by any spending limits.

Before 1980, these regulatory expenditures had grown out of control. More pages were published in the *Federal Register* in 1980 than during the entire period between 1936 and 1945—the first 10 years of the *Register.* Paperwork burdens had grown such that by 1980, almost two billion hours were expended annually by businesses and individuals to satisfy the Federal government. Estimates are that Federal government regulations imposed costs of over $100 billion annually by 1980, adding significantly to the burden imposed on the economy by excessive Federal spending. It has become essential that tools be developed to plan the rational evolution of Federal regulatory requirements.

In 1981, I issued Executive Order No. 12291 setting forth my regulatory principles and, under the Paperwork Reduction Act, my Administration mounted an attack to reduce the paperwork burden. These efforts have helped to reverse the trend of more intrusive and burdensome Federal regulations and paperwork. But more was needed.

The Regulatory Program is a critical step in this process. In order to see that the laws are faithfully executed, and that the policies of this Administration are reflected in the regulations issued under those laws, I issued Executive Order No. 12498 initiating this Regulatory Program. The Program covers the decisions that are within the scope of discretion afforded to the Executive agencies by law and describes the underlying policies and priorities that will influence those decisions.

To set goals and priorities for different programs, government officials must choose the right regulatory tools and identify legitimate needs for regulation as opposed to those that merely benefit special interests. Because some complex regulations take years to develop, involving studies, surveys, and the identification and selection of regulatory options, it is important that senior Federal officials be able to review regulatory options early in the rulemaking process and plan regulatory actions over a longer time horizon. It is also important that they examine and reexamine the nearly 200 volumes of existing regulations to see what regulations need to be modified or have outlived their usefulness.

This year's Regulatory Program is the first in an annual series that will document the efforts of my Administration to manage Federal regulatory programs. This should lead to an increased level of predictability, consistency, accountability, and rationality in Federal regulatory activity.

The objectives of the Regulatory Program are to:

—Create a coordinated process for developing on an annual basis the Administration's Regulatory Program;

—Establish Administration regulatory priorities;

—Increase the accountability of agency heads for the regulatory actions of their agencies;

—Provide for presidential oversight of the regulatory process;

—Reduce the burdens of existing and

future regulations;

—Minimize duplication and conflict of regulations; and

—Enhance public and congressional understanding of the Administration's regulatory objectives.

All of this cannot be accomplished simply by publishing a book. This Regulatory Program is the end product of a long process of agencies planning their regulatory activities: gathering and reviewing information, evaluating past progress and program effectiveness, and setting goals and priorities.

The publication of the Regulatory Program for 1985 is, however, only the first step in this annual planning process. The next step is for each agency to implement its part of this first Program, as planned and on schedule.

My goal remains to have a government that regulates only where necessary and as efficiently and fairly as possible.

RONALD REAGAN

The White House,
August 8, 1985.

Executive Order 12528—Presidential Board of Advisors on Private Sector Initiatives
August 8, 1985

By the authority vested in me as President by the Constitution and laws of the United States of America, and in order to establish, in accordance with the provisions of the Federal Advisory Committee Act, as amended (5 U.S.C. App. I), an advisory committee on private sector initiatives, it is hereby ordered as follows:

Section 1. Establishment. (a) There is established the Presidential Board of Advisors on Private Sector Initiatives. The Board shall be composed of not more than 30 members, to be appointed or designated by the President.

(b) The President shall designate a Chairman and Vice Chairman from among the members of the Board. The Deputy Assistant to the President and Director of Private Sector Initiatives shall serve as Secretary to the Board.

Sec. 2. Functions. (a) The Board shall advise the President and the Secretary of Commerce, through the White House Office of Private Sector Initiatives, with respect to the objectives and conduct of private sector initiative policies, including methods of increasing public awareness of the importance of public/private partnerships; removing barriers to development of effective social service programs which are administered by private organizations; strengthening the professional resources of the private social service sector; and studying options for promoting the long-term development of private sector initiatives in the United States.

(b) The Board shall seek the advice, ideas, and recommendations of the White House Office of Private Sector Initiatives and such other government offices as the President may deem appropriate in order to fulfill its responsibilities under this Order.

(c) In performance of its advisory responsibilities, the Board shall report to the President from time to time as requested.

Sec. 3. Administration. (a) The heads of Executive agencies shall, to the extent permitted by law, provide the Board such information with respect to private sector initiative issues and such other support as it may require for purposes of carrying out its functions.

(b) Members of the Board shall serve without compensation for their work on the Board. However, members appointed from among private citizens of the United States shall be allowed travel expenses, including per diem in lieu of subsistence, as authorized by law for persons serving intermittently in the government service (5 U.S.C. 5701–5707).

981

(c) The Department of Commerce shall, to the extent permitted by law and subject to the availability of funds, provide the Board with such administrative services, funds, and other support services as may be necessary for the effective performance of its functions.

Sec. 4. General. (a) The Board shall terminate two years from the date of this Order, unless sooner extended.

RONALD REAGAN

The White House,
August 8, 1985.

[*Filed with the Office of the Federal Register, 2:44 p.m., August 8, 1985*]

Remarks at the Signing Ceremony for the International Security and Development Cooperation Act of 1985
August 8, 1985

The President. Well, first of all, thank you, gentlemen, for being here—and to all of you. We're here for the signing of the foreign assistance authorization bill, and it's the first one that I have had to sign since 1981, and I am particularly pleased.

The Congress has approved renewed aid to the Nicaraguan freedom fighters and replaced the so-called Clark amendment—or repealed it and provided support for the Philippines and Guatemala. And these gentlemen have my deep gratitude for that. These measures are important in signaling American resolve and support for freedom.

And I must say with the substantial reduction, however, in the support levels, the security assistance has been disappointing. These reductions, plus the reduction in the defense, I think, reduce our effectiveness and the effectiveness of our foreign policy. And I realize that the budget pressures have been very severe, and there's a general lack of enthusiasm for foreign aid, and that made the job more difficult. We have to make the people aware that these programs are the most effective instruments we have for a more secure international environment, and I hope that we can all work together in the months ahead to reinvigorate the program.

And now, I'm going to sign Senate bill 960. I'll do the same thing now with the statement. All right, that does it.

Reporter. Mr. President, what message have you given Mr. McFarlane about South Africa?

The President. No. This is the purpose of this meeting here, and I'm not going to take any questions now in this photo opportunity to take away from this.

Q. Let me try again on something else. Is the NSC directing any *contra* operations, and if so, is that in violation of the current law today prohibiting exchange of intelligence?

Principal Deputy Press Secretary Speakes. Ira [Ira R. Allen, United Press International], he said no questions.

The President. That's a question that kind of traps me—in one that we're not violating any laws.

Thank you all.

Note: The President spoke at 1:15 p.m. in the Oval Office at the White House. Among those attending the ceremony were the Vice President, Secretary of State George P. Shultz, Senator Richard G. Lugar of Indiana, chairman of the Senate Foreign Relations Committee, and Representative William S. Broomfield of Michigan, ranking Republican on the House Foreign Affairs Committee. During the informal exchange at the end of the remarks, a reporter referred to Robert C. McFarlane, Assistant to the President for National Security Affairs. S. 960, approved August 8, was assigned Public Law No. 99–83.

Statement on Signing the International Security and Development Cooperation Act of 1985
August 8, 1985

Today I am signing into law S. 960, the International Security and Development Cooperation Act of 1985. This act authorizes appropriations for security and development assistance programs and related activities and makes certain substantive changes in the statutory requirements governing these programs.

S. 960 is the first foreign assistance authorization bill since 1981 to be passed by both Houses of the Congress and presented to me for signature. I am pleased that the authorization process on foreign aid is back on track. Enactment of foreign assistance legislation is never easy, and I appreciate the tough decisions Members made in their support of it. In helping our allies and friends meet their security, development, and humanitarian needs, we directly support U.S. interests and objectives. Our foreign assistance programs, despite any perceptions to the contrary, are manifestly in our own national interest.

S. 960 authorizes appropriations for both fiscal years 1986 and 1987. I understand the desire of the Congress to enact a 2-year authorization, and I support it. I will, of course, assess the requirements for foreign aid programs in preparing the fiscal year 1987 budget and will transmit to the Congress any additional authorizations that are required to support our national interests.

I am concerned about the sizable reductions made in S. 960 to my fiscal year 1986 requests for security assistance programs. Security assistance enables us to help our friends deter aggression, deepen bilateral ties, build forces which are more compatible with our own, and develop the confidence necessary for advancing peace and stability. These reductions, coupled with legislated earmarkings of numerous programs for individual countries and international organizations, will necessitate severe cuts in other programs that are critical to U.S. security interests. I will review the impact of these reductions and determine whether additional funding in fiscal year

1986 will be required in support of these interests.

Security assistance is, quite simply, the most effective instrument we have for helping to shape a more secure international environment. And yet since the decades of the fifties and sixties, the resources committed to these programs have shrunk drastically in real terms. I invite the Congress to work with us to see how we might best go about reinvigorating this important area. We need to strengthen our security assistance partners so as to give them the confidence and the capability to better defend our common interests. Foreign assistance resources are essential to a successful foreign policy. One of our highest national security priorities in the years ahead must be to reinvigorate our foreign assistance program. At a time of defense reductions, we must pay particular attention to our most compelling international security needs.

I am pleased that S. 960 contains many of the substantive legislative provisions that I proposed over the past 2 years; in particular, the main policy recommendations of the National Bipartisan Commission on Central America. Although it has required extensive debate and compromise on all sides, I believe that this bill sets forth a viable policy framework for Central America, which enjoys strong bipartisan support. It will guide our assistance programs as we seek the goals of peace, democracy, and development in that region of such great importance to the United States. The reductions in security assistance levels, however, will inhibit our ability to achieve these goals in fiscal years 1986 and 1987.

Equally important, S. 960 authorizes vital humanitarian assistance for the democratic resistance in Nicaragua. This aid is an important element in our overall efforts to assist neighboring countries in their defense against Nicaraguan attack and subversion. Unfortunately, the provision unduly and unnecessarily restricts efficient management and administration of the program. Nevertheless, I will continue to work with the Congress to carry out the program as effectively as possible and take care that the law be faithfully executed.

I am gratified by the assistance authorized in this bill for the Afghan people and the non-Communist opposition in Cambodia who are resisting foreign aggression and occupation groups. The repeal of the Clark amendment relating to Angola is also welcome, eliminating a symbol of unnecessary and inappropriate restrictions in the conduct of U.S. foreign policy.

On the other hand, I do have serious reservations about sections 717 and 1302 of S. 960. In spirit both sections are consistent with my foreign policy. Section 717 directs the Secretary of State to enter into negotiations with the Government of Mexico over certain trade issues. I am deeply committed to efforts to facilitate international commerce and welcome congressional attention to this matter. Similarly, section 1302(a) correctly describes U.S. policy not to recognize or negotiate with the Palestine Liberation Organization (PLO) so long as the PLO does not recognize Israel's right to exist and does not accept United Nations Security Council Resolutions 242 and 338. This administration reaffirms that policy and welcomes congressional support for it.

I am compelled, however, as a matter of principle, to reiterate my refusal to accept any congressional effort to impose legislative restrictions or directions with respect to the conduct of international negotiations which, under article II of the Constitution, is a function reserved exclusively to the President. I will therefore consider sections 717(b) and 1302(b) as constituting only nonbinding expressions of congressional views on these issues.

I also wish to mention the new certification requirement relating to arms sales to Jordan. I believe that this requirement is unnecessary and inappropriate in light of King Hussein's recent public statements confirming Jordan's commitment to the recognition of Israel and to negotiate promptly and directly with Israel under the basic tenets of United Nations Security Council Resolutions 242 and 338. Furthermore, the King has made and is continuing to make significant and courageous efforts in putting these principles into practice by moving Jordan toward direct negotiations with Israel.

Finally, I would note that the bill contains a number of other restrictions and requirements that the administration must meet in carrying out its foreign affairs programs; for example, tieing security assistance for Greece and Turkey to an arithmetic formula ignores the changing conditions in the region and unnecessarily limits our flexibility to respond. None of these restrictions by itself is unacceptably onerous, but in the aggregate, they seriously constrain my ability to carry out foreign policy, particularly in rapidly changing situations. I believe that rigid, detailed, prescriptive provisions of law can also frustrate the desires of the Congress. Thus, I plan to work with Congress to minimize such constraints in the future.

The programs authorized by S. 960 are central to attaining U.S. foreign policy objectives and to promoting international security and stability by helping our allies and friends to achieve economic growth, to deal with problems requiring humanitarian assistance, and to deter and defend against military threats. It is therefore imperative that we join in a mutual effort with Congress to ensure the success of these programs during the years ahead.

Note: S. 960, approved August 8, was assigned Public Law No. 99–83.

Nomination of Craig C. Black To Be a Member of the National Science Board
August 9, 1985

The President today announced his intention to nominate Craig C. Black to be a member of the National Science Board, National Science Foundation, for a term expiring May 10, 1990. He would succeed David V. Ragone.

Since 1975 Dr. Black has been director of the Los Angeles County Museum of Natural History. Previously, he was director of the museum and professor of geosciences at Texas Tech University (1972–1975); associate professor, department of systematics and ecology, University of Kansas (1970–1972); and curator (1962–1970) and associate curator (1960–1962) of vertebrate fossils at the Carnegie Museum of Natural History. He has served as president of the American Association of Museums and the Association of Science Museum Directors. He is a fellow of the Geological Society of America and a member of the Society for the Study of Evolution and the Paleontological Society.

Dr. Black graduated from Amherst College (A.B., 1954; M.A., 1957) and Harvard University (Ph.D., 1962). He has two children and resides in Los Angeles, CA. He was born May 28, 1932, in Peking, China.

Nomination of Dennis Miles Kass To Be an Assistant Secretary of Labor
August 9, 1985

The President today announced his intention to nominate Dennis Miles Kass to be an Assistant Secretary of Labor. He would succeed Donald L. Dotson.

Mr. Kass is managing director of the Equitable Investment and Management Corp. in New York City. Previously he was vice president of Dean Witter Reynolds, Inc., in 1982–1983. He served at the White House as Special Assistant to the President for Policy Development and Executive Secretary of the Cabinet Council on Commerce and Trade in 1981–1982. In 1977–1980 he served as manager for corporate finance, energy industry, at Citicorp Investment Bank.

He graduated from Principia College (B.A., 1972) and Massachusetts Institute of Technology (M.S., 1977). He is married, has two children, and resides in Rye, NY. He was born October 5, 1950, in Englewood, NJ.

Nomination of Roger A. Yurchuck To Be a Director of the Securities Investor Protection Corporation
August 9, 1985

The President today announced his intention to nominate Roger A. Yurchuck to be a Director of the Securities Investor Protection Corporation for a term expiring December 31, 1987. This is a reappointment.

Since 1973 Mr. Yurchuck has been a partner with the law firm of Vorys, Sater, Seymour and Pease in Columbus and Cincinnati, OH. In 1971–1973 he served as vice president and general counsel of the Federal Home Loan Mortgage Corporation in Washington, DC. Previously he was a partner with Vorys, Sater, Seymour and Pease.

He graduated from Northwestern University (B.A., 1959) and Harvard Law School (LL.B., 1962). He has two children and resides in Cincinnati, OH. He was born June 9, 1938, in Amityville, NY.

Nomination of Two Members of the United States Advisory Commission on Public Diplomacy
August 9, 1985

The President today announced his intention to nominate the following individuals to be members of the United States Advisory Commission on Public Diplomacy:

E. Robert Wallach, to serve for a term expiring July 1, 1988. This is a reappointment. Mr. Wallach is an attorney in San Francisco, CA. He has served as dean of the Hastings Center for Trial & Appellate Advocacy and as adjunct professor of the Hastings College of Law. He graduated from the University of Southern California (B.A., 1955) and the University of California at Berkeley (Boalt, LL.B., 1958). He was born April 11, 1934, in New York City and now resides in San Francisco.

Herbert Schmertz, to serve for a term expiring April 6, 1988. This is a reappointment. Mr. Schmertz is a director of Mobil Corp. and a director and vice president of Mobil Oil Corp. He joined Mobil in 1966 and has served in various capacities, including manager of the corporate labor relations department and as vice president for public affairs. He has served as a member of the President's Commission on Broadcasting to Cuba. He graduated from Union College (A.B., 1952) and Columbia University (LL.B., 1955). He is married, has four children, and resides in New York City. He was born March 22, 1930, in Yonkers, NY.

Radio Address to the Nation on the 40th Anniversary of the End of the Second World War in the Pacific
August 10, 1985

My fellow Americans:

In a few days, we'll be commemorating V–J Day, the 40th anniversary of the end of the war in the Pacific, which brought to a close the most destructive and widespread conflagration in the history of mankind. Over 3 million American airmen, soldiers, sailors, and marines served in the Pacific and Asian theaters between 1941–1945. They endured some of the most savage combat of the war, from the frozen Aleutian Islands in the north to the jungles of Guadalcanal and the volcanic sands of Iwo Jima.

Our fighting forces came back from the defeat at Pearl Harbor and slugged their way across the Pacific, island by island. General Douglas MacArthur wrote of the American fighting man in the Pacific: "He plods and groans, sweats and toils. He growls and curses. And at the end, he dies, unknown, uncomplaining, with faith in his heart, and on his lips, a prayer for victory." Well, the victory was won, and our freedom and way of life were preserved because of the courage and honor of those who put their lives on the line four decades ago.

The Americans who went through this ordeal of storm and sacrifice, just as their counterparts who battled our enemies in Europe, deserve a special place in the hearts of all those who love liberty. Vice President Bush might be a little embarrassed if he knew I was going to say this, but he's one of those Americans I'm talking about. As a young fighter pilot in the Pacific, his plane was shot down on a military mission. He came perilously close to losing his life. If you know any veterans of the Second World War, you might take the time on August 14th to thank them. There are so many heroes among us, and I'm sure they'd like to know how much we appreciate them.

The veterans of the Pacific war should take special pride that today the Pacific rim is blessed with stability and bustling with enterprise and commerce. The hard-fought battles of the Pacific laid the foundation for what is becoming one of the most vibrant regions of the world. The devastation and rubble of the war have given way to great centers of human progress, futuristic metropolises with vast industrial complexes, modernistic transportation systems, and impressive institutions of culture and learning.

Nowhere is this more evident than in Japan, now a close and reliable friend and one of our most important allies. In these last 40 years, the Japanese have transformed bombed-out ruins into a great industrial nation. With few natural resources of their own, they now produce over 10 percent of all the world's goods and services. They've accomplished this economic miracle with hard work, free enterprise, and low tax rates. The Japanese are today in so many ways our partners in peace and enterprise. Our economic ties are a great boon to both our peoples. Our good will and cooperation will be maintained by a mutually beneficial trading relationship based on free trade and open markets on both sides of the Pacific.

The great strides forward being made in the Pacific rim bode well for the United States. We are, after all, a Pacific rim country. Already our trade with Pacific and East Asian countries is greater than with any other region of the world. We can look forward to the future with anticipation of a better tomorrow. The people of our country will be in the forefront of the economic renaissance of the Pacific.

Liberty not only spawns progress, but it is the genesis of true peace as well. As free peoples, it is unthinkable that the Japanese and Americans will ever again go to war. Where there are differences, as there are in the relations of any two great nations, they can be settled in the spirit of good will.

Those brave Americans who fought in the Pacific four decades ago were fighting for a better world. They believed in America and often they gave the last full measure of devotion. One such man was Marine Lieutenant David Tucker Brown from Alexandria, Virginia. While in the Pacific, he wrote home: "I am more than ever convinced that this is Thomas Jefferson's war, the war of the common man against tyranny and pride. It is really a war for democracy and not for power or materialism." Well, Lieutenant Brown was later killed in action in Okinawa, one of so many brave and courageous young Americans who made the supreme sacrifice.

I think if those brave men were with us today they'd be proud of what has been accomplished. At war's end, with victory in hand, we looked forward, not back. We lived up to our ideals, the ideals of heroes like Lieutenant David Tucker Brown. And we worked with our former enemies to build a new and better world, a world of freedom and opportunity. That's the America we're all so proud of.

Until next week, thanks for listening, and God bless you.

Note: The President spoke at 12:06 p.m. from the Oval Office at the White House.

Appointment of M.B. Oglesby, Jr., To Assume Additional Responsibilities While Serving as Assistant to the President for Legislative Affairs
August 12, 1985

The President today announced his intention to appoint M.B. Oglesby, Jr., to assume the responsibilities of Max Friedersdorf, who will take a new position within the administration in the fall. Mr. Oglesby will continue to serve as Assistant to the President for Legislative Affairs. In his position, he will serve as the President's chief liaison with the United States Congress.

Previously Mr. Oglesby has served as Deputy Assistant to the President for Legislative Affairs and as minority staff associate for the House Energy and Commerce Committee, dealing principally with railroad, environmental, and commerce-related legislation. Mr. Oglesby also served as deputy and acting director of the State of Illinois Washington office and as executive assistant to Congressman Edward Madigan (R-IL). Prior to coming to Washington, he served in Illinois State government as an assistant to Gov. Richard Ogilvie and as executive assistant to the speaker of the house. Mr. Oglesby also spent 3½ years in management positions with Illinois Bell Telephone Co.

He attended the University of Illinois in Champaign. He is married, resides in Bethesda, MD, and was born October 1, 1942, in Flora, IL.

Appointment of Mitchell Daniels, Jr., as Assistant to the President for Political and Intergovernmental Affairs
August 12, 1985

The President today announced his intention to appoint Mitchell Daniels, Jr., as Assistant to the President for Political and Intergovernmental Affairs. He will succeed Edward J. Rollins, who will depart in the fall.

Mr. Daniels has been Deputy Assistant to the President and Director, Office of Intergovernmental Affairs, since March 1985. Previously he served as executive director of the National Republican Senatorial Committee in 1983–1985. He was administrative assistant to Senator Richard Lugar of Indiana (1977–1982) and chief aide to then Mayor Richard Lugar of Indianapolis (1974–1976).

He graduated from the Woodrow Wilson School of Public and International Affairs at Princeton University in 1971 and received a J.D. degree from the Georgetown University Law Center in 1979. He is married, has three children, and resides in Fairfax Station, VA. He was born April 7, 1949, in Monongahela, PA.

Proclamation 5361—Polish American Heritage Month, 1985
August 13, 1985

By the President of the United States of America

A Proclamation

The history of Polish Americans is an inspiring part of our Nation's heritage. The first massive wave of Polish immigrants came to America to flee the political and economic oppression thrust upon their homeland by the 19th century imperial powers of Eastern and Central Europe. While they came with few material possessions, they brought something much more important—a deep faith in God and a determination to succeed in this land of opportunity. And succeed they did. They established churches, schools, and fraternal benefit societies. They worked hard in the mines, steel mills, and stockyards. They understood the importance of education, so that today, the children and grandchildren of the first immigrants can be found in America's leading businesses and educational institutions.

Americans of Polish descent have made, and continue to make, enormous contributions to the culture, economy, and democratic political system of the United States. The names of Tadeusz Kosciuszko and Kazimierz Pulaski, heroes of the American Revolution, have left a lasting imprint upon our history. Highways, bridges, and towns dedicated to the preservation of their memory dot our countryside. In the future, other public facilities and institutions will be named for today's prominent Polish Americans, such as those serving our Nation in the Executive branch, in Congress, the armed services, and in state capitols and city halls from coast to coast.

The dedication of Polish Americans from all walks of life to the ideals of freedom and independence, which Kosciuszko and Pulaski fought for in America and in Poland, and which their worthy successors within the Solidarity movement are struggling for in Poland today, serves as a model for all Americans. That struggle remains alive today and two Polish leaders of international stature—Pope John Paul II and Lech Walesa—provide inspiring examples of moral leadership for us all.

The Congress, by House Joint Resolution 106, has designated August 1985 as "Polish American Heritage Month" and authorized and requested the President to issue a proclamation in observance of this month.

Now, Therefore, I, Ronald Reagan, President of the United States of America, do hereby proclaim August 1985 as Polish American Heritage Month. I urge all Americans to join their fellow citizens of Polish descent in observance of this month.

In Witness Whereof, I have hereunto set my hand this thirteenth day of August, in the year of our Lord nineteen hundred and eighty-five, and of the Independence of the United States of America the two hundred and tenth.

RONALD REAGAN

[*Filed with the Office of the Federal Register, 11:13 a.m., August 15, 1985*]

Note: *The proclamation was released by the Office of the Press Secretary on August 14.*

Proclamation 5362—National Neighborhood Crime Watch Day, 1985
August 13, 1985

By the President of the United States of America

A Proclamation

A Nation promising justice for all must ensure that its citizens are free from fear of crime in their homes and on the streets. Yet crime continues to be a substantial problem for American society. Twenty-three million households were touched by crime in 1984 and felt, in varying degrees, the pain, economic loss, sense of violation, and frustration that accompany crime victimization.

Fewer households were victims of crime in 1984 than in any of the previous nine years, due in part to greater public awareness and understanding of crime. This Administration is committed to increasing that awareness and understanding, thereby assisting in our Nation's effort to combat crime.

We recognize the effectiveness and the growth of local crime watch organizations throughout the country and the major role they have played in turning the tide against crime. By working together and in cooperation with their local law enforcement agencies, citizens have always been one of our most effective deterrents against crime. Such citizen action reaffirms those values of community, respect for the law, and individual responsibility that are so much a part of our national heritage.

It is important that all of the citizens of this Nation are aware of the significance of community crime prevention programs and the valuable impact that their participation can have on reducing crime in their neighborhoods. A "National Night Out" campaign will be conducted on August 13, 1985 to call attention to the importance of community crime prevention programs. All Americans will be urged to spend the hour between 8–9 p.m. on that evening on their lawns, porches, and steps in front of their homes to signify that neighbors looking out for one another is the most effective form of crime prevention.

Participation in this nationwide event also will demonstrate the value and effectiveness of police and community working together in a partnership on crime prevention. It will generate support for, and participation in, local crime watch programs; strengthen neighborhood spirit in the anticrime effort; and send a message to criminals that neighborhoods across America are organized and watching. This is a unique effort to remind the American people of the crucial role they can play in making their streets and neighborhoods safer. Strong, safe communities don't just happen. They are built by people who care and volunteer their time and energy to make the community a good place to live.

The Congress, by Senate Joint Resolution 168, has designated August 13, 1985, as "National Neighborhood Crime Watch Day" and authorized and requested the President to issue a proclamation in observance of this event.

Now, Therefore, I, Ronald Reagan, President of the United States of America, do hereby proclaim August 13, 1985, as National Neighborhood Crime Watch Day. I call upon the people of the United States to spend the period from 8 to 9 o'clock p.m. that day with their neighbors in front of their homes to demonstrate the importance and effectiveness of community participation in crime prevention efforts.

In Witness Whereof, I have hereunto set my hand this thirteenth day of August, in the year of our Lord nineteen hundred and eighty-five, and of the Independence of the United States of America the two hundred and tenth.

RONALD REAGAN

[Filed with the Office of the Federal Register, 11:14 a.m., August 15, 1985]

Note: The proclamation was released by the Office of the Press Secretary on August 14.

Statement on the Death of John Willard Marriott
August 14, 1985

J.W. Marriott was a living example of the American dream. From modest beginnings in Ogden, Utah, he rose to become one of the world's most successful and respected businessmen, but he never lost the values of honesty, decency, and hard work instilled in him as a youth. He built an enterprise and raised a family, both of which are models for us all.

No one ever had an unkind word about Bill Marriott—only words of praise and admiration for a man who never stopped caring about others. He never quite got used to the trappings of status that his hard-earned success brought, preferring instead the quiet and unpretentious world of life on his farm with his beloved family.

Nancy and I will always remember Bill Marriott's friendship and many kindnesses. We will miss him and extend our deepest sympathy to his family.

Executive Order 12529—President's Commission on Americans Outdoors
August 14, 1985

By the authority vested in me as President by the Constitution and statutes of the United States of America, including the Federal Advisory Committee Act, as amended (5 U.S.C. App. I), and in order to revise the name of a presidential advisory commission to better describe its areas of responsibility, and to extend the date within which the commission must complete its responsibilities, it is hereby ordered that Executive Order No. 12503 is amended as follows:

The title of the Order and Section 1(a) are amended by deleting "Presidential Commission on Outdoor Recreation Resources Review" and inserting in lieu thereof "President's Commission on Americans Outdoors"; and

Section 4(b) of the Order is revised to provide as follows:

"The Commission shall submit its report no later than December 31, 1986, and shall terminate 30 days after its report.".

RONALD REAGAN

The White House,
August 14, 1985.

[*Filed with the Office of the Federal Register, 10:51 a.m., August 16, 1985*]

Note: The Executive order was released by the Office of the Press Secretary on August 15.

Appointment of 14 Members of the President's Commission on Americans Outdoors, and Designation of the Chairman
August 15, 1985

The President today announced his intention to appoint the following individuals to be members of the President's Commission on Americans Outdoors. The President intends to designate Lamar Alexander as Chairman upon his appointment.

Lamar Alexander is Governor of the State of Tennessee. He graduated from Vanderbilt University (B.A., 1962) and New York University (J.D., 1965). He is married, has four children, and resides in Nashville. He was born July 3, 1940, in Knox County, TN.

Frank M. Bogert is mayor of Palm Springs, CA. He attended the University of California at Los Angeles. He is married, has three children, and resides in Palm Springs. He was born January 1, 1910, in Mesa, CO.

Sheldon Coleman is chairman of the Coleman Co., Inc., in Wichita, KS. He graduated from Cornell University. He is married, has three children, and resides in Wichita, KS. He was born November 15, 1901, in Fort Worth, TX.

Derrick A. Crandall is president and chief executive officer of the American Recreation Coalition in Washington, DC. He graduated from Dartmouth College (A.B., 1973). He is married, has two children, and resides in Fairfax, VA. He was born July 16, 1951, in East Orange, NJ.

Gilbert Melville Grosvenor is president of the National Geographic Society in Washington, DC. He graduated from Yale University (B.A., 1954). He is married, has three children, and resides in McLean, VA. He was born May 5, 1931, in Washington, DC.

J. Bennett Johnston is a United States Senator from Louisiana. He graduated from Louisiana State University (LL.B., 1956). He is married, has four children, and resides in McLean, VA. He was born June 10, 1932, in Shreveport, LA.

Charles R. Jordan is director of the parks and recreation department for the city of Austin, TX. He graduated from Gonzaga University (B.S., 1961). He is married, has two children, and resides in Austin, TX. He was born September 1, 1937, in Longview, TX.

Wilbur F. LaPage is director of the division of parks and recreation for the State of New Hampshire. He graduated from the University

991

of New Hampshire (B.A., 1960; M.A., 1962) and Syracuse University (Ph.D., 1975). He is married, has three children, and resides in Rye, NH. He was born February 1, 1935, in Jaffrey, NH.

Rex Maughan is president and chief executive officer of Forever Living Products, Inc., in Phoenix, AZ. He graduated from Arizona State University. He is married, has three children, and resides in Mesa, AZ. He was born November 20, 1936, in Logan, UT.

Patrick Francis Noonan is president of the Nature Conservancy in Arlington, VA. He graduated from Gettysburg College (B.A., 1965), Catholic University (M.A., 1968), and American University (M.B.A., 1971). He is married, has two children, and resides in Potomac, MD. He was born December 2, 1942, in St. Petersburg, FL.

Stuart Northrop is chairman of the board of Huffy Corp. in Dayton, OH. He graduated

from Yale University (B.A., 1948). He is married, has two children, and resides in Haverford, PA. He was born October 21, 1925, in New Haven, CT.

Morris King Udall is a Member of the U.S. House of Representatives from Arizona. He graduated from the University of Arizona (LL.B., 1949). He is married, has six children, and resides in McLean, VA. He was born June 15, 1922, in St. Johns, AZ.

Barbara Farrell Vucanovich is a Member of the U.S. House of Representatives from Nevada. She attended Manhattanville College of the Sacred Heart. She is married, has five children, and resides in Alexandria, VA. She was born June 22, 1921, in Camp Dix, NJ.

Malcolm Wallop is a United States Senator from Wyoming. He graduated from Yale University (B.A., 1954). He is married, has four children, and resides in McLean, VA. He was born February 27, 1933, in New York City.

Statement by Assistant to the President for National Security Affairs McFarlane on Apartheid in South Africa
August 15, 1985

Apartheid is a system that has long plagued South Africa, and it must be ended. A cycle of violence and repression has engulfed South Africa; this too must end. South Africa must find peace with itself and develop a system of government which accommodates the legitimate rights and needs of the black majority and provides for justice, equality, respect for fundamental rights, and, most importantly, government based on consent.

The South African President has made an important statement, and we are studying it carefully. We hope that the steps President Botha has outlined will advance the end of apartheid. He has called for negotiations on a new constitutional structure and has rec-

ognized the principle of participation and the responsibility of all South Africans in their country's future. We look for early implementation of those principles through a process of negotiations between the South African Government and the leaders of South Africa's other communities. The President's statement advances new ideas on citizenship. These ideas and other ideas contained in the speech must be clarified.

The tragedy of South Africa can only be resolved if negotiations begin quickly and produce concrete progress. The United States looks to the South African Government and all South Africans to explore every opportunity for negotiation and reconciliation.

Proclamation 5363—Modification of the Effective Date for Increased Rates of Duty for Certain Pasta Articles From the European Economic Community
August 15, 1985

By the President of the United States of America

A Proclamation

1. On June 20, 1985, I determined pursuant to section 301(a) of the Trade Act of 1974, as amended (the Act) (19 U.S.C. 2411(a)), that the preferential tariffs granted by the European Economic Community (EEC) on imports of lemons and oranges from certain Mediterranean countries deny benefits to the United States arising under the General Agreement on Tariffs and Trade (GATT) (61 Stat. (pts. 5 and 6)), are unreasonable and discriminatory, and constitute a burden or restriction on U.S. commerce. I further determined, pursuant to section 301 (a) and (b) of the Act, that the appropriate course of action in response to such practices is to withdraw concessions with respect to certain imports from the EEC and to increase the U.S. import duties on the pasta articles provided for in items 182.35 and 182.36 of the Tariff Schedules of the United States (TSUS) (19 U.S.C. 1202) that are the product of any member country of the EEC. Accordingly, in Proclamation 5354 of June 21, 1985 (50 F.R. 26143), the increased duties with respect to such pasta articles from the EEC were proclaimed to be effective on or after the date that was 15 days after the date on which that proclamation was signed.

2. In light of discussions currently being conducted between the United States and the EEC, I have decided that it is appropriate to delay the effective date of the increased rates of duty with respect to such pasta articles in order to encourage a mutually acceptable solution to the situation.

Now, Therefore, I, Ronald Reagan, President of the United States of America, acting under the authority vested in me by the Constitution and the statutes of the United States, including but not limited to sections 301 (a) and (b) and section 604 of the Trade Act of 1974, do proclaim that:

1. Proclamation 5354 of June 21, 1985, is superseded to the extent inconsistent with this proclamation.

2. The increased duties imposed by Proclamation 5354 are suspended with respect to articles entered, or withdrawn from warehouse for consumption, on or after July 6, 1985, and before November 1, 1985. Any articles entered, or withdrawn from warehouse for consumption, on or after the effective date of Proclamation 5354 and before November 1, 1985, shall be subject to duty and the entries thereof liquidated or reliquidated as if the increased duties imposed by the proclamation were not in effect.

3. The United States Trade Representative is hereby authorized to suspend, modify, or terminate the increase in U.S. import duties on pasta articles, which was imposed by Proclamation 5354, upon the publication in the *Federal Register* of his determination that such suspension, modification, or termination is justified by actions taken by the EEC toward a mutually acceptable resolution of this dispute.

4. This proclamation shall be effective on and after the date of its signing.

In Witness Whereof, I have hereunto set my hand this fifteenth day of August, in the year of our Lord nineteen hundred and eighty-five, and of the Independence of the United States of America the two hundred and tenth.

RONALD REAGAN

[Filed with the Office of the Federal Register, 2:21 p.m., August 19, 1985]

Note: The proclamation was released by the Office of the Press Secretary on August 16.

Nomination of Jennifer Joy Manson To Be an Assistant Administrator of the Environmental Protection Agency
August 16, 1985

The President today announced his intention to nominate Jennifer Joy Manson to be an Assistant Administrator of the Environmental Protection Agency (External Affairs). She would succeed Josephine Cooper.

Miss Manson is presently serving as executive assistant to Senator John Warner. Previously she was executive assistant to Gov. John Dalton of Virginia (1978–1982). Prior to that time she worked on the Dalton committee and in the Governor's transition office. She served at the White House as administrative aide to the Deputy Special Assistant to the President (1976–1977).

She graduated from the University of North Carolina (B.A., 1974). She was born January 10, 1953, in Naples, Italy, and now resides in Alexandria, VA.

Nomination of M. Alan Woods To Be a Deputy United States Trade Representative
August 16, 1985

The President today announced his intention to nominate M. Alan Woods to be a Deputy United States Trade Representative with the rank of Ambassador. He would succeed Robert Emmet Lighthizer.

Mr. Woods is president of the International Service Corp. in Washington, DC. Previously he was vice president of technology, Sears World Trade, in Washington, DC, in 1983–1985. He was vice president of DGA International in Washington in 1977–1983. He served at the Department of Defense as Assistant Secretary for Public Affairs (1976–1977); Special Assistant to the Secretary and Deputy Secretaries (1975–1976); and Principal Deputy Assistant Secretary (1975). He was Deputy Director of Presidential Personnel at the White House in 1974–1975. Prior to that time he was executive assistant to the Governor of Missouri in 1973–1974 and vice president of Bradley, Woods and Co. in 1970–1972.

He graduated from American University (B.A., 1964). He is married and resides in Washington, DC. He was born October 31, 1945, in St. Louis, MO.

Appointment of 10 Members of the Advisory Committee for Trade Negotiations
August 16, 1985

The President today announced his intention to appoint the following individuals to be members of the Advisory Committee for Trade Negotiations for terms of 2 years:

Barbara McConnell Barrett will succeed Gerald J. Lynch. She is presently serving as special counsel in the law firm of Evans, Kitchel & Jenckes in Phoenix, AZ. Previously she was Vice Chairman of the Civil Aeronautics Board. She graduated from Arizona State University (B.S., 1972; M.A., 1975; J.D., 1978). She was born December 26, 1950, in Indiana County, PA, and now resides in Phoenix, AZ.

John R. Faust, Jr., will succeed Vincent McDonnell. He is a partner of the law firm of Schwabe, Williamson, Wyatt, Moore & Roberts in Portland, OR. He is also a director of Western Savings & Loan Association. He graduated from the University of Oregon (B.S., 1953; J.D.,

1958). He was born June 16, 1932, in Portland, OR, where he now resides.

Murray Howard Finley is a reappointment. He is president of the Amalgamated Clothing & Textile Workers Union. Previously he was general president of the Amalgamated Clothing Workers of America. He graduated from the University of Michigan (B.A., 1946) and Northwestern University (J.D., 1949). He was born March 31, 1922, in Syracuse, NY, and now resides in Guttenberg, NJ.

Simon C. Fireman is a reappointment. He is chairman of the board of Aqua Leisure Industries in Avon, MA. Previously he was president and chief executive officer of Marine Hardware and Supply Co., Inc. He graduated from Harvard University (B.S., 1968). He was born September 10, 1925, in Boston, MA, and now resides in Avon, MA.

Leonard A. Lauder is a reappointment. He has been serving as president and chief executive officer of Estee Lauder, Inc., in New York City since 1972. Previously he was executive vice president of Estee Lauder, Inc. He graduated from the University of Pennsylvania (B.S., 1954). He was born March 19, 1933, in New York City, where he now resides.

Kenneth A. Lazarus is a reappointment. He is a partner of the law firm of Ward, Lazarus, Grow and Cihlar in Washington, DC. He has served as an adjunct professor at Georgetown University Law Center. He graduated from Dayton University (B.A., 1964), the University of Notre Dame (J.D., 1967), and George Washington University (L.L.M., 1971). He was born March 10, 1942, in Passaic, NJ, and now resides in Lovettsville, VA.

Harold M. Messmer, Jr., will succeed Stanley Ebner. He is president of Pacific Holding Corp. and vice chairman of its subsidiary, Cannon Mills Co. In addition, he serves as a director of Castle & Cook, Inc., and a partner of the law firm of O'Melveny & Myers. He graduated from Loyola University (A.B., 1967) and New York University Law School (J.D., 1970). He was born February 20, 1946, in Jackson, MS, and now resides in Pacific Palisades, CA.

Edmund T. Pratt, Jr., is a reappointment. He is chairman of the board and chief executive officer of Pfizer, Inc., in New York City. He is chairman of the New York State Council on International Business. He graduated from Duke University (B.S., 1947) and Wharton School of Commerce and Finance, University of Pennsylvania (M.B.A., 1949). He was born February 22, 1927, in Savannah, GA, and now resides in Port Washington, NY.

J. Steven Rhodes will succeed John T. Dailey. He is presently serving as vice president for public finance at Smith Barney in New York City. Previously he served at the White House as Assistant to the Vice President for Domestic Policy (1983–1985) and Special Assistant to the President for Intergovernmental Affairs (1981–1983). He was born September 29, 1951, in New Orleans, LA, and now resides in New York City.

Don A. Sebastiani will succeed Robert Ivie. He has been a California State assemblyman since 1980. He is also a vintner at the Sebastiani Vineyards. He graduated from the University of San Francisco (B.A., 1975). He was born February 15, 1953, in Sonoma, CA, where he now resides.

Statement on Signing the Supplemental Appropriations Act, 1985
August 16, 1985

I have signed H.R. 2577, the Supplemental Appropriations Act for 1985. The act provides additional funding for a number of important programs, including economic aid to several nations in the Middle East, essential humanitarian aid to the Nicaraguan democratic resistance, funding for improving security at our Embassies and facilities abroad, and start-up funding for several water projects.

H.R. 2577 provides funds that I requested to support the Nation's foreign policy. It will contribute significantly to our ability to provide urgently required aid to our friends in the Middle East and will support our efforts to bring peace to the region. I would note in particular the funds it appropriates for both Israel and Egypt, as well as for Jordan. All three of these nations have a vital role to play if there is to be peace in the Middle East.

Moreover, the act contains $27 million in funding for humanitarian assistance to the Nicaraguan democratic resistance. While the program that has been approved is more modest than I believe necessary, we have clearly won bipartisan support on this very critical issue as well as recognition and humanitarian support for those fighting the Sandinista dictatorship. This is an important element in our overall effort to assist neighboring countries to defend themselves against Nicaraguan attack and subversion. Unfortunately, the provision unduly and unnecessarily restricts efficient management and administration of the program. Nevertheless, I will continue to work with the Congress to carry out the program as effectively as possible and will take care to ensure that the law is faithfully executed.

H.R. 2577 is also an important first step in reforming and revitalizing the Nation's water resources development program. Little progress has been achieved in recent years due mainly to the impasse over the proper Federal role in water projects and the amount of cost sharing that local project sponsors should assume. This act acknowledges that the traditional Federal role is no longer appropriate and that project beneficiaries must contribute a larger share of costs for water projects. It allows for progressive and essential new approaches to the financing of projects, while retaining a significant Federal role and demonstrating commitment to implementation of viable water projects. I commend the Congress' efforts in this matter. The act represents only the first of two steps that must be taken to reform national water policy. I anticipate that the Congress will soon be addressing a comprehensive water policy and project authorization bill that could set national policy for years to come. This administration has already demonstrated flexibility in working out a reasonably implementable cost-sharing agreement with the Congress. I am confident that the Congress will act in this matter in a prompt and responsible manner.

I am concerned that the act mandates a specific and excessive number of new grants to be awarded by the National Institutes of Health (NIH). Such requirements not only undermine the flexibility essential to the continued success of the NIH but also threaten the long-run stability of biomedical research funding. In signing this bill, it is my understanding that the Congress will take future appropriations action to restore programmatic flexibility and budgetary stability to the NIH.

This act authorizes the Federal Emergency Management Agency (FEMA) to establish a national board to oversee an emergency food program. I am deeply concerned about the membership of the board. If read literally, the act would permit six private organizations to appoint members of the board. As members, these persons would be officers of the executive branch because the board will perform executive functions. Such appointments by private organizations is in clear violation of the Appointments Clause of the Constitution (U.S. Constitution, Article II, Section 2, Clause 2). In order to avoid this constitutional infirmity, I direct the Director of FEMA to construe this provision as granting him complete discretionary authority to determine who should be appointed to the national board. The organizations mentioned in the act may make recommendations, but only the Director, as the "head of a department," *id.*, is authorized to appoint members to the board.

I am disappointed that the bill provides more funds than I believe necessary. I must urge the Congress to exercise greater restraint if Federal spending is to be brought under effective control.

Note: H.R. 2577, approved August 15, was assigned Public Law No. 99–88.

Radio Address to the Nation on the Farm Industry
August 17, 1985

My fellow Americans:

August is a happy time for most of us, a time of vacations and State fairs. A number of America's farmers will be showing their livestock and produce at those fairs, and this month they'll have more to show than ever. It's been another bumper-crop year on the farms, and that's good news for America's consumers, but a mixed blessing for our farmers. Big crops mean weaker prices, and under current conditions, that means more financial strain for some of those who grow the food that feeds our country.

It's no secret that American agriculture is facing hard times. And it's particularly painful to know that those affected are among our most productive and hard-working citizens. American farmers are the backbone of our country. Their crops and stock and related industries account for nearly one-fifth of our gross national product and almost one-fifth of our exports.

Now, not all farmers are in trouble; many are not. And it's important to note that those whose crops are the beneficiaries of governmental programs are worse off than those who operate without such assistance. Current farm problems arise from a host of reasons. There were the shocks of the seventies: grain embargoes, double-digit inflation, and record interest rates at 21 percent. Some farmers borrowed large sums of money based on inflated land values, and when we brought inflation down, those farmers were left with declining land values to cover their loans. But a major contributor to the problem is the Federal program designed to help farmers. For years now, Federal farm programs have distorted the market and sent confusing signals to farmers. Interventionist commodity programs have encouraged farmers to produce more than the market will bear while attempting to prop up prices.

Today we find ourselves with farmers who grow more than they can sell, and the result is low commodity prices and a depressed rural economy—and this, in spite of how much we've spent. In 1979, for instance, the Federal Government was purchasing less than 1 percent of all dairy products at a cost of $250 million. Just 4 years later, in 1983, it was purchasing 12 percent of those products at a cost to the taxpayer of well over $2½ billion a year. And it's not just the dairy program. From 1981 through this year, we will have spent just under $59 billion on farm price supports. That's nearly 3½ times what we spent from 1976 to 1980. Our administration has spent more on the farm program than any other administration in history. If spending more money on agriculture would solve the problem, we already would have solved it by now.

We've got to create a future for the farmer that's every bit as bright as the future is for the rest of our economy. A big part of that is keeping inflation and interest rates down. We've made progress on these fronts, as you know, and it's helped farmers control their own costs. Farm production costs were rising fast in the 1970's, but now they've been stable since 1981.

The other half of the job is to free ourselves from the quagmire created by Federal farm programs. I support long-term policies that will enable the American farmer to enter the 21st century stronger than ever before. The world market holds the potential for increasing opportunities for our products, but we must have a farm policy that maintains our competitiveness. Through our trade policies, we must ensure that farmers have full and fair access to all foreign markets. That is one of the Federal Government's greatest responsibilities; another is to provide stability in programs. Much of the farm problem stems from the past practice of lurching from one emergency program to another, coming up with so-called solutions that never solve anything.

The answer to our farm problems cannot be found in sticking with discredited programs and increasing government controls. The answer can only be found in our ability to help our entire agriculture industry stand on its own feet again. You know, this country is nothing without the farmer, and those who work the land have the right to know that there's a future in farming. Their children have the right to know that they'll still be able to work the family farm generations from now and make a decent living.

The law governing our farm program expires September 30th. I'm eager to sign historic legislation that will put American agriculture on a sound course for the future. In writing farm legislation, I expect the Congress to stay within its own budget goals. I need your help to send Congress an unmistakable message that change in our farm policy is not only desired but essential.

Until next week, thanks for listening, and God bless you.

Note: The President spoke at 9:06 a.m. from Rancho del Cielo, his ranch near Santa Barbara, CA.

Statement on Signing the Foreign Relations Authorization Act, Fiscal Years 1986 and 1987
August 17, 1985

I have signed H.R. 2068, the Foreign Relations Authorization Act, Fiscal Years 1986 and 1987. H.R. 2068 authorizes appropriations for the conduct of our foreign affairs during fiscal years 1986 and 1987. These appropriation authorizations and several new authorities in this legislation are vital to the national security of the United States. Appropriations authorized by this act will enable the State Department to manage our diplomatic and consular establishment abroad, participate in and provide contributions to important international organizations, and extend humanitarian refugee assistance. The act also continues our important information, exchange of persons, and radio broadcasting efforts through the United States Information Agency and the Board for International Broadcasting. It provides continued authority for the United States Arms Control and Disarmament Agency, as we proceed with arms control negotiations.

A few serious problems are raised, however, by several other provisions of the act, the foremost of which pertain to our relations with the United Nations and its specialized agencies. These provisions establish conditions that may be impossible to meet within the period of time indicated, thereby requiring reductions in U.S. payments of assessed and voluntary contributions. Activities of these organizations of importance to the United States could be deleteriously affected as a result.

I note in particular that section 143 places contingent limitations on our payments unless the United Nations adopts weighted voting on budgetary matters by fiscal year 1987. I am asking Secretary [of State] Shultz to begin discussions toward that end. He will stay in close contact with the Congress as he proceeds. Depending on the outcome of those discussions, it may be necessary to seek legislative changes.

Section 113 prohibits contributions by the United States to the United Nations High Commissioner for Refugees (UNHCR) after June 1986 unless the High Commissioner provides for annual audits by an independent consultant. The Department of State will begin to work immediately with the High Commissioner to see if this requirement can be satisfied, since the limitation could put the United States in a position of being unable to respond adequately through the UNHCR to life-threatening emergencies such as those found in Africa and Southeast Asia. If it cannot, legislative relief may also have to be sought.

Similar difficulties may also result from section 151, which assumes that the United Nations can determine whether and the extent to which some U.N. employees are required to pay part or all of their salaries to their respective governments. This provision also assumes that the United Nations can correct such a practice and requires a reduction to U.S. payments of its assessed contributions to the United Nations to the extent that the practice continues. The difficulties in administering section 151 may require some modification of it at a later date.

I am also concerned about the numerous earmarkings of appropriation authorizations for particular activities included in this act. I understand the intent of the Congress in setting out these amounts. Nevertheless, they may severely limit our ability to meet other important program needs within the limited appropriation amounts that are likely to be enacted by the Congress. In this regard, I am particularly concerned about earmarkings enacted for refugee assistance and for the United States Information Agency. Because of the lack of clarity in the earmarkings of the exchange of persons program of USIA, I am asking the Director of that agency to plan on program levels of $148 and $159 million in 1986 and 1987, respectively. Because of the large number of earmarkings found in the bill, the Secretary of State and the Director of USIA will have to work closely with both authorization and appropriations committees as fiscal years 1986 and 1987 progress so that interests of the Congress and priority foreign affairs needs can best be accommodated.

Note: H.R. 2068, approved August 16, was assigned Public Law No. 99-93.

Nomination of Clyde D. Taylor To Be United States Ambassador to Paraguay
August 19, 1985

The President today announced his intention to nominate Clyde D. Taylor, of Maryland, a career member of the Senior Foreign Service, Class of Minister-Counselor, as Ambassador to the Republic of Paraguay. He would succeed Arthur H. Davis, Jr.

Mr. Taylor worked at Americans United as director of the film department in Washington, DC, from 1959 to 1961. He joined the Foreign Service as a junior officer in 1961. He served from 1962 to 1964 in the Bureau of Security and Consular Affairs. In 1964 he went to the U.S. Embassy in Panama as vice consul and served there until 1966, when he became economic/commercial officer at the U.S. Embassy in Canberra, Australia. He returned to the Department in 1968 as an international economist in the Commodities, Industrial and Strategic Materials Division of the Bureau of Economic Affairs. He then became chief of the economic and commercial section of the U.S. Embassy in San Salvador, El Salvador, from 1972 to 1975. In 1975 Mr. Taylor went to the U.S. Embassy in Tehran, Iran, as economic development and financial officer, where he served until 1979 when he became acting counselor for economic and commercial affairs in Tehran. From 1979 to 1980, he attended the National War College. In July 1980, he became Director of the Office of Program Management in the Bureau of International Narcotics Matters and in November of 1980 was named Deputy Assistant Secretary in that Bureau, where he has served until the present time.

Mr. Taylor was born September 30, 1937, in Colombia, South America (American parents). He received his B.A. in 1959 from Wheaton College and his M.A. in 1961 from American University. His foreign language is Spanish. Mr. Taylor is married to the former Virginia L. Lundberg, and they have two children.

Nomination of Natale H. Bellocchi To Be United States Ambassador to Botswana
August 19, 1985

The President today announced his intention to nominate Natale H. Bellocchi, of New York, a career member of the Senior Foreign Service, Class of Minister-Counselor, as Ambassador to the Republic of Botswana. He would succeed Theodore C. Maino.

After graduating from Georgia Tech, Mr. Bellocchi worked as an industrial engineer at the Burlington Mills Corp. in Allentown, PA, from 1948 to 1950. He joined the Foreign Service as a diplomatic courier in 1955. From 1960 to 1961, he was an administrative assistant in Hong Kong. From 1961 to 1963, he served as general services officer in Vientiane, Laos. He took Chinese language training in Taichung, Taiwan, from 1963 to 1964 and then became assistant commercial attaché in Taipei, Taiwan, where he served until 1968. From 1968 to 1969, he was chief of the commercial unit in Hong Kong. He returned to Washington in 1970 to take economic training. From 1971 to 1972, he was commercial attaché in Saigon, Vietnam, and from 1973 to 1974, he was commercial counselor in Tokyo, Japan. He attended the senior seminar in Washington, DC, from 1974 to 1975 and thereafter was detailed as a special assistant in OASIA, Department of the Treasury, Washington, DC. Mr. Bellocchi then went to New Delhi, India, as economic counselor until 1979, when he returned to Hong Kong as deputy principal officer. From 1981 to the present, he has been Deputy Assistant Secretary of State for Current Analysis in the Bureau of Intelligence and Research.

Mr. Bellocchi was born July 5, 1926, in Little Falls, NY. He received his B.S. in 1948 from Georgia Tech (industrial management) and his M.A. in 1954 from Georgetown University. He served in the United States Army from 1950 to 1953. His foreign language is Chinese-Mandarin. Mr. Bellocchi is married to Sujr (Lilan) Liu, and they have two children.

Statement on the Retirement of Senator Paul Laxalt of Nevada
August 19, 1985

It was with sincere regret that I learned of Paul Laxalt's decision to retire from the Senate after 12 years of honorable service. Paul Laxalt has been a dedicated public servant who has given more than 20 years of his life serving the people of Nevada and this nation, first as district attorney of Ormsby County, then as Lieutenant Governor, then as Governor, and now as U.S. Senator from Nevada. His friendship and support have been invaluable to me over the years.

Senator Laxalt has agreed at my request to remain as general chairman of the Republican National Committee through 1988, and I will continue to rely on Paul's advice and counsel in the years ahead.

Nancy and I offer our thanks and best wishes to Paul and Carol as they continue to serve the people of Nevada, and in their future endeavors.

Statement by Principal Deputy Press Secretary Speakes on Antisatellite Weapons Testing
August 20, 1985

The President today submitted to the Congress, in accordance with the 1985 Department of Defense Authorization Act, the certification required by the Congress prior to a test against an object in space of the nonnuclear miniature vehicle antisatellite (ASAT) system which is now in development. The miniature vehicle is launched from an F-15 aircraft. In the certification, the President attests to the Congress that:

—The United States is endeavoring in good faith to negotiate with the Soviet

Union a mutual and verifiable agreement with the strictest possible limitations on antisatellite weapons consistent with the national security interests of the United States;

—Pending agreement on such strict limitations, testing against objects in space of the F–15-launched miniature homing vehicle ASAT warhead is necessary to avert clear and irrevocable harm to the national security;

—Such testing would not constitute an irreversible step that would gravely impair prospects for negotiations on antisatellite weapons;

—Such testing is fully consistent with the rights and obligations of the United States under the 1972 antiballistic missile treaty, as those rights and obligations exist at the time of testing.

The Soviet Union has for many years had the world's only operational antisatellite system. There is also a growing threat from present and prospective Soviet satellites which are designed to support directly the U.S.S.R.'s terrestrial forces. The United States must develop its own ASAT capability in order to deter Soviet threats to U.S. and allied space systems and, within such limits imposed by international law, to deny any adversary advantages arising from the offensive use of space-based systems which could undermine deterrence. Systematic,

continued testing is necessary for us to be able to proceed with ASAT development and finally to validate operational capability, in order to restore the necessary military balance in this area.

A number of serious problems, including definitional and monitoring difficulties plus the need to counter existing Soviet targeting satellites, contribute to the conclusion that a comprehensive ban on development, testing, deployment, and use of all means of countering satellites is not verifiable or in our national security interest. Moreover, no arrangements or agreements beyond those already governing military activities in outer space have been found to date that are judged to be in the overall interest of the United States and its allies and that meet the congressionally mandated requirements of verifiability and consistency with the national security. We will continue to study possible ASAT limitations in good faith to see whether such limitations are consistent with the national security interests of the United States.

The United States is presently engaged in negotiations with the Soviet Union at Geneva on nuclear arms reductions, defense and space issues. We believe that ASAT testing can constitute an incentive to the Soviet Union to reach agreements on a wide range of issues.

Appointment of 13 Members of the National Highway Safety Advisory Committee
August 21, 1985

The President today announced his intention to appoint the following individuals to be members of the National Highway Safety Advisory Committee for the terms indicated:

For terms expiring March 15, 1987:

Cecelia K. Bros will succeed Joanne Corday Kozberg. She is president of the American Ethnic League United Hungarian Fund in Washington, DC. She was born March 1, 1934, in Jyor, Hungary, and now resides in Springfield, VA.

Frederick Edward (Fritz) Hitchcock, Jr., will suc-

ceed Michael L. Johnson. He is owner and operator of several new car dealerships in City of Industry, CA. He was born October 24, 1939, in Des Moines, IA, and now resides in Palos Verdes Estates, CA.

Candy Lightner will succeed Stanley J. Preebe. She is president and chief executive officer of MADD (Mothers Against Drunk Drivers). She was born May 30, 1946, in Pasadena, CA, and now resides in Arlington, TX.

Frank E. (Gene) Raper will succeed Russell I. Brown. He is president of the United Packaging Corp. He was born January 18, 1946, in Portsmouth, VA, and now resides in Hacienda

Heights, CA.

John F. Sammons, Jr., will succeed William B. Snyder. He is mayor of the city of Temple, TX, and president of Temple Supply Co. He was born June 21, 1949, in Temple, TX, and still resides in Temple.

For terms expiring March 15, 1988:

Thom L. Holmes will succeed Paul R. Meyer, Jr. He is president and chief executive officer of HJT Industries and Associates. He was born January 30, 1946, in Texarkana, AR, and currently resides in Los Angeles, CA.

Eric Harrison Jostrom will succeed Harold Coker. He is vice president of Eaton Vance Management. He was born March 1, 1942, in Newton, MA, and currently resides in Essex, MA.

Vern McCarthy, Jr., will succeed Michael J. Hermreck. He is president of Vern McCarthy, Ltd. He was born May 12, 1927, in Melrose Park, IL, and currently resides in Oak Brook, IL.

Thomas G. McGuire will succeed Henry Edward Hudson. He is the retired chairman of the board of Industrial Indemnity Insurance. He was born March 15, 1907, in Santa Rosa, CA, and currently resides in Borrego Springs, CA.

Andrew S. Natsios will succeed Lexie E. Herrin. He is chairman of the Massachusetts State Republican Committee. He was born September 22, 1949, in Philadelphia, PA, and currently resides in Holliston, MA.

Edward F. Reilly, Jr., will succeed Evie Teegen. He is a Kansas State senator. He was born March 24, 1937, in Leavenworth, KS, and currently resides in Leavenworth.

Oswaldo Gonzalez Rodriguez will succeed Walter W. Gray. He is the owner of Comput Income, Inc. He was born December 26, 1932, in Cardenas, Cuba, and currently resides in West New York, NJ.

A. Starke Taylor, Jr., will succeed John A. Kraeutler. He is the mayor of Dallas, TX. He was born July 2, 1922, in Paris, TX, and currently resides in Dallas, TX.

Nomination of Michael Sotirhos To Be United States Ambassador to Jamaica
August 22, 1985

The President today announced his intention to nominate Michael Sotirhos as Ambassador of the United States of America to Jamaica. He would succeed William Alexander Hewitt.

Mr. Sotirhos began his career as a partner with Ariston Sales Co., Ltd., New York, NY, in 1948. In 1958 he became founder and chairman of Ariston Interior Designers, Inc., of New York, and in 1983 became chairman of the board and consultant. In 1973–1975 Mr. Sotirhos was a member of the National Voluntary Service Advisory Council and Chairman of the International Operations Committee, Peace Corps. In 1976 he served as a member of the National Advisory Council of the Small Business Administration. He has also been chairman of the National Republican Heritage Groups Council. In 1983 he received the Man of the Year Award from the National Republican Heritage Groups Council.

Mr. Sotirhos was born November 12, 1928, in New York. He received his B.B.A. in 1950 from the City College of New York, Bernard M. Baruch School of Business and Civic Administration. His foreign languages are Greek and Spanish. Mr. Sotirhos is married to the former Estelle Manos, and they have two children.

Nomination of Robert G. Houdek To Be United States Ambassador to Uganda
August 22, 1985

The President today announced his intention to nominate Robert G. Houdek, a career member of the Senior Foreign Service, Class of Minister-Counselor, as Ambassador of the United States of America to the Republic of Uganda. He would succeed Allen Clayton Davis.

Mr. Houdek entered the Foreign Service in 1962. In 1963–1965 he was a junior officer trainee at the U.S. Embassy in Brussels, Belgium. He served as political officer in Conakry, Guinea, in 1965–1967 and then returned to the Department as a staff officer in the Executive Secretariat in 1967–1969. Mr. Houdek then went to the National Security Council as a special assistant to the national security adviser in 1969–1971. He attended the Woodrow Wilson School as a Mid-Career fellow at Princeton University in 1971–1972. In 1972 he became deputy

chief of mission at the U.S. Embassy in Freetown, Sierra Leone, where he served until 1976 when he went to Jamaica as political counselor. In 1976 he served as Deputy Director of the Office of West African Affairs in the Department and then Director of the Office of Intra-African Affairs in 1978–1980. In 1980 he became deputy chief of mission in Nairobi, Kenya, where he served until 1984 when he returned to the Department as a member of the executive seminar in national and international affairs.

Mr. Houdek was born February 26, 1940, in Chicago, IL. He received his B.A. in 1961 from Beloit College and his M.A. in 1962 from the Fletcher School of Law and Diplomacy. His foreign language is French. Mr. Houdek is married to the former Mary Elizabeth Wood, and they have two children.

Nomination of Jean Broward Shevlin Gerard To Be United States Ambassador to Luxembourg
August 22, 1985

The President today announced his intention to nominate Jean Broward Shevlin Gerard to be Ambassador of the United States of America to Luxembourg. She would succeed John E. Dolibois.

Mrs. Gerard began her career as an attorney with Cadwalader, Wickersham & Taft in New York in 1977–1981. In 1981 she was named the United States Permanent Representative to the United Nations Educational, Scientific, and Cultural Organization at Paris, France, and accorded the rank of Ambassador by the President during the tenure of her service in this position. In 1982–1985 she was U.S. member of the Executive Board of UNESCO and vice president of the Board in 1983–1985. In 1984 she served as chairman of the U.S. delegation at the preparatory conference for the

1985 United Nations Decade for Women World Conference in Vienna, Austria. In 1983 Mrs. Gerard was chairman of the U.S. delegation to the 4th Extraordinary UNESCO General Conference in Paris, France, and vice chairman of the U.S. delegation to the 22d UNESCO General Conference in Paris. She was chairman of the U.S. delegation to the 2d UNESCO Conference on World Cultural Policies in Mexico City in 1982.

Mrs. Gerard as born March 9, 1938, in Portland, OR. She received her A.B. in 1959 from Vassar College and her J.D. in 1977 from Fordham University School of Law. Her foreign languages are French, Italian, and German. Mrs. Gerard is married to James Watson Gerard II, and they have two children.

Nomination of Edwin J. Feulner, Jr., To Be a Member of the United States Advisory Commission on Public Diplomacy, and Designation as Chairman
August 22, 1985

The President today announced his intention to nominate Edwin J. Feulner, Jr., to be a member of the United States Advisory Commission on Public Diplomacy for a term expiring July 1, 1988. This is a reappointment. The President also intends to redesignate Mr. Feulner as Chairman upon his confirmation by the Senate.

Since 1977 Mr. Feulner has been serving as president of the Heritage Foundation. Previously, he was executive vice president of the Heritage Foundation in 1977; executive director of the Republican Study Com-

mittee in the U.S. House of Representatives, in 1974–1977; president of the Robert M. Schuchman Memorial Foundation in 1973–1974; and legislative assistant, administrative assistant, and special assistant to Representative Philip M. Crane in 1970–1977.

He graduated from Regis College (B.S., 1963) and the Wharton School, University of Pennsylvania (M.B.A., 1974). He is married, has two children, and resides in Alexandria, VA. He was born August 12, 1941, in Chicago, IL.

Remarks at a California Republican Party Fundraising Dinner in Los Angeles
August 22, 1985

Governor Deukmejian, Members of the Congress who are here, Chairman Antonovich, ladies and gentlemen, and a special thanks to Margaret Brock for all she's done to make this the successful dinner that it is. And I'm more than a little overwhelmed now that I know that that building is—what its name is going to be. Up until now, the only thing named after me was a pub in Ballyporeen, Ireland. [*Laughter*] Now you're going to make me respectable. [*Laughter*]

Well, California is always in the forefront of new trends, and perhaps this idea of a before-dinner speech—I'll make it a short one, though—will catch on. I was happy to see our friend John Gavin, our Ambassador to Mexico, and Jack, as you know, has done a superlative job there. I think he's one of the best Ambassadors this country has ever had, and we're enormously pleased that he's going to stay on in his post and continue his great work.

I can't tell you how much of a pleasure it is for Nancy and me to be here with old

friends and back in California. I've told [British Prime Minister] Margaret Thatcher on several occasions that if only their people had come across the other ocean first, the Capitol would be in California. [*Laughter*]

This is the first time that I've been with many of you since spending a little time in Bethesda, and Nancy and I want you to know how much your prayers and well-wishes and good wishes meant to us. We sat together and read many of the get well cards that you sent. Knowing you were with us in spirit was the best medicine of all. Some of those cards were pretty special and pretty memorable. Just one in particular said, "Dear Mr. President, I was very concerned to hear that the doctors took two feet out of your inner workings. How did those two feet get in there?" [*Laughter*]

This was my second serious visit to the hospital since getting to Washington, and I'm not a bit discouraged or anything about it. My father told me that optimism, and as Duke pointed out just a few moments ago, is something that is probably a part of my Irish heritage. As a matter of fact, there's a story that illustrates that. You knew that I'd get around to telling a story, didn't you? [*Laughter*] Had to do with a young Irishman that was bandaged from toes to nose as a result of an accident, couldn't move a muscle. He was in court suing, and he won the suit for $4 million. And the lawyers for the insurance company went over immediately afterward. And they said: "You're not going to enjoy a penny of this. We know you're faking. We're going to follow you 24 hours a day, and the first time you move, we'll have you." And he said: "Will you now? Well, let me tell you what's going to happen to me. In a few minutes, they're coming in with a stretcher. They're taking me out of here and downstairs, they're putting me in an ambulance. We're going straight to Kennedy Airport. There, on the stretcher, they're putting me in an airplane, and we're flying straight to Paris, France. They're taking me off the plane on a stretcher, putting me in another ambulance, and we're driving straight to the Shrine of Lourdes. And there, you're going to see the greatest miracle you ever—[*inaudible*]." [*Laughter*]

Seriously, though, I am feeling fine. And when we get back to Washington, there's going to be full steam ahead. And if we're going to succeed, we'll need your help. I can count on you, can't I? [*Applause*] I was hoping you'd do that.

We've been through a great many political battles together. Mike Antonovich and Pat Nolan were just kids back in those days when I was making my first run for the Governor's office. They were walking precincts for Youth for Reagan. And they called their gang the Brown Is Out To Lunch Bunch. [*Laughter*] I've still got the T-shirt they gave me. Well, now those same young people are assuming leadership positions in State government, and some hold positions of responsibility in our administration in Washington.

Perhaps the most heartening development in recent years is that today's crop of young people is turning to our party as never before. I used to say—sometimes discouraged back in an earlier time—that every time I went to a Republican affair, I

thought the only young people there looked like they couldn't join anything else— [*laughter*]—but not anymore. In that '84 campaign, all the way across the country and on a great many campuses—and I could remember when if I went to a campus, I started a riot—but this time, to see them all filled with energy and idealism at our Republican rallies all across America. Young voters will continue supporting us as long as we offer the way to a better future, as long as we're the can-do party with an agenda for an opportunity-filled tomorrow, the party with a positive strategy for freedom and growth.

And today the Republican Party is the party of the open door. Here in California, as in other States, we're reaching out to Asians, Hispanics, blacks; and it's making a difference. I know, for example, that a big factor in Bob Dornan's race for Congress was his going to the Hispanic community even though he was told why they belong to the other party. Well, they got almost 50 percent of the Hispanic vote. Inroads are being made in the Asian community. You see, the other party looks at all those groups and others and says they're ethnic groups. Well, we look at them, and we see Americans. More and more Democrats are realizing they have more in common with our goals than those targeted with the leadership of their own party.

And today we're a major political force for change in America. That's evident by the terrific job that Governor Deukmejian is doing here in California. And, believe me, we're seeing it all across the country. Now, I hope—indeed, I know that all of you are going to do your best to reelect him next year, and I'll bet I know what his wish would be if he were blowing out birthday candles right now. It would be: Send him a legislature that he can work with—more Republicans.

And while you're at it, why not send another Republican to Washington as a Senator to join the Republican Senator we already have there. Now, I hear there are quite a few people interested in the job— [*laughter*]—and there's nothing wrong with that. And I'm sure that practically any one of them would be an improvement. [*Laugh-*

ter] But may I make a suggestion? Twenty years ago our party in California gave a priceless gift to Republicans everywhere—the 11th commandment: "Thou shalt not speak ill of another Republican." Have a spirited primary, but don't campaign against each other. Campaign against the incumbent and then stand united behind our party's choice. And I mean, not just talk about, as we have maybe for too many years, but let's go back to what it was like in that first year, 20 years ago, when the candidates themselves pledged to observe it and when Republican groups and organizations like the Federated Women said they would only support a candidate who subscribed to the 11th commandment. Let's bring that back and do it again, and maybe this time it will catch on all over the country. I've been trying to spread the word about it for a long time, and we'll get them everyplace.

By being here tonight, you're contributing to a registration drive that will give Governor Deukmejian the leverage he needs up in Sacramento to help us build a new coalition for opportunity and freedom. The other side would like to believe that our victory last November was due to, oh, something other than our philosophy or anything of that kind. They talked about personalities and things like that. I just hope they keep believing that. There's a change happening in America. Realignment is real. What the American people see is that the other party just keeps going in circles. And that's just like, you know, when you get lost in the woods; if every time you come to a decision you lean to the left, you will wind up going in circles. [Laughter]

Now, in contrast, we're going forward with confidence and with gusto. Gusto—that's Republican for vigor. You'll remember vigor back a couple of administrations ago. [Laughter] We're not going to stop till we get the job done. Now, I know that some of the same people who thought that we would be co-opted by the permanent Government when we got to Washington a little over 4½ years ago now think that the second term is going to be little more than a holding action. Well, let me clear that up. Yes, we're proud of what we've accomplished so far, but we've got an agenda for the next few years and to borrow a phrase from that '84 campaign, "You ain't seen nothin' yet."

This fall we're going to campaign for the most extensive tax overhaul this country has had since the 1920's. It will bring down the rates and close the loopholes. It'll be fair. And once in place, it will energize our economy, spurring investment and enterprise. People will have an incentive to channel their resources into job-creating businesses and commercial investment rather than nonproductive shelters and tax dodges. We're going to take our case directly to the people. It's a choice between the special interest and the general interest. This is a big one, and with your help, we're going to win it for America.

Looking to the future, we're moving forward with research on a project that offers us a way out of our nuclear dilemma—the one that has confounded mankind for four decades now. The Strategic Defense Initiative research program offers us the hope of protecting ourselves and our allies from a nuclear ballistic missile attack. This will permit us to shift our focus to saving lives, rather than avenging them. We seek an antinuclear shield, using technology to make us safer. Our success will be measured by the number of people we can save, not destroy. We keep hearing some self-declared experts and some of those blame-America-first crowd saying that our SDI concept is unfeasible and a waste of money. Well, if that's true, why are the Soviets so upset about it? As a matter of fact, why are they investing so many rubles of their own in the same technologies?

One of the reasons the American people have turned to us is that we don't waver from our commitment to do what's necessary to keep our country safe and to secure the blessings of liberty for our children and our children's children. That is the Republican goal, and nowhere is this clearer than in Central America. We've turned around a desperate situation in these last 4½ years. One of the proudest accomplishments of this administration has happened slowly and quietly with little recognition. When we first got to Washington the question we heard everywhere was, "Will El Salvador fall to the Communists?" Well, today the question is, "Will democracy win in Nicaragua?" And tomorrow the question will be, "How soon?" We've held firm. We'll continue to do what needs to be done to protect our country's security and help the people of Central America build free, prosperous, and democratic countries.

Today we have so many reasons to be grateful. Nancy and I have said a few prayers of thanks in these last few weeks, but all of us can be thankful that we're citizens of this blessed land. I want to thank all of you for what you're doing to keep it the good and decent land that God intended it to be. And I'm sorry we can't spend the rest of the evening here with you, but I appreciate—and I know Nancy does—this opportunity, at least for this limited time, to be here with you. Just seeing you here like this makes me sure we'll preserve this last best hope of man on Earth.

God bless you all. Thank you all for all you're doing.

Note: The President spoke at 6:40 p.m. at the Century Plaza Hotel. In his opening remarks, the President referred to California State Republican Party Chairman Michael Antonovich and Republican Party activist Margaret Brock. He also referred to the announcement that the new California State Republican Party headquarters in Burbank was to be named in his honor. The President remained at the hotel overnight.

Proclamation 5364—Women's Equality Day, 1985
August 23, 1985

By the President of the United States of America

A Proclamation

Women's Equality Day is celebrated each year on August 26 because it was on that day in 1920 that the 19th Amendment, guaranteeing women the right to vote, became part of our Constitution. This was an accomplishment of great practical and symbolic importance, since it recognized women as full participants in our democratic system of self-government.

The adoption of the 19th Amendment was a tremendous victory for the ideals of democracy, but its consequences have not been confined to our political system. In every field of endeavor, women have made notable contributions to our national life. Their achievements have shown that America's women are a tremendous human resource for our Nation—an inexhaustible reserve of talent, imagination, and ambition.

Today, women have an unparalleled degree of opportunity to decide what they want to achieve in their lives. Whether they devote themselves to raising families or to pursuing careers, their contributions to America are leaving an indelible mark on our Nation's life. In the years ahead, their accomplishments will continue to shape profoundly our Nation's destiny.

Now, Therefore, I, Ronald Reagan, President of the United States of America, do hereby proclaim August 26, 1985, as Women's Equality Day. I call upon all Americans to mark this occasion with appropriate observances.

In Witness Whereof, I have hereunto set my hand this twenty-third day of August, in the year of our Lord nineteen hundred and eighty-five, and of the Independence of the United States of America the two hundred and tenth.

RONALD REAGAN

[Filed with the Office of the Federal Register, 11:31 a.m., August 23, 1985]

Radio Address to the Nation on Education
August 24, 1985

My fellow Americans:

As summer draws to a close our thoughts naturally turn to the coming school year. Few things could be more central to the life and health of our nation than the education of our children. Our schools hold the future of America in their hands. They will decide whether that future is enlightened, free, and informed, or shrouded in the darkness of ignorance.

From the beginning, our administration has made excellence in education a top priority, and from the beginning, we've recognized that excellence is formed in the classroom by teachers, administrators, and parents working closely together to give their children the very best education possible, not by bureaucrats in the far-off city of Washington. When it comes to education, it's the classroom, not Washington, where the real action is.

That's why, starting in the next couple of weeks, Bill Bennett, our Secretary of Education, will be traveling to eight elementary, middle, and senior high schools across the country and teaching a class in each one. Secretary Bennett will not only be honoring the teaching profession and paying tribute to the art of teaching, he should be having something of a learning experience for himself as well. Now, I remember from my own school days the tough time we used to give substitute teachers, and I warned Bill he might be getting in over his head. But he said he's had a lot of practice dealing with unruly groups like the Congress. Still, I'm going to ask all of you kids who may be in his class—as a favor to me—go easy on him.

A recent Gallup Poll found that an overwhelming majority of Americans want their schools to do two things above all else: to teach students how to speak and write correctly and, just as important, to teach them a standard of right and wrong. They want their schools to help their children develop, as Thomas Jefferson said, "both an honest heart and a knowing head." Unfortunately, parents today all too often find themselves confronted with so-called experts and a large battery of misguided opinion that says their children's education should be what they call value-neutral. Well, to me, and I bet most Americans, a value-neutral education is a contradiction in terms. The American people have always known in their bones how intimately knowledge and values are intertwined. We don't expect our children to rediscover calculus on their own, but some would give them no guidance when it comes to the even more fundamental discoveries of civilization: our ethics, morality, and values. If we give our children no guidance here, if we give them only a value-neutral education, we're robbing them of their most precious inheritance—the wisdom of generations that is contained in our moral heritage.

Our Founding Fathers weren't neutral when it came to values. "We hold these truths to be self-evident," they wrote in the Declaration of Independence, "that all men are created equal," and that they're "endowed by their Creator with certain unalienable Rights." Our forefathers found their inspiration, justification, and vision in the Judeo-Christian tradition that emphasizes the value of life and the worth of the individual. It most certainly was never their intention to bar God from our public life. And, as I have said before, the good Lord who has given our country so much should never have been expelled from our nation's classrooms.

Around the country, the educational picture is improving. Violence in schools is dropping, and test scores are up. Most important, community pride and involvement in our schools is way up. My message to parents is simply this: Your school system exists to serve you; keep getting involved. The more parents get involved with their children's schooling and education, the better it will be and the brighter the future of our country will be.

Finally, I'd like to address a few words to all you students. If you're anything like me when I was in school, you're looking forward to the beginning of the school year with mixed feelings. You've probably got those "end-of-summer blues" now, but soon you'll be wrapped up in the excitement of your classes. But you, too, can help make America's educational system second to none. If your teachers don't give you homework, ask them why not. If discipline is lax, see how you can help to make it better. It's your right to learn, your right to the opportunities that a good education can bring.

Remember, you're not only studying for yourself but for your family, your community, your country, and your God. So, go for it, kids. Give it your best effort.

Until next week, thanks for listening, and God bless you.

Note: The President spoke at 9:06 a.m. from Rancho del Cielo, his ranch near Santa Barbara, CA.

Telephone Interview With Lockwood R. Doty of Washington Broadcast News, Inc.
August 24, 1985

Mr. Doty. Good morning, Mr. President.

The President. Good morning, Dick. Haven't talked to you since our lunch at the White House.

Mr. Doty. That's right, sir. And that was a good experience and this will be, too. And I thank you very much for talking to us.

The President. I'm pleased to do it.

Tax Reform and the Federal Budget

Mr. Doty. Mr. President, you said you will launch a hard campaign to get Congress to pass your tax reform package when you and Congress return to Washington. What will you do first?

The President. Well, we're working on the schedule of appearances and so forth. I will be taking this issue to the people. I think they're the ones who have to show us exactly what they think. And according to all the evidence we have so far, the people are pretty much united that tax reform is exactly what we need. I think they have been misinformed to a certain extent by some pressure groups that want one item or the other taken out of the tax reform program. But we feel we have a good reform there, and it'll be the first one, literally, that we've ever had in the income tax.

Mr. Doty. How do you plan to persuade Congress to accept both budget cuts and tax reform, particularly now that you're getting some negative reaction, not only from Democrats but also from Republicans in both House and Senate?

The President. Well, let me point out one thing: Actually, on tax reform there is no argument about whether we should have it or not in the Congress. The approach is completely bipartisan. The only areas of disagreement have to do with some features of the program—whether it should do one thing or the other.

Now, the same thing is true of the budget. It is true that they have gotten together, and before they went home they passed a budget resolution in the Congress. It's a nonbinding resolution; it is a compromise. I still think that the budget we originally submitted was the best for dealing with the deficit problem and reducing government spending. But we now have this one, and, again, if there is disagreement, it would be over particular items—where to cut, for example, and how much. I'm going to be watching it very carefully because each one of the features has to be augmented by legislation and appropriation bills, and I'm prepared to veto at any time if they start to add in things that would increase the deficit. And I know that there are a number of spending bills that are still before the Congress.

Mr. Doty. President Harry Truman once kept Congress in session when the Members wanted to go home. Do you have any plans for keeping them in session, perhaps through Christmas and New Year's, in order to force tax reform or spending cuts?

The President. No. And, Dick, I think I'd have to tell you that if I did have any ideas of that kind, I don't think I would mention them now. But, no, we haven't considered that. We've just thought that we're going to do everything we can to aid the Congress in dealing with these and getting the plate cleared this year.

South Africa

Mr. Doty. Mr. President, here in Washington, the uproar over apartheid in South Africa is reaching something of a crescendo and there's talk of economic sanctions against South Africa. If Congress passes such sanctions, what will be your reaction: veto or no veto?

The President. Well, Dick, I've always refused to say whether I will specifically veto something before it gets to my desk because you never know just exactly what it's going to look like when it gets there. I will tell you that I am basically opposed to the idea of punitive sanctions. I think in this particular case—South Africa—they would hurt the very people we want to help. They would have an effect on the economy that would result in more unemployment, setbacks in the gains that have been made by labor and by the blacks in South Africa. And so, I can tell you I'm standing back and looking with a kind of jaundiced eye at what may come to me. But then, the final decision as to whether to veto or not will depend on exactly what does hit my desk.

Protectionism

Mr. Doty. What do you plan to do about foreign footwear imported into this country: leave it alone or cut it back?

The President. Well, that's a decision that I have to give an answer to in the next several days. I'll answer that in a broad brush stroke also. I am opposed to protectionism. Protectionism is a two-way street, and you may help some particular industry with protectionism or some group of employees, and you find that you've done it at the expense of other employees. And I recall very well in the Great Depression back in the early thirties when this country did turn to protectionism with the mistaken belief that it might help somehow in the Depression. It was then the Smoot-Hawley tariff bill, and all it did was expand the Depression more worldwide than it was and make it worse and prolong it. So, I have to tell you, basically, I don't think that protectionism is the way to go. We're trying to talk to our trading allies about a meeting to get trade more open, more fair, between all countries—open markets in all countries.

U.S.-Soviet Relations

Mr. Doty. Mr. President, when you meet with Soviet leader Gorbachev, are there proposals that you'll make to him to ease U.S.-Soviet tension?

The President. Well, I'm looking forward to the talks with him, and I hope that it won't be just a session of trying to make some agreements on particular, specific issues, but that we can get right down to discussing the problems between us and an agenda for the future so that we can eliminate the hostilities and the suspicions, if that's possible. There's no question but that the Soviet Union has made it plain that they are embarked on an expansionist program. They believe in the one-world Communist state, the world revolution. But at the same time, you have to wonder if this is not based on their fear and suspicion that the rest of us in the world mean them harm.

Now, I think that we can present evidence to show that we have no such intention and if we could discuss things from the standpoint that we're the only two nations in the world, I believe, that could start world war III. We're also the only two nations in the world that could bring about world peace, and I would think that that would be our task in history—to deal with that problem. And I'm going to do my best to present the evidence that would show and prove that this country has no intention of taking hostile action against them and also, however, that we believe we have good reason to believe—to think—that they do have hostile intent—their expansionism worldwide, their invasion of Afghanistan, and so forth. But I wish we could get that out on the table and, hopefully, reduce the suspicions between us.

Mr. Doty. Thank you, Mr. President, very,

very much. It's been——

The President. Thank you, Dick. My best to your wife.

Mr. Doty. ——a pleasure to talk to you again, sir. Thank you.

Note: *The interview was conducted at 9:16 a.m. from the Washington, DC, studios of Washington Broadcast News. The President was at Rancho del Cielo, his ranch near Santa Barbara, CA. A tape was not available for verification of the content of this interview, which was released by the Office of the Press Secretary on August 26.*

Telephone Interview With Bob Mohan of WSB Radio in Atlanta, Georgia
August 24, 1985

Mr. Mohan. Good morning, Mr. President. This is Bob Mohan with WSB Radio in Atlanta, Georgia.

The President. Yes. Good morning, Bob. Good to talk to you.

South Africa

Mr. Mohan. Thank you so very much, Mr. President, for this opportunity to talk with you this morning. Since time is at a premium, I have a three-part question regarding South Africa, sir. In view of the increased unrest in South Africa, Mr. President, do you anticipate any change in our policies in South Africa?

The President. No, not really, because I have to look at what has been accomplished so far. Our relationship with South Africa, which has always over the years been a friendly one—we have made it plain, in spite of that, that apartheid is very repugnant to us and that they should go down the path of reform and bringing about a more perfect democracy in their country. And our present relationship has, we believe, resulted in some very substantial changes: the very fact that now the blacks have ability—being in labor unions or even having their own labor unions; the fact they can buy property in the heretofore white areas; that they can own businesses in some 40 white-dominated business districts. They have eliminated the segregation that we once had in our own country—the type of thing where hotels and restaurants and places of entertainment and so forth were segregated—that has all been eliminated. They recognize now interracial marriages and all.

But we believe that for us to take an action now such as some are suggesting, turning our backs and walking away, would leave us with no persuasive power whatsoever. We think that if we continue we can help the present administration there, which is a reformist administration as evidenced by the things that I have just mentioned.

Mr. Mohan. Mr. President, what is your reaction to Reverend Jerry Falwell's statement that Bishop Tutu is a phony who does not represent the interests of South African blacks?

The President. Well, I was very pleased to see his clarifying statement—yesterday, I believe it was—and what he had to say about that and his apology to Bishop Tutu. It seems from what I could read that his original statements were based on more, not his judgment, but on quotations from those people that he had met with in South Africa—both blacks and whites. You know, we must recognize that the black majority in South Africa is a combination of minorities. There are at least 10 tribal divisions there. And so, he heard that some considered Bishop Tutu a leader; others rejected him as a leader. And this is what he was trying to say. But I was very pleased when he went public and said that his use of the word "phony" was really an unfortunate choice of words, and he certainly had never meant in any way to describe the character or the beliefs or philosophy of Bishop Tutu. He was trying—he used mistakenly, the word to describe the thing that he had found—that he was not recognized as a black leader of all the blacks.

Mr. Mohan. Mr. President, do you fear a pro-Communist government may take power in South Africa if the present government fails? This is a fear that many people who call my talk show express. How do you feel about that?

The President. I have to say that for us to believe the Soviet Union is not, in its usual style, stirring up the pot and waiting in the wings for whatever advantage they can take—we'd be very innocent, naive, if we didn't believe that they're there——

Mr. Mohan. Yes.

The President. ——ready to do that.

Tax Reform

Mr. Mohan. Okay. The next question I have regards tax reform, Mr. President. Several members of the Georgia congressional delegation are saying that tax reform will be the first order of business when Congress reconvenes. After all the gnashing of teeth, debate, and compromise, can the American people expect any reform in the tax system this year?

The President. I have to be optimistic and believe they can, because we're going to push very hard for it. You see, if we don't do it this year, then we've got to wait a whole other year, another year before this can be implemented. I think there are such advantages to the program, the tax reform program that we've presented: the simplification, the fairness, the advantage to the family. I was greatly encouraged when a committee of the House, dominated by the opposing party, came forth the other day with a statement that this tax plan as we've presented it offers the most advantages to the American family of any of the tax proposals that have been made. So, we're going to try very hard. I know that with the Congress it isn't so much an outright opposition as it is their concern that they've got too much on the plate to get to this in time.

Mr. Mohan. Mr. President, I have one more question I've been allowed. You have been very kind to allow me to ask you some

questions. Since my listening audience comprises about 36 States, I would like to afford you an opportunity to ask them something that they can discuss with me during my show on Monday night. Is there something you would like to ask them?

The President. Oh, my. [*Laughter*] I wish I'd have had some warning about that. I could probably think of several things.

Mr. Mohan. You'll probably think of a thousand things afterwards. I know that's sort of slipping it in the back door. I didn't check with Sue Mathis on that, but I thought perhaps you would have something that you might like to ask them because they'll be talking to me on Monday night.

The President. Well, there are a couple of things where I think there's a possibility of great misinformation: one we've just been talking about—the tax reform. I know that the people have been told where we're eliminating a number of so-called tax deductions and so forth in return for the much lower rates; that if the people have any questions as to exactly how this would come out for them regarding what the fairness would be—would their taxes be increased or reduced? They, in fact, will be reduced. The only people who have to fear this are those people who've been avoiding their fair share of taxation by taking advantage of certain tax shelters and loopholes and so forth—but if they would ask, so that they would know and understand.

Mr. Mohan. Thank you very much for this opportunity.

The President. All right.

Mr. Mohan. Thank you.

The President. Thank you.

Note: The interview was conducted at 9:24 a.m. from the Atlanta studios of WSB Radio. The President was at Rancho del Cielo, his ranch near Santa Barbara, CA. In the final question, Mr. Mohan referred to Susan K. Mathis, Deputy Director of Media Relations. A tape was not available for verification of the content of this interview, which was released by the Office of the Press Secretary on August 26.

Telephone Interview With Tomas Regalado of WRHC Radio in Miami, Florida
August 24, 1985

Mr. Regalado. Good morning, Mr. President.

The President. Good morning, Tomas. It's great to hear your voice again.

The President's Health

Mr. Regalado. Sir, first of all, how do you feel?

The President. I feel just fine. I really do. As a matter of fact, as soon as you and I are finished here, I'm going over and saddle up a horse and take a ride.

Mr. Regalado. Well, Mr. President, we're very glad.

U.S.-Cuba Relations

Mr. Regalado. Sir, 2 years ago in the White House, I asked you about the Kennedy-Khrushchev agreement, and you said that as far as you're concerned, that agreement has been abrogated many times by the Russians and Cuba. My question, sir, is are you prepared to denounce that agreement publicly and officially?

The President. Now, are we talking about the agreement of—did I understand—of the Kennedy-Khrushchev agreement after the missile crisis in Cuba?

Mr. Regalado. Yes, sir.

The President. Ah. Well, actually, that was an agreement, an informal agreement; it had no legal standing. And it is true that the Soviet Union have observed the most important part, which was not replacing the nuclear missiles in Cuba or having any there. They have observed that. Almost from the beginning, however, there are other facets of that kind of informal agreement that have been violated: the use of Castro's forces throughout the world, such as in Angola and all; his interference in Central America and Latin America in attempts to get overthrows of legitimate, democratic governments and all. So, I don't see where there's any need to take action with regard to that particular agreement, but simply to deal with each issue as it comes up and what they are doing and what they're not doing. And what they're

doing with regard to stirring up revolution in Central America is wrong for all the Americas, and I think all of us should oppose it.

Mr. Regalado. Mr. President, as you have said, Castro has been waging war on the U.S. for 26 years, exporting terrorism and suppression in this hemisphere and now trafficking with drugs. Isn't it self-defense to take measures to counter those attacks by Castro?

The President. Yes. And I think we are in dealing with it where he is attacking, such as right now in Nicaragua. We did it before that in El Salvador. When we first came into this administration, the whole question was whether Salvador was going to go Communist. Well, now we have a democracy there. There have been several elections, supervised elections in which we know that they were free of any corruption. Democracy is on the march in other areas, and right now the sore spot is Nicaragua. And we're going to continue our help and support of the freedom fighters.

Mr. Regalado. Mr. President, by the way, speaking to the OAS in 1982, you said that freedom cannot survive if our neighbors lived in misery and oppression. Can you tell us if the Cubans can expect some kind of help from the United States to seek freedom for Cuba?

The President. We have—on more than one occasion—we have heard some proposals from the present Cuban Government about wanting a better relationship and wanting to discuss with us how that could come about. We've responded, and then we've found that, really, they had no concrete proposal. They were offering nothing. I do not believe that armed overthrow is the answer, but I believe that we should continue some of the restraints and restrictions that we have with regard to our relations with Cuba but, at the same time, make it evident that any time that they want to prove by deed, not just word, that they are willing and want to come back to the community of American nations, as they once were, we'd be very happy to help and to help open the door for that. But at the present time, they are openly a satellite of the Soviet Union and taking their orders from the Soviet Union, and we see no opening for us to be of help.

Democracy in Latin America

Mr. Regalado. Mr. President, do you think that when you finish your second term, among your legacy to history will be a Central America and a Caribbean free of communism entirely?

The President. I don't know whether we can accomplish that "entirely"—to qualify that word—but I think that the progress that is being made in Latin America with regard to democracy is far more outstanding than many of us have realized over these past couple of years. Right now about 50 percent of the people in Latin America live in democracies or in countries that are rapidly moving toward democracy. That has never been true before, and we're going to continue helping in every way we can to keep that trend going. But I think great progress has been made.

Soviet Policies in Latin America

Mr. Regalado. Mr. President, one final question. Would you be discussing the situation on the activities of Cuba and Nicaragua with Mr. Gorbachev in Vienna?

The President. I would think that that subject could very well come up, because, as I view these talks with Mr. Gorbachev and our effort to try and lessen the hostility and see if we can't eliminate some of the suspicion that exists between the two countries there, I think very much that we would point out to him the contrast between our own conduct and what he is doing with regard to the Americas—or what his country is doing with regard to the Americas—by way of Cuba principally, and get that out on the table as one of the facets of the relationship that we think stands in the way of any better relationship with the Soviet Union.

Mr. Regalado. Thank you very much, Mr. President.

The President. Well, thank you. Been a pleasure.

Note: The interview was conducted at 9:31 a.m. from the Miami studios of WRHC Radio. The President was at Rancho del Cielo, his ranch near Santa Barbara, CA. A tape was not available for verification of the content of this interview, which was released by the Office of the Press Secretary on August 26.

Statement on the 1984 Census Bureau Report on the Poverty Rate
August 27, 1985

The Census Bureau has just released news for which every American can be thankful. Some 1.8 million Americans escaped from poverty last year, the largest single drop since 1968. Four hundred thousand black Americans moved up and out of poverty, as did more than half a million children. The poverty rate among the elderly in the United States is lower than it has ever been in American history. I believe these numbers are further proof that the greatest enemy of poverty is the free enterprise system.

The success of 1984 does not mean that the battle against poverty in this country is over; it does mean that America—after a difficult decade—is once again headed in the right direction.

Statement on the Denial of Import Relief for the Nonrubber Footwear Industry
August 28, 1985

Today we increasingly find ourselves confronted with demands for protectionist measures against foreign competition, but protectionism is both ineffective and extremely expensive. In fact, protectionism often does more harm than good to those it is designed to help. It is a crippling cure, far more dangerous than any economic illness. Thus, I am notifying the Congress today of my decision not to impose quotas on nonrubber footwear imports.

As President, it is my responsibility to take into account not only the effect of quotas on the shoe industry but also their broader impact on the overall economy. After an extensive review, I have determined that placing quotas on shoe imports would be detrimental to the national economic interest. While we support the principle of free trade, we must continue to insist of our trading partners that free trade also be fair trade. In that regard, I have instructed our Trade Representative to take action to initiate investigations under section 301 of the Trade Act of 1974, as amended, to root out any unfair trade practices that may be harming U.S. interests.

With respect to the footwear industry, the Council of Economic Advisers estimates that quotas on nonrubber shoe imports would cost the American consumer almost $3 billion. Low-income consumers would be particularly hard hit as shoe prices rose and less expensive imports were kept off the market. Instead of spending billions of consumers' dollars to create temporary jobs, I am directing the Secretary of Labor, through the Job Training Partnership Act, to develop a plan to retrain unemployed workers in the shoe industry for real and lasting employment in other areas of the economy.

There is also no reason to believe that quotas would help the industry become more competitive. Between 1977 and 1981, U.S. footwear manufacturers received protection from foreign imports, but emerged from that period even more vulnerable to international competition than before. In fact, while unprotected by quotas, the shoe industry has begun to show positive signs of adjustment. Producers have invested in state-of-the-art manufacturing equipment, modernizing their operations, and diversifying into profitable retail operations.

While bringing no lasting benefit to the shoe industry, quotas or other protectionist measures would do serious injury to the overall economy. The quotas proposed by the International Trade Commission could cost over $2 billion in compensatory claims under GATT and could invite retaliation from our trading partners. The result would be an immediate and significant loss of American jobs and a dangerous step down the road to a trade war, a war we fought in 1930 with the infamous Smoot-Hawley tariffs and lost. Our economy is truly interwoven with those of our trading partners. If we cut the threads that hold us together, we injure ourselves as well. If our trading partners cannot sell shoes in the United States, many will not then be able to buy U.S. exports. That would mean more American jobs lost. Thus, we find that the true price of protectionism is very high indeed. In order to save a few temporary jobs, we will be throwing many other Americans out of work, costing consumers billions of dollars, further weakening the shoe industry, and seriously damaging relations with our trading partners.

The United States can set an example to other countries. We must live according to our principles and continue to promote our prosperity and the prosperity of our trading partners by ensuring that the world trading system remains open, free, and, above all, fair.

Note: Clayton Yeutter, United States Trade Representative, read the President's statement at 2 p.m. to reporters in the Briefing Room at the White House.

Memorandum Announcing the Denial of Import Relief for the Nonrubber Footwear Industry
August 28, 1985

Memorandum for the United States Trade Representative

Subject: Nonrubber Footwear Import Relief Determination

Pursuant to Section 202(b)(1) of the Trade Act of 1974 (P.L. 93–618; 19 U.S.C. 2252(b)(1)), I have determined the action I will take with respect to the report of the United States International Trade Commission (ITC), transmitted to me on July 1, 1985, concerning imports of nonrubber footwear. This investigation covered items 700.05 through 700.45, inclusive, 700.56, 700.72 through 700.83 inclusive, and 700.95 of the Tariff Schedules of the United States.

While the escape clause provisions of the Trade Act of 1974 require the ITC to determine the question of whether a domestic industry has been seriously injured as a result of increased imports, I am charged with the responsibility of determining whether the provision of import relief to the domestic industry is in the national economic interest. After considering all relevant aspects of the case, including those set forth in Section 202(c) of the Trade Act of 1974, I have determined that granting import relief would not be in the national economic interest. I believe my decision today will promote our national economic interest by encouraging an open, nondiscriminatory and fair world economic system, a system in which jobs are created and prosperity grows through increased productivity and competitiveness in an open market. My decision is based on the following reasons:

First, import relief would place a costly and unjustifiable burden on U.S. consumers and the U.S. economy. The Council of Economic Advisers estimates that the global quota remedy recommended by the ITC would create between 13,000 to 22,000 jobs with an average annual wage of $14,000. However, the cost to consumers to create these jobs would be $26,300 per job, amounting to a total cost which could be as high as $2.9 billion over the next five years. Moreover, these jobs would not provide permanent employment and would be likely only to last during the 5-year relief period.

Second, import relief would result in serious damage to U.S. trade in two ways. If the ITC global remedy were imposed U.S. trade would stand to suffer as much as $2.1 billion in trade damage either through compensatory tariff reductions or retaliatory actions by foreign suppliers. This would mean a loss of U.S. jobs and a reduction in U.S. exports. U.S. trade would also suffer because of the adverse impact import relief would have on major foreign suppliers, such as Brazil, who are heavily indebted and highly dependent on footwear exports. Import relief would lessen the ability of these foreign footwear suppliers to import goods from the United States and thus cause an additional decline in U.S. exports.

Third, I do not believe that providing relief in this case would promote industry adjustment to increased import competition. While imports of nonrubber footwear have increased rapidly over the last 12 months, I believe that the industry has been and is in the process of successfully adjusting to increased import competition. An industry that was once characterized by many small firms with limited manufacturing capability, has now emerged as an industry led by larger, more efficient producers who have invested in state of the art manufacturing equipment, diversified into profitable retail operations, and filled out their product lines with imports to respond to rapidly changing consumer taste.

In order to address the difficult problems faced by workers in the industry, I have directed the Secretary of Labor to work with State and local officials to develop a retraining and relocation assistance program specifically designed to aid workers in the nonrubber footwear industry. Appropriate programs of the Job Training Partnership Act are to be used to the fullest extent possible under U.S. law.

This determination shall be published in the *Federal Register*.

RONALD REAGAN

[Filed with the Office of the Federal Register, 3:08 p.m., August 28, 1985]

Message to the Congress Reporting on the Denial of Import Relief for the Nonrubber Footwear Industry
August 28, 1985

To the Congress of the United States:

In accordance with Section 203(b)(2) of the Trade Act of 1974 (19 U.S.C. 2253(b)(2)), I am writing to inform you of my decision today to direct the Secretary of Labor to develop a plan to utilize the Job Training and Partnership Act of 1982 to aid dislocated workers in the nonrubber footwear industry. At the request of the Senate Finance Committee, the United States International Trade Commission (ITC) instituted an investigation to determine whether increasing imports of nonrubber footwear were injuring the domestic nonrubber footwear industry. The ITC found that nonrubber footwear imports are a substantial cause of serious injury, or threat thereof, to the domestic footwear industry.

While the escape clause provisions of the Trade Act of 1974 require the ITC to determine the question of whether a domestic industry has been seriously injured as a result of increased imports, I am charged with the responsibility of determining whether the provision of import relief to the domestic industry is in the national economic interest. After considering all relevant aspects of the case, including those set forth in Section 202(c) of the Trade Act of 1974, I have determined that granting import relief would not be in the national economic interest. I believe my decision today will promote our national economic interest by encouraging an open, nondiscriminatory and fair world economic system, a system in which jobs are created and prosperity grows through increased productivity and competitiveness in an open market. As my determination does not provide import relief to the industry, I am setting forth the reasons for my decision.

First, import relief would place a costly and unjustifiable burden on U.S. consumers and the U.S. economy. The Council of Economic Advisers estimates that the global quota remedy recommended by the ITC would create between 13,000 to 22,000 jobs with an average annual wage of $14,000. However, the cost to consumers to create these jobs would be $26,300 per job, amounting to a total consumer cost which could be as high as $2.9 billion over the next five years. Moreover, these jobs would not provide permanent employment and would be likely only to last during the 5-year relief period.

Second, import relief would result in serious damage to U.S. trade in two ways. If the ITC global remedy were imposed, U.S. trade would stand to suffer as much as $2.1 billion in trade damage either through compensatory tariff reductions or retaliatory actions by foreign suppliers. This would mean a loss of U.S. jobs and a reduction in U.S. exports. U.S. trade would also suffer because of the adverse impact import relief would have on major foreign suppliers, such as Brazil, who are heavily indebted and highly dependent on footwear exports. Import relief would lessen the ability of these foreign footwear suppliers to import goods from the United States and thus cause an additional decline in U.S. exports.

Third, I do not believe that providing relief in this case would promote industry adjustment to increased import competition. While imports of nonrubber footwear have increased rapidly over the last 12 months, I believe that the industry has been and is in the process of successfully adjusting to increased import competition. An industry that was once characterized by many small firms with limited manufacturing capability, has now emerged as an industry led by larger, more efficient producers who have invested in state of the art manufacturing equipment, diversified into profitable retail operations, and filled out their product lines with imports to respond to rapidly changing consumer taste.

In order to address the difficult problems faced by workers in the industry, I have directed the Secretary of Labor to work with State and local officials to develop a retraining and relocation assistance program specifically designed to aid workers in the nonrubber footwear industry. Appropriate programs of the Job Training Partnership Act are to be used to the fullest extent possible under U.S. law.

RONALD REAGAN

The White House,
August 28, 1985.

Message to the Congress Transmitting an Alternative Plan for Federal Civilian Pay Increases
August 29, 1985

To the Congress of the United States:

Under the Federal Pay Comparability Act of 1970, the President is required to make a decision each year on what, if any, pay adjustment should be provided for Federal employees under the General Schedule and the related statutory pay systems.

My pay advisors have reported to me that an increase in pay rates averaging 19.15 percent, to be effective in October 1985, would be required under existing procedures to raise Federal pay rates to comparability with private sector pay rates for the same levels of work. However, the law also empowers me to prepare and transmit to the Congress an alternative plan for the pay adjustment if I consider such an alternative plan appropriate because of "national emergency or economic conditions affecting the general welfare."

Accordingly, after reviewing the reports of my Pay Agent and the Advisory Committee on Federal Pay, and after considering the adverse effect that a 19.15 percent increase in Federal pay rates might have on our continuing national economic recovery, I have determined that economic conditions affecting the general welfare require the following alternative plan for this pay adjustment:

In accordance with section 5305(c)(1) of title 5, United States Code, the pay rates of the General Schedule and the related statutory pay schedules as adjusted by Section 1 of Executive Order No. 12496 of December 28, 1984, shall remain in effect without change.

Accompanying this report and made a part hereof are the pay schedules that will remain in effect under this alternative plan, including, as required by section 5382(c) of title 5, United States Code, the rates of basic pay for the Senior Executive Service.

RONALD REAGAN

The White House,
August 29, 1985.

Letter to President José Napoleón Duarte of El Salvador on the Investigation of the Murder of United States Citizens in San Salvador
August 29, 1985

Dear Mr. President:

I was gratified to hear from you of the important accomplishments of your government's ongoing investigation of the murder of thirteen persons, including American and Salvadoran citizens, in a brutal raid in San Salvador on June 19, 1985. I congratulate you on the speed and professionalism of the arrest of William Celio Rivas Bolanos, Juan Miguel Garcia Melendez, and Jose Abraham Dimas Aguilar. On behalf of the victims' families and the United States, I personally thank all involved.

Terrorism is the antithesis of democracy. By brutal acts against innocent persons, terrorists seek to exaggerate their strength and undermine confidence in responsible government, publicize their cause, intimidate the populace, and pressure national leaders to accede to demands conceived in violence. Where democracy seeks to consult the common man on the governance of his nation, terrorism makes war on the common man, repudiating in bloody terms the concept of government by the people.

I am proud that the Special Investigative Unit, which we in the U.S. worked with you to develop, is playing an active role in the investigation. I shortly will be consulting with Congress to find new ways to assist Central American nations in their laudable efforts to overcome the scourge of terrorism. I hope that, with the support of the Congress, we can help police and military units to respond consistently with the maturity, professionalism, and respect for the law shown by your police in this case. We must not compromise with criminals. Appeasement only invites renewed attack. Terrorists merit only swift, certain justice under the rule of law.

The people of El Salvador and the people of the United States stand together against terrorism. Each defeat for the terrorist makes the world safer and more just for everyone.

Sincerely,

/S/RONALD REAGAN

Note: The original was not available for verification of the content of this letter.

Nomination of F. Keith Adkinson To Be a Member of the Advisory Committee for Trade Negotiations
August 29, 1985

The President today announced his intention to nominate F. Keith Adkinson to be a member of the Advisory Committee for Trade Negotiations for a term of 2 years. This is a reappointment.

Since July 1982, Mr. Adkinson has been an attorney in the law offices of F. Keith Adkinson. Previously he was with the law firm of Seyfarth, Shaw, Fairweather & Geraldson in 1979–1982. From 1974 to 1979, he served as counsel, U.S. Senate Permanent Subcommittee on Investigations, in Washington, DC. Mr. Adkinson was an associate attorney with the law firm of Wyman, Bautzer, Rothman and Kuchel in Los Angeles and Washington, DC, from 1969 to 1974.

He graduated from the University of Virginia (B.A., 1966) and the University of Virginia Law School (J.D., 1969). He resides in Wheaton, MD, and has one child. He was born May 26, 1944, in Brooklyn, NY.

Nomination of Michael A. McManus, Jr., To Be a Member of the Board of Directors of the Communications Satellite Corporation
August 29, 1985

The President today announced his intention to nominate Michael A. McManus, Jr., to be a member of the Board of Directors of the Communications Satellite Corporation until the date of the annual meeting of the Corporation in 1987. He replaces Robert M. Garrick, whose term has expired.

Since March 1985, Mr. McManus has been executive vice president of MacAndrews & Forbes Group, Inc., in New York, NY. Previously he served as Assistant to the President and Deputy to the Chief of Staff at the White House in 1982–1985. From 1977 to 1982, he was corporate counsel and general counsel at Pfizer, Inc. He served as an assistant to Secretary Elliot Richardson at the U.S. Department of Commerce in 1975–1977. Mr. McManus was an attorney with Cadwalader, Wickersham and Taft from 1970 to 1974. He served in the United States Army in 1968–1970.

He graduated from the University of Notre Dame (B.A., 1964) and Georgetown University Law Center (J.D., 1967). He is single and was born March 11, 1943, in Boston, MA.

Nomination of Francis J. Ivancie To Be a Commissioner of the Federal Maritime Commission
August 29, 1985

The President today announced his intention to nominate Francis J. Ivancie to be a Commissioner of the Federal Maritime Commission for the remainder of the term expiring June 30, 1987. He replaces Robert Setrakian, who has resigned.

Since November 1984 Mr. Ivancie has been president of Ivancie and Associates in Portland, OR. Previously he served as the mayor of Portland, OR, from 1980 to 1984. Mr. Ivancie has held various public offices in Portland, serving as a member of the Portland City Council for four consecutive terms beginning in 1966 when he was also elected commissioner of public affairs. In 1957–1966 he served as executive assistant to Portland Mayor Terry Schrunk. Previously he was a teacher and school administrator for 8 years. Mr. Ivancie served in the United States Air Force in 1942–1943.

Mr. Ivancie graduated from the University of Minnesota (B.A., 1948) and the University of Oregon (M.A., 1955). He is married, has 10 children, and resides in Portland, OR. He was born June 19, 1924, in Marble, MN.

Nomination of Charles L. Hosler To Be a Member of the National Science Board
August 29, 1985

The President today announced his intention to nominate Charles L. Hosler to be a member of the National Science Board, National Science Foundation, for the remainder of the term expiring May 10, 1988. He replaces John H. Moore.

Since 1965 Dr. Hosler has served as dean of the College of Earth and Mineral Sciences at Pennsylvania State University. Previously he served as head of the department of meteorology in 1961–1965. Since 1960 he has been professor of meteorology at the university. Prior to that he was associate professor. He started his career at Pennsylvania State University as a graduate assistant in meteorology in 1947–1948. He served in the U.S. Navy in 1943–1946.

He graduated from Pennsylvania State University (B.S., 1947; M.S., 1948; Ph.D., 1951). He is married and has four children. He was born June 3, 1924, and resides in State College, PA.

Selection of Two Members of the Board of Directors of the National Railway Passenger Corporation
August 29, 1985

The President today announced his intention to select the following individuals to be members of the Board of Directors, National Railway Passenger Corporation (Amtrak):

Samuel H. Hellenbrand, to serve for a term of 2 years. This is a reappointment. Mr. Hellenbrand is currently director of Security Capitol Corp. Previously he was vice president of real estate operations of International Telephone and Telegraph Corp., a position he held from 1971. From 1968 to 1971, he was vice president for real estate and industrial development for the Penn Central Corp. From 1942 to 1968,

Mr. Hellenbrand was with the New York Central Railroad Co. He graduated from Brooklyn Law School of St. Lawrence University (1941) and was admitted to the New York Bar in 1942. He was born November 11, 1916, in New York, NY.

Frank W. Jenkins, to serve for a term of 2 years. This is a reappointment. Mr. Jenkins is an attorney in Pennsylvania who is active in Republican politics. He graduated from the University of Pennsylvania (B.A., 1947) and the University of Pennsylvania Law School (L.L.B., 1949). He is married and has four children. Mr. Jenkins was born May 8, 1926, in Philadelphia, PA.

Appointment of Five Members of the National Advisory Council on Adult Education
August 29, 1985

The President today announced his intention to appoint the following individuals to be members of the National Advisory Council on Adult Education:

Thelma P. Duggin, to serve for a term expiring July 10, 1988. She succeeds Nancy H. Hill. Ms. Duggin is currently director of government relations, Comprehensive Benefits Services Co. Previously she was coordinator of minority affairs at the Department of Transportation. Ms. Duggin graduated from Edgewood College in Madison, WI (B.A., 1971). She was born December 23, 1949, in Mobile, AL.

Nicholas M. Nikitas, to serve for a term expiring July 10, 1988. He succeeds Mary Elizabeth Strother. Mr. Nikitas is president of Nikitas Family Inns Property Development, Management and Operations. He graduated from Dartmouth College (B.A., 1972) and currently

resides in Boston, MA. He was born February 26, 1950, in Fitchburg, MA.

Donald F. Shea, to serve for a term expiring July 10, 1988. He succeeds Kathleen McCullough. Mr. Shea is a Catholic priest in residence at St. Anthony's parish in Falls Church, VA. He graduated from DePauw University (B.A., 1947), University of Michigan (M.A., 1947), and Loyola University (Ph.D., 1956). He was born September 24, 1925, in Maywood, IL.

Abraham Shemtov, to serve for a term expiring July 10, 1988. This is a reappointment. Rabbi Shemtov is national director, Friends of Lubavitch. He did his undergraduate and graduate work at Lubavitcher Rabbinical College, Brooklyn, NY, and was ordained in 1960. He is married and has six children. Rabbi Shemtov was born February 16, 1937, in Wilno, Poland.

Henry Yee, to serve for the remainder of the

term expiring July 10, 1986. He succeeds Ronna Romney. Mr. Yee is a certified public accountant. He graduated from California State University in Los Angeles (B.S., 1958). He is married and has six children. Mr. Yee was born August 3, 1927, in Los Angeles, CA.

Executive Order 12530—Establishment of Nicaraguan Humanitarian Assistance Office
August 29, 1985

By the authority vested in me as President by the Constitution and laws of the United States of America, including section 722 of the International Security and Development Cooperation Act of 1985 (Public Law 99–83) (the Act), Chapter V of the Supplemental Appropriations Act, 1985 (Public Law 99–88) (the Supplemental Act), the Foreign Assistance Act of 1961, as amended (22 U.S.C. 2151 *et seq.*) (the FAA), including but not limited to sections 621, 632, and 633 thereof (22 U.S.C. 2381, 2392, 2393), and section 301 of title 3 of the United States Code, it is hereby ordered as follows:

Section 1. Establishment. (a) There is hereby established the Nicaraguan Humanitarian Assistance Office (the Office).

(b) The Office shall, unless otherwise extended, terminate on April 1, 1986, or one week following completion of disbursement of the funds made available under section 722(g) of the Act by Chapter V of the Supplemental Act, whichever date is later.

Sec. 2. Functions. The Office shall, in accordance with the FAA, section 722(g) of the Act, Chapter V of the Supplemental Act, and the provisions of this Order, administer the program of humanitarian assistance to the Nicaraguan democratic resistance authorized thereunder. The Office may, to the extent permitted by law and the provisions of this Order, enter into such grant agreements and contracts and take such other actions as may be necessary to implement the program effectively.

Sec. 3. Policy guidance. In accordance with the FAA, and to the end that such programs and activities are effectively integrated with and supportive of the foreign policy of the United States, the Secretary of State shall be responsible for the continuous supervision and general direction of the programs and activities carried out by the Office.

Sec. 4. Administration. (a) At the head of the Office there shall be a Director, who shall be an officer of the United States designated by the President. The Director shall exercise immediate supervision and direction over the Office.

(b) The Director may, to the extent permitted by law, including but not limited to section 621 of the FAA (22 U.S.C. 2381), employ such staff from Federal agencies as may be necessary, except that the staff shall be limited to twelve supervisory personnel, plus appropriate support personnel. No personnel from the Department of Defense or the Central Intelligence Agency may be detailed or otherwise assigned to the Office.

(c) The Secretary of State shall provide the Office with such administrative services, facilities, and other support as may be necessary for the performance of its functions. Funds made available under section 722(g) of the Act by Chapter V of the Supplemental Act shall be provided to the Office through the Department of State.

(d) At the request of the Director, and to the extent otherwise permitted by law, the agencies of the Executive Branch shall provide such information, advice, additional administrative services, and facilities as may be necessary for the fulfillment of the Office's functions under this Order.

Sec. 5. Classification Authority. In accordance with section 1.2(a)(2) of Executive Order No. 12356 of April 2, 1982, the Director is hereby designated as an agency official with authority to classify information originally as Top Secret. The Director shall ensure that the Office establishes and maintains controls for the safeguarding of classified information as provided in part 4 of that Order.

Sec. 6. Delegation of Functions. Subject to the provisions of this Order and Executive Order No. 12163 of September 29, 1979, as amended, and to the extent necessary to the efficient and effective implementation of this Order, there are hereby delegated to the Director the functions conferred upon the President (and not reserved to him) by sections 632(a) and 635(b) of the FAA and other provisions of that Act (including but not limited to those set forth in Part III of the FAA) that relate directly and necessarily to the conduct of the programs and activities vested in or delegated to the Director.

Sec. 7. Procurement. (a) In accordance with the provisions of section 633 of the FAA (22 U.S.C. 2393), it is hereby determined to be in furtherance of the purposes of the FAA that the functions authorized thereunder, as set forth in section 2 of this Order, may be performed by the Director without regard to the provisions of law and limitations of authority specified in Executive Order No. 11223 of May 12, 1965, as amended.

(b) It is directed that each specific use of the waivers of statutes and limitations of authority authorized by this section shall be made only when determined in writing by the Director that such use is necessary to the efficient and effective implementation and in furtherance of the purposes of this Order and in the interest of the United States.

Sec. 8. Reports. The Director shall assist the President in preparing the reports required by section 722(j)(2) of the Act, including a detailed accounting of the disbursements made to provide humanitarian assistance with the funds provided pursuant to section 722(g) of the Act. The Director shall keep the President informed about the implementation of the program.

RONALD REAGAN

The White House,
August 29, 1985.

[*Filed with the Office of the Federal Register, 2:25 p.m., September 3, 1985*]

Note: The Executive order was released by the Office of the Press Secretary on August 30.

Statement on the Establishment of the Nicaraguan Humanitarian Assistance Office
August 30, 1985

I have signed an Executive order which establishes the Nicaraguan Humanitarian Assistance Office. This Office will administer the distribution of humanitarian assistance to the Nicaraguan democratic resistance as provided for in the International Security and Development Cooperation Act of 1985 and the Supplemental Appropriations Act, Fiscal Year 1985.

The democratic resistance in Nicaragua was born and has grown in response to the steady consolidation of a totalitarian and interventionist Marxist-Leninist regime in Nicaragua since 1979. Most of the members of the armed and unarmed opposition supported the overthrow of General Anastasio Somoza and expected that a democratic, pluralist government would follow. Very quickly, however, it became clear that the Sandinistas intended to make Nicaragua a one-party state. There would be no room for those who opposed the Sandinistas or who sought through democratic elections to challenge the Sandinistas' right to absolute rule. There would be collaboration with Cuba and the Soviet bloc in assisting revolutionary groups seeking to subvert and overthrow the democratic governments of neighboring countries.

The good will that had existed between the Sandinista front and the Nicaraguan people who had welcomed the new government soon began to crumble. Prominent leaders who served in the government after the revolution and who had led the opposition to Somoza fled the country and broke publicly with the Sandinista regime. By 1982 significant numbers of Nicaraguans were compelled to pursue the last resort for civil resistance of bearing arms against the government because there was no other choice. Their numbers have grown steadily. In recent months, with the resistance forces desperately short of weapons, ammunition, food, and supplies, volunteers kept coming. The resistance could not even provide boots, but people from all walks of life left their homes to join the cause. Tens of thousands of Nicaraguans have gone to refugee camps in Costa Rica and Honduras rather than continue to live under the Sandinistas. Many of these people are poor, simple peasants—the very people the Sandinistas claim to be helping—yet under the Sandinistas they lost too much. They lost their individuality, they lost their freedom, they lost the opportunity to control their own destiny.

The $27 million appropriated by the Congress for humanitarian assistance to the democratic resistance recognizes the serious nature of the conflict in Nicaragua and the desperate conditions which have forced people to choose armed opposition and the hard life of warfare and refugee camps over the controlled life offered by the Sandinistas. As Americans who believe in freedom, we cannot turn our backs on people who desire nothing more than the freedom we take for granted. By providing this humanitarian assistance, we are telling the people of Nicaragua that we will not abandon them in their struggle for freedom.

This administration is determined to pursue political, not military solutions in Central America. Our policy is and has been to support the democratic center against extremes of right and left and to secure democracy and lasting peace through internal reconciliation and regional negotiations. In El Salvador, the opening of the political system has led to impressive reconciliation and the beginning of a dialog between President Duarte and the Salvadoran guerrillas. In Nicaragua we support the united Nicaraguan opposition's call for a church-mediated dialog, accompanied by a cease-fire, to achieve national reconciliation and representative government.

We oppose the sharing of power through military force, as the guerrillas in El Salvador have demanded; the Nicaraguan democratic opposition shares our view. They have not demanded the overthrow of the Sandinista government; they want only the right of free people to compete for power in free elections. By providing this humanitarian assistance, we help keep that hope for freedom alive.

As with any foreign assistance program, the mandate of the Nicaraguan Humanitarian Assistance Office will be carried out under the policy guidance of the Secretary of State. Program funds will be provided through the State Department, which will also be responsible for providing administrative services and facilities. Other agencies of the United States Government will be able to provide advice, information, and personnel; however, by the terms of this Executive order, no personnel from the Central Intelligence Agency or the Department of Defense will be assigned or detailed to this Office. I have ordered that the Director of the Nicaraguan Humanitarian Assistance Office shall be an officer of the United States designated by the President, and the staff of the Office shall be limited to 12 officials, plus support staff. The Director will be responsible for assisting the President with reporting requirements, including the detailed accounting required by the law. Authority for this Office will terminate on April 1, 1986, or when all the funds to be distributed are disbursed, whichever is later.

I am proud to establish the Nicaraguan Humanitarian Assistance Office by this Executive order and to begin providing the humanitarian assistance needed to help those people who are fighting for democracy in Nicaragua. I value the support that Congress has shown for this important measure and will ensure that the implementation of the program is fully in accord with the legislation the Congress has enacted.

Nomination of Roger Kirk To Be United States Ambassador to Romania
August 30, 1985

The White House today announced the President's intention to nominate Roger Kirk, of the District of Columbia, a career member of the Senior Foreign Service, Class of Career Minister, as Ambassador to the Socialist Republic of Romania. He would succeed David B. Funderburk.

Mr. Kirk served as a general services assistant in Moscow from 1949 to 1951. He was appointed a Foreign Service officer in 1955 and was assigned to the Department's Executive Secretariat until 1957. He then went to Rome as political officer until 1959. He returned to the Department in 1959 to serve as staff assistant to the Counselor of the Department, followed by special assistant to the Secretary of State from 1960 to 1961. From 1961 to 1962, he was public affairs adviser in the Office of Soviet Union Affairs, Bureau of European Affairs. He then studied the Russian language in Oberammergau, Germany (Soviet area and language school), from 1962 to 1963. From there he served as consular officer in Moscow (1963–1964), to be followed as political officer in Moscow (1964–1965), New Delhi (1965–1967), and then Saigon (1967–1969). From 1969 to 1971, he was assistant to the Deputy Assistant Secretary on Vietnam in the Department. He then attended the senior seminar until 1972 when he was sent on detail to the U.S. Arms Control and Disarmament Agency as Deputy Assistant Director for International Relations. He was appointed Ambassador to the Somali Democratic Republic in 1973, where he served until 1975 when he became Deputy Director of the Bureau of Intelligence and Research in the Department. In 1978 he was appointed the U.S. Permanent Representative to the United Nations system organizations in Vienna, Austria, with the rank of Ambassador. He served there until 1983 when he was asked to serve as Senior Deputy Assistant Secretary in the Bureau of International Organization Affairs.

Mr. Kirk was born November 2, 1930, in Newport, RI. He received his B.A. in 1952 from Princeton University, where he graduated magna cum laude. In 1953 he attended the Johns Hopkins School of Advanced International Studies. He served in the United States Air Force from 1952 to 1955. Mr. Kirk is fluent in Russian, Italian, and French. He is married to the former Madeleine Yaw, and they have four children.

Nomination of Malcolm Richard Wilkey To Be United States Ambassador to Uruguay
August 30, 1985

The President today announced his intention to nominate Malcolm Richard Wilkey, of Texas, as Ambassador to the Oriental Republic of Uruguay. He would succeed Thomas Aranda, Jr.

Mr. Wilkey began his career in 1948 as an associate with Butler, Binion, Rice & Cook in Houston, TX, where he was employed until 1954. He then entered government service as special assistant to the attorney general in Houston in 1953. In 1954 he became United States Attorney for the Southern District of Texas, and in 1958 he was named Assistant Attorney General in the Office of the Legal Counsel in Washington, DC. In 1959 he became Assistant Attorney General in the Criminal Division until 1961. In 1959 he also served as a U.S. delegate to the United Nations Conference on Judicial Remedies in Buenos Aires, Argentina. From 1961 to 1963, he was a partner with Butler, Binion, Rice & Cook, and from 1963 to 1970, he was general counsel, associate general counsel, and secretary with Kennecott Copper Corp. in New York. From 1969 to 1973, Mr. Wilkey was a member of the Advisory Panel on International Law for the Legal Adviser in the Department of State. From 1970 until he retired in 1985, he was U.S. Circuit Judge for the District of Columbia Circuit. From 1975 to 1979, he served on the Judicial Conference of the U.S. Committee on Rules for Admission to Practice in the Federal Courts. Since early 1985 Mr. Wilkey has been a visiting fellow at Wolfson College in Cambridge, England.

Mr. Wilkey was born December 6, 1918, in Murfreesboro, TN. He received his A.B. in 1940 from Harvard College and his J.D. in 1948 from Harvard Law School. He served in the United States Army from 1941 to 1945 and in the U.S. Army Active Reserve from 1948 to 1954. His foreign language is Spanish. Mr. Wilkey is married to the former Emma Secul.

Executive Order 12531—Establishing an Emergency Board To Investigate a Dispute Between the United Transportation Union and Certain Railroads Represented by the National Carriers' Conference Committee of the National Railway Labor Conference
August 30, 1985

A dispute exists between the United Transportation Union and certain railroads represented by the National Carriers' Conference Committee of the National Railway Labor Conference designated on the list attached hereto and made a part hereof.

The dispute has not heretofore been adjusted under the provisions of the Railway Labor Act, as amended ("the Act").

This dispute, in the judgment of the National Mediation Board, threatens substantially to interrupt interstate commerce to a degree such as to deprive a section of the country of essential transportation service.

Now, Therefore, by the authority vested in me by Section 10 of the Act, as amended (45 U.S.C. § 160), it is hereby ordered as follows:

Section 1. Establishment of Board. There is hereby established, effective August 30, 1985, a board of three members to be appointed by the President to investigate this dispute. No member shall be pecuniarily or otherwise interested in any organization of railroad employees or any carrier. The board shall perform its functions subject to the availability of funds.

Sec. 2. Report. The board shall report its finding to the President with respect to the dispute within 30 days from the date of its creation.

Sec. 3. Maintaining Conditions. As provided by Section 10 of the Act, as amended, from the date of the creation of the board and for 30 days after the board has made its report to the President, no change, except by agreement of the parties, shall be made by the carriers or the employees in the conditions out of which the dispute arose.

Sec. 4. Expiration. The board shall terminate upon the submission of the report provided for in Section 2 of this Order.

RONALD REAGAN

The White House,
August 30, 1985.

[*Filed with the Office of the Federal Register, 2:26 p.m., September 3, 1985*]

Note: The attachment listing the designated railroads was printed in the Federal Register *of September 5.*

Announcement of the Establishment of Emergency Board No. 208 To Investigate a Railroad Labor Dispute
August 30, 1985

The President announced today that he has established, effective August 30, 1985, Presidential Emergency Board No. 208 to investigate and make recommendations for settlement of a current dispute between the United Transportation Union and most of the Nation's major railroads represented by the National Railway Labor Conference. The President, by Executive order, established the Emergency Board on the recommendation of the National Mediation Board. The situation appears to the President to be extremely critical.

The impact of a nationwide railroad strike would have an immediate effect on the public. The Nation's railroads move more than one-third of all intercity freight traffic, or more than 100 million tons each month. A strike against the railroads could result in the layoff of hundreds of thousands of employees, who would be idled. Cessation of operations on the freight railroads would halt the flow of $750 million worth of goods each day.

A nationwide railroad strike would have a materially adverse effect on basic industries served by the railroads. The coal industry, for example, relies heavily on rail transport. In 1984 the railroad industry hauled close to 60 percent of total U.S. coal production. Cessation of rail service would force shut-

downs of some mines almost immediately. The automobile industry relies on rail service for transportation of some essential materials for parts production and for distribution of a large share of the finished products. The disruption of supply channels during a rail strike would result in the layoff of thousands of employees. Railroads are one of the primary transporters of Department of Defense freight traffic. A strike would severely limit the Department of Defense's ability to move this freight. Finally, although the National Railroad Passenger Corporation (Amtrak) is not a party to this dispute, its passenger service may be curtailed because it contracts with other railroads for train and engine crews. The railroads also operate trains carrying 150,000 commuters each day, more than three-quarters of them in and around Chicago, IL.

Consequently, the President has invoked the Emergency Board procedures of the Railway Labor Act, which in part provide that the Board will report its findings and recommendations for settlement to the President within 30 days from the date of its creation. The parties must then consider the recommendations of the Emergency Board and endeavor to resolve their differences without engaging in self-help during a subsequent 30-day period.

Proclamation 5365—To Implement Reductions in U.S. Rates of Duty Pursuant to the United States-Israel Free Trade Area Agreement, and for Other Purposes
August 30, 1985

By the President of the United States of America

A Proclamation

1. Section 4 of the United States-Israel Free Trade Area Implementation Act of 1985 (the FTA Act) (19 U.S.C. 2112 note)

confers authority upon the President to proclaim changes in tariff treatment which the President determines are required or appropriate to carry out the schedule of duty reductions for products of Israel set forth in Annex 1 to the Agreement on the Establishment of a Free Trade Area between the

Government of the United States of America and the Government of Israel (the Agreement), entered into on April 22, 1985, and submitted to the Congress on April 29, 1985. I have determined that the modifications to the Tariff Schedules of the United States (TSUS) (19 U.S.C. 1202) set forth in Annexes I, VIII, IX, and X to this Proclamation are required or appropriate to carry out such duty reductions.

2. Previously, pursuant to Title V of the Trade Act of 1974, as amended, (the Trade Act) (19 U.S.C. 2461, *et seq.*), I designated certain articles provided for in the TSUS as eligible articles under the Generalized System of Preferences (GSP) when imported from designated beneficiary developing countries, and determined that limitations on the preferential treatment for eligible articles from certain beneficiary developing countries were necessary or appropriate. Previously, pursuant to section 503(a)(2)(A) of the Trade Agreements Act of 1979 (the Trade Agreements Act) (19 U.S.C. 2119 note), I determined that certain articles provided for in the TSUS are not import sensitive and, if the product of a least developed developing country (LDDC), are eligible for full tariff reductions pursuant to certain trade agreements without staging. Previously, pursuant to sections 211 and 218 of the Caribbean Basin Economic Recovery Act (the CBERA) (19 U.S.C. 2701, 2706), I designated certain articles provided for in the TSUS as eligible articles under the CBERA when imported from designated beneficiary countries.

3. In order to provide, for purposes of the GSP, for the continued designation of eligible articles and beneficiary developing countries (including least developed beneficiary developing countries, pursuant to section 504(c)(6) of the Trade Act (19 U.S.C. 2464(c)(6)), and associations of countries to be treated as individual countries for purposes of limitations on preferential treatment), and for the continuation of existing limitations on preferential treatment for articles from certain beneficiary developing countries, and in accordance with Title V of the Trade Act, as amended, it is appropriate that such preferential treatment and designations be set forth in this Proclamation.

4. Section 604 of the Trade Act (19 U.S.C.

2483) confers authority upon the President to embody in the TSUS the substance of the relevant provisions of that Act, of other Acts affecting import treatment, and of actions taken thereunder. In addition, section 8(b)(2) of the FTA Act (which amends Title V of the Trade Act) confers authority upon the President to embody in the TSUS, by proclamation, actions taken with respect to the GSP. In order to implement the duty reductions authorized by the FTA Act and to facilitate the administration of the preferential tariff regimes described above, it is necessary or appropriate to incorporate the duty treatment provided pursuant to the relevant provisions of the GSP, the Trade Agreements Act, the CBERA, and the FTA Act, in a rate of duty column in the TSUS entitled "Special", and to make other necessary and conforming changes as set forth in Annexes I through XI to this Proclamation.

5. In Proclamation 5291 of December 28, 1984, I determined that modifications in the TSUS were appropriate in order to provide duty-free coverage comparable to the expanded coverage provided by other signatories to the Agreement on Trade in Civil Aircraft (31 UST (pt. 1) 619). Through technical error, the staged reductions in rates of duty for certain tariff items redesignated by the Proclamation were omitted. Accordingly, I have determined that due to the implementation of Proclamation 5291 that further modifications to Annex III to Proclamation 4707 of December 11, 1979, set forth in Annex XII to this Proclamation, are appropriate in order to ensure the application of such reductions in customs duties for articles classified in those tariff items.

6. In order to make technical corrections in the preferential treatment under the GSP for articles that are imported from countries designated as beneficiary developing countries consistent with the changes to the TSUS which have resulted from the implementation of Proclamation 5291 of December 28, 1984, and Proclamation 5305 of February 21, 1985, I have determined that the technical corrections to Executive Order No. 11888 of November 24, 1975, as amended, and general headnote 3 set forth in sections A and B, respectively, of Annex XIII to this Proclamation, are appropriate.

7. In Proclamation 5133 of November 30, 1983, as amended by Proclamation 5142 of December 29, 1983, and Proclamation 5308 of March 14, 1985, I designated certain countries and territories as "beneficiary countries" under section 212 of the CBERA. Section 213(c)(2)(A) of the CBERA provides that duty-free treatment under the CBERA for sugar and beef products that are the product of a beneficiary country shall be suspended if such beneficiary country, within the ninety-day period beginning on the date of its designation as a beneficiary country, does not submit a stable food production plan to the President. I have not received stable food production plans from five beneficiary countries (Antigua and Barbuda, Montserrat, Netherlands Antilles, St. Lucia, and St. Vincent and the Grenadines) within the required ninety-day period. As provided by section 213(c)(3) of the CBERA, I have entered into consultations with these five beneficiary countries. These countries do not export sugar or beef products to the United States and, therefore, have determined not to submit stable food production plans at this time. Should they wish to export either sugar or beef products in the future, they may submit a stable food production plan for review by the United States Government at that time. In accordance with section 213(c)(2)(A) of the CBERA, I am suspending duty-free treatment extended under the CBERA to sugar and beef products that are the product of these five beneficiary countries. I will terminate the suspension of duty-free treatment under the CBERA imposed by this Proclamation with regard to any affected beneficiary countries which take appropriate action to remedy the factors on which the suspension was based.

8. In Proclamation 5021 of February 14, 1983, as amended by Proclamation 5291 of December 28, 1984, I proclaimed temporary duty reductions on certain articles pursuant to legislation implementing the Nairobi Protocol to the Florence Agreement on the Importation of Educational, Scientific, and Cultural Materials. And, pursuant to section 604 of the Trade Act, I modified the Appendix to the TSUS by inserting a new part 4 to such Appendix providing temporary duty reductions for such articles which were entered, or withdrawn from warehouse for consumption, on and after February 11, 1983, and before the close of August 11, 1985, as set forth in the Annex to Proclamation 5021. The effective period for the temporary reduction of such duties having expired on August 11, 1985, I am modifying the Appendix to the TSUS, pursuant to section 604 of the Trade Act, by deleting part 4 thereof.

Now, Therefore, I, Ronald Reagan, President of the United States of America, acting under the authority vested in me by the Constitution and the statutes of the United States, including but not limited to sections 4 and 8(b)(2) of the FTA Act, section 213(c) of the CBERA, and section 604 of the Trade Act, do proclaim that:

(1) The rate of duty column in the TSUS entitled "LDDC" is retitled "Special" each place it appears, including part 1B of the Appendix to the TSUS.

(2) Part 1 of the Appendix to the TSUS is further modified by inserting a rate of duty column entitled "Special", following the rate of duty column numbered 1, opposite each item for which a rate of duty column entitled "LDDC" is not set forth.

(3) The column in the TSUS entitled "GSP" is deleted.

(4) The modifications to the TSUS made by Annex I to this Proclamation, including the designations of eligible articles and beneficiary developing countries and the limitations on preferential treatment necessary to continue existing GSP treatment incorporated therein, and the suspension of duty-free treatment extended under the CBERA to sugar and beef products of certain beneficiary countries, shall be effective with respect to articles entered, or withdrawn from warehouse for consumption, on and after the effective date of this Proclamation.

(5) Products of Israel provided for in TSUS items which are enumerated in Annex VIII to this Proclamation and which are imported into the customs territory of the United States in accordance with general headnote 3 of the TSUS (as modified by Annex I to this Proclamation) on or after the effective date of this Proclamation are eligible for duty-free treatment, and a rate of duty of "Free" applicable to such prod-

ucts is inserted in the column in the TSUS entitled "Special" followed by the symbol "I" in parentheses.

(6) Products of Israel provided for in TSUS items which are enumerated in Annex IX to this Proclamation and which are imported into the customs territory of the United States in accordance with general headnote 3 (as modified by Annex I) on or after the effective date of this Proclamation are subject to duty as described in such Annex IX, and the rate of duty applicable to such products is inserted in the column in the TSUS entitled "Special" followed by the symbol "I" in parentheses.

(7) Products of Israel provided for in TSUS items which are enumerated in Annex X to this Proclamation and which are imported into the customs territory of the United States in accordance with general headnote 3 (as modified by Annex I) on or after January 1, 1995, are eligible for duty-free treatment, and a rate of duty of "Free" applicable to such products shall be inserted on such date in the column in the TSUS entitled "Special" followed by the symbol "I" in parentheses. Until January 1, 1995, products of Israel provided for in the TSUS items enumerated in Annex X are subject to the rate of duty in column numbered 1 of the TSUS unless the tariff treatment of such products is expressly modified in accordance with section 5(c)(2) of the FTA Act.

(8) In order to provide duty-free treatment to articles hereby designated as eligible articles for purposes of the GSP when imported from any designated beneficiary developing country, for each of the TSUS items enumerated in Annex III to this Proclamation, a rate of duty of "Free" is inserted in the column in the TSUS entitled "Special" followed by the symbol "A" in parentheses for each such item.

(9) In order to provide duty-free treatment to articles hereby designated as eligible articles for purposes of the GSP, except when imported from the designated beneficiary countries set forth opposite those TSUS items enumerated in general headnote 3 (as modified by Annex I to this Proclamation), for each of the TSUS items enumerated in Annex IV to this Proclamation, a rate of duty of "Free" is inserted in the column in the TSUS entitled "Special" followed by the symbol "A*" in parentheses for each such item.

(10) For each of the TSUS items which are enumerated in section A of Annex V to this Proclamation, the rates of duty set forth for each item in such section A of Annex V is inserted in the column in the TSUS entitled "Special" followed by the symbol "D" in parentheses.

(11) For each of the TSUS items which are enumerated in sections B and C of Annex V to this Proclamation, effective as of the dates provided in such sections B and C, the rates of duty set forth for each item in such sections B and C of Annex V shall be inserted in the column in the TSUS entitled "Special" followed by the symbol "D" in parentheses.

(12) For each of the TSUS items which are enumerated in Annex VI to this Proclamation, a rate of duty of "Free" is inserted in the column in the TSUS entitled "Special" followed by the symbol "E" in parentheses.

(13) For each of the TSUS items which are enumerated in Annex VII to this Proclamation, a rate of duty of "Free" is inserted in the column in the TSUS entitled "Special" followed by the symbol "E*" in parentheses.

(14) For each of the TSUS items which are enumerated in Annex XI to this Proclamation, the rate status set forth for each item in such Annex XI is inserted in the column in the TSUS entitled "Special".

(15) Annex III to Proclamation 4707 of December 11, 1979, is amended as set forth in Annex XII to this Proclamation effective as to articles entered, or withdrawn from warehouse for consumption, on and after the effective date specified in Annex XII to this Proclamation.

(16) Annexes II and III of Executive Order No. 11888, as amended, and general headnote 3 are further amended as set forth in sections A and B, respectively, of Annex XIII to this Proclamation effective with respect to articles both: (1) imported on or after January 1, 1976, and (2) entered, or withdrawn from warehouse for consumption, on and after the effective dates specified in sections A and B of Annex XIII to

this Proclamation.

(17) Annex III of Proclamation 4707 and Annex III of Proclamation 4768 of June 28, 1980, are amended as set forth in Annex II to this Proclamation as of the effective date of this Proclamation.

(18) Except for articles provided for in items which are enumerated in Annex IV to Proclamation 4707 and Annex IV to Proclamation 4768 and which are not enumerated in Annex V to this Proclamation, Annex IV to Proclamation 4707 and Annex IV to Proclamation 4768 are superseded by Annex V to this Proclamation, to the extent inconsistent therewith, as of the effective date of this Proclamation.

(19) Executive Order No. 11888, as amended by subsequent Executive orders for purposes of the GSP, and as amended by subsequent proclamation to the extent they amend Executive Order No. 11888 for purposes of the GSP, is superseded by this Proclamation as of the effective date of this Proclamation.

(20) Proclamations 4707, 4768, 5133, 5142, 5291, 5305, and 5308, are superseded to the extent inconsistent with this Proclamation.

(21) Part 4 of the Appendix to the TSUS is deleted effective August 12, 1985.

(22) Except as provided in paragraphs (11), (15), (16), and (21), the provisions of this Proclamation shall be effective as to articles entered, or withdrawn from warehouse for consumption, on and after September 1, 1985.

In Witness Whereof, I have hereunto set my hand this thirtieth day of August, in the year of our Lord nineteen hundred and eighty-five, and of the Independence of the United States of America the two hundred and tenth.

RONALD REAGAN

[*Filed with the Office of the Federal Register, 2:22 p.m., September 3, 1985*]

Note: The annexes were printed in the Federal Register of September 5.

Radio Address to the Nation on Free and Fair Trade
August 31, 1985

My fellow Americans:

Last Wednesday I notified Congress of my decision not to impose either quotas or tariffs on foreign shoe imports into this country. I'd like to talk with you about that decision because the case of shoe imports illustrates why so-called protectionism is almost always self-destructive, doing more harm than good even to those it's supposed to be helping.

Advocates of protectionism often ignore its huge hidden costs that far outweigh any temporary benefits. The Council of Economic Advisers estimates that the quotas on shoe imports that I turned down would have cost the American consumer nearly $3 billion, and there are other costs. Quotas would have entitled our trading partners to another $2 billion in compensation, or they would have retaliated, slapping quotas or tariffs on the products we sell to them. That

would mean an immediate loss of American jobs and a dangerous step down the road to a trade war. Also, if our trading partners can't sell their products here, they can't afford to buy our exports and that means more lost jobs for Americans.

Protectionism almost always ends up making the protected industry weaker and less able to compete against foreign imports. Between 1977 and 1981, U.S. footwear manufacturers received protection from foreign imports, but at the end of that time they were more vulnerable to foreign competition than before. Instead of protectionism, we should call it destructionism. It destroys jobs, weakens our industries, harms exports, costs billions of dollars to consumers, and damages our overall economy.

Of course, free trade also means fair trade. We will move vigorously against unfair trading practices, using every legal recourse available to give American manufacturers a fair shake at home and open markets abroad. The balance of trade has become a very emotional issue; some claim our trade deficit has cost us millions of jobs. Congress is awash in bills calling for trade sanctions and retaliation. But look at the facts: In 1980 we had a trade surplus, and about 99 million Americans had jobs. Today we have a trade deficit, and almost 107 million Americans are working. Despite a growing trade deficit, we've gained over 7½ million new jobs since 1980. Our free, open, and growing economy has put more Americans to work in 1985 than ever before in our history. We've created more jobs in the last 3 years than Europe and Japan combined.

The surest way to destroy those jobs and throw Americans out of work is to start a trade war. And one of the first victims of a protectionist trade war will be America's farmers, who have it tough enough already. A news story the other day said protectionist fervor on the Hill is stronger than it has been since the 1930's. Well now, some of us remember the 1930's, when the most destructive trade bill in history, the Smoot-Hawley tariff act, helped plunge this nation and the world into a decade of depression and despair. From now on, if the ghost of Smoot-Hawley rears its ugly head in Congress, if Congress crafts a depression-making bill, I'll fight it. And whether it's tax, trade, or farm legislation that comes across my desk, my primary consideration will be whether it is in the long-run economic interest of the United States. And any tax hike or spending bill or protectionist legislation that doesn't meet the test of whether it advances America's prosperity must and will be opposed.

America is getting stronger, not weaker. Our 23-percent tax rate cuts have given us 2½ years of economic expansion, a dramatic increase in after-tax personal income, and the most dramatic drop in poverty in 10 years. We must not retreat into the failed policies of the past, whether they be protectionism or higher taxes. Let's go forward by cutting income tax rates again and building opportunity. On Monday we'll be recognizing America's working men and women. We've created over 7 million jobs in the last 4½ years. On this Labor Day, let's challenge ourselves to create 10 million more in the next four. To do that, we're going to have to be courageous, hopeful, hard working, and proud, which pretty well sums up what it means to be an American. There is one quality I left out: faith in the loving God who will continue to guide us on the optimistic course we've set.

Enjoy your Labor Day holiday. Until next week then, thanks for listening, and God bless you.

Note: The President spoke at 9:06 a.m. from Rancho del Cielo, his ranch near Santa Barbara, CA.

Statement on the Fifth Anniversary of the Solidarity Movement in Poland
August 31, 1985

In the history of Eastern Europe since World War II, there have been few events whose anniversaries can be celebrated with any sense of pride or satisfaction. The lot of these countries has been one of repression, of sacrifice, of waiting for a better day that never comes. Five years ago, however, in a unique, spontaneous, and overwhelming expression of the public will, the working people of Poland exacted from their government the right to form their own free trade unions. The myth of the "worker state," as Communist governments so misleadingly characterize themselves, was thereby shattered for all time.

During the ensuing 15 months, some 10 million Polish citizens banded together under the banner of the Solidarity movement, to be joined by 4 million farmers who created their own union along similar lines.

Their goals were no different from those of the working class throughout the world—decent working conditions, a fair wage, an economic system that works, and a genuine voice in shaping the society of which they form the foundation. They pursued those goals then, as they do today, not with force, for they had no weapons other than indomitable courage, steadfast will, and a readiness to accept high risks in pursuit of their cause. Not one drop of blood was shed when Polish workers gained their victory, and Solidarity has consistently eschewed violence in any form ever since.

These brave aspirations were brought to a temporary standstill in December 1981, when, pressured by Moscow, Gen. Wojciech Jaruzelski used the Polish Armed Forces to impose martial law on his own people, to arrest most of Solidarity's leaders and many of the rank and file, to force others into hiding, and to withdraw from the union its legal right to exist. Since that day, the alienation of the Polish Government from the people it professes to represent has become all too evident.

But Solidarity has not died, nor have the principles for which it came into existence become any less urgent in the minds of the Polish people. Despite all oppressive measures, provocations, imprisonment, police brutality, and even killings, this, the only free trade union in the entire Communist world, has continued its struggle by peaceful means to persuade its government to provide all elements of the society a role in shaping Poland's destiny. Although Solidarity's voice has been muted by being forced underground, its message—whether via underground radio, clandestine publications, public demonstrations, or by simple word of mouth—continues to be heard clearly throughout Poland and throughout the world, wherever there are people who value freedom.

We here in the United States have also heard Solidarity's message and respond to it with all our hearts. We call upon the Polish Government to do likewise. This is not a subversive organization. It asks only that basic human rights be observed and that Poland be governed by responsible and responsive leaders. It asks those leaders to seek participation of workers, managers, and technocrats, academicians and intelligentsia, and the cohesive strength of the church in grappling with the massive economic and societal problems which must be solved if Poland is to assume its rightful place within the brotherhood of nations. Should such a reconciliation take place, the traditional hand of American friendship will be ready and unreservedly extended to Poland, just as it has been throughout the last 200 years. Meanwhile, we shall continue to support the legitimate hopes of our Polish brothers and sisters who are defending our common values.

Message on the Observance of Labor Day, 1985
September 1, 1985

On this Labor Day, I proudly join my fellow citizens in saluting our Nation's working men and women.

As we celebrate the historic role of our nation's free labor movement, we are reminded that workers have contributed as much to America's social greatness as they have to our economic strength. Their dedication to humanitarian goals, conscientious craftsmanship and technical excellence have improved virtually every aspect of our lives—from jobs and working conditions to education, national defense, housing, medical care and transportation. Because of the quality of the goods and services they produce, we enjoy one of the highest standards of living in the world.

Labor Day, 1985, finds the American wage earner better off than in many years, with inflation down, a vibrant economy creating many opportunities, and employment running at record levels. But we must not slacken in our efforts to resolve the continuing problems facing those whose skills have become obsolete and young people seeking entry level jobs. Labor and management must also work hand in hand to improve the position of American products in foreign markets. Increased exports means more jobs for American workers, more growth, more opportunity. Doing its part, this Administration is committed to keeping open foreign markets and removing obstacles to free trade.

These challenges require the best efforts of all of us because we all have a stake in the success of these efforts. By shaping a better future for our workers, we can and will assure continued progress and even greater opportunity for all Americans.

RONALD REAGAN

Remarks at the Santa-Cali-Gon Days Celebration in Independence, Missouri
September 2, 1985

The President. Thank you very much. And before I begin my remarks, I think out of deference to those who accompany me here on the wagon, I'm going to dictate a change in the wardrobe of the day.

[*At this point, the President removed his jacket.*]

Well, Governor Ashcroft and Mayor Potts, the distinguished guests here on the platform, and all of you ladies and gentlemen, thank you very much. It's wonderful to be in Independence, and I'm especially pleased to be here for the 13th annual Santa-Cali-Gon Days celebration. I was born in the Midwest, oh, sometime back—[*laughter*]—well, not that long ago. There's no truth to the rumor that I waved goodbye to the Donner party when they headed west. [*Laughter*] But the trails that we remember today were still being used up until around the turn of the century. And when I was born, stories of the pioneers and what they went through were still close to our experience. The spirit that won the West is still, in my opinion, very much with us in this country, and that's good. We have great challenges ahead of us, and we're going to need it.

Now, this is the first time that I've really been out on the stump since I was in the hospital, and I missed doing this. I missed it. I even miss hecklers. [*Laughter*] I'm very happy to be in Truman country on this Labor Day. I want to talk about—[*applause*]. I have to digress for a moment because there was a wonderful sign down here that just told me to give 'em hell. [*Laughter*] And I'm very proud, and I learned directly from President Truman that he had not said that. Someone had said it to him, and his reply was, "I'll tell them the truth, and they'll think it's hell." [*Laughter*]

Well, I want to talk about tax reform, and I wanted to be here with you, the men and women who work hard to support yourselves and your families with your weekly paychecks. You're always there when your neighbors need help, when the community needs help. It's the working men and women of America who pay the taxes, foot the bills, and make the sacrifices that keep this country going. And I'm here to talk to you about a long overdue change in our tax laws, a change that is aimed at benefiting you.

Now, tax reform has its enemies, especially among the people who have vested interests in the status quo. Status quo—that's a Latin name for the mess that we're in with our present tax structure. Those vested interests just hate it when we talk about reform, and they loved it when they thought I was laid up and out of action. Well, I'm back and rarin' to go, up for the battle that's only just begun. In fact, when I think of all the good people who've pleaded with the Federal Government for years to clean up our tax structure, I'm reminded of a recent, very popular movie. And in the spirit of Rambo, let me tell you, we're going to win this time.

I've been thinking about ways to sum up exactly how disgusted I am by our current tax structure, and I read a little story Harry Truman once told when he rejected a bit of bad policy. He vetoed a bill, and in doing so he said: "I intended to veto it all along. In fact, I feel like the blacksmith on the Missouri jury. The judge asked him if he was prejudiced against the defendant, and he said, 'Oh, no, judge. We ought to give the bum a fair trial before we string him up.'" [*Laughter*] Well, let me tell you why we ought to take our current tax system out and string it up. It's been tried and found unfair, unworkable, and unproductive. It is a system that yields great amounts of revenues, but even greater amounts of discontent, disorder, and disobedience. It's a system that yields a lot of things that we have to have—of course, that money—but a lot of things we don't need at all.

Our current tax system is antifamily: It gives a measly little deduction of just over a thousand dollars for each dependent. Our current system is an assault on personal improvement and effort: It taxes you at such rapidly increasing rates when you work overtime that the harder you work, the smaller the share of your income that you take home. Our current tax law is anti-growth: It discourages enterprise, and it discourages productive investment. Our current tax law is unfair: It clobbers people who don't have a team of legal advisers and accountants to look after their interests. It's supposed to be progressive—meaning the highest earners are supposed to pay a greater percentage of their earnings than, say, the typical mid-class family. But does it work out that way?

Audience. No!

The President. Recently the Treasury Department completed a study on the taxes paid by those in the top brackets. It wasn't a very pretty sight. True, nearly half paid the heavy tax, but a sizable number took advantage of the so-called loopholes and tax shelters. In the year 1983 there were 260,000 persons who had incomes from all sources of a quarter of a million dollars a year or more; almost 30,000 of them paid virtually nothing at all. There were 28,000 people who made a million dollars or more

in 1983; more than 900 of them didn't pay a dime in taxes, and 3,000 of them paid less than 5 percent of their million-dollar-plus incomes.

Treasury added it all up, and they found that 17,000 taxpayers whose income was anywhere from a quarter of a million dollars a year to millions of dollars a year paid taxes of less than $6,272 apiece. Now, the reason I used that figure, it just happens that $6,272 is just about the tax that is paid by a family of four with two workers in the family and an income of $45,000 a year. Now, undoubtedly some of these high-income people had legitimate losses from bad investments, or maybe there were cases of lawsuits and legal decisions that went against them. But for a great many, it was simply the opportunities provided in the present tax law, with all its complexities, its shelters to hide in, loopholes to get lost in—the legal scams that are worked by people who don't want to pay their fair share. And the middle class gets stuck paying most of the bills.

Now, we all agree that the current system is bad, but we've never quite reformed it. Why? Well, one reason is a good, healthy skepticism on the part of our people. They've heard too many promises by too many politicians about how their lives are going to be made better. They have been hurt too many times by elected officials who promised better and delivered worse. Well, maybe another reason we haven't changed the tax structure is that in a democracy like ours, it's hard for us to get worked up and united over something unless it's truly dramatic, like, say, a very sensational murder. Well, our present tax code is not a sensational murder—it's more like a daily mugging, and we've begun to get used to it. But another, and maybe the biggest, reason we haven't changed the tax structure is that change has been resisted at every point and is being resisted today by vested interests, those who profit from the status quo—organizations that enjoy special tax advantages, special interests, and various professionals who are doing just fine, thank you, under the present, unfair system.

There's a whole slew of people and lobbying groups who share a kind of self-righteous self-interest. They're well represented in Washington, and they're not dumb. They never say, "We're against tax reform because we're in Fat City." Their favorite word is "but." "We're against tax reform"— well, they say, "I like it, but we can't lose State and local tax deductions." Then they say, "I like it, but I don't like the capital gains part," or whatever other part it is they don't like. Well, all I can say to the I-like-it-buts is: Our tax reform bill isn't for special interests; it's for the general interest. And I'm here to declare to the special interests something they already know and something they hope you won't find out. Our fair share tax program is a good deal for the American people and a big step toward economic power for people who've been denied power for far too long.

We have just received a report from Congress, from the House of Representatives, which is controlled, as you know, by the Democratic Party. The House Select Committee on Children, Youth, and Families has called our tax plan the most profamily of all the tax proposals before Congress. Now, this congressional committee says it is fair to low-income working families, fair to large families, single-parent families, and average-income families. Now, that sounds like a pretty fair appraisal. And it doesn't come from the people in my own party; it's coming from the majority party, the Democrats. On this issue, I'm pleased to say that apparently we're not Republicans and Democrats on this; we're Americans, and we've got something to do for America.

Under our plan, middle-class earners will be helped by an increase in the personal exemption from the present $1,040 a year to a more reasonable $2,000. Take a family of four, that means $8,000 is untaxed because of exemptions, and another $4,000 is untaxed because of the standard deduction, which we're raising to $4,000. So, in all, that family of four will find the first $12,000 of earnings won't be taxed one penny. We're going to keep the itemized deductions that speak directly to how Americans live their lives—the mortgage interest deduction on the house you live in and a deduction on charitable contributions and medical expenses. But silly or unproductive tax shelters will be eliminated in our tax reform.

Another reason for tax reform: Even as we clean up the current system, we will be lowering rates for the vast majority of Americans. Lower rates will mean more money stays with you in your hands, more money for savings, more money for investment and economic growth. For each added dollar that you earn up to $29,000 of taxable income, you get to keep 85 cents out of each dollar. Above $29,000 and up to $70,000, you keep 75 cents out of each dollar. And above $70,000, you keep 65 cents of every additional dollar. The highest percentage of tax cut goes to those who earn from $20,000 a year or less. They get a cut of 18 percent. The next biggest cut goes to those who earn from $20,000 to $50,000. They get a tax cut of 7 percent. And the lowest tax cut goes to those who make $50,000 or more. They get a cut of just less than 6 percent.

Now, we think this is quite an improvement over the present complicated 14 tax brackets. Did you know that Einstein actually said he couldn't understand the Form 1040? [*Laughter*] But still it remains, as you can see, that some of the progressive features are retained of the present. But all this means an America bursting with economic opportunity, an America rolling out new jobs the way we used to roll Model T's off the assembly line. And all of that means a better chance for our kids and a first chance for those who've been denied economic power for much too long. If our fair share tax plan didn't bear within it the promise of more justice, more equity for every American, I would never support it.

A few minutes back I mentioned Americans' skepticism about politicians. And when I did, I have a hunch you said to yourself, "Look who's talking." Well, it's true I've been in public office for more than a dozen years now, with roughly 3 years and 4 months to go, the Lord willing. And since the Constitution limits a President to only two terms, there are no more elections for me, and, therefore, no need for political considerations in any decision that I'm called on to make. So, like you, I'll be living the rest of my life with everything that we do in Washington in these next few years. And that's why I want tax reform for all of us.

Now, what can you do? Will you write your Congresswoman or Congressman? Will you write your Senators? Believe me, having been there a few years I can tell you they do read the mail—they count the mail. [*Laughter*] And you do have an effect. They need to hear from you. Tell them to go for it. And if you do, I promise you we are going to win this time.

Well, thank you, and God bless you. And may I just add quickly here: As I said, I've been thinking a lot about Harry Truman. I remember when he took a step toward tar-geting tax reductions to help the poor and those in lower income groups. And I'm proud to be talking about this good deal in the home of the father of the Fair Deal. And I just figure we're taking another step toward independence in Independence. I think Harry would be very pleased.

Thank you all very much. God bless you all. Thank you.

Note: The President spoke at 2:12 p.m. at the Jackson County Courthouse. Following his remarks, the President returned to Washington, DC.

Statement by Principal Deputy Press Secretary Speakes on Soviet General Secretary Mikhail Gorbachev's Interview With Time Magazine
September 3, 1985

We welcome General Secretary Gorbachev's statement that he is prepared to submit serious proposals at the meeting with President Reagan in November. For the United States, the President is taking a serious approach to the relationship, and he is willing to meet the Soviets halfway in an effort to solve problems. The President hopes that the meeting in Geneva will lay the groundwork to address the issues that face our two nations. Our views of the causes of present U.S.-Soviet tensions are quite different from that presented by Mr. Gorbachev, but we do not intend to enter into a debate in the media. Preparations for the meeting in Geneva are best conducted in confidential diplomatic channels.

We are pleased that Mr. Gorbachev was able to present his views to the American public. The interview is a prime example of the openness of the American system and the access the Soviets enjoy to the American media. If President Reagan had a comparable opportunity to present his views to the Soviet people through the Soviet media, this would doubtless improve our dialog and indicate Soviet willingness to accept a degree of reciprocity in an important aspect of improving our relations. Direct access for President Reagan to the Soviet people would go far in improving understanding between our people. The objective of such an exchange would not be to debate, but to make clear the views of each side.

Note: Larry M. Speakes read the statement to reporters in the Briefing Room at the White House during his daily press briefing, which began at 12:08 p.m.

Letter to the Speaker of the House and the Chairman of the Senate Foreign Relations Committee Reporting on the Cyprus Conflict
September 3, 1985

Dear Mr. Speaker: (Dear Mr. Chairman:)

In accordance with Public Law 95–384, I am submitting herewith a bimonthly report on progress toward a negotiated settlement of the Cyprus question.

Since my previous report, United Nations Secretary General Perez de Cuellar has continued his efforts, begun last fall, to obtain the two Cypriot communities' acceptance of an agreement containing the elements of a comprehensive Cyprus settlement. He endeavored to overcome the difficulties that had arisen during the January 1985 summit meeting by incorporating components of the documentation into a consolidated draft agreement. His expressed intention was to bring greater clarity to its various elements and to devise procedural arrangements for follow-up action, while preserving the substance of the documentation. The Secretary General reported to the Security Council in June, a copy of which is attached, that the Greek Cypriot side had replied affirmatively to his revised documentation and that he was awaiting the Turkish Cypriot response to his efforts. The Secretary General added that, "provided both sides manifest the necessary goodwill and co-operation, an agreement can be reached without further delay."

The Turkish Cypriots postponed replying to the Secretary General while they proceeded with a constitutional referendum on May 5, a presidential election on June 9, and parliamentary elections on June 23. The Turkish Cypriots stated that the referendum and elections would not preclude their participation in a federal Cypriot state. We have repeatedly registered with both communities our conviction that actions which might impede the Secretary General's efforts to negotiate an agreement should be avoided and have reiterated our policy of not recognizing a separate Turkish Cypriot "state."

Since my last report to you, American officials in Cyprus have met regularly with leaders of both Cypriot communities. Department of State Special Cyprus Coordinator Richard Haass visited Cyprus, Greece, and Turkey in July. He discussed the Cyprus issue with the two Cypriot parties and the Governments of Greece and Turkey and expressed our support for the Secretary General's initiative. We continue to urge flexibility by all parties and are encouraged that they continue to support a negotiated settlement under the Secretary General's good offices mandate.

Sincerely,

/S/RONALD REAGAN

Note: Identical letters were sent to Thomas P. O'Neill, Jr., Speaker of the House of Representatives, and Richard G. Lugar, chairman of the Senate Foreign Relations Committee. The original was not available for verification of the content of this letter.

Message to the Senate Transmitting the Vienna Convention for the Protection of the Ozone Layer
September 4, 1985

To the Senate of the United States:

I transmit herewith, for the advice and consent of the Senate to ratification, the Vienna Convention for the Protection of the Ozone Layer. The report of the Department of State, the final act of the conference that adopted the Convention, and an environmental assessment and finding of no significant impact are enclosed for the information of the Senate.

The Convention provides a foundation for global multilateral undertakings to protect the environment and public health from the potential adverse effects of depletion of stratospheric ozone. The Convention addresses this important environmental issue primarily by providing for international cooperation in research and exchange of information. It could also serve as a framework for the negotiation of possible protocols containing harmonized regulatory measures that might in the future be considered necessary to protect this critical global resource.

The Convention, which was negotiated and adopted under the auspices of the United Nations Environment Program (UNEP), will be an important step toward protecting and enhancing public health and the quality of the global environment. The United States played a leading role in the negotiation of the Convention. Expeditious ratification by the United States will demonstrate our continued commitment to progress on this significant environmental issue.

I recommend that the Senate give early and favorable consideration to the Convention and give its advice and consent to ratification.

RONALD REAGAN

The White House,
September 4, 1985.

Nomination of William R. Barton To Be Inspector General of the General Services Administration
September 4, 1985

The President today announced his intention to nominate William R. Barton to be Inspector General, General Services Administration. He would succeed Joseph A. Sickon.

Since 1982 Mr. Barton has been serving as Deputy Director of the United States Secret Service. He has been with the United States Secret Service since 1953 and has served as Assistant to the Director (1979–1982); special agent in charge, Los Angeles field office (1978–1979); Deputy Assistant Director, Office of Protective Research (1977–1978); Deputy Assistant Director, Office of Inspection (1976–1977); special agent in charge, Foreign Dignitary Protection Division (1972–1976); Inspector (1970–1972); special agent in charge, Milwaukee field office (1964–1970); and special agent (1953–1964).

He graduated from Michigan State University (B.A., 1953). He is married, has two children, and resides in Fairfax, VA. He was born August 18, 1925, in Detroit, MI.

Nomination of Carol G. Dawson To Be a Commissioner of the Consumer Product Safety Commission
September 4, 1985

The President today announced his intention to nominate Carol G. Dawson to be a Commissioner of the Consumer Product Safety Commission for a term of 7 years from October 27, 1985. This is a reappointment.

Since 1984 Ms. Dawson has been serving as a Commissioner of the Consumer Product Safety Commission. Previously, she was Deputy Special Assistant to the Secretary of Energy (1982–1984); Deputy Press Secretary at the Department of Energy (1981–1982); senior staff assistant on the Reagan-Bush transition team (1980–1981); a real estate sales associate with Latham Realtors (1977–1980); and a freelance writer (1972–1977).

She graduated from Dunbarton College (B.A., 1959). She has four children and resides in Oakton, VA. She was born September 8, 1937, in Indianapolis, IN.

Nomination of Edward V. Hickey, Jr., To Be a Commissioner of the Federal Maritime Commission, and Designation as Chairman
September 4, 1985

The President today announced his intention to nominate Edward V. Hickey, Jr., to be a Federal Maritime Commissioner for the remainder of the term of 5 years expiring June 30, 1986. He would succeed Alan Green, Jr. Upon his confirmation, the President intends to designate him as Chairman.

Since 1982 Mr. Hickey has been serving as Assistant to the President and Director of Special Support Services. In 1981 he was commissioned as Deputy Assistant to the President and Director of Special Support Services. Previously he served as acting counselor for administration at the U.S. Embassy in London. Mr. Hickey served as senior regional security officer for the U.S. Embassies in the United Kingdom, Ireland, and Iceland in 1978–1980; Assistant Director of the Office of Security at the Department of State in 1975–1978; executive director of the California State Police in 1969–1975; and a special agent of the U.S. Secret Service in 1964–1969.

Mr. Hickey graduated from Boston College (B.S., 1960). He served in the United States Army in 1954–1956. He is married to the former Barbara Burke, and they have seven sons. He was born July 15, 1935, in Dedham, MA, and now resides in Falls Church, VA.

Appointment of the Membership of Emergency Board No. 208 To Investigate a Railroad Labor Dispute, and Designation of the Chairman
September 4, 1985

The President has appointed the following individuals to be members of Presidential Emergency Board No. 208, created by Executive Order 12531 of August 30, 1985:

Harold M. Weston, of New York, to serve as Chairman. He is an independent arbitrator and attorney in New York City. Previously he was an attorney with the firm of Cabble, Meddinger, Forsyth and Decker in New York City. He was born June 4, 1912, in New York City and now resides in Hastings-on-Hudson, NY.

Richard R. Kasher, of Pennsylvania, is an attorney and arbitrator in Bryn Mawr. Previously he was director of labor relations for the Consolidated Rail Corp. in Philadelphia. He was born May 30, 1939, in New York City and now resides in Bryn Mawr, PA.

Robert E. Peterson, of New York, is an independent arbitrator in Briarcliff Manor. Previously he was chief personnel officer for the Long Island Rail Road. He was born December 5, 1929, in Bronxville, NY, and now resides in Briarcliff Manor, NY.

Remarks to the Students and Faculty at North Carolina State University in Raleigh
September 5, 1985

The President. Thank you, Governor Martin. Thank you, Lieutenant Governor Jordan, Senator Helms, Congressmen Cobey, Broyhill, McMillan, and Coble, and Chancellor Poulton, all the members of the administration and the faculty, and you, the students, and my fraternity brothers. I think the first thing I'm going to do is pull rank. And I believe that I can dictate the uniform of the day, and out of sympathy for all these distinguished guests here on the platform, I'm changing the uniform of the day.

[*At this point, the President removed his jacket.*]

Well, it is great to be here with all of you at North Carolina State. Matter of fact, nothing could be finer than to be in Carolina in the morning. Last time that I was in North Carolina was about a year ago in the middle of the campaign. And may I tell you that my warmest and happiest memory of that campaign is of young people, college students like yourselves, who came to our campaign rallies. It wasn't always this way, and your generation is something special. You are the future of America. You're urging this country on toward a vision of optimism, hope, and prosperity. And I've come here today to seek your support, because with your support we can make that vision real.

We have before the Congress a plan that would completely overhaul our nation's tax code, knocking down the barriers to achievement and making America's future as big and open and bright as our dreams. It's a good plan, a fair plan that helps families and spurs economic growth. It will mean more jobs, bigger paychecks, and smaller taxes for those who now pay too much. And it will give America a powerful boost ahead in the world competition. Somehow, I just had a sneaky idea that you've been thinking a little bit about the America that you'll meet, diploma in hand, and figure an America with a fair tax plan that lets you keep a bigger share of what

you earn is better than a legal shakedown by Big Brother.

Now, the biggest obstacle between America and the future she deserves is—and I think you've already guessed it—special interests. Everybody agrees that our proposal would be better than the current disgrace we call our tax system, but a lot of cynics in Washington are laying odds against getting our fair share tax plan. Our plan has too many enemies, they say, enemies among those with a vested interest in the status quo. Status quo—that's Latin for the mess that we call our present tax system. [*Laughter*] Well, the special interests may think they have this one locked up tight, and we may be starting this battle for tax fairness as underdogs, but you students of North Carolina State know a thing or two about starting out as underdogs and going on to victory. You began the '83 basketball season near the bottom of the polls, but you never lost heart. You gave it all you had through that final second of play when a dunk shot won you the championship. Well, what I want to do is bring a little more of that Wolfpack spirit to Washington this fall and win one for America.

Now, many of you, I'm sure, have already had your first job, which means that you've had your first experience with the incredible shrinking paycheck. [*Laughter*] You have to see it to believe it. There in one box it tells you your gross pay. And then you have all those other little boxes with the taxes taken out. [*Laughter*] The Federal tax, the withholding, the State tax, the Social Security tax. The list seems endless. And the end of all of it is the figure for your net income. You may have wondered at that point whether you were working for yourself or the Government. And that's a good question, but what we need is a good answer.

The way our tax system is structured, the harder you work and the more you earn, the less you get to keep. One of the first priorities of our tax overhaul is to make sure that more of your hard-earned dollars end up where they belong—in your wallets and not in Uncle Sam's pockets. Now, letting you keep more of what you work for, that's one thing that fairness means. And that's one reason that America needs tax fairness before this semester's seniors graduate. We need America's tax plan this year, in 1985.

Fairness also means opportunity, and opportunity means a vital and growing economy. And that's another priority of our fair share tax plan: to keep our economy humming, creating jobs and opportunity, not only for you seniors but for the juniors, sophomores, and freshmen, too. Our first 25-percent across-the-board tax rate cut has helped give us 32 straight months of growth and helped create nearly 8 million new jobs. Well, on the theory that you can't have too much of a good thing, we're going to cut tax rates again. Our goal is a decade of economic expansion and 10 million more jobs in the next 4 years. And that's 10 million very good reasons why our nation simply can't afford a tax increase that would hurt economic growth. No matter what they call it, no matter how they disguise it, no tax increase will cross my desk without my writing a great big veto on it.

The present system, with all its shelters and loopholes, is not only unfair; it is dumb economics. The economic misuse of the real estate provision of our tax code alone is mind-boggling. Many of our nation's business districts are beginning to look more like ghost towns, with huge see-through skyscrapers. They're built, but not finished—no partitions. That's why they're called see-throughs. They were constructed largely for tax reasons and never occupied. The return to the owners was in tax write-offs, not in profit on an investment. The waste is in the multibillions, and we, the American people, must pay for it with higher taxes and lower economic growth. I say it is time we pulled our money out of tax shelters and invested it in America's future.

By closing loopholes and making sure that everybody pays their fair share, we can lower the tax rates for everybody. With lower personal and corporate rates and another cut in the capital gains tax, small and

entrepreneurial businesses will take off. Americans will have an open field to test their dreams and challenge their imaginations, and the next decade will become known as the age of opportunity.

Fairness also means giving some much-needed relief to the long-suffering American family by raising the standard deduction to $4,000 and nearly doubling the personal exemption to $2,000. This means that a family of four with two wage earners will pay no tax on the first $12,000 of earnings. This summer I received a report card. The House Select Committee on Children, Youth, and Families graded all the different tax plans according to their effect on children and families. Our fair share tax plan came out at the top of the class. That's better than I did when I was in college. And what's especially important, that report card came from the Democratically controlled House of Representatives, not from my own party. I believe that this can be one of those great moments when we stop being Democrats and Republicans and for a time are just Americans.

Audience. U.S.A.! U.S.A.! U.S.A.!

The President. Thank you.

Fairness also means a fair deal for the poor. Our tax plan would immediately take the working poor or any of the blind or elderly Americans living at or below the poverty line off the Federal tax rolls with not one penny of tax to pay. The fact is, years of runaway government spending in the sixties and seventies produced an inflationary binge that threw millions of people into poverty. And that runaway government spending was for a program the Government called the War on Poverty. Well, poverty won. [*Laughter*] And then our first tax cut took effect and ignited one of the strongest economic expansions in history. Between 1983 and 1984, poverty dropped faster and farther than it had in over 10 years. Those figures proved conclusively that big government, big spending, and inflationary policies create poverty, and that tax cuts, less government, and a thriving private sector promote self-sufficiency and prosperity.

You know, I have to inject something here. One of my favorite stories about runaway bureaucracy was a fellow—this is for true—the fellow who sat there in one of our large departments, and his job was, when the papers came there, he was to look at them, whatever was sent to him, and decide where it went in the agency, initial it, and send it on. And one day a classified paper marked "secret" came there. Well, it arrived there and was handed to him. So, he figured out where it should go and wrote his initials on it and sent it on. Twenty-four hours later it came back to him with a memo attached that said, "You weren't supposed to see this. Erase your initials—[*laughter*]—and initial the erasure." [*Laughter*]

You know, the Constitution limits a President to two terms, so there are no more elections for me.

Audience. Awww!

The President. Well now, wait a minute. No, no. They're—nope—there isn't any need for me to take political considerations into account. All I have to think about when I make a decision now is what's good for America. Because I, like so many of you and in about the same number of years, we'll be out there in the world. I'll be living out there with you and with what we've been able to accomplish in these next few years in Washington. And that's why I'm going all out for this simple tax reform, and will you help me?

Audience. Yes!

The President. We can do it, but we're going to need your very strong and vocal support. The walls of Congress are pretty thick. You're going to have to speak up if you want them to hear you. Do we want a tax system that's fairer and simpler with lower tax rates for most Americans?

Audience. Yes!

The President. I can hear you, but make sure those gentlemen and ladies of the press back there can hear you, too. Do we want a decade of prosperity and 10 million new jobs before 1990?

Audience. Yes!

The President. Do we want record growth, record business starts, and an entrepreneurial renaissance of invention and productivity that'll keep America number one in world competition?

Audience. Yes!

The President. Do we want America's tax plan, a fair share tax plan for everyone?

Audience. Yes!

The President. Something tells me I came to the right place. [*Applause*]

All right. Now, the present income tax has 14 brackets. And in these recent years of high inflation, a worker would get a cost-of-living increase to keep pace with inflation. Did he or she keep pace? All too often the increased number of dollars pushed the worker into a higher bracket, leaving him or her with less purchasing power than before the pay raise. Of course, the Government got a raise, a tax increase without having to pass one. Well, we fixed that in our 1981 tax bill. Now the brackets are indexed according to the inflation rate. You don't go into a higher bracket unless you've gotten a real increase in purchasing power.

But our tax reform will reduce those 14 brackets to 3 brackets—15 percent, 25 percent, and 35 percent. An earner will keep 85 cents out of each taxable dollar up to $29,000. From there up to $70,000, you keep 75 cents out of each taxable dollar earned, and above $70,000, you keep 65 cents out of every additional dollar that you earn. Now, in my adult lifetime, I have seen and worked during top tax brackets of 94 percent. That, to be true, was in wartime. But when peace came, it was only reduced to 91. Go ahead, work harder, earn more dollars, and the Government would let you keep less than a dime out of each dollar. When our administration began in Washington, there was a 70 percent bracket; now it's 50 percent. And under our reform plan, that top bracket will be down to 35 percent.

Today we're being called to a second American revolution of hope and opportunity. Our country has never been stronger or our economy so vital. We're at the dawn of a technological revolution which will soon be shining its light into every aspect of our lives. If I have one piece of advice for you: Dare to dream big dreams. Follow your star. Maybe some of you dream of striking out on your own some day as entrepreneurs, starting your own business, or joining a new start-up venture with exciting ideas. Well, there's never been a better time.

There'll always be the naysayers, people who tell you it can't be done. Let me just tell you about one. Just recently I met a young woman with her young husband. She was fairly recently out of college. She had aspired to a career as a classic pianist, and then, shortly after graduation, developed a tendonitis that made the career that she trained for and wanted impossible. She no longer could play. There she was at home; she didn't know what to do. Some of her relatives knew that she'd had a kind of personal recipe for brownies, and while she was there they said, "Well, while you're waiting to see what you're going to do, why don't you make those brownies and sell them to the nearby grocery stores here and at least have a little spending money." So, she did. Last year her business, Nancy's Brownies, sold to gourmet restaurants, to delicatessens, to airlines, and so forth—did $2½ million in business.

I met a couple of young fellows the other day who have an electrical business. They did a million dollars business last year as partners. They got together; they figured that a company with their names put together might just have a pretty good chance. Their names are Cain and Abel.

[*Laughter*]

Well, when our administration sees some of these things, this is why we think what our biggest responsibility is wherever it's in your way—to get government out of your way. Those naysayers that I mentioned a little while ago, those gloom artists, just remind them that this is America and that there are no limits except those that we put on ourselves. We're free to follow our imaginations into a future of abundant promise. Like the final line in that movie "Back to the Future," where we're going, we don't need any roads, just an open heart and a trusting soul to map the way and those standard American qualities of hard work, determination, and faith in the loving God who has so blessed this land beyond any place else.

Thank you. God bless you all. Thank you very much.

Note: The President spoke at 11:30 a.m. at the William Neal Reynolds Coliseum. Following his remarks, the President went to the Special Editions Restaurant at the University Student Center, where he had lunch with members of the chancellor's liaison council. Following the luncheon, the President returned to Washington, DC.

Nomination of Marshall Jordan Breger To Be Chairman of the Administrative Conference of the United States
September 5, 1985

The President today announced his intention to nominate Marshall Jordan Breger to be Chairman of the Administrative Conference of the United States for the term of 5 years. He would succeed Loren A. Smith.

Since December 1983 Mr. Breger has been serving as Special Assistant to the President for Public Liaison with specific responsibility for liaison with the academic and the Jewish community. Prior to that appointment, Mr. Breger was associated with the New York Law School as an associate professor of law, from which institution he is presently on leave. In 1982–1983 he was a visiting and then a senior fellow in

legal policy at the Heritage Foundation, Washington, DC. In 1980 he was a member of the Reagan-Bush transition team. Mr. Breger has taught law at the State University of New York at Buffalo Law School and the University of Texas Law School. In 1975–1978 he served as a member of the Board of Directors of the Legal Services Corporation. In 1981 he served as visiting professor of law at the Bar-Ilan University, Ramat-Gan, Israel.

He graduated from the University of Pennsylvania (B.A., M.A., 1967; J.D., 1973) and received a B.Phil. (Oxon) degree in 1970 from Oriel College, Oxford University.

Mr. Breger is married to the former Jennifer Anne Stern, and they have one daughter. He was born August 14, 1946, in New York City.

Message on the Observance of Grandparents Day, 1985
September 6, 1985

From the earliest days of our Republic the most important institution in American life has been the family. The bonds and values nurtured in the loving atmosphere of the family sustain and uplift us as a people. Although it is not often recognized, grandparents play a critical role in family life.

Grandparents give their grandchildren gifts no one else can give. From them grandchildren learn of times long before their own and of the values that can sustain one through the changes and challenges of a long, full life. Children can see in their grandparents the continuity of family life through the generations. Grandparents give to their grandchildren the same love and counsel, enriched by long experiences they gave to their own children a generation earlier.

The grandparent-grandchild relationship brings together the wisdom of maturity and the curiosity of youth in a special loving way. Many grandparents bring their special wisdom and love to the broader community in the many volunteer efforts of which we Americans are rightly proud. Such sharing deserves great praise, because it enriches the whole of society with the same loving generosity that binds our families together.

In recognition of the important role of grandparents in our families and communities, Congress has proclaimed the first Sunday after Labor Day as National Grandparents Day. Nancy joins me in urging all Americans to take time to honor their grandparents on September 8.

RONALD REAGAN

Remarks Announcing the Latest Employment Statistics and a Question-and-Answer Session With Reporters
September 6, 1985

The President. Why weren't you all in North Carolina? [*Laughter*]

Q. We were.

The President. I know.

Well, I was delighted to learn the exciting news this morning that our unemployment rate has dropped to 6.9 percent, the lowest level in over 5 years. 332,000 more Americans were working last month, and today employment in the United States stands at an all-time high. And I believe that's not only in the amount of numbers but also in the percentage of the overall labor pool. It's interesting to note that this nation which believes in lower taxes and free and fair trade has created more than 8 million jobs now in 33 months. We're seeing the proof

that America's economy is packing new power. We can keep driving our unemployment rate down; we can keep opening up opportunities for our future if all of us unite in working for an America where government doesn't grow, prosperity does.

In the days ahead, I urge the Congress to join with me with renewed energy in our shared responsibilities: to control all unnecessary spending; to work for a freer and fairer trading system; and to pass a new tax plan for America, a fair-share tax plan for all.

Now, let me add that we're still discussing the subjects of trade and South Africa. Let me direct your questions on the economy to Beryl Sprinkel, because I have to be getting back to the office. The schedule was planned before we knew that I would be coming in here.

South Africa

Q. We thought you were going to announce some trade sanctions, Mr. President.

The President. No. As I say, those things are still under discussion, and as quickly as we have something to report on those discussions, we will.

Q. What do you intend to do——

Q. Today?

Q. ——about South Africa?

The President. I can't say that it will be today. I doubt that it would be.

Q. Have you changed your mind, sir, about sanctions against South Africa? There's some indication that you want to try and head off a bruising battle with Congress on——

The President. I said both those subjects, trade and South Africa, we're in consultations now on both of those. And when we can, and I know it won't be too long, we'll be——

Q. Why did you say, sir——

Farm Credit

Q. Will you do something about farm credit? You've got to do something right away on that, haven't you?

The President. That's what we're meeting on. As I say——

South Africa

Q. Are you having any second thoughts, Mr. President, about your policy of constructive engagement?

The President. I think it's the only thing that's shown any signs of improvement in that whole situation as yet.

Q. Do you really believe that all segregation has been eliminated in South Africa, Mr. President? You said that in your radio interview.

The President. No, and I didn't intend to say that. I did know that all the people that have been coming back here have been reporting to me on how widespread was this, and I'm sorry that I carelessly gave the impression that I believed that it had been totally eliminated. There are areas where it hasn't.

Q. Well, what do you believe is the case in South Africa regarding people's ability to live, to move about freely, to vote?

The President. You'll hear about all of this as soon as we finish these consultations.

Q. Are you still against the sanctions, Mr. President? Still against sanctions?

The President. Beryl is waiting impatiently here to take your questions.

Q. Why do you think you were so misinformed about the state of the situation in South Africa in terms of whites and blacks?

The President. Helen [Helen Thomas, United Press International], I will answer that one question, and then I'm going to walk out of here, and Beryl's going to take over.

Q. Don't you have a lot of briefers?

The President. I was not nearly as ill-informed as many of you have made it out that I was. I may have been careless in my language in that one thing, but I was talking about improvements that actually do exist there and have been made. But, as I say, I know that segregation has not been eliminated totally and in some areas there's been no improvement. But there has been a great improvement over what has ever existed before.

Q. Well, there's no vote there. No participation as citizens.

The President. No, no, no. I was talking about the specific things of segregation, of labor, and the new things that have taken place with regard to labor and things of that kind.

Tax Reform

Q. What about the tax reform plan in the House Ways and Means Committee, sir?

Q. Will you get tax reform this year?

The President. You've been hearing me talk about tax reform. You'll hear me some more.

Soviet General Secretary Gorbachev

Q. What about Gorbachev, Mr. President? Do you have a reaction to the interview in *Time* magazine? We haven't heard from you on that yet.

The President. I know. [*Laughter*]

Q. How about a press conference next week?

The President. I'll take it up with him in November.

Americans Missing in Lebanon

Q. Mr. President, can you tell us if there's anything new about the Americans still missing in Lebanon?

The President. We're working just as hard as we can in every channel that we can about that. It's a far different situation than the hostages. And the fact that there isn't anything out there every day, as there was on the hostage situation, doesn't mean that that is not the most important thing for us. And we are doing everything——

Q. But you see no progress at all in that?

The President. We don't know.

The President's Health

Q. How are you feeling, sir? Any aches or pains?

The President. No. You all should have seen me—no, I feel fine. As a matter of fact, my biggest problem's with the doctors that are still trying to shorten down the riding time.

Q. When are you going back out to Bethesda, Mr. President, for the checkups? Do you know?

The President. I don't know, but pretty soon. I know that's a routine thing that has to be done.

Note: The President spoke at 10:34 a.m. in the Briefing Room at the White House. Following the President's remarks, Beryl W. Sprinkel, Chairman of the Council of Economic Advisors, continued to answer reporters' questions.

Nomination of Alan L. Keyes To Be an Assistant Secretary of State
September 6, 1985

The President today announced his intention to nominate Alan L. Keyes to be an Assistant Secretary of State (International Organization Affairs). He would succeed Gregory J. Newell.

Since 1983 Ambassador Keyes has been serving as U.S. Representative on the Economic and Social Council of the United Nations, with the rank of Ambassador. He was a teaching fellow at Harvard University in 1974–1978. In 1978 he was TV-radio news secretary with the Bell for Senate Committee in New Jersey and that same year entered the Foreign Service. In 1979–1980 he was consular officer in Bombay. In the Department he was Zimbabwe desk officer in 1980–1981 and a member of the policy planning staff in 1981–1983. In 1983 he resigned from the Foreign Service.

He received his B.A. (1972) from Harvard College and his Ph.D. (1979) from Harvard University. His foreign languages are French, Spanish, and Italian. He is married, has one child, and resides in Guttenberg, NJ. He was born August 7, 1950, in New York City.

Nomination of Ronald E. Robertson To Be General Counsel of the Department of Health and Human Services
September 6, 1985

The President today announced his intention to nominate Ronald E. Robertson to be General Counsel of the Department of Health and Human Services. He would succeed Juan A. del Real.

He recently served as chief counsel for the Reagan-Bush '84 Committee. Previously he was a partner in the law firm of Musick, Peeler & Garrett in Los Angeles, CA. He was a professor of law at Pepperdine University (1978–1981) and at Mississippi College (1975–1978). He was vice president and general counsel of Amcord, Inc. (formerly American Cement Corp.), in 1971–1975.

Mr. Robertson graduated from California State University at Los Angeles (B.S., 1961) and the University of California at Los Angeles School of Law (J.D., 1964). He is married, has two children, and resides in Vienna, VA. He was born November 8, 1935, in Long Beach, CA.

Nomination of Lawrence J. Jensen To Be an Assistant Administrator of the Environmental Protection Agency
September 6, 1985

The President today announced his intention to nominate Lawrence J. Jensen to be an Assistant Administrator (Water Programs) of the Environmental Protection Agency. He would succeed Jack E. Ravan.

Since 1981 he has been Associate Solicitor at the Department of the Interior. Previously he was an associate with the law firm of Jones, Waldo, Holbrook and McDonough in Salt Lake City, UT (1979–1981), and a trial attorney in the Civil Division at the Department of Justice (1976–1979).

He graduated from the University of Utah (B.A., 1973) and Brigham Young University (J.D., 1976). He is married, has three children, and resides in Woodbridge, VA. He was born January 17, 1950, in Salt Lake City, UT.

Nomination of James P. McNeill To Be an Associate Director of the Federal Emergency Management Agency
September 6, 1985

The President today announced his intention to nominate James P. McNeill to be an Associate Director (Training and Fire Programs) of the Federal Emergency Management Agency. He would succeed Fred Joseph Villella.

Since 1984 Mr. McNeill has been serving as senior planning officer, international security affairs, at the Department of Defense. Previously he was an assistant campaign director for the Reagan-Bush '84 Committee. He was with the Federal Emergency Management Agency (FEMA) in 1977–1983, serving as senior planning officer, Civil Security Division (1981–1983); senior planning officer, Continuity of Government Division (1980–1981); and associate superintendent, National Fire Academy (1977–1980). In 1971–1976 he was with the U.S. Postal Service as director, Northeast Regional Management Institute.

He graduated from Cathedral College (B.A., 1955) and New York University (M.B.A., 1962). He is married, has four children, and resides in Olney, MD. He was born April 9, 1933, in New York City.

Appointment of James M. Crawford as a Member of the National Highway Safety Advisory Committee
September 6, 1985

The President today announced his intention to appoint James M. Crawford to be a member of the National Highway Safety Advisory Committee for a term expiring March 15, 1987. He will succeed Anatole Milunas.

Mr. Crawford is president and chairman of City Mortgage Corp. in Anchorage, AK. Previously he was president of City Deposit Corp. in Anchorage. He was with the Alaska State Housing Authority as deputy executive director in 1979–1981 and manager of Groh Investments in 1978–1979. He was coordinator for the Alaska offices of U.S. Senator Ted Stevens in 1975–1978.

He is married, has one child, and resides in Anchorage, AK. He was born July 10, 1948, in Anchorage.

Appointment of Two Members of the National Commission on Innovation and Productivity, and Designation of the Chairman
September 6, 1985

The President today announced his intention to appoint the following individuals to be members of the National Commission on Innovation and Productivity. These are new positions.

Marshall Turner, Jr., will be designated as Chairman upon his appointment. He is general partner in Taylor & Turner Associates, Ltd., in San Francisco, CA. He graduated from Stanford University (B.S., 1964; M.S., 1965) and Harvard University (M.B.A., 1970). He is married, has three children, and resides in Belvedere, CA. He was born October 10, 1941, in Santa Monica, CA.

William A. Barnstead is president and treasurer of Consolidated Machine Corp. and Scotty Fabricators, Inc., in Allston, MA. He is also an inventor, holding several U.S. and foreign patents. He is married, has two children, and resides in Lexington, MA. He was born November 4, 1919, in Cambridge, MA.

Appointment of Therese Dozier as a Member of the Commission on Presidential Scholars
September 6, 1985

The President today announced his intention to appoint Therese Dozier to be a member of the Commission on Presidential Scholars during her tenure as National Teacher of the Year. She will succeed Sherleen Sue Sisney.

Mrs. Dozier has been a teacher at Irmo High School in Columbia, SC. She graduated from the University of Florida (B.A., 1974; M.A., 1977). She is married and resides in Columbia, SC. She was born June 17, 1952, in Saigon, Vietnam.

Appointment of Nicholas A. Zoto as a Member of the President's Commission on White House Fellowships
September 6, 1985

The President today announced his intention to appoint Nicholas A. Zoto to be a member of the President's Commission on White House Fellowships. This is an initial appointment.

Mr. Zoto is founder and owner of Zoto's, Inc., a restaurant in Hatfield, PA. He was appointed to the board of directors of the Philadelphia Industrial Development Corp.

in 1983 and to the board of directors of the Philadelphia Small Business Investment Corp. in 1982. He served as chairman of the Small Business Advisory Council in Philadelphia in 1980.

Mr. Zoto is married, has three children, and resides in Huntingdon Valley, PA. He was born May 29, 1937, in Philadelphia, PA.

Appointment of Seven Members of the National Council on Vocational Education
September 6, 1985

The President today announced his intention to appoint the following individuals to be members of the National Council on Vocational Education. These are new positions.

For terms expiring January 17, 1986:

Marilyn D. Liddicoat is an attorney in Watsonville, CA. Previously she was chairman of the Santa Cruz County Board of Supervisors. She served on the Santa Cruz County Board of Education for 6 years. She graduated from the University of California at Los Angeles (B.A.) and the University of Southern California (J.D.). She was born October 2, 1931, in Los Angeles, CA, and now resides in Watsonville, CA.

Joe C. Nunez is executive director of the Latin American Research Service Agency in Denver, CO. Previously he was an investigator for the Colorado Department of Labor. He graduated from the University of Northern Colorado (B.A., 1959) and the Inter American University of Puerto Rico (M.A., 1976). He was born April 5, 1937, in Greeley, CO, and now resides in Englewood, CO.

Ray Shamie is founder and chairman of the Metal Bellows Corp. in Sharon, MA. He is a director of the Massachusetts High Technology Council and an adviser and trustee of the National Schools Committee for Economic Education. He is the founder and chairman of Productivity Communication Center, a nonprofit educational foundation based in Boston. He

was born February 14, 1921, in Brooklyn, NY, and now resides in Walpole, MA.

Arthur E. Vadnais is supervisor of education coordination for the Minnesota State Board of Vocational-Technical Education in St. Paul. He graduated from the University of Minnesota (B.S., 1962). He was born December 23, 1928, in Chicago, IL, and now resides in Minneapolis, MN.

For terms expiring January 17, 1987:

George Johnston Ames is president of Asa Properties in San Antonio, TX. He is a member of the board of directors and secretary/treasurer of the Southwest Food Industry Association. He graduated from Trinity University in San Antonio, TX. He was born July 28, 1940, in Gladewater, TX, and now resides in San Antonio.

Pier A. Gherini, Jr., is executive vice president of Westpac Shelter Corp. in Santa Barbara, CA. Previously he was president of Cow Hollow Investment Co. in San Francisco. He graduated from the University of San Francisco (B.A., 1965). He was born December 28, 1942, in Pecos, TX, and now resides in Santa Barbara.

William C. Hayes is president of Windsor Financial Corp., a real estate development company, in Encino, CA. He graduated from Brigham Young University (B.S., 1963). He was born July 25, 1941, in Los Angeles, CA, and now resides in Woodland Hills, CA.

Remarks at a White House Luncheon for Elected Republican Women Officials
September 6, 1985

Thank you all very much. Welcome to the White House. It's always good to see some old friends, but to have a chance also to make some new ones. And it's always a pleasure to be joined by two of the most important women in my life, Nancy and Maureen. We don't often have lunch together.

It may be September, but here in Washington it is still hot and muggy, as you have discovered. They don't know whether we are going to break the record. The record is 7 straight days of this kind of a heat wave, and I think we're up to 5 now or maybe I haven't counted them all. But I remember, as a boy, a preacher in our church one Sunday, in the dog days of summer, told us that because of the heat he was going to preach the shortest sermon that we had ever heard. And he said just seven words: "If you think it's hot now, wait." [*Laughter*] So, I am going to follow his example. I'll run a little bit over seven words, but I'll try to keep it short.

I'm sure you've heard of our plan to completely overhaul the Federal tax structure. This is the most burning issue facing the American people, I think, in this decade. I'm going to be out on the stump all fall bringing our case for tax fairness and economic growth to the American people and rallying their support. I'll be in many of your States, possibly many of your communities. And I'll be looking for your help, because it's at the grassroots level that our tax proposal will find the energy, determination, and willpower needed to topple the status quo. Now, I used that term because every place I've been going, like yesterday to the students of North Carolina State University, I explained status quo—that that's a Latin term for the mess we're in. [*Laughter*] And the present system is a mess.

As State legislators, I'm not going to tell you about the pleadings of lobbyists. You're very familiar with that. The siren songs of special interests are heard in every legislative hall. But this time we can work for the special interests of all the American people to create a fair and equitable tax system, one which will be a double boon to the economy because it will both close wasteful loopholes and cut tax rates. It's time for Americans to take their money out of tax shelters and invest that money in America's future. Every day we live with the present tax code, we're slowing economic growth, sacrificing jobs that could've been created, and unfairly burdening families and perpetuating an unjust system that only breeds cynicism and resentment in the American people.

I was out on the road twice this week. I was in Missouri on Labor Day and yesterday at North Carolina State, as I told you—State University, and talking to those college students brought home the urgency of this issue. The room was just electrified with their hope and energy and enthusiasm. I just said at the table and will repeat—the 21st century is going to be in good hands. How unfair it would be to chain them to the failed policies of the past. One of our proudest accomplishments as Republicans is the way we've been able to draw more and more young people into our ranks. I've repeatedly said that I can remember back a time talking to Republican fundraisers, and so forth, when I'd come home and say the only young people present look like they couldn't join anything else. [*Laughter*] But not anymore.

We've swept aside the pessimism and the resignation that gripped the elected leadership of this country not too long ago, and we've opened up the doors to the future. Like the American people, we Republicans believe that America is still young, still vital, still strong. And what we have accomplished goes beyond just words. We've backed our words, I think, with decisive and dramatic action. Our 25-percent across-the-board tax reduction gave new life and substance to the American spirit of optimism. An entrepreneurial renaissance is spreading across our land. A powerful eco-

1051

nomic expansion is lifting America out of the devastation of a decade of high tax policies and enabling us to build on a solid base of noninflationary growth.

Now, here's a piece of good news you may not have heard about, but then, knowing some of the people on our team that have been talking to you so far today, maybe they mentioned it. The Democratically controlled House Select Committee on Children, Youth, and Families rated all the different tax plans that are floating around and found that ours was, by far, the most profamily of all of them. By raising the standard deduction to $4,000 for a married couple filing jointly and nearly doubling the personal exemption to $2,000, we'll make it so that a family of four doesn't pay one penny in Federal income tax on the first $12,000 of earnings. We're also giving non-wage-earning spouses equal access to the IRA's, those nontaxable savings accounts. And this, coupled with the pension reform that was passed in the last Congress, will go a long way toward alleviating poverty by allowing women the means to care for themselves in their retirement years.

Another report may be of special interest to you as State legislators. Our proposal to eliminate the State and local tax deduction has been getting a lot of flack from some quarters—been talking about it here at this table. Well, it turns out that the New York State government has a study by its comptroller that found that taxpayers in New York would save $588 million a year in taxes under our proposal. And that's the point. If the individual taxpayers in your States benefit, your States and localities as a whole benefit. There's no logic to fighting tax fairness and fighting a plan that would increase economic growth, create jobs, give families a much-needed break, and take the working poor off the tax rolls all together.

Of course, we still have a job to do in Congress getting spending under control. In that connection, on the revenue side, I'd like it known that I could immediately deposit $1.2 billion in cash in the Treasury if Congress will support this administration's decision to sell Conrail back to the private sector, where it belongs, and get the Federal Government out of the business of owning a railroad. I was only a kid the last time the Government tried to run the railroads. That was in World War I. And it was a disaster for the country and for the railroads. Everett Dirksen might have said, "A billion here, a billion there, and pretty soon it adds up." [*Laughter*] Well, some in Congress seem to think that they can proceed as usual, indiscriminately spending taxpayer dollars, and that sooner or later they'll be bailed out with a tax hike. Well, not for at least 3½ years they won't be bailed out with a tax hike. Using Navy terms, I'll say as many times as I have to, there will be no tax hike on my watch.

We Republicans have always looked for long-term solutions, and this tax plan is one of those which will be working long after we've left office. As State legislators, you know the programs closer to home are more cost-efficient, better planned, and offer more assistance. But the gluttonous Federal tax system has robbed you of the base for local programs. We must continue to move this wheel of government in the interest of what's right for America. And this is the time for which all of us have worked, the moment in which together we can build a partnership between the levels of government with a growing economy to give America the momentum for the next century.

And with that, I'm going to say thank you, and God bless you all. And we're going to eat dessert. [*Laughter*] Thank you all.

Note: The President spoke at 12:50 p.m. in the State Dining Room at the White House. In his opening remarks, the President referred to the First Lady and his daughter Maureen.

Radio Address to the Nation on Free and Fair Trade
September 7, 1985

My fellow Americans:

In my last radio address, I discussed my decision not to impose quotas or tariffs on footwear imports. Protectionism, I said, costs consumers billions of dollars, damages the overall economy, and destroys jobs. Instead of closing down markets at home and throwing Americans out of work, we should be stepping up our efforts to open markets abroad and create American jobs by increasing exports. I instructed the United States Trade Representative to begin investigations of unfair trading practices on the part of our trading partners. We have the authority to counter unfair trading practices by initiating investigations, entering negotiations, and taking active countermeasures if those negotiations are unsuccessful.

Therefore, I'm directing the U.S. Trade Representative to start proceedings in three cases of unfair trade: one, against a Korean law that prohibits fair competition of U.S. life and fire insurance firms in the Korean market in direct contradiction of treaty obligations; two, against a Brazilian law that has restricted U.S. exports of computers and related products and squeezed out some American computer firms operating there; and three, against restrictive practices dealing with tobacco products in Japan that unfairly block U.S. entry into that market. I've also ordered acceleration of ongoing efforts to open up Japanese markets in leather and leather footwear and to challenge the European Community's subsidies on canned fruit. On these two cases we're setting a deadline of December 1, 1985. I have directed that a list be prepared of countermeasures which will be taken if these disputes are not resolved by then.

We hope that through these negotiations we will be able to convince our trading partners to stop their unfair trading practices and open those markets that are now closed to American exports. We will take countermeasures only as a last resort, but our trading partners should not doubt our determination to see international trade conducted fairly with the same rules applicable to all. I'm committed to and will continue to fight for fair trade. American exporters and American workers deserve a fair shake abroad, and we intend to see they get it. Our objective will always be to make world trading partnerships freer and fairer for all. So, while we will use our powers as a lever to open closed doors abroad, we will continue to resist protectionist measures that would only raise prices, lock out trade, and destroy the jobs and prosperity trade brings to all. There are no winners in a trade war, only losers.

As we take these important steps to make our trading system freer and fairer, let's also look at the subject of trade in its broader context. Some point to our trade deficit with alarm, but our share of world exports has not declined. In 1980 our share of world exports was just below 12 percent; in 1984 it was just over 12 percent. We have a trade deficit not because exports are declining but because imports are rising at a much more rapid pace. Why? Because our economy is, in a sense, out of balance with many of our trading partners. The strong growth of the U.S. economy has simply not been matched by many countries abroad.

Our tax cuts ignited a noninflationary economic expansion that has put over 8 million Americans to work in the last 33 months alone. In fact, numbers released yesterday showed a dramatic drop in overall unemployment to 6.9 percent, the lowest in 5 years. Contrast that to Europe where a mix of protectionist policies and continued high tax rates have produced economic anemia and where they've actually lost jobs overall in the last 10 years. And many developing countries with massive debts, high taxes, and low or negative growth find it difficult to afford U.S. exports; some look to our strong dollar as the culprit. And, yes, a strong dollar does make it harder for American firms to sell their products abroad, but the strong dollar is a reflection of America's economic strength. Low taxes and low inflation make America an attractive place to invest. We can either balance the trade deficit up by encouraging our trading partners to adopt the high-growth policies of tax cuts and open markets, or we can balance down by adopting the nogrowth policies of tax hikes and protectionism.

The choice is clear. Let's take the high road to prosperity by fighting for an open, free, and fair trading system with our economic partners and by encouraging them to adopt low tax, high employment growth policies. And let's keep our engines of growth humming here at home, too, by passing a new tax plan for America, a fair share tax plan for all.

Until next week, thanks for listening. God bless you all.

Note: The President spoke at 12:06 p.m. from Camp David, MD.

Remarks and a Question-and-Answer Session With Reporters on Signing the Executive Order Prohibiting Trade and Certain Other Transactions Involving South Africa
September 9, 1985

The President. I want to speak this morning about South Africa and about what America can do to help promote peace and justice in that country so troubled and tormented by racial conflict. The system of apartheid means deliberate, systematic, institutionalized racial discrimination, denying the black majority their God-given rights. America's view of apartheid is simple and straightforward: We believe it's wrong. We condemn it, and we're united in hoping for the day when apartheid will be no more.

Our influence over South African society is limited, but we do have some influence, and the question is how to use it. Many people of good will in this country have differing views. In my view, we must work for peaceful evolution and reform. Our aim cannot be to punish South Africa with economic sanctions that would injure the very people we're trying to help. I believe we must help all those who peacefully oppose apartheid, and we must recognize that the opponents of apartheid, using terrorism and violence, will bring not freedom and salvation, but greater suffering and more opportunities for expanded Soviet influence within South Africa and in the entire region.

What we see in South Africa is a beginning of a process of change. The changes in policy so far are inadequate, but ironically, they've been enough to raise expectations and stimulate demands for more far-reaching, immediate change. It's the growing economic power of the black majority that has put them in a position to insist on political change. South Africa is not a totalitarian society. There is a vigorous opposition press, and every day we see examples of outspoken protest and access to the international media that would never be possible in many parts of Africa or in the Soviet Union, for that matter.

But it is our active engagement, our willingness to try that gives us influence. Yes, we in America, because of what we are and what we stand for, have influence to do good. We also have immense potential to make things worse. Before taking fateful steps, we must ponder the key question: Are we helping to change the system? Or are we punishing the blacks, whom we seek to help? American policy through several administrations has been to use our influence and our leverage against apartheid, not against innocent people who are the victims of apartheid. Being true to our heritage does not mean quitting, but reaching out, expanding our help for black education and community development, calling for political dialog, urging South Africans of all races to seize the opportunity for peaceful accommodation before it's too late.

I respect and share the goals that have motivated many in Congress to send a message of U.S. concern about apartheid. But in doing so we must not damage the economic well-being of millions of people in South and southern Africa. If we genuinely wish— as I do—to develop a bipartisan basis of consensus in support of U.S. policies, this is the basis on which to proceed. Therefore, I'm signing today an Executive order that will put in place a set of measures designed and aimed against the machinery of apartheid without indiscriminately punishing the people who are victims of that system, measures that will disassociate the United States from apartheid but associate us positively with peaceful change.

These steps include a ban on all computer exports to agencies involved in the enforcement of apartheid and to the security forces; a prohibition on exports of nuclear goods or technology to South Africa, except as is required to implement nuclear proliferation safeguards of the International Atomic Energy Agency or those necessary for humanitarian reasons to protect health and safety; a ban on loans to the South African Government, except certain loans which improve economic opportunities or educational housing and health facilities that are open and accessible to South Africans of all races. I'm directing the Secretary of State and the United States Trade Representative to consult with our major trading partners regarding banning the importation of Krugerrands. I'm also instructing the Secretary of the Treasury to report to me within 60 days on the feasibility of minting an American gold coin which could provide an alternative to the Krugerrand for our coin collectors.

I want to encourage ongoing actions by our government and by private Americans to improve the living standards of South Africa's black majority. The Sullivan code, devised by a distinguished black minister from Philadelphia, the Reverend Leon Sullivan, has set the highest standards of labor practices for progressive employers throughout South Africa. I urge all American companies to participate in it, and I'm instructing the American Ambassador to South Africa to make every effort to get companies which have not adopted them— the Sullivan principles—to do so. In addition, my Executive order will ban U.S. Government export assistance to any American firm in South Africa employing more than 25 persons which does not adhere to the comprehensive fair employment principles stated in the order by the end of this year.

I'm also directing the Secretary of State to increase substantially the money we provide for scholarships to South Africans disadvantaged by apartheid and the money our Embassy uses to promote human rights programs in South Africa. Finally, I have directed Secretary Shultz to establish an advisory committee of distinguished Americans to provide recommendations on measures to encourage peaceful change in South Africa. The advisory committee shall provide its first report within 12 months.

I believe the measures I'm announcing here today will best advance our goals. If the Congress sends me the present bill as reported by the conference committee, I would have to veto it. That need not happen. I want to work with the Congress to advance bipartisan support for America's policy toward South Africa, and that's why I have put forward this Executive order today.

Three months ago I recalled our Ambassador in South Africa for consultations so that he could participate in the intensive review of the southern African situation that we've been engaged in. I have just said goodbye to him. I'm now sending him back with a message to State President Botha underlining our grave view of the current crisis and our assessment of what is needed to restore confidence abroad and move from confrontation to negotiation at home.

The problems of South Africa were not created overnight and will not be solved overnight, but there is no time to waste. To withdraw from this drama or to fan its flames will serve neither our interests nor those of the South African people. If all Americans join together behind a common program, we can have so much more influence for good. So, let us go forward with a clear vision and an open heart, working for justice and brotherhood and peace.

And now, I'm going to sign the Executive order.

Q. Mr. President, why did you change your mind on sanctions?

The President. Helen [Helen Thomas, United Press International], I haven't. I thought here I tried to explain. I am opposed and could not sign the bill if it came to me containing the economic sanctions which, as we have repeatedly said, would have harmed the very people we're trying to help.

Q. But much of that's in your order——

The President. But there are—no, there were many things in that bill——

Q. Right.

The President. ——that we could agree with and many of those are incorporated in this Executive order.

Q. But those are basic sanctions, aren't they?

The President. Not in the sense of the economic kind of sanctions that the bill called for and that, as I say, would have hurt the economy there.

Q. And this won't hurt the economy?

The President. No, I don't believe so.

Q. Mr. President, you've basically put the weakest measures in the congressional package. Why should this satisfy those in Congress who want a strong message sent to South Africa?

The President. Well, we have consulted with some of them and found that there's a great deal of improvement for what we're doing here, and they see the intent of this.

Q. Mr. President, South Africa's business leaders have been talking about meeting with its black political leaders, but President Botha has described this as disloyal. What do you think?

The President. Well, we happen to believe that negotiation is the thing that must take place, and we hope that maybe we can persuade them that they should—with the responsible black leaders—they should negotiate with regard to the solution of the problems.

Q. Mr. President, can you still call your policy constructive engagement now?

The President. What's that?

Q. Can you still call your policy toward South Africa constructive engagement?

The President. Yes. You might add the word "active" to constructive. But, yes, I do think it is.

Q. But what changes——

The President. It is similar to what we have been doing in the past.

Q. What changes would have to take place in South Africa for you to lift these measures?

The President. Well, I think the negotiations that lead toward the steps necessary to bring about political participation by all the citizens of South Africa, and when they start those constructive steps, as I've said, there isn't anything that's going to be achieved overnight. And——

Q. So, a dialog would be enough?

The President. No, I think out of that dialog then would come further steps leading toward, as soon as possible, the end of apartheid.

Q. But at what point would you feel free to lift what you have done today?

The President. Well, that would be hard for me right now to say. I think you have to see the intent and see whether the steps are being taken in a forthright manner or whether there is some trying to give in here and there but still hold off from the ultimate results. So, let us wait and see what happens.

Q. What are you saying in your letter to Botha?

The President. Well——

Q. Basically, is it the same premise?

The President. I assured him of our desire to be of help in this and to be of help in the further progress that we hope they intend to make.

Q. Well, what kind of reaction do you think your reactions are sending to South Africa?

The President. What is that?

Q. How would you describe the kind of message you think this action is sending to South Africa?

The President. I think the same kind that we've been using before. It is persuasion, but also indicating that the American people can get impatient with this, that we all feel very strongly about the changes that are needed in that society.

Q. You know, Mr. President, since the bill is so similar to what you are proposing, why would you veto it?

The President. Because, as I say, there were features in there——

Q. What? Which ones?

The President. You see, this wouldn't have been necessary if I had what a President should have, which is line-item veto. I could have signed the bill and line-item vetoed out the——

Q. What don't you like?

The President. What?

Q. What don't you like?

The President. Well, as I say, basically, let me just sum it up and say the actual economic provisions that we thought would have militated against the chance for prosperity and good living of the people we want to help. But now, I think I've taken enough here because George Shultz is waiting in the press room to take your questions and to brief you more thoroughly on this whole problem.

Q. Would you tell us, however, if you have discussed this matter with Congress and what kind of response you are going to get? Aren't you in effect stealing their thunder a bit here with what you are doing?

The President. No, we have discussed this with leaders of Congress and have been very pleased with the reaction that we got.

Q. If these sessions don't bring progress, the kind of progress you are looking for, will you take stiffer sanctions then?

The President. Well, that we'll look at when that comes. But remember, we're talking about a sovereign nation, and there are limits to what another country can do. We can't give orders to South Africa. We're trying to be helpful to them, knowing that there is a large element in South Africa which also wants an answer to this problem.

Q. Do you intend to keep the Ambassador there?

The President. What?

Q. He was recalled several months ago because of displeasure over policy. Will he remain in South Africa?

The President. Yes. I said goodbye this morning.

Q. Have you spoken personally to President Botha about these actions?

The President. What?

Q. Have you spoken personally to President Botha about——

The President. No, I've written him.

Now, I think George——

Q. Are you going to fire Don Regan?

The President. ——must be getting very impatient.

What?

Q. Are you going to fire Don Regan?

The President. [*Laughing*] Are you talking about the Redskin football player? [*Laughter*]

Q. Not quite. I'm talking about the Post articles on the schism in your hierarchy.

The President. If I fired anybody, it would be the Post. [*Laughter*]

Okay, go join George.

Q. I shouldn't have mentioned their name. [*Laughter*] Oh, excuse me.

Q. How are you feeling, sir?

The President. What?

Q. How are you feeling?

The President. I feel just fine. Don't I look it? [*Laughter*]

Q. Are we going to be looking forward to more vetoes after this one?

The President. What's that?

Q. If you're talking about vetoing this bill, are you going to veto others, too? Is this going to be a rough session?

The President. Oh, I don't know. That'll depend a lot on the fellows on the Hill. I don't want it to be rough, but I've never——

Q. Don't forget your veto pen.

The President. What?

Q. Don't forget your veto pen.

The President. [*Laughing*] I'll just leave it there for future use.

All right.

Q. Thank you.

Note: The President spoke at 10:30 a.m. in the Oval Office at the White House. George P. Shultz was Secretary of State, and Donald T. Regan was Assistant to the President and Chief of Staff.

Executive Order 12532—Prohibiting Trade and Certain Other Transactions Involving South Africa
September 9, 1985

By the authority vested in me as President by the Constitution and laws of the United States of America, including the International Emergency Economic Powers Act (50 U.S.C. 1701 *et seq.*), the National Emergencies Act (50 U.S.C. 1601 *et seq.*), the Foreign Assistance Act (22 U.S.C. 2151 *et seq.*), the United Nations Participation Act (22 U.S.C. 287), the Arms Export Control Act (22 U.S.C. 2751 *et seq.*), the Export Administration Act (50 U.S.C. App. 2401 *et seq.*), the Atomic Energy Act (42 U.S.C. 2011 *et seq.*), the Foreign Service Act (22 U.S.C. 3901 *et seq.*), the Federal Advisory Committee Act (5 U.S.C. App. I), Section 301 of Title 3 of the United States Code, and considering the measures which the United Nations Security Council has decided on or recommended in Security Council Resolutions No. 418 of November 4, 1977, No. 558 of December 13, 1984, and No. 569 of July 26, 1985, and considering that the policy and practice of apartheid are repugnant to the moral and political values of democratic and free societies and run counter to United States policies to promote democratic governments throughout the world and respect for human rights, and the policy of the United States to influence peaceful change in South Africa, as well as the threat posed to United States interests by recent events in that country,

I, Ronald Reagan, President of the United States of America, find that the policies and actions of the Government of South Africa constitute an unusual and extraordinary threat to the foreign policy and economy of the United States and hereby declare a national emergency to deal with that threat.

Section 1. Except as otherwise provided in this section, the following transactions are prohibited effective October 11, 1985:

(a) The making or approval of any loans by financial institutions in the United States to the Government of South Africa or to entities owned or controlled by that Government. This prohibition shall enter into force on November 11, 1985. It shall not apply to (i) any loan or extension of credit for any educational, housing, or health facility which is available to all persons on a nondiscriminatory basis and which is located in a geographic area accessible to all population groups without any legal or administrative restriction; or (ii) any loan or extension of credit for which an agreement is entered into before the date of this Order.

The Secretary of the Treasury is hereby authorized to promulgate such rules and regulations as may be necessary to carry out this subsection. The initial rules and regulations shall be issued within sixty days. The Secretary of the Treasury may, in consultation with the Secretary of State, permit exceptions to this prohibition only if the Secretary of the Treasury determines that the loan or extension of credit will improve the welfare or expand the economic opportunities of persons in South Africa disadvantaged by the apartheid system, provided that no exception may be made for any apartheid enforcing entity.

(b) All exports of computers, computer software, or goods or technology intended to service computers to or for use by any of the following entities of the Government of South Africa:

    (1) The military;

    (2) The police;

    (3) The prison system;

    (4) The national security agencies;

    (5) ARMSCOR and its subsidiaries or the weapons research activities of the Council for Scientific and Industrial Research;

    (6) The administering authorities for the black passbook and similar controls;

    (7) Any apartheid enforcing agency;

    (8) Any local or regional government or "homeland" entity which performs any function of any entity described in paragraphs (1) through (7).

The Secretary of Commerce is hereby authorized to promulgate such rules and regulations as may be necessary to carry out this subsection and to implement a system of end use verification to ensure that any computers exported directly or indirectly to South Africa will not be used by any entity set forth in this subsection.

(c)(1) Issuance of any license for the export to South Africa of goods or technology which are to be used in a nuclear production or utilization facility, or which, in the judgment of the Secretary of State, are likely to be diverted for use in such a facility; any authorization to engage, directly or indirectly, in the production of any special nuclear material in South Africa; any license for the export to South Africa of component parts or other items or substances especially relevant from the standpoint of export control because of their significance for nuclear explosive purposes; and any approval of retransfers to South Africa of any goods, technology, special nuclear material, components, items, or substances described in this section. The Secretaries of State, Energy, Commerce, and Treasury are hereby authorized to take such actions as may be necessary to carry out this subsection.

(2) Nothing in this section shall preclude assistance for International Atomic Energy Agency safeguards or IAEA programs generally available to its member states, or for technical programs for the purpose of reducing proliferation risks, such as for reducing the use of highly enriched uranium and activities envisaged by section 223 of the Nuclear Waste Policy Act (42 U.S.C. 10203) or for exports which the Secretary of State determines are necessary for humanitarian reasons to protect the public health and safety.

(d) The import into the United States of any arms, ammunition, or military vehicles produced in South Africa or of any manufacturing data for such articles. The Secretaries of State, Treasury, and Defense are hereby authorized to take such actions as may be necessary to carry out this subsection.

Sec. 2. (a) The majority of United States firms in South Africa have voluntarily adhered to fair labor principles which have benefitted those in South Africa who have been disadvantaged by the apartheid system. It is the policy of the United States to encourage strongly all United States firms in South Africa to follow this commendable example.

(b) Accordingly, no department or agency of the United States may intercede after December 31, 1985, with any foreign government regarding the export marketing activity in any country of any national of the United States employing more than 25 individuals in South Africa who does not adhere to the principles stated in subsection (c) with respect to that national's operations in South Africa. The Secretary of State shall promulgate regulations to further define the employers that will be subject to the requirements of this subsection and procedures to ensure that such nationals may register that they have adhered to the principles.

(c) The principles referred to in subsection (b) are as follows:

(1) Desegregating the races in each employment facility;

(2) Providing equal employment opportunity for all employees without regard to race or ethnic origin;

(3) Assuring that the pay system is applied to all employees without regard to race or ethnic origin;

(4) Establishing a minimum wage and salary structure based on the appropriate local minimum economic level which takes into account the needs of employees and their families;

(5) Increasing by appropriate means the number of persons in managerial, supervisory, administrative, clerical, and technical jobs who are disadvantaged by the apartheid system for the purpose of significantly increasing their representation in such jobs;

(6) Taking reasonable steps to improve the quality of employees' lives outside the work environment with respect to housing, transportation, schooling, recreation, and health;

(7) Implementing fair labor practices by recognizing the right of all employees, regardless of racial or other distinctions, to self-organization and to form, join, or assist labor organizations, freely and without penalty or reprisal, and recognizing the right to refrain from any such activity.

(d) United States nationals referred to in subsection (b) are encouraged to take reasonable measures to extend the scope of their influence on activities outside the workplace, by measures such as supporting the right of all businesses, regardless of the racial character of their owners or employees, to locate in urban areas, by influencing other companies in South Africa to follow the standards specified in subsection (c) and by supporting the freedom of mobility of all workers, regardless of race, to seek employment opportunities wherever they exist, and by making provision for adequate housing for families of employees within the proximity of the employee's place of work.

Sec. 3. The Secretary of State and the head of any other department or agency of the United States carrying out activities in South Africa shall promptly take, to the extent permitted by law, the necessary steps to ensure that the labor practices described in section (2)(c) are applied to their South African employees.

Sec. 4. The Secretary of State and the head of any other department or agency of the United States carrying out activities in South Africa shall, to the maximum extent practicable and to the extent permitted by law, in procuring goods or services in South Africa, make affirmative efforts to assist business enterprises having more than 50 percent beneficial ownership by persons in South Africa disadvantaged by the apartheid system.

Sec. 5. (a) The Secretary of State and the United States Trade Representative are directed to consult with other parties to the General Agreement on Tariffs and Trade with a view toward adopting a prohibition on the import of Krugerrands.

(b) The Secretary of the Treasury is directed to conduct a study to be completed within sixty days regarding the feasibility of minting and issuing gold coins with a view toward expeditiously seeking legislative authority to accomplish the goal of issuing such coins.

Sec. 6. In carrying out their respective functions and responsibilities under this Order, the Secretary of the Treasury and the Secretary of Commerce shall consult with the Secretary of State. Each such Secretary shall consult, as appropriate, with other government agencies and private persons.

Sec. 7. The Secretary of State shall establish, pursuant to appropriate legal authority, an Advisory Committee on South Africa to provide recommendations on measures to encourage peaceful change in South Africa. The Advisory Committee shall provide its initial report within twelve months.

Sec. 8. The Secretary of State is directed to take the steps necessary pursuant to the Foreign Assistance Act and related legislation to (a) increase the amount of internal scholarships provided to South Africans disadvantaged by the apartheid system up to $8 million from funds made available for Fiscal Year 1986, and (b) increase the amount allocated for South Africa from funds made available for Fiscal Year 1986 in the Human Rights Fund up to $1.5 million. At least one-third of the latter amount shall be used for legal assistance for South Africans. Appropriate increases in the amounts made available for these purposes will be considered in future fiscal years.

Sec. 9. This Order is intended to express and implement the foreign policy of the United States. It is not intended to create any right or benefit, substantive or procedural, enforceable at law by a party against the United States, its agencies, its officers, or any person.

RONALD REAGAN

The White House,
September 9, 1985.

[Filed with the Office of the Federal Register, 11:59 a.m., September 9, 1985]

Message to the Congress Reporting on the Prohibition of Trade and Certain Other Transactions Involving South Africa
September 9, 1985

To the Congress of the United States:

Pursuant to section 204(b) of the International Emergency Economic Powers Act, 50 U.S.C. 1703(b), I hereby report to the Congress that I have exercised my statutory authority to declare that the policies and actions of the Government of South Africa constitute an unusual and extraordinary threat to the foreign policy and economy of the United States and to declare a national emergency to deal with that threat.

Pursuant to this and other legal authorities, I have prohibited certain transactions, including the following: (1) the making or approval of bank loans to the South African Government, with certain narrow exceptions; (2) the export of computers and related goods and technology to certain government agencies and any apartheid enforcing entity of the South African Government; (3) all nuclear exports to South Africa and related transactions, with certain narrow exceptions; (4) the import into the United States of arms, ammunition, or military vehicles produced in South Africa; and (5) the extension of export marketing support to U.S. firms employing at least twenty-five persons in South Africa which do not adhere to certain fair labor standards.

In addition, I have directed (6) the Secretary of State and the United States Trade Representative to consult with other parties to the General Agreement on Tariffs and Trade with a view toward adopting a prohibition on the import of Krugerrands; (7) the Secretary of the Treasury to complete a study within 60 days regarding the feasibility of minting U.S. gold coins; and (8) the Secretary of State to take the steps necessary to increase the amounts provided for scholarships in South Africa for those disadvantaged by the system of apartheid and to increase the amounts allocated for South Africa in the Human Rights Fund; and (9) the Secretary of State to establish an Advisory Committee to provide recommendations on measures to encourage peaceful change in South Africa.

Finally, this Order (10) commends the efforts of U.S. firms in South Africa that have voluntarily adhered to fair labor, nondiscrimination principles and encourages all U.S. firms to do likewise.

I am enclosing a copy of the Executive Order that I have issued making this declaration and exercising this authority.

1. I have authorized these steps in response to the current situation in South Africa. It is the foreign policy of the United States to seek peaceful change in South Africa, and in particular an end to the repugnant practice and policy of apartheid and the establishment of a government based on the consent of the governed. Recent developments in South Africa have serious implications for the prospects for peaceful change and the stability of the region as a whole, a region of strategic importance to the United States. The recent declaration of a state of emergency in 36 magisterial districts by the Government of South Africa, the mass arrests and detentions, and the ensuing financial crisis are of direct concern to the foreign policy and economy of the United States. The pace of reform in South Africa has not fulfilled the expectations of the world community nor the people of South Africa. Recent government actions regarding negotiations on the participation of all South Africans in the government of that country have not sufficiently diffused tensions and may have indeed exacerbated the situation.

Under these circumstances, I believe that it is necessary for this Nation to recognize that our foreign policy of seeking change through peaceful means is seriously threatened. In order for this Nation successfully to influence events in that country, it is necessary for the United States to speak with one voice and to demonstrate our opposition to apartheid by taking certain actions directed specifically at key apartheid policies and agencies.

2. The above-described measures, many of which reflect congressional concerns, will

immediately demonstrate to the South African Government the seriousness of our concern with the situation in that country. Furthermore, this declaration mobilizes the influence of the private sector to promote an improvement in the economic prosperity, freedom, and political influence of blacks and other nonwhites in South Africa.

RONALD REAGAN

The White House,
September 9, 1985.

Appointment of Dennis Stanfill as a Member of the Board of Trustees of the John F. Kennedy Center for the Performing Arts
September 9, 1985

The President today announced his intention to appoint Dennis Stanfill to be a member of the Board of Trustees of the John F. Kennedy Center for the Performing Arts, Smithsonian Institution, for the remainder of the term expiring September 1, 1988. He would succeed Frances Breathitt.

Mr. Stanfill is president of Stanfill, Doig & Co., an investment company in Los Angeles, CA. Previously Mr. Stanfill was chairman of the board and chief executive officer of Twentieth Century-Fox in 1971–1981. He joined Twentieth Century-Fox in 1969 as executive vice president for finance and as a member of the company's board of directors and executive committee. Previously he was vice president for finance at the Times Mirror Co., Los Angeles. He is chairman of the board of directors of KCET, public television for southern California; a trustee and member of the executive committee of the California Institute of Technology; and a member of the board of governors of the Performing Arts Council of the Music Center.

Mr. Stanfill graduated from the U.S. Naval Academy (B.S., 1949). He was selected for a Rhodes scholarship to Oxford University (England), where he received a M.A. in 1953. He is married, has three children, and resides in San Marino, CA. He was born April 1, 1927, in Centerville, TN.

Appointment of Six Members of the Commission on Presidential Scholars
September 9, 1985

The President today announced his intention to appoint the following individuals to be members of the Commission on Presidential Scholars. These are initial appointments:

Dennis V. Alfieri is vice president for development at Alken Construction Co. in Arcadia, CA. He graduated from the University of Southern California (B.S., 1980). He is married and resides in Arcadia, CA. He was born November 20, 1958, in Pasadena, CA.

Anna C. Chennault is president of TAC International in Washington, DC. She graduated from Ling Nan University, Hong Kong (B.A., 1944), Chungang, Seoul, Korea (Litt. S., 1967), and Lincoln University (LL.D., 1970). She has two children and resides in Washington, DC. She was born June 23, 1925, in Peking, China.

Wells B. McCurdy is chairman and chief executive officer of Pacific Factors, Ltd., in Seattle, WA. He graduated from the University of Washington (B.A., 1941). He is married, has three children, and resides in Seattle, WA. He was born June 24, 1919, in Seattle.

Joseph R. Reppert is president of AmeriFirst Mortgage Corp. in Miami, FL. He graduated from Kansas State University (B.A., 1966; M.A., 1970). He is married, has two children, and resides in Coral Gables, FL. He was born March 8, 1943, in Anna, IL.

Rodney W. Rood is vice president emeritus of Atlantic Richfield Corp. in Los Angeles, CA. He graduated from the University of California (B.A., 1938). He is married, has two children, and resides in La Canada Flintridge, CA. He was born October 1, 1915, in Minneapolis, MN.

Mae Sue Talley was a member of the United States Advisory Commission on Public Diplomacy in 1979. She was also a United States delegate to the UNESCO Conference in Nairobi, Kenya, in 1976. She has two children and resides in Washington, DC. She was born November 27, 1923, in Hampton, VA.

Appointment of William Lucas as a Member of the Commission on the Bicentennial of the United States Constitution
September 9, 1985

The President today announced his intention to appoint William Lucas to be a member of the Commission on the Bicentennial of the United States Constitution. This is a new position.

He was elected Wayne County (Michigan) executive in 1982 and took office in January 1983. Previously he served in Wayne County as sheriff (1969–1983) and under-sheriff (1968–1969). Prior to that time, he was a special agent for the Federal Bureau of Investigation in Washington, DC, Cincinnati, and Detroit.

Mr. Lucas graduated from Manhattan College (B.A., 1952) and Fordham Law School (J.D., 1961). He is married, has five children, and resides in Detroit, MI. He was born January 5, 1928, in New York City.

Appointment of John H. Mackey as a Member of the National Council on Vocational Education
September 9, 1985

The President today announced his intention to appoint John H. Mackey to be a member of the National Council on Vocational Education for a term expiring January 17, 1986. This is a new position.

Mr. Mackey is president of the International Longshoremen's Association in Savannah, GA. Previously he was vice president of the South Atlantic and Gulf Coast District, International Longshoremen's Association.

He is married, has three children, and resides in Savannah, GA. He was born October 26, 1921, in Savannah, GA.

Nomination of Esther Kratzer Everett To Be a Member of the National Advisory Council on Women's Educational Programs
September 9, 1985

The President today announced his intention to nominate Esther Kratzer Everett to be a member of the National Advisory Council on Women's Educational Programs for a term expiring May 8, 1987. She would succeed Marie Sheehan Muhler.

Mrs. Everett is president of Emil A. Kratzer Co., Inc., insurance, real estate, mutual funds, and other financial services, in Amherst, NY. She is a former supervisor and teacher of business management and accounting candidates at the University of

Buffalo.

She graduated from the University of Buffalo (M.A., 1955). She is married, has three children, and resides in Amherst, NY. She was born January 5, 1929, in Buffalo, NY.

Statement on the Conference on Confidence and Security Building Measures and Disarmament in Europe
September 9, 1985

On September 10th the Conference on Disarmament in Europe will reconvene in Stockholm for its seventh session. The Stockholm Conference can contribute importantly to creating a more stable and secure Europe and to improving the East-West relationship. The coming months will determine whether the Conference will be successful in fulfilling its great potential as an instrument for enhancing peace in Europe. The issues before the Stockholm Conference are important and complex. They directly affect the vital security interests of the participants—the United States, Canada, plus 33 European nations. If these issues are to be resolved and a meaningful agreement achieved in time for the review meeting next year of the Conference on Security and Cooperation in Europe (CSCE), serious and detailed negotiations on concrete confidence-building measures must begin very soon.

Towards this end, the members of the Atlantic alliance worked together in Stockholm to put forward six specific proposals which meet the mandate of the Conference to enact practical, concrete, militarily significant measures to reduce the risk of military confrontation and surprise attack in Europe. These Western proposals go well beyond the modest confidence-building measures enacted in Helsinki 10 years ago. They are aimed at increasing openness in relations among all the participating states, reducing the suspicion and mistrust which divide East from West, and lowering the risk of conflict arising from miscalculation, misunderstanding, or misinterpretation.

In preparing for this new round, the United States delegation has consulted closely with our allies to explore how best to advance the work of the Conference. The alliance remains flexible and open to constructive ideas from others. We are in close contact with the other participating states and look forward to continuing this substantive dialog in the upcoming round. The U.S. delegation to the Stockholm Conference continues to have the full support of my administration in its efforts to achieve an agreement which will promote the security of all.

Interview With Representatives of College Radio Stations
September 9, 1985

Central America

Q. Mr. President, many students fear that we will become involved in a war outside our borders. Although you cannot tell us under what specific circumstances we would have a military intervention in Nicaragua, what can you say to address the students' fears?

The President. I would like to address those fears by telling them that we certainly have no plans whatsoever for ever landing military forces in Latin America. As a matter of fact, all our friends down there have told us, and repeatedly, they don't want our forces there to help them, although they want our help in training, in providing the weapons they need and do not have at the present for themselves. But the memories of the big Colossus of the North and that early gunboat diplomacy era are still so much in their minds that just politically they don't want it, and we agree with them.

Q. Would this continue to be our policy even if there is a Soviet or Cuban threat?

The President. Well, now, you could get into hypothetical cases in which—suppose this entire hemisphere were endangered by an all-out invasion—literally we'd be talking about a world war. Now that, I think, would be a much different picture, and we'd probably all find ourselves allied. But that's such a hypothetical, and I don't think I should even be talking about it because we're doing everything we can to see that there won't be that kind of world conflict.

Tax Reform

Q. Mr. President, your tax reform drive has important implications for all of our futures, particularly young people. You've attacked special interests that are fighting to maintain the tax breaks they currently receive in the tax code, but some of your critics have accused your administration of bowing to certain special interests before the plan was submitted to Congress. They note that between the time of the release of the first Treasury tax plan and the unveiling of your plan that larger breaks were reinstated for oil and gas interests, for capital gains, and for the restaurant industry's three-martini lunch. Is there a conflict between these changes and the image you've nurtured as the defender and protector of the little guy during the tax reform debate?

The President. No, not really, and the plan as it came from the Treasury Department contained a number of things which they themselves frankly knew were options. The idea of being able to reduce the rates sizably has to be based on the elimination of many deductions that have—the so-called loopholes—that have grown into situations where, without doing anything illegal, individuals and even corporations have been able to avoid their fair share of taxes through these so-called tax shelters. And, no, the things that we looked at and some of those options had to do with things that could have been inimical to our own eco-

nomic recovery. We're a country that still has to, for example, import a large share of our oil—fuel our industry and our transportation and all. And, so, we looked at some of those things and found that the supposed gains from them would not be enough to justify the setback we might be giving to businesses and to industries that were essential to our own welfare.

Now, listening to some of the talk shows on the weekend, on Sunday, I was a little upset to see some or hear some demagoguery from some individuals about how we were—our tax program, they admitted, benefited the people at the lower end of the bracket, but in the middle bracket, we were penalizing those people to benefit the so-called rich, the people of the upper end. The truth of the matter is we're tying to cut from 14 tax brackets down to 3—a 15 percent, a 25 percent, and a 35 percent. In order to do that, we eliminate many of these cuts. We have found that the average tax cut in the lower bracket will be somewhere in the neighborhood of around 13 percent. The average cut for the middle class will be 7-plus percent. The lowest cut will be in the upper bracket. So, they were misstating—they just plain didn't know what they were talking about on the air with some of those people that were talking about what we're trying to do. We want a program that'll be revenue neutral.

Incidentally, with regard to capital gains, every time we have reduced the capital gains tax we have found that the Government's revenues from capital gains increases, that more people are then induced into using the capital gains or making investments and so forth. And the result is there's more activity and more tax even though the rate is lower. You have to recognize that a number of our trading partners in the world don't even have a capital gains tax. That's a kind of peculiarly American institution.

Q. Does the use of the capital gains tax and also the oil and gas tax break to produce domestic exploration conflict with the goal that you'd set, that the tax system should not be used to promote other social or economic purposes, that it should be a level playing field for all?

The President. I don't think that we violated that, except that when you talk about charitable deductions. Of course, that's something that I think all of us want to keep in our country. We're rather unique in the world in the amount of good that is done by private, voluntary contributions and voluntarism in various social affairs. But like, for example, the oil and gas thing, we did away with one great tax inducement that has existed for a long time. And that began originally to inspire the finding of oil and gas here in our own country. But the thing that we did retain, the break we did retain is for the smaller, the independent wildcatter and so forth out there. And we need that because most of our exploration is done by those independents.

Liberal Arts Education

Q. Mr. President, I'd like to know what you see as the value of a liberal arts education in today's fast-moving, increasingly high-tech society.

The President. Well, I have one myself, and I've been trying to figure how it set me back. No, I'll tell you, I believe very much in it. I think it is the basis, and I deplore the tendency in some places, in some institutions, to go directly toward training for a trade or profession or something and ignoring the liberal arts. I think it is the foundation of education—a good, round liberal arts training. And I think you'll find that in many great companies and corporations and institutions that many of them say that, rather than having someone that has tried to train themselves specifically for that line, whatever line of work they're hiring him to do, they believe in the broad, liberal arts education. Many employers will tell you that they believe they can do the training in their particular line of work or company themselves that needs to be done, but they would like to have a well-rounded, educated individual.

Q. I'm happy to hear you say that because that's the degree I'm pursuing. So, thank you.

The President. Well, I majored in economics and sociology and then found that my careers in the bulk of my adult life came from my extracurricular activities. I always was—you know, all the class plays and belonged to the drama club and loved that sort of thing. And my other love was football, mainly, but athletics in general. And I played football for 8 years in high school and college. So, the first two careers that I had were as a sports announcer and then as an actor. And finally I got around to a job, when I was talked into running for Governor, where I could use, maybe, the economics and sociology.

U.S.-Soviet Relations

Q. Mr. President, White House officials have requested equal time for you to speak to the Russian people. If you were granted 2 minutes on live TV, what would you tell the Soviet citizens?

The President. Well, I don't know whether you can bring it down to 2 minutes or not. I remember a speaker, once, who was to be hired, and they asked his fee. And he said, "A thousand dollars." And the people who were asking him said, "Oh, but we only want a 5-minute speech." He said, "That'll be $5,000. It's that much harder to do a 5-minute speech than a lengthy one."

No, I think the thing is—I've always believed that a lot of troubles would go away if people would talk *to* each other instead of *about* each other. And there's no question but that the people in the Soviet Union hear mainly what their government wants them to hear. And they have little impact on that government, unlike our own country and our people here. I think I would try the best I could to disabuse them from the idea that not only our own country but others of the capitalist world here in the Western World have designs on them and feel an enmity toward the people of Russia, but that their government policies, their expansionism, has led us to fear them. And I would appeal for all of us to be able to get together and know each other and find out that we're the only two countries in the world, I think, that can start a world war. We're also the only two countries—the Soviet Union and the United States—that can preserve the peace.

Q. Do you feel that you would realistically be able to accomplish that, noting, like, the different Soviet press papers that speak of your administration differently? Would that be a realistic accomplishment?

The President. Well, you couldn't do it all at once, no. But maybe you might spark some doubt in their own minds as to what they were being fed by way of their journalism.

U.S. Foreign Policy

Q. Mr. President, the presiding bishop of the Episcopal Church, John Morey Allen, said in a speech on September 7th that America in the 1980's in his view has come to be seen as "a bully preoccupied with profits and self-protection and military power." How would you respond to this view, and how can the United States possibly improve its image for the future among allies and among developing nations particularly?

The President. Well, again, and I have to take issue with the reverend on a statement of that kind. First of all, if we were a bully, if we had aggressive intent, when World War II was over, and we were the only major nation in the world whose industry had not been destroyed by bombings and so forth, and we were the only ones who had the ultimate weapon—the nuclear weapon—if we were a bully, that would've been our time. We could have dominated the world, and there wasn't anyone who could've stopped us. We didn't. What we did instead was a thing called the Marshall plan, in which we set out to not only rebuild our allies and reinstate them but our enemies as well. And today two of our staunchest allies, West Germany and Japan—well, we could make it three, Italy— are, as I say, our staunchest allies now, these erstwhile enemies.

But, also, in the whole world of helping the lesser developed countries, in opening ourselves up to trade to stimulate business and industry on their part so they can have an economy, we do as much as the rest of the world put together. In the feeding of the starving in Africa, again, we are the giver that equals or tops everything that anyone is doing.

Now, that's not only from government. Again, as I say about the voluntarism in our own country, I had an interesting experience here at a dinner one night in the White House. I won't name the country, but an Ambassador's wife was one of my dinner partners. And I was talking about something and the voluntarism and what our people were doing here on their own in this country. And God bless her, she spoke up, this Ambassador's wife from another country. And she said, "Yes, but you must understand, that is unique with the United States." And I said, "What do you mean?" She said, "You're the only country, really, that does that to the extent that you do." She said, "In all our other countries," she said, "all the rest of us, we look to government for doing things of that kind." But she said, "You," and then I thought back to de Tocqueville, 130-odd years ago, who said that in America, if there's a problem, somebody goes across the street, talks to a neighbor. Pretty soon a committee is formed, and the next thing you know the problem is solved and the bureaucracy never had anything to do with it.

So, I think to refer to us in that way— who have we bullied? We're still playing catch-up with the Soviet Union. All the talk about nuclear weapons and all—they still top us by great percentages. Fifty percent more nuclear missile submarines, about 35 percent more land-based missiles—the warheads, I should say. Talk about—that's where the money is—warheads. But—and we're not trying to become superior to them—we want a deterrent. One of our military bases out on the west coast has a sign over the entrance gate to the post. This is a military base of ours. And the sign says, "Peace is our business."

Job Training

Q. Sir, what specific plans does the administration have to aid the blue-collar worker in this transition to a high-tech era?

The President. Specific plan to aid the blue-collar worker. It is true that since 1979 about 1,600,000 factory jobs have been lost in America, lost mainly because of improvement in technology to where robotics and improved machinery does what men used to, and women used to, do by hand before. Also there are industries that become obsolete as new things come along, such as our Silicon Valleys and so forth. So, we have a program in which we help fund the retraining of people who are in those industries or who lose their jobs because a machine has taken their place. We also have in that fund provision for relocating these people to areas, then, where the new jobs they're being trained for are available. It must be fairly successful because where we've lost, since 1979, 1,600,000 jobs in factories, we have in service industries and in transportation, we have added 9,000,000 new jobs. And today we have the highest percentage of the employment pool that has ever been employed in our country is employed today.

What is called the labor pool—they aren't really all looking for jobs—but it is everyone from 16 to 65, male and female in America, is known as the total potential labor pool. And ,as I say, the highest percentage of that pool that has ever been employed is employed. We have the greatest number of people employed today, and in the last 33 months we have created almost 8,000,000 new jobs. Last month alone—when I hear some of the protectionist talk I think of this—last month, the month of August, we put 332,000 more people to work in this country. So, we are making every effort to replace those who, through no fault of their own, find themselves unemployed.

U.S.-Soviet Relations

Q. Mr. President, we realize that we have to maintain a tough bargaining stance with the Soviet Union, but the picture that has been painted by your administration seems pretty bleak. What are your realistic and specific goals for the summit meeting?

The President. Well, it's a little bit like your question about what would I say if I had a few minutes on their television. I believe that, again, the thing that I said about the two countries, the two superpowers, that hold so much of the fate of the world in their hands—that we've got to recognize that. Now, if the Soviet Union, in all of its talk that we represent a threat to them, that we're the aggressor and so forth—if there is any element of real belief in that, if that isn't just propaganda, and they really believe that, then I would like, as I did here a moment ago, I would like to talk a little bit, well, or give them facts to try and show them by deed, not word, that we're not an aggressor.

On the other hand, at the same time, I would like to reveal to them why we believe that they represent a threat to us and to the Western World. There is their expansionism in Africa, Ethiopia, the Cubans' troops that the Soviet Union is maintaining, and they really are, in Angola, but—Afghanistan. But, also, go back as far as you want to go, all the way to Lenin, and every Russian leader at some time or other—the present one hasn't had time yet—but every one of them has, over and over again, restated their goal of a one-world Socialist revolution, a one-world Communist state. And invariably, they have declared that the United States is the final enemy.

Lenin made an eloquent statement. He said, "We must take Eastern Europe." And they certainly have now; there it is behind the Iron Curtain. He said, "We will organize the hordes of Asia." Well, they tried in China. They haven't done too well there, but look at Cambodia and Vietnam, North Korea. And then they said, "We will move into Latin America." And they said, "Then we will not have to take the last bastion of capitalism, the United States. It will fall into our outstretched hand like overripe fruit." But since then, Brezhnev made a statement; he said that the Soviets had gained enough through détente that by the middle-eighties they would be able to have their way wherever in the world they wanted to. Well, in the last few years, with our buildup and our determination to not let that happen, they can't have their way wherever they want to.

And, so, I know that we have differences. We're not going to like their system. They're not going to like ours, but we're not out to change their system. If that's what they want, let them go forward with their foolishness—but to convince them that it is in their best interest also to have peace. Right now, to maintain their armaments, they have reduced the standard of living for their people to a point that—well, Mr. Gorbachev was talking great reforms to try and do something about reinstating their commerce, the consumer items that the people can't buy. Do you know that in Russia today, the average time spent by a Russian in line waiting to buy things is greater than the time they spend in working at their job?

So, I—the only thing—I think, for example, arms control and arms limitation, I don't think about that so much as a thing to take up in the summit as to eliminate the things that are preventing arms control.

Q. Is it realistic, though, to try to prevent them from thinking that we are not aggressive, when they, in fact, their main goal is expansionism? Isn't it kind of difficult to change their view on that?

The President. Well, the only thing that I think that I'd like to try is to prove to them that, or show them that, as I said earlier here, when we had an opportunity to be successfully aggressive, we weren't, but that they have created suspicion in all our minds. Now, if they really mean what they've said about—be the last ones to start a war, that they don't want a war, maybe they don't. Maybe they'd like to win what they want by threatening war, and then they could only do that if they were so far superior to us in armaments. Well, we're not going to let them have that superiority. But I'm hopeful that they'll just see—if we can show them that—well, the cartoon told it all. When we started building up our—refurbishing our arms and our military—when there was a cartoon of two Russian generals, and one of them was saying to the other, "I liked the arms race better when we were the only ones in it." I don't know whether we can or not. I don't know whether they are so indoctrinated with their policy of expansionism that they won't listen, but at least they will know where we're coming from and how we view things and what our determination is.

Administration Goals

Q. Mr. President, what specific goal would you most like to accomplish during the remainder of your administration but realize that you will be unable to?

The President. I'm an optimist. I don't know that I'm admitting anything will be impossible. The things that I would like to see done are the continuation of what we've started already.

First of all, with the arms talks—maybe it might be impossible; I don't know, but I would like to see the end of nuclear weapons. I would like to envision the Soviet Union and the United States agreeing, and then verifiably eliminating those weapons, and then being able to turn to lesser nations, or other nations that maybe have some, and saying, "Look, we've done this now. Come on, get in line. You do it, too. Let's rid the world of this nightmare and this threat." But that'll be something we'll continue to try to do.

But in these next 3 years, I would like to see us continue to where the Federal Government is finally back in the harness where it should be; that authority and autonomy that has been over the years seized by the Federal Government from States and local communities, that it is returned to them; that we return to them also the tax sources that have been preempted by the Federal Government. And I would like to see a start made—this couldn't be accomplished—but I would like to see us come to, with all of this, the elimination of the deficit, a balanced budget. Then an amendment down the road at the proper date that there will be no more deficit spending, and see this country embark, however modestly, on a program to start paying off the national debt. I don't think it's very much of a heritage for us to pass on to all of you.

Q. You mentioned that specific sequence. Do you believe, then, that a balanced budget amendment would have to come after the budget was in balance——

The President. Yes, yes.

Q. ——Rather than trying, imposing it right now?

The President. Well, no, you could do it in advance. Picture this: There's no way that you could balance the budget in 1 year. It is too far out of—[*inaudible*]. And, remember, this unbalanced budget goes back a half a century. And there were many of us, over the years, who were complaining and saying this is wrong and someday it's going to get out of hand.

Well, first of all, in the sixties we had the great War on Poverty passed. And you saw immediately a great increase—1965 there was a $1.6 billion deficit. The whole budget was $118 billion. No, it wasn't 1.6, it was 1.16—was $118 billion. Fifteen years later, in 1980, the budget was almost five times as great as it had been in '65, but the deficit was 38 times as big as the deficit had been then. Now, in 1974 the Congress got together and passed a thing that was called the Budget and the Impoundment Act that supposedly was to give more control over the budget and handle things. Well, since 1974 til now is when the great deficit simply got uncontrollable.

Now, the plan that has been proposed, and even the compromise that we approved, will show that as we increase in our growth, our estimates are that next year the deficit would be 4 percent of gross national product. The following year it would be 3 percent, maybe a fraction of a point above either one of those—3 percent. By 1988 it would be 2 percent. Now, if you envision that line of decline in the deficit, by 1990 it would be even. So, suppose you embarked on a plan right now that said 5 years to balance the budget and in 5 years the balance the budget amendment goes into effect—and work toward that end.

Ms. Mathis. We only have time for one last question.

The President. Oh, dear, did you have more than—I've talked too long, I know, but—[*laughter*]—I don't very often get a chance like this.

Education

Q. Okay, I guess I'd like to close with the fact that it seems that a few of my fellow students are choosing to enter the teaching profession these days while many professional teachers are leaving. What changes should be made so that the teaching profession can compete with private enterprise for the biggest and best, brightest students?

The President. Well, for one thing, I'd like to see a lot of things changed. And some of them are being changed now, after we appointed, a few years ago, our Commission on Excellence in Education. And the States have jumped in with both feet and taken up many of the recommendations that commission made, and there is being an improvement all along the line. But I would like to see for teachers, merit pay. I would like to see where there is recognition of a good teacher or someone not so good—that they could achieve and they could look and see where there was a possibility for in-

crease instead of seeing a fixed income and that was that forevermore, like being on a pension early. I think that that would be one thing that could be done.

Q. Who do you see putting this into effect? It'd come from the State government, Federal Government, any government at all?

The President. Yes, well, basically, education is run at the local end. And, in cooperation with the States, and—either they're—one or the other, but between them is where it should be done. The thing that we have turned around, and I'm very proud of this, is that Federal aid to education never amounted to more than 8 percent of the cost of education. But for that 8 percent, the Federal Government was usurping much of the authority that belonged back at the local and State level where it always has been in our educational system. And I wanted to get Uncle Sam out from the business of—the redtape and pulling the strings and running things in return for its 8 percent, and much of that has been done.

See, having been a Governor, I know what it's like out at that end to get those supposedly government aid programs, but complete with all the rules and regulations. I know that in one change we made here in our administration, having to do with such programs, such grants, we found that we had reduced 805 pages of regulations imposed on the local levels of government by [to] only 30 pages of regulations. Even that maybe is too much, but I think it was quite an improvement. So, yes, that's——

Q. I'm curious. Don't you see it as the—that the Federal Government is the means of ensuring that a poor child in Mississippi—whatever, a poor section of Mississippi is going to get the same opportunity for an education as someone from, say, Shaker Heights, Ohio?

The President. Through all the many social programs that we have, that is taken care of. For example, starting school with a breakfast or a school lunch and so forth, aid to students, as we talked about earlier here, some $9 billion that we're spending now to aid, for secondary education.

No, there are some things, of course, the Federal Government under the Constitution has to see to certain equalities for all our citizens. But the actual running of schools—when you get a bureaucracy back at the national level that tries to make rules that fit all of this country, that ignores the great diversity in this country, that our States aren't all alike. You can't set a figure, for example, that would be adequate for, let's say, the great metropolitan centers where costs are much higher and, at the same time then, have it be right for some States, more rural States where prices and cost-of-living standards and so forth are much lower. So, the best thing is to give this back—the actual running back to those elements that are close at hand, and in a community where parents can be involved, and they know what they want for the education of their children.

———

Is this all that I am going to be able to do? Wait a minute. Could I just then volunteer something else?

We have done a lot of talking here, and your generation is subject to more informa-tion than any generation in history. It is coming at you through the airwaves. They have even fixed it so you can jog and hear it, and you get speakers on your campuses and in the schools and literature of all kinds. And I have been talking to you a lot, and I have been citing a lot of things that I have claimed are facts and figures and so forth. Let me just suggest one thing. Don't let me get away with it. Check me out, but check everybody else out. Don't just take it for granted because you read it someplace or because someone stood up in a lecture course and told you from a lecture plat-form. Check it out. Don't be the sucker generation. You are the brightest and the best, and make sure that you are hearing the facts, not just somebody's opinions. And as I say, that goes for me, too. Check me out.

Q. Thank you very much, Mr. President.

Note: The interview began at 4:31 p.m. in the Roosevelt Room at the White House. Susan K. Mathis was Deputy Director of Media Relations.

Remarks at the Welcoming Ceremony for Prime Minister Poul Schlüter of Denmark
September 10, 1985

The President. Prime Minister Schlüter, Mrs. Schlüter, today it's a great pleasure to welcome you.

Denmark is an old friend and an ally in NATO and an active trading partner; ties between our two countries run long and deep. Denmark recognized the United States as a free and independent nation shortly after our Declaration of Independ-ence. Ever since that act of friendship, rela-tions between the Danish and American people have continued to grow to our mutual benefit. Commerce between our two countries, for example, has been a boon on both sides of the Atlantic, underscoring the need for free and open international trade. I look forward, Mr. Prime Minister, to discussing with you the need to strength-en and broaden the international trading system, perhaps through a new round of comprehensive trade negotiations. At a time when our countries are enjoying im-proving economic conditions, protectionism looms as a threat. Working together, we can see to it that our international markets stay open and that this avenue to progress and well-being is not blocked.

In the past century many Danes immi-grated here to look for the American dream. With their hard work and good citi-zenship, they not only made that dream real, they helped build a great nation as well. So many Danes came here around the turn of the century; in fact, it's said that every Dane in Denmark has a relative in America. Whether that's true or not, clearly we are of the same family of free peoples. We're bound together by our common dedication to the principles of human liberty and our mutual commitment to the preservation of peace. Our countries have both recognized that the blessings of peace can only be secured by free peoples who are strong and stand together. This fundamental truth is at the heart of the NATO alliance in which Denmark has played an active role for nearly four decades. The collective deterrence of NATO has given Denmark and all of Europe 40 years of peace. We in the United States are proud to have played a role in preserving European peace and are grateful that Denmark has committed her moral weight and made a military contribution to the success of the Western alliance.

As we face new and complex challenges to our mutual security, it is ever more important that we reaffirm the trust and friendship which has served us so well. By strengthening our common defense and standing united in our efforts to achieve effective and verifiable arms reductions, we can make ours a safer planet. We can, must, and will have not just four decades of peace but a century of peace—a more stable peace which is what we want most next to the preservation of our own freedom. And independence will not be secured by wishful thinking or public relations campaigns; free people must be mature, vigilant, and stand in solidarity.

We have already reached out in the cause of a safer world on numerous occasions, and we will continue to do so. We have offered to reduce the number of intermediate-range missiles in Europe to zero. We have offered major reductions in strategic and intermediate weapons as well as a lowering of the level of conventional forces. We look forward to the coming meeting in Geneva, not for an end of all that has been wrong between East and West, but a beginning point for better relations, a starting point for progress.

Mr. Prime Minister, I'm certain you agree with me that democratic governments are naturally inclined toward peace. Freedom brings people of diverse backgrounds together as friends. I hope that during the time you spend in the United States you'll feel, through our welcome to you, the warmth and friendship that Americans share for the Danish people.

Perhaps something that best exemplifies this is the unique Fourth of July celebration that takes place every year in Denmark. In the hills of Rebild, thousands of Danes and Americans celebrate together the birth of the United States and the values we share. The American and Danish flags fly together in honor of democracy and freedom. We had the wonderful pleasure—Nancy and I— of sharing that day in Denmark in 1972 when we personally participated in the Rebild Fourth of July festivities. And the warmth and friendship we felt that day reflected something between our two peoples that is very special, and we shall never forget it.

It's an honor for me at this time, Mr. Prime Minister, to return to you the good will and hospitality that was extended to us then. On behalf of all of our citizens, welcome to America.

The Prime Minister. Mr. President, Mrs. Reagan. I wish to thank you, Mr. President, for your very kind words of welcome.

Relations between Denmark and the United States of America have always been close and friendly. When Denmark as early as in 1801 established diplomatic relations with the United States, we were among the very first countries to do so. Over the years, the dynamic creativity of the new nation tempted, as you mentioned, thousands of Danes looking for challenges and opportunities. The contribution by Danish immigrants to the building of America has been one of the pillars of Danish-American relations.

The American engagement in Europe in two world wars and American support for European recovery after World War II have become basic elements in our relationship in the second half of the 20th century. The presence of American troops in Europe is visible proof of the U.S. commitment to the Atlantic alliance, which for almost four decades now has protected its members against war and secured their freedom. The solidarity of the Atlantic alliance has also provided the necessary background for our endeavors to seek a more secure and confident relationship between East and West.

We wish that the upcoming meeting in

November with General Secretary Gorbachev will lead to the beginning of a more constructive East-West relationship, benefiting the United States, the Soviet Union, the alliance, and the world. We all have, as you also expressed, Mr. President, one major goal in common—survival. As free societies, we have always been able to discuss openly; a free and open debate serves mutual understanding and unity in cooperation.

Mr. President, you have not only been a strong supporter of NATO; I would also like to pay tribute to your support to our econo-my. Protectionism is indeed, as you have said, destructionism.

I'm looking very much forward to our talks today, Mr. President, and to meet members of the American administration. Thank you very much, Mr. President.

Note: The President spoke at 10:11 a.m. at the South Portico of the White House, where the Prime Minister was accorded a formal welcome with full military honors. Following the ceremony, the President and the Prime Minister met in the Oval Office.

Nomination of Seven Members of the United States Sentencing Commission, and Designation of the Chairman
September 10, 1985

The President today announced his intention to nominate the following individuals to be members of the U.S. Sentencing Commission:

For terms of 6 years:

William W. Wilkins, Jr., of South Carolina. The President also intends to nominate Judge Wilkins to be Chairman. He has been serving as U.S. District Judge for the District of South Carolina since 1981. He graduated from Davidson College (B.A., 1964) and the University of South Carolina School of Law (J.D., 1967). He is married, has three children, and resides in Greenville, SC. He was born March 29, 1942, in Anderson, SC.

Ilene H. Nagel, of Indiana. She is a professor of law at Indiana University School of Law in Bloomington. She graduated from Hunter College (B.A., 1968) and New York University (M.A., 1973; Ph.D., 1974). She is married, has three children, and resides in Bloomington, IN. She was born June 14, 1946, in New York City.

For terms of 4 years:

Michael K. Block, of Arizona. He is associate professor of management and economics in the School of Business and Public Administration at the University of Arizona. He graduated from Stanford University (B.A., 1964; M.A., 1969; Ph.D., 1972). He is married, has two children, and resides in Tucson, AZ. He was born April 2, 1942, in New York City.

Helen G. Corrothers, of Arkansas. Since 1984 she has been serving as a United States Parole Commissioner for the western region. She graduated from Roosevelt University (B.A., 1965). She has two children and resides in Foster City, CA. She was born March 19, 1937, in Montrose, AR.

George E. MacKinnon, of Maryland. Judge MacKinnon has been serving as United States Circuit Judge for the District of Columbia Circuit since 1969. He graduated from the University of Colorado and the University of Minnesota (LL.B., 1929). He is married, has three children, and resides in Potomac, MD. He was born April 22, 1906, in St. Paul, MN.

For terms of 2 years:

Stephen G. Breyer, of Massachusetts. He has been serving as United States Circuit Judge for the First Circuit since 1980. He graduated from Stanford University (A.B., 1959), Oxford University (B.A., 1961), and Harvard Law School (LL.B., 1964). He is married, has three children, and resides in Cambridge, MA. He was born August 15, 1938, in San Francisco, CA.

Paul H. Robinson, of New Jersey. He is a professor of law at Rutgers University. He graduated from Rensselaer Polytechnic Institute (B.S., 1970), the University of California at Los Angeles (J.D., 1973), and Harvard University (LL.M., 1974). He is married and resides in Collingswood, NJ. He was born November 12, 1948, in Waterbury, CT.

Attorney General Edwin Meese III has designated Ronald L. Gainer, of Virginia, an Associate Deputy Attorney General at the Department of Justice, to serve as his designee to the U.S. Sentencing Commission.

Toast at the State Dinner for Prime Minister Poul Schlüter of Denmark
September 10, 1985

Prime Minister Schlüter, Mrs. Schlüter, and distinguished visitors, welcome to the White House. It's been a pleasure to have you as our guests. As one would expect between close allies, our meeting today with the Prime Minister was straightforward, useful, and reflected the genuine friendship of our countrymen.

I was happy to have had the opportunity to congratulate you, Prime Minister Schlüter, on the success that you've had in your country in putting in place economy-building measures, including a far-reaching tax reform program. [*Laughter*] I can well imagine how difficult that task has been. [*Laughter*] Our efforts at tax reform remind me of one of Denmark's better known fairy tales. When I talk about reforming the tax shelter—or system, I should say, I can visualize a beautiful swan. All the special interests see is an ugly duckling. [*Laughter*] I think the national debate over tax reform reflects the strength and soul of our democracy. The outcome is still in doubt. Every citizen is free to participate in the decision-making process. All sides are going to the people to muster support, and once the issue has been voted on and settled, there will be no recriminations. The losers won't be sent to some gulag. Everyone—winners and losers—will feel proud to live in a country committed to freedom of speech and press and dedicated to the principles of representative government.

This is what binds not just Americans but the free citizens of all lands, especially the people of our two countries. That bond is evident in so many ways. Perhaps the most impressive is in the magnificence of one of the resounding monuments to American freedom—the great stone carvings on Mount Rushmore in South Dakota. There, the son of Danish immigrants, Gutzon Borglum, immortalized in granite the faces of Washington, Jefferson, Roosevelt, and Lincoln. He died before he saw the completion of his work, but his son carried on. And today it stands as a tribute to the flame of liberty that burns red hot in the soul of a man with roots in America and Denmark.

One of the greatest threats to freedom is that it will never be taken for granted—or, pardon me, I should say, it will be taken for granted is the threat. It never should be. But there are many reasons for confidence. And a story I came across recently truly inspired me, and I'd like to share it with you. Ms. Drake is here in the audience, who brought this story to my attention. Natalia and Nels Mortensen, both in their eighties, live in a small town of Marstal on the island of Aero in Denmark. For the last 40 years, they have been tending the gravesite of a young man they never met. They dig the weeds out, they place flowers—red, white, and blue ones—on the grave, and always there is a small American flag, and when it gets too worn, they replace it with another.

They're watching over the final resting place of U.S. Air Force Sergeant Jack Elwood Wagner, who died when his plane was shot down off the coast of that island, fell into the sea after a bombing raid over enemy territory on June 20th, 1944. Jack Wagner's body washed up on shore in occupied Denmark 18 days after his bomber crashed, and the word spread quickly. When the Nazi occupation troops finally arrived to bury the young American, they found nearly the whole town of 2,000 had been waiting at the graveyard since early that morning to pay tribute and homage to the young American flyer. The path had already been lined with flowers. And when the enemy troops—they, incidentally, had removed his identification before the troops had arrived—when the troops had laid him in his grave and left, then the townspeople placed two banners of red, white, and blue flowers on the grave. They conducted a funeral service. One of the banners had a ribbon which read, "Thank you for what you have done."

Jack Wagner was a 19-year-old American from Snyder County, Pennsylvania. They'd never met him, yet the people of the small town—thousands of miles from his home—felt they knew him, because they said he was a young man who gave his life for their freedom. The Mortensens have tended his grave four decades now, just as if he were a member of the family. We invited them to be here tonight, but they wrote and told me that, at their age, they didn't believe that they could take on such a long trip. But Jack Wagner's sister is here tonight—Mrs. Woll, would you stand for just a second and let us—[applause]. She has been to Denmark to meet the Mortensens and to thank them for what they've done.

Let all of us learn from their devotion. After our meeting today and the heartfelt good will of this evening, I think we can all be certain that in the future our two peo-

ples will continue to stand side by side as members of the same family—the family of free people. Incidentally, I should have added that, with the age of the Mortensens, the village in which they live has already officially made it plain that when they can no longer care for the grave, the village will take it over as an official function of that village.

So, I think we shall have two toasts tonight. First, a toast to Her Majesty, the Queen of Denmark—to the Queen. And would you also join me in a toast to Prime Minister and Mrs. Schlüter and to our Danish friends and allies.

―――――――――

Pete Rose has been at bat twice, and he hasn't hit yet. [*Laughter*]

Note: The President spoke at 9:51 p.m. in the State Dining Room at the White House. Following the toast, the President referred to Cincinnati Reds baseball player Pete Rose, who was one hit away from breaking Ty Cobb's record for the most career base hits.

Remarks at a Senior Citizens Forum on Tax Reform in Tampa, Florida
September 12, 1985

The President. Thank you, Paula. Ladies and gentlemen here on the dais and you ladies and gentlemen, before I begin my formal remarks today, I have something that I think many citizens of Florida will be glad to hear. As they say in the news business, "This is just in."

I am today making eligible for Federal assistance those parts of your State which suffered so much at the hands of Hurricane Elena—those are Franklin, Levy, Pinellas, and Manatee Counties. And the entire Nation watched with you as this disastrous storm made not one, but two passes at the Florida Gulf course. And I want to assure you that we in Washington—did I say—you know, gulf stream came out—or gulf coast came out like a golf course—[*laughter*]—

believe me, that was a Freudian slip. [*Laughter*] But I want to assure you that we in Washington will work closely with your State officials, with Senator Hawkins, and your congressional delegation to see that every resource of the Federal Government that's available under law is placed at your disposal. We want those who face the brunt of this storm to have a helping hand to begin rebuilding their homes, their businesses, and their lives.

Now, it's great to be back in Florida, and I am going to dare to say the Sunshine State even though it's a little cloudy out there. I'm happy to have a few kids my own age to play with. [*Laughter*] May I say what an honor it is to be here with your fine Senator, Paula Hawkins; your Congressmen—

Sam Gibbons, Mike Bilirakis, Andy Ireland, and Bill Young; and your mayor, Bob Martinez.

You know, last fall I fought the last election of my political life, and for the rest of my time in this high office, there can be no doubt that all decisions will be guided by a single question: What's best for America? I've tried to do that all along, but no one really believes it of a politician. But now they can't doubt it because I am not going any place. [*Laughter*] My friends, in this regard you and I have a lot in common. We've lived out the great part of our lives. As we look to the past, our hearts are filled with gratitude for the blessings that this great nation has bestowed upon us. And as we look to the future, we want our children and grandchildren to know the same freedom and opportunity, the same greatness of spirit that we as Americans have cherished.

Of course, we intend to live the rest of our own lives to the fullest, but more and more, we do find ourselves asking what's best for the next generation? What's best for America? In this spirit, I'd like to talk to you about a subject of vital importance for the decades ahead. I know you have already heard some specifics about it—tax reform—and I'll hope that I won't replow ground that's already been plowed here today.

But today our administration, as you know, has before the Congress a plan for a dramatic tax reform. It's a reform that would make it easier for Americans to keep more of their own earnings; that would create new jobs by fostering economic growth; and that would make it easier for our children and grandchildren to raise families of their own. Any reform this major is bound to have its opponents, and our tax plan is no exception. The special interests have already dug in around Capitol Hill and are prepared to do battle. They want to preserve certain tax shelters and loopholes and make the rest of us pay for the special treatment that they and their big-money clients receive.

Well, if we're going to out-flank those special interests and get this tax reform passed, a certain senior citizen is going to need your help. He's a fellow named Ronald Reagan. So, with your permission, I'd like to present our case. I want you to know what's wrong with the present system, what our new plan would do, and how each of you can lend a hand. As I've traveled the country to talk about taxes, I've discovered that the American people have a few strong opinions of their own. Let me ask you here in Florida a question that I've asked elsewhere, and I wonder if you'd answer loud enough so all of those way back in Washington can hear you. My friends, don't you believe that our taxes are too high, too complicated, and utterly unfair?

Audience. Yes! [*Applause*]

The President. Thank you. Looks as though I came to the right place. [*Laughter*] The tax code we're saddled with today is the result of almost 75 years of political wheeling and dealing. When the income tax first became law back in 1913, the tax code amounted to just about 15 pages—I may have been the only 2-year-old to read it cover to cover. [*Laughter*] Well, today the tax code runs to 4 volumes and more than 4,000 pages. And one standard interpretation of the code—you know that isn't enough, just the code; you got to have it explained—and that explanation includes 18 volumes, weighs 87 pounds, and takes up 6 feet of shelf space. Just think of it—the Bible contains all the wisdom we need to lead our lives and is perhaps 2 inches thick. You know, the complete works of William Shakespeare—plays and poetry that have enriched life in the English-speaking world for almost four centuries—can be bound in a single volume. But just to explain the tax code to the United States—18 volumes and 6 feet of shelf space—I think you'll agree it's not exactly a major contribution to Western civilization.

The sheer length and complexity of the tax code is bad enough, but the unfairness is worse. Every year many Americans pay more in Federal income taxes than the giant corporations they work for. Some individuals go on so-called educational ocean cruises or purchase sky boxes at sports arenas and write them off as business expense. Now, I've been preaching the merits of free enterprise for years. Business people provide jobs and create wealth; I have nothing against them—on the contrary, they have my heartfelt admiration. What I am against is a tax system that allows some to take perfectly legal deductions that by any standards of fairness are an outrage. I think you agree with that.

For individuals, the current system means you have to pay just too darned much. Maybe one of your grandchildren just got a job and showed you his or her paycheck. One box shows the actual salary—not a bad figure. Then there are all the boxes that show taxes taken out—Federal tax, State tax, and on and on and on. And when you get to the box that shows take-home pay, it's a mere fraction of the starting figure. It's like one of those horror movies from the 1950's—"The Incredible Shrinking Paycheck." [*Laughter*] And I'm sure your grandchild might wonder who he or she is working for—for him or herself or the Government. I still remember—the first one in my family—a daughter, she'd been with that kind of campus liberalism at the time that was going around. Then she brought home her first paycheck. She was pale and horror stricken. And I tried to explain to her that's what her old man had been making speeches about all these years. [*Laughter*] Well, you know, we can tell our children and grandchildren that there was a time when taxes were lower and simpler, and it doesn't stop there. If your grandchildren work hard and get a raise, they'll find out now that they get to keep less of each dollar.

When it comes to families, the present system is shameful. The standard deduction for married couples and the exemption for dependents—so crucial to household finances—were never big to begin with. After the inflation of the seventies, they're downright puny. The tax code has, in effect, made it more and more expensive to care for older parents or to give children the good upbringing and education they deserve.

Today's tax system means that precious resources—often scarce investment capital—are spent on useless tax dodges. It means business districts that look like ghost towns, with huge, unfinished skyscrapers constructed largely for tax reasons—they're called see-through buildings because they haven't finished them and put in the parti-

tions. It means punishment instead of rewards for hard work and achievement; growing pressure on the American family; and high taxes for everybody who can't afford a lobbyist on Capitol Hill. Those see-through buildings—I should have finished and pointed out—they're not finished on purpose, because the purpose in building them were the tax deductions that were made available from that which far exceeded any reason for going after a profit.

You know, the tax code sort of reminds me of Jack Benny's old Maxwell car—it puffs and wheezes and squeaks and squeals and gives everybody a lousy ride. I seem to remember one time when the Maxwell car on the Benny show ran out of gas and Jack Benny's line was, "I don't understand. The gas gauge reads full." And then it was Rochester, his sidekick there on the show, who answered and says, "Well, it's painted that way." [*Laughter*] Well, my friends, today we have a Maxwell car tax code. It's painted fair and simple, but in truth, it's unfair, unjust, and complicated to the point of absurdity. Isn't it time we junked that old heap and got ourselves a better model that's brand new? Now, our tax plan calls for us to close loopholes and make sure that everybody pays his fair share. But this, then, enables us to lower the rates across the board for everyone.

Permit me to say a few words right here about Social Security. I've been accused—oh, boy, have I been accused—of wanting to tamper with Social Security more times than I've had birthdays, and that's getting to be a pretty big number. [*Laughter*] Well, it just ain't so. As long ago as the 1976 campaign—I was saying then that correcting the problems of Social Security must be done without reducing the benefits for those who are receiving them. I mention this, first of all, because I think all of us would like to know that nothing in our tax plan will affect your Social Security checks in any way—period.

Now, to return to our tax plan, the corporate tax rate will come down. The capital gains tax will come down, spurring new investment. On personal income taxes, we'll replace the present tangle of 14 brackets and a top rate of 50 percent with just 3 brackets at 15, 25, and 35 percent. And for the majority of Americans, personal taxes will not only be simpler but lower. With these lower personal, corporate, and capital gains tax rates, new jobs will be created, new technologies will be developed, and living standards will rise. Once again, our country will be a land of true opportunity. And, my friends, isn't that what we want for our children and grandchildren? For families, our plan will raise the standard deduction for married couples to $4,000 and nearly double the personal exemption of $2,000. And with these measures in place, a family of four won't pay one penny in Federal tax on the first $12,000 of its earnings. Won't it be good news when our tax code stops punishing families and starts giving them a helping hand?

Now, last weekend on television, a prominent national figure said that our tax plan would hurt the middle class while it benefited the rich. I finished watching that show on the ceiling, looking down. Well, if I may use a word that people our age will remember, "balderdash." [*Laughter*] Now, there are some earthier words, but balderdash will have to do. [*Laughter*] As I've said, we intend to cut personal income tax rates and raise deductions and exemptions for the family. This means that every group in America will be better off, and anybody who tells you otherwise just doesn't understand or deliberately doesn't want to understand.

Regarding our proposal to eliminate the deduction for State and local taxes, it turns out that there's an important new study by the comptroller of the State of New York, which ranks certainly near the top among States with regard to tax rates. That study concludes that under our proposal, taxpayers in that State would save $588 million a year. And that's the point. If individuals are better off, States are better off, and America is better off.

And our fair share tax plan includes relief for millions of the needy. Under our plan, the poor and all blind, elderly, or disabled Americans living in poverty or at that poverty level would be completely removed from the Federal tax rolls—not one penny of tax to pay. The fact is that years of runaway government spending in the seventies produced an inflationary binge that threw millions into poverty. You remember the Government's War on Poverty? Well, sad to announce, poverty won. Then, our first tax cut took effect and ignited one of the strongest economic expansions in American history. Between 1983 and 1984, poverty dropped faster and farther than it had in more than a decade. Among us senior citizens alone, more than 400,000 have been lifted out of poverty. Now, this experience proves beyond all doubt that prosperity isn't created by big government. Prosperity is created by lower taxes, less government, and more economic growth. You know, I mentioned a moment ago three tax brackets. I think what I've just described to you indicates there are really going to be in our plan four tax brackets—15, 25, 35, and zero.

But we can make the tax plan, this fair tax plan, a reality. But I'll need your help. Please spread the word among your neighbors and, most important, make your views known in Washington. Tell folks up there that it's time for a change, and let them know that you support and want America's tax plan. You know, you and I have lived a good part of the history of this nation. And many of you, no doubt, are the sons and daughters of immigrants who came to this country with nothing. Many, like me, were getting our first jobs during the hard times of the Great Depression—began in '29 and in the early '30s, grew worse. All of us have seen what hard work and determination can accomplish. All of us know from firsthand experience just how much economic growth means to this nation.

To return to my original question of what's best for America, you and I know the answer. It's freedom and opportunity. And today we have a chance to give these precious gifts to the next generation, to our children and grandchildren. Let us work to give them the fair share tax. And together, my friends, I know that we can succeed.

Thank you, and God bless you all.

Note: The President spoke at 11:44 a.m. at the Curtis Hixon Convention Center. He was introduced by Senator Paula Hawkins. The forum was sponsored by Americans for Tax Reform.

Message to the Congress Transmitting the China-United States Fishery Agreement
September 12, 1985

To the Congress of the United States:

In accordance with the Magnuson Fishery Conservation and Management Act of 1976 (Public Law 94–265; 16 U.S.C. 1801 *et seq.*), (the Act), I transmit herewith the text of the Governing International Fishery Agreement between the Government of the United States and the Government of the People's Republic of China, which was signed at Washington on July 23, 1985.

This agreement is one of a series negotiated in accordance with the Act. It is the first such agreement to be concluded that incorporates the 1984 amendments to the Act, clearly establishing the relationship be-tween a foreign nation's allocations requests and its contributions to the development of the U.S. fishery in which it is requesting allocations. This agreement will further the objectives of the Act and will serve to enhance relations between the United States and the People's Republic of China.

I recommend that the Congress give favorable consideration to this agreement at an early date.

RONALD REAGAN

The White House,
September 12, 1985.

Message to the Congress Transmitting the Poland-United States Fishery Agreement
September 12, 1985

To the Congress of the United States:

In accordance with the Magnuson Fishery Conservation and Management Act of 1976 (Public Law 94–265; 16 U.S.C. 1801 *et seq.*), (the Act), I transmit herewith the text of the Governing International Fishery Agreement between the Government of the United States and the Government of the Polish People's Republic, which was signed at Washington on August 1, 1985.

This agreement is one of a series negotiated in accordance with the Act. It is a re-negotiated agreement that will allow the fisheries relationship between the United States and the Polish People's Republic to continue when the agreement currently in force expires on December 31, 1985. It incorporates the 1984 amendments to the Act that clearly establish the relationship be-tween a foreign nation's allocations requests and its contributions to the development of the U.S. fishery in which it is requesting allocations. This agreement will further the objectives of the Act and will permit the fishing industries of the United States and the Polish People's Republic to continue without interruption the cooperative fishery arrangements that have developed since the first such agreement was signed with the Polish People's Republic in 1977.

I recommend that the Congress give favorable consideration to this agreement at an early date.

RONALD REAGAN

The White House,
September 12, 1985.

Nomination of William Robert Graham To Be Deputy Administrator of the National Aeronautics and Space Administration
September 12, 1985

The President today announced his intention to nominate William Robert Graham to be Deputy Administrator of the National Aeronautics and Space Administration. He would succeed Hans Michael Mark.

Mr. Graham is senior associate at R&D Associates in Marina Del Ray, CA. He has been with R&D Associates since 1971 serving as director of computing operations (1971–1973); division manager (1973–present); and corporate program manager (1977–1981). Prior to joining R&D Associates, he was a member of the technical staff, physics department, at the Rand Corp. in 1965–1971; project officer of the Air Force Weapons Laboratory in 1962–1965; and a member of the technical staff of the Hughes Aircraft Corp. Research Laboratory in 1961–1962 and 1959–1961. Since 1982 he has been serving as Acting Chairman of the President's General Advisory Committee on Arms Control and Disarmament. He also serves as a member of the Defense Nuclear Agency Scientific Advisory Group on Effects and as a consultant to the Defense Nuclear Agency. In 1970–1981 he served as a consultant to the Office of the Secretary of Defense.

He graduated from the California Institute of Technology (B.S., 1959) and Stanford University (M.S., 1961; Ph.D., 1963). He is married, has two children, and resides in Mammoth Lakes, CA. He was born June 15, 1937, in San Antonio, TX.

Message on the Observance of the Jewish High Holy Days
September 13, 1985

Rosh Hashanah marks the beginning of the year 5746 in the Jewish Calendar. It is also the beginning of the Jewish High Holy Days, which conclude with the observance of Yom Kippur, the Day of Atonement.

This is the most sacred time of the year in the Jewish tradition, and it is also a time when we are reminded of the depth of our Nation's inheritance from that tradition. During this period, members of the Jewish community look both forward and back in a spirit of repentance. This theme of repentance is one that all Americans can understand because it is an inextricable part of America's oldest traditions. The Jewish High Holy Days provide us all with an opportunity to reflect on our responsibilities toward God and our fellowman and to resolve to do better in the future in meeting those responsibilities than we have done in the past.

This time of year also reminds us of the close and enduring relationship between the United States and Israel. Our two nations are joined not by the fragile strands of temporary interests but rather by the deep bonds of our common values. The Jewish High Holy Days remind us of the permanence and depth of those values. As the shofar's call ushers in the new year, let us all pray that the values of this season will be reflected in our own lives and in the creation of a world at peace.

RONALD REAGAN

Statement on the Nation's Economy
September 13, 1985

This morning we have received more very encouraging news about our nation's economy. Retail sales for the month of August rose sharply, while our standard measure for inflation at the producer level actually declined. Sales for August rose a robust 1.9 percent. Much of that gain came from an impressive 7.8 percent increase in new car sales, and other sales categories also showed increases. In the midst of this healthy consumer activity, we also saw prices at the wholesale level for August fall 0.3 percent while industrial production in the manufacturing sector rose 0.5 percent, the largest increase in a year. Industrial production overall climbed 0.3 percent.

All of this good news follows a drop in our unemployment rate of three-tenths of 1 percent and the Census Bureau's announcement that 1.8 million fewer Americans are living in poverty. This is further evidence of the miraculous powers of American enterprise. If the Congress will help me to control domestic spending, to work for freer and fairer trade, and to reduce tax rates further by passing our fair share tax plan for all Americans, then we can reach our goal—we can unleash a decade of growth and create 10 million new jobs in the next 4 years.

Statement on the Soviet-United States Nuclear and Space Arms Negotiations
September 13, 1985

I met today with my senior negotiators to the nuclear and space arms talks in Geneva—Ambassadors Max Kampelman, John Tower, and Maynard Glitman. I gave them my instructions for the third round of the negotiations, which begins on September 19, and discussed with them the prospects for progress in this round.

I reiterated to Ambassadors Kampelman, Tower, and Glitman my strong desire to move with renewed effort to reduce nuclear arms. Achieving real reductions in both strategic and intermediate nuclear forces is our overriding objective in Geneva. We have placed a number of positive and far-reaching proposals on the table for significant and verifiable reductions. Our negotiators have unprecedented authority for give and take in trying to reach these objectives. There is no reason why a serious reduction process cannot begin promptly, as these nuclear arms exist today and are of considerable concern to both sides. At the same time, I have emphasized my desire to strengthen the dialog with the Soviets in Geneva on the full range of issues involving defense and space arms.

I am hopeful that we may indeed be able to move forward in this round. Soviet leaders have recently given public indications that they may be considering significant nuclear reductions, and we have encouraged them to translate this expression into concrete proposals at the negotiating table in Geneva. Now is the time for them to spell out their intentions; now is the time for both sides to move forward. Concrete Soviet proposals would get the talks moving and would make a positive contribution to the intensified U.S.-Soviet dialog which has been underway in recent months. I am looking forward to my meeting with General Secretary Gorbachev in November. Arms control will, of course, be one of the important parts of our agenda at that meeting, and progress at the negotiating table in Geneva in this round would provide a positive, additional stimulus to a productive discussion in November.

As I have stressed before, my administration is committed to bringing down dramatically the levels of nuclear arms through equitable and verifiable agreements. We have made serious proposals, we are patient, and we are ready for serious give and take. With a comparable Soviet attitude, much can be accomplished and soon.

Nomination of Paul Freedenberg To Be an Assistant Secretary of Commerce
September 13, 1985

The President today announced his intention to nominate Paul Freedenberg to be an Assistant Secretary of Commerce (Trade Administration). He would succeed Lawrence J. Brady.

Since 1981 Mr. Freedenberg has been staff director of the Subcommittee on International Finance and Monetary Policy, U.S. Senate Banking Committee. Previously, he was minority counsel to the International Finance Subcommittee; on the minority professional staff of the U.S. Senate Banking Committee in 1977–1979; minority counsel, U.S. Congress Joint Committee on Defense Production, in 1977.

He graduated from the University of Illinois (B.A., 1965) and the University of Chicago (Ph.D., 1972). He was born February 17, 1943, in Chicago, IL, and now resides in Silver Spring, MD.

Nomination of Jeffrey I. Zuckerman To Be General Counsel of the Equal Employment Opportunity Commission
September 13, 1985

The President today announced his intention to nominate Jeffrey I. Zuckerman to be General Counsel of the Equal Employment Opportunity Commission for a term of 4 years. He would succeed David L. Slate.

Since 1984 he has been chief of staff of the Equal Employment Opportunity Commission. Previously, he was special assistant to the Assistant Attorney General, Antitrust Division, U.S. Department of Justice, in 1981–1984 and associate to the law firm of Sullivan & Cromwell in 1974–1981.

He graduated from the City College of New York (B.A., 1969) and Yale Law School (J.D., 1972). He is married, has three children, and resides in Silver Spring, MD. He was born January 15, 1950, in New York City.

Nomination of Joseph A. Grundfest To Be a Member of the Securities and Exchange Commission
September 13, 1985

The President today announced his intention to nominate Joseph A. Grundfest to be a member of the Securities and Exchange Commission for the term expiring June 5, 1990. He would succeed Charles L. Marinaccio.

Since 1984 Mr. Grundfest has been serving on the Council of Economic Advisers as counsel and senior economist. Previously, he was an associate with the law firm of Wilmer, Cutler & Pickering in 1979–1984; consultant to the firm of Peat, Marwick &

Mitchell in 1979–1980; and an economist and consultant to the Rand Corp. in 1973–1979.

He graduated from Yale University (B.A., 1973) and Stanford University (J.D.). He is married and resides in Washington, DC. He was born October 8, 1951, in New York City.

Nomination of Ford Barney Ford To Be a Member of the Federal Mine Safety and Health Review Commission, and Designation as Chairman
September 13, 1985

The President today announced his intention to nominate Ford Barney Ford to be a member of the Federal Mine Safety and Health Review Commission for a term of 6 years expiring August 30, 1990. He would succeed Frank F. Jestrab. Upon his confirmation, the President intends to designate him as Chairman.

Since 1983 Mr. Ford has been serving as Under Secretary of the Department of Labor. He was Assistant Secretary of Labor for Mine Safety and Health in 1981–1983. Previously he was vice president of the California Institute for Industrial and Governmental Relations and served as president of the Oilquip Marketing Corp. He was chairman and public member of the California Occupational Safety and Health Appeals Board in 1973–1978; deputy secretary, California Resources Agency, in 1967–1973; executive director and chief consultant, the Senate Fact Finding Committee on Natural Resources, in 1959–1967; associate administrative analyst, Joint Legislative Committee, in 1955–1959; and an inspector with the Coca-Cola Bottling Co. in 1948–1955.

He graduated from the University of California (B.S., 1948) and attended Virginia Military Institute. He served in the U.S. Army in 1943–1946. He is married, has two children, and resides in Woodbridge, VA. He was born November 19, 1922, in Norton, VA.

Nomination of James M. Stephens To Be a Member of the National Labor Relations Board
September 13, 1985

The President today announced his intention to nominate James M. Stephens to be a member of the National Labor Relations Board for the term of 5 years expiring August 27, 1990. He would succeed Robert P. Hunter.

Since 1981 Mr. Stephens has been labor counsel to the Senate Committee on Labor and Human Resources. Previously, he was associate minority labor counsel to the House Committee on Education and Labor (1977–1981); an associate in the law firm of Roetzel and Andress in Akron, OH (1973–1977); and law clerk for Judge Leo A. Jackson, Ohio Court of Appeals, Eighth Appellate District, in Cleveland, OH (1971–1973).

He graduated from Wittenberg University (A.B., 1968) and Case Western Reserve University (J.D., 1971). He is married, has one child, and resides in Arlington, VA. He was born September 16, 1946, in Syracuse, NY.

Nomination of William J. Merrell, Jr., To Be an Assistant Director of the National Science Foundation
September 13, 1985

The President today announced his intention to nominate William J. Merrell, Jr., to be an Assistant Director (Astronomical, Atmospheric, Earth and Ocean Sciences) of the National Science Foundation. He would succeed Floyd James Rutherford.

Dr. Merrell is presently serving as director of the division of atmospheric and marine sciences and associate dean of the College of Geosciences at Texas A&M University. He also serves there as a professor in the department of oceanography. Previously, he has served at Texas A&M University as director of the Earth Resources Institute of the College of Geosciences (1983–1984); associate professor (1981–1985) and deputy department head (1981–1983) of the department of oceanography. He was pro-

gram manager of the Gulf of Mexico topographic features synthesis in 1981–1983 and oceanographer and manager, Climate and Coastal Zone Branch Science Applications, Inc., in 1979–1980. He was with Texas A&M University as associate director of the Earth Resources Institute (1978–1979); assistant to the dean of geosciences (1978–1979); deputy sea grant director (1977–1978); and lecturer and deputy department head, department of oceanography (1977–1979).

He graduated from Sam Houston State College (B.S., 1965; M.A., 1967) and Texas A&M University (Ph.D., 1971). He is married, has two children, and resides in Bryan, TX. He was born February 16, 1943, in Grand Island, NE.

Remarks at a White House Luncheon for Elected Republican Women Officials
September 13, 1985

Thank you, and good afternoon, and welcome to the White House. It's always good to see some old friends and have a chance to make new ones. And it's always a pleasure to be joined by two of the most important women in my life, Nancy and Maureen.

Well, it may be September, but here in Washington it's been plenty warm until just a couple of days ago. We turned this off just for this particular—*[laughter]*—gathering. And these past few weeks, I guess we broke the record here for the length of a hot spell just a few days ago, before the reduction in temperature, and it reminded me when I was a kid of our minister one hot summer Sunday morning. And he said that he was going to keep his sermon short, and he did—just seven words. He said: "If you think it's hot now, wait." *[Laughter]* Well, today I'll follow his example, though I may slip a few more in than seven.

But I'm sure you've heard of our plan to overhaul the Federal tax program. This is the most burning issue that's facing the American people, I think, in this decade. I'm going to be out on the stump all fall bringing our case for tax fairness and economic growth to the American people and rallying their support. I'll be in many of your States; indeed, in many of your communities. And I'll be looking for your help, because it's the grassroots level that our tax proposal will find the energy, determination, and willpower needed to topple the status quo. Status quo—that's Latin for the mess we're in. *[Laughter]* And the present system is a mess.

As State legislators, you don't need to hear about the pleadings of lobbyists, and the siren songs of special interests are heard in every legislative hall from Capitol Hill out through all the 50 States. But this time we can work for the special interests of all the American people to create a fair and equitable tax system, one which will be a double boon to the economy because it'll both close wasteful loopholes and, at the same time, cut tax rates. It's time for Americans to take their money out of tax shelters and invest the money in America's future. Every day we live with the present tax code, we're slowing down economic growth, sacrificing jobs that would have been created, unfairly burdening families, and perpetuating an unjust system that only breeds cynicism and resentment in the American people.

You know, last week I spoke about tax reform at North Carolina State University. And talking to those college students brought home to me the urgency of this issue. The room was electrified with their hope and energy and enthusiasm. Believe me, having served as a Governor during the time of the Vietnam riots and all, when, if I went to a campus, they'd burn down a building—to see these young people today has just made me sure—and I'm glad to tell you—the 21st century's going to be in good hands. And one of our proudest accomplishments as Republicans is the way we've been able to draw more and more young people into our ranks.

We've swept aside the pessimism and resignation that gripped the elected leadership of this country not too long ago, and we've opened our doors to the future. Like the American people themselves, we Republicans believe that America is still young, still vital, and still strong. What we've accomplished together goes beyond words. We've backed our words with decisive and dramatic action. Our 25-percent across-the-board tax reduction gave new life and sustenance to a spirit of optimism. An entrepreneurial renaissance is spreading across our land. A powerful economic expansion is lifting America out of the devastation of a decade of high tax policies and enabling us to build on a solid base of noninflationary growth.

Here's a piece of especially good news. The Democratically controlled House Select Committee on Children, Youth, and Families rated all the different tax plans that are presently floating around up there on the

Hill and found that ours was by far the most profamily of all of the tax proposals. By raising the standard deduction to $4,000 for a married couple filing jointly and nearly doubling the personal exemption to $2,000, we'll make it so that a family of four doesn't pay one penny in Federal income tax on the first $12,000 of earnings. We're also giving nonwage-earning spouses equal access to IRA's, those tax deductible savings accounts. Someone's got to be very brave to suggest that a homemaker is not working. But alongside the pension reform passed in the last Congress, this will go a long way toward alleviating poverty by allowing women the means to care for themselves in retirement years.

Another report may be of special interest to you as State legislators. Our proposal to eliminate the State and local tax deduction has been getting a lot of flack from some quarters. Well, it turns out that the New York State government has a study by its own comptroller. It found that under our proposal, taxpayers in New York would save $588 million a year. So, that's the point. If the individual taxpayers in your States benefit, your States and localities as a whole benefit. There's no logic to fighting tax fairness, to fighting a plan that would increase economic growth, create more jobs, give families a much-needed break, and take the working poor off the tax rolls completely.

Of course, we still have a job to do in Congress getting spending under control. In that regard, on the revenue side, I'd like it known that I could immediately deposit $1.2 billion in cash in the Treasury if Congress will support this administration's decision to sell Conrail back to the private sector, where it belongs. I was only a small boy the first time the Federal Government tried to run the railroads. That was during World War I, and it was a disaster. If the war'd gone on a little longer, I don't think we'd have had any trains left. [*Laughter*] So, we have an offer of that amount already. We can sell, if they'll only give the word. As Everett Dirksen might have said, "A billion here and a billion there and pretty soon you're talking real money." Some in Congress seem to think they can proceed as usual, indiscriminately spending taxpayer dollars, and that sooner or later they'll all be bailed out with a tax hike. Well, for at least 3½ years they won't. There'll be no tax hike on my watch.

We Republicans have always looked for the long-range solutions, and this tax plan is one of those which will be working long after we've left office. As State legislators, you know that programs closer to home are more cost-efficient, better planned, and offer more assistance. But the gluttonous Federal tax system has robbed you of the base for local programs. We must continue to move this wheel of government in the interest of what's right for America. And this is the time for which all of us have worked, the moment in which we can build a partnership between the levels of government with a growing economy to give America the momentum for the next century. And, my friends, I'm convinced that together we can succeed.

And now I'm going to—you know, in the business I was always in, you wanted a tag line to get off that would be popular—[*laughter*]—appreciated. It is, we're going to have dessert now. [*Laughter*]

Note: The President spoke at 12:55 p.m. in the State Dining Room at the White House. In his opening remarks, the President referred to the First Lady and his daughter Maureen.

Nomination of Roger Dale Semerad To Be an Assistant Secretary of Labor
September 13, 1985

The President today announced his intention to nominate Roger Dale Semerad to be an Assistant Secretary of Labor (Employment and Training). He would succeed Frank C. Casillas.

Mr. Semerad is presently serving as executive vice president of the Brookings Institution. Previously he was chairman and president of Semerad Associates, Inc. He was executive secretary to the Policy Advisory Councils of the Republican National Committee in 1977–1980; executive director of the Committee on Resolutions of the 1980 Republican National Convention in 1979–1980; and a member of the National Advisory Council on Vocational Education in 1976–1979.

Mr. Semerad graduated from Union College (B.A., 1962). He is married, has one child, and resides in Kensington, MD. He was born September 9, 1940, in Troy, NY.

Nomination of Mark L. Edelman To Be a Member of the Board of Directors of the African Development Foundation
September 13, 1985

The President today announced his intention to nominate Mark L. Edelman, an Assistant Administrator of the Agency for International Development, to be a member of the Board of Directors of the African Development Foundation for a term expiring September 22, 1991. This is a reappointment.

Since 1983 Mr. Edelman has been serving as the Assistant Administrator for the Bureau of African Affairs at the Agency for International Development. From 1981 to 1983, he was Deputy Assistant Secretary, Bureau of International Organization Affairs, at the Department of State. In 1981 he served as a program analyst, Agency for International Development. Mr. Edelman was the legislative assistant to Senator John

C. Danforth in 1977–1981. In 1975–1976 he served as deputy commissioner of administration, Office of Administration, Jefferson City, MO. In 1973–1976 he served as director, Division of Budget, Office of Budget, Jefferson City, MO. Mr. Edelman was the budget examiner, Bureau of the Budget, Office of Management and Budget, from 1968 to 1972.

Mr. Edelman graduated from Oberlin College (B.A., 1965). He did graduate work in public administration at George Washington University in 1965–1966. He was born June 27, 1943, in St. Louis, MO. Mr. Edelman is married and currently resides in Washington, DC.

Nomination of Neal B. Freeman To Be a Member of the Board of Directors of the Communications Satellite Corporation
September 13, 1985

The President today announced his intention to nominate Neal B. Freeman to be a member of the Board of Directors of the Communications Satellite Corporation until the date of the annual meeting of the Corporation in 1988. This is a reappointment.

Since 1976 Mr. Freeman has been president of Jefferson Communications, Inc., a radio-television production and media consulting firm in Reston, VA. During this time, he has also served as consulting editor, Washington Post Writers Group, 1977–1980; contributing editor, the Advocates, 1977–1979; Washington editor, National Review, 1978–1981; and senior consultant, ACTION/Peace Corps, 1981. Prior

to founding Jefferson in 1976, Mr. Freeman was for 9 years an executive with the Hearst Corp. in New York. In 1967 he joined the King Features division of Hearst as editor in charge of newspaper relations, becoming executive editor in 1968 and director of King Features Television Productions, Inc., in 1970. From 1972 to 1976, he was vice president and editor of the Hearst division and responsible for division performance.

Mr. Freeman graduated from Yale College (B.A., 1962). He was born July 5, 1940, in New York, NY. He is married, has three children, and currently resides in Vienna, VA.

Nomination of Barbara J.H. Taylor To Be a Member of the National Commission on Libraries and Information Science
September 13, 1985

The President today announced his intention to nominate Barbara J.H. Taylor to be a member of the National Commission on Libraries and Information Science for a term expiring July 19, 1990. She would succeed Gordon M. Ambach.

Mrs. Taylor was appointed as the U.S. National Commissioner for UNESCO in 1982 and served as a senior adviser to the United States delegation, 22d General Conference of UNESCO in Paris, France (1983). She

also represented the United States at the 15th General Assembly of the International Social Science Council, Paris, France, in 1983. She is chairman of the Daughters of the American Revolution Schools for Underprivileged Children.

She attended the Georgetown University School of Foreign Service. She is married, has one child, and resides in Potomac, MD. She was born September 9, 1934, in Providence, RI.

Appointment of William M. Taylor as a Member of the National Highway Safety Advisory Committee
September 13, 1985

The President today announced his intention to appoint William M. Taylor to be a member of the National Highway Safety Advisory Committee for a term expiring March 15, 1987. He will succeed Taras G. Szmagala.

Since 1982 he has been president of Bill Taylor & Associates, Inc., a corporate and governmental relations firm, in Jacksonville, FL. Previously he was vice president—sales for George Washington Life Insurance Co. in 1966–1967. He was superintendent, general agencies, for Peninsular Life Insurance Co. in 1964–1966.

Mr. Taylor attended Arizona State University. He is married, has two children, and resides in Jacksonville, FL. He was born May 11, 1923, in Thomasville, GA.

Appointment of Barrie S. Ciliberti as a Member of the National Graduate Fellows Program Fellowship Board
September 13, 1985

The President today announced his intention to appoint Barrie S. Ciliberti to be a member of the National Graduate Fellows Program Fellowship Board for a term of 6 years. This is a new position.

Since 1965 he has been a professor at Bowie State College. He is also owner of Reston Town & County School in Reston, VA. He is president of the local chapter of the American Association of University Professors.

He graduated from Ursinus College (B.A., 1951), Georgetown University (M.A., 1961), and Catholic University (Ph.D., 1975). He has three children and resides in Rockville, MD. He was born July 27, 1936, in Philadelphia, PA.

Radio Address to the Nation on the Farm Industry
September 14, 1985

My fellow Americans:

Recent economic reports confirm our economy is moving smartly ahead with solid expansion in the job market and inflation being held down. Our future looks good, but one group is still having difficulty. Far too many farmers are seeing hard times. Prices for corn, wheat, and soybeans have been weak and getting weaker. Demand for exports has dropped as production here and in other countries has steadily increased, and foreign suppliers have filled markets that once were ours.

Our great success in bringing down inflation has helped farmers by ending double-digit price increases for fuel, fertilizer, and other supplies, but there's been a down side. Many farmers took out loans in the late seventies when inflation was soaring, assuming the value of the land they were pledging as collateral would keep on rising. Unfortunately, the opposite happened. When inflation plunged, land values plunged, too. And when inflation stayed down, defying the experts' predictions, those loans farmers were carrying became more and more difficult to finance. How can we not open our hearts to these people in distress who mean so much and give so much to America? We know that, while farmers account for only 3 percent of the work force, farming and related industries generate $660 billion a year or almost 18 percent of our gross national product. We know that these industries are responsible for 21 million workers, nearly 20 percent of the work force. We can be thankful that agriculture, one of the few industries with a strong, positive trade balance, provides employment for 630,000 nonfarm workers through its yearly exports.

These facts and figures are convincing in their own right. Yet facts and figures don't tell the whole story. They don't convey the strength and nobility of values, the deep faith in God, and love of freedom and independence, the many years of hard work and caring for friends and neighbors that began on the farm and made America the greatest Nation on Earth. Farming is hard work, maybe the hardest. The strength of our farmers has always been the strength of their dreams for the future—dreams that a son or a daughter working the fields, tending the herds, might decide to stay on that farm and be able to make a go of it. There is no price tag on traditions like these, only the stark realization that to lose our farmers would be to lose the best part of ourselves, the heart and soul of America. Well, we cannot let that happen. We cannot permit the dreams of our farmers to die. We must have compassion for these men, women, and their families, so important to all of us.

I'm asking Congress to join me in planting fresh seeds of hope for America's farmers. We might begin by seeing and avoiding the one threat that could make today's problems far worse. Some 300 protectionist bills await action in Congress. To enact them would be to invite certain retaliation against our farm exports, heightening the risk of a farm catastrophe which would send shock waves throughout our economy. Believe me, protectionism is farmers' enemy number one, and that enemy is stalking our gate. Let us work aggressively for freer and fairer markets. But more than that, let us have the courage to urge that more countries start doing what America has begun doing so well. Go for growth by adopting low-tax, free-market policies that will increase jobs, raise their people's standard of living, thereby strengthening demand for our products. Nations which have stagnated their economies with high taxes are weak importers, and this problem must be recognized.

We do not seek an America that is closed to the world; we seek a world that is open to America. We do not dream of protecting America from others' success; we seek to include everyone in the success of the American dream. I'm asking Congress to unite with me for intelligent policies that provide farmers needed help, without doing harm to the budget limitations adopted by Congress, and greater freedom for them to grow and sell their crops in the marketplaces of the world. By working in this spirit, we can avoid budget-busting legislation which repeats the mistakes of the past, legislation I would not hesitate to veto. We must meet our responsibility to America's farmers and pass a farm bill that provides hope, not measured doses of despair.

Until next week, thanks for listening, and God bless you.

Note: The President spoke at 12:06 p.m. from Camp David, MD.

Proclamation 5366—National Hispanic Heritage Week, 1985
September 14, 1985

By the President of the United States of America

A Proclamation

One of the greatest strengths of our Nation is its rich mixture of people from various cultural backgrounds. Americans of Hispanic heritage have made an immense and unique contribution. In thousands of communities across the land, Hispanics are a vital element in fostering America's achievements in fields as diverse as the arts and industry, agriculture and education, religion and business, science and politics.

People from Spain were among the first explorers and settlers in the New World, long before the United States became an independent Nation. They came in search of a better life for themselves and their children, and they have helped to create a richer life for all of us.

In our international relations, Hispanic Americans also contribute to our Nation's identity—our own perception of who we are and our role in the world. The strong family and cultural ties which bind Hispanics in the United States with our nearest neighbors are an important element of strength, unity, and understanding in the Western Hemisphere. The freedom of our neighbors is our freedom. Their security is our security. We Americans seek justice, economic progress, the spirit of good neighborliness throughout the hemisphere, and we count on Americans of Hispanic heritage for special insight and leadership as we work together toward these goals.

In recognition of the many achievements of the Hispanic American community, the Congress, by Joint Resolution approved September 17, 1968 (Public Law 90–498), has authorized and requested the President to issue annually a proclamation designating the week which includes September 15 and 16 as "National Hispanic Heritage Week."

Now, Therefore, I, Ronald Reagan, President of the United States of America, do hereby proclaim the week beginning September 15, 1985, as National Hispanic Heritage Week, in recognition of the Hispanic individuals, families, and communities that enrich our national life. I call upon the people of the United States, especially the educational community, to observe this week with appropriate ceremonies and activities.

In Witness Whereof, I have hereunto set my hand this fourteenth day of September, in the year of our Lord nineteen hundred and eighty-five, and of the Independence of the United States of America the two hundred and tenth.

RONALD REAGAN

[*Filed with the Office of the Federal Register, 11:13 a.m., September 16, 1985*]

Interview With Guillermo Descalzi of the Spanish International Network
September 13, 1985

Tax Reform

Mr. Descalzi. Mr. President, the major focus of your Presidency has been the reactivation of the economy, and many would, of course, arguably say that you've been very successful at that. So, the question now is: Why now with the project of tax reform?

The President. Well, what we've started with the economy and the growth that we've had—the increase in prosperity here—I think is only a beginning. I think there's further to go, and so the tax reform, I think, could contribute to economic growth. But the main thing is, even without that, our present tax system is unfair. It is so complicated that a great many people can't determine how much they owe the Government without getting expensive legal help. And we believe it's long overdue that we have a tax system that is more fair; that is simpler, more easily understood by the people; and that, at the same time, can lower the tax rates in the simplification, removing some of the loopholes that have led to unfair deductions by some, the use of tax shelters to avoid, legally, a fair share of tax.

Mr. Descalzi. Now, the question is: If through simplification and through the new tax system the average amount of money that the individual is going to contribute to the IRS is going to diminish, how, then, is the Government going to compensate for the diminishing tax returns that it will take?

The President. Well, we aren't going to diminish the total tax revenues the Government gets. It's true we'll lower the rates; it's true that individuals will pay less tax than they're presently paying. The difference will be made up in part by what we think will be more growth in the economy, and the more the economy grows, the more tax revenues there'll be. But mainly it's because right now there are a great many people who have taken advantage of some well-intentioned tax loopholes, as we call them, to reduce their personal tax burden, and this has resulted in a great unfairness. For example, we have people today who are paying a higher income tax as individuals than the great corporations they work for are paying as their total tax. So, once we change that, the difference will mainly be made up by those tax revenues that are being avoided by some, and that's where the fairness comes in. Everybody will be paying their fair share.

Mr. Descalzi. And we're also banking on the growth of the economy. Talking about the primary focus of this reform, many see the family as the main concern of yours, and I would like to ask you about which is the main focus of this project of yours.

The President. Well, we think it is aimed at the family, and we think that the family is the most important unit in our whole social structure. As the family goes, so goes the Nation. But what we are going to do in addition to lowering the rates, we are going to make the personal deduction for a wage earner $4,000. We are going to almost double the increase exemption—or deduction for dependents to $2,000 because it hasn't nearly kept up with inflation over the years—that deduction that used to be $600 and then came to $1,040. Well, now it's going to be $2,000 under our plan, and thus we feel particularly the families at the lower end of the earning scale—we could see an average family of four that wouldn't have to pay a penny on the first $12,000 of earnings. Also we are going to see people that are near the poverty line that are going to be dropped from the tax rolls entirely.

Mr. Descalzi. Now, Mr. President, tax reform is a very serious and complex issue,

and there have been many attempts in the past. There is opposition in Congress, and I would like to ask you, in here, which are the political angles of tax reform, or are there any political angles to it?

The President. I think the main political angles have to do with specific changes we want to make—some of those deductions I am talking about removing—that there are special interest groups that will try to preserve those, and they will get here and there some congressional support in behalf of one or the others of those features. But I believe that overall this may be one of those times when we see there are no Democrats or Republicans, just Americans, because overall there is a bipartisan feeling that tax reform is necessary.

Mr. Descalzi. Well, among the Americans, we have Hispanic Americans, and, of course, as you know, most of Hispanic America—not most, a large proportion of Hispanic America is in the modest-income category. You already talked a little bit about how people with a modest income would benefit, but talking specifically about Hispanic Americans, most of them in a modest-income category, how would modest-income and middle-income Americans benefit from this proposal?

The President. They would benefit most of all, particularly at the lower end of the earnings. Right now, you know, there are 14 tax brackets that people, based on their earnings, fall into. We're reducing that to 3—a 15-percent bracket, a 25-percent bracket, and a 35-percent bracket. But in reality, there's a fourth bracket—zero. The people at the very lowest end and there around the poverty line will find they no longer have any taxes at all to pay. And elderly people that are in that particular bracket, some of the handicapped people, and then those that are just earning but around that location—they won't have any tax to pay at all.

Nicaragua

Mr. Descalzi. Mr. President, let me go to another major concern of your Presidency. I remember interviewing you in Los Angeles in 1980, and you mentioned as one of your big concerns the spread of communism in this hemisphere, in the Caribbean and Central America. Well, one of your most notable successes in foreign policy has been Grenada; however, we still have Nicaragua, and it continues unabated. My question now is: What can you tell us that will give us confidence that the problems presented now by the Sandinista regime in Nicaragua will be solved in the future?

The President. Well, I'm optimistic about what's going to happen there. Right now we have a totalitarian government—the Sandinista government—in Nicaragua. This came out of the revolution to overthrow the dictator, Somoza. But the people who are fighting as the *contras* against the Sandinista government now are mainly the people who were part of the revolution also against Somoza. They came together to overthrow that particular regime.

In 1979 those revolutionaries, including the Sandinistas, went to the Organization of American States and asked that organization to appeal to Somoza to step down so the killing could stop. The Organization of American States asked them: Well, what were the goals of their revolution? The promise was given that it was to have democracy, to have free labor unions, a free press, free speech—all the things that we associate with democracy and government by and of and for the people. And then the revolution was over. Well, the Sandinistas were probably the most organized. They had been a pro-Communist organization for years back. They ousted from the revolution those who had fought with them. Some of the leaders had to flee into exile; some of them were imprisoned; some of them, I'm afraid, were executed.

And we have this totalitarian government. It is literally a satellite of Cuba, the Communist regime in Cuba, and that means it's indirectly a satellite of the Soviet Union. It has made it plain that its revolution knows no borders, that it is going to be the centerpiece here in the Western Hemisphere for spreading that kind of Communist regime throughout the hemisphere. Their military has been furnished, and their weapons—well, they're furnishing weapons to the guerrillas in their neighboring country, El Salvador, where there is a democrat-

ic government. So, we think that in helping, as we have been trying to help, the *contras*—and we've seen them grow as the dissatisfaction in Nicaragua with the Sandinistas spread among the people; the forces of the *contras* have grown to around 20,000 in number. They're getting stronger. Deserters from the Nicaraguan Army, the Sandinista army, are turning up and volunteering as *contras*.

So, we think that those people who were simply striving for the original promises of the revolution to be kept should have our help. That does not mean, however, military forces from the United States. All of our friends in Latin America have made it plain to us—maybe with some memories of a far distant past—that no, they have the manpower; they don't need American manpower. They do need our help in supplies and weapons and training and so forth, and that we're giving them. And, so, I know that the *contras* have progressed to the point that they have several times offered to lay down their arms and negotiate a settlement with the Sandinistas, their former allies in the revolution, and the Sandinistas have repeatedly refused. But we think they deserve our help.

Mr. Descalzi. Well, you say that we are giving them help, and, yes, we are; however, Congress has wavered constantly on this issue. It's teeter-tottered between the Boland amendment and no aid to the *contras.* And right now there is limited humanitarian aid. Has Congress been playing politics with the security of this hemisphere?

The President. Well, I hesitate to say that. Some may; I don't know. I think maybe the rest were well intentioned, and they're suffering from something I call the Vietnam syndrome. I think too many of them, still remembering our entanglement there 10,000 miles away from our own land, in that that this might lead to our military involvement. And, so, they have been cautious about what we can do. As I've already explained, we have no intention of military involvement nor do I think it is needed. And I think as more of them come to see that, and also as more of them have come to realize the real nature of the Sandinista government—that it is a totalitarian, Communist government—that that opposition is lessening.

Immigration Reform

Mr. Descalzi. Mr. President, another very important issue for Hispanic Americans is that of immigration. As you know, there have been attempts in the past at immigration reform. This is the third time that Senator Simpson is pushing his own version of immigration reform through Congress—and Congressmen Rodino and Mazzoli in the House—do you support this? Are you behind this attempt? Would you sign into law a Simpson-Rodino-Mazzoli bill if it comes to be?

The President. I have to say that, beginning back in 1981, I supported the principle of reform in our immigration laws because we, in a way, have lost control of our borders. Right now, I have to say with regard to the Simpson bill that—and we've informed of this—that we support generally his bill, but there are some amendments that we think are necessary. For one, we very much need in any immigration bill—we need protection for people who are in this country and who have not become citizens, for example, that they are protected and legitimized and given permanent residency here. And we want to see some things of that kind added to the immigration bill.

Hispanic Americans

Mr. Descalzi. Mr. President, this is my last question, really, and I want to ask you simply if you have any messages for the Hispanic community in America that's listening to you.

The President. Well, yes, I do. Our whole country is made up of people who came here from someplace else, either the individuals themselves or, like myself—in my case it was grandparents, others it's their parents—but we represent the cultures and the diversity of the whole world. And we've come together in what some people called a melting pot and created a whole new breed of human being called an American. And I have to say, I think America's great success in the world has been the result of this diversity and this understanding and coming together of such diverse peoples. And I just have to say that our Hispanic Americans—their contribution to America is not surpassed by that of any other people. They have brought a great warmth, and they have brought great traditions of family. In our wars, they have brought great service and great heroism and loyalty to this country. And all I would like to say to them is, God bless them all, and *vaya con Dios.*

Mr. Descalzi. And *vaya con Dios, tambien, Senor Presidente. Muchas gracias.*

The President. *Gracias.*

Mr. Descalzi. Thank you very much.

Note: The interview began at 3:25 p.m. in the Map Room at the White House. The transcript was released by the Office of the Press Secretary on September 16.

Nomination of Two Members of the Board of Regents of the Uniformed Services University of the Health Sciences
September 16, 1985

The President today announced his intention to nominate the following individuals to be members of the Board of Regents of the Uniformed Services University of the Health Sciences, Department of Defense, for terms expiring June 20, 1991.

Mario Efrain Ramirez would succeed William R. Roy. Dr. Ramirez is in the private practice of medicine in Rio Grande City, TX. He is a char-

ter fellow of the American Academy of Family Physicians and a charter member and diplomate of the American Board of Family Practice. He graduated from the University of Texas (B.A., 1945) and the University of Tennessee (M.D., 1948). He is married, has five children, and resides in Roma, TX. He was born April 3, 1926, in Roma, TX.

Carol Johnson Johns would succeed Lauro F. Cavazos. Dr. Johns is associate professor, assistant dean, and director of continuing education at Johns Hopkins University. She is a full-time faculty member of Johns Hopkins University in the respiratory division. She graduated from Wellesley College (B.A., 1944) and Johns Hopkins University (M.D., 1950). She is married, has three children, and resides in Baltimore, MD. She was born June 18, 1923, in Baltimore, MD.

Appointment of Stanley M. Freehling as a Member of the President's Committee on the Arts and the Humanities
September 16, 1985

The President today announced his intention to appoint Stanley M. Freehling to be a member of the President's Committee on the Arts and the Humanities. He will succeed Gabriele Murdock.

He is a partner in Freehling and Co. in Chicago, IL. He also serves as a trustee of the Art Institute of Chicago. He was chairman of the board of the Illinois Arts Council in 1971–1973. He has been an active member of the Chicago Theatre Group, the National Corporation Theatre Fund, and Sadler's Wells Theatre Association in London.

He graduated from the University of Stockholm (B.A., 1947). He is married, has three children, and resides in Chicago, IL. He was born July 2, 1924, in Chicago.

Nomination of Hazel M. Richardson To Be a Member of the National Advisory Council on Women's Educational Programs
September 16, 1985

The President today announced his intention to nominate Hazel M. Richardson to be a member of the National Advisory Council on Women's Educational Programs for a term expiring May 8, 1988. She would succeed Eleanor Thomas Elliott.

She is vice chancellor of government affairs at the University of California at Santa Barbara. Previously she was deputy regional campaign director for Reagan-Bush '84. She has served as regional chairman, chancellor's council, at the University of California at Santa Barbara.

She graduated from the University of California at Los Angeles (B.A., 1967). She has two children and resides in Santa Barbara. She was born February 15, 1947, in Redlands, CA.

Appointment of Thomas W. Moses as a Member of the Advisory Committee on the Arts
September 16, 1985

The President today announced his intention to appoint Thomas W. Moses to be a member of the Advisory Committee on the Arts (John F. Kennedy Center for the Performing Arts, Smithsonian Institution). This is an initial appointment.

Since 1969 Mr. Moses has been serving as chairman of the board of the Indianapolis Water Co. Previously he was chairman of the board of the First National City Bank of Minneapolis. He serves as chairman of the board and director of Compucom Development Corp.; director of Merchants National Bank & Trust Co.; director of Merchants National Corp.; and director of Park Fletcher, Inc. He is vice chairman of the capital fund for the Indianapolis Ballet League and honorary chairman of the capital fund for the Indianapolis Art League.

He graduated from Washington & Lee University (A.B., 1939) and Yale University (LL.B., 1942). He is married, has three children, and resides in Indianapolis, IN. He was born January 30, 1919, in Benton, IL.

Appointment of L. William Mc Nutt, Jr., as a Member of the Board for International Food and Agricultural Development
September 16, 1985

The President today announced his intention to appoint L. William Mc Nutt, Jr., to be a member of the Board for International Food and Agricultural Development for a term expiring December 6, 1987. He will succeed Ernest T. Marshall.

Mr. McNutt is director and chief executive officer of the Collin Street Bakery in Corsicana, TX. He also serves as a director of Interfirst Bank of Corsicana, Navarro Pecan Co., Data Dallas Corp., and Dexter Lloyds Insurance Co.

He graduated from Vanderbilt University (B.A., 1949). He is married, has four children, and resides in Corsicana, TX. He was born June 16, 1925, in Corsicana.

Appointment of Benjamin Frank as a Member of the Advisory Committee for Trade Negotiations
September 16, 1985

The President today announced his intention to appoint Benjamin Frank to be a member of the Advisory Committee for Trade Negotiations for a term of 2 years. This is a reappointment.

Since 1971 Mr. Frank has been with Allied Stores Corp. and is currently senior vice president. He served as executive vice president of the Hament Corp. in 1969–1971 and deputy commissioner of the Office of General Services of the State of New York in 1967–1969. He was in the private practice of law with the firm of Dubow, Frank & Dubow in New York in 1963–1967.

He graduated from Boston University (B.Sc., 1958) and New York University School of Law (J.D., 1961). He is married, has three children, and resides in New York City. He was born February 10, 1934, in Montreal, Canada.

Remarks and a Question-and-Answer Session With Regional Editors and Broadcasters
September 16, 1985

The President. Good afternoon, and welcome to the White House. Like millions of Americans, Nancy and I recently returned from our summer vacation. My horse and I got reacquainted, and I had time to reflect once again on the old truth inherited from the cavalry that there's nothing so good for the inside of a man as the outside of a horse. Now, fall is nearly here, and the Nation's begun another season of work and achievement. I can't think of a better way to begin the new season here at the White House than by speaking to you, the representatives of newspapers and television and radio stations out there in the real America, and through you, I hope, to the communities that you serve.

Today our country's at peace, and our economy is in good health. The inflation rate, which was in double digits when we first took office, is under 4 percent, sizably so. Interest rates have dropped dramatically and are still easing down. And already this year we've seen the creation, this year, so far of more than 900,000 jobs. And last month the Census Bureau reported that between 1983 and '84, the poverty rate in America showed the sharpest drop in 16 years. In all, more than 1,800,000 Americans were lifted out of poverty. Gains were shared by virtually every major group, including children, the elderly, and blacks. Income among Hispanic families rose by a remarkable 6.8 percent, and that was more than double the percent for the rest of us. It all goes to show that the answer to poverty is not more government programs and redistribution. The answer to poverty is economic growth through greater freedom.

And despite all this good news, we can do even better. And I'd like to spend just a moment on our historic new initiative. I'm sure you've heard about it—tax reform. When the income tax first became law back in 1913, the tax code amounted to just 15 pages. Today it runs four volumes, and the complexity alone is staggering. But worse is the unfairness, the simple injustice that the complexity engenders. You just know that with a tax code that complicated, there are going to be accountants and lawyers who know how to make it work to their clients' advantage and that ordinary Americans who can't afford such high-paid advice will end up paying for it with higher taxes.

Today some individuals are able to take so-called educational cruises, ocean luxury liners, to buy sky boxes at sports arenas, and write it all off as business expense. Many Americans pay more in Federal income taxes each year than the giant corporations they work for. Now, I've been preaching the gospel of the enterprise system for more years than I can remember. Business people are the ones who provide many of our jobs, create much of America's wealth, and they have my enduring admiration. What I am against is the unfair tax system that allows some businesses to take perfectly legal deductions that by any standards of fairness are ridiculous.

The key idea in our proposal is that by ironing out the complexities, closing loopholes, making everyone pay their fair share, we can lower tax rates, almost double the personal exemption, make the system more equitable, and do it all without a loss in revenue. Lower tax rates, nearly doubling the personal exemption, end the loopholes—it all adds up to fairness, stronger growth, more jobs, and renewed hope for our future. Well, next summer's a long way off, but if you thought your vacation was good this year, just wait till next August. You see, after being on a horse, the next best thing for a man is lower tax rates. [*Laughter*]

Thank you again for joining us here today. And I'm going to quit with the monolog, and you perhaps have some questions that——

Farm Industry

Q. Mr. President, you have repeatedly warned Congress that you will veto any budget-busting farm bill. A lot of farmers in Minnesota are concerned as to what price to farmers does this administration intend to hold the line on farm spending? And will you, at some point, be forced to either rescue the Farm Credit System or approve a farm bill that exceeds budgetary limits?

The President. First, let me just say that more has been spent since our administration's been here on farm programs than ever in the history of our country. And what we have right now—we believe, incidentally, that the Government programs are the cause of much of the farmers' problem. And we believe that we can't pull the rug out from under an industry that has gotten used to this government participation. That wouldn't be right. But we have an obligation to not only correct what is wrong but to do it in such a way as to not penalize the farmers.

We have a short-term problem—or answer. We're going to do something with regard to those farmers who borrowed—and under the double-digit inflation the land prices were high. Now they've come down with the corraling of inflation, left many farmers out on a limb. We're going to have a short-term program of loans and financial aid for those farmers.

But we want to embark—and this is what we want to work with Congress on—is to have a long-term program that will be pointing to a date certain down the line where we can say to the farmers, as of that point, we're going to phase these programs out, these regulations, and so forth and have you out in the free marketplace as of such and such a year. And we think that this can work, because the two-thirds of farming that is not and never has been included in the Government programs is not part of the great crisis today and is not having the trouble. They have known a consistent increase in the per capita consumption of their produce, where the rest of farming has known a per capita decrease in that consumption.

So, we think that is the way to help the farmers and, at the same time, do all that we can out in the world markets and so forth to see that they get a fair shot at export markets and all.

Q. Mr. President——

The President. Let me take him and then I'll be back——

Central American Conflict

Q. Mr. President, as another priority of your administration, Central America. This weekend, Nicaragua again attacked Honduras. And I wonder, and also know that Honduras wonders, what can the United States do if these attacks continue against Honduras and Costa Rica?

The President. Well, I don't say that I—or I wouldn't talk if I did have anything about a specific thing that we would do. But I thought that Honduras behaved nobly and was well within their rights, because Honduras responded against that battery that, as I understand it, caused casualties on their

side of the border with an aerial strike and took it out. We have been supportive of Honduras and Costa Rica and Guatemala, the other Central American countries. There's no question but all of them have, to a certain extent, been preyed upon by the Sandinista government.

We are, as you know—continue to be supportive of the *contras,* and they are gaining in strength every day. They now number some 20,000. Their goal is to restore the true revolution. The Sandinista government is a totalitarian, Communist government here in the mainland of the Americas, and we feel that all of us have a stake in seeing that they're not allowed to export that revolution to other Latin American countries.

I think there's more of a support and an agreement between the countries of Latin America and the United States than we've known in many years. And we'll do what we can. We have no plans for military action of our own in any Latin American country nor do we think it's necessary; in fact, it isn't wanted by our friends down there. And we're continuing to support the Contadora process and its 21 goals.

Federal Employees

Q. Mr. President, your administration has tried to bring business practices to government to make it run more like a business. The guiding principle of many successful businesses is to treat employees like winners and problemsolvers. Yet as President, many times you've gone on television in speeches around the country and blamed the bureaucrats for the Government's problems that may have been caused by past Presidents or past Congresses. How do you feel about the Federal employee, and what message do you have for them?

The President. I think there are thousands and thousands of Federal employees that are performing a great service for this country and for their fellow citizens, and they're doing a great job. On the other hand, there are some ills of bureaucracy that cannot be overlooked, that programs many times that are started by government in the best of intentions—and then the bureaucracy that is created to manage that program, its first priority becomes to preserve the bureaucracy. And we have to be ready to deal with that. But that isn't to overlook the fact, as I say, of the great service performed by so many government employees. We have reduced the number of government employees, without any loss of service to the people, by—I guess it's around a hundred thousand by now. And we feel that the elected representatives of government have got to determine the policy of government, not the permanent structure.

U.S.-Soviet Relations

Q. Mr. President, first of all, I'm Bill Sharp from Charleston, South Carolina. We would like to have you there. If you would like to come, I have an extra bedroom in the house if you and Mrs. Reagan need a place to stay.

In your upcoming talks with Mr. Gorbachev, do you believe that dealing with a Communist is a Communist is a Communist? That is to say, whether it's Mr. Gorbachev or anybody else, essentially it is dealing with the Communists. And also do you take or seek Mr. Nixon's advice in the upcoming summit?

The President. I have frequently talked with President Nixon. He had great experience and I think is most knowledgeable on international affairs. And certainly he had a number of—well, he had a leader that was there while he was there and had a number of meetings, both in this country and there, with that leader. My problem for the first few years was they kept dying on me. *[Laughter]*

No, I feel, though, that there's one thing that you have to recognize: There are great differences between our two systems. And they're not going to like ours, and we don't like theirs, but we have to live in the world together. And I think one line recently written by former President Nixon was very true. He said of our country, we want peace; he said the Soviet Union needs peace. And they do, with this great, massive buildup, the greatest the world has ever seen in military might.

We have augmented our forces and, I think, have given them reason to believe that we're not going to allow them to get such a superiority in weapons that they can

someday lay down an ultimatum. But I think the thing of the summit and what we would hope to do is to make them recognize that we both have to live in the world together, and it doesn't mean that we have to love each other or that we have to change each other's system, but that we can—there are areas where we can—we're the only two nations in the world, I think, that could start another world war. We're also the two that could prevent one from starting. And we're going to try to find a way to deal practically with them.

Nicaragua

Q. Mr. Reagan, you referred to Nicaragua a while back. The *contras* you're supporting, are they not merely remnants of the Somozista government down there which was in and of itself totalitarian?

The President. I'm glad you asked that question. No, they aren't. There are some there, some that were formerly connected with the National Guard, but there are also a great many who were part of the revolution. What the Sandinistas did—that wasn't their revolution alone, they were just one factor in it of the groups that had come together to oust Somoza. But once they got in, they do what the Communists have traditionally done. Now, their idea of a consensus government is for them to run it. And they ousted other revolutionary leaders; they took over for themselves. Some were exiled; some, I think, were executed; some were imprisoned.

And you have many of the former revolutionaries that are now in the *contras.* And what they're after is reinstituting the goals. Remember that the revolutionaries, 1979, went to the Organization of American States. And they asked the Organization to appeal to Somoza to step down and let the killing end. And the Organization asked, what are the goals of your revolution, and they were given. And the goals were: pluralistic society, democracy, freedom of speech, free labor unions, freedom of press—all the things that go with a democracy. They have never kept one of those promises. As I say, they ousted the rest, and it became the—well, the Sandinista government was a pro-Communist organization before there was a revolution. So, this is what we're trying to bring about, and it isn't just a case of the Somozistas trying to get back in at all.

Q. Mr. President——

Ms. Mathis. One more question.

The President. I promised someone here—then there will be one more after this one.

Tax Reform

Q. Mr. President, according to figures from the Massachusetts Department of Revenue, when you take Social Security tax increases, only the very wealthy will actually be getting decreases according to your tax plan. Now, granted that those Social Security tax increases were passed before you came into office, still, it doesn't seem consistent with your goal of fairness.

The President. The Social Security tax, of course, is—and as you say, has been increased at a time when it looked like—when we came here, we gave Social Security until July of '83—then it would be broke. And then after using the issue in '82 politically, our opponents, shortly after the election, came to us and said, now, what are we going to do about Social Security. They denied it had any problems. And we had a bipartisan commission that reorganized Social Security and has put it on a sound financial footing. The Social Security tax, there's no question many people are paying a higher tax there than they are in the income tax. But there will be a sizable decrease in the overall tax because while they'll still be paying that, they'll be paying much less in their income tax.

Right now our estimate is that between $15,000 and $20,000 a year incomes, the individuals will be getting about a 13½ percent average decrease in taxes. From 20 to 30,000, that will drop to a little under 9 percent, 8.7 percent by our estimates. And as you go up in the income tax brackets—actually the average deduction or cut in taxes is going to get less. So, we think that this is fair from top to bottom. We talked about 3 instead of 14 brackets—15, 25, and 35. There is a fourth bracket—zero—because those people who are down at or near the poverty line are going to be off the tax rolls all together and not pay any tax at all.

So, we think there's no way they can distort the figures. The other day, with all the campaign that's being waged in New York with regard to the one feature of the program—tax, State and local tax deduction—the comptroller of New York has done a study and has estimated that New Yorkers will get $588 million a year in tax cuts. So, I think that we can stand on ours that it is going to be fair and it is going to result in individual as well as a certain business tax decrease. Where we're going to remain revenue neutral is we're going to have some people paying taxes that are not now paying their fair share.

Ms. Mathis. Last question.

Q. Mr. President——

Q. Mr. President, despite your——

The President. I heard this voice a couple of times here before.

Free and Fair Trade

Q. Thank you, Mr. President. Mr. President, everybody believes you're going to veto the textile import after it comes to your desk. Let me ask you, sir, are you going to veto it if it does, and what would you say to textile workers in places like the Carolinas and Virginia who believe that their jobs depend on a bill which would limit foreign imports?

The President. I should have taken one of the—[*laughter*]. Well, first of all, let me say, I have a rule. I never say veto or not veto until something reaches my desk, because what started out be an apple might arrive there an orange. So, I'll wait till that to answer that part of your question.

But now, let me say one thing about this whole idea of protectionism. And, with regard to those employees in industries where they think their—the possibility of losing their jobs, we have a program and we're supporting a program of providing funds for retraining and relocation of people who lose their jobs because of industries of this kind. Remember, also, that we have a lot of people losing their jobs, not because of this, but in other industries because of change in the industries—modern technology that has now made the industry use fewer employees; some things that are just out of date, but other new industries have come along. The truth of the matter is, with regard to jobs, we have the highest percentage of the labor pool employed that we've ever had in the history of our country, the labor pool being everyone in the country, male and female, from 16 to 65—highest percentage of those. Last month 332,000 people found jobs. In the last 33 months, new jobs have been created for more than 8 million people.

So, yes, this can happen. But with protectionism to favor one industry over another, no one ever looks over their shoulder at the retaliation that, then, throws people out of work in other jobs. So, let me say this one thing about protectionism: that it's good to be old enough to remember the Great Depression, which I do. I was looking for my first job in 1932. The Smoot-Hawley tariff was passed, a great protectionist measure. It spread the Depression worldwide; it prolonged it and kept it in existence until World War II after about 10 years—was the only thing that ended the Great Depression. More than a thousand economists appealed to Herbert Hoover to veto the Smoot-Hawley tariff. But there was a classic example of protectionism, overall protectionism, and its result.

Now, I'd like to say a word or two about it. Looking at these last 33 months, 8 million new jobs without the protectionist things that we're asking. And I'd like to point out that this, in coupling with the trade deficit, that has so many people concerned—it'd be nice if we didn't have one, but we're the biggest exporters it is in the world. In these 33 months, we've had this great trade deficit. And I hear this linked to people losing jobs, but we gained 8 million new jobs. In the Great Depression—every one of those 10 years of the Great Depression—we had a trade balance that was in surplus on our side, and yet we had the greatest depression we've ever had in this country.

But protectionism—we want to do, as I say—we will try to help the people that, through no fault of their own, are—if there is a cutback and are going to lose jobs. But, at the same time, we want fair trade, and we've already announced the things we're going to do to try and see that the world can be out there in the free marketplace competing on even ground. We'll do all those things. We will take actions against countries that are unfairly militating against us, keeping us out of their markets or whatever. But there's no way that you can go for protectionism without having it a two-way street and retaliation. And the retaliation will be against others in other industries.

The American farmer knows that most of all—there was a farm question. The American farmer knows—he's one of our biggest exporters now—and he knows that the easiest way to retaliate is against farm exports. So, we're just going to continue to try for free and fair markets and believe that that's the answer that we should have.

Ms. Mathis. Thank you, Mr. President.

Q. Mr. President——

The President. They've told me I've got to—in fact, I am late, aren't I? I've kept you here too long, and I'm sorry. It's just like on those other press conferences—there's always more hands than there are answers. And I'm sorry that I can't get to all of you here, but again, I appreciate very much your being here. It's good to have you from outside the beltway and have a chance to meet with you here. And I hope the briefings you've been getting have been helpful to all of you. And now, I'd better get out of here, or I'll get scolded. [*Laughter*]

Note: The President spoke at 1:12 p.m. at a luncheon for the editors and broadcasters in the State Dining Room at the White House. Susan K. Mathis was Deputy Director of Media Relations.

Nomination of Two Members of the Board of Directors of the United States Institute of Peace
September 16, 1985

The President today announced his intention to nominate the following individuals to be members of the Board of Directors of the United States Institute of Peace for terms of 4 years expiring January 19, 1989. These are new positions.

Dennis L. Bark, of California, is professor of history, emeritus, at the Hoover Institution in Stanford, CA. He served at the Hoover Institution in various capacities including deputy director and senior fellow and executive secretary of the National Peace and Public Affairs Fellows Program. He graduated from Stanford University (B.A., 1964) and the Free University of Berlin (Ph.D., 1970). He was born March 30, 1942, in Appleton, WI, and now resides in Stanford, CA.

Evron M. Kirkpatrick is president of the Helen Dwight Reid Educational Foundation in Washington, DC. Previously he served as executive director of the American Political Science Foundation. He graduated from the University of Illinois (M.A., 1932), Yale University (Ph.D., 1939), and Indiana University (LL.D., 1977). He was born August 15, 1911, in Raub, IN, and now resides in Washington, DC.

Proclamation 5367—Citizenship Day and Constitution Week, 1985
September 16, 1985

By the President of the United States of America

A Proclamation

In this, the commencement year of the 100th anniversary renovation of the Statue of Liberty, Americans are called on to renew and deepen their appreciation of the unique and precious heritage passed on to us by our Founding Fathers. This heritage finds its most sustained and formal expression in the United States Constitution. It is truly a marvel that a group of people assembled from a small population could develop a document capable of guiding the course of this Nation through nearly 200 years of growth to become the greatest on earth. The wisdom and foresight of the architects of the Constitution is manifest in the fact that this dynamic document has required so few amendments over the 198 years of its existence, and has remained a powerful governing tool throughout.

The kind of society our Constitution has created—free and fair and reformable—helps to explain the desire of many foreign nationals to become United States citizens. Last year, over a quarter of a million people, more than ever before in a single year, took the oath of United States citizenship. Clearly the fire of liberty enshrined in the Constitution is not only a hearth to warm, it remains a beacon that draws people from every continent.

How grateful to God all Americans should be that our Constitution remains as Judge David Davis observed more than a century ago: "A law for rulers and people, equally in war and peace, and covers with the shield of its protection all classes of men, at all times, and under all circumstances."

In recognition of the importance of our Constitution and the role of our citizenry in shaping our government, the Congress, by Joint Resolution of February 29, 1952 (36 U.S.C. 153), designated September 17 of each year as Citizenship Day and authorized the President to issue annually a proclamation calling upon officials of the government to display the flag on all government buildings on that day. The Congress, by Joint Resolution of August 2, 1956 (36 U.S.C. 159), also requested the President to proclaim the period beginning September 17 and ending September 23 of each year as Constitution Week.

Now, Therefore, I, Ronald Reagan, President of the United States of America, call upon appropriate government officials to display the flag of the United States on all government buildings on Citizenship Day, September 17, 1985. I urge Federal, State and local officials, as well as leaders of civic, educational, and religious organizations, to conduct appropriate ceremonies and programs that day to commemorate the occasion.

I also proclaim the period beginning September 17 and ending September 23, 1985, as Constitution Week, and I urge all Ameri-

cans to observe that week with fitting ceremonies and activities in their schools, churches, and other suitable places.

In Witness Whereof, I have hereunto set my hand this sixteenth day of September, in the year of our Lord nineteen hundred and eighty-five, and of the Independence of the United States of America the two hundred and tenth.

RONALD REAGAN

[Filed with the Office of the Federal Register, 11:59 a.m., September 17, 1985]

Nomination of United States Representatives and Alternate Representatives to the 40th Session of the United Nations General Assembly
September 17, 1985

The President intends to nominate the following individuals to be Representatives and Alternate Representatives of the United States of America to the 40th Session of the General Assembly of the United Nations:

To Be Representatives:

Vernon Walters, of Florida, Representative of the United States of America to the United Nations and the Representative of the United States of America in the Security Council of the United Nations;

Herbert Stuart Okun, of the District of Columbia, Deputy Representative of the United States to the United Nations;

Gerald B.H. Solomon, United States Representa-

tive from the State of New York;

Daniel A. Mica, United States Representative from the State of Florida; and

John Davis Lodge, of Connecticut, former United States Ambassador to Switzerland (1983–1985).

To Be Alternate Representatives:

Robinson Risner, of Texas, brigadier general, USAF (ret.);

Patricia Mary Byrne, of Ohio, Deputy Representative of the United States in the Security Council of the United Nations—designate;

Joseph V. Reed, of New York, United States Representative to the United Nations Economic and Social Council—designate; and

Hugh Montgomery, of Virginia, Alternate United States Representative to the United Nations for Special Political Affairs.

Appointment of Richard B. Morris as a Member of the Permanent Committee for the Oliver Wendell Holmes Devise
September 17, 1985

The President today announced his intention to appoint Richard B. Morris to be a member of the Permanent Committee for the Oliver Wendell Holmes Devise for a

term of 8 years. He will succeed Philip B. Kurland.

Dr. Morris is the Gouverneur Morris professor emeritus of history at Columbia University. Prior to teaching at Columbia, he was a professor at City University. He was a visiting professor at the University of Hawaii and Princeton University; a distinguished professor at the Free University of Berlin; and a Fulbright research scholar at the Sorbonne. He has served as president of the American Historical Association and of the Society of American Historians. He received a New York State special citation for historic preservation in 1982.

He graduated from City College of New York (A.B., 1924), Columbia University (A.M., Ph.D., 1925, 1930), and Hebrew Union College (L.H.D., 1963). He received his Litt.D. in 1976 from Columbia University and Rutgers University. He is married, has two children, and resides in Mount Vernon, NY. He was born July 24, 1904, in New York City.

The President's News Conference
September 17, 1985

The President. Good evening. Please be seated. I have a statement here.

Economic Growth

We've been pleased to see mounting evidence of new strength in our economy. By following policies of lower taxes and free and fair trade, America has led the world with 33 straight months of growth and more than 8 million new jobs. Inflation has been held under 4 percent. And, meanwhile, nations clinging to high taxes and protectionist policies have not only failed to match our performance, they've lost jobs and seen their investment flow to the United States.

Opportunity is our engine of progress. So, I'm asking Congress to work with me and not against me to control Federal spending, to pass our fair share tax plan lowering rates further, open up closed markets overseas, and urge other nations to cut their high tax rates to strengthen their economies and ability to buy American products. We need stronger growth not just at home but throughout the world. And we must have free and fair trade for all. This is the path of cooperation and success that will make our people more productive and that can lead to a decade of growth and 10 million new jobs in the next 4 years.

But there's another path that can only lead away from opportunity and progress: A mindless stampede toward protectionism will be a one-way trip to economic disaster. That's the lesson of the Smoot-Hawley tariff in 1930, which helped to trigger a world-wide trade war that spread, deepened, and prolonged the worst depression in history. And I know; I lived through that period. I've seen and felt the agony this nation endured because of that dreadful legislation. If we repeat that same mistake, we'll pay a price again. Americans whose jobs depend upon exports of machinery, commercial aircraft, high-tech electronics, and chemical products could well be the first targets of retaliation. Agriculture and industry, already in great difficulty, would be even more vulnerable. Protectionist tariffs would invite retaliation that could enliven a—or deliver, I should say, an economic death blow to literally tens of thousands of American family farms.

We've begun doing many good things for America these last 4½ years. Much remains to be done and can be done. So, let us not place all that progress, all our hopes for the future at risk by starting down on a slippery slope of impulsive acts and imprudent judgment. And this is a time for cool heads and clear vision, and now my vision says that I should call on you, Helen [Helen Thomas, United Press International].

Strategic Defense Initiative

Q. Mr. President, as you head toward the summit, one of the big questions is whether you would be willing to explore the possibility of a tradeoff on the space weapons or big cuts in the Soviet arsenal. And I'd like to follow up.

The President. Helen, no, we're talking

about the Strategic Defense Initiative now. I'm sorry that anyone ever used the appellation Star Wars for it because it isn't that. It is purely to see if we can find a defensive weapon so that we can get rid of the idea that our deterrence should be the threat of retaliation, whether from the Russians toward us or us toward them, of the slaughter of millions of people by way of nuclear weapons. And rather than that kind of negotiation, I think at this summit meeting what we should take up is the matter of turning toward defensive weapons as an alternative to this just plain naked nuclear threat of each side saying we can blow up the other. And I would hope that if such a weapon proves practical, that then we can realistically eliminate these horrible offensive weapons—nuclear weapons—entirely. And I also have to point out that with regard to whether that would be a bargaining chip—which I don't see it as that at all—is the fact that the Soviet Union is already ahead of us in this same kind of research. They have been doing it much longer than us, seeking a defensive weapon also.

Q. And you're really saying, then, that you are not going to negotiate and that you really want to test just to see if it's practical. But aren't you really paving the way toward a militarization of the heavens, because the Soviets are bound to build up a weapon—offensive to counter the Star Wars.

The President. No, the strategic defense that we're seeking is something that can, just as an antiaircraft gun once could protect you against bombers, could be used against these offensive weapons—the missiles. And it doesn't mean no negotiation at all. As a matter of fact, the side that has not been negotiating—with all of our months and months of meetings in Geneva and the arms talks—is the Soviet Union. We have offered at least six versions of a possible reduction and six different ways to enlist their interest in negotiating with us in a reduction of warheads. They have come back with nothing. They simply won't discuss it or negotiate.

But the original idea of weapons in space dealt with the thought that, in addition to the present missiles that we have, that

somebody would place weapons of that kind in orbit in space with the ability to call them down on any target wherever they wanted to in the world, and we agreed. This isn't anything of what we're talking about. We're talking about a weapon that won't kill people; it'll kill weapons. And, as I say, they have been exploring this, but there's a great deal of room for negotiation. The room would be if and when such a weapon does prove feasible, then prior to any deployment, to sit down with the other nations of the world and say, "Here. Now, isn't this an answer?" I don't see it as being something that we would add to our arsenal to increase our ability over them. I see it as the time then that you could say, "Isn't this the answer to any of us having nuclear weapons?"

Federal Support for AIDS Research

Q. Mr. President, the Nation's best-known AIDS scientist says the time has come now to boost existing research into what he called a minor moonshot program to attack this AIDS epidemic that has struck fear into the Nation's health workers and even its schoolchildren. Would you support a massive government research program against AIDS like the one that President Nixon launched against cancer?

The President. I have been supporting it for more than 4 years now. It's been one of the top priorities with us, and over the last 4 years, and including what we have in the budget for '86, it will amount to over a half a billion dollars that we have provided for research on AIDS in addition to what I'm sure other medical groups are doing. And we have $100 million in the budget this year; it'll be 126 million next year. So, this is a top priority with us. Yes, there's no question about the seriousness of this and the need to find an answer.

Q. If I could follow up, sir. The scientist who talked about this, who does work for the Government, is in the National Cancer Institute. He was referring to your program and the increase that you proposed as being not nearly enough at this stage to go forward and really attack the problem.

The President. I think with our budgetary constraints and all, it seems to me that $126 million in a single year for research has got to be something of a vital contribution.

U.S.-Soviet Summit Meeting

Q. Mr. President, why has the United States consistently played down expectations of what will happen at the summit meeting when you meet with Mr. Gorbachev in November, even as the Soviet Union has insisted that summit meetings are for grand and important decisions and sought to raise our expectations. And I'd like to follow up, sir.

The President. Well, it worries me a little bit that they go out of their way to try and raise expectations, in view of summits in the past and what has come of them. Maybe we were overly concerned, but we were worried that there might build up a euphoria and that people would be expecting something of a near miracle to come out of that summit. But I don't mind saying right now, we take this summit very seriously. And we're going to try to get into real discussions that we would hope could lead to a change in the relationship between the two countries—not that we'll learn to love each other; we won't—but a change in which we can remove this threat of possible war or nuclear attack from between us and that we can recognize that, while we don't like their system and they don't like ours, we have to live in the world together and that we can live there together in peace. And we're going to be very serious about that.

Q. Well, sir, that implies that you think that you will be able to reach some sort of agreement. Can you reach agreement? Or do you think that this will be used mainly to get acquainted?

The President. No. This has got to be more than get acquainted, although, that's important, too. As you know, I've said before, I believe that you start solving problems when you stop talking about each other and start talking to each other. And I think it's high time that we talk to each other.

Antisatellite Weapons Testing

Q. Mr. President, the United States has just had its first successful test of an antisatellite weapons system. We showed the Soviet Union that we could do it. Would this not be an ideal time to stop further ASAT tests and negotiate a ban on such weapons?

The President. Well, here again, this is going to take a lot of verification if you're going to try to do that, because, here again, we were playing catch-up. They already have deployed an antisatellite missile. They can knock down and have knocked down satellites that have been sent up in their testing, and they've completed all of that testing. And this was our test, and I don't know whether others are necessary to complete the thing, but we couldn't stand by and allow them to have a monopoly on the ability to shoot down satellites when we are so dependent on them for communication, even weather and so forth.

Gary [Gary Schuster, Detroit News]?

U.S.-Soviet Nuclear and Space Arms Negotiations

Q. Mr. President, thank you. You sent the arms negotiators back to Geneva for the start of the third round of talks that begin in 2 days. Did you send them with any new proposals?

The President. No, because they have a great flexibility, and I sent them back with the same thing that we sent them in in the first place, and that is that we are to be flexible. We know that there is a difference in the Soviet Union's—the emphasis they place on various weapons systems. They have all the same ones we do—airborne, submarine launched, and so forth. Theirs is a little different strategy than ours. So, we said that we proposed a number of warheads as an opener for discussion, that we would reduce to a certain number. As I said earlier, we have presented at least six different ways in which that could be done, and we have made it plain that we're willing to meet whatever are their specific problems with regard to their mix of weapons, that we would find ways to accommodate the differences between us in our strategies.

And so far, they have not made a single comment or proposed a different number. They have just been there. And I don't know how much more flexible we can be, but we're there waiting for them to say,

"Well, that number's wrong; let's try another number," or make a proposal of their own. And in spite of the language that's been used in some of the international broadcasts recently by leaders in the Kremlin, none of those proposals, nothing of that kind has ever come to the table for negotiations.

Sam [Sam Donaldson, ABC News]?

Antisatellite Weapons Testing

Q. Mr. President, we did conduct an antisatellite weapons test the other day, and the Soviets said that that showed you were not serious about curbing the space race and that it complicated the summit. Why was it necessary to make that test now? Couldn't it have waited until after the summit, sir?

The President. No, I don't think so, because, as I said, we're playing catch-up. We're behind, and this was on the schedule that we hoped that we could keep with regard to the development of this weapon. And it wasn't done either because of or with the summit in mind at all. It was simply time for the test. They've been doing it, and we didn't call them any names.

Soviet General Secretary Gorbachev

Q. On the summit, sir, British Prime Minister Margaret Thatcher met Mr. Gorbachev and said, "I like Mr. Gorbachev. We can do business together." Is it necessary, do you think, that you and Gorbachev like each other at the summit in order to do business?

The President. Well, I wasn't going to give him a friendship ring or anything. [*Laughter*] No, seriously, I believe this. I think she made an observation out of this, and our own people who've been over there—our recent group of Senators who met with him found him a personable individual. I'm sure I will, too. It isn't necessary that we love or even like each other. It's only necessary that we are willing to recognize that for the good of the people we represent, on this side of the ocean and over there, that everyone will be better off if we can come to some decisions about the threat of war. We're the only two nations in the world, I believe, that can start a world war. And we're the only two that can pre-

vent it. And I think that's a great responsibility to all of mankind, and we'd better take it seriously.

Chris [Chris Wallace, NBC News], your question the same one as this morning?

Q. No, actually, Helen asked that question. But I've got another one, Mr. President.

The President. All right.

Q. Some people believe that the Soviets are winning the propaganda war leading up to the summit, that Mr. Gorbachev, in recent days, has made a number of proposals for test moratoria, for a chemical free zone in Europe, while the U.S. is testing an antisatellite weapon and, we learned today, a test of a component of SDI. With them talking peace while we're testing weapons of war, is Mr. Gorbachev beating you at your own game?

The President. Well, I've not engaged in a propaganda game. I'm getting ready to go to the meeting and take up some things I think should be discussed. I do think that this is a continuation of a long-time campaign aimed mainly at our allies in Europe and in an effort to build an impression that we may be the villains in the peace and that they're the good guys. I don't think it has registered with our allies, and I'm not going to take it seriously at all. He can practice whatever tactics he wants to. We're going to meet, and we're seriously going to discuss the matters that I've just mentioned here.

Strategic Defense Initiative

Q. Sir, if I could follow up, actually, on Helen's question. You're known as a pretty good negotiator, and some people think that even if you were willing to negotiate on SDI, you wouldn't tell us now; you'd wait for Geneva. Are you telling the American people tonight that you are ruling out any deal with the Soviets at this point on testing, deployment, research, development of SDI?

The President. I'm saying that the research to see if such a weapon is feasible is not in violation of any treaty. It's going to continue. That will one day involve, if it reaches that point, testing. On the other hand, I stop short of deployment, because, as I said then, I'm willing to talk to our allies, talk to them, and talk to the Soviets—to anyone about the meaning of it, if it could be used in such a way as to rid the world of the nuclear threat.

Q. But development and testing—you're ruling out any deal on that? You're ruling out a deal on testing or development?

The President. I think that's a legitimate part of research, and, yes, I would rule that out. I don't mind saying here—and normally I don't talk about—as you said, what's going to be your strategy in negotiations. But in this, this is too important to the world to have us be willing to trade that off for a different number of nuclear missiles when there are already more than enough to blow both countries out of the world.

President's Relationship with Congress

Q. Thank you, Mr. President. You won reelection in an unprecedented landslide, and your personal popularity is standing at an all-time high, yet members of your own party in Congress have failed to follow your leadership on two key policies—South Africa and trade. How do you account for the difference between your popularity and the willingness of the members of your own party to follow your lead, sir?

The President. Oh, I don't think that that's unusual. You're dealing with a Congress and 535 people up there on the Hill who also have their own ideas. I think we're getting along pretty well right now, and we've had meetings on most of these subjects. I made my position clear on the matters that you mentioned—trade and South Africa and all. And as a matter of fact, I thought that our own side, the Republicans, rallied around pretty well when one of the authors of the sanction bill gave that up and heartily approved of my proposed Executive order. So, I don't anticipate too much friction.

Q. May I follow up, Mr. President? On both those issues, you seem to have moved closer to the position of those in Congress. Are you afraid of losing your leadership at a key point in what you call your fall offensive?

The President. No, I'm not afraid of that. And, no, I saw in that bill things that I could say to them, "If that bill came down

without this and this and this, but with these things, I could happily sign it." And then it occurred to me that I could also prove that by writing an Executive order that included those things plus a few of our own, and they seemed to accept it.

South Africa

Q. Mr. President, your sanctions against South Africa seem to have drawn criticism from many sides. Bishop Tutu called you a racist; President Botha says they will impede U.S. efforts to help in the region, and many in Congress are still pressing for stronger measures. What is your answer to these charges, and do you plan to appoint a special envoy to the region as you have in Central America?

The President. I think that when you're standing up against a cellophane wall and you're getting shot at from both sides, you must be doing something right. And if it had all come from one direction, I would have looked again and said, "Well, did I miss something here?" But the very fact that both factions are unhappy—one says it goes too far, and the other one says it doesn't go far enough—I must be pretty near the middle. And what I tried to do was to avoid the kind of sanctions, economic sanctions, that would have militated against the people we're trying to help. And there have been other leaders over there and leaders against apartheid who have been gratified by what we did. So, we'll see what happens.

I've got to call on somebody in a red dress here or Nancy will never forgive me.

U.S. Trade Deficit

Q. Thank you, sir. Thank you, Mr. President. You're looking well, and I'm sure the American people are happy to see you——

The President. Thank you.

Q. ——looking so well. But I have a question. For the first time in 70 years, we have become a deficit nation—since 1914. Does this disturb you? Throughout your political life, you have decried deficit spending and our secondary posture in the world of trade. Do you have a solution for this?

The President. You used the word "deficit"; you mean our trade imbalance?

Q. Yes, the fact that we have become a debtor nation for the first time since 1914.

The President. Are we? I think this false impression that's being given that a trade imbalance means debtor nation. This isn't our government that is expending more than it is for imports than it is getting back in exports. These are the people of our country and the businesses and the corporations and the individual entrepreneurs. On one hand, the American people are buying more than the American people are selling. Incidentally, those figures of export and import have some failings in them, some weak spots. They don't include on exports anything that we're getting back for services. There's a lot of technical things I won't get into, because they get too complicated here, about the difference in the two figures.

But let me point something out about this. The deficit that I'm concerned about, that is the most important, and that can be the biggest problem for us and that must be solved, is the deficit in Federal spending— here, our domestic spending. This is the threat to everything that we hold dear.

But the trade imbalance—from 1890—or 1790 to 1875, this country, all that 85 years, ran a trade imbalance. And in those years, we were becoming the great economic power that we are in the world today. Now, we come up to the present. And in the last 33 months, we have seen more than 8 million new jobs created. Yes, we've lost since 1979 1.6 million jobs in manufacturing, but we've added 9 million new jobs in travel and service industries. We've had this great recovery; we've brought inflation down; the interest rate is coming down—all of these things that we want. This recovery, the greatest one we've known in decades, has been done with this same trade imbalance. Now, in the 1930's, in that depression that I mentioned earlier in my remarks, in that depression, 25-percent unemployment—the worst depression the world has ever known—we had a trade surplus every one of those 10 years until World War II ended the depression.

So, I think this has been exaggerated, and it isn't a case of us being a debtor nation. Another thing we don't count is that from abroad, that is not counted in our export figures are the billions of dollars of foreign capital that has been invested in the United States, invested in our private industries, invested in our government bonds, if you will, things of this kind, because we are the best and safest investment in the world today.

School Attendance of Children With AIDS

Q. Mr. President, returning to something that Mike [Mike Putzel, Associated Press] said, if you had younger children, would you send them to a school with a child who had AIDS?

The President. I'm glad I'm not faced with that problem today. And I can well understand the plight of the parents and how they feel about it. I also have compassion, as I think we all do, for the child that has this and doesn't know and can't have it explained to him why somehow he is now an outcast and can no longer associate with his playmates and schoolmates. On the other hand, I can understand the problem with the parents. It is true that some medical sources had said that this cannot be communicated in any way other than the ones we already know and which would not involve a child being in the school. And yet medicine has not come forth unequivocally and said, "This we know for a fact, that it is safe." And until they do, I think we just have to do the best we can with this problem. I can understand both sides of it.

Back there, back——

Strategic Defense Initiative

Q. Mr. President, why couldn't all the weapons and all the technology that are currently under rubric of the Strategic Defense Initiative be used offensively as well as defensively and thereby defeat your rationale for a strategic defense? Why couldn't lasers and electronic beam weapons be used offensively and defeat the purpose of the program?

The President. Well, I'm sure there must have been some research in things of that kind, but we're definitely seeking a defensive weapon. And one of the things that I believe should be taken up at the summit is to make it plain that we're both willing to look at certainly a mix and see if we can't place more dependence on defensive weapons, rather than on destructive weapons that could wipe out populations.

Q. But, sir, isn't it fair to assume that the Russians, out of their own sense of military security, are bound to consider the possibility that weapons developed under SDI could be used offensively as well as defensively?

The President. Well, I'm not a scientist enough to know about what that would take to make them that way. That isn't what we are researching on or what we're trying to accomplish. And at the moment I have to say the United States—in spite of some of the misinformation that has been spread around—the United States is still well behind the Soviet Union in literally every kind of offensive weapon, both conventional and in the strategic weapons. And we think that we have enough of a deterrent, however, that the retaliation would be more than anyone would want to accept.

So, for 40 years we've maintained the peace, but we've got more years to go, and this threat hangs over all of us worldwide, and some day there may come along a madman in the world someplace—everybody knows how to make them anymore—that could make use of these. It's like when we met in 1925, after the horror of World War I, and in Geneva decided against poison gas anymore as a weapon in war. And we went through World War II and down to the defeat of our enemies without anyone using it, because they knew that everyone had it. But they also knew something else. We outlawed poison gas in 1925, but everybody kept their gas masks. I think of this weapon as kind of the gas mask.

Jerry [Jeremiah O'Leary, Washington Times]?

President Machel of Mozambique

Q. Mr. President, this week you'll be meeting with President Machel of Mozambique, who is a Marxist, but he has turned his back on his Soviet allies to cut off the lines of infiltration from the African National Congress to South Africa. What is the *quid pro quo* in this meeting? In other words, what will you do to make President Machel's action worth what it has probably cost him?

The President. Well, all I know is that for some time now there has been an indica-

tion that he, who had gone so far over to the other camp, was having second thoughts. We just think it's worthwhile to show him another side of the coin, and we think it's worth a try to let him see what our system is and see that he might be welcome in the Western World. And that's why I'm meeting with him.

I know I should go over here. Yes.

Espionage

Q. Mr. President, I'd like to turn, if I might, to the subject of the recent spy scandals and ask you a two-part question. Do the string of West German defections mean that the United States must cut back the amount of sensitive information it shares with NATO? And secondly, does the Walker spy scandal in the United States suggest to you that perhaps we should reduce the Soviet presence in this country?

The President. Well, we've always been aware of the fact that the Soviets had, undoubtedly, more agents in this country than any personnel that we had in theirs; this has been very much on our minds. I don't know just how you can evaluate what might have been compromised. The Walker case somehow doesn't seem to look as big as it did a short time ago now with what we've seen happening in the other countries. I think that if there has been damage, it's been done already with what they could have conveyed both ways in this. You know, England, at the same time, has got the defectioners from the KGB that have now come to them with information that certainly must make a lot of agents throughout the world wonder when they're going to feel a tap on their shoulder. And we just have to play with this the best we can and hope that, together and between us all, we can establish some means of identifying better those who are loyal.

Q. Can I follow up on that and ask again the first part of the question, and that is whether you feel that now, given these defections in West Germany, that perhaps it's time for us to reevaluate just how much information we share with some of our allies in Europe?

The President. Oh, I think there's reevaluating that's going on all over the world on that, and I'm sure here, too.

Free and Fair Trade

Q. Yes, Mr. President, just returning to trade specifically for a minute. Members of Congress who support the so-called Textile and Apparel Protection Act claim that the U.S. adherence to free trade and our allies' adherence to unfair trade practices has not only cost the jobs of 300,000 workers since 1980 but forced companies here to close down even the newest, most efficient plants in the world. Now, if the shoe were on the other foot, Mr. President, and you represented a textile apparel producing State, how would you explain the President's reluctance to support a bill that seems to be the last, best hope for those industries and also for the 2 million remaining workers in those industries?

The President. Well, again, protectionism is a two-way street. And there is no way that you can try to protect and shield one industry that seems to be having these competitive problems without exposing others. No one ever looks over their shoulder to see who lost their job because of protectionism. We do know the history of the Smoot-Hawley tariff and what it did. There were over a thousand economists that sought the President out at the time and begged him to veto that bill. But in this one with a single industry, if there is an unfairness—and we've already made that plain and made it evident—we are going to, if they're taking advantage in some way in another country, competing unfairly with us—we're going to take action on those items. For almost 2 years now, I have been begging our allies and trading partners in the GATT, the general tariff program, to join with us in another round of trade talks to again eliminate whatever holdovers there are of discrimination against someone else's products getting into their country or subsidizing sale at less than production cost in other countries. These things we'll do and we'll do vigorously.

But just plain protectionism—let me point out another problem that no one has considered. You take one product—that kind—and you look at the list of countries, and then you find out we're the biggest exporter in the world. Then you find out that in some of these countries, if we punish them for that one product, we happen to have a trade surplus in that country. How can they stand by on the one thing they're exporting successfully and then say, "But we're buying more from you than we're selling to you in your country." So, there just is no excuse for protectionism that is simply based on legitimate competition and curbing that competition.

Q. May I follow up, Mr. President? If the current bills which are on the Hill now seeking sweeping trade protectionism were enacted, do you foresee somewhat of a, might say, reenactment of Smoot-Hawley which led to the Depression or certainly deepened it? Do you feel there is a cause and effect there?

The President. I don't know. I think there are probably some individuals that haven't learned the lesson or haven't lived long enough to have been around when the Great Depression was on. That's one of the advantages of being a kid my age.

Ms. Thomas. Thank you, Mr. President.

Note: The President's 32d news conference began at 8 p.m. in the East Room at the White House. It was broadcast live on nationwide radio and television.

Remarks at a White House Reception for Members of the Future Farmers of America
September 18, 1985

The President. Well, and already I've met someone from my hometown, Dixon, Illinois. Thank all of you. It is wonderful to have you visit here in the Rose Garden, where you can still see a little of the summer's crop is left.

I have been very interested in the Future Farmers of America, your program of building our American communities. And I commend all of you individually for your wonderful work in helping our rural communities. It's gratifying to me to see young people like yourselves volunteering your time to keep these communities strong. And everything you've done, including OPERATION: Care and Share and working with local churches and various groups and other private sector initiatives, is indispensable to the future of our farm communities.

I want you to know that I've been thinking about the problems of the farm these past few years. In fact, we're, all of us here in this big house, constantly concerned about the challenges faced by American farmers during these difficult days. We're a farming nation. We always have been. The American farmer not only feeds this country that is 238 million strong, the American farmer feeds the world. And so when we contemplate the problems farmers are facing these days, we realize that we are dealing with a problem that speaks to the heart of how America lives and what America is.

A while back I received a letter from a daughter of a farmer in Louisiana. She wrote of how she remembered her father—up at last light, no time for breakfast, out milking the cows, gathering eggs, feeding the dogs. She spoke of how always in a farmer's day something will break down, and her father would have to fix it. And then he would hit the fields with the tractor and the earth tiller, and he wouldn't mind because "a farmer is part of the ground he works." But she ended it with these words addressed to all: "Don't you think it is time to say thanks to the farmer? After all, you stick your feet under his table every day." Well, those are wonderful words, and they shine with truth. But we do thank the farmer. And when you go home, will you tell your parents how we feel?

We've been trying to encourage a national farm bill that will help the farmer and ensure that you have a future in farming by making American agriculture more competitive. We want to put the agriculture industry on a firm and sound basis once and for all so that by the time you're ready to own and work a farm, you can count on being part of a strong and vibrant industry. And my great hope for you, for those of you who do aspire to farm for a living, is that you will be as wonderful as your parents are—those people who are feeding a great nation and the world. They are the mainstay, the backbone of a great country. And I've got a little special place in my heart that's devoted to them alone.

It's been wonderful to have you here, and I thank you all for coming. I'd like to just add something here. You know, about 135 years ago a Frenchman came to this country because this country had already become the great economic powerhouse that it has continued to be. His name was Alexis de Tocqueville, and he toured all over this country, as he said, looking for the secret of our greatness. And he told some wonderful things. We are pretty unique in all the world with things like you, yourselves, are doing—volunteer programs where people set out to help others, to help their neighbors. It's pretty traditionally American. And he described it as how, he said, a man would see a problem, and he wouldn't call the Government. He'd cross the street and talk to a friend, and pretty soon a committee would be formed. And, he said, they would solve the problem. And then in his book to his own countrymen in France, he said, and you won't believe this, but there wouldn't be a bureaucracy involved at any time in solving that problem. But he found the secret of America, and he also put this in his book. He said he had looked in the busy harbors; he'd looked in our industrial cities; he'd looked all over for the secret of our greatness. And then he said he looked in our churches, and he heard our pulpits aflame with righteousness. And he said America is great because America is good. And if America ever ceases to be good, America will cease to be great.

Well, I've taken more than my time here because I've got to get in Marine One out there on the South Lawn in just a few minutes and head off for New Hampshire with some of our people and talk to the people up there. And you are all invited to go on over there and—you girls, it will kind of blow your hairdos a little bit when we take off. [*Laughter*] We'll shortly be taking off in Marine One, as it's called, out to get on Air Force One.

So, again, thank you all for being here. God bless all of you.

Mr. Meredith. Mr. President, you have long been recognized as having a tremendous desire to serve both education and agriculture, a desire reflected by the appointment of Secretaries Bennett and Block to serve this nation. As young people preparing for careers in the agriculture industry, and as part of a vocational education program in agriculture, we're excited about our futures. In particular, we are pleased to have you as a part of this national FFA conference on community development and would like to present you with this special gift from the Future Farmers of America and R.J. Reynolds Industries, Incorporated, and invite you to attend the 58th National FFA Convention, with over 22,000 members in attendance, November 14 through the 16th, in Kansas City, Missouri. Thank you.

[*At this point, the President was presented with a clock.*]

The President. Well, thank you all very much. I am very proud and pleased to have this. I have to tell you that there have been times when I hear a ticking I worry a little bit. [*Laughter*] In this case I figure it must be all right. But thank you all very much, and this will see that I get on the helicopter on time, as well as everyplace else. Thank you all.

Note: The President spoke at 9:14 a.m. in the Rose Garden at the White House. Paul Kidd Meredith was assistant director of the Future Farmers of America.

Remarks to Citizens in Concord, New Hampshire
September 18, 1985

The President. Governor Sununu, Senators Humphrey and Rudman, Mayor Coeyman, and you have two fine Congressmen—Smith and Gregg—whose wives are representing them here. But instead of coming here, they had to stay on the floor of the House of Representatives and defend yours and my interests, which they are now doing. And all of you ladies and gentlemen. You know, I was told that some time ago Lafayette spoke here. And I wasn't around at the time—[*laughter*]—but they said that his crowd was bigger than the crowd today. I don't know about that, but I'll bet he wasn't any happier than I am today.

It's a great pleasure to be with so many old friends. New Hampshire has a special place in my heart. I came here, as the Governor told you, in 1980 asking for your help. I know that many of you were active in that campaign, and together we started something that has changed the face of the Nation. And I'm going to continue trying to keep that change going until the Federal Government looks a little bit more like New Hampshire. Let me just take this opportunity to express to you my heartfelt appreciation. Thank you, New Hampshire.

A lot of political pros come up here to test the waters. And I don't know why—I'm going to let that remind me of a story. I heard about one who was driving on a back road up here. And he looked out and noticed that there was a chicken running alongside the car, and he couldn't believe what he was seeing. So, he stepped on the gas, and the chicken kept up with him. Then he spurted ahead to about 70 miles an hour, and all of a sudden the chicken went by him and turned down a side road. Well, now he was really intrigued because he thought the chicken looked like it had three legs. So, he turned down the side road and found himself in a farmer's barnyard, and the farmer was standing there. And he pulled up, and he said, "Pardon me, but did you see a chicken go by here?" And he says, "Yep. It's one of mine." Well, he said, "I don't know whether I'm crazy or not, but tell me, it looked like it had three legs." And the farmer says, "Yes, I breed them that way." He says, "You breed them that way. Why?" "Well," he says, "I like the drumstick; Ma likes the drumstick; and now we got Junior, and he likes the drumstick. I just got tired of fighting over them." [*Laughter*] And the fellow says, "Well, how did it taste?" He says, "I don't know. We haven't been able to catch one yet." [*Laughter*]

Well, I hope that, unlike that farmer, the American people are beginning to enjoy the fruits of what we set out to do. There was a monster loose in our land back in 1980; inflation was running at double digits for 2 years in a row. It was destroying the economic well-being of our people and tearing at the fabric of our free society. But we've put that monster in a cage and brought inflation under control. The latest figures have it running something well under 4 percent, and we're not going to stop until there isn't any inflation at all. Have we made a difference? You bet we have.

Our economy was in serious trouble, and today we've enjoyed 33 straight months of economic growth. Retail sales are up; personal income is up; overall unemployment is down to 6.9 percent, and more Americans are working than ever before in our history. And if someone cynically says, "Well, that's because there are more Americans today"—no, the employment pool is considered to be everyone, male and female, between the ages of 16 and 65 are part of the employment pool. Well, today the highest percentage of that employment pool is employed than ever in the history of our nation.

I think there's reason for optimism on the trade front as well. American industry has become vastly more efficient in the last few years. There's been a jump in worker productivity, and our tax rate reductions have stimulated heavy investment in new technology. This is the way to a more competitive America and lasting progress. What we can't be nor do is be stampeded into the dark hole of protectionism, igniting a trade war that will undercut everything we've accomplished and, in the long run, throw mil-

lions of Americans out of work. The last trade war we fought was back in the 1930's. We brought it on ourselves with the Smoot-Hawley tariff. It was called the Great Depression. I was looking for my first job in that Great Depression. What we must do, and what we're committed to do, is to see to it that there is free and fair and open trade on both sides of the ocean.

We have created more than 8 million new jobs since this recovery began 33 months ago. Many of those jobs flowed from a tidal wave of new small business activity. Well over a million businesses were incorporated in the last 2 years, most of them small operations, each the entrepreneurial dream of one individual. The grassroots free enterprise can keep America number one. On November 22d there will be a meeting of the White House Conference on Small Business here in Concord to get New Hampshire's input on how to further expand the opportunities on Main Street America. I urge you to participate and to make your voices heard.

New Hampshire already has a strong voice in Washington, and I want to thank you for sending one of the best delegations of any State to Washington. Senators Humphrey and Rudman and Representatives Smith and Gregg are doing a terrific job in your behalf and in behalf of America.

The way to progress is not, as some in the Nation's Capital would have us believe, to harness the energy of the American people by centrally directing it from Washington. Do any of you want to be harnessed by the Government planners?

Audience. No-o-o!

The President. The way to a better life for all Americans is to free the energy of our citizens, to let you the people make decisions with your own lives, and to do that by getting the Government out of your way. That's the plan for a more prosperous future. With freedom and the profit motive, there's nothing we can't do. It's frightening to think of where we would be now had we permitted government policies of the last decade, with their disastrous economic consequences, to continue. Instead, together we set America on a new course, and because we stuck to our principles, life is improving.

One of the accomplishments of which I am most proud is the turnaround that we've seen in poverty. When I campaigned here and throughout the country back in 1980, I said, and still firmly believe, the best cure for poverty is a strong and growing economy. The answer to helping those in need is not more welfare, government programs, and dependency; the answer is growth, jobs, and opportunity. Well, after years of progress, the number of poor people in America surged sharply upward in 1979, as the tax, tax, spend, and spend philosophy of the previous administration came on line. Well, it took time to put our program in place, time to reverse previous trends, but as our program began to take hold in 1983, when it was finally fully in place—contrary to certain news accounts—that increase in poverty, which had continued since 1979 and increased, ground to a halt. And last year we witnessed one of the largest reductions in the number of people living in poverty in history—1.8 million people lifted into new lives of progress and hope.

One of the cornerstones of our economic program was a 25-percent across-the-board reduction in the tax rates. In the years before we got to Washington, taxes had been skyrocketing. The Federal tax take doubled just between 1976 and 1981, siphoning off strength and resources from the private sector and undermining any chance for economic growth. Our economy was being bled dry, and the liberals acted surprised when they found the patient was barely breathing. Well, we put a stop to the tax spiral by offsetting tax increases built into the system. Without our changes, an average family of four with two earners in America would have paid $2,544 more in taxes in these last few years. I'm sure that being able to keep $2,544 more of your money has been good for you and for your family. Offsetting the built-in tax increases was a good start, and it's paid off with more investment, more jobs, and better times for everyone.

Well, that was step one; now it's time to finish the job. Taxes are still too high. The system is unfair and too complicated. It encourages people to channel their resources

into tax shelters rather than job-creating investment. It's a boon to the tax experts and accountants and a drag on just about everyone else. There are politicians in Washington—some of the same ones who constructed this tax code monstrosity—who say that you, the American people, are not interested in tax reform. Well, that's why I came here. I want to simplify the system and overhaul it from top to bottom. I want to bring down the rates and close up the loopholes. Are those politicians right when they say you don't care?

Audience. No-o-o!

The President. Can I count on your support to finish the job that we began in 1981?

Audience. Yes!

The President. Thank you. You just made my day. Your representatives here and I will give them in Washington your message personally.

We propose to reduce the 14 tax brackets down to 3—15 percent, 25 percent, and 35 percent. Virtually everyone will be paying at a lower rate. At the same time, we'll be closing loopholes that distort economic choices, do nothing to improve our economy, and are downright unfair. Now, let's not blame those who are using legal but unfair loopholes and writeoffs. Let's just change the system so all of us are treated the same.

Now, one of the writeoffs we're talking about concerns State taxes. Less than 40 percent of all taxpayers—usually the more well-to-do—use this writeoff. The majority use the short form and don't itemize; so you don't get advantage of that as a deduction. So, even for the people within the same State and within the same community, it is unfair. It is even more unjust for those who live, as you do, in low-tax States. Thanks to the responsible leadership of Governors like John Sununu and his predecessors, New Hampshire is, as I said, one of the low-tax States. So, in effect, the current system rewards rich States with big budgets and high taxes. You people who've been responsible and kept your budgets low don't receive an equal benefit, and that's no way to run a Federal tax system.

What we want is a tax system that encourages prudent management of resources, a system that rewards those who work by permitting them to keep more if they produce more. We want the ingenuity and creative talents of the American people channeled into beating the competition instead of focusing on beating the tax collector with schemes and maneuvers. We want a system that's good for the American family. We want a new tax system for all Americans, a fair share tax plan for everyone. So, we propose raising the standard deduction for the American family to $4,000 and nearly doubling the personal exemption to $2,000. The political establishment back in Washington says you don't care about these things. Well, I say the Washington establishment is out of touch with the American people. America wants tax reform, and America deserves tax reform, and if we stand together, America is going to get tax reform.

You know, one cannot come to this spot without remembering what New Hampshire has meant to America. The tranquility of your countryside, your lakes and forests, the majesty of your wooded hills and mountains gave birth to a new breed of people—people respectful of God, fiercely independent, and unafraid to stand up and be counted. In 1976, and then again in 1980, I traveled through your beautiful State, speaking at city halls and school gymnasiums and town meeting halls. And if anyone doubts that democracy is alive and well, let them come to New Hampshire. "Live free or die" is more than a motto. It's more than a motto; it's a way of life that we're bound and determined to preserve. And you know something? I don't think you'd be unhappy if a lot more of the other 49 neighboring States would adopt that same motto and we'd adopt it in Washington.

The American Revolution that began here never died. It, too, started over unjust taxation. King George underestimated how much the people cared about this issue. Don't you think it's time for a second American revolution? And we'll win this one, too, together. We'll overhaul our tax structure. We'll continue building a society where people are free and opportunity is unlimited—one nation under God, with liberty and justice for all.

And now, before I thank you for letting me be here today, I just have a little news note. There has been some information already that has leaked out about it. And I can tell the press that they're supposed to wait around because you're going to get a briefing from some others. I'm pleased to inform you, if you haven't heard, that Reverend Benjamin Weir, who was held hostage for 18 months in Lebanon, has now been released. I talked with Reverend Weir on Air Force One this morning. And I'm happy for him and his family. But I will not be satisfied and will not cease our efforts until all the hostages, the other six, are released.

The Vice President plans to meet with the families of the six remaining hostages on Friday, when they will be in Washington. And, as I said, a briefing for the press will occur here after I depart. But I want to tell you that, on the plane, knowing about this and knowing that we had him back in America, safe with his family, I wasn't going to say anything because we were going to make the announcement from Washington at 12:30 p.m. And then when I saw that someplace along the line some information had leaked and that I would be here until about 12:20 p.m., I thought, well, I'll just jump the gun on the fellows in Washington and tell you about it. So, we were trying to keep it so quiet because we don't want to do anything that endangers the chances of the other six.

But now, God bless you all, and thank you for letting me be with you here today. Thank you very much.

Note: The President spoke at noon outside the statehouse. He was introduced by Gov. John H. Sununu. Following his remarks, the President returned to Washington, DC.

Statement by the Deputy Press Secretary for Foreign Affairs on the Release of Reverend Benjamin Weir in Lebanon
September 18, 1985

We are pleased to inform you that Reverend Benjamin Weir has been released 18 months after he was taken hostage in Lebanon. We are obviously happy for Reverend Weir and his family and friends, but we will not be satisfied and will not cease our efforts until all hostages—American, French, and British—have been released. This is top priority for the Reagan administration. Since the first American was seized, the President has been directly engaged in intensive efforts to liberate our citizens. He will remain involved until all of our citizens have been liberated.

This morning the President spoke to Reverend Weir, expressing relief at his release and determination to see the others freed. While there was no linkage between the release of the Atlit prisoners and the freeing of our hostages, we have hoped that repatriation of the Atlit prisoners would improve the atmosphere in the region. We, therefore, intensified our efforts when the Atlit release occurred. Thus far, these efforts have resulted in the liberation of Reverend Weir, for which we are grateful. Our efforts are continuing in order to obtain the release of the other six hostages. I am not going into any further detail on the release of Reverend Weir or what measures we are taking to obtain the release of the others because it might interfere with these efforts.

The Vice President plans to meet with the families of the six remaining hostages on Friday, when they will be in Washington. He will review for them what can be shared on our efforts to obtain release of the remaining hostages and to assure them of the administration's determination to continue these efforts.

Note: Edward P. Djerejian read the statement to reporters at 12:35 p.m. during a press briefing in the statehouse cafeteria in Concord, NH.

Nomination of Mary L. Walker To Be an Assistant Secretary of Energy
September 18, 1985

The President today announced his intention to nominate Mary L. Walker to be an Assistant Secretary of Energy (Environment, Safety, and Health). She would succeed William Addison Vaughan.

Since 1984 Ms. Walker has been serving as Deputy Solicitor of the Department of the Interior. Previously, she was Deputy Assistant Attorney General, Land and Natural Resources Division, Department of Justice, in 1982–1984; associate (1976–1979) and partner (1979–1982) in the law firm of Richards, Watson, Dreyfuss & Gershon in Los Angeles, CA; and an attorney with Southern Pacific Transportation Co. and subsidiaries in 1973–1976.

Ms. Walker graduated from the University of California at Berkeley (A.B., 1970) and Boston University Law School (J.D., 1973). She was born December 1, 1948, in Dayton, OH, and now resides in Bethesda, MD.

Accordance of the Personal Rank of Ambassador to John J. Crowley, Jr., While Serving as Head of the United States Delegation to the Annual Meeting of the Inter-American Council for Education, Science, and Culture
September 18, 1985

The President today accorded the personal rank of Ambassador to John J. Crowley, Jr., in his capacity as head of the U.S. delegation to the annual meeting of the Inter-American Council for Education, Science, and Culture. Mr. Crowley is presently Deputy Permanent Representative of the United States of America to the Organization of American States as well as the U.S. Representative to the 16th meeting of the Inter-American Council on Education, Science, and Culture.

He served in the United States Army in 1946–1948. He was an instructor at the University of Puerto Rico in 1950–1952. Mr. Crowley joined the Government in 1952 as a public affairs assistant in Maracaibo, Venezuela, with the International Communication Agency. He entered the Foreign Service in 1955 and became consular and political officer in Lima, Peru. In 1959–1960 he attended advanced labor and economic studies at the University of Wisconsin and then served as labor and political officer in Brussels, Belgium, in 1960–1964. He then

returned to the Department as an international relations officer until 1966 when he went to serve as deputy chief of mission in Quito, Ecuador, until 1969. Mr. Crowley then attended the National War College. In 1970–1974 he served as deputy chief of mission in Santo Domingo, Dominican Republic. In 1974 he was assigned in the Department as Director of the Office of Northern European Affairs until 1977 when he became deputy chief of mission in Caracas, Venezuela. In 1980 he was appointed Ambassador to the Republic of Suriname and served there until 1981 when he became a senior inspector in the Department. Since 1982 he has been Deputy Permanent Representative of the United States to the Organization of American States.

Mr. Crowley was born February 10, 1928, in Albuquerque, NM. He graduated from West Virginia University (A.B., 1949) and Columbia University (M.A., 1950). His foreign languages are French and Spanish. Mr. Crowley is married to the former Ileana Cintron and has two daughters.

Remarks at a White House Barbecue for Members of Congress
September 18, 1985

The President. Thank you very much, and welcome to the White House. I'm glad you could all make it here this evening. And Mickey is the sometime cowboy to an urban cowboy. That was just wonderful, and thank you very much. You know, we have a music hall here in Washington, too. It's up there on a hill; it's called the Capitol. [*Laughter*] And we got lots of vocal talent, but— [*laughter*]—but we're not always so good when it comes to carrying the harmony. [*Laughter*] That's why I always enjoy these get-togethers with Congress. Rest of the

year we have our differences, but times like these allow us just a moment to stop being Republicans and Democrats and just eat— [*laughter*]—and enjoy.

Now, you won't mind, will you, if I tell them a little thing here that I understand happened at Mickey Gilley's restaurant?

Q. Did we lose the mike?

The President. Did we?

That one sounds better than this one, or maybe I'll get a feedback if I get to use them all? [*Laughter*]

Well, anyway, I understand that a real

tough young cowboy came in one night and said to one of your waiters there, "I want a real rare steak." In about 3 minutes, the waiter was back with a platter and a steak on it, and the kid took one look at it and says, "Take it back." And he said, "You said you wanted a real rare steak." And the kid said, "I've seen cows hurt worse than this get up and walk away." [*Laughter*]

Now, I only did that as an excuse to just tell a little something that I saw in the Milwaukee Journal not too long ago that actually might—you could stretch it, and it might apply to the activities of all of us—our friends out here and myself and things we go through. This was a woman that's been reading about all the crime and the violence and so forth and became frightened enough that she started studying judo. And she really did; she studied and she went through all the stages of that till she was a master of the art all the way to the very top. And then one night, the thing she dreaded happened. She was walking down the street—it was about 9:30—and a fellow stepped out of a doorway and grabbed her, this judo expert. She hit him over the head with her umbrella. [*Laughter*]

So, again, I just want to say that, because although the executive branch may complain about the legislative branch a lot and vice versa, the U.S. Congress remains the greatest invention in self-government this world has ever seen, and all of you in the Senate and the House do it proud. Maybe it's natural that in the heat of legislative combat we focus on our differences, but this season let's also try to remember how much we have in common—the great love we have for this blessed land of ours and our desire that comes before all else to do what's best for America. As I said, we've got a lot of work to do this fall.

Speaking for Nancy and myself, let me just say again what a great pleasure it is to have all of you here. And now, once again, and I think speaking for all of you—and this time you won't mind if I speak for you—and that is, Mickey and all of your talented artists here, God bless you, and thank you very much for the generous and warm way you've entertained us.

Note: The President spoke at 7:59 p.m. on the South Lawn of the White House. The entertainment for the barbecue was provided by country singer Mickey Gilley.

Nomination of John A. Gaughan To Be Administrator of the Maritime Administration
September 19, 1985

The President today announced his intention to nominate John A. Gaughan to be Administrator of the Maritime Administration, Department of Transportation. He would succeed Harold E. Shear.

Mr. Gaughan is presently serving as Deputy Assistant Secretary for Governmental Affairs at the Department of Transportation. Previously, he was Director of the Office of External Affairs, Maritime Administration, in 1984; congressional relations officer in the Office of the Secretary of Transportation in 1981–1984; an attorney for the Federal Maritime Commission in 1980–1981; Deputy Chief, Legislative Division, in the Office of the Chief Counsel at the U.S. Coast Guard Headquarters in 1978–1979; and on the U.S. Coast Guard House/Senate Liaison staff, U.S. Coast Guard Headquarters, in 1973–1978.

Mr. Gaughan graduated from the U.S. Coast Guard Academy (B.S., 1970) and the University of Maryland Law School (J.D., 1977). He is married and resides in Bethesda, MD. He was born March 29, 1947, in Washington, DC.

Remarks Following Discussions With President Samora Moises Machel of Mozambique
September 19, 1985

President Reagan. It has been a pleasure for me today to meet with President Machel of Mozambique. At a time when much attention is focused on southern Africa, my meeting with the President underscores the determination of the United States to continue playing an active and constructive role in this volatile portion of the globe. The United States prides itself as a force for freedom and progress and stability, and this is true in southern Africa, as in other parts of the world. We seek to encourage the development of democratic government in all the nations of southern Africa. Democracy and the respect for fundamental human liberties are not only consistent with our values as a free people but are also the surest pathway to economic progress, internal reconciliation, and international peace.

President Machel, you have already taken a step toward peace. And because of your personal foresight and courage, cross-border violence in the region has been reduced and a more constructive relationship with South Africa has begun. These efforts already have proven to be a great boon to the well-being of your people. We know that economic recovery and development will require the restoration of peace, a process which will call upon all the statesmanship of Mozambique's leaders.

Mozambique has suffered greatly in the last decade from drought, domestic violence, and economic dislocation. I was impressed today with President Machel's sincere desire to improve the lot of his people. The United States, as is true in other African countries, is doing what it can to alleviate the worst effects of the drought. We are now also involving ourselves in a major effort to rebuild Mozambique's shattered economy. We welcome Mozambique's decision to cooperate with the International Monetary Fund and the World Bank to design a program of economic stabilization and development. Encouraging Western investment and strengthening Mozambique's private sector is a formula for economic advancement and improving the quality of life. We know you will find, President Machel, that the freer people are in the arena of economics, the more enterprising they become and the more benefits are enjoyed by the society as a whole.

I was glad to have had this opportunity today to express personally to President Machel America's good will toward the people of his country. We look forward to the success of his economic initiatives and movement toward national unity. Thank you, President Machel, for your visit to the United States.

President Machel. Thank you very much. We have come here on an official visit at the invitation of President Ronald Reagan. We say a sincere thank you for this friendly gesture. Our aim in this visit is to strengthen existing bilateral relations and define a basis for the long-term development of these relations. I have just had a very positive, fruitful, and constructive meeting with President Ronald Reagan. I had the opportunity to express our appreciation for the food and development aid that the United States of America has granted us.

Mozambique is an independent and nonaligned African country. We value our independence. We are proud of our independence. We are intransigent in the defense of our national interest. We firmly believe that, like ourselves, each people must determine the destiny of its own country. Our chief concern is to solve the basic problems of our people and to make the region where we live one of peace, stability, good-neighborliness, cooperation, and development.

In this context, we signed with the Republic of South Africa the Nkomati agreement, an essential condition for peace and development. The People's Republic of Mozambique has strictly complied with the Nkomati agreement. The need for the urgent elimination of apartheid is a matter of common concern. Mozambique took a positive view of the efforts of the international community, including the United States, in this regard. We hope that such efforts continue and that they lead to the independence of Namibia, to peace and stability for the whole of southern Africa.

Mozambique is still a backward and underdeveloped country, but one with vast potential and natural resources. We seek the participation of the United States and of its private sector in putting those resources at the service of our economic and social development. I am convinced that the meeting I have just had with President Ronald Reagan has established a solid basis for long-term cooperation in all fields between Mozambique and the United States. With mutual respect and reciprocal advantages, we shall develop the friendship which we all seek. So, thank you very much, Mr. President.

Note: President Reagan spoke at 1:25 p.m. at the South Portico of the White House. President Machel spoke in Portuguese, and his remarks were translated by an interpreter. Earlier, the two Presidents met in the Oval Office.

Interview With Pat Robertson of the Christian Broadcasting Network
September 19, 1985

Administration Accomplishments

Mr. Robertson. The 40th President of the United States. When historians write about the Reagan administration, what do you want them to say?

The President. You know, I've been asked that, and I guess I have to say, I've never thought that far ahead. I'm so busy thinking about what we want to accomplish. I guess maybe just that I helped perpetuate this great American dream.

Administration Goals

Mr. Robertson. What do you hope for in the next 3 years?

The President. There are so many things. I would like to get us definitely on the pattern of reducing the deficit so that the balanced budget is in view. I would like to have, then, going into effect at that time a balanced budget amendment so we could never again go a half a century, as we have, of regularly deficit spending each year. And I would like to see us also have some plan for beginning installments to start reducing the national debt, as we have done many times in the past. There are a number of things that I would like to see—resolve the problem of prayer in schools and have us on the road, a good solid road that could make us optimistic about the chances for peace.

Budget Deficit and Tax Reform

Mr. Robertson. On the budget deficit, it seems as if members of your own party are not totally in accord with you. The Congress hasn't supported you. Are you optimistic? David Stockman said maybe this is the last chance, but you're optimistic about the future?

The President. Yes, I am. There's no way that anyone could ever balance the budget in 1 year. This budget, over the years, has been structurally built into our budgeting process. And the difficulty, of course, is getting agreement not on the need to reduce it—everyone seems to agree on that—but then trying to get them to agree on, well, where do you apply the tourniquet and shut off that hemorrhage of funds. But I think that we're on the beginning of a track where we can see a progression of reducing the deficit as a percentage of gross national product.

You know, if you just count the deficit in dollars—and it looks so horrifying—and you say, "How did this ever happen?" Well, if you look at it back over these 50 years of deficit spending on the basis of what it is as a percentage of gross national product, that, too, has been growing bigger. So, it isn't as far out of line with past deficits; some of them were just about as big as this one is in that percentage. But if we can get on a percentage to where, for these next 3 years—what we have in mind is if we can get it next year down to 4 percent of the gross national product, 3 percent the following year, 2 percent the next year, we think that that progression will point us to, by 1990, a balanced budget and then you could have go into effect the balanced budget amendment.

Mr. Robertson. I spoke to an influential Republican Senator on Sunday who felt that, possibly, the tax reform measure might be diverting attention away from deficit reduction. Do you see that as a complement to it or possibly a stimulant for it?

The President. Actually, a stimulant for it in a way, because if you look back, not just in our administration and what we did in 1981 when we implemented—or began implementing our tax cuts, but go back to President Kennedy's across-the-board tax cut, before that to President Coolidge and the tax cuts that he implemented—in every instance the economic growth has resulted in the Government getting more revenues at the lower rates than it was getting at the higher rates. So, I think this tax reform very definitely would help. It isn't aimed at being a part of that, but it would help in that it would stimulate economic growth and I think would actually, thus, result in increased revenues.

Mr. Robertson. This has been spoken of as a profamily tax measure. How will that help the families in your estimate?

The President. Well, let's start right off with someone down there at the lower end of the earning scale. One of the features of this is that the personal exemption is increased to $4,000 and then the deduction for dependents is almost doubled to $2,000 apiece instead of the present 1,040. So, you take a family of four, you've got $8,000 of nontaxable income to begin with right there. And that plus the reduced rates—we believe that—and first of all, so many of our people can't and don't take advantage of many of the loopholes that others have been able to use to reduce their fair share of the tax burden. So, it is very definitely aimed at families and that was sort of proven the other day when the Democratic

majority in the House of Representatives— so, I'm not just citing a Republican measure—in the Committee on Children, Youth, and Family have made a study of this tax proposal plus all the others that are before the Congress and said flatly this one is the most profamily of all of the tax proposals.

Mr. Robertson. Is the $2,000 personal exemption, dependent's exemption, is that a non-negotiable feature? Would you veto a bill if it didn't have that in it?

The President. I think it just has to have it, and let me give you my thinking on that. Some years ago, as you know, that deduction was $600 and then inflation took hold and has kept coming on. And finally, someone got around to increasing the 600 to 1,040. But right now, actually, if we had kept up with inflation, the deduction should be $2,700. Now, we couldn't remain revenue neutral and go that high, but going to $2,000 is eminently justified simply on the matter of—that actually, in purchasing power, that's smaller than the $600 was back in 1948.

Mr. Robertson. There's no lobby for it, though; among the people, the vast numbers will help. So would you, in a sense, be their champion and go the mount on that issue?

The President. Yes, and I have to say, though, that I haven't heard here, from Democrats or Republicans, any objection to those figures. There have been some of the loopholes or deductions, other areas that people have thought should be retained, and there's been argument about that. But I haven't heard anyone raise a complaint about these personal exemptions.

Administration Accomplishments

Mr. Robertson. One oblique question. I read that the reason that you and Franklin Roosevelt were so tremendously popular is because you gave the American people hope. Looking down the road, what cause do you have for hope?

The President. Well, I'm an eternal optimist, I know; but I can't help but have hope. Just a few years ago, we were seeing our streets torn up with rioting and demonstrations of various kinds, but we also were seeing a lack of hope. We were hearing talk that we were no longer a nation of growth and so forth; that we must begin to limit ourselves in our expectations, and our government itself was telling that to the people. And here, today, in these few short years, double-digit inflation is down to less than 4 percent and still on its way down; interest rates, the prime rate had reached 21½ percent, and it is down to far less than a half of that now, and still, I believe, they're going down. In the last 33 months, we have created more than 8 million new jobs. And today—you know what is referred to as the employment pool is everyone in the United States—male and female between the age of 16 and 65 are known as the potential labor pool—that if all of them sought work—they're all employable. The highest percentage of that labor pool is employed now than has ever been employed before in our history. And the growth in the recovery has been the greatest that we've known in any recovery from any previous recession or depression.

But even more than that, there is something out there—you get out on the road and talk to the people. There is a spirit. Our young people, who once were, as you know, totally disillusioned with government and so forth over the Vietnam war—the resurgence of patriotism among them. And now with our volunteer military—no longer having to have a draft—I don't know of anything I am more proud of than our young men and women in uniform and their spirit.

Nancy Reagan

Mr. Robertson. I ask you a question for the women viewers in our audience. You've just gone through a very critical medical problem, and we know how close you and your wife Nancy are. It is almost a fabled love affair—better than Hollywood could do it. What was her reaction? How did she handle this crisis?

The President. Well, she is very courageous, and once upon a time when she was younger she was one of those—what did they call them—those nurses aides that—during war time and all. So, that part, she was on the job. But she also is a very great worrier, and let me put it this way: I've recovered quicker than she did.

Mr. Robertson. It was a terrible crisis. This is the second one. Some of your very close friends from California have gone back into private enterprise or gone back home. Are you turning more to your wife for counsel? She's a very wise lady.

The President. Oh, listen, we have always talked over everything together. I couldn't imagine it being otherwise. But as to the people leaving the administration, I've expected that. I had 8 years experience in California. And I made it plain from the beginning that these people—I would take them even if it was only for a year or 2 years and then find someone else if and when they had to return to their own careers. And I think it should be that way if you're going to get—well, I always put it this way. I wanted people in government that really didn't want a job in government, but that were willing to come and serve rather than those that were seeking government jobs. And the result is, you know that they will have to go back to their own careers sooner or later.

But, no, Nancy and I—we don't have any secrets from each other.

American Hostages in Lebanon

Mr. Robertson. We were very heartened to learn that Reverend Weir had been released from Lebanon, and word reached us that a member of the White House staff was dispatched on Sunday, I believe, to Iran to seek the release of the remaining six—and actually it was seven at that time. Is there any word on that that might give hope to us?

The President. Well, I can't really talk about what we are doing, because I don't want to do anything that will endanger the prospects of the others being freed. I can only say that we have explored every avenue. We've been working for this for all the time since the first one, Mr. Buckley, was kidnaped. And I know that some of the families have grown impatient, because if they don't see things in the paper, they don't think we're doing anything. But going public and being in the paper is not the way to get a Reverend Weir back or any of the others.

Mr. Robertson. Could we say cautiously

optimistic, or is there anything that we can say to characterize it?

The President. I have to remain cautiously optimistic. And we are continuing the efforts that—and we've explored and been trying in every avenue that is open to us. But, again, it's something I can't talk about because, as I say, there is a risk in all of this for them.

Soviet Propoganda

Mr. Robertson. You're getting ready for the summit. Is the American press—and a free press is so important in our nation—but is it from time to time being manipulated by the Soviet Union to sort of stack the deck against you in this summit meeting?

The President. Well, I did begin to feel there for a while that when the summit started they'd be rooting for the other side; that he was wearing the white hat, and I was wearing the black hat. You know, that's an old Hollywood expression, that you identify the villain as——

Mr. Robertson. I know.

The President. ——by the color of the hat. I think what should be better understood by our people—and this isn't any criticism of our press—the Soviet Union has a worldwide disinformation network, and it's very effective. And they can get many things published and broadcast and so forth to suit their ends and in their drives, for example, to try to create some friction among us and our allies. And I don't think we have anything comparable to that.

Free and Fair Trade

Mr. Robertson. One last question. I see that our time has run out. If the Congress gives you a trade protectionist bill having either a tariff or a surcharge or some other name, will you veto it?

The President. I'll have to. That's one of the advantages of being my age. I was looking for work in the Great Depression, and I know what the Smoot-Hawley bill did, the world trade war that it created. There is no way that that can win—protectionism for,

say, a particular industry—no one ever looks over their shoulder to see how many people in other industries lost their jobs—because it's a two-way street, and retaliation sets in. We are still the greatest exporter in the world. And even though there is a great trade imbalance right now, that we're importing far more than we're exporting, that is not because we have reduced our exports, as big as they ever were. We have increased our imports because of the value of our dollar and the fact that our trading partners have not had the economic recovery we've had, so their prices are low. And you can't blame people for picking up a bargain.

Mr. Robertson. What they need is a dose of Reaganomics in Europe, is that what you say?

The President. Exactly. As a matter of fact, they themselves admit that in their systems there are so many rigidities in labor laws and everything else that have been built in that they have not had the recovery. Indeed, when I was at the recent economic summit, the last summit in May, they called to my face, they called what we have is the miracle of America. So, we've tried to pass on to them information that we think would help them have some miracles.

Mr. Robertson. Mr. President, thank you so much. This has been wonderful.

The President. Well——

Mr. Robertson. God bless you.

The President. Well, thank you very much, and, in saying that, let me tell you, when you asked about the future and why I was optimistic and all, I am convinced this is a nation under God and as long as we recognize that, believe that, I think he'll help us.

Mr. Robertson. There's no question about it. That's the greatest cause for optimism I know of. Thank you very much, sir.

The President. Thank you.

Note: The interview began at 4:44 p.m. in the Map Room at the White House.

Nomination of the United States Representative and Alternate Representatives to the 29th Session of the International Atomic Energy Agency General Conference
September 20, 1985

The President today announced his intention to nominate the following individuals to be the Representative and Alternate Representatives of the United States of America to the 29th Session of the General Conference of the International Atomic Energy Agency:

Representative:

Danny J. Boggs, of Kentucky, is Deputy Secretary at the United States Department of Energy. Previously he was Special Assistant to the President and Assistant Director, Office of Policy Development, at the White House. He graduated from Harvard University (B.A., 1965) and the University of Chicago Law School (J.D., 1968). He was born October 23, 1944, in Havana, Cuba, and now resides in Arlington, VA.

Alternate Representatives:

Richard T. Kennedy, of the District of Columbia, is Ambassador at Large, United States Representative to the International Atomic Energy Agency, Department of State. Previously he was Ambassador at Large, Department of State, in 1982–1984. He graduated from the University of Rochester (B.A., 1941), Harvard University (M.B.A., 1953), the U.S. Army Command and General Staff College (1959), and the National War College (1965). He was born December 24, 1919, in Rochester, NY, and now resides in Washington, DC.

Nunzio J. Palladino, of Pennsylvania, is Chairman of the Nuclear Regulatory Commission. Previously he was dean of the College of Engineering at Pennsylvania State University. He was Alternate Representative to the General Conference of the International Atomic Energy Agency in 1984. He graduated from Lehigh University (B.S., 1938; M.S., 1939). He was born November 16, 1916, in Allentown, PA, and now resides in Washington, DC.

Bruce Chapman, of Washington, is Representative of the United States of America to the Vienna office of the United Nations and Deputy Representative of the United States of America to the International Atomic Energy Agency in Vienna, Austria. Previously he was Deputy Assistant to the President and Director of the Office of Planning Evaluation in 1983–1985. He graduated from Harvard College (B.A., 1962). He was born December 1, 1940, in Evanston, IL, and now resides in Washington, DC.

Nomination of Two Members of the National Transportation Safety Board
September 20, 1985

The President today announced his intention to nominate the following individuals to be members of the National Transportation Safety Board:

Kenneth John Hill, of Virginia, for the remainder of the term expiring December 31, 1986. He would succeed Donald D. Engen. He was director of governmental relations and Armed Forces liaison for the 50th Presidential Inaugural Committee in 1984. Previously he was the White House staff liaison to the 1984 Summer Olympics. He served in the Foreign Service in the Bureau of Administration in 1982–1983 and as Deputy Chief, Dignitary Protection Division, in 1978–1982. He graduated from Rollins College (B.A., 1968). He was born September 7, 1946, in Trenton, NJ, and now resides in Alexandria, VA.

John K. Lauber, of California, for the term expiring December 31, 1989. He would succeed George Herbert Patrick Bursley. He is Chief of the Aeronautical Human Factors Research Division at NASA—Ames Research Center. Previously he was the project psychologist for the training analysis and evaluation group at the Naval Training Devices Center in Orlando, FL.

He graduated from Ohio State University (B.S., 1965; M.A., 1967; Ph.D., 1969). He was born December 13, 1942, in Archbold, OH, and now resides in Palo Alto, CA.

Designation of Three Members of the Board of Governors of the United Service Organizations, Incorporated
September 20, 1985

The President today announced his intention to designate the following individuals to be members of the Board of Governors of the United Service Organizations, Incorporated, for terms of 3 years. These are reappointments:

Fred H. Gottfurcht, of California, is president of Gottfurcht Investment Securites Co. He graduated from Detroit City College (1931) and Wayne University (1935). He is married, has four children, and resides in Los Angeles, CA. He was born May 8, 1910, in Vienna, Austria.

Mary Carol Rudin, of California, is a member of the board of directors of the South Coast Foundation, the Blue Ribbon Club for the Los Angeles Music Center, and the Hereditary Disease Organization. She graduated from the University of California at Los Angeles (B.A., 1969) and California State University (M.A., 1974). She is married, has four children, and resides in Santa Monica, CA. She was born April 1, 1944, in Ellenburg, WA.

Gordon D. Walker, of California, is vice president of Smith Barney, Harris Upham, Inc., in Beverly Hills. Previously he was president of Dowalco, Inc., in 1962–1965. He graduated from the University of Southern California. He is married, has four children, and resides in Los Angeles. He was born June 3, 1923, in East Orange, NJ.

Radio Address to the Nation on Foreign Policy
September 21, 1985

My fellow Americans:

During the next 10 days at the White House, matters of central importance to our country's role in the world and to the peace and prosperity of all nations will be dealt with.

This week I will meet President Mubarak of Egypt; next week with King Hussein of Jordan. In both meetings, one item will dominate the agenda—peace between Israel and her neighbors. King Hussein has made clear his wish for a peaceful solution to the Arab-Israeli conflict which has plagued the Middle East and the world for so long. He foresees a peace negotiated directly between Israel and a Jordanian-Palestinian delegation and is committed to begin those negotiations, if possible, by the end of the year. We're doing all we can to support the efforts to make this vision a reality. Egypt, President Mubarak's nation, has already proven that peace between the Israelis and Arabs is possible and now faces other problems—a troubled economy at home and danger on some of its borders. We're doing all we can to help Egypt meet these challenges because we know that a secure and prosperous Egypt is the cornerstone of peace and stability in that region.

King Hussein, President Mubarak, and I will also discuss the war between Iran and Iraq. America and other nations have worked for years now to bring this war to an end—so far, to no avail. Yet if we cannot end the fighting, we and close friends like Egypt and Jordan can keep it from spreading. In particular, we're determined to preserve the free shipment of oil through the Persian Gulf.

Next Friday I'll meet the new Soviet Foreign Minister Eduard Shevardnadze. He and I will discuss human rights, regional conflicts such as the Soviet invasion of Afghanistan, bilateral issues such as trade between our two countries, and security matters including our efforts to achieve genuine, verifiable reductions in nuclear arms. As Mr. Shevardnadze and I meet, it will be 6 months since Mr. Gorbachev became the new Soviet leader, and this will give our meeting special significance.

As you know, the Soviet Union frequently has been bent upon expansion. Indeed, since the 1970's the Soviet Union has been engaged in a military buildup which far exceeds any rational definition of its defensive needs. These policies have inflicted bitter costs upon the Soviet peoples. Every week Russian soldiers are dying in Afghanistan, while their standard of living has suffered accordingly. Mr. Gorbachev can change this; he can set in train a policy of arms reductions and lasting peace. By shifting resources from armaments to people, he can enable his nation to enjoy far more economic growth. Given the nature of the Soviet system and its ideology, we must not raise false hopes, but during my meeting with Mr. Shevardnadze, I will express the good will of the United States and search for signs of a Soviet willingness to engage in genuine give and take.

Mr. Shevardnadze and I will both have in mind the approaching meeting between myself and Mr. Gorbachev. Again, with regard to this meeting, we must not raise false hopes. The differences between communism and democracy are profound. There will inevitably be competition between us, but it's the central responsibility of the leaders of the United States and the U.S.S.R. to ensure that this competition is peaceful. In these meetings, we will make clear to the Soviet leaders that we are determined to protect Western interests, but willing at the same time to do our part to improve American-Soviet relations. If there's comparable seriousness and flexibility on the Soviet part, cooperation between our two great nations will be enhanced. Already many in our administration are toiling on preparations. On Friday I will tell Mr. Shevardnadze how genuinely we wish this meeting to bear fruit.

Turning from foreign affairs to international trade, in recent weeks there has been sentiment growing in the Congress for some form of protectionism—legislation which would make it difficult or impossible for us to exchange whole categories of goods with our trading partners. On Monday I'll address our absolute commitment to trade that is both free and fair. For now, let me simply state that the answer to our trade problems isn't antitrade legislation; it's more economic growth worldwide.

My friends, the dangers to world peace and prosperity are ever present. But I believe that with your support, during the next 10 days, we'll be able to promote peace and advance the cause of free and fair international trade.

Now, in closing, I want to talk about the tragedy of the Mexican earthquake, which has brought a great outpouring of sympathy and offers of assistance from the American people. We greatly admire the bravery and resolve of the Mexican people to dedicate all their resources to overcome this calamitous event. A tragedy like this reminds us that the desire to be a good neighbor is basic to the American character and to our foreign policy. We have already provided some technical assistance, as requested by the Mexican Government, and stand ready to help in every way in the days and months ahead. To aid in that effort, Nancy will go to Mexico within the next few days to express the support of the American people for our courageous friends in Mexico and to explore how we can lend a hand in this ordeal.

Until next week, thanks for listening, and God bless you.

Note: The President spoke at 12:06 p.m. from Camp David, MD.

Remarks at a White House Meeting With Business and Trade Leaders
September 23, 1985

Thank you very much, and welcome to the White House. I'm pleased to have this opportunity to be with you to address the pressing question of America's trade challenge for the eighties and beyond. And let me say at the outset that our trade policy rests firmly on the foundation of free and open markets—free trade. I, like you, recognize the inescapable conclusion that all of history has taught: The freer the flow of world trade, the stronger the tides for human progress and peace among nations.

I certainly don't have to explain the benefits of free and open markets to you. They produce more jobs, a more productive use of our nation's resources, more rapid innovation, and a higher standard of living. They strengthen our national security because our economy, the bedrock of our defense, is stronger. I'm pleased that the United States has played the critical role of ensuring and promoting an open trading system since World War II. And I know that if we ever faltered in the defense and promotion of the worldwide free trading system, that system will collapse, to the detriment of all.

But our role does not absolve our trading partners from their major responsibility: to support us in seeking a more open trading system. No nation, even one as large and as powerful as the United States, can, by itself, ensure a free trading system. All that we and others have done to provide for the free flow of goods and services and capital is based on cooperation. And our trading partners must join us in working to improve the system of trade that has contributed so much to economic growth and the security of our allies and of ourselves.

And may I say right here to the leaders of industry that my admiration for business in the United States is stronger than ever. You know, sometimes in Washington, there are some who seem to forget what the economy is all about. They give me reports saying the economy does this and the economy will do that, but they never talk about business. And somewhere along the way, these folks in Washington have forgotten that the economy is business. Business creates new products and new services; business creates jobs; business creates prosperity for our communities and our nation as a whole. And business is the people that make it work, from the CEO to the workers in the factories. I know, too, that American business has never been afraid to compete. I know that when a trading system follows the rules of free trade, when there is equal opportunity to compete, American business is as innovative, efficient, and competitive as any in the world. I also know that the American worker is as good and productive as any in the world.

And that's why to make the international trading system work, all must abide by the rules. All must work to guarantee open markets. Above all else, free trade is, by definition, fair trade. When domestic markets are closed to the exports of others, it is no longer free trade. When governments subsidize their manufacturers and farmers so that they can dump goods in other markets, it is no longer free trade. When governments permit counterfeiting or copying of American products, it is stealing our future, and it is no longer free trade. When governments assist their exporters in ways that violate international laws, then the playing field is no longer level, and there is no longer free trade. When governments subsidize industries for commercial advantage and underwrite costs, placing an unfair burden on competitors, that is not free trade.

I have worked for 4 years at Versailles and Williamsburg and London and last at Bonn to get our trading partners to dismantle their trade barriers, eliminate their subsidies and other unfair trade practices, enter into negotiations to open markets even further, and strengthen GATT, the international accord that governs worldwide trade. I will continue to do these things. But I also want the American people and our trading partners to know that we will take all the action that is necessary to pursue our rights and interests in international commerce under our laws and the GATT to see that other nations live up to their obligations and their trade agreements with us. I believe that if trade is not fair for all, then trade is free in name only. I will not stand by and watch American businesses fail because of unfair trading practices abroad. I will not stand by and watch American workers lose their jobs because other nations do not play by the rules.

We have put incentives into our own economy to make it grow and create jobs, and, as you know, business has prospered. We have created over 8 million new jobs in the last 33 months. Just since 1980 manufacturing production has increased 17 percent. But I'm not unmindful that within this prosperity, some industries and workers face difficulties. To the workers who have been displaced by industrial shifts within our society, we are committed to help. To those industries that are victims of unfair trade, we will work unceasingly to have those practices eliminated.

Just a few weeks ago, I asked the United States Trade Representative to initiate unfair trade practice investigations. It's the first time a President has done this. And, as you know, we have self-initiated three such cases that will investigate a Korean law that prohibits fair competition for U.S. insurance firms, a Brazilian law restricting the sale of U.S. high technology products, and Japanese restrictions on the sale of U.S. tobacco products. I have also ordered the United States Trade Representative to accelerate the ongoing cases of Common Market restrictions of canned fruit and Japanese prohibitions on imports of our leather and leather footwear.

But I believe more must be done. I am, therefore, today announcing that I have instructed Ambassador Yeutter to maintain a constant watch and to take action in those instances of unfair trade that will disadvantage American businesses and workers. I have directed the Secretary of the Treasury to work with the Congress to establish a $300 million fund that will support up to a billion dollars in mixed-credit loans. These funds will counter our loss of business to trading partners who use what, in effect, are subsidies to deprive U.S. companies of fair access to world markets. And I've asked that these initiatives be continued until unfair credit subsidies by our trading partners are eliminated through negotiations with them. I have further instructed Treasury Secretary Jim Baker to inform the participants at the International Monetary Fund and World Bank conferences in Seoul that we will take into consideration the trading practices of other nations in our deliberations and decisionmaking.

A major factor in the growth of our trade deficit has been the combination of our very strong economic performance and the weak economic performance of our major trading partners over the last 4 years. This has limited our exports and contributed to the weakening of other currencies relative to the dollar, thereby encouraging additional imports by the United States and discouraging our exports. Yesterday I authorized Treasury Secretary Baker to join his counterparts from other major industrial countries to announce measures to promote stronger and more balanced growth in our economies and thereby the strengthening of foreign currencies. This will provide better markets for U.S. products and improve the competitive position of our industry, agriculture, and labor.

I have ordered the Secretary of State to seek time limits on negotiations underway to open up markets in specific product areas in Japan. I have instructed the United States Trade Representative to accelerate negotiations with any and all countries where the counterfeiting and piracy of U.S. goods has occurred to bring these practices to a quick end. And I look forward to working with the Congress to increase efforts to protect patents, copyrights, trademarks, and other intellectual property rights. And finally, I am today directing that a strike force be established among the relevant agencies in our government whose task it will be to uncover unfair trading practices used against us and develop and execute strategies and programs to promptly counter and eliminate them.

I'm also looking forward to working with the Congress to put into place any necessary legislation that would help us promote free and fair trade and secure jobs for American workers. Among the topics that we should jointly consider are authority to support our new trade negotiating initiatives that would, among other things, reduce tariffs and attempt to dismantle all other trade barriers; to protect intellectual property rights, including trade in articles that infringe U.S. process patents, longer terms for agricultural chemicals, and eliminating Freedom of Information Act abuses that will help our businesses protect their proprietary property; to improve our antidumping and countervailing duty laws so that a predictable pricing test covers nonmarket economies, enabling our companies to have protection against unfair dumping from those countries. We should also improve these laws so that business can have full and rapid protection in receiving help against unfair imports—to amend our trade laws to put a deadline on dispute settlement and to conduct a fast-track procedure for perishable items. We should no longer tolerate 16-year cases and settlements so costly and time consuming that any assistance is ineffective.

I am also directing the Secretary of Labor to explore ways of assisting workers who lose jobs to find gainful employment in other industries, and I look forward to working with Congress in this vital task. Additionally, I welcome the suggestions of the Members of Congress on other potential legislation that has as its object the promotion of free and fair trade. I will work with them to see that good legislation is passed. Conversely, I will strongly oppose and will veto measures that I believe will harm economic growth, cause loss of jobs, and diminish international trade.

But I do not want to let this discussion pass without reminding all of our ultimate purpose: the expansion of free and open markets everywhere. There are some, well-meaning in motive, who have proposed bills and programs that are purely protectionist in nature. These proposals would raise the costs of the goods and services that American consumers across the land would have to pay. They would invite retaliation by our trading partners abroad; would in turn lose jobs for those American workers in industries that would be the victims of such retaliation; would rekindle inflation; would strain international relations; and would impair the stability of the international financial and trading systems. The net result of these counterproductive proposals would not be to protect consumers or workers or farmers or businesses. In fact, just the reverse would happen. We would lose markets, we would lose jobs, and we would lose our prosperity.

To reduce the impediments to free markets, we will accelerate our efforts to launch a new GATT negotiating round with our trading partners. And we hope that the GATT members will see fit to reduce barriers for trade in agricultural products, services, technologies, investments, and in mature industries. We will seek effective dispute settlement techniques in these areas. But if these negotiations are not initiated or if insignificant progress is made, I'm instructing our trade negotiators to explore regional and bilateral agreements with other nations.

Here at home, we will continue our efforts to reduce excessive government spending and to promote our tax reform proposal that is essential to strengthening our own economy and making U.S. business more competitive in international markets. Further, we will encourage our trading partners, as agreed upon at the Bonn summit, to accelerate their own economic growth by removing rigidities and imbalances in their economies. And we will encourage them to provide sound fiscal and monetary policies to have them fully participate in the growth potential that is there for all. We will seek to strengthen and improve the operation of the international monetary system. And we will encourage the debt burdened, less-developed countries of the world to reduce and eliminate impediments to investments and eliminate internal restrictions that discourage their own economic growth.

Let me summarize: Our commitment to free trade is undiminished. We will vigorously pursue our policy of promoting free and open markets in this country and around the world. We will insist that all nations face up to their responsibilities of preserving and enhancing free trade everywhere. But let no one mistake our resolve to oppose any and all unfair trading practices. It is wrong for the American worker and American businessman to continue to bear the burden imposed by those who abuse the world trading system. We do not want a trade war with other nations; we want other nations to join us in enlarging and enhancing the world trading system for the benefit of all. We do not want to stop other nations from selling goods in the United States; we want to sell more of our goods to other nations. We do not dream of protecting America from others' success; we seek to include everyone in the success of the American dream.

Thank you very much, and thank you for coming.

Note: The President spoke at 11:30 a.m. in the East Room at the White House. Also attending the meeting were Members of Congress, the Cabinet, the President's Export Council, and the Advisory Committee on Trade Negotiations. Clayton Yeutter was the United States Trade Representative.

Appointment of 21 Members of the President's Export Council
September 23, 1985

The President today appointed the following individuals to be members of the President's Export Council:

Joseph A. Boyd, of Florida, is chairman and chief executive officer of Harris Corp. in Melbourne, FL. He was born March 25, 1921, in Oscar, KY, and now resides in Indialantic, FL.

Edward A. Brennan, of Illinois, is president and chief operating officer of Sears, Roebuck and Co. in Chicago, IL. He was born January 16, 1934, in Chicago and now resides in Burr Ridge, IL.

Philip Caldwell, of Michigan, is retired chairman of the board of Ford Motor Co. in Bloomfield Hills, MI. He was born January 27, 1920, in Bourneville, OH, and now resides in Bloomfield Hills.

Colby H. Chandler, of New York, is chairman and chief executive officer of Eastman Kodak Co. in Rochester, NY. He was born May 15, 1925, in Strong, ME, and now resides in Honeoye Falls, NY.

Douglas D. Danforth, of Pennsylvania, is chairman and chief executive officer of Westinghouse Electric Corp. in Pittsburgh, PA. He was born September 25, 1922, in Syracuse, NY, and now resides in Venetia, PA.

Russell L. Hanlin, of California, is president and chief executive officer of Sunkist Growers, Inc., in Sherman Oaks, CA. He was born November 18, 1932, in Sioux Falls, SD, and now resides in Pasadena, CA.

Arthur H. Hausman, of California, is chairman of AMPEX Corp. in Redwood City, CA. He was born November 24, 1923, in Chicago, IL, and now resides in Atherton, CA.

Edward G. Jefferson, of Delaware, is chairman and chief executive officer of E.I. DuPont de Nemours and Co. in Wilmington, DE. He was born July 15, 1921, in London, England, and now resides in Wilmington.

James E. Jenkins, of California, is president of Transworld Group Limited in Washington, DC. He was born September 12, 1923, in Oklahoma City, OK, and now resides in Arlington, VA.

Whitney MacMillan, of Minnesota, is chairman and chief executive officer of Cargill, Inc., in Wayzata, MN. He was born September 25, 1929, in Minneapolis, MN, and now resides in Wayzata.

Lee L. Morgan, of Illinois, is chairman and chief executive officer of Caterpillar Tractor Co. in Peoria, IL. He was born January 4, 1920, in Aledo, IL, and now resides in Peoria.

John J. Murphy, of Texas, is chairman, chief executive officer, and president of Dresser Industries, Inc., in Dallas, TX. He was born November 24, 1931, in Olean, NY, and now resides in Dallas.

J. Bonnie Newman, of New Hampshire, is president of the Business and Industry Association of New Hampshire in Concord. She was born June 2, 1945, in Lawrence, MA, and now resides in Durham, NH.

Robert W. Page, Sr., of Texas, is chairman and chief executive officer of Kellogg Rust, Inc., in Houston, TX. He was born January 22, 1927, in Dallas, TX, and now resides in Houston.

Van P. Smith, of Indiana, is chairman and president of Ontario Corp. in Muncie, IN. He was born September 8, 1928, in Oneida, NY, and now resides in Muncie, IN.

George J. Stathakis, of Connecticut, is president and chief executive officer of General Electric Trading Co. in New York City. He was born April 22, 1930, in Martinez, CA, and now resides in New York City.

Stephen M. Studdert, of Utah, is president of Commerce Consultants International, Ltd., in Washington, DC. He was born November 17, 1948, in Pataluma, CA, and now resides in Morgan, UT.

David S. Tappan, Jr., of California, is chairman and chief executive officer of Fluor Corp. in Irvine, CA. He was born May 27, 1922, in Hainan, China, and now resides in Newport Beach, CA.

Charles Parry Tyson, of California, is former Deputy Assistant to the President for National Security Affairs. He was born July 25, 1941, in San Diego, CA, and now resides in Madrid, Spain.

Thornton A. Wilson, of Washington, is chairman and chief executive officer of the Boeing Co. in Seattle, WA. He was born February 8, 1921, in Sikeston, MO, and now resides in Seattle.

David C. Scott, currently serves as Chairman. He has been a member of the Council since August 13, 1981.

Letter to President Miguel De la Madrid Hurtado on the Earthquake in Mexico
September 23, 1985

Dear Miguel:

On behalf of the American people, Nancy and I want to convey once more to you and the Mexican people our sympathy and support as you struggle mightily with the tremendous tragedy that has befallen Mexico.

It was Nancy's strong desire to travel to Mexico to let your people know of our respect and admiration for Mexico's vigorous response in meeting its great human needs. The resiliency of your citizens is truly extraordinary.

During this time of need, I am confident that the global community will generously respond in supporting Mexican efforts to overcome this tragic earthquake.

You can be sure that the United States will accelerate our efforts in providing appropriate assistance, as identified by the Mexican Government. We stand ready to assist you and the Mexican people as you undertake this heroic effort to relieve the misery wrought by the earthquake. And, beyond your immediate needs, as you formulate your longer term reconstruction plans, we will want to consult with you about how we and other members of the international community can be of help.

Nancy and I will have you, Paloma, and the Mexican people in our prayers in the days ahead.

Sincerely,

/S/ RONALD REAGAN

Note: The original was not available for verification of the content of this letter.

Remarks at a Symposium at the University of Tennessee in Knoxville
September 24, 1985

Well, thank you, Dr. Reese, distinguished panelists and guests. Thank you all—and Senator Baker, Congressmen Duncan, Quillen and Ford—all of you. It's wonderful to be here in the Volunteer State at the university of volunteers.

Governor Alexander couldn't make it today; I'll miss him because he's been one of the staunchest and most eloquent supporters of America's fair share tax plan. Right now he's on his way to the East looking for opportunities to expand Tennessee's links to the Asian market. He pointed out to me that Tennessee has a significant concentration of Japanese capital investment and that the future of this State, as well as every other State in our nation, is dependent on an open, free, and fair trading system. And that's why he's abroad right now aggressively promoting Tennessee's interests. He's trying to increase world trade, not block it out. I'm glad to see Governor Alexander taking this positive approach to prosperity through free trade.

When I was in Tennessee last year, the Governor and Senator Baker briefed me on the proposals for a high-tech corridor in Knoxville. They talked about soon competing with Silicon Valley. And when I see the impressive strides Tennessee has made in just the last few years, all I know—they weren't just whistling Dixie. [*Laughter*] As all of you know so well, advances in technology are almost synonymous with advances in knowledge, and that's one reason why improving America's educational system must be a high priority for our nation.

Last year scholastic aptitude test scores rose four points nationwide. And this year we have even better news to report; yesterday we learned that the SAT scores were up nine points over a year ago. I like that trend; that's the biggest single jump since 1963. We're making a powerful comeback from the two decades of educational decline that began in the 1960's, but we have more to do if we're going to fully prepare our nation to lead the world into the 21st century. So, let's keep up the good work.

Now, I've really come here today to listen to you. I can't wait to hear about your plans and the progress that you've made, and afterward I may say a few words about how America's fair share tax plan will promote high-tech investment and—[*laughter*]—and the prosperity that it brings here in Knoxville.

[*At this point, symposium participants discussed developments in the partnership between the State of Tennessee, the private sector, and the university. At the conclusion of the symposium, the President delivered the following remarks.*]

Well, first of all, I am fascinated by what I've heard, and at the same time, here we've all heard concrete examples that explain some of the statistics about which I like to speak now and then, such as how we could, since 1979, lose 1,600,000 manufacturing jobs. And in one of the talk shows over the weekend there was someone from government that was making quite a point of this—neglected to answer why at the same time, since 1979, we have added more than 9 million new jobs to transportation industries, to service industries, and so forth. And I've seen here the examples of what we're talking about.

When I was young, which was quite a while ago everybody reminds me—[*laughter*]—high technology then probably referred to a Model T that could make it up a hill. But we've come a long way. I think we're standing at the beginning of a new era of technological revolution that will transform all our lives for the better. And it's more than just the personal computers that have found a place in so many of our homes and offices. Every facet of industry, as has been evidenced here at this table today—the manufacturing, agriculture, science, health care—is being improved, made more efficient and productive by technology. Our healthy increases in productivity are in great part attributable to the efficiencies that technology brings. And technology also strengthens our national security and has given us the hope that within the next generation the human race can strengthen and ensure for the long term our ability to deter nuclear war with nonnuclear defense systems that would allow us to protect against missiles without threatening innocent civilians.

But while we celebrate the beginning of this new era, we should remember that misguided tax policies in the late sixties and seventies almost destroyed America's position as the leader of the high-tech revolution. Not just the tax policies—I know that you were sure you were going to hear me say something about that—but when I first became a part of government, I did so imbued with the feeling that, among other things, government had developed a kind of adversarial relationship with its own business community, where government and its business community should be partners, and not with government being the senior partner, by any means. And I say—we'd almost wiped out the venture capital markets in this country with tax rates, plus the high rate of inflation. Entrepreneurs were forced to look abroad for financing.

You gave an example of someone who couldn't find what was needed here. There was a fellow named Gene Amdahl, the inventor of what many consider the most successful computer that was ever built. And back in the seventies, he was going to start his own company. He couldn't find the venture capital that he needed in this country, and he was forced to go to Japan to a large, high-tech competitor. And they gave him the money all right—in exchange for his ideas.

High tax rates were literally producing an exodus of American high tech to foreign countries and creating tax refugees out of some of our best minds and talents and most successful entrepreneurs. One figure that just explains this—just a few years ago, in the late seventies, there was only $39 million—in I believe the year was 1979, of venture capital available in the United States. Today there is $4 billion in venture capital that is available. And I think that one of the basic rules of economics was proven: that if you tax something, you get less of it. So, this was the result, I think, of our cutting the taxes and, certainly, the taxes on capital gains and so forth. High rates discourage work and risk-taking and initiative and imagination. And they're really a tax on hope and optimism and our faith in the future, and they penalize many of the people that give us the most—the risk takers, the entrepreneurs who create whole new businesses and industries and often do it out of no more than a dream and some hard work, as this little bottle also

evidences.[1]

Cutting the tax rates has opened the floodgates on entrepreneurship in our country. That's why, on the theory that you can't have too much of a good thing, we're going to propose more tax cuts in our fair share tax plan, and we're going to cut the capital gains tax rate again to encourage more venture capital and fuel the fires of technological innovation. Equally important for entrepreneurs in small business, though, we're bringing down the top personal tax rate to 35 percent, and that's just half of what it was 5 years ago. We're going to close wasteful loopholes. And we'll be able to lower tax rates on America's businesses. We think it's time that America pulled its money out of tax shelters and started investing in the future. This tax cutting has given the economy new blood and new life. And in the last 33 months, we have created 8 million new jobs alone. And I believe that this tax plan that I'm out on the road talking about—and will be talking about it in Athens in a little while—will give us a decade of economic expansion, and we foresee creating 10 million more new jobs in the next 4 years. Now, I'll bet you anything a whole bunch of those jobs are going to be created right here in Tennessee. Incidentally, I had the privilege of driving the prototype of the new car that is going to be built here. I don't get to do that very often—only drive the Jeep when I'm up at the ranch and—[*laughter*]—8 years as Governor, when we finally left the Governor's office and went home, I remember one night Nancy and I were invited out to dinner. We went out and got in the back seat of the car and waited for somebody to get in and drive us. [*Laughter*] But driving that Saturn, I must say, was an experience. [*Laughter*] Having driven for a lot of years—you're really going to be making something very remarkable here.

Well, the best way, I think, to stay number one is to lower tax rates further and give all of our business community and

[1] *The President referred to a vial containing a small plant used in tissue propogation given to him by Randolph Henke, president of Phyton Technologies, Inc.*

our people a chance. You can feel the excitement, and I felt it here at this table down here in Tennessee; it's the excitement of progress. Your Congressman here, John Duncan and his colleagues Jimmy Quillen and Harold Ford and I are not going to let Washington obstruct the road to the future. So, you let these people know how you feel, and we'll pass this tax bill in this year of 1985 and open the future to hope and opportunity.

This whole idea of your partnership here—it's government, education, private sector—I've had some experience with that. When I became Governor of California, I invited what had to be the top industrialists and business and labor people—well, the leadership of the State of California to a luncheon. The room wasn't much bigger than this one and probably no more people than are here today. And I suggested to them an idea, and that was would they volunteer their services to be formed into task forces to go into every agency and department of the State government and come back and tell us how modern business practices could be put to work to make it more efficient, more economic—and to a man and woman, they volunteered. And for the next period of virtually a year, these busy people gave an average of more than 3 days a week to this task. They appointed among themselves an executive committee to put things together, and they delivered to us 1,200 specific recommendations. And by the time I had left the governorship, we had implemented more than 800 of those for a visible savings of billions of dollars to government, and it vastly reduced the size of the government, while the population of California was increasing faster than any other State.

We've done something of the same kind at the Federal level, and that partnership does work. And the private sector, in every way—and this country of ours has made us unique in all the world. It's possible that some of the deterioration of our technology and all that has been mentioned here, maybe that was a result of World War II, where everything of ours remained intact and the rest of the world—our industrial partners and neighbors—had theirs virtually destroyed in the war, and then we set out to help them rebuild. And they rebuilt in a different period of time and with all the newer things that were available.

Well, we don't have to bomb everything here to catch up with them, just do what several of you here have been suggesting that you have been doing. And I see my job, and that of John's and the others here in government, to get out of your way, to be a partner but not a senior partner, and to have policies that we are sure are not going to hinder the practice of the free economy. I think we've discovered in this land more than anyplace else, freedom really works.

Well, I've gone on for too long here. I'll stop talking and listen some more.

Note: The President spoke at 10:50 a.m. and 11:25 a.m. at the Carolyn P. Brown University Center. He was introduced by Jack E. Reese, chancellor of the University of Tennessee. Following the symposium, the President had lunch with students, faculty, and private sector representatives in the Executive Dining Room. He then traveled to Athens, TN.

Remarks to Citizens in Athens, Tennessee
September 24, 1985

The President. Thank you very much, and thank you, Congressman Duncan. Believe me, it is wonderful to be here. You know, I always wanted to speak on democracy and good government in Athens. Now, it is absolutely not true that I taught Plato all he knew. [*Laughter*] So, I thank you for this opportunity. It's good to see my friends, Senator Baker and Congressman Quillen and Congressman Ford and Mayor Brake-bill. Governor Alexander wanted to be here, but he's off finding new business opportunities for Tennessee. And I suspect that he will have the same success on this trip as he did in recent dealings with a company in Detroit.

But I want to speak to you today about changing our tax system. I'm going to speak briefly so I don't hold you up too much from your day, but I'm going to—you know, I learned once a very important lesson about the importance of brevity in a speech. I was making a speech, and in the audience was a minister from Oklahoma, Bill Alexander, who had been quite well known around the country. And Bill told me, after I had spoken, about his first sermon, and I've always thought there was a connection between my speech and his story.

He said that he had been ordained, and then he was invited to speak at a little church out in the country. And he worked for weeks on that first sermon, and then stood up in that little country church that was empty except for one lone little fellow sitting out there among all the empty pews. Well, he went down, and he said: "My friend, you seem to be the only member of the congregation that showed up. I'm just a young preacher getting started. Should I go through with it?" And the fellow said: "Well, I don't know about that sort of thing. I am just a little old cowpoke out here in Oklahoma. But I do know this—if I loaded up a truckload of hay, take it out on the prairie, and only one cow showed up, I'd feed her." [*Laughter*] Well, Bill thought that was a cue. So, he got back up in the pulpit with his carefully prepared sermon, and an hour and a half later said, "Amen." And then he went down again and said: "My friend, you seem to have stuck with me. I'm a young preacher, like I told you, just getting started. What did you think?" And he said: "Well, like I told you, I don't know about that sort of thing, but I do know this—if I loaded up a truckload of hay, took it out on the prairie, and only one cow showed up, I sure wouldn't give her the whole load." [*Laughter*]

Well, to start with, the whole struggle for tax reform in our country is a kind of drama, with good guys and bad guys and even a damsel in distress. But like all dramas, it occurs in a certain context, and here's ours: Our economy, the American economy, has never been stronger, never been bigger, and never been better. Since the economic recovery began, we've created over 8 million new jobs. Well over a million new businesses were incorporated in the last 2 years alone. The American standard of living has increased. Our tax cuts put more money back in the American wallet. Interest rates are down from 21½ percent to 9½ percent; so we can build houses and make big purchases again. And most important, in the past 5 years, we chased inflation. We caught it; we wrestled it to the ground and stopped it from robbing the American consumer. That's a long way of saying that inflation, when we got to Washington, was 12 percent, and so far this year, it has only been 3.3 percent, and for the last 4 months, it has only been 2½ percent. And we're not going to stop until we get it even lower and eliminate it entirely.

So, we're in good shape, and because of that we can afford, finally, to turn to one big area of American life that's been a mess for years now. I'm talking about our current tax system. Now, I sometimes do an informal poll about what the people think about taxes, and if you'll cooperate—do you love our current tax system?

Audience. No-o-o!

The President. Well, do you like our current tax system?

Audience. No-o-o!

The President. Well, how about this? Do you find our present tax system utterly disgusting and demoralizing?

Audience. Yes!

The President. Well, I'm with you. [*Laughter*] A system that penalizes people for working overtime, a system that allows some to unfairly shelter their income from taxation—well, that's a system that just doesn't deserve to survive. What we want to put in its place is a tax system that, to begin with, will reduce the 14 tax brackets we have now down to 3. We want to simplify the system and make it loophole-free. We want to see that everyone pays their fair share, but no one pays more than that.

Our tax plan is aimed at helping the

family. We're raising the personal exemption for each dependent from about $1,040 to $2,000. We're going to raise the standard deduction to $4,000 for a married couple filing jointly. And under our plan, a family of four won't pay one cent in Federal income tax on the first $12,000 of earnings. Now, we're also giving nonwage-earning spouses an equal chance to have an IRA, the tax-deductible savings account. You'd have to be pretty brave or awfully foolish to suggest that a housewife, a homemaker, isn't working. You bet you are.

Well, one of the keys to our tax proposal is that we went in with the clear intent to try to lower the personal income taxes faced by the American people. So, we devised a system in which a full 79 percent of the taxpayers of our country would either get a tax cut or see their taxes for now remain unchanged. Barely 20 percent would face a tax increase, and they are mostly the folks who've been using shelters and loopholes and such to avoid paying their fair share. By the way, there's been a little inaccurate information provided by some of our opponents on this. They say that under our plan the rich will benefit the most; they have it exactly backward. Under our proposal, those who make $20,000 a year or less will enjoy the biggest tax cut. It will average about 18 percent. The second biggest tax cut goes for those who earn from $20,000 to $50,000 a year, and they will get a cut that averages 7 percent. And the smallest cut, but still a cut, nonetheless, goes to those who make $50,000 a year or more, and their tax cut averages a little less than 6 percent.

And I want to be very clear on why we think it's important to keep trying, to keep striving to get your tax bills lower. I want you to think about the cash that you've got in your pocket right now, in your wallet or your purse. The money that is in there you earned. The less of it the Government takes from you, the more freedom you will have. You can take that money and spend it and give a boost to retail sales and encourage Miller's and Proffitt's to hire more workers. [*Laughter*] You can take it and save it and add to the capital available for all kinds of investment. Or you can take it and ultimately invest it in a business or a new firm

or a new idea of your own. But whatever you do—spend, save, or invest—you'll be making a wonderful contribution to the quality of life of your fellow citizens; you'll be creating jobs.

You may have heard that our Council of Economic Advisers has just done a study of the expected economic impact of our tax plan. They said the economic growth it will inspire should create the equivalent of almost 4 million new full-time jobs. They found that the personal economic gain for each household will be about $600 a year for every household in America. And they came up with something else that was pretty interesting. There are some people who go around saying the American people are undertaxed and we can't give them a break now because it will lower the amount of revenues coming into the Government. And I know that people are concerned about the deficit, and we are. And we are going to do something about it. But what we are going to do something about is—or the something we are going to do is reduce government spending, not increasing taxes.

Now, the funny thing is that our tax plan, by reducing individuals and businesses—their taxes—will ultimately bring a lot more money into the Government. With the rates lower, the revenues become greater because of economic growth and increased prosperity. One reason is that every time we cut tax rates in one area, say on capital gains, we bring in more capital gains revenues because the cut in rates stimulates economic activity. When we cut, in 1981, the top tax rate of 70 percent down to 50 percent, actually the people paying in that bracket ended up paying more money to government at 50 percent than they had been at 70, because there was an incentive now for them to go out and do better and earn more and not try to find ways just to evade their taxes, but to pay them because they got to keep more of the share of the dollar. There's another element that figures in here. Our plan closes unproductive loopholes and eliminates the welter of shelters, and that will cut down on legal tax avoidance.

A few minutes ago I said that tax reform is a drama with heroes and villains and a damsel in distress. Well, the heroes are the citizens across this country who are asking for tax justice. The villains are the special interests, "the I-got-mine gang," and the damsel in distress, well, that's a lass named endless economic growth, and she's tied to the tracks and struggling to break free. What do you say? Will you help us untie her? [*Applause*] Thanks, I needed that.

I want to mention something that is kind of funny, and I hope you can help me with it. I've been going all over the country talking about tax reform, and wherever I go the people tell me they are frustrated by the current system, and they back our plan, and then they ask me what can they do to help? Well, it's up to us together. Now, maybe you can help me and Congressmen Duncan and Quillen and Ford. Maybe we can make Washington listen. Do you want a fairer tax system?

Audience. Yes!

The President. Washington is kind of far away. I'm not sure they can hear you, and our friends there in the press, they want to know if you really want a fairer tax system?

Audience. Yes!

The President. I think I've just fallen in love with Tennessee. Well, I'm not surprised; Andrew Jackson started here—that couldn't have been me [*referring to a noise on the public address system*]. Andrew Jackson started here, and he was a President who cared about the average American. He knew you weren't so average. And this great town, Athens, the friendly city, you have a history of standing up to special interests. I guess you just can't stop Athens and McMinn County from backing justice and fairness.

I'll tell you what you've done here today—and with these Congressmen here to carry the message back to Washington in person, even if some of them didn't hear you way back there, I'm sure they tried. I've heard from so many up on the Hill that said: "Well, we just haven't heard anything from the people yet about tax reform. We don't know whether they're very interested or not." Well, everyplace I've gone it's been just like this: You are interested, and you want what tax reform means—a reduction of the rates, making it simpler so that you don't have to hire an expert to tell you how to pay your tax, making it simpler and making it fairer—all of this. And we can go back to Washington now and tell them that out here, in the real America, we found out the people do want something done about this hodgepodge tax system that's been growing like a jerry-built something or other for the last several decades.

Well, your support means a lot to me; I know it means a lot to them. And we're going to do everything we can to see if we can't get this passed this year so you'll know in a hurry that Aprils from here on are going to be a little happier around the 15th than they've been.

Audience member. Thank you, Mr. President!

The President. Well, just saw a sign—I love you, too. Somebody had a sign up. Yes. Thank you for letting me come here, and thank you for listening to me. God bless you all, and God bless Tennessee. Thank you very much.

Note: The President spoke at 1:37 p.m. at the McMinn County Courthouse.

Informal Exchange With Reporters in Knoxville, Tennessee
September 24, 1985

Q. Tell us what you think about Shevardnadze's proposal for "star peace"? Will you join him for "star peace"?

The President. I have already seen some items that suggest to me that I was misunderstood in trying to call an answer over

here. First of all, we have received no proposal officially of a 40-percent cut as I was asked about, and when I made a remark that I wish it were more if he had done it, I was doing that in the context of the fact that both Mr. Gorbachev and myself said that we would both like to see the missile done away with entirely. But I was not turning down any offer; we've received no offer, either here or our negotiators in Geneva have received no proposals.

Q. Would you go for deeper cuts than the 40 percent which seems to be bandied about and he may propose to you this week?

The President. Well, all I know is that no one on our side has heard anything, but just this report that he has said this.

Q. But would you go for deeper cuts?

The President. I told you, our goal, if we could make it, would be total elimination, but we are perfectly prepared to take whatever mutual reduction we can get with the idea of eventually getting there to zero.

Q. What do you think of this "star peace" proposal?

The President. That again, I have just heard that it was said in a speech. I'll wait until we get together and I hear exactly what they are talking about.

Q. Mr. President, Shevardnadze specifically said that the Soviet side has given detailed proposals in Geneva and has heard nothing back in substance from the United States.

The President. I'm sorry, but our negotia-

tors there have had numbers out on the table that we have put there as to a reduction in weapons, and there have been no counteroffers as yet to those other numbers suggested or any thing of the kind. There has been no negotiating position presented by the Soviets.

Q. How do you think this tit for tat bodes for Friday and your meeting with Gorbachev?

The President. No, you mean Shevardnadze. No, I'm going to see what we say to each other, but I'm not going to pay any attention to statements that are made publicly until they are presented to us formally.

Q. Are they lying about having put anything on the table in the way of—[*inaudible*].

The President. What?

Q. Are they lying?

The President. As far as I know they have unless something has been done since I have talked to our people. Our people have never had any numeral count suggested to them either agreeing or suggesting a difference from the figures we've presented.

Q. Thank you.

Note: The exchange began at 2:45 p.m. at McGhee Tyson Airport. The President then returned to Washington, DC.

Nomination of Charles J. Cooper To Be an Assistant Attorney General
September 25, 1985

The President today announced his intention to nominate Charles J. Cooper to be an Assistant Attorney General (Office of Legal Counsel), Department of Justice, vice Theodore B. Olson, resigned.

Since 1982 Mr. Cooper has served as Deputy Assistant Attorney General, Civil Rights Division, Department of Justice. Previously he was special assistant to the Assistant Attorney General, Civil Rights Division,

Department of Justice. From 1979 to 1981, he was an attorney with the law firm of Long & Aldrige in Atlanta, GA. In 1978 Mr. Cooper served as a law clerk to Justice William H. Rehnquist at the Supreme Court of the United States.

Mr. Cooper graduated from the University of Alabama (B.A., 1974; J.D., 1977). He was born March 8, 1952, in Dayton, OH, and currently resides in Alexandria, VA.

Nomination of Stephen J. Markman To Be an Assistant Attorney General
September 25, 1985

The President today announced his intention to nominate Stephen J. Markman to be an Assistant Attorney General (Office of Legal Policy), Department of Justice, vice Harold J. Lezar, Jr.

Since 1978 Mr. Markman has served as chief counsel and staff director of the Senate Subcommittee on the Constitution, except for 1983 when he left to serve as deputy chief counsel, Senate Committee on Judiciary. From 1975 to 1978, he was legis-

lative assistant to Representative Tom Hagedorn. In 1978 Mr. Markman was legislative assistant to Representative Edward Hutchinson on the House Judiciary Committee.

Mr. Markman graduated from Duke University (B.A., 1971) and the University of Cincinnati College of Law (J.D., 1974). He was born June 4, 1949, in Detroit, MI. He is married and currently resides in Alexandria, VA.

Nomination of Charles Fried To Be Solicitor General of the United States
September 25, 1985

The President today announced his intention to nominate Charles Fried to be Solicitor General of the United States, Department of Justice, vice Rex E. Lee, resigned.

Since 1985 Mr. Fried has served as Deputy Solicitor General and counselor to the Solicitor General at the Department of Justice. Previously he was special assistant to the Attorney General. From 1961 to 1984, he held various positions at Harvard University Law School including Carter professor of general jurisprudence (1981–1984); lecturer on medical ethics at Harvard

Medical School (1974–1975); professor of law; and assistant professor (1961–1965). From 1960 to 1961, Mr. Fried was law clerk to Justice John Harlan, United States Supreme Court.

Mr. Fried graduated from Princeton University (A.B., 1956), Oxford University (B.A., 1958; M.A., 1960), and Columbia University Law School (J.D., 1961). He is married to the former Anne Summerscale, and they have two children. Mr. Fried was born April 15, 1935, in Prague, Czechoslovakia, and currently resides in Washington, DC.

Appointment of Carl A. Anderson as Special Assistant to the President for Public Liaison
September 26, 1985

The President has appointed Carl A. Anderson to be Special Assistant to the President for Public Liaison. Mr. Anderson will have responsibility for domestic issues.

Since 1983 Mr. Anderson has been serving in the Office of Policy Development. Previously he was counselor to the Under

Secretary of Health and Human Services in 1981–1983. He served as legislative assistant to Senator Jesse Helms in 1976–1981. He was a member of the Presidential transition team in the office of the President-elect in 1980–1981. Mr. Anderson is an attorney admitted to practice in the State of Washington and the District of Columbia.

Mr. Anderson graduated from Seattle University (B.A., 1972) and the University of Denver College of Law (J.D., 1975). He is married to the former Dorian Lounsbury, and they have four children. He was born February 27, 1951, in Torrington, CT, and currently resides in Arlington, VA.

Nomination of Fred L. Hartley for the Rank of Ambassador While Serving as Commissioner General of the United States Exhibition for the International Exposition in Vancouver, Canada
September 26, 1985

The President today announced his intention to nominate Fred L. Hartley, of California, for the rank of Ambassador during the tenure of his service as Commissioner General of the United States Exhibition for the International Exposition, Vancouver, BC, Canada, 1986. The nomination of Mr. Hartley reflects the importance the United States attaches to the Vancouver Exposition.

Since 1939 Mr. Hartley has been employed by the Union Oil Co. of California (Unocal Corp.) as an engineering trainee at the San Francisco refinery. He has remained in the employ of the Union Oil Co. of California progressing through many job assignments to his present title of chairman and president. Among numerous member- ships he is presently also chairman of the American Petroleum Institute, trustee of the California Institute of Technology, and a member of the British-North American Committee. Mr. Hartley was appointed earlier this year as Commissioner General of the United States Exhibition for the International Exposition in Vancouver by Director Wick of the United States Information Agency.

Mr. Hartley received his bachelor of applied science in chemical engineering at the University of British Columbia in Vancouver in 1939. He is married to the former Margaret Alice Murphy, and they have two children. He was born January 16, 1917, in Vancouver, BC, Canada.

Nomination of Ross O. Swimmer To Be an Assistant Secretary of the Interior
September 26, 1985

The President today announced his intention to nominate Ross O. Swimmer to be an Assistant Secretary of the Interior (Indian Affairs). He would succeed Kenneth L. Smith.

Since 1975 Mr. Swimmer has been principal chief of the Cherokee Nation of Oklahoma in Tulsa. He also served as president of the First National Bank of Tahlequah, OK, in 1975–1984. He was general counsel of the Cherokee Nation of Oklahoma in 1972– 1975 and an attorney with the law firm of Hanson, Peterson and Thompkins in Oklahoma City, OK, in 1967–1972. He was a member of the Presidential Commission on Indian Reservation Economies in 1983– 1984. He serves in Oklahoma on the Economic Development Commission and on the board of trustees of the Oklahoma Health Sciences Foundation. He is also president of the Cherokee National Historical Society.

He graduated from the University of Oklahoma (B.A., 1965) and University of Oklahoma School of Law (J.D., 1967). He is married, has two children, and resides in Tulsa, OK. He was born October 26, 1943, in Oklahoma City, OK.

Statement on the Mutual and Balanced Force Reduction Negotiations
September 26, 1985

Today in Vienna members of NATO and the Warsaw Pact will resume their efforts to negotiate reductions and limitations on conventional forces in central Europe. The Vienna talks are an important part of the United States commitment to achieve concrete progress in arms reductions on a broad front—in the areas of conventional, chemical, and nuclear forces.

In Geneva U.S. negotiators are striving to reduce the risk of nuclear war through significant reductions of nuclear weapons that will create a more stable deterrence. Also in Geneva, the American negotiators continue our effort to achieve a comprehensive, global, and verifiable ban on chemical weapons, as we proposed last year at the 40-nation Conference on Disarmament. And at the Stockholm Conference on Confidence and Security Building Measures in Europe, the U.S., in conjunction with its NATO allies, will continue to press for agreement on confidence-building measures designed to reduce the risk of surprise attack in Europe.

The U.S. and its NATO allies in Vienna will actively pursue every avenue of possible agreement in the upcoming negotiating round in order to achieve a verifiable agreement that reduces conventional forces in central Europe in an equitable manner. The U.S. delegation will give close scrutiny to proposals on the table as part of its ongoing search for mutually acceptable solutions to the difficult issues that underlie the talks. We hope for a similar approach from the Warsaw Pact. Ambassador Robert Blackwill, our representative to these negotiations, can count on my support and keen interest in reaching a meaningful agreement that will add to the security of both sides.

Appointment of Three Members of the Advisory Committee for Trade Negotiations
September 26, 1985

The President today announced his intention to appoint the following individuals to be members of the Advisory Committee for Trade Negotiations for terms of 2 years:

Maurice R. Greenberg, of New York, will succeed Charles H. Pillard. He is president and chief executive officer of the American International Group in New York City. Previously he was vice president of Continental Casualty Co. He graduated from New York Law School (LL.B., 1950). He is married, has four children, and resides in New York City. He was born May 4, 1925, in New York City.

Henry Y. Hwang, of California, is a reappointment. Mr. Hwang is chairman and president of the Far East National Bank in Los Angeles, CA.

He graduated from National Taiwan University (B.A., 1950) and Linfield College (B.A., 1951). He is married, has three children, and resides in Pasadena, CA. He was born November 28, 1929, in Shanghai, China.

Nancy Clark Reynolds, of Virginia, will succeed LeGree S. Daniels. Ms. Reynolds is president of Wexler, Reynolds, Harrison and Schule, Inc., in Washington, DC. Previously she was vice president at the Bendix Corp. She served as Representative of the United States of America on the Commission on the Status of Women of the Economic and Social Council of the United Nations in 1981. She graduated from Goucher College (B.A., 1949). She has four children and resides in Arlington, VA. She was born June 26, 1927, in Pocatello, ID.

1141

Appointment of Three Members of the Intergovernmental Advisory Council on Education, and Designation of the Chairperson
September 26, 1985

The President today announced his intention to appoint the following individuals to be members of the Intergovernmental Advisory Council on Education for terms expiring July 27, 1989:

Paul M. Jenkins, of California, will succeed Emlyn Irving Griffith. Mr. Jenkins is a resource teacher in the achievement goals program at the Baker School of Music in San Diego, CA. He is married, has two children, and resides in La Mesa, CA. He was born March 5, 1948, in Santa Monica, CA.

Sterling R. Provost, of Utah, will succeed Esther Rushford Greene. Mr. Provost is assistant commissioner for veterans education and proprietary school affairs in the State of Utah. He graduated from the University of Utah (B.A., 1955; M.S., 1957) and Brigham Young University (Ed.D., 1966). He is married, has two children, and resides in Salt Lake City, UT. He was born August 13, 1929, in Provo, UT.

Sylvia B. Wagner, of Nebraska, will succeed Norman A. Murdock. Mrs. Wagner has been a city council member in Omaha since 1981. She graduated from the University of Nebraska (B.S., 1946). She is married, has three children, and resides in Omaha, NE. She was born August 4, 1925, in Omaha.

The President today also designated Anne Lindeman to chair the Intergovernmental Advisory Council on Education. She will succeed Joseph C. Harder. She has served as a member of the Council since August 6, 1985.

Statement by Principal Deputy Press Secretary Speakes on Trade With Canada
September 27, 1985

The President spoke by telephone with Prime Minister Mulroney on September 26, 1985, and warmly welcomed the offer from the Prime Minister to explore the scope and prospects for bilateral trade negotiations between our two countries. The President is firmly committed to the pursuit of free and fair trade. The Canadian offer could provide opportunities for both countries to facilitate trade and investment flows.

Canada is our largest trading partner with two-way trade in 1984 exceeding $110 billion. Canada takes nearly one-fifth of our total exports, accounting for close to $45 billion in U.S. exports. The Canadian expression of interest is in keeping with the desire expressed by the President and Prime Minister at the Quebec summit to explore ways to reduce and eliminate all existing barriers to trade between our two countries.

The U.S. Trade Representative, Ambassador Clayton Yeutter, will begin informal consultations with the Senate Finance and the House Ways and Means Committees on the advisability of entering negotiations. The administration will also seek advice from the private sector on the desirability and objectives of any bilateral negotiations. In addition, the administration will request advice from the U.S. International Trade Commission on the economic impact on U.S. industry of a bilateral trade agreement with Canada.

Note: Larry M. Speakes read the statement to reporters in the Briefing Room at the White House during his daily press briefing, which began at 9:20 a.m.

Nomination of Robert L. Barry for the Rank of Ambassador While Serving as United States Representative to the Conference on Confidence and Security Building Measures and Disarmament in Europe
September 27, 1985

The President today announced his intention to nominate Robert L. Barry, of New Hampshire, a career member of the Senior Foreign Service, Class of Career Minister, for the rank of Ambassador during the tenure of his service as United States Representative to the Conference on Confidence and Security Building Measures and Disarmament in Europe. He would succeed James E. Goodby.

Mr. Barry served in the United States Navy as lieutenant in 1957–1960. He entered the Foreign Service in 1962 and was vice consul in Zagreb in 1963–1965. In 1965–1967 he was in the Department as international relations officer in the Office of Soviet Union Affairs. He studied the Russian language at Munich (Garmisch) in 1967–1968. He was consular officer, then political officer in Moscow (1968–1970), political officer at the United States Mission to the United Nations in New York, NY (1970–1971), and deputy principal officer in Leningrad (1971–1973). He was on detail to the International Communication Agency as Di-

rector of U.S.S.R. Division of the Voice of America in 1973–1975. Mr. Barry returned to the Department as Deputy Director of the Office of Soviet Union Affairs (1975–1977), Director of the Office of United Nations Political Affairs (1977–1978), Deputy Assistant Secretary of State for International Organization Affairs (1978–1979), and Deputy Assistant Secretary of State for European Affairs (1979–1981). He was appointed Ambassador to Bulgaria in 1981 and served in Sofia until 1984, when he became a John Sloan Dickey fellow (Dartmouth College) and Distinguished Visitor of the W. Averell Harriman Institute for Advanced Study of the Soviet Union (Columbia University).

He graduated from Dartmouth College (B.A., 1956) and Columbia University (M.A., 1962). He attended Oxford University (England) in 1956–1957. His foreign languages are Russian, Serbo-Croatian, Bulgarian, and French. He is married to the former Margaret Crim, and they have two children. He was born August 28, 1934, in Pittsburgh, PA.

Nomination of Francis S.M. Hodsoll To Be Chairman of the National Endowment for the Arts
September 27, 1985

The President today announced his intention to nominate Francis S.M. Hodsoll to be Chairman of the National Endowment for the Arts, National Foundation on the Arts and the Humanities, for a term of 4 years. This is a reappointment.

Since 1981 Mr. Hodsoll has been serving as Chairman of the National Endowment for the Arts. Previously he was at the White House as Deputy Assistant to the President and Deputy to the Chief of Staff. He was a

Foreign Service officer and Deputy U.S. Special Representative for Nonproliferation at the Department of State (1978–1980). He was Deputy Assistant Secretary of Commerce for Energy and Strategic Resource Policy and Assistant to the Under Secretary of Commerce. He has previously been a Special Assistant to the Administrator of EPA.

He graduated from Yale University (B.A., 1959), Stanford University (J.D., 1964), and

Cambridge University (M.A., LL.B., 1963). He is married, has two children, and resides in Arlington, VA. He was born May 1, 1938, in Los Angeles, CA.

Appointment of Richard Chavez as a Member of the Architectural and Transportation Barriers Compliance Board
September 27, 1985

The President today announced his intention to appoint Richard Chavez to be a member of the Architectural and Transportation Barriers Compliance Board for a term expiring December 3, 1988. This is a reappointment.

Mr. Chavez is president of Educational Designs, Inc., in City of Commerce, CA. Previously he was founder and executive director of Chavez and Associates Institute. He was the Federal representative for California to the 1977 White House Conference on the Handicapped and was a member of the California Governor's Committee for Employment of the Handicapped.

He is married, has two children, and resides in Whittier, CA. He was born August 28, 1943, in Los Angeles, CA.

Appointment of Cynthia Boich as a Member of the Advisory Committee on Small and Minority Business Ownership
September 27, 1985

The President today announced his intention to appoint Cynthia Boich to be a member of the Advisory Committee on Small and Minority Business Ownership. She will succeed Al Cardenas.

Ms. Boich presently serves as a consultant to Cynthia Boich & Associates, a corporate art marketing firm in Phoenix, AZ. She was founder and served as president of the firm in 1981–1984. Previously, she was with Armour-Dial, Inc., in product management (1977–1981); and with J. Walter Thompson Co. as an account executive in 1974–1976.

She graduated from Bethany College (B.A., 1969) and the American Graduate School of International Management (M.A., 1973). She was born November 10, 1947, in Steubenville, OH, and now resides in Scottsdale, AZ.

Appointment of Two Members of the Commission on Presidential Scholars
September 27, 1985

The President today announced his intention to appoint the following individuals to be members of the Commission on Presidential Scholars. These are initial appointments.

Carlos Benitez, of Florida, is president of United Schools of America in Miami. Previously he was president of Loyola School in Miami. He graduated from Miami Dade Junior College (A.A., 1965) and the University of Miami (B.B.A., 1968). He is married, has three children, and resides in Miami, FL. He was born May 11, 1942, in Havana, Cuba.

Marvin A. Pomerantz, of Iowa, is president of the Mid-America Group in West Des Moines, IA.

Previously he was with International Harvester as president of the diversified group. He graduated from the University of Iowa (B.S., 1953).

He is married, has four children, and resides in Des Moines, IA. He was born August 6, 1930, in Des Moines.

Appointment of Sally Ann Gumaer Ranney as a Member of the President's Commission on Americans Outdoors
September 27, 1985

The President today announced his intention to appoint Sally Ann Gumaer Ranney to be a member of the President's Commission on Americans Outdoors. This is a new position.

She is founder and president of the American Wilderness Alliance in Englewood, CO. She also serves as executive director of the Island Foundation and of the Crystal Island Foundation. She is a member of the Advisory Board of the World Wilderness Congress and is coordinator for the National Wilderness Research and Management Conference. She served as a resource policy analyst for the Wilderness Society in 1975–1977.

She graduated from Western State College of Colorado (B.A., 1970; M.A., 1972). She has one child and resides in Englewood, CO. She was born July 2, 1947, in Denver, CO.

Proclamation 5368—National Sewing Month, 1985
September 27, 1985

By the President of the United States of America

A Proclamation

The sewing industry annually honors approximately fifty million people who sew at home and approximately forty million people who sew at least part of their wardrobes. Their initiative, creativity, and self-reliance are characteristic of the people of our Nation.

The home sewing industry generates an estimated $3,500,000,000 annually for the economy of the United States. Home sewing also has enhanced career opportunities for many Americans in fields such as fashion, retail merchandising, design, patternmaking, and textiles. Learning the art of sewing in the home or in elementary school home economics classes started many on careers in these fields.

In recognition of the importance of home sewing to our Nation, the Congress, by Senate Joint Resolution 173, has designated the month of September 1985 as "National Sewing Month," authorizing and requesting the President to issue a proclamation in observance of this month.

Now, Therefore, I, Ronald Reagan, President of the United States of America, do hereby proclaim September 1985 as National Sewing Month. I call upon the people of the United States to observe this month with appropriate ceremonies and activities.

In Witness Whereof, I have hereunto set my hand this twenty-seventh day of September, in the year of our Lord nineteen hundred and eighty-five, and of the Independence of the United States of America the two hundred and tenth.

RONALD REAGAN

[*Filed with the Office of the Federal Register, 10:58 a.m., September 30, 1985*]

Proclamation 5369—National Adult Day Care Center Week, 1985
September 27, 1985

By the President of the United States of America

A Proclamation

The people of this Nation are striving to help older Americans to avoid being institutionalized unnecessarily and to remain independent in their homes. The rapid growth of adult day care centers is a reflection of the increasing interest in the development of long-term community care alternatives for the elderly. These centers offer comprehensive personal, medical, and therapeutic assistance to older people and to the handicapped, thus helping them to maintain a great degree of independence. The centers also offer support for families who are willing to care for their loved ones at home, but who welcome the opportunities the centers afford for wider human contacts among people often consigned to loneliness.

The many adult day care centers throughout America are to be commended for recognizing the vital needs of older people and for striving to meet those needs.

To increase public awareness of the importance of adult day care centers, the Congress, by House Joint Resolution 229, has designated the week beginning September 22, 1985, as "National Adult Day Care Center Week" and authorized and requested the President to issue a proclamation in observance of this occasion.

Now, Therefore, I, Ronald Reagan, President of the United States of America, do hereby proclaim the week beginning September 22 through September 28, 1985, as National Adult Day Care Center Week, and I call upon all government agencies, national organizations, community groups, and the people of the United States to observe this week with appropriate programs, ceremonies, and activities.

In Witness Whereof, I have hereunto set my hand this twenty-seventh day of September, in the year of our Lord nineteen hundred and eighty-five, and of the Independence of the United States of America the two hundred and tenth.

RONALD REAGAN

[*Filed with the Office of the Federal Register, 10:59 a.m., September 30, 1985*]

Nomination of Russell A. Rourke To Be Secretary of the Air Force
September 27, 1985

The President today announced his intention to nominate Russell A. Rourke to be Secretary of the Air Force. He would succeed Verne Orr.

Since 1981 Mr. Rourke has been serving as Assistant Secretary of Defense (Legislative Affairs). Previously he was administrative assistant to Representative Harold S. Sawyer (R–MI) in 1977–1981. In 1976–1977 he served as Special Assistant to the President (Legislative Affairs). Mr. Rourke was Deputy to Presidential Counsellor John O. Marsh, Jr., in 1974–1976. In 1974 he was the Republican-Conservative nominee for Congress in the 36th District of New York. Mr. Rourke served in 1965–1974 as administrative assistant to Representative Henry P. Smith III (R–NY). In 1960–1964 he was administrative assistant to Representative John R. Pillion (R–NY). Mr. Rourke was associated with the firm of Keogh, Carey and Costello in 1959–1960.

He graduated from the University of Maryland (B.A., 1953) and Georgetown University Law Center (LL.B., 1959). He is married, has three children, and resides in Annapolis, MD. He was born December 30, 1931, in New York City.

Nomination of Julius W. Becton, Jr., To Be Director of the Federal Emergency Management Agency
September 27, 1985

The President today announced his intention to nominate Julius W. Becton, Jr., to be Director of the Federal Emergency Management Agency. He would succeed Louis O. Giuffrida.

Since January 1984 General Becton has been serving as the Director of the Office of Foreign Disaster Assistance at the Agency for International Development. In 1983 General Becton retired from the U.S. Army after nearly 40 years of distinguished service. In his last Army post, he reported directly to the Army Chief of Staff and was responsible for institutional training and education in over 300 specialties. In 1978–

1981 he commanded the largest U.S. Army Combat Ready Force in the free world (VII Corps) located in Stuttgart, West Germany. He was commander of the U.S. Army Operational Test and Evaluation Agency in 1976–1978, commander of the 1st Cavalry Division (1975–1976), and deputy commander of the U.S. Army Training Center in 1972–1975.

He graduated from Prairie View A&M (B.S., 1960) and the University of Maryland (M.A., 1967). He also attended the National War College. He is married, has five children, and resides in Springfield, VA. He was born June 29, 1926, in Bryn Mawr, PA.

Nomination of Two Members of the National Commission on Libraries and Information Science
September 27, 1985

The President today announced his intention to nominate the following individuals to be members of the National Commission on Libraries and Information Science for terms expiring July 19, 1990:

Lee Edwards, of Maryland, would succeed Paulette H. Holahan. Mr. Edwards is editor of Conservative Digest and president of the Center for International Relations in Washington, DC. Mr. Edwards graduated from Duke University (B.A., 1954) and received a certificate from the Sorbonne in Paris, France. He is married, has

two children, and resides in Bethesda, MD. He was born December 1, 1932, in Chicago, IL.

Frank Gannon, of New York, would succeed Charles William Benton. Mr. Gannon is presently serving as editor of Saturday Review in Washington, DC. He is also president of Frank Gannon Productions, a communications consulting company. He graduated from Georgetown University (B.S., 1964), the London School of Economics (M.S., 1965), and Oxford University (Ph.D., 1968). He was born August 11, 1942, in Jamaica, NY, and now resides in Washington, DC.

Statement on United States Arms Sales to Jordan
September 27, 1985

I have today notified the Congress of my intention to provide the Kingdom of Jordan with the tools it needs to help defend its people as King Hussein courageously pursues peace with Israel. The provision of these defensive arms to Jordan is essential

for two reasons: first, it conveys in the near term a powerful message of U.S. political support for King Hussein's efforts to bring about a comprehensive, lasting peace settlement between Israel and the Arab world; and second, in the longer term, it will meet

Jordan's most pressing military deficiency; namely, its ability to provide adequate air defense against an external attack and military intimidation by the adversaries of peace. It will not directly counter the cruel acts of the terrorists, whose bombs and assassination attempts are even now trying to turn Hussein from his quest for peace.

Nevertheless, as firm evidence of America's support, this package will strengthen Jordan as a force for stability and moderation in the Middle East. By giving Jordan's small armed forces the ability to deter the threat of conventional attack, we provide King Hussein the flexibility and confidence he needs to continue toward negotiations with Israel.

For the past 15 years, Jordan has successfully denied the use of its own territory to terrorists from abroad seeking to attack Israeli targets across the Jordan River. More recently, King Hussein has renewed diplomatic relations with Egypt, the first Arab state to do so; he has enlisted the Palestinians in his peace initiative in order to dissuade them from their earlier policies of confrontation and hostility toward Israel; and he has publicly recognized Israel's right to exist and stated his desire to commence peace talks this year.

I remain totally committed to helping Israel to ensure its security, survival, and well-being and to maintaining its decisive advantage over any combination of potential adversaries. The arms transfer which I am proposing for Jordan does not jeopardize this policy. Indeed, a strong, stable Jordan able to defend itself against radical pressures is in Israel's interests, as well as our own. I am convinced that this support by the United States is an absolute necessity if we are ultimately to achieve the peace which we all so fervently desire.

Statement by Principal Deputy Press Secretary Speakes on the Policy for Release of Sensitive Information Derived From Federally Funded Research
September 27, 1985

President Reagan has issued guidance to the various agencies of the Federal Government which outlines procedures concerning the releasability of scientific, technical, and engineering information generated as a result of federally funded fundamental research in universities, colleges, and laboratories. This policy addresses a widespread concern that efforts to reduce the flow of sensitive technologies to potential adversaries could restrain free and open exchange of fundamental scientific information. It is included in a directive to the heads of executive branch departments and agencies.

The new policy states that: It is the policy of this administration that, to the maximum extent possible, the products of fundamental research remain unrestricted. It is also the policy of this administration that, where the national security requires control, the mechanism for control of information generated during federally funded fundamental research in science, technology, and engineering at colleges, universities, and laboratories is classification. Each Federal Government agency is responsible for: (a) determining whether classification is appropriate prior to the award of a research grant, contract, or cooperative agreement and, if so, controlling the research results through standard classification procedures; (b) periodically reviewing all research grants, contracts, or cooperative agreements for potential classification. No restrictions may be placed upon the conduct or reporting of federally funded fundamental research that has not received national security classification, except as provided in applicable U.S. statutes.

Our goal is to maintain the free and open exchange of unclassified research so necessary to a free society and an expanding economy.

Proclamation 5370—National Historically Black Colleges Week, 1985
September 27, 1985

By the President of the United States of America

A Proclamation

The one hundred and two historically black colleges and universities in the United States have contributed substantially to the growth and enrichment of the Nation. These institutions have a rich heritage and tradition of providing high quality academic and professional training, and their graduates have made countless contributions to the progress of our complex technological society.

Historically black colleges and universities bestow forty percent of all degrees earned by black students in the United States. They have awarded degrees to sixty percent of the black physicians, sixty percent of the pharmacists, forty percent of the attorneys, fifty percent of the engineers, seventy-five percent of the military officers, and eighty percent of the members of the judiciary. Throughout the years, these institutions have helped many underprivileged students to develop their full talents through higher education.

Recognizing that the achievements and aspirations of historically black colleges and universities deserve national attention, the Congress of the United States, by Senate Joint Resolution 186, has designated the week of September 23 through September 29, 1985, as "National Historically Black Colleges Week" and authorized and requested the President to issue a proclamation in observance of this event.

Now, Therefore, I, Ronald Reagan, President of the United States of America, do hereby proclaim the week of September 23 through September 29, 1985, as National Historically Black Colleges Week. I ask all Americans to observe this week with appropriate ceremonies and activities to express our respect and appreciation for the outstanding academic and social accomplishments of the Nation's black institutions of higher learning.

In Witness Whereof, I have hereunto set my hand this twenty-seventh day of September, in the year of our Lord nineteen hundred and eighty-five, and of the Independence of the United States of America the two hundred and tenth.

RONALD REAGAN

[*Filed with the Office of the Federal Register, 11 a.m., September 30, 1985*]

Note: The proclamation was released by the Office of the Press Secretary on September 28.

Radio Address to the Nation on the President's Meeting With Foreign Minister Eduard Shevardnadze of the Soviet Union
September 28, 1985

My fellow Americans:

During the past week we've been working hard to advance the Middle East peace process and to try to improve U.S.-Soviet relations. I met with our good friend President Mubarak of Egypt, and I'll be holding discussions this coming week with another longtime friend of the United States, King Hussein of Jordan. I hope to talk to you more about the Middle East next week.

But today let me speak about our efforts to build a more constructive and stable long-term relationship with the Soviet Union. Both Secretary Shultz and I met with the new Soviet Foreign Minister Eduard Shevardnadze this past week. These meetings covered a broad global agenda, including the four major areas of the U.S.-Soviet dialog: human rights, regional and bilateral issues, and security and arms control matters. They enabled us to discuss at the most senior levels the key issues facing our two nations. I told the Foreign Minister I'm hopeful about my upcoming meeting with General Secretary Gorbachev, and I put forward some new ideas as well as my plans and expectations for that meeting. The Soviet Foreign Minister indicated that Mr. Gorbachev also is looking forward to these discussions. Furthermore, we agreed to set up a series of senior level discussions between our experts in preparation for the Geneva meeting.

Let's be clear, however, that success will not come from one meeting. It must come from a genuine, long-term effort by the leadership of the Soviet Union as well as ourselves. The differences between us are fundamental in political systems, values, and ideology as well as in the way we conduct our relations with other countries. The United States must and will be forthright and firm in explaining and defending our interests and those of our allies. I went over with Mr. Shevardnadze Soviet actions in various parts of the world which we feel undermine the prospects for a stable peace, and I discussed with him the need for the Soviet Union to work with us seriously to reduce offensive nuclear arms. These weapons exist today, and there's no reason why real reductions cannot begin promptly.

Finally, I emphasized the need for a more productive Soviet response to our efforts in Geneva to begin a U.S.-Soviet dialog now on how to fashion a more stable future for all humanity if the research in strategic defense technologies, which both the U.S. and the U.S.S.R. are conducting, bears fruit. Mr. Shevardnadze indicated that the Soviet negotiators will present a counterproposal in Geneva to the initiatives we've taken there. We welcome this. It is important that the counterproposal address our concerns about reductions and stability just as we've sought to address Soviet concerns. And we hope it'll be free of preconditions and other obstacles to progress. We're ready for tough but fair negotiating. You, the people, can distinguish diplomatic progress from mere propaganda designed to influence public opinion in the democracies.

All too often in the past, political and public opinion, and sometimes government policy as well, have taken on extreme views of the U.S.-Soviet relationship. We have witnessed sometimes a near euphoria over a supposed coming together, at other times a feeling that the U.S. and the U.S.S.R. may somehow be at the brink of conflict. By holding to the firm and steady course we set out on 5 years ago, we've shown that there is no longer any reason for such abrupt swings in assessing this relationship. Our differences are indeed profound, and it is inevitable that our two countries will have opposing views on many key issues. But we've intensified our bilateral dialog and taken measures, such as the recent upgrading of the crisis hotline, to ensure fast and reliable communications between our leaders at all times.

Above all, I emphasized to the Foreign Minister, and will do so with Mr. Gorbachev, that the overriding responsibility of the leaders of our two countries is to work for peaceful relations between us. So, what we're engaged in is a long-term process to solve problems where they're solvable, bridge differences where they can be bridged, and recognize those areas where there are no realistic solutions, and, where they're lacking, manage our differences in a way that protects Western freedoms and preserves the peace. The United States stands ready to accomplish this. Much more must be done, but the process is underway, and we will take further steps to show our readiness to do our part. With equal determination by the Soviets, progress can be made. We will judge the results as Soviet actions unfold in each of the four key areas of our relations. And I will be reporting to you further as preparations for the November meeting proceed.

Until next week, thanks for listening, and God bless you.

Note: The President spoke at 12:06 p.m. from the Oval Office at the White House.

Remarks in an Interview With Representatives of Le Figaro of France, Together With Written Responses to Questions
September 26, 1985

Views on the Presidency

Q. There was a question I wanted to ask, Mr. President, which is: At a time when everybody would love to retire, how is it that you still feel you've got to run the biggest country in the world and the enormous burden that it represents?

The President. Well, I only sought this job because I thought there were some things that needed to be done and that maybe I could help bring them about, and I just don't want to leave the job unfinished.

Q. What time in your career, which has been a long—political career, I mean, did you feel that you could run for the White House if it possibly was offered to you and that you would win in the end?

The President. Well, I've always said that you don't decide, the people tell you. The truth is I never sought or thought I ever would seek public office. I, as a performer, as an entertainer, I always thought that you kind of pay your way; so, I supported causes and candidates that I approved of. And, being an entertainer, I could attract an audience and so forth and, therefore, be useful at a fundraiser—things of that kind.

Never did I ever dream in my wildest time that I would ever even want to be in public life. And then, at a time in our country when our party was greatly divided— and all the friction, there was a group that came to me. And my first reply was a refusal. This group that came wanted me to seek the governorship. And finally, they convinced me I had an obligation, I should do it and that I could win, and so, I ran. And I found out after I had won and was in the office that where I had thought that I was giving up a career, which I did love—in the other business—and that I'd find this very dull, I found out it wasn't at all. And then, subsequent to 8 years in the Governor's office, there were people that came and, on that basis, said that I should try for this. So, I did.

Q. Is the American President, in fact, impeded by the fact that he can't run more than twice for the office?

The President. I think that this country should look very seriously at that recent change in the Constitution which limits the President to two terms and see if they don't feel that they have taken something away from democracy. After all, if the people—as they did in this country the one time for Roosevelt—want someone to serve them, they should have the right to vote for them.

Q. It means that you could put forward or present an amendment against the 22d amendment?

The President. Well, if I did that, I would do it at such a time to make it very plain that I was not doing it with myself in mind, I was doing it for whoever would be President from now on.

Q. Which would be, I suppose, the Republican Party?

The President. Who knows. The only time it was ever four terms, extended, it was Franklin Delano Roosevelt, a Democrat.

Q. Thank you very much.

The President. Good to see you.

The President's Responses to Questions Submitted by Le Figaro

NATO Alliance

Q. Mr. President, before going to Geneva, Mikhail Gorbachev will visit Paris on October 2. You have often denounced the Soviet attempts to seduce Western Europe. Do you think, nevertheless, that the results of this trip can be useful to your November meeting or, on the contrary, that it represents a threat for the NATO alliance?

The President. I think General Secretary Gorbachev's visit to France can be very useful both in its own right and with regard to my meeting with him in Geneva. It is particularly important that Mr. Gorbachev realize that our alliance stands strong and that the Soviet Union has to do its part—as we are ready to do ours—in a serious, honest effort to build more constructive relations. I am sure this will be made clear to the General Secretary during his visit to France. I know from my many meetings with President Mitterrand that he is a very forceful advocate of his views; that he favors a strong, united, and secure West; and that he has no illusions about the Soviet system.

The Soviet Union has long sought to divide the Western allies from each other and the people from their governments. They have never succeeded because the Western democracies have a partnership based on equality, common values, and a shared vision of the future. These ties have kept us strong, united, and determined to defend our mutual interests. We and our allies want to establish a more stable relationship, but we cannot be lulled into a illusory peace that masks or ignores the real causes of tension between us. What we want is a just and secure peace.

I will be looking with great interest at General Secretary Gorbachev's visit to France. This will be his first trip to the West as a leader of the Soviet Union, and I'll be interested in President Mitterrand's impressions. And, of course, I look forward to hearing what the General Secretary will have to say on all the issues between East and West, including nuclear arms reductions. I have read often in the press that General Secretary Gorbachev is a new style of Soviet leader. I very much hope that, if true, then, he will pursue policies which will lead to a more constructive East-West relationship.

U.S.-Soviet Relations

Q. Depending on the outcome of the conversations that President Mitterrand and the General Secretary will have, would you be susceptible to modifying the United States position for the Geneva summit?

The President. Of course, I welcome President Mitterrand's views as well as the views of our other allies. This is an important part of the preparations for my meeting with the General Secretary. We are prepared to listen to any positive, concrete proposals the Soviets may have, and we want to engage in a dialog on the full scope of the U.S.-Soviet relationship. My meeting with the General Secretary in November, and President Mitterrand's next week, are important steps in a process that all of us in the West have been pursuing for a number of years—to build a more constructive relationship with the Soviet Union and a more secure future. We have not come as far as I would have liked, and we should ask why that is.

Does it serve the long-term Soviet interest or the interest of peace for them to keep well over 100,000 troops in Afghanistan against the wishes of that country's people? Is it in the long-term interest of a just world for the Soviet Government to ignore the obligations it assumed under the Helsinki accords and other international agreements, to deny its people some of the basic human rights that we in the West take for granted? Is it in the long-term interest of peace and stability for the Soviet Union to continue to build up its military forces beyond defensive needs and to such levels that NATO has no choice but to respond by strengthening its own defenses?

One of my objectives for Geneva is to put these kinds of questions to Mr. Gorbachev, in hopes that we can clear away some of the misunderstanding and narrow differences wherever possible. But I also hope that, even before then, we can make as much progress as possible in all areas of our relations: human rights, regional issues such as Afghanistan, bilateral questions, and arms control. Arms control is, understandably, one of the central issues between us, but it is not the only one. We need to look hard at the fundamental sources of tension in our relationship if we are to be true to our responsibilities to the peoples of our countries and the world.

European Security and the Strategic Defense Initiative

Q. From the point of view that the setting of a nuclear shield in the United States seems to put in question the principle of linkage, do you foresee a defense of Europe by conventional means? In your opinion, if there were to be a threat to European security and integrity, what would be the role of the French deterrent?

The President. Let me make clear that there is no thought whatever of calling into question the principle of linkage between the U.S. and its European allies. The U.S. remains fully committed to the defense of its European allies, and our research under the Strategic Defense Initiative seeks to strengthen that unalterable commitment. It will be years before we can make a judgment about the feasibility of defensive technologies. Meanwhile, we must continue to rely on our existing deterrent forces. NATO's strategy of flexible response remains as valid today as when it was first adopted.

The Strategic Defense Initiative does not replace the current energetic efforts to improve the conventional defenses of the alliance. Moreover, by countering ballistic missile threats against all members of the alliance, including the United States, strategic defenses would strengthen the credibility of U.S. extended deterrence and NATO's flexible response doctrine by reducing the vulnerability of United States reinforcements to Europe. Finally, the United States fully supports the independent French nuclear deterrent force, and the Strategic Defense Initiative does not weaken or call into question that support.

Q. A corollary question, how do you intend to convince Europe, and especially West Germany, that SDI can improve their security?

The President. Research into new technologies which could provide effective defenses against nuclear attack is both prudent and necessary. Indeed, defensive systems are consistent with a policy of deterrence, both historically and in practical terms. Moreover, the Soviet Union clearly believes in defenses. They continue to improve their ballistic missile defense system in place around Moscow. Their activities have violated the ABM treaty and raise even more serious questions about their future intentions. They have an extensive and longstanding strategic defense research program which is exploring many of the areas in which the United States is interested, and they have a sizable headstart. Thus, the question should be, can we afford not to pursue this research? Effective defenses against ballistic missiles have the potential for enhancing deterrence by increasing an aggressor's uncertainties and helping reduce or eliminate the apparent military

value of nuclear attack to an aggressor. The U.S. will continue its close consultations with our allies regarding SDI research. We would ultimately make a decision on whether to deploy strategic defense systems only after consultations with our allies and negotiations with the Soviet Union, as envisioned by the ABM treaty.

Q. Is the Strategic Defense Initiative, to which you intend to associate your European allies, only an update of the ABM system, or does it further mean a revision by the United States of its commitment to a nuclear protection of Europe?

The President. The Strategic Defense Initiative is a research program to pursue vigorously important new technologies that may be used to create a defense against ballistic missiles, which could strengthen deterrence and increase the security not only of the United States but of our allies as well. The prevention of war through deterrence is fundamental to U.S. and NATO defense policy. If our research bears fruit, increasing reliance on defensive systems which threaten no one would be fully compatible with that objective. In our SDI research, we seek to reduce the incentives—now and in the future—for Soviet aggression and thereby to ensure effective deterrence for the long term. This represents a reaffirmation, not a revision, of the U.S. commitment to the protection of Europe.

Defensive technologies, should they prove feasible, would counter the threat posed by the massive growth of Soviet offensive nuclear forces during a period in which the United States exercised considerable restraint. For it is a fact that while the United States significantly reduced the number of weapons in our nuclear arsenal, the Soviet Union was continually adding to its arsenal. SDI also responds to the Soviets' longstanding and extensive strategic defense efforts. In the near term, then, SDI is a direct response to the Soviet efforts, which include longstanding advanced research in many of the areas we are now exploring, as well as the world's only deployed antiballistic missile (ABM) system. Our program provides a powerful deterrent to any Soviet decision to break out of the ABM treaty, which in fact the Soviets are already violating. Our SDI research, however, is fully compatible with the terms of the ABM treaty.

Because the security of the United States is inextricably linked to that of our friends and allies, the SDI program is not confining itself solely to an examination of technologies with the potential to defend against intercontinental ballistic missiles, but it is also carefully examining promising technologies with potential against shorter range ballistic missiles as well. An effective defense against short-range ballistic missiles would have a significant impact on deterring aggression against Europe. By reducing or eliminating the military effectiveness of such ballistic missiles, defensive systems have the potential for enhancing deterrence against both nuclear and conventional attacks on any members of our alliance.

Q. Would the fact that France has clearly shown its doubts towards this project, despite your administration's approval of the Eureka program, mean that its scientists and firms will be excluded from this trans-Atlantic cooperation?

The President. No, certainly not. The United States has made very clear that we do not see any competition between SDI research and the Eureka program. We welcome participation in SDI research by allied, including French, institutions and companies.

Q. The Germans and the British are on the eve of being associated with the SDI program. At which level, at which stage of its development would you require their participation?

The President. Although the United States welcomes the participation of its allies in the various stages of SDI research, it is a decision for each ally. We have invited such participation and are convinced that such participation will bring real benefits for participating allies, for the research program itself, and for the security of the alliance as a whole.

U.S.-France Relations

Q. During the visit to the United States of President François Mitterrand, in the spring of 1984, you said that France was the best ally of your country. Is this statement still valid?

The President. In the hearts of the American people, France has always had a special place, with profound ties of affection and respect. France was America's first ally, joining us in the fight for independence. Our two constitutions stand on a shared foundation of liberty and democracy, and our peoples are bound by common political and cultural traditions. Among the traditions which we both hold dear are respect for individual human rights and equality of all peoples. We share and respect these values, and they link us more strongly than any political agreement can. Since the days of Lafayette and through two world wars, Frenchmen and Americans have fought side by side in defense of our values. I was poignantly reminded of that bond two summers ago when I visited the Normandy beaches where so many Frenchmen and Americans gave their lives as brothers-in-arms. Today our two countries and peoples still stand together, both in the Atlantic alliance and around the world, and I have every confidence that we will continue to do so in the years to come.

U.S. Foreign Policy

Q. The interest of the United States for the Pacific nations is more and more obvious and geopolitically somehow natural. Does this mean that in the future, Europe and Africa have a chance of losing the major role they have had in American diplomacy since World War II?

The President. The NATO alliance remains the cornerstone of U.S. foreign policy. It not only embodies a fundamental security interest; it represents a community of moral and political values. It is no accident that one of America's most durable peacetime alliances is with our fellow democracies of the Atlantic world.

The Pacific nations are indeed growing in importance in political, security, and especially economic terms, but our strengthened relations with Asia have not diminished our traditional ties to Europe. Indeed, a major foreign policy accomplishment of this administration is its success in encouraging the industrialized democracies in Europe, Asia, and North America to cooperate in developing global, not parochial, solutions to our common economic and security problems. The United States has sought not merely to strengthen our bilateral ties with Asia and Europe but to encourage greater interaction among all members of the community of advanced industrialized democracies. This new and more cohesive allied consensus has been in evidence in the economic summit meetings, where the leaders of the seven largest industrialized democracies of North America, Europe, and Asia meet to discuss a vast range of political, economic, and security problems.

U.S. International Trade

Q. Commercial relations between the United States and the European Community are marked, and have been marked, by tensions and their quota of mutual accusations, but Congress is more and more pressing for measures against what it thinks are unfair practices. Do you think you would be able to reduce its appetite for protectionism?

The President. It's true some highly protectionist ideas are circulating in Congress right now. I recently rejected proposals to restrict footwear imports, and I will continue to fight protectionism. We remain dedicated to free trade; however, to remain free, trade must also be fair. Many of our industries face unfair trade practices by other nations. Unless our trading partners stop these practices, support in the United States for free trade will be undercut. I recently outlined a series of initiatives which my administration is going to take to eliminate such practices. We mean business on this question of fairness; it is fundamental to freedom and to avoiding the disastrous mis-

take of protectionism. I anticipate that the Congress and the administration will be working together on this problem.

Q. Do you think a new GATT round could terminate the commercial war which is flaring up between the United States and its occidental allies?

The President. The GATT has been the linchpin of the postwar trade system. It hasn't worked perfectly, but until recently it has kept the world trade system working relatively well. Now, we and our trading partners need to take a fresh look at the GATT and the new kinds of barriers that have been raised against trade. Early launching of a new GATT trade round is needed to shore up the open trading system. We think some parts of the GATT, for example the dispute settlement process, can be improved. Now, I know that improving the system won't solve all our trade problems, but I think it will help. There are many other things to negotiate in a new round as well, such as establishing rules for trade in services, breaking barriers to agricultural trade, improved protection of intellectual property rights, and the elimination of many nontariff barriers. I don't expect the new round to end all the trade disputes between the United States and Europe or Japan, but we will all be better off negotiating than closing our markets to one another in frustration over outdated and ineffective rules.

Note: A tape was not available for verification of the context of the oral portion of this interview, which was released by the Office of the Press Secretary on September 30.

Informal Exchange With Reporters on Secretary of Health and Human Services Margaret M. Heckler
September 30, 1985

Q. Mr. President, will you fire Margaret Heckler today or soon?

The President. There's never been any thought in my mind of firing Margaret Heckler. I don't know where these stories

have come from. They are not true.

Q. You're perfectly satisfied with her performance, then?

The President. Yes. That does not mean I don't have something else that I want her to do.

Q. So, she may be finding a new job soon? Another appointment?

The President. You'll hear in due time.

Q. Will you have the decision for meeting with Palestinian delegation? At the end of this meeting will you arrive at any decision?

The President. We'll wait until we have the meeting.

Q. Sounds like you are letting her go from the Cabinet.

The President. It'll all be explained soon, but you have been given a great deal of misinformation——

Q. When you——

Q. No one's risen to her defense lately.

The President. Pardon?

Q. No one's risen to her defense from here lately.

The President. Well, it's just burst in the last couple of days.

Q. Do you think that you will send her to an ambassadorial position or something of that kind in the near future?

The President. As I said, no further answer to this today. I would only suggest— I know I can't shut off the leaks, but you ought to be more astute at recognizing whether the leaks are true or not.

Q. Has anyone recommended, like Mr. Regan, for example—would you consider another position for her?

The President. No more comments on that.

Q. ——the visit of His Majesty, are you satisfied with his address at the United Nations especially—said we are prepared. Does that mean Jordan and PLO and the Arab world or what?

The President. Well, we're going to be discussing all those matters here together.

Note: The exchange began at 10:10 a.m. in the Oval Office at the White House, prior to discussions with King Hussein I of Jordan. Donald T. Regan was Assistant to the President and Chief of Staff. A tape was not available for verification of the content of this exchange.

Remarks Following Discussions With King Hussein I of Jordan
September 30, 1985

The President. I have just had a very productive meeting with King Hussein of Jordan. Jordan has been moving steadily and courageously forward in a search for a peaceful, negotiated settlement of the conflict in the Middle East. Jordan has not wavered from this course despite terrorist attacks against its diplomats and its interests abroad and the threat of worse to come. I told His Majesty in May that he could count on us for the economic and security assistance Jordan would need to address the risks that it is taking. Indeed, over the summer, the Congress improved an important package of economic aid for Jordan; but on Friday I notified the Congress that I would now be proposing a package of defensive arms. And these arms are important in meeting Jordan's proven defense needs and as evidence that those who seek peace will not be left at the mercy of those who

oppose it.

But peace, not arms, has been the focus of our discussions with our Jordanian friends. And all of us—Jordan, the United States, and Israel—share the same realistic objective: direct negotiations under appropriate auspices before the end of this year. There are complex and sensitive issues which must be resolved before actual negotiations can begin, but I believe these issues can be resolved.

Let me repeat that the United States is dedicated to achieving a just and durable peace between Israel and all its Arab neighbors. We'll do all that we can to maintain the momentum already achieved, much of it the result of King Hussein's personal courage and vision. The goal is peace and stability for Jordan, Israel, and all states in the Middle East. The way to that goal is through direct negotiations on the basis on

U.N. Security Council Resolutions 242 and 338. The time to begin is now. I know that His Majesty shares this aim, and I am proud to work with him in this noble endeavor of peace.

Your Majesty, once again, you have my thanks and the thanks of all our people.

The King. I wish to thank my dear and great friend, President Reagan, for his kind words. I value his friendship and the long-standing relations which happily exist between our two countries and which are based on our joint commitment to the common values and principles of liberty, freedom, equality, and human rights.

I have had a very useful meeting with the President. Our discussions were as frank and honest as our friendship dictates. I have reiterated to him Jordan's commitment to a negotiated settlement of the Arab-Israeli conflict within the context of an international conference to implement Security Council Resolution 242. I repeated to the President what I stated in my address to the United Nations 3 days ago; namely, Jor-

dan's unwavering position and condemnation of terrorism, irrespective of its nature and source. Jordan condemns violence and is committed to a peaceful resolution of the Arab-Israeli conflict. We are prepared to join all parties in pursuing a negotiated settlement in an environment free of belligerent and hostile acts.

I have also expressed Jordan's satisfaction with the positive development of our bilateral relations, especially in the economic and military fields. We endeavor to strengthen our ties and hope to continue our close cooperation in all areas. I wish you, Mr. President, continued good health, happiness, and success. And may the Almighty God bless you and grant you strength to lead this bastion of democracy to ever greater heights.

Thank you, sir.

Note: The President spoke at 10:52 a.m. at the South Portico of the White House. Earlier, the President and King Hussein met in the Oval Office.

Remarks at a Farewell Ceremony for General John W. Vessey, Jr., Chairman of the Joint Chiefs of Staff
September 30, 1985

Jack, I hope you weren't embarrassed by that uniform with the World War I helmet. The way I look at it, you're almost old enough now to run for President. [*Laughter*] But, as I say, Jack, don't let the uniform upset you, because, you know, we enlisted in the reserves at about the same time, and believe me, you should have seen my uniform—I was in the horse cavalry, which brings up an important point. You know, ladies and gentlemen, I recently disclosed that the real reason I ran for President was to bring back the horse cavalry. And when I took office some people told me I was now the most powerful man in the world. So, now that you're retiring, Jack, maybe you can tell me why every time I've brought up the horse cavalry in the Oval Office, you and Cap [Secretary of Defense Weinberger] would just smile and nod and say, "Yes, Mr.

President," and nothing would happen. [*Laughter*]

Ladies and gentlemen, we're here today to honor and thank Jack Vessey for his years of service and devotion to America. As you've heard, Jack Vessey's military career has taken him right to the top: four-star general, Vice Chief of Staff of the United States Army, and ultimately Chairman of the Joint Chiefs of Staff—and all of this after receiving a battlefield commission. I know Jack was proud of every rank and command he held; in each he performed with skill, competence, and devotion to duty. And yet for Jack Vessey, I suspect the title of which he was proudest was the first one he every held during his 46—count them—46 years of military service, the one he earned the day he joined the Minnesota National Guard, the title that said, "Jack

1157

Vessey, soldier."

General Vessey will be remembered for many things: as a battlefield hero—you've heard today about North Africa, Monte Cassino, Anzio, and that grim night with the 2d Battalion in Vietnam; he'll be remembered as a man of patriotism and deep religious belief, an officer who brought character and credit to every billet he ever held; as a military leader who always spoke his mind to civilian authority, respectfully but candidly; as the Chairman of the Joint Chiefs of Staff who presided over the restoration of America's military strength and power at a moment critical to the fate of freedom and his country's security. In all these things, he bore the marks of greatness.

But there's one accomplishment that is not there in Jack Vessey's personnel file, yet it's an accomplishment that made the difference in the lives of so many GI's over so many years in so many places around the globe. Jack Vessey always remembered the soldiers in the ranks; he understood those soldiers are the backbone of any army. He noticed them, spoke to them, looked out for them. Jack Vessey never forgot what it was like to be an enlisted man, to be just a GI.

Mark J. Neal, of Las Cruces, New Mexico, remembers. In January of 1975, he was a private at Fort Carson, a member of the drill team there. He said recently that after one drill team event, he was in his residence doing dishes—before the volunteer army, way back when Jack and I enlisted, it seems to me they had another name for doing dishes. Anyway, Mark Neal was told the commanding general wanted to see him. He was scared, of course, but he found his meeting and friendly chat with the general something he would always remember. After that, Mark Neal followed General Vessey's career. Hearing about his retirement, he wrote to him recently: "This short meeting made a lasting impression on me. It was amazing to me that you even knew I was on the premises . . . even more amaz-

ing that you would want to meet me. That moment of thoughtfulness for a lonely enlisted man back at Fort Carson proved the truth of your reputation as a real soldier's general." There were many Mark Neals in Jack Vessey's career, and Jack Vessey made their lives a little easier, a little less lonely. And he made them a little prouder to wear their country's uniform and defend freedom.

Jack, in the 5 years or so that I've been doing events like this, I've learned something about people like you. A career like yours, combining as it does heroism, patriotism, competence, wisdom, and kindness, doesn't need elaboration from commanders in chief or President; it speaks enough all by itself. And today I'll let history be your valedictorian, not me.

But what I can do today is thank you. On behalf of your friends here today who've had the honor of working with you and on behalf of some others who couldn't be here—all your fellow Americans, if they had the chance to be here, they would express their gratitude to you for making their lives and the lives of their children safer and more secure. And then, there's that other group I'm standing in for today. I know all of them would want to be remembered to you. I'm talking, of course, about those young people who wore the uniform for Jack Vessey, had the privilege of having their own GI general. So, from all of us, Jack—your friends, your fellow Americans, but especially the soldiers who stood a little taller because of you—thanks, thanks from a great and grateful nation. May God bless you and give you and Avis many more rich, fruitful, and happy years together.

And now, ladies and gentlemen, it is my honor to present to you a great soldier, a great general, a great GI—Jack Vessey.

Note: The President spoke at 11:57 a.m. in Hangar No. 2 at Andrews Air Force Base, MD.

Proclamation 5371—National Employ the Handicapped Week, 1985
September 30, 1985

By the President of the United States of America

A Proclamation

Today disabled men and women are entering the American labor force in unprecedented numbers, finding personal fulfillment and contributing to our society and our economy. The reasons for this welcome development are not hard to find: enhanced enforcement of laws that prohibit discrimination against the handicapped; actions by employers to provide more accessible work places and transportation; improved education and training; more innovative job accommodations; and better attitudes toward the disabled. The most important reason of all is the outstanding work record people with disabilities are achieving at their jobs.

But none of this should make us complacent. Much remains to be done if we are to bring brighter days to all the disabled people of our country.

All of us must constantly strive for full acceptance of disabled people, so that we begin to see people rather than disabilities. We must first learn, and then seek to inculcate in others, especially the young, a deep respect for the human person, whatever that person's handicaps. By doing so, we reaffirm the timeless American principle of equality of opportunity and help build a future in which the unique attributes of every citizen are recognized and allowed to develop for the good of all.

The Congress, by Joint Resolution approved August 11, 1945, as amended (36 U.S.C. 155), has called for the designation of the first full week in October of each year as "National Employ the Handicapped Week." This special week is a time for all Americans to join together to renew their dedication to meeting the goal of full opportunities for disabled citizens.

Now, Therefore, I, Ronald Reagan, President of the United States of America, do hereby designate the week beginning October 6, 1985, as National Employ the Handicapped Week. I urge all governors, mayors, other public officials, leaders in business and labor, and private citizens to help meet the challenge of the future by ensuring that disabled people have the opportunity to participate fully in the economic life of the Nation.

In Witness Whereof, I have hereunto set my hand this thirtieth day of September, in the year of our Lord nineteen hundred and eighty-five, and of the Independence of the United States of America the two hundred and tenth.

RONALD REAGAN

[*Filed with the Office of the Federal Register, 4:19 p.m., September 30, 1985*]

Executive Order 12533—President's Advisory Committee on Mediation and Conciliation
September 30, 1985

By the authority vested in me as President by the Constitution and laws of the United States of America, including the Federal Advisory Committee Act, as amended (5 U.S.C. App. I), and in order to extend the life of the President's Advisory Committee on Mediation and Conciliation and clarify the status of its members, it is hereby ordered that Executive Order No. 12462, as amended, is further amended as follows:

Section 1 is amended by deleting the word "twelve" and inserting in its place the word "thirteen" and by adding the following sentence at the end thereof:

"The members of the Committee other than the Chairman shall serve as representatives of labor and of management, and labor and management shall be equally represented among its members."

Section 4(b) is amended to read: "The Committee shall terminate on December 31, 1986, unless sooner extended."

RONALD REAGAN

The White House,
September 30, 1985.

[*Filed with the Office of the Federal Register, 11:50 a.m., October 1, 1985*]

Executive Order 12534—Continuance of Certain Federal Advisory Committees

September 30, 1985

By the authority vested in me as President by the Constitution and statutes of the United States of America, and in accordance with the provisions of the Federal Advisory Committee Act, as amended (5 U.S.C. App. I), it is hereby ordered as follows:

Section 1. Each advisory committee listed below is continued until September 30, 1987:

(a) Advisory Committee on Small and Minority Business Ownership; Executive Order No. 12190 (Small Business Administration).

(b) Committee for the Preservation of the White House; Executive Order No. 11145, as amended (Department of the Interior).

(c) Federal Advisory Council on Occupational Safety and Health; Executive Order No. 12196 (Department of Labor).

(d) President's Commission on White House Fellowships; Executive Order No. 11183, as amended (Office of Personnel Management).

(e) President's Committee on the Arts and the Humanities; Executive Order No. 12367 (National Endowment for the Arts).

(f) President's Committee on the International Labor Organization; Executive Order No. 12216 (Department of Labor).

(g) President's Committee on Mental Retardation; Executive Order No. 11776 (Department of Health and Human Services).

(h) President's Committee on the National Medal of Science; Executive Order No. 11287, as amended (National Science Foundation).

(i) President's Council on Physical Fitness and Sports; Executive Order No. 12345, as amended (Department of Health and Human Services).

(j) President's Economic Policy Advisory Board; Executive Order No. 12296 (Office of Policy Development).

(k) President's National Security Telecommunications Advisory Committee; Executive Order No. 12382, as amended (Department of Defense).

(l) President's Export Council; Executive Order No. 12131 (Department of Commerce).

Sec. 2. Notwithstanding the provisions of any other Executive Order, the functions of the President under the Federal Advisory Committee Act that are applicable to the committees listed in Section 1 of this Order, except that of reporting annually to the Congress, shall be performed by the head of the department or agency designated after each committee, in accordance with guidelines and procedures established by the Administrator of General Services.

Sec. 3. The following Executive Orders, which established committees that have terminated or been abolished by statute or whose work is completed, are revoked:

(a) Executive Order No. 12502, establishing the Chemical Warfare Review Commission.

(b) Executive Order No. 12369, establishing the President's Private Sector Survey on Cost Control in the Federal Government.

(c) Executive Order No. 12395, establishing the International Private Enterprise

Task Force.

(d) Executive Order No. 12433, establishing the National Bipartisan Commission on Central America.

(e) Executive Order No. 12335, establishing the National Commission on Social Security Reform.

(f) Executive Order No. 12332, establishing the National Productivity Advisory Committee.

(g) Executive Order No. 12412, establishing the Peace Corps Advisory Council.

(h) Executive Order No. 12426, establishing the President's Committee on Women's Business Ownership.

(i) Executive Order No. 12499, establishing the President's Blue Ribbon Task Group on Nuclear Weapons Program Management.

(j) Executive Order No. 12428, establishing the President's Commission on Industrial Competitiveness.

(k) Executive Order No. 12400, establishing the President's Commission on Strategic Forces.

(l) Executive Order No. 12439, establishing the President's Task Force on Food Assistance.

(m) Executive Order No. 12421, establishing the Presidential Commission on the Conduct of United States-Japan Relations.

(n) Executive Order No. 12401, establishing the Presidential Commission on Indian Reservation Economies.

(o) Executive Order No. 12468, establishing the Presidential Advisory Council on the Peace Corps.

Sec. 4. Executive Order No. 12399 and Executive Order No. 12489 are superseded.

Sec 5. This Order shall be effective September 30, 1985.

RONALD REAGAN

The White House,
September 30, 1985.

[Filed with the Office of the Federal Register, 11:51 a.m., October 1, 1985]

Letter Accepting the Resignation of Edward J. Rollins, Jr., as Assistant to the President for Political and Governmental Affairs
September 30, 1985

Dear Ed:

It is with deep regret that I accept your resignation as Assistant to the President for Political and Governmental Affairs, effective October 1, 1985.

The poet who wrote that "parting is such sweet sorrow" never said whether leave-takings get any easier when they're done twice. The first time I accepted your resignation, in October 1983, it was with considerable regret, but at least I had the consolation of knowing that you would be near at hand at the Reagan-Bush '84 Committee if I ultimately decided to seek reelection to a second term. Having counted on your professional experience and wise counsel throughout my first years in office, I was reassured to know that our effort to get out a message of hope and opportunity to the American people would be under such capable direction.

As the adage goes, the rest is history. But I think our success, which in so many ways is your success, flowed from a quality that you have exemplified at every stage of your career. And that is a recognition that neither effective government nor successful campaigns really depend on the delivery of messages to the people. Rather they depend on their willingness to hear the message of the people, and to give voice to their deepest aspirations of freedom, dignity, and self-government. In those long hours of travel and strategy meetings, from great cities to the smallest plots of this good American earth, you helped us all keep in mind the fundamental principles that brought our team to office in 1981.

I'm not surprised, then, that a time should come when you would move on to the private sector where those principles can be practiced to the fullest. I know that

1161

your consummate skill and professionalism will serve you well in all your endeavors. But please don't expect that those endeavors will forever be to the exclusion of public life: I intend to call on you frequently in the months ahead for the advice, wisdom, wit and, most of all, friendship you've provided over the last five years.

From the bottom of my heart, Ed, thank you for all you have done for me and for our beloved America. Nancy joins me in sending you our warmest wishes for every future success and happiness.

Sincerely,

/s/RON

September 18, 1985

Dear Mr. President:

This letter is probably one of the most difficult I will ever write because the decision it represents is the most difficult I've ever made.

Effective October 1, 1985, I am resigning my position as your Assistant for Political and Governmental Affairs.

After nearly five years in the White House and the campaign and 16 years of service at the local, state and federal levels of government, I've decided it's time to move on to the private sector and give Reaganomics a chance to work for me. As you have often said, if we start referring to the government as we, instead of them, then we've been here too long. I'm starting to think like "them" and obviously I've been here too long.

However, it is with a mixture of nostalgia, pride and regret that I will be leaving.

Nostalgia, because in looking back over the past five years, I can say without hesitation that they have been the most exciting, rewarding and inspirational of my career.

Pride, because I have had the privilege of serving a man who has been touched by destiny and whom destiny will not let go.

Regret, because it isn't over until it's over, and I firmly believe during the next three years you will continue to earn a place in history as one of this nation's greatest Presidents.

When the history books are written on you, Mr. President, your Presidency will be seen as a time of turning.

A time when America turned from excessive government and renewed the strength of its economy and the vigor of its people.

A time when we as a country moved off the defensive in the world and began to promote the ideals of liberty, peace, trade and democracy that nurtured our forefathers before us.

A time when the life of ordinary Americans improved, a time when they dared to dream again.

But most of all, Mr. President, your time in office will be viewed as a period when the Presidency worked. A period in which leadership and courage prevailed. Mr. President, you might not realize it but a whole generation of young Americans grew up in the last 20 years who never knew a successful Presidency. Now they know a successful two-term Presidency. That alone will help re-write history.

When Americans look back on these years, our gratitude for you will be even more profound than it already is.

Mr. President, I can never thank you enough for the privilege of serving you over the last five years. I am honored that I was able to be a small part of your team during this time of choosing and this time of changing. I will always take pride in having been a member of your staff during this critical period when you made America—Prouder, Stronger and Better—for ourselves, our families and the future.

Thank you, Mr. President and my prayers and best wishes for your success.

Sincerely,

/s/ED

P.S. I'm still sorry about not winning Minnesota—if you had a decent campaign manager, you would have won all 50 states.

Note: The originals were not available for verification of the content of these letters.

Statement on Congressional Action on Fiscal Year 1986 Appropriations Bills
September 30, 1985

I am pleased that the Congress has passed H.J. Res. 388, an acceptable continuing resolution. Now action on the regular fiscal year 1986 appropriations bills must proceed without delay.

I urge the Congress to pass all the individual bills promptly within the levels assumed in the congressional budget resolution and to present to me bills that are consistent with both the need for restraint in domestic spending and support of the defense and international interests of the Nation. As we meet with the Soviets to discuss sensitive and important arms control issues, it is particularly important that we not be hindered by lack of congressional action on or inadequate support for our FY '86 national security programs.

If the Congress cannot hold spending at its own budget resolution guidelines, we will not have meaningful deficit reduction. The performance to date is not encouraging. Only two of the House-passed appropriations bills for domestic programs are within the guidelines of the budget resolution. We will be working with the Congress to achieve a more responsible outcome.

Note: H.J. Res. 338, approved September 30, was assigned Public Law No. 99-103.

Statement on Signing the Federal Highway Funding Bill
October 1, 1985

I have signed S. 1514, which will approve the Interstate Cost Estimate (ICE) and the Interstate Substitute Cost Estimate (ISCE). Signing this bill will permit the timely release of about $4.8 billion in Federal aid highway funds. My administration has consistently urged the passage of a clean ICE and ISCE approval bill to permit the release of about $4.8 billion in highway user fees. In the past 2 years, delays in approval of the ICE and ISCE have tended to disrupt highway construction plans. We must continue to keep the highway program free of costly special interest projects that hamper our ability to fund the national Federal interest highway system. It is with great pleasure that I sign S. 1514.

Note: S. 1514, approved September 30, was assigned Public Law No. 99-104.

Message to the Congress Reporting Budget Deferrals
October 1, 1985

To the Congress of the United States:

In accordance with the Impoundment Control Act of 1974, I herewith report 23 new deferrals of budget authority for 1986 totaling $1,628,765,311. The deferrals affect accounts in Funds Appropriated to the President, the Departments of Agriculture, Defense-Military, Defense-Civil, Energy, Health and Human Services, Justice, and State, the Pennsylvania Avenue Development Corporation, and the Railroad Retirement Board.

The details of these deferrals are contained in the attached report.

RONALD REAGAN

The White House,
October 1, 1985.

Note: The attachment detailing the deferrals was printed in the Federal Register *of October 8.*

Message to the Congress Reporting Budget Deferrals
October 1, 1985

To the Congress of the United States:

In accordance with the Impoundment Control Act of 1974, I herewith report two new deferrals of budget authority for 1985 totaling $10,438,657 and two revised deferrals now totaling $1,433,548,866. The deferrals affect accounts in Funds Appropriated to the President and the Departments of Health and Human Services and State.

The details of these deferrals are contained in the attached report.

RONALD REAGAN

The White House,
October 1, 1985.

Note: The attachment detailing the deferrals was printed in the Federal Register *of October 8.*

Proclamation 5372—United Nations Day, 1985
October 1, 1985

By the President of the United States of America

A Proclamation

The founders of the United Nations, meeting in San Francisco 40 years ago, set forth in the U.N. Charter the fervent hope that humanity might experience peace and international cooperation in the era after the greatest and most costly war ever experienced. The ideals expressed in the Charter were that all member states would work together to maintain international peace and security, encourage human rights, and cooperate in dealing with the economic, social, humanitarian, and technical problems that afflict our planet.

The United Nations and its family of international organizations have sought, constructively, to improve the human condition. Many people today live under better conditions because of work done in the name of these organizations. That hope for international cooperation, expressed 40 years ago, has been achieved most often in the U.N.'s technical, development, and humanitarian agencies. The United Nations Children's Fund (UNICEF), the World Health Organization (WHO), the International Civil Aviation Organization (ICAO), the World Meteorological Organization (WMO), the International Atomic Energy Agency (IAEA), and the World Food Program (WFP), for example, have made major contributions to the safety and welfare of people everywhere.

On this the United Nation's 40th Anniversary, it is appropriate that all member states reflect not only on the achievements of the organization, but also its shortcomings, its unfulfilled promise, and yes, even its failures. We do so in a positive spirit, seeking constructive solutions to those problems that prevent the U.N. from realizing its full potential and fully embodying the ideals of the Charter. We believe that by facing those problems realistically and working together, many can be solved. The tasks before us are not easy. It will require both patience and dedication to the ideals of the U.N. Charter. We owe it to ourselves, however, to our children, and to all future generations to make this effort.

To the American people and their elected representatives, the United Nations plays an important role in the search for peace with justice. It provides a forum where member states can discuss and try to resolve their differences peacefully, in the spirit of the Charter. We will continue to do all we can to support that process within the U.N., within recognized regional fora, and in direct bilateral dialogue. As we encourage more responsible international behavior, we strengthen the United Nations and the prospect for achieving the goals of its Charter. But much more can and must be done. We look to all member states to support the sound principles upon which the U.N. was founded. These include respect for the rights and views of states that may find themselves in the minority, and support for recognized regional associations as provided for in the Charter, as well as the wise use of its own resources and established procedures.

The people and the government of the United States take satisfaction in the very substantial moral, political, and financial support we have given to the United Nations since its founding. We remain firmly committed to the noble ideals set forth in the Charter; they are entirely consonant with the ideals embodied in our own political institutions. The United Nations continues to stand as the symbol of the hopes of all mankind for a more peaceful and productive world. We must not disappoint those hopes.

Now, Therefore, I, Ronald Reagan, President of the United States of America, do hereby proclaim Thursday, October 24, 1985, as United Nations Day and urge all Americans to acquaint themselves with the activities of the United Nations, its accomplishments, and the challenges it faces. I have appointed Peter H. Dailey to serve as 1985 United States Chairman for United Nations Day and welcome the role of the United Nations Association of the United States of America in working with him to celebrate this special day.

In Witness Whereof, I have hereunto set my hand this first day of October, in the year of our Lord nineteen hundred and eighty-five, and of the Independence of the United States of America the two hundred and tenth.

RONALD REAGAN

[*Filed with the Office of the Federal Register, 11:57 a.m., October 1, 1985*]

Nomination of C. Everett Koop To Be Surgeon General of the Public Health Service
October 1, 1985

The President today announced his intention to nominate C. Everett Koop to be Surgeon General of the Public Health Service, Department of Health and Human Services, for a term of 4 years. This is a reappointment.

Since 1981 Dr. Koop has been serving as Surgeon General of the Public Health Service. Previously he was Deputy Assistant Secretary of Health, Department of Health and Human Services. He was surgeon-in-chief of Children's Hospital of Philadelphia, PA, and professor of pediatric surgery at the University of Pennsylvania Medical School. He began his association with the University of Pennsylvania in 1941. He is a member of the Commission on Cancer, American College of Surgeons; the Surgical Steering Committee; Children's Cancer Study Group; and the Cancer Committee, American Pediatric Surgical Association. He has received many honorary degrees and is the author of more than 170 articles and books on the practice of medicine.

Dr. Koop graduated from Dartmouth College (A.B., 1937), Cornell Medical School (M.D., 1941), and the Graduate School of Medicine of the University of Pennsylvania (Sc.D., 1947). He is married, has four children, and resides in Bethesda, MD. He was born October 14, 1916, in New York City, NY.

Nomination of Richard Schifter To Be an Assistant Secretary of State
October 1, 1985

The President today announced his intention to nominate Richard Schifter to be Assistant Secretary of State for Human Rights and Humanitarian Affairs. He would succeed Elliott Abrams.

Mr. Schifter is a partner in the law firm of Fried, Frank, Harris, Shriver and Kampelman in Washington, DC. Since 1981 he has been serving as U.S. Representative to the United Nations Commission for Human Rights. He was Deputy U.S. Representative in the Security Council of the United Nations with the rank of Ambassador in 1984–1985; Alternate Representative for the United Nations Commission on Human Rights in 1981–1982; United States Representative, Committee on Conventions and Recommendations, UNESCO, in 1981–1982; and a member of the President's Task Force on American Indians in 1966–1967. He has been a member of the United States Holocaust Council since 1980.

Mr. Schifter graduated from the College of the City of New York (B.S., 1943) and Yale Law School (LL.B., 1951). He is married, has five children, and resides in Bethesda, MD. He was born July 31, 1923, in Vienna, Austria.

Executive Order 12535—Prohibition of the Importation of the South African Krugerrand
October 1, 1985

By the authority vested in me as President by the Constitution and laws of the United States of America, including the International Emergency Economic Powers Act (50 U.S.C. 1701 *et seq.*), in order to take steps additional to those set forth in Executive Order No. 12532 of September 9, 1985, to deal with the unusual and extraordinary threat to the foreign policy and economy of the United States referred to in that Order, and in view of the continuing nature of that emergency, the recommendations made by the United Nations Security Council in Resolution No. 569 of July 26, 1985, and the completion of consultations by the Secretary of State and the United States Trade Representative directed by Section 5(a) of Executive Order No. 12532, it is hereby ordered that the importation into the United States of South African Krugerrands is prohibited effective 12:01 a.m. Eastern Daylight Time October 11, 1985. The Secretary of the Treasury is authorized to promulgate such rules and regulations as may be necessary to carry out this prohibition.

RONALD REAGAN

The White House,
October 1, 1985.

[*Filed with the Office of the Federal Register, 4:45 p.m., October 1, 1985*]

Message to the Congress on the Prohibition of the Importation of the South African Krugerrand
October 1, 1985

To the Congress of the United States:
On September 9, 1985, I informed the Congress pursuant to Section 204(b) of the International Emergency Economic Powers

Act, 50 U.S.C. 1703(b), that I had exercised my statutory authority to prohibit certain transactions involving South Africa (Executive Order No. 12532). I also informed the Congress that the Executive Order directed the Secretary of State and the United States Trade Representative to consult with other parties to the General Agreement on Tariffs and Trade with a view toward adopting a prohibition on the import of Krugerrands.

In order to deal with the unusual and extraordinary threat to the foreign policy and economy of the United States referred to in Executive Order No. 12532, and in view of the continuing nature of that emergency, and in view of the successful completion of those consultations, I have issued an Executive order, a copy of which is attached, exercising my statutory authority to

prohibit such imports effective October 11, 1985.

All of the measures I have adopted against South Africa are directed at apartheid and the South African Government, and not against the people of that country or its economy. The Krugerrand measure ordered was taken in recognition of the fact that the Krugerrand is perceived in the Congress as an important symbol of apartheid. This view is widely shared by the U.S. public. I am directing this prohibition in recognition of these public and congressional sentiments.

RONALD REAGAN

The White House,
October 1, 1985.

Message to the Congress Transmitting the Soviet-United States Fishery Agreement
October 1, 1985

To the Congress of the United States:

In accordance with the Magnuson Fishery Conservation and Management Act of 1976 (the Act) (16 U.S.C. 1801 *et seq.*), I transmit herewith an exchange of Diplomatic Notes, together with the present agreement, extending the Governing International Fishery Agreement between the United States and the Union of Soviet Socialist Republics, signed at Washington on November 26, 1976, until December 31, 1986. The exchange of notes, together with the present agreement, constitutes a Governing Inter-

national Fishery Agreement within the requirements of Section 201(c) of the Act.

In order to prevent the interruption of joint fishery arrangements between the United States and the Union of Soviet Socialist Republics when the current agreement expires on December 31, I urge that the Congress give favorable consideration to this extension at an early date.

RONALD REAGAN

The White House,
October 1, 1985.

Remarks to Business Leaders During a White House Briefing on Tax Reform
October 1, 1985

Thank you, and good afternoon, and welcome to the White House. It's an honor to be able to greet so many leaders of American business. You provide our nation with

jobs, direct the creation of much of our wealth, and oversee the development of innovations which keep our economy vibrant. Now, you've come together to perform a further service to our nation by supporting America's fair share tax plan.

Permit me to congratulate you, first of all, for taking out that full-page newspaper ad last week. Believe me, it's not often that I get so much pleasure from opening the Washington Post. [*Laughter*] Your efforts on behalf of our tax reform plan represent an important contribution to the national debate. Many already understand that our plan will lower Federal income taxes for most individuals, but there has been confusion—some of it sown intentionally—over just what our plan would mean to American business. Well, permit me to set the record straight.

For small business, our plan will represent a substantial tax break. Unincorporated small businesses, as you know, are taxed according to the personal incomes of their owners. As our plan reduces personal income tax rates for most individuals, therefore, it will be doing the same for many unincorporated small businesses. The top individual rate alone will come down from 50 to just 35 percent. Incorporated small businesses will receive graduated rates of 15, 18, 25, and 33 percent—a measure that will prove of particular benefit to businesses that are just getting started. This tax relief will benefit our entire economy as small businesses multiply and grow. From late 1982 to late 1984, industries in which small businesses predominated created new jobs at the rate of more than 11 percent. Under our progrowth plan, new jobs could be created even more quickly.

For big business, America's tax plan will mean a lower maximum corporate tax rate—down from 46 to 33 percent. Countless provisions for special treatment will be reduced or eliminated. Compare this to the present system. The corporate tax structure today represents a vast maze of deductions, credits, and allowances for those industries and corporations who happen to be favored by Capitol Hill. It encourages competition of the worst kind, not to produce better products at lower prices, but to assemble ever bigger, more clever terms of lobbyists—or teams of lobbyists, I should say, or to hire lawyers more skilled in taking advantage of tax code ambiguities. It all amounts to a so-called industrial policy—

that's a fancy name for Washington using the tax code to tell you how to run your business.

Every man and woman in this room must know a gifted fellow worker whose career has been spent entirely on tax policy or political calculations. Think of that person as I assert that in making taxes simpler and lower we'll be engaging in a great act of liberation, and the countless individuals who now waste their talents on tax considerations will be set free—free to participate in the ennobling work of creating new goods, services, and techniques. My friends, isn't it time that we let American business get back down to business?

For capital formation, our plan envisions a cut in the top rate on capital gains to just 17½ percent. This measure is founded on clear-cut, recent experience. During the seventies, you remember that capital formation suffered. High rates on capital gains combined with raging inflation nearly wiped out sources of venture capital and turned many of our best entrepreneurs into tax refugees. One story concerns Gene Amdahl, the inventor of what many consider the most successful computer ever built. Back in the seventies he decided to start his own company. He searched America for capital; he couldn't find enough. In the end he was forced to go to a large high-technology firm in Japan. They gave him capital—in return for the rights to his ideas.

And then in 1978 taxes on capital gains were cut, and in 1981 we cut them again. The number of dollars committed to venture capital has exploded, from just $39 million available in 1977 has grown to more than $4 billion last year. Today entrepreneurs like Gene Amdahl are able to get the capital they need here at home. Indeed, former Massachusetts Senator Paul Tsongas said of the 1978 cut in the capital gains tax rate—and listen carefully to these words of his: "That bill, which I did not support, did more for the economy of my State than anything I did as a Congressman." When we cut the tax on capital gains again this year, capital formation will climb still higher. Perhaps the most significant aspect of our plan is that it will be good for business, employees and customers, and the

American people.

And I have already mentioned that we'll lower the rates for most individuals. In addition, we'll increase to $4,000 the standard deduction for married couples filing jointly, and nearly double the personal exemption from just over $1,000 all the way to $2,000. The American people will have more money in their pockets, more with which to purchase your goods, more to save, and more to invest. History is clear: When we pit industry against industry in a costly combat for special tax treatment, when we diminish disposable income by shifting the tax burden onto individuals and families, then we choke off the sources of economic growth and innovation. America's tax plan will do the reverse. It will promote fairness by making certain that everyone—corporations and individuals alike—pays his fair share. It'll increase disposable income and foster capital formation. It will, I'm convinced, inaugurate a new era of economic opportunity and growth.

Recently, the Council of Economic Advisers completed a study of our proposal's long-term economic impact. Using conservative estimates, the Council found that America's tax plan would increase gross national product by 2½ to 3.2 percent over the next 10 years, and that's the equivalent of providing 11 years of growth in just a decade. That translates into the equivalent of almost 4 million additional new jobs over the next 10 years and from $600 to $900 a year in additional income for every American household. My friends, I think that's growth of historic proportions. Needless to say, these growth estimates are based on America's tax plan, and I intend to fight for our plan: a top corporate rate of 33 percent; a top capital gains rate of 17½ percent; 15, 25, 35 percent rates for individuals; a standard deduction of $4,000; and a nearly doubled personal exemption of $2,000.

To those who say that we can't get tax reform passed this year, I have a simple answer. The word I'd like to use was a favorite of Harry Truman's, and Bess didn't like it much—[*laughter*]—and I'm afraid Nancy doesn't approve, either. [*Laughter*] And since I can't think of an acceptable substitute word anywhere as eloquent as Harry's, I'll just use more words and say,

yes, it can be passed this year if all of us do what we know is the statesmanlike thing to do and quit playing political games.

Tax reform is among the most pressing issues facing the country. There can be no greater demand upon the time and attention of the Congress. For delay in enacting it, there can be no excuse. In the words of Congressman Rostenkowski: "To those who are preparing to stand against the change, I have a warning," he said. "Don't underestimate the public. Demand for reform is growing." I've kind of guessed that myself. I've gone out, as you know, and a few places—and we'll be doing it again this week to talk about this to crowds. And when you go into a town of 14,000 for an outdoor rally and see more than 20,000 people standing in the hot sun and had been there for a couple of hours waiting, and they had made great banners hailing the tax reform, and you're applauded on just about everything that you say about it, I think that Rostenkowski is right: The public is further along on this than some of the boys on the Hill are giving them credit for.

Well, permit me one final thought. The practice of business is, in large measure, a moral endeavor; a practice in which men and women give of themselves, their strength, their intelligence, and imagination to unlock the mysteries of the material world on behalf of their fellow man. To inhibit this process through an oppressive system of taxation is, in a fundamental sense, to inhibit human development. What we're dealing with in the matter of tax reform is not there for a mere collection of facts and figures, but the liberation of the human spirit.

And speaking about the opportunities created by recent tax cuts, George Gilder, author of the "Spirit of Enterprise," has stated, and I'll read his words: "Opportunities summon initiatives. Initiatives develop character and a sense of responsibility, a feeling of optimism. The future looks more open and promising to our young people than it did before, for the simple reason that it is more open and promising. We've had a doubling of business starts in the last seven years. There has been a riot of new technologies; there has been a convergence of policy and technology that has changed the spirit of America." My friends, by enacting this historic tax reform, we can make America's spirit brighter still. And with your help, I'm confident we will.

Thank you for what you're doing. Thank you for being here, and God bless you.

Thank you very much. Now, Don says I got to get back to work.

Note: The President spoke at 1:30 p.m. in the East Room at the White House. In his closing remarks, the President referred to Donald T. Regan, Assistant to the President and Chief of Staff.

Remarks Announcing the Nomination of Margaret M. Heckler To Be United States Ambassador to Ireland and a Question-and-Answer Session With Reporters
October 1, 1985

The President. I've come here to make an announcement and also to say a few words with regard to that announcement. I am delighted and happier than I've been in a long time that Margaret Heckler has agreed to my request that she become the Ambassador to Ireland.

And in saying this, I would like to say— and I'm sorry that I didn't start saying it sooner—that the malicious gossip, without any basis in fact, that had been going on for the last several days about this is without any basis in fact. She has done a fine job at HHS. As a matter of fact, if she hadn't done such a good job, I wouldn't have been so eager to seek her out to be the Ambassador to Ireland. And whoever finally replaces her there, as she goes on to her new duties, will find that that agency is in great shape as a result of her direction and her leadership.

And it has been absolutely unjustified— whoever has been leaking these falsehoods and intimating—well, for one thing, I certainly have never thought of the Embassies as dumping grounds. And, therefore, if she hadn't been doing as well as she has been doing, I certainly would not have picked Ireland, or any Embassy for that matter, but Ireland especially, for her to take that post. And, as I say, I'm delighted that—she had to give it some thought, of course, leaving the country, and a whole new post—but I had been putting on quite a sales pitch because this was my idea, and I wanted her very much to do that.

Q. What is the malicious gossip, sir, that you refer to? You mean the fact that leaks, coming mainly from your administration, said that she'd be appointed Ambassador to Ireland?

The President. No, the leaks that we were doing this in some way because we were unhappy with what she was doing where she was.

Q. You were not unhappy?

The President. No.

Q. Have you reprimanded any members of your staff or talked to them about any of these reports?

The President. This sort of thing has been going on—and they tell me that it's kind of typical of the territory—this has been going on for some time; Margaret isn't the first. This has been happening with others—not only Cabinet members but the staff members and so forth. And to this day, I've never been able to find the individuals responsible for this. And——

Q. Sir, if you're not unhappy with the job that she's been doing, why doesn't Mrs. Heckler stay in that position?

The President. Well, because we have a need for an Ambassador, and Ireland is getting very impatient, and I thought that she might like a change of pace. It was my desire for her, and I think that she will be just great in that particular spot.

Q. How much of a selling tactic do you have to do, Mr. President? We understood that as of the other day Mrs. Heckler didn't want the job.

The President. I think Mrs. Heckler was justifiably upset by the kind of gossip that was going around, and——

Q. Are you appointing Jack Svahn as her replacement?

The President. No.

Q. Speak to some of that gossip, Mr. President. The word is that she wasn't conservative enough, that she wasn't true enough for the "true believers" in your administration, particularly Mr. Regan.

The President. No, Don was my messenger in carrying the word to her that I wanted her to be the Ambassador, and this was some time ago.

Q. Mr. President, since you're here, do you agree with——

Q. Could you let him finish, please, Andrea [Andrea Mitchell, NBC News]?

The President. No, I don't know, as I say, where this was coming from. But, as I say, it was malicious; it was false. No——

Q. Well, is she conservative enough? Just speak to that point, sir?

The President. Yes, you bet she is, and she's executed the policies that I have wanted for that particular agency, and, as I say, it is in great shape. She has done a fine job, and if she hadn't, well, then I don't think I would have asked her to be an Ambassador.

Q. Is this a promotion, Mr. President?

The President. What?

Q. Is this a promotion, sir?

The President. I don't know whether one job is better or greater than another, but I think that there is a distinction to an ambassadorship. The title is retained for life, and, after all, when you come down to the Embassies, the Ambassadors are the personal representatives of the President.

Q. Mr. President, since you're here, could you tell us, do you agree with the administration officials who've said that they feel the Soviet offer is unbalanced because it locks in their superiority, particularly in terms of strategic missiles and because it would prevent us from deploying the D–5, the Midgetman, the MX, some of the things that are coming on line?

The President. Andrea, I am not going to comment on this, and I don't think anyone should. This is in the hands now of the ne-

gotiators, and I just don't think that you, from outside, get into public discussions about things of that kind. But I am not going to take any more questions on any other subject.

Q. Mr. President, do you condone the Israeli raid, sir, the Israeli raid into Tunis? Do you condone the Israeli raid into Tunisia?

The President. Sam [Sam Donaldson, ABC News], I will take other questions later on, but not today.

Q. Were U.S. planes involved?

The President. We're due at a Cabinet meeting. Would you like to say something?

Secretary Heckler. All right. Yes.

Q. Were U.S. planes involved, Mr. President? Could you clear up that one issue? Were U.S. planes involved in the Israeli raid?

The President. I'm not going to comment on that at all, Chris [Chris Wallace, NBC News], and I don't know. I don't know the facts.

Q. Because there has been a prohibition, as you know, in the past against using U.S. planes for offensive purposes.

Principal Deputy Press Secretary Speakes. He said he wasn't going to comment, Chris.

The President. Yes, I am not going to comment. No.

Secretary Heckler. May I just say, Mr. President——

Q. Do you have a successor for Mrs. Heckler?

The President. Madame Ambassador.

Secretary Heckler. Not quite. Mr. President, I'd like to say that I have had a really rewarding and challenging career in public service. In serving as a Member of Congress for 16 years and having the honor of being appointed by you, sir, to represent you, carry your portfolio of health and human services—these have been very important opportunities for public service which has really been my life.

Now that you have offered me the post of Ambassador to the Republic of Ireland, I see a new opportunity for public service. And I think every American of Irish ancestry can appreciate the special place that Ireland is to each of us. It is especially special at this time as we hoped there will be some movement toward the reconciliation of the most serious and difficult issue in that country. I look upon your trust in me as a new facet of a public service career. I thank you, Mr. President, for the faith that you have reposed in me. It has been an honor to represent you in the role that I have played. And as I look to the new day in the future, it will be as an honor and a very exciting challenge to represent you as Ambassador to Ireland. And I thank you for the opportunity.

Q. Mrs. Heckler, what changed your mind, because you said in August that this was a job that you didn't want? What changed your mind?

Secretary Heckler. When the Great Communicator—[*laughter*]—our leader, the President of the United States, asks one to take on an assignment that is significant and important—not only in his eyes but, truly, in terms of its external impact as well as internal impact, important to many Americans of Irish background—it is, in my view, irresponsible for one who has served in public office for all these years—or public service—to have said no to the President at his request.

Q. Did Don Regan kick you out, Mrs. Heckler? Did Don Regan force you out of the White House?

Secretary Heckler. The President and I are the only two who have discussed the issue of my service in both the Cabinet and my service as Ambassador to Ireland. I feel very strongly that the President, in offering me an opportunity for a new dimension in service, he reposed in me a special degree of trust. I looked upon this assignment with new eyes having heard the presentation that he made and having also his assurance that it was my choice to stay on as Secretary of HHS or to become Ambassador to Ireland.

Q. Mrs. Heckler, what do think of the political whispering against you?

Q. Mrs. Heckler, Mrs. Heckler, what do think of these reports that you were not up to the job?

Q. You've heard the whispering campaign—excuse me, Chris—you've heard the whispering campaign against you. What do you think of that whispering campaign which said either that you are not conservative enough or that you are not a good administrator? Speak to it.

Secretary Heckler. I'm very proud of my record as Secretary of Health and Human Services. I'm proud of the fact that we inaugurated the perspective payment plan; we've inaugurated a new direction in health policy; I have carried the President's portfolio and been faithful to his philosophy and to his directives. I'm very proud of what I leave behind and would expect that the new drug approval process at FDA and the other changes that I've inaugurated will actually be implemented by my successor. I would expect these things to happen. But I am also very proud of the fact that this President, whom I consider to be a great leader, has now asked me to take on a new challenge, a new direction in my life.

Q. Is this a promotion or a demotion, Mrs. Heckler?

Q. So, you don't consider yourself incompetent, as that whispering campaign would have it?

Secretary Heckler. I am proud of my service in all regards. And, frankly, I am proud of the team who has helped me and the individuals at HHS who have made my service, I believe, as distinguished as it is.

Q. Mr. President, any other changes——

Q. Was it your understanding that you could have stayed on as Secretary of HHS?

Secretary Heckler. That was clearly my understanding.

Q. Mr. President, have you spoken to Mr. Regan about the furor that this caused, and do you hold him, in any way, responsible?

The President. No. He and I have talked about this and how to resolve this and, no, he's——

Q. You don't think he had anything to do with stirring this up?

The President. No. He's on our side.

Q. Could she have stayed on, Mr. President, as she said?

The President. Yes.

Q. If she had turned this down, she could have stayed on at HHS?

The President. Yes.

Q. Who's the successor?

The President. We have not made a selection yet.

Q. When will you?

Q. Any other Cabinet changes, Mr. President?

Q. Housing?

Q. Any other Cabinet changes?

Q. Housing?

The President. No, I don't think of any right now. But I do——

Q. Mrs. Heckler, how do you figure that a $16,000 pay cut's a promotion?

Secretary Heckler. I've never chosen my occupation based on the compensation it afforded because, as you know, considering the hours one spends in Congress serving people, or in a Cabinet post, there is no correlation between the hours that you invest in your job and the salary that it actually accrues. In this case, however, there is, if one wants to be totally financial, the fact that the Ambassador's salary is not taxable. [*Laughter*]

Q. Mr. President, Soviet diplomats have been kidnaped in Lebanon, sir——

The President. We've got to go to the Cabinet Room——

Q. Is that a tax loophole? [*Laughter*]

Q. Soviet diplomats have been kidnaped in Lebanon, and two of them may have been murdered. Do you have a statement to make on that terrorism?

The President. Well, I will break my own self-imposed rule only to say this: That terrorism, that kind of violence, is, I think, the most cowardly, the most vicious thing the world is faced with today, regardless of who the victims are.

Q. Would the Soviets have a right to retaliate——

Q. Would we cooperate with the Soviets?

Q. ——clearly, just as much as the Israelis have a right to retaliate?

The President. Anyone has if they can pick out the people who are responsible.

Q. Do you think the Israelis did pick out the right people?

The President. Well, I've always had a great faith in their intelligence capabilities.

Note: The President spoke to reporters at 1:54 p.m. in the Briefing Room at the White House. John Svahn was Assistant to the President for Policy Development, and Donald T. Regan was Assistant to the President and Chief of Staff.

Appointment of Two Members of the National Commission for Employment Policy
October 1, 1985

The President today announced his intention to appoint the following individuals to be members of the National Commission for Employment Policy for terms expiring September 30, 1988:

Paul A. Russo, of Virginia, will succeed Roderick R. Paige. Mr. Russo is president of Capitol Consultants in Alexandria, VA. He served on the Reagan-Bush '84 Committee and the 50th Presidential Inaugural Committee. He was Deputy Under Secretary for Intergovernmental Affairs at the Department of Labor in 1983–1984 and as Special Assistant to the President in 1981–1983. He graduated from Ohio State University (B.S., 1966). He was born July 21, 1943, in Cleveland, OH, and now resides in Alexandria, VA.

Jerry J. Naylor, of California, will succeed Roberto Cambo. Mr. Naylor is president and owner of the Jerry Naylor Co. The Jerry Naylor Co. is a public relations organization in Westlake Village, CA. He attended the University of Maryland. He is married, has three children, and resides in Agoura, CA. He was born March 6, 1939, in Erath County, TX.

Appointment of Kay A. Orr as a Member of the Advisory Committee on the Arts
October 1, 1985

The President today announced his intention to appoint Kay A. Orr to be a member of the Advisory Committee on the Arts (John F. Kennedy Center for the Performing Arts, Smithsonian Institution). This is an initial appointment.

Mrs. Orr is presently serving as State treasurer for the State of Nebraska. Previously she was executive assistant to Gov. Charles Thone in 1979–1981. She serves as a member of the National Association of State Treasurers and was vice chairman for the midwest region in 1984–1985. She is a member of the President's Council at Hastings College.

She is married, has two children, and resides in Lincoln, NE. She was born January 2, 1939, in Burlington, IA.

Remarks at a White House Ceremony Honoring the Winners in the Secondary School Recognition Program and the Exemplary Private School Recognition Project
October 1, 1985

Thank you all, and welcome to the White House. You know, I have been out of school for some time now, but I still get nervous around so many principals. [*Laughter*] Actually, one of the advantages of being 39 years old as long as I have is that you develop a different perspective on life. I have come to realize that principals and Presidents have a great deal in common; both of us have to keep a lot of people happy. You have school boards, and I have the administration. You have the PTA, and I have the voters. You have unruly children; I'd better not name any names. [*Laughter*]

Seriously, it is a great honor to have you here today. I don't think it's an exaggeration to say that we are seeing a renaissance in American education, and it's people like you in communities like yours who are making it happen. Not too long ago, much of the news we heard about education was bad. From 1963 to 1980, scholastic aptitude test scores underwent a virtually unbroken decline. Science and achievement scores of 17-year-olds were dropping, and an alarming number of those 17-year-olds were dropping out. Crime was on the rise in our nation's schools; teachers and students lived in fear of violence. Our educational system, the very underpinning of our free society, appeared to be breaking apart. Well, as we used to say when I was in school: That's all ancient history. No, we haven't solved all of the problems yet. In public and private schools throughout the country, administrators, teachers, and parents still labor like heroes against tremendous odds. But today there is a new spirit of optimism in our land, and, as Secretary Bennett has said, American education is on the mend.

Last year I issued a challenge to America's students and educators. By the end of this decade, I said scholastic aptitude test scores should regain at least half of what they've lost in the last 20 years. Well, that is 42 points—7 points a year—a big challenge. I bet a lot of people were saying to themselves at the time that it couldn't be done. Well, I've learned one thing as President of this great country: Never underestimate the American people. Secretary Bennett told me just last week that the SAT scores for 1985 are up 9 whole points over last year— 2 points above the yearly increase we need to meet our challenge. So, congratulations to you. Congratulations to all educators out there who are doing their part to build a better America. Congratulations to parents who care, all parents who are involved in their children's education. And let's give credit where credit is due—to America's students. Well done, and keep up the good work!

You know, I have been on a number of campuses recently, and, granted, I am talking about those who are up there on the college level, but from all those appearances, and after having gone through the years of the sixties when it was quite different, I have come back with the firm conviction that the 21st century is going to be in good hands. Well, one of the most heartening things I've witnessed in these last 4½ years is the pride and exuberance with which our young people have taken up the call to America's future. I don't think there's ever been a younger generation with more spirit or promise. America's a team effort, and as we've seen with these recent SAT scores, America's young people are some of our star players.

We have a challenge at the Federal level as well: to reform programs that stand in the way of educational excellence. That's why we're going to make our program for teaching English to limited English-speaking students more flexible, allowing local districts to use the teaching methods that they know from experience work best. And in our compensatory education program, we're going to give parents of disadvantaged children the right to choose the school that gives their children the best education. Affluent Americans already have that choice; why shouldn't the poor and the minorities, too?

There can no longer be any question that an education founded on the basics works; that higher standards produce higher achievement; and that an orderly, disciplined classroom is a prerequisite for learning. And we're also finding out again the value of values. A recent Gallup Poll found that the overwhelming majority of parents want their schools to do two things above all: to teach their children to speak and write correctly and, just as important, to teach them a standard of right and wrong—in other words, to teach them values; teachers agree. In another recent poll, 92 percent of teachers polled said that schools should emphasize the development of ethical character in students. Unfortunately, some so-called experts in the field still insist that education should be what they call value neutral. Well, as I've said before, a value-neutral education is a contradiction in terms. If we fail to instruct our children in values of justice and liberty, we'll be condemning them to a world without virtue, a life in the twilight of civilization where the great truths have been forgotten.

In many schools, students are being taught the economic burdens of our national defense. Fair enough, but while being taught about the cost of defending freedom, shouldn't they also learn that the price will be far greater if we fail to defend freedom? Yes, our schoolchildren should know about their country's faults, but they should also be taught that by any objective measure, we live in the freest, most prosperous nation in the history of the world. As Jeane Kirkpatrick once said, "We must learn to bear the truth about our society no matter how pleasant it may be." [*Laughter*] America's schools do not and cannot exist in isolation from the rest of our society; and that brings me to an important point.

As we work to rid our schools of crime, drugs, and violence, isn't it time that everybody in the media and entertainment industries followed the leadership of those who've accepted their responsibility to our nation's youth? Isn't it time that those who have so much influence over young minds stop glorifying violence and promiscuous sex? As a matter of fact, I heard a clergyman one day from the pulpit ask, "When did promiscuity become 'sexually active'?" [*Laughter*] Let's start being a little more blunt with this wonderful language of ours and using words that describe what we're talking about. Aren't we tired of people who plead first amendment rights when it's as clear as day that what they're really talking about is big profits for themselves? America's young people have rights, too. They have a right to grow up without being constantly bombarded by images of violence and perversity. Let's give our children back their childhood. Let's give them the support all children need—the support of traditional values like family, faith, hope, charity, and freedom.

And maybe in this modern age our schoolchildren need a little extra support; maybe like the rest of us, sometime during the day they need that extra support of prayer. I can't help but thinking that if some of those people who spend all their time trying to keep God out of our nation's schools spent just as much time trying to keep out drugs and violence, well, they'd certainly be doing our children a lot more good.

Now, I realize, here—and speaking to you particularly—I'm "preaching to the choir." [*Laughter*] You here today represent the best in American education. You're in the vanguard of educational reform, and every vanguard needs a flag. So, I'm going to hand over the podium to the only substitute teacher I know of with Cabinet rank—[*laughter*]—our Secretary of Education, Bill Bennett, and he is going to hand out your awards. Fly these flags with pride; you've earned them.

And now, I'll do what the little girl told me to do in a P.S. to a letter she wrote, telling me all the problems that had to be solved, and then the P.S. was, "Now get back to the Oval Office and get to work."[*Laughter*] So, congratulations, and God bless you all. Thank you.

Note: The President spoke at 3:01 p.m. on the South Lawn of the White House. Following his remarks, 281 principals were presented with American flags, honoring the achievements of their schools.

Proclamation 5373—General Pulaski Memorial Day, 1985
October 1, 1985

By the President of the United States of America

A Proclamation

General Casimir Pulaski's life was committed to the cause of freedom. Before coming to America in 1777, he fought bravely and tirelessly for the independence of his beloved Poland. Here, he devoted all his energy and skill to the American War of Independence. His personal contribution to the Revolutionary Army on the field of battle, his tactical innovations, and his creation of a highly effective corps of dragoons, known informally as the Polish Legion, won him the title: "Father of American Cavalry."

On October 11, 1779, General Pulaski gave his life in our struggle for freedom. He died from wounds suffered bravely in the battle of Savannah. Although he died before the goal of a free and independent America had been achieved, his heroic example has inspired Polish and American patriots for over two centuries. George Washington's words written to the Continental Congress in 1778 memorialize General Pulaski: "The Count's valor and active zeal on all occa-sions have done him great honor."

As we gratefully reflect on the life of this great champion of freedom, we are moved to salute all Americans of Polish descent, who from the settlement in Jamestown through the Revolutionary War and on to the present have contributed so greatly and so generously to the realization of the American dream. Generations of Polish Americans have left a lasting imprint on American life in every field of human endeavor: from science and the arts to politics, sports, and religion. Their achievements have enriched the lives of all Americans.

Now, Therefore, I, Ronald Reagan, President of the United States of America, do hereby proclaim Friday, October 11, 1985, as General Pulaski Memorial Day, 1985, and I direct the appropriate Government officials to display the flag of the United States on all Government buildings on that day. In addition, I encourage the people of the United States to commemorate this occasion as approriate throughout the land.

In Witness Whereof, I have hereunto set my hand this first day of October, in the year of our Lord nineteen hundred and eighty-five, and of the Independence of the

United States of America the two hundred and tenth.

RONALD REAGAN

[*Filed with the Office of the Federal Register, 10:40 a.m., October 3, 1985*]

Note: The proclamation was released by the Office of the Press Secretary on October 2.

Remarks to the 54th General Assembly of Interpol, the International Criminal Police Organization
October 2, 1985

I wanted to stop by briefly today and extend my good wishes to each of you. The United States is honored and proud that you would choose our Capital as the site of your convention. And we're especially pleased that you have extended to one of our distinguished public servants, John Simpson, the privilege of serving as your president.

John, who is a good friend, will tell you, if he hasn't already, about the priority that our administration has placed on the war against the crime syndicates—syndicates that in recent years have grown in power and sophistication. Here in the United States, for example, prosecutions of traditional organized crime families, as well as some of the newer groups of drugs traders, have gone up dramatically. And for the first time, we feel we're making significant headway. In addition to dramatically increasing the number of prosecutors and Federal agents working in these areas, we have taken many other steps. One of them is our Presidential Commission on Organized Crime, which is currently working with your member nations to bring to light problems like money laundering, especially its international dimensions. And that word "international" is, of course, the point. Whether it's organized crime, narcotics trafficking, terrorism, or any other area of criminal activity, the increasing sophistication and power of criminal syndicates calls for a response from those who are pledged to uphold the law and protect society from the hardened criminal. And this is the work of Interpol.

You know, I'm sure a good many of you've heard of that international celebrity, Inspector Maigret—the celebrated French detective from the pen of Georges Simenon, who in so many of his stories relied on information from his counterparts in other police forces throughout the world to solve his cases. Well, as is often the case, fiction does reflect reality. It is Interpol that institutionalizes and makes vastly easier those professional contacts and vital exchanges of information that each of you needs to serve the people of your country. Interpol's record of achievement in these areas is unparalleled, and let me stress today that the United States Government pledges to you and your organization its full support.

And now, if you will permit, I'd like to leave you on a personal note. You know, I've spoken to many law enforcement groups throughout my time in public life, and I doubt that I have ever failed to mention that yours is one of the most difficult of any profession in civilized society. And yet there is no work more vital to the safety and freedom of your fellow citizens. The nature of your work frequently brings you in contact with your fellow citizens when they have been victimized by crime or committed a crime themselves. So frequently you see people only when they're hurting or in trouble. I hope you will not permit this to discourage you too much about human nature or to change your perspective on society as a whole. I hope you will remember that not only are most people upstanding and law-abiding citizens, but they are also on your side in the fight against lawlessness and are very grateful to you for the work you do. And that's why I think there is great cause for hope in the war against crime.

Georges Simenon has also said that sometimes "the truth is too simple for intellectuals." Well, we all remember a time when some elaborate theories excusing criminal wrongdoing were very fashionable, a time when there was a great loss of will in apprehending and bringing to justice professional wrongdoers. And now all of this is changing. Increasingly, the people of my own country and yours are coming to appreciate again the truth of old verities like: Right and wrong do matter, individuals should be held accountable for their actions, and society has the right to be protected from those who prey on the innocent.

This trend is no better evidenced than in the growth and renewed strength of Interpol. So, again, I want to pledge the American people's full support. And I want to wish each of you well in your professional lives, in your stay here in the United States; and I want to convey to you the warmest welcome and the kindest regards of the American people. And thank you for letting me have these few minutes with you here. God bless you all.

Note: The President spoke at 11:27 a.m. at the Departmental Auditorium. John R. Simpson was Director of the United States Secret Service.

Nomination of Joseph Ghougassian To Be United States Ambassador to Qatar
October 2, 1985

The President today announced his intention to nominate Joseph Ghougassian, of California, as Ambassador to the State of Qatar. He would succeed Charles Franklin Dunbar.

Mr. Ghougassian began his career as an instructor of philosophy and psychology at the University of San Diego in 1966. Since then and to date, he has been an assistant professor and then associate professor of philosophy at the University of San Diego. He was a law student at the University of San Diego School of Law in 1979–1980. He joined the law office of Bruce Harrison in San Diego in 1980–1981. From February 1981 to September 1981, Mr. Ghougassian was a member of the Office of Policy Development at the White House. In June 1981 he also served as Special Assistant for Public and Private Liaison, Office of Refugee Resettlement, Department of Health and Human Services. From January 1982 to July 1982, he was a consultant with the Immigration and Naturalization Service, Department of Justice. Since 1982 he has been director of the Peace Corps in the Yemen Arab Republic.

He received his B.A. (philosophy) in 1964 and his M.A. in 1965 at the Gregorian University in Rome, Italy. In 1966 he received his Ph.D.c. and in 1969 his Ph.D. (philosophy) from Louvain University in Belgium. In 1974 he received his B.Sc. (family studies) from Louvain University and his M.A. in 1977 (international relations) from the University of San Diego and his J.D. from the University of San Diego School of Law. His foreign languages are Arabic, Armenian, French, Italian, and Spanish. He is married to the former Zena S. Yasmine, and they have three children. He was born March 5, 1944, in Cairo, Egypt.

Message to the Senate Transmitting the Sri Lanka-United States Taxation Convention
October 2, 1985

To the Senate of the United States:

I transmit herewith for Senate advice and consent to ratification the Convention between the Government of the United States of America and the Government of the Democratic Socialist Republic of Sri Lanka for the Avoidance of Double Taxation and the Prevention of Fiscal Evasion with Respect to Taxes on Income, signed at Colombo on March 14, 1985. I also transmit the report of the Department of State on the Convention.

The Convention is the first income tax treaty to be negotiated between the United States and Sri Lanka. It is based on model income tax treaties developed by the Department of the Treasury and the Organization for Economic Cooperation and Development. The Convention deviates from these models, however, in several signifi-

cant respects, as indicated in the attached report of the Department of State, to reflect Sri Lanka's status as a developing country. These deviations generally provide for broader source country right to tax than is found in the model treaties.

Among the principal features of the Convention are provisions to prevent third-country residents from taking unwarranted advantage of the treaty. Also included are the usual articles on nondiscrimination, mutual agreement, and exchange of information.

I recommend that the Senate give early and favorable consideration to the Convention and give its advice and consent to ratification.

RONALD REAGAN

The White House,
October 2, 1985.

Statement on the Death of Actor Rock Hudson
October 2, 1985

Nancy and I are saddened by the news of Rock Hudson's death. He will always be remembered for his dynamic impact on the film industry, and fans all over the world will certainly mourn his loss. He will be remembered for his humanity, his sympathetic spirit, and well-deserved reputation for kindness. May God rest his soul.

Announcement of the Establishment of the Trade Strike Force
October 2, 1985

The President announced the creation of an administration Trade Strike Force designed to uncover unfair trading practices used against the United States and to develop strategies to counter and eliminate them. It will identify barriers to U.S. exports, as well as unfair export subsidies. The Strike Force will be chaired by Commerce Secretary Malcolm Baldrige. Other mem-

bers will be the Secretaries of the Treasury, State, Transportation, Agriculture, and the United States Trade Representative.

The Strike Force was first mentioned in the President's trade speech delivered on September 23 to members of the President's Export Council, select Members of Congress, and invited business leaders in the East Room of the White House. The

1179

President said at that time: "I will not stand by and watch American businesses fail because of unfair trading practices abroad. I will not stand by and watch American workers lose their jobs because other nations do not play by the rules."

The Strike Force will report its findings to the President through his Economic Policy Council, along with a recommended plan of action, on a regular basis. The appropriate executive branch agencies will then be responsible for execution of the plan. Working groups chaired by Commerce Under Secretary for International Trade Administration Bruce Smart will be established under the Strike Force.

Note: Larry M. Speakes, Principal Deputy Press Secretary to the President, read the announcement to reporters in the Briefing Room at the White House during his daily press briefing, which began at 12:02 p.m.

Nomination of Three Members of the Board of Governors of the United States Postal Service
October 3, 1985

The President today announced his intention to nominate the following individuals to be members of the Board of Governors of the United States Postal Service for the terms indicated:

J.H. Tyler McConnell, of Delaware, for the remainder of the term expiring December 8, 1989. He would succeed David E. Babcock. Mr. McConnell is retired chairman and chief executive officer of Delaware Trust Co. He currently serves on the board of directors of Delaware Trust Co. He graduated from Virginia Military Institute (B.A., 1936) and the University of Virginia (LL.B., 1939; J.D., 1970). He is married, has three children, and resides in Wilmington, DE. He was born November 23, 1914, in Richmond, VA.

Barry D. Schreiber, of Florida, for the remainder of the term expiring December 8, 1992. He would succeed Frieda Waldman. He is a member of the board of county commissioners in Miami, FL. He is of counsel to the law firm of Broad & Cassel in Bay Harbor Islands, FL. He is a member of the State Association of County Commissioners and the Dade League of Cities. He graduated from Yeshiva University (B.A., 1964) and the University of Maryland (J.D., 1967). He is married, has three children, and resides in North Miami Beach, FL. He was born April 17, 1943, in Richmond, VA.

Robert Setrakian, of the District of Columbia, for the term expiring December 8, 1993. He would succeed William J. Sullivan. Since 1983 he has been serving as a Commissioner of the Federal Maritime Commission. Previously he was president of Midstate Horticultural Co. He was a director of FN Financial Corp. in 1976–1983. He graduated from Stanford University (B.A., 1949). He has four children and resides in Washington, DC. He was born January 21, 1924, in Fresno, CA.

Nomination of W. Scott Thompson To Be a Member of the Board of Directors of the United States Institute of Peace
October 3, 1985

The President today announced his intention to nominate W. Scott Thompson to be a member of the Board of Directors of the United States Institute of Peace for a term of 4 years expiring January 19, 1989. This is a new position.

Dr. Thompson is a professor of international politics at the Fletcher School of Law and Diplomacy. He was a research fellow at the Center for International Affairs at Harvard University in 1979–1980. In 1975–1976 he was assistant to the Secretary of Defense while serving as a White House fellow and was also a member of the State Department Promotion Board. Dr. Thompson is a founding member of the board of the Committee on the Present Danger and is a member of the Council on Foreign Relations and of the International Institute for Strategic Studies. He serves on the Board of the Foreign Policy Research Institute and the Institute for Strategic Trade. He is the author of many books on U.S. global strategy.

He graduated from Stanford University (B.A., 1963) and Oxford University (Ph.D., 1967). He is married, has three children, and resides in Washington, DC. He was born January 1, 1942, in Providence, RI.

Proclamation 5374—Leif Erikson Day, 1985
October 3, 1985

By the President of the United States of America

A Proclamation

Sent by King Olav in the year 1000 to bring Christianity to the Nordic settlers in Greenland, Leif Erikson set out on a daring and danger-filled voyage that began a centuries-long relationship between the Nordic peoples and the lands of North America. "Leif the Lucky," as his contemporaries knew him, sailed well beyond the tip of Greenland to the shores of the North American mainland. His enthusiastic account of his voyage describes a fertile land abounding in fruit, grain, and timber.

Hundreds of years later, millions of Nordics followed in the wake of Leif Erikson, crossing the Atlantic to make their homes in this land of opportunity. Pressing westward, they settled across the continent, making important contributions to American agriculture and industry. Prizing personal freedom, hard work, and family values, these hardy God-fearing pioneers played a key role in shaping the American character. Today, cultural exchanges, commercial ties, and cordial diplomatic relations with the countries of Denmark, Finland, Iceland, Norway, and Sweden continue to enrich the lives of all Americans.

To commemorate the courage of Leif Erikson and in recognition of our long and fruitful relationship with the peoples of northern Europe, the Congress of the United States, by a joint resolution approved on September 2, 1964 (78 Stat. 849, 36 U.S.C. 169c), has authorized and requested the President to proclaim October 9 of each year as Leif Erikson Day.

Now, Therefore, I, Ronald Reagan, President of the United States of America, do hereby proclaim October 9, 1985, as Leif Erikson Day, 1985, and I direct the appropriate government officials to display the flag of the United States on all government buildings that day. I also invite the people of the United States to honor Leif Erikson and our Nordic-American heritage by holding appropriate exercises and ceremonies in suitable places throughout the land.

In Witness Whereof, I have hereunto set my hand this third day of October, in the year of our Lord nineteen hundred and eighty-five, and of the Independence of the United States of America the two hundred and tenth.

RONALD REAGAN

[*Filed with the Office of the Federal Register, 11:31 a.m., October 4, 1985*]

1181

Remarks to Employees at the Ivorydale Soap Manufacturing Plant in St. Bernard, Ohio
October 3, 1985

Thank you very much, Brad, and thank you all very much, and thanks for the tour of your plant. It was 99⁴⁴⁄₁₀₀ percent pure fascinating. [*Laughter*] But I have to say, Ed, I appreciate the introduction because I once had an experience, back in that other life of mine, when I was on television every week. And on a New York street one day, a fellow suddenly, from 30 feet away, says, "I know you. I see you." And he started toward me and everybody on the street stopped. And I'm kind of being stalked by him as he comes toward me. And he's getting a piece of paper and a pen out and got right up to me and told me he saw me all the time and wanted my autograph—Ray Milland. [*Laughter*] So, I signed Ray Milland. There was no sense in—[*laughter*]——

But it's great to be back in the Cincinnati area. I was out here last year, visiting Procter and Gamble during the campaign; didn't get exactly here, though. It hardly seems possible now that there was actually a Presidential candidate back then who promised the first thing he'd do if elected was raise your taxes. Well, the American people held a little referendum on that idea and sent a message loud and clear to Washington that America wants less government, less taxes, and more prosperity. And that's why leaders of the other party have now joined us in our effort to overhaul our nation's creaky tax code and replace it with a streamlined version, one that cuts personal and business tax rates, closes unfair loopholes, and spurs economic growth.

America's fair share tax plan is now working its way through the House of Representatives. It's up to them to send a bill to the Senate as quickly as possible so that we can pass a fairer, progrowth tax plan this year, in 1985. It's a challenge, I know, but I just don't think that America should have to wait for fairness and the increased growth that lower tax rates will bring. And if we have to, we're going to send Mr. Clean down there to keep an eye on them— [*laughter*]—and make sure they do the job right.

From the beginning, Procter & Gamble has been an important ally in our fight for tax reform. I was talking to one of your executive officers earlier, and he had kind of a funny way of talking, but I couldn't have agreed more with what he was saying. He said there's a rising Tide of good Cheer and Joy in the land. [*Laughter*] We see new Zest in the economy every day. [*Laughter*] And all we need now is a Bold new Dash to Safeguard the gain we've made already. [*Laughter*] I said thanks and congratulated him on the Top Job that you're all doing— [*laughter*]—in support of tax fairness.

Well, seriously, this company exemplifies the forward-looking, executive—or expansive philosophy, I should say, that has made America the number one economic power in the world, the kind of positive thinking behind America's fair share tax plan. Your president, John Smale, testified before the House Ways and Means Committee that, although Procter & Gamble would be affected by our loophole closing, you support the initiative because you know lower tax rates mean greater growth and more jobs. And this company has the vision to look beyond the ledger books and see what's good for America is good for individual businesses and every one of their employees and customers, too.

Let me also take a moment to recognize the contributions of your Congressman, Bill Gradison. He's been an effective, untiring supporter of tax reform in the House. And if every Congressman were as supportive as Bill Gradison, we'd have tax fairness today. Bill and his Ohio colleagues—Tom Kindness and Bob McEwen, and one who was going to be with us, but then got interrupted by the press of things in the House and couldn't, Del Latta—they understand one thing that is all too often forgotten in Washington: that a tax overhaul that doesn't make life easier for America's working men and women isn't worth the paper it's printed on. That's why our profamily initiatives are the heart and soul of America's fair share tax plan.

Some people in Washington are saying that people aren't very worked up about tax reform. Well, I think the people just don't know yet what it is we're talking about. We're going to make it affordable to raise children again. You hear a lot about tax shelters, well, the one shelter we approve of is the family home. The truth is, the profamily measures of our tax plan are there to right a great historical injustice. Throughout the great tax explosion of the sixties and seventies, everybody with a paycheck got hit, and hit hard, by taxes; but those trying to raise families got clobbered. Not only did their taxes skyrocket, their personal exemption, the real value of the deduction they were allowed to take for themselves and each one of their dependents, was steadily knocked down by inflation.

Let me insert here just some figures that would give you an idea of how everyone was victimized. In 1977—Henry Hazlett, the economist, has done a study of this—the average median income—that's the halfway mark, half the people are above it and half the people are below it—was $189 a week—1977. By now its up to $299 a week. And that means, of course, the individual that's making that many more dollars is paying considerably more income tax, has moved up through the tax brackets. But figure out that earnings in 1977 dollars. If the dollar today had the same purchasing power it had in 1977—that $299 only has $171 of purchasing power compared to $189 in 1977. But, in addition to that, because the tax is based on the number of dollars, not their value, that individual has moved up through a number of tax brackets and is paying a higher percentage of less purchasing power than he was before. In other words, families were getting a double whammy, double tax hikes. It wouldn't be an exaggeration to say that the colossal growth of government over the last two decades was financed by raiding the dwindling bank accounts of America's families.

If the personal exemption, which was $600 in 1948, had kept pace with inflation, it would be worth $2,700 today. But we plan to almost double the current exemp-

tion—we can't go all the way, but our plan would make it $2,000 to make up for some of what families lost over the years. And to me that is only fair, and what's fair is worth fighting for. I hope you're with me on that. Well, we're also increasing the standard deduction of $4,000—or to $4,000 I should say, for joint returns, and this will mean that families as well as the elderly, the blind, or the disabled living at or below the poverty line will be completely scratched from the Federal income tax rolls. The U.S. Government will no longer tax families into poverty.

Our profamily measures will mean that a family of four doesn't have to pay one single cent of Federal taxes on the first $12,000 of income. And because saving is so essential to families but so very difficult with all these expenses, we're expanding the tax-free savings accounts, the IRA's, the individual retirement accounts, so that they are fully available to nonwage-earning spouses. We figure that the housewife is also working a full 40-hour week. Now, you shouldn't have to be affluent to experience the blessings of a home life, and that's a right to which every American is entitled.

I am glad to say that the Democratically controlled House Select Committee on Children, Youth, and Families has rated our tax proposal the most profamily tax proposal before the Congress, more profamily than any other proposal around and light years ahead of the present tax system. Now, this goes beyond economics, and, although, in my opinion, profamily policies are the best economics there is. This gets to the moral core of our nation. America has a responsibility to the future, and our children are our future. We're a nation of immigrants who've labored and sacrificed to give their children a better life. And that's the American dream. And we can't let American tax policies and big government policies kill that dream.

You know, our forefathers got so riled up over a tea tax, among other things, that they started a revolution. And now we have a tax on families, a tax on achievement, success, and aspiration—a tax on the American dream. I think I know what Thomas Jefferson would have said about that, because Thomas Jefferson only had one line of criticism when the Constitution was adopted. He said, it lacks one important thing: a provision preventing the Federal Government from borrowing money. Well, I think it's time we had another revolution, a peaceful one this time, called America's fair share tax plan. We need your support. Let Congress know that you're progrowth, profairness, and profamily. And America's fair share tax plan is a gift that we owe to our children. And with your help and with this company's support and with these fine Representatives in the House that I've mentioned who are here with me, it's a gift that—we all do our part—we'll have wrapped up by Christmastime. And, then, maybe we can sing "Joy to the World" with extra feeling.

I mentioned here this—some people have suggested publicly, lately, that I'm so concerned about the tax plan that I'm not concerned about the deficit, the Federal deficit that we're trying to correct. Well, don't let anybody fool you. Both of these things are important, but there's nothing more important than eliminating the deficit in Federal spending. And right now a few of our Senators and us are talking about a long-range plan—not just every year trying to whittle a dollar here or a dollar there out, but a plan aimed at a balanced budget. And then we will obey the wisdom of Mr. Jefferson and see if we can't get a provision in the Constitution that says the Government, from then on, can't spend any more than it takes in.

Well, God bless you all. Thank you all. It's been a great pleasure to be here with you.

Note: The President spoke at 12:35 p.m. Prior to his remarks, he toured the plant and had lunch with plant employees in the cafeteria. In his opening remarks, the President referred to Owen B. Butler, chairman of the board of Procter & Gamble.

Informal Exchange With Reporters in St. Bernard, Ohio
October 3, 1985

Q. Mr. President, Gorbachev has made his plans public. Does that harm serious negotiations?

The President. No, I don't believe so. The details have not been spelled out, and the proposal has been put before the negotiators in Geneva and that's where it will be——

Q. Mr. President, he has said there will be a——

Q. Well, what's he doing, Mr. President? He's trying to put you on the defensive, isn't he?

Q. ——he said there will be a——

The President. Now, wait a minute. She said it first. Then I'll get to you, Bill [Bill Plante, CBS News].

What?

Q. He said that there will be a cap on SS–20's back to the June '84 level, that they will dismantle the launchers in Europe, and that he wants separate negotiations with the British and French. Isn't that quite a big change in their position?

The President. Yes. Everything they're saying is a change in their position. Well, with regard to the British and the French, that is up to the Soviet Union and the British and the French. Certainly, the United States cannot negotiate with the Soviets about what they're going to do with regard to the nuclear missiles of other countries. With regard to the remarks he made about the intermediate-range missiles in Europe, this was the—when we acceded to the European request and provided missiles for them to have, intermediate missiles, in defense against these missiles aimed at them—this is what caused the Soviets, more than a year ago, to walk out for more than a year from the negotiations, because we had put those missiles in Europe. Now, they're back negotiating, and they now, I understand, have made a suggestion about reducing the number of their weapons. This, too, will have to be negotiated.

Q. Well now, why do you think they're doing that, sir? Are they trying to put you on the defensive with the Europeans?

The President. Oh, I don't know whether they're trying to do that or not. It would be nice to hope that they may have gotten religion.

Q. Well, how do you look at them? How do you look at these——

The President. Well——

Q. ——at the Gorbachev appearance to the press?

The President. As I say, I'm not going to discuss the terms they're proposing because that's going to be dealt with by our negotiators in Geneva.

Q. Yes, but what do you think of him in trying——

The President. But with regard to this latest statement about the SS–20's, which are their multiwarhead missiles that are aimed at European targets, and in response to which we had put the Pershings and the cruise missiles in Europe. As I understand it, the only proposal they've made is one that would not be destroying any of their weapons; it would simply be moving them. Well, that missile, the SS–20, is a mobile missile. It is transported; it can move from place to place. To simply drive them up into the Ural Mountains or someplace else and then say that they're not a threat to Europe makes no sense.

Q. Well, he did say dismantle——

The President. They can be brought back any time they want to turn on the gas.

Q. He did say dismantle the launchers for the first time, Mr. President.

The President. Well——

Q. Doesn't that change the nature of the movement between European and Asian SS countries?

The President. If they truly mean that, but then, again, we'll leave that to our negotiators in Geneva.

Q. Well, Gorbachev says, sir, that if you don't——

Q. ——going to our European allies——

Q. Gorbachev says if you don't give up SDI, there'll be hard times in the world.

The President. Well, he could probably feel that way because the Soviet Union is about 10 years ahead of us in developing a defensive system themselves, and they're very upset at the idea that they might not be the only ones that have a defense against nuclear weapons as well as having the offensive nuclear weapons. Now, we're working so that we, too, can have a defensive shield that kills weapons, not people. And I'm sure that is upsetting to them, but we're not going to retreat from the research that could deliver to the world a defense against these nuclear weapons and finally bring us to the realization that we should eliminate the nuclear weapons entirely.

Q. And the testing, sir? And the testing?

The President. That goes along with research.

Q. What about the fact that these separate negotiations might——

Principal Deputy Press Secretary Speakes. We've had a lot of questions——

Q. ——undercut the U.S.-Soviet negotiations in Geneva? If they go off on their own and deal with the British and the French, doesn't that drive a wedge between us and our allies?

The President. No, I don't believe so at all. It certainly would drive a wedge if we arrogantly decided that we would negotiate on behalf of other countries and without their consent. No, this is between them and the Soviet Union. And more power to them. I've got to go on.

Q. Anything more on the Israeli raid in Tunisia? Do you still——

The President. No——

Q. ——think it's understandable?

Q. The PLO——

The President. ——no more comments.

Note: The exchange began at 12:50 p.m. following the President's visit to the Ivorydale Soap Manufacturing Plant. He then traveled to Cincinnati. A tape was not available for verification of the content of this exchange.

Remarks to Business Leaders in Cincinnati, Ohio
October 3, 1985

Thank you, Dr. Barrett, and thank you all. This is quite a wonderful reception. You know, for a minute there, I thought maybe you thought I was Pete Rose. [*Laughter*] Well, it's great to be back in Cincinnati and a genuine honor to share the platform with your Congressman, Bill Gradison, and his Ohio colleagues, Tom Kindness and Bob McEwen. Del Latta would have been with us but, as things happen in Washington, something happened that interfered with his getting here. And I know that someplace out there with you is a companion of mine of years back when we were Governors together—Jim Rhodes. There you are, Jim. I remember a story back from my Jim Rhodes days, my Governor days in California. I was on the way to the office one morning, had the car radio on. And there was a disc jockey on playing songs and so forth and suddenly, I heard him saying— now, we were having some problems at the time—I heard him saying something that endeared him to me. He said, "Every man should take unto himself a wife, because sooner or later, something is bound to happen that you can't blame on the Governor." [*Laughter*]

Well, the last time I visited here it was August 1984, the middle of the Presidential campaign. And I spoke to you that day about my dreams for America and my plans for this second term. And I told you: "We're going to simplify the tax system, actually make it understandable and clear and fair. And when we do that, your tax rates are going to come down, not go up." Well, my friends, today I've come back to Cincinnati to help make good on that promise. We now have before the Congress a sweeping proposal to reform our entire Federal system of taxation. It has its roots deep in the American tradition of limited government, individual achievement, and economic growth.

During the 1920's for example, Presidents Harding and Coolidge instituted a series of tax cuts that reduced the top rate on individuals from 73 percent to just 25 percent.

Today we remember the boom that followed as the Roaring Twenties. In the 1960's John F. Kennedy cut taxes again, and again the economy responded with great vigor and great growth. In 1981 our own first-term tax cuts were enacted, and in 1983, when those installments—because it was an installment plan of tax cuts—went into effect and began to take full effect, America took off on this recovery. I understand that here in Cincinnati, in 1984 alone some 20,000 new jobs were created. And during the last 18 months, greater Cincinnati has seen the creation of more than 1,400 businesses. No wonder the press has coined the term "Cincynomics." I knew the program was succeeding when they stopped calling it Reaganomics. [*Laughter*] Today the American expansion is in its 34th consecutive month, and across the country, we've seen the creation of more than 8 million new jobs.

My friends, history is clear: Lower tax rates mean greater freedom, and whenever we lower the tax rates, our entire nation is better off. Freedom for people to grow is as American as apple pie and the Cincinnati Reds. America's fair share tax plan will give us a new burst of economic achievement. Now, many already understand that our plan will mean lower Federal income taxes for most individuals, but there's been some confusion about just what it would mean for business. Well, permit me to set the record straight. For business, America's tax plan will mean growth.

Those of you here with the Cincinnati Institute for Small Enterprise Division of the Greater Cincinnati Chamber should be aware that for small businesses our plan will represent a substantial tax break. Unincorporated small businesses, taxed according to the personal incomes of their owners, will benefit as we reduce and simplify personal income tax rates. The top personal rate alone will come down from 50 percent to just 35 percent. Incorporated small businesses will receive graduated rates of 15, 18, 25, and 33 percent, a measure especially helpful to businesses just getting started. As you know, small businesses create most of our new jobs. From late 1982 to late 1984, industries dominated by small businesses created new jobs at the remarkable rate of more than 11 percent. Under our pro-growth plan, I'm convinced that small businesses will form, grow, and create new jobs even more quickly.

Those of you here with the Cincinnati Business Committee represent larger concerns, such giants as Procter & Gamble and Kroger Company and Federated Department Stores. Well, it's no mistake that this wonderful town is called the "Blue Chip City." For corporations like your own, America's fair share tax plan will mean a lower top corporate rate, down from 46 to just 33 percent. In addition, the system will dramatically be simplified as countless provisions for special treatment are reduced or eliminated. Take a moment to compare this simplified, low-tax rate future to the present arrangement. The corporate tax structure today represents a jungle of deductions, credits, and allowances. The only ones who can hack their way through it with ease are those with friendly guides on Capitol Hill. The whole weed-ridden, overgrown arrangement encourages competition of the worst kind—not to produce better products at lower prices, but to hire bigger and bigger teams of lobbyists and lawyers evermore skilled in taking advantage of the tax code. My friends, great American corporations should not be strapped by a system that is tied to the stake of tax shelters. It should be set free to make better products than any other industry, in any country of the world. And that's what America's tax plan, we think, is going to do.

For capital formation, our plan envisions a cut in the top rate on capital gains to just 17½ percent. Now, here again, history is our guide. Back in 1977 the number of dollars committed to venture capital, the funding so important to business start-ups, was just $39 million. And then, in 1978 taxes on capital gains were cut, and in 1981 we cut them again. And last year, venture capital commitments were over $4 billion. Even early opponents of tax cuts on capital gains can now see how the new availability of

venture capital has spurred our economic growth. Indeed, former Massachusetts Representative and then Senator, Paul Tsongas, said of the 1978 tax cut: "That bill, which I did not support, did more for the economy of my State than anything I ever did as a Congressman." When we cut the tax on capital gains again this year, we can expect capital formation and new business starts to hit new highs.

As businesspeople, you'll understand that by far the most significant aspect of our plan is that it will be good for your employees and customers, the American people. As I've said, rates for most individuals will come down. To benefit the family, we'll increase to $4,000 the standard deduction for married couples filing jointly and nearly double the personal exemption from just over $1,000 all the way to $2,000. The American people will have new incentives—more money in their pockets, more with which to purchase your goods, to save, and to invest.

Just last month, the Council of Economic Advisers completed a study of what our long-term impact would be. Using conservative estimates—that's the only kind I approve of—[*laughter*]—the Council found that America's fair share tax plan would increase our gross national product by about 2½ to 3.2 percent over the next 10 years. Now, that's the same as providing 11 years worth of growth in just 10 years, in a decade. That translates into the equivalent of almost 4 million additional new jobs over the next 10 years and from $600 to $900 a year in additional income for every American household. Needless to say, these growth estimates are based on our own proposal. And I've said it before and I'll say it again: I intend to fight for our plan—a top corporate rate of 33 percent; a top capital gains rate of 17½ percent; 15, 25, and 35 percent rates for individuals, in exchange for the 14 tax brackets we have today; a standard deduction of $4,000; and a nearly doubled personal exemption of $2,000.

Now, of course, there are those who say that getting tax reform through Congress this year will be impossible. Well, if everybody on Capitol Hill worked as hard for tax reform as your own outstanding Congressman, Bill Gradison, we wouldn't have to worry. But for those who are predicting the defeat of America's fair share tax plan, I have a few other choice predictions I'd like them to consider. In 1899 Charles H. Duell, Commissioner of the U.S. Patent Office, said this: "Everything that can be invented has been invented." And he suggested we should do away with the Office. [*Laughter*] And with the advent of sound tracks for motion pictures in the twenties, Harry Warner, one of my old bosses at Warner Brothers, said this: "Who the hell wants to hear actors talk." [*Laughter*] Do you know that Fulton tried to sell the steamboat for warships to Napoleon. And do you know what Napoleon said about it? "You're telling me that you can make a ship go against the tide and the wind and the current by building a bonfire under the deck? I won't listen to such foolishness." [*Laughter*]

Well, here's one for a great baseball town like Cincinnati. In 1921 Tris Speaker of the Cleveland Indians said this: "Babe Ruth made a big mistake when he gave up pitching." [*Laughter*] My friends, today, naysayers will soon take their place beside Tris Speaker in the Great Mistakes Hall of Fame. Just as sure as Ruth could hit home runs and Rose can break records, during this session of the Congress, America's tax plan will become law; but it's going to take all of us and all of you letting the folks in Washington know that you want this change made.

I'm going to inject something here because lately I've seen some remarks or some—no, philosophy attributed to me that somehow I am concerned only with this and that I'm not paying any attention to the national deficit, the deficit spending that the Government is doing. Thirty years ago, out on the mashed-potato circuit, I was saying we had to interrupt this 50-year span that we've had of deficit spending and which over the years we were told was necessary to prosperity. And I kept saying it would blow up and get out of control. And it has, but I'd like to just tell you something about that.

That's a top priority with us, and in our wing over there, at the West Wing of the White House, we have been talking about not just each year trying to get further cuts

in the budget with the hope that someday we can get down to a balanced budget; we have been discussing a plan—over a period of years, to start a plan of spending cuts that will bring the percentage of gross national product that the deficit is today down 4, then 3 percent, then 2 percent, and on down to zero in a several-year period—not too many years—and then our dream is, at the end of that, that year you implement a constitutional amendment that denies the Federal Government the right to borrow money.

Well, just recently we discovered that two of our Senators up on the Hill, and in fact one of your Congressmen, Del Latta, were engaged in discussions of exactly the same thing. Now, we hadn't said a word about what we were talking about; they hadn't told us either what they were talking about. But we found out that we were sure thinking alike. I don't know whether the ESP was going from them to us or us to them or whether it crossed on the way, but we have gotten together, and we are now in discussions with the people up on the Hill about that kind of a plan, to exert the discipline that is needed in Washington so that for someone to stage a big fight for his particular spending and overspending that he wanted to do or she wanted to do— instead they would be breaking the pattern of a plan, over extended years, to bring about a balanced budget. So, we're in agreement on that, and we're going to be talking about that.

And I just want to say to you my gratitude for what so many of you have done. You know, I've talked about the things that have happened there—for the last 4 months inflation has only been 2½ percent. I'd spoke about the capital money, the venture capital that is available. We know that interest rates are coming down. We know about the 8 million jobs that I mentioned. And we didn't do all of that; America did all of that, and I think the greatest contribution we made was, we tried to get government out of your way. And we're going to keep on trying to do that.

Thank you all very much. God bless all of you, and God bless Cincinnati.

Note: The President spoke at 1:35 p.m. at the Cincinnati Clarion Hotel. In his opening remarks, the President referred to James M. Barrett, chairman and chief executive officer of the Western-Southern Life Insurance Co., and Cincinnati Reds baseball player Pete Rose. The event was sponsored by the Cincinnati Business Committee and the Cincinnati Institute for Small Enterprise, the small business division of the Greater Cincinnati Chamber of Commerce. Following his remarks, the President returned to Washington, DC.

Remarks Announcing Bipartisan Support for Balanced Budget and Emergency Deficit Control Legislation
October 4, 1985

The President. Good morning. I'm announcing today what may well be an historic agreement to bring Federal spending under control and, at long last, put the United States on the course to a balanced Federal budget.

Over the years, sincere efforts have been made by men and women of good will in both parties to solve the chronic problem of overspending by the Federal Government. But the problem has not been solved. This week, Congress faces the unhappy task of raising the debt ceiling to over $2 trillion. We cannot escape the simple truth that the budget process has failed nor will we avoid the harsh verdict of history if we cannot summon the political courage to put our national house in order and finally live within our means. The great saving strength of democracy is that we can confront the truth about ourselves. Individuals of vision, courage, and leadership can set things right.

Well, we're going to set things right. We're going to begin amending the budget process today. Many Members of Congress are joining the Senate authors—Phil Gramm, who's been working with us on this issue since Gramm-Latta in 1981, and Warren Rudman; Democratic chief sponsor, Fritz Hollings; and the House chief sponsors, Connie Mack and Dick Cheney—in this important deficit control measure. I'm delighted with the leadership support of Senate Majority Leader Bob Dole; Bob Michel, who's in Illinois today; House Republican Whip Trent Lott; as well as the Republican Budget Committee leaders, Pete Domenici and Del Latta.

Let me also thank all of you here today, of both parties, who are joining in support of the Balanced Budget and Emergency Deficit Control Act of 1985. This legislation will impose the discipline we now lack by locking us into a spending reduction plan. It will establish a maximum allowable deficit ceiling beginning with our current 1986 deficit of $180 billion, and then it will reduce that deficit in equal steps to a balanced budget in calendar year 1990. One of the reasons I like this Gramm-Rudman bill is because it attacks budget deficits the right way, not by raising taxes, but by restraining spending. I want it clearly understood that while spending discipline must and will be enforced, we will honor our commitments on Social Security. We will maintain a strong defense, and I expect the Congress to live up to its previous commitments on defense.

Under this legislation, no budget may be submitted with a deficit greater than the maximum allowable as set out in law, and neither House may consider any budget that violates these ceilings. Speaking for myself, I would like to make an additional request—that Congress work with me to put in place a balanced budget constitutional amendment to begin taking effect in 1991. It will make permanent our plan to have no deficits at the Federal level.

If Congress cooperates and passes this legislation, we can send a clear and compelling message to the world: The United States Government is not only going to pay its bills, but we're also going to take away the credit cards. From now on it'll be cash and carry. And I believe it's critical that the Senate vote today because the debt-limit authority expires on Monday. If we move with bipartisan unity to pass this dramatic but responsible plan to bring Federal spending securely under control and, just as important, unite to bring personal and business tax rates further down, there will be no barriers to America's progress. There'll be no limits to the American dream. And the time is now to move on. So, let's get started.

―――――

Reporter. Mr. President, can you tell us any more about Mr. Buckley and whether or not the statement that he has been killed is true?

The President. Well, that changes the subject here a little bit. But, no, we have no word, no way to confirm. He is the one who had been kidnaped in March of '84. We have no confirmation, and until we know something definite, why, we're not going to comment.

Q. Are you worried by your allies' failure to agree to come and see you in New York to discuss matters before the summit?

The President. Well, I'm sorry there seems to be a misunderstanding. This is simply the summit, seven that meet every year. And it was just our thought that since they were going to be here, with the opening of the U.N. and all, that we'd have an extra summit meeting of the kind that we usually have.

Q. Mitterrand has rejected the request for separate negotiations with the Soviets, does that please you or affect you in any way?

The President. That's his decision to make, and I'll have no comment on it. That's――

Q. Well, what about the full appeal that Gorbachev is making to Europe? It seems to be a very powerful appeal.

The President. Well, I'm just going to wait until we get to Geneva to see how things come out.

Note: The President spoke at 9:32 a.m. in the State Dining Room at the White House.

Remarks at a State Republican Fundraising Luncheon in Parsippany, New Jersey
October 4, 1985

Thank you very much, and thank you very much, Governor Tom Kean. My friends, Frank Holman, Members of the Congress, it's great to see you all. You know, I have a spot in my heart for Governors―*[laughter]*―due to about 8 years of that experience. And just recently, I was—well, as a matter of fact, yesterday I was telling a story I hadn't told for a long time about my own days as Governor. I'd come into a situation in California as a newcomer, and the situation was just about as bad as it was at the Federal level in 1980. And I was on my way to work one morning with the car radio on, and I heard a disc jockey. And out of the clear blue sky he spoke a line that endeared him to me forever. He said, "Every man should take unto himself a

wife, because sooner or later something is bound to happen that you can't blame on the Governor." *[Laughter]*

But I've come here just to let you know that I have officially appropriated the saying of the State across the river there, and I just want to say, I love New Jersey! It's wonderful to be here. I saw Tom Kean a few months ago when I was visiting Bloomfield, and I told him I wanted to come back soon, and he very conveniently arranged this fundraiser just to accommodate me. Wasn't that sweet of him? *[Laughter]* Incidentally, I should apologize to—and I should have done this when I first started talking here—about keeping you waiting for so long. But, you know, the whole hitch was that the plan called for an airplane from

Washington to here and then a helicopter closer to here and then an automobile for the last few minutes, and the helicopter had to be canceled. But if it will encourage you, this gray stuff is all the way to Washington—[*laughter*]. And I can tell you from having been up there, if you just want to go 2,000 feet straight up, you're in the clear sunshine. [*Laughter*] It's that low.

Well, it used to be that, centuries ago, that New Jersey was said to be a valley of humility between two mountains of pride. Well, if that is still true, and humility is a virtue, then I think, Jersey, you'd better be aware of the important place that you hold in our White House. I want you to know—and I'm serious about this—I've been watching New Jersey these past few years and seeing it as a bellwether for the national recovery. There are reasons for this. In many ways New Jersey is a perfect reflection of our country as a whole. You're both industrial and agrarian; you're a big manufacturing State, and you're the ninth largest State in population, and you have one of the lowest unemployment rates in the country. And as your Governor just told you, you just passed yourselves a tax cut bill, a State tax cut bill. So, New Jersey is in good shape; it's in great shape. You've got the Giants and the Jets, Springsteen and Sinatra, and the single most popular Governor in the history of the State of New Jersey.

I'm here to tell you that I am keen on Kean. [*Laughter*] But I know that he's one of the most decent and able administrators, leaders, and political figures and Governors in America. Now, that's just my humble opinion. [*Laughter*] Let me ask—you're an impartial nonpartisan group—[*laughter*]—does New Jersey like Tom Kean, too? [*Applause*] Well, I'm with you. And there's another great race in this great State. It's been mentioned already, the race for "Assembly Majority '85." The Republican Party of New Jersey is within five seats of control of the State assembly, and you're going to win it this year, and you're going to make Chuck Hardwick majority leader, and you're going to return the GOP to the dominance that it deserves.

This, too, is an experience that I shared, because as Governor of California for 8 years, 7 of those had a majority of the other party. If the people of the State believe enough in the things that Tom Kean is doing, then they ought to give him the help that he needs and the capital to get those things done, instead of making an uphill fight for him. And then next year, I'd like to talk to you about another body. [*Laughter*] But the race for the State assembly and the race for the Governor's mansion won't be easy. They'll require all your commitment, your time, your efforts, and, as well, some of your cash. [*Laughter*] But it's going to be a good cause. Ultimately, it's going to help the party that stands for economic growth and economic justice; the party that cares that the poor get a piece of the pie; the party that has finally put an end to the tax enslavement of the middle class in America. It's our party that has worked for years now to get government spending down.

And I want you to know that I have just come from Washington where this morning we announced an historic agreement to put our nation on the road to a balanced budget. We are uniting with the leaders of the Senate to support the balanced budget and emergency deficit control act of 1985. This is a measure that will lock us into spending reductions and lead us to a balanced budget by 1990.

Let me just tell you something unusual about this. Over in the west wing of the White House, we have been huddling over the idea of a plan—that it isn't good enough just each year to see if we can haggle the budget down and get a little more money out of it. We needed a plan leading toward a balanced budget, and so we were talking about looking for 5 years of a declining pattern of deficits. There's no way this deficit can be eliminated in 1 year, we know, but 5 years—and then at the end of the 5 years, let's get that balanced budget amendment that the Federal Government will have to stop spending more than it takes in after we get it. But while we were doing that in the White House, all of a sudden, a few days ago, we discovered that up on the Hill, two of our Senators were working on exactly the same kind of plan—5 years and then our balanced budget. And so, this morning

1191

was to announce that—I don't know whether the extrasensory perception was going that way, from the White House or from the Hill down to us, but we were all on the same track, and we are working together now with the Congress to bring this about and pass as quickly as we can this 5-year plan so that from now on, when somebody wants to bust the budget for some particular spending program, they will be breaking into a well-organized plan that is aimed at, as I say, the balanced budget.

But the GOP is, in my view, the party of the American family; the party whose tax reform proposals, to touch on another subject, would expand the personal exemption, increase the standard deduction, and make IRA's—you know, those are those individual retirement accounts—equally available to those who work both inside and outside the home. The GOP is the party that adheres to the old Jeffersonian philosophy that that government governs best that governs least. Incidentally, Thomas Jefferson made a little-known statement about the Constitution just about the time it was being ratified. He said it only had one flaw: It did not contain a provision preventing the Federal Government from borrowing money. [*Laughter*] Well, we're going to make Tom Jefferson, wherever he is, happy. [*Laughter*]

Well, it's the GOP that would keep political power near the true roots of that power—in the neighborhood, the town, the county, and then the State. Such an approach to governmental justice demands creativity on the part of the local elements who would lead and govern. Happily, it's the Republican Party that strives for creativity on the local level, that encourages and develops it. The Republican Party sees the challenges of the world with clear eyes and recognizes the difference between the totalitarians and the freedom fighters and rejects the former and hails the latter.

And finally, it's the Republican Party that has stood up, with the help of many Democrats, for SDI, our strategic space shield. They call it Star Wars; there's nothing in that, descriptive of what we're talking about. We're talking about a defensive shield that won't hurt people, but will knock down nuclear weapons before they can hurt people. We will go forward with seeing if it cannot be made into a great protector of our people and the people of the world. It could be the device, if the research pans out—we can perfect this—it could be the thing that would eliminate nuclear weapons because they wouldn't have any use any more. Demands to abandon a program with real potential for strengthening deterrence and enhancing Western security do not deal with the real issue of peace. What we need are good-faith discussions, and we're seeking to discuss even now with the Soviets in Geneva the vital relationship between strategic offense and defense. I see where he made a statement in a recent interview, where he said that he did not believe that the God above could have done something—would prevent the people of the world from doing something for themselves. And I have to believe if he's talking to God we ought to be able to get along, because so am I.

But much is at stake when we talk about the principles of our party. And much is at stake when we ask New Jersey to get out there and elect a Republican assembly. It'll be another step toward the political realignment that's been going on for a few years now and that needs an extra push from your wonderful State. And remember the whole country will be watching. What you do in a few weeks will make a difference. And I just want to thank all of you for caring and sharing your time. You're the troops of a mighty movement, you are the movement, and God bless you all.

And I thank you kindly for your reception here today. I was here, as I say, just a few months ago, and I'll be back again soon. I love New Jersey!

Note: The President spoke at 2:40 p.m. in the Grand Ballroom at the Hilton Hotel. He was introduced by Gov. Thomas H. Kean. Following his remarks, the President attended a reception at the hotel for major donors to the State Republican Party. He then returned to Washington, DC.

Statement on Signing the Bill Expressing Support for the Earthquake Victims in Mexico
October 4, 1985

The tragedy that has unfolded in Mexico in the past several days is of historic proportion. Thousands have lost their lives; thousands more have been injured. The devastation done to one of the world's great cities is massive. Nancy went to Mexico City and saw the damage firsthand. She saw the depth of the suffering, the extent of the destruction, and the courage and determination of the Mexican people to overcome the catastrophe that has befallen them.

I am signing House Joint Resolution 394 that expresses our sympathy as a nation for the people and Government of Mexico. The United States is already providing emergency medical, water storage, and communications supplies to help alleviate the immediate suffering from this tragic event. In addition, we stand ready to cooperate with Mexico in long-term efforts to recover from the effects of the earthquake. A global effort will surely be needed and will surely be forthcoming. The United States will fully support such an undertaking.

This resolution reflects the spontaneous support that has come from all sectors in the United States. State and local governments, church groups, schools, businesses, labor unions, and individual citizens have given generously and freely in an effort to relieve the evident human suffering. With pride and dignity, the people of Mexico have accepted this help from their neighbors as they have carried out an impressive effort of their own to save lives and to protect the well-being of those affected. This tragedy has demonstrated dramatically that, indeed, we are more than neighbors; we are brothers. Their pain is our pain; their loss is our loss. Throughout the past several days as citizens of Mexico waited, citizens of the United States also waited for news of loved ones. Hundreds of thousands called our Department of State to learn the fate of friends and family members in the earthquake zone.

This tragedy, the shared sorrow, the spontaneous acts of friendship and assistance— all of these things clearly demonstrate that our lives, our fortunes, and our futures are inextricably intertwined. We will respond with sympathy knowing that were the situation reversed, Mexicans would react with the same compassion for us. As I have said many times, we are all Americans. And today I say again, *todos somos Americanos.*

Note: H.J. Res. 394, approved October 4, was assigned Public Law No. 99–116.

Proclamation 5375—Child Health Day, 1985
October 4, 1985

By the President of the United States of America

A Proclamation

This year, we mark the golden anniversary of the landmark maternal and child health legislation, Title V of the Social Security Act. Under that authority, the Federal government has sponsored a wide variety of training, demonstration, research, and related special activities that have made a great contribution to our effectiveness in providing health care to American mothers and their children.

Even more important, I believe, is the fact that for 50 years we have provided assistance to the States through formula grants and, more recently, through the Maternal and Child Health Services Block Grant. Through this approach, States have matched Federal funds and have assumed full responsibility for program administration. We can all take pride in this relationship that has supported a wide range of vital preventive and therapeutic services for mothers and infants and children and adolescents, including highly sophisticated help to children with special needs, such as those with handicaps and chronic illness. We can take pride in the services provided and, especially, in the way they are provided, for the nature, scope, location, and timing of these services are determined as they should be—at the State and community levels, and by the medical professionals at the scene. These are the people who know firsthand what the greatest needs are and how best to respond to them.

On this Child Health Day, 1985, as we celebrate 50 years of cooperative endeavor in support of maternal and child health, we should rededicate ourselves to the expansion of State and local responsibility in this extremely important field. We must do everything necessary to protect the health of our mothers and children. We must remember that the best way to do this is to entrust the responsibilities and the needed resources to the States and communities in which they live.

Now, Therefore, I, Ronald Reagan, President of the United States of America, pursuant to a joint resolution approved May 18, 1928, as amended (36 U.S.C. 143), do hereby proclaim Monday, October 7, 1985, as Child Health Day.

In Witness Whereof, I have hereunto set my hand this fourth day of October, in the year of our Lord nineteen hundred and eighty-five, and of the Independence of the United States of America the two hundred and tenth.

RONALD REAGAN

[*Filed with the Office of the Federal Register, 10:59 a.m., October 7, 1985*]

Note: The proclamation was released by the Office of the Press Secretary on October 5.

Proclamation 5376—Columbus Day, 1985
October 4, 1985

By the President of the United States of America

A Proclamation

We are privileged each year to pay honor to the great explorer whose epic voyages of discovery led to the development of the Western Hemisphere. Christopher Columbus won an imperishable place in history and in the hearts of all Americans by challenging the unknown and defying the doubters. In doing so he set in motion a chain of events which transformed the world and led to the birth of the great country in which we live.

Columbus' achievement lies not only in his daring navigational exploits but also in the practical outgrowth of his efforts. More than a great seaman, he was a man of vision who could see the opportunities that lay beyond the horizon. Indeed, the results of his quest were far grander than he could have envisioned. Those who followed in the path he had opened built a new world whose economic, political, and social development have been marvels of human energy and ingenuity. People from across the globe have come to America to find freedom, justice, and economic opportunity.

Columbus exemplified a spirit which still inspires all Americans—a spirit of reaching out, expanding the frontiers of knowledge, a spirit of undaunted hope. In the words of Joaquin Miller, "He gained a world; he gave that world its grandest lesson: 'On! Sail On!'" Like Columbus, we Americans are ready to take risks in pursuit of our goals. We understand that boundless opportunities await those who dare to strive.

Our tribute to Columbus has special meaning to Americans of Italian descent. This son of Genoa was the first of many great Italian travelers to the New World. Millions of his countrymen would later settle in the new land, adding their pre-ious contribution to the developments that stemmed from Columbus' voyages. Columbus was the first link in a chain which today binds the United States to Italy in a special relationship.

This remembrance is also particularly important for those of Spanish descent. Columbus' achievement depended on the vision and energy of a newly united Spain. This was only the first of Spain's many cultural and economic contributions to the New World. We share with our Spanish-speaking neighbors this heritage and our debt of gratitude to Spain.

In the coming years this commemoration of the voyage of 1492 will take on heightened significance, because we are approaching the 500th anniversary of that great event. The Christopher Columbus Quincentenary Jubilee Commission, a distinguished group of Americans assisted by representatives from Spain and Italy, will plan, encourage, and carry forward the commemoration of Columbus' great voyages of discovery. The Committee held its initial meeting on September 12, and will report within two years its recommendations for observance of the celebration.

In tribute to Columbus' achievement, the Congress of the United States, by joint resolution approved April 30, 1934 (48 Stat. 657), as modified by the Act of June 28, 1968 (82 Stat. 250), has requested the President to proclaim the second Monday in October of each year as Columbus Day.

Now, Therefore, I, Ronald Reagan, President of the United States of America, do hereby proclaim Monday, October 14, as Columbus Day. I invite the people of this Nation to observe that day in schools, churches, and other suitable places with appropriate ceremonies in honor of this great explorer. I also direct that the flag of the United States be displayed on all public buildings on the appointed day in honor of Christopher Columbus.

In Witness Whereof, I have hereunto set my hand this fourth day of October, in the year of our Lord nineteen hundred and eighty-five, and of the Independence of the United States of America the two hundred and tenth.

RONALD REAGAN

[*Filed with the Office of the Federal Register, 11 a.m., October 7, 1985*]

Note: The proclamation was released by the Office of the Press Secretary on October 5.

Radio Address to the Nation on the Budget Deficit and the Middle East
October 5, 1985

My fellow Americans:

Today I'd like to talk to you about two matters: a dramatic new legislative proposal and recent events in the Middle East.

First, the new proposal: Yesterday I gave my enthusiastic support to what might well become historic legislation—the Balanced Budget and Emergency Deficit Control Act of 1985—introduced by Senator Phil Gramm of Texas and Senator Warren Rudman of New Hampshire. This legislation will impose the discipline our government has so long lacked to control its insatiable appetite to spend. Under this proposal the Federal Government, by law, would be required to lock in a deficit reduction path leading to a balanced budget. This would be achieved without raising taxes, without jeopardizing our defenses, and without breaking our commitments on Social Security. The proposal would establish a maximum allowable deficit ceiling, beginning with the current level of $180 billion, and then mandate that this deficit be reduced—by equal amounts each year—until we reach a balanced budget in calendar year 1990. Moreover, I personally believe in, and I've asked Congress to put in place, a balanced budget amendment to the Constitution to take effect in 1991. By doing this, we could make sure that our progress would not be lost.

The importance of the proposal to eliminate deficit spending can hardly be overstated. For decades Federal spending has been growing virtually out of control. It took 173 years, from the establishment of our government in 1789 to the Kennedy administration in 1962, for the annual budget of the United States to reach $100 billion. It took only the next 9 years for the budget to double to 200 billion, and in the 14 years since, it has more than quadrupled to over 900 billion. Not surprisingly, as the Government has been spending like a drunken sailor, it's taken our country deeper and deeper into the red. Indeed, today the Federal deficit amounts to more than $211 billion.

Now, this deficit has not—and I repeat, not—developed because of our tax cut. On the contrary, government revenues have actually been rising rapidly since we cut tax rates—42 percent since we started, but spending has increased by 60 percent. But overall, since our tax cut, government has still spent more than it has taken in. It sort of reminds me of that old definition of a baby—an enormous appetite at one end and no sense of responsibility at the other. Well, with the passage of the bill I endorsed yesterday, the Government of the United States can show that, at long last, we are growing up, and we're gaining that sense of responsibility. The Senate is debating this proposal today, and I strongly urge them to approve it before the debt limit authority expires on Monday.

Let me add here a personal caveat: While spending control is vital to the economic well-being of this nation, the highest priority of any American Government is preservation of the national security. The maintenance of a national defense second to none, indeed, the only legitimate justification for running a large annual deficit—as we ran every year of World War II—is preservation of the Nation, itself. When the spending cuts are made by this administration, as they must be made, the security of this country, its allies, and its friends will not be put at risk. The Congress has agreed, and next year I will propose those amounts already accepted as necessary for keeping the peace.

Permit me now to turn to recent events in the Middle East. In shock and dismay we've watched murderous attacks on Israeli civilians, and in response, an Israeli military raid on a PLO headquarters in a country that is an old friend of the United States. Now we hear that one of our American hostages in Lebanon may have been murdered, as was a Soviet citizen earlier this week. This return to violence is abhorrent. All the more so because it's so useless. Armed struggle has solved nothing. There is no military option for resolving the difficult conflicts of the Middle East. The only way to bring a lasting end to this dreadful cycle of violence is to deal with the circumstances that underlie it through negotiations—direct, peaceful negotiations among the parties concerned.

Permit me to close by mentioning the gifted statesman whose country was affected by this week's violent events, President Habib Bourguiba of Tunisia. Farseeing and wise, President Bourguiba has been a true friend to America for decades. There is a particularly bitter irony about events of the past week because President Bourguiba was one of the very first to urge a negotiated settlement of the Arab-Israeli conflict. Our hearts go out to him and to the innocent Tunisians swept up in this violence. In this horror, our hope lies in statesmen like President Bourguiba and King Hussein, President Mubarak and Prime Minister Peres. They are men of vision and peace; they deserve our support and our prayers.

Until next week, thanks for listening, and God bless you.

Note: The President spoke at 12:06 p.m. from Camp David, MD.

Statement Urging Senate Approval of the Balanced Budget and Emergency Deficit Control Bill
October 6, 1985

This is a momentous day for the United States Senate. Zero hour is approaching. By tomorrow, the Federal Government's cash balances will be virtually exhausted and we will be facing a financial emergency. The choice before the Senate is clear: to meet its responsibilities by approving the Gramm-Rudman-Hollings amendment to bring deficits down, thereby permitting the debt ceiling increase to pass, or to resort to a temporary quick fix that will only postpone the day of reckoning and raise the price all of us must pay. This latter course would be imprudent, unwise, and unsatisfactory. The American people have grown very weary of delays, excuses, and inaction.

They cannot accept that this government is incapable of living within a reasonable budget, when their families can and do live within their budgets.

I'm confident that the people are united with me, the Republican leadership, and many other Republicans and Democrats in urging the Senate: Seize this moment of opportunity, move now to pass the historic Gramm-Rudman-Hollings amendment that will deal decisively with deficits and give our nation a balanced budget by 1990. There is no problem that we Americans cannot fix if only we have the faith, unity, and courage to act. The days of delays have run out.

Nomination of James R. Richards To Be Inspector General of the Department of the Interior
October 7, 1985

The President today announced his intention to nominate James R. Richards to be Inspector General, Department of the Interior. He would succeed Richard Mulberry.

Since 1981 he has been serving as Inspector General at the Department of Energy. Previously, he was general counsel and vice president of the National Legal Center for the Public Interest in 1980–1981; vice president of the Capital Legal Foundation in

1978–1980; consultant to the National Legal Center for the Public Interest in 1977; and Director of the Office of Hearings and Appeals, Department of the Interior, in 1974–1977.

He graduated from Western State College (B.A., 1955) and the University of Colorado School of Law (LL.B., 1960). He was born November 21, 1933, in Kinder Post, MO, and now resides in Arlington, VA.

Nomination of William J. Doyle III To Be Inspector General of the Railroad Retirement Board
October 7, 1985

The President today announced his intention to nominate William J. Doyle III to be Inspector General, Railroad Retirement Board. This is a new position.

Since 1981 Mr. Doyle has been serving as

Inspector General for ACTION. Previously, he was with the Law Enforcement Assistance Administration, Department of Justice, as executive assistant to the Administrator (1979–1981) and executive management adviser to the Administrator (1976–1979); at the Department of Housing and Urban Development as senior management adviser to the Executive Director of the Commission on Federal Paperwork in 1975–1976.

Mr. Doyle graduated from Catholic University (M.A., 1969; Ph.D., 1981). He has two children and resides in Davidsonville, MD. He was born May 18, 1941, in Gainesville, FL.

Nomination of C.M. Naeve To Be a Member of the Federal Energy Regulatory Commission
October 7, 1985

The President today announced his intention to nominate C.M. Naeve to be a member of the Federal Energy Regulatory Commission, Department of Energy, for a term expiring October 20, 1989. He would succeed Oliver G. Richard III.

Since 1984 Mr. Naeve has been serving as an attorney with the law firm of Skadden, Arps, Slate, Meagher and Flom in Washington, DC. Previously, he was vice president of the Mid-Continent Oil & Gas Association in 1982–1984; manager for Federal public affairs at Aminoil USA, Inc., in 1980–1982;

legislative director for Senator Lloyd Bentsen (1978–1980); a member of the professional staff of the U.S. Senate Committee on Environment and Public Works in 1977–1978; and in the division of planning coordination, office of the Governor of Texas, in 1972–1974.

He graduated from the University of Texas (B.S., 1970; M.P.A., 1972) and George Washington University (J.D., 1984). He is married, has two children, and resides in Alexandria, VA. He was born May 25, 1947, in Rapid City, SD.

Nomination of Ralph W. Tarr To Be Solicitor of the Department of the Interior
October 7, 1985

The President today announced his intention to nominate Ralph W. Tarr to be Solicitor of the Department of the Interior. He would succeed Frank K. Richardson.

Since 1984 Mr. Tarr has been serving as Acting Assistant Attorney General at the Department of Justice. Previously he was at the Department of Justice as principal Deputy Assistant Attorney General in 1982–1984. Since 1982 he has also been a member of the Administrative Committee of the Federal Register, representing the

Department of Justice. He was with Baker, Manock & Jensen in Fresno, CA, as director and member of the executive committee (1981–1982) and associate attorney (1977–1981).

He graduated from Dartmouth College (B.S., 1970), California State University (M.A., 1973), and the University of California, Hastings College of Law (J.D., 1976). He is married and resides in Vienna, VA. He was born September 29, 1948, in Bakersfield, CA.

Nomination of Dennis Eugene Whitfield To Be Under Secretary of Labor
October 7, 1985

The President today announced his intention to nominate Dennis Eugene Whitfield to be Under Secretary of the Department of Labor. He would succeed Ford Barney Ford.

Mr. Whitfield is presently serving as Chief of Staff to the Secretary of Labor. Previously he was with the Republican National Committee as regional political director for the Southeast, then as director of education and training, and later, director of political affairs. He was director of the Republican National Committee's 1979 and 1980 voter registration program.

He graduated from the University of Georgia (B.A., 1971). He is married and resides in Alexandria, VA. He was born July 9, 1948, in Albany, GA.

Remarks at a White House Meeting With Reagan-Bush Campaign Leadership Groups
October 7, 1985

Thank you all very much, and welcome to your home, America's home. It sure looks good to see this old room filled with the sons and daughters of the Grand Old Party.

This is a real treat for me today. It's a treat because while you may not know it, you're the ones I think of whenever those jaded voices start telling us what we can't do and why we shouldn't even try. I think you know who I mean. Weren't you the ones who rebelled against the notion that America was becoming a sick old bird, too wobbly to walk or fly? Seems to me you were saying, don't hold us down, don't get in our way. America is still an eagle, and she's ready to soar again. And, yes, you not only said the American people want to win, the people will win again because we offer a vision of victory. You did all that. At an important moment in our history, we set forth together to awaken our nation and rally her spirit. We said, let the opposition have their entrenched elites, their power brokers, and let them play their special interest politics. Let them have all that; we just want the people, and we're winning the people—millions of converts to our cause, millions of new Republicans uniting under bright banners of freedom and opportunity, turning a Grand Old Party into a grand new party, making GOP the great opportunity party for every American.

When we asked the people to help out and cut spending and tax rates, bring down inflation and interest rates, to index taxes so government can never again profit from inflation at the people's expense—when we won each of those great victories, we did it with the people's help, and all of the people have been helped. When we asked the people to help America meet great new challenges through renewed excellence in education and developing new frontiers in space and technology, we were declaring that the Republican Party does not fear the future; that the Republican Party embraces the future with confidence, a clear vision, and an open heart. And when we say we're the party of opportunity, we mean to draw attention to a modern miracle: nearly 8½ million—wait a minute, I can update that figure as of this morning—more than 9 million new jobs in the last 34 months; 378,000 more people went to work last month than had been working. If you take the employment pool, as defined as everyone—male and female, from 16 to 65—the highest percentage of that potential pool is employed than has ever been employed in the United States before.

Now, more can be done to squeeze this

bloated Federal Establishment, and believe me, more will be done. We're going to bring deficits down, and we're going to bring them down the right way—with greater growth and spending restraint and not higher taxes. We're backing—[applause]—I was just worried there for a split second. [Laughter] I hoped you were with me on that last part. [Laughter] We're backing what I believe can be an historic proposal: the Gramm-Rudman-Hollings amendment in the Senate that will lock in spending reductions and lead, at long last, to a balanced Federal budget. And believe me, that's one proposal that is worth fighting for.

But this amendment is being held hostage to a wrangling over the debt ceiling, putting the Federal Government in an emergency situation. The business of our nation must go forward. We need the debt ceiling increase passed. Now, I know it's true that we Republicans have swallowed hard, and we have regretted every time we've had to sign an increase in that, but we weren't responsible for the 50 years of deficit spending that was a matter of policy on the part of our opponents and that brought this all about. We've now inherited the bomb that we always said was there with a lighted fuse in all of that deficit spending, and we're going to do something about it—on a permanent basis. And we need the Gramm-Rudman-Hollings amendment passed so we can reach a balanced budget without hurting our senior citizens who are on Social Security and without raising taxes. Let's just make one thing very plain: We don't have a deficit problem because the American people are not paying enough in taxes. We have a deficit problem because the Federal Government is spending too much of the people's money.

I hope you didn't tell them this figure because I'm going to tell it anyway, again. You know, we've gone through some recent periods here—1965 until 1980, the last year before our administration, the Great Society and the War on Poverty, which poverty won, went into effect—[laughter]—it went into effect in the latter part of the sixties and then the seventies. And in those 15 years, the budget multiplied just about 5 times in 1980 what it was in 1965, 15 years

before; but the deficit multiplied 50 times what it had been in 1965, which explains and means that it is built in; it is structural. And that's why we're going to set out to change the structure with this plan that I have just mentioned, which is a 5-year plan.

Now, I'm appealing for your help on that plan and on another pressing matter, too. We have another historic opportunity to overhaul our tax code—to knock down the barriers to achievement, to make America's future as big and open and bright as your dreams. We can replace an unfair system of 14 tax brackets with a simple 3-bracket system of 15, 25, and 35 percent so that more of what the people earn stays in their pockets, not Uncle Sam's pockets. We can reduce business rates to 15, 18, 25, and 33 percent and enable our firms to outcompete, outproduce, and outsell anybody, anywhere in the world. We can be the American family's most faithful friend by nearly doubling the personal exemption to $2,000 for each dependent; increasing the standard deduction to $4,000; by providing the full benefit of IRA's, those are the amounts of earnings that could be deducted and put into a savings account and be tax deductible until the time of cashing in. And we want to extend that to both spouses, those working inside the home as well as those working outside the home. I don't think anyone can ever convince anyone in their right mind that a spouse working within the home is not working.

Under our profamily plan, a family of four won't have to pay a single cent of tax on their first $12,000 of earnings. So, really, it's more than a 3-bracket system; we've got a fourth bracket—zero. Families in every income group would be better off than today. And I happen to believe that as the family goes, so goes the Nation. And those in Washington should put the needs of family budgets ahead of the wants of the Federal budget. Passage of our fair share tax plan, as submitted, would increase economic growth by some 3 percent above our projections, create the equivalent of nearly 4 million more jobs, and provide from $600 to $900 a year in added income for every American household. And more people paying taxes means less red ink.

I'm convinced that an historic reform of this magnitude would be the most precious gift that we could give to our children—an America striding with confidence into the sunlight of human progress, leading a world that hungers for liberty, prosperity, and peace. Here in Washington, rumor has it that this tax issue doesn't excite the people's passion. Well, that's not the impression I get out in the grassroots. As a matter of fact, one of my most recent appearances out there—it was in a town of 14,000 and 20,000 of the 14,000 had come—[*laughter*]—for the rally. So, let me ask you. Are you with us? [*Applause*] Okay. With your strong support in your communities, contacting your representatives and the media, we can forget what the cynics say and pass America's fair share tax plan this year.

But even that great step won't be enough to get us where we want to be. We know there are pockets of great pain in America, with casualties lining the roadsides stretching back for too many years. Well, we're the party of Lincoln, born in the deep, rich soil of the plains, born and bred of hurdy-sturdy stock—the hardest working, most productive people in the world. And only by keeping our family farmers strong and only by keeping our family businesses strong will our Republican Party remain strong. When anxiety and despair knock at our door, we must answer with a willing hand, reaching out with support; we must answer with tax policies that ensure robust growth at home and with trade policies that pry open markets that are closed to American exports abroad; and we must answer with monetary policies that ensure a sound dollar, low inflation, low interest rates, and stable exchange rates. Incidentally, the inflation rate for the last 4 months has been 2½ percent. We have learned that without such stability, as I've just mentioned, free trade is a fantasy. Now, all this we must work for and more.

To those in our inner cities, in our ghettos and barrios, we say, "Our progress cannot be complete until the dream is real for all." The party of Lincoln will not be whole until those who were with us once before rejoin us again, until they taste the emancipation of full economic justice and economic power. Let us make one thing plain: It is we who are battling for a true jobs agenda with enterprise zones and the youth opportunity wage. But if we're to open these doors for millions of whites, blacks, and Hispanics, if we're going to help people off unemployment, off welfare, and into the decent jobs they deserve, then we need to ask them for their support. We need to elect more Republicans to the United States Congress. You know, in 1990 there'll be another reapportionment. And do you know that, I believe, it's been more than 50 years since Republicans have been in charge of reapportionment. I think in our own State out in California the only Republican district they've left us is south of the border. [*Laughter*]

My friends, when we say that we're going forward and taking America's heritage with us, we're saying that the values of our fellow citizens deserve to be respected and not patronized. For us, words like faith, family, work, and neighborhood are not slogans to be dragged out of the closet at election time; they're values we cherish and live by every day. For us, the right of an unborn child to be brought into the world, the right of children to pray and acknowledge God in their schools, the right of parents to guide the education and moral development of their children—these are not fringe issues to be forever shunted aside; these are questions that go to the core of who we are and what we stand for. And these rights must and will be proudly carried forward by our party.

I can't leave without reminding you that America must remain freedom's staunchest friend, for freedom is our staunchest ally. It's America's responsibility and the responsibility of the Republican Party to stand with people that are being persecuted for their beliefs, to stand with people risking their lives for liberty, from Afghanistan to Angola to Nicaragua. Supporting them is not only morally right, it is the way of honor; to abandon these brave souls would be to condemn America to eternal shame. By pushing forward the frontiers of freedom, we reinvigorate the forces for democracy and peace.

At the same time, we will continue trying to work with the Soviet Union to solve problems, work for an agreement to reduce the weapons of war in a manner that is equitable and verifiable, and build a foundation for a safer world. I'm going to do my part—after Time magazine, I'm going to wear my pinstriped suit to Geneva. [*Laughter*]

Seriously, that's why I'm determined to pursue our research program to explore the feasibility of strategic defenses, a security shield that could protect the United States and our allies from a missile attack. Why should this effort fill us with hope? Because it would not kill people, it would destroy weapons; because it would not militarize space, it would help demilitarize the arsenals of Earth; because it's the essence of science and spirit joining for mankind's highest ideal—peace on Earth. It must go forward; it will go forward. It is not a bargaining chip, and we will go forward.

Thank you, and God bless you.

Note: The President spoke at 11:46 a.m. in the East Room at the White House.

Nomination of Donald J. Bouchard To Be an Assistant Secretary of State
October 7, 1985

The President today announced his intention to nominate Donald J. Bouchard to be an Assistant Secretary of State (Administration). He would succeed Robert E. Lamb.

He is presently serving as executive assistant to the Under Secretary for Management, Department of State. He joined the State Department in 1962 and served in various administrative officer positions in Africa until 1972. He was special assistant to the Under Secretary for Management in 1972–1976; administrative counselor at the U.S. Embassy in Ottawa (1976–1979); administrative counselor at the U.S. Embassy in Madrid (1979–1981); Executive Director, Bureau of Inter-American Affairs (1981–1984); and Deputy Assistant Secretary of State for Personnel in 1984–1985.

He attended the University of California at Berkeley. He is married, has two children, and resides in Fairfax, VA. He was born June 18, 1937, in Waterville, ME.

Designation of Terry Calvani as Acting Chairman of the Federal Trade Commission
October 7, 1985

The President today designated Terry Calvani to be Acting Chairman of the Federal Trade Commission. He has served as a member since November 16, 1983.

Prior to becoming a member of the Federal Trade Commission in 1983, Mr. Calvani was of counsel to the law firm of North, Haskell, Slaughter, Young & Lewis in Birmingham, AL (1980–1983); on the staff of Vanderbilt University School of Law as professor (1980–1983), associate professor (1977–1980), and assistant professor (1974–1977); and an associate with the law firm of Pillsbury, Madison & Sutro in San Francisco, CA (1973–1974). He was a senior research associate at the Vanderbilt Institute for Public Policy Studies in 1977–1983.

He graduated from the University of New Mexico (B.A., 1970) and Cornell University (J.D., 1972). He has two children and resides in Washington, DC. He was born January 29, 1947, in Carlsbad, NM.

Nomination of Paul H. Lamboley To Be a Member of the Interstate Commerce Commission
October 7, 1985

The President today announced his intention to nominate Paul H. Lamboley to be a member of the Interstate Commerce Commission for a term expiring December 31, 1989. This is a reappointment.

Since 1984 Mr. Lamboley has been serving as a member of the Interstate Commerce Commission. Previously he was in the private practice of law in 1970–1982.

Mr. Lamboley graduated from the University of Notre Dame (B.S., 1962) and the University of Wisconsin (J.D., 1967). He is married, has two children, and resides in Chevy Chase, MD. He was born July 17, 1940, in Monroe, WI.

Nomination of Two Members of the Board for International Broadcasting
October 7, 1985

The President today announced his intention to nominate the following individuals to be members of the Board for International Broadcasting for a term expiring April 4, 1988:

Michael Novak, of Washington, DC, is a reappointment. Mr. Novak presently holds the George Frederick Jewett Chair in religion and public policy at the American Enterprise Institute. In 1981 and 1982 he served as chief of the United States delegation to the United Nations Human Rights Commission in Geneva. He has written numerous books and articles on philosophy, theology, and culture. He graduated from Stonehill College (A.B., 1956), the Gregorian University in Rome (B.T., 1958), and Harvard University (M.A., 1965). He is married, has three children, and resides in Washington, DC. He was born September 9, 1933, in Johnstown, PA.

Edward Noonan Ney, of New York, is a reappointment. Mr. Ney is chairman of Young and Rubicam, Inc., in New York City. He first joined Young and Rubicam in 1951 as an account executive. He was named a vice president in 1959; senior vice president in 1963; executive vice president and director of international in 1967; president of international in 1968; president and chief executive officer in 1970; and chairman in 1972. He is a member of the boards of trustees of the National Urban League, the Museum of Broadcasting, and the United States Council for International Business. He graduated from Amherst College (B.A., 1946). He is married, has three children, and resides in Pound Ridge, NY. He was born May 26, 1925, in St. Paul, MN.

Nomination of Warren J. Baker To Be a Member of the National Science Board
October 7, 1985

The President today announced his intention to nominate Dr. Warren J. Baker to be a member of the National Science Board, National Science Foundation, for a term expiring May 10, 1988. He would succeed Marian E. Koshland.

Dr. Baker has been serving as president of California Polytechnic State University since 1979. Previously he spent 12 years at the University of Detroit, joining the College of Engineering faculty in 1966. In 1973 he became the Chrysler professor and dean of the College of Engineering and in 1977 became the chief academic officer and vice president of the university. He was the National Science Foundation visiting fellow at the Massachusetts Institute of Technology in 1971–1972.

He graduated from the University of Notre Dame (B.A., 1960; M.S., 1962) and the University of New Mexico (Ph.D., 1966). He is married, has four children, and resides in San Luis Obispo, CA. He was born September 5, 1938, in Fitchburg, MA.

Proclamation 5378—Twenty-fifth Anniversary Year of the Peace Corps
October 7, 1985

By the President of the United States of America

A Proclamation

The American people throughout our history have shown their commitment and concern for the welfare of their fellow men and women, both in their own communities and around the globe. Nowhere has the proud American tradition of voluntarism been better illustrated than through the Peace Corps, which has begun a year-long observance of its twenty-fifth anniversary.

For a quarter of a century, the Peace Corps has recruited and trained volunteers to serve in countries of the developing world, helping people help themselves in their quest for a better life. More than one hundred and twenty thousand Americans have served in the Peace Corps in more than ninety countries. Their projects and programs have built bridges of understanding between the people of the United States and the peoples of the countries they have been privileged to serve.

Peace Corps volunteers have returned to their communities enriched by the experience, knowing more of the world, its complexities, and its challenges. They continue to communicate with people in the countries where they served, thereby strengthening the ties of friendship and mutual understanding.

The Peace Corps' call for service has renewed importance today, as American volunteers help others overseas seek long-term solutions to the complex human problems of hunger, poverty, illiteracy, and disease. The generous response to this call continues to exceed the Peace Corps' recruitment requirements.

The Congress, by House Joint Resolution 305, has designated the period from October 1, 1985, through September 30, 1986, as the twenty-fifth anniversary of the Peace Corps and authorized and requested the President to issue a proclamation on this occasion to honor Peace Corps volunteers past and present.

Now, Therefore, I, Ronald Reagan, President of the United States of America, do hereby proclaim October 1, 1985, through September 30, 1986, the Twenty-fifth Anniversary Year of the Peace Corps. I call upon public and private international voluntary organizations, development experts, scholars, the business community, individuals and leaders in the United States of America and overseas, and past and present Peace Corps volunteers to reflect upon the achievements of the Peace Corps during its twenty-five years, as well as to consider ways that talents and expertise of its volunteers may be used even more effectively in the future. During this time, I invite all Americans to honor the Peace Corps and its volunteers past and present, and reaffirm our Nation's commitment to helping people in the developing world help themselves.

In Witness Whereof, I have hereunto set my hand this seventh day of October, in the year of our Lord nineteen hundred and eighty-five, and of the Independence of the United States of America the two hundred and tenth.

RONALD REAGAN

[*Filed with the Office of the Federal Register, 2:20 p.m., October 8, 1985*]

Proclamation 5377—Suspension of Entry as Nonimmigrants by Officers or Employees of the Government of Cuba or the Communist Party of Cuba
October 4, 1985

By the President of the United States of America

A Proclamation

In light of the current state of relations between the United States and Cuba, including the May 20, 1985, statement that the Government of Cuba, had decided "to suspend all types of procedures regarding the execution" of the December 14, 1984, immigration agreement between the United States and Cuba, thereby disrupting normal migration procedures between the two countries, I have determined that it is in the interest of the United States to impose certain restrictions on entry into the United States of officers or employees of the Government of Cuba or the Communist Party of Cuba.

Now, Therefore, I, Ronald Reagan, by the authority vested in me as President by the Constitution and laws of the United States of America, including section 212(f) of the Immigration and Nationality Act of 1952, as amended (8 U.S.C. 1182(f)), having found that the unrestricted entry of officers or employees of the Government of Cuba or the ·Communist Party of Cuba into the United States would, except as provided in Section 2, be detrimental to the interests of the United States, do proclaim that:

Section 1. Entry of the following classes of Cuban nationals as nonimmigrants is hereby suspended: (a) officers or employees of the Government of Cuba or the Communist Party of Cuba holding diplomatic or official passports; and (b) individuals who, notwithstanding the type of passport that they hold, are considered by the Secretary of State or his designee to be officers or employees of the Government of Cuba or the Communist Party of Cuba.

Sec. 2. The suspension of entry as nonimmigrants set forth in Section 1 shall not apply to officers or employees of the Government of Cuba or the Communist Party of Cuba: (a) entering for the exclusive purpose of conducting official business at the Cuban Interests Section in Washington; at the Cuban Mission to the United Nations in New York; or at the United Nations in New York when, in the judgment of the Secretary of State or his designee, entry for such purpose is required by the United Nations Headquarters Agreement; (b) in the case of experts on a mission of the United Nations and in the case of individuals coming to the United States on official United Nations business as representatives of nongovernmental organizations when, in the judgment of the Secretary of State or his designee, entry for such purpose is required by the United Nations Headquarters Agreement; or (c) in such other cases or categories of cases as may be designated from time to time by the Secretary of State or his designee.

Sec. 3. This Proclamation shall be effective immediately.

In Witness Whereof, I have hereunto set my hand this 4th day of Oct., in the year of our Lord nineteen hundred and eighty-five, and of the Independence of the United States of America the two hundred and tenth.

RONALD REAGAN

[*Filed with the Office of the Federal Register, 2:19 p.m., October 8, 1985*]

Note: The proclamation was released by the Office of the Press Secretary on October 8.

Proclamation 5379—Mental Illness Awareness Week, 1985
October 7, 1985

By the President of the United States of America

A Proclamation

At some time in their lives, millions of Americans in all walks of life suffer from some form of mental illness. The cost of such illness to society is staggering, totaling billions of dollars for treatment, support, and lost productivity each year.

The emotional costs to those who suffer, and the anguish it causes their families and friends, are beyond reckoning. Because of the unwarranted stigma too often associated with mental illness—a by-product of fear and misunderstanding—many victims do not seek the help they need.

But help is available. Treatment can bring relief to many. Scientific advances in recent decades have led to a variety of effective treatments, using modern drugs as well as behavioral and psychosocial therapies: the lows of a depressive disorder can be ameliorated; suicide prevented; hallucinations and delusions dispelled; and crippling anxieties eased. Those who suffer can be healed and again become productive members of society.

In recognition of the unparalleled growth in scientific knowledge about mental illnesses and the need to increase awareness of such knowledge, the Congress, by Senate Joint Resolution 67, has designated the week beginning October 6, 1985, as "Mental Illness Awareness Week" and authorized and requested the President to issue a proclamation in observance of this event.

Now, Therefore, I, Ronald Reagan, President of the United States of America, do hereby proclaim the week beginning October 6, 1985, as Mental Illness Awareness Week. I call upon all health care providers, educators, the media, public and private organizations, and the people of the United States to join me in this observance.

In Witness Whereof, I have hereunto set my hand this seventh day of October, in the year of our Lord nineteen hundred and eighty-five, and of the Independence of the United States of America the two hundred and tenth.

RONALD REAGAN

[Filed with the Office of the Federal Register, 2:21 p.m., October 8, 1985]

Note: The proclamation was released by the Office of the Press Secretary on October 8.

Remarks at the Welcoming Ceremony for Prime Minister Lee Kuan Yew of Singapore
October 8, 1985

The President. It gives me great pleasure to welcome Prime Minister Lee Kuan Yew and Mrs. Lee to Singapore. We greet you today, Mr. Prime Minister, not only as the leader of Singapore but also as a friend and as a senior world citizen—a statesman.

The dazzling success of Singapore in these last two decades shines as a tribute to the hard work and ingenuity of its people and also as a monument to the wise leadership that you have provided your country-men over your 26 years in office. Mr. Prime Minister, today it is common to hear of the vitality and progress of the Pacific rim; perhaps more than any other, your country exemplifies the spirit which is catapulting Pacific rim nations into a new age. The people of the United States, Mr. Prime Minister, are committed to being part of this great experiment in enterprise and freedom. We are and will remain a Pacific rim country.

Consistent with this, our two countries

enjoy ever-broadening commercial ties. Two-way trade between us continues to grow rapidly. The United States is now the largest foreign investor in Singapore—over 400 United States corporations have a presence there. Our people are joined together in a multitude of profitmaking enterprises that benefit all concerned. As in many parts of the world, Singapore is struggling to overcome the effects of the international economic downturn, yet your people are free, with every reason to have faith in tomorrow. Freedom is the mainspring of progress that has enriched the lives of our people. Competition, the profit motive, low tax rates that increase incentives to work, save, and invest—these have accomplished much. It is the way to better lives, not only for people in the developed nations but, as you've proven, in the developing nations as well.

The well-being and happiness of our two peoples is living evidence of the rightness of this past. I'm certain that you will agree, Prime Minister Lee, that relatively free and open trade has been a key element of our success. Your country has one of the most open trading markets on the planet. A principal foreign policy objective of the United States is to protect and expand free trade by opening markets now closed or unfairly regulated. This will be a major goal at the next round of trade talks. In striving to accomplish this, I hope, as has been true in so many other areas of common concern, that we can stand shoulder to shoulder. Protectionism is a threat to the living standards our people have worked so hard to build. Once unleashed, it will set in motion a cycle of reaction and paralysis, eventually destroying those it claims to protect.

Mr. Prime Minister, I look forward to our discussion today. I'm confident that people of good will working together can make our international trading system work, defeat protectionism, and tear down unfair trade barriers. And, Mr. Prime Minister, you can be proud that under your leadership, Singapore has not only moved forward economically, but it has also stood for democratic government, human rights, and international peace. As a country, like the United States, composed of citizens with many philosophies and religions, your democratic institutions encourage social harmony by protecting the rights of the minority and offering peaceful resolution to differences and conflict. As a genuinely nonaligned nation, Singapore is independent and beholden to no country; we respect this, Mr. Prime Minister. We also admire that, although nonaligned and independent, you have demonstrated a sense of responsibility that few can match—playing a constructive role in the world community of nations and in the Asian-Pacific region.

Mr. Prime Minister, most heartening has been the stand Singapore and its colleagues in the Association of South East Asian Nations have taken against the Vietnam occupation of Cambodia and ASEAN's reasonable proposal for a political settlement returning self-determination to the Cambodian people. You and other ASEAN nations have waged a successful diplomatic offensive, rightfully denying international respectability to the Cambodian puppet regime. At the same time, support has been provided to the non-Communist resistance to this aggression. The United States applauds and supports this courageous effort by its ASEAN friends.

Our two peoples, though separated by thousands of miles, have much in common. We both cherish our political and economic freedom. Our populations are composed of people who are fiercely competitive, who strive for and expect perpetual progress. We're builders, entrepreneurs, people of wisdom. It's natural for us to be friends and to work together, and I'm grateful to have this opportunity to meet with you and discuss a broad range of issues and to renew our personal friendship.

Prime Minister Lee, welcome to America.

The Prime Minister. Mr. President, it is an honor to be received by you. I'm delighted to find you as robust as ever. Great leaders mirror the qualities of the nations they lead, and I see in your demeanor an America at peace, prosperous, and facing the future with confidence.

Since 1945 American leadership has been a constant factor in an ever-changing world. What the leader of the world's most powerful country and the world's largest economy does affects Singapore and the rest of East and Southeast Asia. Twenty years ago there was no external power that could have challenged the preeminence of the United States in Southeast Asia. In 1975, when the Communists captured South Vietnam, Laos, and Cambodia, the outlook turned bleak. Few dared to believe that American resolve to stay in power in the region would not melt, that the U.S. fleet and Air Force would continue to be based in the region.

What is more, America's economy has boosted growth in the non-Communist countries of Southeast Asia and made them peaceful, prosperous, and confident societies. Out of the travail in Vietnam and its tragic ending, the non-Communist countries of Southeast Asia came to understand the imperative of self-reliance and of cooperation between themselves. They grew closer together in political and economic cooperation as member states of the Association of South East Asian Nations. They have sustained stability and achieved rapid economic growth.

I first visited the White House 18 years ago, when I was welcomed by President Lyndon Johnson. Since then, the bonds of common interests between Singapore and the United States have grown deeper and more extensive. Mr. President, I look forward to my discussions with you and your colleagues, and I'm sure that our discussions will be positive and constructive. The ties between the United States and Singapore will strengthen, for it is an association that rests easily on both of us and our governments and brings mutual benefits.

Thank you, Mr. President, for this warm welcome.

Note: The President spoke at 10:12 a.m. at the South Portico of the White House, where the Prime Minister was accorded a formal welcome with full military honors. Following the ceremony, the President and the Prime Minister met in the Oval Office.

Nomination of Gregory J. Newell To Be United States Ambassador to Sweden
October 8, 1985

The President today announced his intention to nominate Gregory J. Newell, of Virginia, as Ambassador to Sweden. He would succeed Franklin S. Forsberg.

Mr. Newell attended the Church College of Hawaii (now Brigham Young University, Hawaii) in 1967–1968. He was then associated with Brigham Young University in 1971–1974 and 1977. In 1974–1975 he was a planning analyst at the Alexander Hamilton Life Insurance Corporation of America in Farmington Hills, MI. He then became coordinator, evaluation department, language training mission, Brigham Young University, in Provo, UT, in 1977–1978. Mr. Newell entered government service in 1975 as a staff assistant to President Ford. In 1979 he was director of the advance office, U.S. Senator Robert Dole primary (Presidential campaign). In 1979–1980 he was deputy administrative assistant to Gov. Richard Thornburg, Harrisburg, PA. In 1980 he became director of Presidential scheduling, Reagan-Bush Committee, Arlington, VA. In 1980–1981 he was a staff member of the Presidential Transition Foundation, Washington, DC. He then served as Special Assistant to President Reagan. In 1982 Mr. Newell was appointed Assistant Secretary of State for International Organization Affairs.

Mr. Newell was born August 30, 1949, in Geneseo, IL. He is married to the former Candilynne Jones, and they have four children.

Nomination of Allen Weinstein To Be a Member of the Board of Directors of the United States Institute of Peace
October 8, 1985

The President today announced his intention to nominate Allen Weinstein to be a member of the Board of Directors of the United States Institute of Peace for a term of 4 years expiring January 19, 1989. This is a new position.

Mr. Weinstein is president of the Center for Democracy in Washington, DC. Previously he was university professor at Georgetown University. He also served at Georgetown's Center for Strategic and International Studies in the following positions: executive editor of the Washington Quarterly, senior fellow for American institutions and values, and executive director of the CSIS

bipartisan congressional policy group in international communications. He served as Vice Chairman on the United States delegation to the UNESCO World Conference on Cultural Policies held in Mexico City in 1982. He was a member of the editorial board of the Washington Post in 1981 and served as professor of history at Smith College in 1966–1981.

Mr. Weinstein graduated from the City College of New York (B.A. and Ph.D.) and Yale University (M.A.). He is married, has two children, and resides in Washington, DC. He was born September 1, 1937, in New York City.

Statement by Principal Deputy Press Secretary Speakes on the Senate's Delay in Confirming Presidential Nominations
October 8, 1985

The President is deeply displeased that 70 key appointments touching virtually every area of the executive branch are being deliberately held up by Senate Democratic Leader Robert Byrd. These are Assistant Secretaries, Ambassadors, Federal circuit and district judges, and members of important agencies, commissions, and boards. Over 5,000 midlevel career military personnel alone are being denied promotions and pay raises. It is the largest backlog of Presidential appointments in modern history.

Senator Byrd has decided to block these and other nominations because of what he terms his "deep concern" about the seven recess appointments made last August. The President's power to make recess appointments is grounded in the Constitution, and this issue was decided long ago. George Washington made three recess appointments between the sessions of the First Congress. President Carter made 17 direct appointments during temporary Senate

breaks, including a Cabinet member. Fifteen recess appointments have been made to the United States Supreme Court, including one sitting Justice.

President Reagan did not evade the Senate's power to confirm. The individuals he appointed had already been nominated before the recent Senate recess. The Senate just hadn't acted on the nominations. And those appointees were renominated when the Senate returned. The Constitution speaks without equivocation on the power and right of the President to make recess appointments. The courts have held the President has the power, and history dating to the first President confirms it. These individuals stand ready to serve.

The President respectfully requests Senator Byrd's cooperation in freeing up his nominations without further delay.

Note: Larry M. Speakes read the statement to reporters at 12:22 p.m. in the Briefing Room at the White House.

Toasts at the State Dinner for Prime Minister Lee Kuan Yew of Singapore
October 8, 1985

The President. Prime Minister Lee and Mrs. Lee, honored guests who are here tonight, Nancy and I welcome you to the White House.

It was a great pleasure for me today to renew a valued friendship with Prime Minister Lee. I first met the Prime Minister on a trip that I took on behest of President Nixon. And when we stopped in Singapore, I was amazed at the dynamic society that I found there. How could a country with such a small area and few resources be making such strides? And then I met Prime Minister Lee, and my questions were answered. He is a man of principle and vision. His leadership has provided the vigorous and creative people of Singapore the means to move ahead, to achieve, and to build.

Singapore's experience has been in stark contrast to developing countries where political power has been derived from terror and brute force. Instead, Prime Minister Lee's authority has rested on his capacity to mold the opinion of his countrymen and build consensus. He has used his position to free the talents and energy of his people so they could be channeled into constructive, society-building activity. Fortunately, Prime Minister Lee's sound judgment does not stop at the water's edge. American leaders, including this one, have frequently benefited from his wise counsel. Our meetings today were no less beneficial. Our exchange was cordial, reflecting a mutuality of interests and a harmony of views.

Mr. Prime Minister, I want to express my personal admiration for your recognition of the contributions America makes to world peace. As the world's most powerful democracy, our people carry a heavy military and diplomatic burden and often thankless task. But you have demonstrated an appreciation and understanding that makes it all worthwhile. This spirit of mutual respect was evidenced in our meetings today. None of this should be reason for surprise. Our two peoples may, at first glance, seem worlds apart, both in geographic location and culture; but

a closer look reveals that Singapore and the United States are nations made up of hardworking immigrants and their descendants, who came to a new homeland to improve their lot and build a decent life for their families. We're both democratic nations committed to peace and to the preservation of human liberty. And these bonds are being bolstered by continued cultural and educational exchanges and, of course, the many commercial ties between our peoples.

Mr. Prime Minister, we're aware that your people are now faced with severe challenges brought on by international economic conditions. The United States faced economic adversity not long ago; tough decisions had to be made. It's heartening to see that you're moving forward, Mr. Prime Minister, with an eye toward the long-run well-being of your people. I understand full well this is not always easy to do, but I want you and your citizens to know that the people of the United States want you to succeed and prosper. Our meetings today confirmed again the people of Singapore, as we say here, are our kind of people.

So, would you all join me in toasting the people of Singapore and the distinguished leader, Prime Minister Lee, and Mrs. Lee.

The Prime Minister. Mr. President, Mrs. Reagan, ladies and gentlemen, my wife and I are much honored and delighted to be here with you, enjoying your warm hospitality. We would like to express our special thanks to Mrs. Reagan, for we learned of her personal interest in the preparations for this splendid occasion. It is a rare and gracious First Lady who would personally settle and approve the menu, the wines, the floral arrangements, and the entertainment.

I read of Mrs. Reagan and her campaign against drug abuse. Her personal efforts and her attention to the details of the cause that she has championed has won her wide acclaim. I watched her on television, standing amidst the rubble of Mexico City a few days after the earthquake, bringing succor and comfort to the victims. After nearly 5 years in the White House, I notice the latest opinion poll puts her approval rating at 71 percent—[*laughter*]—ahead of the President's—[*laughter*]—and by 9 percent. [*Laughter*] Mr. President, your staff has to shape up—[*laughter*]—or you may have to borrow the First Lady's staff. [*Laughter*]

Mr. President, I have been a regular visitor of the United States for about two decades. It was an ordeal to watch America writhe in the self-inflicted agony at home during the years she tried to fight a war in Vietnam. And even after the war, she did not bounce back from her depression. And morale dropped to a new low when American hostages were held in Tehran. When you were taking your oath of office as President, the hostages were released. It was proof to me that the Iranian mullahs were not as crazy as the media had made them out to be. [*Laughter*]

You made your fellow Americans and your friends feel proud and optimistic by the confidence you radiated. You have never allowed any problem, however daunting, to weigh you down. Now, as imports surge into America because of an over-strong dollar, Congress, in its pessimism, moves towards protectionism. You have not yielded to such despair. You will astound your critics yet again when you turn the spell of apparent adversity to advantage by opening up foreign markets and creating new jobs for Americans. The Reagan years will surely be a noticeable landmark in American history, for you have restored American leadership in the maintenance of a just and equitable world order.

Mr. President, I have been privileged to share some of your thoughts today. The friendly relations between the United States and Singapore are at their best, indeed, as they should be. I have been a privileged guest in these surroundings under different Presidents, as I explained to the young lady so judiciously selected to be my companion tonight. [*Laughter*] I have never felt more relaxed and more at home, and I think I owe that to the other attractive young lady on my left. I have been here and have been impressed. Tonight, I have been here and have enjoyed myself. [*Laughter*]

Mr. President, ladies and gentlemen, may I now ask you to join me in a toast to the President and the First Lady to wish them good health and happiness.

Note: The President spoke at 10:12 p.m. in the State Dining Room at the White House.

Message to the Congress Transmitting the Annual Report of the Railroad Retirement Board
October 9, 1985

To the Congress of the United States:

I hereby submit to the Congress the Annual Report of the Railroad Retirement Board for Fiscal Year 1984, pursuant to the provisions of Section 7(b) 6 of the Railroad Retirement Act, enacted October 16, 1974, and Section 12(1) of the Railroad Unemployment Insurance Act, enacted June 25, 1938.

Railroad Retirement Board actuaries inform me that, while the Railroad Retirement Solvency Act of 1983 has removed immediate cash-flow problems threatening the rail pension fund, "the long-term stability of the railroad retirement system is still questionable." Despite the 1983 legislation, the rail sector unemployment fund is insolvent and currently owes some $700 million to the rail pension fund. Extending Federal/State unemployment insurance coverage to rail employment, as proposed, would provide comprehensive, soundly financed unemployment insurance coverage for rail workers, and would ensure that rail pensioners' assets are protected and all debts to the rail pension are repaid.

RONALD REAGAN

The White House,
October 9, 1985.

Remarks at a Fundraising Luncheon for Virginia Gubernatorial Candidate Wyatt Durrette in Arlington, Virginia
October 9, 1985

Thank you, Wyatt, very much. Thank all of you very much—the Members of the Congress, our former Governors, our visiting Governor Dick Thornburgh of Pennsylvania, and our Governor-to-be.

I've just come a short distance to be here today, but I feel worlds away from that town across the river. It's estimated that nearly 60 percent of all Virginians identify with the conservative philosophy. My only question is, what happened to that other 40 percent? [*Laughter*] And how are we going to help them see the light? I guess we all know the answer to that. He's sitting right here—Wyatt Durrette, the candidate for Governor. He ranks right up with the finest of the fine Governors that have governed this great Commonwealth of Virginia. And that's why so many of Virginia's most respected elected officials have come out strongly for Wyatt. And Wyatt's support extends beyond the State and crosses party lines. I know at least two former Democrats who are giving Wyatt Durrette their wholehearted endorsement. One is Harry Byrd, who served this State so ably for so many years, and the other one is the current leader of the Republican Party—me. [*Laughter*] When I was a child, I spake as a child, I thought as a child. And when I became a man, I put aside—[*laughter*]—childish things. [*Laughter*]

Well, Virginia needs Wyatt Durrette's strong, principled leadership. But you all know that already, and I'm here today to tell you that America needs him, too, because it's only if we pull together at both the State and national levels that we can give America the bright future of expanding hope and opportunity that she deserves. Wyatt understands that the road to that future is not paved with government programs. He knows it's freedom that creates economic growth and prosperity, and all over the world we are seeing more and more freedom works.

He knows, in addition to that, that it's not another new State office boondoggle paid for by higher taxes that we need for any of the problems that confront us. He knows the way to give minorities a fair shake is to open up with enterprise zones and a youth opportunity wage for teenagers. He understands the transportation needs of Northern Virginia, and he knows that the way to educational excellence is through incentives for achievement, higher standards for our students, and merit pay for teachers.

I've been following this race in Virginia pretty closely, and in many ways it reminds me of that campaign I was going through not too long ago. Last year, too, we heard promise after promise for billions of dollars of new government spending programs, but at least my opponent, then, admitted that he wanted to raise your taxes. Well, the American people let it be known last November what they thought about that idea, and I am convinced come November 5th, the people of this great State are going to repeat that message loud and clear when they elect Wyatt Durrette Governor of Virginia.

While I'm on that subject of taxes, let me interject a note here about the national scene. I'm going to let you in on a little-known fact. There are people in Washington—some of them even hold elected office—who still harbor a secret desire, way down deep in their hearts, to raise your taxes. Now, I know you may find this hard to believe, but it's true. They pine for the old days, when the special interests were lined up 10 deep at the Federal trough gorging on taxpayer dollars; some even want to pervert our fair share tax plan and turn it into a sneaky way of raising America's taxes. Well, they can keep on dreaming because there isn't going to be any tax hike.

I've said it before, and I'll keep on saying it as many times as it takes: No matter how it's disguised or packaged, if Congress sends me a tax hike I'll send it right back with a big veto written across it. And for those who are trying to torpedo tax fairness, let's remind them exactly what's on the line. America's fair share plan, as submitted, would increase the gross national product by about 3 percent above projections; that translates into nearly 4 million more new jobs and $600 to $900 a year in added income for every American household. Now, those are the benefits of America's fair share tax plan, and those are the standards by which any alteration of the plan will be judged. Any plan that is less progrowth, any plan that is less profamily will be robbing America of the jobs and prosperity that are rightfully theirs.

Now, last Friday I announced our support for an historic deficit-busting measure called the Balanced Budget and Emergency Deficit Control Act of 1985. It would put the force of law behind deficit reduction, locking us into a spending reduction path that will bring the budget into balance by 1990. And then I think we should honor the words and the complaint of another great Virginian, Thomas Jefferson, who, when he looked at the ratification of our Constitution, said: "It lacks only one thing—a provision to prevent the Federal Government from borrowing." Well, let's have that come 1990 with our balanced budget. [*Applause*] Well, it sounds like an awfully good idea to me, and I gather from your reaction, you agree.

It's funny how some of those who've been screaming the loudest about deficits are now obstructing and delaying, doing everything they can to try and sink this bill, which will be coming to a vote, I understand, in the Senate this afternoon. Now, I'm not accusing anybody of insincerity, but the next time one of those folks gets up and complains about the deficit, they'd better have a smile on their face. You know, there's been a lot of jousting and hustling going on there across the river in the Capital. You learn that when you get between

the hog and the bucket, you get jousted about a bit. [*Laughter*]

But when we talk about the future of Virginia and the future of America, we're really talking about something more fundamental than dollars and cents. Wyatt understands that underneath all these issues lie basic questions of values. The big spending pressures that we still have to fight against on both the State and national levels are really an attempt to artificially pump up a failed and exhausted liberal ideology. It's an ideology that looks on America with despair and that has spent the last several decades trying to unravel the social order that binds us together as a nation and as a people. When it looks abroad, it is an ideology that, in Jeane Kirkpatrick's famous phrase, always "blames America first," while too often making excuses for the enemies of freedom. At home, it erects walls to lock out God and keep Him away from our schoolchildren, but has trouble locking up drug pushers, thieves, and murderers. Well, I just have to say—and I think you'll agree with me—that the real walls of separation we need in this country are prison walls that will keep criminals off the streets and away from our children.

You know, I often think the real heroes of today are the parents trying to raise their children in an environment that seems to have grown more and more hostile to family life. Music and the media floods their children's world with glorifications of drugs and violence and perversity, and there's nothing they can do about it, they're told, because of the first amendment. Well, I don't think James Madison, author of the Bill of Rights and one of Virginia's proudest sons, ever imagined that his great document of liberty would be twisted into a pretext for license. I don't believe that our Founding Fathers ever intended to create a nation where the rights of pornographers would take precedence over the rights of parents and the violent and malevolent would be given free rein to prey upon our children.

I guess one of the things that I like best about Wyatt is that he has common sense enough to know the value of values. Family, faith, freedom, and opportunity aren't just campaign slogans for him; they're the foundation upon which his political philosophy is built. Wyatt is an experienced, principled leader that Virginia can depend on and trust.

You know, back in 1977 I spoke at my first fundraiser for Wyatt, and by coincidence the day of the fundraiser just happened to be my birthday. So, the event turned into a kind of a dual celebration. There I was 39 years old—[*laughter*]—for the 27th time. [*Laughter*] Wyatt, I just want to make sure that when I reach 40 next year—[*laughter*]—you can give me a birthday call from the Governor's office. You know, I learned a little truism about this talk of age and everything else, in addition to having 39th birthdays from here on out, and that is someone told me very wisely that getting old is 15 years from wherever you are now. [*Laughter*]

Well, you know, ladies and gentlemen, Virginia is one of the greatest States of the greatest Nation on Earth. Virginia deserves the very best—John Chichester for lieutenant governor, Buster O'Brien for attorney general, and Wyatt Durrette for Governor. And all of them, I know, endorse the fact that we must never forget that our very freedom is based on this fact: that this nation is a federation of sovereign States, and they must never be reduced to administrative districts of the Federal Government, as some in Washington would have us do.

Thank you. God bless you all.

Note: The President spoke at 12:30 p.m. at the Marriott Gateway Hotel. He was introduced by Mr. Durrette.

Executive Order 12536—Board of the Foreign Service
October 9, 1985

By the authority vested in me as President by the Constitution and laws of the United States of America, including section 153 of Public Law 99–93, it is hereby ordered that Section 9(e) of Executive Order No. 12293, as amended, relating to the appointment of the Chairman of the Board of the Foreign Service, is revoked, and that Section 9(f) of that Order is redesignated as Section 9(e).

RONALD REAGAN

The White House,
October 9, 1985.

[*Filed with the Office of the Federal Register, 10:34 a.m., October 10, 1985*]

Proclamation 5380—Fire Prevention Week, 1985
October 9, 1985

By the President of the United States of America

A Proclamation

Fire controlled is one of man's greatest friends; unchecked, it is our deadly enemy. Each year, millions of fires kill thousands of Americans and destroy billions of dollars of property.

Carelessness and apathy are fire's greatest allies. But an informed public aware of fire hazards and ways to prevent and combat fire can bring the problem under control.

Thanks to the efforts in both the public and private sectors, our annual fire loss has been declining in recent years. But we must not become complacent. We must build on the progress that has been made.

I urge every American to join the fight against fire. During Fire Prevention Week, communities should begin initiatives for fire prevention and control that can be implemented throughout the year. I encourage all citizens to join in local efforts to marshal the forces of the entire community—local government, the fire service, business leaders, civic organizations, and service groups—to redouble their efforts to prevent and control fire and minimize its toll of life and property.

One place we can all start is with this year's Fire Prevention Week theme, "Fire Drills Save Lives." Everyone should plan ahead noting the most convenient fire exits. Families should install and maintain smoke detectors in their homes to provide early warning of fire. Your local fire fighters can provide you with more detailed recommendations and will be happy to do so. And let us not forget to thank them for the great job they do to protect us, our homes, our businesses, and our belongings. Daily they risk their lives to protect our communities. It is most fitting that the culmination of National Fire Prevention Week will be the observance of the National Fallen Firefighter Memorial Service in Emmitsburg, Maryland. The observance will honor the scores of brave firefighters who last year gave their lives in service to others.

We also must recognize and commend the efforts of all organizations concerned with fire prevention and control, and in particular the National Fire Protection Association, the International Association of Firefighters, the International Association of Fire Chiefs, the National Volunteer Fire Council, the International Society of Fire Service Instructors, the Fire Marshals Association of North America, and all the members of the Joint Council of National Fire Service Organizations.

Now, Therefore, I, Ronald Reagan, President of the United States of America, do hereby proclaim the week of October 6, 1985, as Fire Prevention Week, and I call upon the people of the United States to plan and actively participate in fire prevention activities during this week and throughout the year.

In Witness Whereof, I have hereunto set my hand this ninth day of October, in the year of our Lord nineteen hundred and eighty-five, and of the Independence of the United States of America the two hundred and tenth.

RONALD REAGAN

[*Filed with the Office of the Federal Register, 10:29 a.m., October 10, 1985*]

Proclamation 5381—National School Lunch Week, 1985
October 9, 1985

By the President of the United States of America

A Proclamation

Since 1946, the National School Lunch Program has made it possible for our Nation's children to enjoy nutritious, well-balanced, low-cost lunches. Now in its 39th year, the National School Lunch Program stands as an outstanding example of a successful partnership between Federal and State governments and local communities to make food and technical assistance available in an effort to provide a more nutritious diet for students.

The youth of our Nation are our greatest resource, and the school lunch program demonstrates our commitment to the promotion of their health and well-being. Under its auspices, over 23 million lunches are served daily in nearly 90,000 schools throughout the country. The success of this effort is largely due to resourceful and creative food service managers and staff, working in cooperation with government personnel, parents, teachers, and members of civic groups.

By joint resolution approved October 9, 1962, the Congress has designated the week beginning on the second Sunday of October in each year as "National School Lunch Week" and authorized and requested the

President to issue a proclamation in observance of that week.

Now, Therefore, I, Ronald Reagan, President of the United States of America, do hereby proclaim the week beginning October 13, 1985, as National School Lunch Week, and I call upon all Americans to give special and deserved recognition to those people at the State and local level who, through their dedicated and innovative efforts, have contributed so much to the success of the school lunch program.

In Witness Whereof, I have hereunto set my hand this ninth day of October, in the year of our Lord nineteen hundred and eighty-five, and of the Independence of the United States of America the two hundred and tenth.

RONALD REAGAN

[*Filed with the Office of the Federal Register, 10:31 a.m., October 10, 1985*]

Proclamation 5382—White Cane Safety Day, 1985
October 9, 1985

By the President of the United States of America

A Proclamation

Americans admire courage and respect independence. Every day some of our neighbors renew our appreciation of these qualities. They are the Americans who set forth about their daily business bearing the white cane.

The white cane is the badge of courage carried by those blind and visually impaired citizens who believe freedom and independence are meant for all Americans. The white cane tells the world that its bearer expects not pity but fairness and consideration—on the street, on the job, and everywhere Americans' paths cross.

In recognition of the significance of the white cane, the Congress, by joint resolution approved October 6, 1964, has authorized the President to designate October 15 of each year as "White Cane Safety Day."

Now, Therefore, I, Ronald Reagan, President of the United States of America, do hereby proclaim October 15, 1985, as White Cane Safety Day. I urge all Americans to salute the courage of those who carry the white cane and consider how each of us, in our work and in our daily rounds, can show our respect for these proud and able Americans.

In Witness Whereof, I have hereunto set my hand this ninth day of October, in the year of our Lord nineteen hundred and eighty-five, and the Independence of the United States of America the two hundred and tenth.

RONALD REAGAN

[*Filed with the Office of the Federal Register, 10:32 a.m., October 10, 1985*]

Statement by Principal Deputy Press Secretary Speakes on the *Achille Lauro* Hijacking Incident
October 9, 1985

While we welcome the release of the passengers and crew of the *Achille Lauro,* we are saddened and outraged at this brutal killing of an innocent American, the second such terrorist murder in 3 months. We are particularly distressed that there has been no announcement yet that those responsible will be turned over to the appropriate authority for prosecution and punishment.

From the outset the United States Government made it clear to the Government of Egypt and the Government of Italy our opposition to negotiations with the terrorists and our expectation that the terrorists would be apprehended, prosecuted, and punished. The United States remains determined to see that those responsible for this heinous act be brought to justice and punished to the maximum extent. There must be no asylum for terrorists or terrorism.

Note: Larry M. Speakes read the statement to reporters at 8:16 p.m. in the Briefing Room at the White House. The murdered American was Leon Klinghoffer, a passenger on the ship.

Proclamation 5383—National Spina Bifida Month, 1985
October 9, 1985

By the President of the United States of America

A Proclamation

Spina bifida is one of the most common birth defects. It affects between one and two of every 1,000 babies born in the United States. Infants with spina bifida may have partially developed spinal cords and often suffer nerve damage, muscle paralysis, and spine and limb deformities. Most develop hydrocephalus—a potentially dangerous buildup of fluid and pressure within the brain.

A generation ago, the majority of children with spina bifida died. Today, their survival rate and long-term outlook have improved dramatically. Carefully planned programs of biomedical research have led to advances in neurosurgery that help alleviate some physical problems. Through research, physicians now are able to control brain and bladder infections more effectively. Scientists have also developed lighter braces and splints to give patients greater mobility.

Further improvements in treating this crippling birth defect can be expected to result from research supported by the Federal government's National Institute of Neurological and Communicative Disorders and Stroke and the National Institute of Child Health and Human Development. Achieving the long-sought goal of prevention now appears more likely. Collaborating in this vital effort are a number of private, voluntary health agencies including the Spina Bifida Association of America, the March of Dimes Birth Defects Foundation, and the National Easter Seal Society. The combined energies of these Federal and private agencies assure the Nation of continued progress toward the conquest of spina bifida.

So that we as a Nation may increase our sensitivity to the needs of spina bifida children and the difficulties faced by their parents, the Congress, by Senate Joint Resolution 111, has designated October 1985 as "National Spina Bifida Month" and authorized and requested the President to issue a proclamation in observance of this month.

Now, Therefore, I, Ronald Reagan, President of the United States of America, do hereby proclaim October 1985 as National Spina Bifida Month, and I call upon all government agencies, health organizations, and the people of the United States to observe this month with appropriate ceremonies and activities.

In Witness Whereof, I have hereunto set my hand this ninth day of October, in the year of our Lord nineteen hundred and eighty-five, and of the Independence of the United States of America the two hundred and tenth.

RONALD REAGAN

[*Filed with the Office of the Federal Register, 11:05 a.m., October 11, 1985*]

Note: The proclamation was released by the Office of the Press Secretary on October 10.

Proclamation 5384—Oil Heat Centennial Year, 1985
October 9, 1985

By the President of the United States of America

A Proclamation

It was just 100 years ago that American ingenuity developed oil heat as a practical reality. On August 11, 1885, the Patent Office granted to David H. Burrell of Little Falls, New York, a patent for the first technically sound oil burner—a furnace that could burn liquid and gaseous fuels. By 1893 oil burners were used for the first time in major public exhibit buildings at the Columbian Exposition in Chicago. By the 1970s oil burner technology had been adapted to the heating needs of more than 15 million Americans, providing comfort for homes, schools, businesses, and factories.

There is hardly an area of the Nation where this great resource has not been a critical development factor. The oil heat industry is, and always has been, made up of a large and diverse group of competitive small businesses, many of which are in the forefront of the new energy-efficient technologies of the 1980s. They are helping develop higher-efficiency oil heat, new conservation techniques, solar heating, and other technologies.

In recognition of the many thousands of men and women who have contributed to this important industry in our Nation over the past 100 years, the Congress, by Senate Joint Resolution 115, has designated 1985 as "Oil Heat Centennial Year" and authorized and requested the President to issue a proclamation to commemorate this event.

Now, Therefore, I, Ronald Reagan, President of the United States of America, do hereby proclaim 1985 as Oil Heat Centennial Year. I call upon the people of the United States to observe the occasion with appropriate ceremonies and activities.

In Witness Whereof, I have hereunto set my hand this ninth day of October, in the year of our Lord nineteen hundred and eighty-five, and of the Independence of the United States of America the two hundred and tenth.

RONALD REAGAN

[*Filed with the Office of the Federal Register, 11:06 a.m., October 11, 1985*]

Note: The proclamation was released by the Office of the Press Secretary on October 10.

Informal Exchange With Reporters on the *Achille Lauro* Hijacking Incident
October 10, 1985

Q. Right here, Mr. President——

Q. Mr. President, do you think they should let the hijackers go?

The President. Let me just say something if I can, first. I know that all of us were pleased, of course, when the hijackers were apprehended and the hostages were all freed, but then, I know how sorry all of us were to learn that one, an American, Klinghoffer, had been murdered—brutally murdered—by the hijackers. Now, it is possible and certainly is apparent at this time, or seems to be, that they have been allowed to depart Egypt and—to parts unknown. But we're doing everything we can to see if they cannot be brought to justice. We think that no nation, responsible nation, should give shelter to these people, should make them available to whichever country has the proper jurisdiction for prosecution—if that is us, because the victim was American, fine; or Italy, because it was on an Italian ship, or—I'm not a lawyer, the legal niceties of that sort of thing, but we're going to do everything we can to see that they are brought to justice.

Q. Are you mad at Egypt for letting them go, Mr. President?

The President. Apparently, from what we know so far—it's been rather difficult getting all the information—apparently the Egyptians did not know that a hostage had been murdered, that there'd been a crime committed at that time, before they were turned over to the PLO, which evidently was the arrangement, would get them off the ship and free the hostages.

Q. Mr. President, Arafat has them now. How are we going to bring them to justice if Arafat and the PLO has them?

The President. I think certainly a demand should be made. Mr. Arafat has said the PLO had nothing to do with this. I would think that we should make a demand to him, then, to turn them over to whichever country should have proper jurisdiction.

Q. Arafat doesn't——

Q. Didn't you say the same thing about the TWA hijackers? And yet nothing has happened there.

The President. Yes. The problem was—we all know the situation in Lebanon. The Government seems to have very little authority with all the conflicting groups that are there battling each other. But we feel that they could be—[*inaudible*]—which we have—we continue to try and find out, to apprehend those original two hijackers who committed the murder on TWA flight——

Q. Arafat says that he'll punish them. Is that good enough for you?

The President. Well, I would think that if he believes that their organization has enough of a—sort of a kind of a national court set up, like a nation, that they can bring them to justice and carry that out, all right; but just so they are brought to justice.

Q. But you'd let the PLO punish them, then?

The President. What? Yes, I said if they were determined to do that.

Q. Do you really believe that the PLO has nothing to do with this?

The President. I have no way of knowing one way or the other on that. With the factions that are existing there within the Palestinians, I have no way to know that.

Q. But, sir, if you would let the PLO punish them, wouldn't that be, in effect, recognizing the PLO as a governing nation, which we don't do?

The President. I don't think that would necessarily follow.

Q. Is the U.S. willing to take action itself, Mr. President? Would the U.S. take military action to bring these people to justice?

The President. You're now talking about whether we would invade a friendly nation—[*inaudible*]. No, we're going to try to do this in a legal manner. The time for action, which could have been taken by us, is passed and was ended when the rescue was made.

Q. Mr. President, even if they had not murdered an American, would it have been right to offer them free passage, in your opinion?

The President. Well, you know our position has always been—and we've tried to persuade all the other countries that had an interest in this, were involved—that you do not negotiate or bargain with terrorists.

Q. [*Inaudible*]

The President. Yes, they did.

Q. What do you think of that?

The President. Well, I'm not going to comment on it. They made a judgment based on——

Q. What is bringing them to justice? Just giving them a 6-month jail term or something?

The President. No. This is trying them for murder, a very brutal murder, and the threat of murder to others. In our country that would be capital punishment.

Q. What does this do to the peace process, sir? Does this end the peace process for the time being?

The President. I don't think that this has any effect on the peace process. We're continuing with that. But I've got to go.

Note: The exchange began at 10:36 a.m. at O'Hare International Airport in Chicago, IL. The President then traveled to Deerfield.

Remarks to Employees at the Kitchens of Sara Lee in Deerfield, Illinois
October 10, 1985

Thank you Chairman Bryan, Governor Thompson, Representatives Porter, O'Brien, Martin, and Hyde—thank you all. And I just was greeted out at the helicopter by the Deerfield High School student body, and now I see the band is in here also. Well, bless you. And I'd like to recognize also the founder of Sara Lee, Charles Lubin. Charles, you've made it very difficult for a lot of people to stick to their diets.

But it's great to be here in Deerfield and at the Kitchens of Sara Lee. You're the expert when it comes to baking, but I thought I'd bring you a recipe of my own. It's a recipe for tax relief, as you've just heard here from Chairman Bryan, for working families and prosperity for our country, and we call it America's fair share tax plan. Now, the main ingredients are tax rate cuts for individuals and businesses, loophole closings, and a near doubling of the personal exemption for you and every dependent in your family. And all of it adds up to increased incentives for work and achievement, rising real incomes, and a bigger economic pie for our country.

America's fair share tax plan is a plan for a growing, dynamic nation. You know, using that symbol of a pie, economic pie—for too many years in this country, we've had a lot of people around government that have been trying to say that they want to make someone's share smaller, his slice of pie, so they can make someone else's slice bigger. The simple answer is let's make the whole pie bigger, and everybody gets a bigger slice. Lower, flatter tax rates will give Americans more confidence in the future. It'll mean that if you work overtime, get a raise or a promotion, or if your company does well and raises your salaries, more of your extra earnings will end up where they belong—in your wallet and not in Uncle Sam's pocket.

Let's get specific: Our very conservative, long-time estimates show that our tax plan will add three percentage points to our gross national product. And that translates into the equivalent of 4 million new jobs and from 600 to 900 extra real dollars of income for every household, every family in America. And the immediate benefits of our plan are even more dramatic: We are hiking the standard deduction and raising the personal exemption, the deduction that the taxpayer can take for himself and every one of his dependents, to $2,000. Now, that'll mean that a family of four wouldn't pay one penny of Federal tax on the first $12,000 of income.

We also know how hard it is these days for families to save, so we're going to make it a lot easier. We're expanding the tax-free savings of IRA's, you know, those are those tax deductible savings that you can deposit for your own retirement some day and no tax to be paid until the payoff day comes. Well, we're now enlarging those so that they will fully cover both spouses working inside or outside the home or members of the Sara Lee team. But we figure that the housewife—it better be recognized—she's working too and, therefore, she can take out the money for that.

Now, those are some of the reasons that the Democratic-controlled House Select Committee on Children, Youth, and Families, and I emphasize that it is Democratic-controlled because that committee—to show you that there are people on both sides of the aisle for this tax plan—rated our tax plan the most profamily of any of the tax programs that've proposed to the Congress. Our proposals to give families a break from excessive taxation are really the heart and soul of America's fair share tax plan. It's our objective to make it affordable to raise families again. I've been all over this country stumping for tax fairness, and everywhere I go the American people are enthusiastically embracing tax fairness, just as you apparently have. I saw, and was reading as fast as I could, all those signs you were holding up, as well as the larger signs that you have. In fact, it wouldn't be too much of an exaggeration to say, "Nobody doesn't like

America's fair share tax plan."

But the truth is that many people don't know the real story about our tax overhaul, because for the last month our fair share tax plan hasn't been given much space by the national media. They say that's because they've already reported that I've been saying this—these things—so they don't have to report it again. But I was thrilled to see a poll in the paper USA Today this week. It showed that in Cincinnati, where I went to talk about our tax plan last week, support for America's fair share plan among those who had heard the explanation of what the plan does shot up 14 points to an overwhelming 68 percent majority. Now, that's because the local media did its job and did it well. When the people hear all the facts, when they hear the case for tax fairness, as well as the case against it, America's fair share tax plan wins a landslide victory. The American people know a good deal when they see one. Now, I'd like to be able to visit every city and town in this country to talk about our fair share plan. I'd like to be able to go door to door, tell every American how our proposal will benefit them. But there's just not enough time if we're going to pass tax fairness this year, in 1985. So, we've just got to rely on the media to get the information out to the American people. Let them hear the facts and let the American people decide for themselves. A fellow named Thomas Jefferson once said, "If the people know all the facts, the people will never make a mistake."

Five years ago, one of the first things we did when we came into office was pass an across-the-board 25-percent cut in tax rates. Those tax cuts saved our economy from shipwreck and put us on a steady course of economic growth with increasing productivity, rising real wages, and declining inflation. And ever since 1984, the first full year that all of our tax elements were in place— you will remember it came in three installments—our expanding economy has brought in increasing amounts of revenue to the United States Government. The fact is, you can cut the rates but increase the total revenue because of the increase in prosperity and the number of people working and all those things. In the first

months—11 months—of fiscal 1985, revenues grew an astounding 10 percent at the fully reduced rates. The tax rate cuts and profamily measures of America's fair share tax plan are the next necessary steps to prosperity.

But we must also do something about the deficit timebomb that is ticking away, threatening to destroy all the progress that we've made. It's clear that tax hikes are not the answer—they're like cooking the goose that lays the golden egg; they just slow the economy and shrink revenues. Tax cutting and economic growth are already bringing in, as I mentioned, sizable revenue increases. The problem is, for all the talk about the deficit, some in Congress are still spending and spending like mad. They gobble up that added 10 percent and still want more. The time has come to match all that deficit talk with action. It's time to stop complaining about the deficit and to simply reduce it.

Now, last week I announced my support for a Senate bill—the Gramm-Rudman amendment—that will put the force of law behind deficit reduction, locking us into a downward deficit path that will bring the budget into balance by 1990. Yesterday the Senate took a major step toward this proposal and should be commended. But some who've been talking the loudest about deficits would obstruct this bill. It seems that some would do anything not to have to kick their spending habit, even if it threatens the well-being of our nation and undermines the economic security of every American. Well, they may try to obstruct and delay, but I've got news for them—the American people aren't going to put up with it.

Deficit reduction and America's fair share tax plan—a sure recipe for a vibrant, surging economy into the 21st century. Chairman Bryan has been one of the most determined and eloquent supporters of our plan in the business community. He's been stumping the country, too, in an all-out effort for tax fairness. And, John, I thank you, and America thanks you. John has the vision to see that what's good for America's working men and women is good for American business and vice versa. America is a team, the best team there is, and if we all pull together, there ain't no stopping us now. And there's something else you all should be proud of. I've heard that you've achieved 68 percent participation in our U.S. Savings Bond drive. Well, congratulations, and keep up the good work.

Now, there's no reason that we shouldn't have a tax fairness bill through the Congress by the end of December. We're urging the House to conclude their work so that the Senate has time to act before the end of the year. Tax fairness will be America's Christmas present to ourselves, and we shouldn't let any Grinch steal our Christmas this year. Give the people in Washington a piece of your mind, and you might let those ladies and gentlemen in the press know how you feel, too—who are right there with you. [*Laughter*] Let's do what's right for America. Let's pass tax fairness this year.

And let me just interject something—in all of the conversation, and we talked about the deficit and all the attempts now going around to try and spread the blame around for who's responsible for the deficit—oh, I've come in for my share of that. This deficit has been building and growing—I've been talking out of the mashed-potato circuit 30 years ago. We've been deficit spending virtually every year for the last 50 years. And when some of us spoke up and said, "We ought to end this; we ought to spend no more than we take in," the voices from Washington back over those 50 years said, "Oh, it's quite all right; a little deficit spending makes for prosperity," and that, "after all, it's all right, we owe it to ourselves." Well, let me just tell you what happened with this—it's built into the struc-

ture. And that's why you can't all at once pull the rug out from under it and why we've got a 5-year plan pending to do this and bring it down, then level it off, and then have a constitutional amendment that says from now on government will spend no more than it takes in.

Let me give you a figure that would show you where trying to pin the deficit comes— 1965 to 1980—15 years. By 1980 the budget was just about 5 times greater than it had been in 1965. The deficit was 50 times greater than it had been in 1965. Well, that's just stupid; that's foolishness. And we're not going to take 15 years; we're going to take 5. And we're going to get the job done for all of you.

Thank you. God bless you all. Thank you, thanks very much.

[*At this point, a large Sara Lee pound cake was presented to the President by Thomas MacLeod, president of Sara Lee Corp., and Earl Ritchie, plant manager of the Kitchens of Sara Lee.*]

Thank you very much, thank you. I'll obey your instructions. First of all, Nancy wouldn't let me eat it all. [*Laughter*] But if I could make just one little correction, when I take it up on Capitol Hill, can I use it to blackmail them into doing what we want? [*Laughter*] All right. Thank you all.

Note: The President spoke at 11:15 a.m. In his opening remarks, he referred to John H. Byran, Jr., chairman of the board of directors and chief executive officer of the Sara Lee Corp., Gov. James R. Thompson, and Representatives John Edward Porter, George M. O'Brien, Lynn Martin, and Henry J. Hyde.

Informal Exchange With Reporters on the *Achille Lauro* Hijacking Incident
October 10, 1985

The President. Listen, I'm just going to take a second. I've got 30 people waiting in there to have lunch. But apparently there's a little confusion, and maybe I'm responsi-

ble, I don't know, with regard to the PLO and their part in this hostage setup. I did not mean to imply that I favored them giving a trial or attempting to do justice to the hijackers. I really believe that the PLO, if the hijackers were in their custody, should turn them over to a sovereign state that would have jurisdiction and could prosecute them as the murderers that they are. And that is reality—what I think should be done and what we would make every effort to see would be done.

Q. Well, sir, if they won't turn them over, how can we make them turn them over?

The President. That is a problem we'll have to look at and find out. And if I had an answer to that specifically right now, I wouldn't make it public.

Q. Are you satisfied that the PLO does have control of the hijackers in Tunisia now?

The President. I would have to tell you that there had been so many things spoken and left unanswered in this—and this and then I'm going to go into lunch, after I say this—that I'm hesitant about saying anything positive. It was our understanding that they were put in their custody. And where they are now or whether they have them, I don't really know. And I'm just trying to keep in touch with our sources of information, our Ambassador there, to try and stay abreast of what the situation is.

Q. Are you satisfied they're out of Egypt, though, sir?

The President. No. I'm not even satisfied with that. All I know is they're off the boat, and they're someplace over there, and our people are safe.

Q. But no trial by the PLO?

Q. ——Mubarak said——

The President. What?

Q. No trial by the PLO?

The President. No, I don't think——

Q. Mr. President——

The President. They are not a sovereign nation, and I don't think that they would have a machinery that——

Q. So, you would not be——

Q. Despite what Mubarak——

Q. ——satisfied—as you said before—you would not be satisfied if they punish them? You said that you would be satisfied, but now you're saying you would not be satisfied?

The President. Well, no. And I shouldn't have made a statement of that kind. I think that I was thinking kind of—as mad as I am—vengeance instead of justice and——

Q. But any sovereign nation?

The President. What?

Q. Any sovereign nation?

The President. Well, I think that there's a possibility of our own because it was our citizen, but Italy because it was an Italian ship. I think because the crime began in Egypt there could be a—I think that you could find a reason for more then one sovereign nation to have jurisdiction in this case.

Q. Mr. President, the Israelis——

Q. Mubarak says that they're out of Egypt.

The President. What?

Q. But President Mubarak says they're out of Egypt. Don't you believe him?

The President. The case is whether he has all the same information or the information he should have, too. Earlier, in his work to get the hostages freed, he did not know that a crime had been committed either.

Q. He said they were all safe.

Q. Mr. President, the Israelis say that——

The President. What?

Q. ——Yasser Arafat knew in advance of the raid. Is that your understanding, sir?

The President. That what?

Q. The Israelis say Yasser Arafat knew in advance of the hijacking.

The President. I wouldn't have any way of knowing whether that's true or not.

Q. They say you were planning a military operation to free the hostages if they had not been freed.

The President. Now, Sam [Sam Donaldson, ABC News], you know that that's something I can't talk about either.

Q. Have a nice lunch.

Note: The exchange began at 11:36 a.m. in the cafeteria of the Kitchens of Sara Lee in Deerfield, IL. The President then returned to Chicago.

Remarks and a Question-and-Answer Session With Students and Faculty at Gordon Technical High School in Chicago, Illinois
October 10, 1985

The President. Reverend clergy, Governor Thompson, Representatives Porter and O'Brien and Martin and Hyde—and I've got to stop on one of those names there. Congresswoman Martin represents the district in Illinois that contains a town called Tampico, where I was born, and a town called Dixon, where I grew up. So, I didn't think the rest would mind if I gave a special mention here. I can still call her my Congresswoman. But you the faculty and the students—I thank all of you very much. Believe me, it's great to be in Chicago; it's my kind of town. And it's wonderful to be at Gordon Tech and the home of the Rams.

Now, you know, it'd be awfully tempting to say, "Beat Loyola," but then, again, in my present job I'm not supposed to take sides within the country that way.

Audience. Boo-o-o!

The President. But let me tell you what I will say. I remember back playing football at Eureka College down here in the center of the State, and I remember one night in a chalk talk—I guess maybe today they're called skull sessions—but anyway, in this chalk talk the conversation got around—I don't know how—now, I'd always known that I never started a football game without asking somebody's help. And I wouldn't have said that out loud; I'd have been afraid to. But I was amazed that, one by one, we found there wasn't a man in the squad that didn't pray before a game. We got comparing notes on what we prayed and what we asked, and somehow all of us, on our own, had figured out we couldn't ask God to help us win, because he couldn't take sides either. But we found that we'd finally worked it out for ourselves that each one of us was praying that no one would get hurt, be no injuries, that everyone would do their best, that the best team would win, and we'd have no reason for regret at how it turned out. So, I'll pass that prayer on to all of you for the game at Loyola.

But I've come here not just to talk to you, but to talk with you and to have a little give and take about some of your concerns and your hopes and dreams for the future. But first let me just say a few words about the kind of future that I hope for you, and it is a nation that prospers in a world that is free. This is the America that we've been trying to—well, maybe—I was going to say create, but no; I think it's the kind of America we have created. And I looked at some of your signs up here, and I know something about your student body. Did you ever realize how unique you are and we are in all the world?

Audience. Yes!

The President. All of us. All of us—either by ourselves, on our own, or by way of our ancestors, our parents, grandparents, or great-grandparents—all of us came here from someplace else in the world, and it meant that somebody in our family had an inner spirit, a desire and love for freedom, and the courage to pick up and leave a homeland and come here to a strange land and start all over again and become a whole new breed of people called Americans. And we all retain, as the signs indicate, a feeling with regard to the land of our heritage. You know, a man doesn't have to give up his mother because he takes a wife; so, it's a little bit that way with us. Yes, we're Americans, but, yes, we have a feeling of kinship with those places from whence we came, and there isn't any other place on Earth like it.

Now, a few years ago when we first started in Washington, we found that we had a broken economy that needed a little fixing—government had grown so big, taxing and spending were out of control, families were struggling to get by, a web of regulations were so thick that businesses were spending most of their time filling out forms instead of tending to business and rather than keeping America number one in the world. So we tried to use some common sense. We put the people back in charge and cut the increase in government spending nearly in half. We cut the growth of regulations by about a third, and we're still whittling at those. And we passed the first across-the-board tax cut for everyone since 1964, and then we indexed the tax rates to inflation.

And maybe some of you haven't thought about what that means. The income tax is based on the number of dollars you earn, not their purchasing power. And so, when we were going through these long decades of inflation that continued to erode the value of the dollar and when people had to get cost-of-living pay raises to make them keep even with inflation, they didn't keep even because the number of dollars increased, and Uncle Sam pushed you into higher tax brackets, and you found out you were paying a higher tax, year after year, just for trying to keep even with the depreciating value of your money. Well, we've indexed that now, so that can't happen again. Government can't get any tax increases for free by just simply moving you up into higher tax brackets. The brackets now are indexed along with inflation.

But we also did something about inflation. It was about 12½ percent when we came here, came to Washington. For the last 4 months it's been 2½ percent, and we're going to get that down. We've had 34 months of economic growth, and we've created about 8½ million new jobs. Our trading partners in Europe—the European Community, 10 nations there—have not increased or had a new job created in any of the countries there in over the last 10 years. We've had a record number of new business incorporations.

But our job isn't finished; the Government is still spending too much. If your families can live within a reasonable budget, the Federal Government ought to be able to do the same thing. So, I'm supporting a thing that the Senate was taking action on yesterday—and maybe it's one of the reasons why our friend, Congressman Rostenkowski, couldn't be here today, because now it's over to the House—and that is a plan called the Gramm-Rudman amendment that would force the Government to control spending and give the United States a balanced budget. In other words, to bring the deficits down over a period of 5 years, and by 1990, we would

balance the budget. And then it is my dream that we adopt a constitutional amendment that says henceforth the Federal Government cannot spend more than it takes in.

And so with the help of your fine Congressman Dan Rostenkowski, we're going to do that, and we're going to overhaul that complicated tax system and make it shine with fairness for everyone and make it simple. The present tax system has 14 different brackets in which you earn a few more dollars and the Government shoves you automatically up into another bracket. Well, our proposal will only have 3 brackets—15 percent, 25 percent, and 35 percent. Well, there will be a fourth bracket that we haven't talked about. That'll be zero because there'll be a lot of people down at the lower end of the earning scale that won't have to pay any tax at all.

So, taxable income all the way up to $29,000 a year, you'll keep 85 cents out of every dollar you earn. And from $29,000 up to $70,000 a year, you'll keep 75 cents in that bracket out of everything that you earn. And above $70,000, you'll keep about 65 cents out of every dollar that you earn. When we began 5 years ago, the top bracket was 70 percent, not 35 percent. We've lowered it to 50. And it's been 50 now for these few years, but we want to come down some more; that top bracket should be 35 percent.

We think our plan is also very profamily, because one of the important reforms we'd make is in the personal exemption. Now, you know, each one of you—you're an exemption. When your parents sit down to figure out the income tax every year, they get to deduct, now, $1,040 from their taxable income for each one of you. Well, we think that isn't enough any more, after the inflation we've had. We're holding out now that it be $2,000. Now, some of the people in the Congress want to cut that down. They don't want to make it $2,000. I think we've got a pretty good argument—because back in 1948, when it was $600, and then, to try and keep pace with inflation, it went up to $1,040 as it is now—well, to tell you the honest truth, if we'd really kept up with inflation, that exemption would be $2,700, but we're only asking for $2,000. But we're sure going to have an argument against anybody that wants to cut it back.

But there's more than just doing something about the economy. It's also renewing America's mind and heart and spirit. And some of that renewal has evidently been going on right here, from what I've heard. We're determined to stand up for the rights of the family, to strengthen the community, to acknowledge that we're a nation under God that gives all children the right to pray in their schools. And that's why we're determined to renew excellence in education, to help restore discipline to schools, to reward teachers of merit, to make sure all our students learn English, and to put parents back in charge of their own families. Now, we've been making some gains in that educational field because those SAT scores—you know, the scores that you take in the examinations with regard to college entrance—well, they have been up now for 3 of the last 4 years, after 20 years of straight decline. And this year's jump was the biggest jump since 1963. Now, there's one other reform that we want. We've tried, and we haven't gotten it so far, but we're going to keep trying because it's right and it's fair. We believe for parents who are sending young people to schools like yours, they are entitled to a tuition tax credit.

Well, these are some of the things that we're trying to do, including the fact, yes, that we feel there is a right for every unborn child to be born. And we're going to strive for that. We also want to leave you a world that is at peace. And some people seem to misunderstand the job that we have been doing in these last few years of refurbishing our armed forces to the point that we can stand in the world with a deterrent to war. As a matter of fact, one of our large military bases in this country has a sign over their entrance gate that says, "Our business is peace."

But you tempted me beyond my strength, and I talked longer than I was supposed to. But we're going to have a dialog now instead of a continued monolog, and I know that you have chosen some for questions. And I'll start with the right microphone and then switch back and forth—take your questions.

The President's Visit to the School

Q. I have a question I'd like to ask you. Why did you choose to come to this school?

The President. Why did I choose to come to this school? Well, I'd have to ask them—no, I'd have to ask some people that were doing some of the scheduling. But all I can tell you is that I keep needling those people that put a schedule on my desk and tell me what I'm going to do. I keep needling them to let me come to more schools, because I like what I've seen of young America. But you also were picked on the basis of some of the things that you have accomplished and we know you're here, and we tied that into our trip here to Chicago to come and see you.

Hijacking of the Achille Lauro

Q. I'm a junior here at Gordon Tech. What is your comment on the hostage crisis this past week?

The President. The comment this last week on the hostage question? First, a general comment: This terrorism and this thing that is going on in the world is the most frustrating thing to deal with. You know you want to say retaliate when this is done get even. But then what do you say when you find out that you're not quite sure that a retaliation would hit the people who were responsible for the terror and the crime and you might be killing innocent people and so you swallow your gorge and don't do it.

But in this last situation, we had moved, we were ready and prepared, and then this thing that happened with the Egyptian Government offering to release the hostages. They did not know at the time that a murder had been committed. I can only say about this one that we are making every effort to see if those hostages cannot be—or not the hostages, those terrorists, the four of them, cannot be located and turned over to one of the governments—our own or Italy or Egypt—the governments that would have a legitimate right to prosecute them and bring them to the court of justice for the murder.

Q. Thank you very much, Mr. President.

The President. Thank you.

The President's Visit to the School

Q. I'm a freshman. My question is what are your feelings now that you have seen Gordon Tech?

The President. You turned down a little away from the microphone, there. Say that again; I lost you.

Q. What are your feelings now that you have seen Gordon Tech?

The President. What are my feelings now that I've seen Gordon Tech? You saw me have to tilt the mike up. I grew 3 inches since I came in the room here. I must say, I was somewhat prepared. You have friends who told me that I would find a great spirit here, told me some other things about your school, your accomplishments. But believe me, I heartily approve, and I think, looking at all of you, the 21st century is in good hands.

Student Financial Aid

Q. I'm a junior at Gordon Tech. Mr. President, my question is: What about more financial aid to college students?

The President. What about more financial aid to college students? All right. Well, as one who worked his way through college, believe me, I have a sympathy for those who could not go without having some kind of help. As a matter of fact, one of the better jobs I've ever had was working my way through college. I washed dishes in the girls' dormitory. But there seems to have been some misunderstanding. I know why you ask about us and our approach to that very subject. First of all, we found when we arrived in Washington that there were people who were getting grants and loans whose family income was such that they weren't justified. We thought that the help should be aimed more directly to those who would actually have to have help if they were to go to school.

So, we did make some changes. And there were some people, then, that on the basis of income were ruled out as to getting this help. And we have directed more to those with the incomes that made it necessary. But, also, the idea that in these changes that somehow we have cut back— we have reduced requests for more spending, but we right now are spending more on that program of college aid to students

than has ever been spent in the country's history. And right this year, we're spending around $9 billion on college aid, and more than 40 percent of the college students in this country are getting some kind of Federal help. So, I think we're doing—in the situation we're in, what with deficits and all—as much as could be expected of the Federal Government.

Views on the Presidency

Q. I'm a freshman from homeroom 114, and my question is: What is it like to be the President of the United States?

The President. What is it like to be the President? Well, I have to say, first of all, I view the Presidency as—you know, some people become President, but I've always thought of it that temporarily you are given custody of an institution called the Presidency. And you must then return the custody of that or hand it on to someone else when your turn is over.

Obviously, there is a great pride and there's a great thrill to serving the people of this great country, and I feel it very deeply. I have to say, also, there are moments of great stress when decisions have to be made. I don't know of a strain on a President or a problem that could be greater and more anguishing than to some day have to put the young men and women in uniform in our country out where they face the risk of wounds or death. And I made such a decision with regard to the invasion of Grenada. I have made decisions of that kind with regard to terrorism and then found that the exercises didn't need to be carried out. But you have moments, things that you will never forget, such as the death of our marines at the hands of a fanatic terrorist in Lebanon. Those things you have to learn to live with. Well, all I can tell you is that every morning when I wake up I thank God for having given me the opportunity to serve.

Q. Mr. President, we have time for two more questions.

The President. Thank you, Father.

Military Strength and Deterrence

Q. I'm a sophomore. Mr. President, my question is: Will you continue to stand by your strategy of peace through strength?

The President. Yes, we're a peace-loving people, and out of the wars we've been in, we haven't taken additional territory or conquered other lands. We've had peace for 40 years, and I believe that peace is based on two things: a deterrent capacity, and the other is that after wars—and there've been four in my lifetime—after previous wars, peace would come and, yet, in the terms of the peace we would lay the foundation for the next war. The hatreds, the rivalries would still pertain. And 40 years ago, our country—when we came to the end of the World War II—our country set out to help all the war-ravaged nations, including our enemies. And today those enemies—Japan, West Germany, Italy—they are our staunchest and strongest allies. And we believe that part of the 40 years of peace has been due to the fact that we, for once, helped in bringing about a peace that erased the hatreds and rivalries, rather than just smoothing them over until there would be another chance to express them.

When we came into office, we found that our military had been allowed to decline. We had, as you know, the draft, and we have now a volunteer army. Do you know that we meet our quotas every year on enlistment. We do better on reenlistment than has ever been done. But do you also know that we have the highest percentage of high school graduates in uniform in this country than we have ever had in the history of the United States.

And I can sum up why it must be peace through strength. We tried over the years in unilateral disarmament. I saw some signs of some demonstrators outside that were asking for that very thing. We tried détente and letting our military decline and not building weapons, canceling the B–1 bomber, and so forth. Instead, the enemy kept on—or the adversaries, I'm not going to call them an enemy anymore—an adversary who is contesting with us continued to build up to where there was a dangerous imbalance that was growing. And I think the greatest proof came in a cartoon I saw of two Russian generals when we started to rearm. And one of them was saying to the other, "I liked the arms race better when we were the only ones in it." Well, they're not going to be the only ones in it. We're going to do everything we—[*inaudible*]. This will be one of our goals in Geneva next month—to reveal to them that we both can bring down those mountains of armaments if we are willing to agree that neither one of us should be responsible for starting a war. But that if they're going to insist on building up these tremendous arsenals of offensive weapons, which they are, then they might as well face it—we are not going to let them get enough advantage that they can ever make war.

The President's Future Plans

Q. I would like to know what you plan to do after you finish your final term of President.

The President. What do I intend to do after I finish my final term as President? Well, this is the final term. Well, for one thing, I'll go back to the ranch and catch up on a little ranch work that I haven't been able to do much of. Oh, people keep telling me I'll write a book. They say it's the proper thing to do. But, no, I think then—as you know, I've been 39 years old 33 times now. [*Laughter*] I think that I will try to do just whatever I can, as a citizen, to help whoever is in government keep on with the things that need to be done to keep our nation great.

I wish I'd have forgotten the opening remarks so we could have taken more questions here; I love to do this. And I just want to tell you I also have received from your student council a document, a letter containing a lot of things and subjects that you are interested in. Many of them did not come up in the limited questioning so far today, but I'm going to take that back with me. I just received it today and saw it for the first time. I'm going to take it back and I'm going to write an answer to that letter to your student council for all of you.

Thank you very much. Thank you.

Note: The President spoke at 2:15 p.m. in the school gymnasium. Following his remarks, the President returned to Washington, DC.

Nomination of Manuel H. Johnson To Be a Member of the Board of Governors of the Federal Reserve System
October 10, 1985

The President today announced his intention to nominate Manuel H. Johnson of Virginia, District 5, to be a member of the Board of Governors of the Federal Reserve System for a term of 14 years from February 1, 1986, vice J. Charles Partee term expiring.

Dr. Johnson is currently Assistant Secretary for Economic Policy at the Department of the Treasury. He previously served as Deputy Assistant Secretary for Economic Policy, 1981–1982. He was an associate pro-

fessor of economics at George Mason University in Fairfax, VA, 1980–1981, and an assistant professor of economics, 1977–1980. He was an instructor and research associate at Florida State University in the Department of Economics, 1973–1976.

Dr. Johnson graduated from Troy State University (B.S., 1973), Florida State University (M.S., 1974; Ph.D., 1977). He was born February 10, 1949, in Troy, AL, is married, and has two children. Dr. Johnson resides in Fairfax, VA.

Nomination of Wayne D. Angell To Be a Member of the Board of Governors of the Federal Reserve System
October 10, 1985

The President today announced his intention to nominate Wayne D. Angell of Kansas, District 10, to be a member of the Board of Governors of the Federal Reserve System for the unexpired term of 14 years from February 1, 1980, vice Lyle Elden Gramley resigned.

Dr. Angell is currently Director, Federal Reserve Bank of Kansas City. He was first elected to the Bank in 1979. He has been a professor of economics at Ottawa Universi-

ty, Ottawa, Kansas, since 1956, and dean of the college, 1969–1972. Dr. Angell has served on the Advisory Committee to the staff of the Federal Reserve Board of Governors, 1972–1973.

He graduated from Ottawa University (B.A., 1952) and the University of Kansas (M.A., 1953; Ph.D., 1957). He was born June 28, 1930, in Liberal, KS, is married, and has three children. Dr. Angell resides in Ottawa, KS.

Nomination of James Curtis Mack II To Be Deputy Administrator of the National Oceanic and Atmospheric Administration
October 10, 1985

The President today announced his intention to nominate James Curtis Mack II to be Deputy Administrator, National Oceanic and Atmospheric Administration, Department of Commerce. He would succeed Anthony Calio.

Mr. Mack served as executive director of Citizens for the Republic in Santa Monica,

CA, in 1979–1985. Previously he served at the Veterans Administration regional office in Los Angeles as assistant to the Regional Director and assistant veterans services officer in 1973–1979. Since 1984 he has served as a Commissioner on the President's Commission on White House Fellowships. He is also a director of Brentwood Square Savings and Loan Association in Los Angeles.

Mr. Mack graduated from the University of Southern California (B.A., 1967; M.P.A., 1969; M.A., 1976). He was born December 22, 1944, in Los Angeles, CA, where he now resides.

Nomination of Adele Langston Rogers To Be an Alternate United States Representative to the 40th Session of the United Nations General Assembly
October 10, 1985

The President today nominated Adele Langston Rogers to be an Alternate Representative of the United States of America to the 40th session of the General Assembly of the United Nations.

Mrs. Rogers has been involved in civic and charitable activities for many years. She graduated from Cornell University (A.B., 1933; LL.B., 1936) and attended Stanford Law School (1934–1935).

Mrs. Rogers is married, has four children, and resides in Bethesda, MD. Mrs. Rogers was born August 15, 1911, in Wenonah, NJ.

Statement by Principal Deputy Press Secretary Speakes on the *Achille Lauro* Hijacking Incident
October 10, 1985

At the President's direction, U.S. military forces intercepted an aircraft over international airspace that was transporting the *Achille Lauro* terrorists. The aircraft was diverted to the airbase at Sigonella, Italy. In cooperation with the Government of Italy, the terrorists were then taken into Italian custody for appropriate legal proceedings. Earlier today, upon learning that the terrorists would be flown from Egypt to their freedom, the President directed that U.S. forces intercept the aircraft and escort it to a location where the terrorists could be apprehended by those with appropriate jurisdiction. U.S. F-14 aircraft, flying from the carrier *Saratoga*, detected the aircraft in international airspace and intercepted it. They instructed it to follow them and escorted it to the military airbase at Sigonella, Italy. This operation was conducted without firing a shot. The aircraft landed with Italian consent and was surrounded by American and Italian troops. The terrorists aboard were taken into custody by Italian authorities. The Egyptian aircraft, with its crew and other personnel on board, is returning to Egypt.

We have been assured by the Government of Italy that the terrorists will be subject to full due process of law. For our part, we intend to pursue prompt extradition to the United States of those involved in the crime. This action affirms our determination to see that terrorists are apprehended, prosecuted, and punished. This episode also reflects our close cooperation with an exemplary ally and close friend—Italy—in combating international terrorism. The American Government and people are grateful to Prime Minister Craxi, his Government, and the Italian people for their help. We are also grateful to the Government of Tunisia for its refusal to permit the aircraft transporting the terrorists to land in Tunis.

Finally, we must at this point note our gratitude to the Government of Egypt for its efforts to end this dangerous crisis without additional loss of life. We strongly disagreed with the Government of Egypt, however, on disposition of the terrorists.

From the onset, the United States Government made clear to all the Governments involved our firm opposition to negotiations with the terrorists or concessions to them. We also made clear our expectation that the terrorists would be brought to justice. We were, therefore, deeply distressed to learn that those responsible for the death of Leon Klinghoffer might be permitted to go free. We said yesterday that we were determined to see justice done and that we would use every appropriate means to that end.

The decision on ending the hijacking was an independent one by the Government of Egypt. When we were consulted, we advised strongly against any arrangements which would permit the terrorists to escape justice. Since the time the terrorists were taken off the ship, we have continued intensive contacts with the Government of Egypt to pursue that point. The United States wants to emphasize the fundamental and durable interests that the United States and Egypt share, interests which transcend this difficult incident. These have been trying times for both our governments. We will do all we can to ensure that the basic U.S.-Egyptian relationship—in which both our countries have taken so much pride for so long—remains unaffected.

In closing, the President wants to emphasize once again that the international scourge of terrorism can only be stamped out if each member of the community of civilized nations meets its responsibility squarely—passing up no opportunity to apprehend, prosecute, and punish terrorists wherever they may be found. We cannot tolerate terrorism in any form. We will continue to take every appropriate measure available to us to deal with these dastardly deeds. There can be no asylum for terrorism or terrorists.

Note: Larry M. Speakes read the statement to reporters at 11:15 p.m. in the Briefing Room at the White House.

Remarks and a Question-and-Answer Session With Reporters
October 11, 1985

The President's Health

The President. Before making the announcement and the business that has brought me here and knowing your great concern and not wanting you to lose any sleep at night—[*laughter*]—let me explain the patch on my nose. I figured you might ask. The doctor has been keeping track of me since the first operation for skin cancer on my nose and felt that there was some additional work needed. So, yesterday afternoon when we came back from Chicago, I went over there in the White House to the doctor's office, and he did the additional work. And a biopsy revealed there were some cancer cells. And now I have a verdict of—my nose is clean.

Hijacking of the Achille Lauro

So, listening to all the questions and comments regarding my thoughts on last night's events, I felt it might be helpful to take a moment here to make a comment, and then I'd ask Bud McFarlane to be here to provide answers to all the questions that you may have.

Events of the past 24 hours reinforce the determination of all of those who share the privileges of freedom and liberty to join together in countering the scourge of international terrorism. All civilized peoples welcome the apprehension of the terrorists responsible for the seizure of *Achille Lauro* and the brutal murder of Leon Klinghoffer. The pursuit of justice is well served by this cooperative effort to ensure that these terrorists are prosecuted and punished for their crimes.

I want to point out the crucial role played by the Italian Government in bringing this operation to a successful and peaceful conclusion. Throughout, Prime Minister Craxi has been courageous in his insistence that those apprehended shall be subject to full due process of law. I also want to note my gratitude that the Government of Egypt was able to end the crisis without additional loss of life, although I disagreed with their disposition of the terrorists. And, additionally, I wish to praise President Bourguiba's forthright decision to refuse the entry of the fugitives.

Most of all, I am proud to be the Commander in Chief of the soldiers, sailors, airmen, and marines who deployed, supported, and played the crucial role in the delivery of these terrorists to Italian authorities. They and the men and women of our foreign service and intelligence community performed flawlessly in this most difficult and delicate operation. They have my gratitude and, I'm sure, the gratitude of all of their countrymen. These young Americans sent a message to terrorists everywhere. The message: You can run but you can't hide.

End of statement.

Q. Mr. President, Mr. President, does your action last night increase the danger for other Americans being held hostage in the Middle East?

The President. I don't believe so. I don't think that there's any increase that could be made. I think that Americans are, as well as many other people from other countries—as was evidenced in the passenger list of that ship—are targets of continued terrorism.

Q. Mr. President, we were told you'd answer a few questions. If I might ask one. The Egyptians are apparently holding on to the *Achille Lauro,* the ship that the hijacking took place on. What do you know about that? Is there any tie to the fact that Italy is now holding the Egyptian plane, and what are you going to do to try to get that ship released? There are apparently still Americans on it.

The President. I really don't know whether that is being held there for anything other than just simply it is berthed there at this time. I don't know whether the other passengers who were away from Port Said—they are waiting for them to come aboard or anything—whatever might be true of that. I just don't know.

Q. Mr. President, can you tell us about your attitude now toward Egypt, and can you tell us whether we intercepted this plane without any help from Egyptian authorities, either the top officials of the Government or lower down or whether in fact they did give us some sort of help?

The President. Knowing that we could not risk a leak of any plans of this kind—this plan was ours, and the decision was made yesterday afternoon on Air Force One coming back from Chicago.

Q. You're telling us, sir, if I may follow up, you're telling us that Egypt then didn't know we were going to do it and didn't sanction it in any way?

The President. And nor did the Italians know we were going to do it, as far as I'm aware.

Q. Mr. President, you say the decision was made on Air Force One. Can you tell all of us exactly what you did on this yesterday? What went through your mind, what decisions exactly you made, and what it was like for you yesterday?

The President. Well, I can't answer exactly on some of those things, on the decisions that were made. The operation, as it was carried out, was the operation that I ordered and approved of. But the reason I don't want to answer any more specifically on things of that kind is because terrorism and fighting terrorism is an ongoing thing, and again, as we've said before, I don't want to make public decisions that we've made as to what we would or would not do in events of that kind, because I think it's for the terrorists to wonder what we're going to do.

Q. But was it difficult for you or easy for you? Can you give us some sense of your own state of mind?

The President. I don't know whether a decision like that can ever be called easy, but I had complete faith in our forces, and the opportunity was there, and I believed that the mission was possible, and I didn't think there was any way that I could not approve a mission of that kind with what was at stake.

Q. Mr. President, what kind of message do you think this sends regarding your resolve? You've been criticized in the past for not taking action against terrorists. How does this fit the profile of what you think is possible, feasible, and what kind of message for the future?

The President. Well, our problem in the past has not been a lack of will. Our problem has been in terrorist attacks that have taken place in the past. First of all, in a number of them, such as the terrible tragedy with the marines, the perpetrators of the act went up with the bomb. They were suicides, so, there wasn't—you couldn't—you were faced with, well, who were their collaborators, who were behind them, how do you retaliate—they're gone. And the other thing is in a number of incidents where to retaliate would simply be an act of violence without any knowledge that you were striking the perpetrators of the deed and you might be attacking many innocent people. This has been our great problem with terrorism. But here was a clear-cut case in which we could lay our hands on the terrorists.

Q. Well, since you know that these were the criminals and since you knew there were not innocent people around, were you prepared to fire? Were you prepared to shoot that plane down?

The President. This, again, is one of those questions, Andrea [Andrea Mitchell, NBC News], that I'm not going to answer. That's for them to go to bed every night wondering.

Q. Mr. President, on extradition, will you press to extradite the terrorists to the United States if the Italians do give them what you consider to be justice, knowing that there is no capital punishment in Italy?

The President. Well, we think this is the proper thing to do because—I'm not a lawyer, and I don't intend to get into too many legal areas where I might be caught short—but they could be tried in both countries, and in this country they would be tried for murder, where in Italy they will probably be tried on the basis of piracy because of the taking over of the Italian vessel. So, this is why we have put in a request for extradition.

Q. Well, do you want two trials, or would you be satisfied if the Italians give them, say, a long prison sentence?

The President. That remains to be decided as to how far we go or how far we pursue this. What we want is justice done.

Q. Does that mean death?

The President. What?

Q. Does that mean death to the hijackers?

The President. Well, I'm just going to say justice done.

Q. Mr. President, there were reports that there was disagreement between yourself and Prime Minister Craxi about the disposition of these terrorists—how they'd be tried, where they'd be tried. Is there any truth to that?

The President. No. We had a phone call last night. He told me what his situation was with regard to them, and I told him what ours was. And I told him that we would introduce an extradition request. He told me what their legal process was with regard to that, that it wasn't something that he could just give an opinion on himself, any more than I could if the situation was reversed. And, no, we had full cooperation.

But now, I think the few are finished. I know there are many hands, and I'm going to turn them all over to Bud McFarlane.

The President's Health

Q. Well, can you just tell us about your nose, Mr. President? Does——

The President. What?

Q. Can you tell us what—[*laughter*]—forgive us, but what kind of finding the biopsy you had, what level of cancer?

The President. Oh, I thought I answered that—that there were——

Q. Well, there are different levels. Was it melanoma? Was it basal cell?

The President. ——there were some cancerous cells found——

Q. Let him——

The President. ——and now, following that, the examination following the little minor operation, there is such that, as I say, I can stand before you proudly and say, "My nose is clean."

Q. Do you mean cancer cells found yesterday, sir, or are you referring to the original swatch a month ago?

The President. There were a few found yesterday. This was, as I say—the doctor had felt that there was additional work that he needed and wanted to do.

1233

Hijacking of the Achille Lauro

Q. Well, Mr. President, are you concerned that this act may endanger the other six American hostages—that the action taken yesterday may endanger the other six?

The President. I have no way of knowing that or what they're thinking. All I know is that we are still doing everything we can, and investigating every channel we can, to try and get back the other six hostages.

Q. Are you——

The President's Health

Q. ——basal cell or a melanoma, sir? Can you tell us the diagnosis?

The President. I heard the term. I'm not medical, and I'm not a lawyer. And I'm not medical, either, but I did hear the term basal cell.

Hijacking of the Achille Lauro

Q. Are you angry at Mubarak?

The President. Pardon?

Q. Are you angry at President Mubarak for his conduct in this whole affair?

The President. No. As I say, we disagreed, but we have had too firm a relationship between our two countries, and there's too much at stake with regard to peace in the Middle East for us to let a single incident of one kind or a disagreement of this kind color that relationship.

Q. But did he not lie to you, sir?

Q. ——lie to the U.S.

Q. ——Mubarak——

Q. Did he not lie about where the hijackers were to the United States?

The President. I have no way of knowing that, either, or in knowing what that——

Q. Did the Egyptians assist in any way, Mr. President?

Q. Did you call the Klinghoffer——

Q. Did the Egyptians assist in any way in this operation? Did the Egyptians in any way assist you in this operation?

The President. No. As I say, we did this all by our little selves.

Q. Mr. President, are you satisfied that all the perpetrators are in custody?

Q. Have you talked to Mubarak——

Q. Mr. President, are you satisfied that all of the perpetrators are in custody?

The President. I don't think any one of us could answer that. We have no way of knowing that. We know that the four that were on the ship were the ones that perpetrated the crime. Very obviously, they are part of a splinter group from the PLO and have their own goals and aims, and how many were involved in planning or supporting such a mission of this kind, we don't know.

Q. But, sir, it is said that there are two additional Palestinians——

Q. Have you called the Klinghoffer family yet, sir? Have you called the Klinghoffer family yet?

The President. That's what I'm going to the office to do, and you're making me late.

Q. ——two additional Palestinians on that plane; one of them is said to be one of the murder experts for the PLO, who has organized many raids of this type.

The President. All of these things, I think, will be answered in the investigation leading to prosecution.

Q. Thank you.

Note: The President spoke at 12:25 p.m. in the Briefing Room at the White House. Following the President's remarks, Assistant to the President for National Security Affairs Robert C. McFarlane briefed reporters and answered questions.

Proclamation 5385—National Learning Disabilities Month, 1985
October 11, 1985

*By the President of the United States
of America*

A Proclamation

The crowning wonder of our marvelous universe is the human brain. This organ of awesome complexity usually functions so dependably that thoughts can be transmitted from one person to another across the centuries, across the barriers of language, custom, and place. In all our daily transactions, we assume that others will comprehend and respond to the symbols of logic and language that are processed through the instrumentality of the brain.

Yet many Americans do not always find our language, numbers, and symbols natural and logical. They exhibit learning disabilities. In a sense, they are most aware of the deep complexity of our mental processes, for they must struggle to make the connections that, for most of us, are effortless habits.

While science still knows little about the biochemical and structural differences in brain function that may account for the various anomalies we call learning disabilities, our educators are finding alternative methods of teaching which help the learning disabled enjoy a greater use of their mental potential despite the difficulties they may face in reading, calculating, and other forms of mentation and expression. Meanwhile, scientific observation of the difficulties and the successes of learning-disabled persons is helping researchers gain greater understanding of both the learning process and the functioning of the brain.

Awareness of learning disabilities is one of the most important advances in education in recent years. As more and more Americans become aware, our citizens with learning disabilities will have even greater opportunity to lead full and productive lives and to make a contribution to our society.

The Congress, by House Joint Resolution 287, has designated the month of October 1985 as "Learning Disabilities Awareness Month" and has authorized and requested the President to issue a proclamation in honor of this observance.

Now, Therefore, I, Ronald Reagan, President of the United States of America, do hereby proclaim the month of October 1985 as Learning Disabilities Awareness Month, and I call upon all Americans to observe this week with appropriate ceremonies.

In Witness Whereof, I have hereunto set my hand this eleventh day of October, in the year of our Lord nineteen hundred and eighty-five, and of the Independence of the United States of America the two hundred and tenth.

RONALD REAGAN

[*Filed with the Office of the Federal Register, 4:15 p.m., October 11, 1985*]

Proclamation 5386—National Down Syndrome Month, 1985
October 11, 1985

*By the President of the United States
of America*

A Proclamation

Over the past decade, Americans have become increasingly aware of the accomplishments and the potential of the developmentally disabled. Nowhere has this become more evident than in the changed attitudes and perceptions regarding Down Syndrome.

Just a few short years ago, this condition carried with it the stigma of hopeless mental retardation. There were few options available other than institutionalization or other forms of custodial care. Today, great progress has been made on all fronts. Through advances in medical science, the basis for the condition has been uncovered, raising hopes for eventual prevention. Already, treatment can minimize the effects of the condition and increase the life span of people with Down Syndrome.

Through the efforts of concerned physicians, teachers, and parent groups, such as the National Down Syndrome Congress, programs are being put into place to assure access to appropriate medical treatment, education, rehabilitation, and employment. Such programs can have a dramatic impact on the lives of those with this disorder, respecting their intrinsic worth as individuals and maximizing the contributions they can make to society. These efforts include developing special education classes within the context of mainstream school programs; providing vocational training in preparation for competitive employment in the work force; and preparing young adults with Down Syndrome for independent living.

In addition, parents of babies with Down Syndrome are receiving the education and support they need to understand this condition and acquire new hope for the future of their children. We must work together to increase the awareness of the American public as a whole to the true nature of this condition and dispel the stubborn myths about the degree to which it is disabling.

The Congress, by Senate Joint Resolution 40, has designated the month of October 1985 as "National Down Syndrome Month" and authorized and requested the President to issue a proclamation in observance of this month.

Now, Therefore, I, Ronald Reagan, President of the United States of America, do hereby proclaim the month of October 1985 as National Down Syndrome Month. I invite all concerned citizens, agencies and organizations to unite during October with appropriate observances and activities directed toward resolution of the condition of Down Syndrome and toward assisting affected individuals and their families to enjoy to the fullest the blessings of life.

In Witness Whereof, I have hereunto set my hand this eleventh day of October, in the year of our Lord nineteen hundred and eighty-five, and of the Independence of the United States of America the two hundred and tenth.

RONALD REAGAN

[*Filed with the Office of the Federal Register, 4:18 p.m., October 11, 1985*]

Proclamation 5387—Lupus Awareness Week, 1985
October 11, 1985

By the President of the United States of America

A Proclamation

Systemic lupus erythematosus (also known as lupus or SLE) is a potentially serious, complicated, inflammatory connective tissue disease that can produce changes in the structure and function of the skin, joints, and internal organs. More than 500,000 Americans are estimated to have lupus; approximately 90 percent of these are women. One of the most frequent serious disorders of young women, lupus is characterized by periods when the disease is active alternating with periods of remission.

In recent years, the outlook for lupus patients has become progessively brighter as a result of advances from biomedical research. Positive findings have emerged from such diverse projects as studies of the immune system; research on genetic and environmental factors; investigations of hormonal effects; and evaluations of the course and treatment of the disease and its complications. The Federal government and private voluntary organizations have developed a strong and enduring partnership committed to research on lupus. Working together, our objective must be to eradicate lupus and its tragic consequences.

In order for us to take advantage of the knowledge already gained, to increase public awareness of the characteristics and treatment of lupus, and to point up the urgent need for continuing research, the Congress, by Senate Joint Resolution 57, has designated the week beginning October 20, 1985, through October 26, 1985, as "Lupus Awareness Week" and authorized and requested the President to issue a proclamation in observance of this event.

Now, Therefore, I, Ronald Reagan, President of the United States of America, do hereby proclaim October 20 through October 26, 1985, as Lupus Awareness Week. I urge the people of the United States and educational, philanthropic, scientific, medical, and health care organizations and professionals to observe this week with appropriate ceremonies and programs.

In Witness Whereof, I have hereunto set my hand this eleventh day of October, in the year of our Lord nineteen hundred and eighty-five, and of the Independence of the United States of America the two hundred and tenth.

RONALD REAGAN

[*Filed with the Office of the Federal Register, 4:19 p.m., October 11, 1985*]

Nomination of Bruce Marshall Carnes To Be a Deputy Under Secretary of Education
October 11, 1985

The President today announced his intention to nominate Bruce Marshall Carnes to be Deputy Under Secretary for Planning, Budget and Evaluation, Department of Education. He would succeed Gary L. Bauer.

Mr. Carnes is presently serving as assistant to the Secretary of Education. Previously, he was at the National Endowment for the Humanities as Director of the Office of Planning and Budget in 1983–1985; Acting Director of Administration in 1985; and Assistant Director of the Office of Planning in 1979–1983. He was a member of the planning staff and program officer in the Office of Education, HEW, in 1976–1979.

He graduated from the University of Colorado (B.A., 1966) and Indiana University (M.A., 1969; Ph.D., 1971). He is married, has two children, and resides in Springfield, VA. He was born May 19, 1944, in Xenia, OH.

Nomination of Jennifer Lynn Dorn To Be an Associate Deputy Secretary of Transportation
October 11, 1985

The President today announced his intention to nominate Jennifer Lynn Dorn to be Associate Deputy Secretary of Transportation. This is a new position.

Since 1984 Ms. Dorn has been serving as Director of the Office of Commercial Space Transportation, Department of Transportation. Previously, she was Special Assistant to the Secretary of Transportation in 1983– 1984; a professional staff member of the U.S. Senate Committee on Appropriations in 1981–1983; and legislative assistant to Senator Mark O. Hatfield in 1977–1981.

Ms. Dorn graduated from Oregon State University (B.A., 1973) and the University of Connecticut (M.A., 1971). She was born December 7, 1950, in Grand Island, NE, and now resides in Silver Spring, MD.

Nomination of Edward H. Fleischman To Be a Member of the Securities and Exchange Commission
October 11, 1985

The President today announced his intention to nominate Edward H. Fleischman to be a member of the Securities and Exchange Commission for the remainder of the term expiring June 5, 1987. He would succeed James C. Treadway, Jr.

Mr. Fleischman is a partner in the firm of Gaston Snow Beekman & Bogue in New York City. He was a member of the American Law Institute in 1976–1985 and the American College of Investment Counsel in 1982–1985. He served at New York University Law School as an adjunct professor in securities regulation (1976–1985).

Mr. Fleischman graduated from Harvard College (B.A., 1953) and Columbia Law School (LL.B., 1959). He is married, has two children, and resides in Glen Rock, NJ. He was born June 25, 1932, in Cambridge, MA.

Proclamation 5388—Myasthenia Gravis Awareness Week, 1985
October 11, 1985

By the President of the United States of America

A Proclamation

Myasthenia gravis is a harrowing neuromuscular disorder that enfeebles as many as 250,000 of our citizens, most of them in their prime years. It debilitates strength and destroys vigor. Extreme muscle weakness and abnormal fatigue weigh down its victims, sapping their ability to stand, to walk, to pick up a glass and drink from it, and—in critical cases—even to breathe.

Myasthenia gravis can strike anyone at any time. While its exact cause is unknown, scientists have found evidence that a chemical needed to stimulate muscle movement is somehow blocked, leaving muscles unable to contract. Such new knowledge suggests the possibility of one day preventing myasthenia gravis by replenishing the missing chemical and restoring the transmission of nerve impulses. To this end, scientists supported by the Federal government's National Institute of Neurological and Communicative Disorders and Stroke and by private voluntary groups—notably the Myasthenia Gravis Foundation, Inc., and the Muscular Dystrophy Association—are diligently investigating the basic neurological processes that underlie voluntary movement. Studies of immune system function are also underway to help scientists understand why myasthenia gravis patients seem more susceptible than others to infections.

Thanks to previous investigations, several drugs have been developed that can help many myasthenia gravis patients regain muscle strength and resume a fairly normal life. More research is needed, however, to find ways of liberating patients and their families from rigid medication schedules and from the side effects that accompany long-term drug use.

To acquaint the public with the tragedy of myasthenia gravis and the hope that research holds for eliminating this disorder, the Congress, by Senate Joint Resolution 183, has designated the week of October 6, 1985, through October 12, 1985, as "Myasthenia Gravis Awareness Week" and authorized and requested the President to issue a proclamation in observance of this week.

Now, Therefore, I, Ronald Reagan, President of the United States of America, do hereby proclaim the week beginning October 6, 1985, as Myasthenia Gravis Awareness Week. I call upon all government agencies, health organizations, communications media, and people of the United States to observe this week with appropriate ceremonies and activities.

In Witness Whereof, I have hereunto set my hand this eleventh day of October, in the year of our Lord nineteen hundred and eighty-five, and of the Independence of the United States of America the two hundred and tenth.

RONALD REAGAN

[*Filed with the Office of the Federal Register, 10:39 a.m., October 15, 1985*]

Note: The proclamation was released by the Office of the Press Secretary on October 12.

Proclamation 5389—National Housing Week, 1985
October 11, 1985

By the President of the United States of America

A Proclamation

A gratifying sign of our continuing economic upswing is the greatly improved housing picture. The strength and ingenuity of private enterprise, the efficiency and liquidity of our capital markets, and sound government policies have brought decent and affordable housing to the overwhelming majority of Americans. The opportunity to own a home or to live in decent rental housing strengthens the family, the community, and the Nation. It gives individual Americans a stake in the local community and encourages responsible political involvement.

Since World War II, the housing industry has made an immense contribution to the economic prosperity of the United States. It has created millions of productive jobs, creating demand for goods and services, and generated billions of dollars in tax revenues.

Shelter is one of the most basic human needs, and therefore encouraging the production of decent affordable housing must be a primary concern at all levels of government. It is, then, fitting to reaffirm our national commitment to livable housing and family home ownership and to recognize the multiple economic benefits engendered by the current housing recovery.

The Congress, by Senate Joint Resolution 197, has designated the week beginning October 6, 1985, through October 13, 1985, as "National Housing Week" and authorized and requested the President to issue a proclamation in observance of this event.

Now, Therefore, I, Ronald Reagan, President of the United States of America, do hereby proclaim the week beginning October 6, 1985, as National Housing Week. I call upon the Governors, Mayors of our cities, and people of this Nation to observe this week with appropriate ceremonies and activities.

In Witness Whereof, I have hereunto set my hand this eleventh day of October, in the year of our Lord nineteen hundred and eighty-five, and of the Independence of the United States of America the two hundred and tenth.

RONALD REAGAN

[*Filed with the Office of the Federal Register, 10:40 a.m., October 15, 1985*]

Note: The proclamation was released by the Office of the Press Secretary on October 12.

Radio Address to the Nation on Soviet Strategic Defense Programs
October 12, 1985

Last week our State and Defense Departments released the most comprehensive report yet on the strategic defense programs of the Soviet Union. You can obtain a copy of—it's called "Soviet Strategic Defense Programs"—by writing the Department of Defense in Washington, DC. This report shows that the Soviets not only continue to build up their offensive nuclear forces at an unprecedented rate, they're also spending almost as much on strategic defense.

For years, we have deterred aggression through the threat of nuclear retaliation, but we virtually ignored our defensive needs. While the Soviets were expanding their own involvement in strategic defense, we were virtually standing still. At this point, their buildup of offensive weapons combined with their very extensive strategic defense programs is threatening the security of the West. We must respond in three ways: first, by modernizing our own strategic forces, the forces on which deterrence depends; second, by doing our part to get an agreement with the Soviets in Geneva for equitable and verifiable reductions in offensive nuclear forces; and third, by investigating the possibilities of nonnuclear defenses to help protect the United States and our allies from attack.

It's our hope that this research and testing under our Strategic Defense Initiative, or SDI, may, in fact, point the way to advanced defenses that could protect millions of people. We've got to restore military balance between the United States and the Soviet Union, and we need your support for both a strong defense and a strong deterrent against aggression. In a democracy, no policy can be sustained without such public support, but the Soviet Union is not a democracy. We see this in its internal structure, in its treatment of the individual, and in the way it conducts its foreign affairs. The Soviets refuse to admit they have any strategic defense program at all. This is not only deception, its dangerous deception, for without a full picture of what is going on, the people of the world cannot know what they need to know to keep the peace.

Let me give you just a few details about Soviet strategic defense programs. First of all, unlike our own, Soviet activities go well beyond research. The Soviet Union today has the world's only operational antiballistic missile system. The Soviet Union also has the world's only operational antisatellite system and the world's most extensive strategic air defense network. Beyond that, the Soviets are engaged in a number of activities that raise questions about their commitment to the antiballistic missile treaty of 1972, including the construction of a new radar in central Siberia, which is an out-and-out violation of the treaty. But that's not all. The Soviets have for a long time been doing advanced research on their version of SDI. They don't talk about that; all they say about SDI is that the United States shouldn't have it, but as many as 10,000 Soviet scientists and engineers are believed to be working on research related to SDI. They're doing so well, our experts say they may be able to put an advanced technology defensive system in space by the end of the century.

When you look at what the Soviets are doing in both strategic offense and defense, you realize that our SDI research program is crucial to maintain the military balance and protect the liberty and freedom of the West. America's research and testing is being conducted within the terms of the ABM treaty. I want to make it clear that we welcome the day when the Soviet Union can shoot down any incoming missile, so long as the United States can shoot down any incoming missile, too. Our SDI research offers the hope that we can enhance U.S. and allied security through greater reliance on defenses which threaten no one, rather than on offensive nuclear weapons which could kill millions. What I'm speaking of is a balance of safety, as opposed to a balance of terror. This is not only morally preferable, but it may result in getting rid of nuclear weapons altogether. It would be irresponsible and dangerous on our part to deny this promise to the world.

And so, we're dealing with the real issue of peace, with the real issue of how to free the entire world from the nuclear threat. And this is why we want the Soviets to join us now in agreeing to equitable and verifiable reductions, and I mean significant reductions in offensive nuclear arms. And it's why we're seeking to discuss with the Soviet Union, even now in Geneva, our hopes for the creation of a world with more

defense and less and less offense. The sooner the Soviet Union comes clean about its own strategic defense programs and joins with us in a real dialog to reduce the risk of war, the better it will be for the world. Write the Defense Department and ask for the "Soviet Strategic Defense Programs."

Until next week, thanks for listening, and God bless you.

Note: The President spoke at 12:06 p.m. from Camp David, MD.

Statement by Principal Deputy Press Secretary Speakes on the Murder of Iskander Odeh
October 12, 1985

The Santa Ana office of the Arab American Anti-Discrimination Committee was bombed October 11, killing the center's director, Mr. Iskander (Alex) Odeh. The administration deeply deplores this tragic event and condemns in the strongest possible terms the criminal use of violence and terrorism to achieve political ends. To think even for a moment that there exists a justification for such heinous acts does grave

injustice to the principles of political freedom upon which this country was founded.

The President extends his sincere condolences to Mr. Odeh's widow Norma and his three small daughters, as well as to other members of the family. The President has instructed that appropriate Federal authorities provide the fullest possible support to the local police investigation now underway.

Statement by Principal Deputy Press Secretary Speakes on the Italian Government's Release of Palestinian Terrorist Abu el Abbas
October 13, 1985

The U.S. Government finds it incomprehensible that Italian authorities permitted Abu el Abbas to leave Italy despite a U.S. Government request to the Italian Government for his arrest and detention. Abbas is one of the two Palestinians who accompanied the four *Achille Lauro* hijackers on the plane that was intercepted after leaving Egypt Thursday night. A U.S. Federal judge Friday issued a warrant for Abbas' arrest, charging him with violation of 18 U.S.C. 1203, hostage taking, as well as piracy and conspiracy to commit both offenses. The Italian Government was notified, and the U.S. requested Italy to arrest Abbas provi-

sionally pending transmission of a formal request for extradition.

Abbas, also known as Abu Khaled, is one of the most notorious Palestinian terrorists and has been involved in savage attacks on civilians. Evidence at hand strongly suggests that Abbas was criminally implicated in the hijacking of the *Achille Lauro;* indeed, that he planned and controlled the operation. The Italian Government has informed us, however, that its judicial authorities did not consider this evidence legally strong enough to support provisional arrest of Abbas while awaiting a formal U.S. request for his extradition. The U.S. Government is astonished at this breach of any reasonable standard of due process and is deeply disappointed.

Remarks on Arrival in Boise, Idaho
October 15, 1985

The President. Well, it's great to be back here in Idaho again and to be here in support of your fine Senator, Steve Symms.

You know, our country is enjoying peace and prosperity, and this just didn't happen by accident. We got rid of some irresponsible policies that have been kicking around Washington for a while, and we put in a growth-oriented program in their place. And that couldn't have been done without a Republican Senate. When we got to Washington, when Steve got there to the Senate and I got there in the White House, we found that inflation was more than 12 percent. It's now, for the last 4 months, been 2½ percent. We lowered the income tax rates by 25 percent. And the prime interest rate was 21½ percent, and it's now down to less than half of that. And Steve Symms was a soldier in the frontline of the battle that brought these things about, and that battle is still being fought.

We're going to end something that's been going on ever since World War II, and that is deficit spending, and we're going to get a hold of it once and for all.

Audience member. Way to go with the PLO!

The President. And we're going to have a tax reform that will make the tax program fairly understandable and I think a little bit cheaper. And it'll be fair, which isn't true of the present system. And we're going to do this, and in spite of some critics to the contrary, we're going to do it at the same time we keep our military forces strong, as they should be.

So, I know I've got to go into town—there's some people waiting there—but I just wanted to say to you, you keep Steve Symms right there in Washington where he belongs for this next Senate term. You need him, and our country needs him, and I'll guarantee you, I need him.

So, thank you all for coming out here. Thank you. God bless you all.

Note: The President spoke at 11:30 a.m. at the Boise Air Terminal.

Remarks at a Fundraising Event for Senator Steven D. Symms in Boise, Idaho
October 15, 1985

Thank you, Steve, and thank you, Senator McClure and Lieutenant Governor Leroy, Congressman Craig, and all of you, the distinguished people up here. And, especially, I want to mention these two grandstands filled with these wonderful young people up here. This is what these contests are all about. And a special congratulations to Veronica Barnes for her award-winning essay on why she's proud to be an American.

Well, it's a pleasure for me to be here in support of a champion of liberty, a tough advocate for the interests of Idaho and for all of America—Senator Steve Symms. Somebody asked me earlier today how it feels to be leaving Washington for a visit to Idaho. Well, I said, it's a little like coming home to old friends after a trip through the Twilight Zone. [*Laughter*] And it really does feel like being home with friends. Steve mentioned this already, but I haven't forgotten the 66-percent and the 72-percent majorities the Gem State gave me in 1980 and 1984. And all I can say is: Thank you, Idaho! You not only helped me get my present job, you also sent to Washington one of this country's finest and most responsible Senators, Steve Symms. And along with Senator Jim McClure and Congressman Larry Craig, they're all doing a terrific job. I need them. Can I count on you to keep them there? [*Applause*] All right.

A little over 4½ years ago, we set out to revitalize our country and to turn around some ominous trends. Inflation was raging, our economy was declining, and our military strength was getting weaker by the day. With the help of hard-working, concerned citizens like yourselves, we've put America back on track. Now, some of the experts said that it would take 10 years to wring inflation out of our economy. Well, you know what an expert is? That's someone who can tell you every reason why something can't be done. We didn't listen to the naysayers and neither did Steve Symms. And now, instead of the 12-percent inflation rate we inherited last—well, last month, and as it's been for most of the last 3 years, inflation was under 4 percent, and for the last 4 months, it has been 2½ percent. Now, that's good for you, it's good for Idaho, and it's good for America.

The drop in the inflation rate is only part of the picture. The prime interest rate was 21½ percent before we got to Washington; today it's under 10. Productivity has jumped, real take-home pay has increased, and that's real, not just pay that was raised to keep pace with inflation. And we've had 34 straight months of economic growth. Unemployment is down to 7.1 percent, and this year we have had a higher percentage of our working-age population employed than at any time in our nation's recorded history. Last month 378,000 more people found jobs in America. Now, this couldn't have been accomplished without effective Senators like the two that are here, like Jim McClure and like Steve Symms.

The progress that we've enjoyed has not been, as our liberal opposition would like the public to believe, as a result of luck or personality or the celestial effects of Halley's Comet. America is back because we discarded wrongheaded solutions that relied on big government, high taxes, and more Federal regulation. Instead, we put power back in the names [hands] of the people. Your success proves the best thing that anyone can do for the American people is to get the Government off your backs and out of your way. Our program, aimed at private sector growth rather than more government and higher taxes, stood in stark contrast to failed liberal policies of the past two decades. It was about as popular with the Washington establishment, that program of ours, as a skunk at a lawn party. [*Laughter*] So, it hasn't been easy. I've had to rely heavily on individuals with courage, energy, and principle. And you know now I'm talking about Steve Symms. Steve has been a linchpin, a driving force behind our efforts to keep our country free, prosperous, and at peace.

And today we're on the verge of a landmark victory for America's economic future. Last week, as Steve told you, the Republican Senate, with the support of a majority of Democrat Senators, adopted the Gramm-Rudman-Hollings deficit reduction plan. This farsighted legislation puts in place a fair, enforceable method of reducing the budget deficit by equal amounts each year, mandating a balanced budget by 1990. And then, I hope we'll be able to get a constitutional amendment to ensure that from then on the Federal Government doesn't spend any more than it takes in. Maybe over the weekend, on some of the talk shows, you have seen some people—without mentioning them—snidely calling this some kind of a gimmick, this Gramm-Rudman-Hollings plan, and some kind of a trick to cover up the fact of the deficits.

Well, it's no such thing. Let me just take a second and tell you briefly what it is. From the moment we got there, we've been trying to reduce the deficits and eliminate them and get them down to the balanced budget. If we had gotten all the spending cuts that we asked for in 1981, the deficit would be $50 billion less than it is right now. And so, each succeeding year, you got back to the same old fight, asking some of those in Congress who have favorite programs that are supported by special interest groups, trying to get further reductions in the spending of government. Well, finally, the idea came, let's have a program—we're on a path, right now, started on a path of decline in the deficits in proportion to the gross national product. So, we said, why don't we have a 5-year plan in which we keep this downward path of deficits to the point that it arrives at the balanced point? And then, instead of battling that same old battle every year, anyone who tries to bust the budget with a spending program will be violating an adopted 5-year program. And that's what that amendment does.

And, of course, it's now over in the House. Friday, the House of Representatives took a step in the right direction, but we still have a large hurdle to get over. In a few days, the House-Senate conferees will meet to iron out their differences. And they need to know, back in Washington, how you feel about it and what you want. So, don't hesitate to take pen in hand or a telegram or a wire. The American people will not tolerate, I don't believe, any attempt to scuttle this last, best hope to come to grips with the budget deficit. The days of the big spender are over. The House-Senate conference committee should realize the American people are watching.

Steve Symms has fought long and hard against the profligate spending that Gramm-Rudman-Hollings will finally put behind us. One indication of the respect his colleagues have for Steve is his membership on the critical Senate Finance Committee. It is a tribute for a freshman Senator to get a coveted seat on that committee. And it, along with his Budget and Environment and Public Works Committee assignments, allows him effectively to represent the needs and views of Idaho in our Nation's Capital. For instance, as chairman of the Senate Transportation Subcommittee, he has worked hard and successfully to keep up this State's and the Nation's infrastructure, making certain that your roads and bridges are in tiptop shape. Effective as he has been for your State, Steve has never lost sight of the fact that what's best for Idaho is what's best for America.

We've come a long way, but there's still much more to do. I know that here in Idaho some of your key industries are still struggling. Quick fixes aren't the answer. We've had a half a century of that. We're opposed to any policy that raises trade barriers against our products. With our farmers under stress as they are now, we must not hurt them further with a trade policy that cuts them off from the foreign markets that are the key to a recovery for our agricultural economy. Now is not the time to be closing markets and retreating; now is the time to let the world know we mean business. The era of the all-providing, never-complaining America is over. Fair trade means fair trade for us, too. I don't care if we're talking about microchips, potatoes, chemicals, or any other product. It has to be free, fair, and open trade for all.

Restoring America's economic vitality was priority number one for this administration. To do that we had to come to grips with economy-destroying levels of taxation. We cut the Federal income tax rates 25 percent across the board, offsetting tax increases that were built into the system. And then, we indexed taxes so they wouldn't increase because of inflation.

Some idea of what had happened to you in the years just a few years before—let me give you just one little set of figures here. Indexing, and what does it mean? Maybe some of our young people who haven't paid an income tax yet don't know that as inflation was raging back over the last decade and a half or so, and we were getting pay raises to try and keep pace with inflation—not to increase our income, but just to stay even—well, you're taxed on the number of dollars you earn, not on their value. So, you get a cost-of-living increase and you're pushed up into another one of those 14 tax brackets. And you pay a higher rate of tax, but you hadn't improved yourself at all, and you're worse off than you were back there before you got the cost-of-living pay raise.

Well, this is what is cured with indexing; now it can't happen. Now, it'll be really done away with when we get tax reform. But right now with the present tax system, that is indexed so that, as you get cost-of-living pay raises, you don't go up into another tax bracket. You stay in the same bracket you were until you actually get a real raise. But the figures I was going to mention—in 1977 the average weekly wage in America was $189. By 1985 that had gone to $299. That sounds like a pretty hefty raise, doesn't it? But if you count that 299 in 1977 dollars, without the intervening inflation, the 299 was only equal to $171 in the 1977 purchasing power. And yet think how many tax brackets that 189 to 299 had taken you up, so that the Government could profit by your bad fortune. Well, thanks to the hard work of Steve and Jim and Larry and others, we also dramatically brought down the inheritance tax so families, especially family farmers and small businessmen, won't lose through taxation what they spent a lifetime building.

Now it's time for step two. Our taxes are still too high. The system is unfair, as I've just pointed out, and too complicated. We propose to overhaul the system from top to bottom, bringing down the tax rates, simplifying the process, and making it more fair. Now, some of the Washington cynics who are opposing this say that you don't really care. I say it's time for a change. Can we count on your help to get the job done? [*Applause*] Thank you, you just made my day. I've always had the sneaking suspicion that not only can Americans run their own affairs better than government can, they can probably run the Government better than the bureaucrats and politicians.

You know, I've read a lot of the constitutions of other countries, including the Soviet Constitution. And I was amazed to find that it has a lot of things in there that it promises, that our own Constitution promises. Of course, they don't keep those promises over there, but they're in there. But then, I was trying to figure out, what is the great difference between our two constitutions? And for these young people, if they've ever wondered, I want them to listen clearly. All those other constitutions I read said, we, the government allow you, the people, the following rights and privileges. Our Constitution says, we, the people, will allow the Government to do the following things, and nothing more than we have allowed them.

Now, some of the important issues that we face as a people concern our own national security. During the last decade we permitted our military strength to erode.

The Soviets, at the same time, rushed ahead with one of the most massive peacetime strategic and conventional buildups in history. No one in a free country likes to spend money on weapons. I'd much rather see that money left in the hands of those who work for it, but as long as I'm President, I will not see our free country relegated to a position of weakness or inferiority to any other country. Now, this does not have to mean, necessarily, more and more weapons. One way out is reaching arms agreements which will reduce the number of nuclear weapons threatening mankind to equal and verifiable levels. If we're resolute in our search for an agreement while, at the same time, firm in protecting our own interests, arms reduction can be a reality. But let's not kid ourselves, progress in this arena will not come from weakness or vacillation. If the United States negotiates with anyone, it must be from a position of strength.

As the world has been reminded repeatedly in recent weeks, we're involved in a major research effort to see if it is feasible to build a system, a security space shield, which would protect us against missile attacks, against those giant intercontinental ballistic missiles. This program is an historic turning point. For the first time, energy and resources are being put to use in an attempt to find new technology that is aimed at saving lives. If we're successful, it will improve the opportunity for arms reduction because missiles, no longer the ultimate weapon they are today, will be more negotiable. You wouldn't know it from what they've been saying about the American research effort, but the Sviets have had an expensive, ongoing strategic defense research program of their own for years before we ever started such a thing. Well, the idea of using American technological genius to develop a system to protect us against nuclear missiles is moral and in the fundamental interest of the United States and our allies and the cause of peace. We will not bargain this research and testing program away when we get to Geneva.

Technological advances, like developing a space shield, offer us new options. Yet we should never forget that our independence and freedom ultimately depend on our courage, determination, and strength of character. And I think there's reason for optimism here, too. There is a new patriotism alive in our country. I've been in a few schools recently, doing what I am doing here and talking to some students. And I've been on a few campuses recently, and I've seen something that back when I was Governor and those rioting days were going on that I haven't seen. And I have to tell you, as you look at these young people up here, I have come to the conclusion the 21st century is going to be in good hands.

There's a new patriotism alive in our country. And, something about which I'm most proud, those brave men and women who are defending our way of life have no doubt that their fellow countrymen appreciate their dedication. As a former marine, Steve knows how important that is. He understands that the fellows who intercepted those terrorists last week need to know that we are behind them all the way. And I can tell you, I'm mighty proud of the job they did, as I know you are. They didn't have more than an hour's notice, and yet out there over the Mediterranean, with all the aerial traffic that is going on in that area, in the dark of night, they were able to pick out the target plane and persuade it to land where they wanted it to land. Any time, now and then, if you see someone in uniform—it only takes a couple of steps out of the way—you might want to say hello and give them a smile and tell them how proud we are. Do you know that today we have in our military the finest young men and women that I think we've ever had? As a matter of fact, we have the highest percentage of the military that are high school graduates that we have ever had in our nation's history—91 percent are graduates.

We're building an America that is confident and proud, where every citizen enjoys the fruits of peace and prosperity. Steve Symms and I know that our greatest days are still ahead. There's no limit to what free men and women can do, and there's no limit to how far America can go.

Thank you all. God bless you, and send these fellows back. Thank you very much.

Note: The President spoke at 12:05 p.m. at the Morrison Center for the Performing Arts at Boise State University. He was introduced by Senator Symms. Following his remarks, the President attended a reception at the center for major donors to Senator Symms' reelection campaign. He then traveled to Milwaukee, WI.

Remarks at a Fundraising Dinner for Senator Robert W. Kasten, Jr., in Milwaukee, Wisconsin
October 15, 1985

Thank you, Bob, and ladies and gentlemen here on the dais with me and all of you, thank you very much. You know, in the business that I used to be in, I don't think I can top what's already happened here. I should maybe take a bow and leave.

But it's great to be back here in the great city of Milwaukee. I noticed on the way that there were some protesters outside. Bob, I always think of protesters as a good luck sign. We had them all through last fall's campaign, and as I remember that election turned out fair to middling. [*Laughter*] Now, that means, then, that 1986 is going to be a victory year for Bob Kasten, too. I just know that a State whose motto is "Forward" and whose official song is "On Wisconsin" is going to want a fighter, a man with bold vision for the future and the imagination, willpower, and just plain guts to take us there. And that man is Bob Kasten. He's just one of the best Senators your State has ever had. Incidentally, I want you to know that I have a few little pangs, too, when I said, "On Wisconsin." I played football south and a little west of here, Dixon, Illinois, in our high school. And like so many high schools, our song was "Onward Dixon," and it sounded an awful lot like "On Wisconsin"—[*laughter*]—in both lyrics and music.

Well, in the battle to control Federal spending and make our tax system fairer, as Bob was telling you, Bob is leading the charge. He's effective because he works hard, knows the issues inside and out, and really cares about the people of Wisconsin. And when it comes to delivering for Wisconsin and America, you can count on Bob Kasten. He'll always come through for you. Wisconsin needs Bob Kasten, but you know that already. I'm here to tell you America needs him, too. Bob has been a leader in America's economic renaissance, keeping our nation on an upward path of economic growth and prosperity. You know, I've heard that there is a new version of Trivial Pursuit, that game; it's called the economist's edition. In this one there are 100 questions, 3,000 answers. [*Laughter*] But Bob has learned one lesson well from history: The one great nonanswer in economics is tax increases.

Tax rates in this country long ago passed the point where they became counterproductive, stunting economic growth and actually bringing in less revenue than the tax rate cuts that spur growth and draw investment out of wasteful loopholes and back into productive economy. Look at the effect of our first across-the-board 25-percent tax cut. Now, I've heard some voices of the cynics in Washington suggesting that that contributed to the deficits. Not on your life! First of all, that was the principal cause of the economic recovery that we've been having. But second of all, would it interest you to know that the revenues for government have increased as the rates were reduced. Everything—you know, it was a 3-year installment plan—our program, economic program—and finally, it was all in place. And so, 1984 was really the first year when all the elements were there so you would see what had been happening—and the tax revenues were increasing at a rapid pace. In the first 11 months of fiscal '85, this year, Federal revenues grew a remarkable 10 percent, and that's quite unusual.

Let me suggest that over the long haul, the Federal Government simply can't raise revenue any faster than by cutting tax rates and then cutting tax rates again. It stimulates everybody to do better and more

people go to work. You know, as the great Yogi Berra once said, "You can observe a lot just by watching." [*Laughter*] He's full of those. [*Laughter*]

Well, Bob Kasten knows these issues inside out, and that's why he's in the forefront of the fight for our tax overhaul. He's going to make sure that we get a tax system that's profamily, profairness, and progrowth. And incidentally, in the House just a short time ago, the Democratic-dominated committee having to do with youth and family and all said that, in their study of all the tax proposals before the Congress, this one is the most profamily. And that's one good reason I'm confident that come November 1986, the people of Wisconsin are going to say, "Six more years for Bob Kasten in the United States Senate." Bob knows that the economy is more than numbers; the economy is people, their hopes and dreams, their hard work, and their faith. He knows that high taxes are more than just an economic mistake; they're a human mistake. They destroy our dreams; they dash our hopes; they make our hard work futile; and they undermine our faith. And he knows that America's economic renaissance didn't come about through government programs; it is the spirit of America unleashed, a spirit that knows no bounds, that can scale any heights.

If I had to give just one brief phrase as to what was at the bottom of and the best description of what our economic program was beginning in 1981 is: We just tried to get government out of your way. I mentioned a moment ago about what tax cuts, I thought, had done in regard to the recovery. Well, we have had one of the strongest economic expansions in our nation's history. We have helped put nearly 8½ million more people to work—new jobs—in this country in the last 34 months alone. And after trailing behind so much in the years just immediately following World War II, when our Marshall plan had set up the economies of so many other countries, now a Japanese study shows that United States plant and equipment is, today, newer than Japan's, and that's for the first time since World War II. And that came about because more businesses and industries and more people had more money to invest. And that's what does it.

Just a few years ago, there was only $39 million available in venture capital in the United States. And last year there was $4 billion of venture capital available for investment in business and industry in the United States. America is the world's leader in job creation, growth, and technological innovation. And I can tell you it was a big thrill for me just recently—well, last year's economic summit with the other six countries that are in that summit with us—and when I got there—and instead of them jumping on me for this or that or the value of the dollar, they said, "What explains the American miracle?" And so, I had the pleasure of sitting there and telling them how they, too, could have a miracle—cut spending in their governments and do away with some of the rigidities that were harassing their economic programs and their private industry. And they all listened. Now, we'll see if they'll do it. [*Laughter*]

Let's continue to build the American dream by passing a fair, progrowth American tax plan this year, in 1985. And just as a free society needs laws, so, too, a free economy needs the assurance of a stable dollar, a dollar that will be worth as much tomorrow as it is today, so that savings can't be stolen away by inflation and Americans can invest in the future with confidence. This stealing away of the people's money—and government contributed to that also. In 1977 the average income in the United States was—the weekly wage—was $189; this year that average is $299. But wait a minute. Let me tell you what's been done to all of you—this was throughout those years, that great spiral of inflation—well, that $299 in '77 dollars has only $171 as compared to the 189 in 1977. And yet by going up to $299, how many tax brackets did you go up through? That's why we've indexed the tax brackets for the future, so government can never again make a profit on your cost-of-living pay raises.

Now, we've got another thing in Washington that's cooking right now. Let's put the force of law behind the deficit reduction with the Gramm-Rudman-Hollings bill. Last week the Republican Senate, with the support of a majority of Democrat Senators,

adopted the Gramm-Rudman-Hollings deficit reduction plan. This farsighted legislation puts in place a fair, enforceable method of reducing the budget deficit by equal amounts each year, mandating a balanced budget by the end of 1980—or 1990; I'm sorry. 1980 is kind of Freudian with me; something happened then, too. [*Laughter*]

Well, Friday the House of Representatives took a step in the right direction, but we still have a large hurdle to get over. I know that there are some critics now that are saying this is some kind of gimmick. Well, ever since 1981 we have been trying to whittle at the deficits by attacking government spending. And then, those who wanted to defend particular pet spending programs—Senator Russell Long once said, you know, "The game in Washington is don't cut you and don't cut me, cut that fellow behind the tree." [*Laughter*] Well, then, every year we've had the same battle, trying to whittle down spending to reduce the deficits.

What this bill does is make this a 5-year program, a program in which we start a deficit decline that by 1990 will bring us to the even stage. And, then, I pray that we'll have the sense to have a constitutional amendment that says from 1990 on the Federal Government will not spend more than it takes in. You see what this does now? This makes it so that somebody that tries to bust the budget now in the future will be going against a plan that has been put into effect by law. And we won't have to every year fight that same futile and frustrating fight with the big spenders. In a few days, the House-Senate conferees will meet to iron out their differences. The American people I don't think will tolerate any attempt to scuttle this last, best hope to come to grips with the budget deficit. The days of the big spender are over. The House-Senate conference committee should realize the American people are watching.

America's future never held more promise, but we need Bob Kasten in the Senate to make that promise real. Our agenda is full: fair taxes, balanced budgets, and, beyond the economy, excellence in education and the end to government-sanctioned discrimination and, important above all, using our technology, in which we're the world's leader, to make peace more secure for generations to come.

I know you've heard all about it. First of all, a hostile voice was raised and called our defense plan that we're working on Star Wars. Well, it isn't anything of the kind. Then, we've been going by SDI, which is the Strategic Defense Initiative. Well, I tell you what I prefer to call it. It is the strategic space shield, a nonlethal weapon that is not going to kill people, but that is going to kill antiballistic missiles before they can reach their target. Today our deterrent, our war deterrent, is based on: They have missiles, we have missiles; and if they fire their missiles and kill millions of our people, we will fire ours and kill millions of theirs. That's no way to go. How long can the American people stand still for a strategy that threatens so many innocent lives? But our goal is that once we can prove and establish—we can with this research—that the kind of weapon we're talking about, a defensive weapon aimed at missiles, is effective, then, we really can do away with nuclear weapons in the world once and for all, because they'll be useless from then on.

We're searching for the most cost-effective means of providing for our defense based on rapid advances in technology, and that's the American way. We are high tech and the highest tech in the world today. Computers that, not so long ago, used to fill whole rooms and cost millions of dollars are today outperformed by little silicon chips smaller than your thumbnail and costing only a fraction of a penny. Technology is getting more productive and cheaper every day. Doesn't a cost-effective defense, allied with high technology, make sense in this day and age? The semiconductor industry is discovering a world of seemingly unlimited possibility in the infinitely small recesses of a grain of sand. Our technological achievements of the past few years are one of the greatest stories ever told, and if we can bring this great resource of knowledge and wisdom to bear in creating a more secure and peaceful world, it may be one of the greatest blessings that mankind has ever received.

Well, it's been a real pleasure coming— oh, I'm going to interrupt for a second and just tell you something. We have a new head at the United Nations, you know, former General Walters. And General Walters recently—he's Ambassador Walters now—was on a mission for us to China. And there they were speaking critically to him of this strategic shield that I have mentioned, and they didn't seem very optimistic about it. And then one of the government officials there said to him, "We have a problem here in China that we often speak of." He said, "If a man has invented a spear that can penetrate any shield, and another man has invented an impenetrable shield and they meet, what happens?" And Ambassador Walters said, "I don't know the answer to that. But," he said, "I do know what happens if a man with a spear that can penetrate anything meets a man who doesn't have a shield at all—I know what happens then. They sort of changed their mind about our defense program."

Well, it's been a real pleasure coming out to this beautiful State once again. Pretty soon I am going to have to be getting back to Washington, and I'm just hoping that the people of Wisconsin will send Bob Kasten back there to keep me company. Bob is the Senator Wisconsin needs to represent it into the 1990's, and he's the kind of leader America needs to carry us proudly into the 21st century. So, you elect Bob Kasten in 1986 and that would really make my day. And it would make America's day, too.

And I just want to thank you all. God bless you, and we'll both be there to thank you in Washington.

Note: The President spoke at 6:32 p.m. in Bruce Hall at the Milwaukee Convention Center. He was introduced by Senator Kasten. Prior to his remarks, the President attended a reception at the center for major donors to Senator Kasten's reelection campaign. Following his remarks, the President returned to Washington, DC.

Proclamation 5390—National Forest Products Week, 1985
October 15, 1985

By the President of the United States of America

A Proclamation

From the dense stands of hardwoods in New England to the towering redwoods of California, America has been blessed with an abundance of forestland. There is much to praise in the beauty of our forests and much to be thankful for. John Muir once said of the forests of America that they "must have been a great delight to God; for they were the best He ever planted." They are also a great boon to man. Besides their beauty, they act as protectors of our drinking water and wildlife and provide us with abundant opportunities for recreation. They bring us cooling shade in summer and break the icy winter winds.

America's forests also are an unparalleled resource. For the past three centuries they have contributed greatly to the economic and social development of our Nation. From our forests come the lumber we use to build our houses and the paper for the books, magazines, and newspapers we read. Though we may sometimes overlook the fact in this age of technological breakthroughs, wood is an enduring and invaluable part of our everyday lives.

The Pennsylvania Dutch have a saying: "We don't inherit the land from our ancestors, we borrow it from our children." That is a profound insight we cannot afford to ignore. Fortunately, Americans have proven time and again that we see ourselves as the stewards of this abundant land of ours. We well understand that we cannot take our forests for granted. From the time of Gifford Pinchot, the Nation's first American-born trained forester, Americans have sought and found ways to insure the health and improve the management of our forests. Today, we have reached a point where the growth of our forests exceeds the harvest. This has come about thanks to the continuing efforts of our Nation's forestry

and natural resource schools, hundreds of trained foresters, and other resource specialists, working with private firms and local, State, and Federal agencies such as the United States Forest Service.

Through the success of sustained-yield forestry, Americans can enjoy the splendor of our Nation's woodlands, as well as benefit from an abundant supply of the numerous products that come from trees. The forests provide jobs for millions of people, and they afford a healthy environment for the many who take to the woods in their leisure time. Even though forests provide us with a variety of products today, we will still have—thanks to proper management—millions of acres of forest as a living legacy for generations to come.

To promote greater awareness and appreciation of the manifold benefits of our forest resources to our economy and the world economy, the Congress, by Public Law 86–753 (36 U.S.C. 163), has designated the week beginning on the third Sunday in October of each year as National Forest Products Week.

Now, Therefore, I, Ronald Reagan, President of the United States of America, do hereby proclaim the week beginning October 20, 1985, as National Forest Products Week and request that all Americans express their appreciation for the Nation's forests through suitable activities.

In Witness Whereof, I have hereunto set my hand this fifteenth day of October, in the year of our Lord nineteen hundred and eighty-five, and of the Independence of the United States of America the two hundred and tenth.

RONALD REAGAN

[*Filed with the Office of the Federal Register, 4:20 p.m., October 16, 1985*]

Note: The proclamation was released by the Office of the Press Secretary on October 16.

Proclamation 5391—Veterans Day, 1985
October 15, 1985

*By the President of the United States
of America*

A Proclamation

Veterans Day is a special day for all Americans. It is a time to reflect on the many sacrifices and the great achievements of the brave men and women who have defended our freedom, and to salute them for their loyal and valiant service.

The blessings of liberty which our ancestors secured for us, and which we still enjoy, are ours only because, in each generation, there have been men and women willing to bear the hardships and sacrifices of serving in the military forces we need to preserve our freedom.

These fine men and women have not sought glory for themselves, but peace and freedom for all. They exemplify the spirit that has preserved us as a great Nation, and they deserve our recognition for everything they have done. With a spirit of pride and gratitude, we honor and remember our veterans today.

I urge all Americans to recognize the valor and sacrifice of our veterans through appropriate public ceremonies and private prayers. I urge the families and friends of our sick and disabled veterans to visit them and extend to them a grateful Nation's promise that they will not be forgotten. I ask all Americans, whether or not a family member or friend is a veteran, to find ways to pay a special sign of respect to a veteran in their community on this day.

I also call upon Federal, State, and local government officials to display the flag of the United States and to encourage and participate in patriotic activities throughout the country. I invite the business community, churches, schools, unions, civic and fraternal organizations, and the media to support the national observance with suitable commemorative expressions and programs.

In order that we may pay meaningful tribute to those men and women who proudly served in our Armed Forces, Congress has provided (5 U.S.C. 6103(a)) that November 11 shall be set aside each year as a legal public holiday to honor America's veterans.

Now, Therefore, I, Ronald Reagan, President of the United States of America, do hereby invite the American people to join with me in a fitting salute on Veterans Day, 1985, Monday, November 11, 1985. Let us resolve anew to keep faith with those whose love of country has placed their names on a well-deserved roll of honor.

In Witness Whereof, I have hereunto set my hand this fifteenth day of October, in the year of our Lord nineteen hundred and eighty-five, and of the Independence of the United States of America the two hundred and tenth.

RONALD REAGAN

[*Filed with the Office of the Federal Register, 4:21 p.m., October 16, 1985*]

Note: *The proclamation was released by the Office of the Press Secretary on October 16.*

Proclamation 5392—OPERATION: Care and Share, 1985
October 15, 1985

*By the President of the United States
of America*

A Proclamation

Since the days of our Founding Fathers, the American people have banded together to meet the needs of their communities. This spirit of neighbor helping neighbor is one of the Nation's finest traditions. Generosity and awareness of community needs are traits that have kept our country strong. Voluntary service remains as important today as it was in earlier decades, and personal involvement lends a warmth to giving and sharing that no government or institution by itself can.

During the holiday season, I call upon all Americans to join in partnership with others to help provide food for those who are in need. The agriculture and food industries, churches, civic and fraternal organizations, corporations, and nonprofit groups can each play a vital role in reaching out to their fellow Americans. Let the caring and sharing that stems from private sector initiatives reach out across this great land of ours like the warming rays of dawn and bring to all the blessings of compassion and goodwill, to those who give as much as to those who receive.

Now, Therefore, I, Ronald Reagan, President of the United States of America, do hereby proclaim the forthcoming holiday season to be a time in which partnerships are forged under OPERATION: Care and Share. Further, I proclaim that November 25, 1985, should be a day upon which each of us should focus upon our fellow citizens and collect and distribute food to those in need.

In Witness Whereof, I have hereunto set my hand this fifteenth day of October, in the year of our Lord nineteen hundred and eighty-five, and of the Independence of the United States of America the two hundred and tenth.

RONALD REAGAN

[Filed with the Office of the Federal Register, 4:22 p.m., October 16, 1985]

Note: The proclamation was released by the Office of the Press Secretary on October 16.

Statement by Principal Deputy Press Secretary Speakes on Free and Fair Trade
October 16, 1985

President Reagan is today instructing Ambassador Yeutter to initiate proceedings under the General Agreement on Tariffs and Trade (GATT) against wheat export subsidies offered by the European Community. He is also asking Ambassador Yeutter to begin an investigation under section 301 of the Trade Act of 1974 of Korea's practices for protecting intellectual property rights.

The President is also pleased to announce today that consultations between the American Institute in Taiwan and the Coordination Council for North American Affairs have resulted in an agreement by Taiwan to improve access to its market for American beer, wine, and cigarettes. Ambassador Yeutter will report to the President by December 31, 1985, on Taiwan's progress in implementing these changes. This market-opening step by Taiwan is particularly gratifying because it represents the kind of response we would hope to receive from all nations to our request for elimination of trading practices that prohibit free and fair competition between the goods and services produced by all nations.

Through the actions we have already taken and the further actions we are announcing today, we are asking all nations to live up to their responsibility to preserve and enhance free trade. Our objective continues to be to enlarge and enhance the world trading system for the benefit of all.

Note: Larry M. Speakes read the statement to reporters at 10 a.m. in the Briefing Room at the White House. Also present to answer reporters' questions was Michael B. Smith, Acting U.S. Trade Representative.

Message to the Congress Transmitting the Annual Report on Radiation Control for Health and Safety
October 16, 1985

To the Congress of the United States:

In accordance with Section 360D of the Public Health Service Act (42 U.S.C. 263 1), I am transmitting the report of the Department of Health and Human Services regarding the administration of the Radiation Control for Health and Safety Act. The report discusses the progress of the Food and Drug Administration's (FDA) Center for Devices and Radiological Health toward the accomplishment of its objectives during calendar year 1984.

The report recommends that Section 360D of the Public Health Service Act that requires the completion of this annual report be repealed. All of the information found in this report is available to the Congress on a more immediate basis through congressional committee oversight and budget hearings and the FDA Annual Report. This annual report serves little useful purpose and diverts Agency resources from more productive activities.

RONALD REAGAN

The White House,
October 16, 1985.

Note: The report was entitled "1984 Annual Report on the Administration of the Radiation Control for Health and Safety Act of 1968, Public Law 90–602."

Proclamation 5393—World Food Day, 1985
October 16, 1985

By the President of the United States of America

A Proclamation

One of the most encouraging results of World Food Day, which the Food and Agriculture Organization (FAO) of the United Nations inaugurated in 1980, has been the rising tempo of public interest in the world food situation. Last year in the United States alone, millions of people in more than 3,000 communities participated in a wide variety of World Food Day activities.

Yet even this great outpouring paled before the American response to the terrible famine in Africa, especially in Ethiopia and Sudan.

For many years, the United States has shared its agricultural abundance and technical expertise with nations in need. We have led the effort to alleviate world hunger. Yet it is clear that charitable assistance in the form of emergency food deliveries, no matter how extensive, treats only the symptoms of malnourishment, not the causes.

The persistent problem of underfed people has deep roots that unfortunately are too often nourished by government policies that discourage economic growth and progress, put obstacles in the way of international trade, and inhibit a free market system. Governments dictate urban food prices at the expense of farmer income, and the farmer's judgement on the type of crops to plant and harvest is ignored.

Although some American farmers have recently suffered economic reverses, this Nation has not wavered in its commitment to aid the developing nations of the world to improve their agricultural methods and to provide food relief during emergencies. Our assistance has paid dividends to the recipient countries. Since 1954, when the Eisenhower Food For Peace program was adopted by the United States, food production per person has increased an average of 21 percent in the developing countries. Food consumption in the same areas has

1253

increased an average of 7.5 percent per person since 1963. We are especially proud that America has taken the lead in the promotion and distribution of oral rehydration therapy. This simple technology saved the lives of half a million children around the world last year.

In recognition of the continuing problem and of the need to continue focusing public awareness on means to alleviate world hunger, the Congress, by Senate Joint Resolution 72, has designated October 16, 1985, as "World Food Day" and authorized and requested the President to issue a proclamation in observance of that day.

Now, Therefore, I, Ronald Reagan, President of the United States of America, do hereby proclaim October 16, 1985, as World Food Day, and I call upon the people of the United States to observe that day with appropriate activities to explore ways in which our Nation can further contribute to the elimination of hunger in the world.

In Witness Whereof, I have hereunto set my hand this sixteenth day of October, in the year of our Lord nineteen hundred and eighty-five, and of the Independence of the United States of America the two hundred and tenth.

RONALD REAGAN

[*Filed with the Office of the Federal Register, 4:23 p.m., October 16, 1985*]

Remarks at a Dinner Honoring Senator Russell B. Long of Louisiana
October 16, 1985

Ladies and gentlemen, one of the things I've been trying to figure out is why anyone as young as Russell Long would want to retire. [*Laughter*] Now, of course, that's only a cue for a story I want to tell you, because, you know, in my position anymore I have to be very careful of whether there is any ethnic note to any jokes that I tell, but I find that I can still tell jokes about people getting old. [*Laughter*] They know I'm not picking on anyone. So, this doesn't have any bearing on his being too young to retire.

But it is a story about an elderly couple who were getting ready for bed one night, and she said, "Oh, I just am so hungry for ice cream, and there isn't any in the house." And he said, "I'll get some." "Oh," she said, "you're a dear." And she said, "Vanilla with chocolate sauce." He says, "Vanilla with chocolate sauce." She says, "Write it down. Now, you'll forget, dear." He says, "I won't forget." She said, "With some whipped cream on top." And he said, "Vanilla with chocolate sauce, whipped cream on top." And she said, "And a cherry." And he said, "And a cherry on top." Well, she said, "Please write it down. I know you'll forget." And he said, "I won't forget. Vanil-

la with chocolate sauce, whipped cream, and a cherry on top." And away he went. By the time he got back, she was already in bed, and he handed her the paper bag. She opened it and there was a ham sandwich. [*Laughter*] And she said, "I told you to write it down. You forgot the mustard." [*Laughter*]

But, ladies and gentlemen, I'm delighted that I could be here tonight to salute one of the most important presences in the United States Senate for, yes, over 36 years. There's one thing about being able to talk first, and before you all have dinner because then no one can—well, maybe I'm taking some material away from some others—[*laughter*]. But the simple facts about Russell Long are that he's the son of an American political legend. He ran a celebrated campaign for student body president at Louisiana State University. He earned four battle stars in his country's service in World War II; was elected in 1948 to the United States Senate, and that was the day before he turned 30; and he became one of the most powerful Senators in that body's history, including a committee chairmanship and a leadership post.

Now, these are the simple facts, but, you

know, in a curious way, they don't really tell the whole story. You see, for those who really know Washington well, Russell Long is regarded as one of the most skillful legislators, compromisers, and legislative strategists in history. Lyndon Johnson, Richard Nixon, and many others who knew the Congress intimately fully appreciated the enormous weight and power that Russell Long wielded on Capitol Hill and the tremendous savvy that he brought to any legislative enterprise. For example, Senator Long is famed for his capacity to anticipate the truly critical moments in the legislative process. He was the one legislator who had his mind on the conference, one observer noted, when the others were worrying about the floor debate. Indeed, it's true that this son of a political legend has become a legend on his own.

Russell Long is not one of the truly important Senators of our time simply because he's a skillful statesman or was a fine political mind. He also has a great capacity for personal friendship and a warmth and candor that has won him many friends. For example—and I shouldn't be telling this until after the session is over—he used to ask, and I am quoting him, "What is a loophole?" [*Laughter*] And he answered, "That is something that benefits the other guy. If it benefits you, it's tax reform." [*Laughter*]

But to be serious, we're not here this evening simply because Russell Long was and is a distinguished and important United States Senator. We're here tonight because Russell Long, throughout one of the longest and most substantive careers in public life, has been a friend of ours, a friend of his country, and of the American people. Russell, I assure you that I speak not only for your friends on Capitol Hill but for the people of Louisiana and for the American people who say "thank you" for your devotion to duty, for the years of service to your country. You won four battle stars making amphibious landings in North Africa, Italy, and southern France. And if the truth be known, you won many more battle stars in your country's service on Capitol Hill. I want you to know how grateful we are to you. And, Carolyn, I especially want to thank you for your years of devotion to your family and your country.

Thank you all, and God bless you.

Note: The President spoke at 8:17 p.m. at the Madison Hotel.

Nomination of Charles Roger Carlisle for the Rank of Ambassador While Serving as United States Negotiator on Textile Matters
October 17, 1985

The President today announced his intention to nominate Charles Roger Carlisle, of Vermont, for the rank of Ambassador during his tenure of service as United States Negotiator on Textile Matters in the Office of the United States Trade Representative. He would succeed Richard H. Imus.

Mr. Carlisle entered the Foreign Service in 1956 as an international economist in the Trade Agreements Division in the Bureau of Economic Affairs. He was political officer in Bogotá, Colombia (1958–1960), and commercial officer in Melbourne, Australia (1960–1962). In 1962–1963 he attended advanced economic studies at Harvard University and was assigned as minerals officer in Santiago, Chile, in 1963. Mr. Carlisle then returned to the Department as an economic planning officer in the Office of Cuban Affairs (1963–1966) and senior staff assistant to the Assistant Secretary for Inter-American Affairs (1966–1967). In 1967 he was economic officer at the United States Mission to the North Atlantic Treaty Organization in Paris and Brussels. In the Department he was chief of the Industrial and Strategic Materials Division in the Bureau of Economic and Business Affairs (1967–1968) and special assistant to the Under Secretary of State for Economic Affairs (1969–1970). He resigned from the Foreign Service in 1970. In 1970–1971 he was director of the international action branch of the United Nations Conference on Trade and Development and chairman of the Lead-Zinc Producers Committee in 1971–1974. He was vice president of St. Joe Minerals Corp. in 1974–1983 and president of Man-Made Fibers Producers Association, Inc., in 1983–1984. In 1984 he became special negotiator in the Office of the Assistant Secre-

tary for Economic and Business Affairs, Department of State.

He graduated from the University of Cincinnati (B.A., 1953) and Harvard University (M.P.A., 1963). His foreign languages are Spanish and French. He is married to the former H. Nadeane Howard, and they have two children. He was born April 11, 1929, in Marietta, OH.

Nomination of Jerry Lee Calhoun To Be a Member of the Federal Labor Relations Authority, and Designation as Chairman
October 17, 1985

The President today announced his intention to nominate Jerry Lee Calhoun to be a member of the Federal Labor Relations Authority for the remainder of the term expiring July 29, 1987. He would succeed Barbara Jean Mahone. Upon his confirmation, the President intends to designate him Chairman.

Mr. Calhoun is presently serving as Acting Assistant Secretary and Principal Deputy Assistant Secretary of Defense for Manpower, Installations and Logistics, Department of Defense. Previously he was Deputy Assistant Secretary of Civilian Per-

sonnel Policy and Requirements in the Office of the Assistant Secretary of Defense (Manpower, Installations and Logistics). Prior to joining the Department of Defense, he was manager of industrial and labor relations with the Boeing commercial airplane company in Seattle, WA. He also taught on the faculty of the University of Washington School of Business.

He graduated from Seattle University (B.A., 1967) and the University of Washington (M.A., 1975). He has two children and resides in Washington, DC. He was born September 9, 1943, in Ludlow, MA.

Nomination of Gerald Ralph Riso To Be an Assistant Secretary of the Interior
October 17, 1985

The President today announced his intention to nominate Gerald Ralph Riso to be an Assistant Secretary of the Interior (Policy, Budget and Administration). He would succeed J. Robinson West.

Mr. Riso most recently served as vice president of the health care division of Korn-Ferry International in New York City (1984–1985). Previously, he was at the Department of Justice as Deputy Commissioner of the Immigration and Naturalization Service in 1982–1984; vice president, health and medical division, at Booz-Allen & Ham-

ilton in New York City in 1978–1982; with Touche Ross & Co. in New York City in 1977–1978; managing director of the American Lung Association in 1974–1977; and managing director of Knight, Gladieux & Smith in 1973–1974.

Mr. Riso graduated from Lafayette College (B.A., 1953) and Wharton School of Business and Finance, University of Pennsylvania (M.B.A., 1956). He is married, has four children, and resides in Scarsdale, NY. He was born January 31, 1930, in New York City.

Designation of Charles D. Hobbs as Director of the Office of Policy Development
October 17, 1985

Charles D. Hobbs, Deputy Assistant to the President for Policy Development, has been designated as the Director of the Office of Policy Development, replacing Dr. Roger B. Porter, who has left the administration to return to the faculty at Harvard University.

Mr. Hobbs has served on the White House staff since April 1984. From 1972 to 1984, he was president and principal consultant of Charles D. Hobbs, Inc., a California-based public policy and management consulting firm. His company served a wide variety of Federal, State, and local government agencies in the development of public service programs and management plans. Mr. Hobbs was chief deputy director of social welfare in California from 1970 to 1972 and also served on then-Governor Reagan's tax limitation and local government task forces in 1973 and 1974. He was a delegate to the Economic Summit Conference on Inflation in 1975. Mr. Hobbs designed and managed the development of computer-based information and command/control systems from 1958 to 1970.

He graduated from Northwestern University (B.S., 1955) and was a Woodrow Wilson fellow at UCLA in 1958 and 1959. He was the distinguished military graduate at Northwestern in 1955 and served 3 years as an officer in the U.S. Air Force. He was born September 2, 1933, in Kansas City, MO, and now resides in Arlington, VA.

Appointment of Donald A. Clarey as Special Assistant to the President and Deputy Director of the Office of Cabinet Affairs
October 17, 1985

The President today announced his intention to appoint Donald A. Clarey to be Special Assistant to the President and Deputy Director of the Office of Cabinet Affairs.

Mr. Clarey has served as Associate Director of the Office of Cabinet Affairs since August 1983. Previously he was a consultant to the State Department for the 1983 Williamsburg Summit of Industrialized Nations Task Force. Prior to joining the Reagan administration, Mr. Clarey served as administrative assistant to the majority leader of the New York State Senate from 1980 to 1983. In 1977–1980 he was a program associate in the office of the Senate majority leader. In both 1980 and 1982 he was a Republican/Conservative candidate for the New York State Assembly. From 1973 to 1976, he was executive assistant to the Director for Congressional Affairs at the Federal Energy Administration. In 1972 he served on the staff of Congressman Howard W. Robison (R-NY).

Mr. Clarey graduated from Union College (B.A., 1972) and the Kennedy School of Government at Harvard University (M.P.A., 1977). He is married to the former Wendy Allen and resides in Alexandria, VA. He was born on February 8, 1950, in Johnson City, NY.

Appointment of Deborah Steelman as Deputy Assistant to the President and Director of the Office of Intergovernmental Affairs
October 17, 1985

The President today announced his intention to appoint Deborah Steelman as Deputy Assistant to the President and Director of the Office of Intergovernmental Affairs.

Since April 1983, Ms. Steelman has been serving in the Office of Intergovernmental Affairs at the White House, handling policy matters. Ms. Steelman served as Director of Intergovernmental Affairs at the Environmental Protection Agency in 1983–1985. Previously, she was legislative director to Senator John Heinz of Pennsylvania; deputy director of the Missouri Department of Natural Resources under Governor Christopher S. (Kit) Bond; and campaign manager for the reelection effort of Attorney General John Ashcroft. She began her career as assistant public defender in Kansas City, MO.

She graduated from the University of Missouri (B.A., 1976; J.D., 1978). She was born February 4, 1955, in Salem, MO, and now resides in Alexandria, VA.

Appointment of Cecilia Cole McInturff as Special Assistant to the President for Political and Intergovernmental Affairs
October 17, 1985

The President today announced his intention to appoint Cecilia Cole McInturff as Special Assistant to the President for Political and Intergovernmental Affairs.

She currently serves at the White House in the Office of Intergovernmental Affairs, acting as liaison between the White House and State legislators. Ms. Cole McInturff served as director of communications for the National Republican Senatorial Committee in 1983–1984. Previously she served as press spokesman for Senator Bill Armstrong of Colorado.

She attended the University of Florida College of Journalism and Communications in 1974–1978. She is married and resides in Alexandria, VA. She was born November 19, 1956, in Ocala, FL.

Nomination of Robert Logan Clarke To Be Comptroller of the Currency
October 17, 1985

The President today announced his intention to nominate Robert Logan Clarke to be Comptroller of the Currency, Department of the Treasury, for a term of 5 years. He would succeed C.T. Conover.

Since 1968 Mr. Clarke has been an attorney with the law firm of Bracewell & Patterson in Houston, TX. He serves as head of the banking section of Bracewell & Patterson, which he formed in 1972. He is a director of Allied Beltway Bank in Houston and an advisory director of the Centerville State Bank in Centerville, TX. He served as a captain in the United States Army in 1966–1968.

He graduated from Rice University (B.A., 1963) and Harvard Law School (LL.B., 1966). He is married, has one child, and resides in Houston, TX. He was born June 29, 1942, in Tulsa, OK.

Remarks to Representatives of Ethnic and Fraternal Benefit Organizations During a White House Briefing on Tax Reform
October 17, 1985

Well, thank you all, and welcome to the White House. I just stopped and stuck my head in the door of a meeting that's going on down the hall you'd have liked very much. They range from about that high on up to that high. They were the Young Astronauts. This is the first anniversary of the Young Astronauts Program. Well, a special greeting to Virgil Dechant and Al Mazewski—two men that I know have done a great deal in support of our fair share tax plan.

Washington, I'm glad to say, is cooling off now that it's fall, but the battle for tax fairness is just beginning to heat up. As someone once said, government is too big and important to be left to the politicians. The same could be said of our struggle to overhaul our tax system. We need you, America needs you to get actively involved and to help get the message out to the American people and, through them, back to Congress that we want a progrowth, profairness, and profamily tax bill this year, in 1985.

I've been all around this country stumping for tax fairness, and everywhere I go, the American people enthusiastically embrace our proposals. I was thrilled to see a poll in USA Today recently—where I went to talk about our tax plan earlier this month; that was in Cincinnati. Support for America's fair share plan among those who had read or heard my explanation of what the plan does shot up 14 points to an overwhelming 68-percent majority. I have complained that I think one of the reasons there isn't more action from the people is that there just isn't enough information out there about what the plan will do. When the people hear all the facts, when they hear the case for tax fairness as well as the case against it, America's fair share tax plan wins a landslide victory. The American people know a good deal when they see one, but you have to show it to them first.

Now, I'd like to be able to visit every city and town in this country and talk about our fair share tax plan. I'd like to be able to go door to door and tell every American how our proposal will benefit them, but there's just not enough time if we're going to pass tax fairness in 1985. And that's why you were asked here to the White House today. We can't rely on the media to tell the good news of America's fair share tax plan to the American people. They've got all kinds of news to report and just can't take that on. But you represent ethnic and fraternal benefit organizations all across our country. You are the grassroots that everyone talks about. You are America. You can get the message out directly to the American people that if we want our nation to achieve its full potential, if we want America to be first in economic growth and technological innovation, if we want to save the American family from being crushed under the burden of Federal taxation, and if we want our children to have the bright and prosperous future they deserve, we must restructure our nation's tax system; we must pass America's fair share tax plan. I know you've had some briefings and some talk already, but I hope I won't be plowing plowed ground, but let me get into a few specifics of our plan.

First, we see no reason to start up a new tax on America's fraternal benefit organizations. We should be bolstering and encouraging, not taxing and discouraging these essential organizations that mean so much to the private life of our nation. But let me also tell you some of the specifics of how we plan to make it easier for families, because our profamily initiatives are the heart and soul of America's fair share tax plan. The historians Will and Ariel Durant once wrote that the family "is the nucleus of civilization." Well, they were right, but for the past several decades, the Federal Government has been treating the family almost as if it didn't matter. Throughout the great tax explosion of the sixties and the seventies, everybody with a paycheck got hit and hit hard by taxes, but those trying to raise families got clobbered. Not only did their taxes skyrocket, their personal exemption, the real value of the deduction they were allowed to take for themselves and each one of their dependents, was steadily being knocked down by inflation. In other words, families were getting a double whammy, a double tax hike.

It wouldn't be an exaggeration to say that the colossal growth of government over the last two decades was financed by raiding the dwindling bank accounts of America's families. If the personal exemption, which was $600 in 1948, had kept pace with inflation, it would be worth $2,700 today. So, there's a tax increase the people didn't even know was being imposed on them. We plan to almost double the current exemption to $2,000. We can't go all the way, but our plan would raise the exemption in order to make up for some of what the families lost over those years. To me, that's only fair, and what's fair is worth fighting for. And I hope you're with me on that. [Applause] Thank you.

Now, we are also increasing the standard deduction for joint returns to $4,000, and our proposal will mean that families as well as the elderly, the blind, and the disabled living at or below the poverty line will be completely scratched from the Federal income tax rolls. The United States Government will no longer tax families into poverty. Our profamily measures will mean that a family of four doesn't have to pay one single cent of Federal taxes on the first $12,000 of income. And because saving is so essential to families but so very difficult with all these expenses, we're expanding the tax-free savings accounts of the IRA's so that they are fully available to nonwage-earning spouses. We figure that the housewife is also working a full 40 hours a week and probably much more. So, let's have an end to treating homemakers like second-class citizens.

Our profamily initiatives are designed to make it affordable to raise families again. You shouldn't have to be affluent to experience the blessings of home life, and that's a right to which every American is entitled. I'm glad to say that the Democratic-controlled House Select Committee on Children, Youth, and Families has rated our tax proposal the most profamily tax proposal before the Congress, more profamily than any other proposal that's around and light years ahead of the present system. Now—and this goes beyond economics, although in my opinion profamily policies are the best economics there is—this gets to the moral code—or core of our nation. America has a responsibility to the future, and our children are our future. We're a nation of immigrants who've labored and sacrificed to give our children a better life, and we can't let big government, high tax policies take away what we've worked so hard to achieve.

You know, our forefathers got so riled up over a tea tax, among other things, that they started a revolution. Now, today we have a tax on families, a tax on achievement, success, and aspiration—a tax on the American dream. Well, I think it's time we had another revolution, a peaceful one this time, called America's fair share tax plan. This fair share tax plan is a gift that we owe to ourselves and to our children. And with your help, mobilizing support out there in the grassroots, we'll have it wrapped up by the holiday season, and then we'll really have something to celebrate on New Year's Day.

So, thank you all for being here. God bless you all. Thank you. When I first got here, a little 11-year-old girl wrote me a letter, and she told me all the things that I should do. And by golly, she had a pretty good grasp on what was needed. But I've always remembered her letter. She wound up and said, "Now get back over to the Oval Office and go to work." [Laughter]

Note: The President spoke at 1 p.m. in Room 450 of the Old Executive Office Building.

Remarks Following Discussions With Prime Minister Shimon Peres of Israel
October 17, 1985

The President. It has been a special pleasure for me to welcome Prime Minister Peres to the White House, both as a personal friend and the leader of the Government of Israel. It's a great honor for me to receive the Weizmann Institute's honorary degree of doctor of philosophy. The Weizmann is synonymous with humanitarianism and the pursuit of excellence. For Israel, the institute is a symbol of an old intellectual tradition that has survived even the ravages of the Holocaust. The institute made a magnificent contribution to the future state of Israel, helping to assure its leading role in the vanguard of peaceful democratic nations leading the world toward the 21st century. And I'm very pleased to have been honored by this award.

Our talks today have been in the tradition of the close regular dialog that we have with Israel, a reflection of the warm and enduring relationship between our two nations. In our talks, we paid special attention to two issues: our commitment to Israel's security and well-being and our shared desire to move forward together toward a just and lasting peace between Israel and all its Arab neighbors. Prime Minister Peres and I fully agreed to press ahead in this search. We recognize there are obstacles, significant obstacles to peace, but we also recognize that there is a better opportunity for real progress now than there has been for some time and a better chance than we may have for some time to come; much progress has already been made.

Prime Minister Peres has made clear Israel's desire for direct negotiations without preconditions, and King Hussein stated here at the White House on September 30 that he welcomes the prospect of beginning negotiations with Israel promptly and directly. This kind of determination and good faith gives the United States confidence that the hurdles to peace can be overcome. Prime Minister Peres and I are also fully agreed that a strong, secure Israel is a shared interest. In the year since the Prime Minister's last visit, Israel and the United States have strengthened and expanded our security cooperation, which furthers a number of common objectives, including the maintenance of Israel's qualitative military advantage against any combination of adversaries.

We also discussed the evil scourge of terrorism which has claimed so many Israeli, American, and Arab victims and has brought tragedy to many others. Terrorism is the cynical, remorseless enemy of peace, and it strikes most viciously whenever real progress seems possible. We need no further proof of this than the events of the last few weeks. The Prime Minister and I share a determination to see that terrorists are denied sanctuary and are justly punished. Furthermore, and just as important, Prime Minister Peres and I agreed that terrorism must not blunt our efforts to achieve peace in the Middle East.

Prime Minister Peres and I also have reviewed many other issues on our common agenda. We took stock with real satisfaction of what Israel and the United States have accomplished together. Among other things, we've concluded a free trade area agreement, the first of its kind for us. In this regard, I salute Prime Minister Peres and his government for their courage in adopting an economic reform program that holds promise if effectively implemented for leading Israel to strong and steady non-inflationary growth. We agreed last year that growth is the main objective. And we will continue to explore in our joint economic group and elsewhere ways to promote Israel's strong economic potential.

Mr. Prime Minister, I thank you very much for your visit. It's been an occasion to renew a friendship and to review and enhance the strength of our unique bilateral relationship.

The Prime Minister. Mr. President, I'm grateful for the opportunity of expressing to you the admiration and the gratitude of the people of Israel. In our country, pluralistic as it is, where the national consensus is reserved for very rare occasions, you have achieved it—an admiration of all parts in our country, all people, who came, really, to learn to know you and to admire you.

We admire your leadership because it gave American greatness a new dimension; because it has introduced a new solidarity to the free world; because it has enhanced the desire for knowledge in the realm of science; because it has demonstrated a moving friendship for the new and old Israel. On a personal note, may I add that one who has had to take decisions affecting the lives of young soldiers, I appreciate both your correct instinct and decisive reaction to the unfolding drama in the east Mediterranean last week as it was manifested in real leadership and real courage.

Twelve months ago, Mr. President, when we met here, I felt that I was standing at a new beginning. You then extended your support for some of Israel's ambitious plans. Since then, we have removed the Lebanese wall from the agenda of Arab-Israel relations. We tightened our belts in order to stabilize our economy, reduce inflation, and deficits. We have begun a process meant to transform the peace treaty into a viable precedent for the whole region—I'm referring to the peace treaty with Egypt. We have changed our policy on the West Bank. We confronted the agony of terrorism without losing hope that peace would destroy terror before terror would destroy peace. Today we stand ready to take bold steps in a no less challenging direction, and I trust, Mr. President, that we shall have the benefit of your continued support.

The first objective is the most challenging of all: making peace. With our hand of peace extended across the Jordanian River, we call upon our eastern neighbor to heed and accept this sincere invitation. We should not miss the opportunity of putting an end to belligerency and of entering honorable and direct negotiation. We are ready to meet without preconditions, without losing time, at any suitable location—be it in Amman, in Jerusalem, or Washington. We are prepared to consider any proposal put forward by the Jordanians. Let us bear the cost of peace in preference to the price of war. Our second objective is to move economically from stabilization to growth.

We are grateful for your continued support in reaching both objectives, particularly in the light of our heavy security burden and lack of natural resources, save for a highly motivated people. Finally, Mr. President, we would like to join hands with the United States in an appeal to the heart of our fellow men. We welcome the opportunity to participate in amplifying the voice of democracy and echoing its values as we address those who are denied its reality, yet yearn for it. In so doing, we reaffirm our commitment to strive for a world free of discrimination, free of oppression, free of terror.

Mr. President, Chaim Weizmann, a world-renowned scientist, was our first president. He believed that ancient prophecy and modern science, together reaching across the gulf of generations, could set our small nation on the road to development at its highest values. In recognition of your proven ability to lead a great country to even greater heights by seeking the new horizons of real and great promise, the Weizmann Institute, which has gained high repute, was proud to bestow on you, Mr. Ronald Reagan, an honorary doctorate. Your search for a more stable and safer world has unleashed human curiosity in pursuit of wisdom and knowledge as well as of untold opportunity.

Mr. President, as always, it was a great pleasure and honor to meet with you to discuss in a real friendly way and free spirit our common problems and hopes. And again, thank you for your support, and I'm sure we shall be able to cooperate in the future in the same good way that our two countries were working together for such a long period of time.

The President. The feeling is mutual.

The Prime Minister. Thank you very much.

———————

Reporter. Mr. President, Italy says we violated their airspace. Did we, sir? Italy, violated their airspace, plane.

The President. I'm not going to take questions or get into a debate on what took place. I am satisfied with what we did.

Q. Does the PLO still have a place in the

peace process?

Q. What would you expect——

Q. Should Hussein go ahead without the PLO?

The President. I'm not going to take your questions on these things.

Q. What about the Jordanian arms sale,

sir? Is Israel going to support us?

Note: The President spoke at 3:12 p.m. at the South Portico of the White House. Earlier, the President and the Prime Minister met in the Oval Office.

Proclamation 5394—National High-Tech Month, 1985
October 17, 1985

By the President of the United States of America

A Proclamation

National High-Tech Month provides an opportunity for all Americans to learn how technological advances contribute to our economic growth and rising standard of living and to reaffirm our national commitment to maintain the leadership of the United States in high-technology development. Technology is crucial to our physical well-being, a strong national defense, and economic growth. It is transforming not just industry, but medicine, agriculture, education, communications—indeed, virtually every field of human endeavor.

History has demonstrated that progress in technology is essential to maintaining competitiveness, creating new products, and improving productivity. Enhanced productivity lowers unit costs, thereby increasing profits and allowing industries to reduce prices and capture a larger share of the market. Technology-induced productivity gains help hold down inflation, make American products more competitive in world markets, and raise our standard of living.

I am calling upon all Americans to open themselves to the opportunities presented by the incorporation of technology into their lives and livelihoods. First, government policies should not penalize but rather improve incentives for the entrepreneurial development of new technology so critical to maintaining industrial leadership. Second, American business should redouble its efforts to channel investment into promising research and development projects. Third, American labor and management must recognize and welcome the opportunities provided in a high-technological

economy and actively cooperate in adapting to the changing work environment, availing themselves of the benefits to their working lives that will come with enhanced productivity and innovation.

Finally, we must pay attention to the education of American youth—education that will give them the skills and insights they need to grow and develop in a high-technology future. School systems from the elementary level to graduate school must conscientiously seek opportunities to educate our young people about the benefits of technology and to encourage development of the basic knowledge our citizens will require if they are to function successfully in tomorrow's world.

In recognition of the importance of high technology to our lives, the Congress, by House Joint Resolution 128, has designated the month of October 1985 as "National High-Tech Month" and authorized and requested the President to issue a proclamation in observance of this event.

Now, Therefore, I, Ronald Reagan, President of the United States of America, do hereby proclaim the month of October 1985 as National High-Tech Month, and I request all Federal, State, and local officials to cooperate in its observance.

In Witness Whereof, I have hereunto set my hand this seventeenth day of October, in the year of our Lord nineteen hundred and eighty-five, and of the Independence of the United States of America the two hundred and tenth.

RONALD REAGAN

[Filed with the Office of the Federal Register, 10:29 a.m., October 18, 1985]

Announcement of the 1986 President's Volunteer Action Awards Program
October 17, 1985

The President today announced the fifth annual President's Volunteer Action Awards to honor outstanding volunteer achievement by individual citizens and organizations. The President will present the awards at a White House ceremony in April. Award categories include arts and humanities, education, the environment, health, human services, international volunteering, mobilization of volunteer, public safety, youth, and the workplace.

In a unique cooperative effort between the private sector and government, VOLUNTEER: The National Center, a private nonprofit volunteer support organization, and ACTION, the Federal agency for volunteering, are cosponsoring the program for the fifth year. Funding for the program is provided by private sector corporate and foundation sponsors. In announcing the program, the President said: "Citizens from every walk of life volunteer their time, energy, and resources to help those less fortunate than themselves. We can never fully measure the positive effects that each kind word or deed has upon this great and wonderful land of ours."

VOLUNTEER is the primary national organization supporting greater citizen involvement in community problem-solving, providing technical assistance to volunteer-involving organizations, public agencies, unions, and corporations. It works closely with a network of over 225 associated Volunteer Action Centers and more than 1,000 other local, State, and national organizations. ACTION serves to stimulate voluntarism and to demonstrate the effectiveness of volunteers in addressing social problems. Its major programs include the Foster Grandparent, Retired Senior Volunteer, and Senior Companion programs for the elderly and a variety of programs for youth. ACTION also promotes private sector initiatives by providing short-term grants to innovative volunteer projects in such areas as literacy and drug abuse.

Among the corporations and foundations providing support for the 1986 program are Aid Association for Lutherans, Avon Products, Inc., Keyes Martin and Co., Knights of Columbus Supreme Council, the Mayflower Hotel, the Mutual Benefit Life Insurance Co., Rexnord, Inc., and Tenneco, Inc. President Reagan presented the fourth annual awards to 15 individuals and groups, 1 labor union, and 2 corporations at a White House luncheon on April 22, 1985.

Nomination forms can be obtained by writing: The President's Volunteer Action Awards, P.O. Box 37488, Washington, DC 20013. The deadline for submission for nominations for the 1986 awards is January 25, 1986.

Remarks to Business Leaders During a White House Briefing on the Federal Budget and Deficit Reduction
October 18, 1985

Thank you, and it's a pleasure to add my welcome to the others that I know you've already had.

Change in a free society is never easy, and the battle for a balanced budget is no exception. And that's why we have asked

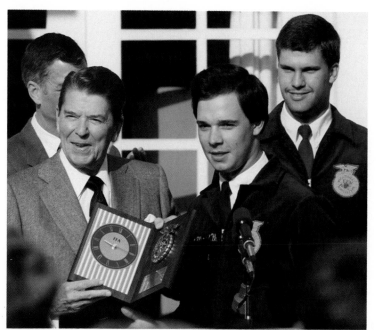

Overleaf: Addressing a joint [ ]
of Congress following the [ ]
Soviet-U.S. summit meeting [ ]
Geneva, November 21. *Left* [ ]
reception for the Future Fa[ ]
America in the Rose Garde[ ]
September 18. *Below left:* A [ ]
Carolina State University in [ ]
Raleigh, September 5. *Righ* [ ]
Accepting an Indian quilt f[ ]
Chief Wallace Wells in the [ ]
Office, September 9. *Below* [ ]
With Their Royal Highnesse[ ]
Prince and Princess of Wale[ ]
Residence, November 9.

Greeting the World Series
[champi]on Kansas City Royals in the
[Rose G]arden, October 31. *Left:*
[with S]oviet General Secretary
[Gorbac]hev at the summit meeting
[in Gen]eva, November 19. *Right:*
[walkin]g with Soviet General
[Secreta]ry Gorbachev during the
[summi]t meeting in Geneva,
[Novem]ber 19.

NEW HAMPSHIRE WELCOMES
PRESIDENT REAGAN
WHERE IT ALL BEGAN

...elivering a speech outside ...ehouse in Concord, NH, ...ber 18. *Above right:* ...ng a gift from the citizens of ... TN, September 24. *Right:* ...g to President Assad of ... telephone from the Oval ...July 1. *Overleaf:* ...aphing a picture for a White ...visitor, October 7.

you here today—or have you guessed that? We need some help from the first string. Many of us have been slugging it out on the issue of deficit spending for a number of years, many years. I think that we now have a window of opportunity to establish— or accomplish what we have so long strived for. We cannot let this opportunity pass, and I hope I can count on every one of you to maximize your efforts in the days ahead.

The Gramm-Rudman-Hollings deficit reduction plan, if passed, will be a landmark victory for responsible government. The need for structural reform has been evident to some of us for quite some time, and that's why we've been raising our voices in support of a balanced budget amendment. What we haven't realized, however, and what is clear now is that there is also need for a transition to that point where structural change is possible. And that's what Gramm-Rudman-Hollings is all about. This farsighted and practical proposal gives us an enforceable method of reducing the budget deficit each year, leaving us with a balanced budget by 1990. An end to deficits can be made permanent with an amendment to the U.S. Constitution requiring a balanced budget and preventing us from ever getting behind the eight ball again.

The passage of Gramm-Rudman-Hollings will be an affirmation to the entire country—well, yes, even to the world—that we Americans have finally gotten serious about deficit spending. Gramm-Rudman-Hollings will replace "no way" with "can do." We can, if we have the will to do it, bring the deficit down without raising taxes and without undermining our national security. Now, let me just underscore that last point. No one should look at our energetic support of Gramm-Rudman-Hollings as an indication that America's military strength is going to be weakened. There's too much at stake. We must keep this country strong and at peace. We'll continue spending what is necessary in this vital area, but no more, no less.

During the last election much was said on this issue. I think any political figure who declaimed in front of the voters against the deficit owes it to the people to support this bipartisan approach or explain him or herself. I'm counting on each of you to help me

let our fellow citizens know who's standing in the way and who's clearing the way. Or, put in the vernacular of the 1960's, who's part of the solution or who's part of the problem. By being here today, we figure that you're part of the solution. The big spenders, still trying to hold on to the free-wheeling days of the past, have got to realize how serious the American people are about this. The American people are watching, and I don't think they'll tolerate obstructionism. Those politicians who try to scuttle this reform in the fall of 1985 do so at their own peril.

But I must tell you, I am optimistic. I think we can be proud of the foursquare example the Senate has set on this issue. The Gramm-Rudman-Hollings amendment passed the United States Senate with the support of a majority of members of both parties and is now in a House-Senate conference committee. If you hear some unusual noises floating in through the window, that's what's going on. [*Laughter*] Our elected representatives must know that on this issue, no one is anonymous; everyone is on record. If they understand this, then we'll be on the edge of an historic victory. But your perseverance is needed, and we can't afford to wait a day. I hope you'll be up on the Hill this afternoon to let them know how high a priority Gramm-Rudman-Hollings is on your agenda. And as I have said already today to another group of individuals who you might run into up on the Hill, it isn't necessary that you make them see the light, just make them feel the heat. [*Laughter*]

Having worked in my current job going on 5 years now, I have a perspective on our country I'd like to share. As I mentioned earlier, change is never easy in a democracy. I'm proud of the changes that we've made. But each time we've succeeded, it's always been due to the efforts of the people. Certainly, political leaders have meetings and talk about differences, but when fundamental change happens, it's because the people are involved, giving leverage to those that are fighting for the right. In this particular case, the American people want us to end this deficit spending that has been mortgaging the future of our children and undercutting confidence in our own. We have it in our power to put this problem behind us. When we do, I predict a new surge of optimism will be felt throughout our land. It will sweep us into a time of prosperity as never imagined. And pardon me for using a phrase from the campaign, but when we get deficit spending under control, as far as the economic progress we've enjoyed so far, well, you ain't seen nothin' yet!

I've been telling some people some figures—and I just will close with this—that prove—I know there's a great deal of controversy and everybody's expressing opinions out there—well, who's to blame for the deficit? The deficit is built into the structure of our government. And the greatest proof of that I can give you is that 1965 to 1980—15 years—in those 15 years, the budget increased to five times what it was in 1965; the deficit increased to 50 times what it was in 1965. And that rate of increase has continued through the years

we've been here. In spite of our efforts to cut, all we've been able to do is reduce the increase in spending. We've fought every year for a number of cuts, and now we've come to the conclusion that this thing of instead of every year, trying to whittle away here and there and hope we can get enough votes to do so and hope that one day the budget deficit will disappear.

But today the idea is—with this amendment I've been talking about—is a 5-year plan in which you look at the rate of decrease in the deficit and you can point to a year down here in which sticking to this plan—that is the balanced budget and, then, we get that constitutional amendment and make sure that Uncle Sam gets off his sailor's binge and stays within the limits of the revenues.

Well, thank you all for being here. Go get 'em! And God bless you.

Note: The President spoke at 1:14 p.m. in Room 450 of the Old Executive Office Building.

Proclamation 5395—National CPR Awareness Week, 1985
October 18, 1985

By the President of the United States of America

A Proclamation

Heart attack is the number one cause of sudden death in the United States. More than a million and a half Americans will experience heart attacks this year, of which over a half million will be fatal. We are making progress: Mortality from heart attacks has declined significantly over the past decade. But since heart attacks remain by far the leading cause of death in America, much remains to be done.

Heart attacks sometimes cause the heart to stop pumping, and cardiopulmonary resuscitation (CPR) then becomes a critical and potentially life-saving first-aid procedure. Trained individuals applying CPR can often preserve the life of a heart attack victim until proper medical care can be obtained. Tens of thousands of Americans who

have had heart attacks are leading productive lives today only because someone trained in CPR quickly and effectively applied this life-saving technique.

Cardiopulmonary resuscitation may also be life-saving first aid for other conditions that cause sudden cessation of the heartbeat or cut off the delivery of oxygen into the lungs. Medical authorities are in agreement that a person adequately trained in CPR can make all the difference between life and death in many emergencies. But they stress that CPR is effective only when employed by people who are properly trained.

Because of the effectiveness of CPR, the number of sudden deaths from heart attacks and other emergencies could be reduced still further if more Americans were trained in this procedure. Facilities for CPR training are widespread, and I am pleased to acknowledge the contribution by those who train others. I urge all qualified Americans to take advantage of this training and to become certified in the use of CPR. This could be a life-saving decision.

To reinforce this message and to increase awareness among all Americans that people trained in CPR can be an effective means of reducing mortality from heart attacks, the Congress, by Senate Joint Resolution 175, has designated the week beginning October 20 through October 26, 1985, as "National CPR Awareness Week" and authorized and requested the President to issue a proclamation in observance of this event.

Now, Therefore, I, Ronald Reagan, President of the United States of America, do hereby proclaim the week of October 20 through October 26, 1985, as National CPR Awareness Week. I invite the Governors of the States, the Commonwealth of Puerto Rico, the officials of other areas subject to the jurisdiction of the United States, and the American people to join with me in acknowledging the benefits of this valuable life-saving technique and to undergo training in its use.

In Witness Whereof, I have hereunto set my hand this eighteenth day of October, in the year of our Lord nineteen hundred and eighty-five, and of the Independence of the United States of America the two hundred and tenth.

RONALD REAGAN

[*Filed with the Office of the Federal Register, 4:10 p.m., October 18, 1985*]

Radio Address to the Nation on the 40th Anniversary of the United Nations General Assembly
October 19, 1985

My fellow Americans:

Next week Nancy and I will be traveling to New York City. We'll be joining some 80 world leaders and other distinguished guests from around the globe to commemorate the 40th anniversary of the United Nations General Assembly. I'll be meeting with many of these leaders, and I want to share with you my thoughts and hopes on this special occasion.

I can remember vividly the high hopes and expectations we all shared when the United Nations was created in 1945. The nations of the world, exhausted and devastated after the most destructive war in history, came together to lay the foundation for a better world, one free of war. President Harry Truman declared on behalf of all Americans our solemn dedication to fight for the principles of the U.N. Charter: peace, freedom, and an end to tyranny, hunger, and human suffering.

Americans have never stopped striving to uphold and defend those principles. The American people have held high the torch of freedom for all those fighting for liberty around the world. Our farmers have provided food for millions of needy people across the globe. We helped rebuild the nations ravaged by the Second World War. We and our allies have worked to prevent a third. We've come to the aid of our friends threatened by aggression in Korea, Vietnam, Pakistan, El Salvador, and Grenada. And we've worked to bring about peace in the Middle East and offered far-reaching proposals to reduce nuclear arsenals. For 40 years, we have honorably carried out our responsibilities to the U.N. Charter, and we have not hesitated to stand firm against those who've sought to undermine peace and freedom for their own sinister ends.

In the coming weeks, we will have a new opportunity to pursue the charter's lofty goals. On Monday, Nancy will be meeting with 31 other first ladies at the U.N. to continue the cooperative efforts she began last spring to focus world attention on the devastating problem of drug abuse. This is a problem which affects the well-being of virtually every country and can only be solved through the kind of cooperative efforts the United Nations was intended to foster. In 1 month, I will be meeting with Soviet leader Mikhail Gorbachev. I intend to discuss with him, openly and frankly, the obstacles to peace and to suggest how, together, we can remove some of them. If he's receptive, our discussions can go a long way toward building a safer world and realizing the ideals of the U.N. Charter.

The United Nations' founders understood that true peace must be based on more than just reducing the means of waging war. It must address the sources of tension that provoke men to take up arms. True peace is based on self-determination, respect for individual rights, open and honest communications, and that is the kind of peace we want. We want countries to stop trying to expand their power and control through armed intervention and subversion. We have the opportunity—in fact, we have the mandate—to reduce the danger of nuclear war by drastic reduction of nuclear arsenals. And that's why we've proposed radical, verifiable, and balanced reductions of offensive nuclear weapons and why we're pursuing research and testing to identify defensive technologies which threaten no one.

We must defend human rights every-where, since countries which respect human rights are unlikely to unleash war or to impose their will on others. And that's why we insist that the Helsinki accords and other international commitments be observed. We must establish better communication between our societies, since misunderstandings make the world more dangerous. These will be the subjects of my discussion with General Secretary Gorbachev. I hope that our discussions will contribute to building true peace, to guaranteeing a safe path into the 21st century. But whether this comes to pass will depend on the Soviet willingness to address the real sources of tension in the world and, in particular, their conduct in the world, their treatment of their own citizens, and their continuing and longstanding arms buildup. In preparing for my meeting with General Secretary Gorbachev, I'll be seeking the advice and counsel of our allies and friends, some of whom will be in New York with me. With their support and yours, we can set a course now for a safer future.

Until next week, thanks for listening, and God bless you.

Note: The President spoke at 12:06 p.m. from the Oval Office at the White House.

Remarks During a White House Briefing for United States Attorneys
October 21, 1985

Well, I'm delighted to have this opportunity to be with you today. Actually, I was thinking on the way over that this is the second gathering of attorneys I've addressed in the last few months. When I spoke to the American Bar Association a short time ago, I said how disappointed I was that the White House counsel wouldn't let me accept the honorarium. [*Laughter*] I was really looking forward to the first time I ever talked to a group of lawyers and came home with the fee. [*Laughter*]

Well, I'm told there won't be any honorarium this morning, either. [*Laughter*] But, you know, that's not quite right either, be-cause there will be honorariums today, except this time it's the speaker who is going to be handing them out. By that I mean I just wanted to be here today to say how grateful I am to all of you, to each one of you. All of you are on the front line; each one of you holds one of the toughest jobs there is in law enforcement. You know, sometimes when I've spoken to police officers, I've reminded them to be cautious about drawing too many conclusions based on their daily work, to remember that too often they only see their fellow citizens when they've committed a crime or been victimized by one, when they're hurting or in trouble. It's easy to forget the people they don't see every day—that great majority of Americans who are law-abiding citizens and who are proud of those in law enforcement, grateful to them and anxious to give them their full support.

Well, not only do you have to deal with the criminals and their victims every day, you also have to deal with judges and juries and other lawyers. And all of that, I know, demands the utmost in professional skill and dedication from each one of you. I'm sure there are moments of enormous frustration, and I'm sure there are times when you feel unappreciated. But I hope that in such moments in the future you'll remember the fellow who lives in public housing just across the street here and spoke to you once about your work and its meaning, a fellow who, on behalf of millions of your fellow Americans who never get the chance, wants to say to you today: We're mighty appreciative and mighty grateful to you and proud of you also. I want to underscore a point that I know the Attorney General has regularly made. You and your assistants are in large measure the Justice Department. Our job here in Washington is to support you, to give you the tools that you need to do your job.

Now, I don't want to keep you too long, so let me just touch quickly on a few items of mutual interest. As you know, there was some speculation that this second term might turn out to be a caretaker Presidency, a quiet time that saw little in the way of reform or action. And I just happen to think that the work you're doing is one bit of strong evidence to the contrary.

For example, you're cutting deeply into the infrastructure of the mob by prosecuting major crime bosses. You are not—as one longtime crusader against organized crime, Professor Robert Blakey, of Notre Dame, said about past government prosecutions—picking off the retired or wounded. In fact, organized crime convictions are running at a rate quadruple what they were in 1981. This means we're finally doing something about a black mark on our national history, one that's been there roughly since the turn of the century.

And you know, I've heard some people wonder about the sudden appearance of the powerful new drug rings, but no one should really be surprised. In many ways these new criminal syndicates are a result of our past failure to deal effectively with the older organized crime rings who have attempted to corrupt so much of American life. The new groups see in these older syndicates their prototype, an example to emulate, an inspiration to follow. And that's why we have to act as promptly and as effectively as we can against the syndicates, old and new.

I always steer away from questions about any kind of a personal legacy I'd like to leave America after 8 years in office. Answering questions like that sound a bit pompous, and right now, thank you very much, I think such thoughts are just a bit premature. [*Laughter*] But just this once I'll break my rule, and I'll tell you. Some years ago, many of us in Hollywood saw organized crime at work when it attempted to infiltrate and corrupt unions there; indeed, the union of which I later became president. And we've never forgotten. And believe me, there is nothing I'd like better than to be remembered as a President who did everything he could to bust up the syndicates and give the mobsters a permanent stay in the jailhouse, courtesy of the United States Government. The American people feel just as strongly on this issue, a fact sometimes forgotten by too many in American politics. But if you look at the careers of Tom Dewey, Estes Kefauver, John and Robert Kennedy, and others in public life, I think you will see evidence the American people have always cared deeply about this issue and approved of public officials who spoke and acted responsibly in dealing with it.

So, let me repeat what I said to you the last time we were together. We are in this thing to win. There will be no negotiated settlements, no détente with the mob. It's war to the end where we're concerned. Our goal is simple: We mean to cripple their organization, dry up their profits, and put their members behind bars where they belong. They've had a free run for too long a time in this country. And that's the end of quoting myself. [*Laughter*] One other thing, after due process has been done, after you're certain the defendant's rights have been protected and a fair trial has been held, should the jury return a guilty verdict and the court ask you for a sentencing recommendation, will you do me and the millions of Americans who are fed up with professional gangsters and career criminals—do us the favor of asking His Honor to throw the book at them?

And while we're on the subject, let me bring up another area you have to deal with: waste and fraud against the United States Government, which has been unrelenting national scandal. Well, now that we've reinvigorated the Inspector Generals' program as well as instituted reforms that have uncovered items like $400 hammers, that scandal may be starting to relent, but only a bit. Believe me, we're still a long way from home. Frankly, I can think of few criminals more contemptible than those who for selfish ends would cheat our service men and women out of the best we can give them to defend America or those who for personal gain would corrupt a social welfare program designed to benefit the less fortunate members of our society. So, I encourage you to prosecute fraud against the government cases and seek severe penalties against those who seek to cheat the taxpayers by shortchanging the armed services or depriving the truly needy.

You know, about that, let me just say one thing that maybe hasn't been called to your attention. These $400 hammers and expensive toilet covers and a few things like that—these have been portrayed generally as if our people and this administration is somehow responsible. Well, we are responsible—for finding them. They've been going on for a long time, and every time they have come to public attention, it's because we brought them to public attention by digging them out and doing something about it. And we're going to keep on doing that, and we'll take your help whenever we can get it.

And finally, let me speak about another matter that comes up from time to time, and that's the selection of Federal judges. I'm very proud of our record of finding highly qualified individuals who also adhere to a restrained and truly judicious view of the rule of the courts—or the role of the

courts under our Constitution. The independence of the courts from improper political influence is a sacred principle. It must always be guarded. And let me assure you, it always will be guarded while this administration is in office. But as you know, the Founding Fathers knew that, like any other part of the Government, the power of the judiciary could be abused. They never intended, for example, that the courts preempt legislative prerogatives or become vehicles for political action or social experimentation or for coercing the populace into adopting anyone's personal view of utopia. So, to make sure the courts weren't misused in this way and did not set themselves up as an institution entirely removed from the society they're intended to serve, the Founding Fathers provided for checks and balances, one of which was to place the appointive power for the judiciary in the hands of those who are in office as a result of popular election.

Now, during the past two Presidential elections, I've made it clear to the American public that I felt the courts had sometimes gone too far in interfering with the constitutional prerogatives of other branches of government, even while they neglected their constitutional duty of protecting society from those who prey on the innocent. Well, this is still my belief. So, I intend to go right on appointing highly qualified individuals of the highest personal integrity to the bench, individuals who understand the danger of short-circuiting the electoral process and disenfranchising the people through judicial activism. I want judges of the highest intellectual standing who harbor the deepest regard for the Constitution and its traditions, one of which is judicial restraint.

So, again, my thanks to each one of you, and please tell all of those working with you in your offices and in the investigative agencies how proud and grateful I am. And that is just an echo of how the people of this country feel about you and the way you serve. Thank you. Thank all of you, and God bless you.

Note: The President spoke at 11:46 a.m. in Room 450 of the Old Executive Office Building.

Appointment of David A. Bockorny as Special Assistant to the President for Legislative Affairs (House)
October 21, 1985

The President today appointed David A. Bockorny to be a Special Assistant to the President for Legislative Affairs (House). He will succeed Tom Donnelly.

Mr. Bockorny has been on the staff of the National Association of Realtors since 1981 serving most recently as staff vice president of political and legislative liaison. In 1977–1981 he served as legislative assistant to Senator James Abdnor (R–SD) during Mr. Abdnor's tenure in the House of Representatives.

Mr. Bockorny graduated from Dakota State College (B.S., 1976) and the University of South Dakota (M.B.A., 1978). He is married, has one daughter, and resides in Annandale, VA. He was born August 24, 1954, in Huron, SD.

Appointment of J. Edward Fox as Special Assistant to the President for Legislative Affairs (House)
October 21, 1985

The President has appointed J. Edward Fox to be a Special Assistant to the President for Legislative Affairs (House). He will succeed Henry Gandy.

Mr. Fox most recently served as Principal Deputy Assistant Secretary of State for Legislative and Intergovernmental Affairs. Previously he served as the Department's Deputy Assistant Secretary in charge of liaison with the House of Representatives in 1983–1984. He was a minority staff consultant with the House of Representatives Committee on Foreign Affairs in 1975–1982. He also served as legislative assistant to Representative John R. Rousselot (R–CA) in 1974–1975 and as research assistant to Representative John Ashbrook (R–OH) in 1973–1974.

He graduated from Ohio State University (B.A., 1972) and George Washington University (M.A., 1976). He is married, has three children, and resides in Washington, DC. He was born December 1, 1948, in Columbus, OH.

Appointment of Merlin P. Breaux as Special Assistant to the President for Public Liaison
October 21, 1985

The President has appointed Merlin P. Breaux as a Special Assistant to the President for Public Liaison. Mr. Breaux will have responsibility for economic issues.

Mr. Breaux most recently served as vice president of industrial relations for Gulf Oil Corp. in Houston, TX. Previously, he was vice president of human resources (1975–1976), director of labor relations (1968–1975), labor negotiator (1967–1968), and industrial relations assistant (1966–1967) at Gulf. He graduated from Lamar University in Beaumont, TX, in 1958, where he is currently vice chairman of the board of regents. He served in the United States Air Force in 1951–1953. He was recently appointed by President Reagan to the President's Advisory Committee on Mediation and Conciliation. He has been a member of the Business Roundtable and served on several of its committees.

Mr. Breaux is married and has five children. He was born January 15, 1932, in Edgerly, LA.

Appointment of Thomas F. Gibson III as Special Assistant to the President and Director of Public Affairs
October 21, 1985

The President has appointed Thomas F. Gibson III to be Special Assistant to the President and Director of Public Affairs.

For the past 2 years, Mr. Gibson has served as an Associate Director of the White House Office of Cabinet Affairs. From 1982 to 1983, he was an editor on the opinion staff of USA Today. From 1979 to 1981, Mr. Gibson was director of government relations for the Brick Institute of America, and from 1978 to 1979, he was a legislative assistant to United States Senator Dewey F. Bartlett. He was a freelance political illustrator for a number of publications from 1977 to 1982.

Mr. Gibson graduated from Princeton University (B.A., 1977) and Harvard University (M.P.A., 1982). He was born January 23, 1955, in Indianapolis, IN, and now resides in Alexandria, VA.

Appointment of Susan K. Mathis as Special Assistant to the President and Director of Media Relations
October 21, 1985

The President has appointed Susan K. Mathis to be Special Assistant to the President and Director of Media Relations.

Ms. Mathis has served in the Media Relations Office since 1981, first as Deputy Director, then Acting Director. Prior to joining the administration, she was a television and radio correspondent in Washington for Cox Communications. In 1976 Ms. Mathis was a press assistant with the Ford-Dole committee. From 1973 to 1976, she anchored a daily newscast on cable television in East Lansing, MI, and produced public affairs programs. From 1971 to 1973, she was a secondary school communications instructor and coached drama, debate, and forensics in Roseville, MI. She was also a newspaper columnist and freelance writer.

Ms. Mathis graduated from the University of Michigan (B.A., 1971). She was born June 21, 1949, in Detroit, MI, and now resides in Alexandria, VA.

Appointment of Agnes M. Waldron as Special Assistant to the President and Director of Research
October 21, 1985

The President has appointed Agnes M. Waldron to be Special Assistant to the President and Director of Research. This is a new position.

Miss Waldron most recently served as a professional staff member of the Senate Republican Policy Committee in 1977–1984. She served at the White House in the Office of the Press Secretary (1970–1973); Director of Research (1973–1976); and as

Deputy Director of Communications in 1976.

She graduated from the University of Connecticut (B.S., 1946) and Catholic University (M.S.W., 1949). She was born October 2, 1924, in New Canaan, CT.

Statement Following a Meeting with Solidarity Movement Representative Jerzy Milewski on the Situation in Poland
October 21, 1985

I had the pleasure today to meet Mr. Jerzy Milewski, the distinguished representative in Brussels of the Polish labor union Solidarity and a close friend of Nobel Peace Prize Laureate Lech Walesa. We discussed a subject of great interest to me, the situation in Poland.

I told Mr. Milewski of my high hopes that the amnesty declared in July 1984 would represent a giant step toward national reconciliation. Unfortunately, most of the recent news from Poland has not been good. The number of persons detained for purely political reasons has once again risen sharply. Amendments to the penal code have gone into effect which empower the authorities to make summary judgments on a wide variety of so-called crimes. A new law on higher education impinges severely upon traditional academic freedoms. Amendments to the 1982 trade union law effectively rule out de jure trade union pluralism for the foreseeable future. The parliamentary elections just concluded, and like elections before them, have failed to provide a genuine public mandate for Poland's legislative representatives.

Mr. Milewski and other thoughtful observers of the Polish scene understandably feel deep concern over this trend of events. History proves that increased repression only aggravates current problems and sows the seeds of future discontent. I continue to believe that a genuine dialog between the government and important elements of society, including free and independent trade unions, is the only way to solve Poland's serious problems. The release of political detainees would certainly be a prerequisite, both for improving conditions within Poland and for pursuing that country's relations abroad. Mr. Milewski's work in keeping the Western World abreast of his countrymen's efforts to bring their needs and aspirations to the attention of their government is thus extremely important.

Note: The President met with Mr. Milewski at 11:30 a.m. in the Oval Office at the White House.

Remarks in an Interview With J.N. Parimoo of the Times of India, Together With Written Responses to Questions
October 21, 1985

Mr. Parimoo. Good afternoon, Mr. President.

The President. Well, hello there. Pleased to see you.

South Asia and Nuclear Weapons

Mr. Parimoo. I thank you, sir. I believe you are making some certification to Congress on Pakistan. Is it your judgment that Pakistan doesn't have the bomb?

The President. Well, we have no evidence that they do—and this is required. We're very hopeful that south Asian countries will forgo nuclear weapons—all of the countries there. And yet at the same time, we want to be of assistance with regard to legitimate energy needs, and that is a source of energy, but should not be a coverup for bombs and the making of nuclear weapons. As a matter of fact, we're going to try our best to see if we, at the level of the Soviet Union and ourselves, cannot do something about curbing those, and I would like to think that they might one day eliminate them all.

Mr. Parimoo. Mr. Gandhi, the Prime Minister, has suggested in Newsweek in an interview that this Symington amendment waiver need not be extended. Why should it be extended any further? You know, it's the waiver of the Symington amendment——

The President. I don't——

Mr. Parimoo. ——which allows sale of arms to Pakistan. See, because otherwise— that's a law, Symington law, which will not allow sale of arms to Pakistan because of this ex-nuclear weapons waiver. But you have granted the waiver that—and that waiver will expire in September in '87. He says it need not be extended. Why should it be extended?

The President. We hope by that time that we definitely know that there are no nuclear weapons—not going to be any, because that's what we've tried to, as I say, to impress on both the major countries there— and on all of south Asia or, for that matter, the rest of the world.

India

Mr. Parimoo. Are you coming to India, sir?

The President. What?

Mr. Parimoo. You accepted an invitation to India, to come visit India? Will you and Mrs. Reagan be visiting?

The President. If we can work out a schedule to do that, we would like it very much.

Mr. Parimoo. India is the largest democracy of——

The President. My only experience in your country was one in which I wasn't even aware of it. I was on a flight from Taiwan to London, England, on my way home from some tours that I'd had over there in the Far East, and it seems like long before dawn, early in the morning, the plane dropped down in New Delhi for refueling——

Mr. Parimoo. Oh, is that right?

The President. ——and I was sound asleep—[*laughter*]—so at least I slept a few moments in India. But no, we'd like that very much.

Mr. Parimoo. We'll be very happy to see you there. You already visited China once——

The President. Yes.

Mr. Parimoo. ——but you did not visit India, so it's time that you also visited India. India is the largest democracy of the world.

The President. I know. We'd like that very much.

Mr. Parimoo. And you are the leader of that democratic world.

The President. Thank you. Good to see you.

Mr. Parimoo. Thank you, sir.

The President. Looking forward to seeing your Prime Minister in the next couple of days.

Mr. Parimoo. Yes. He's really concerned about Pakistan's program. He has been——

The President. Well, we'll have a good talk about it.

Mr. Parimoo. Thank you, sir.

The President. You bet.

The President's Responses to Questions Submitted by the Times of India

U.S.-Soviet Relations

Q. Mr. President, in the postwar era, no two leaders came to the summit with so much political support at home and with such charisma. We in India look upon the next month's meeting between you and Mr. Gorbachev as a unique opportunity for disarmament and durable peace. Do you share that view?

The President. I believe that our meeting offers a unique opportunity to set U.S.-Soviet relations on a more constructive course for years to come. I have no illusions. I understand well the difficulties involved, but I feel an obligation to make a sincere effort at least to narrow some of the profound differences between us. If we can make any progress toward that goal, I believe that all peoples throughout the world will benefit. General Secretary Gorbachev and I will surely discuss our respective ideas of how best to bring about deep reductions in arms levels. If the Soviets are ready for the give and take that an arms agreement will require, they'll find us ready as well.

I think it is also important to remember that arms, whether nuclear or conventional, do not come to exist for no reason. They exist because nations have very real differences among themselves and suspicions about each other's intentions. Thus, a frank discussion of our concerns about Soviet behavior, particularly its attempts to expand its influence by force and subversion, is an important part of our effort to focus on the sources of world tension, not just the symptoms. To establish the foundation for a truly more constructive relationship, I want to talk with General Secretary Gorbachev not only about arms control but also about regional tensions, about our bilateral relationship, and about the obligation of both our nations to respect human rights—all of these issues are as important to us as the question of nuclear arms. I will go to Geneva ready to make whatever progress the Soviets will allow toward resolving them.

May I add that I am aware the people of India and of many other nations sometimes feel that they have no control over what the big powers do in matters that affect all mankind. I want to do my part to dispel this impression. I am very aware of the way people around the globe will be watching our decisions in Geneva, and I can assure them that I will have their concerns in mind when I sit down at the table with General Secretary Gorbachev. I only hope that the General Secretary will come to our talks with a similar attitude. And in my speech to the United Nations General Assembly this week, I will be spelling out in more detail just how I believe we can make real progress toward easing the world tensions that are of concern to us all.

Q. Important as it is, arms control by itself cannot resolve the geopolitical rivalries of the two superpowers. Would the summit agenda next month include a discussion on some more abiding ways of resolving these differences?

The President. I think you are right in viewing arms control in this broader context. As anyone who has studied the differences between the Western democracies

and the Communist system realizes, we have fundamentally different views of the world and fundamentally different ways of behaving in it. My hope would be to find ways with Mr. Gorbachev to ensure that our differences continue to be peaceful. In some other areas, serious discussions may permit the bridging of differences. In those areas, if the Soviets are willing, we can make immediate progress. This progress may lead, in turn, to agreements in other, more contentious areas.

I hope that Mr. Gorbachev and I can reinforce the intensive regional dialog that we and the Soviets have had since the beginning of this year. As you know, our regional experts have already met to discuss Afghanistan, the Middle East, Africa, and east Asia. Later this month in Washington, we'll have talks on Central America and the Caribbean. Although these talks haven't resulted in any solutions to problems in those parts of the world, they have been useful for two reasons. First, by clarifying our respective positions on regional issues, we lessen the chance of miscalculations or misunderstandings between us. Second, these talks give us an opportunity to make clear what we, our allies, and our friends consider important.

Regional Conflicts

Q. Regional conflicts in south Asia, the Middle East, South Africa, Central America, and Southeast Asia could escalate into a world war. Even if an arms control agreement were to be reached at Geneva, these regional conflicts would continue to threaten world peace. Would you not like to propose next month some restraint on the political conduct of superpowers to defuse these regional conflicts?

The President. Our regional exchanges with the Soviets have covered and will continue to cover these points. Let me suggest briefly how the Soviets can advance the cause of peace in one of these regions, your very own. In Afghanistan, we are witnessing a brutal war simply because the Afghan people are determined to resist an attempt by outsiders to impose a government on them. It's clear that the Afghan spirit of independence cannot be crushed; that continued war will only mean more bloodshed;

and that only a political solution is possible. The Soviets claim that they, too, believe in a negotiated settlement. I will be asking General Secretary Gorbachev in Geneva whether, if that is so, he is willing to address the crucial issue: withdrawal of the more than 100,000 Soviet troops in Afghanistan and the restoration of that country's independence and nonalignment.

I know the Soviet Union has concerns about the countries on its border, but Afghanistan poses no threat to Soviet security. We Americans also have neighbors, and neighbors that do not always agree with us; however, look at our borders with Canada and Mexico. They stretch for thousands of miles, and not an inch of them is defended. Bear in mind, too, that both of these countries have very independent political systems and foreign policies, and, in fact, Mexico is one of the leaders of the nonaligned movement. The way to solve regional problems is through dialog and negotiations, not invasion and occupation.

Arms Sales and Nuclear Weapons

Q. Former President Nixon has suggested that one of the ways to reduce world tensions is for the two superpowers to stop supplying sophisticated arms to poor developing countries. Do you agree with this view, and would you like to propose a moratorium on such arms supplies at the next summit?

The President. To my mind, poor nations are entitled to security just as rich nations are. That ought to be obvious. The hard question is, what really *promotes* their security? To answer that, we need a more sophisticated approach than simply trying to cut off military sales and assistance; that has its place in an overall strategy, but it doesn't seem like quite the right place to start. Instead, I think we have to look at the underlying conflicts and ask how to ease them and to build confidence among neighboring states that have known only hostility and mistrust. If such a process takes root, outside states may well be able to help it along in various ways, perhaps by limiting arms supplies; perhaps by providing assurances of some sort or by helping the parties to integrate themselves more successfully into the world economy; perhaps simply by

offering what the diplomats call "good offices."

Start with the real sources of conflict and see how they can most realistically be overcome—that's our approach. I might add that it hasn't been everyone's approach. Over the past 10 years, a growing source of instability and war in the developing world has been the imposition of new regimes—Marxist-Leninist ones—that are, almost from the day they take over, at war with their own people, and then before very long, at war with their neighbors. This is a problem that simply has to be addressed, a pattern that has to be broken if we are to avoid the further spread of conflict. The Soviet Union, as we see it, is too often supporting, and sometimes directing, these wars. In such cases, the flow of arms from outside *is* a major concern, and we want to do something about it. I'll speak on this subject this week at the United Nations and, of course, with General Secretary Gorbachev when I meet him in Geneva.

Q. In view of the danger of proliferation and the graver risk of miniaturization of nuclear weapons, which could bring such weapons within the reach of terrorists, would you not like to put some more determined restraint on countries that have an advanced nuclear weapons-making program?

The President. Our concern about the proliferation of nuclear weapons is a matter of public record. We have been working with a number of countries, including the Soviet Union, to control access to both weapons and technology, in good part because of the kind of concerns you mention. It really is a grave threat, both proliferation and miniaturization, and restraining proliferation is a big part of our effort to reduce the threat of nuclear war or nuclear accident or incident. We recognize that a country's sense of insecurity may lead it to look for a nuclear option, yet if one pauses to think, one has to agree that possession of nuclear weapons actually adds to the insecurity. We hope that the countries of south Asia will set an example by forgoing nuclear weapons.

At the same time, we have always supported the legitimate energy needs of developing countries. The United States has shared its know-how with many nations around the world, starting with the Atoms for Peace program in the 1950's. However, we strongly believe that energy programs must not provide a cover for the development of nuclear weapons.

Terrorism

Q. Recently, the Soviet Union also came in for attack from the terrorists—one of its diplomats was killed in the Middle East. Countries like the United States and India have been facing the problem of international terrorism. Would you not like to bring this up and make a joint declaration from the summit pronouncing terrorism and abetment of terrorism an international crime?

The President. We have condemned the kidnaping of Soviet diplomats in Beirut. The murder of one of the Soviets was an abhorrent act, and we have expressed our regret to the Soviet Union. In turn, we note with satisfaction their condemnation of the *Achille Lauro* terrorists. We hope that this is a sign that their own recent experiences may have made them aware that terrorism knows no international boundaries and lead them to reassess their policy of support for terrorist organizations and states. India for its part has suffered the terrible loss of a great national leader, Madame Gandhi. The U.S. also has suffered terribly from terrorism and is determined to combat it vigorously. We would be pleased if the Soviets would join us in a common effort to stamp out terrorism. Unfortunately, we believe some of their policies actually encourage terrorism.

Strategic Defense Initiative

Q. Mr. President, it is believed that your stand on the Strategic Defense Initiative, which has come to be known as the Star Wars system of defense, is crucial to the success of the summit next month. What is SDI, and why does the United States have to change from deterrence to defense?

The President. For at least the past 30 years, deterrence has rested on the threat of offensive nuclear retaliation; the United States and the Soviet Union have been hostage to each other's nuclear forces. Our re-

taliatory deterrent has enabled us to live in peace with freedom; however, the ability to deter rests on an equitable and stable strategic balance. That balance is now being increasingly threatened by the continuing Soviet buildup in offensive nuclear forces, a buildup which began in the early seventies, as well as deep Soviet involvement in strategic defense. Our Strategic Defense Initiative is a prudent response to these Soviet programs. It is a research program, being conducted in conformity with our treaty obligations, which seeks to establish whether in the future deterrence could be based increasingly on defensive systems which threaten no one, rather than on the threat of offensive retaliation.

I began this intensified research effort on March 23, 1983, when I proposed that we explore the possibility of countering the awesome Soviet missile threat with defensive systems that could intercept and destroy missiles before they strike their targets. Such a defense-oriented world would not be to any single nation's advantage, but would benefit all. And the research and testing of SDI would move us toward our ultimate goal of eliminating nuclear weapons altogether from the face of the Earth. By necessity, this is a very long-term goal. For years to come, we will have to continue to base deterrence on the threat of nuclear retaliation, but there is no reason why we should not begin now to seek a safer, more stable world.

Q. Does SDI violate any U.S. treaty obligations? Specifically, does it violate article 5 of the ABM treaty of 1972, which prohibits not only deployment but also development of space-based antiballistic missiles?

The President. I have directed that the SDI research program be conducted in a manner fully consistent with all U.S. treaty obligations, including the ABM treaty. We are and intend to remain in full compliance with the ABM treaty and to seek Soviet compliance as well.

Q. Sir, you have said that new technologies are now at hand which make possible a truly effective nonnuclear defense, and for that reason you have launched the SDI. Do you believe that the U.S.A. will continue to have a lasting lead in these technologies?

Don't you think that the Soviet Union will catch up as it did in the case of the MIRV technology, which was a U.S. monopoly in the sixties?

The President. It is not a question of the Soviet Union catching up with U.S. technologies. For over two decades, the Soviet Union has pursued an intensive research program in many of the same basic technological areas that our research program will address. For example, more than 10,000 Soviet scientists and engineers are engaged in their advanced laser research program. A comprehensive report on Soviet strategic defense programs has just been released by our State and Defense Departments. If we do not respond to Soviet strategic defense efforts, Soviet programs in both offense and defense could seriously threaten our ability to deter attack.

Q. The first nation to achieve both defensive and offensive capabilities might well be tempted to launch a devastating nuclear first strike. Since decisionmaking in the Soviet political system is secret and highly centralized, as distinct from the open system of governance in the U.S.A., the U.S.S.R. could well be that nation. By advocating SDI, therefore, sir, are you not promoting the first-strike capabilities of the Soviet Union?

The President. If the Soviet Union were to achieve overwhelming superiority in both offensive and defensive systems, it could come to believe that it could launch a nuclear attack against the U.S. or its allies without fear of effective retaliation. That is why the U.S. is concerned over the massive Soviet investment in both offensive and defensive systems. SDI is, in part, a response to the danger from these Soviet military programs. It is aimed precisely at strengthening deterrence and stability by reducing the danger that the Soviets might be tempted to think in terms of a nuclear first strike.

Q. Mr. President, do you share the apprehension that SDI would give a new dimension to the arms race by taking nuclear weapons into outer space and that this could heighten tensions at the decisionmaking levels of both the superpowers, making the world more unstable and insecure?

The President. No, I'm certain the impact of SDI will be quite the opposite. Given the hope it offers the world, it will ease tensions, not increase them.

Q. Some strategists have suggested that while the U.S.A. moves close to actual deployment of a defensive space weapons system, the Soviet Union would be under an increasingly desperate temptation to strike while it still has a chance. For that reason, would you not like to launch a joint superpower initiative for research in defensive space weapons so that the fears and suspicions raised by SDI are obviated?

The President. As I said earlier, we are seeking agreement in Geneva on ways to strengthen deterrence through the introduction of defensive systems into the force structures of both sides, if the technologies which we are *both* investigating prove feasible and cost-effective. Our negotiators at Geneva are prepared to discuss how such a transition could be carried out in a stable manner. And I want very much to explain personally to General Secretary Gorbachev how important it is for him not to let this chance to set arms control on a more hopeful course pass by.

Q. What is the Soviet Union doing in the field of strategic defense? Do you think that the Soviet opposition to SDI is merely pre-summit posturing similar to their opposition to cruise missile deployment in Western Europe?

The President. Posturing is a good word. Although they have been treating strategic defenses as if they were solely an American invention, the Soviets, over the past 20 years, have spent roughly as much for strategic defense as they have for their massive offensive buildup. During this time, it has been the Soviets who have built the world's most extensive network of civil defenses and the most widespread air defense system; who have deployed the world's only operational ABM and antisatellite systems; and who have devoted extensive resources to investigating many of the very same technologies we are now examining in our SDI research. Some of these Soviet efforts, such as their construction of a large phased-array radar in central Siberia, are in clear violation of the 1972 ABM treaty; others are questionable under the treaty.

In light of all this, Soviet criticism of SDI

is more than a little hypocritical. It is quite clear that the Soviets are intent on undermining the U.S. SDI program, while minimizing any constraints on their own ongoing strategic defense activities. For our part, we believe that it is important that our two countries get down to a serious, no-nonsense dialog about the questions of how we might together enable our mutual interest in strategic defenses to lead to a more stable balance.

Developing Countries

Q. All the ills of the world are not due to Russia. If there were no Russia, the problems of poverty and underdevelopment of most of the world would still be there. Next month, the two strongest leaders of the world are meeting in Geneva. Is this not an opportunity to cry halt to the deployment and development of all new nuclear weapons and to divert the resources thus saved to improve the lot of the poorest countries of the world?

The President. I certainly would like to see a world in which there are no nuclear weapons and plentiful resources devoted to the eradication of world poverty. I suspect that I won't see such an ideal world during my lifetime, but I will do all I can to help this dream come true. If General Secretary Gorbachev and I can address some of our differences frankly, we will perhaps have taken one small step towards this goal, and no one should underestimate the importance of that.

Although the Soviet Union is not the source of all the troubles of the developing world, we do think that the Soviet Government has too often supported forces intent on imposing their rule by violence. This not only creates untold suffering and halts economic and social development but often introduces an East-West element in the disputes when there should be none. These practices must stop if we are to create a safer and better world. All nations are entitled to work out their destinies free from force and violence, particularly that coming from other countries.

Let me suggest, then, one immediate way that the peoples of the West and the Soviet

Union can help the poorer nations: by keeping the competition of ideas peaceful. Let there be competition by example—no subversion of free governments, no invasion, no occupation, no injection of foreign troops to support factions in internal disputes. Developing habits of solving problems peacefully would benefit all. We already are observing those principles, because they are the only ones consistent with our vision of the future.

Perhaps I can close by saying a word about that vision as it applies to the developing nations. As you know, the United States has contributed billions of dollars to economic and social development in all regions of the globe; most of this aid has gone to nations that won their independence during the past few decades. Hundreds of thousands of Third World students, many of them from India, have received American university educations. Both the U.S. Government and private American donors are contributing great sums today to famine relief in especially needy countries.

But, to be frank, aid levels aren't the heart of the matter. The future of the developing nations, both economic and political, really depends on the resolution of a broader issue; that is, whether those institutions of freedom are created that are the best, and in the long term the only source of economic growth and guarantee of individual dignity. India's great victory in the past 40 years has been to protect those institutions through good times and bad. The benefits you win from them are probably only just beginning. They are the basis of so much of the cultural vigor and economic dynamism that we see in your country now. Free institutions, however, aren't just a freak of history, something that only a few peoples can ever hope to enjoy. There's no reason they can't take deeper root throughout the Third World. If they do—well, almost anything will be possible.

Note: A tape was not available for verification of the content of the oral portion of this interview, which was released by the Office of the Press Secretary on October 22.

Nomination of John R. Bolton To Be an Assistant Attorney General
October 22, 1985

The President today announced his intention to nominate John R. Bolton to be an Assistant Attorney General (Office of Legislative and Intergovernmental Affairs), Department of Justice. He would succeed Robert A. McConnell.

Since 1983 Mr. Bolton has been a partner in the law firm of Covington & Burling in Washington, DC. Previously, he was executive director of the Committee on Resolutions (Platform) at the Republican National Committee in 1983–1984; Assistant Administrator for Program and Policy Coordination at the Agency for International Development in 1982–1983; General Counsel at the Agency for International Development in 1982–1983; and an associate with Covington & Burling in 1974–1981.

He graduated from Yale College (B.A., 1970) and Yale Law School (J.D., 1974). He was born November 20, 1948, in Baltimore, MD, and now resides in Arlington, VA.

Nomination of Alexander Hansen Good To Be Director General of the United States and Foreign Commercial Service
October 22, 1985

The President today announced his intention to nominate Alexander Hansen Good to be Director General of the United States and Foreign Commercial Service, Department of Commerce. He would succeed Kenneth S. George.

Mr. Good is presently serving as Principal Deputy Assistant Secretary, International Economic Policy, Department of Commerce. Previously, he was Deputy Solicitor of the Department of the Interior in 1983; Associate Solicitor for Energy and Resources, Department of the Interior, in 1981–1983; and with the law firm of O'Melveny and Myers in 1976–1981.

He graduated from the University of California (A.B., 1972) and Loyola University in Los Angeles (J.D., 1975). He was born December 5, 1949, in Glendale, CA, and now resides in Washington, DC.

Nomination of Charles Edward Horner To Be an Associate Director of the United States Information Agency
October 22, 1985

The President today announced his intention to nominate Charles Edward Horner to be an Associate Director for Programs of the United States Information Agency. He would succeed Charles E. Courtney.

Mr. Horner has been serving as Deputy Assistant Secretary of State for Science and Technology since October 1981. Previously, he served as U.S. Deputy Representative to the United Nations Conference on Law of the Sea (1981); at Georgetown University as a member of the adjunct faculty at the School of Foreign Service and as an associate of the Landegger program in international business diplomacy; as senior legislative assistant to Senator Daniel Moynihan; and on the staff of the Senate's Subcommittee on National Security and International Operations. He has written on international issues for various publications, including the Wall Street Journal, Commentary, and American Spectator.

He graduated from the University of Pennsylvania (B.A., 1964) and the University of Chicago (M.A., 1967). He studied in the Far East at National Taiwan University and then at Tokyo University. He is married, has two children, and resides in Washington, DC. He was born April 8, 1943, in New York City.

Nomination of Sam A. Nixon To Be a Member of the Board of Regents of the Uniformed Services University of the Health Sciences
October 22, 1985

The President today announced his intention to nominate Sam A. Nixon to be a member of the Board of Regents of the Uniformed Services University of the Health Sciences, Department of Defense, for a term expiring June 20, 1991. He would succeed Caro Elise Luhrs.

Dr. Nixon is currently director of the University of Texas Health Science Center in Houston. He has been a practicing physician specializing in family medicine and surgery since 1954 and was chief of staff at Memorial Hospital, Floresville, TX, 1968–1972. Dr. Nixon served in the U.S. Army Medical Corps in Korea, Japan, and Texas, 1950–1954.

He graduated from Texas A&M University (B.S., 1946) and the University of Texas Medical Branch (M.D., 1950). Dr. Nixon is married, has four children, and resides in Houston, TX. He was born June 28, 1927, in Galveston, TX.

Appointment of Joyce Lee Gorringe as a Member of the National Advisory Council on Adult Education
October 22, 1985

The President today announced his intention to appoint Joyce Lee Gorringe to be a member of the National Advisory Council on Adult Education for a term expiring July 10, 1988. This is a reappointment.

Mrs. Gorringe has been owner and manager of Farm Business since 1959. She has also been a schoolteacher in elementary and secondary schools in the Chicago area, 1965–1972. Mrs. Gorringe has been active in a number of civic programs for adult education and has served as a counselor for crisis intervention and family relations.

Mrs. Gorringe graduated from Northwestern University (B.M., 1949) and has done graduate work at Valparaiso and Northwestern Universities. Mrs. Gorringe is married, has four children, and resides in Naperville, IL. She was born August 8, 1928, in Hammond, IN.

Appointment of Six Members of the President's Commission on White House Fellowships
October 22, 1985

The President today announced his intention to appoint the following individuals to be members of the President's Commission on White House Fellowships:

Betty H. Brake has been active in political and civic activities in Oklahoma for many years. She graduated from the University of Oklahoma (B.A., 1942). She was born May 14, 1920, in Oklahoma City, OK.

Francis Winford Cash is executive vice president of Marriott Corp. Prior to Marriott, he spent 10 years with Arthur Anderson & Co. He graduated from Brigham Young University (B.A., 1965). He was born March 16, 1942, in Buena Vista, VA, and currently resides in Potomac, MD. He is married and has five children.

LeGree S. Daniels has most recently served as chairman of the National Black Republican Council. Previously she was employed by the Bureau of Motor Vehicles, Commonwealth of Pennsylvania. She was born February 29, 1920, in Denmark, SC, and attended Temple University. She is married and has 15 foster children. She currently resides in Harrisburg, PA.

Robert Elliott Freer, Jr., is a partner with the law firm of Wheeler and Wheeler. Previously he served as general counsel of Roswell, Kimberly-Clark Corp. He graduated from Princeton University (B.A., 1963) and the University of Virginia (J.D., 1966). He was born February 19, 1941, in Washington, DC. He is married, has four children, and currently resides in Chevy Chase, MD.

Lester Bernard Korn is chairman of the board and chief executive officer of Korn/Ferry International. From 1960 to 1969, he was a partner with Peat, Marwick, Mitchell & Co. He graduated from UCLA (B.S., 1959; M.B.A., 1960). He was born January 11, 1936, in New York, NY, and currently resides in Los Angeles, CA. He is married and has two children.

Judith Anne Walter is Deputy Comptroller for Operations, Office of the Comptroller of the Currency. Her previous positions with Comptroller of the Currency include Director, Strategic Planning; Acting Director, Strategic Analysis; and Deputy Director, Strategic Analysis. She graduated from the University of Wisconsin (B.A., 1964); University of California at Berkeley (M.A., 1968; M.B.A., 1975). She was born February 14, 1941, in Ames, IA, and currently resides in Washington, DC. She is married and has two children.

Appointment of Two Delegates to the National White House Conference on Small Business
October 22, 1985

The President today announced his intention to appoint the following individuals to be delegates to the National White House Conference on Small Business:

Scott A. (Casey) Clugston is currently president of the Clugston Companies, Inc., a consulting firm. Previously Mr. Clugston was president of Oklahoma Energy Shutters, Inc., and from 1972 to 1980, was vice president of Loveless Manufacturing Co. Mr. Clugston graduated from Kansas State College (B.S., 1967) and served in the United States Army, 1968–1972. He was born October 13, 1945, in Pittsburg, KS, and currently resides in Tulsa, OK. He is married and has two children.

Henry Hammond Stith, Jr., is president and general manager of Stith Equipment Co. He graduated from Georgia Tech University (B.S., 1958). He was born August 3, 1936, in Atlanta, GA, and currently resides in Atlanta. He is married and has one child.

Appointment of Frances Barrett Hammer as an Alternate United States Member of the Roosevelt Campobello International Park Commission
October 22, 1985

The President today announced his intention to appoint Frances Barrett Hammer to be an alternate member on the part of the United States on the Roosevelt Campobello

International Park Commission. She will succeed Grace Tully.

Mrs. Hammer is a member of the Amazing Blue Ribbon 400 and is on the board of directors of the Armand Hammer United World College of the American West. She has participated in the Armand Hammer Conferences for Peace and Human Rights as well as other projects for improvements in human and cultural needs. Mrs. Hammer is one of the founders of the International Student Center at UCLA. She is also a recipient of the Award of the American Women for International Understanding and Peace.

Mrs. Hammer was born April 4, 1902, in Chicago, IL. She is married and resides in Los Angeles, CA.

Letter to the Speaker of the House and the President of the Senate on the Removal of Portugal as a Trade Beneficiary Developing Country
October 22, 1985

Dear Mr. Speaker: (Dear Mr. President:)

I am writing to inform you of my intent to remove Portugal from the list of beneficiary developing countries under the Generalized System of Preferences (GSP) Program, effective January 1, 1986.

This action is required by section 502(b) of Title V of the Trade Act of 1974, as amended (the Act), which states that no member state of the European Communities may be designated as eligible for GSP benefits. Portugal will become a member state of the European Communities on January 1, 1986.

This notice is being provided pursuant to section 502(a)(2) of the Act.

Sincerely,

RONALD REAGAN

Note: Identical letters were sent to Thomas P. O'Neill, Jr., Speaker of the House of Representatives, and George Bush, President of the Senate.

Proclamation 5396—A Time of Remembrance, 1985
October 23, 1985

By the President of the United States of America

A Proclamation

The problem of terrorism has become an international concern that knows no boundaries—religious, racial, political, or national. Thousands of men, women, and children have died at the hands of terrorists in nations around the world, and the lives of many more have been blighted by the fear and grief that terrorist attacks have caused to peace-loving peoples. Today, unfortunately, terrorism continues to claim many innocent lives.

Recent events in the Middle East, including the piratic seizure of the ACHILLE LAURO and the brutal murder of Leon Klinghoffer, only serve to remind us of the intolerable threat from terrorists. All Americans share the sorrow of the families of their victims, and we are determined that those responsible be brought to justice.

October 23 is the second anniversary of the date on which the largest number of Americans was killed in a single act of terrorism—the bombing of the United States compound in Beirut, Lebanon on October 23, 1983, in which 241 United States servicemen lost their lives. These brave soldiers died defending our cherished ideals of freedom and peace. It is appropriate that we honor these men and all other victims of terrorism. Let us also offer our profound condolences to the families and friends of the victims of these unprovoked and contemptible acts of violence.

The Congress, by Senate Joint Resolution 104, has designated October 23, 1985, as "A Time of Remembrance" and authorized and requested the President to issue a proclamation in observance of this event.

Now, Therefore, I, Ronald Reagan, President of the United States of America, do hereby proclaim October 23, 1985, as A Time of Remembrance. I urge all Ameri-cans to take time to reflect on the sacrifices that have been made in the pursuit of peace and freedom.

In Witness Whereof, I have hereunto set my hand this twenty-third day of October, in the year of our Lord nineteen hundred and eighty-five, and of the Independence of the United States of America the two hundred and tenth.

RONALD REAGAN

[*Filed with the Office of the Federal Register, 11:38 a.m., October 23, 1985*]

Toast at a Luncheon for the Heads of Delegations to the 40th Session of the United Nations General Assembly in New York, New York
October 23, 1985

Well, Mr. Secretary General and distinguished guests, on behalf of the people of the United States, I'm honored to be with you today to commemorate the 40th anniversary of the United Nations. The world is a busy place. It's full of movement and action, and it's good for us to get away from things for an hour or two and meet in the quiet of this great room, consider the meaning of the United Nations, its past and its future. There are a great number of distinguished world leaders here today. I believe, Mr. Secretary General, that their presence bears witness to the enduring vitality of the idea of the United Nations. I believe it also bears witness to the success of your leadership during a challenging time for both the U.N. and the world.

This anniversary, for all of us—a time for reflection as well as celebration. The nations and the peoples of the world value the United Nations for many things, but most, perhaps, for what it symbolizes. The U.N. began as a symbol of hope and reconciliation 40 years ago after the worst war in history; it's no less a symbol today. The United Nations is still a symbol of man's great hope that some day he'll be able to resolve all disputes through peaceful discussion and never again through the force of arms. The United Nations is a symbol of man's long struggle to rise beyond his own flawed nature and live by the high ideals that the best of mankind have defined and declared down through the ages.

As the host country, the United States believes in the United Nations and in what it symbolizes. We have criticized it sometimes in the past when we felt that it was not all it could be and should be. And we have on occasion been frustrated, but we have never stopped believing in its possibilities, and we've never stopped taking the United Nations seriously. That is why we are determined to see to it that the United Nations lives up to its noble potential to further the cause of freedom, defend individual rights, increase economic growth and well-being, and strengthen the rule of law.

And so, today, 40 years after the birth of the United Nations and 15 years before the end of the century whose tribulations inspired it, let us, together, seize the moment. Let us recapture the vision of the charter and recall the principles upon which the U.N. was founded. Let us resolve to make this organization and the world it represents a better, safer place. And let us renew our commitment, individually and together, to peace and justice and the rights of man.

And may I presume to suggest a toast to the Secretary General and what he has accomplished and what he is doing for all of us.

Note: The President spoke at 2:45 p.m. in

the North Delegate's Lounge at the United Nations in response to a toast by Secretary General Javier Perez de Cuellar de la Guerra.

Address to the 40th Session of the United Nations General Assembly in New York, New York
October 24, 1985

Mr. President, Mr. Secretary General, honored guests, and distinguished delegates, thank you for the honor of permitting me to speak on this anniversary for the United Nations. Forty years ago, the world awoke daring to believe hatred's unyielding grip had finally been broken, daring to believe the torch of peace would be protected in liberty's firm grasp. Forty years ago, the world yearned to dream again innocent dreams, to believe in ideals with innocent trust. Dreams of trust are worthy, but in these 40 years too many dreams have been shattered, too many promises have been broken, too many lives have been lost. The painful truth is that the use of violence to take, to exercise, and to preserve power remains a persistent reality in much of the world.

The vision of the U.N. Charter—to spare succeeding generations this scourge of war—remains real. It still stirs our soul and warms our hearts, but it also demands of us a realism that is rockhard, clear-eyed, steady, and sure—a realism that understands the nations of the United Nations are not united. I come before you this morning preoccupied with peace, with ensuring that the differences between some of us not be permitted to degenerate into open conflict, and I come offering for my own country a new commitment, a fresh start.

On this U.N. anniversary, we acknowledge its successes: the decisive action during the Korean war, negotiation of the nonproliferation treaty, strong support for decolonization, and the laudable achievements by the United Nations High Commissioner for Refugees. Nor must we close our eyes to this organization's disappointments: its failure to deal with real security issues, the total inversion of morality in the infamous Zionism-is-racism resolution, the politicization of too many agencies, the misuse of too many resources. The U.N. is a political institution, and politics requires compromise. We recognize that, but let us remember from those first days, one guiding star was supposed to light our path toward the U.N. vision of peace and progress—a star of freedom.

What kind of people will we be 40 years from today? May we answer: free people, worthy of freedom and firm in the conviction that freedom is not the sole prerogative of a chosen few, but the universal right of all God's children. This is the universal declaration of human rights set forth in 1948, and this is the affirming flame the United States has held high to a watching world. We champion freedom not only because it is practical and beneficial but because it is morally right and just. Free people whose governments rest upon the consent of the governed do not wage war on their neighbors. Free people blessed by economic opportunity and protected by laws that respect the dignity of the individual are not driven toward the domination of others.

We readily acknowledge that the United States is far from perfect. Yet we have endeavored earnestly to carry out our responsibilities to the charter these past 40 years, and we take national pride in our contributions to peace. We take pride in 40 years of helping avert a new world war and pride in our alliances that protect and preserve us and our friends from aggression. We take pride in the Camp David agreements and

1285

our efforts for peace in the Middle East, rooted in resolutions 242 and 338; in supporting Pakistan, target of outside intimidation; in assisting El Salvador's struggle to carry forward its democratic revolution; in answering the appeal of our Caribbean friends in Grenada; in seeing Grenada's Representative here today voting the will of its own people; and we take pride in our proposals to reduce the weapons of war. We submit this history as evidence of our sincerity of purpose. But today it is more important to speak to you about what my country proposes to do in these closing years of the 20th century to bring about a safer, a more peaceful, a more civilized world.

Let us begin with candor, with words that rest on plain and simple facts. The differences between America and the Soviet Union are deep and abiding. The United States is a democratic nation. Here the people rule. We build no walls to keep them in, nor organize any system of police to keep them mute. We occupy no country. The only land abroad we occupy is beneath the graves where our heroes rest. What is called the West is a voluntary association of free nations, all of whom fiercely value their independence and their sovereignty. And as deeply as we cherish our beliefs, we do not seek to compel others to share them.

When we enjoy these vast freedoms as we do, it's difficult for us to understand the restrictions of dictatorships which seek to control each institution and every facet of people's lives—the expression of their beliefs, their movements, and their contacts with the outside world. It's difficult for us to understand the ideological premise that force is an acceptable way to expand a political system. We Americans do not accept that any government has the right to command and order the lives of its people, that any nation has an historic right to use force to export its ideology. This belief, regarding the nature of man and the limitations of government, is at the core of our deep and abiding differences with the Soviet Union, differences that put us into natural conflict and competition with one another.

Now, we would welcome enthusiastically a true competition of ideas; welcome a competition of economic strength and sci-

entific and artistic creativity; and, yes, welcome a competition for the good will of the world's people. But we cannot accommodate ourselves to the use of force and subversion to consolidate and expand the reach of totalitarianism. When Mr. Gorbachev and I meet in Geneva next month, I look to a fresh start in the relationship of our two nations. We can and should meet in the spirit that we can deal with our differences peacefully. And that is what we expect.

The only way to resolve differences is to understand them. We must have candid and complete discussions of where dangers exist and where peace is being disrupted. Make no mistake, our policy of open and vigorous competition rests on a realistic view of the world. And therefore, at Geneva we must review the reasons for the current level of mistrust. For example, in 1972 the international community negotiated in good faith a ban on biological and toxin weapons; in 1975 we negotiated the Helsinki accords on human rights and freedoms; and during the decade just past, the United States and the Soviet Union negotiated several agreements on strategic weapons. And yet we feel it will be necessary at Geneva to discuss with the Soviet Union what we believe are violations of a number of the provisions in all of these agreements. Indeed, this is why it is important that we have this opportunity to air our differences through face-to-face meetings, to let frank talk substitute for anger and tension.

The United States has never sought treaties merely to paper over differences. We continue to believe that a nuclear war is one that cannot be won and must never be fought. And that is why we have sought for nearly 10 years—still seek and will discuss in Geneva—radical, equitable, verifiable reductions in these vast arsenals of offensive nuclear weapons. At the beginning of the latest round of the ongoing negotiations in Geneva, the Soviet Union presented a specific proposal involving numerical values. We are studying the Soviet counterproposal carefully. I believe that within their proposal there are seeds which we should nurture, and in the coming weeks we will seek to establish a genuine process of give and take. The United States is also seeking to discuss with the Soviet Union in Geneva the vital relationship between offensive and defensive systems, including the possibility of moving toward a more stable and secure world in which defenses play a growing role.

The ballistic missile is the most awesome, threatening, and destructive weapon in the history of man. Thus, I welcome the interest of the new Soviet leadership in the reduction of offensive strategic forces. Ultimately, we must remove this menace, once and for all, from the face of the Earth. Until that day, the United States seeks to escape the prison of mutual terror by research and testing that could, in time, enable us to neutralize the threat of these ballistic missiles and, ultimately, render them obsolete.

How is Moscow threatened if the capitals of other nations are protected? We do not ask that the Soviet leaders, whose country has suffered so much from war, to leave their people defenseless against foreign attack. Why then do they insist that we remain undefended? Who is threatened if Western research and Soviet research, that is itself well-advanced, should develop a nonnuclear system which would threaten not human beings but only ballistic missiles? Surely, the world will sleep more secure when these missiles have been rendered useless, militarily and politically; when the sword of Damocles that has hung over our planet for too many decades is lifted by Western and Russian scientists working to shield their citizens and one day shut down space as an avenue of weapons of mass destruction. If we're destined by history to compete, militarily, to keep the peace, then let us compete in systems that defend our societies rather than weapons which can destroy us both and much of God's creation along with us.

Some 18 years ago, then-Premier Aleksei Kosygin was asked about a moratorium on the development of an antimissile defense system. The official news agency, TASS, reported that he replied with these words: "I believe the defensive systems, which prevent attack, are not the cause of the arms race, but constitute a factor preventing the death of people. Maybe an antimissile system is more expensive than an offensive system, but it is designed not to kill people,

but to preserve human lives." Preserving lives—no peace is more fundamental than that. Great obstacles lie ahead, but they should not deter us. Peace is God's commandment. Peace is the holy shadow cast by men treading on the path of virtue.

But just as we all know what peace is, we certainly know what peace is not. Peace based on repression cannot be true peace and is secure only when individuals are free to direct their own governments. Peace based on partition cannot be true peace. Put simply: Nothing can justify the continuing and permanent division of the European Continent. Walls of partition and distrust must give way to greater communication for an open world. Before leaving for Geneva, I shall make new proposals to achieve this goal. Peace based on mutual fear cannot be true peace, because staking our future on a precarious balance of terror is not good enough. The world needs a balance of safety. And finally, a peace based on averting our eyes from trouble cannot be true peace. The consequences of conflict are every bit as tragic when the destruction is contained within one country.

Real peace is what we seek, and that is why today the United States is presenting an initiative that addresses what will be a central issue in Geneva—the issue of regional conflicts in Africa, Asia, and Central America. Our own position is clear: As the oldest nation of the New World, as the first anticolonial power, the United States rejoiced when decolonization gave birth to so many new nations after World War II. We have always supported the right of the people of each nation to define their own destiny. We have given $300 billion since 1945 to help people of other countries, and we've tried to help friendly governments defend against aggression, subversion, and terror.

We have noted with great interest similar expressions of peaceful intent by leaders of the Soviet Union. I am not here to challenge the good faith of what they say. But isn't it important for us to weigh the record as well? In Afghanistan, there are 118,000 Soviet troops prosecuting war against the Afghan people. In Cambodia, 140,000 Soviet-backed Vietnamese soldiers wage a war of occupation. In Ethiopia, 1,700 Soviet advisers are involved in military planning and support operations along with 2,500 Cuban combat troops. In Angola, 1,200 Soviet military advisers involved in planning and supervising combat operations along with 35,000 Cuban troops. In Nicaragua, some 8,000 Soviet-bloc and Cuban personnel, including about 3,500 military and secret police personnel.

All of these conflicts—some of them underway for a decade—originate in local disputes, but they share a common characteristic: They are the consequence of an ideology imposed from without, dividing nations and creating regimes that are, almost from the day they take power, at war with their own people. And in each case, Marxism-Leninism's war with the people becomes war with their neighbors. These wars are exacting a staggering human toll and threaten to spill across national boundaries and trigger dangerous confrontations. Where is it more appropriate than right here at the United Nations to call attention to article II of our charter, which instructs members to refrain "from the use or threat or use of force against the territorial integrity or political independence of any state. . . "? During the past decade, these wars played a large role in building suspicions and tensions in my country over the purpose of Soviet policy. This gives us an extra reason to address them seriously today.

Last year, I proposed from this podium that the United States and Soviet Union hold discussions on some of these issues, and we have done so. But I believe these problems need more than talk. For that reason, we are proposing and are fully committed to support a regional peace process that seeks progress on three levels.

First, we believe the starting point must be a process of negotiation among the warring parties in each country I've mentioned, which in the case of Afghanistan includes the Soviet Union. The form of these talks may and should vary, but negotiations and an improvement of internal political conditions are essential to achieving an end to violence, the withdrawal of foreign troops, and national reconciliation.

There is a second level. Once negotia-

tions take hold and the parties directly involved are making real progress, representatives of the United States and the Soviet Union should sit down together. It is not for us to impose any solutions in this separate set of talks; such solutions would not last. But the issue we should address is how best to support the ongoing talks among the warring parties. In some cases, it might well be appropriate to consider guarantees for any agreements already reached. But in every case, the primary task is to promote this goal: verified elimination of the foreign military presence and restraint on the flow of outside arms.

And finally, if these first two steps are successful, we could move on to the third: welcoming each country back into the world economy so its citizens can share in the dynamic growth that other developing countries, countries that are at peace, enjoy. Despite past differences with these regimes, the United States would respond generously to their democratic reconciliation with their own people, their respect for human rights, and their return to the family of free nations. Of course, until such time as these negotiations result in definitive progress, America's support for struggling democratic resistance forces must not and shall not cease.

This plan is bold; it is realistic. It is not a substitute for existing peacemaking efforts; it complements them. We're not trying to solve every conflict in every region of the globe, and we recognize that each conflict has its own character. Naturally, other regional problems will require different approaches. But we believe that the recurrent pattern of conflict that we see in these five cases ought to be broken as soon as possible. We must begin somewhere, so let us begin where there is great need and great hope. This will be a clear step forward to help people choose their future more freely. Moreover, this is an extraordinary opportunity for the Soviet side to make a contribution to regional peace which, in turn, can promote future dialog and negotiations on other critical issues.

With hard work and imagination, there is no limit to what, working together, our nations can achieve. Gaining a peaceful resolution of these conflicts will open whole new vistas of peace and progress—the discovery that the promise of the future lies not in measures of military defense or the control of weapons, but in the expansion of individual freedom and human rights. Only when the human spirit can worship, create, and build, only when people are given a personal stake in determining their own destiny and benefiting from their own risks, do societies become prosperous, progressive, dynamic, and free.

We need only open our eyes to the economic evidence all around us. Nations that deny their people opportunity—in Eastern Europe, Indochina, southern Africa, and Latin America—without exception, are dropping further behind in the race for the future. But where we see enlightened leaders who understand that economic freedom and personal incentive are key to development, we see economies striding forward. Singapore, Taiwan, and South Korea, India, Botswana, and China—these are among the current and emerging success stories because they have the courage to give economic incentives a chance.

Let us all heed the simple eloquence in Andrei Sakharov's Nobel Peace Prize message: "International trust, mutual understanding, disarmament and international security are inconceivable without an open society with freedom of information, freedom of conscience, the right to publish and the right to travel and choose the country in which one wishes to live." At the core, this is an eternal truth; freedom works. That is the promise of the open world and awaits only our collective grasp. Forty years ago, hope came alive again for a world that hungered for hope. I believe fervently that hope is still alive.

The United States has spoken with candor and conviction today, but that does not lessen these strong feelings held by every American. It's in the nature of Americans to hate war and its destructiveness. We would rather wage our struggle to rebuild and renew, not to tear down. We would rather fight against hunger, disease, and catastrophe. We would rather engage our adversaries in the battle of ideals and ideas for the future. These principles emerge from the innate openness and good character of our people and from our long struggle and sacrifice for our liberties and the liberties of others. Americans always yearn for peace. They have a passion for life. They carry in their hearts a deep capacity for reconciliation.

Last year at this General Assembly, I indicated there was every reason for the United States and the Soviet Union to shorten the distance between us. In Geneva, the first meeting between our heads of government in more than 6 years, Mr. Gorbachev and I will have that opportunity. So, yes, let us go to Geneva with both sides committed to dialog. Let both sides go committed to a world with fewer nuclear weapons, and some day with none. Let both sides go committed to walk together on a safer path into the 21st century and to lay the foundation for enduring peace. It is time, indeed, to do more than just talk of a better world. It is time to act. And we will act when nations cease to try to impose their ways upon others. And we will act when they realize that we, for whom the achievement of freedom has come dear, will do what we must to preserve it from assault.

America is committed to the world because so much of the world is inside America. After all, only a few miles from this very room is our Statue of Liberty, past which life began anew for millions, where the peoples from nearly every country in this hall joined to build these United States. The blood of each nation courses through the American vein and feeds the spirit that compels us to involve ourselves in the fate of this good Earth. It is the same spirit that warms our heart in concern to help ease the desperate hunger that grips proud people on the African Continent. It is the internationalist spirit that came together last month when our neighbor Mexico was struck suddenly by an earthquake. Even as the Mexican nation moved vigorously into action, there were heartwarming offers by other nations offering to help and glimpses of people working together, without concern for national self-interest or gain.

And if there was any meaning to salvage out of that tragedy, it was found one day in a huge mound of rubble that was once the Juarez Hospital in Mexico City. A week after that terrible event, and as another day of despair unfolded, a team of workers heard a faint sound coming from somewhere in the heart of the crushed concrete. Hoping beyond hope, they quickly burrowed toward it. And as the late afternoon light faded, and racing against time, they found what they had heard, and the first of three baby girls, newborn infants, emerged to the safety of the rescue team. And let me tell you the scene through the eyes of one who was there. "Everyone was so quiet when they lowered that little baby down in a basket covered with blankets. The baby didn't make a sound either. But the minute they put her in the Red Cross ambulance, everybody just got up and cheered." Well, amidst all that hopelessness and debris came a timely and timeless lesson for us all. We witnessed the miracle of life.

It is on this that I believe our nations can make a renewed commitment. The miracle of life is given by One greater than ourselves, but once given, each life is ours to nurture and preserve, to foster, not only for today's world but for a better one to come. There is no purpose more noble than for us to sustain and celebrate life in a turbulent world, and that is what we must do now. We have no higher duty, no greater cause as humans. Life and the preservation of freedom to live it in dignity is what we are on this Earth to do. Everything we work to achieve must seek that end so that some day our prime ministers, our premiers, our presidents, and our general secretaries will talk not of war and peace, but only of peace. We've had 40 years to begin. Let us not waste one more moment to give back to the world all that we can in return for this miracle of life.

Thank you all. God bless you all.

Note: The President spoke at 10:08 a.m. in the General Assembly Hall at the United Nations. Upon his arrival at the United Nations, the President was greeted by Secretary General Javier Perez de Cuellar de la Guerra.

Informal Exchange With Reporters Prior to a Meeting With Soviet Foreign Minister Eduard Shevardnadze in New York, New York
October 24, 1985

Q. Mr. President, why were you so tough in outlining Soviet misdeeds today?

The President. You haven't been around for previous photo ops, but I've made it a rule today not to take any questions.

Q. Mr. Shevardnadze, what did you think of the President's speech, sir?

The Foreign Minister. Well, I've outlined it in my speech today.

Q. It sounded like you didn't like it.

Q. Are you going to talk to Mr. Shevardnadze about your plan for settling regional conflicts in this meeting?

The President. No answers, Sam [Sam Donaldson, ABC News].

Q. Mr. President, [Nicaraguan President] Ortega says that your speech flew in the face of peace.

The President. Never have I regretted so much that I'm not giving an answer as on that one.

Q. Is there any questions you will answer?

Q. Mr. Shevardnadze, what, sir, do you think of the President's plan for settling regional conflicts?

The Foreign Minister. That's what we shall be discussing.

Q. In this meeting here?

Q. Does it make arms control——

The Foreign Minister. I don't think we shall be able to discuss it today because of the shortage of time—all of it today.

Q. But does it have some positive aspects?

The Foreign Minister. If there were no positive seeds, we would not have met at all.

Q. Do you think it makes arms control less important, Mr. Shevardnadze?

Mr. Weinberg. Let's go, Andrea [Andrea Mitchell, NBC News]. We're done.

Note: The exchange began at 4 p.m. at the

Waldorf-Astoria Hotel. Mark Weinberg was Assistant Press Secretary to the President. A tape was not available for verification of the content of this exchange.

Nomination of Laurence William Lane, Jr., To Be United States Ambassador to Australia and Nauru
October 24, 1985

The President today announced his intention to nominate Laurence William Lane, Jr., of California, as Ambassador to Australia and to serve concurrently as Ambassador to the Republic of Nauru. He would succeed Robert Dean Nesen.

From 1946 to the present, Mr. Lane has been with the Lane Publishing Co. in Menlo Park, CA, serving in various positions such as marketing representative, salesman, editorial assistant, sales manager, vice president, president, and chairman of the board. He is also publisher of Sunset magazine. From 1965 to the present, he was a member of the advisory board for Liberty Mutual Insurance Company of Northern California; 1967 to the present, a member of the board of directors of the California Water Service Co. in San Jose; 1971 to the present, a member of the board of directors of Crown Zellerbach Corp. in San Francisco; and 1980 to the present, a member of the board of directors of Pacific Gas and Electric Co. in San Francisco. Mr. Lane's government service has included chairman-

ship of the Water Panel, Governor's "California Changing Environment" in 1969; 1972, Chairman, President's Commission for National Parks Centennial; 1973–1974, member, President's National Advisory Committee on Oceans and Atmosphere; 1974–1985, member, Secretary of the Interior Advisory Council for National Parks; 1975, Ambassador/Commissioner General of the U.S. Exhibition at the International Ocean Exposition in Okinawa, Japan; 1976–1981, chairman of the Pacific Area Travel Association, USTS/Commerce; and 1981–1983, a member of the National Productivity Advisory Committee. He was also mayor and councilman, town council of Portola Valley, CA.

Mr. Lane graduated from Stanford University (B.A., 1942). He served in the United States Navy from 1942–1946. His foreign language is Spanish. He is married to the former Donna Jean Gimbel and has three children. He was born November 7, 1919, in Des Moines, IA, and currently resides in Portola Valley, CA.

Nomination of John Edwin Upston To Be United States Ambassador to Rwanda
October 24, 1985

The President today announced his intention to nominate John Edwin Upston, of Virginia, as Ambassador to the Republic of Rwanda. He would succeed John Blane.

Mr. Upston was an associate with Draper, Gaither, and Anderson in Palo Alto, CA, from 1959 to 1964. In 1964 he became a

member of the management planning staff (West Africa) with the Department of State. From 1966 to 1968, he was a member of the permanent U.S. delegation to the United Nations in New York and an adviser in the Bureau of International Organization Affairs in the Department. In 1969 he was an associate with the investment banking firm of Burnham and Co. Mr. Upston then returned to the Department in 1971 to serve as special assistant to the Under Secretary of State for Management, where he remained until 1973 when he became Executive Director of the United States National Commission for Educational, Scientific and Cultural Organization (UNESCO), United Nations, in the Department. In 1981 he was a Presidential delegate to the independence celebration of Antigua and Barbuda. In 1981 he also served as a member of the White House Puerto Rico Task Force. Since 1981 he has been Department of State Coordinator for Caribbean Affairs.

Mr. Upston graduated from Stanford University (A.B., 1958). He has four children. He was born April 17, 1935, in Maxwell Field, AL, and currently resides in Leesburg, VA.

Nomination of Helen M. Witt To Be a Member of the National Mediation Board
October 24, 1985

The President today announced his intention to nominate Helen M. Witt, of Pennsylvania, to be a member of the National Mediation Board for the term expiring July 1, 1988. This is a reappointment.

Mrs. Witt has been a member of the National Mediation Board since 1983. Previously, she was assistant to the chairman, board of arbitration, USS/USWA, in 1975–1982; special arbitrator, U.S. Steel Corp. and United Steelworkers of America, in 1974; on the first expedited arbitration panel formulated by Coordinating Committee Steel Companies and the United Steelworkers under the 1971 basic agreements in 1972; and in the private practice of law with the firms of Cleland, Hurtt & Witt and Witt & Witt in 1970–1974.

Mrs. Witt graduated from Dickinson College (B.A., 1955) and the University of Pittsburgh School of Law (J.D., 1969). She is married, has five children, and resides in Washington, DC. Mrs. Witt was born July 13, 1933, in Atlantic City, NJ.

Appointment of Stephen I. Danzansky as Special Assistant to the President for National Security Affairs and Senior Director of International Economic Affairs for the National Security Council
October 24, 1985

The President today announced the appointment of Stephen I. Danzansky as Special Assistant to the President for National Security Affairs and Senior Director of International Economic Affairs

Mr. Danzansky is a partner in the Washington office of the law firm of Willkie Farr & Gallagher, where he served as managing partner. He has been appointed under three Presidents and elected Chairman of the District of Columbia Law Revision Commission; has been an adjunct professor at George Washington University School of Law; and is a member of the D.C. Bar Association, International Trade Commission Trial Lawyers Committee, and the International Law Institute Advisory Board. He was appointed by President Reagan to serve as a member of the Advisory Committee for Trade Negotiations. Mr. Danzansky has also served as an officer and director of numerous civic and cultural organizations.

He graduated from Washington & Lee University (B.A., 1961) and George Washington University School of Law (J.D., 1964). He is married to Joan Winston Cox. They have two children and reside in Washington, DC. He was born July 31, 1939.

Appointment of Ronald Keith Sable as Special Assistant to the President for National Security Affairs and Senior Director of Legislative Affairs for the National Security Council
October 24, 1985

The President today announced the appointment of Ronald Keith Sable as Special Assistant to the President for National Security Affairs and Senior Director of Legislative Affairs for the National Security Council. He will succeed Christopher M. Lehman.

Mr. Sable has served since December 1983 as Director of Legislative Affairs for the National Security Council. Previously he served as special assistant to Kenneth M. Duberstein, Assistant to the President for Legislative Affairs. Prior to that time, Mr. Sable served as Chief of Air Operations, Office of the Secretary of the Air Force, 1979–1982, and Air Force advance agent for Presidential travel from 1974 to 1978. Mr. Sable, a commercial and military pilot, is retired from the Air Force (colonel). He graduated from Iowa Wesleyan College (B.S., 1963) and Southern Illinois University (M.S., international relations, 1975). He also studied international security affairs at Harvard University. He is a recipient of the Valley Forge Freedoms Foundation George Washington Honor Medal, the Defense Superior Service Medal, the Distinguished Flying Cross, the Meritorious Service Medal, and the Air Medal.

Mr. Sable is married and has one child. He was born May 8, 1941, in Farmington, IA, and currently resides in Alexandria, VA.

Appointment of Raymond F. Burghardt as Special Assistant to the President for National Security Affairs
October 24, 1985

The President today announced his intention to appoint Raymond F. Burghardt as Special Assistant to the President for National Security Affairs. Mr. Burghardt will succeed Constantine C. Menges as Senior Director of Latin American Affairs on the National Security Council staff.

Mr. Burghardt has served on the National Security Council staff since March 1984 as Director of Latin American Affairs, with responsibility for Central America and the Caribbean region. Prior to joining the National Security Council staff, Mr. Burghardt, a career Foreign Service officer, was chief of the political section at the American Embassy in Honduras. His earlier Latin American experience included an assignment as political officer in Guatemala, 1973–1975. Before joining the Foreign Service in 1969, Mr. Burghardt spent 1 year as a Peace Corps volunteer in Colombia. Mr. Burghardt also has had extensive experience in east Asia, including assignments in Saigon and Hong Kong and in the State Department's Bureau of East Asian Affairs.

Mr. Burghardt graduated from Columbia College (B.A., 1967) and attended Columbia University's School of International Affairs. He is married to the former Susan Day, and they have two children. He was born on May 27, 1945, in New York City and resides in Great Falls, VA.

Radio Address to the Nation on International Stability
October 26, 1985

My fellow Americans:

As you know, Nancy and I were in New York City this week to help mark the 40th anniversary of the United Nations. I remember well that summer in 1945 when, out of the great devastation of World War II, the United Nations was born.

Well, this week also marks another important anniversary. Just 2 years ago, the United States came to the rescue of democracy and of hundreds of American students in Grenada. All of us can be proud of the swift response of our country, together with Grenada's democratic Caribbean neighbors to the SOS from Grenada's Governor General Paul Scoon. He appealed for our help to restore order in his country, threatened by the machinery of dictatorship. The scores of Communist-bloc advisers that we found on the island, not to mention the supplies of Soviet arms and files of secret treaties with Communist states, showed the world what the people of Grenada had learned firsthand how Communist revolutionaries can hijack an entire country. Today Grenada is free, and we're helping rebuild their economy. Their democratically elected leader, Herbert Blaize, told me there's more to be done, but "thanks to America, we will make it work."

Well, the deep desire to be free moves people everywhere to resist oppression, from Afghanistan to Cambodia, Angola, Ethiopia, and Nicaragua. Make no mistake, the attempt to impose repressive dictatorships subordinated to Soviet objectives is a fundamental source of tension in many regions of the world. This is why our support for struggling resistance forces shall not cease, why in my address to the U.N. I proposed a three-part initiative to resolve regional conflicts: First, negotiations among warring parties to end the violence and to bring about the democratic reforms and respect for human rights essential for national reconciliation. Second, once progress is made by those directly involved, the United States and the Soviet Union should negotiate the elimination of all foreign military

presence and flow of outside arms. Third, when progress is made through negotiations to end the violence, to bring about democratic reforms and to eliminate the foreign military presence, the United States will ask other nations to join in supporting economic recovery and reconstruction.

When I meet with General Secretary Gorbachev in Geneva, I intend to make our regional peace initiative a key part of our discussions. How can we discuss the goal of a more peaceful and civilized world without discussing those places where peace is being violated and innocent people are being killed? Does the Soviet Union share our conviction that true peace must rest on the right of all people to choose their destiny, to grow and develop free from coercion and fear? Well, we shall see in Geneva. Secretary of State Shultz will be taking up these and other issues on his forthcoming trip to Moscow.

We Americans are practical. We seek practical solutions to problems that seemed intractable, from achieving the universal immunization of children to finding new ways to protect civilization against missile attack. Talking about a safer world is not good enough; we must make it happen. I had detailed discussions with some of our allied leaders this past week. Our conversations convinced me more than ever that we are on the right track. We're negotiating hard with the Soviet Union on reducing offensive nuclear weapons. We have proposals on the table for deep reductions and are examining their counterproposal. We're also determined to move ahead on research and testing of our Strategic Defense Initiative to see whether an effective nonnuclear defense against a nuclear attack is feasible.

Finally, we're combating the deadly menace of international terror. Our action weeks ago to apprehend the Palestinian hijackers was not our last. We're working with all peace-loving nations to create a united front against terrorism, and we're fighting the international narcotics traffickers poisoning our youth. The First Lady's drug conference at the United Nations, which Nancy hosted this week, bringing together 31 first ladies from around the world, will raise global awareness and hopefully touch the conscience of the world.

This has been an important week. We have held high our banner for personal freedom, human progress, and global peace.

Now we must go forward to do what is not only practical and beneficial but what is right and just.

Until next week, thanks for listening.

Note: The President spoke at 12:06 p.m. from Camp David, MD.

Remarks on Receiving the Final Report of the President's Private Sector Survey on Cost Control in the Federal Government
October 28, 1985

I'm delighted that all of you are here today. First, the distinguished leaders of the Grace Congressional Caucus—Chairman Beau Boulter and Cochairman Buddy Roemer and Gordon Humphrey—also, representatives from Associations United To Cut Federal Spending—38 trade organizations led by Wayne Smith, who advised the caucus—and lastly, former members of the Grace commission and of another of my favorite organizations, Citizens Against Government Waste, cochaired by Peter Grace and Jack Anderson. You know, Peter, every time you're here I start thinking about how the Grace contingent keeps growing in numbers, in power, and in influence. Believe me, nothing delights me more, because we need a people's lobby here in Washington.

All of you are here today because of your deep concern about a problem in government that's easy to talk about in terms of saving billions of dollars a year. The war against waste and inefficiency is worth waging on just these grounds alone, but I know your involvement goes even beyond this. The people who came before us in this nation put a heavy emphasis on what is today almost a forgotten virtue. I remember back in Dixon, Illinois, when I was growing up, it was called thriftiness. Thriftiness was a quality appreciated as a kind of signal about the maturity and judgment of a person or institution, an indication that deeper values were there. Some of you in business have noticed that when a company gets in trouble, there are more serious

problems than simple inefficiency—all sorts of projects and activities that are wasteful or marginal and a neglect of those products or services that made the firm successful in the first place.

Well, government is no different. And as the people here know better than most, the Federal Government was headed a few years ago in much the same direction. It was neglecting essential tasks like protecting our nation's security abroad and upholding the law at home while it built gigantic bureaucracies to handle all sorts of problems, problems it was neither competent nor intended to handle. I used to use an example in some of my mashed-potato circuit days about the town that decided that they would have better traffic safety if they raised the height of their traffic signs and various warning signs from 5 feet above the ground to 7 feet above the ground. And then, the Federal Government stepped in and said they had a department to come in and help them, and their plan was to lower the streets 2 feet. [*Laughter*]

Well, then these special interests became involved. Pretty soon the way to a prospering political career was to vote for higher appropriations and for grand, new spending schemes that appeal to this or that voting bloc. And if this pattern of putting politics over country sounds familiar, that's because it is. Historians have frequently seen in this "bread and circuses" climate the signs of government in decline and a nation in decay. Faith in our democratic system—and without that faith democracy simply can't work—was being undermined. As James Madison said, "It's the gradual and silent encroachments of governments, not sudden revolutions, that prove to be the threat to freedom." So, it was the average citizen who harbored enormous feelings of resentment toward government and an enormous sense of frustration. They believed the only voices that were heard in this city were those of the organized lobbies or special interests, not the taxpayers.

Those of you associated with the Grace commission have forthrightly and without apologies helped change all of this. You've shown that citizens from every walk of life could come to the Capitol and not only make their voices heard but persuade and, yes, push and prod government to change its ways. The Grace commission stood back and took a look at government, concluded that the Federal Government had lost its moorings, came up with concrete proposals on how to recover those moorings. But, as I know Peter believes, the most important part of the job is upon us—making sure that the Grace commission is not remembered as just another government commission and that its recommendations don't become just another pile of reports gathering dust in the Library of Congress; in short, implementing as many recommendations as possible.

And on this point, I've just come from a meeting with the Domestic Policy Council. I've received a final report that shows we are going forward with over 80 percent—as a matter of fact, 83 percent of the commission's recommendations. Many have already been implemented; others included in the '86 budget; and a number will be proposed in the '87 budget. Even with the recommendations deferred at this time, we have every intention of trying to implement as many of them as possible in the future. I've asked Jim Miller to have OMB continue to monitor our progress and report to me periodically through the Domestic Policy Council. I also thanked Peter Grace at the close of the meeting, and let me do so now again publicly.

Peter, I can think of few Americans who have done more to make the people's voice heard in Washington. You shook this city up. You put the issue of waste and inefficiency front and center on the public

agenda, and I am grateful to you and so is America. But now, we must work together to get your recommendations through the Congress, and that's what this people's lobby of yours is all about. It's why the Congressional Caucus leaders who are here today are so important. Imagine the courage of these Members of Congress who would dare to associate themselves with such a clear-cut effort to thwart the special interests. And I want to thank each one of them who are here today.

In carrying on this battle, you're going to need the help of the largest pressure group of all—the taxpayers. And that's why the multimillion-dollar, nonpartisan campaign by the Advertising Council is so important in helping to inform and educate the taxpayers. And finally, that's why the work of the trade associations and Citizens Against Government Waste are also vital—vital in the battle against budget deficits and vital to the strength and resiliency of the democratic system and public confidence in our government.

So, I want to congratulate you on all that you've done. You know, I've mentioned this to you before, but I can well remember a time when waste and inefficiency were thought of as issues without any political appeal, issues that stirred little interest in the media or among the seers and sayers of Washington. Well, all of that has changed. Government management—mismanagement, I should say, is a hot story, and the Grace commission has played a key role in bringing the change about. In fact, I want you to know the vigor with which you've pursued this fight has inspired me on other closely related matters, and once again, the issue is your issue—making government responsive to the people.

First, I must warn the Congress that their unwillingness to deal with the debt ceiling and to take responsible action on the deficit is creating a large and unnecessary problem. We're running up against the possibility that we may have to disinvest the Social Security Trust Fund, shortchanging that trust fund of accumulated interest, all because of the inexcusable dithering and delay in meeting the responsibilities about raising the debt ceiling. So, please help us convince them—present company exempted; they're convinced—that the time for political gamesmanship was over long ago.

All of us know the importance of an effective resolution this year to our deficit problem, and I happen to think the Gramm-Rudman-Hollings proposal is an excellent one. This proposal is linked closely to what you're doing, because if we can adopt the plan, we can maintain our commitment to a strong defense while providing a framework for the Grace reforms and a device for flushing out waste and inefficiency. Congress must not fail the people on this.

And second, I think some of you know that we have a tax reform plan on the agenda this fall. It's a plan I'm certain has the support of the American people. Right now, Congress is in deliberation on this matter, and that deliberative process is something I deeply respect. I will await its outcome attentively. But let it be said today, I believe that the essential items of tax reform, as I've outlined them, have the support of the American people. And I want action on this plan; I want action this year and so do the people. Believe me, if necessary, I'm prepared to spend a lot more time with Congress at Christmas this year than either of us originally anticipated. [*Laughter*]

Well, let me conclude by, again, thanking Peter Grace and all those thousands of patriotic Americans who gave unstintingly of their time, their efforts, and their talents to help the Government. And let me assure you that we, for our part, will not rest in the fight to have their recommendations implemented.

So, again, thank all of you. God bless you.

Note: The President spoke at 11:45 a.m. in the Rose Garden at the White House.

Proclamation 5397—National Hospice Month, 1985
October 28, 1985

By the President of the United States of America

A Proclamation

Hospices play an important role in our national medical care system. Terminally ill hospice patients receive expert medical care while they and their families can develop essential emotional and spiritual support.

Hospices have shown their ability to provide appropriate, competent, and compassionate care. Under the hospice concept, each program has a team of physicians, nurses, social workers, pharmacists, psychological and spiritual counselors, and community volunteers—all trained to assist the terminally ill. The team works together to care for patients and their families, especially helping them to cope with their pain and grief.

Hospices are rapidly becoming full partners in our health care system. In November 1983, hospice care benefits became available to people under Medicare. Many private insurance carriers and employers have also recognized the value of hospice care and included hospice benefits in their health care plans.

The Congress, by Senate Joint Resolution 155, has designated the month of November 1985 as "National Hospice Month" and authorized and requested the President to issue a proclamation in observance of this event.

Now, Therefore, I, Ronald Reagan, President of the United States of America, do hereby designate the month of November 1985 as National Hospice Month, and I direct the appropriate government officials, all citizens, and interested organizations and associations to observe this month with activities that recognize this important event.

In Witness Whereof, I have hereunto set my hand this twenty-eighth day of October, in the year of our Lord nineteen hundred and eighty-five, and of the Independence of the United States of America the two hundred and tenth.

RONALD REAGAN

[*Filed with the Office of the Federal Register, 3:09 p.m., October 28, 1985*]

Proclamation 5398—National Farm-City Week, 1985
October 28, 1985

By the President of the United States of America

A Proclamation

American farmers are the most productive in the world. But without farm machinery, fuel, electric power, chemical products, and other supplies from industry, our farms could never have achieved this remarkable level of efficiency.

American consumers have the widest variety and the most plentiful supply of food and fiber products that can be found anywhere. But without adequate transportation, processing, and marketing, our consumers could not reap the full benefits of our bounteous farms, orchards, and ranches.

It is the successful synergism of farms, towns, cities, industry, and business that makes the United States a cornucopia for its own citizens, able to share its superabundance with a world where large regions suffer from critical shortages of food, often because of policies that discourage initiative and thwart progress.

To arrive at a better appreciation of how our American system works—with its cooperation between farm workers and city workers—we set aside in each November a Farm-City Week. During this time we seek to highlight the contributions that farmers and city dwellers, working together, make to the bounty, vitality, and strength of our Nation.

Now, Therefore, I, Ronald Reagan, President of the United States of America, do hereby proclaim the week beginning November 22, 1985, through November 28, 1985, as National Farm-City Week. I call upon all Americans, in rural areas and in cities alike, to join in recognizing the accomplishments of our productive farmers and of our urban residents in working together in a spirit of cooperation and interdependence to create abundance, wealth, and strength for the Nation.

In Witness Whereof, I have hereunto set my hand this twenty-eighth day of October, in the year of our Lord nineteen hundred and eighty-five, and of the Independence of the United States of America the two hundred and tenth.

RONALD REAGAN

[*Filed with the Office of the Federal Register, 3:10 p.m., October 28, 1985*]

Proclamation 5399—National Family Week, 1985
October 28, 1985

By the President of the United States of America

A Proclamation

America's families are America's greatest strength. Just as American society is more than the sum of its parts, families are more than just collections of individuals.

It is within the family that we first gain an understanding of who we are; that we learn to give and receive love; that we learn to respect the individuality of others; that we grow to be strong, healthy adults able to take our place in the larger families of community, country, and the world.

Through the family we pass on our traditions, our rituals, and our values. From our families we receive the love, encouragement, and education needed to meet life's challenges. Family life also provides a stimulus for the spiritual growth that fosters probity of character, generosity of spirit, and responsible citizenship.

It is important that we dedicate ourselves to the promotion of strong families for, with their strength, commitment, and loyalty, they form the hearth and heart of our national life. As an eminent American educator has wisely observed: "The security and elevation of the family and of family life are the prime objects of civilization, and the ultimate ends of all industry." Special concern is due to troubled families, for we recognize that any chain is only as strong as its weakest link. At their best, strong families are small communities of love. Let us help them prosper.

National Family Week gives us a chance to honor all families and especially to honor those Americans who have extended the love and support of their families to a child through adoption or foster care. By giving the shelter of their loving arms to such a child on a temporary or permanent basis, these Americans demonstrate in a special way the unconditional love that only families can provide.

The Congress, by Senate Joint Resolution 31, has designated the week of November 24 through 30, 1985, as "National Family Week" and authorized and requested the President to issue a proclamation in observance of this week.

Now, Therefore, I, Ronald Reagan, President of the United States of America, do hereby proclaim the week of November 24 through November 30, 1985, as National Family Week. I invite the Governors of the several states, the chief officials of local governments, the leaders in industry, and all Americans to observe this week with appropriate ceremonies and activities. As we celebrate this Thanksgiving Week, I also invite all Americans to give thanks for the many blessings that they have derived from their family relationships and to reflect upon the importance of maintaining strong families.

In Witness Whereof, I have hereunto set my hand this twenty-eighth day of October, in the year of our Lord nineteen hundred and eighty-five, and of the Independence of the United States of America the two hundred and tenth.

RONALD REAGAN

[*Filed with the Office of the Federal Register, 3:11 p.m., October 28, 1985*]

Remarks on Signing the Bill Designating the Centennial Year of Liberty in the United States
October 28, 1985

Three very nice young people. I will speak about them in a few moments. Lee Iacocca, chairman of the Statue of Liberty-Ellis Island Foundation, honored guests, and ladies and gentlemen, on this date in 1886, President Grover Cleveland stood on an island in New York Harbor to dedicate a statue entitled "Liberty Enlightening the World." Ninety-nine years later, the statue is known by a more familiar affectionate name, the Statue of Liberty or simply Miss Liberty. She's cherished across America, and the torch that she bears is recognized throughout the world as a symbol of human freedom.

The Statue of Liberty was conceived and created by the French sculptor Frederic Bartholdi. Legend has it that as he worked, he modeled the statue's face—that face of utter calm and nobility—on the features of his own mother. Completed, the statue rose more than 150 feet and was constructed of 200,000 pounds of hand-hammered copper sheathing hung on an iron frame engineered by Gustav Eiffel, who later designed the Eiffel Tower. On July 4th, 1884, the statue was presented to the American Ambassador to France. Built using funds donated by the French people, she was then dismantled and shipped to the United States. Then, she was rebuilt using funds donated by the American people, including money raised by schoolchildren. Ever since, she's stood on her island in that great harbor lighting the way to freedom.

Just a few hundred yards away, there's a second island, Ellis Island. Between 1892 and 1954, nearly 17 million immigrants to the New World passed through the Ellis Island checkpoint. Most immigrants moved through the checkpoint in a few hours to begin their new lives in America and freedom. And I like to picture the scene as a boatload of immigrants leaving Ellis Island for New York, they pass Miss Liberty and crowd the rails to gaze. Someone on board knows English, he reads and translates the inscription that the statue bears, words that have proclaimed the meaning of America for millions of immigrants, for shiploads of returning soldiers in two great wars, for every family that has ever visited that glorious statue. And those words: "Give me your tired, your poor, your huddled masses yearning to breathe free, the wretched refuse of your teeming shore. Send these, the homeless, tempest-tost, to me. I lift my lamp beside the Golden Door." Well, many of those immigrants remain at the rails until Miss Liberty is lost in the fog. It would be no surprise if some shed tears of joy.

In recent years, it became all too apparent that Ellis Island and Miss Liberty, herself, were being ravaged by the passing of decades. Nearly half of all Americans can trace their ancestry to someone who passed through the Ellis Island checkpoint. But that island, which should be a proud memorial to our forebearers, had instead become a sad and ramshackled place. Miss Liberty, for her part, had been badly corroded by decades of salt air; her iron supports had weakened; in places, she'd become pocked with jagged, rusty holes.

Well, then, in 1982 the Statue of Liberty-Ellis Island Foundation was formed to restore Miss Liberty and rebuild Ellis Island, and to do so with private funds. This effort has become one of the largest private sector initiatives in American history. Across America, everyone is lending a hand; major

corporations are making contributions; small businesses are helping out. And I'm pleased to say that just as schoolchildren helped raise the money to build her pedestal and install Miss Liberty back in the 1880's, today, a century later, they're holding bake sales and car washes to see to it that she gets the restoration she needs.

Let me give you just three of many stirring examples. Michael Haverly, of Indianapolis, Indiana, has raised over $5,000 for the statue by going door to door with an appeal to help Miss Liberty. Well, I'm proud to be in Michael's company here in the Rose Garden today. And then, there is Amy Nessler, of West Deptford Township, New Jersey, who brought a jar of 365 pennies into her first-grade class to help raise money for the Statue of Liberty. The pennies had been collected 15 years earlier by Amy's mother, who, day by day, put one into a jar to mark the time that her fiance was in Vietnam. And now, after all these years, they felt it was only appropriate to give these special coins to Lady Liberty, who symbolizes what Amy's dad fought for—freedom. Well, I'm very happy that Amy, her mother, and father are here with us today. And finally, there is Donna Daley, a 13-year-old from Ridgeland, South Carolina. When Donna's hometown learned that she was losing her sight to an incurable eye disease, they pitched in to raise money to send her and her family to visit the Statue of Liberty. However, Donna, in the spirit of generosity, donated part of this contribution to the Liberty Restoration Project. And, Donna, you're a fine example to us all.

So far, this private sector initiative has raised more than $170 million, well on its way to its goal of 230 million. Today Miss Liberty and Ellis Island are surrounded by scaffolding; workers are on the sites 24 hours a day. Among countless other repairs, they're giving the statue new iron supports and fitting her pedestal with the tallest hydraulic elevator in America. On Ellis Island, they're giving the main building a new roof, replacing the copper towers, and completely restoring the interiors. Much has been accomplished, but there's still a great deal to be done in order to reopen Ellis Island and the Statue of Liberty by the only appropriate date—the Fourth of July, 1986.

And mindful of this need, the Congress has passed a resolution which it is my honor to sign today. The resolution reads in part: "Whereas, the nation will celebrate the Statue of Liberty's 100th anniversary through commemorative events scheduled to take place during the Fourth of July weekend in 1986, and on October 28, 1986; now therefore be it resolved—that the 12-month period ending on October 28, 1986, is designated as the centennial year of liberty. . ."

Well, I'm looking forward to attending the Liberty Weekend celebration next July and the hundredth anniversary a year from today. David Wolper, who is producing the Liberty Weekend activities, has promised to outdo himself, which won't be easy, after seeing the superb job he did with the 1976 bicentennial and the 1984 Olympics. And Ambassador Mosbacher has planned quite a display himself with the tall ships of Operation Sail.

Throughout this Centennial Year of Liberty, let us join in the great work of restoring the Statue of Liberty and Ellis Island, perhaps our nation's most moving and powerful symbols of freedom. And drawing inspiration from these symbols, let us rededicate ourselves to the great cause of human liberty throughout the world.

I thank you, and God bless you. And now I'm going to sign that resolution.

Note: The President spoke at 2 p.m. in the Rose Garden at the White House. H.J. Res. 407, approved October 28, was assigned Public Law No. 99–136.

Proclamation 5400—Centennial Year of Liberty in the United States
October 28, 1985

By the President of the United States of America

A Proclamation

She remains a Wonder of the World—an uncanny fusion of art and engineering. She is the result of a unique collaboration between two freedom-loving Frenchmen with a profound affection for America: a great sculptor, Frederic-Auguste Bartholdi, and the greatest structural engineer of his time, Alexandre Gustave Eiffel. Next year she will be 100 years old.

Nineteen hundred and eighty-six marks the Centennial of the Statue of Liberty. Originally called "Liberty Enlightening the World," the Statue was a generous gift from the people of France to the people of the United States. It represents the close and cordial relationship that traditionally has existed between our countries and our common devotion to freedom and democracy.

She rises majestically 151 feet above the magnificent base designed by Richard M. Hunt, the preeminent American architect.

But she is much more than her awesome dimensions and her physical splendor. For millions of anxious immigrants, the forebears of countless millions of today's Americans, she was the first glimpse of America. She was assurance of journey's end, safe harbor reached at last, and the beginning of a new adventure in a free and blessed land. For them she was a dream come true, the Lady with the Lamp, a warm welcome to a new world and a new life.

The gifted American poet, Emma Lazarus, hailing her as the "New Colossus," put the message of the Statue of Liberty in unforgettable words:

Keep ancient lands, your storied pomp,
Give me your tired, your poor,
Your huddled masses yearning to breathe free,
The wretched refuse of your teeming shore.
Send these, the homeless, tempest-tost, to me.
I lift my lamp beside the Golden Door.

Since its dedication on October 28, 1886,

the Statue of Liberty has held high the beacon of freedom, hope, and opportunity to welcome millions of immigrants and visitors from foreign lands. From that time she has been one of the proudest symbols of the American ideal of liberty and justice for all.

Today, the Statue of Liberty and nearby Ellis Island are being restored from the ravages of time and weather by the Statue of Liberty-Ellis Island Centennial Foundation, Inc.

The United States will celebrate the one hundredth anniversary of the Statue of Liberty through commemorative events scheduled to take place during the Fourth of July Weekend in 1986 and on October 28, 1986.

In recognition of the importance of the Statue of Liberty to the American people, the Congress, by House Joint Resolution 407, has designated the twelve-month period ending on October 28, 1986, as the "Centennial Year of Liberty in the United States" and authorized and requested the President to issue a proclamation in observance of this occasion.

Now, Therefore, I, Ronald Reagan, President of the United States of America, do hereby proclaim the twelve-month period ending on October 28, 1986, as the Centennial Year of Liberty in the United States, and I call upon the people of the United States to observe this year with appropriate ceremonies and activities.

In Witness Whereof, I have hereunto set my hand this twenty-eighth day of October, in the year of our Lord nineteen hundred and eighty-five, and of the Independence of the United States of America the two hundred and tenth.

RONALD REAGAN

[*Filed with the Office of the Federal Register, 10:40 a.m., October 29, 1985*]

Executive Order 12537—President's Foreign Intelligence Advisory Board
October 28, 1985

By the authority vested in me as President by the Constitution and statutes of the United States of America, and in order to enhance the security of the United States by improving the quality and effectiveness of intelligence available to the United States, it is ordered as follows:

Section 1. There is hereby established within the White House Office, Executive Office of the President, the President's Foreign Intelligence Advisory Board (the "Board"). The Board shall consist of not more than fourteen members, who shall serve at the pleasure of the President and shall be appointed by the President from among trustworthy and distinguished citizens outside the government who are qualified on the basis of achievement, experience, and independence. The President shall establish the terms of the members upon their appointment. To the extent practicable, one-third of the Board at any one time shall be comprised of members whose current term of service does not exceed two years. The President shall designate a Chairman and Vice Chairman from among the members. The Board shall utilize full-time staff and consultants as authorized by the President. Such staff shall be headed by an Executive Director, appointed by the President.

Sec. 2. The Board shall assess the quality, quantity, and adequacy of intelligence collection, of analysis and estimates, of counterintelligence, and other intelligence activities. The Board shall have the authority to continually review the performance of all agencies of the Federal government that are engaged in the collection, evaluation, or production of intelligence or the execution of intelligence policy. The Board shall further be authorized to assess the adequacy of management, personnel, and organization in the intelligence agencies.

Sec. 3. The Board shall report directly to the President and advise him concerning the objectives, conduct, management, and coordination of the various activities of the agencies of the intelligence community. The Board shall report periodically, but at least semiannually, concerning findings and appraisals and shall make appropriate recommendations for actions to improve and enhance the performance of the intelligence efforts of the United States.

Sec. 4. The Board shall receive, consider, and recommend appropriate action with respect to matters, identified to the Board by the Director of Central Intelligence, the Central Intelligence Agency, or other government agencies engaged in intelligence or related activities, in which the support of the Board will further the effectiveness of the national intelligence effort. With respect to matters deemed appropriate by the President, the Board shall advise and make recommendations to the Director of Central Intelligence, the Central Intelligence Agency, and other government agencies engaged in intelligence and related activities, concerning ways to achieve increased effectiveness in meeting national intelligence needs.

Sec. 5. The Board shall have access to the full extent permitted by applicable law to all information necessary to carry out its duties in the possession of any agency of the Federal government. Information made available to the Board shall be given all necessary security protection in accordance with applicable laws and regulations. Each member of the Board, each member of the Board's staff, and each of the Board's consultants shall execute an agreement never to reveal any classified information obtained by virtue of his or her service with the Board except to the President or to such persons as the President may designate.

Sec. 6. Members of the Board shall serve without compensation, but may receive transportation, expenses, and per diem allowance as authorized by law. Staff and consultants to the Board shall receive pay and allowances as authorized by the President.

Sec. 7. Executive Order No. 12331 of October 20, 1981 is revoked.

RONALD REAGAN

The White House,
October 28, 1985.

[*Filed with the Office of the Federal Register, 10:41 a.m., October 29, 1985*]

Statement by Principal Deputy Press Secretary Speakes on the Export of Alaskan Oil
October 28, 1985

On the recommendation of his Economic Policy Council, the President has decided to permit the export of a small quantity of Alaskan oil produced at Cook Inlet. This administrative action does not permit export of oil from the North Slope of Alaska, which is a question to be addressed in a Commerce Department study that will be submitted to Congress next April.

This decision is consistent with the administration's market-oriented policy of removing barriers to trade and encouraging others to do likewise. U.S. interests will be well served because of the reduced oil transportation costs associated with shipping oil to Asia rather than to U.S. refining terminals. This will generate higher revenues to producers, thereby generating higher Federal and Alaska State tax revenues. In addition, the incentive to explore and develop oil reserves in the Cook Inlet area will increase. The President, in making his decision, sought nothing in exchange. We have made it clear to our friends in Asia that we would like to see them move more rapidly in opening their markets to U.S. products.

This action has long been recommended by Senator Frank Murkowski, and the President has expressed his utmost appreciation to the Senator for his advice on the issue. Furthermore, the administration will be consulting with Congress to ensure that these benefits to the U.S. are well understood.

Proclamation 5401—National Sudden Infant Death Syndrome Awareness Month, 1985
October 28, 1985

By the President of the United States of America

A Proclamation

Sudden Infant Death Syndrome (SIDS), the sudden and unexpected death of apparently healthy babies, is the major cause of death of infants between the ages of one month and one year. Between 5,000 and 6,000 babies die of SIDS annually in the United States. Most die unobserved in their sleep. Despite two decades of aggressive biomedical and behavioral research, supported in large part by the Federal government, the exact cause of SIDS remains elusive. From what we have learned through research, choking, neglect, infection, and heredity have been ruled out as probable causes, and today the syndrome is attributed to a combination of subtle physiological deficiencies in the infant.

The parents and families of SIDS victims frequently experience intense and traumatic grief, often accompanied by unwarranted feelings of guilt that can result in psychosocial and even physical problems. It is extremely important that the facts about SIDS be widely disseminated and understood in order to banish myths and misconceptions. By working together, parents, schools, private and voluntary organizations, and government at all levels can bring about a greater public understanding of this tragic syndrome.

The Congress, by House Joint Resolution 322, has designated the month of October 1985, as "National Sudden Infant Death Syndrome Awareness Month" and authorized and requested the President to issue a proclamation in observance of this event.

Now, Therefore, I, Ronald Reagan, President of the United States of America, do hereby proclaim the month of October 1985, as National Sudden Infant Death Syndrome Awareness Month.

In Witness Whereof, I have hereunto set my hand this twenty-eighth day of October, in the year of our Lord nineteen hundred and eighty-five, and of the Independence of the United States of America the two hundred and tenth.

RONALD REAGAN

[*Filed with the Office of the Federal Register, 11:05 a.m., October 29, 1985*]

Nomination of Francis Anthony Keating II To Be an Assistant Secretary of the Treasury
October 29, 1985

The President today announced his intention to nominate Francis Anthony Keating II to be an Assistant Secretary of the Treasury (Enforcement and Operations). He would succeed John Walker, Jr.

Mr. Keating is a partner in the law firm of Pray, Walker, Jackman, Williamson, and Marler in Tulsa, OK. Previously he was a partner in the law firm of Leonard, Snider and Keating and a trustee of the Heller Co. He was United States Attorney for the Northern District of Oklahoma and Chairman of the Attorney General's Advisory Committee for United States Attorneys in

1981–1983 and partner in the law firm of Blackstock, Joyce, Pollard, Blackstock, and Montgomery in 1972–1981. In 1972–1981 he served as a member of the Oklahoma House of Representatives and later a member of the Oklahoma State Senate.

Mr. Keating graduated from Georgetown University (B.A., 1966) and the University of Oklahoma (J.D., 1969). He is married, has three children, and resides in Tulsa, OK. He was born February 10, 1944, in St. Louis, MO.

Appointment of Joseph C. Harder as a Member of the Intergovernmental Advisory Council on Education
October 29, 1985

The President today announced his intention to appoint Joseph C. Harder to be a member of the Intergovernmental Advisory Council on Education for a term expiring July 27, 1989. This is a reappointment.

Since 1961 Mr. Harder has been serving as a State senator in Kansas. In the senate he serves as chairman of the senate education committee; chairman of the master planning commission; a member of the senate ways and means committee; and a member of the commercial and financial institutions committee. From 1972 to 1976, he was the majority floor leader of the Kansas senate. In 1979 Mr. Harder served as educator in residence at the University of Kansas in Lawrence. He was manager of the Moundridge Telephone Co. in 1962–1978.

He is married, has one child, and resides in Moundridge, KS. He was born February 1, 1916, in Hillsboro, KS.

Nomination of Nanette Fabray MacDougall To Be a Member of the National Council on the Handicapped
October 29, 1985

The President today announced his intention to nominate Nanette Fabray MacDougall to be a member of the National Council on the Handicapped for a term expiring September 17, 1987. This is a reappointment.

Mrs. MacDougall is an actress. She is also active in organizations benefiting the hearing handicapped and other disabled persons. She serves on the boards of the National Captioning Institute, the Better Hearing Institute in Washington, DC, the Ear Research Institute, and the Museum of Science and Industry in Los Angeles. She is past chairman of the National Easter Seal Society for Crippled Children, the National Mental Health Association, and the National Advisory Committee for Education of the Deaf. She has received many awards for her service, including the President's Distinguished Service Award in 1971 and the Eleanor Roosevelt Humanitarian Award in 1964.

Mrs. MacDougall has one child and resides in Pacific Palisades, CA. She was born October 27, 1920, in San Diego, CA.

Appointment of Six Members of the Commission of Fine Arts
October 29, 1985

The President today announced his intention to appoint the following individuals to be members of the Commission of Fine Arts for a term of 4 years:

Neil H. Porterfield, of Missouri, will succeed Sondra Gelb Myers. Mr. Porterfield is professor and head of the Department of Landscape Architecture at Pennsylvania State University. He graduated from Pennsylvania State University (B.S., 1958) and the University of Pennsylvania (M.S., 1964). He is married, has three children, and resides in St. Louis, MO. He was born August 15, 1936, in Murrysville, PA.

Pascal Regan, of California, will succeed John S. Chase. Mrs. Regan, a sculptress, is well known for sculpturing glass by hammer and chisel. She is married, has one child, and resides in Beverly Hills, CA. She was born March 19, 1914, in Miles City, MT.

J. Carter Brown, of the District of Columbia, is a reappointment. Mr. Brown has been serving as Director of the National Gallery of Art since 1969. He graduated from Harvard University (A.B., 1956; M.B.A., 1958) and the Institute of Fine Arts, New York University (M.A., 1962). He is married, has two children, and resides in Washington, DC. He was born October 8, 1934, in Providence, RI.

Carolyn Deaver, of California, will succeed Alan Novak. Mrs. Deaver is a consultant to Mary Pettus & Associates in Washington, DC. She also is a council member of the Phillips Collection in Washington. She graduated from the University of California, Berkeley (B.A., 1960). She is married, has two children, and resides in Washington, DC. She was born January 17, 1939, in San Francisco, CA.

Diane Wolf, of New York, will succeed Edward Durell Stone, Jr. She served as founder and chairman of the Junior Committee of the Metropolitan Museum of Art in 1979–1983 and as a member of the Friends Council of the Whitney Museum in 1978–1982. She graduated from the University of Pennsylvania (B.A., 1976) and Columbia University (M.A., 1980). She was born March 16, 1954, in Cheyenne, WY, and now resides in New York City.

Roy M. Goodman, of New York, will succeed Harold Burson. He has been serving as a State senator in New York for 17 years. He serves as vice chairman of the Senate Special Committee on the Cultural Industry. He graduated from Harvard College (1951) and Harvard Graduate School of Business Administration (M.B.A. 1953). He is married, has three children, and resides in New York City. He was born March 5, 1930, in New York City.

Appointment of Two United States Commissioners on the International Commission for the Conservation of Atlantic Tunas
October 29, 1985

The President today announced his intention to appoint the following individuals to be United States Commissioners on the International Commission for the Conservation of Atlantic Tunas:

Michael B. Montgomery, of California, will succeed Frank Eberle Carlton. He is president of Mr. B. Montgomery Properties, Inc., in San Marino, CA. He also serves as a director of the following corporations: Majestic Housing Corp., Los Angeles, CA; Pacific Waste Management Co.; and Natural Energy Conservation Management, Inc. Mr. Montgomery graduated from the University of California at Los Angeles (B.S., 1960) and the University of Southern

California Law School (J.D., 1963). He is married, has three children, and resides in South Pasadena, CA. He was born September 12, 1936, in Santa Barbara, CA.

Leon John Weddig, of Maryland, will succeed John S. McGowan. He has been serving as executive vice president of the National Fisheries Institute since 1977. Previously he was executive director of the National Fisheries Institute in 1975–1977 and 1967–1973. In 1973–1974 he was president of C.L. Watt, Inc., and president of Financial Management Services, Inc., both in Dayton, OH. He graduated from Marquette University (B.S., 1956). He is married, has two children, and resides in Rockville, MD. He was born September 22, 1935, in Fond du Lac, WI.

Remarks to Religious Leaders at a White House Meeting on Tax Reform
October 29, 1985

Thank you all very much, and welcome to the White House. I always feel self-concious when I say that, and I say that every time I'm in here, but somehow, technically—and that just kind of explains some of the problems of government—that this Old Executive Office Building is part of the White House. I haven't put my clothes in a single closet over here.

Well, I'm glad to welcome members of the clergy and lay leaders to Washington. I've always assumed that men of the cloth can visit this town and really see how it works without returning home feeling the need to pray fervently, and let me tell you, we need all the help we can get. I also feel a certain kinship with those of you who are members of the clergy. Now, this is a comparison that isn't always made, but politicians and clergy do have a lot in common. We both have to make speeches and keep our audiences interested, and I know I'm running a risk in telling members of the clergy a story about their own profession, but maybe it will be new to some of you.

It has to do with a young minister who was very disturbed because sometime, particularly on those hot Sunday or summer mornings—Sunday mornings, he'd see his group nodding off while he was preaching his sermon. And he told about his distress to more experienced and older clergyman who said that he'd had that same problem, but he'd found an answer to it. He said, "When you see them and their eyes beginning to close," he said, "you just insert a line in your sermon and say, 'Last night, I held another man's wife in my arms.'" [*Laughter*] And he said, "They'll wake up." [*Laughter*] Well, it happened. There came a hot Sunday morning, and there they were and the eyes were closing, and remembering, he said the line: "Last night, I held in my arms a woman who was not my wife." Well, the first minister had told him that after he got them awake, he was to then say, "That woman was my dear mother." And this young fellow said the line and

then said, "I can't remember who she was." [*Laughter*] Well, I hope I have better luck today. [*Laughter*]

I've come to talk to you about our efforts to overhaul our nation's tax code, but I first want to stress our commitment to solving the school dropout problem and youth unemployment. The two subjects aren't unrelated because a vital, growing economy, liberated from high tax rates and an unfair and restrictive tax code, is the best way to provide opportunity for all. For the special problem of our unemployed young people, a youth employment opportunity wage is also vital. Now, if you haven't heard that term expressed, it's something we've asked of the Congress and asked that they do. The figures reveal that every time the minimum wage has increased, the number of jobs available for teenagers, young people, has gone down—those afterschool jobs, those weekend, and those summer jobs. The jobs are simply priced out of existence. They aren't that necessary, and we've made the cost too high. The school dropout problem is more complex, but I think that we can all agree that it's at least attributable in part to the increase in family breakdown. But one of the common causes of dropout from school also is a need or desire to be earning some money.

In this modern age, families are subject to intense pressures from all sides. And sad to say, the Federal Government, instead of helping, has been adding to the burden of families. Throughout the great tax explosion of the sixties and seventies, everybody with a paycheck got hit and hit hard by taxes, but those trying to raise families really got clobbered. Not only did their taxes skyrocket, their personal exemption, the real value of the deduction that they were allowed to take for themselves and each one of their dependents, was steadily knocked down by inflation. If the personal exemption, which was $600 in 1948, had kept pace with inflation, that exemption today would be $2,700.

Now, this is where the profamily initiatives of America's fair share tax plan come in. We're not going to go to the $2,700—or haven't asked to do that—but in our tax plan we have asked to almost double it, to raise it to $2,000 in order to make up for some of what the family has lost over those years. We're also increasing the standard deduction to $4,000 for joint returns. Our proposal will mean that families, as well as the elderly, the blind, and the disabled, living at or below the poverty line will be completely scratched from the Federal income tax rolls. The U.S. Government will no longer tax families into poverty. And under our proposal, a family of four wouldn't have to pay one single cent of Federal income taxes on the first $12,000 of income. And because saving is so essential to families, but so very difficult with all those expenses, we're expanding the tax-free savings accounts of IRA's, the individual retirement accounts, so that they're fully available to nonwage-earning spouses. We think they're working, too.

America's fair share tax plan has received commendations from some unexpected quarters. The Democratically controlled House Select Committee on Children, Youth, and Families rated our plan more profamily than any other tax proposal around and light years ahead of the present system. And then, there's Pat Moynihan, the Democratic Senator from New York. He said that our profamily provisions will "do more for the poor than Lyndon Johnson ever did during the years of the Great Society." So, I guess the question is: Are we going to give up and stick with a tax system loved only by the special interests and their high-priced tax attorneys, or are we going to stop making excuses and give the poor the break from unfair taxation they so very urgently need? Indeed, giving everyone a break from this unfair tax situation.

You know, the Lord has told us that his share is a tenth of what we earn, and He has told us that if we prosper 10 times as much, we will give 10 times as much. But when we start computing Caesar's share under our present tax policy, you can prosper 10 times as much and find you're paying 50 times as much tax. So, I think what's fair for the Lord ought to be more reasonably fair for Caesar, also. [*Laughter*]

Opportunity also means economic growth, and the best way to achieve that's by cutting tax rates still further. One of the great economic lessons of the last few years is the beneficial effect of tax rate reductions. We've seen that as tax rates go down, all the negative economic indicators, like poverty and inflation, go down, too; and all the positive economic indicators, like productivity, disposable income, and employment, go up. Something else also goes up when marginal tax rates are cut—believe it or not—at the lower rates, government revenue increases; it does not go down with the cut in the rates.

Tax rates in this country, long ago, passed the point where they became counterproductive, stunting economic growth and actually bringing in less revenue than tax rate cuts that spur growth and draw investment out of wasteful loopholes and back into the productive economy. Just a few years ago, before our present tax cut—the one that we launched in 1981—before that, there was only $39 million in America available for what is called venture capital—to be invested into new ventures and new business and so forth. Well, last year, after our tax cuts were in effect, there was $4 billion available for such investment.

Our first tax cut—you can see the across-the-board thing—it was 25 percent. And since 1984—that was the first year that all of the three installments of our tax cut were in place—we found that the tax revenues have been increasing at a rapid pace. And in fiscal year 1985, which ended October 1st, Federal revenues continued to grow at the remarkable rate of 10 percent. Now, let me suggest that over the long haul, the Federal Government simply can't raise revenue any faster than by cutting tax rates and, then, cutting them again. So, it doesn't make much sense to blame the deficit on tax cuts, and even less to ask for economy-busting tax hikes as a cure. The deficit is quite clearly caused by overspending. The government Gargantua has been eating up those extra revenues from our tax cut and pounding on the table demanding more. Well, we're going to put Gargantua on a diet, the Gramm-Rudman-Hollings diet. It would pare $36 billion a year off its overating, resulting in a balanced budget by 990. All we're asking is that Congress take little over one-half the extra $60-odd bilon in revenue generated by our tax cuts nd economic growth and use it to reduce he deficit.

And the way some people in government pend the public's money also reminds me f a story. And again, it's about a clergyman ·ho had gone to a small hamlet about a undred miles from his own parish to ·reach at a revival meeting. And driving 1to the village, he noticed a man from his ·wn community. The fellow was known, a ttle bit, for his drinking. And he was siting on the front steps of the general store, nd he had a bottle of beer in his hands. .nd the preacher stopped his car, and he sked the drinker why he was so far from ome. And the man told him that beer was cents a bottle cheaper where they were hen. Well, the minister pointed out the ost of travel back and forth, the price for a

hotel room. And the beer drinker retorted, "I'm not stupid, Reverend, I just sit here and drink till I show a profit." [*Laughter*]

Well, we're seeing an economic renaissance in this country, but we need two things to keep it going: cuts in the deficit and cuts in the tax rates. Both are in the Congress now, and we need your support to keep their noses to the grindstone. As for America's fair share tax plan, we're shooting for Christmastime. Economic growth and tax fairness are gifts we owe ourselves and our children, and with your help, we'll have them all wrapped up by the holiday season, ready to take effect in 1986. And then we'll really have something to celebrate on New Year's Day.

I thank you all, thank you for being here. God bless you all.

Note: The President spoke at 1:02 p.m. in Room 450 of the Old Executive Office Building.

Remarks at a Reception for the McLaughlin Group
October 29, 1985

I've always wanted to be on a McLaughlin show. [*Laughter*] I was in the neighbor1ood and thought I'd just drop in. [*Laugher*] Let's cut the nonsense and get down to 1eltway business. [*Laughter*] Issue one— *laughter*]—the McLaughlin Group, 3 years unning strong and getting stronger, seen 1—well, you've just heard how many mar:ets. And now we know that next year it's ;oing to play the big towns. [*Laughter*] In ust 3 short years, the McLaughlin Group 1as distinguished itself on three fronts. ·irst, it became a stable—staple—[*laugher*]—that was a Freudian slip—[*laughter*]— 1 America's diet of political commentary. ts intellectual nutritional values fall somevhere between potato chips and Twinkies. *Laughter*] Second, the McLaughlin Group 1lso serves as the most tasteful programning alternative to professional wrestling— *laughter*]—live from Madison Square ¡arden. And third, it's also been an obedi·nce school for White House staffers.

Issue two, political potpourri. [*Laughter*] We're talking about the four horsemen of the political apocalypse and their now-famous rotating chair. By the way, Pat Buchanan rotated all the way to a windowless office down the hall in the west wing just across from the broom closet. [*Laughter*]

Well, I can dish it out, as well as take it. [*Laughter*] I'm going to give it to you with the bark on. [*Laughter*] That's McLaughlin Group talk. [*Laughter*] Robert Novak, the Prince of Darkness. [*Laughter*] I only said that because he's so darn liberal. [*Laughter*] Morton Kondracke, neoconservative, neoliberal, one of the best open minds in the business. [*Laughter*] Jack Germond, everything Geraldine Ferraro is today she owes to Jack. [*Laughter*] But don't laugh, at least he got Minnesota right. [*Laughter*] And John McLaughlin, Mr. T of TV journalism. [*Laughter*] I once described John by saying the United States needs a tax increase like John McLaughlin needs assertiveness training. [*Laughter*] John took a simple Sunday morning discussion format out of the issues of our day and, using the insight, skill, and great humility that have become his trademarks—[*laughter*]—managed to turn it into a political version of "Animal House." [*Laughter*]

One last word in keeping with the format of the show—I'd like to offer a prediction. [*Laughter*] I predict that besides your current outlets, you're going to be carried by at least one other major city—"Miami Vice," watch out. [*Laughter*] As you've

heard, the group promises real mayhem, and this kid McLaughlin, he means business. [*Laughter*] Well, thank you for making that half hour every weekend something very special to look forward to. I wouldn't miss it. I can't afford to. [*Laughter*]

God bless you all. Thank you.

Note: The President spoke at 6:46 p.m. at the Ritz-Carlton Hotel. In his remarks, the President referred to Patrick J. Buchanan, Assistant to the President and Director of Communications.

Interview With Brian Widlake of the British Broadcasting Corporation
October 29, 1985

U.S.-Soviet Summit Meeting

Mr. Widlake. Mr. President, your meeting with Mr. Gorbachev is only 3 weeks away now; everyone regards it as crucial. What do you hope, personally, to get out of the summit with Mr. Gorbachev?

The President. Well, I think that the most that we could get out is if we could eliminate some of the paranoia, if we could reduce the hostility, the suspicion that keeps our two countries particularly—but basically, should we say, the Warsaw bloc and the West—at odds with each other. And while I know everyone is looking toward and emphasizing a reduction in arms—this is vital and important, but I see reduction in arms as a result, not a cause. If we can reduce those suspicions between our two countries, the reduction of arms will easily follow because we will reduce the feeling that we need them.

Mr. Widlake. Mr. Shultz is off to Moscow on Saturday to do the groundwork for this summit fully aware, as he himself admits, that there are major differences between the United States and Russia. Apart from the paranoia which you talked about, what are those differences as you see them?

The President. Oh, my heavens. Here are two systems so diametrically opposed that— I'm no linguist, but I've been told that in the Russian language there isn't even a

word for freedom. And two nations everyone's referring to as the "superpowers" obviously are competitive and our philosophies and our ideas on the world—and that probably can't be corrected, but we can have a peaceful competition. We have to live in the world together. There's no sense in believing that we must go on with the threat of a nuclear war hanging over the world because of our disagreements. We don't like their system; they don't like ours, but we're not out to change theirs. I do feel sometimes they're out to change ours—but if we could get along. They have a system of totalitarian government and rule of their people; we have one in which we believe the people rule the government. And there isn't any reason why we can't coexist in the world. Where there are legitimate areas of competition, compete; but do it in a manner that recognizes that neither one of us should be a threat to the other.

Mr. Widlake. When Mr. Shultz talks to Mr. Gorbachev and Mr. Shevardnadze, what will be the topics of discussion? Will it be trying to find some groundwork, for example, on arms control and reduction?

The President. No, I would think that probably the main point in their meeting ahead of the major meeting is to establish an agenda. In other words, Secretary [of State] Shultz would tell them the things that we feel are important to be discussed. Minister Shevardnadze will probably have a list of things that are on their agenda, so that we can plan and neither one of us be caught by surprise at the summit with having a subject come up that hadn't even been considered. So, I think that this is probably the main, useful purpose that will be served by their getting together.

Mr. Widlake. Is there any chance at all that the discussions Mr. Shultz has in Moscow might enable you to produce an initiative before you go to Geneva?

The President. Right now we are in the position of studying what we call a counterproposal. In Geneva, where our arms control delegations are meeting and have been meeting for a long time, we have had a proposal for a reduction of nuclear weapons. Now, for the first time, the Soviet Union has made a counterproposal. We have put that in the hands of our people in Geneva now for them to look at; we ourselves are studying it. There are some elements in there that are—well, we've called them "seeds to nurture," things that we look at and say, "Yes, these could very easily be acceptable." At the same time, in their proposal there are some things that we believe are so disadvantageous to us that they should be negotiated and some changes made.

And with all of this going on, I'm not in a position to say now at what point will we make our reply to their counteroffer and state where we are or where we differ and so forth, and then, that should be the area in which negotiations would take place. Now, whether that doesn't happen prior to the summit meeting or whether our team in Geneva tables it before they adjourn for their recess that is coming up, that I can't answer; that still remains to be seen.

Mr. Widlake. But I must tell you, Mr. President, that Mrs. Thatcher has already told the leader of the opposition—and she said this today in the House of Commons—that you were going to come up with an initiative before Geneva. Has she been talking to—[*inaudible*]?

The President. Well, I'm personally hopeful of that, also. So, she's right that that is what we're striving to do.

Strategic Defense Initiative

Mr. Widlake. Now, can we look at some of the things which obviously are going to affect Geneva, but particularly I'd like to talk to you about the Strategic Defense Initiative and how important that is going to be. Can anything be achieved in Geneva without some understanding from both sides in this area?

The President. Probably not, but I think there can be an understanding when they hear what we have in mind. I believe that this is something that is probably one of the most momentous things in a century. We have a team that, within the terms of the ABM treaty, is researching to see if there is a defensive weapon, the possibility of a defensive weapon that could intercept missiles before they reach their target, instead of having a deterrent to war, as we have now, which is both sides with massive weapons of destruction—nuclear missiles—and the only thing deterring war is the threat we represent to each other of killing millions and millions of citizens on both sides.

Now, if we can come up with a defensive weapon, then, we reach—and we know that we have it, that it is there, that it is practical, that it will work—then, my idea is that we go to the world, we go to our allies, we go to the Soviet Union, and we say, "Look, we are not going to just start deploying this at the same time we maintain a nuclear arsenal. We think this weapon, this defensive weapon—we would like to make available, and let's have the world have this for their own protection so that we can all eliminate our nuclear arsenals." And the only reason, then, for having the defensive weapon would be, because since everyone in the world knows how to make one, a nuclear weapon—we would all be protected in case some madman, some day down along the line, secretly sets out to produce some with the idea of blackmailing the world, and the world wouldn't be blackmailed because we would all be sitting here with that defense. I've likened it to what happened in 1925, after World War I—all the nations got together and outlawed poison gas, but everybody kept their gas masks. So, we would have a world with some nuclear gas masks, and we could sleep at night without thinking that someone could bring this great menace of the nuclear threat against us.

Mr. Widlake. When you say, Mr. President, you'd go to the world once you had proved—satisfactory to yourself—that here was a weapon which would actually work. If you go to the world, would you include Russia in that?

The President. Yes. I think that—what could be safer than—today everything is offensive weapons. It's the only weapon I know of that's ever been developed in history that has not brought about a defense against it. But what would be safer than if the two great superpowers, the two that have the great arsenals—both of us sat there with defensive weapons that ensured our safety against the nuclear weapons and both of us eliminated our nuclear missiles.

Mr. Widlake. But the Russians, presumably, would have to make their own SDI. You wouldn't offer it to them, would you, off the shelf?

The President. Why not? And I think this is something to be discussed at the summit as to what kind of an agreement we could make in the event. I would like to say to the Soviet Union, we know you've been researching for this same thing longer than we have. We wish you well. There couldn't be anything better than if both of us came up with it. But if only one of us does, then, why don't we, instead of using it as an offensive means of having a first strike against anyone else in the world, why don't we use it to ensure that there won't be any nuclear strikes?

Mr. Widlake. Are you saying then, Mr. President, that the United States, if it were well down the road towards a proper SDI program, would be prepared to share its technology with Soviet Russia, provided, of course, there were arms reductions and so on on both sides?

The President. That's right. There would have to be the reductions of offensive weapons. In other words, we would switch to defense instead of offense.

Mr. Widlake. That, of course, is quite a long way away——

The President. Yes.

Mr. Widlake. ——this idealistic world of yours, if I may say so.

The President. Yes, although we're optimistic. We've had some good breakthrough in our research so far.

Mr. Widlake. It's going well, is it?

The President. Yes.

Mr. Widlake. And is the research going so well as to suggest to you that a defensive weapon of this kind is really practical now?

The President. As a matter of fact, very leading scientists who are involved in this have said that, that they can foresee us achieving this weapon.

Mr. Widlake. Will it take long?

The President. Oh, I think we're talking a matter of years.

Mr. Widlake. Let us say, though, this isn't going to come about, as you say, for a matter of years. And Mr. Gorbachev, as we all know, is very worried about SDI. Would you be prepared to negotiate on SDI at Geneva?

The President. Well, negotiate in the sense of coming to an agreement, which we are bound by in the future for whenever that weapon happens—bound to this matter of worldwide sharing.

Mr. Widlake. I wonder if you'd be kind enough to clear up one point on the SDI, and it's this: Mr. Gorbachev, I think, accepts the idea that you could do nothing about research because it's not really verifiable; testing, on the other hand, worries him. Now, does testing, in your view, come within the ABM treaty?

The President. Yes, I believe it does. I think that we're well within it and within a strict adherence to the treaty, although you could have a more liberal interpretation of the treaty that I believe is justified. But rather than have any debate or argument about that, we are staying within the strict limits of the treaty.

Mr. Widlake. Do you think the SDI is likely to be a stumbling block at Geneva, bearing in mind what Mr. Gorbachev thinks about it, these reservations?

The President. I think it should be the other way around. I think it should be one of the most helpful things in erasing some of that paranoia I mentioned or that hostility or suspicions between us.

Mr. Widlake. You have a horror of nuclear weapons and that's why you say that SDI s a good thing. If we had SDI worldwide, vould there still be nuclear weapons available?

The President. I wouldn't see any need or them at all. I wouldn't know why a aation would strap itself to invest in them. But, as I say, there is always the possibility of a madman coming along, and, as I say, ou can't eliminate the knowledge about building those weapons—who might seize apon them. We've had an experience in our ifetime of a madman in the world who caused great tragedy worldwide. And so, I vould think that this would be our gas mask.

Regional Conflicts

Mr. Widlake. Mr. President, can we turn now to some of the things you said in your J.N. speech? One of the central themes you brought up there concerned those areas of regional conflict, such as Afghanistan, in which the Soviets have a hand. Are you going to bring these up with Mr. Gorbachev? And, if so, do you expect him to respond positively?

The President. Well, I would think that this is very much a part of trying to rid the world of the suspicions. They claim that they fear that we of the Western World threaten them, that somehow we're lying here in wait for a day when we can eliminate their method of government and so forth. There is no evidence to sustain that. If you look back to the end of World War II, our country, for example, absolutely undamaged—we hadn't had our industries destroyed through bombings and so forth—and we were the only nation with the bomb, the nuclear weapon. We could have dictated to the world; we didn't. We set out to help even our erstwhile enemies recover. And today those erstwhile enemies are our staunchest allies in the NATO alliance.

They, on the other hand, have created—well, they've gone through the biggest military buildup in the history of man, and it is basically offensive. Now, we, therefore, claim we've got some right to believe that we are threatened; not the other way around. Now, to eliminate that suspicion or that fear, if they really want to live in a peaceful world and be friends and associate with the rest of the world, then, we need

more than words. And the deeds could be the stopping of their attempt to—either themselves or through proxies and through subversion—to force their system on other countries throughout the world. And that could be one of the greatest proofs there is that——

Mr. Widlake. Do you think you were being a bit optimistic in your U.N. speech? You proposed the idea that these areas of regional conflict should be discussed. But, of course, you took them much further than that. What you actually said—they should be discussed up to the point when they're just eliminated. Now, do you think you're being optimistic when you recognize the fact that the fellow sitting opposite you is Mr. Gorbachev, and he's tied up in these things.

The President. Yes. But on the other hand, he has some practical problems in his own country, some problems of how long can they sustain an economy that provides for their people under the terrific cost of building up and pursuing this expansionist policy and this great military buildup.

Mr. Widlake. His economic problems.

The President. Yes. And if we can show him that he can resolve those economic problems with no danger to themselves, convince him that we represent no threat, then I could see us—as I've said before, we don't like each other's systems, maybe we don't like each other; but we're the only two nations that can probably cause a world war. We're also the only two nations that can prevent one.

Human Rights

Mr. Widlake. Will you want to talk to him about human rights? You've probably heard that Mrs. Yelena Bonner has just been granted a visa——

The President. Yes.

Mr. Widlake. ——to come to the West so she can get medical treatment, but she'll have to go back to Russia, of course. Do you see that as a propaganda move by the Russians? Or is it a step along the road?

The President. I would like to feel it's a step along the road, and there needs to be more. I don't think, however, that the human rights thing should be a kind of a

1313

public discussion and accusing fingers being pointed at each other and their claim that this is an internal matter with them. But I think it should be explained that some of these violations—well, first of all is the violation of the Helsinki pact. This was one of the main reasons why we are signatories to that pact is this agreement about not separating families and so forth, allowing people freedom to choose. What they have to understand is that in some of the major areas where we could seek agreement, we have a better chance in our type of society of getting the approval that we need from our Congress, from our people of some of these agreements if these issues, these human rights problems are not standing in the way. And maybe I can point that out.

U.S.-Soviet Relations

Mr. Widlake. Mr. President, there have been fears expressed in Europe that arms control will be pushed right down the agenda at Geneva in favor of issues like regional conflict and human rights, which we've been discussing. Can you give an assurance that that is not the case?

The President. I certainly can, as far as I'm concerned. But, as I've said, that follows another thing. The effort is to arrive at an understanding about our ability to live in the world together and at peace and the other—that can follow. Someone—if I can only remember the quote correctly—the other day said: "Nations aren't suspicious of each other because of their arms. They are armed because they are suspicious."

Soviet General Secretary Gorbachev

Mr. Widlake. There is a feeling, Mr. President, that Mr. Gorbachev has seized the initiative in Europe. European leaders have undoubtedly been impressed by his performance. Mrs. Thatcher, as you know, said that he is someone she can do business with. What do you think about it?

The President. Well, I don't know him as yet, but he seems to have shown more of an interest in the people, the man in the street, than other Soviet leaders have. He has expressed great concern about the economic problems and the improvements that he feels that should be made there. And he's younger and more energetic than some

of the more recent leaders have been. And I'm optimistic by nature, but I have to be optimistic that he is looking at the entire picture. On the other hand, I don't think we should believe that he is not dedicated to the principles of their system, to communism and so forth. If he wasn't, he wouldn't be where he is.

Mr. Widlake. Do you think he's, in terms of youth, energy, if you like, intelligence, and obviously a powerful grasp of public relations—do you think he is a pretty formidable Russian leader to deal with compared with his predecessors?

The President. Well, I don't know. On the public relations thing, he did far better with some of our own press than he did with the French press on his recent visit when he was there. I can't judge him on that. Sometimes public relations are made by those reporting, not by those doing.

Terrorism

Mr. Widlake. Can I take one or two other areas with you, Mr. President? The first is terrorism. We know how you handled the *Achille Lauro* affair, but does that carry the risk of alienating friendly governments? Egypt, if you remember, wasn't too pleased.

The President. Well, I know, and yet we felt that we had no choice in the matter if we were going to prevent those terrorists from suddenly, as so many in past have, disappearing into the rabbit warrens that abound the Middle East, Lebanon and so forth; and therefore they would escape being brought to justice. They had murdered a man, a helpless individual. We felt we had to do it. But I'm pleased to say, now, that I think the flurry is over and that both Egypt and Italy want to continue the warm relationship that we've had. And so, that has worked out all right.

Mr. Widlake. Mr. President, would you do it again, even if it meant, say, violating international law?

The President. Well, it actually didn't violate international law. Well——

Mr. Widlake. But, say, could in the future?

The President. It could, I suppose. It's a hypothetical question.

Mr. Widlake. But terrorism is always with

us.

The President. Yes. And I think that you'd have to judge each case on its own as to the need to bring terrorists to justice; the need to convince them that terrorism is not going to be successful, it is not going to make governments, like your own or our own, change their policies out of fear of terrorism. If that ever happens, then, the world has gone back to anarchy. So, you would have to judge that against how much you would be violating international law to achieve your goal.

Mr. Widlake. But if it was necessary, I take it you would.

The President. Yes.

Mr. Widlake. And you would pursue terrorism as hard as you can, as often as you can?

The President. Yes. It's been very frustrating for a number of the things that have happened, and I've been taken to task by members of the press that I talked, but I didn't take action. But just look at the nature of some of those terrorist acts. The terrorist blows himself up with all the innocent people that he also kills at the same time. So, there's no way you're going to punish him. You now seek to find—well, who does he belong to? What group brought this about? Well, there the difficulty is almost insurmountable. But also, even if you do get some intelligence that indicates it's a certain group, they're in some foreign city and you say, "Well, how do we punish them without blowing up a neighborhood and killing as many innocent people as they did?" And this has been our problem up until this last time when we had a very clear-cut case.

Administration Accomplishments

Mr. Widlake. Mr. President, this may be a difficult question for you to answer, but what would you most like to be remembered for by history?

The President. Well, 5 years ago when we came here, the United States had allowed its defenses to decline. The United States economy—I remember attending my first economic summit in Ottawa, Canada—and that was just in the spring of the year, my first year here—and I remember our friends and allies, the heads of state of the other summit nations there, beseeching me to stop exporting our inflation and our recession to their countries in this world of international trade and all—that we were exporting bad economic situations to the rest of the world. The Soviet Union—again, as I say, through surrogates or on their own— there was Afghanistan, there was Ethiopia, South Yemen, Angola, Nicaragua, and they had forced governments of their choosing into all of those countries.

Well, it's been 5 years now. We have the greatest recovery, economic recovery that we've ever had in our history. It is not we who are exporting inflation anymore. Inflation is down from those double-digit figures—well, for the last 5 months it's only been 2½ percent, and none of our trading partners can match that. Our interest rates are down. We have created almost 9 million new jobs over these 5 years with our economic recovery.

And in the world abroad, the Soviet Union has not stepped in or created a government of its kind in any new country in these 5 years. It's not moved under one additional inch of territory, and I just like to feel that maybe some of the things we did here—the American people, their spirit was down, they had heard talks, prior to our arrival, that maybe we should give up our high expectations, that never again could we look toward the future as we had in the past, lower our expectations, and so forth.

Today we have a volunteer military, we exceed our enlistment quota every year. We have the highest level of education in the military, in this volunteer military, that we've ever had in our history, even in wartime drafts. The American people have rallied, and with a spirit of voluntarism, voluntarily stepping into problems that once they just let go by and thought somebody in the Government would take care of them. And as I say, the economy—last year some 600,000 new businesses were incorporated in our country.

I would like to be remembered not for doing all those things—I didn't do them; the American people did them. All I did was help get government out of their way and restore our belief in the power of the people and that government must be limited in its powers and limited in its actions. And that part I helped in—I'd like to be remembered for that.

The President's Health

Mr. Widlake. One final question, Mr. President, it's about your health. How do you feel, and what do the doctors say?

The President. The doctor said that I'd had a 100 percent recovery. I'm riding horses regularly now, as I've always done, and I'm doing my exercises in the gym every day at the end of the day. I have a little gymnasium upstairs and some weight and so forth, and I'm doing all those things. And I've just never felt better.

Mr. Widlake. Well, it's a pleasure—you look remarkably fit. It's been a pleasure to talk to you. Thank you.

The President. Well, my pleasure, and thank you.

Note: The interview began at 2:35 p.m. in the Oval Office at the White House. The transcript was released by the Office of the Press Secretary on October 30.

Nomination of Wendell L. Willkie II To Be General Counsel of the Department of Education
October 30, 1985

The President today announced his intention to nominate Wendell L. Willkie II to be General Counsel, Department of Education. He would succeed Maureen E. Corcoran.

Mr. Willkie has been serving as Chief of Staff at the Department of Education since February of this year. Previously, he was at the White House as Associate Counsel to the President in 1984–1985; General Counsel at the National Endowment for the Humanities in 1982–1984; and an associate with the firm of Simpson, Thacher & Bartlett in 1978–1982.

Mr. Willkie graduated from Harvard College (B.A., 1973), Oxford University, England (M.A., B.A., 1975), and the University of Chicago (J.D., 1978). He was born October 29, 1951, in Indianapolis, IN, and now resides in Washington, DC.

Nomination of Walter J Shea To Be a Member of the Board of the Panama Canal Commission
October 30, 1985

The President today announced his intention to nominate Walter J. Shea to be a member of the Board of the Panama Canal Commission. He would succeed William Sidell.

Mr. Shea is vice president of the International Brotherhood of Teamsters. Previously he served as executive assistant to two general presidents of the International Brotherhood of Teamsters in 1967–1982. He joined the International Brotherhood of Teamsters in 1957 as a member of the research department of the eastern conference. In 1960–1967 he was assistant to the eastern conference director.

Mr. Shea was appointed to the President's Commission on Alcohol Abuse in 1983. He is married, has six children, and resides in Annapolis, MD. He was born November 30, 1929, in Brooklyn, NY.

Message to the Congress Transmitting a Report on the Exclusion of Certain Federal Employees From the Performance Management and Recognition System
October 30, 1985

To the Congress of the United States:

Supervisors and management officials in GS–13, 14, and 15 positions throughout the Federal government are covered by the Performance Management and Recognition System as required by Chapter 54, Title 5, U.S. Code, unless otherwise excluded by law.

Upon proper application from the heads of affected agencies and upon the recommendation of the Director of the Office of Personnel Management, I have excluded, pursuant to 5 U.S.C. 5402(b)(1), three agencies, units of agencies, and classes of employees from coverage under the Performance Management and Recognition System.

In accordance with Section 205(d) of P.L. 98–615, any agency or unit of an agency that was excluded from merit pay immediately prior to enactment of this legislation is excluded from coverage under the Performance Management and Recognition System for the 12-month period beginning on the date of enactment. However, such exclusion may be revoked at any time in accordance with 5 U.S.C. 5402(b)(5). Upon request of the heads of the affected agencies and upon recommendation of the Director of the Office of Personnel Management, I have revoked the exclusion of seven agencies and units of agencies so that they may implement the Performance Management and

Recognition System in fiscal year 1986.

Attached is my report describing the agencies to be excluded and the reasons therefor. I am also providing the names of those agencies for which the exclusion is revoked.

RONALD REAGAN

The White House,
October 30, 1985.

Note: The exclusions affected certain employees of the Board of Veterans Appeals, Veterans Administration; NATO Supreme Headquarters Allied Powers Europe; NATO International Staff (Evere, Belgium); NATO Integrated Communications System Management Agency; NATO Supply Center (Cappellen, Luxembourg); SHAPE; and the Bureau of Indian Affairs and Indian Arts and Crafts Board, Department of the Interior. The revocations of exclusions affected the Advisory Committee on Historic Preservation; the Committee for Purchase from the Blind and Other Severely Handicapped; the Commission of Fine Arts; the Foreign Claims Settlement Commission; the Japan-United States Friendship Commission; the Office of Hearings and Appeals, Department of the Interior; and the United States Architectural and Transportation Barriers Compliance Board.

Message to the Senate Transmitting the Hague Convention on the Civil Aspects of International Child Abduction
October 30, 1985

To the Senate of the United States:

With a view to receiving the advice and consent of the Senate to ratification, I transmit herewith a certified copy of the Hague Convention on the Civil Aspects of International Child Abduction, adopted on October

24, 1980 by the Fourteenth Session of the Hague Conference on Private International Law and opened for signature on October 25, 1980.

The Convention is designed to secure the prompt return of children who have been abducted from their country of habitual residence or wrongfully retained outside that country. It also seeks to facilitate the exercise of visitation rights across international borders. The Convention reflects a worldwide concern about the harmful effects on children of parental kidnapping and a strong desire to fashion an effective deterrent to such conduct.

The Convention's approach to the problem of international child abduction is a simple one. The Convention is designed promptly to restore the factual situation that existed prior to a child's removal or retention. It does not seek to settle disputes about legal custody rights, nor does it depend upon the existence of court orders as a condition for returning children. The international abductor is denied legal advantage from the abduction to or retention in the country where the child is located, as resort to the Convention is to effect the child's swift return to his or her circumstances before the abduction or retention. In most cases this will mean return to the country of the child's habitual residence where any dispute about custody rights can be heard and settled.

The Convention calls for the establishment of a Central Authority in every Contracting State to assist applicants in securing the return of their children or in exercising their custody or visitation rights, and to cooperate and coordinate with their counterparts in other countries toward these ends. Moreover, the Convention establishes a judicial remedy in wrongful removal or retention cases which permits an aggrieved parent to seek a court order for the prompt return of the child when voluntary agreement cannot be achieved. An aggrieved parent may pursue both of these courses of action or seek a judicial remedy directly without involving the Central Authority of the country where the child is located.

The Convention would represent an im-

portant addition to the State and Federal laws currently in effect in the United States that are designed to combat parental kidnapping—specifically, the Uniform Child Custody Jurisdiction Act now in effect in every State in the country, the Parental Kidnapping Prevention Act of 1980, the 1982 Missing Children Act and the Missing Children's Assistance Act. It would significantly improve the chances a parent in the United States has of recovering a child from a foreign Contracting State. It also provides a clear-cut method for parents abroad to apply for the return of children who have been wrongfully taken to or retained in this country. In short, by establishing a legal right and streamlined procedures for the prompt return of internationally abducted children, the Convention should remove many of the uncertainties and the legal difficulties that now confront parents in international child abduction cases.

Federal legislation will be submitted to provide for the smooth implementation of the Convention within the United States. This legislation will be consistent with the spirit and intent of recent congressional initiatives dealing with the problem of interstate child abduction and missing children.

United States ratification of the Convention is supported by the American Bar Association. The authorities of many States have indicated a willingness to do their part to assist the Federal government in carrying out the mandates of the Convention.

I recommend that the Senate give early and favorable consideration to the Convention and accord its advice and consent to ratification, subject to the reservations described in the accompanying report of the Secretary of State.

RONALD REAGAN

The White House,
October 30, 1985.

Appointment of Five Delegates to the National White House Conference on Small Business
October 30, 1985

The President today announced his intention to appoint the following individuals to be delegates to the National White House Conference on Small Business. These are new positions.

William H. Marumoto, of Virginia, is president and founder of the Interface Group, Ltd., of Washington, DC, a management consulting firm. He graduated from Whittier College (B.A., 1957). He is married, has four children, and resides in McLean, VA. He was born December 16, 1934.

B.F. (Chip) Backlund, of Illinois, is president and chief executive officer of Bartonville Bank in Peoria, IL. He graduated from Washburn University (B.A., 1946) and the University of Colorado (LL.B., 1949). He is married, has three children, and resides in Peoria, IL. He was

born May 31, 1924, in Stromsburg, NE.

Vincent G. Bell, Jr., of Pennsylvania, is chairman of the board and president of Safeguard Business Systems, Inc., in Fort Washington, PA. He graduated from Lehigh University (B.S., 1949). He is married, has three children, and resides in Radnor, PA. He was born November 30, 1925, in Wilkes-Barre, PA.

Thomas Norman Innes, of Virginia, is president of Brooks & Innes, Inc., realtors in Richmond, VA. He graduated from the University of Richmond (B.A., 1971). He is married, has two children, and resides in Richmond, VA. He was born October 9, 1949, in Somers, NY.

Milo Eugene Smith, of Indiana, is president of M.E. Smith, Inc., a real estate firm in Columbus, IN. He attended the University of Indiana. He has two children and resides in Columbus, IN. He was born July 18, 1950, in Columbus.

Letter to the Speaker of the House and the President of the Senate on Copper Production Restraints
October 30, 1985

Dear Mr. Speaker: (Dear Mr. President:)

In accordance with Section 247(c)(2) of the Trade and Tariff Act of 1984 (P.L. 98–573), I am writing to inform you of my decision not to seek to negotiate voluntary production restraints on copper.

Section 247(b) conveyed the sense of Congress that I should negotiate "with the principal foreign copper-producing countries to conclude voluntary restraint agreements with those governments for the purpose of effecting a balanced reduction of total annual foreign copper production for a period of between three and five years . . ." In light of this provision, an interagency task force, chaired by the Office of the United States Trade Representative, was formed to take another look at the possibility of negotiating such restraints—which had been considered, and rejected, in the context of the determination made on September 6, 1984, on import

relief in accordance with Section 202(b)(1) of the Trade Act of 1974.

The task force reviewed all questions relevant to the issue of voluntary production restraints, including:

1. The consistency of voluntary production restraints with the basic policies of this Administration.

2. The situation of the U.S. copper industry.

3. The extent of subsidization or unfair trade practices in the world copper economy.

4. The probable economic effects of production restraints.

5. The feasibility of negotiating and implementing such restraints.

The findings of the task force are outlined in the attached report.

In light of this review, I have determined that it would be inappropriate for this Government to seek to negotiate voluntary production restraint agreements with the governments of the principal foreign copper-producing countries.

An attempt to negotiate such restraints would be inconsistent with the overall, market-oriented trade and economic policy objectives of this Administration. It would set an undesirable precedent in light of both our efforts to increase the responsiveness of the domestic and international economy to market forces and our continued opposition to cartels or other arrangements aimed at controlling world markets. Moreover, any effort by this Government, in the context of production restraint negotiations, to give foreign producers assurances regarding the intentions of U.S. copper producers would raise serious antitrust concerns.

Efforts to raise world copper prices through the restraint of foreign production would also be inefficient and expensive for the U.S. economy; they would incur losses to U.S. consumers substantially in excess of any gains accruing to U.S. producers.

Finally, I do not believe it would be feasible either to conclude or to implement production restraint agreements. The major copper-producing countries have made it clear that they are opposed to the negotiation of such restraints—largely because they do not feel that such actions would be effective in improving the longer term situation in the world copper market. Moreover, past experience shows that production restraint agreements are extremely difficult to implement effectively and that any benefits from restraints tend to be eroded or reversed in the years following their termination.

While I do not believe that the negotiation of restraints is an appropriate course of action, I have asked the United States Trade Representative to continue to follow closely developments in the world copper market and to explore other possibilities for improving the situation of the U.S. copper industry. I also continue to be deeply concerned about the problems facing many workers in the U.S. copper industry. In re-

sponse to my directives of September 6, 1984, the Department of Labor has developed, and begun to implement, a plan for a special effort to assist workers displaced from the copper industry.

This plan consists of three elements. First, of the funds reserved by the Secretary under Title III of the Job Training Partnership Act (JTPA), $5.0 million has been earmarked specifically for retraining programs to assist copper workers in heavily impacted States and localities. To assure that a maximum effort is made in the States to assist copper workers, the States have been asked to contribute an amount equivalent to twice the Federal allocation to support these projects. In total this will amount to approximately $15 million in new training and employment services for copper workers. In addition, the 12 States targeted by this plan already have been allocated almost $38 million of title III grant resources which they have matched with some $25 million in State support. These combined resources totalling almost $63 million are also available for States to use in assisting dislocated copper workers.

Second, a team of senior Department of Labor staff has been made available to work with those State and local governments that request assistance to help establish programs of retraining, relocation, and related assistance for displaced copper workers.

Finally, Secretary Brock, working closely with representatives of industry and labor and officials from all levels of government, is monitoring these efforts and seeking ways to improve upon them. A more detailed report on the Department of Labor's efforts to assist dislocated copper workers is attached.

Sincerely,

RONALD REAGAN

Note: Identical letters were sent to Thomas P. O'Neill, Jr., Speaker of the House of Representatives, and George Bush, President of the Senate.

Proclamation 5402—National Foster Grandparent Month, 1985
October 30, 1985

By the President of the United States of America

A Proclamation

This year, we celebrate the 20th Anniversary of the Foster Grandparent Program. In its first year of operation, 782 foster grandparents carried out 33 projects in 27 States. Today, some 19,000 foster grandparents are serving some 65,000 children through 245 projects in all 50 States, Puerto Rico, the Virgin Islands, and the District of Columbia. The program, which has achieved both great success and great acceptance, is administered by ACTION, a Federal agency that promotes voluntarism.

Most of us have been fortunate enough to have enjoyed a very special relationship with our grandparents. They were the living bridge to the past. They handed down to us the hard-won lessons they had learned from life and the wisdom they had received from their own grandparents. They provided us with the patient, unquestioning love and understanding that gave us the strength to face the future with confidence and hope.

Today, the elderly and retired participants in the Foster Grandparent Program provide unique, personal guidance and care to tens of thousands of physically, emotionally, and mentally handicapped children as well as those who have been abused, neglected, or who are in the juvenile justice system, or in need of other special help.

Love is the only thing we have more of the more we give it away. And these volunteers who give of themselves, of their wisdom, and of their time, reap rich benefits. They rejoice in a newfound independence. Their loneliness and fear of isolation disappear. In many cases, their health improves. Their sense of self-worth is enhanced as they find themselves deeply involved with others who depend on them. They experience a new fulfillment in performing a much-needed community service which taps all their reserves of understanding, creativity, and warmth.

The children in the program blossom under the golden glow of counsel and caring that foster grandparents bring into their lives. This program has truly worked wonders for hearts young and old.

I urge all Americans to join me in applauding the activities of these foster grandparent volunteers. Their service encourages positive attitudes about the abilities of the elderly. It demonstrates how greatly society benefits when it calls on the experience and seasoned judgment of older persons.

The Congress, by Senate Joint Resolution 92, has designated the month of October 1985 as "National Foster Grandparent Month" and authorized and requested the President to issue a proclamation in observance of this event.

Now, Therefore, I, Ronald Reagan, President of the United States of America, do hereby proclaim the month of October 1985 as National Foster Grandparent Month. I invite all citizens and appropriate agencies and organizations to unite during October with appropriate observances and activities to honor these volunteers and the children they serve.

In Witness Whereof, I have hereunto set my hand this thirtieth day of October, in the year of our Lord nineteen hundred and eighty-five, and of the Independence of the United States of America the two hundred and tenth.

RONALD REAGAN

[Filed with the Office of the Federal Register, 10:48 a.m., October 31, 1985]

Proclamation 5403—American Education Week, 1985
October 30, 1985

By the President of the United States of America

A Proclamation

From their very beginnings, the colonies that later were to form the United States of America set great store by the education of the young, and with the birth of the New Nation this commitment to education deepened. Our Founding Fathers shared the insight of an ancient sage that "only the educated are free," and they took to heart the inspired maxim that it is the truth which sets us free. To them it was clear that since here the people would rule, the people must have the means to understand the issues and to make wise decisions. As James Madison put it: "On the diffusion of education among the people rest the preservation and perpetuation of our free institutions."

American Education Week offers all Americans an invitation to reflect on the importance of education to our Nation, not only to its prosperity but to the proper functioning of our whole system of government. It invites each of us to play a part in the national commitment to sound education and to the constant striving to improve the institutions that provide education at every level, from pre-school through graduate school. American Education Week is a time for all Americans to seek to do something to further the cause of education— whether by involvement in parent-teacher groups, contributions to private educational institutions, serving on local school boards, participation in adult education programs, furthering the utilization of libraries and museums, or any similar activity. For educators it is a time to rededicate themselves to what is surely one of the noblest of callings; and to students it is a challenge to make the best use of the manifold educational opportunities this country offers.

Now, Therefore, I, Ronald Reagan, President of the United States of America, do hereby proclaim the week beginning November 17, 1985, and the first full week preceding the fourth Thursday of November of each succeeding year, as American Education Week, and to observe this time with appropriate ceremonies and activities.

In Witness Whereof, I have hereunto set my hand this thirtieth day of October, in the year of our Lord nineteen hundred and eighty-five, and of the Independence of the United States of America the two hundred and tenth.

RONALD REAGAN

[*Filed with the Office of the Federal Register, 10:49 a.m., October 31, 1985*]

Statement on the Death of John Davis Lodge
October 30, 1985

Nancy and I are deeply saddened by the loss of our friend, John Davis Lodge. His death is not only a personal loss to those of us who trusted in his friendship and advice but to the country he served so patriotically throughout his long and full life.

John was a man of great and varied talents who excelled in each of his chosen occupations. We will never forget the young lawyer-cum-movie star who acted in such film classics as "Little Women" and "The Scarlet Empress" and who continued his acting career on the stage. But we shall always be most grateful to John Davis Lodge, the able public servant. As a Congressman and Governor of Connecticut, Ambassador to Spain, Argentina, and Switzerland, and in many other important positions, John was a tireless fighter against communism and a constant friend of freedom, both at home and abroad. At the time of his death, John was still serving his nation and the cause of humanity as a delegate to the United Nations. He will be sorely missed by his friends and by the country to which he gave such a full measure of his devotion.

On behalf of all Americans, Nancy and I extend our heartfelt sympathy to the Lodge family.

Remarks Congratulating the Championship Kansas City Royals Following the World Series
October 31, 1985

The President. Well, I thank you all. Welcome to the White House and back to the White House for some of you. It's a great pleasure to have you here, just as it was a great pleasure to watch these gentlemen perform in the World Series, and all of my words of welcome are intended for all of you, also.

In that Interstate 70 series, the "Show Me" spirit really came through. Your team showed the world, and you did it royally. You've proved to America what a never-say-die spirit can do. Even after losing the first two games of the series at home, you met the challenge, and you kept America in suspense for seven full games and rallied to bring the World Series trophy to Kansas City. Only five other teams in World Series history have managed to overcome such a margin.

Now, look at how enthusiastic I'm being in—I pitched in a World Series, but I was with the Cardinals at the time. [*Laughter*] Three games—it was the 1926 World Series, but I was doing it in 1952 in a movie. [*Laughter*] I had an edge on all of you in the sense that I knew the script in advance, so I knew it was going to come out right. [*Laughter*]

Well, Dick Howser, you may not have the words to describe it, but in the words of Bret Saberhagen, it was a dream come true. And what a dream it's been for Bret—a 20 and 6 regular season record—at 21, the youngest player ever to win the World Series Most Valuable Player, a leading candidate for the Cy Young Award, and a proud papa to brand-new Drew William. You're not only a hot pitcher, Bret, but I understand you're a pretty good coach, too. [*Laughter*] And if you don't think so, just ask Jeannine.

The Royals have some super talented players. George Brett, the third baseman who has captured the essence of hitting, has become something of a Kansas City institution. He's an inspiration for future ballplayers all across the country. Then, there's Willie Wilson, who batted .367 in the series; Frank White, the ever-steady second baseman; slugger Steve Balboni and Hal McRae; and, of course, Dan Quisenberry, the premier relief man, whom I called Jim on the phone the other night. [*Laughter*] Heads will roll in the west wing for that. [*Laughter*]

But it's the Royals' team play, a combination of the great spirit and hard work of every one of you on the roster, that brought you this championship. I always like to point to experience as a major element of success, but it's hard in this case when you could add up the ages of three of the five starting pitchers and come up with fewer birthdays than I've seen. [*Laughter*] Seriously, you've fought long and hard throughout the season. And your dedication has paid off. And now that you've proved you're the champions of the world, what do you do for an encore?

Mr. Howser. Next year.

The President. All right. Congratulations. God bless all of you.

[*At this point, the President was presented with a Royals jacket and cap.*]

Reporter. Mr. President, have you sent your new arms proposal to Gorbachev?

The President. I'm making an announcement this afternoon.

Q. Right here?

Q. ——a letter, sir?

Q. Are we going to see you in the Briefing Room, sir?

The President. Yes.

Q. Fifty-percent cut?

The President. I'll see you soon.

Q. Have a nice day!

Q. It's a date.

Q. Make it early!

Note: The President spoke at 11:52 a.m. in the Rose Garden at the White House. Dick Howser was the manager of the team.

Nomination of William R. Kintner To Be a Member of the Board of Directors of the United States Institute of Peace
October 31, 1985

The President today announced his intention to nominate William R. Kintner to be a member of the Board of Directors of the United States Institute of Peace for a term of 2 years expiring January 19, 1987. This is a new position.

Dr. Kintner currently is a professor of political science at the Wharton School of the University of Pennsylvania. In 1973–1975 he was the United States Ambassador to Thailand. He served at the Foreign Policy Research Institute in Philadelphia as president (1976), director (1969–1973), and deputy director (1961–1969). He was a member of the Board of Foreign Scholarships in 1970–1973 and a member of the academic board of the Inter-American Defense College in 1967–1972. Dr. Kintner also is the author of many books on military policy.

He graduated from the United States Military Academy (B.S., 1940) and Georgetown University (Ph.D., 1949). He is married, has four children, and resides in Bryn Athyn, PA. He was born April 21, 1915, in Lock Haven, PA.

Nomination of Michael H. Mobbs To Be an Assistant Director of the United States Arms Control and Disarmament Agency
October 31, 1985

The President today announced his intention to nominate Michael H. Mobbs to be an Assistant Director of the United States Arms Control and Disarmament Agency (Bureau of Strategic Programs). He would succeed Henry F. Cooper, Jr.

Mr. Mobbs is currently special counsel to the head of the U.S. delegation to negotiations on nuclear and space arms, International Security Policy, Office of the Secretary of Defense. Previously he was representative of the Secretary of Defense to strategic arms reduction talks in 1982–1985. He was senior associate with the law firm of Stroock & Stroock & Lavan in Washington, DC (1977–1981), and an associate with the law firm of Bradley, Arant, Rose & White in Birmingham, AL (1974–1977).

Mr. Mobbs graduated from Yale University (B.A., 1971) and the University of Chicago Law School (J.D., 1974). He is married, has one child, and resides in Leesburg, VA. He was born December 25, 1948, in Lawrenceburg, TN.

Nomination of James J. Carey To Be a Commissioner of the Federal Maritime Commission
October 31, 1985

The President today announced his intention to nominate James J. Carey to be a Federal Maritime Commissioner for the term expiring June 30, 1990. This is a reappointment.

Mr. Carey was appointed Commissioner of the Federal Maritime Commission in 1981 and was elected Vice Chairman of the Commission in 1983. Prior to this time, he was a business development manager with Telemedia, Inc. He was a management consultant to Telemedia in 1978–1979. He was

president, Coordinated Graphics, in 1976–1978; executive vice president, Total Graphic Communication, Inc., in 1974–1976; and president of the Chicago Offset Corp. in 1972–1974.

He served in the U.S. Navy in 1962–1965 as an officer in the First and Seventh Fleets and held three commands. He graduated from Northwestern University (B.A.). He is married, has two children, and resides in Arlington, VA. He was born April 9, 1939, in Berlin, WI.

Remarks Announcing the Presentation of a New United States Proposal at the Nuclear and Space Arms Negotiations With the Soviet Union
October 31, 1985

The President. I have instructed our negotiators in Geneva at the nuclear and space talks to present a new United States proposal designed to advance the prospects for achieving real reductions in nuclear arms, enhancing stability, and addressing the legitimate concerns of the United States and our allies as well as of the Soviet Union. I have also asked our negotiators to seek Soviet agreement to extend this round of the negotiations into next week so that our negotiating team can make a full presentation of our proposal and have a real give-and-take with the Soviets on its details. Finally, I have written to the leaders of allied nations and have transmitted a personal letter to General Secretary Gorbachev on this subject.

History has shown that progress is more surely made through confidential negotiations; therefore, I'm not going into any details about our proposal. Suffice to say that our proposal is serious, it is detailed, and it addresses all three areas of the negotiations. It builds upon the very concrete reductions proposals, which our negotiators had tabled

earlier, as well as the Soviet counterproposal.

The Soviet counterproposal was first presented to me by Foreign Minister Shevardnadze at our White House meeting in September, following which it was tabled at Geneva by the Soviet negotiators. Since that time, our arms control experts have analyzed the Soviet counterproposal extremely carefully. This analysis now completed, I have met with my senior advisers, decided on our response, and have instructed our negotiators to make this move. During our careful review, we measured the Soviet counterproposal against our concrete proposals for deep, equitable, and verifiable reductions which we already had on the table and against the criteria which we have long held for attaining effective arms control agreements. We have made clear that, measured against these criteria, the Soviet counterproposal, unfortunately, fell significantly short in several key areas. At the same time, as I indicated in my address to the United Nations General Assembly last week, the counterproposal also had certain positive seeds which we wish to nurture.

Our new proposal builds upon these positive elements and calls for very significant balanced reductions of comparable nuclear systems, particularly those that are the most destabilizing. It's my hope that our new proposal will enable both of our nations to start moving away from ever-larger arsenals of offensive forces. At the same time, we seek in Geneva to undertake with the Soviets a serious examination of the important relationship between offensive and defensive forces and how people everywhere can benefit from exploring the potential of non-nuclear defenses which threaten no one. I'm pleased that we seem to have made a successful start on this long process. The Soviet response to our earlier proposals and the new proposal which we're making are important milestones in moving these negotiations forward.

Additionally, I hope we can achieve progress in the other key areas of the broad agenda which Mr. Gorbachev and I will discuss in Geneva—human rights, regional issues, and bilateral matters. Strengthening the peace and building a more constructive, long-term U.S.-Soviet relationship requires that we move ahead in all of these areas. I believe progress is, indeed, possible if the Soviet leadership is willing to match our own commitment to a better relationship.

Now, I'm going to leave here because I can't discuss the details or answer any questions on it since it will be introduced tomorrow and then all of those things will be available.

Reporter. What about a general question?

The President. Just let me—just sum up. What I wanted to say is that I would characterize our arms control position as deep cuts, no first-strike advantage, defensive research—because defense is safer than offense—and no cheating.

Q. Let me ask you a question that is—sir, could we ask you a question that is general?

Q. Mr. President, do you think anything can be accomplished in time for the Geneva summit?

The President. What?

Q. Do you think anything can be accomplished on arms control on this new counterproposal in time for a broad statement of principles at the Geneva summit?

The President. Well now, this is all I'm going to respond to and simply say—because it touches on something I said here and explains. Since they were scheduled—the negotiations—to recess, they will do that, but hopefully a week late. Naturally, both sides are going to have to agree to that. We're asking our people to extend it by a week, but it will give them time to table this and at least be able to see back and forth. After all, it isn't that deep a document, but the figures and where they are. And then they will find the relationship between the counterproposal and our original proposal.

Q. ——the Soviet journalists——

Q. ——no give on Star Wars, sir—no give on Star Wars, sir?

Q. ——in time for the Geneva summit, which was the question—in time for you and Mr. Gorbachev to actually announce something?

The President. No, I don't—they may say something about it, but you'll have all the facts and figures——

Q. Sir, you told the——

Q. Are you going to ask——

Q. ——no give on Star Wars, Mr. President?

Q. ——you told the Soviet journalists, Mr. President——

Q. No give on Star Wars, Mr. President?

Q. Sir, if I may ask——

The President. In my statement, I said that defense and—I hope that we can arrive at a discussion of defensive weapons.

Q. Mr. President, do you intend to go ahead with Star Wars?

Q. You told the Soviet journalists that you hoped for concrete achievements at Geneva. Just a couple of days ago you told a BBC interviewer that perhaps the hope was that the paranoia might be lessened. It sounds like you're more optimistic about actually coming out with something?

The President. I'm always optimistic, Sam [Sam Donaldson, ABC News].

Q. Yes, but do you hope for concrete results, meaning some sort of broad framework of at least the principles?

The President. Well, I was answering—I think that some of you have misinterpreted the answer that I gave in that BBC interview. The question had been what was my hope—what I thought—felt would come out and so forth. And I was simply putting in place that arms control is a result; that first, you've got to eliminate the suspicions and the paranoia between us and so forth, and then, you find out that arms control can come easily. But to just simply dwell on arms control—if both of you are sitting there suspiciously saying how can we keep an advantage—each side saying the same thing to itself, well, then, it doesn't really matter how many missiles you've counted.

Q. Is [Secretary of State] Shultz going to ask for regular summit meetings when he goes to Moscow?

The President. I can't speak for him of what's going to be——

Q. Will you be actually negotiating with Mr. Gorbachev when you meet with him—arms control negotiations?

The President. Well, yes, of course. That's one of the main features.

Q. You mean you'll be talking figures?

The President. ——will be negotiated at Geneva, but I'm quite sure that there will be—they'll want to discuss this and why they've taken certain positions and so forth.

Note: The President spoke to reporters at 3 p.m. in the Briefing Room at the White House.

Message to the Congress Reporting on Economic Sanctions Against Nicaragua
October 31, 1985

To the Congress of the United States:

On May 1, 1985, in Executive Order No. 12513, I declared a national emergency to deal with the threat to the national security and foreign policy of the United States posed by the policies and actions of the Government of Nicaragua. In that order, I prohibited: (1) all imports into the United States of goods and services of Nicaraguan origin; (2) all exports from the United States of goods to or destined for Nicaragua except those destined for the organized democratic resistance; (3) Nicaraguan air carriers from engaging in air transportation to or from points in the United States; and (4) vessels of Nicaraguan registry from entering United States ports.

The declaration of emergency was made pursuant to the authority vested in me as President by the Constitution and laws of the United States, including the International Emergency Economic Powers Act, 50 U.S.C. 1701 et seq., and the National Emergencies Act, 50 U.S.C. 1601 et seq. I reported the declaration to the Congress on May 1, 1985, pursuant to Section 1703(b) of the International Emergency Economic Powers Act.

The Office of Foreign Assets Control of the Department of the Treasury issued the Nicaraguan Trade Control Regulations implementing the prohibitions in Executive Order No. 12513 on May 8, 1985, 50 Fed. Reg. 19890 (May 10, 1985). I am enclosing a copy of these regulations with this report.

It should be noted that Section 540.505 permits the issuance of licenses authorizing the export of goods from the United States to Nicaragua in certain circumstances involving contractual obligations which the exporter incurred prior to May 1, 1985. The regulation provides that such exports may be authorized only through October 31, 1985. Once this deadline has passed, licenses for exports on prior contractual grounds will no longer be available.

The policies and actions of the Government of Nicaragua continue to pose an unusual and extraordinary threat to the national security and foreign policy of the United States. I shall continue to exercise the powers at my disposal to apply economic sanctions against Nicaragua as long as these measures are appropriate, and will continue to report periodically to the Congress on significant developments, pursuant to 50 U.S.C. 1703(c).

RONALD REAGAN

The White House,
October 31, 1985.

Nomination of Charles L. Woods To Be a Member of the National Mediation Board
October 31, 1985

The President today announced his intention to nominate Charles L. Woods to be a member of the National Mediation Board for the remainder of the term expiring July 1, 1986. He would succeed Robert Oberndoerfer Harris.

Since 1975 he has been serving as the airline representative to the Teamsters Airline Division. Previously, he was an airline pilot (captain) for United Air Lines (1947–1975) and a copilot for United (1944–1947).

He is married, has three children, and resides in Manhattan Beach, CA. He was born May 10, 1915, in Redlands, CA.

Appointment of John George Pappajohn as a Member of the Advisory Committee on the Arts
October 31, 1985

The President today announced his intention to appoint John George Pappajohn to be a member of the Advisory Committee on the Arts (John F. Kennedy Center for the Performing Arts, Smithsonian Institution). This is an initial appointment.

He is president of Equity Dynamics, Inc., in Des Moines, IA. Previously he was president of Guardsman Life Investors Co.

Mr. Pappajohn graduated from the University of Iowa (B.S.C., 1952). He is married, has one child, and resides in Des Moines, IA. He was born July 31, 1928, in St. Lukes, Greece.

Nomination of Paul Matthews Cleveland To Be United States Ambassador to New Zealand
November 1, 1985

The President today announced his intention to nominate Paul Matthews Cleveland, of Florida, a career member of the Senior Foreign Service, Class of Minister-Counselor, as Ambassador to New Zealand. He would succeed H. Monroe Browne.

Mr. Cleveland served with the Department of Navy as a management analyst in the Office of Management in 1956–1957. He entered on duty as a Foreign Service officer with the Department of State in 1957 and became a staff aide to the Deputy Assistant Secretary for Operations in 1958. In 1959 Mr. Cleveland went to Canberra, Australia, as economic, then political officer, where he served until 1962. He then became Ambassador's aide in Bonn, Germany, in 1963–1964. In 1964–1965 he took academic training and received his M.A. from the Fletcher School of Law and Diplomacy. From there he went to Jakarta, Indonesia, as economic officer, where he served until 1968, when he returned to the Department as an economic officer in the

Office of Fuels and Energy. In 1970 he became special assistant to the Assistant Secretary for East Asian Affairs, departing in 1973 to become political/military officer, then political counselor at the U.S. Embassy in Seoul, Korea. In 1977 he was named Deputy Director and Director of Regional Affairs in the Bureau of East Asian Affairs in the Department. In 1980–1981 Mr. Cleveland was Director of Thai Affairs, and in 1981–1982 he was Director of Korean

Affairs. Since 1982 he has been deputy chief of mission at the U.S. Embassy in Seoul, Korea.

Mr. Cleveland graduated from Yale University (B.A., 1953) and the Fletcher School of Law and Diplomacy (M.A., 1965). He was a pilot in the United States Air Force in 1953–1956. His foreign language is German. He is married to the former Carter Sellwood, and they have four children. He was born August 25, 1931, in Boston, MA.

Notice of the Continuation of the Iran Emergency
November 1, 1985

On November 14, 1979, by Executive Order No. 12170, the President declared a national emergency to deal with the threat to the national security, foreign policy, and economy of the United States constituted by the situation in Iran. Notices of the continuation of this national emergency were transmitted by the President to the Congress and the *Federal Register* on November 12, 1980, November 12, 1981, November 8, 1982, November 4, 1983, and November 7, 1984. Because our relations with Iran have not yet returned to normal and the process of implementing the January 19, 1981, agreements with Iran is still underway, the national emergency declared

on November 14, 1979, must continue in effect beyond November 14, 1985. Therefore, in accordance with Section 202(d) of the National Emergencies Act (50 U.S.C. 1622(d)), I am continuing the national emergency with respect to Iran. This notice shall be published in the *Federal Register* and transmitted to the Congress.

RONALD REAGAN

The White House,
November 1, 1985.

[*Filed with the Office of the Federal Register, 4:19 p.m., November 1, 1985*]

Message to the Congress Reporting on the Continuation of the Iran Emergency
November 1, 1985

To the Congress of the United States:

Section 202(d) of the National Emergencies Act (50 U.S.C. 1622(d)) provides for the automatic termination of a national emergency unless, prior to the anniversary date of its declaration, the President publishes in the *Federal Register* and transmits to the Congress a notice stating that the emergency is to continue in effect beyond the anniversary date. In accordance with this provision, I have sent the enclosed notice, stating

that the Iran emergency is to continue in effect beyond November 14, 1985, to the *Federal Register* for publication. Similar notices were sent to the Congress and the *Federal Register* on November 12, 1980, November 12, 1981, November 8, 1982, November 4, 1983, and November 7, 1984.

The crisis between the United States and Iran that began in 1979 has not been fully resolved. Although the international tribunal established to adjudicate claims of U.S.

1329

nationals against Iran and of Iranian nationals against the United States continues to function, full normalization of commercial and diplomatic relations between the United States and Iran will require more time. In these circumstances, I have determined that it is necessary to maintain in force the broad authorities that may be needed in the process of implementing the January 1981 agreements with Iran and in the eventual normalization of relations with that country.

RONALD REAGAN

The White House,
November 1, 1985.

Radio Address to the Nation on the Soviet-United States Nuclear and Space Arms Negotiations
November 2, 1985

My fellow Americans:

Yesterday in Geneva American negotiators presented to their Soviet counterparts new proposals designed to achieve real reductions in the nuclear arsenals of both the United States and the Soviet Union. My instructions to our negotiators also asked that this round of the negotiations be extended into this coming week so that our team can make a full presentation of our new proposals and so that the Soviets have the opportunity to ask questions about them. I am very pleased that the Soviet Union has agreed to this extension of the talks. I know you join me in hoping that this will be a productive week in Geneva. Our new proposals address all three areas of these negotiations: strategic nuclear arms, intermediate-range nuclear forces, and defense and space systems. They build upon the concrete reduction proposals American negotiators have had on the table since early in the talks, and they take into account expressed Soviet concerns.

Our objective since the start of the administration in 1981 has been to achieve real progress in reducing not only nuclear arms but conventional forces and chemical weapons as well. We've been firm and consistent in our arms control approach. Just as important, we have placed great value on maintaining the strength and unity of our alliances and ensuring that the security interests of our allies are enhanced in these negotiations. And we've demonstrated flexibility in taking legitimate Soviet interests into account. I'm pleased to report to you

that our strategy has been working. I believe we've laid the groundwork for productive negotiations in Geneva. The first sign of this was when Soviet Foreign Minister Shevardnadze presented to me at our White House meeting in September a Soviet counteroffer to our own earlier proposals. The Soviet negotiators then presented this in detail in Geneva, and our negotiators and our experts here at home have had a chance to analyze it carefully.

Based on this analysis, I decided upon the new U.S. proposals and instructed our negotiating team to present them in Geneva. Judged against our very careful criteria for reaching sound arms control agreements, we found that the Soviet counterproposal had some flaws and in some ways was one-sided. But as I made clear in my speech to the United Nations, the Soviet move also had certain positive seeds which we wish to nurture. Our new proposals build upon these positive elements. One of them is the Soviet call for 50-percent reduction in certain types of nuclear arms. For more than 3 years we've been proposing a reduction of about half in the strategic ballistic missiles of both sides. We therefore have accepted the 50-percent reduction proposed by the Soviets.

At the same time, we're making it clear that we have a safer and more stable world. And if we're to have that, reductions must be applied to systems which are comparable, and especially to those which would give either side a destabilizing first-strike advantage. We not only want to bring nuclear arms way down to equal levels in a stable way, we also want to decrease our mutual reliance for security on these extremely destructive offensive arsenals. Thus, we're seeking to discuss at the same time with the Soviets in Geneva how together we can try to help make the world a safer place by relying more on defenses which threaten no one, rather than on these offensive arsenals. Each of us is pursuing research on such defenses, and we need to be talking to each other about it.

I have written to both allied leaders and Soviet General Secretary Gorbachev about our new proposals. And I have informed Mr. Gorbachev how much I am looking forward to our meeting later this month in Geneva. He and I will have a broad agenda at our meeting, one that includes human rights, regional issues, and contacts between our peoples, as well as the Geneva and other arms control negotiations. If we hope to succeed in our efforts to create a safer world and to bring about a fresh start in the U.S.-Soviet relationship, progress will be

needed in all of these areas. And this can only be accomplished if the Soviet leaders share our determination. We're encouraged because after a long wait, legitimate negotiations are underway.

Now, we've had a proposal on the table in Geneva for quite a while. Now the Soviet Union has offered a counterproposal, and we, in turn, have a new proposal now reflecting some of the elements of both of the others. And this is what negotiation is all about. I can't give you any more details about our new arms control proposals because we have to let the negotiators work this out behind closed doors in Geneva. But I want to leave you with the four key objectives our American negotiators are seeking: deep cuts, no first-strike advantages, defensive research—because defense is much safer than offense—and no cheating.

Until next week, thanks for listening. God bless you.

Note: The President spoke at 12:06 p.m. from Camp David, MD.

Remarks in an Interview With Representatives of Soviet News Organizations, Together With Written Responses to Questions
October 31, 1985

The President. May I welcome you all. It's a pleasure here, and I appreciate very much the opportunity to be able to speak, in a sense, to the people of your country. I've always believed that a lot of the ills of the world would disappear if people talked more to each each other instead of about each other. So, I look forward to this meeting and welcome your questions.

Q. Mr. President, we appreciate greatly this opportunity to ask to you, personally, questions after you kindly answered our written questions. We hope that they will be instructive and will facilitate success for your forthcoming meeting with our leader.

The President. Well, I'm looking forward to that meeting. I'm hopeful and optimistic that maybe we can make some concrete achievements there.

Q. We are planning to ask our questions

in Russian. I think you don't mind.

The President. No.

Nuclear and Space Arms Negotiations

Q. Mr. President, we have become acquainted with the answers which you furnished to our written questions. They basically reflect the old U.S. proposals, which have been evaluated by the Soviet side as being unbalanced and one-sided in favor of the U.S. side, and you have not answered concerning the new Soviet proposal. And this reply to the new Soviet proposal is what is of greatest interest before the meeting in Geneva.

The President. When this interview is over, later this afternoon at 3 o'clock, I will be making a statement to our own press—well, to all the press—to the effect that we have been studying the Soviet proposal, and tomorrow in Geneva our team at the disarmament conference will be presenting our reply, which will be a proposal that reflects the thinking of the original proposal that we had, but also of this latest. Indeed, it will show that we are accepting some of the figures that were in this counterproposal by the Secretary General. There are some points in which we have offered compromises between some figures of theirs and some of ours, but all those figures will be available tomorrow, and I will simply be stating today that that is going to take place tomorrow in Geneva. But it is a detailed counterproposal to a counterproposal, as is proper in negotiations, that will reflect, as I say, the acceptance on our part of some of this latest proposal as well as compromises with earlier figures that we'd proposed.

Strategic Defense Initiative

Q. I'd like to have another question for you, Mr. President. According to a survey taken by the Washington Post and ABC on Tuesday, it was found that 74 percent of the American people, as compared to 20 percent, said that they would like the U.S. and the Soviet Union to reduce their nuclear arsenals and not to have the U.S. develop space weapons. This seems to be the choice which the American people have made. It seems clear that without stopping the development of weapons in space there can be no reduction of nuclear weapons. This is the position of the Soviet side. So, how then will you react, Mr. President, to this opinion expressed by the American public?

The President. Well, for one thing, it is based on a misconception. The use of the term Star Wars came about when one political figure in America used that to describe what it is we're researching and studying, and then our press picked it up, and it has been worldwide. We're not talking about Star Wars at all. We're talking about seeing if there isn't a defensive weapon that does not kill people, but that simply makes it impossible for nuclear missiles, once fired out of their silos, to reach their objective—to intercept those weapons.

Now, it is also true that—to show that this is a misconception on the part of the people when you use the wrong terms—not too long ago there was a survey taken, a poll of

our people, and they asked them about Star Wars. And similar to the reaction in this poll, only about 30 percent of the people in our country favored it, and the rest didn't. But in the same poll they then described, as I have tried to describe, what it is we're researching—a strategic defensive shield that doesn't kill people, but that would allow us one day—all of us—to get rid of nuclear weapons, and over 90 percent of the American people favored our going forward with such a program.

Now, this is one of the things that we will discuss. We are for and have for several years now been advocating a reduction in the number of nuclear weapons. It is uncivilized on the part of all of us to be sitting here with the only deterrent to war—offensive nuclear weapons that in such numbers that both of us could threaten the other with the death and the annihilation of millions and millions of each other's people. And so that is the deterrent that is supposed to keep us from firing these missiles at each other. Wouldn't it make a lot more sense if we could find that—as there has been in history for every weapon—a defensive weapon? Weapon isn't the term to use for what we're researching. We're researching for something that could make it, as I say, virtually impossible for these missiles to reach their targets. And if we find such a thing, my proposal is that we make it available to all the world. We don't just keep it for our own advantage.

Q. Mr. President, with the situation as it stands today in the international arena, attempts to create such a space shield will inevitably lead to suspicion on the other side that the country creating such a space shield will be in a position to make a first strike. This is a type of statement whose truth is agreed to by many people. Now, it's apparent that the American people have indicated their choice, that if it comes down to a choice between the creation of such a space system and the decrease in nuclear arms, they prefer a decrease in nuclear arms. So, it seems to be a realistic evaluation on the part of the American people. And I would like to ask how the American government would react to the feelings of the American people in this regard.

The President. Well, in the first place, yes, if someone was developing such a defensive system and going to couple it with their own nuclear weapons, offensive weapons, yes, that could put them in a position where they might be more likely to dare a first strike. But your country, your government, has been working on this same kind of a plan beginning years before we ever started working on it, which, I think, would indicate that maybe we should be a little suspicious that they want it for themselves. But I have said and am prepared to say at the summit that if such a weapon is possible, and our research reveals that, then our move would be to say to all the world, "Here, it is available." We won't put this weapon—or this system in place, this defensive system, until we do away with our nuclear missiles, our offensive missiles. But we will make it available to other countries, including the Soviet Union, to do the same thing.

Now, just whichever one of us comes up first with that defensive system, the Soviet Union or us or anyone else—what a picture if we say no one will claim a monopoly on it. And we make that offer now. It will be available for the Soviet Union as well as ourselves. And if the Soviet Union and the United States both say we will eliminate our offensive weapons, we will put in this defensive thing in case some place in the world a madman some day tries to create these weapons again—nuclear weapons—because, remember, we all know how to make them now. So, you can't do away with that information, but we would all be safe knowing that if such a madman project is ever attempted there isn't any of us that couldn't defend ourselves against it. So, I can assure you now we are not going to try and monopolize this, if such a weapon is developed, for a first-strike capability.

U.S. Troops Stationed Abroad

Q. Mr. President, I would like to ask you about some of the matters which concern mutual suspicion and distrust. And you indicated at your speech at the United Nations that the U.S. does not have troops in other countries, has not occupied other countries, but there are 550,000 troops, military personnel, outside of the United States; in 32 countries, there are 1,500 military bases. So, one can see in this way which country it is that has become surrounded. And you have agreed that the Soviet Union has the right to look out for the interest of its security. And it is inevitable that the Soviet Union must worry about these bases, which are around it. The Soviet Union, in turn, has not done the same. So, how do you in this respect anticipate to create this balance of security, which you have spoken about?

The President. Well, I can't respond to your exact numbers there that you've given. I don't have them right at my fingertips as to what they are, but we're talking about two different things. We're talking about occupying a country with foreign troops, such as we see the Soviet Union doing in Afghanistan, and there are other places, too—Angola, South Yemen, Ethiopia.

Yes, we have troops in bases. The bulk of those would be in the NATO forces, the alliance in Europe along the NATO line, there in response to even superior numbers of Warsaw Pact troops that are aligned against them. And the United States, as one of the members of the alliance, contributes troops to that NATO force. The same is true in Korea in which, at the invitation of the South Korean Government, we have troops to help them there because of the demilitarized zone and the threatening nature of North Korea, which attacked them without warning. And that was not an American war, even though we provided the most of the men; that war was fought under the flag of the United Nations. The United Nations found North Korea guilty of aggression in violation of the charter of the U.N. And finally, South Korea was defended, and the North Koreans were defeated, but they still have maintained a sizable, threatening offensive force. Other places—we have bases in the far Pacific; we've had them for many years in the Philippines. We lease those; those are bases we rent. In fact, we even have a base that is leased on Cuba, that was there long before there was a Castro in Cuba, a naval base.

But this, I think, is a far cry from occupying other countries, including the nations in the Warsaw Pact. They never were allowed the self-determination that was agreed to in the Yalta treaty—the end of World War II. So, I think my statement still goes: that there is a difference in occupation and a difference in having bases where they are there in a noncombat situation, and many where they are requested by the parent country.

Guantanamo Bay Naval Base

Q. If there's a referendum and the Cuban people decide that the base at Guantanamo should be evacuated, would it be evacuated?

The President. No, because the lease for that was made many years ago, and it still has many years to run, and we're perfectly legal in our right to be there. It is fenced off; there is no contact with the people or the main island of Cuba at all.

U.S. Foreign Policy

Q. Mr. President, you have mentioned Afghanistan. I would like to say that in Afghanistan, Soviet troops are there at the invitation of the Afghan Government to defend the Afghan revolution against the incursions of forces from abroad that are funded and supported by the United States. In the United Nations and in your written replies to our questions, you have indicated that the United States has not attempted to use force but has fostered the process of democracy by peaceful means. Now, how does this reply fit in with the use of force by the United States in many countries abroad, beginning with Vietnam, where seven million tons of weapons were dropped—seven million tons more than were in the Second World War, and, also, Grenada? I ask this not to dwell on the past, but simply to clarify this issue.

The President. And it can be clarified, yes. First of all, with regard to Afghanistan, the government which invited the Soviet troops in didn't have any choice because the government was put there by the Soviet Union and put there with the force of arms to guarantee. And in fact, the man who was the head of that government is the second choice. The first one wasn't satisfactory to the Soviet Union, and they came in with armed forces and threw him out and installed their second choice, who continues

to be the governor. Now, there are no outside forces fighting in there. But, as a matter of fact, I think there are some things that, if they were more widely known, would shock everyone worldwide. For example, one of the weapons being used against the people of Afghanistan consists of toys—dolls, little toy trucks, things that are appealing to children. They're scattered in the air, but when the children pick them up, their hands are blown off. They are what we call boobytraps; they're like landmines. This is hardly consistent with the kind of armed warfare that has occurred between nations.

Vietnam? Yes, when Vietnam—or let's say, French Indochina—was given up as a colony, an international forum in Geneva, meeting in Geneva, established a North Vietnam and a South Vietnam. The North Vietnam was already governed by a Communist group and had a government in place during the Japanese occupation of French Indochina. South Vietnam had to start and create a government. We were invited, with instructors, to help them establish something they had never had before, which was a military. And our instructors went in in civilian clothes; their families went with them; and they started with a country that didn't have any military schools or things of this kind to create an armed force for the Government of South Vietnam. They were harassed by terrorists from the very beginning. Finally, it was necessary to send the families home. Schools were being bombed. There was even a practice of rolling bombs down the aisles of movie theaters and killing countless people that were simply enjoying a movie. And finally, changes were made that our people were allowed to arm themselves for their own protection.

And then, it is true that President Kennedy sent in a unit of troops to provide protection. This grew into the war of Vietnam. At no time did the allied force, and it was allied—there were more in there than just American troops—at no time did we try for victory. Maybe that's what was wrong. We simply tried to maintain a demilitarized zone between North and South Vietnam. And we know the result that has occurred now. And it is all one state of Vietnam. It was conquered in violation of a treaty that was signed in Paris between North and South Vietnam. We left South Vietnam, and North Vietnam swept down, conquered the country, as I say, in violation of a treaty.

But this is true of almost any of the other places that you mentioned. I've talked so long I've forgotten some of the other examples that you used.

Q. Grenada.

The President. What?

Q. Grenada.

The President. Grenada. Ah, we had some several hundred young American medical students there. Our intelligence revealed that they were threatened as potential hostages and the Government of Grenada requested help, military help, not only from the United States but from the other Commonwealth nations—island nations in the Caribbean—from Jamaica, from Dominica, a number of these others. They in turn relayed the request to us because they did not have armed forces in sufficient strength. And, yes, we landed, and we found warehouses filled with weapons, and they were of Soviet manufacture. We found hundreds of Cubans there; there was a brief engagement. We freed the island. And in a very short time, our troops came home after rescuing our students, rescuing the island. There are no American troops there now. Grenada has set up a democracy and is ruling itself by virtue of an election that was held shortly thereafter among the people, and of which we played no part.

And there is the contrast: The Soviet troops have been in Afghanistan for 6 years now, fighting all that time. We did what we were asked to do—the request of the Government of Grenada—and came home.

ABM Treaty

Q. Mr. President, with relation to the ABM treaty, which was signed in 1972, article V of that treaty indicates, and I quote, "that each side will not develop or test or deploy antiballistic missile components or systems which are sea-based, air-based, space-based, or mobile land-based." Now, some administration representatives say that the treaty is such that it permits all of these things—the development, the testing, and deployment of ABM systems. Such an interpretation of that treaty certainly cannot help achieve agreement. What is the true position of the American administration with regard to the interpretation of this treaty? Will the U.S. abide by the treaty or not? And certainly the results of your meeting with General Secretary Gorbachev will depend a great deal on that fact.

The President. There are two varying interpretations of the treaty. There is an additional clause in the treaty that would seem to be more liberal than that paragraph 5— or clause 5. The other hand, we have made it plain that we are going to stay within a strict definition of the treaty, and what we are doing with regard to research—and that would include testing—is within the treaty. Now, with regard to deployment, as I said earlier, no, we are doing what is within the treaty and which the Soviet Union has already been doing for quite some time, same kind of research and development. But when it comes to deployment, I don't know what the Soviet Union was going to do when and if their research developed such a weapon, or still if it does. But I do know what we're going to do, and I have stated it already. We would not deploy—it is not my purpose for deployment—until we sit down with the other nations of the world and those that have nuclear arsenals and see if we cannot come to an agreement on which there will be deployment only if there is elimination of the nuclear weapons.

Now, you might say if we're going to eliminate the nuclear weapons, then why do we need the defense? Well, I repeat what I said earlier. We all know how to make them, the weapons; so it is possible that some day a madman could arise in the world—we were both allies in a war that came about because of such a madman— and therefore, it would be like in Geneva after World War I when the nations all got together and said no more poison gas, but we all kept our gas masks. Well, this weapon, if such can be developed, would be today's gas mask. But we would want it for everyone, and the terms for getting it and the terms for our own deployment would be the elimination of the offensive weapons, a switch to maintain trust and peace between us of having defense systems that gave us security, not the threat of annihilation—that one or the other of us would annihilate the other with nuclear weapons.

So, we will not be violating this treaty at any time, because, as I say, it is not our purpose to go forward with deployment if and when such a weapon proved practical.

U.S.-Soviet Relations

Q. Mr. President, we've about run out of time unless you had something in conclusion you wanted to state.

The President. All right. We haven't covered—I guess I've filibustered on too many of these questions here with lengthy answers. I know you had more questions there. I'm sorry that we haven't time for them.

But I would just like to say that the Soviet Union and the United States—well, not the Soviet Union, let us say Russia and the United States have been allies in two wars—the Soviet Union and the United States, allies in one, the last and greatest war, World War II. Americans and Russians died side by side, fighting the same enemy. There are Americans buried on Soviet soil. And it just seems to me—and what I look forward to in this meeting with the General Secretary—is that people don't start wars, governments do. And I have a little thing here that I copied out of an article the other day, and the author of the article uttered a very great truth: "Nations do not distrust each other because they are armed. They arm themselves because they distrust each other." Well, I hope that in the summit maybe we can find ways that we can prove by deed—not just words, but by deeds—that there is no need for distrust between us. And then we can stop punishing our people by using our wherewithal to build these arsenals of weapons instead of doing more things for the comfort of the people.

Q. Thank you very much, Mr. President, and——

The President. Thank you.

Q. ——it's a pity, sir, too, that there can't be enough time to have your answers for all our questions.

The President. Well, all right. Okay.

Q. Thank you, Mr. President.

Q. Unfortunately, Mr. President, we cannot discuss with you the history of questions which we just asked already, because we have sometimes a very different attitude of that. But no time.

Q. As you know, the world is sort of different.

The President. I was waiting for a question that would allow me to point out that, under the détente that we had for a few years, during which we signed the SALT I and the SALT II treaties, the Soviet Union added over 7,000 warheads to its arsenal. And we have fewer than we had in 1969. And 3,800 of those were added to the arsenal after the signing of SALT II. So——

Q. But still you have more warheads——

The President. No, we don't.

Q. ——Mr. President.

The President. Oh, no, we don't.

Q. Yes, you have—well, to 12,000——

Q. You know, it's an interesting phenomenon, because in '79, after 7 years of very severe—I would say the researching in SALT II, President Carter and other specialists told that there was a parity in strategic and military. And then you came to the power, and you said it sounded that the Soviet Union is much ahead. Then, recently, in September, you said almost the same, though the Joint Chiefs of Staffs told this year that there is a parity. What is the contradiction?

The President. No, there really isn't. Somebody might say that with the sense of that we have sufficient for a deterrent, that, in other words, we would have enough to make it uncomfortable if someone attacked us. But, no, your arsenal does outcount ours by a great number.

Q. People say that—[*inaudible*]. [*Laughter*] The generals, your generals say that they wouldn't——

Q. Okay.

Q. ——switch, you know, with our generals, your arsenal.

Q. I would like to tell you also that those stories about dolls in Afghanistan. I was in Afghanistan there a little bit——

Principal Deputy Press Secretary Speakes. He's—maybe we'll have another opportunity——

Q. Yes, we hope so.

Mr. Speakes. And he's got to go down and tell the General Secretary, through our press, what he's going to do.

Q. Thank you very much, Mr. President, and we wish you certainly success and good achievements in your meeting with Mr. Gorbachev. We hope for this.

Q. Thank you very much, Mr. President.

The President. Thank you.

The President's Responses to Questions Submitted by Soviet News Organizations

U.S.-Soviet Relations

Q. The forthcoming meeting between General Secretary Gorbachev and you, Mr. President, is for obvious reasons looked upon as an event of special importance. Both sides have stated their intention to make an effort to improve relations between our two countries, to better the overall international situation. The Soviet Union has, over a period of time, put forward a whole set of concrete proposals and has unilaterally taken steps in various areas directly aimed at achieving this goal. What is the U.S., for its part, going to do?

The President. I fully agree that my meeting with General Secretary Gorbachev has special significance, and I am personally looking forward to it very much. I sincerely hope that we will be able to put relations between our two countries on a safer and more secure course. I, for my part, will certainly do all I can to make that possible.

We, of course, study every Soviet proposal carefully, and when we find them promising, we are happy to say so. If, on the other hand, we find them one-sided in their effect, we explain why we feel as we do. At the same time we, too, have made concrete proposals, dozens of them, which also cover every sphere of our relationship, from the elimination of chemical weapons and resolution of regional conflicts to the expansion of contacts and exchanges, and we hope these receive the same careful attention that we give to Soviet proposals. Let me give you a few examples.

One thing that has created enormous tension in U.S.-Soviet relations over the last few years has been attempts to settle problems around the world by using military force. The resort to arms, whether it be in

Afghanistan, Cambodia, or in Africa, has contributed nothing to the prospects for peace or the resolution of indigenous problems and has only brought additional suffering to the peoples of these regions. This is also dangerous, and we need to find a way to stop attempts to solve problems by force. So, I have proposed that both our countries encourage parties to these conflicts to lay down their arms and negotiate solutions, and if they are willing to do that, our countries should find a way to agree to support a peaceful solution and refrain from providing military support to the warring parties. And if peace can be achieved, the United States will contribute generously to an international effort to restore war-ravaged economies, just as we did after the Second World War, contributing to the recovery of friends and erstwhile foes alike, and as we have done on countless other occasions.

Both of our governments agree that our nuclear arsenals are much too large. We are both committed to radical arms reductions. So, the United States has made concrete proposals for such reductions: to bring ballistic missile warheads down to 5,000 on each side and to eliminate a whole category of intermediate-range missiles from our arsenals altogether. These have not been take-it-or-leave-it proposals. We are prepared to negotiate, since we know that negotiation is necessary if we are to reach a solution under which neither side feels threatened. We are willing to eliminate our advantages if you will agree to eliminate yours. The important thing is to begin reducing these terrible weapons in a way that both sides will feel secure and to continue that process until we have eliminated them altogether.

Events of the past 10 to 15 years have greatly increased mistrust between our countries. If we are to solve the key problems in our relationship, we have to do something to restore confidence in dealing with each other. This requires better communication, more contact, and close attention to make sure that both parties fulfill agreements reached. That is why we have made literally 40 to 50 proposals to improve our working relationship, expand communication, and build confidence. For example, we have proposed an agreement to cooperate on the peaceful use of space. The Apollo-Soyuz joint mission was a great success in 1975, and we should try to renew that sort of cooperation. We have also made several proposals for more direct contact by our military people. If they talked to each other more, they might find that at least some of their fears are unfounded. But most of all, ordinary people in both countries should have more contact, particularly our young people. The future, after all, belongs to them. I'd like to see us sending thousands of students to each other's country every year, to get to know each other, to learn from each other, and most of all to come to understand that, even with our different philosophies, we can and must live in peace.

Obviously, we are not going to solve all the differences between us at one meeting, but we would like to take some concrete steps forward. Above all, I hope that our meeting will give momentum to a genuine process of problemsolving and that we can agree on a course to take us toward a safer world for all and growing cooperation between our countries.

Q. The Soviet Union stands for peaceful coexistence with countries which have different social systems, including the U.S. In some of your statements, the point has been made that in spite of differences between our countries, it is necessary to avoid a military confrontation. In other words, we must learn how to live in peace. Thus, both sides recognize the fact that the issue of arms limitation and reduction is and will be determining in these relations. The special responsibility of the U.S. and U.S.S.R. for the fate of the world is an objective fact. What in your opinion can be achieved in the area of security in your meeting with Gorbachev?

The President. Well, first of all, I would say that we think *all* countries should live together in peace, whether they have the same or different social systems. Even if social systems are similar, this shouldn't give a country the right to use force against another.

But you are absolutely right when you say that we must learn to live in peace. As I have said many times, a nuclear war cannot be won and must never be fought. And this means that our countries must not fight any type of war. You are also right when you say that our countries bear a special responsibility before the world. This is the case not only because we possess enormous nuclear arsenals but because as great powers, whether we like it or not, our example and actions affect all those around us.

Our relations involve not only negotiating new agreements but abiding by past agreements as well. Often we are accused by your country of interfering in your internal affairs on such questions as human rights, but this is a case in point: Ten years ago we both became participants in the Helsinki accords and committed ourselves to certain standards of conduct. We are living up to those commitments and expect others to do so also. Soviet-American relations affect, as well regional conflicts, political relations among our friends and allies, and many other areas.

The fact that our countries have the largest and most destructive nuclear arsenals obliges us not only to make sure they are never used but to lead the world toward the elimination of these awesome weapons. I think that my meeting with General Secretary Gorbachev can start us on the road toward the goal our countries have set: the radical reduction of nuclear weapons and steps to achieve their complete elimination. We can do this by finding concrete ways to overcome roadblocks in the negotiating process and thus give a real impetus to our negotiators. Of course we will also have to deal with other problems, because it will be very hard to make great progress in arms control unless we can also act to lower tensions, reduce the use and threat of force, and build confidence in our ability to deal constructively with each other.

Nuclear and Space Arms Negotiations

Q. As is well known, the U.S. and the U.S.S.R. reached an understanding last January in Geneva that the top priority of the new negotiations must be the prevention of the arms race in space, but now the American delegation in Geneva is trying to limit the discussion to consideration of the question of nuclear arms and is refusing to talk about the prevention of the arms race in space. How should we interpret this American position?

The President. You have misstated the January agreement. Actually, our Foreign Ministers agreed to work out effective agreements aimed at preventing an arms race in space and terminating it on Earth, at limiting and reducing nuclear arms, and at strengthening strategic stability. Further, they agreed that the subject of negotiations will be a complex of questions concerning space and nuclear arms, both strategic and medium range, with all these questions considered and resolved in their interrelationship. Since your question reflects a misunderstanding of the United States position, let me review it for you:

First, we believe that the most threatening weapons facing mankind today are nuclear weapons of mass destruction. These are *offensive* weapons, and they exist today in numbers that are much too high. Our most urgent task therefore is to begin to reduce them radically and to create conditions so that they can eventually be eliminated. Since most of these weapons pass through space to reach their targets, reducing them is as important to prevent an arms race in space as it is to terminate an arms race on Earth. As I noted earlier, we have made concrete, specific proposals to achieve this. Recently your government finally made some counterproposals, and we will be responding in a genuine spirit of give-and-take in an effort to move toward practical solutions both countries can agree on.

Second, we believe that offensive and defensive systems are closely interrelated and that these issues should be treated, as our Foreign Ministers agreed, as interrelated. Our proposals are fully consistent with this understanding. We are seeking right now with Soviet negotiators in Geneva a thorough discussion of how a balance of offensive and defensive systems could be achieved and how, if scientists are able to develop effective defenses in the future, we might both use them to protect our countries and allies without threatening the other. And if we ever succeed in eliminating nuclear weapons, countries are going to require a defense against them, in case some madman gets his hands on some and

tries to blackmail other countries.

Specifically, we have proposed:

On strategic nuclear arms, a reduction of each side's nuclear forces down to 5,000 warheads on ballistic missiles—that would be a very dramatic lowering of force levels in a way that would greatly enhance strategic stability. We have also offered to negotiate strict limits on other kinds of weapons. Because our force structures are different and because the Soviet Union has complained about having to reconfigure its forces, we have offered to seek agreements which would balance these differing areas of American and Soviet strength.

On intermediate-range nuclear forces, we believe the best course is to eliminate that entire category of forces, which includes the 441 SS–20 missiles the Soviet Union has deployed and our Pershing II and ground-launched cruise missiles. If this is not immediately acceptable, we have also offered an interim agreement, which would establish an equal number of warheads on U.S. and Soviet missiles in this category at the lowest possible level.

In the area of space and defense, we are seeking to discuss with Soviet negotiators the possibility that new technology might allow both sides to carry out a transition to greater reliance on defensive weapons, rather than basing security on offensive nuclear forces. So that there would be no misunderstandings about our research program on new defensive systems, which is being carried out in full compliance with the ABM treaty, I sent the director of our strategic defense research program to Geneva to brief Soviet negotiators. Unfortunately, we have not had a comparable description of your research in this area, which we know is longstanding and quite extensive.

Frankly, I have difficulty understanding why some people have misunderstood and misinterpreted our position. The research we are conducting in the United States regarding strategic defense is in precisely the same areas as the research being conducted in the Soviet Union. There are only two differences: First, the Soviet Union has been conducting research in many of these areas longer than we have and is ahead in some; second, we are openly discussing our program, because our political system requires open debate before such decisions are made. But these differences in approaches to policy decisions should not lead to erroneous conclusions. Both sides are involved in similar research, and there is nothing wrong in that; however, this does make it rather hard for us to understand why we should be accused of all sorts of aggressive intentions when we are doing nothing more than you are. The important thing is for us to discuss these issues candidly.

In sum, what we are seeking is a balanced, fair, verifiable agreement—or series of agreements that will permit us to do what was agreed in Geneva in January: to terminate the arms race on Earth and prevent it in space. The United States has no tricks up its sleeve, and we have no desire to threaten the Soviet Union in any way. Frankly, if the Soviet Union would take a comparable attitude, we would be able to make very rapid progress toward an agreement.

U.S. Foreign Policy

Q. Mr. President, officials of your administration claim that the U.S., in its international relations, stands for the forces of democracy. How can one reconcile statements of this kind with the actual deeds of the U.S.? If you take any current example, it seems that when a particular country wants to exercise its right to independent development, whether it be in the Middle East, in southern Africa, in Central America, in Asia, it is the U.S., in particular, which supports those who stand against the majority of the people, against legitimate governments.

The President. Your assertion about U.S. actions is totally unfounded. From your question, one might think that the United States was engaged in a war in some other country and in so doing had set itself against the majority of the people who want self-determination. I can assure you that this is not the case. I am proud, as are all Americans, that not a single American soldier is in combat anywhere in the world. If every country could say the same, we would truly live in a world of less tension and danger.

Yes, we are very supportive of democracy. It is the basis of our political system and our whole philosophy. Our nation was not founded on the basis of one ethnic group or culture, as are many other countries, but on the basis of the democratic ideal. For example, we believe that governments are legitimate only if they are created by the people and that they are subordinate to the people, who select in free elections those who govern them. But democracy is more than elections in which all who wish can compete. In our view there are many things that even properly elected governments have no right to do. No American government can restrict freedom of speech or of religion, and no American government can tell its people where they must live or whether they can leave the country or not. These and the other individual freedoms enshrined in our Constitution are the most precious gift our forefathers bequeathed us, and we will defend them so long as we exist as a nation.

Now, this doesn't mean that we think we are perfect; of course we are not. We have spent over 200 years trying to live up to our ideals and correct faults in our society, and we're still at it. It also doesn't mean that we think we have a right to impose our system on others; we don't because we believe that every nation should have the right to determine its own way of life. But when we see other nations threatened from the outside by forces which would destroy their liberties and impose the rule of a minority by force of arms, we will help them resist that whenever we can. We would not be true to our democratic ideals if we did not.

We respond with force only as a last resort and only when we or our allies are the victims of aggression. For example, in World War II we took a full and vigorous part in the successful fight against Hitlerism, even though our country was not invaded by the Nazis. We still remember our wartime alliance and the heroism the peoples of the Soviet Union displayed in that struggle. And we also remember that we never used our position as one of the victors to add territory or to attempt to dominate others. Rather we helped rebuild the devastated countries, friends and erstwhile foes alike, and helped foster democracy where there was once totalitarianism. Have we not all benefited from the fact that Japan and the Federal Republic of Germany are today flourishing democracies and strong pillars of a stable and humane world order? Well, the German and Japanese people deserve the most credit for this, but we believe we helped along the way.

In the areas you mention, we are heartened by trends we see, although there are still many troubling areas. In the southern part of Africa, Angola is torn by civil war, yet we have determined not to supply arms to either side and to urge a peaceful settlement. In South Africa the system of apartheid is repugnant to all Americans, but here as well, we seek a peaceful solution, and for many years we have refused to supply arms or police equipment to the South African Government. In Latin America great progress in the transition from authoritarian to democratic societies has been made, and now on that continent there exist only four countries that do not have democratically elected governments. Since 1979 seven Latin American countries have made major strides from authoritarian to democratic systems. Over the years we have been a leading voice for decolonization and have used our influence with our closest friends and allies to hasten this process. We are gratified by the nearly completed process of decolonization and take pride in our role.

I should emphasize that our aim has been to encourage the process of democratization through peaceful means. And not just the American government but the American people as a whole have supported this process with actions and deeds.

American society has long been characterized by its spirit of voluntarism and by its compassion for the less fortunate. At home we are proud of our record of support for those who cannot manage for themselves. It is not simply that the government but the American people, through a host of voluntary organizations, who bring help to the needy—the victims of floods and fires, the old, the infirm, and the handicapped. Americans have been no less generous in giving to other peoples. I remember the efforts of Herbert Hoover in orga-

nizing the American relief effort to feed Soviet victims of famine in the 1920's. And these efforts continue to this day, whether it be food for the victims of famine in Ethiopia or of earthquakes in Mexico.

Nuclear Weapons

Q. The Soviet Union has unilaterally taken a series of major steps. It has pledged not to be the first to use nuclear weapons. It has undertaken a moratorium on any kind of nuclear tests. It has stopped deployment of intermediate-range missiles in the European part of its territory and has even reduced their number. Why hasn't the U.S. done anything comparable?

The President. Actually, we have frequently taken steps intended to lower tension and to show our good will, though these were rarely reciprocated. Immediately after World War II, when we were the only country with nuclear weapons, we proposed giving them up altogether to an international authority so that no country would have such destructive power at its disposal. What a pity that this idea was not accepted. Not only did we not use our nuclear monopoly against others, we signaled our peaceful intent by demobilizing our armed forces in an extraordinarily rapid way. At the end of the war in 1945, we had 12 million men under arms, but by the beginning of 1948 we had reduced our forces to one-tenth of that number—1.2 million. Since the 1960's we have unilaterally cut back on our own nuclear arsenal. We now have considerably fewer weapons than in 1969 and only one-third of the destructive power which we had at that time.

The United States and the NATO allies have repeatedly said that we will never use our arms, conventional or nuclear, unless we are attacked. Let me add something that might not be widely known in the Soviet Union. In agreement with the NATO countries, the United States since 1979 has removed from Europe well over 1,000 nuclear warheads. When all of our withdrawals have been completed, the total number of warheads withdrawn will be over 2,400. That's a withdrawal of about 5 nuclear weapons for every intermediate-range missile we plan to deploy. It will bring our nuclear forces in Europe to the lowest level in some 20 years. We have seen no comparable Soviet restraint.

If the Soviet Union is now reducing its intermediate-range missiles in Europe, that's a long overdue step. The Soviet Union has now deployed 441 SS–20 missiles, each with 3 warheads—that is 1,323 warheads. I don't have to remind you that this Soviet deployment began when NATO had no comparable systems in Europe. We first attempted to negotiate an end to these systems, but when we could not reach agreement NATO proceeded with a limited response which will take place gradually. Today the Soviet Union commands an advantage in warheads of 7 to 1 on missiles already deployed. Our position remains as it has always been: that it would be better to negotiate an end to all of these types of missiles. But even if our hopes for an agreement are disappointed and NATO has to go to full deployment, this will only be a maximum of 572 single-warhead missiles.

Moreover, President Carter canceled both the enhanced-radiation warhead and the B–1 bomber in 1978, and the Soviet Union made no corresponding move. In fact, when asked what the Soviet Union would reduce in response, one of your officials said, "We are not philanthropists." In 1977 and 1978 the United States also tried to negotiate a ban on developing antisatellite weapons; the Soviet Union refused a ban and proceeded to develop and test an antisatellite weapon. Having already established an operational antisatellite system, the Soviet Union now proposes a freeze before the U.S. can test its own system. Obviously that sort of freeze does not look very fair to us. If the shoe were on the other foot, it wouldn't look very fair to you either.

The issues between our two countries are of such importance that the positions of each government should be communicated accurately to the people of both countries. In this process the media of both countries have an important role to play. We should not attempt to score points against each other, and the media should not distort our positions. We are committed to examining every Soviet proposal with care, seeking to find areas of agreement. It is important that the Soviet Government do the same in regard to our proposals. The important thing is that we both deal seriously with each other's proposals and make a genuine effort to bridge our differences in a way which serves the interests of both countries and the world as a whole. It is in this spirit that I will be approaching my meeting with General Secretary Gorbachev.

Note: The interview began at 2:05 p.m. in the Oval Office at the White House. Participants included Genrikh Borovik of Novosti, Stanislav Kondrashov of Izvestia, Vsevolod Ovchinnikov of Pravda, and Gennadiy Shishkin of TASS. The questions were asked in Russian and translated by an interpreter. The interview was released by the Office of the Press Secretary on November 4.

Nomination of Sylvester Robert Foley, Jr., To Be an Assistant Secretary of Energy
November 4, 1985

The President today announced his intention to nominate Sylvester Robert Foley, Jr., to be an Assistant Secretary of Energy (Defense Programs). He would succeed William W. Hoover, who has resigned.

Admiral Foley most recently served as Commander in Chief of the U.S. Pacific Fleet, 1982–1985. During his 35 years with the U.S. Navy, Admiral Foley served as Deputy Chief of Naval Operations (Plans, Policy and Operations), 1980–1982; Commander, U.S. Seventh Fleet, 1978–1980; and Deputy Director, Strategic Plans and Policy Division of the Navy staff, 1975–1977.

Admiral Foley graduated from the United

States Naval Academy (B.S., 1950) and George Washington University (M.S., 1968). He is married, has four children, and resides in Chester, MD. Admiral Foley was born September 19, 1928, in Manchester, NH.

Nomination of J. Steven Griles To Be an Assistant Secretary of the Interior
November 4, 1985

The President today announced his intention to nominate J. Steven Griles to be an Assistant Secretary of the Interior (Land and Minerals Management). He would succeed Garrey Edward Carruthers, who has resigned.

Mr. Griles has been Acting Assistant Secretary for Land and Minerals Management and Deputy Assistant Secretary for Land and Water Resources since 1983; Deputy Director, Office of Surface Mining, 1981–1983, at the Department of the Interior. Previously, Mr. Griles served in the Virginia Department of Conservation and Economic Development as executive assistant, 1978–1981, and as programs administrator, 1977–1978.

Mr. Griles graduated from the University of Richmond (B.S., 1970). He is married, has three children, and resides in Reston, VA. Mr. Griles was born December 13, 1947, in Clover, VA.

Appointment of Bernard Eugene Smith, Jr., as a Member of the Advisory Board of the National Air and Space Museum
November 4, 1985

The President today announced his intention to appoint Bernard Eugene Smith, Jr., to be a member of the Advisory Board of the National Air and Space Museum, Smithsonian Institution. He would succeed Richard H. Jones.

Since 1978 Mr. Smith has been a partner with Lawrence, O'Donnell & Co., a stock brokerage firm in New York, NY. From 1967 to 1978, he was a partner with Lasker, Stone and Stern and from 1950 to 1967, a partner with LaMorte Maloney & Co., also stock brokerage firms. Mr. Smith served in the United States Navy, 1946–1949 and 1951–1952.

Mr. Smith graduated from the United States Naval Academy (B.S., 1946). He was born December 20, 1924, in New York, NY. He is married, the father of seven children, and resides in New York, NY.

Message to the Senate Transmitting Protocols to the Oil Pollution Damage Conventions
November 5, 1985

To the Senate of the United States:
I transmit herewith, for the advice and consent of the Senate to ratification, the Protocol of 1984 to Amend the International Convention on Civil Liability for Oil Pollution Damage, 1969 (Civil Liability Convention) and the Protocol of 1984 to Amend the International Convention on the Estab-

lishment of an International Fund for Compensation for Oil Pollution Damage, 1971 (Fund Convention). The Department of State has prepared a Technical Report on the Protocols, which is attached for the information of the Senate.

The 1984 Protocols to the Civil Liability and Fund Conventions are intended to revise and update the international system of liability and compensation for damage caused by vessel source oil pollution. In light of worldwide experience with costly oil spills since the conventions were first negotiated, they both required substantial amendment to raise their liability and compensation limits. The maximum liability and compensation limits contained in the new Protocols are approximately four times higher than in the original conventions and are now deemed sufficient to compensate all legitimate claimants with regard to any oil spill likely to occur in waters off the coasts of the United States. These new limits would provide substantially greater levels of compensation for United States citizens who sustain oil pollution damage than is currently available under existing domestic statutes or voluntary industry mechanisms.

A United States understanding of the term "pollution damage" and declarations by which the United States would exercise the option under the Protocols to delay the effective date of our instruments of ratification, are included in the Technical Report of the Department of State for consideration of the Senate. If approved, these declarations and understanding would be appended to the United States instruments of ratification.

Expeditious ratification of the 1984 Protocols would demonstrate not only our interest in assuring compensation for United States citizens who sustain oil pollution damage, but also our commitment to higher, uniform international standards for mitigating such damage which can be generally accepted worldwide.

I recommend that the Senate give early and favorable consideration to the 1984 Protocols to the Civil Liability and Fund Conventions and give its advice and consent to ratification.

RONALD REAGAN

The White House,
November 5, 1985.

Proclamation 5404—National Drug Abuse Education Week, 1985
November 5, 1985

By the President of the United States of America

A Proclamation

Only a decade ago, many people believed that drug abuse was an insurmountable problem. Throughout America, parents, educators, law enforcement officials, and other community leaders are proving that the fight against drugs can be won. Law enforcement and international cooperation are reducing the availability and supply of illegal drugs. Research and experience have given us new insight into the causes and treatment of drug and alcohol abuse. Most important, Americans have changed their attitudes toward both drugs and drug users. Negative attitudes have been replaced with understanding, and drug abuse is seen for what it really is: destructive of life's potential and a tragic waste of health and opportunity.

We have developed a sense of responsibility, collectively and individually. Today, we hold the key to creating a drug-free society: prevention of drug abuse through awareness and education.

Many people have contributed to this improved situation. During the past four years, all segments of American society have worked together to stop drug abuse among our young and have brought about new laws and public policies. Young people everywhere are moving away from drug-taking behavior and embracing positive goals such as excellence in education, physical fitness, and personal integrity.

Parents have banded together, and young people are receiving strong support for behavior that is anti-drug, pro-achievement, and that recognizes individual responsibility. These efforts are creating an environment that nurtures our Nation's greatest asset—our children.

But while much has been done, we cannot let up on our efforts against illicit drugs and those who would profit from the havoc they wreak.

We must continue to work together to address drug and alcohol problems in our homes and families. We must carry these concerns into our schools, churches, workplaces, and community life. By heightening awareness, we can gather the moral strength to do what is right and channel it into effective measures against this menace.

To encourage widespread participation in efforts directed at preventing drug abuse, the Congress, by House Joint Resolution 126, has designated the week of November 3 through November 9, 1985, as "National Drug Abuse Education Week" and authorized and requested the President to issue a proclamation in observance of this occasion.

Now, Therefore, I, Ronald Reagan, President of the United States of America, do hereby proclaim the week of November 3 through November 9, 1985, as National Drug Abuse Education Week. I call upon all Americans to join me in observing this week with personal dedication and a public commitment to protect the future of our Nation by eliminating drug abuse.

In Witness Whereof, I have hereunto set my hand this fifth day of November, in the year of our Lord nineteen hundred and eighty-five, and of the Independence of the United States of America the two hundred and tenth.

RONALD REAGAN

[*Filed with the Office of the Federal Register, 10:36 a.m., November 6, 1985*]

Note: The proclamation was released by the Office of the Press Secretary on November 6.

Remarks at a White House Meeting With 1984 Reagan-Bush Campaign Supporters
November 6, 1985

Good morning, and welcome. It's a pleasure to look out on this audience and see so many old and loyal friends. I seem to recall that we shared a great moment on this date 1 year ago. And I can't think of anyone I'd rather be celebrating this anniversary with than each one of you.

We worked hard during the campaign of 1984, you and I. There were funds to be raised, voters to be registered, rallies to be planned, and speeches to be given. By the way, I can't help but recalling that at about my 10th or 20th speech that I was reminded of something an old boss of mine once said, that was Harry Warner of Warner Brothers, when I was under contract there. And back during the twenties when sound pictures were just coming in, when the "talkies" were coming in, Harry Warner demanded to know who the heck wants to hear actors talk? [*Laughter*]

While I was taking our message around the country, you were taking it to the most important level of all—the grassroots. And that message, that historic message, went like this: Four years before, when our party had first won the White House and the Senate, we'd inherited the disastrous results of two vast and prolonged experiments.

The first experiment, a domestic endeavor, had begun during the thirties and had been renewed on a massive scale during the sixties. And based upon the premise that the answer to virtually every problem was government intervention, this experiment involved an ever-growing tax burden, an endless proliferation of government regulations, and a Federal budget that took in more and more of our gross national product. By the late seventies, the results of this domestic experiment had become clear. Inflation was spiraling up at double-digit numbers, interest rates were sky-high, and the basis for sustained growth in our economy and standard of living had been undermined.

The second experiment had involved foreign affairs. We'd allowed our military capabilities to erode. Indeed, with regard to the Navy alone, by 1980 our fleet had fallen from nearly a thousand battle-ready ships to fewer than 500. And then we had waited for the Soviets to demonstrate their good faith by doing the same. We're trusting souls. [*Laughter*] The Soviets, however, had embarked upon the biggest arms buildup in the history of the world. And while American liberals had treated the realm of foreign affairs like a dream world, the grim realities had been felt in places like Afghanistan and Poland.

But our administration, we told the people, had brought those experiments to an end. In foreign affairs, we'd begun the rebuilding of our military. We had boldly restated the fundamental, moral difference between democracy and communism. And in 1983 we had begun the Strategic Defense Initiative, an initiative aimed at knocking down weapons, not people. Here at home, we'd weeded out needless regulations, supported a sound monetary policy, and enacted an across-the-board cut in personal income tax rates of 25 percent. By mid-1984 our economy had been expanding for 19 months, our gross national product was soaring, productivity was up, interest rates were down, and inflation was headed toward the lowest level in over a decade.

We took this message to the people, and we asked them to make a fundamental decision: Forward or back? Our opponent, you may remember—I said may remember—[*laughter*]—actually promised the American people that he would raise their taxes. He told the people that we wanted to reform the system to make tax rates even lower—we told you that, not he. Well, spreading that message was exciting, but exhausting. And on this date 1 year ago, we'd given it everything we had, all of us in this room. There was nothing to do but wait. And by

the wee hours of the next morning, we'd heard the final news. My friends, I'm sure you'll agree, 49 out of 50 ain't bad. The American people had answered loud and clear: Forward, full throttle, to more limited government, stronger defenses, and still greater economic growth.

With your help, we've worked hard to put that mandate into effect in this second term. In foreign affairs, we're determined and strong. Indeed it's precisely because of our continued strength that the Soviets may well prove ready to engage in a genuine give-and-take at the upcoming meeting in Geneva. And permit me to add that—as we made clear just last month—the United States of America isn't about to be pushed around by the nickel-and-dime cowards who commit acts of terror.

In domestic policy, we continue to face two great challenges, two challenges on which our administration will continue to need your help. The first is deficit spending. This autumn the Congress has faced the unhappy task of raising the debt ceiling to over $2 trillion. With only a few days left before that deadline, Congress must realize that by failing to act they're entering very dangerous territory. Already they have forced us to redeem prematurely the Social Security and other trust funds in order to make payments to recipients. Never before in our history has the Federal Government failed to honor its financial obligations. To fail to do so now would be an outrage, and the Congress must understand this and bear full responsibility. And the final date is the 15th of this month.

But there's hope. By an overwhelming vote the Senate has initiated the Gramm-Rudman-Hollings amendment, a bipartisan measure that would lock the Federal Government onto a path to eliminate the budget deficit in 1990. And to protect that achievement, I will ask the Congress to enact a balanced budget amendment to the Constitution to take effect in that break-even year. The reason that I so strongly support the Gramm-Rudman-Hollings proposal is that it attacks budget deficits the right way—not by raising taxes, but by restraining spending. It will enable us to enforce spending restraint while at the same time we honor our commitments on Social Security and defense.

Just last week the House produced a version which, unfortunately, missed the opportunity. But I believe it's essential that the House and Senate agree on a version of Gramm-Rudman-Hollings that provides for an assured path to a balanced budget without tax increases and without attacking our defenses. We agreed with the Congress in the budget resolution to the 0–3–3 arrangement on defense spending, and we expect them to live up to it; 0–3–3 means that in 1986 defense spending will be zero as to real increase over 1985. It will, however, be allowed the difference in inflation. And 3–3, those 2 years, there will be allowed a real increase in defense spending of 3 percent each year.

Now, this brings me to the other great challenge—tax reform. Yes, tax reform has its ups and downs—so do all proposals of consequence. But to paraphrase Mark Twain, reports of its death are greatly exaggerated. You see, the American people, I believe, want tax reform; many Members of the Congress want tax reform; and it so happens that this administration, overwhelmingly sent back to office 1 year ago today, wants tax reform, too. Tax reform is very much alive on the Hill, and I'm convinced we can get it and get it this year. But once again, we'll need to turn up the heat. Can I count on your help to do that? [*Applause*] All right. We need the kind of tax reform that we originally proposed and not with some of the waterings down that are taking place as they discuss it up there.

My friends, these are historic times for the Republican Party and the ideals that unite us. On every front, from foreign policy to education to economic growth, it is the Republican Party that is moving forward with intelligence and vigor. Our numbers are growing; indeed, for the first time in 27 years, back in my home State, as many Californians consider themselves now Republicans as consider themselves Democrats. I remember 8 years when I wished that had happened then. [*Laughter*] And in the country at large, the polls show that we hold a commanding lead among Americans between the ages of 18 and 24. We hold a lead, in other words, on the years ahead.

Not too long ago, sitting where you're sitting were 150 officeholders, elected officials from all over the country, who had all, since their election, switched from being Democrats to being Republicans. It was quite an inspiring gathering. So it is that we stand poised to become the party of the future and party of ideas, the party of a new and durable governing coalition. All this—all that we've accomplished, all of our noble hopes for the future—has been built by your intelligence, dedication, and willingness to give and to work. Each of you is a participant in history, and from my heart, I thank you. I know George [Bush] has already told you how much he appreciates it. God bless you all, and now some of us are going to go back to work.

Thank you.

Note: The President spoke at 10:46 a.m. in the East Room at the White House.

Appointment of Barber B. Conable, Jr., as a Member of the President's Blue Ribbon Commission on Defense Management
November 6, 1985

The President today announced his intention to appoint Barber B. Conable, Jr., to be a member of the President's Blue Ribbon Commission on Defense Management. This is a new position.

Mr. Conable was a U.S. Congressman from the 30th District of New York from 1965 to 1984. At the time of his retirement he was ranking Republican on the House Ways and Means Committee. He is now a professor at the University of Rochester in New York.

Mr. Conable graduated from Cornell University (A.B., 1942; LL.B., 1948). He is married, has four children, and resides in Alexander, NY. He was born November 2, 1922, in Warsaw, NY.

Appointment of Five Members of the National Advisory Committee on Oceans and Atmosphere
November 6, 1985

The President today announced his intention to appoint the following individuals to be members of the National Advisory Committee on Oceans and Atmosphere for terms expiring July 1, 1988.

Gordon Snow, of California, is a reappointment. He is assistant secretary for resources, California Resources Agency, in Sacramento. He graduated from Chico State College (A.B., 1951; M.A., 1952) and Oregon State College (Ph.D., 1956). He is married, has one child, and resides in El Macero, CA. He was born February 11, 1925, in Rush Springs, OK.

Richard T. Leier, of Minnesota, is a reappointment. He is a mineral processing engineer at the Reserve Mining Co. in Silver Bay, MN. He graduated from the University of Minnesota (B.S., 1974). He is married, has two children, and resides in Silver Bay, MN. He was born July 1, 1951, in St. Paul, MN.

Stanley W. Legro, of California, will succeed John N. Moore. He is the principal officer in the firm of Potomac Capitol in Washington, DC. He graduated from the United States Naval Academy (B.S., 1959) and Harvard University (J.D., 1966). He is married, has two children, and resides in Washington, DC. He was born July 3, 1936, in Muskogee, OK.

John J. Real, of California, will succeed Donald Walsh. He is a former president and chief executive officer of Star Kist Foods, Inc. He graduated from Loyola University (A.B., 1939; J.D., 1943). He is married, has three children, and resides in San Pedro, CA. He was born July 4, 1917, in Wilmington, CA.

Alan D. Hutchison, of Nevada, will succeed William Brewster. He is president of Marlborough Investments, Ltd., in Reno, NV. He graduated from Ohio State University (B.S., 1956) and George Washington University (J.D., 1960). He is married, has three children, and resides in Reno, NV. He was born January 23, 1931, in New York City.

Statement on the Death of Spencer W. Kimball
November 6, 1985

Spencer W. Kimball spent a long and full life devoted to his church and the service of his fellow man. As a young man, he combined dedication to work with an active role in charitable and community work, exemplifying the Mormon ethic of rugged free enterprise and mutual aid. Following in the footsteps of his grandfather, a contemporary of Joseph Smith, Spencer Kimball went on to 30 years of service in his church's governing Council of Twelve Apostles, before becoming president in 1973.

Nancy and I note with sorrow the passing of one of the important figures of our generation. Our deepest sympathy goes out to his wife and family.

Interview With Representatives of the Wire Services
November 6, 1985

U.S.-Soviet Summit Meeting

Q. Secretary [of State] Shultz did give rather a bleak news conference in Moscow and seemed to have struck out, coming back empty-handed. That may or may not be true; maybe you're getting private information otherwise. But is it so, and do you think that the Soviets are being very hard-line? And what are your maximum and minimum goals for this summit? What do you really think you can get out of it?

The President. Oh, Helen [Helen Thomas, United Press International], I haven't tried to pin it down to success or failure or terms of that kind. We're going there to try and basically eliminate if we can or certainly reduce the distrust between our two countries. We have to live in the world together. And it is that distrust that causes the problems and causes the situation with regard to arms negotiations. As I cited to our Russian friends when they were in here the other day that statement—it isn't mine, I wish it were—but a statement that I read in the press the other day that summed it up so succinctly; and that is that nations do not distrust each other because they're armed, they are armed because they distrust each other.

Q. Well, do you think you can get anywhere near a semblance of an arms agreement? Will you negotiate Star Wars at all? Any aspects?

The President. Well, I will be presenting the same thing that I told those others. My concept of the strategic defense system has been one that, if and when we finally achieve what our goal is, that is a weapon that is effective against incoming missiles— not a weapon, a system that's effective against incoming weapons—missiles—then rather than add to the distrust in the world and appear to be seeking the potential for a first strike by rushing to implement, my concept has always been that we sit down with the other nuclear powers, with our allies and our adversaries and see if we cannot use that defensive system for the elimination of nuclear weapons.

And that, certainly, I will discuss there and try to impress upon them how firmly we believe in this. I don't think the negotiation of facts and figures about which weapon and how many and numbers and so forth in weaponry should take place at the summit. I think that belongs where we have already put it and that is with the arms control negotiators that are already in Geneva. That's their kind of figuring that should go on. We shouldn't be doing that with all of the things we have to discuss at the summit meeting. At that meeting there are a number of things—some of them I hinted at in the speech in the U.N.—regional situation. In other words, try to, as I say, eliminate the distrust that exists between us.

Q. Well, that's the maximum goal, then?

The President. Yes, because the other things would automatically follow.

Strategic Defense Initiative

Q. Mr. President, if I could pursue the SDI a little bit more. Considering what you told the Soviet journalists when they were here last week, there seems to be some discrepancy between your comments to them and your comments today about what the conditions for deployment would be. Could you explain it to us now?

The President. Yes, because I have already explained that to our allies at the United Nations, and this was the first misunderstanding that I have seen about it. I went through the transcript of that interview, and I mentioned it three or four times through there, in the transcript. And I think it was someone just jumped to a false conclusion when they suggested that I was giving a veto to the Soviets over this; that, in other words, if that thing that I've just described to you, that meeting, took place and we couldn't get satisfaction, that I would say, "Well, then, we can't deploy this defensive system." I couldn't find any place where that was anything but an erroneous interpretation of what I'd been saying.

Obviously, if this took place, we had the

weapon—I keep using that term; it's a defensive system—we had a defensive system and we could not get agreement on their part to eliminate the nuclear weapons, we would have done our best and, no, we would go ahead with deployment. But even though, as I say, that would then open us up to the charge of achieving the capacity for a first strike. We don't want that. We want to eliminate things of that kind. And that's why, frankly, I think that any nation offered this under those circumstances that I've described would see the value of going forward. Remember that the Soviet Union has already stated its wish that nuclear weapons could be done away with.

Q. You say today that you would go ahead with deployment if you had the system and there weren't international agreement on mutual deployment. The other day you said that that deployment would be only on condition of what you call disarmament. This misunderstanding, it seems to me, on whoever's part has caused a lot of confusion. Does that disrupt your negotiations with Gorbachev, and what can he expect when you have said this to his journalists and now you are telling us something different?

The President. No, I'm not telling something different. I'm saying that reading that transcript of what I told to the journalists— someone has jumped to an erroneous conclusion. I don't find anything in there— maybe it's because I've talked about this with so many individuals, as I've said, at the U.N. and all—that maybe having more of an understanding of it, I see it more clearly than some others might. But I have not— and I have had others now that look at this transcript and they don't get that interpretation, that I'm giving anyone a veto over this defensive system.

Q. May I ask you, Mr. President, it seems that in the recent weeks you have been more flexible in the way you have talked about the SDI. You have not said that it could not be a bargaining chip, as you used to say it very often before. Are you more flexible? Do you want your message to be seen as more flexible? Is there room for compromise?

The President. Well, this is the point where flexibility, I think, is not involved.

The demands that have been made on us already with regard to arms control are that we stop the research and any effort to create such a defensive system. And I have said that there's no way that we will give that up, that this means too much to the world and to the cause of peace if it should be possible to have an effective defensive system. In discussions here in the office, I've likened it many times to the gas mask—1925, when all the nations of the world after World War I and the horror of poison gas in that war. When it was over, all the nations got together in Geneva and ruled out the use of poison gas, but we all had gas masks, and no one did away with their gas masks. Well, this, in a sense, is how I see what this could be. The defense that would—it would be so practical and sensible for any country, including the Soviet Union, to say, why go on building and maintaining and modernizing these horrible weapons of destruction if there is something that can be implemented that makes them useless?

U.S.-Soviet Relations

Q. Mr. President, Secretary [of State] Shultz held a press conference in Iceland today on his way back to report to you and with him was a senior official—not identified, but we can guess who it is—who held a background briefing for reporters. And he said that the impression that the American delegation got during this weekend's talks in Moscow was that Mr. Gorbachev was concerned that U.S. policy was influenced by a small circle of anti-Soviet extremists. Now, if Mr. Gorbachev said that to you personally, how would you respond, Mr. President?

The President. I would respond with the truth as clearly as I could enunciate it. This is one of the things that I feel with regard to the distrust, that the Soviet Union tends to be distrustful and suspicious that things that are presented to them are perhaps concealing some ulterior motive. And I want to discuss with him the record—our own record, that if this were true, that if the United States was guided by some desire to one day assault the Soviet Union, why didn't we do it when we were the most powerful military nation on Earth right after World War II. Our military was at its height. We had not had the great losses in the millions that the other nations had had that had been there longer. Our industry was intact. We hadn't been bombed to rubble as all the rest had, and we were the only ones with the ultimate weapon, the nuclear weapon. We could have dictated to the whole world, and we didn't. We set out to help the whole world.

And the proof of it is, today, that our erstwhile enemies—and there could never have been more hatred in the world than there was between the enemies of World War II and ourselves—they are today our staunchest allies. And yet here is a former ally—there are Americans buried in the soil of the Soviet Union that fought side by side against the same enemies. And so, I think we can prove by the record that any fair-minded person would have to see that we did not have expansionism in mind. We never took an inch of territory as a result of the victory of World War II or of World War I, for that matter. And on the other hand, to point out to him why we are concerned about them—that their expansionist policy is very evident. The gunfire hasn't stopped for a moment in Afghanistan. We could name all the other spots where they or their surrogate troops are in there. So, this is my hope, that I can convince him, if he's a reasonable man—and there's every indication that he is—would see that if we both want peace, there'll be peace.

Soviet General Secretary Gorbachev

Q. Mr. President, your remark that you think Mr. Gorbachev is a reasonable man brings me to another question. I assume that you have been doing a lot of reading about Mr. Gorbachev, the man, and Gorbachev, the leader of the Soviet Union, and that perhaps you've even seen some videotapes of him in action. What sort of an opponent do you expect to face across the table at Geneva?

The President. Ralph [Ralph Harris, Reuters], I would think that any Soviet leader who reaches the office that he holds would be a formidable opponent. If he does not subscribe to the party philosophy, he wouldn't be in that position.

Soviet Defectors

Q. Mr. President, this [Vitaly] Yurchenko case is very puzzling, baffling to everyone.
The President. Yes.
Q. Is it baffling to you?
The President. Yes.
Q. And also—yes? Have you ordered an investigation of the CIA handling? And have you gone even further to order an investigation of handling by any agency of defectors per se?
The President. Well, right now the Justice Department is investigating the INF and their——
Q. Right.
The President. ——or INS, I mean, and their handling of the [Miroslav] Medvid incident down in New Orleans to see just what led to all of that. I have to say that—coming as they do together—these three particular incidents, you can't rule out the possibility that this might have been a deliberate ploy or maneuver. Here you have three separate individuals in three different parts of the world who defected and then recanted and, of their own free will, said they wanted to return to the Soviet Union. And in every one of the three incidents, we insisted on and did secure the last word, the final meeting with each one of them, to make sure that they understood completely that they were welcome here, that we would provide safety and sanctuary for them here in the United States. And in every incident that was repudiated, and we had to say that, of their own free will, as far as we could see——
Q. So——
The President. ——and for whatever reason, they wanted to go back.
Q. So, were we had by Yurchenko? Was he not a true defector? And is this a sort of a disinformation plan to disrupt——
The President. Well, Helen, as I say, there's no way that you can prove that that isn't so. On the other hand, there's no way you can prove that it is. So, you just have to accept that we did our best in view of their expressed desires, and then they did what other defectors before them have not done, and they—oh, I think here and there, there's been one or two that went back. So, you can't rule out personal desire, home-

sickness, whatever it might be. I'm sure that, as has been suggested by someone discussing this, that people who go through that must be under quite some strain, and it must be a traumatic experience to step forth from the land of your birth and denounce it and say you want to live someplace else, in another country. But there's no way to establish this. Either they honestly did feel they wanted to defect and then changed their minds, or the possibility is there that this could have been a deliberate ploy.

Q. It sounds like you're leaning toward the latter, that there has been something very systematic——

The President. No, maybe I spent more time explaining why I didn't think you could rule that out but——

Q. But you said at the outset that there seemed to be a deliberate——

The President. No, no. I said there is this suspicion that has been voiced by more people than me——

Q. But you don't agree with the——

The President. ——and all I have to say is we just have to live with it because there's no way we can prove or disprove it.

Q. Do you think that that makes the information that he did give the CIA worthless or perhaps even, you know, that it was misinformation?

The President. Well, actually, the information that he provided was not anything new or sensational. It was pretty much information already known to the CIA.

Q. Oh, really? So, that would tend to support your thought that perhaps this whole thing was cooked.

The President. [*Laughing*] If you want to take it that way. I'm not going to comment on that one way or the other.

Q. Would you say you're perplexed by it?

The President. Yes. I think anyone is perplexed by this. I think it's awfully easy for any American to be perplexed by anyone that could live in the United States and would prefer to live in Russia.

Q. Mr. President, if I may——

Principal Deputy Press Secretary Speakes. You'd better tell them one more time that there's no way to tell either way. You said it about four times, but the questions keep coming back.

The President. [*Laughing*] Yes.

Q. We got it. [*Laughter*]

U.S.-Soviet Summit Meeting

Q. If I may come back to the——

Mr. Speakes. I want to read the lead before you go——

Q. ——to the summit preparation. What do you expect from the summit on the human rights issue? You have been very cautious on the human rights issue in the Soviet Union. Is it because you sense that there might be something positive coming out and you don't want to——

The President. I have always felt that there are some subjects that should remain in confidence between the leaders discussing them. In this world of public life and politics, if you try to negotiate on the front page—some items—you have almost put the other fellow in a corner where he can't give in because he would appear in the eyes of his own people as if he's taking orders from an outside government. And the greatest success that, I think, has been had in this particular area has been with predecessors of mine who have discussed these subjects privately and quietly with——

Human Rights

Q. Are you encouraged by Yelena Bonner being allowed to have medical treatment in the West, or do you think it's just something to defuse the issue before the summit?

The President. I don't know, but I welcome it. It's long overdue, and we're pleased to see it happen. But let me point out also this does not mean that human rights will not be a subject for discussion. They will be very much so. They're very important to the people of our country and, in their view, of a relationship with the Soviet Union. But I don't think that it is profitable to put things of this kind out in public where any change in policy would be viewed as a succumbing to another power.

Espionage

Q. Mr. President, talking of spies, some months ago—I forget the date—in one of your Saturday radio speeches, you said there were too many Soviet and East European diplomats in this country and too many spies among them.

The President. Yes.

Q. And you said, in effect or perhaps precisely, that you were going to cut these numbers down. Could you brief us on what has happened since then, sir?

The President. Well, we're having discussions about that and reducing numbers. We recognize that when we do anything of this kind there's going to be retaliation, but what we're trying to do is to simply arrive at agreements that will be mutual and with regard to reductions of staff and numbers in each other's countries.

Q. So, when you say you're having discussions, you mean with the Soviet Union and East European countries——

The President. Yes, this has——

Q. ——or within this administration?

The President. ——this has been done at a ministerial level.

Q. Oh, I see.

Mr. Speakes. If you could go quickly, we can get one more round, but you've got to do it quickly.

The President. All right.

Secretary of Defense Weinberger / Libyan Chief of State Qadhafi

Q. Is Weinberger trying to sabotage the summit? And are you trying to overthrow Qadhafi? [*Laughter*]

The President. [*Laughing*] Oh, let me——

Q. One at a time. [*Laughter*]

The President. Let me simply say no. Secretary Weinberger isn't trying to sabotage anything of the kind. He's been most helpful in all of the meetings that we have had on this. And all of the talk that we unhappily read about feuds and so forth; again, this is a distortion or misinterpretation of my desire for what I've always called Cabinet-type government, where I want all views to be frankly expressed, because I can then make the decision better if I have all those viewpoints. And the fact that we have debate and discussion in that regard, in that way, should not be construed as feuds and battles and so forth. I want all sides.

Q. You want it—it's okay in the public? It's okay in public and on the front page?

The President. Well, not the way it's been portrayed on the front page. It's been por-

trayed——

Q. You've been quoted.

The President. Well, but it'd been portrayed not in the spirit in which I just spoke of it. It's been portrayed as animus and anger and so forth, and it isn't that kind. It's the devil-advocate type of thing where I hear all sides.

Now, with regard to Qadhafi, let's just say we don't have a very personal relationship.

Q. What? Were you going to try to overthrow him indirectly?

The President. No, no comment on——

Q. No comment on are you trying to overthrow him?

The President. No. I never like to talk about anything that might be being done in the name of intelligence.

The President's Health

Q. Mr. President, your health is vital to the long-range success of any progress that you make at the summit. Why won't you permit the release of the test results from your periodic examinations to reassure the public that there is no recurrence of the cancer?

The President. Well, for heaven's sakes. First of all, that term "the recurrence of cancer"—you've given me an opportunity to give an answer I've wanted to give for some time. I'm deeply appreciative of the concern of people and all the letters of condolence and good wishes and so forth that I've received. But I feel the people have been doing this under a little misapprehension. The whole thing has been portrayed as that I was a sufferer of cancer, I had cancer. And then an operation took place, and now I have had a good recovery. No, the truth of the matter was, I had a polyp. There are two kinds of polyps in the intestines, and one kind, if allowed to go on, eventually becomes cancerous and then would spread. I had a polyp removed. It is true that it, within itself, had begun to develop a few cancer cells, but it was still a self-contained polyp. The only way that type of polyp can be removed is by major surgery. So, in reality, the only real illness that I suffered in any way and at any time was the incision. And my healing was not a healing of cancer; mine was a healing of a 10- or 12-

inch incision. So, I'm delighted to get this out and on the table before you.

Yes, they gave me a complete schedule, and they said we will want to do this down the line periodically, and then, it gets farther and farther apart as time goes on. It would mainly be an examination, periodically, to see if any further polyps of that kind—if one could start, then, I suppose another could start. And then, if so, you'd want to get rid of them. The examinations that I have had are also spaced out, like this last time, are part of the kind of annual physical that I've had for many years and long before I came here. Where, once I used to go into the hospital for a few days and have all the whole physical done, well, now we do it in bits and parts. So, this last one, mainly I went in and they simply examined the incision—wanted to see how the healing was coming—and then I had some x-rays of the lungs, which had nothing to do with the operation, but that are a normal part of the general physical that I have. Now, there will be another trip there coming up in the near future and that will be the first trip for a look at the intestines for the possibility of polyps.

And so, when the doctors come out and when the doctors—they say the same thing to me that has been said to you—maybe I'll have them say it to you instead of me repeating it—when they stand there in front of me and say, "You've had 100-percent recovery. Everything is just fine. You're as healthy as you could possibly be." I go out and tell you that and you think I'm covering something up.

Q. I just would suggest that, while I'm not suggesting we don't believe you, it would be reassuring to a lot of people to see the test results and know what's being done and how it's being done and——

The President. Well, the test result, in the cases of this kind, is simply to tell you what happened. For example, if they do the examination to see—to check if there's another polyp—well, the only test is they say to you—[*laughter*]—there wasn't one or there is one; whichever way it comes out. So, it's a case of verbalizing. There isn't any report to be given you that—oh, incidentally, I also had the blood check taken this time also with the x-rays. But that was done

here a few days before, not at Bethesda. They take a little blood, see what it is. And that would be done, this would have been done, now, even without any physical examination. They always do this prior to a trip abroad, make sure that they know what's there, and in the event of an accident or anything, they know what could be needed.

Angola

Q. Mr. President, we were talking about Qadhafi, but do you think the U.S. should give some aid to the rebels in Angola, as it is doing in Nicaragua or in Afghanistan?

The President. We were embarked on a plan of trying to negotiate the Cubans out of Angola and the independence of Namibia, and this also involved that in that there would be a reconciliation between UNITA, the Savimbi forces and the present government, which, more or less, was installed by the presence of the Cuban troops. Now, with the elimination of the Clark amendment, we are still most supportive of that, that we believe a settlement in Angola should involve UNITA, and the people of that country have a choice in making a decision as to the government they wanted to have. And so, all of this is going forward.

Q. So, you don't envision your covert aid to rebels in Angola because of the Clark amendment, as you mentioned, having been——

The President. No, I think there are some areas where we could be of help to them.

Q. I have no further questions, Mr. President.

The President. All right.

Administration Goals

Q. Well, how do you feel on the anniversary of your reelection?

The President. Well, I feel just fine. I wish the Congress would have a sharp memory of it as they're discussing tax reform and some other things.

Q. Do you have any particular goals for the next 3 years?

The President. Oh, yes, and you know most of them: tax reform, a program that will set us, even longer than 3 years, on a course for the elimination of the deficit;

then, the achievement of a balanced budget amendment, so that once and for all we'll be free of this. And I've had one tucked away in the back of my mind for a long time, that once we can do that, then, I would like to see us start on the reduction of the national debt.

Q. Well, then, would you veto the House version of the Gramm-Rudman as it stands now?

The President. Now, you know, Helen, I never comment on whether I will or will not veto until it——

Q. Except for tax increases.

The President. Well, that's a general thing; this is talking about a particular piece of legislation. I'm going to wait and see what it is.

Q. Thank you.

Note: The interview began at 11:35 a.m. in the Oval Office at the White House. Also participating in the interview were Mike Putzel of the Associated Press and Pierre Rousselin of Agence France Presse. The transcript of the interview was released by the Office of the Press Secretary on November 7.

Remarks at the Presentation Ceremony for the Presidential Medal of Freedom
November 7, 1985

The President. Welcome. The Medal of Freedom is our nation's highest honor for those outside the Armed Forces who've rendered outstanding service to their country. It acknowledges discipline, courage, high standards, and moral character. The three Americans we honor today have contributed among them more than a century of public service. They have been personally involved in answering the great questions of their day, questions of war or peace in a nuclear age. And today we underscore their impressive contributions with a token of appreciation from their fellow countrymen.

Paul Nitze brought unmatched experience and expertise to his current responsibilities. He has served so long and so faithfully in the highest councils of state that his presence has been almost taken for granted. Today we acknowledge for all the world that Paul is indeed an exceptional individual, a great man and a great public servant. And Paul Nitze played a key role in the design and implementation of the Marshall plan. He was a principal architect of our security strategy after World War II, helping us understand what it would take in resources and commitment to meet the new challenges emerging in the postwar world. Paul, we may need to call on you to give our current foreign assistance program

the same boost that you gave to Harry Truman's.

Paul Nitze has held numerous positions of high responsibility—Secretary of the Navy, Assistant Secretary of Defense, and Deputy Secretary of Defense. For the past 15 years he's played a special role in the Nation's search for ground arms policy. He worked in government to ensure our approach was right. When he saw things headed in the wrong direction, he worked outside the Government to alert his fellow citizens. Paul is now playing an indispensable role in our efforts to forge a bold and creative arms control policy. Peace and equilibrium are terms we associate with international affairs, and yet they also describe Paul Nitze, the man who seeks them. He is consistently shrewd, but never cynical; impressively erudite, yet never pedantic; immensely dignified, yet never stuffy; always hopeful, and yet ever realistic. We're happy, then, to honor him for what he has done and, even more, for what he is.

Now, we also honor Roberta and Albert Wohlstetter, two of the finest strategic analysts and security specialists our country has known. In saying this, however, we only begin to describe their work in helping citizens and statesmen to understand fundamental relationships in this nuclear age be-

1355

tween technology, politics, history, and psychology. It's been the good fortune of our country to have these two brilliant people help us make sense of the unprecedented security problems we've faced in our modern age.

Roberta Wohlstetter, a generation ahead of her time, asserted her influence in areas dominated by and, in some cases, reserved for men. She rose above all obstacles and has had a profound influence. Her inquiries went to the heart of the system of our society, focusing on essential questions. Her analysis of the problems of terrorism, intelligence, and warning and, with Albert, the problem of nuclear deterrence broke new ground and opened new alternatives for policymakers. I daresay that she has blankly enjoyed posing the same penetrating questions to her husband that she has to the intellectual and political leaders of the country. And that is certainly one explanation for the clarity and persuasiveness of his own voluminous words on strategy, politics, and world affairs.

Albert Wohlstetter is a brilliant man with enormous strength of character. His intellectual integrity is renowned, and his analytical standards have been increasingly and unceasingly rigorous. He's been a steady hand in an uncertain time. His understanding on many levels has been indispensable to the well-being of the free world. In these last 30 years, Albert has been influential in helping to design and deploy our strategic forces—an awesome task. He's sought ways to make our forces safer from attack, less destructive, and thereby less dangerous to us all. Many of the basic concepts and requirements for deterrence in the nuclear age—analysis on which we've operated—can be traced to this outstanding individual. And his work on the problem of nuclear proliferation gave us the insight we needed to better curb the irresponsible flow of sensitive material and technology.

Albert has always argued that in the nuclear age technological advances can, if properly understood and applied, make things better; but his point, and Roberta's, has been a deeper one than that. He has shown us that we have to create choices and, then, exercise them. The Wohlstetters have created choices for our society where others saw none. They've taught us that there is an escape from fatalism.

Those we honor today continue to make contributions. Their genius has made it possible for us to start on a new path which can free mankind of the fear of nuclear holocaust. These three people began their work in far different times, four decades ago when our national success was far from certain. Who would have foreseen the extraordinary achievements of the past generation, not the least of these a general peace, which has remained intact for 40 years. We praise these three extraordinary individuals who played a significant role in the most successful of all peace movements. They gave us strength through clarity; security through preparedness; and progress through intellect. They were the engineers and architects of a system that works and has served mankind well. They are the innovators who are leading mankind to the next step forward: Peace, based on protection, rather than retaliation.

Jonathan Swift, author of "Gulliver's Travels," once wrote, "Who'er excels in what we prize, appears a hero in our eyes." Well, these individuals are indeed American heroes.

I will now read the citations, which accompany our expression of gratitude for all that our honorees have done.

[At this point, the President read the citations which accompanied the medals. The texts of the citations follow.]

Paul H. Nitze:

In a career spanning nine Presidencies, Paul Nitze has made enormous contributions to the freedom and security of his country. Paul Nitze exemplifies the powers of mind, commitment, and character needed to fulfill America's world responsibilities. He was present at the creation of the strategy that has kept us at peace for 40 years. His deep understanding of the issues of war and peace, his discharge of high public assignments, and his advice to those in authority have been invaluable to our national well-being. He remains the most rigorous, demanding, and independent of analysts and the wisest of counselors.

Paul, congratulations, and thank you.

Ambassador Nitze. Thank you, Mr. President. Mr. President, I'm deeply honored at having received and you having awarded me the Medal for Freedom. There is, I think, the task that gives the greatest opportunity for development and for doing things is service in this government. You, today, have really a marvelous team helping you on foreign policy and national security, led by Secretary [of State] Shultz and Bud McFarlane, but they're also supported by an able team of negotiators, a most able team of negotiators, in Geneva. And we all thank you for your leadership.

Thank you, Mr. President.

The President. Thank you.

Now, Roberta and Albert Wohlstetter— one citation, but two medals.

Participants in the nuclear era's most momentous events, Roberta and Albert Wohlstetter have shaped the ideas and deeds of statesmen, and have helped create a safer world. Over four decades, they have marshaled logic, science, and history and enlarged our democracy's capacity to learn and to act. Through their work, we have seen that mankind's safety need not rest on threats to the innocent, and that nuclear weapons need not spread inexorably. Their powers of thought and exposition are, in themselves, among the Free World's best defenses.

I want to make sure I have these right. Albert, to you. All right.

Mrs. Wohlstetter. Thank you, Mr. President.

The President. And now—all right. Thank you both, and congratulations.

Mrs. Wohlstetter. Thank you. I'm dazzled and very deeply honored. Thank you very much.

Mr. Wohlstetter. Mr. President, I receive this great honor not only for myself but for the brilliant and devoted research men and students with whom I've been lucky enough to work for nearly 35 years. I take particular pride in being given this Medal of Freedom from a President who's stressed that it's freedom that we're defending, that we have to defend it without bringing on a holocaust that would end both free and unfree societies. I'm most grateful and honored, Mr. President. Thank you very much.

Note: The President spoke at 11:05 a.m. in the East Room at the White House.

Nomination of Otis R. Bowen To Be Secretary of Health and Human Services
November 7, 1985

The President today announced his intention to nominate Otis R. Bowen to be Secretary of Health and Human Services. He would succeed Margaret M. Heckler.

Dr. Bowen is presently serving as the Lester D. Bibler professor of family medicine and director of undergraduate family practice education at the Indiana University School of Medicine. He was Governor of Indiana in 1973–1981. He was a member of the Indiana House of Representatives in 1957, 1958, and 1961–1972, serving as minority leader in 1965–1966 and speaker from 1967 to 1972. Dr. Bowen has served on a number of Federal advisory commissions, including the Advisory Council on Social Security (Chairman, 1982–1984); the Presidential Advisory Committee on Federalism (member, 1981–1982); the Education Commission of the States (member, 1973–1981; Chairman, 1978–1979); the Republican Governors Association (member, 1973–1981; Chairman, 1978–1979); the President's Committee on Science and Technology (member, 1976–1977); and as a member of the Advisory Council of the United Student Aid Fund. Dr. Bowen is the recipient of many awards for his contributions to the field of public health. He has written extensively on health issues.

He graduated from Indiana University (A.B., 1939) and Indiana University School of Medicine (M.D., 1942). He is married and has four children. He was born February 26, 1918, in Richland Center, IN.

Nomination of Two Members of the Board of Directors of the National Institute of Building Sciences
November 7, 1985

The President today announced his intention to nominate the following individuals to be members of the Board of Directors of the National Institute of Building Sciences:

Philip D. Winn, of Colorado, will succeed Rudard Jones. Mr. Winn is chairman of Philip D. Winn & Associates, Inc., a real estate development company, in Englewood, CO. Previously he was senior vice president of Witkin Homes/U.S. Home Corp. in 1964–1976. He graduated from the University of Michigan (B.A., 1948). He is married, has two children, and resides in Englewood, CO. He was born February 1, 1925, in New Britain, CT.

Fred E. Hummel, of California, will succeed Herbert H. Swinburne. He is an architect, planner, and consultant in Sacramento, CA. He served as a member of the National Capital Committee of the American Institute of Architects (1973–1974) and was chairman of the California State Building Standards Coordination Council in 1970–1971. He graduated from the University of California at Berkeley (B.A., 1951). He is married, has seven children, and resides in Carmichael, CA. He was born January 10, 1927, in Sheridan, NY.

Appointment of Two Members of the Advisory Committee for Trade Negotiations
November 7, 1985

The President today announced his intention to appoint the following individuals to be members of the Advisory Committee for Trade Negotiations for terms of 2 years:

J. Kenneth Robinson, of Virginia, will succeed Russell Hanlin. He was a United States Congressman from the Seventh District of Virginia from 1970 to 1985. He is now an orchardist in Winchester, VA. He graduated from Virginia Polytechnic Institute (B.S., 1937). He is married, has six children, and resides in Winchester, VA. He was born May 14, 1916, in Winchester.

Robert P. Visser, of Virginia, is a reappointment. He is a partner in the firm of Barnett & Alagia in Washington, DC. Previously he was president and chief executive officer of Vistra International, Inc., in Washington, DC. He graduated from the City College of New York (B.S., 1963) and George Washington University (J.D., 1966). He is married, has three children, and resides in Vienna, VA. He was born October 7, 1940, in New York City.

Statement on the Taxation of Multinational Corporations by States
November 8, 1985

Since early in this administration, we have been working with the States, the business community, and foreign governments in an effort to resolve issues related to State use of the worldwide unitary method of taxation. At this time I believe it appropriate for the Federal Government to state its support for the concept of legislation that would:

1. Effect a requirement that multinationals be taxed by States only on income derived from the territory of the United States ("the water's edge requirement"); and

2. Address the question of equitable taxation of foreign source dividends.

We hoped that by this time these principles would have been enacted by the various States that have unitary taxation. Since

States have not universally accepted these principles, I am instructing the Secretary of the Treasury to initiate the process of crafting Federal legislation to incorporate these principles into law and to work with the Congress for passage and also, where appropriate, to enter into negotiations to amend double taxation agreements. I am also instructing the Secretary of the Treasury to pursue enactment of the domestic "spread-sheet" legislation, which has been previously proposed and which is designed to assist nonunitary States with tax enforcement respecting multinational corporations in order to promote full taxpayer disclosure and accountability. Further, I am instructing the Attorney General to ensure that the United States interests are represented in appropriate controversies and cases consistent with this approach.

Nomination of Rockwell Anthony Schnabel To Be United States Ambassador to Finland
November 8, 1985

The President today announced his intention to nominate Rockwell Anthony Schnabel, of California, as Ambassador to the Republic of Finland. He would succeed Keith Foote Nyborg.

Mr. Schnabel began his career in the international investment banking field in 1959 with Quincy Cass Associates in Los Angeles. In 1965 he joined Bateman Eichler, Hill Richards Group (members N.Y.S.E.), and held various positions to president. Since 1983 Mr. Schnabel has been deputy chairman of Morgan, Olmstead, Kennedy & Gardner, Inc. (investment bankers). He also is a director of a number of U.S. and foreign corporations. Mr. Schnabel has been active in a number of civic and political organizations, including Citizens for America, Americans for Responsible Government, the Los Angeles World Affairs Council, and the Los Angeles Olympic Organizing Committee. This year Mr. Schnabel received the Medal of Honor of The Netherlands Olympic Committee. During 1983–1984 he was the Los Angeles Olympic Committee's envoy to The Netherlands.

Mr. Schnabel was born December 30, 1936, in Amsterdam, The Netherlands, where he attended Trinity College. He served in the U.S. National Guard in 1959–1965. Mr. Schnabel is married to the former Marna Belle Del Mar, and they have three children. They reside in Malibu, CA.

Appointment of Elizabeth I. Board as Special Assistant to the President and Director of the Television Office
November 8, 1985

The President has appointed Elizabeth I. Board to be Special Assistant to the President and Director of the Television Office at the White House.

Since January 1985 Miss Board has served as Director of the Television Office at the White House. Miss Board worked for NBC News in 1979–1984, first as senior unit manager and later as network news editor. Previously she was director of creative services for WMAL Radio and executive producer of the Washington Redskins Radio Network. She was also an account executive at WRC Radio and producer of "Empathy" on WWDC Radio.

Miss Board graduated from the University of Colorado (B.A., 1974), the Stanford University Broadcasting and Film Institute, and

George Washington University (M.B.A., 1981). She now resides in Washington, DC, where she serves on the board of directors for Big Sisters.

Message to the House of Representatives Returning Without Approval the Health Research Extension Bill
November 8, 1985

To the House of Representatives:

I am returning herewith without my approval H.R. 2409, the "Health Research Extension Act of 1985," which would extend and amend the biomedical research authorities of the National Institutes of Health (NIH).

My action on this bill should in no way be interpreted as a lessening of this Administration's strong commitment to the biomedical research endeavors of NIH. In fact, I want to underscore my personal support and the support of my Administration for biomedical research and for the NIH. For over 40 years, the NIH has enjoyed unparalleled success. Enormous progress in research and the improved health of the American people attest to that success. An appropriations bill or a continuing resolution will provide uninterrupted funding for NIH activities in fiscal year 1986.

I believe that instead of fostering a strong Federal biomedical research effort, H.R. 2409 would adversely affect the pursuit of research excellence at NIH by:

—imposing numerous administrative and program requirements that would interfere with the ability to carry forward our biomedical research activities in the most cost-effective manner and would misallocate scarce financial and personnel resources;

—establishing unneeded new organizations, which would lead to unnecessary coordination problems and administrative expenses while doing little to assist the biomedical research endeavors of NIH; and

—imposing a uniform set of authorities on all the research institutes, thus diminishing our administrative flexibility to respond to changing biomedical research needs.

Although H.R. 2409 is overloaded with objectionable provisions that seriously undermine and threaten the ability of NIH to manage itself and is therefore unacceptable, I recognize there are areas in which the Administration can step forward to strengthen specific research efforts.

As Senator Hatch pointed out when introducing the NIH reauthorization bill in the Senate in June of this year, arthritis afflicts some 49 million of this Nation's citizens and "all of us suffer, at some time in our life, from some form of arthritis." Further, arthritis, along with musculoskeletal and skin diseases, "collectively result in an extraordinary loss to our economy from lost productivity as well as from medical expense."

In recognition of the plight of the millions of arthritis victims and society's costs, I have directed the Secretary of Health and Human Services to establish administratively a separate National Institute of Arthritis and Musculoskeletal and Skin Diseases that will meet the continuing need for coordinated research in this important area. This directive is consistent with the Department's recommendation to me that this Institute be established.

At the same time, I do not believe that the establishment of a nursing research center at NIH is appropriate, for a very basic reason—there is a lack of compatibility between the mission of such a center and the mission of NIH. The biomedical research activities of NIH are concerned with discovering the etiology of and treatment for diseases. In contrast, nursing research uses substantive scientific information and methodology and focuses on their relevance to nursing practice and administration. This research is important, but neither it nor disease-oriented research are served by the provisions of the bill.

H.R. 2409 manifests an effort to exert undue political control over decisions regarding scientific research, thus limiting the ability of the NIH to set this Nation's biomedical research agenda. I do not believe that it is either necessary or wise to restrict the flexibility under which the NIH has operated so successfully. In 1984, I rejected a very similar bill, and once again I find no reasonable justification for the extensive changes to the NIH mandated by H.R. 2409. In order to allow NIH to continue to provide excellence in biomedical research and in its management, I am disapproving this bill.

RONALD REAGAN

The White House,
November 8, 1985.

Note: H.R. 2409, which passed over the President's veto on November 20, was assigned Public Law No. 99–158.

Proclamation 5405—National Alzheimer's Disease Month, 1985
November 8, 1985

By the President of the United States of America

A Proclamation

For more than two million Americans with Alzheimer's disease, each day is fraught with fear and frustration. Fear of getting lost in one's own neighborhood; of not recognizing members of one's immediate family; of not being able to perform simple, familiar chores. For the victims of this disease, tying shoes or setting a table can be overwhelming tasks. As our elderly population grows, more and more people will be affected by this malady.

Alzheimer's disease is the major cause of the confusion, erratic behavior, and forgetfulness once believed to be a "normal" part of old age. This "senility" is actually the result of the destruction of certain brain cells.

As the afflicted person loses the ability to function intellectually, the family faces growing emotional, physical, and financial burdens. Eventually, many victims require specialized professional care. Fifty percent of all nursing home residents in America suffer from Alzheimer's disease or other serious, irreversible forms of dementia.

The medical research community is focusing special attention on Alzheimer's disease in an effort to discover its causes and develop effective treatments. Recently, a Department of Health and Human Services task force defined the current state of medical knowledge of Alzheimer's disease and recommended future research directions. Organizations leading this research include the National Institute of Neurological and Communicative Disorders and Stroke; the National Institute on Aging; the National Institute of Mental Health; and the National Institute of Allergy and Infectious Diseases. For Alzheimer's patients and their families, this intensive research is the greatest source of hope.

But until a way to prevent Alzheimer's disease is found, these families need our support and understanding. I commend the superb services provided by voluntary health organizations, notably the Alzheimer's Disease and Related Disorders Association.

To enhance public awareness of Alzheimer's disease, the Congress, by Senate Joint Resolution 65, has designated the month of November 1985 as "National Alzheimer's Disease Month" and authorized and requested the President to issue a proclamation in observance of this month.

Now, Therefore, I, Ronald Reagan, President of the United States of America, do hereby proclaim the month of November 1985 as National Alzheimer's Disease Month, and I call upon the people of the United States to observe that month with appropriate observances and activities.

In Witness Whereof, I have hereunto set my hand this 8th day of November, in the year of our Lord nineteen hundred and eighty-five, and of the Independence of the United States of America the two hundred and tenth.

RONALD REAGAN

[*Filed with the Office of the Federal Register, 11:15 a.m., November 12, 1985*]

Radio Address to the Nation and the World on the Upcoming Soviet-United States Summit Meeting in Geneva
November 9, 1985

My fellow Americans:

We're expanding the format of our radio broadcast today. During the next 10 minutes, I'll be speaking to the citizens of the Soviet Union over the Voice of America about the upcoming Geneva summit. My words will be directed to them, but I want you to hear what I say. My speech is also being broadcast to over 50 nations by the Worldnet Television Network.

So, good evening, this is Ronald Reagan, President of the United States, speaking to you from Washington about my upcoming meeting with General Secretary Gorbachev in Geneva and my hopes for a better relationship between our two governments. Your leaders can freely appear on American radio and television and be interviewed by our magazines and newspapers. So, I was grateful for my recent and rare opportunity to speak with representatives of the Soviet press. While I appreciate that, only parts of the interview were published in Izvestia, and much of what was left out I think is important. So, I wish to speak to you personally as a husband, father, and grandfather who shares your deepest hopes—that all of our children can live and prosper in a world of peace.

I grew up in a small town in America's heartland where values of faith in God, freedom, family, friends, and concern for one's neighbors were shared by all—values you also share. During my school years I worked during vacations, for a time on construction and then for several summers as a lifeguard at a river beach. After finishing my education I became a radio sports announcer, which led to acting in Hollywood where I was elected head of our actor's guild. I'm the only American President who was also president of a labor union. Back then I had no intention of engaging in national politics, but America's a great country filled with opportunities. In the years that followed, including my years as Governor of California and as President, I have not forgotten the values I learned as a boy nor have my fellow Americans.

Now, I know that much has been written in your press about America's hostile intentions toward you. Well, I reject these distortions. Americans are a peace-loving people; we do not threaten your nation and never will. The American people are tolerant, slow to anger, but staunch in defense of their liberties and, like you, their country. More than once, our two countries have joined to oppose a common enemy. During our War of Independence, Russia provided assistance to the distant American colonists. A century and a half later, we joined together to defeat the common enemy of fascism; before that, we were allies in World War I.

Even before we entered World War II, America was supplying massive quantities of food and equipment to those fighting the Nazis. We provided 14,795 aircraft to your forces, 7,056 tanks, more than half a million vehicles, and more than 6 million tons of food and other staples. Americans will never forget the valor, the pain, and, at last, the joy of victory that our peoples shared. I remember President Roosevelt's praise for the Russian people's heroism. How can any of us alive then forget that terrible year of 1941 when the Nazis were repulsed at the gates of Moscow, the courage of Leningraders during the 900-day siege, the victory at Stalingrad, or our historic meeting on the Elbe in 1945? Americans fought for 4 years on all fronts. Many lie buried in northern Africa, Europe, Burma, China, the Pacific islands, and at the bottom of the sea. Some are buried on Soviet soil—in the hero city of Murmansk, where they had brought precious supplies through the treacherous convoy route.

Yet after that victory, Americans gave generously to help rebuild war-torn countries, even to former enemies, because we had made war on a vicious ideology, not on a people. And we demonstrated our desire for peace by rapidly demobilizing. At the end of 1945, we had an armed force of almost 12 million men; by 1948 we had reduced that number to less than 1½ million. We were the only country with nuclear weapons. We proposed giving those weapons up altogether to an international authority so that no country would have such destructive power at its disposal. What a pity this idea was not accepted.

Today we must both face the challenge of eliminating nuclear weapons. I have said many times and will say again to you: A nuclear war cannot be won and must never be fought. I pray God that we can rid the world of these dangerous weapons, in part by finding a reliable defense against them. Our negotiators in Geneva are working hard to reach a breakthrough. I am pleased that the Soviet Union finally responded to our original proposals. We studied the response carefully and replied quickly. These are complicated negotiations and satisfactory results will take long, hard work.

Let me be clear about our research and testing program on strategic defense technologies. Our goal is to make the world safer through development of nonnuclear security shields that would protect people by preventing weapons from reaching their targets and, hopefully, render ballistic missiles obsolete. Your own government has been conducting longstanding and extensive programs on its own defensive systems, including advanced research. The United States is just beginning a long process of investigating defenses. If and when our research proves that a defensive shield against nuclear missiles is practical, I believe our

two nations, and those others that have nuclear weapons, should come together and agree on how, gradually, to eliminate offensive nuclear weapons, as we make our defensive system available to all. We ought to start talking about this process at the Geneva arms talks.

We must live together in peace. America's whole history has been a search for peace and opportunity by pioneers seeking freedom, many from the old European order. We're proud of the Russians, the Ukrainians, the Jews, the Armenians, and many others who sailed by our Statue of Liberty and reached our shores. Diversity is one of our great strengths. This is partly why we're confusing to outsiders. Our government is elected by the people; it is not above the people or above the law. We believe the truth is found through debate and discussion. Truth does not burn in the fire or drown in the water. Our system is often uncomfortable for elected officials, because one of our proudest institutions is a free press. The press criticizes me, and sometimes it hurts, but that is their role—to raise difficult questions and keep officials accountable to the people. But no one should mistake our freedoms for weakness. We favor free and open dialog not just for Americans, but for all peoples. We believe in freedom of the individual. Freedom of worship, freedom of speech, freedom of the press are, as our Declaration of Independence says, unalienable rights of all men.

Ten years ago the United States and the Soviet Union, along with 33 other countries, signed the Helsinki accords. We all pledged to respect human rights, permit our citizens freedom of speech and travel, and improve communication among the peoples of the signatory nations. America asks the world's leaders to abide by what they have committed themselves to do. As the world's two strongest nations, we owe it to the rest of humanity not only to keep our word but to help find peaceful settlements to local and regional conflicts in Afghanistan, Africa, Latin America, and elsewhere.

We must also join forces against terrorism. There is no place in a civilized world for assassinations, terrorist bombings, and other mindless violence. I strongly urge you and your government to join us in combating terrorism and ensuring that no country will offer succor or comfort to terrorists.

We have much to learn from each other. Americans have long been enriched by your cultural giants. The works of Tolstoy, Dostoyevsky, Turgenev, Chekov, and Pasternak are taught in many American universities; just as American authors from James Fenimore Cooper, Mark Twain, and Jack London to Ernest Hemingway and William Faulkner are popular in your country. I want expanded contacts between our two great societies, wherever there is mutual interest. I am particularly interested in increasing exchanges among our young people, for they are our future. We should open a dialog between our nations, so leaders of each country would have the same chance to communicate to the people of the other on television. If more of your citizens visited us, you would understand that our people want peace as fervently as you do.

I hope my discussions with Mr. Gorbachev in Geneva will be fruitful and will lead to future meetings. We seek peace not only for ourselves but for all those who inhabit this small planet. We share borders with three countries—Mexico, Canada, and the Soviet Union. We pride ourselves on our friendly relations and open borders with our two North American neighbors. And I hope the day will come when that narrow chain of islands stretching from Alaska to the eastern shore of Siberia will symbolize the ties between our two great peoples, not the distance between us.

Everything has a season. Let us hope as we near Christmas and the New Year that this will be the season for peace. Thank you for welcoming me into your homes. God bless you.

Note: The President spoke at 12:06 p.m. from the studios of the Voice of America.

Statement by Principal Deputy Press Secretary Speakes on Soviet Jamming of the President's Radio Address on the Upcoming Soviet-United States Summit Meeting in Geneva
November 9, 1985

The President's address to the Soviet people today via the Voice of America was monitored by Russian language-qualified officers of the American Embassy in Moscow and the American consulate in Leningrad. They report that in Moscow, two and possibly three frequencies were clearly audible and probably not jammed; the signal on one of them was as clear as a local station, according to the Embassy monitoring report. On another 15 frequencies, there were varying degrees of jamming. In Leningrad, one Russian-language frequency was received loud and clear. All others were jammed. A Lithuanian broadcast of the speech was also received clearly in Leningrad; however, this same frequency may have been jammed in Lithuania.

Atmospheric conditions on November 9 were conducive to good reception of shortwave signals in the Soviet Union. English-language broadcasts, which are not normally jammed, were well received. We are pleased and hope that this development will set a precedent which will allow the Soviets to put a permanent end to jamming on all frequencies. A free flow of information would be a very positive development in people-to-people communications between the two nations.

Toasts at a White House Dinner for the Prince and Princess of Wales
November 9, 1985

The President. Your Royal Highnesses, Sir Oliver and Lady Wright, and Ambassador and Mrs. Price, ladies and gentlemen, Nancy and I are deeply honored to welcome the Prince and Princess of Wales to the White House. Permit me to add our congratulations to Prince Charles on his birthday, just 5 days away, and express also our great happiness that we have been able to have this affair with Princess Diana, here on her first trip to the United States—that we should be able to share in that first trip.

In his 1941 address before a Joint Session of the United States Congress, Prime Minister Churchill remarked, "I cannot help reflecting that if my father had been American and my mother British, instead of the other way around, I might have got here on my own." [*Laughter*] But Your Royal Highnesses, the reception you've received here suggests that if you had been American, you might well have gotten to this house on your own. [*Laughter*]

Our two countries are bound together by innumerable ties of ancient history and present friendship. Our language, our law, our democratic system of government, our fierce belief in the God-given right of men to be free—all of these we owe to you. We've stood together through two great world conflicts. Today we go on, shoulder to shoulder, in an alliance to protect freedom and democracy.

This evening we've gathered on a happy occasion, a celebration of the "Treasure Houses of Britain," perhaps the most magnificent exhibition ever mounted and five centuries of British achievement, five centuries of elegance, beauty, and charm; I should add, wit. When Nancy and I toured the exhibition, we were struck by a settee from Balmoral Castle, constructed almost entirely of deer antlers. I've been wondering ever since whether something like that could be done with cattle horns out on the ranch. [*Laughter*] But one misadventure in the corral one day has taught me that it might be more painful than pleasant, so—

[*laughter*]. The "Treasure Houses of Britain" truly is a great gift from the houses' owners, the British people, and you, the exhibition's patrons. I speak for all Americans when I say a heartfelt "thank you."

Your Royal Highnesses, in the eyes of my countrymen, you and your family hold a place of high honor; your devotion to duty commands our esteem. Americans join our British cousins in looking upon you with affection and respect. And in that same 1941 address, Winston Churchill said: "It is not given to us to peer into the future. Still I avow my hope and faith, sure and inviolate, that in the days to come, the British and American people will, for their own safety and for the good of all, walk together in majesty, in justice, and in peace." And today that noble hope is a glorious reality.

Would you please join me in a toast to Her Majesty, the Queen. To the Queen.

Prince Charles. Mr. President, Mrs. Reagan, ladies and gentlemen, if I may say so, Mr. President, you really have touched both my wife and myself most deeply this evening by your extremely kind words. And we can't possibly, both of us, thank you enough for your immense hospitality and your great kindness in having us here this evening and in making us feel so unbelievably welcome.

I would think one of the most marvelous things about coming to the United States is that you have this extraordinary gift for making people feel welcome. And apart from the friendliness with which you greet everybody, it really does warm the heart to come here and be made to feel welcome. I can't tell you what it means to us both. It really does. As you know, we've flown in hesitant stages from Australia and tried to stop on the way in order to regain our strength. And all that's happened is we're suffering terribly from jet lag. [*Laughter*] And I've yet to discover a foolproof method for actually getting one over the problems of this particular affliction.

However, we are greatly looking forward

to the opportunity of seeing this exhibition, the "Treasure Houses of Britain," which we are both very proud to be patrons of. And we hear from all sides just how stupendous this particular exhibition is. I think if you go and look at most of the country houses in Britain at the moment, you'll find them completely empty—[*laughter*]—of all the furniture and pictures, some emptier than others and, no doubt, with rather dirty marks on the walls where the pictures were. I only hope that they manage to get them all back in the right place at the right time. [*Laughter*]

I'm also very much looking forward, myself, to going to the Congress Library on Monday and discussing something about the Constitution, of which I know you celebrate the bicentenary in 1987. And I was very intrigued to discover that of the 55 delegates that came to the Federal convention in 1787, nearly all of them were in their thirties, which just goes to show what an extremely good age the midthirties is. [*Laughter*] I keep telling myself that because you reminded me about my birthday, and I'm not sure I need reminding. [*Laughter*]

I would also just like to say that coming, as we have, down from Australia, it is one of the more interesting aspects, I think, of the pioneering spirit of the English-speaking peoples. That here were two great continents—Australia and the United States of America, the former having developed about 150 years later than this great country—and in many ways there are similarities between the two. And I think that one of the things that becomes most obvious about Australia and America is that personal independence becomes a very dominant feature, particularly, I think, in American life. And one Englishman observed in 1796 that Americans tend to pass their lives without any regard to the smiles or frowns of men in power. However, in your case, Mr. President, I'm sure it's completely different.

So, if I may, finally, again say what an enormous pleasure it gives both of us to be here and how proud we are to be able to represent Britain here in America. As you say, it does, I think, emphasize the very strong links that do exist between our two countries—always have done, and I'm sure always will. And in the end, that bond between our two peoples is one of the most important and enduring features of this Earth.

Mr. President, thank you very much.

Note: The President spoke at 10:09 p.m. in the State Dining Room at the White House. In his opening remarks, he referred to Sir Oliver Wright, British Ambassador to the United States, and Charles H. Price II, U.S. Ambassador to the United Kingdom.

Remarks at the Veterans Day Wreath-Laying Ceremony at Arlington National Cemetery
November 11, 1985

Secretary Weinberger, Harry Walters, Robert Medairos, reverend clergy, ladies and gentlemen, a few moments ago I placed a wreath at the Tomb of the Unknown Soldier, and as I stepped back and stood during the moment of silence that followed, I said a small prayer. And it occurred to me that each of my predecessors has had a similar moment, and I wondered if our prayers weren't very much the same, if not identical.

We celebrate Veterans Day on the anniversary of the armistice that ended World War I, the armistice that began on the 11th hour of the 11th day of the 11th month. And I wonder, in fact, if all Americans' prayers aren't the same as those I mentioned a moment ago. The timing of this holiday is quite deliberate in terms of historical fact but somehow it always seems quite fitting to me that this day comes deep in autumn when the colors are muted and the days seem to invite contemplation.

We are gathered at the National Cemetery, which provides a final resting place for the heroes who have defended our country since the Civil War. This amphitheater, this place for speeches, is more central to this cemetery than it first might seem apparent, for all we can ever do for our heroes is remember them and remember what they did—and memories are transmitted through words. Sometime back I received in the name of our country the bodies of four marines who had died while on active duty. I said then that there is a special sadness that accompanies the death of a serviceman, for we're never quite good enough to them—not really; we can't be, because what they gave us is beyond our powers to repay. And so, when a serviceman dies, it's a tear in the fabric, a break in the whole, and all we can do is remember.

It is, in a way, an odd thing to honor those who died in defense of our country, in defense of us, in wars far away. The imagination plays a trick. We see these soldiers in our mind as old and wise. We see them as something like the Founding Fathers, grave and gray haired. But most of them were boys when they died, and they gave up two lives—the one they were living and the one they would have lived. When they died, they gave up their chance to be husbands and fathers and grandfathers. They gave up their chance to be revered old men. They gave up everything for our country, for us. And all we can do is remember.

There's always someone who is remembering for us. No matter what time of year it is or what time of day, there are always people who come to this cemetery, leave a flag or a flower or a little rock on a headstone. And they stop and bow their heads and communicate what they wished to communicate. They say, "Hello, Johnny," or "Hello, Bob. We still think of you. You're still with us. We never got over you, and we pray for you still, and we'll see you again. We'll all meet again." In a way, they represent us, these relatives and friends, and they speak for us as they walk among the headstones and remember. It's not so hard to summon memory, but it's hard to recapture meaning.

And the living have a responsibility to remember the conditions that led to the wars in which our heroes died. Perhaps we can start by remembering this: that all of those who died for us and our country were, in one way or another, victims of a peace process that failed; victims of a decision to forget certain things; to forget, for instance, that the surest way to keep a peace going is to stay strong. Weakness, after all, is a temptation—it tempts the pugnacious to assert themselves—but strength is a declaration that cannot be misunderstood. Strength is a condition that declares actions have consequences. Strength is a prudent warning to the belligerent that aggression need not go unanswered.

Peace fails when we forget what we stand for. It fails when we forget that our Republic is based on firm principles, principles that have real meaning, that with them, we are the last, best hope of man on Earth; without them, we're little more than the crust of a continent. Peace also fails when we forget to bring to the bargaining table God's first intellectual gift to man: common sense. Common sense gives us a realistic knowledge of human beings and how they think, how they live in the world, what motivates them. Common sense tells us that man has magic in him, but also clay. Common sense can tell the difference between right and wrong. Common sense forgives error, but it always recognizes it to be error first.

We endanger the peace and confuse all issues when we obscure the truth; when we refuse to name an act for what it is; when we refuse to see the obvious and seek safety in Almighty. Peace is only maintained and won by those who have clear eyes and brave minds. Peace is imperiled when we forget to try for agreements and settlements and treaties; when we forget to hold out our hands and strive; when we forget that God gave us talents to use in securing the ends He desires. Peace fails when we forget that agreements, once made, cannot be broken without a price.

Each new day carries within it the potential for breakthroughs, for progress. Each new day bursts with possibilities. And so, hope is realistic and despair a pointless little sin. And peace fails when we forget to pray to the source of all peace and life and happiness. I think sometimes of General Matthew Ridgeway, who, the night before D-day, tossed sleepless on his cot and talked to the Lord and listened for the promise that God made to Joshua: "I will not fail thee, nor forsake thee."

We're surrounded today by the dead of our wars. We owe them a debt we can never repay. All we can do is remember them and what they did and why they had to be brave for us. All we can do is try to see that other young men never have to join them. Today, as never before, we must pledge to remember the things that will continue the peace. Today, as never before, we must pray for God's help in broadening and deepening the peace we enjoy. Let us pray for freedom and justice and a more stable world. And let us make a compact today with the dead, a promise in the words for which General Ridgeway listened, "I will not fail thee, nor forsake thee."

In memory of those who gave the last full measure of devotion, may our efforts to achieve lasting peace gain strength. And through whatever coincidence or accident of timing, I tell you that a week from now when I am some thousands of miles away, believe me, the memory and the importance of this day will be in the forefront of my mind and in my heart.

Thank you. God bless you all, and God bless America.

Note: The President spoke at 11:30 a.m. after laying a wreath at the Tomb of the Unknown Soldier. In his opening remarks, the President referred to Secretary of Defense Caspar W. Weinberger, Harry N. Walters, Administrator of Veterans Affairs, and Robert Medairos, national commander of AMVETS.

Proclamation 5406—National Reye's Syndrome Week, 1985
November 11, 1985

By the President of the United States of America

A Proclamation

There is a potentially deadly disorder that affects our children called Reye's Syndrome. It is one of the top ten killers among all diseases affecting young people aged one to ten. Each year in the United States, a number of healthy children under age nineteen are afflicted with Reye's Syndrome, and many victims die or become crippled within several days.

We did not recognize Reye's Syndrome as a specific illness until 1963, and we still do not know what causes it or how to prevent it. Diligent research has identified its symptoms: severe vomiting, delirium, lethargy, unusual drowsiness, and belligerence. During last winter's flu season, only 171 cases of Reye's Syndrome were reported in the United States, down from the 422 cases reported as recently as 1980. A variety of factors have contributed to this sharp decline, which is an encouraging chapter in the annals of American medicine. Experience has taught us that quick medical intervention usually can avert death or disability.

But much remains to be learned. Federal scientists, supported by the National Institute of Neurological and Communicative Disorders and Stroke and other units of the National Institutes of Health such as the National Institute of Allergy and Infectious Diseases, the National Institute of Child Health and Human Development, and the National Institute of Arthritis, Diabetes, and Digestive and Kidney Diseases, are untiring in their efforts to understand this lethal disorder. They are assisted in this endeavor by their Federal colleagues at the Food and Drug Administration and Centers for Disease Control, who monitor the occurrence of Reye's Syndrome throughout the country.

In recent years, the medical community and groups of concerned citizens have brought Reye's Syndrome into the public eye. Volunteer organizations such as the American Reye's Syndrome Association and the National Reye's Syndrome Foundation have launched effective public education campaigns. We must build upon these efforts to acquaint all parents and medical professionals with the dangers of this illness. We must stimulate further scientific investigation of the origin of this enigmatic killer in the biomedical research arena, where our greatest hope of conquering this disease lies.

To focus public and professional attention on the seriousness of Reye's Syndrome, the Congress, by Senate Joint Resolution 29, has designated the week of November 11 through November 17, 1985, as "National Reye's Syndrome Week" and authorized and requested the President to issue a proclamation in observance of that week.

Now, Therefore, I, Ronald Reagan, President of the United States of America, do hereby proclaim the week of November 11 through 17, 1985, as National Reye's Syndrome Week. I call upon all government agencies, health organizations, communications media, and people of the United States to observe that week with appropriate ceremonies and activities.

In Witness Whereof, I have hereunto set my hand this 11th day of November, in the year of our Lord nineteen hundred and eighty-five, and of the Independence of the United States of America the two hundred and tenth.

RONALD REAGAN

[*Filed with the Office of the Federal Register, 11:02 a.m., November 13, 1985*]

Note: The proclamation was released by the Office of the Press Secretary on November 12.

Nomination of Lois Burke Shepard To Be Director of the Institute of Museum Services
November 12, 1985

The President today announced his intention to nominate Lois Burke Shepard to be Director of the Institute of Museum Services, National Foundation on the Arts and the Humanities. She would succeed Susan E. Phillips.

Mrs. Shepard served as chairman of Republicans Abroad at the Republican National Committee in 1981–1985 and was director of Americans Abroad for Reagan/Bush '84. She was the first representative for overseas Americans at the 1982 White House Conference on Aging.

She graduated from Hartford College (A.A., 1957) and Vassar College (B.A., 1959). She is married, has two children, and resides in Potomac, MD. She was born February 1, 1938, in Hartford, CT.

Interview With Foreign Broadcasters on the Upcoming Soviet-United States Summit Meeting in Geneva
November 12, 1985

Q. Mr. President, thank you very much for receiving us at the White House, just a week before your meeting with Mikhail Gorbachev. I'm Claude Smadja, from the Suisse Television. Let me introduce my colleagues: Martin Bell, from the BBC; Giuseppe Lugato, from RAI; Dieter Kronzucker, from ZDF; and Jacques Abouchar, from AN–2.

Mr. President, 1 week before the summit in Geneva, the prospects seem quite bleak. Do you still expect to strike a deal in Geneva, and, in fact, are you going to strike a deal in Geneva?

The President. Well, I'm not as pessimistic as that. I understand, of course, that it's not going to be easy. There's a long history of meetings between our two countries and, many times, without much result. But I'm going to make every effort to try and reduce the mistrust and suspicion that seems to exist between our—well, not only our two nations but sort of the East and the West. And I believe there are possibilities. We're going to try to deal in some four areas—arms control, of course, is one; the regional disputes that are going on in the world and where the major powers are involved. Bilateral issues, a number of kind, that are between us probably would be the easiest thing that we'll face in those meetings. And we'll just carry on, see what we can do.

Q. Mr. President, I wonder, on arms control, are you going with a set negotiating position—some counterproposals to Mr. Gorbachev's proposals—and is your team of advisers finally united behind you?

The President. Yes, we are united, and I think that there's been some distortion as to whether we weren't. In our government here, I solicit and encourage varying opinions and ideas. I think it helps to make a decision when I hear all viewpoints. But I don't envision this meeting as being one where we will get down to specific numbers and so forth. We have a team of negotiators, each side, in Geneva that have been negotiating on the possibility of nuclear arms reductions for some time.

We have had a proposal on the table in those talks for a considerable period of time, and finally, the Soviet Union came back with a counterproposal. And we have now offered a counter to that. We found encouragement in their counterproposal; there were numbers that we could agree with. And so, the proposal that we've made in response is one that kind of compromises between our original proposal and theirs, accepting some of their figures—in fact, some of the main figures on basic numbers and so forth—and then, our view on some of the complex issues about the mix of weapons and so forth. And to me, this is legitimate negotiations.

But I would think what we should be dealing with at the summit is, as I said earlier, the elimination of suspicion and mistrust to the point that we could turn the specific numbers over to those other negotiators, but that they could have a signal from both sides, from their government and ours from us, have a knowledge that we want them to continue and to arrive at an agreement.

Q. Mr. President, over the last few days and even now here, you continue to sound optimistic about the summit in Geneva, though we know now there will be no substantial agreement, there will be no arms agenda, and even, probably, there would be no joint communique. Now, what would it be—just a get-acquaintance meeting? And in this case, even the atmosphere, I think it's a bit strange, considering the last occurrences. So, what's the reason of your optimism?

The President. Oh, no, I don't think this is just a get-acquainted meeting, important though that may be. But I think there are many areas for agreement here. And as I say, I'm not pessimistic about them. Look at the one situation that has both of us continuing to build these arsenals of weapons. The Soviet Union claims that they fear that we mean harm to them, that somehow we're nursing a plan of invading them or attempting to change their system. On the other hand, we believe, and I think with some evidence, that their policy has been expansionist; that's evidenced by Afghanistan, Ethiopia, South Yemen, Angola.

And I think that if we sit and face each other and lay our cards on the table as to the fact that they don't like us or our system and we don't like theirs. But we're not going to try to change theirs, and they better not try to change ours. But we have to live in the world together. And we're the only two countries that probably could start world war III. We're also the two countries that could prevent world war III from happening. And I think that a little common sense should make us find out that we can continue to be competitive in the world, but in a peaceful way and without the threat of annihilation hanging over the world as it does now.

Q. Mr. President, scientific results show up to now that your space defense shield is not as impenetrable as originally thought.

Does this make SDI more of a bargaining chip? Could you compromise on this system?

The President. Not compromise in the sense of giving up on the research. Now, the truth of the matter is there've been some breakthroughs that have a number of scientists quite optimistic about this research, and since this research is all going on within the bounds of the ABM treaty, we're going to continue, because I think it would be the greatest thing in this century if we could come up with the idea that, at last, there is a defensive measure, a system against nuclear missiles. Nuclear missiles—these are the only weapons in the history of man that have not given birth, so far, to a defense against them, but this, as I say, would be the greatest thing for peace. If we could switch from a setup today in which peace is maintained on the basis that we can destroy each other, totally offensive weapons, each with a great arsenal and the threat that, well, if one starts, the other will retaliate. Doesn't it make much more sense if we could come up with a defensive system and then sit down with all the nuclear powers in the world and say, "Look, let us get to less of an offensive nature and let us take up the idea of reassurance for ourselves on a basis of defensive systems, not offensive weapons"?

And so, this isn't a bargaining chip in that sense—of being willing to trade off the research and stop what we're doing in order to get *x* number of missiles eliminated; we'll continue with that. Then, as I've said many times, I think if the research, and when the research, would show that such a weapon is practical, then, before deployment, I think we sit down together and decide how we use this to bring about the elimination of nuclear weapons, offensive weapons, and to make the world safer.

Q. Mr. President, you have described Mr. Gorbachev as a formidable opponent. Did his Paris meeting with the French President give you a new light on the Soviet leader's personality and did that change your approach of the summit in any way?

The President. Well, no, but some of our own people, now, have met with Mr. Gorbachev. Unfortunately, President Mitterrand couldn't be at the U.N. meeting, where I managed to meet with the heads of state of our other economic summit allies. And so, I heard secondhand, however, from some of them who had had an opportunity and then from Margaret Thatcher and then, as I say, with our own people who've met with him. I recognize all they say. On the other hand, I just told our people this morning that there will be another first in these meetings. It'll be the first time we've ever had someone on our side of the table who's older than the fellow on the other side of the table. So, maybe I can help this young man with some fatherly advice.

Q. Mr. President, you have set regional conflict high on the agenda. What will be your approach to Mr. Gorbachev on this regional conflict? The substance of your talk will be enough is enough? Will it be kind of fist-on-the-table approach to Mr. Gorbachev?

The President. Well, I believe if we're going to eliminate or reduce the tensions or the mistrust between us, it's going to have to be by deeds rather than words. And I enunciated what I believe about the regional things in my speech to the United Nations, that here are these conflicts, people are being killed, such as is going on in Afghanistan. And it is true that there is a government in Afghanistan that is on the side of the Soviet Union. It also is true that the Soviet Union installed that government there; it was not chosen by the people of Afghanistan. Now, my thought is that if we can take these up as examples of the expansionism that I mentioned and see if we together, these two great powers together, cannot withdraw foreign forces and then help and perhaps get international custodial forces while they settle peacefully the dispute within each one of these regions.

This is what we've been trying to do in Nicaragua, where, again, the Soviet Union is—no question—they're involved with advisers, trainers, and great amounts of weaponry, more than any Central American country needs for its own defense. So, you have to believe that they, too, are looking toward spreading beyond their borders this totalitarianism. But we have urged the *contras* and the Sandinista government of Nicaragua to come together, lay down their weapons, declare a truce and come together, and then, we suggested there the church overall supervise or mediate while they seek to settle their differences without further bloodshed. So far the *contras* have agreed. The Sandinista government is the—and so has the church—the Sandinista government has said no.

But this is the type of thing that we think should be the answer to these regional problems, not only out of humanitarianism and a desire to see people be able to live peacefully in their countries but because those regional conflicts run the risk of spreading and leading to confrontation between major powers.

Q. Mr. President, Mrs. Thatcher described you last night as our champion; that is, you're going in to bat at Geneva for the Europeans as well as the Americans. Is that so, and what can you do for us?

The President. Well, I think the world is pretty much divided right now, certainly Europe and our own hemisphere here between East and West and the NATO alliance—that NATO line does seem to be a dividing line between that and the Warsaw Pact, and there's no way that I could go there and deal with the subjects before us without having in mind the best interests of our allies also, because in the event of catastrophe they are there on the front line, they would be the first to feel that. So, yes, I expect to have their interests very much in mind.

Q. Sir, this is in a way a followup on Martin Bell's question. I should say that the Europeans have a great nostalgia of détente, and what's your message to them at the eve of Geneva, and what's your vision of a new détente? Limits also?

The President. If it is a real détente, if it is based on the elimination or reduction of the suspicions that now exist—but in the past, under the guise of détente, we saw the Soviet Union engage in the greatest military buildup in world history and at the same time that we were supposed to be talking as if we had friendly relations and had achieved some kind of a détente. And what was really, finally, going on was an arms race, because when they achieved an imbalance so great that we felt our own security was threatened, we had to get into the arms

race. I've often told of a cartoon that appeared in one of our papers when we started our refurbishing of our military power. And it was a cartoon of two Soviet generals, and one was saying to the other, "I liked the arms race better when we were the only ones in it." And I know that Mr. Brezhnev at one point, to his own people, publicly made the statement that through détente they had gained enough that they would soon, shortly, be able to have their way and work their will throughout the world. Well, that isn't really détente.

Q. Mr. President, if SDI is not negotiable at the moment, so there might be no compromise also on ballistic missiles, could you envision an understanding with Mr. Gorbachev in the area of theater nuclear weapons already in Geneva?

The President. Well, yes, as you say, this is already in Geneva. And this is definitely one of the topics we will take up there at the summit. As you know, our original proposal was—we were willing to cancel all of them. The Soviets were sitting with SS–20's in great numbers, multiple-warhead missiles targeted on Europe. And Europe had asked us—before my arrival here—had asked my predecessor for weapons to counter those. And the agreement was made that we would. And I inherited the job when I got in here of providing those weapons. They had not yet been delivered. We at no time ever were delivering an equal number of what the Soviets had, but we did propose zero-zero. And on that case, the Soviets met us halfway—zero for us and they'd continue to have their SS–20's. But, yes, we would like to see that, as we're negotiating in Geneva, as treated separately from the intercontinental ballistic missiles, the strategic weapons, to see if we could not eliminate those medium-range weapons that could target each other in a matter of just a few minutes.

Q. So, you should be closer in this area?

The President. Well, I know that the Soviets have talked about such things as a nuclear-free zone in Europe. And we're willing to engage them, and will, in conversation on that kind of a subject.

Q. Mr. President, in the past, you have referred to the Soviet Union as an "evil empire." Then, lately, you avoided the expression. Have you changed your opinion, or do you still consider that Gorbachev, U.S.S.R., is still a totalitarian regime?

The President. Well, it is a totalitarian regime. They don't see freedom for their people as the democracies do. But as I've said before, we're not trying to change their system internally. What I think it's necessary to do is to let them know that the democratic world is not going to hold still for their expansionism into other parts of the world and to our own countries. Yes, I used the term the "evil empire." There've been some things that have gone on that— and yet I have a few quotes of my own that they have said; one in which they even called us "cannibals." So, I think both of us have stopped that language, thinking that we'll get farther at the meetings if we come together to try and eliminate the need for such talk.

Q. Mr. President, the summit of Geneva will be the first in 6 years, and you will have about 8 hours of discussion with Mr. Gorbachev, which is not so much. So, what kind of approach will you try on him? Will you try a kind of man-to-man approach to try to convince, to get your point?

The President. Yes. As a matter of fact, there are some meetings scheduled where it will just be one on one, the two of us. And I will do my utmost, with the evidence at hand, to prove to them that if he does nurse any suspicion that we mean him harm—I think the presentation of some facts such as at the end of World War II, when we were the only nation whose industry and capacity had not been bombed to rubble, when we were the only ones with the nuclear weapon, we could have been pretty dictatorial, ourselves, in the world. But we weren't; we didn't do that—and then point out to him how we see their expansionist policies and so forth and see if we can't come together and recognize that this—when I said deeds, this is how we can eliminate the suspicion. I think the theme that I will take was cited by someone—the line is not original with me—who said that nations do not distrust each other because they are armed, they're armed because they distrust each other. So, we'll see if we can't work on that last half.

Q. Mr. President, this is obviously the most important meeting of your Presidency. You're up against a very formidable figure. I wonder, are you nervous at all?

The President. Not really, no. Maybe I'm relying on past experience. Long before I ever thought I would be in public life in this way—for about 20 years, I did the negotiating for the union of which I was president for 6 of those 20 years, our contract negotiations, repeatedly, with management. I'm the first President of the United States who was ever president of a labor union. And I think I know something about negotiating, and I intend to go at it in the same manner.

Q. Mr. President, do you really want an agreement with the Soviets, and considering the situation and the differences, the gap between the two systems, what kind of an agreement do you want? On what basis? Naturally, this is in perspective, not only Geneva. Let's see Geneva as the starting point.

The President. Well, an overall agreement that we do understand the positions that we're in as the two so-called superpowers and that we have a great responsibility to maintain peace in the world and that it doesn't mean that we interfere with each other's internal policies at all, but that we agree to exist in the world and compete peacefully. And that's the overall tone I think that should come out of the summit. But as I say, it can't just be based on each of us making a promise and saying we feel that way. There have to be some things done, some deeds that really prove that we mean our words.

Q. Mr. President, do you already have a forward copy of the new book of Mr. Gorbachev, "Time for Peace," which will come to the market this week?

The President. No, I don't have that. I'll look forward to that.

Q. Mr. President, do you intend to meet Mr. Gorbachev regularly, maybe on an annual base?

The President. I think whether it's on an annual basis or back and forth and so forth, I think those are things to be settled at this summit. But I definitely think that a great measure of success would be if we came away from this meeting with a decision that we were going to continue meeting and discussing the problems between us.

Q. Mr. President, it has been said that there will be no final communique, but will you bet, at least, on a set of guidelines to give a new impetus to the arms talk?

The President. Yes, I'm not a great fan of communiques, the sort of settling on a statement in advance. And I know we discussed this with them. I think that it'd make far more sense if each one of us came forth and gave our own view of the meetings and what had been achieved, told frankly what had been accomplished and what hadn't. I have agreed with the heads of state of our NATO allies that on the day that we leave Geneva to come home, I'm going by way of Brussels, and if they will be there, I'm going to give a briefing right then. And then, when I arrive here that night, I am going to go directly from the plane to the Congress and before a Joint Session of our Congress and on television to the people of the United States, report on the meetings. And I think that's a better thing to do. If there are things that we haven't been able to agree on, let's be willing to say it, but say we'll keep on trying—but not have a communique which all too often seems to want to gloss over the things that weren't accomplished.

Q. So, how will we know whether you have failed or succeeded? Will it be whether you have managed to set up another meeting?

The President. Well, I think it'll be on the basis of when I report, judgment of the outcome of the things that I will specify that were done or the things that were left undone or the things, then, that we've agreed to go on talking about.

Q. Sir, apparently, according to several reports, Mr. Shultz came back from Moscow with quite a bad impression of Mr. Gorbachev. Do you share that opinion?

The President. Now, who did you say came away with the——

Q. Mr. Shultz——

The President. Oh.

Q. ——according to several reports——

The President. No, no, as a matter of fact, he told me that they kind of went at it and that he was argumentative and interrupted at times. But then he said he, [Secretary of State] George Shultz, interrupted also and found out that it wasn't resented, that it was that kind of a free-for-all discussion. And he said that he was very set in his ways—or I mean, about his views on the aims of his country and so forth. And, well, we're very set on ours.

Q. Mr. President, in the second debate with the then-candidate of the Democrats, Mr. Mondale, you said that, even possibly, you would share the results of the scientific research on SDI with the Russians in order to make the world safer. Do you still consider in doing that, finally?

The President. Maybe I didn't make it clear. That's what I meant in my earlier answer—not just share the scientific research with them. Let me give you my dream of what would happen. We have the weapon. We don't start deploying it. We get everybody together, and we say, "Here, here it is. And here's how it works and what it'll do to incoming missiles." Now, we think that all of us who have nuclear weapons should agree that we're going to eliminate the nuclear weapons. But we will make available to everyone this weapon. I don't mean we'll give it to them. They're going to have to pay for it—[*laughter*]—but at cost. But we would make this defensive weapon available.

Now, some can say, "Well, if you're going to do away with the nuclear offensive weapons, then, why does anyone need this?" Well, because we all know how to make it. And someday there may be a madman in the world, as there have been before, who would start in secretly to produce these weapons. But it's like when in Geneva in 1925 all the nations of the world after World War I got rid of poison gas—everybody kept their gas masks. Well, the same thing—this is kind of the gas mask thing. We could say, "Look, we'll never, any of us, have to fear that maybe some one of us cheating or maybe there is going to be that madman someday if we all have the ability to defend ourselves against nuclear missiles." And I think this would make far more sense than for us to say, "Oh, we found it. We'll go ahead and deploy it now while we still keep our other missiles." The world would have a right to expect that maybe we were thinking first blow.

Q. And if the Soviets don't share that view, what will happen?

The President. I certainly don't believe that we could stand by and let them veto our use or implementation of a defensive weapon.

Q. Mr. President, what's your feeling when some of your allies, France, but not only France, are either reluctant or openly opposed to the SDI? What can you tell them?

The President. Well, I think there was some misunderstanding about it and where we were going with it. And I know in the meetings up at New York, at the U.N. opening this time, there was a great change on the part of a number of them when I explained what our view of this was. And so I think that there is not that great opposition

to it. And a number of the countries where they, as governments, did not want to become involved, for whatever reasons they had, but would not object to their own scientists, their own private business firms and so forth, or industries getting involved and joining in with us in this research and development.

Q. Mr. President, on behalf of my colleagues here, I would like to thank you very much for granting us this interview and sharing your views just a week before your summit meeting in Geneva with the Soviet leader. Thank you very much, Mr. President.

The President. Well, I'm greatly honored that you all wanted to do this, and thank you very much. I appreciate it.

Q. Thank you.

Note: The interview began at 2:30 p.m. in the East Room at the White House.

Proclamation 5407—High Blood Pressure Awareness Week, 1985
November 12, 1985

By the President of the United States of America

A Proclamation

High blood pressure is a disease that affects as many as 60 million Americans and is a major contributing factor in 1.25 million heart attacks and half a million strokes that take place every year in the United States. More than half a million of those who have a heart attack will die this year, and the economic cost to the Nation in direct medical costs, lost work days, and lost production is estimated to be in excess of ten billion dollars annually.

There are many encouraging signs that we are making progress in bringing this disease under control. The death rates from heart attacks and stroke have been declining dramatically over the past decade and more. From 1972 to 1984, for example, the death rate for heart attack dropped by 33 percent, and for stroke by 48 percent.

At least one of the factors responsible for this decline is an enhanced awareness

among the medical profession and the public of the dangers of high blood pressure and the steps that must be taken to control it. This growing awareness has been brought about with the assistance of the National High Blood Pressure Education Program, a coordinated effort involving the Federal government; community volunteer organizations; medical associations; industry and labor; State and local public health agencies, and many other groups. Since the program began in 1972, public understanding of high blood pressure, the number of people being treated, and the number of those effectively controlling their high blood pressure has increased considerably.

Often called the "silent killer" because it usually has no easily detectable symptoms, high blood pressure is an insidious condition that may lead to heart attack, stroke, or kidney damage. It is one of three major risk factors, along with cigarette smoking and elevated blood cholesterol, for cardiovascular diseases. All of these factors can be controlled or eliminated.

High blood pressure can be detected using the familiar inflatable arm cuff and stethoscope. The test takes only a few moments and is painless. Once detected, high blood pressure can be very effectively controlled. Sometimes this can be accomplished by such measures as weight loss, salt restriction, and exercise. When these do not work, the physician can select an appropriate treatment program from a wide range of drug therapies.

I urge all Americans to take advantage of the high blood pressure screening activities in their communities, their work places, and their public health facilities. They should ask their physicians how often they should have a blood pressure check. All Americans should be aware of the dangers of this very widespread condition and they should also know that these dangers can be eliminated by proven methods.

To stimulate awareness among Americans of the importance of having their blood pressure measured, the Congress, by Senate Joint Resolution 130, has designated the week beginning November 10, 1985, as "High Blood Pressure Awareness Week" and authorized and requested the President to issue a proclamation in observance of this week.

Now, Therefore, I, Ronald Reagan, President of the United States of America, do hereby proclaim the week beginning November 10, 1985, as High Blood Pressure Awareness Week. I invite the American people to join with me in reaffirming our commitment to the resolution of the problem of high blood pressure.

In Witness Whereof, I have hereunto set my hand this 12th day of November, in the year of our Lord nineteen hundred and eighty-five, and of the Independence of the United States of America the two hundred and tenth.

RONALD REAGAN

[*Filed with the Office of the Federal Register, 11:03 a.m., November 13, 1985*]

Statement by Principal Deputy Press Secretary Speakes on the Failure of Congress To Pass Appropriations and National Debt Ceiling Bills
November 13, 1985

Because of failure by Congress to act on appropriations bills and on legislation to raise the ceiling on the national debt, our country faces an unprecedented crisis in our history. It is an unnecessary crisis, and it can be avoided. But the President cannot stand by and wait for the worst to happen, including dishonoring the Government's checks.

We cannot avoid some serious damage. However, to mitigate the problem, the President has authorized the Director of the Office of Management and Budget, Jim Miller, to instruct the Federal agencies, starting Friday, to stop issuing any new checks if the debt ceiling is not raised by then. The Government would continue to function, but it would temporarily stop paying its bills—to vendors, to its own employees, to individuals receiving government benefits, to State and local governments—until this crisis is resolved. We are not going to issue checks that will bounce.

The hardship this will cause would be solely the result of congressional failure to do what everyone knows is necessary. We trust that Congress will understand the consequences of its inaction.

Note: Larry M. Speakes read the statement to reporters at 10:50 a.m. in the Briefing Room at the White House.

Nomination of John C. Layton To Be Inspector General of the Department of Energy
November 13, 1985

The President today announced his intention to nominate John C. Layton to be Inspector General of the Department of Energy. He would succeed James R. Richards.

Since 1984 Mr. Layton has been Inspector General of the Department of the Treasury. Previously, he was Deputy Inspector General of the National Aeronautics and Space Administration (NASA) in 1983–1984; OIG Center Director, NASA Office of Inspector General, in 1982–1983; regional director of investigations, NASA Office of Inspector General, in 1980–1982; and on the investigative staff of the U.S. Senate Committee on Appropriations in 1972–1980.

Mr. Layton graduated from Rider College (B.A., 1966). He was born October 9, 1944, in East Stroudsburg, PA, and now resides in Woodbridge, VA.

Appointment of Kathleen Osborne as Special Assistant to the President
November 13, 1985

The President today announced the appointment of Kathleen Osborne to be Special Assistant to the President. Ms. Osborne will remain in the personal office of the President, where she has served as his personal secretary for 4 years, and will continue carrying out her duties in that capacity.

While President Reagan was Governor of California, Ms. Osborne was assistant personal secretary to the Governor for approximately 2 years and was also personal secretary to the First Lady of California, Mrs. Ronald Reagan, for approximately 2 years. In 1975 she opened her own business, a ladies apparel store, in Sacramento, CA, and managed it until she was appointed in October 1981 to be the President's personal secretary. Ms. Osborne closed her business in December 1984.

A native of Sacramento, CA, Ms. Osborne currently resides in Arlington, VA, with her 11-year-old daughter, Shelley. Her 18-year-old son, Scott, is a freshman in college in Sacramento, CA.

Appointment of Linas J. Kojelis as Special Assistant to the President for Public Liaison
November 13, 1985

The President today announced the appointment of Linas J. Kojelis as Special Assistant to the President for Public Liaison. Mr. Kojelis will head the division of foreign policy and defense issues in the Office of Public Liaison. He has served 2½ years as Associate Director in the same office.

In 1981–1983 Mr. Kojelis served at the Department of Defense in the Office of European and NATO Affairs in the Office of International Security Policy. In 1981 he served on the staff of the Assistant to the President for Political Affairs. Before joining the administration, Mr. Kojelis was a legislative assistant for former Pennsylvania Senator Richard S. Schweiker (R–PA).

Mr. Kojelis received his bachelor's degree in history (highest departmental honors) and economics at the University of California, Los Angeles (1976). He earned a master of public affairs degree, specializing in international relations, from the Woodrow Wilson School of Public and International Affairs at Princeton University in 1978, where he was a McConnel Foundation fellow. A native of Los Angeles, CA, Mr. Kojelis currently resides in the District of Columbia.

Appointment of Nancy J. Risque as Deputy Assistant to the President for Legislative Affairs
November 13, 1985

The President today announced his intention to appoint Nancy J. Risque to be Deputy Assistant to the President for Legislative Affairs.

Ms. Risque has served as Special Assistant to the President for Legislative Affairs since 1982 and currently serves as Deputy Director of the Office of Legislative Affairs. She was designated a member of the U.S. delegation to the World Conference To Review and Appraise the Achievements of the United Nations Decade for Women, which was held last July in Nairobi, Kenya. Ms. Risque is also a member of the President's Interagency Committee on Women's Business Enterprise.

Ms. Risque has been with the Reagan administration since January 1981. Previously, she was a government affairs representative for private industry; a Ford administration appointee at the Commerce Department; and a publicist. She also worked in program and campaign development for the Republican Party. She has a bachelor of arts degree from Radford College and currently resides in Virginia.

Statement on Signing the Fair Labor Standards Amendments of 1985
November 13, 1985

Today I have signed S. 1570, the "Fair Labor Standards Amendments of 1985." This law once again permits State and local governments and their employees the flexibility to serve their citizens effectively. It is the culmination of a vigorous effort by State and local governments, their employees, and a bipartisan coalition in the Congress. All these efforts have had the strong support of my administration. While this law does not fully restore State and local governments to the position they held prior to the Supreme Court's decision in *Garcia* v. *San Antonio Metropolitan Transit Authority*, it does recognize, in significant measure, their special burdens, responsibilities, and character.

Without this legislation, the cost of services that State and local governments provide—police, firefighters, and other services necessary to the success of any community—would have increased by as much as $3 billion per year. The new law provides important relief to State and local governments, their employees, and all American taxpayers. The law contains an effective date of April 15, 1986, eliminating the unexpected back pay liability for overtime pay dating from the court's decision. It enables all State and local governments to accept offers of voluntary service from civic-minded citizens, and it allows the continuation of a longstanding practice by legitimizing the use of compensatory time as a substitute for cash in paying overtime hours.

Although real improvement has been brought about by this legislation, I believe the constitutional principles of federalism must be recognized so that limits are placed on Federal regulation of State and local governments in a manner consistent with their special status in our system of government. In this and in other regards, federalism will remain a major priority of my administration.

I commend all those officials and workers in State and local governments and all those in the Congress who worked to secure this much-needed legislative success. Secretary of Labor William Brock; Attorney General Edwin Meese III; Senators Orrin Hatch, Don Nickles, Howard Metzenbaum, and Pete Wilson; Representatives Gus Hawkins, Jim Jeffords, Austin Murphy, Tom Petri, and Steve Bartlett all provided essential leadership. I am especially grateful to Senator Nickles, whose early leadership and hard work were essential to the enactment of the legislation.

Note: The President signed the bill at 2:30 p.m. at a ceremony in the Oval Office at the White House. S. 1570, approved November 13, was assigned Public Law No. 99–150.

Proclamation 5408—National Diabetes Month, 1985
November 13, 1985

By the President of the United States of America

A Proclamation

Each year, an estimated 500,000 more Americans are told by their physicians that they have diabetes. This chronic disease interferes with the body's ability to derive energy from glucose, a type of sugar and an important product of digested food. When diabetes strikes children, it is in a form that can soon be fatal without daily injections of the life-saving hormone insulin. Most people with diabetes have another form of the disease that begins in adulthood and that, over the years, can insidiously and progressively damage the heart, eyes, kidneys, and nervous system.

The acute illness and long-term complications of diabetes cost the country an estimated $14 billion each year in medical outlays, disability payments, and loss of income. Individuals and families suffer an inestimable drain on their emotional and economic resources in coping with this disease.

Hope for the future lies in research. In recent years, scientists have laid the groundwork for an eventual cure for diabetes. Basic research has provided the tools with which scientists are describing the genetic, immunologic and biochemical mechanisms that underlie diabetes. Through research, we now know that diabetes has multiple causes, and scientists are developing the means to understand and correct these defects in ways specific to each cause. Research is also clarifying how best to treat diabetes. This research, along with efforts to transmit the most up-to-the-minute knowledge to health practitioners and to individuals who might be affected by diabetes, is helping to preserve the health of its potential victims.

Only through the continued commitment and cooperation of the Federal government, the scientific community, and the private agencies and citizens dedicated to the fight against diabetes can progress continue.

To increase public awareness of diabetes and to emphasize the need for continued research and educational efforts aimed at controlling and one day curing this disease, the Congress, by Senate Joint Resolution 145, has designated the month of November 1985 as "National Diabetes Month" and authorized and requested the President to issue a proclamation in observance of this month.

Now, Therefore, I, Ronald Reagan, President of the United States of America, do hereby proclaim the month of November 1985 as National Diabetes Month. I call upon all government agencies and the people of the United States to observe this month with appropriate programs and activities.

In Witness Whereof, I have hereunto set my hand this thirteenth day of November, in the year of our Lord nineteen hundred and eighty-five, and of the Independence of the United States of America the two hundred and tenth.

RONALD REAGAN

[*Filed with the Office of the Federal Register, 10:23 a.m., November 14, 1985*]

Proclamation 5409—National Women Veterans Recognition Week, 1985
November 13, 1985

By the President of the United States of America

A Proclamation

We Americans are justly indebted to all who have served in uniform in the cause of our national defense. It is an honor for me to invite special attention to the unique contributions made to that cause by women veterans.

Throughout our Nation's history, American women have answered duty's call, even when that call exacted a great price. Many women have become casualties in their country's service, and countless more have suffered family disruptions and dislocations caused by commitments to the armed services.

The nearly 1.2 million women veterans living in the United States today have contributed immeasurably to restoring and maintaining the peace. Their performance in a wide range of demanding specialties in all branches of service has been in the proudest traditions of our Armed Forces, and it is altogether fitting that we as a Nation pause to express our appreciation.

The Congress, by Senate Joint Resolution 47, has designated the week beginning November 10, 1985, as "National Women Veterans Recognition Week" and authorized and requested the President to issue a proclamation in observance of that week.

Now, Therefore, I, Ronald Reagan, President of the United States of America, do hereby proclaim the week beginning November 10, 1985, as National Women Veterans Recognition Week. I call upon the American people, the Federal government, and State and local governments to celebrate this week with appropriate observances.

In Witness Whereof, I have hereunto set my hand this thirteenth day of November, in the year of our Lord nineteen hundred and eighty-five, and of the Independence of the United States of America the two hundred and tenth.

RONALD REAGAN

[*Filed with the Office of the Federal Register, 10:24 a.m., November 14, 1985*]

Nomination of C. Dale Duvall To Be Commissioner of the Bureau of Reclamation
November 13, 1985

The President today announced his intention to nominate C. Dale Duvall to be Commissioner of Reclamation, Department of the Interior. He would succeed Robert N.

Broadbent.

Mr. Duvall is presently serving as Secretary-Treasurer of the Overseas Private Investment Corporation. Previously, he served as White House liaison at the Community Services Administration in 1981 and before that as a member of the staff in the office of the President-elect (1980–1981).

From 1965 to 1980, he was partner and managing partner at Morris, Lee & Co. in Spokane, WA.

Mr. Duvall graduated from Kinman Business University, Spokane, WA, in 1960. He is married, has four children, and resides in Arlington, VA. He was born May 11, 1933, in Spokane, WA.

Nomination of David M.L. Lindahl To Be Director of the Office of Alcohol Fuels
November 13, 1985

The President today announced his intention to nominate David M.L. Lindahl to be Director of the Office of Alcohol Fuels, Department of Energy. He would succeed James G. Sterns.

Since 1972 Mr. Lindahl has been serving at the Congressional Research Service, Library of Congress, as a specialist in energy policy. Previously, he was Federal representative for the National Petroleum Council in 1978–1980; Assistant Director for Research and Analysis, Office of Energy Transportation, Department of Energy (1978). Since 1973 he has also served as a consultant to the National Geographic Society.

Mr. Lindahl graduated from the University of Indiana (B.Sc., 1967) and Western Michigan University (M.A., 1968). He is married, has two children, and resides in Springfield, VA. He was born August 6, 1944, in Fort Wayne, IN.

Message to the Congress Reporting on the National Emergency With Respect to Iran
November 13, 1985

To the Congress of the United States:

Pursuant to Section 204(c) of the International Emergency Economic Powers Act (IEEPA), 50 U.S.C. Section 1703(c), I hereby report to the Congress with respect to developments since my last report of April 22, 1985, concerning the national emergency with respect to Iran that was declared in Executive Order No. 12170 of November 14, 1979.

1. The Iran-United States Claims Tribunal, established at The Hague pursuant to the Claims Settlement Agreement of January 19, 1981 (the "Algiers Accords"), continues to make progress in arbitrating the claims before it. Since my last report, the Tribunal has rendered 25 more decisions, for a total of 194 final decisions. Of these, 146 have been awards in favor of American claimants; 101 were awards on agreed terms, authorizing and approving payment of settlements negotiated by the parties; and 45 were adjudicated decisions. As of October 15, 1985, total payments to successful American claimants from the Security Account stood at approximately $368 million. In cases between the governments, the Tribunal has issued two decisions in favor of each government, dismissed one claim that had been filed by the United States, and dismissed four claims that had been filed by Iran. In addition, Iran has withdrawn fifteen of its government-to-gov-

ernment claims, while the United States has withdrawn only three.

2. My last report noted various changes in the composition of the Tribunal, including the designation of Karl-Heinz Bockstiegel as President of the Tribunal and Chairman of Chamber One. During the past six months, Swiss lawyer Robert Briner and French law professor Michel Virally have assumed their new positions as Chairmen of Chambers Two and Three, respectively. Shortly before Messrs. Briner and Virally assumed their new positions, Tribunal proceedings had been briefly disrupted because of travel difficulties allegedly encountered by Iranian respondents in connection with the Iran-Iraq war. With these alleged difficulties having abated, and the two new arbitrators having assumed their roles as Chairmen, the Tribunal has resumed normal operations.

3. The Tribunal continues to make progress in the arbitration of claims of U.S. nationals for $250,000 or more. More than 36 percent of the claims for over $250,000 have now been disposed of through adjudication, settlement, or voluntary withdrawal, leaving 330 such claims on the docket. The Tribunal issued long-awaited orders in claims involving dual United States-Iranian nationals, allowing these claimants to resume actively arbitrating their claims by demonstrating their dominant and effective U.S. nationality. The Chambers have also made significant awards to several American claimants, including a $7.3 million contested award to Sylvania Technical Systems, Inc. The *Sylvania* decision also purports to set forth a uniform standard for awarding interest in Tribunal cases. In another important decision, the Tribunal decided that, at least in the context of that case, the Treaty of Amity, Economic Relations and Consular Rights between Iran and the United States governs the standard of compensation in claims for expropriation of property, and determined that the claimant in that case was entitled to recover the fair market value of the going concern that had been expropriated by Iran. Settlement discussions continue to proceed between numerous American claimants and Iranian respondents.

4. The Tribunal has made significant progress in the arbitration of the claims of U.S. nationals against Iran of less than $250,000 each. As described in my last report, in addition to 18 test cases, the Tribunal has selected 100 other claims for active arbitration. As of October 15, 1985, the Department of State had submitted Supplemental Statements of Claim in 85 of these claims, containing more than 25,000 pages of text and evidence. Additional pleadings are being filed weekly. Although Iran repeatedly seeks extensions of time within which to file its responsive pleadings to these claims, the Tribunal has continued to press for their resolution. At the Tribunal, three senior legal officers and a law clerk work exclusively on these claims. The first three test case hearings have been set for December, and six additional cases have been set for hearing during the spring of 1986. The Department of State remains optimistic that the Tribunal will issue its first decision in a fully arbitrated small claim in early 1986. Finally, since my last report, another two small claimants have received awards on agreed terms, bringing the total to twelve.

5. The Department of State continues to coordinate the efforts of concerned governmental agencies in presenting U.S. claims against Iran as well as responses by the U.S. Government to claims brought against it by Iran. Since my last report, the Department has filed pleadings in six government-to-government claims based on contracts for the provision of goods and services. The Tribunal held one hearing in a major contract dispute on whether it could hear approximately 1,500 cases under the Iranian Foreign Military Sales Program closed before October 1, 1978.

In addition to work on the government-to-government claims, the Department of State, working together with the Department of the Treasury and the Department of Justice, filed five pleadings in disputes concerning the interpretation and/or performance of various provisions of the Algiers Accords. The Tribunal issued one significant decision in an interpretive dispute, ruling that—subject to a limited exception, which Iran has stated does not apply to any of its claims—the Tribunal lacks jurisdiction over claims brought by Iran against U.S. banks for allegedly unpaid deposits and for interest on transferred deposits. This, together with the Tribunal's earlier decision that it lacked jurisdiction over standby letter of credit claims asserted by Iran against U.S. banks, has resulted in the dismissal of more than 400 of Iran's claims against such banks.

Since my last report, Iran has initiated two new interpretive disputes. The first concerns the purported obligation of the U.S. Government to satisfy Tribunal awards issued in favor of Iran against private U.S. claimants. The second concerns the Tribunal's jurisdiction over indirect claims for losses incurred by corporations (and similar entities) that lack U.S. nationality, but which are controlled by U.S. nationals. The Department of State is now preparing responsive pleadings in both these proceedings.

6. The Algiers Accords also provide for direct negotiations between U.S. banks and Bank Markazi Iran concerning the payment from Dollar Account No. 2 (the interest-bearing escrow account established at the Bank of England in January 1981 with the deposit of $1.418 billion of previously blocked Iranian funds) of nonsyndicated debt claims of U.S. banks against Iran. Since my last report, Continental Illinois National Bank and Trust Company of Chicago reached a settlement with Iran, bringing to 30 the total number of bank settlements involving payments from Dollar Account No. 2. About 16 banks have yet to settle their claims. In addition, a number of those banks that have already reached settlements with Iran have reserved claims against Dollar Account No. 2.

As mentioned in my previous report, attorneys from the Department of the Treasury and the Federal Reserve Bank of New York have been negotiating an "Agreed Clarification" with Bank Markazi to allow for the payment from Dollar Account No. 2 of certain amounts still owing on Iran's syndicated debt. Agreement on the text of this "Agreed Clarification" was reached in June, and Treasury instructed the Federal Reserve Bank of New York, as fiscal agent of the United States, to sign the document; however, the Bank Markazi representatives

were not prepared to sign. They claimed the delay was due to the need to obtain additional formal clearances in Tehran and that there was no substantive problem with the agreement. The Department of the Treasury is hopeful that the necessary approval in Tehran will be forthcoming.

7. There have been no changes in the Iranian Assets Control Regulations since my last report.

8. Pursuant to a June 7, 1982, Directive License from the Department of the Treasury, the Federal Reserve Bank of New York had been deducting two percent from amounts received from the Security Account in satisfaction of awards rendered by the Tribunal in favor of U.S. claimants. The purpose of the deduction was to reimburse the U.S. Government for a portion of the expenses incurred in connection with the arbitration of claims of U.S. persons against Iran before the Tribunal and the maintenance of the Security Account from which such claims are paid. In ordering the deduction of this user fee, Treasury relied solely on the authority of the Independent Offices Appropriation Act (the "IOAA"). The amounts deducted, which as of August 16, 1985, totaled $7.3 million, had been paid into the Treasury as miscellaneous receipts. Last May, in a case brought by Sperry Corporation, the U.S. Claims Court issued a bench ruling holding that the two percent fee did not comply with the requirements of the IOAA and hence was invalid. No judgment has yet been issued, and, in light of the new legislation described below, it is unlikely that one will be issued.

On August 16, 1985, the President signed the Foreign Relations Authorization Act for Fiscal Years 1986 and 1987, Public Law 99–93, Title V of which deals with claims against Iran. Section 502 of this legislation directs the Federal Reserve Bank of New York to deduct one and one-half percent from the first $5 million awarded on each claim paid from the Security Account, and one percent from any amount over $5 million, and to deposit the amounts deducted into the Treasury to the credit of miscellaneous receipts. The constitutionality of this legislation has been challenged, however, in a continuation of the litigation by Sperry.

By its terms, Section 502 is effective as of June 7, 1982. Consequently, the Department of the Treasury is in the process of refunding to those claimants that have received awards paid from the Security Account the difference between the two percent fee already deducted and the one and one-half/one percent fee authorized by Section 502 of Public Law 99–93. These refunds will total approximately $2.6 million.

Title V of Public Law 99–93 also grants standby authority to the Foreign Claims Settlement Commission to determine the validity and amounts of any claims against Iran that are settled en bloc by the United States and Iran, and provides certain limited exceptions to the disclosure provisions of the Freedom of Information Act for Tribunal-related documents within the possession of the U.S. Government.

9. Financial and diplomatic aspects of the relationship with Iran continue to present an unusual challenge to the national security and foreign policy of the United States. In particular, the Iranian Assets Control Regulations, issued pursuant to Executive Order No. 12170, continue to play an important role in regulating that relationship and in enabling the United States properly to implement the Algiers Accords. I shall continue to exercise the powers at my disposal to deal with these problems and will continue to report periodically to the Congress on significant developments.

RONALD REAGAN

The White House,
November 13, 1985.

Statement Following a Meeting With the United States Delegation to the Nuclear and Space Arms Negotiations With the Soviet Union
November 14, 1985

I met today with the senior American negotiators at the Geneva nuclear and space arms talks, Ambassadors Max Kampelman, John Tower, and Maynard Glitman. The meeting provided an opportunity for our chief negotiators to brief me on the just concluded round of negotiations in Geneva and on their perspectives for future developments in the talks.

This past round in Geneva, the third in the negotiations which began this past March, has been useful. It was marked by the Soviet presentation, in late September, of a counterproposal to the concrete reductions offers which the U.S. had put forward at the outset of the talks. Drawing on the counsel of our negotiating team and of our experts in Washington, we analyzed this Soviet counteroffer very carefully, making clear both its positive elements and the areas in which it fell seriously short of the criteria which we have established for an effective and equitable arms reduction agreement. As I have emphasized before, these necessary criteria are deep cuts; no first-strike advantages; research on defense,

because defense is much safer than offense; and no cheating—that is to say, full compliance.

Building upon these criteria, as well as the positive seeds in the Soviet counterproposal, I instructed, on November 1, our negotiators to table a new set of proposals in Geneva. These new U.S. proposals cover all three areas of the negotiations: strategic nuclear arms, intermediate nuclear forces, and defense and space arms. These new developments in the Geneva negotiations demonstrate that a serious give-and-take process can now take place. We welcome this, and we are determined to do our part to bring about the real nuclear reductions that the world desires and deserves. If there is equal determination and flexibility on the Soviet part, this can be done. I therefore hope that my coming meeting with General Secretary Gorbachev will give further momentum to this process.

Finally, I expressed the gratitude of all Americans to Ambassadors Kampelman, Tower, and Glitman for their highly professional and very patient negotiating efforts in Geneva, and my own appreciation for the wise counsel they have provided to me. Their continued efforts and advice will be vital in the days and months ahead, as we strive for radical, equitable, and verifiable cuts in nuclear arms.

Appointment of Joseph A. Latham, Jr., as Staff Director of the Commission on Civil Rights
November 14, 1985

The President today announced his intention to appoint Joseph A. Latham, Jr., to be Staff Director of the Commission on Civil Rights. He will succeed Linda Chavez Gersten.

Since 1983 Mr. Latham has been serving as Chief Counsel at the National Labor Relations Board. Previously he was an attorney with the law firm of Paul, Hastings, Janofsky and Walker of Atlanta, GA, and Los Angeles, CA, in 1976–1983.

He graduated from Yale University (B.A., 1973) and Vanderbilt University (J.D., 1976). He is married and resides in Alexandria, VA. He was born September 16, 1951, in Kinston, NC.

Nomination of Thomas A. Bolan To Be a Member of the Board of Directors of the Overseas Private Investment Corporation
November 14, 1985

The President today announced his intention to nominate Thomas A. Bolan to be a member of the Board of Directors of the Overseas Private Investment Corporation, United States International Development Cooperation Agency, for a term expiring December 17, 1988. This is a reappointment.

Mr. Bolan has been a member of the Board of Directors of the Overseas Private Investment Corporation since March 2, 1982. He is counsel to the law firm of Saxe, Bacon, and Bolan in New York City. He joined the firm, then Saxe, Bacon and O'Shea, in 1959 as an associate and became a partner in 1960 and counsel in 1972.

He graduated from St. John's University (B.A., LL.D.). He is married, has five children, and resides in Flushing, NY. He was born May 30, 1924, in Lynn, MA.

Designation of John R. Trice as a Member of the Board of Governors of the United Service Organizations, Incorporated
November 14, 1985

The President today announced his intention to designate John R. Trice to be a member of the Board of Governors of the United Service Organizations, Inc., for a term of 3 years. This is a reappointment.

Mr. Trice is in the private practice of law in Carrollton, TX. He is a member of the Reserve Officers Association of the United States and serves on the national executive committee and the building committee. He is former chairman of the Central Texas Salvation Army Advisory Committee and former member of the board of directors of the Dallas County Mental Health Association.

He has two children and resides in Carrollton, TX. He was born September 28, 1932, in Houston, TX.

Appointment of Carol A. Morrow as a Delegate to the National White House Conference on Small Business
November 14, 1985

The President today announced his intention to appoint Carol A. Morrow to be a delegate to the National White House Conference on Small Business. This is a new position.

Ms. Morrow is owner of C&M Consultants, real estate consultants, in Burbank, CA. Previously she was vice president of Betty Zane Corp. in San Dimas, CA. Ms. Morrow has also served on the board of trustees of the California Agriculture Foundation.

She graduated from the University of Alabama (B.A., 1962). She has one child and resides in Burbank, CA. She was born September 10, 1939, in Miami, FL.

Appointment of Susan Schiffer Stautberg as a Member of the Commission on Presidential Scholars
November 14, 1985

The President today announced his intention to appoint Susan Schiffer Stautberg to be a member of the Commission on Presidential Scholars. This is a new position.

Mrs. Stautberg is director of communications for Touche Ross & Co. in New York City. Previously, she served as executive assistant to the president of Morgan Stanley & Co. in 1980–1982; vice president of Fraser Associates, Washington, DC, in 1980; director of communications, McNeil Consumer Products Co., in Fort Washington, PA, in 1978–1980; and Director of Communications, U.S. Consumer Product Safety Commission, in 1976–1978. She was a White House fellow in 1974–1975.

Mrs. Stautberg graduated from Wheaton College (B.A., 1967) and George Washington University (M.A., 1970). She is married, has one child, and resides in New York, NY. She was born November 9, 1946, in Bryn Mawr, PA.

Appointment of Four Members of the National Advisory Council on Continuing Education
November 14, 1985

The President today announced his intention to appoint the following individuals to be members of the National Advisory Council on Continuing Education for terms expiring September 30, 1988:

Richard O. Brinkman is a reappointment. He is president emeritus, Clark Technical College, in Springfield, OH. Mr. Brinkman has also served as president of the Ohio College Association. He is married, has two children, and resides in Springfield, OH. Mr. Brinkman graduated from Wittenberg University (B.A.), Kent State University (M.A.), and the Harvard Institute for Educational Management. He was born February 8, 1926, in Springfield, OH.

Morris Hadley Mills is a reappointment. He is currently a State senator in Indianapolis, IN, (1973-present) and a partner in Mills Brothers Farms (1962-present). Since 1973 Mr. Mills has served on higher education, secondary, and elementary committees in the Indiana senate. Mr. Mills is married, has three children, and resides in Indianapolis, IN. He was born September 25, 1927, in West Newton, IN.

Indiana Retana would succeed W. Hughes Brockbank. She has been president of Conroy's Florist in Bell, CA, since 1982. Previously, Ms. Retana has worked in management capacities with the engineering firms of EON Corp.

(1977–1979) and Bechtel Corp. (1972–1975). She graduated from West Los Angeles College, 1980. Ms. Retana has one child and resides in Los Angeles, CA. She was born May 6, 1949, in Managua, Nicaragua.

Donald L. Smith would succeed David O. Martin. He is currently an assemblyman in Anchorage, AK (1975-present); owner of a printing business; and publisher of the Alaska Register. He served as a representative in the State legislature in 1965–1969. Mr. Smith has four children and resides in Anchorage, AK. He was born March 14, 1939, in Anchorage, AK.

Nomination of Truman McGill Hobbs To Be a Member of the Harry S. Truman Scholarship Foundation
November 14, 1985

The President today announced his intention to nominate Truman McGill Hobbs to be a member of the Harry S. Truman Scholarship Foundation for a term expiring December 10, 1991. This is a reappointment.

Since 1980 Mr. Hobbs has been serving as U.S. District Judge for the Middle District of Alabama. Previously he had a private law practice in Alabama, 1949–1980, and during that time he served as president of the Ala-

bama Bar Association, 1970–1971; the Montgomery Bar Association, 1965–1966; and the Alabama Trial Lawyers Association, 1964–1965.

Mr. Hobbs graduated from the University of North Carolina at Chapel Hill (1942) and Yale Law School (LL.B., 1948). He is married, has four children, and resides in Montgomery, AL. Mr. Hobbs was born February 8, 1921, in Selma, AL.

Letter to Congressional Leaders Transmitting a Report on the Central American Conflict
November 14, 1985

Dear Mr. Speaker: (Dear Mr. President:) (Dear Mr. Chairman:)

The enclosed report is transmitted in compliance with the requirements of Section 722(j) of the International Security and Development Cooperation Act of 1985 (P.L. 99–83), and Section 104 of Chapter V of the Supplemental Appropriations Act, 1985 (P.L. 99–88).

The report, with appropriate background, describes efforts by the United States and others, including developments in the Contadora process, to promote a negotiated settlement in Central America and Nicaragua;

alleged human rights violations by the democratic resistance and the Government of Nicaragua; and disbursement of humanitarian assistance to the democratic resistance (with a classified annex).

During the period covered by the report, the Sandinistas have continued their refusal to engage in dialogue with the democratic opposition and have adopted an intransigent position in Contadora negotiations. The October 15 suspension of civil liberties dramatically reflected the Sandinistas' continued repression of human rights and their desire to silence their opponents rather than pursue internal reconciliation.

The events of the ninety days covered by the attached report clearly show the need for continued support for the Nicaraguan democratic resistance. Only it can provide the sharp pressure needed to move the Sandinistas toward serious negotiations and prevent the consolidation of a totalitarian state allied with Cuba and the Soviet bloc in Central America.

An identical letter with a copy of the attached report has also been forwarded to the President of the Senate and the Chairmen of the Senate and House Select Committees on Intelligence.

Sincerely,

RONALD REAGAN

Note: Identical letters were sent to Thomas P. O'Neill, Jr., Speaker of the House of Representatives; George Bush, President of the Senate; Barry Goldwater, chairman of the Senate Select Committee on Intelligence; and Edward P. Boland, chairman of the House Permanent Select Committee on Intelligence.

Address to the Nation on the Upcoming Soviet-United States Summit Meeting in Geneva
November 14, 1985

My fellow Americans:

Good evening. In 36 hours I will be leaving for Geneva for the first meeting between an American President and a Soviet leader in 6 years. I know that you and the people of the world are looking forward to that meeting with great interest, so tonight I want to share with you my hopes and tell you why I am going to Geneva.

My mission, stated simply, is a mission for peace. It is to engage the new Soviet leader in what I hope will be a dialog for peace that endures beyond my Presidency. It is to sit down across from Mr. Gorbachev and try to map out, together, a basis for peaceful discourse even though our disagreements on fundamentals will not change. It is my fervent hope that the two of us can begin a process which our successors and our peoples can continue—facing our differences frankly and openly and beginning to narrow and resolve them; communicating effectively so that our actions and intentions are not misunderstood; and eliminating the barriers between us and cooperating wherever possible for the greater good of all.

This meeting can be an historic opportunity to set a steady, more constructive course to the 21st century. The history of American-Soviet relations, however, does not augur well for euphoria. Eight of my predecessors—each in his own way in his own time—sought to achieve a more stable and peaceful relationship with the Soviet Union. None fully succeeded; so, I don't underestimate the difficulty of the task ahead. But these sad chapters do not relieve me of the obligation to try to make this a safer, better world. For our children, our grandchildren, for all mankind—I intend to make the effort. And with your prayers and God's help, I hope to succeed. Success at the summit, however, should not be measured by any short-term agreements that may be signed. Only the passage of time will tell us whether we constructed a durable bridge to a safer world. This, then, is why I go to Geneva—to build a foundation for lasting peace.

When we speak of peace, we should not mean just the absence of war. True peace rests on the pillars of individual freedom, human rights, national self-determination, and respect for the rule of law. Building a safer future requires that we address candidly all the issues which divide us and not just focus on one or two issues, important as they may be. When we meet in Geneva, our agenda will seek not just to avoid war, but to strengthen peace, prevent confrontation, and remove the sources of tension. We should seek to reduce the suspicions and mistrust that have led us to acquire mountains of strategic weapons. Since the dawn of the nuclear age, every American President has sought to limit and end the dangerous competition in nuclear arms. I have no higher priority than to finally realize that dream. I've said before, I will say again: A nuclear war cannot be won and must never be fought. We've gone the extra mile in arms control, but our offers have not always been welcome.

In 1977 and again in 1982, the United States proposed to the Soviet Union deep reciprocal cuts in strategic forces. These offers were rejected out-of-hand. In 1981 we proposed the complete elimination of a whole category of intermediate-range nuclear forces. Three years later, we proposed a treaty for a global ban on chemical weapons. In 1983 the Soviet Union got up and walked out of the Geneva nuclear arms control negotiations altogether. They did this in protest because we and our European allies had begun to deploy nuclear weapons as a counter to Soviet SS–20's aimed at our European and other allies. I'm pleased now, however, with the interest expressed in reducing offensive weapons by the new Soviet leadership. Let me repeat tonight what I announced last week. The United States is prepared to reduce comparable nuclear systems by 50 percent. We seek reductions that will result in a stable balance between us with no first-strike capability and verified full compliance. If we both reduce the weapons of war there would be no losers, only winners. And the whole world would benefit if we could both abandon these weapons altogether and move to nonnuclear defensive systems that threaten no one.

But nuclear arms control is not of itself a final answer. I told four Soviet political commentators 2 weeks ago that nations do not distrust each other because they're armed; they arm themselves because they distrust each other. The use of force, subversion, and terror has made the world a more dangerous place. And thus, today there's no peace in Afghanistan; no peace in Cambodia; no peace in Angola, Ethiopia, or Nicaragua. These wars have claimed hundreds of thousands of lives and threaten to spill over national frontiers. That's why in my address to the United Nations, I proposed a way to end these conflicts: a regional peace plan that calls for negotiations among the warring parties—withdrawal of all foreign troops, democratic reconciliation, and economic assistance.

Four times in my lifetime, our soldiers have been sent overseas to fight in foreign lands. Their remains can be found from Flanders Field to the islands of the Pacific. Not once were those young men sent abroad in the cause of conquest. Not once did they come home claiming a single square inch of some other country as a trophy of war. A great danger in the past, however, has been the failure by our enemies to remember that while we Americans detest war, we love freedom and stand ready to sacrifice for it. We love freedom not only because it's practical and beneficial but because it is morally right and just.

In advancing freedom, we Americans carry a special burden—a belief in the dignity of man in the sight of the God who gave birth to this country. This is central to our being. A century and a half ago, Thomas Jefferson told the world, "The mass of mankind has not been born with saddles on their backs . . . " Freedom is America's core. We must never deny it nor forsake it. Should the day come when we Americans remain silent in the face of armed aggression, then the cause of America, the cause of freedom, will have been lost and the great heart of this country will have been broken. This affirmation of freedom is not only our duty as Americans, it's essential for success at Geneva.

Freedom and democracy are the best guarantors of peace. History has shown that democratic nations do not start wars. The rights of the individual and the rule of law are as fundamental to peace as arms control. A government which does not respect its citizens' rights and its international commitments to protect those rights is not likely to respect its other international undertakings. And that's why we must and will speak in Geneva on behalf of those who cannot speak for themselves. We are not trying to impose our beliefs on others. We have a right to expect, however, that great states will live up to their international obligations.

Despite our deep and abiding differences, we can and must prevent our international competition from spilling over into violence. We can find, as yet undiscovered, avenues where American and Soviet citizens can cooperate fruitfully for the benefit of mankind. And this, too, is why I'm going to Geneva. Enduring peace requires openness, honest communications, and opportunities for our peoples to get to know one another directly. The United States has always stood for openness. Thirty years ago in Geneva, President Eisenhower, preparing for his first meeting with the then Soviet leader, made his Open Skies proposal and an offer of new educational and cultural exchanges with the Soviet Union. He recognized that removing the barriers between people is at the heart of our relationship. He said: "Restrictions on communications of all kinds, including radio and travel, existing in extreme form in some places, have operated as causes of mutual distrust. In America, the fervent belief in freedom of thought, of expression, and of movement is a vital part of our heritage."

Well, I have hopes that we can lessen the distrust between us, reduce the levels of secrecy, and bring forth a more open world. Imagine how much good we could accomplish, how the cause of peace would be served, if more individuals and families from our respective countries could come to know each other in a personal way. For example, if Soviet youth could attend American schools and universities, they could learn firsthand what spirit of freedom rules our land and that we do not wish the Soviet people any harm. If American youth could do likewise, they could talk about their interests and values and hopes for the future with their Soviet friends. They would get firsthand knowledge of life in the U.S.S.R., but most important, they would learn that we're all God's children with much in common. Imagine if people in our nation could see the Bolshoi Ballet again, while Soviet citizens could see American plays and hear groups like the Beach Boys. And how about Soviet children watching "Sesame Street."

We've had educational and cultural exchanges for 25 years and are now close to completing a new agreement. But I feel the time is ripe for us to take bold new steps to open the way for our peoples to participate in an unprecedented way in the building of peace. Why shouldn't I propose to Mr. Gorbachev at Geneva that we exchange many more of our citizens from fraternal, religious, educational, and cultural groups? Why not suggest the exchange of thousands of undergraduates each year, and even younger students who would live with a host family and attend schools or summer camps? We could look to increased scholarship programs, improve language studies, conduct courses in history, culture, and other subjects, develop new sister cities, establish libraries and cultural centers, and, yes, increase athletic competition. People of both our nations love sports. If we must compete, let it be on the playing fields and not the battlefields. In science and technology, we could launch new joint space ventures and establish joint medical research projects. In communications, we'd like to see more appearances in the other's mass media by representatives of both our countries. If Soviet spokesmen are free to appear on American television, to be published and read in the American press, shouldn't the Soviet people have the same right to see, hear, and read what we Americans have to say? Such proposals will not bridge our differences, but people-to-people contacts can build genuine constituencies for peace in both countries. After all, people don't start wars, governments do.

Let me summarize, then, the vision and hopes that we carry with us to Geneva. We go with an appreciation, born of experience, of the deep differences between us— between our values, our systems, our beliefs. But we also carry with us the determination not to permit those differences to erupt into confrontation or conflict. We do not threaten the Soviet people and never will. We go without illusion, but with hope, hope that progress can be made on our entire agenda. We believe that progress can be made in resolving the regional conflicts now burning on three continents, including our own hemisphere. The regional plan we proposed at the United Nations will be raised again at Geneva. We're proposing the broadest people-to-people exchanges in the history of American-Soviet relations, exchanges in sports and culture, in the media, education, and the arts. Such exchanges can build in our societies thousands of coalitions for cooperation and peace. Governments can only do so much. Once they get the ball rolling, they should step out of the way and let people get together to share, enjoy, help, listen, and learn from each other, especially young people.

Finally, we go to Geneva with the sober realization that nuclear weapons pose the greatest threat in human history to the survival of the human race, that the arms race must be stopped. We go determined to search out and discover common ground— where we can agree to begin the reduction, looking to the eventual elimination, of nuclear weapons from the face of the Earth. It is not an impossible dream that we can begin to reduce nuclear arsenals, reduce the risk of war, and build a solid foundation for peace. It is not an impossible dream that our children and grandchildren can someday travel freely back and forth between America and the Soviet Union; visit each other's homes; work and study together; enjoy and discuss plays, music, television, and root for teams when they compete.

These, then, are the indispensable elements of a true peace: the steady expansion of human rights for all the world's peoples; support for resolving conflicts in Asia, Africa, and Latin America that carry the seeds of a wider war; a broadening of people-to-people exchanges that can diminish the distrust and suspicion that separate our two peoples; and the steady reduction of these awesome nuclear arsenals until they no longer threaten the world we both must inhabit. This is our agenda for Geneva; this is our policy; this is our plan for peace.

We have cooperated in the past. In both world wars, Americans and Russians fought on separate fronts against a common enemy. Near the city of Murmansk, sons of our own nation are buried, heroes who died of wounds sustained on the treacherous North Atlantic and North Sea convoys that carried to Russia the indispensable tools of

survival and victory. While it would be naive to think a single summit can establish a permanent peace, this conference can begin a dialog for peace. So, we look to the future with optimism, and we go to Geneva with confidence.

Both Nancy and I are grateful for the chance you've given us to serve this nation and the trust you've placed in us. I know how deep the hope of peace is in her heart, as it is in the heart of every American and Russian mother. I received a letter and picture from one such mother in Louisiana recently. She wrote, "Mr. President, how could anyone be more blessed than I? These children you see are mine, granted to me by the Lord for a short time. When you go to Geneva, please remember these faces, remember the faces of my children—of Jonathan, my son, and of my twins, Lara and Jessica. Their future depends on your actions. I will pray for guidance for you and the Soviet leaders." Her words, "my children," read like a cry of love. And I could only think how that cry has echoed down through the centuries, a cry for all the children of the world, for peace, for love of fellow man. Here is the central truth of our time, of any time, a truth to which I've tried to bear witness in this office.

When I first accepted the nomination of my party, I asked you, the American people, to join with me in prayer for our nation and the world. Six days ago in the Cabinet Room, religious leaders—Ukrainian and Greek Orthodox bishops, Catholic church representatives, including a Lithuanian bishop, Protestant pastors, a Mormon elder, and Jewish rabbis—made me a similar request. Well, tonight I'm honoring that request. I'm asking you, my fellow Americans, to pray for God's grace and His guidance for all of us at Geneva, so that the cause of true peace among men will be advanced and all of humanity thereby served.

Good night, and God bless you.

Note: The President spoke at 8 p.m. from the Oval Office at the White House. His address was broadcast live on nationwide radio and television.

Letter to President Belisario Betancur Cuartas Offering Support Following the Volcanic Eruption in Colombia
November 14, 1985

Dear Mr. President:

I was stunned to learn of the devastation following the eruption of the volcano Nevado Del Ruiz. The loss of life and the destruction have caused sorrow to us all. Our prayers are with you and all those who are working to rescue those who have been affected. Colombia is a great friend and ally of the United States. I want you to know in this hour of need, that we want to work with your government and be of help.

Sincerely,

/S/RONALD REAGAN

Note: The original was not available for verification of the content of this letter, which was released by the Office of the Press Secretary on November 15.

Written Responses to Questions Submitted by Japanese Journalists on the Upcoming Soviet-United States Summit Meeting in Geneva
November 14, 1985

Q. Your first meeting with the Soviet party secretary in Geneva has focused worldwide attention upon the subject of U.S.-Soviet relations, greatly raising the expectations of many for possible improvements in this relationship. What do you yourself think that the outcome of the summit meeting will be?

The President. I am optimistic that my meeting with General Secretary Gorbachev can be an important step on the path to a safer, more stable, and more productive East-West relationship—if the Soviets come to Geneva with the same goal in mind. Such an outcome would be an investment in the future, in a safer and better world for ourselves and our children. I think it's clear that the Soviets see things much differently than do we of the democratic world and that those differences will ensure continued competition for years to come. Yet this competition can and must be peaceful.

Arms control is one obvious area where we must limit our competition. I hope that General Secretary Gorbachev shares my determination to go to Geneva with the idea of moving forward the arms control process as well as other areas of our relationship. To establish a more constructive relationship, discussion of arms reductions must be ac- companied by a frank discussion of areas of tension and the causes of those tensions which have led the U.S. and our allies, including the Japanese, to build up our defensive capabilities. Someone once said, "Nations do not distrust each other because they are armed; they are armed because they distrust each other." That's why it's especially important to make progress in all areas, even as we seek to cut our nuclear arsenals.

On October 24 at the United Nations, I proposed a comprehensive approach to dealing with five long-running conflicts—in Afghanistan, Cambodia, Ethiopia, Angola, and Nicaragua. We are also seeking ways to increase contact and communication between the Soviet and American peoples, and we hope the Soviet Union will take practical steps to meet Western concerns on human rights and humanitarian questions. I cannot predict breakthroughs in any of these areas. But I think the meeting will be an important step towards real progress down the road.

Q. Could you discuss the possibility that an even broader, more encompassing framework for arms control negotiations might come about as a result of your meeting with the Soviet leader in Geneva next month? In your view, are there any substantive issues not now included in the arms control talks that should be?

The President. I do not believe that the problem has been in the *structure* of the arms talks. The Geneva nuclear and space forum provides a good framework for us to address the most pressing problems we face: first, to bring about the radical reduction of offensive nuclear weapons to equal levels under verifiable agreements; and second, to discuss with the Soviets the possibilities for moving toward a more stable and secure world in which defenses play an increasingly prominent role, if the technological research being done by the United States and the Soviet Union shows this is feasible.

There are other arms control fora where the United States and our NATO allies are pursuing a broad arms control agenda, for example, the MBFR talks on troop levels in central Europe; the Stockholm CDE Conference; and the Conference on Disarmament, where we have proposed a comprehensive global ban on chemical weapons. On nuclear testing, we think the first step is to improve the verification of compliance with the thresholds set down in the Threshold Test Ban Treaty. I've unconditionally invited Soviet experts to observe one of our nuclear tests, a practical step toward verification of effective limits on underground nuclear testing.

To reach effective arms control agreements requires genuine give-and-take on both sides. For too long the Soviet Union has not been willing to engage in serious negotiations or to make reasonable proposals. And they coupled their massive military buildup with an attempt to win in the streets and parliaments of the democratic world concessions that they couldn't win at the bargaining table. Fortunately, Western governments and public opinion remained steadfast in their insistence that arms control agreements improve stability rather than give unilateral Soviet advantage and that they meet other criteria of a successful agreement, such as significant reductions in nuclear warheads and the most destabilizing missile systems, equitable limits and constraints on other systems, and verifiability.

This steadfastness brought the Soviets back to the negotiating table after their walkout and, more recently, convinced them to table an arms control counterproposal that accepts the principle of deep reductions. Although the Soviet counterproposal is unacceptable to us as is, it includes positive elements. It is for this reason that I instructed American negotiators at Geneva to put forward a new U.S. proposal designed to advance the prospects for achieving real reductions in nuclear arms, enhancing stability and addressing the legitimate concerns of the United States and our allies, as well as the Soviet Union.

Q. Although we can assume that this upcoming summit meeting between the two superpowers might contain a sort of give-and-take process, it seems to us that you have struck a hard or rather nonnegotiable position on behalf of the Strategic Defense Initiative (SDI), to which the Soviet leader is deadly opposed. Are you confident in persuading Mr. Gorbachev to accept this SDI concept, or are you going to take a little bit more flexible stance on this issue?

The President. My vision of the future is of a more stable and secure world in which strategic defenses play a dominant role, one which would neutralize the menace of ballistic missiles and, ultimately, allow us to eliminate nuclear weapons altogether. And since a transition from reliance on offensive to defensive weapons will be neither simple nor quick, it is in everyone's interest to explore now the possibilities for doing so. That's why we have raised with the Soviets the vital relationship between offensive and defensive systems and sought to discuss ways for jointly managing a stable transition to a peace based on defense systems which threaten no one, rather than the threat of nuclear retaliation.

Now, let me speak more specifically about SDI. It is a research program to ascertain the feasibility of defenses against ballistic missiles. SDI research has been and will continue to be conducted within the bounds of the ABM treaty. Incidentally, the Soviets have conducted strategic defense programs since the 1960's. Their research and development program far exceeds ours in this area. When our research is completed, and if strategic defenses prove feasible, we will consult with our allies before deciding whether to develop and deploy strategic defenses. We will discuss and, as appropriate, negotiate with the Soviets prior to deployment, in accordance with the ABM treaty.

Q. Large numbers of Soviet SS–20's have been deployed in the Pacific Far East in recent years, but the Soviets have refused to negotiate their presence. Is the U.S. planning to try to include these SS–20's in the Geneva arms control talks? What is the U.S. position on the strategic importance of the Soviet SS–20's that are stationed in Asia? Do they threaten Western security interests in the Pacific region?

The President. These missiles are included in the Geneva talks. The Soviet SS–20 is more accurate than earlier Soviet intermediate-range forces. It is mobile and thus easily redeployed. It also carries three independently targetable warheads, as opposed to the single warhead of the earlier generation of Soviet intermediate-range missiles; thus, the SS–20 greatly increases the threat to Asia as well as to Europe. In 1981 we advocated that a total elimination of U.S. and Soviet missiles in this category is the best solution, and we have made this proposal to the Soviets in the Geneva arms control talks. As an interim measure, we have proposed reductions to the lowest possible equal number of these U.S. and Soviet missile warheads on a global basis. We have made this position clear in the Geneva talks.

Nuclear weapons that threaten our allies and friends anywhere in the world are, of course, of deep concern to us. We could not, therefore, accept any Soviet proposal in Geneva which would endeavor to address European security by increasing the threat to our friends and allies in Asia. We have consulted and will continue to consult with the Japanese Government as negotiations over Soviet intermediate-range forces proceed.

Q. What kind of progress are you expecting to make in Geneva on regional problems such as Afghanistan and the Middle East? We are particularly interested in what might happen with regards to Afghanistan.

The President. Discussion of our regional differences is an important part of our overall dialog. We have initiated experts' talks on these problems between our regional specialists and their Soviet counterparts. In my speech to the United Nations on October 24, I proposed that we and the Soviets make a special effort to contribute to the resolution of crises in Afghanistan, Cambodia, Ethiopia, Angola, and Nicaragua. Our starting point would be a process of negotiation among the warring parties in troubled countries. In the case of Afghanistan, this would include the Soviet Union; in Cambodia, the Vietnamese. On a second level, once negotiations take hold and the parties involved are making progress, representatives of the United States and the Soviet Union should sit down together and ask how we can best support the ongoing talks among warring parties. Finally, if the first two steps are successful, we would welcome each country back into the world economy, so that its citizens can share in the dynamic growth that other developing countries enjoy.

Actions by the Soviet Union in Asia, Africa, and the Western Hemisphere have been a major cause of tension in our relations over the last decade. Moreover, they could lead to situations that could be hard for either side to control. I hope we will make substantial progress in resolving our differences over our approaches to regional problems. General Secretary Gorbachev can contribute to this progress by bringing a positive response to my U.N. initiative. Afghanistan would be a good place to start. The Soviets say that they agree with us that only a political solution can end Afghanistan's war. If so, they should begin by addressing the critical question: that of the more than 100,000 Soviet troops waging war against the Afghan people. As for the Middle East, the way to peace is through direct negotiations with the parties involved. Unfortunately, the Soviet Union has not shown it is ready to play a constructive role in the Middle East. The Soviet Union consistently attacks the very concept of direct negotiations between the parties.

Q. What do you think is the most important thing on your part to make this summit meeting productive?

The President. The meeting with Mr. Gorbachev is an important part of a process we have long pursued—putting East-West relations on a safer and more productive course. I have no illusions about the difficulties involved. But General Secretary Gorbachev and I have an obligation to try and narrow some of the profound differences between us. If we make progress toward that goal, all of the world will benefit. To establish the foundation for a more constructive relationship, I want to discuss not just arms control but regional tensions, our bilateral relationship, and our mutual obligation to respect human rights. All of these issues are important to us. Even before the meeting, we want to make as much progress as possible in all aspects of our relationship. We are ready to do this and hope the Soviet Union will cooperate.

Obviously, we're not going to solve every difference in the next few weeks. I hope, however, that the meetings will give momentum to a genuine process of problem-solving and that we can agree on a bilateral agenda that will bring dividends in the future. A dedicated approach to a safe future would be the most important thing I can bring home from Geneva.

Q. How might Japan and the other allies countries contribute to the success of the upcoming summit?

The President. You have already made a considerable contribution to peace and East-West stability through your steadfast support of a policy which brought the Soviets back to the bargaining table and convinced them to respond to our arms control proposals with a serious counterproposal of their own. The free world has contributed by maintaining its strength, unity, and sense of purpose. The revival of democratic beliefs in all corners of the world and the expanding global prosperity within the free world has to have made a deep impression in the Soviet leadership. Nowhere is this more apparent than in east Asia, where countries such as Japan, which are dedicated to individual freedom and initiative, have set new standards for social and economic development.

The United States can be proud of its role in the recent history of the Pacific. The evolution of the U.S.-Japanese relationship during the past 40 years, for example, is evidence of the foresight of two generations of American and Japanese statesmen. The support of nations such as Japan, which share our democratic values, has played a crucial role in strengthening our hand as we look to our meeting in Geneva. I have consulted frequently with Prime Minister Nakasone in the months leading up to the meeting and I will continue to do so as our discussions with the Soviets develop.

Note: The questions and answers were released by the Office of the Press Secretary on November 15.

Statement on the United Kingdom-Ireland Agreement Concerning Northern Ireland
November 15, 1985

I am delighted to join with Speaker O'Neill in welcoming the important Anglo-Irish accord announced today by Mrs. Thatcher and Dr. FitzGerald. We applaud its promise of peace and a new dawn for the troubled communities of Northern Ireland. I wish to congratulate my two good friends—and outstanding Prime Ministers—who have demonstrated such statesmanship, vision, and courage.

The peoples of the United Kingdom and of Ireland have made a great contribution to the political and intellectual heritage of the United States and to our economic and social development. We are particularly pleased that these two neighbors, faithful friends of America, so close to the United States in their ties of history, kinship, and commitment to democratic values have joined on a common causeway toward hope and harmony in Northern Ireland. All Americans—and above all those of Irish descent who have prayed for an end to violence in the land of their ancestry—can take pride in this important step forward.

We view this agreement as a clear demonstration of British and Irish determination to make progress concerning Northern Ireland and in their bilateral relations. Given the complex situation in Northern Ireland, all may not applaud this agreement. But let me state that the United States strongly supports this initiative, which pledges to both communities in Northern Ireland respect for their rights and traditions within a society free from violence and intimidation. On a number of occasions, we have joined the Irish and British Governments in condemning violence and discord in Northern Ireland and calling on all Americans not to assist, either with money or moral support, those misguided efforts that prolong the nightmare of terrorism and hatred. Our call is even more compelling now that a framework for peace has been agreed upon. I wish to reconfirm and reinforce our condemnation of terrorism wherever it may take place.

Now that a framework has been established, the work of constructing a durable peace must proceed. This will involve rebuilding what has been destroyed by hatred and violence and giving hope to those who have been tempted by despair. We have often encouraged Americans to let their foreign investments and vacation dollars, and the employment opportunities that accompany such spending, find their way to the Emerald Isle. I am proud that Northern Ireland enterprises in which American money is involved are among the most progressive in promoting equal opportunity for all.

The British and Irish Governments have pledged their cooperation in promoting the economic and social development of those areas, in both parts of Ireland, which have suffered from the instability of recent years. It is entirely fitting that the United States and other governments join this important endeavor. As President Carter said on August 30, 1977, "In the event of a settlement, the U.S. Government would be prepared to join with others to see how additional job-creating investment could be encouraged, to the benefit of all the people of Northern Ireland."

There are many in Congress who have shown their concern and sympathy for the people of Northern Ireland. And I will be working closely with the Congress, in a bipartisan effort, to find tangible ways for the United States to lend practical support to this important agreement. The Speaker, who has kindly joined me at the White House today, and I have already discussed how the United States could assist in promoting peace, friendship, and harmony between the two great Irish traditions.

In closing, permit me to underscore our heartfelt support for this courageous and determined effort to promote peace and reconciliation in Northern Ireland.

Remarks on the United Kingdom-Ireland Agreement Concerning Northern Ireland
November 15, 1985

The President. The Speaker and I are very pleased this morning to be able to tell you that we have each issued a statement about what has taken place today between the Taoiseach of Ireland and the Prime Minister of England in regard to Northern Ireland in trying to finally settle the tragic internecine warfare going on there. We're delighted that this has come about, and we hope that, in a bipartisan way, that we can go forward with anything we can do to help—and they have agreed to—the two governments, other two governments—to help in restoring sound economics there— and anything we can do to encourage private investment that will provide prosperity and employment for their people. But it has been, we think, a great breakthrough which shows great promise. Now, Tip.

Speaker O'Neill. Well, thank you, Mr. President. I think it was very courageous on the part of the leaders of the English Government and the Government of Ireland to get together to try to work out and solve the problems of Northern Ireland. There, in the land of cultures, yet 90 miles from the European Continent, there have been hundreds of killings and thousands of woundings, and it has showed through the years that bullets and bombs are not the answer—the answer is talking the question over. And I'm glad that both of these countries appreciate the severity of the questions. America has flourished because of diversity, and there's no reason that Northern Ireland can't be the same way. And so, I stand here beside the President of the United States, part of the fact that we both support the leaders of those two great nations—the Taoiseach and the Prime Minister.

And I want to assure you how delighted I am that America is backing a policy which all Presidents have said, that if we could bring this to an end, we would do everything that we humanly could. And I speak for the House, Mr. President—any means that we can use in the Congress of the United States to help bring peace in Northern Ireland, I assure you that we'll have the full cooperation of the Congress; there's no question in my mind.

So, again, we congratulate the people of Ireland, the leaders and the people of England, Mrs. Thatcher, their Prime Minister. And our hope and our prayers and our best wishes and our support is with them that this venture will be a success.

Reporter. Mr. President, Speaker O'Neill is predicting major results at the summit in Geneva next week. Do you agree with him?

The President. I'm—this is almost—this was that knuckleball I was talking about yesterday, to throw something—I was prepared not to take any questions. We're not going to take questions here at this particular occasion; statements have been issued. But when you ask one like that with the Speaker standing here, yes, I am very pleased and delighted with what he had to say.

Speaker O'Neill. I want you to know that we wish you all the success and happiness and best wishes, and you come home with the greatest results—everyone in America. You're our leader, and we know that you're going to have results.

Q. Mr. President, Mr. Arbatov, today in Geneva calls you a "Grade B movie actor."

The President. Well, he's never seen "King's Row." [*Laughter*]

Note: The President spoke at 9:54 a.m. in the Oval Office at the White House. Sir Oliver Wright, British Ambassador to the United States, and Padraic McKernan, Irish Ambassador to the United States, were also present. In the final question, a reporter referred to Georgiy Arbatov of the Soviet Union, director of the Institute for the Study of the United States of America and Canada. A tape was not available for verification of the content of these remarks.

Nomination of Arnold I. Burns To Be Associate Attorney General
November 15, 1985

The President today announced his intention to nominate Arnold I. Burns to be Associate Attorney General, Department of Justice. He would succeed D. Lowell Jensen.

Since 1960 Mr. Burns has been a partner in the law firm of Burns, Jackson, Miller, Summit & Jacoby in New York City. Previously, he was an associate with the firm of Dewey, Ballantine, Bushby, Palmer & Wood in New York City.

He graduated from Union College (A.B.,

1950) and Cornell University (J.D., 1953). He is married, has two children, and resides in New York, NY. He was born April 14, 1930, in Brooklyn, NY.

Nomination of Arch L. Madsen To Be a Member of the Board for International Broadcasting
November 15, 1985

The President today announced his intention to nominate Arch L. Madsen to be a member of the Board for International Broadcasting for a term expiring April 28, 1987. This is a reappointment.

Mr. Madsen is president of Bonneville International Corp., an independent broadcast organization wholly owned by the Mormon Church, in Salt Lake City, UT. He has served as chairman of the international committee, National Association of Broadcasters, and is a member of the Broadcasters Foundation. In 1981 he was recognized by the National Association of Broadcasters for his achievements in broadcasting.

He is married, has five children, and resides in Salt Lake City, UT. He was born December 4, 1913, in Provo, UT.

Appointment of 14 Members of the President's Foreign Intelligence Advisory Board, and Designation of the Chairman and Vice Chairman
November 15, 1985

The President today announced his intention to appoint 14 members to the President's Foreign Intelligence Advisory Board (PFIAB) for 2-year terms. The Board was recently reconstituted by the President on October 28, 1985, by Executive Order 12537. The most significant change in the new Board is that it establishes a limit of 14 members. The existing PFIAB, with 21 members, had grown to a size that made it difficult to carry out its advisory responsibilities.

The PFIAB is a permanent, nonpartisan body of distinguished Americans who perform a continuing and objective review of the performance of the intelligence community. The Board reports directly to the President and has full access to all information necessary to advise the President on the conduct, management, and coordination of the various agencies of the intelligence community.

The PFIAB (then known as the Board of Consultants on Foreign Intelligence Activities) was first established by President Eisenhower in 1956. The Board was continued by each President thereafter until its termination in 1977 by President Carter. The PFIAB was reconstituted by the President on October 20, 1981, by Executive Order 12331.

Under the new Board, Anne Armstrong will remain as Chairman and Leo Cherne as Vice Chairman. The following are the members who will be reappointed to the new Board:

Anne Legendre Armstrong is currently chairman of the advisory board of the Georgetown University Center for Strategic and International Studies. She was United States Ambassador to Great Britain in 1976–1977 and served as Counsellor to the President in 1973–1974. She is married, has five children, and resides in Armstrong, TX.

Leo Cherne is an economist and currently serves as executive director of the Research Institute of America in New York City. He was a member of the President's Foreign Intelligence Advisory Board in 1973–1976 and served as chairman in 1976–1977. He is married, has one daughter, and resides in New York City. He was born September 8, 1912.

Howard H. Baker, Jr., is a senior partner in the law firm Vinson & Elkins in Washington, DC. He served as a United States Senator from Tennessee from 1966 to 1985. He was minority leader in 1977–1981 and majority leader in 1981–1985. He is married, has two children, and resides in Washington, DC. He was born November 15, 1925.

William O. Baker is a research chemist and was chairman of the board of Bell Telephone Laboratories. He was a member of the President's Foreign Intelligence Advisory Board in 1959–1977. He is married, has one son, and resides in Morristown, NJ. He was born July 15, 1915.

W. Glenn Campbell has been director, Hoover Institution on War, Revolution and Peace, Stanford University, since 1960 and has served as the chairman of the President's Intelligence Oversight Board since 1981. He was a member of the National Science Board, National Science Foundation, in 1972–1978. He is married, has three children, and resides in Stanford, CA. He was born April 29, 1924.

John S. Foster, Jr., is vice president, science and technology, TRW, Inc. He was Director of Defense Research and Engineering for the Department of Defense in 1965–1973. Mr. Foster served as a member of the President's Foreign Intelligence Advisory Board in 1973–1977. He is married, has five children, and resides in Cleveland, OH. He was born September 18, 1922.

Henry A. Kissinger is chairman of Kissinger and Associates, Inc. He was Secretary of State in 1973–1977 and served as the Assistant to the President for National Security Affairs from 1969–1974. He is married, has two children, and resides in New York City. He was born May 27, 1923.

Clare Boothe Luce was a member of the President's Foreign Intelligence Advisory Board in 1973–1977. She is a playwright and journalist. She was also a Member of Congress in 1943–1947 and Ambassador to Italy in 1953–1957. She resides in Washington, DC.

William French Smith is a partner in the firm of Gibson, Dunn and Crutcher of Los Angeles. Previously he served as Attorney General of the United States in 1981–1985. He is married, has four children, and resides in San Marino, CA. He was born August 26, 1917.

Albert D. Wheelon is senior vice president and group president of the Space and Communications Group of Hughes Aircraft Co. He was Deputy Director for Science and Technology at the Central Intelligence Agency in 1962–1964. He is married, has two children, and resides in Los Angeles, CA. He was born January 18, 1929.

The following are the four new members who will be appointed to the Board:

Jeane J. Kirkpatrick was the representative of the United States to the United Nations and a member of the Cabinet (1981–1985). She has resumed her position as Leavey professor at Georgetown University and as senior fellow at the American Enterprise Institute. She is married, has three children, and resides in Bethesda, MD.

Bernard A. Schriever was commander of the U.S. Air Force Systems Command in 1961–1966. He retired from the Air Force with the rank of general. He was Chairman of the President's Advisory Council on Management Improvement and is currently serving as a member of the National Commission on Space. He is married, has three children, and resides in Washington, DC. He was born September 14, 1910.

James Q. Wilson is Henry Lee Shattuck professor of government at Harvard University and James Collins professor of management at UCLA. He is chairman of the board of directors of the Police Foundation and former chairman of the White House Task Force on Crime and the National Advisory Council on Drug Abuse Prevention. He is married, has two children, and resides in Belmont, MA. He was born May 27, 1931.

Albert J. Wohlstetter is director of research at PAN Heuristics, Marina del Rey, CA. He held the university professorship for 15 years at the University of Chicago and before that was a member of the research council and assistant to the president at RAND Corp. He is married, has one child, and resides in Los Angeles, CA. He was born December 19, 1913.

Statement on the Veto of the Treasury Department, Postal Service, and Certain Independent Agencies Appropriations Bill
November 15, 1985

Today I am vetoing H.R. 3036, which makes appropriations for the Treasury Department, the United States Postal Service, and certain Independent Agencies for the fiscal year 1986. Last night, under emergency conditions, I signed two pieces of temporary legislation to prevent the Federal Government from shutting down and having its checks dishonored.

This is an unacceptable situation in two respects. First, the temporary bills on appropriations and the debt ceiling again illustrate the failure of the budget process. I have received only 4 of the required 13 appropriations bills, though all were supposed to be passed by September 30th. We have known for months that the debt limit would have to be increased, yet legislative inaction forced us to accelerate the redemption of securities in the Social Security and other trust funds and waste millions of taxpayer dollars.

Second, this episode is just the latest example of an ingrained incapacity to tackle the large budget deficit. Although a budget resolution was finally produced 2½ months behind schedule, its presumed savings have not been achieved. The old propensity to spend and spend and to capitulate to one interest group after another continues unabated. The solution to solving the deficit problem is not to be found in spending more money. The need to veto this unacceptable measure is proof positive of the need to sign acceptable legislation to improve the budget process, such as the amendment proposed by Senators Gramm, Rudman, and Hollings.

Many Members of Congress share my frustration. That is why the Senate passed in early October the Gramm-Rudman-Hollings legislation to force hard decisions and set us on a course toward a balanced budget. We need this legislation urgently, just as we need the line-item veto. There is still ample time to enact both before this session of Congress ends. This chronic budgetary crisis, and the inexcusable waste of taxpayer dollars that it entails, highlights once again the pressing need for basic reform of the congressional budget process. But there can be no gain for our prosperity or our security if Congress approves the version of Gramm-Rudman-Hollings passed by the House—a distorted version that takes unacceptable risks with our national security.

In my budget last February I proposed a commonsense path toward lower deficits by reforming, reducing, or eliminating about 50 domestic spending programs. The Congress has accepted very few of these proposals, and every nondefense appropriations bill will far exceed my budget. The bill I am vetoing today is a case in point. For discretionary programs the bill is more than $900 million above my budget and $180 million for budget authority and other discretionary resources above the level for this bill implied in the budget resolution. Its language contains provisions that are purely and simply bad policy, and one section of the bill raises serious constitutional concerns with respect to Presidential appointments.

The Presidential veto is an instrument to be used with care. But unless and until a genuine effort is made to control spending, the veto is an instrument I shall not hesitate to employ.

Message to the House of Representatives Returning Without Approval the Treasury Department, Postal Service, and Certain Independent Agencies Appropriations Bill
November 15, 1985

To the House of Representatives:

I am returning herewith without my approval H.R. 3036, making appropriations for the Treasury Department, the United States Postal Service and certain Independent Agencies for the fiscal year 1986.

In my budget last February I proposed reforms, reductions, and terminations in some 50 domestic programs to start us on a sensible path to lower budget deficits. Because Congress has accepted very few of these proposals, it is now clear that all of the non-defense appropriations bills will be far above my budget.

However, in the interest of accommodation, I have indicated that I would accept appropriations bills, even if above my budget, that were within the limits set by Congress' own budget resolution. This bill does not meet that test.

For discretionary programs the bill provides $900 million more than my budget and is $180 million above the level for budget authority and other discretionary resources implied in the budget resolution. For example, my budget proposed a major paring of the remaining postal subsidies, and the Congressional budget resolution en-

visaged a lesser saving. This bill provides $820 million for these subsidies, which represents little saving from current levels and is $72 million above the budget resolution level.

Apart from its spending levels, this bill contains a number of language provisions that are highly objectionable. Among them are provisions blocking performance-based regulations for civil servants issued by the Office of Personnel Management, curbing the authority of the General Services Administration to contract out certain services to the private sector, forbidding review by the Office of Management and Budget of marketing orders for agricultural products, and one section of the bill raises serious constitutional concerns with respect to presidential appointments.

The presidential veto is an instrument to be used with care. But until the Congress comes to grips with the problem of the large budget deficit, it is an instrument that I shall not hesitate to employ.

RONALD REAGAN

The White House,
November 15, 1985.

Proclamation 5411—National Adoption Week, 1985
November 15, 1985

By the President of the United States of America

A Proclamation

The basic unit of our society is the family. Families transmit the values and traditions of the past. They are the primary civilizing agent, preparing the young for good citizenship. It is, therefore, fitting that we give special recognition to those generous families that encourage and take part in adoption.

Children who live in a permanent home with caring adoptive parents are far less likely to develop emotional and psychological problems. We must encourage the effort to promote the adoption of all children without families—with particular emphasis on those who are older, handicapped, or members of minority groups. Whenever possible, the adoption process should work to keep siblings together as they are placed in new families.

1401

Through promotional efforts in the workplace and through inclusion of adoption benefits in employee benefit plans, the American corporate sector has been supporting the adoption of children with special needs. Furthermore, through the Adoption Assistance and Child Welfare Act, many children with special needs have been adopted who otherwise might not have been.

National Adoption Week should remind us that no woman need fear that the child she carries is unwanted. It is a sad paradox that while thousands of American couples desperately desire to adopt a baby, many women who undergo abortions every year in the United States are unaware of all the couples eager to share their home with a newborn and to give that child all the love and care they would give if they had been its natural parents. Adoption is an alternative that provides family life for children who cannot live with their biological parents, and it is especially fitting that at Thanksgiving time we emphasize the importance of family life through the observance of National Adoption Week.

This week provides an opportunity to reaffirm our commitment to give every child waiting to be adopted the chance to become part of a family. During this holiday season, let us work to encourage community acceptance and support for adop-

tion, and take time to recognize the efforts of adoptive parent groups, companies, organizations, and agencies that assure adoptive placements for waiting children. We also pay tribute to those magnanimous people who have opened their homes and hearts to children, forming the bonds of love that we call the family.

The Congress, by Senate Joint Resolution 51, has designated the week of November 24 through November 30, 1985, as "National Adoption Week" and authorized and requested the President to issue a proclamation in observance of this week.

Now, Therefore, I, Ronald Reagan, President of the United States of America, do hereby proclaim the week of November 24 through November 30, 1985, as National Adoption Week, and I call on all Americans and governmental and private agencies to observe the week with appropriate activities.

In Witness Whereof, I have hereunto set my hand this fifteenth day of November, in the year of our Lord nineteen hundred and eighty-five, and of the Independence of the United States of America the two hundred and tenth.

RONALD REAGAN

[*Filed with the Office of the Federal Register, 10:41 a.m., November 18, 1985*]

Proclamation 5412—Thanksgiving Day, 1985
November 15, 1985

By the President of the United States of America

A Proclamation

Although the time and date of the first American thanksgiving observance may be uncertain, there is no question but that this treasured custom derives from our Judeo-Christian heritage. "Unto Thee, O God, do we give thanks," the Psalmist sang, praising God not only for the "wondrous works" of His creation, but for loving guidance and deliverance from dangers.

A band of settlers arriving in Maine in

1607 held a service of thanks for their safe journey, and twelve years later settlers in Virginia set aside a day of thanksgiving for their survival. In 1621 Governor William Bradford created the most famous of all such observances at Plymouth Colony when a bounteous harvest prompted him to proclaim a special day "to render thanksgiving to the Almighty God for all His blessings." The Spaniards in California and the Dutch in New Amsterdam also held services to give public thanks to God.

In 1777, during our War of Independence, the Continental Congress set aside a day for thanksgiving and praise for our victory at the battle of Saratoga. It was the first time all the colonies took part in such an event on the same day. The following year, upon news that France was coming to our aid, George Washington at Valley Forge prescribed a special day of thanksgiving. Later, as our first President, he responded to a Congressional petition by declaring Thursday, November 26, 1789, the first Thanksgiving Day of the United States of America.

Although there were many state and national thanksgiving days proclaimed in the ensuing years, it was the tireless crusade of one woman, Sarah Josepha Hale, that finally led to the establishment of this beautiful feast as an annual nationwide observance. Her editorials so touched the heart of Abraham Lincoln that in 1863—even in the midst of the Civil War—he enjoined his countrymen to be mindful of their many blessings, cautioning them not to forget "the source from which they come," that they are "the gracious gifts of the Most High God . . ." Who ought to be thanked "with one heart and one voice by the whole American People."

It is in that spirit that I now invite all Americans to take part again in this beautiful tradition with its roots deep in our history and deeper still in our hearts. We manifest our gratitude to God for the many blessings he has showered upon our land and upon its people.

In this season of Thanksgiving we are grateful for our abundant harvests and the productivity of our industries; for the dis-coveries of our laboratories; for the researches of our scientists and scholars; for the achievements of our artists, musicians, writers, clergy, teachers, physicians, businessmen, engineers, public servants, farmers, mechanics, artisans, and workers of every sort whose honest toil of mind and body in a free land rewards them and their families and enriches our entire Nation.

Let us thank God for our families, friends, and neighbors, and for the joy of this very festival we celebrate in His name. Let every house of worship in the land and every home and every heart be filled with the spirit of gratitude and praise and love on this Thanksgiving Day.

Now, Therefore, I, Ronald Reagan, President of the United States of America, in the spirit and tradition of the Pilgrims, the Continental Congress, and past Presidents, do hereby proclaim Thursday, November 28, 1985, as a day of national Thanksgiving. I call upon every citizen of this great Nation to gather together in homes and places of worship and offer prayers of praise and gratitude for the many blessings Almighty God has bestowed upon our beloved country.

In Witness Whereof, I have hereunto set my hand this fifteenth day of November, in the year of our Lord nineteen hundred and eighty-five, and of the Independence of the United States of America the two hundred and tenth.

RONALD REAGAN

[*Filed with the Office of the Federal Register, 10:42 a.m., November 18, 1985*]

Executive Order 12538—Imports of Refined Petroleum Products From Libya
November 15, 1985

By the authority vested in me as President by the Constitution and laws of the United States, including Section 504 of the International Security and Development Cooperation Act of 1985 (Public Law 99–83), and considering that the Libyan government actively pursues terrorism as an instrument of state policy and that Libya has developed significant capability to export petroleum products and thereby circumvent the prohibition imposed by Proclamation No. 4907 of March 10, 1982 and retained in Proclamation No. 5141 of December 22, 1983 on the importation of Libyan crude oil, it is ordered as follows:

Section 1. (a) No petroleum product refined in Libya (except petroleum product loaded aboard maritime vessels at any time prior to two days after the effective date of this Executive Order) may be imported into the United States, its territories or possessions.

(b) For the purposes of this Executive Order, the prohibition on importation of petroleum products refined in Libya shall apply to petroleum products which are currently classifiable under Item Numbers: 475.05; 475.10; 475.15; 475.25; 475.30; 475.35; 475.45; 475.65; 475.70 of the Tariff Schedules of the United States (19 U.S.C. 1202).

Sec. 2. The Secretary of the Treasury may issue such rulings and instructions, or, following consultation with the Secretaries of State and Energy, such regulations as he deems necessary to implement this Order.

Sec. 3. This Order shall be effective immediately.

RONALD REAGAN

The White House,
November 15, 1985.

[*Filed with the Office of the Federal Register, 10:43 a.m., November 18, 1985*]

Proclamation 5410—Eugene Ormandy Appreciation Day, 1985
November 15, 1985

By the President of the United States of America

A Proclamation

Eugene Ormandy was a consummate musician and a masterly conductor, as well as a father figure and an inspiration to generations of gifted American musicians.

As music director of the Philadelphia Orchestra for 44 years, he brought that ensemble to a point of such polish and perfection that many esteemed it the very greatest in the world. No one could mistake the "Philadelphia Sound," a perfectly pitched and artfully blended miracle of sonorities that was at once lush and supple. Virgil Thomson, the noted critic, has described Ormandy's goal as "beauty of sound and virtuosity of execution . . . at the service of the music in complete humility."

Maestro Ormandy achieved that goal by dint of patience, persuasion, and example. He persuaded his musicians to do it his way without taunts or tantrums. They knew how much he loved the music, how much he loved the audiences, and how much he loved them. They could not fail him—they did not. And he never stinted in giving his musicians the credit. "They play," he said once "as one great Stradivarius, not as individual musicians."

It was an accurate description and a supreme tribute from a child prodigy whose musicial genius first found expression on the violin—at the age of three! Born in Budapest on November 18, 1899, Eugene Ormandy came to the United States in 1921. His first job was as a violinist with the orchestra of the Capitol motion picture theater in New York City. Soon he became its conductor. Then, after a brief stint with the Minneapolis Symphony, Ormandy succeeded the legendary Leopold Stokowski as director of the Philadelphia Orchestra. It would be his true home for the rest of his life. Under the magic of his baton, conductor and orchestra entered the musical pantheon of the United States and of the world.

Eugene Ormandy brought widespread acclaim to his adopted nation, which he loved with the passion of a patriot. He served as an ambassador of goodwill through the Philadelphia Orchestra's tours of China, the Soviet Union, South America, Europe, and Japan.

To commemorate these magnificent and enduring contributions of Eugene Ormandy to the rich cultural traditions of the United States, the Congress, by Senate Joint Resolution 174, has authorized and requested the President to declare the anniversary of the birth of Eugene Ormandy as "Eugene Ormandy Appreciation Day" and called upon the American people to observe the day with appropriate ceremonies.

Now, Therefore, I, Ronald Reagan, President of the United States of America, do hereby declare November 18, 1985, Eugene Ormandy Appreciation Day.

In Witness Whereof, I have hereunto set my hand this fifteenth day of November, in the year of our Lord nineteen hundred and eighty-five, and of the Independence of the United States of America the two hundred and tenth.

RONALD REAGAN

[*Filed with the Office of the Federal Register, 10:40 a.m., November 18, 1985*]

Note: The proclamation was released by the Office of the Press Secretary on November 16.

Radio Address to the Nation on the American National Red Cross
November 16, 1985

My fellow Americans:

As I speak to you today, I am flying across the ocean to Geneva, Switzerland, on a mission for peace. As you know, I'll be meeting with General Secretary Gorbachev of the Soviet Union. Those meetings may occupy the news for the next few days, but right now I want to talk to you about something closer to home—the American Red Cross.

Actually, the Red Cross was founded in Geneva over a hundred years ago to care for the victims of war. Then Clara Barton, who became known as the "Angel of the Battlefield" during our Civil War, brought the idea to the United States and expanded it to include disaster relief during peacetime. One way or another the Red Cross has touched most of our lives. Last year close to 1½ million volunteers worked for the Red Cross, with many millions more giving blood and participating in their programs for young people. It was with the Red Cross, in fact, that I received training for one of my first jobs—as a lifeguard. And today I'm proud to serve as this noble organization's honorary chairman.

This year has been unprecedented in the history of Red Cross disaster relief efforts, and their resources have been stretched to the limit. In addition to helping our neighbors around the world—in famine-stricken Africa, after the devastating earthquake in Mexico City, and most recently with the eruption of a volcano in Colombia—well,

Red Cross has had its work cut out for it here at home, too. A series of natural disasters has struck the United States since last July 1st. Several of them you probably know by name: Bob, Danny, Elena, Gloria, and Juan. But in addition to these hurricanes, there have been other disasters: fires, evacuations, the Puerto Rican mudslides, and the floods in Virginia, West Virginia, Maryland, and Pennsylvania, which were extremely destructive and have added enormously to the burden of Red Cross relief efforts.

Still, each time disaster struck, the Red Cross volunteers were there. I'm sure that for those people whom the storms made homeless a hot meal, a Red Cross blanket, a soft bed, and a warm smile helped get them through the nightmare and take that first step on the difficult road to rebuilding their lives. I guess the only good thing to come out of natural disasters like these are the stories of self-sacrifice and downright heroism, and so often those heroes turn out to be Red Cross volunteers.

That was the case recently in West Virginia when some volunteers heard a dog barking inside a flooded house. By the time they got there, the water was already rising past the windows. Inside, a man was struggling to save his furniture from the water and had no idea the peril he was in. He was blind and may not have been evacuated if the Red Cross hadn't come to save both him and his dog. Then there was a family in West Virginia marooned in their home; the only way food and supplies could reach them was by a Red Cross boat. And there were the volunteers who dove into a rushing torrent to save a mother and her children just before they got swept away by the current.

The Red Cross is always there for us; now we need to be there for them. You may be surprised to know that, as big as it is, the Red Cross receives no government funding; it is entirely dependent on private contributions for support. Just since the beginning of July, the Red Cross has spent a record $48 million responding to emergencies, and they are quite simply running out of funds. So, they are launching an emergency disaster relief campaign, and they've set a fundraising goal of $20 million. It's now time for all of us to volunteer for the volunteers, to give to those who've given so much of themselves. In recent years we've witnessed a resurgence in the great American spirit of neighbor helping neighbor. Now more of you are volunteering your time and contributing money to charity than any time in our nation's past. We've seen Americans unite to help feed the hungry around the world, provide emergency assistance to disaster victims in foreign lands, and we've seen one of the largest private sector initiatives in history raise funds to restore our great Statue of Liberty. Well, today I ask your help so that others may be helped. Please contact the Red Cross chapter nearest you and ask what you can do to give them a hand.

Till next week, thanks for listening, and God bless you.

Note: The President's remarks were recorded at 1:30 p.m. on November 15 in the Diplomatic Reception Room at the White House for broadcast at 12:06 p.m. on November 16.

Remarks on Arrival in Geneva, Switzerland
November 16, 1985

President Furgler, I would like to extend to you and to the Swiss people my appreciation for helping to make possible the coming meetings between representatives of the United States and the Soviet Union. Nancy and I are delighted to be in this magnificent city on the shores of Lake Geneva. On behalf of the American people, thank you for your warm and friendly welcome.

Mr. President, it is fitting that the meetings of the next few days should take place on Swiss soil, for Switzerland has long been a leader in the search for peace and the defense of human freedom. Again and again, you've provided your territory for international meetings and your good offices in the mediation of disputes. It was the Swiss who founded one of the great humanitarian organizations of our time, the International Red Cross. And it is Switzerland that often represents the diplomatic interests of other nations, including the United States, in lands where these nations have no formal diplomatic relations of their own. Indeed, in your unshakable commitment to independence, democratic government, and human rights, the Swiss Confederation in itself serves as an example to all the world.

The motto on the Great Seal of the United States, Mr. President, is "E Pluribus Unum"—Out of many, one. Well, here in Switzerland, a country of rich religious, cultural, and linguistic variety, you practice just such unity in diversity. Permit me to add that our two countries are bound together by family ties. As early as 1562 a Swiss citizen appeared in Florida, and in 1670 a Swiss settlement was established near Charleston, South Carolina. Ever since, Americans of Swiss descent have pioneered and led the development of our nation. Today Swiss Americans number in the hundreds of thousands, and I would be remiss if I failed to express their affection for you, their Swiss cousins. Indeed, just last month the good will of the American people toward the Swiss was formally expressed in a joint resolution of the Congress of the United States.

And recently, Mr. President, Boston University awarded you an honorary doctorate of laws. In your acceptance address, you stressed the obligations incumbent upon the West to defend its values and its way of life. "It is," you said, "part of the definition and vocation of the human being to be free." Well, Mr. President, each in its own way, our two nations stand at the forefront of this struggle for liberty; each stands determined to defend the freedoms of its own people and to advance the cause of freedom throughout the world; and each rests confident in the knowledge that freedom will endure and prevail.

It is to make certain that this great work on behalf of human freedom can go forward in peace that I have come here today. As I stated last month before the United Nations, I'm convinced that American-Soviet relations need a fresh start—a genuine give-and-take on regional conflicts, on human rights, and on the reduction of arms. American and Soviet differences on these matters run deep. Mr. Gorbachev and I cannot surmount them in only 2 days, but I'm here in the fervent hope that on behalf of all the people of the world, we can at least make a start.

President Furgler, once again, to you and the people of Switzerland, our friendship and our deepest gratitude.

Note: The President spoke at 10:36 p.m. at Cointrin Airport. He was greeted by President Kurt Furgler of Switzerland.

Joint Soviet-United States Statement on the Summit Meeting in Geneva
November 21, 1985

By mutual agreement, President of the United States Ronald Reagan and General Secretary of the Central Committee of the Communist Party of the Soviet Union Mikhail Gorbachev met in Geneva November 19–21. Attending the meeting on the U.S. side were Secretary of State George Shultz; Chief of Staff Donald Regan; Assistant to the President Robert McFarlane; Ambassador to the USSR Arthur Hartman; Special Advisor to the President and the Secretary of State for Arms Control Paul H. Nitze; Assistant Secretary of State for European Affairs Rozanne Ridgway; Special Assistant to the President for National Security Affairs Jack Matlock. Attending on the Soviet side were Member of the Politburo of the Central Committee of the CPSU, Minister of Foreign Affairs E. A. Shevardnadze; First Deputy Foreign Minister G. M. Korniyenko; Ambassador to the United States A. F. Dobrynin; Head of the Department of Propaganda of the Central Committee of the CPSU, A. N. Yakovlev; Head of the Depart-

ment of International Information of the Central Committee of the CPSU L. M. Zamyatin; Assistant to the General Secretary of the Central Committee of the CPSU, A. M. Aleksandrov.

These comprehensive discussions covered the basic questions of U.S.-Soviet relations and the current international situation. The meetings were frank and useful. Serious differences remain on a number of critical issues.

While acknowledging the differences in their systems and approaches to international issues, some greater understanding of each side's view was achieved by the two leaders. They agreed about the need to improve U.S.-Soviet relations and the international situation as a whole.

In this connection the two sides have confirmed the importance of an ongoing dialogue, reflecting their strong desire to seek common ground on existing problems.

They agreed to meet again in the nearest future. The General Secretary accepted an invitation by the President of the United States to visit the United States of America and the President of the United States accepted an invitation by the General Secretary of the Central Committee of the CPSU to visit the Soviet Union. Arrangements for and timing of the visits will be agreed upon through diplomatic channels.

In their meetings, agreement was reached on a number of specific issues. Areas of agreement are registered on the following pages.

Security

The sides, having discussed key security issues, and conscious of the special responsibility of the USSR and the U.S. for maintaining peace, have agreed that a nuclear war cannot be won and must never be fought. Recognizing that any conflict between the USSR and the U.S. could have catastrophic consequences, they emphasized the importance of preventing any war between them, whether nuclear or conventional. They will not seek to achieve military superiority.

Nuclear and Space Talks

The President and the General Secretary discussed the negotiations on nuclear and space arms.

They agreed to accelerate the work at these negotiations, with a view to accomplishing the tasks set down in the Joint U.S.-Soviet Agreement of January 8, 1985, namely to prevent an arms race in space and to terminate it on earth, to limit and reduce nuclear arms and enhance strategic stability.

Noting the proposals recently tabled by the U.S. and the Soviet Union, they called for early progress, in particular in areas where there is common ground, including the principle of 50% reductions in the nuclear arms of the U.S. and the USSR appropriately applied, as well as the idea of an interim INF agreement.

During the negotiation of these agreements, effective measures for verification of compliance with obligations assumed will be agreed upon.

Risk Reduction Centers

The sides agreed to study the question at the expert level of centers to reduce nuclear risk taking into account the issues and developments in the Geneva negotiations. They took satisfaction in such recent steps in this direction as the modernization of the Soviet-U.S. hotline.

Nuclear Non-Proliferation

General Secretary Gorbachev and President Reagan reaffirmed the commitment of the USSR and the U.S. to the Treaty on the Non-Proliferation of Nuclear Weapons and their interest in strengthening together with other countries the non-proliferation regime, and in further enhancing the effectiveness of the Treaty, *inter alia* by enlarging its membership.

They note with satisfaction the overall positive results of the recent Review Conference of the Treaty on the Non-Proliferation of Nuclear Weapons.

The USSR and the U.S. reaffirm their commitment, assumed by them under the Treaty on the Non-Proliferation of Nuclear Weapons, to pursue negotiations in good faith on matters of nuclear arms limitation and disarmament in accordance with Article VI of the Treaty.

The two sides plan to continue to promote the strengthening of the International Atomic Energy Agency and to support the activities of the Agency in implementing safeguards as well as in promoting the peaceful uses of nuclear energy.

They view positively the practice of regular Soviet-U.S. consultations on non-proliferation of nuclear weapons which have been businesslike and constructive and express their intent to continue this practice in the future.

Chemical Weapons

In the context of discussing security problems, the two sides reaffirmed that they are in favor of a general and complete prohibition of chemical weapons and the destruction of existing stockpiles of such weapons. They agreed to accelerate efforts to conclude an effective and verifiable international convention on this matter.

The two sides agreed to intensify bilateral discussions on the level of experts on all aspects of such a chemical weapons ban, including the question of verification. They agreed to initiate a dialogue on preventing the proliferation of chemical weapons.

MBFR

The two sides emphasized the importance they attach to the Vienna (MBFR) negotiations and expressed their willingness to work for positive results.

CDE

Attaching great importance to the Stockholm Conference on Confidence and Security Building Measures and Disarmament in Europe and noting the progress made there, the two sides stated their intention to facilitate, together with the other participating states, an early and successful completion of the work of the conference. To this end, they reaffirmed the need for a document which would include mutually acceptable confidence and security building measures and give concrete expression and effect to the principle of non-use of force.

Process of Dialogue

President Reagan and General Secretary Gorbachev agreed on the need to place on a regular basis and intensify dialogue at various levels. Along with meetings between the leaders of the two countries, this envisages regular meetings between the USSR Minister of Foreign Affairs and the U.S. Secretary of State, as well as between the heads of other Ministries and Agencies. They agree that the recent visits of the heads of Ministries and Departments in such fields as agriculture, housing and protection of the environment have been useful.

Recognizing that exchanges of views on regional issues on the expert level have proven useful, they agreed to continue such exchanges on a regular basis.

The sides intend to expand the programs of bilateral cultural, educational and scientific-technical exchanges, and also to develop trade and economic ties. The President of the United States and the General Secretary of the Central Committee of the CPSU attended the signing of the Agreement on Contacts and Exchanges in Scientific, Educational and Cultural Fields.

They agreed on the importance of resolving humanitarian cases in the spirit of cooperation.

They believe that there should be greater understanding among our peoples and that to this end they will encourage greater travel and people-to-people contact.

Northern Pacific Air Safety

The two leaders also noted with satisfaction that, in cooperation with the Government of Japan, the United States and the Soviet Union have agreed to a set of measures to promote safety on air routes in the North Pacific and have worked out steps to implement them.

Civil Aviation / Consulates

They acknowledged that delegations from the United States and the Soviet Union have begun negotiations aimed at resumption of air services. The two leaders expressed their desire to reach a mutually beneficial agreement at an early date. In this regard, an agreement was reached on the simultaneous opening of Consulates General in New York and Kiev.

Environmental Protection

Both sides agreed to contribute to the preservation of the environment—a global task—through joint research and practical measures. In accordance with the existing U.S.-Soviet agreement in this area, consultations will be held next year in Moscow and Washington on specific programs of cooperation.

Exchange Initiatives

The two leaders agreed on the utility of broadening exchanges and contacts including some of their new forms in a number of scientific, educational, medical and sports fields (*inter alia*, cooperation in the development of educational exchanges and software for elementary and secondary school instruction; measures to promote Russian language studies in the United States and English language studies in the USSR; the annual exchange of professors to conduct special courses in history, culture and economics at the relevant departments of Soviet and American institutions of higher education; mutual allocation of scholarships for the best students in the natural sciences, technology, social sciences and humanities for the period of an academic year; holding regular meets in various sports and increased television coverage of sports events). The two sides agreed to resume cooperation in combatting cancer diseases.

The relevant agencies in each of the countries are being instructed to develop specific programs for these exchanges. The resulting programs will be reviewed by the leaders at their next meeting.

Fusion Research

The two leaders emphasized the potential importance of the work aimed at utilizing controlled thermonuclear fusion for peaceful purposes and, in this connection, advocated the widest practicable development of international cooperation in obtaining this source of energy, which is essentially inexhaustible, for the benefit for all mankind.

Remarks on Issuing the Joint Soviet-United States Statement on the Summit Meeting in Geneva
November 21, 1985

General Secretary Gorbachev. You've already been handed the joint statement. The President and I have done a huge amount of work. We've gone into great detail; we've really done it in depth. And we've done it totally openly and frankly. We've discussed several most important issues. The relations between our two countries and the situation in the world in general today—these are issues and problems the solving of which in the most concrete way is of concern both to our countries and to the peoples of other countries in the world. We discussed these issues basing our discussions on both sides' determination to improve relations between the Soviet Union and the United States of America. We decided that we must help to decrease the threat of nuclear war. We must not allow the arms race to move off into space, and we must cut it down on Earth.

It goes without saying that discussions of these sort we consider to be very useful, and in its results you find a clear reflection of what the two sides have agreed together. We have to be realistic and straightforward and, therefore, the solving of the most important problems concerning the arms race and increasing hopes of peace, we didn't succeed in reaching at this meeting. So, of course there are important disagreements on matters of principle that remain between us; however, the President and I have agreed that this work of seeking mutu-

ally acceptable decisions for these questions will be continued here in Geneva by our representatives. We've also going to seek new kinds of developing bilateral Soviet-American relations. And also we're going to have further consultations on several important questions where, for the most part, our positions, again, are completely different. All this, we consider these forthcoming talks to be very, very useful.

But the significance of everything which we have agreed with the President can only, of course, be reflected if we carry it on into concrete measures. If we really want to succeed in something, then both sides are going to have to do an awful lot of work in the spirit of the joint statement which we have put out. And in this connection, I would like to announce that the Soviet Union, for its part, will do all it can in this cooperation with the United States of America in order to achieve practical results to cut down the arms race, to cut down the arsenals which we've piled up, and produce the conditions which will be necessary for peace on Earth and in space.

We make this announcement perfectly aware of our responsibility both to our own people and to the other peoples of the Earth. And we would very much hope that we can have the same approach from the administration of the United States of America. If that can be so, then the work that has been done in these days in Geneva will not have been done in vain.

I would like to finish by thanking most profoundly the Government of Switzerland for the conditions which they've created for us to be able to work. Thank you for attention.

The President. President Furgler, General Secretary Gorbachev, may I express Nancy's and my deep personal appreciation and that of all Americans to the people of Switzerland for welcoming us so warmly and preparing the foundations for productive discussions. Yours is a long and honorable tradition of promoting international peace and understanding. You should take pride in being the capital for international discussions. So, again, to the Government of Switzerland and to the citizens of Geneva, many, many thanks.

We've packed a lot into the last 2 days. I came to Geneva to seek a fresh start in relations between the United States and the Soviet Union, and we have done this. General Secretary Gorbachev and I have held comprehensive discussions covering all elements of our relationship. I'm convinced that we are heading in the right direction. We've reached some useful interim results which are described in the joint statement that is being issued this morning. In agreeing to accelerate the work of our nuclear arms negotiators, Mr. Gorbachev and I have addressed our common responsibility to strengthen peace. I believe that we have established a process for more intensive contacts between the United States and the Soviet Union. These 2 days of talks should inject a certain momentum into our work on the issues between us, a momentum we can continue at the meeting that we have agreed on for next year.

Before coming to Geneva, I spoke often of the need to build confidence in our dealings with each other. Frank and forthright conversation at the summit are part of this process, but I'm certain General Secretary Gorbachev would agree that real confidence in each other must be built on deeds, not simply words. This is the thought that ties together all the proposals that the United States has put on the table in the past, and this is the criteria by which our meetings will be judged in the future.

The real report card on Geneva will not come in for months or even years, but we know the questions that must be answered. Will we join together in sharply reducing offensive nuclear arms and moving to non-nuclear defensive strengths for systems to make this a safer world? Will we join together to help bring about a peaceful resolution of conflicts in Asia, Africa, and Central America so that the peoples there can freely determine their own destiny without outside interference? Will the cause of liberty be advanced, and will the treaties and agreements signed—past and future—be fulfilled? The people of America, the Soviet Union, and throughout the world are ready to answer yes.

I leave Geneva today and our fireside summit determined to pursue every opportunity to build a safer world of peace and freedom. There's hard work ahead, but we're ready for it. General Secretary Gorbachev, we ask you to join us in getting the job done, as I'm sure you will.

Thank you.

Note: The President spoke at 10:13 a.m. in the International Press Center. In his remarks, he referred to President Kurt Furgler of Switzerland. Following his remarks, the President returned to Washington, DC. A tape was not available for verification of the content of these remarks.

Address Before a Joint Session of the Congress Following the Soviet-United States Summit Meeting in Geneva
November 21, 1985

Mr. Speaker, Mr. President, Members of the Congress, distinguished guests, and my fellow Americans:

It's great to be home, and Nancy and I

thank you for this wonderful homecoming. And before I go on, I want to say a personal thank you to Nancy. She was an outstanding Ambassador of good will for all of us. She didn't know I was going to say that. Mr. Speaker, Senator Dole, I want you to know that your statements of support here were greatly appreciated. You can't imagine how much it means in dealing with the Soviets to have the Congress, the allies, and the American people firmly behind you.

I guess you know that I have just come from Geneva and talks with General Secretary Gorbachev. In the past few days, the past 2 days, we spent over 15 hours in various meetings with the General Secretary and the members of his official party. And approximately 5 of those hours were talks between Mr. Gorbachev and myself, just one on one. That was the best part—our fireside summit. There will be, I know, a great deal of commentary and opinion as to what the meetings produced and what they were like. There were over 3,000 reporters in Geneva, so it's possible there will be 3,000 opinions on what happened. So, maybe it's the old broadcaster in me, but I decided to file my own report directly to you.

We met, as we had to meet. I called for a fresh start, and we made that start. I can't claim that we had a meeting of the minds on such fundamentals as ideology or national purpose, but we understand each other better, and that's a key to peace. I gained a better perspective; I feel he did, too. It was a constructive meeting; so constructive, in fact, that I look forward to welcoming Mr. Gorbachev to the United States next year. And I have accepted his invitation to go to Moscow the following year. We arranged that out in the parking lot. I found Mr. Gorbachev to be an energetic defender of Soviet policy. He was an eloquent speaker and a good listener.

Our subject matter was shaped by the facts of this century. These past 40 years have not been an easy time for the West or for the world. You know the facts; there is no need to recite the historical record. Suffice it to say that the United States cannot afford illusions about the nature of the U.S.S.R. We cannot assume that their ideology and purpose will change; this implies enduring competition. Our task is to assure that this competition remains peaceful. With all that divides us, we cannot afford to let confusion complicate things further. We must be clear with each other and direct. We must pay each other the tribute of candor.

When I took the oath of office for the first time, we began dealing with the Soviet Union in a way that was more realistic than in, say, the recent past. And so, in a very real sense, preparations for the summit started not months ago, but 5 years ago when, with the help of Congress, we began strengthening our economy, restoring our national will, and rebuilding our defenses and alliances. America is once again strong, and our strength has given us the ability to speak with confidence and see that no true opportunity to advance freedom and peace is lost. We must not now abandon policies that work. I need your continued support to keep America strong.

That is the history behind the Geneva summit, and that is the context in which it occurred. And may I add that we were especially eager that our meetings give a push to important talks already underway on reducing nuclear weapons. On this subject it would be foolish not to go the extra mile or, in this case, the extra 4,000 miles. We discussed the great issues of our time. I made clear before the first meeting that no question would be swept aside, no issue buried, just because either side found it uncomfortable or inconvenient. I brought these questions to the summit and put them before Mr. Gorbachev.

We discussed nuclear arms and how to reduce them. I explained our proposals for equitable, verifiable, and deep reductions. I outlined my conviction that our proposals would make not just for a world that feels safer, but one that really is safer. I am pleased to report tonight that General Secretary Gorbachev and I did make a measure of progress here. We have a long way to go, but we're still heading in the right direction. We moved arms control forward from where we were last January, when the Soviets returned to the table. We are both instructing our negotiators to hasten their vital work. The world is waiting for results.

Specifically, we agreed in Geneva that each side should move to cut offensive nuclear arms by 50 percent in appropriate categories. In our joint statement we called for early progress on this, turning the talks toward our chief goal—offensive reductions. We called for an interim accord on intermediate-range nuclear forces, leading, I hope, to the complete elimination of this class of missiles—and all of this with tough verification. We also made progress in combating, together, the spread of nuclear weapons, an arms control area in which we've cooperated effectively over the years.

We are also opening a dialog on combating the spread and use of chemical weapons, while moving to ban them altogether. Other arms control dialogs—in Vienna on conventional forces and in Stockholm on lessening the chances for surprise attack in Europe—also received a boost. And finally, we agreed to begin work on risk reduction centers, a decision that should give special satisfaction to Senators Nunn and Warner who so ably promoted this idea.

I described our Strategic Defense Initiative, our research effort, that envisions the possibility of defensive systems which could ultimately protect all nations against the danger of nuclear war. This discussion produced a very direct exchange of views. Mr. Gorbachev insisted that we might use a strategic defense system to put offensive weapons into space and establish nuclear superiority. I made it clear that SDI has nothing to do with offensive weapons; that, instead, we are investigating nonnuclear defense systems that would only threaten offensive missiles, not people. If our research succeeds, it will bring much closer the safer, more stable world that we seek. Nations could defend themselves against missile attack and mankind, at long last, escape the prison of mutual terror. And this is my dream.

So, I welcomed the chance to tell Mr. Gorbachev that we are a nation that defends, rather than attacks; that our alliances are defensive, not offensive. We don't seek nuclear superiority. We do not seek a first-strike advantage over the Soviet Union. Indeed, one of my fundamental arms control objectives is to get rid of first-strike weapons altogether. This is why we've pro-

posed a 50-percent reduction in the most threatening nuclear weapons, especially those that could carry out a first strike.

I went further in expressing our peaceful intentions. I described our proposal in the Geneva negotiations for a reciprocal program of open laboratories in strategic defense research. We're offering to permit Soviet experts to see firsthand that SDI does not involve offensive weapons. American scientists would be allowed to visit comparable facilities of the Soviet strategic defense program, which, in fact, has involved much more than research for many years. Finally, I reassured Mr. Gorbachev on another point. I promised that if our research reveals that a defense against nuclear missiles is possible, we would sit down with our allies and the Soviet Union to see how together we could replace all strategic ballistic missiles with such a defense, which threatens no one.

We discussed threats to the peace in several regions of the world. I explained my proposals for a peace process to stop the wars in Afghanistan, Nicaragua, Ethiopia, Angola, and Cambodia—those places where insurgencies that speak for the people are pitted against regimes which obviously do not represent the will or the approval of the people. I tried to be very clear about where our sympathies lie; I believe I succeeded. We discussed human rights. We Americans believe that history teaches no clearer lesson than this: Those countries which respect the rights of their own people tend, inevitably, to respect the rights of their neighbors. Human rights, therefore, is not an abstract moral issue; it is a peace issue. Finally, we discussed the barriers to communication between our societies, and I elaborated on my proposals for real people-to-people contacts on a wide scale. Americans should know the people of the Soviet Union—their hopes and fears and the facts of their lives. And citizens of the Soviet Union need to know of America's deep desire for peace and our unwavering attachment to freedom.

As you can see, our talks were wide ranging. And let me at this point tell you what we agreed upon and what we didn't. We remain far apart on a number of issues, as had to be expected. However, we reached agreement on a number of matters, and as I mentioned, we agreed to continue meeting, and this is important and very good. There's always room for movement, action, and progress when people are talking to each other instead of about each other.

We've concluded a new agreement designed to bring the best of America's artists and academics to the Soviet Union. The exhibits that will be included in this exchange are one of the most effective ways for the average Soviet citizen to learn about our way of life. This agreement will also expand the opportunities for Americans to experience the Soviet people's rich cultural heritage, because their artists and academics will be coming here. We've also decided to go forward with a number of people-to-people initiatives that will go beyond greater contact, not only between the political leaders of our two countries but our respective students, teachers, and others as well. We have emphasized youth exchanges. And this will help break down stereotypes, build friendships, and, frankly, provide an alternative to propaganda.

We've agreed to establish a new Soviet consulate in New York and a new American consulate in Kiev. And this will bring a permanent U.S. presence to the Ukraine for the first time in decades. And we have also, together with the Government of Japan, concluded a Pacific air safety agreement with the Soviet Union. This is designed to set up cooperative measures to improve civil air safety in that region of the Pacific. What happened before must never to be allowed to happen there again. And as a potential way of dealing with the energy needs of the world of the future, we have also advocated international cooperation to explore the feasibility of developing fusion energy.

All of these steps are part of a long-term effort to build a more stable relationship with the Soviet Union. No one ever said it could be easy, but we've come a long way. As for Soviet expansionism in a number of regions of the world—while there is little chance of immediate change, we will continue to support the heroic efforts of those who fight for freedom. But we have also agreed to continue, and to intensify, our

meetings with the Soviets on this and other regional conflicts and to work toward political solutions.

We know the limits as well as the promise of summit meetings. This is, after all, the 11th summit of the postwar era and still the differences endure. But we believe continued meetings between the leaders of the United States and the Soviet Union can help bridge those differences. The fact is, every new day begins with possibilities; it's up to us to fill it with the things that move us toward progress and peace. Hope, therefore, is a realistic attitude and despair an uninteresting little vice.

And so, was our journey worthwhile? Well, 30 years ago, when Ike, President Eisenhower, had just returned from a summit in Geneva, he said, ". . . the wide gulf that separates so far East and West is wide and deep." Well, today, three decades later, that is still true. But, yes, this meeting was worthwhile for both sides. A new realism spawned the summit. The summit itself was a good start, and now our byword must be: steady as we go. I am, as you are, impatient for results. But good will and good hopes do not always yield lasting results, and quick fixes don't fix big problems. Just as we must avoid illusions on our side, so we must dispel them on the Soviet side. I have made it clear to Mr. Gorbachev that we must reduce the mistrust and suspicions between us if we are to do such things as reduce arms, and this will take deeds, not words alone. And I believe he is in agreement.

Where do we go from here? Well, our desire for improved relations is strong. We're ready and eager for step-by-step progress. We know that peace is not just the absence of war. We don't want a phony peace or a frail peace. We didn't go in pursuit of some kind of illusory détente. We can't be satisfied with cosmetic improvements that won't stand the test of time. We want real peace.

As I flew back this evening, I had many thoughts. In just a few days families across America will gather to celebrate Thanksgiving. And again, as our forefathers who voyaged to America, we traveled to Geneva with peace as our goal and freedom as our guide. For there can be no greater good than the quest for peace and no finer purpose than the preservation of freedom. It is 350 years since the first Thanksgiving, when Pilgrims and Indians huddled together on the edge of an unknown continent. And now here we are gathered together on the edge of an unknown future, but, like our forefathers, really not so much afraid, but full of hope and trusting in God, as ever.

Thank you for allowing me to talk to you this evening, and God bless you all.

Note: The President spoke at 9:20 p.m. in the House Chamber of the Capitol. He was introduced by Thomas P. O'Neill, Jr., Speaker of the House of Representatives. The address was broadcast live on nationwide radio and television.

Nomination of Chapman B. Cox To Be an Assistant Secretary of Defense
November 22, 1985

The President today announced his intention to nominate Chapman B. Cox to be an Assistant Secretary of Defense (Force Management and Personnel). He would succeed Lawrence J. Korb.

Mr. Cox is presently serving as General Counsel at the Department of Defense. Previously he was Assistant Secretary of the Navy for Manpower and Reserve Affairs in 1983–1984. From 1981 to 1983, Mr. Cox was Deputy Assistant Secretary of the Navy for Logistics.

He graduated from the University of Southern California (B.A., 1962) and Harvard Law School (J.D., 1965). He is married, has two children, and resides in Arlington, VA. He was born July 31, 1940, in Dayton, OH.

Nomination of Robert B. Barker To Be Chairman of the Military Liaison Committee to the Department of Energy
November 22, 1985

The President today announced his intention to nominate Robert B. Barker to be Chairman of the Department of Defense Military Liaison Committee to the Department of Energy. He would succeed Richard L. Wagner.

Since 1983 Mr. Barker has been Deputy Assistant Director, Bureau of Verification and Intelligence, Arms Control and Disarmament Agency. Previously, he was at Lawrence Livermore National Laboratory in Livermore, CA, as assistant associate director in 1982–1983; special projects division leader in 1978–1982; evaluation and planning division leader in 1973–1978; and strategic warhead design group leader in 1971–1973.

He graduated from Dartmouth College (A.B., 1960) and Syracuse University (Ph.D., 1966). He is married and resides in Arlington, VA. He was born March 9, 1939, in New York City.

Nomination of Frank B. Sollars To Be a Member of the Board of Directors of the National Consumer Cooperative Bank
November 22, 1985

The President today announced his intention to nominate Frank B. Sollars to be a member of the Board of Directors of the National Consumer Cooperative Bank for a term of 3 years. This is a reappointment.

Mr. Sollars is chairman of the board of Sollars Brothers Corp., manufacturers of farm equipment, in Washington Court House, OH. He is also on the board of directors of the Nationwide Insurance Co.

and chairman of the board of the Nationwide Mutual Insurance Co. He is a past president of the Ohio Farm Bureau Federation and a past president of the Ohio Federation of Soil and Water Conservation Districts.

He is married, has five children, and resides in Washington Court House, OH. He was born June 29, 1921, in Washington Court House, OH.

Appointment of John H. Rousselot as Chairman of the United States Section of the Permanent Joint Board on Defense, United States and Canada
November 22, 1985

The President today announced his intention to appoint John H. Rousselot to be Chairman of the United States Section of the Permanent Joint Board on Defense, United States and Canada. He will succeed Charles S. Gubser.

Since July 1985, Mr. Rousselot has been serving as chairman of the National Council of Savings Institutions. He was Special Assistant to the President and Deputy Direc-

tor of the Office of Public Liaison in 1983. Prior to that time, he was a partner with the firm of Alcalde, Henderson & O'Bannon in Washington, DC. He served as a United States Congressman from California in 1961–1962 and 1970–1983.

Mr. Rousselot is married, has six children, and resides in Falls Church, VA. He was born November 1, 1927, in Los Angeles, CA.

Appointment of Two Members of the Board of Visitors to the United States Air Force Academy
November 22, 1985

The President today announced his intention to appoint the following individuals to be members of the Board of Visitors to the United States Air Force Academy for terms expiring December 30, 1988. These are reappointments.

Julian Martin Niemczyk, of Missouri, is chairman of the executive committee of People to People headquarters in Kansas City, MO. He graduated from the University of the Philippines (B.A., 1956). He is married and resides in

Kansas City, MO. He was born August 26, 1920, in Fort Sill, OK.

Lynda Smith, of Colorado, has been a member of the University of Colorado Medical Center Advisory Committee in Denver. She also serves as a member of the advisory board to the chancellor of the University of Colorado. She graduated from the University of Texas (B.S., 1962). She is married, has three children, and resides in Colorado Springs, CO. She was born August 1, 1940, in Tyler, TX.

Radio Address to the Nation on the Soviet-United States Summit Meeting in Geneva
November 23, 1985

My fellow Americans:

This has been a busy and eventful week for Nancy and me. Now that the summit in Geneva is behind us, we need to look ahead and ask: Where do we go from here? As I told Congress, we've made a fresh start in U.S.-Soviet relations. Every issue was on the table, and our 15 hours of discussions were tough and lively throughout. I got a better perspective from listening to General Secretary Gorbachev, and I think he went home with a lot to think about, too. I plan to meet Mr. Gorbachev again next year in Washington, but between now and then, we have much work to do. Opportunities to address important problems of Soviet-American relations should not be squandered. We must always be realistic about our deep and abiding differences, but we should be working for progress wherever possible.

On arms control, the Soviets, after several years of resisting talks, have now agreed that each side should cut nuclear arms by 50 percent in appropriate categories. And in our joint statement, we called for early progress on this, directing the emphasis of the talks toward what has been the chief U.S. goal all along: deep, equitable, fully verifiable reductions in offensive weapons. If there's a real interest on the Soviet side, there's a chance the talks can begin to make headway.

Mr. Gorbachev and I discussed our work on SDI, America's Strategic Defense Initiative. I told him that we're investigating nonnuclear defensive systems designed to destroy offensive missiles and protect people. Although reluctant to acknowledge it, the Soviets have been carrying forward a research program, far more extensive than ours, on their own version of SDI. I think it's fair to point out that the Soviets main aim at Geneva was to force us to drop SDI. I think I can also say that after Geneva Mr.

Gorbachev understands we have no intention of doing so—far from it. We want to make strategic defense a strong protector of the peace. A research and testing program that may one day provide a peace shield to protect against nuclear attack is a deeply hopeful vision, and we should all be cooperating to bring that vision of peace alive for the entire world.

Regional conflicts were prominent in our discussions, and we'll be watching very closely for any change in Soviet activities in the Third World. Another resounding vote of the U.N. General Assembly has just called for Soviet withdrawal from Afghanistan. Next month a new round of talks on this question takes place, also under United Nation auspices. If these talks are to succeed, the Soviets must provide a timetable for getting out and recognize that the freedom fighters will not be conquered.

On bilateral and human rights questions, there were some small, encouraging steps before the summit, and in the agreements we reached there, to promote people-to-people contacts. In both areas, we're hoping greater steps will follow. As I also told the Congress, human rights is a true peace issue.

If there is one conclusion to draw from our fireside summit, it's that American policies are working. In a real sense, preparations for the summit started 5 years ago when, with the help of Congress, we began strengthening our economy, restoring our national will, and rebuilding our defenses and alliances. America is strong again, and American strength has caught the Soviets attention. They recognize that the United States is no longer just reacting to world events; we are in the forefront of a powerful, historic tide for freedom and opportunity, for progress and peace.

There's never been a greater need for

courage and steadiness than now. Our strategic modernization program is an incentive for the Soviets to negotiate in earnest. But if Congress fails to support the vital defense efforts needed, then the Soviets will conclude that America's patience and will are paper thin, and the world will become more dangerous again. Courage and steadiness are all important for freedom fighters, too. I made it clear in Geneva that America embraces all those who resist tyranny and struggle for freedom. Breaking faith with freedom fighters would signal that aggression carries no risk, and this we will not allow. My fellow Americans, we are entering a season of hope. If we remain resolute for freedom and peace, if we keep faith with God, then our American family, 238 million strong, will be even more thankful for next year.

Again it's wonderful to be home; so until next week, thanks for listening. God bless you.

Note: The President spoke at 12:06 p.m. from the Oval Office at the White House.

Proclamation 5413—National Day of Fasting To Raise Funds To Combat Hunger, 1985
November 23, 1985

By the President of the United States of America

A Proclamation

At this time of national Thanksgiving, when we thank God for our many blessings, we are especially mindful of those in distress. And we thank God for inviting us to respond with open hearts to the cry of the afflicted and the needy. For in being generous to others we become more like Him Who has been so generous to us. Most recently, we heard the cry for help that came from the rubble of Mexico City and from the people of Colombia whose villages were engulfed by mud slides. We heard and we responded.

Similarly, we hear and we continue to respond to the cry that comes to our ears from the famine-stricken regions of Africa. That famine has already caused the death of hundreds of thousands of people and endangers the lives of millions. The solution to such famine involves not only rushing emergency food and medical supplies to the areas stricken, but also improving agricultural policies and enlisting greater cooperation by certain governments with international relief agencies.

Americans from all walks of life and every part of our country have responded quickly and generously to every famine that has occurred since World War II. And we have already raised more than $120 million for emergency relief for victims of the current famine in Africa. The generosity and compassion of our people deserve to be recognized and commended.

It has been estimated that in Africa 24 people die of starvation each minute; clearly much more must be done.

Various private organizations are organizing a day of fasting as a means by which Americans can show their concern, express solidarity with the plight of fellow human beings suffering from hunger, and draw attention to efforts to raise funds to help the victims of famine.

The Congress, by House Joint Resolution 386, has designated November 24, 1985, as "National Day of Fasting to Raise Funds to Combat Hunger" and authorized and requested the President to issue a proclamation in observance of this event.

Now, Therefore, I, Ronald Reagan, President of the United States of America, do hereby proclaim November 24, 1985, as National Day of Fasting to Raise Funds to Combat Hunger. I call upon the people of the United States to observe such day with appropriate ceremonies and other activities and to consider donating to relief organizations fighting hunger.

In Witness Whereof, I have hereunto set

my hand this twenty-third day of November, in the year of our Lord nineteen hundred and eighty-five, and of the Independence of the United States of America the two hundred and tenth.

RONALD REAGAN

[*Filed with the Office of the Federal Register, 10:27 a.m., November 25, 1985*]

Note: The proclamation was released by the Office of the Press Secretary on November 25.

Statement on United States Arms Sales to Jordan
November 25, 1985

On October 21 I submitted to the Congress a formal notification of the proposed sale of fighter aircraft, air defense missiles, armored vehicles, and other equipment to the Hashemite Kingdom of Jordan. The number and type of arms included in our proposal were selected only after careful study of Jordan's legitimate defensive needs.

I have today signed into law Senate Joint Resolution 228, which provides that no letter of offer for any of the advanced weapons systems, including advanced aircraft and advanced air defense systems, included in our proposed sale to Jordan will be valid before March 1, 1986, unless Jordan enters direct negotiations with Israel before that date. This legislation expresses Congress' belief that the peace process should be our primary concern. Peace remains my main concern, as it is that of King Hussein, Prime Minister Peres [of Israel], and other responsible leaders throughout the Middle East. King Hussein has taken dramatic steps towards peace, steps which have exposed him and the people of Jordan to strong pressure and bloody violence from those adamantly opposed to any peaceful settlement. Our arms proposals are designed to strengthen Jordan's ability to pursue its demonstrated commitment to peace.

In the months between now and March 1, we will continue to work towards achieving the goal we all share, the goal King Hussein outlined in his recent speech to the United Nations General Assembly: prompt, direct negotiations between Jordan and Israel. I remain equally committed to providing Jordan the defensive arms it requires. These weapons are neither a reward nor penalty for Jordan's actions, but tangible proof that we remain committed to providing a good friend of many years with the tools needed to protect itself during the search for peace in a troubled region.

Statement on Signing the Department of Housing and Urban Development-Independent Agencies Appropriations Act, 1986
November 25, 1985

I have today signed H.R. 3038, a bill providing for appropriations for the Department of Housing and Urban Development and several independent agencies, including the Federal Emergency Management Agency (FEMA).

This bill would also authorize FEMA, through a new "national board," to oversee an emergency food and shelter program. I am deeply concerned about the membership of the Board. Under this bill the Board is to be composed of seven members who would be officers of the executive branch because the Board will perform executive functions. If read literally, the bill would permit six private organizations to appoint members of the Board, in violation of the appointments clause of the Constitution (Article II, section 2, clause 2). In order to avoid this constitutional infirmity, I direct the Director of FEMA to construe this provision as granting him complete discretionary authority to determine who should be appointed to the national board. The organizations mentioned in the bill may make recommendations, but only the Director, as the "head of a department," *id.*, is authorized to appoint members to the Board.

The bill also provides, in section 413, that "[n]o part of any appropriation contained in this Act shall be available to implement, administer, or enforce any regulation which has been disapproved pursuant to a resolution of disapproval duly adopted in accordance with the applicable law of the United States." The "applicable law of the United States" includes, of course, the Constitution and the decision of the Supreme Court in *INS* v. *Chadha.* Under the Constitution and that decision, the "resolution of disapproval" referred to in section 413 must be a joint resolution presented to the President for approval or disapproval.

Note: H.R. 3038, approved November 25, was assigned Public Law No. 99–160.

Message to the Congress Transmitting the Sweden-United States Social Security Agreement
November 25, 1985

To the Congress of the United States:

Pursuant to section 233(e)(1) of the Social Security Act, as amended by the Social Security Amendments of 1977 (P.L. 95–216, 42 USC 433(e)(1)), I transmit herewith the Agreement between the United States of America and the Kingdom of Sweden on Social Security which consists of two separate instruments. The Agreement was signed at Stockholm on May 27, 1985.

The U.S.-Sweden agreement is similar in objective to the social security agreements already in force with Italy, the Federal Republic of Germany, Switzerland, Canada, Belgium, Norway, and the United Kingdom. Such bilateral agreements, which are generally known as totalization agreements, provide for limited coordination between the United States and foreign social security systems to overcome the problems of gaps in protection and of dual coverage and taxation for workers who move from one country to the other.

I also transmit for the information of the Congress a comprehensive report prepared by the Department of Health and Human Services, which explains the provisions of the Agreement and provides data on the number of persons affected by the Agreement and the effect on social security financing as required by the same provision of the Social Security Act.

The Department of State and the Department of Health and Human Services join with me in commending the U.S.-Sweden Social Security Agreement and related documents.

RONALD REAGAN

The White House,
November 25, 1985.

Message to the Congress Reporting Budget Deferrals
November 25, 1985

To the Congress of the United States:

In accordance with the Impoundment Control Act of 1974, I herewith report 8 new deferrals of budget authority for 1986 totaling $2,023,327,275. The deferrals affect accounts in Funds Appropriated to the President, the Departments of Commerce, Defense-Military, Health and Human Services, Transportation, and Treasury.

The details of these deferrals are contained in the attached report.

RONALD REAGAN

The White House,
November 25, 1985.

Note: The attachment detailing the deferrals was printed in the Federal Register *of December 2.*

Letter to the Speaker of the House and the Chairman of the Senate Foreign Relations Committee Reporting on the Cyprus Conflict
November 25, 1985

Dear Mr. Speaker: (Dear Mr. Chairman:)

In accordance with Public Law 95–384, I am submitting to you a bimonthly report on progress toward a negotiated settlement of the Cyprus question.

Since my previous report, the United Nations Secretary General has continued to work with the two Cypriot communities to achieve a framework agreement for a comprehensive Cyprus settlement. As I reported to you earlier, the Secretary General announced in June that the Greek Cypriot side had accepted revised documentation incorporating such an agreement. On August 8 the Turkish Cypriot leader, Mr. Denktash, sent the Secretary General a letter with detailed comments on the Secretary General's documentation and expressed willingness to meet with him for further discussion.

The Secretary General invited Mr. Denktash to New York and they met on September 12–13. Following their meetings the Secretary General said he had most useful talks with Mr. Denktash and that these talks would be helpful in deciding the steps to be taken in the near future.

The Security Council heard an oral report from the Secretary General on September 20. He told the Council that his efforts had brought the positions of the two sides closer than ever before; and he expressed his conviction that what had been achieved so far should lead to an early agreement on a framework for a just and lasting settlement of the Cyprus question. The United Kingdom Permanent Representative to the Security Council, speaking as President of the Council, expressed strong support on behalf of its members for the mandate of the Secretary General and called upon all parties to make a special effort in cooperation with the Secretary General to reach an early agreement.

Continuing his consultations, the Secretary General met with President Kyprianou on October 16 and October 25 for discussion of recent developments on the Cyprus issue. The Secretary General also met on October 25 with Turkish Prime Minister Ozal.

During this period, American officials continued their active efforts in support of the Secretary General's good offices mission and urged a cooperative and constructive attitude by all the parties. Ambassador Boehm encouraged support for a negotiated settlement in his meetings with President Kyprianou and Mr. Denktash. Secretary Shultz met with the Secretary General and during the General Assembly with the Greek and Turkish Foreign Ministers. Under Secretary Armacost also had useful talks with senior officials of Greece and Turkey during his October 28–November 3 visit to those countries.

Sincerely,

RONALD REAGAN

Note: Identical letters were sent to Thomas P. O'Neill, Jr., Speaker of the House of Representatives, and Richard G. Lugar, chairman of the Senate Foreign Relations Committee.

Proclamation 5414—National Mark Twain Day, 1985
November 26, 1985

By the President of the United States of America

A Proclamation

Like the comet that startled the night sky at his birth and returned as a bright chariot to "carry him home" 75 years later, the literary achievements of Mark Twain can truly be called an "astronomical" phenomenon.

Born Samuel Langhorne Clemens, November 30, 1835, in Florida, Missouri, he enjoyed an idyllic boyhood in Hannibal, Missouri. There by the banks of the mighty Mississippi, he came to know and love the common people of America. Their crotchets and kindnesses; their exasperating foibles; their endearing loyalties; their dreams and hopes were printed indelibly in his memory. Annealed through time and art, those recollections would be transformed by his genius into immortal characters in masterworks that not only won great popularity in his day but have also stood the test of time.

Today, as we commemorate the 150th anniversary of Mark Twain's birth—and as Halley's Comet again brightens the skies of our planet—the wit, the wisdom, and the inimitable style of Mark Twain continue to delight and instruct young and old—in more than 50 languages.

It is a measure of the richness of Twain's genius and the complexity of his character that debates still go on as to whether he was primarily a humorist, a novelist, a charming spinner of provincial yarns, a cynic, or a sentimentalist. The truth is he was all of these—and more.

He was American to the core and he was also a sophisticated world traveller. He evoked the concrete details of his own time and place as no one else could, and he was also deeply versed in history.

He relished the innocent joys of childhood and the storybook adventures of his young manhood. He knew the fulfillment of a happy marriage and the heady wine of wealth and adulation. The dons of Yale and Oxford honored him with exalted degrees, and when he died the common people wept.

Twain also knew the shattering humiliation of betrayal and bankruptcy. He endured the soul-searing desolation of bereavement, and in the depths of his grief he could sometimes rail like the proverbial village atheist. But he could also write of the saintly Joan of Arc with the awe and ardor of a hagiographer. In many ways Twain remains a riddle. He still awaits a definitive biography. He would probably have been amused at all the fuss that has been made over him and chuckle at some of the theories the critics have spun about him and his works. Self-deprecation was the hallmark of his humor; he loved to puncture pomposity—even his own.

New York, Connecticut, California, and Hawaii are only some of the States that can claim to have shaped his life, but Hannibal, Missouri, where he grew up, will always have a prior claim. And so it is especially fitting that while all Americans celebrate this anniversary, Hannibal—which maintains his boyhood home as a museum—has been the scene of special events starting in May and culminating on November 30, the 150th anniversary of his birth.

The Congress, by House Joint Resolution 259, has designated November 30, 1985, as "National Mark Twain Day" and authorized and requested the President to issue a proclamation in observance of this event.

Now, Therefore, I, Ronald Reagan, President of the United States of America, do hereby proclaim November 30, 1985, as National Mark Twain Day. I call upon the people of the United States to observe such day with appropriate ceremonies and activities.

In Witness Whereof, I have hereunto set my hand this twenty-sixth day of November, in the year of our Lord nineteen hundred and eighty-five, and of the Independence of the United States of America the two hundred and tenth.

RONALD REAGAN

Note: The proclamation was released by the Office of the Press Secretary on November 29.

Radio Address to the Nation on Efforts to Prevent Espionage Against the United States
November 30, 1985

My fellow Americans:

You've heard me say that nuclear war cannot be won and must never be fought. Well, today I wish to speak to you about a struggle which we do wage every day, a struggle we must win if we're to protect our freedom and our way of life. At stake are government secrets essential to our national security. Protecting these secrets against espionage and any hostile intelligence threat to the United States is a heavy responsibility.

Operations to protect America's secrets are usually done quietly with little publicity. Well, lately they've been making big news. Some of you may be wondering if the large number of spy arrests in recent weeks means that we're looking harder or whether there are more spies to find. Well, I think the answer to both questions is yes. The threat is certainly increasing. The number of hostile intelligence officers in the United States and working against us around the world has grown sharply in recent years. Espionage, spying, is not a game. It costs our country secrets and millions of dollars in stolen technology. It can also cost lives and threaten our national survival.

This administration had given high priority to improving our ability to detect and counter any hostile intelligence threat. We've added resources, people, and top-level attention to this task. We will not hesitate to root out and prosecute the spies of any nation. We'll let the chips fall where they may. And we've had impressive results. From 1975 to 1980, the United States apprehended a total of 13 spies. From 1981 through this year, we've apprehended 34. Here, let me add a word of appreciation in particular to the men and women of the FBI who have been working so diligently on this vital and sometimes thankless task.

In the past, we've had some difficulty in readily admitting the intensity of this threat. Today, however, we approach the intelligence threat with a new degree of realism. We recognize that the KGB and others seeking to exploit the openness of our society are not 10 feet tall; neither, however, are they midgets. We're up against aggressive people who take their job seriously. There's no reason to sugar-coat reality. The free world is today confronted with some of the most sophisticated, best orchestrated efforts of theft and espionage in modern history. Today the Soviet intelligence services and secret police, the KGB and the GRU, and their surrogate services among the Soviet-bloc countries—Czechoslovakia, Poland, East Germany, Bulgaria, Cuba, and others—are hard at work. Their activities include classical espionage and what they call active measures. They are employing all the means we associate with spies, including electronic espionage against sensitive communications and other sophisticated techniques, to steal our secrets and technology.

As events of recent days have made clear, many nations spy on the United States. The totality of this threat underscores just how important it is that we protect ourselves. What better time than this Thanksgiving weekend to remember and give thanks that we live in the freest land God has placed on this Earth. Yet even with our freedom, we must have the ability to protect certain vital secrets. So much depends on this: our diplomatic efforts to advance liberty and preserve peace, our own ability to see and hear what is going on in the world, and the readiness of our military forces and their effectiveness in carrying out their mission anywhere in the world.

While our security is tied to protecting certain secrets, there is no need to fight repression by becoming repressive ourselves. Understanding the problem is the first step. The arrests we are seeing now should alert us to the danger we face. Even skeptics should recognize how necessary it is to maintain our top-quality counterintelligence efforts. At the same time, we can learn through each espionage case how to prevent these spies and turncoats from hurting us. In 1981 we began a comprehensive review of counterintelligence, security,

and countermeasures. While much has been done, culminating in additional arrests, there is more we can and must do.

We are currently seeking a broad range of reforms and improvements, including reducing the size of the hostile intelligence threat within our borders, better monitoring of exchange programs, improving government communications and personnel procedures, better analysis, expanding counterintelligence capabilities abroad, and ensuring the security of U.S. Embassies and bases throughout the world. We are working closely with the Congress in addressing many of these needs. I am asking for your understanding and support as we move ahead together to win this struggle and keep America free, secure, and at peace.

Until next week, thanks for listening, and God bless you.

Note: The President spoke at 9:06 a.m. from Rancho del Cielo, his ranch near Santa Barbara, CA.

Remarks at the All-Star Tribute to Ronald "Dutch" Reagan in Burbank, California
December 1, 1985

The President. Well—[*laughter*]—it's good to be Dutch again, and it's wonderful to be surrounded by so many fine and talented friends. To paraphrase Jack Kennedy, there hasn't been so much talent assembled in one room since—well, since the last time Monty Hall hosted "Let's Make a Deal." [*Laughter*] Seriously, Nancy and I have watched these parties over the years, and we're thrilled to be a part of the good work of the Variety Clubs International. And something Lucy [Ball] said last year applies to the way that I feel right now. Let's see if I can quote her accurately: "To those of you who said such nice things about me tonight, I just wish you were all under oath." [*Laughter*] I wish you were all Members of Congress. [*Laughter*]

You know, when I first started in my present job, I'd sometimes put together in my mind my own dream Cabinet—you

know, John Wayne as Secretary of State—[*laughter*]—Clint Eastwood at Defense—[*laughter*]—Jack Benny as Secretary of Treasury—[*laughter*]—Groucho Marx at Education. [*Laughter*] But even Presidents can't have everything, except tonight; tonight, all of you here, well, you've really made my day. [*Laughter*] And as for all of you who were so generous in sharing your talents with us tonight, will you please stand up so that I can applaud you all once more? Come on, those of you—[*applause*]. Thank you. And, Frank——

Mr. Sinatra. Yes, sir.

The President. "Old Blue Eyes," as always, you've been the perfect host. Your voice rings just as pure and clear as ever for all of us guys and dolls who are still young at heart. And speaking of music, Steve and Eydie, I like the songs you sang—not a clinker in the bunch. [*Laughter*] And Dean

Martin, there you go again. [*Laughter*] Dean, I am thrilled that you were able to be here tonight for Burt Reynolds' party. [*Laughter*] And sometime, if they ever have a party for Nancy and me, I hope you can make that one, too. [*Laughter*] And Vin Scully, you brought back a lot of happy memories. And Monty Hall, the voice of Variety Clubs, thank you for your presentation. And Mike Frankovich, you share those words of gratitude; everybody knows how devoted you are to Variety. [*Laughter*] And Ben Vereen, you've danced your way into America's heart. And Emmanuel Lewis, we should never lose sight of what you said—wait a minute—even if sometimes we lose sight of you. [*Laughter*] Well, there you are, Manny. And that was a lovely sentiment that was expressed by the International [National] Children's Choir. And Chuck Heston, I knew you had leadership qualities when I saw you play Moses. You were eloquent and gracious in your remarks about me—that guard on the Eureka varsity—thank you.

To all of you associated with the good work of Variety, you have our eternal gratitude for arranging this party, for all the good work that you have done in your half a century of giving and caring for those who need our help the most, the innocent children of the world. Having my name associated with your good work—the University of Nebraska Medical Center will always have a special place in my heart, and I thank you all very much.

And now, speaking for Nancy as well as myself, to all of you here and to all Americans everywhere, paraphrasing something that Moses said earlier, God shed His grace on each of thee. Thank you.

Note: The President spoke at 7:53 p.m. at the NBC studios. The fundraiser was sponsored by Variety Clubs International. Following his remarks, he attended a dinner for program participants and guests. At the end of the evening, the President went to the Century Plaza Hotel in Los Angeles, CA, where he stayed overnight.

Remarks at a Fundraising Luncheon for Senator Slade Gorton in Seattle, Washington
December 2, 1985

Thank you all very much, and I was delighted to see these young people here, because that's what these elections for the next few times are all about—them and the America that they are going to grow up in. Well, I thank you, Senator Gorton, for your very kind words about party duties. I think I should confess: I'm doing penance for all those wasted years before I—[*laughter*]. Senator Evans, Congressmen Miller, Morrison, and Chandler, Bill Ruckelshaus, and you ladies and gentlemen, it's an honor for me to be here today in support of a courageous champion of good government and fiscal responsibility, your Senator, Slade Gorton.

Slade has been a powerful voice for the State of Washington, and an ally of mine on the major issues of the day. And if I have one message for you, it is: Please send Slade

Gorton back to the United States Senate. I was going to ask if I could count on you to do that, but I think you've already answered that. I didn't think you paid this much for lunch just to hear me talk. [*Laughter*] It's a pleasure to be here to keep Slade in a job in which he has so distinguished himself.

There's a story—you knew I'd have a story—about a fellow who had a different kind of job in mind, but he was out there working for the job. And then he saw an ad in the help wanted ads, where the zoo wanted a worker at the zoo, and he immediately applied because he had always wanted to work and loved to work with animals. And when he got there, though, he found that the job was to put on a gorilla suit, sit in the cage, and be the gorilla for the people who came to visit the zoo. Their old gorilla had died, and they had not yet received delivery of his successor. Well, he was a little upset by that, but then they explained that it would only be temporary and then he would have a legitimate job in the zoo. So, he took the job. And pretty soon he got a little bored just sitting there in that cage and people coming by, so he began doing tricks, particularly for the children that had come by to see the gorilla. And there was a rope in there and he'd get on the rope, and he'd swing around, and he was kind of getting into the act pretty good. And one day, very rambunctious, he swung so far on the rope that he landed in the lion's cage. And the lion started for him, and he stood up, and he started screaming, "Get me out of here! Get me out of here!" And the lion jumped on him and said, "Shut up, or you'll get both of us fired!" [*Laughter*]

Well, seriously though, Slade and I were both elected in 1980 because there was a critical job to do. And thanks to the policies of tax and tax and spend and spend, our country was heading toward an economic catastrophe. We were suffering the ravages of both double-digit inflation and stagnation. Our military strength had been permitted to erode, and our confidence as a people was shaken. Turning around that situation was no easy job, but with the leadership of Senate Republicans like Senator Gorton, we went to work. It took some doing to reverse the decades of more and more government as the answer to every problem and to put our program in place, and even more to stand firm until it had time to produce results. There was enormous pressure to go back to the policies that we'd left behind. Let me just ask you: Were we right to stick to our guns? [*Applause*] You just made my day. [*Laughter*] I think most Americans feel the way you do.

We've now had 3 years of growth. Last quarter the gross national product grew at a healthy 4.3-percent rate. Now, that was higher than had been projected by a great many of the critics and the naysayers in Washington. The economic resurgence has opened new opportunities and a chance for a better life for all people. We have created nearly 9 million new jobs since the recovery began. Almost 2 million businesses, most of them small, independent businesses, have been incorporated in the last 3 years. And during this same time, we've reduced inflation—it's been 3.2 percent for the last 12 months. And there are still some diehards who refuse to acknowledge that the changes we've made have had anything to do with America's dramatic progress in these last few years. They sort of remind me of the fellow who was asked which was worse, ignorance or apathy, and he said, "I don't know, and I don't care." [*Laughter*]

We can all be proud that there's a new spirit alive in America today. We've left cynicism and pessimism behind and recaptured that confidence and optimism that has been a hallmark of our people. We have it within our power to lay the foundation for a generation of prosperity and peace. With the leadership of responsible, hardworking, future-oriented elected officials like Senator Slade Gorton, we'll do just that. We can be proud that since he arrived in our Nation's Capital, Senator Gorton has remained immune to the Potomac disease, which causes too many elected officials to give up a better tomorrow for America in order to placate special interests today. I think that reflects well on you, the people he represents.

For the people of Seattle and the State of Washington, like the people of my home State of California, have always been able to see a great future just beyond the horizon and understand that it is not beyond our power to get there. You are America's doorway to the Pacific rim, the most dynamic region of the planet. We have to keep leading the great advances that are being made there, or we'll be left behind by people who are waiting for no one. While others are overwhelmed by fear and apprehension, you are excited by the vista of new challenges and opportunities. Underscoring this, Senator Gorton has been a timeless defender of free trade. He knows that free trade is a cornerstone of America's prosperity.

I know that there's been much talk of late about America's trade challenges. But we've been leading the way out of a global recession and pulling the world into better times with us. As foreign economies strengthen, their currencies are strengthening, too. As this happens, other nations will buy more from us, and pressure on the trade balance will ease. Short-term protectionist measures now will undermine the chances of economic growth, not only in friendly countries but here as well. Protecting an industry here by imposing these restrictions will inevitably result in countermeasures that will cost the jobs of Americans in other industries. Those who claim to be concerned about the American farmer, for example, should realize that protectionism is the greatest single threat to the well-being of American agriculture, which is one of our main exports.

Instead of shooting ourselves in the foot with job-killing protectionism, what we can, should, and will do is demand that free trade be a two-way street. And I can assure you our representatives are doing just that. The markets must be open on both sides of the ocean. The solution we seek is not decreasing what others send us, but increasing what we send them. Balancing the trade deficit up means a better life for all. Balancing it down through protectionism and weaker economic growth means stagnation and decline. I firmly believe that if the deck is not stacked against us, the American people can outproduce and outcompete anyone in the world. The genius, creative talents, and hard work of our people have always been our greatest assets. With freedom and the profit motive, there's nothing we can't do.

Seattle has a man who exemplifies this spirit: Mr. T. Wilson, a giant of American enterprise. And thanks to the business sense, foresight, and everyday effort of individuals like Mr. Wilson, America is today on the edge of vast new frontiers. The world already marvels at American aircraft and space technology. Our latest aircraft are doing more and using less fuel than ever before. The common man now jets across continents and it's no big thing. Our space shuttle missions now are all but routine, and we're just beginning to touch the commercial use of space, something which, in the not too distant future, will be a tremendous asset to our country. I know that Senator Gorton is one of the Senate's leading advocates of putting space to use to benefit all mankind.

Our technology can also help us leave behind the threat of nuclear holocaust, which has hung over our heads like the sword of Damocles for four decades. Our leading minds have been mobilized to see if it's possible to build a defense system, not to kill people, but to protect them. If successful, our research could usher in a new era of security. A space shield could make arms reduction more feasible by rendering nuclear missiles obsolete, and so they would become more negotiable. I expressed these sentiments to General Secretary Gorbachev during our recent meetings in Geneva. I went to Geneva as a first step. I didn't expect miracles; I did expect progress, an opening, a crack in the door, for improved relations. General Secretary Gorbachev and I spoke frankly, over many hours, about our differences, about a wide range of issues including Soviet expansionism.

As I reported to a joint session of Congress and to you, the American people, when I returned, I was pleased with the results of our sessions. It was the fresh start we wanted. We're not claiming any great breakthroughs and so forth, but—start. As a matter of fact, we had thought before we left that if we could even get agreement from them to continued meetings in the next few years to come that that would make the trip worthwhile. Well, we got that promise from them on a parking lot on the first day we were there. [*Laughter*] It was, as I say, the fresh start that we wanted.

And Geneva let loose a lot of hopes, mine among them; but there've been hopeful times before. We have to understand which policies work and which ones don't. Blurring the issues and ignoring the areas of friction between the Soviet Union and the United States is no way to create a more peaceful world. In fact, the progress we made at Geneva was possible only because in the last 5 years we've been determined to make America stronger. That's how the meeting came about. Because we've spoken out clearly about Soviet policies that threaten peace, that policy is working. I'm confident that if we remain firm in our convictions, realistic in our approach, and strong enough to defend our interests, the competition that we have with the Soviets can remain peaceful. Jefferson is quoted as saying, "Eternal vigilance is the price of liberty." Well, it's as true today as it was two centuries ago.

But just as in Jefferson's day, Americans are preparing themselves for great strides forward. Our technological advances of the last four decades are only the foundation for a new era that is almost beyond imagination. We have just given thanks as a nation to God for all our many blessings, but we should be also grateful for this bright future that lies just over the horizon.

And, again, I have to say to you we have a representative government that represents the will and the desires of the people. And I think it is high time that we not only dwelt on sending someone in charge of the executive branch of government but send those people, as you have sent your two Senators there, to represent the interests of your State and of the people of this country

in seeing that we can put forth the policies that apparently the people of this country have approved. So, 1986—there'll be a November day, and you send Slade Gorton back there to join your junior Senator. And just think, you won't have a situation in which one Senator is canceling out the other Senator's vote for the things that you want done in Washington. There'll be two votes there for all those right things. Send us people back there in the Congress to help with the things that we have started so far, and I think maybe you'll be very pleased with the result.

Thank you all. God bless you all.

Note: The President spoke at 12:54 p.m. in the Grand Ballroom at the Westin Hotel. Prior to his remarks, he attended a reception at the hotel for major contributors to Senator Gorton's reelection campaign. Following his remarks, the President returned to Washington, DC.

Remarks at a White House Ceremony for Participants in the National Initiative on Technology and the Disabled
December 3, 1985

Good afternoon, and welcome to the White House. It's a pleasure to be able to welcome participants in the National Initiative on Technology and the Disabled—men and women who've given so much to their fellow Americans.

This is an age of marvels, technological marvels. And today we have calculators the size of playing cards and computers that can fit inside a suitcase—or a briefcase—boil it down a little. We have home entertainment centers that put the great music and literature of the ages at a family's fingertips. And we have dazzling communications. Indeed, I remember my disbelief—and I still have trouble with this—when I was told one day of a satellite that could transmit the entire Encyclopaedia Britannica in 3 seconds.

Perhaps the central marvel of our age is space travel. It was less than three decades ago that the first U.S. satellite was launched

and less than two decades ago that man first walked on the Moon. And yet today the dream of regular space travel is already becoming a reality, a working part of our everyday lives. It seems like yesterday when Nancy and I watched the space shuttle *Columbia* glide to a magnificent landing in the California desert, 1 of 23 space shuttle missions so far. I think my greatest surprise was, out there in Edwards Air Force Base, to be told to get up on the platform, that it was on its approach. And I said, "Where is it now?" And they said, "Just over Honolulu." [*Laughter*] And it was on its approach. I have to tell you, it was the biggest thrill I'd felt since hearing that Lindbergh had landed in France. [*Laughter*]

But reflecting on the new technology, and in particular on aerospace technology, Secretary [of Health and Human Services] Heckler and others began to wonder about its wider applications. They thought that maybe technology could be applied not just out in space but here on Earth. If we could give astronauts jetpacks, couldn't we give the disabled better wheelchairs? And if we could enable a spacecraft orbiting the Earth to talk to Houston control, couldn't we help those with speech impairments? And so it was that an exciting new partnership between the Government and the private sector was born, the National Initiative on Technology and the Disabled. Already, the initiative is hard at work, encouraging the development of dramatic new technologies.

Our one new device is called Compu-talk and is designed for people incapable of intelligent speech—intelligible speech, I should say. The person simply types the phrase he wants to pronounce, then a computer synthesizes the sound. And the whole unit—that's the one that fits inside a suitcase—it can bring to an end the misery of those who can think clearly but cannot make themselves understood. Another new device is called the blink writer, and this is designed to help persons, like stroke victims, who are completely paralyzed and can neither speak nor write. Imagine the frustration they encounter when trying to communicate. But with the blink writer a paralyzed person can look at a television screen and construct phrases simply by blinking. In a very real sense, the blink writer is a device of liberation, an instrument which sets free men and women who would otherwise be trapped in the isolation of their own minds.

Other new high-tech medical instruments and techniques are being developed every day. There are motorized wheelchairs made of strong, lightweight metal alloys. There are the artificial heart, the pacemaker, and a handheld x-ray device called the Lixiscope. There's an implantable device called the human tissue stimulator which shows great promise for controlling chronic pain, like that associated with arthritis, rheumatism, and cancer. And there's a remarkable arrangement called the programmable implantable medication system or, for short, PIMS. Although still in the testing stages, it's hoped that PIMS can actually be inserted into the patient's body and used to deliver specified doses of medication to particu-

lar parts of the body at carefully chosen times. It holds out enormous hope for people who must receive periodic injections, people like diabetics or patients with inoperable tumors.

To help make certain that these technologies reach the people who need them, you of the National Initiative on Technology and the Disabled are assembling Tech-Net, a national information network that can be consulted by physicians and disabled citizens alike. You're also working on Tech-Team, a network of local technological professionals who are applying their skills, knowledge, and talents to the problems encountered by the disabled. And day in and day out, you're hard at work raising the money to make all these efforts possible. In the last year alone, I understand the Initiative has raised more than $2 million. What it all comes down to is remarkable American know-how being used to help the American people.

Tom Cusworth, on the dais with us today, understands. Five years ago at the age of 19, Tom suffered a swimming accident which left him a paraplegic. But Tom went to a high-technology rehabilitation center in Seattle and overcame his handicap so well that he even learned computer programming. And I have to tell you, Tom, that's a subject we didn't have when I was your age. [*Laughter*] Today, Tom is a computer analyst in Tech-Net. And, Tom, I know I speak for everyone here when I give you my heartfelt congratulations.

Susan Yim is also with us today. She is also someone who understands. While a graduate student in biology at Duke University, Susan suffered a severe brain stem stroke which left her a quadraplegic. She was unable to speak and unable to move any part of her body except her thumbs. But Susan's mind was sound. For months she struggled to communicate, always dependent on others to decipher her thoughts. Then nothing less than a miracle took place. Jim Jaklitsch, a brilliant engineer who's also with us today, designed a computer that could be operated by Susan's thumb movements, and Susan became able to communicate on her own. And today she has retained a large measure of the freedom that she thought was gone forever. And, Susan, you're what it's all about and you make us very proud.

On behalf of Susan and all of the disabled Americans, I want to thank Secretary Margaret Heckler, the Department of Defense, and NASA for bringing the National Initiative on Technology and the Disabled into being. And I know that each of us wants to express his deep gratitude to Robert Kirk, the head of the Initiative's executive committee. But the Initiative would be nothing without its many participants and so it is that I want to thank you, the men and women who have given this Initiative its drive and substance.

Yes, technology can lift hopes and dreams. And so, really, I can say it all—I just want to thank you all for what you're doing, and God bless you all.

Note: The President spoke at 1:34 p.m. in the East Room at the White House.

Proclamation 5415—National Home Care Week, 1985
December 3, 1985

By the President of the United States of America

A Proclamation

Americans have always cared for one another in both good times and bad. When a family has a loved one—elderly, disabled, or a child—needing special care at home, it will inevitably respond by doing everything to keep that person at home. This is the American spirit. Home health care has a long tradition in our Nation. The Federal government, the States, and families are now working in a cooperative way to see that this commitment continues.

No one would suggest that a family can do more for a patient when a hospital or other appropriate institution is clearly needed. But American families go the extra step or mile, if needed, to protect, care for, and serve a member in need. The Federal government has done its share to help. Now, our many States have taken on the initiative to create special programs to enhance home health care. They are to be commended for this humane action.

In addition, there are countless churches, voluntary organizations, and private agencies that assist our families to care for a member at home. Our Nation is learning that, in spite of a time when "doing your own thing" is in, caring for a mother, father, sister, or brother—or any relative or friend—in the home is vastly more important. Independence, under God's loving care and guidance, is to be cherished. Who, then, should care for our own than those who love them best? Once again our long tradition prevails as so many in government, charitable groups, and families work for the well-being of one in need at home.

The Congress, by Senate Joint Resolution 139, has designated the week beginning December 1, 1985, as "National Home Care Week" and authorized and requested the President to issue a proclamation in observance of this event.

Now, Therefore, I, Ronald Reagan, President of the United States of America, do hereby proclaim the week beginning December 1, 1985, as National Home Care Week. I call upon the people of the United States to observe the week with appropriate programs, ceremonies, and activities.

In Witness Whereof, I have hereunto set my hand this third day of December, in the year of our Lord nineteen hundred and eighty-five, and of the Independence of the United States of America the two hundred and tenth.

RONALD REAGAN

[*Filed with the Office of the Federal Register, 11:46 a.m., December 4, 1985*]

Proclamation 5416—National Temporary Services Week, 1985
December 3, 1985

By the President of the United States of America

A Proclamation

The temporary services industry provides employers much needed flexibility to tailor their work forces to meet short-term needs. It also provides important job opportunities for American workers: last year, the temporary services industry provided employment for an estimated five million people.

The temporary services industry currently is the second fastest growing business sector in our economy, in terms of new jobs created. Approximately one out of every two hundred nonagricultural jobs in the United States is provided through temporary services.

It is appropriate that we recognize the many and vital contributions that the men and women of the temporary services industry provide to our economy.

The Congress, by Senate Joint Resolution 195, has designated the week of December 1 through December 7, 1985, as "National Temporary Services Week" and has authorized and requested the President to issue a proclamation in commemoration of this observance.

Now, Therefore, I, Ronald Reagan, President of the United States of America, do hereby proclaim the week of December 1 through December 7, 1985, as National Temporary Services Week, and I call upon the people of the United States to observe this week with appropriate programs and activities.

In Witness Whereof, I have hereunto set my hand this third day of December, in the year of our Lord nineteen hundred and eighty-five, and of the Independence of the United States of America the two hundred and tenth.

RONALD REAGAN

[*Filed with the Office of the Federal Register, 11:47 a.m., December 4, 1985*]

Executive Order 12539—President's Council on Physical Fitness and Sports
December 3, 1985

By the authority vested in me as President by the Constitution and laws of the United States of America, including the Federal Advisory Committee Act, as amended (5 U.S.C. App. I), and in order to increase the membership of the President's Council on Physical Fitness and Sports, it is hereby ordered that Section 2(b) of Executive Order No. 12345, as amended, is further amended by increasing the number of members of the Council from fifteen to eighteen.

RONALD REAGAN

The White House,
December 3, 1985.

[*Filed with the Office of the Federal Register, 11:48 a.m., December 4, 1985*]

Remarks to the Students and Faculty at Fallston High School in Fallston, Maryland
December 4, 1985

Thank you, Alyson, and thank you all very much. Governor Hughes, Senator Mathias, Representative Bentley, and the representatives of the board of education, the administration, the faculty, and you, the student body—believe me, it is good to be here. It's great to be here at Fallston High School, home of the Cougars—[*laughter*]—and the Cougar cheerleaders, who I understand will be competing in a big contest this evening. I hope you can all get out to Sunrise [Rising Sun] for that event. I wish I could be there. [*Laughter*]

You know, I've only been out of school a few years, but—[*laughter*]—they tell me that things have changed quite a bit in the meantime. There's one thing that I bet, though, hasn't changed. When you heard that you'd have to cancel your scheduled class for a special assembly, well, I hope you weren't too disappointed. [*Laughter*] I know I've been looking forward to this chance to speak to you, because I've got a very important mission that I want young Americans to be a part of. Let me first just give a little background.

As you know, Nancy and I returned almost 2 weeks ago from Geneva where I had several lengthy meetings with General Secretary Gorbachev of the Soviet Union. I had more than 15 hours of discussions with him, including 5 hours of private conversation just between the two of us. I found him to be a determined man, but one who is willing to listen. And I told him about America's deep desire for peace and that we do not threaten the Soviet Union and that I believe the people of both our countries want the same thing—a safer and better future for themselves and their children. You know, people don't start wars, governments do. Our meeting should be of special importance to all of you. I know you're concerned about the future, about the growth in nuclear arsenals, about injustice and persecution of fellow human beings, and about threats to peace around the world. Well, it's because I shared that concern that I went to Geneva to begin a dialog for peace with Mr. Gorbachev.

We talked about many things—the need to cut the number of offensive nuclear weapons on each side, the wars of independence being waged by freedom fighters against Soviet-backed regimes around the world, human rights, and how we could improve our overall relationship. I also stressed to Mr. Gorbachev how our nation's commitment to the Strategic Defense Initiative, our research and development of a nonnuclear, high-tech shield that would protect us against ballistic missiles, and how we were committed to that. I told him that SDI was a reason to hope, not to fear; that the advance of technology, which originally gave us ballistic missiles, may soon be able to make them obsolete. I told him that SDI history had taken a positive turn, that men of good will should be rejoicing, that our deliverance from the awful threat of nuclear weapons may be on the horizon, and I suggested to him that I saw the hand of Providence in that. What could be more moral than a system based on protecting human life rather than destroying it? I could no more negotiate away SDI than I could barter with your future. As I told Mr. Gorbachev, as far as I'm concerned, a defense shield is an insurance policy for your future, and I think he understood our sincerity on this issue.

We were realistic going into these meetings with the Soviets. The United States and the Soviet Union are as different as any two nations can be. These differences are based on opposing philosophies and values and no differences could be more profound or meaningful. It is virtually impossible for us to understand their system and how, over these—what—70 years, it has imposed a way of thinking on their people. So, we didn't expect miracles. But we wanted these talks, if possible, to plant the seeds of hope in our relationship, the hope that some day, perhaps, might blossom into a real peace, a lasting peace, resting upon the only foundation on which a true peace can be built—the indestructible foundation of human freedom. And I was determined to see if we could begin to narrow some of our differences and even come to some agreements where there was common ground. I believe that we've made a good start.

This is the mission I've come to speak to you about. One of the most exciting developments to come out of Geneva was Mr. Gorbachev's agreement to people-to-people exchanges. We're still negotiating the specifics, and it remains to be seen how much the Soviets will be willing to open up their closed society. But our objective is massive exchange programs between private citizens in both countries—between people, not government bodies. Let's allow the people of the Soviet Union and the people of the United States to get to know each other, without governments getting in the way. And that's one reason I'm here today—to encourage young people like you from across the country to take part in these people-to-people exchanges as never before in our history. I believe such contacts are an essential part of our building a lasting foundation for peace, because true peace must be based on openness and people talking to each other rather than about each other, and the peace must also be based on understanding. And that's why I proposed to Mr. Gorbachev that we let young people from each country spend time in the other's schools, universities, summer camps, and homes. Americans would be able to see for themselves what life is like in the Soviet Union, and their young people could see for themselves the freedom and openness of our society and that we do not bear the people of the Soviet Union any ill will.

So, we'll establish scholarship funds to make it possible for the best and the brightest of both countries to take part in these exchanges. We will also exchange teachers to impart a deeper understanding of our respective histories, cultures, and languages—where we have much to learn from one another. We'll resume cooperation in cancer research to combat one of the century's most hated diseases. And we can jointly prepare for the demands of the 21st century with a cooperative program

for the development of educational software. It won't be all work and no play. We'll have regular meets in various sports and increased television coverage of these sports events. We can't eliminate competition from our relationship, but we can channel some of it to the playing fields and courts rather than the international arena. These programs and others that may be worked out will not solve all the problems that exist between us, but they can be a beginning to building communities of trust and understanding. If Soviet mistrust of our country is at the bottom of some of the tension between us, then, I know that even a few hours spent with America's open and eager younger generation would dispel mistrust in even the most suspicious soul. So, those who participate in these programs will be our good-will ambassadors to the Soviet Union.

I know that all of you have dreams and hopes for the future. For some, there are dreams of college and a challenging career; for others, a good job, a car, a house of your own. And most of you, I'm sure, plan to marry and raise a family. All these dreams can come true if we have peace. Twice in my lifetime I have seen world wars that robbed our young people of their dreams. And the awesome power of nuclear weapons makes me even more determined to see that it doesn't happen again. As I've said many times before, a nuclear war cannot be won and must never be fought. So, I went to Geneva to set a course for enduring peace. And while I can't say that the path is clear, we've made a start.

Mr. Gorbachev and I agreed to press on in several arms control areas where there is common ground, especially to achieve deep reductions in nuclear arsenals. We will also continue talking about our differences on regional issues. And we had a heart-to-heart talk about human rights. These are the cornerstones on which peace and your future rest. You and young people like you have a vital role in bringing about a better future by keeping America strong and by helping draw the people of the United States and the Soviet Union closer together. And we will continue the dialog begun at Geneva to reach agreements for deep reductions in nuclear arsenals with strict compliance; to help support an end to the regional conflicts that carry the seeds of wider wars; and to uphold the ideal of human rights and justice for all peoples.

Mr. Gorbachev, as the leader of the Soviet Union—the new leader—has held out the promise of change. He has said that he wants better relations between our two nations. Well, what better way than allowing people to travel freely back and forth? Let's begin, at the very least, to draw back the barriers that separate our peoples from one another. We're asking for no more than what the Soviets have already agreed to in the Helsinki accords. Freedom of movement and information, contact between peoples—the Soviet Union has already signed its name to a commitment to these things. We should have no illusions that people-to-people contacts will solve all the problems, however, that exist between us. The Soviet Union is not a democracy. The hopes and aspirations of the Soviet people have little or no direct effect on government policy. But these changes are a beginning to building a better world, one based on better human understanding. You can have a vital role in bringing about this better future, in drawing the people of our two nations closer together. It's an exciting adventure, one that will not be completed this year or next. But we must begin somewhere. And with God's help, we may reach that free and peaceful world that we all desire.

I promise the young people of America that I will see to it that information on these people-to-people exchanges is widely disseminated. I want all of you throughout America to have a chance to meet and get to know your counterparts in the Soviet Union, so that you can tell them all about this great country of ours. And we'll continue our efforts to reach agreements for deep reductions in nuclear arsenals with strict compliance; to help support an end to regional conflicts; and to see to it that human rights are respected. Together we can build a future that will be safer and more secure for you and your children.

I couldn't help but—one point in our discussions privately with General Secretary Gorbachev—when you stop to think that we're all God's children, wherever we may live in the world, I couldn't help but say to him, just think how easy his task and mine might be in these meetings that we held if suddenly there was a threat to this world from some other species, from another planet, outside in the universe. We'd forget all the little local differences that we have between our countries, and we would find out once and for all that we really are all human beings here on this Earth together. Well, I don't suppose we can wait for some alien race to come down and threaten us, but I think that between us we can bring about that realization.

Thank you all. God bless you all.

Note: The President spoke at 10:17 a.m. in the school theater. He was introduced by Alyson Moore, the 9th grade student representative. Prior to his remarks, the President was presented with a stuffed cougar and the school's academic letter, given to those students demonstrating outstanding academic achievement.

Question-and-Answer Session With Students at Fallston High School in Fallston, Maryland
December 4, 1985

The President. Hello, there.

Q. The class of students here at Fallston High School have several questions prepared for you today.

The President. All right.

Q. Would you speak this morning on the Geneva summit? We'd like to——

The President. How come I'm nervous? [*Laughter*] We'll all be seated. Well, it's good to see you, and I'll try my best with the questions that you have. And have you decided who's first?

U.S.-Soviet Relations

Q. Mr. President, my name is Bill Greer. Mr. Gorbachev and yourself are very strong proponents of your respective political systems. It was apparent that the two of you formed a friendship, but there was also a sense of mistrust between you. Do you really believe we can achieve world peace with the Soviets?

The President. Yes, I have to believe that we can, and I'm optimistic and hopeful of it. In spite of the differences between our systems, I think one thing on our side is the Soviet people are virtually obsessed with the desire for peace because of the suffering they underwent in World War II. The Soviets lost 20 million people in that war. And that was not just military; that was the civilians that died as the attacks went into their cities, like at Stalingrad and all. So, there is a great desire for peace there. At the same time there is a mistrust, and we have to at least recognize that. I got the impression that many of them do believe that we have hostile intentions toward them. And I tried to disabuse them of that thought by pointing out that when World War II ended, ours was the only country that our industry hadn't been bombed to rubble in the war. Our military was virtually intact. We had 12½ million people, men and women, in uniform. And we were the only ones with the nuclear weapon. We were the only ones who had the bomb. At that point we could have literally dictated to the world if we'd chosen to do so, and we didn't. We set out to help the other nations in the war, including our enemies. And I pointed this out to him—that we had some evidence on our side that we didn't have hostile intentions. And I can only hope that it registered.

Terrorism

Q. Mr. President, I'm Craig Hatfield. The recent outburst of terrorist actions in the Middle East has shown that both the U.S. and the Soviet Union are victims of terrorism. Have you considered some way the Soviets and we can join forces to prevent further terrorism?

The President. This is one of the things that I think could come out of these meetings that we're having, because now that they, too, have been victims of terrorism, I think that they've got a very definite reason for wanting that. We do cooperate with all the other nations in the world—or most of them. We've managed to establish a contact, exchange information, and so forth on terrorism, and I hope the same thing can happen with them.

You, and then I'll go that way.

Weapons Systems

Q. My name's Troy Baisden. Mr. President, I've been wondering what test you're putting in place to stop a $2 billion failure like the Sergeant York program from happening again.

The President. Well, it isn't a case of putting things in place. You don't want those things to happen, and yet you must realize that in that field, as in so many others, you are going to research. And your research indicates the potential of some weapons system, and you go forward. And now and then you're going to find that defensive abilities have been developing all the time, too. And suddenly, you find that something that looked good when you first planned it and ordered it has now been overtaken by a superior defense. And I don't know any answer to that. Just try our best and see that those kinds of things don't occur.

Nuclear Disarmament

Q. My name is Andrea Hooper. Mr. President, do you believe that a verifiable agreement of nuclear disarmament can ever be accomplished?

The President. A verifiable——

Q. Agreement.

The President. ——agreement?

Q. Yes.

The President. Yes, but it's going to take confidence and trust on both sides. This was one of the first things that I talked to General Secretary Gorbachev about—that for us to start talking, reducing arms, or doing this or that, we would first have to—by deed, not just word—prove that we were losing our distrust of each other. Because as long as we distrust to the point that there are restrictions on whether you can go in and verify what the other fellow is doing, then you're going to have to be suspicious and believe that those restrictions are based on a desire to not keep the agreement. And this was the basis of one of our talks—and made it plain again that it's more than just words. There have to be deeds, both sides, to show that we mean we want to get along. And this was why I offered to them, with our Strategic Defense Initiative—I told him that their scientists could come into our laboratories if ours could come into theirs, where this research was going on, so that they could see exactly what it was we were trying to develop.

Import Quotas

Q. Mr. Reagan, my name is Brenda Cannon. Since the steel imports are still coming into the country above the quotas that were set, what steps are going to be taken to enforce these quotas?

The President. We have the quotas, and, here and there, there are violations, and sometimes there are countries that get into the steel business that haven't been there before. Our whole system is based on equity in trade between the countries, and we just have to pursue that. And wherever we find a violation, why, we then bring that case forward and nail the other country or where that violation is occurring.

I think I should maybe turn this way for a minute, if I'm going to be fair at all, shouldn't I? Yes.

Accomplishments of the Geneva Summit

Q. Mr. President, my name is Valerie Clunk. What do you feel is the most important accomplishment of the summit meeting outside of the cultural exchange?

The President. I think the most important thing was the very fact that we decided to continue having the meetings. We had thought when we left that the Soviets might be so resisting to future meetings that this alone could make the summit a success, if we could get an agreement. And we got it on the first day there, and with no problem at all. He was almost eager for that.

And I think that our agreement—you know, ever since 1946 our country has been proposing controls of weapons and, in more recent years, the controls of nuclear weapons. And we've had negotiators—Vienna, in Stockholm, and in Geneva—on this subject. For the first time, really, now, the Soviets have actually suggested a figure to which, if we can work out the conditions, they would be willing to reduce their numbers. Up till now, we've been the only ones that have had a number and said, let's do away with x number of weapons. And there's never been, in the negotiation, of them coming back and say, well, we're willing to reduce this number, so you could then haggle about it. Now we've both come to the agreement that the idea would be, right now, to start with 50 percent of the nuclear weapons. And so, I think this was an accomplishment, also.

Visits to Educational Institutions

Q. Mr. President, my name is Steve Baliko. I was wondering, why was Fallston High School chosen out of thousands of schools across the country to be honored by your visit?

The President. Well, you're a pretty outstanding high school, and you're also here, within range of the Capital. I'd like to do this in more areas of the United States. But we just thought that this was a pretty good place to start telling your generation about our dreams of people exchanges, and with the hope that we have that it will be your generation that will start these exchanges where we can get better acquainted.

Soviet Views on Human Rights

Q. My name is Scoop Kelly. I'm wondering what position was held by the Russians about the human rights issue.

The President. I have to be a little careful here on that because I talked privately with General Secretary Gorbachev about that. They feel very strongly that they could appear to be yielding to an outside influence if they changed their laws and so forth that we think are so repressive. So, I felt that that was something that we should talk about in private. And I can tell you that he has our full view and understanding of how we feel about the differences between our two nations in that respect. But it isn't something that I think you go public with because of this resistance of anyone in a leadership position in a government about seeming to give in to an outside government. But I can assure you they know how we feel, and they know what we think would be a good move.

U.S.-Soviet Relations

Q. Mr. President, my name is Kim Ey. Do you believe that in the future an economic exchange will be established between the United States and the Soviet Union?

The President. An economic——

Q. Exchange.

The President. Well, there are certain areas of trade now, as you know, between us. And this, too, would come along with this better understanding. Right now, with the conditions the way they are and the arms race that has been going on and their evident desire to be number one militarily, we've had to have restrictions on trading with them things that might help them in their arms race. And those are the restrictions—the only ones that I know—basically, on the trade between us. But there is trade, particularly in our agricultural field, and we want to keep those doors as open as we can.

Q. Thank you.

Q. Mr. President, I'm Ericka Pearce. On the issue of arms reduction, do you believe that there will ever be any significant agreement settled between the U.S. and the Soviet Union, because of the unwillingness on either side to deplete nuclear weapons out of each other's major stockpiles?

The President. I think, as I said before, that we made a pretty good start here on this matter of the nuclear weapons. I think that both sides recognize that as long as we keep building these mountains of armaments higher in an effort to stay even with each other—and here I have to say on our behalf, we are the ones who are trying to catch up. They are the ones who went out ahead and have placed their military emphasis on offensive weapons, where we have thought of them as a deterrent to war, and why we're seeking a defensive shield right now that would render nuclear missiles, if not obsolete, at least more harmless as a threat. But I believe that, for the first time, they recognize, with some of their

problems, that the arms race has helped create those problems for them. They have dwelt so much on military buildup that they've had to deny their people many of the things that you and I think are just everyday—in our ability to go down to the store and buy them. Well, they don't have such privileges. And we hope that with that as a help that maybe we can begin a reduction.

Back in 1980, when I was running for this job, there had been a number of arms agreements, but all of them were limitations on how fast and how much we would increase. And I got pretty outspoken that those weren't the kind of agreements we needed, that we needed an agreement that started reducing them. And so, for the first time, that's what we're proposing and what is going on in Geneva.

Way in the back there.

Q. My name is Jennifer Harrison. How do you and Mr. Gorbachev propose to organize a risk reduction center to prevent accidental nuclear war?

The President. Now, wait a minute. I had a little problem there.

Q. How do you and Mr. Gorbachev propose to organize a risk reduction center to prevent accidental nuclear war?

The President. How do we propose to—you've got to forgive me, I have a little problem.

Q. To organize a risk reduction center.

The President. The risk, oh. Well, this is a thing that we're trying to put together here and have proposed, and they seem very willing to go along with this. And this is to have, again, meeting places where our own military can meet with each other so that there wouldn't be danger of one or the other of us thinking that a hostile action had been taken. This is more information on maneuvers, war games, practice war games, and so forth. And we would have these centers where we could immediately communicate with each other at a military level and know what's going on. So, we are going to go forward with those. And it's kind of a new experiment, so I can't tell you exactly how they'll work out.

Q. As you've said, the Soviet people believe that Americans are looking for war.

What can we as Americans do to help change—[*inaudible*].

The President. I think it comes from our understanding of the basic Marxian principle, because Karl Marx had always said that socialism could never succeed until the whole world was a one-world Communist state. And so, this has caused us to view with alarm, as I say, their outright buildup of offensive weapons. Now, I think this would be one of the things and the type of deeds that we would talk about if they do not still follow that Marxian principle. If they are not aimed at expansionism and conquering or taking over the whole world, then they can help prove that by joining in arms reductions to show that they have no hostile intent. But this is one of the reasons for the basic suspicion between us.

Space Program

Q. Mr. President, Greg Romanski. I have a question concerning a different issue. Due to the success of the crew of the *Atlantis* experiments in the area of space construction, what are your plans concerning a skylab or space station?

The President. We believe that the newest frontier in the world is space, and we believe that the shuttle experiments so far have shown us so many, literally, miracles that can be performed in the weightlessness of outer space—that instead of these just shuttle flights going up with experiments, that we should see if we cannot put together out there a place where then the shuttles could carry workers. And workers in space could develop—let's take in the fields of medicines alone, we have an incurable ailment, diabetes. We have found in the experiments in the shuttle out there that a cell which, in order to have a cure for diabetes, must be able to be divided and split. We can't do it here on Earth as we could do it up there in the weightlessness of space. So, there are other medicines and things of that kind, that from the experiments already conducted, we believe we need a place now not just to experiment, but to actually manufacture. And so, this kind of a space station—I don't particularly like that name—space station. You know, I know some people are toying with things like call it a "universal space camp." "Sta-

tion," again, has a kind of a hard, possibly military, sound to it, and that isn't what it's for.

Views on the Presidency

Q. My name is Beth Biedronski. First, I'd like to thank you for mentioning the cheerleaders' competition at Rising Sun today. I'm a cheerleader. My question to you, Mr. President, is simply: How do you feel now that the effects of any decision you make concerning the Strategic Defense Initiative, or more generally the nuclear arms race, literally affects the lives of billions of people all around the world?

The President. Well, it's something anyone in this position has to live with. It isn't easy, and I have come to understand very much why Abraham Lincoln once said that he had been driven to his knees many times because there was no place else to go. And he said if he didn't believe that he could call on someone who was stronger and wiser than all others, he couldn't meet the responsibilities of his position for a single day. And all you can do is to try to the best of your ability, with all the input and knowledge you get, then hope that the decisions you make are based on what is morally right. And that's all you can do. As I say, I've come to understand very much what Mr. Lincoln meant. He's supposed to be around the White House, you know, now and then. [*Laughter*]

SALT II Agreement

Q. My name's Todd Pegg. I would like to know, what will the United States' position be when the SALT II agreement expires late in December?

The President. We haven't made a decision on that yet. We have compiled a report right now that shows the Soviet Union has committed 23 violations of the SALT II agreement. And we have to decide whether we can have complete agreement on both sides that we're going to abide by it, even though it has never been ratified. Or we're going to have to conduct ourselves on the basis of what they are doing also. There's no way that we could be so one-sided as to be destroying missiles and things of that kind, stay within a limit that they are violating.

This is one of the things—when I talk about an arms buildup and where the race started—when SALT I was agreed upon, from the time of SALT I, the Soviet Union has added 6,000 warheads, nuclear warheads. And since SALT II, 3,850 of those have been added. And this is what I mean about agreements that were aimed at trying to limit the increase instead of flatly saying, "Let's get rid of some of these things." So, we have a decision yet to make on that. And it's going to, in part, depend on our negotiations with them about the present violations of that agreement.

Nuclear Proliferation

Q. Mr. President, my name is Michelle Martin. I was wondering, do you feel that a nation other than the United States or the Soviet Union could possibly start a nuclear war?

The President. That another nation other than the Soviet Union or the United States could start a nuclear war? Well, we know that there are a few other nations—some allies of ours—that have some nuclear weapons. We suspect that, here and there, there have been efforts. Whether they've succeeded yet in creating a missile or not, we don't know. But other countries—and some of them, the countries that are in the Third World and where there is a lot of hostility and instability, wars can start by accident. If you take World War I, it's been called by everyone who ever knew in history, the war that no one wanted. But it started when a terrorist, a radical, threw a bomb at a leader of a European country—assassinated the leader of the European country. And out of that came World War I, which finally included even the United States.

Wars can start accidentally. Wars can spread across borders—regional wars, such as the one in Nicaragua. And this is why this was one of our subjects also for negotiation. We want to help in any way we can to persuade the Soviet Union to withdraw its troops, that they've had there fighting for 6 years, and bring them home and then let the people of Afghanistan, within their country, settle peacefully what kind of a government they want. The present government of Afghanistan was installed there by the Soviet Union, so that's why they're in, defending that government.

Soviet General Secretary Gorbachev

Q. Mr. President, my name is Andrew Llyd. I've heard that first impressions are very important——

The President. A little louder, there, for old dad.

Q. I feel that first impressions are very important. What were your first impressions of General Secretary Gorbachev?

The President. My first impressions of him? A very intelligent man. And, while at the same time I recognize that he, heart and soul, believed in the system that he's grown up in—he's young enough that this is all he's ever known. He grew up from even earlier than you in this system. He has faith in it and believes in it. But, at the same time, having dealt with other leaders—the Soviet Union who can kind of pound the table and get quite excited about things, no. Our discussions, I must say, would be like we're having. He listened well, and I listened to him. And we were affable in this. And it was a case of disagreeing on particular issues, but no hostility, no enmity.

And I had to believe that he believed some of the propaganda that's been going on for 70 years about us, that he—he's never been to the United States—and that his impression of us—he was ready to believe, for example, that our Strategic Defense Initiative, that we're trying to find a defense against nuclear weapons, that, really, out of that research we might develop something that would be a weapon in space for attacking them. And I countered that by telling him that if our research yielded a defensive weapon, we would sit down with them and with our allies—with all the world—and share it, and say, "Look, why don't we all have this, and then none of us have to have nuclear missiles." And I hope that that had some impact on him.

But, no, I think that I have no illusions about him suddenly turning soft about their system or not. He totally believes in—that that's the system that the people should have. And I said to him, "Look, you have your system. We don't like it. And you don't like ours. But we can each have our own systems and still get along together."

Q. Thank you, Mr. President.

Note: The exchange began at 10:50 a.m. in the band room at the school. Following the exchange, the President returned to the White House.

Remarks Announcing the Resignation of Robert C. McFarlane as Assistant to the President for National Security Affairs and the Appointment of John M. Poindexter
December 4, 1985

The President. I have a statement I wish to read to you.

It's with deep regret and reluctance that I have accepted the resignation of Bud McFarlane as my Assistant for National Security Affairs. Bud's more than 30 years of service to his nation have been exemplary in every respect. He has served in peace and war, ranging from his early days at the Naval Academy to Vietnam and to the White House. And few have served with more dedication, none with more loyalty.

A little over 2 years ago, I asked Bud to serve as my national security adviser. He continued his record of distinguished service in this most sensitive and critical assignment. I know of no President who has been better served. Bud has offered me wise counsel and has been a trusted adviser and confidant in carrying out our administration's foreign policy goals and objectives. He has an impressive list of successes of which he can justly be proud: his key role in the preparation for the Geneva summit meeting and his contribution toward greater stability in East-West relations; his unending efforts which have helped strengthen the Western alliance; his service in the Middle East as my personal envoy at a most difficult time and at great personal risk; his key role in carrying out our counterterrorism policies, as exemplified by the TWA hijacking incident and our recent operation leading to the apprehension of the hijackers of the *Achille Lauro.*

Bud, I know that you're eager now to move on to new personal and professional challenges. Let me say that I shall never forget the sacrifices that you and your family have made in the service of your country, and I wish you and your family the best success and happiness in the future. But before you get too comfortable, I should warn you that I'll probably be calling on you from time to time for your wise counsel and advice.

As in all things in life, while Bud's departure is a cause of deep regret for me, I'm pleased to announce that I have appointed Vice Admiral John M. Poindexter to be the new Assistant to the President for National Security Affairs. I appointed John as Deputy Assistant for National Security Affairs on October 17th, 1983. He has served in that capacity in an exemplary manner and has proved to be a truly steady hand at the helm. Since he first joined the National Security Council staff in June 1981 as the Military Assistant, he has played a key role. His naval career began with his graduation at the head of his class at the U.S. Naval Academy. And he was not only first in his class at the Naval Academy but, also, brigade commander, an achievement rarely duplicated. And I know of only one other, and that was Douglas MacArthur at West Point.

In choosing Admiral Poindexter for this key position in our national security affairs structure, I am acknowledging the very important contribution that he has already made to the formulation and carrying out of our major foreign policy objectives. I'm also underscoring the great value I place in the continuity of our foreign policy. For 5 years John has been intimately involved in this administration's national security affairs and is well prepared and able to assume this very important post. So, I welcome you onboard the captain's deck, John, and wish you the very best success.

Admiral Poindexter. Thank you, sir. Mr.

President, I'm greatly honored by this position that you are bestowing upon me. It's going to be very difficult to fill in behind Bud. We've worked together as a team—really, the three of us—for over the past 2 years, and it's always difficult to lose one of the team members. But we've got a very good staff, and we will continue to provide the President with the best advice available.

Mr. McFarlane. Mr. President, John, and colleagues, ladies and gentlemen, I'm deeply grateful, Mr. President, for you have allowed me to serve in your administration at a moment in our history that is terribly exciting, where the opportunity for our country has been enormous. I think philosophers have devoted a great amount of thought to whether or not intrinsic flaws in democracy and free enterprise would, over time, lead such systems to decline. And I think it's fair to say that 5 years ago many were saying that that decline was in fact taking place: We'd lost a war, our economy was in great chaos, the military balance had shifted dramatically against us, and with it the willingness of the Soviet Union to take risks was being expressed from Angola to Ethiopia, Cambodia, Afghanistan, Nicaragua. And yet the importance of your stewardship, Mr. President, has been that those predictions have declined, have been reversed, and that a great national renewal has taken place. Today, 5 years later, we see the expression of that renewal, foremostly, in the reality of peace, that the United States is once more leading and deterring, and an economy that is recovering with impressive pace and quality, and with it the resources going to provide assistance where it's needed to struggling countries that gives them some hope for their own futures.

And so, the recovery and the restoration of American leadership is very, very well along indeed. That's not to say the job is finished. There are very, very fundamental questions to be answered in the next 3 years. For example, can the impressive renewal of the American economic strength be replicated in other democracies? Can the countries of Europe follow this model, reduce government intervention in their economy, reduce consumption of the prod-

uct of their own societies? With regard to developing countries, can the United States—without imposing its model, by sheer example—provide sufficient political, economic, and moral incentives to lead these countries in the post-colonial period to adopt democracy, free enterprise? With regard to East-West relations, after the enormously successful renewal of a stable discourse, can we move beyond to wage peace and wage a peaceful competition with a fundamentally different system at lower levels of arms, with broadened cooperation, but always at peace? Based upon the strength of your leadership, Mr. President, and the support you've engendered from industrial democracies and developing countries in these past 5 years, there's no question in my mind but that your stewardship will include as its legacy continued peace, stability, arms reduction, and an evermore inspiring model for developing countries throughout the world.

For my own part, after 30 years, I can only say how deeply grateful I am for the honor and privilege that you have bestowed upon me to serve at this time. Thank you.

Q. Why are you leaving?

Q. Mr. President, there's been a lot of talk, as you well know, that Mr. McFarlane is really leaving because of personality clashes, turf battles, with Mr. Regan. Could you and Mr. McFarlane both speak to this question of what role the McFarlane-Regan problems had in his decision to leave?

The President. Whether he feels he wants to speak or not about this, let me just say—and I say this with full confidence that he endorses what I'm going to say—you have all been misinformed about that. The reason that has been given is one in which, after 30 years in which this country has been his first priority, he feels a responsibility, that I think all of us feel, toward his family. And the things that he just spoke of here and about what I might have contributed and what has taken place and the change in America in these last few years, he has been a very, very major part of that change. And we're all going to miss him.

Q. Are you saying there is no turf war——

Q. But weren't there problems with Mr.

Regan, sir?

Mr. McFarlane. That's nonsense.

The President. There.

Q. Mr. President, there are those who suggest that you were better served when there were multiplicity of voices competing for attention inside the west wing. And that under Mr. Regan, there will be no point of view funneled to you, which doesn't go through him. What do you say to that, sir?

The President. I can just simply say that the national security adviser reports directly to me and does not go through the chief of staff.

Q. Did you tell him that?

The President. What?

Q. Does he know that?

The President. Yes. Yes.

Q. Mr. Poindexter, do you get along with Mr. Regan? Do you think you will have clashes and turf battles with him?

Admiral Poindexter. Well, as you probably know, the Navy and the Marine Corps always get along well together. [*Laughter*] I don't anticipate any problems. Don and I are good friends. I've known him since he was Secretary of Treasury. And with regard to the last question about access to the President, Don Regan told me that yesterday, that I had direct access. So, it won't be a problem.

Q. Mr. President, in the——

Q. Mr. President, what does this——

Q. ——nearly 6 years of your Presidency——

Q. ——what does this change——

Q. ——an extraordinarily large number of people have either resigned under pressure or of their own volition. Can you tell us why?

The President. I have read stories that have disturbed me probably more than anything that has happened since I've been in this office, things of that kind. I happen to believe in something that might be a little unusual in Washington with regard to the Cabinet structure and staff. And that is that I want to hear all sides of every issue before I make the decision that I have to make. And as I understand it, normally, that's not been the nature of Cabinet and staff workings in this office. Whether that's true or not, I don't know; I only know about ours. But for that to be translated into what I am

desiring—for that to be translated into as somehow friction and every time someone leaves—I said in the very beginning, when I first came here and realized I had appointments to make, that I would take people if they could only stay a year, 2 years, whatever it might be, because the kind of people I wanted were the kind of people who didn't necessarily want government jobs. And I wanted that kind of success in here. And so, every once in a while someone has to move on and have their own obligations, their own responsibilities, and this is the case here.

Q. Mr. President, in terms of Mr. Beggs and others who have had to leave government under your regime, don't you wonder at the clearance policies of the administration, where so many people have had to leave under a cloud?

The President. I don't think it's been so many people, when you stop to think that there are upwards of a thousand people that are appointed. And with regard to Mr. Beggs, I don't know of anyone who could have done a finer job than he has done and is doing at NASA. And we're talking about something that is supposed to have happened prior to government service. And, also, if you read it correctly, not something in which he in any way was doing anything—if he was doing this at all—that would redound to his benefit personally or enrich him in any way. And I believe that everyone is innocent until proven guilty of whatever they're charged with. And——

Q. But you did——

The President. ——I can look over the record——

Q. ——approve of him stepping aside for a while?

The President. What? Well, I think that that is necessary for him because—time requirements that'll be brought about by this. But I think——

Q. Mr. McFarlane, could you tell us where you're going and what you're going to do?

Principal Deputy Press Secretary Speakes. This is going to be the last question.

Mr. McFarlane. I have no plans and I—I don't know. If you've got any leads, let me know. [*Laughter*]

Q. How about an ambassadorship?

Q. How would you feel about appointing him as an Ambassador, Mr. President?

The President. What?

Q. There's been some talk that he might like to be an Ambassador. How would you feel about that?

The President. That—I—what do I say? Yes, anything. But the man has told me and has said that he needs to leave government service now for certain responsibilities that he feels to his family.

Q. Do you support Rostenkowski's tax plan, Mr. President?

The President. What did he say?

Q. Tax plan.

Q. Rostenkowski's tax plan.

Q. Tax plan.

Q. Rostenkowski's tax plan, sir?

The President. I hope that the process goes forward and through the Senate and then into a conference and that we get tax reform.

Q. Does that mean yes?

Q. That's a yes?

Q. Yes, you do?

The President. What?

Q. Yes, you support it?

The President. I just said I want the process to go forward.

Q. Admiral, will we ever see you? [*Laughter*]

Admiral Poindexter. Maybe.

Q. Thank you.

Note: The President spoke to reporters at 2:31 p.m. in the Briefing Room at the White House.

Letter Accepting the Resignation of Robert C. McFarlane as Assistant to the President for National Security Affairs
December 4, 1985

Dear Bud:

It is with deep regret and reluctance that I accept your resignation as Assistant to the President for National Security Affairs. Your more than thirty years of service to the United States have been exemplary in all regards. As a career Marine, you served your country in peace and war—from your days at the Naval Academy to Vietnam.

Your contributions since 1981 have been in the highest tradition of national service. As Counselor to the Secretary of State and as Deputy Assistant to the President for National Security Affairs, you served tirelessly. A little more than two years ago, I asked you to be my National Security Adviser. You continued your record of distinguished service in the most sensitive and critical assignment in the national security area. I know of no President who has been better served. You have offered wise counsel and have been a trusted adviser and confidant. Your kind words to me regarding our national renewal are due in no small part to your own efforts over the last five years.

As you move on to new personal and pro-

fessional challenges, I shall never forget the sacrifices you and your family made in service. I trust you will still permit me to call on you from time to time.

Again, my thanks to you and Jonny. You have truly lived up to the proudest traditions of your beloved Marines Semper Fidelis; a President could ask no more.

Sincerely,

/s/RONALD REAGAN

Dear Mr. President,

It is with a deep sense of gratitude, sadness and fulfillment that I tender my resignation as your national security advisor. Five years ago, without knowing me, you appointed me to serve in your administration. It was an important moment in our history. During the previous five years, a number of historic events had occurred: we had lost a war, with all that implied for our reputation as a reliable ally; our economy was stricken—overseas, leaders were asking whether we could solve our own problems, much less lead in the resolution of theirs; and finally, there had been a dramatic shift in the military balance, and with it a greater willingness on the part of the Soviet Union to challenge us through ambitious excursions from Angola to Ethiopia to Cambodia to Afghanistan to Nicaragua. But it was also a time at which the deep and enduring self-confidence of the American people was reasserting itself in a call for leadership.

Looking back over these five years, it is difficult to encompass the enormity of change. Under your leadership, America has indeed come back. We are deterring, "Not one square inch of territory has been lost . . ." and democracy is once more the ascendant model for developing countries everywhere. There is little doubt that history will record this period of your stewardship as the time when Spengler was disproved. Truly, you have led in the highest

tradition of Churchill and Roosevelt.

As for me, to have been a part of this national renewal has been an honor and privilege beyond expression. For that I am deeply grateful. In the coming years, as you continue to consolidate this foundation of political, economic and military strength and move beyond it to greater stability in East-West relations, I shall be one of the millions of proud Americans out there in support. Hopefully, there will be a little more time for Jonny and the family. But we won't forget that we were a part of something very important. Thanks, Mr. President.

God bless.

/s/BUD

Note: The originals were not available for verification of the content of these letters.

Appointment of John M. Poindexter as Assistant to the President for National Security Affairs
December 4, 1985

The President announced the appointment of John M. Poindexter as the Assistant to the President for National Security Affairs. He will succeed Robert C. McFarlane.

Admiral Poindexter was appointed as the Deputy Assistant to the President for National Security Affairs by President Reagan on October 17, 1983. He was promoted to vice admiral on May 15, 1985. Admiral Poindexter first joined the National Security Council staff in June 1981 as military assistant to the Assistant to the President for National Security Affairs. Immediately before joining the National Security Council staff, he was Deputy Chief of Naval Education and Training and chief of staff of the Naval Education and Training Command in Pensacola, FL. In 1958 he graduated from the U.S. Naval Academy at the head of his class. He was a Burke scholar at the California Institute of Technology in Pasadena, where he earned the degree of doctor of philosophy in nuclear physics in 1964, studying under the Nobel laureate Rudolph

Mossbauer. He was on the personal staff of Secretaries of the Navy John Chafee, John Warner, and J. William Middendorf II from 1971 to 1974, and was executive assistant to the Chief of Naval Operations, Adm. James L. Holloway III, from 1976 to 1978. During his naval career, Admiral Poindexter served aboard a number of surface ships. He commanded the guided missile cruiser U.S.S. *England* (CG–22) and later commanded destroyer squadron *31*. In this capacity, he was a battle group antisurface and antisubmarine warfare commander on deployments to the western Pacific, Indian Ocean, and South Pacific. His decorations include the Legion of Merit with Gold Star in lieu of Second Award, the Meritorious Service Medal, the Navy Expeditionary Medal for service in the Indian Ocean, and the Sea Service Deployment Ribbon.

Admiral Poindexter is married to the former Linda A. Goodwin, has five sons, and resides in Rockville, MD. He was born in Washington, IN, on August 12, 1936.

Statement by Principal Deputy Press Secretary Speakes on the Leave of Absence of James M. Beggs as Administrator of the National Aeronautics and Space Administration
December 4, 1985

James M. Beggs has requested that the President relieve him of his duties as Administrator of the National Aeronautics and Space Administration pending disposition of the charges against Mr. Beggs. While reluctantly acceding to his request, the President has asked Mr. Beggs to assist temporarily in the orderly transition of his responsibilities to his colleagues at NASA to facilitate continuity of management at this critically important agency. Mr. Beggs has agreed to do so. Under Mr. Beggs' leadership the space program has been revitalized, a fact which is accepted by virtually everyone in the field. This important record must be continued.

Appointment of 12 Members of the Presidential Task Force on Project Economic Justice, and Designation of the Chairman
December 4, 1985

The President today announced his intention to appoint the following individuals to be members of the Presidential Task Force on Project Economic Justice. These are new positions.

J. William Middendorf II will be designated Chairman upon his appointment. He is United States Ambassador to the European Economic Community. Previously he was Ambassador to the Organization of American States. He was born September 22, 1924, in Baltimore, MD.

Walter Bish is president of the Independent Steelworkers Union in Weirton, WV. He was born October 12, 1946, in E. Liverpool, OH, and now resides in Weirton, WV.

Robert Dickson Crane is president of Native American International in Vienna, VA. He was born March 26, 1929, in Cambridge, MA, and now resides in Vienna, VA.

Richard A. Derham is Assistant Administrator of the Agency for International Development in Washington, DC. He was born May 29, 1940, in Seattle, WA, and now resides in Washington, DC.

Steve H. Hanke is assistant professor of economics at the Johns Hopkins University in Baltimore. He was born December 29, 1942, in Macon, GA, and now resides in Baltimore, MD.

Norman G. Kurland is president of Norman Kurland & Associates in Arlington, VA. He was born April 27, 1930, in Bridgeport, CT, and now resides in Arlington, VA.

John McClaughry is president of the Institute for Liberty and Community in Concord, VT. He was born September 15, 1937, in Detroit, MI, and now resides in Concord, VT.

Paul W. McCracken is the Edmund Ezra Day university professor of business administration, School of Business Administration, University of Michigan. He was born December 29, 1915, in Richland, IA, and now resides in Ann Arbor, MI.

Michael Novak is the George Frederick Jewett chair in religion and public policy at the American Enterprise Institute in Washington, DC. He was born September 9, 1933, in Johnstown, PA, and now resides in Washington, DC.

Malott White Nyhart is vice president and member of the executive committee of the Nyhart Co., Inc., in Indianapolis, IN. He was born July 6, 1950, in Indianapolis, where he currently resides.

Carlos M. Perez is president of Banana Services, Inc., in Coral Gables, FL. He was born May 28, 1932, in Arte MisaPinar del Rio, Cuba, and now resides in Coral Gables.

Norman A. Weintraub is chief economist and director of the International Brotherhood of Teamsters in Washington, DC. He was born May 24, 1936, in Springfield, MA, and now resides in Alexandria, VA.

Statement on Signing the Intelligence Authorization Act for Fiscal Year 1986
December 4, 1985

I am pleased to sign into law H.R. 2419, the "Intelligence Authorization Act for Fiscal Year 1986." This act represents another positive step in our efforts to revitalize America's intelligence capabilities and to protect our nation from hostile intelligence threats, particularly those of the Soviet Union and its surrogates. It is essential that we authorize sufficient appropriations and provide adequate authorities to enable our intelligence agencies to undertake effectively their vital mission. With this act, the Congress has provided the basis for ensuring that the intelligence community is equipped to deal with the increasingly complex and diverse challenges facing it.

The congressional vote of support for the Unified Nicaraguan Opposition (UNO) reflected in this legislation is a recognition of the threat the repressive Sandinista regime in Managua poses to all the peoples of Central America. H.R. 2419 demonstrates our resolve to support the brave men and women of the Nicaraguan resistance in the crucial campaign to achieve a democratic outcome in Nicaragua. Although the Congress did not authorize the full program requested by the administration to support the democratic forces in Nicaragua and to facilitate the reconciliation of the Nicaraguan people, the legislation is a positive step and furthers important United States policy objectives in this vital region.

I am disappointed that H.R. 2419 is used as a vehicle to amend the National Security Act of 1947 and mandates reporting requirements that are best left to working arrangements and guidelines agreed to by the Congress and the Director of Central Intelligence. Despite my disappointment, I believe, on the whole, that this legislation represents a positive step toward fulfilling our commitment to strengthen our intelligence capabilities.

Note: H.R. 2419, approved December 4, was asssigned Public Law No. 99–169.

Statement Urging the House of Representatives To Support Tax Reform Legislation
December 4, 1985

The House of Representatives is nearing a crucial decision in our historic effort to streamline the Nation's tax code for greater growth, simplicity, and fairness. Both the Ways and Means Committee and the Ways and Means Republicans have developed proposals that, like our own, represent substantial progress from current law. Each would simplify the tax bracket structure, lower individual and corporate rates, remove families living at or near poverty level from the tax rolls entirely, and substantially increase the personal exemption and standard deduction.

We do not want to risk damaging, perhaps irreparably, an entire year's effort to achieve real tax reform, so I strongly believe the legislative process must be allowed to go forward. But let me add this caveat: This can only be considered a good start, not an end product. More can and must be done to broaden the tax base, reduce tax rates further, and lower the cost of capital, so we can strengthen economic growth and personal opportunity for every American. Any legislation that ends up retarding economic growth and thereby diminishing the number of jobs upon which American families depend is not what we mean by tax reform. True tax reform is imperative. The first step must begin with a positive vote in the House of Representatives. I urge Members of the House to act affirmatively on this important matter.

Statement on a NATO Proposal To Reduce Troops in Central Europe
December 5, 1985

Consistent with the Joint Statement issued by General Secretary Gorbachev and me at the conclusion of the Geneva meeting and with our efforts to promote a more constructive East-West relationship, we and our NATO allies are introducing in Vienna today a new proposal designed to break the long deadlock on conventional arms reductions in Europe.

Since the early 1970's, NATO has engaged the Warsaw Pact in discussions aimed at limiting the numbers of troops on both sides in central Europe. These discussions, known as the Mutual and Balanced Force Reduction Talks (MBFR), now constitute one of the longest continuously running arms control negotiations in history. The NATO allies have consistently tried to move these negotiations forward. In 1982 and 1984, the U.S. and the allies presented new proposals designed to achieve progress in the MBFR negotiations. Regrettably, both proposals were rejected by the Warsaw Pact. After extensive national reviews of these talks and their objectives, we and our allies have concluded that a significant and forthcoming new move could provide new impetus to the negotiations.

In an effort to move the negotiations forward, and taking into account expressed Eastern concerns, we have today tabled a new proposal for reductions with effective verification. The proposed package of verification measures is intended to verify the numbers of troops withdrawn as well as the numbers which will remain. Thus, in exchange for a comprehensive and effective package of verification measures, NATO would be willing to accept the general framework of the February 1985 model proposed by the Soviet Union and its allies for a noncomprehensive agreement. We will no longer insist, as we have since the outset of negotiations, that the sides come to an agreement on Eastern troop levels before treaty signature. Nor will we continue to insist, for now, on a comprehensive approach whereby East and West must agree at the outset on all the steps needed to reduce to parity.

In this context, the U.S. is now prepared to accept a reduction of 5,000 U.S. and 11,500 Soviet ground troops in the central European reduction area. These figures reflect the ratio between existing U.S. and Soviet troop levels in the area. As soon as these reductions are completed, NATO is prepared to accept a commitment by both alliances not to increase forces in central Europe. As verified by implementation of the verification measures, this no-increase commitment would last for 3 years.

The new Western proposal builds on key aspects of the Warsaw Pact's ideas of February 1985. These include a time-limited, noncomprehensive agreement; reductions without prior data agreement on Eastern forces; and a no-increase agreement. The main element which NATO has added is in the area of verification. Fair, effective, and reciprocal verification measures are essential so that both sides will be able to know whether the terms of the accord are being complied with. This is especially important if we are to accept a no-increase commitment on troops in the area without prior agreement on the level of those troops. The Soviets have contended that such prior agreement was unnecessary and that Western concerns could be satisfied through implementation of verification measures. This new Western proposal offers them an opportunity to pursue that approach. Agreement on all aspects of the proposed verification measures would, of course, have to be reached prior to the signature of a treaty.

We urge the Soviet Union and the other Warsaw Pact countries to consider carefully the details of our proposal. This NATO initiative can help fulfill the commitments made at the Geneva summit and produce real progress in Vienna which would reduce forces in central Europe.

Proclamation 5417—National Consumers Week, 1986
December 5, 1985

By the President of the United States of America

A Proclamation

Because ours is a free society, we Americans are blessed with many choices. We can choose to live where we want. We can choose our education and our vocation. We are free to speak our minds, to worship God as our conscience prompts us, and to choose our political affiliation. And nowhere else in the world is there a wider variety of goods and services from which to choose, thanks to an open marketplace and the freedom to produce and purchase. This bountiful marketplace has provided us with a standard of living that is the marvel and envy of the world.

The outlook for the future is even brighter. The regulatory reform of recent years is spawning innovation and reinvigorated competition; by opening new markets, it has resulted in even more choices for consumers. This gives buyers both a new opportunity and a new responsibility to make informed decisions about the quality and value of products and services offered for sale.

To make responsible decisions in our dynamic and abundant economy, consumers need both information and education if they are to reap the full benefits of the marketplace. They need information, the facts about the goods and services; they need to be educated so they can analyze those facts before making a purchase. This will enable them to make wise choices whether they are shopping for food, shelter, clothing, transportation, recreation, health care, entertainment, and so on. Prudent, informed, discriminating consumers put pressure on suppliers to keep improving products and services while devising production efficiencies that will permit them to keep their prices competitive.

In light of the central role of the consumer in our free economy, it is especially appropriate to recognize that relationship during National Consumers Week, 1986. The slogan for 1986, "Consumers Rate Quality," acknowledges that consumers, by seeking quality and value, set the standards of acceptability for products and services by "voting" with their marketplace dollars, rewarding efficient producers of better quality products and performance. It is also a ringing declaration that consumers are entitled to and can insist on honest value for their hard-earned income.

Indeed, American businessmen and women are becoming aware that the broadened competition of a global marketplace necessitates attention to quality if they are to succeed. They must do more than just build better products—they must strive to improve marketing, sales, warranties, and service. Quality demands efficient management, productive use of human resources, and responsiveness to consumer needs and preferences.

Now, Therefore, I, Ronald Reagan, President of the United States of America, do hereby proclaim the week beginning April 20, 1986, as National Consumers Week. I urge businesses, educators, community organizations, labor unions, the media, government leaders, and consumers to recognize the pursuit of quality and excellence in every aspect of our lives, and to contribute to consumer and economic awareness during this week.

In Witness Whereof, I have hereunto set my hand this fifth day of December, in the year of our Lord nineteen hundred and eighty-five, and of the Independence of the

United States of America the two hundred and tenth.

RONALD REAGAN

[*Filed with the Office of the Federal Register, 4:24 p.m., December 6, 1985*]

Note: The proclamation was released by the Office of the Press Secretary on December 6.

Proclamation 5418—National Community College Month, 1986
December 6, 1985

By the President of the United States of America

A Proclamation

The more than thirteen hundred community, technical, and junior colleges, public and private, in the United States have contributed enormously to the richness and availability of American higher education. Nearly half of all undergraduate college students in the Nation today are enrolled in such institutions.

By providing educational opportunities at costs and locations accessible to all who are qualified, community, technical, and junior colleges have greatly enhanced the opportunity for every ambitious student, young or old, to enter a postsecondary school program. As community-based institutions, these schools provide varied programs and offer specialized training for more than one thousand occupations.

In recognition of the important contribution of community, technical, and junior colleges to our total educational system, the Congress, by Senate Joint Resolution 158, has designated the month of February 1986 as "National Community College Month" and authorized and requested the President to issue a proclamation in observance of this event.

Now, Therefore, I, Ronald Reagan, President of the United States of America, do hereby proclaim the month of February 1986 as National Community College Month. I ask all Americans to observe this month with appropriate activities that express recognition of the significant contribution these institutions are making to the strength, vitality, and prosperity of our Nation.

In Witness Whereof, I have hereunto set my hand this sixth day of December, in the year of our Lord nineteen hundred and eighty-five, and of the Independence of the United States of America the two hundred and tenth.

RONALD REAGAN

[*Filed with the Office of the Federal Register, 4:25 p.m., December 6, 1985*]

Radio Address to the Nation on the Farm Industry
December 7, 1985

My fellow Americans:

Before I get to my main topic today, I'd like to say a word about tax reform. Next week the House will decide whether the Congress will continue working on this important issue. While the proposals before the House are far from perfect, they do represent an essential step toward a tax code that is fairer, simpler, and encourages greater growth. I hope the House will vote yes next week and allow the Senate to consider debate and to improve this important measure.

Now, permit me to talk about the trouble faced by some of the most important Americans among us: our nation's farmers and those who provide them with goods and services. Here's a letter I received from Debbie Wilson, a farm wife in Bennington, Oklahoma: "Dear Mr. President, we've seen a neighbor lose his farm and we've seen neighbors throw up their hands and quit because they couldn't make enough money to cover their farm expenses. We have felt the devastation those losses inflicted on the children, as well as the parents, because farming is a family endeavor."

Debbie speaks for thousands of farmers from Maine to California. The reason our farmers are facing such hard times are complicated, but three main reasons stand out. First, a dramatic drop in land values as the inflation of the seventies was cut dramatically. Suddenly farmers who used their land as collateral found it much harder to obtain the loans they needed to purchase goods like chemicals, livestock, and tractors. The second major problem involved a fall in the demand for farm exports. The last administration contributed to this by imposing grain embargoes, a failed policy that our administration will never repeat. Later, many countries that had been purchasing large quantities of American farm goods began to purchase less, in large part because their economies had weakened. The third cause involved a sharp drop in the prices of many commodities as inflation slowed. Indeed, in the last year alone, prices that farmers receive for grains have fallen nearly 15 percent. All these problems mean hard times. I'm reminded of the troubles I saw during the Depression, growing up in Illinois, the heart of the Corn Belt, and living later in Iowa. The worst of it then was the hopelessness. Well, I'm determined not to let that terrible hopelessness spread through our farm communities today.

Our farm communities have, as I said, been hurt by grain embargoes and failed policies of other administrations, by past inflation and the difficulty of adjusting to our success in bringing that inflation under control. Well, since government had much to do with causing these problems, government must do its part to help our farm communities get back on their feet. Government should do so, of course, in a manner consistent with its obligation to cut deficit spending. But lend a hand government must.

To bolster farm credit, we proposed and the Senate, under the able leadership of Senators Dole and Helms, has passed a bill to strengthen the farm credit system and put it back on a sound basis. The House Agriculture Committee, under the leadership of Congressmen de la Garza, Madigan, Jones, and Coleman, has reported out a similar bill. I hope to sign an acceptable measure soon. To expand farm exports, Secretaries Block and Baker have been working to open markets and promote stronger economic growth in Europe and the Third World. And Secretary Baker is continually working with his foreign counterparts to ensure that the value of the dollar reflects economic conditions here and abroad. The dollar's decline during the past few months will brighten prospects for agriculture exports. The Congress is also putting together a comprehensive farm bill to guide our agricultural policy for years to come. As they work, the House and Senate must understand that more Federal dollars alone are not the answer. Indeed, during our administration farm price and income supports have more than quadrupled. What's needed is policy reform, including a long-term plan to get government out of farming and establish a more market-oriented farm policy. I call upon the Congress to send me a bill I can sign, one that provides America's farmers with hope.

Perhaps most significant, our administration is continuing the policies that have already done so much to foster economic growth: the encouragement of sound monetary growth, the limiting of government, and the preventing of tax hikes. In the past 3 years, we've enabled America to put 8.8 million more people to work. And in recent months, the news for farmers has been hopeful as interest rates have dropped; indeed, the prime rate has dropped a full point since last spring. And inflation has remained low, helping to hold down the prices farmers must pay for equipment and supplies. Times are still hard, but I'm convinced that a more prosperous future for our farms is beginning to take shape at last.

Until next week, thanks for listening, and God bless you.

Note: The President spoke at 12:06 p.m. from the Oval Office at the White House.

Statement on the Death of Former Supreme Court Justice Potter Stewart
December 7, 1985

Nancy and I are deeply saddened to learn of the death this afternoon of our friend, former Supreme Court Justice Potter Stewart. Potter Stewart was born in 1915 and grew up in Cincinnati, OH, in an atmosphere steeped in the law; indeed, his father, a prominent lawyer and former Cincinnati mayor, once served as a member of the Ohio Supreme Court. Potter went east to study at the Hotchkiss School, Yale, and Yale Law School. But just a few years after receiving his law degree, he returned home to practice in Cincinnati.

In 1954 President Eisenhower appointed Potter to the Sixth U.S. Circuit Court of Appeals, and at 39, Potter became the Nation's youngest Federal judge. Four years later, President Eisenhower raised Potter to the Supreme Court, making Potter, at 43, the second youngest justice to be appointed since the Civil War. On the Court, Potter soon became renowned for his measured and insightful opinions, his wit, and his lucid prose. Always, he strove for complete impartiality and complete fidelity to the Constitution. "The mark of a good judge," Potter once said, "is a judge whose opinion you can read and . . . have no idea if the judge was a man or woman, Republican or Democrat, a Christian or Jew . . . You just know he or she was a good judge." In 1981, after 23 years of untiring service, Potter stepped down from the Supreme Court in order to spend more time with his family. After his retirement, it was my honor to appoint Potter to the President's Commission on Organized Crime.

In a moment of reflection, Potter once remarked, "I never thought of putting a label on myself, except trying to be a good lawyer." It is as a patriot and a good lawyer—indeed, a brilliant man of the law—that we remember Justice Potter Stewart this day. Nancy and I join Potter's family and his close friends, the Vice President and Mrs. Bush, in mourning Potter's death and in cherishing the memory of his magnificent life.

Proclamation 5419—National Drunk and Drugged Driving Awareness Week, 1985
December 7, 1985

By the President of the United States of America

A Proclamation

Motorists who drive while impaired by alcohol or other drugs are one of our Nation's most serious public health and safety problems. Each year, drunk drivers account for tens of thousands of highway fatalities and hundreds of thousands of injuries.

This needless carnage on our streets and highways can be reduced through increased public awareness and a willingness to take the necessary steps to prevent it. We must not wait until personal tragedy strikes to become involved.

Strict law enforcement and just penalties are essential. Contrary to popular opinion, driving is not a right, but a privilege that can and should be withdrawn when a drunken or drugged driver endangers

1451

others. We also need to develop better means of detecting these drivers and getting them off the road before they cause an accident.

Statistics show that a disproportionate number of our young people are involved in accidents in which alcohol and drugs are a contributing factor. In recognition of the considerable evidence that such accidents can be drastically reduced by raising the legal drinking age, the Federal government is encouraging each State to establish 21 as the minimum age at which individuals may purchase, possess, or consume alcoholic beverages. Many States have already raised the legal drinking age, as a result of efforts of dedicated citizen volunteers and the growing awareness that motor vehicle accidents are the leading cause of death among young people. States that have not raised their legal drinking age should review these developments carefully.

We need informed, concerned citizens who are willing to help generate awareness; we need education and action to eliminate drunk and drugged drivers from our highways. With the continued involvement of private citizens and action at all levels of government, we can control the problem of drunken and drugged driving.

In line with the recommendations of the Presidential Commission On Drunk Driving, we have embarked on a long-term sustained effort to focus the resources of our local, State, and Federal governments on this problem.

In order to encourage citizen involvement in prevention efforts and to increase awareness of the seriousness of the threat, the Congress, by Senate Joint Resolution 137, has designated the week of December 15 through December 21, 1985, as "National Drunk and Drugged Driving Awareness Week."

Now, Therefore, I, Ronald Reagan, President of the United States of America, do hereby proclaim the week of December 15 through December 21, 1985, as National Drunk and Drugged Driving Awareness Week. I call upon each American to help make the difference between the needless tragedy of alcohol- and drug-related accidents and the blessings of health and life. I ask all Americans to take this message to heart and to urge others not to drive if they are under the influence of drugs or alcohol.

In Witness Whereof, I have hereunto set my hand this seventh day of December, in the year of our Lord nineteen hundred and eighty-five, and of the Independence of the United States of America the two hundred and tenth.

RONALD REAGAN

[*Filed with the Office of the Federal Register, 11:09 a.m., December 10, 1985*]

Note: The proclamation was released by the Office of the Press Secretary on December 9.

Letter to Members of the House of Representatives Urging Support for Tax Reform Legislation
December 9, 1985

As the House prepares to vote on H.R. 3838, the Tax Reform Act of 1985, let me repeat my strong support for tax reform and for moving a bill forward to the Senate.

The tax reform proposals pending before the House are a substantial improvement over present law and represent a significant and essential first step toward real tax reform. Under both proposals, individual and corporate tax rates are reduced substantially, with the top individual tax rate reduced to its lowest level since 1931. The personal exemption and standard deductions are increased substantially, and millions of working poor families would be removed from the tax rolls. Tax shelters are curtailed, special preferences are eliminated or restricted, and a stiff minimum tax is imposed.

I share the concern many have over particular aspects of the pending bills. As I have said, they can only be considered a good start, not an end product. More can and must be done to reduce tax rates further, and lower the cost of capital, so we can strengthen economic growth and opportunity for every American.

A tremendous amount of work has already gone into the process that has brought us this far. If a bill does not move forward from the House now, it is reasonable to suggest that tax reform might be "dead" for several years. From this perspective, the House vote is essentially a vote on whether or not to sustain the possibility of tax reform—to allow the legislative process to continue in the difficult effort to fashion a satisfactory bill.

To fail to advance a bill now would mean maintaining the status quo—a tax system with all its inequities, complexities, and tendencies to discourage efficient economic growth. That is not what I want. It is not what the American people want. I trust it is not what the House wants.

I strongly urge you to vote for tax reform—the Republican alternative or, should it not prevail, the Ways and Means bill. A vote against final passage in the House would doom our efforts to achieve real tax reform for the American people. We must not allow that to happen.

Note: Larry M. Speakes, Principal Deputy Press Secretary to the President, read the President's letter at 9:17 a.m. to reporters in the Briefing Room at the White House. The original was not available for verification of the content of this letter.

Message on the Observance of Hanukkah
December 9, 1985

I am delighted to send my warmest greetings to everyone marking the joyous feast of Hanukkah, which commemorates one of the most significant and symbolic events in Jewish history.

The story of the Maccabees and their brave struggle has inspired Jewish families down through the ages, calling to mind the valor and zeal of their forebears and bringing to life the rich character of their heritage. Hanukkah provides a fitting opportunity to reflect on the gifts a generous God ever wills to bestow on those who are faithful to Him.

As each candle of the menorah is lighted over the eight days of celebration, Jewish families gratefully remember the miracle of God's sustaining love which has brought them through every trial and persecution. The Miracle of the Flame is a message of hope against great odds, of rededication in the midst of doubt and oppression. It, and all the other beautiful traditions of Hanukkah, remind people everywhere that the light of God's presence can never be extinguished by the night of fear and human malice.

Nancy joins me in wishing His choicest blessings on all who observe this holiday. May the fires of faith and reverence you seek to rekindle on this feast blaze with renewed power the whole year through.

Nomination of H. Lawrence Garrett III To Be General Counsel of the Department of Defense
December 9, 1985

The President today announced his intention to nominate H. Lawrence Garrett III to be General Counsel of the Department of Defense. He would succeed Chapman B.

Cox.

Since 1983 Mr. Garrett has been serving at the White House as Associate Counsel to the President. Previously, he was Regional Director of the Merit Systems Protection Board in Seattle, WA (1982–1983); Executive Assistant to the President and chief operating officer, U.S. Synthetic Fuels Corporation (1981–1982); assistant counsel in the Office of the Counsel to the President at the White House in 1981; senior attorney/

adviser to the Director, Office of Government Ethics (1979–1981). During his Navy service, he served as Force Judge Advocate, Commander, Submarine Force, U.S. Pacific Fleet, Pearl Harbor, HI (1974–1978).

Mr. Garrett graduated from the University of West Florida (B.S., 1969) and the University of San Diego School of Law (J.D., 1972). He is married, has two children, and resides in Oakton, VA. He was born June 24, 1939, in Washington, DC.

Nomination of Jed Dean Christensen To Be Director of the Office of Surface Mining Reclamation and Enforcement
December 9, 1985

The President today announced his intention to nominate Jed Dean Christensen to be Director of the Office of Surface Mining Reclamation and Enforcement, Department of the Interior. He would succeed John D. Ward.

Mr. Christensen is Acting Director of the Office of Surface Mining Reclamation and Enforcement at the Department of the Interior. Previously, he was Deputy Assistant Secretary for Water and Science at the Department of the Interior; staff assistant to

the Commissioner, Bureau of Reclamation, Department of the Interior (1981–1984); finance and administrative services director for the city of Provo, UT (1979–1981); and budget officer in the office of the county manager, Clark County, NV (1977–1979).

Mr. Christensen graduated from Brigham Young University (B.S., 1970) and Arizona State University (M.P.A., 1972). He is married, has three children, and resides in Springfield, VA. He was born March 11, 1945, in Salina, UT.

Nomination of J. Craig Potter To Be an Assistant Administrator of the Environmental Protection Agency
December 9, 1985

The President today announced his intention to nominate J. Craig Potter to be an Assistant Administrator (Air and Radiation) of the Environmental Protection Agency. He would succeed Joseph A. Cannon.

Mr. Potter is currently Acting Assistant Secretary for Fish and Wildlife and Parks at the Department of the Interior. Previously, at the Department of the Interior he was Principal Deputy Assistant Secretary for Fish and Wildlife (1982–1985) and special assistant to the Assistant Secretary for Fish and Wildlife and Parks (1981–1982). He

served on the professional staffs of the U.S. Senate Appropriations Committee (1978–1981) and the U.S. Senate Government Affairs Committee (1977–1978). He was chief counsel of the U.S. Senate Post Office and Civil Service Committee in 1976–1977.

Mr. Potter graduated from the University of Illinois (A.B., 1967) and the University of Wyoming (J.D., 1972). He is married, has one child, and resides in Alexandria, VA. He was born December 23, 1943, in La Jolla, CA.

Appointment of Two Delegates to the National White House Conference on Small Business
December 9, 1985

The President today announced his intention to appoint the following individuals to be delegates to the National White House Conference on Small Business:

Nicholas A. Zoto, of Pennsylvania, is founder and owner of Zoto's, Inc., a family restaurant in Hatfield, PA. He served on the boards of the directors of the Philadelphia Industrial Development Corp. and the Philadelphia Small Business Investment Corp. He is married, has three children, and resides in Huntingdon Valley, PA. He was born May 29, 1937, in Philadelphia, PA.

Bernhardt William Collins, of Arizona, is a partner in charge of emerging business service with the national accounting firm of Coopers & Lybrand, Tucson office. He is also associated with the accounting firm of Turigliatto, Collins, Bitner & Palm in Tucson. He graduated from St. Louis University (B.S., 1956). He has four children and resides in Tucson, AZ. He was born December 28, 1932, in St. Louis, MO.

Nomination of Della M. Newman To Be a Member of the National Advisory Council on Women's Educational Programs
December 9, 1985

The President today announced his intention to nominate Della M. Newman to be a member of the National Advisory Council on Women's Educational Programs for the remainder of the term expiring May 8, 1987. She would succeed Peter Douglas Keisler.

Ms. Newman is president and owner of Village Real Estate, Inc., in Seattle, WA. She is also treasurer of Pacific Factors, Ltd., Inc., and sole proprietor of Braemar Associates, consulting services. She was on the board of directors of the Washington State Council on Economic Education and was secretary/treasurer, on the board of directors and executive committee for the Association of Washington Business.

She is married, has two children, and resides in Seattle, WA. She was born June 6, 1932, in Seattle.

Announcement of Donald R. Fortier as Principal Deputy Assistant to the President for National Security Affairs
December 10, 1985

The President today announced that Donald R. Fortier will serve as the Principal Deputy Assistant to the President for National Security Affairs. He will succeed John M. Poindexter.

Mr. Fortier joined the National Security Council staff in September 1982 as Director for Western Europe and NATO. In June 1983 he assumed the position of Senior Director for Political-Military Affairs and Special Assistant to the President. In December of 1983 he was appointed to the rank of Deputy Assistant to the President with responsibility for policy development. From February 1981 until joining the National Security Council staff, Mr. Fortier served as Deputy Director for Policy Planning at the Department of State. He received the Department's Superior Honor Award for his work in that position. Prior to his service in the Department of State, Mr. Fortier served for 5 years as a senior member of the professional staff of the House Foreign Affairs Committee. Prior to joining the Government, Mr. Fortier also worked as a consultant to the Rand Corp. on national security issues.

Mr. Fortier received a B.A. from Miami University in Oxford, OH, and his M.A. in political science and international relations from the University of Chicago. He was the recipient of a Ford Foundation fellowship in Chicago and served as the executive administrator of the university's symposium on "The Role of the Expert in a Democracy." Mr. Fortier is married, has one child, and resides in Bethesda, MD. He was born January 9, 1947, in Columbus, OH.

Nomination of Morton I. Abramowitz To Be an Assistant Secretary of State
December 10, 1985

The President today announced his intention to nominate Morton I. Abramowitz to be an Assistant Secretary of State (Intelligence and Research). This is a new position.

Mr. Abramowitz is Director of the Bureau of Intelligence and Research at the Department of State. Previously he was United States Ambassador to the Mutual and Balanced Force Reduction talks in 1981–1982. He joined the Foreign Service in 1960 as an economic officer specializing in Chinese affairs. During his career in the Foreign Service, he has progressed to the rank of Career Minister. He was Ambassador to Thailand in 1978–1981; Deputy Assistant Secretary of Defense for International Affairs, on detail from the Foreign Service, in 1974–1978; political adviser to CINC–PAC in 1973–1974; foreign affairs analyst at the State Department in 1971–1973; special assistant in the office of the Deputy Secretary of State in 1969–1971; international economist at the State Department in 1966–1968; political officer, Hong Kong, in 1963–1966; and consular-economic officer in Taipei in 1960–1962. He served with the International Cooperation Administration in 1958–1960.

He graduated from Stanford University (B.A., 1953) and Harvard University (M.A., 1955). He served in the U.S. Army in 1957. He is married, has two children, and resides in Washington, DC. He was born January 20, 1933, in Lakewood, NJ.

Nomination of H. Allen Holmes To Be an Assistant Secretary of State
December 10, 1985

The President today announced his intention to nominate H. Allen Holmes to be an Assistant Secretary of State (Politico-Military Affairs). This is a new position.

Mr. Holmes served in the United States Marine Corps in 1954–1957 as captain. He was an intelligence research analyst in the Department of State in 1958–1959 and entered the Foreign Service in 1959 as consular and political officer in Yaounde. In the Department he was foreign affairs officer (1961–1963) and staff assistant to the Under Secretary of State for Political Affairs (1963). In 1963–1967 he was political officer in Rome and was foreign affairs officer in the Department in 1967–1970. He was Counselor for Political Affairs in Paris in 1970–1974. He attended the executive seminar in national and international affairs at the Foreign Service Institute in 1974–1975 and was Director of the Office of NATO and Atlantic Affairs in the Bureau of European Affairs in 1975–1977. He was deputy chief of mission in Rome in 1977–1979 and Principal Deputy Assistant Secretary of State for European Affairs in 1979–1982. He served as United States Ambassador to Portugal in 1982–1985.

He graduated from Princeton University (A.B., 1954) and received a certificate in 1958 from the University of Paris. His foreign languages are French and Italian. He was born January 11, 1933, in Bucharest, Romania, of American parents.

Nomination of Henry F. Schickling To Be a Member of the Board of Directors of the Overseas Private Investment Corporation
December 10, 1985

The President today announced his intention to nominate Henry F. Schickling to be a member of the Board of Directors of the Overseas Private Investment Corporation, United States International Development Cooperation Agency, for a term expiring December 17, 1988. This is a reappointment.

Mr. Schickling is international president of the International Union of Tool, Die and Mold Makers (IUTDM) and the International Society of Skilled Trades (ISST), labor organizations. Previously he served as president of the IUTDM and ISST.

Mr. Schickling is married, has five children, and resides in Langhorne, PA. He was born December 13, 1926, in Philadelphia, PA.

Appointment of Robert W. McVey as a United States Commissioner of the International Pacific Halibut Commission
December 10, 1985

The President today announced his intention to appoint Robert W. McVey to be a United States Commissioner on the International Pacific Halibut Commission for the term expiring December 12, 1986. This is a reappointment.

Since 1980 Mr. McVey has been Director, Alaska Region, National Marine Fisheries Service (NMFS), in Juneau, AK. Previously

he was Deputy Director, Alaska Region, NMFS (1970–1980). He was assistant fisheries attaché at the U.S. Embassy in Copenhagen, Denmark, in 1966–1979.

He graduated from the University of Missouri (B.A., 1953; M.A., 1955). He is married, has two children, and resides in Juneau, AK. He was born February 19, 1932, in Stockton, KS.

Appointment of John A. Nuetzel as a Member of the President's Committee on the National Medal of Science
December 10, 1985

The President today announced his intention to appoint John A. Nuetzel to be a member of the President's Committee on

the National Medal of Science for a term expiring December 31, 1987. He would succeed John R. Whinnery.

Since 1962 Dr. Nuetzel has been serving as medical director of St. Mary's Health Center in St. Louis, MO. At St. Mary's Health Center he served as director of cardiology (1955–1977) and director of medical service (1955–1962). Since 1954 he has also been affiliated with St. Louis University School of Medicine, where he now serves as clinical professor of internal medicine.

He graduated from Washington University (M.D., 1947). He is married, has six children, and resides in St. Louis, MO. He was born February 16, 1925, in East St. Louis, IL.

Remarks on Signing the Bill of Rights Day and the Human Rights Day and Week Proclamation
December 10, 1985

The President. Well, good afternoon, and welcome to the White House. Today we mark the 37th anniversary of the signing of the Universal Declaration of Human Rights, a document to which virtually every nation on Earth subscribes. It's a day for us to take stock, to survey the globe with an eye not so much to words, as to actual deeds, to measure the world against the noble assertions of the Universal Declaration, and to reaffirm our commitment to the cause of human dignity.

America has, since its founding, been a refuge for those suffering under the yoke of oppression. A belief in the dignity of man and government by the consent of the people lies at the heart of our national character and the soul of our foreign policy. I had the pleasure of explaining that to a gentleman in Geneva not too long ago. [*Laughter*] But here the difference is our documents, such as the Constitution, say we, the people, will allow government to do the following things.

Today, more than ever, we're proud to be champions of freedom and human rights the world over. So, in observing Human Rights Day, we celebrate our commitment to the beliefs and moral teachings on which our own nation is founded, a belief in liberty, in the dignity of man, and in the inalienable rights of free men and women to choose their destinies. We have not hesitated when these rights and freedoms have been threatened. Last month on Veterans Day, I visited the graves of our soldiers who gave their lives so that the rest of us might know the blessings of peace and freedom.

Our sons, brothers, and fathers also lie in cemeteries and fields from Flanders to Manila, under undying testimony to our determination that these rights shall not perish.

We've learned from history that the cause of peace and human freedom is indivisible. Respect for human rights is essential to true peace on Earth. Governments that must answer to their peoples do not launch wars of aggression. That's why the American people cannot close their eyes to abuses of human rights and injustice, whether they occur among friend or adversary or even on our own shores. And we must be particularly appalled that, on the threshold of the 21st century, when man has made gigantic strides in opening the universe of space and finding cures for dread diseases, millions of our fellow men still suffer the grossest abuses. There are regimes, some friendly, some adversarial, that engage in frequent violations of human rights. There are other regimes which by their very nature are built upon the denial of human rights and the subordination of the individual to the state.

In Afghanistan and Cambodia, for example, alien dictatorships, with the support of foreign occupation troops, subject their peoples to unceasing warfare. Today, 6 years after the Soviet invasion of Afghanistan, up to 120,000 Soviet troops remain. They have slaughtered innocent women and children. They have employed poison gas. And they have loaded toys with small explosives, an attempt to demoralize the people by crippling Afghan children. Some 3½ million Afghans, fully one-fourth of the prewar population, have been forced to flee to Pakistan and Iran. The Communist rulers of Vietnam have launched vicious attacks upon Cambodian refugees, refugees who were fleeing a Communist regime in Cambodia itself, which led to the deaths of up to one-quarter of the entire Cambodian population.

In Ethiopia a Marxist government has used famine to punish large segments of its own population. Vice President Bush visited a camp for Ethiopian refugees in the Sudan last March. Men and women of all ages were dying; but the Vice President told me there's something unbearably painful about seeing the eyes of the children, the huge, sad eyes of starving children. And the peoples and governments of the democracies have responded generously to those pleas with tangible evidence of our concern.

In the Western Hemisphere, where so much progress toward democracy has been made, Cuba stands out as the country where institutionalized totalitarianism has consistently violated the rights of the citizens. Unfortunately, the Sandinista regime in Nicaragua seems determined to embark on the same course.

On three continents we see brave men and women risking their lives in anti-Communist battles for freedom. We cannot and will not turn our backs on them. This year the House of Representatives has heeded their call and voted aid to the freedom fighters in Cambodia, Afghanistan, and Nicaragua and repealed a ban on aid to freedom fighters in Angola. Elsewhere we have seen considerable progress toward observance of human rights. In El Salvador, Grenada, and Honduras, freely selected—or elected governments, I should say, represent the best hope of their peoples for the future. And just over the last weekend, a new civilian president was elected in Guatemala—that's the first time in 15 years. We laud those achievements, but our concern remains for those who are still captive and oppressed. This is where our voices must speak for justice, for the force of world opinion can and does make a difference.

One of the more tragic cases today is that of the Baha'i, whose leaders are with us today. The Government of Iran is engaged in rampart religious persecution, especially against the Baha'is. Since 1979, 198 Baha'is have been put to death, 767 are imprisoned, some 10,000 made homeless, and over 25,000 forced to flee their country. Only the continued world outcry can help bring an end to their suffering. In South Africa the inhuman policy of apartheid continues. The declaration of a state of emergency has given the police in that country essentially unlimited powers to silence critics of the government. Thousands of South African citizens have been detained without cause—or charge, I should say, and denied even elementary judicial protection. I have said that apartheid is abhorrent. It's time that the Government of South Africa took steps to end it and to reach out for compromise and reconciliation to end the turmoil in that strife-torn land. In Chile and the Philippines, too, we've shown our strong concern when our friends deviate from established democratic traditions.

In Eastern Europe the hopes and aspirations of millions of people for religious freedoms, civic rights, remain alive despite years of repression. The Solidarity labor union is still outlawed in Poland, and the Polish regime has once again moved to restrict the few freedoms that its people still enjoy. In Romania religious persecution includes the destruction of Bibles, while in Bulgaria the repression of the Turkish minority and the Islamic faith are witness to the unyielding denial of the basic freedom of speech, assembly, religion in this region.

I addressed human rights in my meetings with General Secretary Gorbachev, and I made it very clear to him that human rights are an abiding concern of the American people. We had a long and confidential discussion, and at the conclusion of our meetings, we declared in a joint statement that humanitarian issues would be resolved in a humanitarian spirit. Americans will be watching hopefully to see whether that pledge is observed. Make no mistake about it, human rights will continue to have a profound effect on the United States-Soviet relationship as a whole, because they are fundamental to our vision of an enduring peace.

President Lincoln once called America the last, best hope of man on Earth. Mr.

Lincoln's remark has special poignancy today, when American determination and strength are central to the peace and freedom of the entire democratic world. It is therefore incumbent upon us to work for the expansion of freedom throughout the world. In this great effort, my friends, I deeply believe we have a good cause for hope. Evidence of the triumph of the ideal of freedom and respect for human rights can be seen in every corner of the globe, and this is because freedom is not only morally right but practical and beneficial. Indeed, governments that rest upon the consent of the governed and the rule of law are more successful in fulfilling their people's aspirations for a better life. Democratic government and economic freedom have turned a number of small nations into economic giants. It even appears to have roused a giant nation from its economic slumber.

Permit me in closing to return to Mr. Lincoln: "What defined America, what gave our nation its purpose and mission," he once said, "was something in that Declaration of Independence giving liberty not alone to the people of this country, but hope to the world. It was that which gave promise that in due time, the weights should be lifted from the shoulders of all men." Well, let us always be true to that distinctly American cause. Let us never cease to work and pray that the weights should be lifted from the shoulders of all men.

Thank you, and God bless you, and I will now sign the proclamation designating December 10th as Human Rights Day and December 15th, 1985, as Bill of Rights Day, and the week beginning today is now recognized officially as Human Rights Week.

[At this point, the President signed the proclamation.]

Mr. Nelson. Mr. President, you have mentioned in your remarks the relentless persecution of the Baha'is in Iran. And though the mullahs of that country may choose to perpetuate these atrocities, they must know that because of you and the voices that you will encourage to speak out against it, these cannot now be perpetrated, except in the full light of public opinion. For this we are deeply and eternally grateful. We are aware also, Mr. President, that this is not a one-dimensional commitment; that in addition, you are morally and spiritually committed to the establishment of the peace we all want among the nations of the world—peace, the most pressing of all issues facing humanity today, and for which the Baha'is ardently pray, and that this country will help lead the world out of its current predicament.

Therefore, Mr. President, in recognition of your devotion to human rights, the National Spiritual Assembly presents to you, on behalf of the 100,000 American Baha'is, a commemorative plate. And in recognition of your continuous commitment to world peace, we have the honor, Mr. President, to transmit to you, from the Universal House of Justice, the international governing body of the Baha'is of the world, a statement on world peace. Thank you, Mr. President.

The President. Well, thank you very much, and thank all of you for what you're doing in this. I had the pleasure of quoting a statement of Thomas Jefferson to my colleague there in Geneva, and he called it, after he had heard it, very profound when Thomas Jefferson said, "If the people know all the facts, the people will never make a mistake." So, you, the people, and all of us together, I think, can continue to be a tide that will prove irresistible. Thank you all very much.

Note: The President spoke at 1:47 p.m. in Room 450 of the Old Executive Office Building. James Nelson was chairman of the National Spiritual Assembly of the Baha'is of the United States.

Proclamation 5420—Bill of Rights Day, Human Rights Day and Week, 1985
December 10, 1985

By the President of the United States of America

A Proclamation

On December 15, 1791, the adoption of the first ten amendments to the Constitution of the United States—the Bill of Rights—gave legal form to the noble principles which our Founding Fathers had set forth in the Declaration of Independence as the very basis for the birth of our Nation.

Benjamin Franklin, then 81 years old, in a moving address, reminded the members of the Constitutional Convention that it was God who had seen them safely through the War of Independence and that it was only through His "kind Providence" that they were able to meet in peace to shape "the means of establishing . . . future national felicity. . . . And if a sparrow cannot fall to the ground without His notice," Franklin asked, "is it probable that an empire can rise without His aid?"

Mindful of this, and deeply convinced that fundamental human rights are not a concession from the state but a gift of God, the Founding Fathers knew that government has a solemn obligation to safeguard those rights. That is why they were at pains to devise and ordain a constitutional system that would ensure respect for the dignity and uniqueness of every human being. Thus, they brought into existence a form of limited government—representative democracy—whose powers are circumscribed by law and whose legitimacy derives from the consent of the governed. For the first time in the history of nations, a written Constitution based on the inalienable God-given rights of the individual was promulgated.

It is with sincere thanksgiving that we reflect on the successful efforts of those wise patriots of two hundred years ago who laid the political foundations of our beloved Nation, and also to those millions of citizens ever since who have cherished and defended the Constitution and the principles it embodies. Many have given their lives on the field of battle so that freedom and human dignity might live both at home and abroad; let us never forget our debt to them or fail to honor their sacrifice and courage.

One hundred and fifty-seven years after the adoption of our Bill of Rights, the fundamental concepts enshrined in our Constitution were internationally acknowledged as applying to all peoples when the United Nations adopted the Universal Declaration of Human Rights on December 10, 1948.

Although we can take heart at the number of nations in which human rights are respected and real progress towards democratic self-government is being made, a disturbingly large number of governments continue to commit serious abuses of human rights. In the tradition of our forefathers, we protest against these abuses wherever they occur. We condemn the practice of torture, racial and religious persecution, and the denial of the right of free expression and freedom of movement.

The United States will never cease to be in the forefront of the noble battle for human rights. We have committed our resources and our influence to efforts aimed at extending throughout the world the rights we enjoy, rights which are rightly the prerogative of all people. This Nation must remain and will remain a beacon of hope for all who strive for human dignity. There is no better way of showing our gratitude for our inheritance of liberty.

We believe it is a right, not a privilege, to be allowed to speak freely; to assemble peacefully; to acquire and dispose of private property; to leave the country of one's residence; to form trade unions; to join or not to join groups and associations; and to worship according to one's conscience. Experience teaches us that the best check against tyranny is a government of the people in which leaders are elected in fair and open balloting and where the government's powers are subject to constitutional limitations. We pray that one day all nations of the earth may share with us the joys and rewards of living in free societies, and we resolve not to rest from our labors until the most noble longings of the human spirit, those for freedom of belief and expression, are fully realized.

During this commemorative week, let us rededicate ourselves to the advancement of human rights throughout the world, recalling the words of Alexander Hamilton that "natural liberty is a gift of the beneficent creator to the whole human race . . . and cannot be wrested from any people without the most manifest violation of justice."

Now, Therefore, I, Ronald Reagan, President of the United States of America, do hereby proclaim December 10, 1985, as Human Rights Day, and December 15, 1985, as Bill of Rights Day, and I call upon all Americans to observe the week beginning December 10, 1985, as Human Rights Week.

In Witness Whereof, I have hereunto set my hand this 10th day of December, in the year of our Lord nineteen hundred and eighty-five, and of the Independence of the United States of America the two hundred and tenth.

RONALD REAGAN

[*Filed with the Office of the Federal Register, 10:11 a.m., December 11, 1985*]

Appointment of Three Members of the Advisory Commission on Intergovernmental Relations
December 10, 1985

The President has appointed the following individuals to be members of the Advisory Commission on Intergovernmental Relations:

Robert Boone Hawkins, Jr., of California, for a term of 2 years. This is a reappointment. Mr. Hawkins is president of the Sequoia Institute and Trendsetter Energy Systems, Inc. He was a fellow at the Woodrow Wilson International Center for Scholars, 1975–1976; and he has published several articles on local and Federal Government. He graduated from San Francisco State College (B.S., 1965) and the University of Washington (Ph.D., 1969). He is married and has two children. He was born September 6, 1941, in Berkeley, CA.

Sandra R. Smoley, of California, for a term of 2 years. This is a reappointment. Ms. Smoley serves as supervisor for the third district for the Sacramento County Board of Supervisors. She is active in both civic and community affairs. She graduated from the University of Iowa (B.S., 1959). She is married and has three children. She was born July 8, 1936, in Spirit Lake, IA.

John T. Bragg, of Tennessee, for a term of 2 years. Mr. Bragg currently serves as deputy speaker for the Tennessee House of Representatives, where he has chaired the house finance, ways and means committee since 1973. He graduated from Middle Tennessee State University (B.A.). He has two children. He was born May 9, 1918, in Woodbury, TN.

Nomination of Larry K. Mellinger To Be an Alternate Executive Director of the Inter-American Development Bank
December 10, 1985

The President today announced his intention to nominate Larry K. Mellinger to be an Alternate Executive Director for the Inter-American Development Bank. He would succeed Hugh Foster.

Mr. Mellinger is senior vice president and chief financial officer of GRUMA Corp. in Malibu, CA. Previously, he was with Union

Bank in Los Angeles as senior vice president, planning and development (1983–1985); senior vice president, international banking department (1981–1983); senior vice president, Asia/Pacific (1978–1981); and vice president, Latin America (1974–

1978).

Mr. Mellinger graduated from the University of Kansas (B.A., 1967; B.S., 1968). He is married, has two children, and resides in Malibu, CA. He was born April 28, 1944.

Appointment of Three Members of the National Advisory Council on Indian Education
December 10, 1985

The President today announced his intention to appoint the following individuals to be members of the National Advisory Council on Indian Education for terms expiring September 29, 1988:

Clarence Wallace Skye, of South Dakota. This is a reappointment. Mr. Skye currently serves as executive director of the United Sioux Tribes of South Dakota. He is active in both civic and community activities. He attended the University of South Dakota (B.S.). He is married and has three children. He was born July 26, 1941, in Fort Yates, SD.

Eddie Leon Tullis, of Alabama. This is a reappointment. Mr. Tullis currently serves as utility foreman for the Monsanto Corp. He is active in several American Indian community organizations. He attended Faulkner State Junior College. He is married and has four children. He was born January 9, 1938, in Mobile, AL.

Robert Youngdeer, of North Carolina. This is a reappointment. Mr. Youngdeer currently serves as chief to the Eastern Band of Cherokee Indians. He is married and has two children. He was born April 13, 1922, in Cherokee, NC.

Appointment of T. Marshall Hahn, Jr., as a Member of the President's Export Council
December 10, 1985

The President today announced his intention to appoint T. Marshall Hahn, Jr., to be a member of the President's Export Council.

Mr. Hahn is chairman and chief executive officer of the Georgia-Pacific Corp. He has been with the Georgia-Pacific Corp. since 1973 as director (1973–present); chairman of the board, president and chief executive officer (1984–1985); president and chief executive officer (1983–1984); president and chief operating officer (1982–1983); president (1976–1982); executive vice president, pulp, paper, and chemicals (1975–1976);

and executive vice president, chemicals (1975). Prior to joining the Georgia-Pacific Corp., Mr. Hahn was president of Virginia Polytechnic Institute and State University (1962–1975); dean of arts and sciences at Kansas State University; and head of the physics department at Virginia Polytechnic Institute (1954–1959).

He graduated from the University of Kentucky (B.S., 1945) and the Massachusetts Institute of Technology (Ph.D., 1950). He is married, has two children, and resides in Atlanta, GA. He was born December 2, 1926, in Lexington, KY.

Appointment of John A. Love as a Member of the President's Commission on White House Fellowships
December 10, 1985

The President today announced his intention to appoint John A. Love to be a member of the President's Commission on White House Fellowships. This is an initial appointment.

Mr. Love has been with Ideal Basic Industries, Inc., in Denver, CO, since 1974 and is currently chairman of the board. In 1962 he was elected Governor of Colorado, and he served three consecutive 4-year terms. Mr. Love also served as chairman of the Republican Governors Conference in 1966–1967 and as chairman of the National Governors Conference in 1969–1970. He is a director of Frontier Airlines, the Manville Corp., United Banks of Colorado, and the Denver Chamber of Commerce. He is also a trustee of the University of Denver.

Mr. Love graduated from the University of Denver (A.B., 1938; L.L.B., 1941). He is married, has three children, and resides in Denver, CO. He was born November 29, 1916, in Gibson City, IL.

Statement Endorsing the Congressional Conference Agreement on the Balanced Budget and Emergency Deficit Control Bill
December 10, 1985

I am pleased that the Senate and House conferees have produced a bill that I can support which will bring the Federal budget into balance by 1991. I strongly endorse this measure and urge the Congress to act quickly and make this the law of the land. The American people have made clear their desire to eliminate the Federal deficit, and this bill provides a realistic way to accomplish that goal. Additionally, it is my strong hope that the Congress will build upon this effort to adopt a balanced budget amendment to the Constitution to ensure that these deficit reductions are permanent.

While this proposal is welcome, I am concerned that in the extreme it could have adverse effects on maintaining adequate levels of defense spending. We have no higher priority than maintaining a strong national defense. To that end, I am committed to and will propose budgets that meet this requirement. I look forward to working with Congress to implement our previous agreements on defense spending levels. In pursuing our commitment to a balanced Federal budget, I am pleased that Gramm-Rudman-Hollings does so in the proper way, by providing the incentive to reduce Federal spending, not by raising taxes. As I have said, the budget deficits are not the result of Americans paying too little in taxes; they come from the Federal Government spending too much money.

This agreement is the result of a lot of hard work and determination. In particular, Senators Gramm, Rudman, and Hollings have energetically fought to produce this landmark legislation. Much credit also goes to Senators Domenici and Packwood and Congressmen Foley, Gephardt, and Panetta. They are to be commended for their dedicated efforts to deficit reduction.

Statement by Principal Deputy Press Secretary Speakes on the Canada-United States Free Trade Agreement Negotiations
December 10, 1985

The President today gave formal notification to the Congress of the administration's intention to enter into negotiations leading to a bilateral free trade arrangement with Canada. The notification, required under 1984 amendments to section 102 of the Trade Act of 1974, requires 60 days' notice to the House Committee on Ways and Means and the Senate Committee on Finance.

On September 26, 1985, Canadian Prime Minister Brian Mulroney telephoned the President, followed by a formal letter proposing that the two governments explore more directly the scope and prospects for a new trade agreement ". . . involving the broadest possible package of mutually beneficial reductions in barriers to trade in goods and services." The President thereafter instructed the United States Trade Rep-

resentative (USTR), Clayton Yeutter, to begin the process of informal consultations with the Congress and the private sector. That process having been completed, Ambassador Yeutter recommended that the President proceed with formal notice.

In his notification letters to the congressional committees, the President emphasized that he viewed the initiation of negotiations as an opportunity to significantly enhance U.S. efforts to eliminate trade frictions with Canada. The President also welcomed the Canadian proposal as consistent with administration and congressional efforts to further open foreign markets for U.S. exports. "As you know, Canada is both our largest trading partner and fastest growing export market, representing one-fifth of our total exports," wrote the President.

Written Responses to Questions Submitted by Foreign Publications
December 6, 1985

U.S.-Soviet Summit Meeting

Q. Mr. President, if you would get the possibility of replaying the summit with Mr. Gorbachev, would you change anything in what you did and said in Geneva? Would it have been possible to produce better results?

The President. I met with Mr. Gorbachev for 15 hours, and 5 of those hours were spent in private conversations together, one on one. As Mr. Gorbachev has said, we did a lot of work together. We were both frank and serious in discussing our points of view. I told him exactly what I wanted to, and I found Mr. Gorbachev to be energetic and clear in making his points. I'm ready for the difficult, step-by-step work it will take to achieve lasting results in arms control, human rights, on regional issues, and in bilateral and other vital areas. Important as they were, our words in Geneva were not

as important as the deeds that must follow them if we are to reduce the mistrust and suspicions between us. I believe Mr. Gorbachev and I have made a fresh start.

Strategic Defense Initiative

Q. Mr. President, you are pursuing a military program, the SDI, that will last some years before producing results. How can you be sure that your successor will not abandon the program? How can you assure the allies about the continuity of this initiative?

The President. No freely elected leader can guarantee the actions of his successors. Our allies understand this. They also understand, however, that democracies tend to sustain those defense programs that are vital to their national interests and to the defense of freedom. I believe that the Strategic Defense Initiative is one of those programs. You must keep in mind that SDI is, at this stage, a research program designed to answer basic questions about whether defenses against ballistic missiles are feasible. This effort enjoys broad bipartisan support in the United States. Over the longer term, if we find that strategic defenses are feasible, I believe that SDI will continue to command support because it holds out the promise of effective deterrence through defense, rather than through the threat of massive death and destruction. It will endure because it offers the hope of creating a safer, more stable world and of someday rendering nuclear weapons obsolete.

Italy's International Role

Q. Mr. President, in the last few years, Italy has become more active on the international scene, not always in full agreement with the American policy. How do you assess this more autonomous role of Italy, for instance in the Middle East, and do you see any danger of potential misunderstandings or concerns in U.S.-Italian relations?

The President. We assess Italy's international role as positive. For instance, Italy has played a valued role in Middle East peacekeeping by its participation in the United Nations Interim Force in Lebanon (UNIFIL) and the Sinai multinational force. Italy and the United States sometimes have differing assessments on how best to promote the Middle East peace process. But both Italy and the United States firmly support the peaceful resolution of the Arab-Israeli conflict and Israel's right to exist behind secure and recognized boundaries. I do not see a danger of misunderstandings in Italo-American relations. We will continue to stay in close touch and consult with each other in a manner befitting our very friendly relations. The United States certainly intends to do this, and we are confident Italy has the same desire.

West German Participation in SDI

Q. The Government of the German Federal Republic is at the moment taking a decision about a German participation in SDI and has been attacked by Moscow for doing so. How significant would this kind of partnership in SDI be for the U.S.A. from a political and technological point of view?

The President. The United States appreciates the unique achievements of the Federal Republic of Germany in technologies which could have direct applications in the Strategic Defense Initiative research. The technical expertise and scientific capabilities of German institutions and corporations involved in advanced research would be helpful and very welcome. We believe that the technological results of joint efforts will lead to enhanced security for the alliance as a whole and that the participation of the Federal Republic of Germany and other NATO allies in the research effort itself will foster closer cooperation within NATO.

Chemical Weapons

Q. The question of chemical weapons is becoming a matter of growing anxiety in Europe. Can we expect a new American initiative for a worldwide ban of these weapons in the near future?

The President. We are firmly committed to reaching agreement on an effective, comprehensive, and verifiable global ban on all chemical weapons. As you may know, Vice President Bush tabled a draft chemical weapons treaty at the Conference on Disarmament in April 1984. This treaty would ban chemical weapons throughout the world. Since then, we have worked closely with our allies and others to improve upon our draft provisions and to press for progress in the Geneva Conference on Disarmament negotiations. We feel, however, that the negotiations on that treaty, particularly with regard to the essential verification measures, have not progressed as rapidly as they should.

This was one of the issues which I discussed in Geneva with General Secretary Gorbachev. I was heartened that we could record our agreement in the joint statement to accelerate our efforts to conclude an effective and verifiable global ban. We also agreed to intensify bilateral discussions on all aspects on such a chemical weapons ban, including verification questions. Further, we agreed to initiate a dialog on preventing the proliferation of chemical weapons. The United States has often expressed concern with the spread of chemical weapons, particularly with regard to instances of chemical weapon use. We welcome Mr. Gorbachev's expression of interest in this problem and hope the U.S.S.R. will take concrete steps to help deal with it. Ultimately, the way to stem the spread of chemical weapons is to conclude an effective and verifiable global ban on them. Until such a ban is achieved, it is important that the United States retain a modern and credible deterrent against the existing Soviet chemical weapon capability.

U.S.-Soviet Summit Meeting

Q. Is Mr. Gorbachev a man—to quote Mrs. Thatcher—one can do business with? What has been for you the most surprising aspect and impression of this meeting?

The President. Since I took office, I have sought to deal realistically with the U.S.S.R. We are all aware of the facts of the past 40 years of international relations. The basis for my meeting with General Secretary Gorbachev was 5 years of firm and consistent policies pursued by the United States and its allies. It was on this basis that I came to Geneva, ready for a constructive dialog and to make a fresh start. In Geneva, I spent a good deal of time with Mr. Gorbachev, including 5 hours in one-on-one conversations. I found him an energetic exponent of Soviet policy and a good listener. Our exchanges were lively, open, and serious. We had a lot of give-and-take. We agreed on some things and disagreed on much else. But we agreed that deeds, and not words, will be necessary to make real and lasting progress in our relations. We are ready and eager for step-by-step progress in the months ahead.

Intermediate-Range Nuclear Weapons

Q. When do you expect an agreement on intermediate-range missiles, separate from the other negotiations, and if there will be an agreement before 1988, is there a possibility that Holland won't need to deploy the cruise missile?

The President. As you know, the United States made a new proposal on intermediate nuclear forces (INF) systems at the end of the last round of the Geneva arms talks. This new proposal, drawing on the positive elements of the Soviet INF counterproposal made during the round, establishes an in-

terim ceiling on United States and Soviet longer range INF launchers in Europe or in range of NATO Europe, but allows freedom to mix under that ceiling. The Soviet Union has not yet fully responded to our new proposal, which we intend to pursue when the talks resume in January.

Although there are significant differences which still separate the sides, General Secretary Gorbachev and I have agreed that our arms control negotiators should accelerate their work toward arms control agreements which provide for significant reductions and increased stability and which can be effectively verified. As we noted in our joint statement of November 21, both sides have called for early progress on an interim INF agreement. Further, I would note that the Government of the Netherlands has stated that it would accept its proportional share of cruise missiles under the terms of an INF agreement which provides for reductions in U.S. and Soviet LRINF missiles. If the Soviet Union were to agree to the United States objective in INF, the total ban on LRINF missiles, that would of course be a significant step toward improving stability and prospects for peace.

Trade With the Soviet Union

Q. In the area of more cooperation with the Soviet Union, are you prepared to soften your policy on high-tech exports to Eastern Europe, and is the new American-Russian nuclear fusion project a first step in that direction?

The President. While the United States favors mutually beneficial, nonstrategic trade with the Soviet Union and its allies, we maintain export controls to ensure that American exports to these destinations do not undercut our security interests. In addition, we, our NATO allies, and Japan control strategic exports to the Soviet Union through COCOM. COCOM maintains a list of controlled items with potential military significance which cannot be exported to the Soviet Union or its allies without special approval. Since the Soviet invasion of Afghanistan, we and our COCOM partners have followed a policy of strictly enforcing these controls. We generally do not authorize exports to the Soviet Union of items on the COCOM control list. This policy will be continued. Cooperative fusion research with the Soviets would not result in the transfer of COCOM controlled technology to the Soviet Union. American and allied participation in the fusion project would be carried out within existing COCOM guidelines to prevent transfer of sensitive technology with military potential.

South Africa

Q. If human rights are so important for you, as you pointed out to Mr. Gorbachev, why don't you push harder on human rights for the black majority in South Africa?

The President. We have been doing all we can to foster the development of a just society in South Africa, and will continue to do so. My administration has on repeated occasions publicly condemned the system of apartheid as systematic racial discrimination that denies the black majority its unalienable rights. We have done so even more often in private discussions with officials of the South African Government. American policy is based on ensuring peaceful change in South Africa. Change is inevitable. The issue, in our view, is not whether apartheid is to be dismantled, but how and when. All men of good will want to see it replaced by a just society, not through a racial conflagration where the people could well exchange one oppressor for another. To encourage peaceful change, on September 9, I ordered a set of measures aimed against the machinery of apartheid. We favor actions against the racist system, not actions that would penalize the black population in South Africa or the peoples of the neighboring states.

U.S.-Soviet Relations

Q. Your perceptions of the Soviet leadership, its policies, interests, and long-term aims seem to have changed during your time in office. Is this a normal development, reflecting changing times, preoccupations, and interests in the U.S., or do you see a different type of leadership at work in the Kremlin with a real prospect for change?

The President. Our policy toward the Soviet Union is based on a long-term and realistic understanding of the differences between us. We are all aware of the lessons of the past 40 years. We have no illusions about the nature of communism and Soviet foreign policy. We must not hold out hopes for immediate, dramatic change. Given these facts, our relations with the U.S.S.R. have been and will continue to be essentially competitive. At the same time, we must and will ensure that our competition remains peaceful. As I have said many times, and as General Secretary Gorbachev and I agreed in Geneva, a nuclear war cannot be won and must never be fought. We must strive for real progress in human rights, regional issues, arms control, bilateral and other areas wherever we can. In Geneva, a new Soviet leader and I made a fresh start. I have no illusions, but I do have hope. And I hope and believe Mr. Gorbachev is ready, as I am ready, for the hard, productive work that lies ahead.

United Nations

Q. The Swiss people will vote next spring on whether, finally, to join the United Nations. American skepticism towards this body seems to have grown in the last decade. What is your view of the role the U.N. plays and should play in the modern world?

The President. The United Nations has not been a panacea for all of the world's problems as some expected. Nevertheless, it has been and can be a force for great good. The U.N.'s peacekeeping and peacemaking efforts have been important at many critical times, for example, in Korea, the Congo, Cyprus, and in the Middle East. Many of its specialized agencies have served the purposes for which they were intended and performed valuable services in the fields of health, economic assistance and development, care of refugees, and in various other humanitarian and technical areas. While acknowledging the U.N.'s achievements, we must not close our eyes to its disappointments: its failures to deal effectively with essential security issues, the politicization of too many of its agencies, the misuse of too many resources. Given the divided state of the world, realism demands we recognize the U.N.'s limitations. But we must not overlook its real potential and opportunities, opportunities that for the good of mankind we cannot afford to waste. The principles of the U.N. Charter are as valid today as in 1945 and provide a guide for action. If the member states live up to them, the U.N. can be the means to a better and safer world.

Note: The questions were submitted by Corriere Della Sera, of Italy; Die Welt, of the Federal Republic of Germany; NRC Handelsblad, of the Netherlands; and Neue Zurcher Zeitung, of Switzerland. The questions and answers were released by the Office of the Press Secretary on December 11.

Appointment of Lane A. Carson as a Member of the Architectural and Transportation Barriers Compliance Board
December 11, 1985

The President today announced his intention to appoint Lane A. Carson to be a member of the Architectural and Transportation Barriers Compliance Board for a term expiring December 3, 1988. He will succeed Jackie McSpadden.

Mr. Carson is presently serving as assistant district attorney for St. Tammany Parish in Louisiana. Since 1977 he has also been a partner in the law firm of Carson & Exni-cios. Mr. Carson was elected to serve as a member of the Louisiana Legislature in 1976 and reelected for another 4-year term in 1979.

He graduated from Louisiana State University (B.S., 1971) and Tulane University School of Law (J.D., 1974). He is married, has two children, and resides in Mandeville, LA. He was born August 21, 1947, in New Orleans, LA.

Appointment of Three Members of the National Council on Educational Research
December 11, 1985

The President has appointed the following individuals to be members of the National Council on Educational Research for terms expiring September 30, 1988:

Donald Barr, of Connecticut. This is a reappointment. Mr. Barr is currently the headmaster for Hackley School in Tarrytown, NY. He is the author of several articles on education and has published various children's books. He is married and has four children. He was born August 2, 1921, in New York City.

Robert H. Mattson, of Oregon. Mr. Mattson is currently serving as associate dean and professor of education at the University of Oregon, where he also serves as director for the Center for Educational Policy. He is married with four children. He was born November 11, 1925, in Outlook, MT.

James Harvey Harrison, Jr., of Virginia. This is a reappointment. Mr. Harrison currently serves as Washington area manager for the international systems division. He graduated from Middle Tennessee State College (B.S., 1951). He is married and has two children. He was born September 13, 1927, in Shellyville, TN.

Remarks During a White House Briefing for Supporters of Tax Reform
December 11, 1985

Sorry that I have kept you waiting a few minutes here. I was a little late; I was meeting with some Congressmen. You can't imagine what we were talking about. [*Laughter*] Well, I thank you for being with us here. And I would like to say a few words about the upcoming vote on tax reform. It's a deeply significant vote in our long, uphill climb to streamline the Nation's tax code to make it the strongest possible engine for growth and opportunity and a model for simplicity and fairness. Now, we do not believe that after all our efforts, good-faith efforts on both sides of the aisle, and after today's developments, that our work should be lost for lack of a handful of votes. I hope Members will vote yes on final passage to allow this important issue to move forward.

Both the tax reform proposals before the Congress would reduce corporate and individual tax rates substantially, bringing the top individual rate down to its lowest level since 1931. The minimum tax would be strengthened, even as tax shelters and special preferences are eliminated and restricted. And millions of the working poor would be removed from the tax rolls as the personal exemption and standard deduction are increased.

But I realize there are loyal supporters of mine who have difficulties with the Ways and Means bill, even some with the Republican substitute. But let me say here that despite the good aspects of these proposals, as far as we're concerned, more improvement needs to be done. We continue to insist that true tax reform is imperative, but when we examined the legislation, we did conclude that, in many respects, it is better than the current tax law. It is the beginning, or at least it can be the beginning, of a final product that is true and historic tax reform. And it's your support and help that can give us the chance to move forward now on the tax reform.

We can't afford to wait. If we let tax reform die, I think it will be years before we can bring it back. You only have to look back in your own memories to say, how far back do I have to remember before anyone ever attempted to reform this tax system, which has grown more complex and more cumbersome and more unjust as the years have gone on. So, what I'm saying and urging you today is simply this: Give us the chance to finish the job. Give us the chance to improve this initiative in the Senate based on what I've just said. I thank you for all that you're doing, but we need you more than ever right now.

You know, it's hard to realize that a Senator back in 1913, when they were debating the first income tax amendment, was literally laughed out of politics and lost his office because in opposing the income tax—he said, "Why, the way this is worded," he said, "some day we could find that a government could take even as much as 10 percent of a man's earnings." [*Laughter*] And they thought that was so ridiculous that they literally, as I say, laughed him out of politics. Well, wouldn't it be nice to be back there. The business I used to be in—it was good enough for an agent. [*Laughter*] But there is one other comparison also. The Lord says that His share is a tenth. We believe in tithing, but when you start computing Caesar's share nowadays—[*laughter*]—and the Lord had said, "If I profit you 10 times as much, you will give 10 times as much." Now, in Caesar's case, if he profits you 10 times as much, you give 50 times as much—[*laughter*]—to him.

Well, I don't think Caesar ought to be better than that other friend. So, keep at it, and I'm going back to talk to some more people about tax reform. Thank you all very much for being here.

Note: The President spoke at 3:48 p.m. in Room 450 of the Old Executive Office Building.

Statement on Signing the Bill Increasing the Public Debt Limit and Enacting the Balanced Budget and Emergency Deficit Control Act of 1985
December 12, 1985

Today I have signed H.J. Res. 372, which increases the statutory limit on the public debt and includes the Balanced Budget and Emergency Deficit Control Act of 1985, also known as the Gramm-Rudman-Hollings amendment. With the passage of this landmark legislation, the Congress has made an important step toward putting our fiscal house in order. Deficit reduction is no longer simply our hope and our goal; deficit reduction is now the law. From here to the end of the decade, mandated cuts can put the deficit on a declining path and eliminate governmental overspending by 1991. It is my hope that we will move even one step further to secure the gains we have made by adopting a balanced budget amendment to the Constitution.

Deficits have threatened our economic well-being for too long. For years the Congress has talked about the deficit, and now it has done something about it. But the tough work of controlling Federal spending still lies ahead. It is important that we now cooperate in good faith toward building a solid fiscal foundation for economic growth. This legislation mandates that the President and the Congress work together to eliminate the deficit over the next 5 years. The first step in that process will begin early next year. At that time I anticipate that we will have to take some significant across-the-board reductions in a wide range of programs. That means cutting back on the expansion of government, an expansion which has slowed, but which still continues apace. Whether increased government spending is financed through taxes or borrowing, it imposes a heavy burden on the private economy, the source of our prosperity and the foundation of our hopes for the future. That is why increasing taxes is not an option: Deficit reduction must mean spending reductions. We must also never lose sight of the necessity to maintain a strong national defense. Restoring our defenses has been vital not only to our securi-

ty but to the cause of freedom. Today our once ailing alliances are stronger than before. America is looked upon with renewed admiration around the world, and the principles of human freedom that we embody are no longer in retreat. I am confident that implementing our previous agreements with Congress for steady real growth in defense will keep our defenses secure.

In signing this bill, I am mindful of the serious constitutional questions raised by some of its provisions. The bill assigns a significant role to the Director of the Congressional Budget Office and the Comptroller General in calculating the budget estimates that trigger the operative provisions of the bill. Under the system of separated powers established by the Constitution, however, executive functions may only be performed by officers in the executive branch. The Director of the Congressional Budget Office and the Comptroller General are agents of Congress, not officers in the executive branch. The bill itself recognizes this problem and provides procedures for testing the constitutionality of the dubious provisions. The bill also provides a constitutionally valid alternative mechanism should the role of the Director of the Congressional Budget Office and the Comptroller General be struck down. It is my hope that these outstanding constitutional questions can be promptly resolved.

Similar constitutional concerns are raised by a provision in the bill authorizing the President to terminate or modify defense contracts for deficit reduction purposes, but only if the action is approved by the Comptroller General. Under our constitutional system, an agent of Congress may not exercise such supervisory authority over the President. As the Supreme Court made clear in its *Chadha* decision, Congress can veto Presidential action only through the constitutionally established procedure of passing a bill through both Houses and presenting it to the President.

My administration alerted Congress to these various problems throughout the legislative process in an effort to achieve a bill free of constitutionally suspect provisions. Although we were unsuccessful in this goal, I am nonetheless signing the bill. In doing so, I am in no sense dismissing the constitutional problems or acquiescing in a violation of the system of separated powers carefully crafted by the framers of the Constitution. Rather, it is my hope that the constitutional problems will be promptly resolved so that the vitally important business of deficit reduction can proceed.

In addition, the legislation also increases the debt ceiling so that the Federal Government can continue to meet its financial obligations.

The many Senators and Representatives whose hard work has borne fruit in this bill are to be commended. The American people expect their elected officials to take action now to reduce the size of government and to set upon a reasonable and equitable course to eliminate Federal budget deficits. I am unequivocally committed to that goal. I am hopeful and confident that Congress will act responsibly in meeting its obligations under the bill and thus in future years will render implementation of the automatic budget reduction mechanism unnecessary. Deficit reduction is on the horizon. We are embarked on this promising new path together, and together we will make it work.

Note: H.J. Res. 372, approved December 12, was assigned Public Law No. 99–177.

Remarks at the Presentation Ceremony for the Presidential Distinguished Executive Awards
December 12, 1985

Thank you all very much. Who's tending the store? [*Laughter*] Connie Horner and ladies and gentlemen, good morning, and welcome to the White House. We've assembled today to—if some of you think that's strange, I always have to explain that. I had to have it explained to me—that they technically call this the White House. I know we're across the street. [*Laughter*] But we're assembled here today to honor the best of our Senior Executive Service, those of you whom it is my privilege to bestow distinguished Presidential Rank Awards.

You know, any administration, even one that lasts 8 years, is keenly aware of the ticking of the clock and the calendar pages flipping by as it strives to achieve what it set out to accomplish. Each President, each administration, is a rendezvous with Father Time. Father Time—I did—I went to school with him; he was a classmate. [*Laughter*] But the clock is ticking, and even as our administration has called for government to play a more limited role in American life, we've worked hard to see that government

performs its legitimate functions with greater diligence and efficiency. It's men and women like you who have made this vital effort successful. At Treasury and Justice, in the Army, the Navy, the Air Force, at Agriculture, NASA, and so many others, you've become shining examples of individuals who have delivered on the promises of the Government to the American people.

Now, time won't permit me to discuss each of your achievements, but I do want to mention just, at least, a few. One of you has fought crime by developing a program to help cut drug smuggling in Miami; another helped put Americans on the Moon and is now working to make NASA's space station a reality. Several of you've made advances of critical importance to our national defense. And at this time of battles to bring deficit spending under control, I have to point out that several of you've saved our taxpayers major sums: one, a financial officer at the Agency for International Development, saved the Government more than $4½ million. An award winner at Treasury is credited with saving taxpayers $12 million. And an award winner in the Navy pioneered changes that, it's estimated, will save some $300 million. And you know, even in Washington $300 million is real money. [*Laughter*]

Even more important than these specific savings and advances—each of you has provided an example, an inspiration to others in the civil service, to work hard and to be more conscientious of the great trust that is shared by all in public service. Through your personal achievement, you, whom we honor today, have improved the lives of millions of your fellow citizens throughout our nation. And these awards represent the appreciation that each of us feels for you having accomplished so much for so many.

On behalf of all Americans, permit me to offer my heartfelt congratulations on a job well done. Thank you all, and God bless you. And now, Connie, if you'll get up here and do your chore, I'll step over here and do mine.

Note: The President spoke at 11:30 a.m. in Room 450 of the Old Executive Office Building. Constance Horner, Director of the Office of Personnel Management, read the names of the recipients. The 1985 award recipients were: Valdus V. Adamkus, Richard C. Armstrong, Robert N. Battard, Curtis W. Christensen, James E. Colvard, Guy H. Cunningham III, Angelo J. DiMascio, Anthony R. DiTrapani, Robert I. Dodge III, Barry Felrice, Kenneth M. Fogash, Robert M. Forssell, Gerald D. Griffin, Arthur H. Guenther, Richard L. Haver, David A. Israel, Samuel W. Keller, John C. Keeney, Ruth L. Kirschstein, Michael G. Kozak, Jack W. McGraw, James C. McKinney, Alexia L. Morrison, James W. Morrison, Jr., William Y. Nishimura, R. Max Peterson, Stanley M. Silverman, John A. Simpson, Andrew J. Stofan, Naomi R. Sweeney, Margery Waxman, and Larry G. Westfall.

Statement on the Crash of an Airliner Transporting Members of the 101st Airborne Division
December 12, 1985

Nancy and I are deeply shocked and saddened by the report of the tragic crash of a chartered airliner returning U.S. troops to the United States from peacekeeping duty with the United Nations' Multinational Force and Observers in the Sinai. The loss, tragic at any time, is especially painful at this holiday period. I have been advised by the Secretary of Defense that the full resources of the U.S. Army and the U.S. Government are being made available to assist families of victims however possible. Our hearts go out to the loved ones of these brave soldiers who have paid the fullest price in the service of their country and the cause of peace.

Note: Larry M. Speakes, Principal Deputy Press Secretary to the President, read the President's statement to reporters in the Briefing Room at the White House during his daily press briefing, which began at noon. The airliner, which was en route to Fort Campbell, KY, crashed at 6:45 a.m. in Gander, Newfoundland. There were 248 casualties.

Remarks on Lighting the National Christmas Tree
December 12, 1985

My fellow Americans, thank you for joining Nancy and me on this festive evening. The menorah stands lighted in Lafayette Park, for this is also the time of Hanukkah, and this season is rich in the meaning of our Judeo-Christian tradition. In a moment we'll be lighting the National Christmas Tree, carrying forward what is now a 62-year tradition first begun by Calvin Coolidge.

Tonight we're drawn in warmth to one another as we reflect upon the deeply holy meaning of the miracle we shall soon celebrate. We know that Mary and Joseph reached the stable in Bethlehem sometime after sunset. We do not know the exact moment the Christ Child was born, only what we would have seen if we'd been standing there as we stand here now: Suddenly, a star from heaven shining in our eyes, shining with brilliant beauty across the skies, a star pointing toward eternity in the night, like a great ring of pure and endless light, and then all was calm, and all was bright. Such was the beginning of one solitary life that would shake the world as never before or since. When we speak of Jesus and of His life, we speak of a man revered as a prophet and teacher by people of all religions, and Christians speak of someone greater—a man who was and is divine. He brought forth a power that is infinite and a promise that is eternal, a power greater than all mankind's military might, for His power is Godly love, love that can lift our hearts and soothe our sorrows and heal our wounds and drive away our fears. He promised there will never be a long night that does not end. He promised to deliver us from dark torment and tragedy into the warming sunlight of human happiness, and beyond that, into paradise. He's never been a halfway giver; His generosity is pure and perfect and sure.

This, then, expresses the true meaning of Christmas. If each of us could give but a fraction to one another of what He gave to the whole human family, how many hearts could heal, how much sorrow and pain could be driven away? There's still time for joy and gladness to touch a sad and lonely soul, still time to feed a hungry child, to wrap a present for a kind old man feeling forlorn and afraid, and to reach out to an abandoned mother raising children on her own. There's still time to remember our Armed Forces, to express our profound gratitude to those keeping watch on far-away frontiers of freedom, and to redouble our energies to account for our MIA's. They are not and never will be forgotten. And there's still time to remember the deepest truth of all: that there can be no prisons, no walls, no boundaries separating the members of God's family.

Let us reach out tonight to every person who is persecuted; let us embrace and comfort, support and love them. Let us come together as one family under the fatherhood of God, binding ourselves in a communion of hearts, for tonight and tomorrow and for all time. May we give thanks for an America abundantly blessed, for a nation united, free, and at peace. May we carry forward the happiness of the Christmas spirit as the guiding star of our endeavors 365 days a year. And as we light this magnificent tree, may all the youthful hope and joy of America light up the heavens and make the angels sing.

Merry Christmas, and God bless you all. And now we're going to light the tree.

[At this point, the National Christmas Tree, which was located on the Ellipse, south of the White House grounds, was lighted.]

Merry Christmas!

Note: The President spoke at 5:45 p.m. at the South Portico of the White House during the annual Christmas Pageant of Peace.

Nomination of James L. Malone To Be United States Ambassador to Belize
December 13, 1985

The President today announced his intention to nominate James L. Malone, of Virginia, to be Ambassador to Belize. He would succeed Malcolm R. Barnebey.

Mr. Malone is currently a consultant to the Department of State. He served as an Assistant Secretary of State for Oceans and International Environmental and Scientific Affairs, and in that capacity he was also the Special Representative of the President for the Law of the Sea Conference, with the personal rank of Ambassador, 1981–1985. In 1981 Mr. Malone served as the Acting Director of the U.S. Arms Control and Disarmament Agency. Mr. Malone practiced law with the firm of Doub and Muntzing in Washington, DC, 1978–1981. He served as U.S. Representative to the Conference of the Committee on Disarmament, 1976–1977; General Counsel to the U.S. Arms Control and Disarmament Agency, 1973–1976; Assistant General Counsel, 1971–1973; and senior principal trial attorney for the Federal Maritime Commission, 1970–1971. He was a visiting professor of law, School of Law, University of Texas, in 1969; dean and professor of law, College of Law, Willamette University, in 1967–1968; assistant dean and lecturer in law, School of Law, University of California, Los Angeles, 1961–1967.

Mr. Malone graduated from Pomona College (B.A., 1953), Stanford Law School (J.D., 1959), and Fletcher School of Law and Diplomacy (M.A., 1965). He is married, has three children, and resides in McLean, VA. Mr. Malone was born December 22, 1931, in Los Angeles, CA.

Nomination of Michael A. Samuels To Be a Deputy United States Trade Representative
December 13, 1985

The President today announced his intention to nominate Michael A. Samuels, of the District of Columbia, to be a Deputy United States Trade Representative with the rank of Ambassador. He would succeed Peter Otto Murphy.

Dr. Samuels is currently vice president, international division, at the U.S. Chamber of Commerce, 1981 to the present; and he has also been serving as vice chairman and executive director at the Center for International Private Enterprise, 1978 to the present. He was executive director of the Third World Studies Center for Strategic and International Studies at Georgetown University in 1977–1981. Dr. Samuels served as U.S. Ambassador to Sierra Leone in 1975–1977; as Executive Assistant to the Deputy Secretary of State in 1973–1974; and as legislative management officer at the Department of State in 1970–1973. He was a teacher and supervisor with the Peace Corps in Nigeria in 1962–1964.

Dr. Samuels graduated from Yale University (A.B., 1961) and Teachers College at Columbia University (M.A., 1962; Ph.D., 1965). He is married, has one child, and resides in Washington, DC. Dr. Samuels was born April 4, 1939, in Youngstown, OH.

Nomination of Hugh W. Foster To Be Alternate United States Executive Director of the International Bank for Reconstruction and Development
December 13, 1985

The President today announced his intention to nominate Hugh W. Foster, of California, to be United States Alternate Executive Director of the International Bank for

Reconstruction and Development for a term of 2 years. This is a reappointment.

Mr. Foster has been serving in this position since October 1983, and prior to that he served as Alternate Executive Director for the Inter-American Development Bank in 1982–1983. He was associated with the Wells Fargo Bank in San Francisco, CA, where he last served as vice president and area manager of the bank's Asia Pacific division. Previously, Mr. Foster served as vice president and area manager in Mexico City in 1977–1980; vice president and area manager, China Sea area, in 1975–1977; and assistant vice president and area manager, Australasia area, in 1974–1975. He has held other positions with the Wells Fargo Bank since 1969.

Mr. Foster graduated from Colgate University (A.B., 1965) and Stanford University Graduate School of Business (M.B.A., 1969). He is married, has five children, and resides in Washington, DC. He was born December 13, 1943, in Baltimore, MD.

Designation of Heather J. Gradison as Chairman of the Interstate Commerce Commission
December 13, 1985

The President today announced the designation of Heather J. Gradison, of Ohio, to be Chairman of the Interstate Commerce Commission. She would succeed Reese H. Taylor, Jr.

Mrs. Gradison has been serving as a member of the Interstate Commerce Commission since June 1982. Previously she was with the Southern Railway System in Washington, DC, 1974–1982.

Mrs. Gradison graduated from Radford College (B.A., 1975) and attended George Washington University, 1976–1978. She is married and resides in Washington, DC. Mrs. Gradison was born September 6, 1952, in Houston, TX.

Radio Address to the Nation on Tax Reform and the Situation in Nicaragua
December 14, 1985

My fellow Americans:

I have two subjects to speak about today. First, taxes. I think you know how strongly I want to improve our unfair and complicated tax code. A problem that's grown so monstrous over the years isn't easy to correct. But we're on the edge of a breakthrough that can bring personal income tax rates down to the lowest level in over 50 years. This past week the House began final consideration of crucial reform legislation, but because of a parliamentary impasse, the House was unable to vote. Unless it's overturned, the result can only be a defeat for all Americans, who know taxes are too high and the system is hopelessly unfair. Today I'd like to make a personal request of the House of Representatives. You have the opportunity to provide the relief millions of Americans demand. If, together, Republicans and Democrats would agree to a format for considering this vote, I believe there will be sufficient bipartisan support for tax reform to pass. This is one time politics must be put aside on both sides of the aisle. There are ways to permit this much-needed reform to go forward. There are ample excuses for not going forward; there will be no justification if it does not.

Now, I must address recent disturbing events in a country close to our borders—the Communist dictatorship in Nicaragua. Nicaragua today is an imprisoned nation. It is a nation condemned to unrelenting cruelty by a clique of very cruel men—by a dictator in designer glasses and his comrades, drunk with power and all its brutal applications. They stripped the Nicaraguan people of their rights by a state decree last October 15th, yet that decree only made official, and by their reckoning permissible, the theft of liberty that took place years ago.

No institution more deeply embodies or glorifies or seeks to perfect the moral and spiritual goodness of man than the church in all of its denominations. Yet in Nicaragua, the church is the enemy. Protestant ministers and lay people have been arrested, interrogated, and tormented at secret police headquarters; some forced to stand naked in very cold rooms for long periods. A tiny population of Jews was bullied and driven out. Cardinal Obando y Bravo, a great hero of truth and courage, is prevented from speaking freely to his flock. The state police have expelled foreign priests and drafted seminarians, who are virtual prisoners in the Sandinistas' armed forces. And the Catholic Church's newspaper has been seized and Radio Catolica censored, sometimes shut down entirely. The same dictators who insulted Pope John Paul II also stopped Radio Catolica from broadcasting a letter from the Pope and this beatitude: "Blessed are those who are persecuted for righteousness sake, for theirs is the kingdom of Heaven." The truth is, these men are nothing but thugs, a gang of hardcore Communists to whom the word of God is a declaration of liberation that must be stamped out.

Their denial of rights, their trampling of human dignity, their wrecking of an economy with suffocating socialist controls—all hurt and deeply offend us. But there's a cause for deeper concern: the specter of Nicaragua transformed into an international aggressor nation, a base for subversion and terror. Some 3,000 Cuban military personnel now lead and advise the Nicaraguan forces down to the smallest combat units. The Cubans fly the Soviet assault helicopters that gun down Nicaraguan freedom fighters. Over 7,000 Cubans, Soviets, East Germans, Bulgarians, Libyans, PLO, and other bloc and terror groups are turning Managua into a breeding ground for subversion. A delegation of Nicaraguans is now in Iran. Nicaragua's border violations against Honduras and Costa Rica continue. And Nicaragua's connection with the recent terrorist attack against Colombia's Supreme Court is now unclear.

What are we to do about such aggressions? What are we to do about Cuba's willful disregard of the 1962 Kennedy-Khrushchev understanding of which President Kennedy said, ". . . if Cuba is not used for the export of aggressive Communist purposes, there will be peace in the Caribbean."? Well, the answer is: more than we're doing now. If Nicaragua can get material support from Communist states and terrorist regimes and prop up a hated Communist dictatorship, should not the forces fighting for liberation, now numbering over 20,000, be entitled to more effective help in their struggle for freedom? Yes, and to reinforce this message, I sent my new national security adviser, John Poindexter, this week to visit the Central American democracies and make clear our commitment to a democratic outcome in Nicaragua. Those who struggle for freedom look to America. If we fail them in their hour of need, we fail ourselves as the last, best hope of liberty.

Until next week, thanks for listening. God bless you.

Note: The President spoke at 12:06 p.m. from the Oval Office at the White House.

Remarks at a Dinner for the Board of Governors of the Ronald Reagan Presidential Foundation
December 14, 1985

I have been quite surprised in the last few moments, and every bit of show business instinct in me tells me I ought to keep my mouth shut and sit down. [*Laughter*]

But Nancy and I want to thank all of you for being here tonight and tell you how grateful we are for your kind efforts on behalf of the foundation. Paul Laxalt mentioned the other day how fitting it was that so many old friends there from the beginning should be associated with a project that someday will mark the formal end to 8 years of government, though we pray not an end to the idea and principles for which we stood.

Now, like the good chairman that he is, I think Paul also said something about creating a proper mood for fundraising. Entrepreneurial leverage, I think he called it. [*Laughter*] Shame on you, Paul. [*Laughter*] You're talking bureaucratese. That's a language peculiar to Washington, and there are no interpreters of it. Let me give you an example. Some of you have heard this before, but I'm going to tell it anyway. One day early in my first term a native bureaucrat stood in front of my desk and said, "Action-oriented orchestration of meaningful indigenous decision-making dialog, focusing on multilinked problem complexes, can maximize the vital thrust toward nonalienated and viable urban infrastructure." [*Laughter*] Now, that's pure basic bureaucratese. So, I took a chance and said, "Well, why don't we try busing" and hoped he'd go away. [*Laughter*]

But I look out here tonight and I see so many old friends. I'm gravely tempted to reminisce. I could tell a few stories that I think would interest future historians, but there isn't time for that this evening, except to say the moments that we've spent together are locked away forever in our memory and our hearts. Nancy and I want you to know that we looked forward to this dinner for a special reason: We thought this a particularly good time to extend our thanks, first, because of the season—and we wanted to share the joy of it with you—and second, through this foundation you are helping to guide future generations of Americans to a deeper appreciation of our nation's past.

Now, in that film you just saw, I mentioned how living in the White House can overwhelm you with a sense of the past—so many events, so many Presidents. I know

all of you share this sentiment and this attachment to history, so I think we are here for a good cause and a noble work. But I can assure you in one century or ten, scholars and students looking through these records will find an anecdote of heart or humor or a detail of warmth and wit that will not so much tell the story of one man's Presidency as the story of an entire people, a good and generous people, proud of their heritage of freedom, determined that America shall be, as it was said on that tiny ship, the *Arabella*, off the Massachusetts coast some three centuries ago, "A light unto the nations, a shining city on a hill."

And you know, what we've done as friends and fellow citizens to keep faith with those who came before us, those who won for us the blessings of liberty, is at the heart of our purpose here this evening. Have we had some success? Well, I believe we have. But we haven't won all the battles. Just these last few days we lost a skirmish, but the battle goes on. And it's the nature of this battle, and the other battles in these last 5 years, that has changed. We're no longer the embattled few trying to stem the tide of ever-increasing government growth, fighting to halt the adoption of new programs and the increase of government interference in the people's lives. No, today the debate has switched; it's over how much government should be reduced, which programs should be eliminated, and how best to make government less intrusive in people's lives and less costly.

You know, in a play some years ago called "Benjamin Franklin in Paris," Franklin sits alone in the final act and wonders what he would find if after 200 years: "I, too, should rise up and stand once more on Pennsylvania land and walk and talk and breathe the free air. For I know in my heart it will be free. I know it—I know it even now. What a dream. Two hundred years, and I wonder—I wonder how I should find them then, those Americans to whom the name 'American' will not be new. Will they love liberty, being given it outright in the crib for nothing? And will they know that if you are not free, you are, sir, lost without hope? And will they who reap this harvest of ideas be willing to strive to preserve them as we so willingly strove to plant them—that all men are created equal and that they are endowed by their Creator with certain inalienable rights"? Well, the ham in me makes me think I would have loved to have had a speech like that in a theatrical production. But I think old Ben, were he to make such a visit, might be a little proud of what he would find. And he might even have a word or two of praise for what the American people have achieved. It is those inalienable rights that were threatened not too long ago. And tonight I believe they're safe, made so by we, the people. My every instinct is to turn to you for answers to our problems, and you have always responded. As long as I'm here, I'll turn to you.

In one of the Geneva meetings, I spoke of having read the constitutions of a number of countries, including that of the Soviet Union. And in each, the government enumerated the privileges granted to the citizenry. For the most part, they were very much the same as the privileges that we take for granted here. But I pointed out to the General Secretary that there was one difference between those other constitutions and ours, a difference that's often overlooked and yet a difference so great that it tells the entire story. Those other constitutions are grants to the people by government; our Constitution says we the people grant to government the following powers and government shall have no power or privilege that is not granted in that document by we, the people. This administration, which you have so generously helped, has one guiding thought. I have said it very often to the people surrounding me in the administration. That guiding thought is, when we start talking about government as "we" instead of "they," we've been here too long. For that, and for helping through this foundation to record a part of the American saga, Nancy and I extend to you tonight our heartfelt thanks and wish you the best of the season and a joyous New Year.

Thank you all more than I can say, and God bless you all.

Note: The President spoke at 9:01 p.m. in the Main Ballroom at the Ritz-Carlton Hotel.

Remarks at a Benefit Concert for the Children's Hospital National Medical Center
December 15, 1985

Nancy and I are delighted that so many have lent their talents tonight to help benefit the Children's Hospital National Medical Center here in Washington. On occasions like this, our thoughts reach back to that day 1,985 years ago in Bethlehem. Tom, I hope you won't feel like I'm horning in on your profession, but I'd like to read a contemporary news account of that event 2,000 years ago: "And there were in the same country shepherds abiding in the field keeping watch over their flock by night. And, lo, the angel of the Lord came upon them and the glory of the Lord showed 'round them, and they were sore afraid. And the angel said unto them, 'Fear not, for behold, I bring you good tidings of great joy, which shall be to all people. For unto you is born this day in the City of David a Savior, which is Christ the Lord.'"

So, it's appropriate that in the Christmas season we honor the little children. Like the Savior who first appeared in this world a helpless infant, our children, in their vulnerability, innocence, and trust, carry the light of the world in their hearts. With our children, we literally hold the future in our arms. Let us follow the better angels of our nature and come to see this thing which the Lord has made known to us in the spirit of every little child.

Let me read a little more of that news account: "'And this shall be a sign unto you,' the angel said to the shepherds. 'Ye shall find the babe wrapped in swaddling clothes, lying in a manger.' And suddenly there was with the angel, a multitude of the heavenly hosts, praising God and saying, 'Glory to God in the highest, and on earth, peace, good will toward men.' "

Thank you again for all that you've done for the Children's Hospital. Let us find comfort and joy in our children and with them pray for peace on Earth and good will toward men.

Thank you, and God bless you all.

Note: The President spoke at 5:55 p.m. at the National Building Museum. Tom Brokaw, NBC News correspondent, hosted the concert and introduced the President.

Proclamation 5421—Seventy-fifth Anniversary of the Boy Scouts of America, 1985
December 15, 1985

By the President of the United States of America

A Proclamation

The Boy Scouts of America, our Nation's largest organization for young people, has served our youth since 1910. Thanks to dedicated adult volunteers, more than 70 million young people have learned Scouting's lessons of patriotism, courage, and self-reliance over the past 75 years, and millions more have benefited from the service, inspiration, and leadership of the Boy Scouts.

Former Scouts have gone on to become leaders in all fields, including business, education, and government. The values they learned through Scouting have given them the confidence to make ethical choices and to realize their full potential as active and responsible citizens.

America's young people have always been treasured as our most precious resource. Since Scouting has had a strong positive influence on young people, it has played a vital role in shaping America's future. The Boy Scouts have clearly shown that it is possible to innovate while remaining faithful to their original principles. I am confident that they will continue to play an im-portant role in American society for many years to come, molding our youth with programs that build confidence and competence, and instilling in them principles that can guide them through their lives.

The Congress of the United States, by House Joint Resolution 159, has designated the year 1985 as the "75th Anniversary of the Boy Scouts of America" and has authorized and requested the President to issue a proclamation to commemorate this event.

Now, Therefore, I, Ronald Reagan, President of the United States of America, do hereby proclaim the year 1985 as the Seventy-fifth Anniversary of the Boy Scouts of America.

In Witness Whereof, I have hereunto set my hand this fifteenth day of December, in the year of our Lord nineteen hundred and eighty-five, and of the Independence of the United States of America the two hundred and tenth.

RONALD REAGAN

[Filed with the Office of the Federal Register, 4:27 p.m., December 16, 1985]

Note: The proclamation was released by the Office of the Press Secretary on December 16.

Remarks at a Memorial Service in Fort Campbell, Kentucky, for the Members of the 101st Airborne Division Who Died in the Airplane Crash in Gander, Newfoundland
December 16, 1985

We are here in the name of the American people. The passing of American soldiers killed as they returned from difficult duty abroad is marked by our presence here. At this point the dimensions of the tragedy are known to almost every person in the country. Most of the young men and women we mourn were returning to spend the holidays with their families. They were full of happiness and laughter as they pushed off from Cairo, and those who saw them at their last stop spoke of how they were singing Christmas carols. They were happy; they were returning to kith and kin.

And then the terrible crash, the flags lowered to halfstaff, and the muffled sobs, and we wonder: How this could be? How could it have happened, and why? We wonder at the stark tragedy of it all, the enormity of the lost. For lost were not only the 248 but all of the talent, the wisdom, and the idealism that they had accumulated; lost too were their experience and their enormous idealism. Who else but an idealist would choose to become a member of the Armed Forces and put himself or herself in harm's way for the rest of us? Who but the idealist would go to hard duty in one of the most troubled places of the world and go not as a matter of conquest, but as a force that existed to keep the peace?

Some people think of members of the military as only warriors, fierce in their martial expertise. But the men and women we mourn today were peacemakers. They were there to protect life and preserve a peace, to act as a force for stability and hope and trust. Their commitment was as strong as their purpose was pure. And they were proud. They had a rendezvous with destiny and a potential they never failed to meet. Their work was a perfect expression of the best of the Judeo-Christian tradition. They were the ones of whom Christ spoke when He said, "Blessed *are* the peacemak-

ers: for they shall be called the children of God."

Tragedy is nothing new to mankind, but somehow it's always a surprise, never loses its power to astonish. Those of us who did not lose a brother or a son or daughter or friend or father are shaken nonetheless. And we all mourn with you. We cannot fully share the depth of your sadness, but we pray that the special power of this season will make its way into your sad hearts and remind you of some old joys; remind you of the joy it was to know these fine young men and women, the joy it was to witness the things they said and the jokes they played, the kindnesses they did, and how they laughed. You were part of that, and you who mourn were a part of them. And just as you think today of the joy they gave you, think for a moment of the joy you gave them and be glad. For love is never wasted; love is never lost. Love lives on and sees us through sorrow. From the moment love is born, it is always with us, keeping us aloft in the time of flooding and strong in the time of trial.

You do not grieve alone. We grieve as a nation, together, as together we say goodbye to those who died in the service of their country. In life they were our heroes, in death our loved ones, our darlings. They were happy and singing, and they were right: They were going home. And so, we pray: Receive, O Lord, into your heavenly kingdom the men and women of the 101st Airborne, the men and women of the great and fabled Screaming Eagles. They must be singing now, in their joy, flying higher than mere man can fly and as flights of angels take them to their rest.

I know that there are no words that can make your pain less or make your sorrow less painful. How I wish there were. But of one thing we can be sure—as a poet said of other young soldiers in another war: They will never grow old; they will always be young. And we know one thing with every bit of our thinking: They are now in the arms of God.

God bless you.

Note: The President spoke at 10:38 a.m. at Fort Campbell Army Air Field to family members and friends of the victims. The crash occurred at 6:45 p.m. on December 12.

Statement on Signing the China-United States Nuclear Energy Agreement Implementation Bill
December 16, 1985

I am pleased to sign into law today S.J. Res. 238, in which the Congress states that it favors the agreement for peaceful nuclear cooperation between the United States and the People's Republic of China, which I transmitted to Congress on July 24, 1985. The agreement will have a significant, positive effect on the relations between the United States and the People's Republic of China and will lead to a continuing dialog with China on important nuclear energy and nonproliferation matters. It will further U.S. nonproliferation and other foreign policy interests. I therefore welcome the Congress' support for the agreement. Since I submitted the agreement without exempting it from any requirement in section 123(a) of the Atomic Energy Act, no affirmative legislation was required to permit the agreement to be brought into force after the legally stipulated time periods for congressional review had been completed. The agreement may therefore be brought into force at that time in accordance with the procedure set forth in article 10 of the agreement.

The joint resolution does require a one-time certification and a one-time report before exports to China under the agreement may commence. It assigns exclusively to the President the responsibility to review the matters to be certified to and to decide whether the certification may be made. Three matters must be certified: (1) that the arrangements for visits and exchanges of information made pursuant to article 8 of the agreement are, as called for by this article itself, designed to be effective in ensuring that nuclear exports under the agreement are used solely for intended peaceful purposes; (2) that, after examining all informa-

tion available to the United States Government, including any additional information that China has provided, nuclear exports to China are not precluded under section 129(2) of the Atomic Energy Act; and (3) that the obligation to consider favorably a request to carry out activities described in article 5(2) of the agreement does not prejudice the decision of the United States to approve or disapprove such a request. In addition, the joint resolution requires a report on Chinese nonproliferation policies and practices before exports commence.

The joint resolution also states that U.S. exports are subject to U.S. laws and regulations in effect at the time of export. This is a restatement of existing U.S. law and does not conflict with any obligations undertaken by the United States under the agreement. Finally, the joint resolution contains a section intended to ensure that the provisions in the China agreement that are textually different from provisions of the type contained in other U.S. peaceful nuclear cooperation agreements will not be the starting point for future nuclear cooperation agreement negotiations with other countries.

This joint resolution serves our interests in promoting peaceful nuclear cooperation and a nonproliferation dialog with China. For this reason, I have decided to sign the joint resolution. I appreciate the efforts of Senators Lugar and Cranston and Representatives Fascell, Broomfield, Bonker, Solarz, as well as others, in developing a joint resolution text that both the administration and the Congress could accept. I understand that an amendment relating to the U.S.-China peaceful nuclear cooperation agreement is currently under consideration in the conference on the continuing resolution. I strongly object to that amendment.

Note: S.J. Res. 238, approved December 16, was assigned Public Law No. 99–183.

Remarks at a White House Ceremony Observing National Drunk and Drugged Driving Awareness Week
December 16, 1985

Secretary Dole [of Transportation], ladies and gentlemen, good afternoon, and welcome to the Old Executive Office Building. You know, I can remember when it was the "New" Executive Office Building—*[laughter]*—the carriage entrance. [*Laughter*] But it's an honor to welcome you all here during this National Drunk and Drugged Driving Awareness Week, a week when Americans throughout the country will reflect upon an urgent and worthy cause—the battle against drunk driving.

Year in and year out, drunk driving levies its gruesome toll upon our nation. Every 12 months, it kills some 25,000 Americans— one death every 20 minutes, 70 a day, 500 a week. Every 12 months, drunk and drugged driving injures some 700,000. Every 12 months, it accounts for more than $20 billion in medical costs, insurance payments, and lost production. For young people from 16 to 24, drunk and drugged driving represents now the leading cause of death. Indeed, if a foreign power did to America what drunk drivers do in just a single day, we would consider it an act of war. And to their credit, millions of Americans have done just that, including you—gone to war against drunk driving.

Today in America we have people like Secretary Dole, who is doing all within her power to make our highways safer. We have people like Jim Aducci, the Chairman of the National Commission on Drunk Driving, and John Volpe, the Chairman of the Presidential Commission on Drunk Driving, who are devoting untold hours of their time to studying the problem with a view to recommending specific solutions. Perhaps most important, we have people like Mothers Against Drunk Driving, and thousands of others like them—everyday Americans, mothers and fathers, teachers and students,

who are, frankly, fed up with drunk driving and absolutely determined to bring it to an end. The progress has been encouraging. During our administration, fatalities from drunk driving have fallen to their lowest point in more than two decades. And between 1980 and 1984, the number of fatally injured drunk drivers dropped from 14,000 to 11,000, a decrease of 24 percent. The use of seat belts, the best defense against drunk drivers, is up.

Concern through the country, moreover, has led to the passage of important new laws. Today we have child safety seat laws in all 50 States and the District of Columbia. And a year-and-a-half ago, it was my honor to sign into law a measure encouraging a uniform drinking age of 21 across the country. And I'm pleased to be able to tell you that 37 States have adopted the law and that efforts are afoot to raise the drinking age in still more States. I'm sure you'll agree there's no measure more vital to the safety and well-being of our young people. But perhaps the most effective work against drunk driving has involved not government, but private, volunteer efforts, efforts like the seminars sponsored by Mothers Against Drunk Driving and the work of student groups to reduce drunk driving among young people. Today I'm pleased to announce a new private sector initiative that I know you'll find inspiring.

Jerry Sacks is the president of the Capital Centre sports arena here in the Washington area. Some time ago, Jerry realized that fans at sports events often need to be reminded not to drink and then drive home. So, Jerry founded TEAM, Techniques of Effective Alcohol Management. And under the TEAM plan, those who sell drinks at the Capital Centre put up banners and wear buttons that urge their customers not to drink and drive. And during the game, more reminders are flashed across the scoreboard. The whole atmosphere in the stadium is transformed into one that encourages not only enjoyment but safety. Now, TEAM is going national. In an effort supported by David Stern, the commissioner of the National Basketball Association, the International Association of Auditorium Managers, the National Automobile Dealers' Association, the GEICO Insurance Company, CBS, and the Department of Transportation—six major arenas will join the TEAM plan, which has worked so well here in the Nation's Capital. Beginning tonight, moreover, CBS will air public service announcements during their broadcasts of NBA games. These announcements will feature basketball stars, including one of my favorites, Magic Johnson, of the Los Angeles Lakers. All told, this new team effort will reach millions, and it's just getting started.

To Jerry Sacks and to all of you who've worked so hard to bring TEAM into being, my congratulations.

This holiday season, as American families gather from around the country, they'll be able to drive on roads that are safer than they used to be, and getting safer still. Everyone in this room has helped to make that possible. And now, at the beginning of National Drunk and Drugged Driving Awareness Week, I want to give you—and I think on behalf of an awful lot of people—my heartfelt thanks. And just thank you for what you're doing, and God bless you. Thank you.

Note: The President spoke at 3:36 p.m. in Room 450 of the Old Executive Office Building. He signed Proclamation 5419, which proclaimed National Drunk and Drunk Driving Awareness Week, on December 7.

Proclamation 5422—Wright Brothers Day, 1985
December 17, 1985

By the President of the United States of America

A Proclamation

From the time the first human being glimpsed the first bird, the dream of flight has captivated the human imagination. The great Leonardo da Vinci sketched elaborate designs for flying machines, and the poet Tennyson had a vision of the heavens filled with commerce and "argosies of magic sails."

But it was not until early in this century that the remarkable ingenuity and dogged determination of two young Americans finally made that dream come true. On a sandy strip of the North Carolina coast on the morning of December 17, 1903, Orville Wright, then 32, made the first piloted power-driven flight in a heavier-than-air vehicle. He did it in a 750-pound machine designed and built by him and his older brother, Wilbur. It was the culmination of four years of intensive research by the two inseparable brothers whose talents and temperament complemented each other perfectly.

That first conquest of the sky lasted only 12 seconds and took Orville only 120 feet, far less than the wingspan of today's great jets. But it changed forever the course of human history.

The lives of the Wright Brothers reveal a quintessentially American success story. Their father first sparked their interest in flight when he gave them a toy helicopter powered by rubber bands. Neither of these boys from Dayton, Ohio had ever attended college. Indeed, although they were bright students, neither ever formally graduated from high school. They made a living manufacturing bicycles, but all their spare time was devoted to the conquest of the skies. Wilbur read everything available in the local library and then wrote away to the Smithsonian Institution for more.

But what others had written was not enough. The Wright Brothers experimented for years with kites and gliders. They took detailed notes and made up tables of ratios. To master the challenge of controlling their craft, they designed and built their own wind tunnel and tested hundreds of different wing designs in small scale models.

For all its historic importance, only five people were present that fateful morning eight days before Christmas when Orville at the controls of his 12-horsepower plane took off into a 27-mile-per-hour wind and managed to stay aloft 12 seconds. Later that day with Wilbur piloting it, the craft covered 852 feet in 59 seconds.

Three years after that first flight the Wright Brothers were awarded U.S. Patent No. 821,393. They continued to pioneer developments in flight for as long as they lived. Wilbur died in 1912, while jealous rivals were still contesting their claims to priority and just before the rapid development of aviation. But Orville, who sold the Wright company in 1915, served for many years on the National Advisory Committee for Aeronautics and lived to see his and his brother's claim fully vindicated and universally recognized. Before he died in 1948 the revolution they had set in motion was moving on to new achievements. Jet planes had broken the sound barrier and Bill Odum had flown around the world in just over 73 hours.

That revolution continues, and America has stayed on its cutting edge. This year some 400 million passengers will fly some 334 million miles, and almost 66 percent of all the aircraft they will fly on are made in the U.S.A. America leads in space, reaching the moon and beyond. And today our engineers are working on aircraft that will be able to travel coast to coast in 12 minutes and reach any point on the globe in an hour and a half.

Truly, the age of flight is still young and its greatest achievements are yet to come, but we must never forget those two extraordinary young men, the Wright Brothers. Eighty-two years ago they turned an impossible dream into reality.

To commemorate the historic achievement of the Wright Brothers, the Congress, by joint resolution of December 17, 1963 (77 Stat. 402; 36 U.S.C. 169), has designated the seventeenth day of December of each year as Wright Brothers Day and requested the President to issue annually a proclamation inviting the people of the United States to observe that day with appropriate ceremonies and activities.

Now, Therefore, I, Ronald Reagan, President of the United States of America, do hereby proclaim December 17, 1985, as Wright Brothers Day, 1985, and I call upon the people of this Nation and local and national governmental officials to observe this day with appropriate ceremonies and activities, both to recall the accomplishments of the Wright Brothers and to provide a stimulus to aviation in this country and throughout the world.

In Witness Whereof, I have hereunto set my hand this seventeenth day of December, in the year of our Lord nineteen hundred and eighty-five, and of the Independence of the United States of America the two hundred and tenth.

RONALD REAGAN

[*Filed with the Office of the Federal Register, 3:01 p.m., December 17, 1985*]

Statement on House of Representatives Action on Tax Reform Legislation
December 17, 1985

I want to express my heartfelt thanks to the bipartisan majority of Members of the House of Representatives who, by their vote this afternoon, have allowed tax reform to come before the House of Representatives. As heartened as I was by the vote on the rule, I will not relax until Congress has once and for all cast the final vote that will ensure true tax reform for the American people. Tonight there will be another step in that process. I want to urge all Members of both parties to send a bill on to the Senate, so they can finish the job when they return after Christmas.

Statement on House of Representatives Approval of Tax Reform Legislation
December 17, 1985

Today the House of Representatives moved us one historic step closer toward a new tax code for America. I congratulate the Members of both parties who worked together to enable the long and arduous process of tax reform to go forward. We now look to the Senate to move quickly, and to make all necessary changes, to ensure that the final bill is unequivocally profamily, projobs, and progrowth.

Message to the House of Representatives Returning Without Approval the Textile and Apparel Industries Bill
December 17, 1985

To the House of Representatives:

I am returning herewith without my approval H.R. 1562. It is my firm conviction that the economic and human costs of such a bill run far too high—costs in foreign retaliation against U.S. exports, loss of American jobs, losses to American businesses, and damage to the world trading system upon which our prosperity depends.

At the same time, I am well aware of the difficulties of the apparel, textile, copper, and shoe industries, and deeply sympathetic about the job layoffs and plant closings that have affected many workers in these industries.

As I stated in my trade speech in September, I will not stand by and watch American businesses fail because of unfair trading practices abroad. I will not stand by and watch American workers lose their jobs because other nations do not play by the rules.

I am directing Secretary of the Treasury Baker, as Chairman Pro Tempore of the Economic Policy Council, to investigate the import levels of textiles and apparel to determine if these imports have exceeded those limits agreed upon in international negotiations. I have directed that he report back to me within 60 days and recommend changes in existing administrative and enforcement procedures, if necessary, so that corrective action is taken.

Also, I am directing the Office of the United States Trade Representative to most aggressively renegotiate the Multi-Fiber Arrangement (MFA) on terms no less favorable than present. Our trading partners must be put on notice that we will not allow unfair trading practices to continue. I am further directing Ambassador Yeutter to closely consult with the U.S. textile and apparel industry to ensure that their views will be fully represented during the negotiations.

Finally, I have directed Secretary of Labor Brock to work with the Congress to provide an additional $100 million increase in funds appropriated to help retrain and relocate displaced workers under the Job Training Partnership Act. The Job Training Partnership Act is a more effective way than Trade Adjustment Assistance for the Secretary of Labor to target those American workers and geographic areas most affected. This is the way we can best help dislocated workers—and without pitting one American worker against another.

Free and fair trade policies have helped create nearly 9 million new jobs in the last 3 years and given us the highest rate of employment in our Nation's history. Still, for some workers in troubled industries, these are difficult times. The personal distress of those who lose their jobs is very real. None of us wants to see American workers lose their jobs or American businesses suffer. I pledge to you to do everything possible to combat unfair trade practices. But in so doing we must take wise and positive steps to redress wrongs. To do otherwise would be counterproductive.

Unfortunately, H.R. 1562 would invite immediate retaliation against our exports resulting in a loss of American jobs in other areas. Because this bill is so sweeping in its provisions, we could expect that retaliation to be extensive. The United States exported tens of billions of dollars worth of goods to the countries which would be most affected by this measure, including approximately a third of our farm exports. Workers in agriculture, aerospace, high-tech electronics, chemicals, and pharmaceuticals would be the first to feel the retaliatory backlash, but the damaging effects would soon be felt by every American in the form of lost jobs, higher prices, and shrinking economic growth.

We are pursuing an aggressive trade policy, based on the knowledge that American know-how is still number one and that American industry thrives on fair competition. Where U.S. industries are hurt by unfair practices, we will continue to take vigorous actions. Where foreign trade barriers lock out U.S. exports, we will do everything in our power to knock those barriers down. Our philosophy will always be to increase trade, increase economic growth, and increase jobs. We want to open markets abroad, not close them at home. In a fair and open world market, we know that America can out-produce and out-compete anybody.

RONALD REAGAN

The White House,
December 17, 1985.

Statement on Signing the Gold Bullion Coin Act of 1985
December 17, 1985

I have given my approval today to S. 1639, the "Gold Bullion Coin Act of 1985." I have previously indicated support for legislation to permit the Secretary of the Treasury to mint and sell gold bullion coins. Indeed, when I issued Executive Order No. 12532, concerning South Africa, on September 9, 1985, I specifically requested that the Treasury conduct a study "regarding the feasibility of . . . expeditiously seeking legislative authority to accomplish the goal of issuing such coins." Legislation prepared pursuant to this directive was under review within the administration at the time S. 1639 was passed by the Congress. Although I would have preferred that the Congress defer action on S. 1639 until the administration's proposal could have been submitted and duly considered, I support the principal objectives of this legislation.

I must note, however, that certain provisions are troublesome. Specifically, enactment of this legislation may raise questions about the willingness of the United States to honor its international obligations. In this regard, my administration will strongly support the prompt enactment of appropriate legislative clarifications, should any prove to be necessary. In addition, I am also concerned about a provision of this legislation that would effectively prohibit the Secretary of the Treasury from using gold held in the United States' reserves in producing gold coins. In my view, this restriction denies the United States a potentially major source of revenue. At a time when we have committed ourselves to eliminating the budget deficit over the next several years, a limitation of this nature is especially unfortunate. Therefore, I am instructing the Department of the Treasury to work closely with the Congress to provide the Secretary of the Treasury with authority in minting gold coins to use gold from sources, including the Nation's reserves, that the Secretary deems necessary or appropriate.

Note: S. 1639, approved December 17, was assigned Public Law No. 99–185.

Remarks to Congressional Supporters of the Balanced Budget and Emergency Deficit Control Act of 1985
December 18, 1985

Good morning, and welcome to the White House. There's good news for the American people in the paper this morning. Tax reform is alive and well and kicking. [*Laughter*] What's that I heard about lameduckery? [*Laughter*]

Congratulations are due to all of those in the House who worked so long and hard to bring us to this point. And we can now look forward to a lot more hard work, but today America can feel that a true tax reform is within its grasp. We must not disappoint the American people. We must move forward from here with all deliberate speed to pass a tax reform bill that will spur economic growth, create jobs, and give America's families the long overdue tax relief that they deserve. In this last week, we have begun to put into place a solid, progrowth framework of lowered marginal tax rates and spending restraints. And together, they promise to make our economy fit and trim and competitive for the future.

Now, Phil, Warren, and Fritz, you who have given your names to Gramm-Rudman-Hollings bill, also deserve our congratulations. From now on when the public hears the names Gramm, Rudman, or Hollings, they'll think deficit reduction. And Connie Mack and Dick Cheney, who followed quite quickly in the House, you deserve our thanks. All of you here today who have given so much time and hard work to this bill have earned your country's thanks. The Government Gargantua has been gorging on taxpayer dollars for too long. We plan to get it slimmed down into shape by the end of the decade.

For years we've been warning that the growing deficit reflects a dangerous in-crease in the size of government. Polls, too, demonstrate public concern. Now Gramm-Rudman-Hollings locks in a long-term commitment to lowering and eventually eliminating deficits. It's my hope that history will record last week as the time when the relentless expansion of the Federal Government was finally halted and put into reverse. But we can't afford to be complacent. It's going to take a lot more hard work and many more difficult decisions if we're to live up to the promise of this moment. The law now puts a time limit on governmental overspending. It mandates a balanced budget. But while Gramm-Rudman-Hollings gives us some guidelines and directions, it doesn't take us to our destination. It's essential as we embark on this journey toward a balanced budget that we keep a clear sense of our priorities and hold our first purposes firmly in mind.

We must not allow Gramm-Rudman-Hollings to become an excuse to avoid the tough decisions entailed in cutting back on runaway domestic spending. We will not only be held responsible for cutting the deficit; ultimately, we will be judged on how we reduce the deficit. Will we, for instance, continue to fund welfare for the rich? Will we continue to insist that low-income taxpayers subsidize programs for people who make 10 or 11 times as much money as they do? Will we fund wasteful pork barrel programs at the expense of essential defense requirements? Will we stifle economic growth and kill off our new-found prosperity with a tax increase? Gramm-Rudman-Hollings won't make our decisions any easier, but it will make our choices crystal clear for all to see. Last year, for instance, we said the United States Government had no business running a railroad—and running it, by the way, hundreds of millions of dollars in the red. We proposed eliminating Federal subsidies to Amtrak, but intense lobbying pressure kept money flowing. Next time around, no program will get a free ride. We can abide by the letter of the Gramm-Rudman-Hollings law and still violate its spirit.

If we try to accomplish deficit reduction by tax increases or through just deep cuts in defense that endanger our national security, we will have failed in our paramount duty to the American people—the duty of good and responsible government. Raising taxes in order to reduce the deficit is robbing Peter to pay Paul, and Peter went bankrupt a long time ago. Whether excess spending is financed through taxes or borrowing, it puts a heavy burden on the private economy and slows the engines of prosperity. In fact, by slowing economic growth, a tax increase might well make the deficit bigger, not smaller. And I want you all to know that when I sat at my desk in the Oval Office and signed Gramm-Rudman-Hollings, I kept my veto pen ready in the top drawer. It's sitting there right now waiting for any tax increase that might come my way.

We should also remember that when we passed Gramm-Rudman-Hollings, we didn't absolve ourselves of our first responsibility as the elected representatives of this country to provide for the national defense. The last thing we want to do is return our country to the weakened, vulnerable state in which we found it in 1980. It was a stronger and reinvigorated national defense that allowed the United States to move swiftly and confidently, liberating Grenada from communism and bringing the terrorist murderers of Leon Klinghoffer to justice. It was this renewed sense of purpose and commitment that gave confidence to friends and allies around the globe, and particularly to those struggling for freedom against Soviet-imposed regimes.

And it was our determination to proceed with the modernization of our nuclear deterrent that, through Geneva, has improved the prospects for real arms reduction. Maintaining a strong national defense is not only our obligation to America, it's our duty as the last, best hope of mankind to the cause of human freedom. I feel confident that if Congress abides by its already established agreement for real growth in defense, we can meet our national security requirements. We will meet the Gramm-Rudman-Hollings targets in the budgets that we submit to Congress, and we'll do it the right way—by cutting or eliminating wasteful and unnecessary programs.

I hope that each of us will pledge to follow through in the spirit of Gramm-Rudman-Hollings to see that government does only that which it must do and no more. And I hope that we'll all work together to secure the deficit cutting gains that we make by adopting a balanced budget amendment to the Constitution. So, as I said, the real work of controlling Federal spending has only just begun. We've taken a dramatic step forward; let's keep the momentum going.

Thank you all for coming down here. God bless you all.

Note: The President spoke at 10:50 a.m. in the State Dining Room at the White House.

Nomination of Daniel Oliver To Be a Commissioner of the Federal Trade Commission, and Designation as Chairman
December 18, 1985

The President today announced his intention to nominate Daniel Oliver to be a Federal Trade Commissioner for the unexpired term of 7 years from September 26, 1981.

He would succeed James C. Miller III. Upon his confirmation, the President will designate him Chairman.

Since 1983 Mr. Oliver has been serving as

General Counsel at the Department of Agriculture. He is also a member of the Council of the Administrative Conference of the United States. Mr. Oliver was General Counsel at the Department of Education in 1981–1983. He practiced law in New York City with the firms of Alexander & Green (1976–1979 and 1971–1973) and Hawkins, Delafield & Wood (1967–1970). He served as executive editor of National Review in 1973–1976.

He graduated from Harvard College (A.B., 1964) and Fordham Law School (LL.B., 1967). He is married, has five children, and resides in Washington, DC. He was born March 10, 1939, in New York City.

Message on the Observance of Christmas
December 18, 1985

Nancy and I are pleased to share our warmest greetings with all Americans during the celebration of this Christmas season.

Amid all the hubbub and hustle this time of year always brings, we should not forget the simple beauty of that first Christmas long ago. Joseph and Mary, far from home and huddled in a place barely fit for habitation, felt the universal love that binds all families together and a unique awe at the special purpose for which God had chosen them. Gathering around them first the shepherds and later, the Magi—poor and rich, humble and great, native and foreign—each bowed before the King whose dominion knows no boundaries. Above them was the Star, the guiding light which would shine down through the centuries for everyone seeking the Way, the Truth, and the Life.

In the center of all lay the infant, born in the shadows and straw of a stable in Bethlehem, yet truly the fulfillment of ancient prophecies and the hope of every age to come.

Today, as we celebrate the birth of Christ in our homes and churches, among family and friends, and by our many different traditions, let us accept and share the generous gifts of joy, peace, and love given on that first Christmas. May we honor them in our hearts and keep them through the year.

Nancy and I pray that this Christmas will be a time of hope and happiness not only for our nation but for all people of the world. Merry Christmas, and God bless you.

RONALD REAGAN

Nomination of Joan M. Gubbins To Be a Member of the National Council on Educational Research
December 18, 1985

The President today announced his intention to nominate Joan M. Gubbins to be a member of the National Council on Educational Research for a term expiring September 30, 1988. This is a reappointment.

Mrs. Gubbins is executive director of the Watchman Foundation in Indiana. She was a State senator in Indiana in 1968–1980 and served on the education committee (chairman, 1978–1980); public safety committee (chairman, 1969–1974); public policy committee; public health and welfare committee; and governmental affairs committee. In 1978–1980 she was the Indiana representative to the Education Commission on the States.

She attended the University of Illinois. She is married, has two children, and resides in Noblesville, IN. She was born July 2, 1929, in White Plains, NY.

Statement by Principal Deputy Press Secretary Speakes on Nuclear Testing
December 19, 1985

The Soviet Union has both publicly and through confidential diplomatic channels continued to press its proposal for a moratorium on all nuclear explosions that it made public on July 29. For our part, the President has long advocated a dialog with the Soviet Union to arrive at the improved verification procedures necessary for any testing limitations. It was the President who extended an unconditional invitation to Soviet experts to visit the U.S. nuclear test site to measure the yield of a U.S. nuclear test, with any instrumentation devices they deemed necessary. This initiative was designed with the hope that it might set in motion a process that could increase confidence and cooperation between our nations regarding limitations on nuclear testing. The U.S. would, of course, welcome Soviet willingness to agree to reciprocal visits to nuclear testing sites.

It is through measures of this type that a basis could be created to develop and institute the type of verification measures needed to make effectively verifiable the pending treaties dealing with nuclear testing, namely, the threshold test ban and peaceful nuclear explosions treaties. This is an issue, however, quite separate from that of a moratorium on nuclear explosions.

As we have stated many times previously, the U.S. has learned through experience that moratoria cannot be counted on to lead to the enhanced security desired. The Soviet Union broke a nuclear testing moratorium a quarter of a century ago with the most intensive nuclear test series in history—some 40 explosions over a period of several weeks. We made clear when the Soviets announced their moratorium the reasons for our nuclear testing limitation policy, as well as for continuing the U.S. testing program. U.S. testing is required to ensure the continued credibility and effectiveness of our deterrent and to ensure the reliability and safety of the U.S. arsenal.

While we are actively investigating technologies that may one day make the U.S. less dependent on offensive nuclear weapons for our security, nuclear weapons will remain, for the foreseeable future, the key element of our deterrent. In such a situation, where both the U.S. and our allies must rely upon nuclear weapons to deter aggression, nuclear testing will be required. A comprehensive test ban, however, is a long-term objective of the U.S. in the context of achieving broad, deep, and verifiable arms reductions; substantially improved verification capabilities; expanded confidence-building measures; greater balance in conventional forces; and at a time when a nuclear deterrent is no longer as essential an element as currently for international security and stability. The United States is currently involved in discussions with the Soviet Union in most of these areas.

Letter to the Speaker of the House and the President of the Senate on the Designation of Aruba as a Trade Beneficiary Developing Country
December 19, 1985

Dear Mr. Speaker: (Dear Mr. President:)
 I am writing to inform you of my intent to add Aruba to the list of beneficiary developing countries under the Generalized System of Preferences (GSP) Program, effective January 1, 1986.

Aruba will become independent of the Netherlands Antilles on January 1, 1986.

The Netherlands Antilles is a GSP Beneficiary and this designation will permit Aruba to continue to receive GSP benefits after it becomes independent.

This notice is submitted in accordance with section 502(a)(1) of the Trade Act of 1974.

Sincerely,

RONALD REAGAN

Note: Identical letters were sent to Thomas P. O'Neill, Jr., Speaker of the House of Representatives, and George Bush, President of the Senate.

Appointment of Five Members of the Board of Foreign Scholarships
December 19, 1985

The President today announced his intention to appoint the following individuals to be members of the Board of Foreign Scholarships:

Peter Miller Dawkins, of New York, for the remainder of the term expiring September 22, 1986. He will succeed Milorad M. Drachkovitch. He is managing director of Lehman Brothers Kuhn Loeb, Inc., in New York City. He graduated from the United States Military Academy and Princeton University (M.A., 1969; Ph.D., 1979). He is married, has two children, and resides in New York City. He was born March 8, 1938, in Highland Park, MI.

Forrest McDonald, of Alabama, for the term expiring September 22, 1988. This is a reappointment. He is professor of history at the University of Alabama. He graduated from the University of Texas at Austin (B.A., M.A., 1949; Ph.D., 1955). He is married, has five children, and resides in Coker, AL. He was born January 7, 1927, in Orange, TX.

James Babcock Meriwether, of South Carolina, for the term expiring September 22, 1988. This is a reappointment. He is professor of English at the University of South Carolina. He graduated from the University of South Carolina (B.A., M.A.) and Princeton University (Ph.D., 1952). He is married, has five children, and resides in Columbia, SC. He was born May 8, 1928, in Columbia, SC.

Richard Anderson Ware, of Michigan, for the term expiring September 22, 1988. This is a reappointment. He is president emeritus and trustee of the Earhart Foundation in Ann Arbor, MI. He graduated from Lehigh University (B.A., 1941) and Wayne State University (M.P.A., 1943). He is married, has three children, and resides in Ann Arbor, MI. He was born November 7, 1919, in New York City.

James Robert Whelan, of Virginia, for the term expiring September 22, 1988. He will succeed Marvin G. Kelfer. He is managing director of CBN News in Washington, DC. He graduated from Florida International University (B.A., 1972). He has two children and resides in Arlington, VA. He was born July 27, 1933, in Buffalo, NY.

Appointment of Six Delegates to the National White House Conference on Small Business
December 19, 1985

The President today announced his intention to appoint the following individuals to be delegates to the National White House Conference on Small Business. These are new positions.

Murchison B. Biggs is secretary/treasurer of K.M. Biggs, Inc., in Lumberton, NC. He graduated from North Carolina State University (B.A., B.S., 1977). He was born August 1, 1954, in Lumberton, NC, where he now resides.

William E. Fletcher is president and director of

Termiflex Corp. in Merrimack, NH. He attended the California Institute of Technology and Harvard Business School. He is married, has two children, and resides in Nashua, NH. He was born April 4, 1935, in Los Angeles, CA.

William I. Gulliford, Jr., is president of Pilot Equipment Co. in Jacksonville, FL. He graduated from the University of Florida (B.S., 1966). He is married, has four children, and resides in Atlantic Beach, FL. He was born November 18, 1943, in Deland, FL.

Dean I. Harrison is president of Harrison Chevrolet-Cadillac, Inc., in Dixon, IL. He graduated from the University of Illinois (B.S., 1950). He

is married, has three children, and resides in Dixon, IL. He was born October 3, 1926, in Tama, IA.

Larry Larison is president of Columbia Paint Co. in Spokane, WA. He graduated from Carroll College (B.A., 1965). He is married, has two children, and resides in Spokane, WA. He was born October 17, 1940, in Chicago, IL.

Patsy R. Williams is a partner in Rhyne Lumber Co. in Newport, TN. She graduated from the University of Tennessee (B.S., 1955). She is married, has three children, and resides in Newport, TN. She was born April 6, 1934, in Asheville, NC.

Appointment of Three Members of the Presidential Task Force on Project Economic Justice
December 19, 1985

The President today announced his intention to appoint the following individuals to be members of the Presidential Task Force on Project Economic Justice. These are new positions.

John E. Carbaugh, Jr., is a partner in the law firm of Vance, Joyce, Carbaugh, Huang, Fields, and Crommelin in Washington, DC. He graduated from the University of the South (B.A., 1967), the University of South Carolina (M.A., 1969), Georgetown University (M.A., 1979), and the University of South Carolina (J.D., 1973). He is married, has two children, and resides in Alexandria, VA. He was born September 4, 1945, in Greenville, SC.

Howard J. Wiarda is resident scholar and director

of the Center for Hemispheric Studies at the American Enterprise Institute. He graduated from the University of Miami (B.A., 1961) and the University of Florida (M.A., 1962; Ph.D., 1965). He is married, has three children, and resides in Amherst, MA. He was born November 30, 1939, in Grosse Pointe, MI.

Keith Leonard Miceli is director, Latin American Affairs, and executive vice president of the Association of American Chambers of Commerce in Latin America, U.S. Chamber of Commerce. He graduated from Fordham University (B.A., 1965) and Tulane University (M.A., 1968). He is married, has three children, and resides in Reston, VA. He was born March 29, 1943, in New London, CT.

Appointment of Four United States Commissioners on the Pacific Salmon Commission
December 19, 1985

The President today announced his intention to appoint the following individuals to be United States Commissioners on the United States Section of the Pacific Salmon Commission.

Don W. Collingsworth, to serve for a term of 4 years. He is currently the commissioner of the Alaska Department of Fish and Game in

Juneau, AK. He graduated from California State University at Sonoma (B.A., 1970) and the University of California at Davis (M.S., 1972). He is married, has two children, and resides in Juneau, AK. He was born June 9, 1941, in Glendale, CA.

David A. Colson, to serve for a term of 4 years. He is Assistant Legal Adviser for Oceans for International Environmental and Scientific Affairs, Office of the Legal Adviser, Department of State. He graduated from California State, Hayward (B.A.) and the University of California at Berkeley (J.D.). He is married and resides in Bethesda, MD. He was born August 31, 1943, in Olympia, WA.

Sherman Timothy Wapato, to serve for a term of 2 years. He is executive director of the Columbia River Inter-Tribal Fish Commission in Portland, OR. He attended California State College. He is married, has three children, and resides in Portland, OR. He was born July 18, 1935, in Chicago, IL.

William R. Wilkerson, to serve for a term of 2 years. He is director of the Washington Department of Fisheries in Olympia, WA. He graduated from the University of Washington (B.A., 1968) and the University of Oregon (J.D., 1971). He is married, has one child, and resides in Olympia, WA. He was born March 2, 1946, in Seattle, WA.

Letter to the Chairmen of the Senate Committee on Finance and the House Committee on Ways and Means Transmitting Reports Concerning Trade Barriers on Wine
December 19, 1985

Dear Mr. Chairman:

I am submitting to you the country reports required by Title IX, Section 905(b), of the Trade and Tariff Act of 1984. These reports concern the trade barriers on wine that are maintained by Canada, Japan, Mexico, Trinidad and Tobago, Korea, and Taiwan, countries previously identified by the U.S. Trade Representative.

We have made progress in reducing or eliminating the trade barriers maintained by several of these countries. In particular, Taiwan has agreed to greatly improve market access for U.S. wines. The Japanese Government has agreed to further reduce its tariffs on wine. In all cases, we will continue to work with the concerned Governments to pursue the reduction or elimination of the trade barriers to wine. I am optimistic that more progress can and will be made.

Additionally, I would like to point out that three other countries not cited in the reports have taken action to liberalize their import restrictions on wine. Last winter, as part of our implementation of Title IX, we discussed our concerns about barriers to wine trade with the representatives of many countries. Since that time, the Philippines removed its ban on wine imports, Jamaica eliminated its wine import licensing restrictions, and Switzerland opened its quota for bulk red wine imports to all countries thereby providing access for U.S. products.

As you will note in the enclosed reports, our wine exports face a number of barriers that impede trade but that are not necessarily inconsistent with existing international trade rules. Notably, several countries maintain high tariff barriers. Under current law, I have no tariff-cutting authority to negotiate reductions in foreign tariffs, a problem that also confronts other U.S. exports. As I said in my speech of September 23 on international trade, this is an area where I look forward to working with the Congress to put into place legislation that will help us promote U.S. exports.

Sincerely,

RONALD REAGAN

Note: Identical letters were sent to Robert Dole, chairman of the Senate Committee on Finance, and Dan Rostenkowski, chairman of the House Committee on Ways and Means.

Nomination of Frances M. Norris To Be an Assistant Secretary of Education
December 20, 1985

The President today announced his intention to nominate Frances M. Norris to be Assistant Secretary for Legislation and Public Affairs, Department of Education. She would succeed Anne Graham.

Mrs. Norris is currently serving as Deputy Assistant Secretary for Legislation at the Department of Education. Previously, she was Director for Legislative Education at the Department of Education in 1983; staff assistant in the office of the Republican Whip, Trent Lott, U.S. House of Representatives (1981–1983); staff assistant to Congressman Trent Lott, U.S. House Committee on Rules, in 1979–1980; and legislative assistant to Congressman G.V. Montgomery in 1974–1978.

She graduated from the University of Mississippi (B.S., 1968) and the University of Kentucky (M.S.L.S., 1970). She is married and resides in McLean, VA. She was born March 27, 1946, in Jackson, MS.

Proclamation 5423—Amending the Generalized System of Preferences
December 20, 1985

By the President of the United States of America

A Proclamation

1. Pursuant to section 502(b) of the Trade Act of 1974 (the Trade Act) (19 U.S.C. 2462(b)), as amended, and section 604 of the Trade Act (19 U.S.C. 2483), I have determined that it is appropriate to provide for the termination of preferential treatment under the Generalized System of Preferences (GSP) for articles which are currently eligible for such treatment and which are imported from Portugal. Such termination is the result of the accession of Portugal to the European Economic Community.

2. Section 502(b) of the Trade Act specifies that member states of the European Economic Community are ineligible for such preferential treatment under the GSP.

Now, Therefore, I, Ronald Reagan, President of the United States of America, acting under the authority vested in me by the Constitution and the statutes of the United States of America, including but not limited to sections 502(b) and 604 of the Trade Act, do proclaim that:

(1) General headnote 3(e)(v)(A) to the Tariff Schedules of the United States (TSUS), listing those countries whose products are eligible for benefits of the GSP, is amended by striking out "Portugal."

(2) No article the product of Portugal and imported into the United States after the effective date of this proclamation shall be eligible for preferential treatment under the GSP.

(3) The modifications to the TSUS made by this proclamation shall be effective with respect to articles both: (1) imported on or after January 1, 1976, and (2) entered, or withdrawn from warehouse for consumption, on or after January 1, 1986.

In Witness Whereof, I have hereunto set my hand this 20th day of December, in the year of our Lord nineteen hundred and eighty-five, and of the Independence of the United States of America the two hundred and tenth.

RONALD REAGAN

[*Filed with the Office of the Federal Register, 11:08 a.m., December 23, 1985*]

Statement on Signing the Arts, Humanities, and Museums Amendments of 1985
December 20, 1985

I have today approved S. 1264, the "Arts, Humanities, and Museums Amendments of 1985." The main purpose of this legislation is to extend for 5 years the authorizations for the National Endowment for the Arts and the Humanities, which was proposed by the administration in legislation submitted to the Congress last April. S. 1264 also extends the authorizations for the Institute of Museum Services and contains another amendment to the Museum Services Act about which I wish to comment. Section 201 of the bill contains a clause stating that the National Museum Services Board "may not include, at any time, more than three members from a single State." I have been advised by the Attorney General that this provision applies only to future appointments and that it does not require me, and could not constitutionally require me, to remove any of the present members of the Board in order to comply immediately with that clause. I shall be guided by that advice.

Note: S. 1264, approved December 20, was assigned Public Law No. 99–194.

Radio Address to the Nation on the Major Legislative Achievements of 1985
December 21, 1985

My fellow Americans:

This week the Congress adjourned for the holidays, and today I'd like you to join me in considering the main legislative achievements of 1985. There were many, including the passage of a vital farm bill, but I'd like to draw your attention to three of truly historic importance.

None is of greater significance than the passage 4 days ago in the House of a tax reform bill, a bill which calls for the most sweeping overhaul of the income tax system in more than 40 years. The House bill is broadly based upon the proposal first put forward by our administration. It includes sharp cuts in both personal and corporate income tax rates, a large increase in the standard deduction, and an enlargement of the personal exemption. To help the needy, the bill would remove some 6 million low-income workers from the income tax rolls altogether. It's clear that in working on this bill, the House took to heart what I said in my speeches and you said in your thousands of letters and telegrams: It's time to promote economic growth and give the family a break. Historic as it is, the House bill, unfortunately, contains serious flaws; these the Senate must deal with when the Congress returns to Washington early in 1986. I know you join me in looking to the Senate to perform its work quickly and to make absolutely certain that the final bill is unequivocally profamily, projobs, and profuture.

The passage of the Gramm-Rudman-Hollings amendment, a measure to bring Federal spending under control once and for all, represented a second historic achievement. This legislation mandates steady decreases in the Federal budget deficit every year for 5 years, with the result that in 1991 the Federal Government will have a balanced budget at last. All my political life I've urged the Government to stop spending more than it takes in. So, it was with great pleasure that I signed this measure into law just 9 days ago. It's my hope that history will record that day as the moment when the relentless expansion of the Government was finally brought to a halt. But although Gramm-Rudman-Hollings tells us that we must cut the deficit, it does not altogether tell us how to do so. And that means we still have our work cut out for us.

Will we fund wasteful, pork barrel programs at the expense of our national defense? Will we kill off our prosperity with a tax increase? No matter how intense the political pressures become, the answer to both of these questions must and will remain an unmistakable no. Defense spending must depend not upon this or that guideline, but one consideration alone: the size of the threat with which our adversaries confront us. To sacrifice our defenses in order to balance the budget would be to abdicate the paramount duty of the Government to the people.

As for a tax hike, the lesson is clear: When government raises taxes, incentives for achievement are undermined and economic growth is stifled. My friends, we simply cannot allow that to happen again. I want you to know that my veto pen is inked up and ready to go. I'm just waiting for the first tax hike that has the temerity to come across my desk. We intend to meet the Gramm-Rudman-Hollings requirements in the only proper way—by seeing to it that government fulfills its few and legitimate functions more efficiently at the same time that we eliminate government waste.

The final legislative achievement I want to mention concerns foreign affairs. It involves the emergence in the Congress of a new mood, a new point of view. During this past year, the Congress repudiated isola-tionism and weakness and reasserted America's legitimate world role on behalf of human freedom. Indeed, in July, Congress voted aid to freedom fighters in Cambodia, Afghanistan, and Nicaragua and repealed a ban on aid to the freedom fighters in Angola. This effort marked the appearance of a sober-minded realism, a new willingness to see clearly and to confront the dread effects of Communist expansion upon innocent peoples like those of Afghanistan and Nicaragua. And it's especially significant that aid to freedom fighters was also approved by the Democrat-controlled House. I'm convinced that a new, bipartisan foreign policy consensus is emerging, one based upon realism and which unites Democrats and Republicans alike in support of a strong national defense and help for freedom fighters around the globe.

As so many of us prepare to celebrate Christmas, we can take comfort in the knowledge that, although we must continue our efforts to improve it, the legislative process established by the Founding Fathers is still working. Yes, as 1985 draws to a close, we Americans can take stock of our nation with pride: inflation is down, jobs are up, our country is at peace, and the American spirit is proud and bright.

From the Reagan family to your family, Merry Christmas. And until next week, thanks for listening, and God bless you.

Note: The President spoke at 12:06 p.m. from Camp David, MD.

Remarks at the Signing Ceremony for the Food Security Act of 1985 and the Farm Credit Amendments Act of 1985
December 23, 1985

Thank you all very much. Members of the Congress, ladies and gentlemen: First, I want to thank Secretary [of Agriculture] Block and all the Members, those with us today and those who worked so hard on this but couldn't be here. Thank you all for the Herculean effort you've put forth on behalf of America's farmers.

The plight of so many of our farmers has been a major concern of this administration and of responsible Members of Congress on both sides of the aisle. The level of concern, however, was much higher than the level of agreement on how best to deal with the problem. It's taken extraordinary hard work and cooperation, not to mention the tenacity of a mule, to maneuver these bills through Congress. The two pieces of legislation being signed into law today represent divergent approaches, but on balance, they're a step forward for American agriculture. They underscore the commitment of the legislative and executive branches to make things better for America's farmers, yet we must recognize, even while signing these bills, that there are no quick fixes.

The Food Security Act of 1985 is a comprehensive bill that improves our existing farm programs. It gives the Secretary of Agriculture the flexibility needed to maintain farm price supports at levels consistent with market realities. Unrealistic price supports put many farmers out of the running. This legislation will help put America's farmers back into a competitive position in world markets. America's farmers are the most productive in the world. This bill will help unleash their enormous productive capacity and will help America reclaim lost markets.

Under this bill, farmers will be eased into a market-oriented policy with generous income supports to ensure the viability of the transition. I believe more progress could have been made in keeping down costs, but I recognize that many Members of Congress have made a good-faith effort in this regard. With the signing of this legislation, we are moving away from the failed policies of the past. Our farmers must share in the growth and prosperity that is spreading throughout America. Our reforms will provide new hope for America's hard-working farmers and our rural communities.

This bill includes laudatory conservation measures, provisions for the training of food stamp recipients, and other positive features. On the negative side, it maintains costly and counterproductive government intervention in the dairy industry; encourages surplus production; and mandates export subsidies, which could well backfire on us. It will hurt sugar-producing nations that are our friends and allies. And, ironically, it could actually provide taxpayer subsidies to our adversaries. I intend to work with Congress to rectify these problems, especially in the area of trade.

The second bill being signed today is the Farm Credit Amendments Act of 1985. This law enables the farm credit system to pool its considerable resources in a self-help effort. It establishes a stronger and more complete regulatory oversight system, and it authorizes a backstop system of Federal assistance, although we believe that it will never be necessary. This reform will ensure a steady supply of credit to America's farmers and assure the investors of the safety and soundness of the system. What we do today recognizes that the health of American agriculture is essential to the well-being of the American economy. If things are not going well down on the farm, things cannot continue to go well in our cities and towns.

Members of both parties have managed to work together in passing these bills for the sake of our overall economy and for the sake of those Americans who produce our food and fiber. Cicero said so many centuries ago: "Of all occupations from which gain is secured, there is none better than agriculture. Nothing more productive, nothing sweeter, nothing more worthy of a free man." Well, today I sign these bills with that ancient wisdom in mind.

And now I'll get to the signing.

Note: The President spoke at 11:03 a.m. in the State Dining Room at the White House. H.R. 2100, the Food Security Act of 1985, was assigned Public Law No. 99–198; S. 1884, the Farm Credit Amendments Act of 1985, was assigned Public Law No. 99–205.

Remarks and a Question-and-Answer Session With Broadcasters and Editors on the Food Security Act of 1985 and the Farm Credit Amendments Act of 1985
December 23, 1985

The President. Well, thank you, Secretary [of Agriculture] Block. And as you've been told, I've just come from the White House, where I signed the farm bill, which is formally called the Food Security Act of 1985. I also signed a farm credit act, which promises to have considerable impact on various farming areas throughout the country.

Before I tell you about these bills, I want to mention one thing that's personal. I don't mind saying that, because of your letters and what I've been told and seen myself, few things have made a greater impression on me the past few years than the problems of the farmer. My guiding thought throughout our efforts to put together a truly helpful farm bill has been: We're nothing without the farmers. They're the backbone of this country. And everything we do to help them helps our country and its future. So, with all that in mind, I signed the bills this morning, and now I want to tell you about them.

The 1985 farm bill is, in my opinion and the opinion of a bipartisan majority in the Congress, a clear and obvious improvement over existing farm programs. Perhaps the most helpful thing it does is establish predictable long-term policies so that our farmers will be able to make realistic plans for investment and production. The farm bill gives the Secretary of Agriculture the flexibility he needs to maintain farm price supports at levels that reflect the realities of the market. This will help put our farmers back in a more competitive position in world markets. With this bill, we hope to ease American agriculture away from the heavy hand of government and toward a more market-oriented system. We're trying to free farmers from the influence and directives of government and encourage them to produce for the public market basket and not for government storage bins. The bill also contains income supports that will ease the problems that occur during the transition to a market economy.

The farm bill is comprehensive. It includes some very good conservation measures and provisions to train food stamp recipients. But there are problems with the bill, too. It continues the truly unhelpful Federal involvement in the dairy industry. It also expands government intervention in the area of export subsidies. In fact, the bill mandates subsidized export sales, meaning citizens of other countries could pay less for

American grain than American consumers. Now, these provisions are totally counterproductive, and we'll be working with the Congress to make appropriate changes next year.

The second bill I signed today is the Farm Credit Act Amendments of 1985. This will enable the farm credit system to pool its resources and reorganize with an eye to improving their ability to supply reasonable credit. It will make for a stronger farm credit system with a stronger oversight setup. It also provides a backstop system of Federal assistance should that ever become necessary. The whole point of all this retooling is to help rural Americans who rely on a steady stream of reasonable credit.

I want to note here that the farm bill of 1985 is not exactly what we wanted, but in government you can't let the perfect be the enemy of the good. You can't let your desire for a superior product lead you to kill a bill that's really pretty good. We worked closely with Congress on both these bills. And, as I said, a majority of Republicans and Democrats in both Houses came together to declare these bills the very best they could do. And we've accepted their honest efforts.

I believe that the 1985 farm bill will bring about a long-awaited rebirth and renewed opportunities for American agriculture. It is clear that Congress has heeded the message that our farm policies need fundamental reforms. This bill begins that reform. I believe that these two bills will help lead to a healthy, sustained recovery for those who are engaged in the proud and peerless way of life called American farming. This is the season for new beginnings. And I truly believe today marks a new beginning, a new season of hope for all of American agriculture.

Thanks for listening. And now with the help of the people of the USDA here, we are able to have a sort of satellite news conference. And I guess, Jim Johnson, I'd better throw it back to you.

Mr. Johnson. Thank you, Mr. President. We do have some farm broadcasters and farm editors and writers out on a telephone hookup with us, and so, let's go to those questioners. Our first stop will be in Chicago—Orian Samuelson with WGN. Orian.

Q. Thank you very much, Jim. And, Mr. President, thank you for this opportunity. My question deals with cost, Mr. President, because your administration has been concerned about cutting the budget and budget deficits. How do you reconcile that concern with spending $52 billion—$2 billion over your limit—on a government farm price support program?

The President. Well, because this is what is necessary if we're to do the job. And I would have to tell you that we have—in this administration, in these last few years—while we have been trying to reduce government spending elsewhere, we have spent more with regard to the farm problems than has ever been spent by any American Government heretofore. This particular bill, the $52 billion, is over a 3-year period. And it's true, we had set the figure at—as we said—$50 billion. But we believe that we can live with an increase of this particular amount. But, also, it is necessary if we are to solve the farm problem in the right way. And that is, as I said in my remarks, to get farming more market-oriented and less of a heavy hand of government. But since it's government that's been responsible for many of the farmers' problems, it's also only fair that government now not just abandon but make an effort to help the farmers through this transition.

Mr. Johnson. The next questioner—we'll be going to Philadelphia and Lane Palmer with the Farm Journal. Lane, your question, please.

Q. Thank you. Mr. President, during the congressional debate on the farm credit bill, there were many questions about whether they were talking about enough money or whether they could move it quickly enough to where it's needed. What confidence do we have that the farm credit act really will solve the financial problems being faced by farmers?

The President. Well, we believe that these bills do contain what is necessary to help them. For example, the farm credit bill. The program that we're helping supplies a third of the total credit to farmers in the United States. And we have made that program more practical now and brought it

together where the resources can be directed to the points of greatest need. And I think that, based on our previous experience with things that didn't work too well, I think that we now have a farm program that has eliminated many of the faults of the past and that will bring farming, as we say, back out into the market economy. But recognize also that, with regard to our fights against deficit spending and all, that nothing could be more helpful to that than to take a great industry like agriculture and make it more independent and more capable of realistic earnings and growth.

Mr. Johnson. Our next questioner will be from Indiana—New Palestine, to be exact. The Rural Radio Net—Dan Modland. Dan.

Q. Mr. President, earlier this year, Secretary Block came to Indiana to unveil plans for the conservation reserve. Now that this program is part of the farm bill, what will it mean to American agriculture?

The President. Well, I know that farmers themselves have been very concerned over, for one thing, the erosion of topsoil, which could wipe out great sections of agriculture, if allowed to continue at an excessive rate. And what this program does is make it possible for farmers to take marginal land out of production so that you don't have that erosion. I remember some time ago when a farmer friend of mine in Illinois sent me some snapshots about erosion. They were in the winter, and he was talking about the practice of plowing and leaving the ground exposed, all plowed up, and then the winds would come in the fall and the winter and so forth. And it would be wind erosion was taking this away. And I handed those snapshots over to Secretary Block and said, "What are we going to do about this?" The snapshots were taken after snowfall, and they were taken in two areas: in an area where there was not plowing of the land, to lie there all through the winter, and where it had been done. And what the snapshots revealed was that—in one set of photographs the snow was dark gray; in the others the snow was white, and it was a pretty good example of what wind erosion was doing in those particular areas. So, I think that the farmers, themselves, are going to be the first to benefit from this setting aside of marginal land and knowing that we are saving some of their precious topsoil and hanging on for any future need.

Mr. Johnson. The next questioner we have will be from Illinois—Bill Kilby, Courier Journal, from Jacksonville, Illinois. Bill, your question, please.

Q. Mr. President, the big question bouncing around my area at the present time is: Will this farm legislation benefit the small family farmer, or will it simply further subsidize the large-scale farming operations?

The President. We believe it will help the family farmer. I can turn to Jack to see if he's nodding yes here on that. It will, and it's aimed at doing precisely that. Bill, I hope you'll forgive me of a little nostalgia and a little reminiscence here—when I saw Jacksonville, Illinois, as your home there, and the Courier Journal—my last college football game was played against Illinois College in Jacksonville on a very cold winter day with a frozen field. It isn't a happy memory, particularly because we lost. [*Laughter*]

Mr. Johnson. The next question we have will be from Wichita, Kansas—Larry Steckline with the Mid-America Ag-Net and KSN–TV. So, Larry, your question, please.

Q. Thank you, Jim, and thank you, Mr. President, for this opportunity. Mr. President, is the farm credit act that you signed this morning just an institutional bailout for the farm credit banks or will this bill really help farmers?

The President. Well, this bill will help farmers in the sense that here is a combined source for about one-third of all of the farm credit in America. And it has been managed in such a way that it was scattered and there would be some parts of it with plenty of funds but in an area where there was no demand for them; while in other areas, the way it was locally managed, there wasn't enough for the problems at hand. This has now been brought together under a single administration. And it is now set up so that the money can be directed from all of the resources to wherever it might be needed most. And we think that this, as I

say, since it provides a third of the credit that farming needs, it is going to now be able to be much more practical and much more effective.

Mr. Johnson. I'd like to point out that the fact is that we've gone through five questioners and time is about out. President Reagan does need to leave very soon. Before we do break away, though, I would turn to Secretary Block and see if you have any comments to make at this time with President Reagan right here.

Secretary Block. Well, my only comments would be that we're just delighted that the President would come over here. And Mr. President, as you talked about those snapshots of that soil erosion—I remember well that Cabinet meeting when they came across the table to me. And I do believe that we have done something about soil erosion in this legislation that I'm proud of and I know you are, too. Not only the conservation reserve, which will take this erosive land out of production and set it aside for future generations, but also in this conservation package there's included a provision that effectively says that we believe in conservation so much in this country that if we provide farm program benefits to farmers in future years out there, those farmers are going to be obligated to protect the land. They're not going to be allowed to abuse the land as long as the Government is providing that kind of helping hand. I don't think that's too much to expect, and I think it's also part of this process of trying to save this land for future generations.

It's a pleasure to have you with us, Mr. President.

The President. Well, pleased to be here. And I'm glad to have you help me out on that answer. [*Laughter*]

Secretary Block. You did it just right.

Note: The President spoke at 11:30 a.m. at the Department of Agriculture via the Department's AGNET Farm Network. Jim Johnson was Chief of Radio and Television at the Agriculture Department.

1501

Statement on Signing the Food Security Act of 1985
December 23, 1985

I have today signed H.R. 2100, the Food Security Act of 1985, into law. This legislation reauthorizes virtually all of our farm programs, from the major commodity price support programs to research, credit, food stamp, and export promotion. It represents the culmination of a year-long effort to establish a sound policy to guide U.S. agriculture for the rest of this decade.

Farmers and ranchers, hard-working men and women who till the fields and tend the herds, have always been an important part of our heritage and of our economy. Today, however, our farmers and ranchers and the thousands of small towns and communities in which they live are currently suffering through difficult times. These difficulties have been caused in part by the very same government programs that were designed to help American agriculture. Earlier this year, my administration proposed a market-oriented farm bill designed to correct past farm policies that have often worked at cross purposes. We have encouraged farmers to produce more commodities by artificially propping up prices while, at the same time, forcing farmers to set aside more and more land to reduce production so prices would not drop. As a result of years of such counterproductive farm policies, the American farmer has become less competitive in the international marketplace, the cost of our farm programs has risen to unsustainable levels, and farm income has stagnated. Clearly, our past policies have failed.

The legislation that I have today signed contains some of the needed reforms sought by my administration:

• Crop price support levels that are a major factor in establishing minimum market prices are lowered, thus helping make U.S. commodities more competitive in the international marketplace.

• Planting decisions are partially uncoupled from government program income benefits by making those benefits available if only 50 percent of a farmer's acreage is planted into a price-supported commodity. Planting decisions on the remaining 50 per-

cent of the land will be based on market signals, not government benefits.

• Farmers are discouraged from increasing their planted acreage for the purpose of receiving greater Federal income payments.

American agriculture is the most efficient in the world. This legislation will help our farmers use that efficiency to regain export markets without sacrificing the income they need to operate effectively in our domestic economy.

Unfortunately, however, the bill did not make all of the reforms we requested. By failing to totally uncouple farm income support from planting decisions, and by keeping support prices artificially high, we will encourage more and more farmers to become dependent upon our farm programs. In addition, the legislation includes several highly objectionable features that must be changed. These include:

• A mandatory 3-year payment-in-kind export promotion program which will give away $2 billion worth of commodities to encourage U.S. exports. A program of this size and nature threatens to precipitate an agricultural commodity trade war with our allies. Moreover, it may well be impossible to fulfill the $2 billion goal over the next 3 years without subsidizing exports in a manner which will be contrary to the national security interests of the United States.

• A mandatory reduction in the size of the sugar quota that threatens to severely disrupt the economies of the Caribbean Basin countries and the Philippines. This provision is inconsistent with the foreign policy objectives of our country and may also be violative of our obligations under international trade agreements. I find it difficult to ask other countries to bear the cost of our sugar program while encouraging them to maintain a stable course toward development with democracy.

• The inclusion of a dairy assessment tax, which will tax all milk producers to fund a program that will force the Government to pay farmers to liquidate their dairy herds.

The Government is also required to buy meat above our needs in order to keep prices up while dairy herds are being liquidated.

These programs represent the worst in the way of policy. My administration will seek modifications of these programs next year. Although I have serious reservations about these and other provisions of the conference agreement, I have signed this bill into law because it represents a step in the right direction toward a sound agricultural policy. It promises to make American farm products more competitive in the international marketplace, and it begins to break the link between high government price supports and production decisions. Most importantly, the bill will ensure adequate supplies of reasonably priced food for American consumers and the beginning of renewed hope for America's farmers and our rural communities. They have suffered far too long because of the mistakes of the past. Because I believe this bill represents a promise of a better future, I have signed it into law.

Note: H.R. 2100, approved December 23, was assigned Public Law No. 99–198.

Proclamation 5424—Made in America Month, 1985
December 23, 1985

By the President of the United States of America

A Proclamation

America's current trade problems have caused some to wonder whether this country may not be in danger of losing its reputation as a supplier of high quality products at competitive prices. As America's strong economic growth has led to increased demand for goods and services, imports have become more attractive because of the relative strength of the dollar. U.S. exports have become less attractive to foreign buyers for the same reason. Recently, however, increased growth in the economies of our trading partners and movement of the dollar toward a more sustainable equilibrium give us reason to expect that our trade deficit should ease in the near future. Tough foreign competition, in the last few years, has presented our manufacturers and our work force with a stiff challenge.

But America's producers are responding to that challenge, and it is time for consumers both here and abroad to take a fresh look at what America has to offer. Those who do will find the traditional variety, high quality, and dependability that "Made in the U.S.A." has come to symbolize. They also will find this quality at more competitive prices.

Made in America Month also provides an opportunity for American firms and workers to resolve to take greater advantage of new competitive opportunities both here at home and in overseas markets. We Americans do not shrink from competition; we believe in competition—*fair* competition. Historically, competition constantly creates pressure for innovation, product improvement, and customer satisfaction. The open marketplace makes the consumer the king, and we are all consumers.

In an increasingly competitive world, we Americans must redouble our efforts to make products of the highest quality in the most efficient way and market them aggressively. As we do I have no doubt that more and more Americans and foreigners will be drawn to the products with the proud label: "Made in America."

The Congress of the United States, by Senate Joint Resolution 206, has authorized and requested the President to proclaim December 1985 as "Made in America Month" and authorized and requested the President to issue a proclamation in observance of this event.

Now, Therefore, I, Ronald Reagan, President of the United States of America, do hereby proclaim December 1985 as Made in America Month. I invite the people of the United States to observe this month with appropriate programs and activities to recognize and celebrate the excellence of American products.

In Witness Whereof, I have hereunto set my hand this twenty-third day of December, in the year of our Lord nineteen hundred and eighty-five, and of the Independ-

ence of the United States of America the two hundred and tenth.

RONALD REAGAN

[Filed with the Office of the Federal Register, 10:40 a.m., December 24, 1985]

Letter to the Speaker of the House and the President of the Senate Transmitting a Report on Soviet Noncompliance With Arms Control Agreements
December 23, 1985

Dear Mr. Speaker: (Dear Mr. President:)

In response to Congressional requests as set forth in Public Law 99–145, I am forwarding herewith classified and unclassified versions of the Administration's report to the Congress on Soviet Noncompliance with Arms Control Agreements.

Detailed classified briefings will be available to the Congress early in the new year.

I believe the additional information provided, and issues addressed, especially in the detailed classified report, will significantly increase understanding of Soviet violations and probable violations. Such understanding, and strong Congressional consen-

sus on the importance of compliance to achieving effective arms control, will do much to strengthen our efforts both in seeking corrective actions and in negotiations with the Soviet Union.

Sincerely,

/S/RONALD REAGAN

Note: Identical letters were sent to Thomas P. O'Neill, Jr., Speaker of the House of Representatives, and George Bush, President of the Senate. The original was not available for verification of the content. The text of the President's unclassified report was included in the White House press release.

Memorandum on the Fiscal Year 1987 Budget
December 26, 1985

Memorandum for the Heads of Departments and Agencies

I want to take this opportunity to thank each of you for your efforts during the past several weeks in working with OMB Director Jim Miller and his associates to develop my FY 1987 budget. Preparing the budget is never an easy task, for it requires the balancing of competing priorities and the sacrificing of some goals in order that our overall agenda can go forward. This year's budget was no exception, especially in view of my decision to meet lower deficit targets

without increasing taxes or cutting into defense preparedness.

The true test comes in the spring, however, when we will either succeed or fail in persuading the American people, and their elected representatives, to accept the comprehensive program I will be submitting on February 3. As we move forward in that effort, I know I can count on you to be an able and forceful advocate. Only by working together can we achieve those goals that brought us here in the first place.

RONALD REAGAN

Statement on the Sixth Anniversary of the Soviet Invasion of Afghanistan
December 27, 1985

Today, December 27, marks the sixth anniversary of the Soviet invasion of Afghanistan. Since December 27, 1979, when a massive Soviet force crossed the Afghan frontier to support a faltering Marxist regime, the Afghan resistance has grown increasingly effective. The Soviet-supported regime in Kabul has failed to gain even a modicum of popular support or international acceptance. The Soviets and their Afghan surrogates have resorted to barbaric methods of waging war in their effort to crush this war of national liberation. Indiscriminate air and artillery bombardments against civilian areas, savage reprisals against noncombatants suspected of supporting the resistance, and the calculated destruction of crops and irrigation systems have ravaged the Afghan countryside. Thousands of young Afghans are being shipped to the Soviet Union for reeducation in summer camps, universities, and specialized institutions.

The Afghan people, however, are unswerving in their determination to resist the invader. The resistance fighters are more numerous, better armed, and more effective than ever before. Unable to trust Kabul's forces to counter the enhanced resistance, the Soviets have begun using their own troops in a more active combat role. But the effort has availed them little. Last summer, when fighting was at its peak, resistance forces repeatedly attacked Soviet lines of communication, convoys, barracks and facilities, and mounted their largest, longest, and best coordinated offensive operation of the war. The resistance has also drawn together into a political alliance, which can present Afghanistan's cause to the world in unambiguous terms and coordinate all aspects of the liberation struggle.

Since 1980 the United States has strongly advocated a negotiated political settlement, the only reasonable alternative to the bleak prospect of an open-ended military struggle. Seven United Nations resolutions passed by growing and overwhelming margins since that year show that the United States is not alone in this view. These resolutions call for the withdrawal of foreign troops, the restoration of Afghanistan's independent and nonaligned status, self-determination, and the voluntary and safe return of the refugees. The United States reiterated its support for the U.N.-sponsored talks during the November summit meetings in Geneva. We also indicated that the continued Soviet occupation of Afghanistan remains an obstacle to overall improvement in our relationship. Although we welcome any suggestion that the Soviets are prepared to back U.N.-led peace efforts, we will await positive developments on the ground and concrete evidence of Soviet willingness to agree to a timetable for withdrawal of their troops.

The victims of this war also command American attention. The United States has played, and will continue to play, a major role in the humanitarian efforts to alleviate the suffering of the 2 to 3 million Afghan refugees now living in Pakistan. Since 1980 we have spent over $430 million in aid. In the face of deteriorating conditions inside Afghanistan caused largely by the increasingly widespread Soviet reprisals against civilians suspected of opposing the regime, we have allocated, in the current 2-year timeframe, almost $25 million in assistance to the brave people who remain inside Afghanistan.

When the Soviet Union invaded Afghanistan 6 long and bloody years ago, few in the West knew much about that distant land and its proud people. That certainly has changed, as the Afghan people, in their determination to defend their liberty, have added new chapters to the long annal of human courage in the face of tyranny. Forged in a similar crucible two centuries ago, the United States stands squarely on the side of the people of Afghanistan and will continue its support of their historic struggle in the cause of liberty.

Radio Address to the Nation on the Soviet Occupation of Afghanistan
December 28, 1985

My fellow Americans:

Today I'd like to talk to you about a matter of vital importance to our country and the world: the struggle for a free Afghanistan. It's been 6 years since the Soviet Union invaded that nation, 6 years of utter hell for the Afghan people who still fight on in the name of the ideals upon which our own nation was founded: freedom and independence. To demoralize and defeat the Afghans, the Soviets have unleashed the full force of their modern weaponry. Poison gas has been razed down from the air upon Afghan settlements. Massive attack helicopters have been used against mere villages. Hundreds of thousands of innocent civilians have been injured or killed, and countless tiny mines have been strewn across the countryside to maim and blind Afghan children.

Today Soviet troops inside Afghanistan number nearly 120,000. And in the face of this brutal onslaught, the Afghan people still refuse to surrender—is surely a miracle. And in this holiday season of renewed faith in miracles, it is surely fitting for us to honor and pray for those brave men and women. These courageous people have shown the world that the Soviets can never achieve the outright subjugation of the Afghan mind and spirit that they seek. The Afghan people are too proud, too fiercely determined to fight on. The Soviets understand this. They know that, in a sense, the battle for Afghanistan has shifted from the mountains of Afghanistan itself to the wider field of world opinion. So it is that the Soviets are prolonging the war and blacking out news about the daily atrocities which they're committing. They're waiting for world attention to slip, for our outrage to wane. Then, they believe the support which the free world has been providing to the freedom fighters will dwindle. The Soviets at that point will have effectively cut off the freedom fighters' lifelines, and although the mujahidin may never surrender, the Soviets will have achieved indisputable con- trol of the country. An entire nation will have been strangled.

My friends, in the name of human free- dom, we cannot, we must not, allow that to happen. From the first, the United States has insisted on a settlement of the Afghan conflict that ensures the complete with- drawal of all Soviet troops. We're doing all that we can to see that a settlement comes about. Indeed, in my discussions with Mr. Gorbachev in Geneva, I made it clear that the presence of Soviet forces in Afghanistan represent an obstacle to the improvement of American-Soviet relations. As long as the Soviets insist upon a policy of aggression, they must face the fact that free men will oppose them. The Soviet Union has always presented itself as a champion of anticolon- ialism and national liberation; history pre- sents a different picture.

But if, at any time, the Soviets choose to withdraw from Afghanistan, we will place no barriers in their way. The sixth round of United Nations negotiations aimed at achieving a political settlement in Afghani- stan has just come to an end with no signifi- cant change. If the Soviets want progress, they must simply put forward a timetable for the withdrawal of their forces from Af- ghanistan and for the restoration of the rights of the Afghan people. As I said, the United States will do everything in its power to make this the course which the Soviets choose. Indeed, we're prepared to serve as a guarantor of a comprehensive Afghan settlement so long as it includes the complete withdrawal of foreign forces within a fixed timetable; ensures genuine independence, not de facto Soviet control over the Afghan people and their govern- ment; and allows the millions of Afghan ref- ugees to return to their homeland in safety. Only then can the process of national rec- onciliation and rebuilding Afghanistan begin and the killing of Russians and Af- ghans alike come to an end.

My friends, I want to ask for your help to make sure that those who struggle in Afghanistan receive effective support from us. Indeed, such support is a compelling, moral responsibility of all free people. What takes place in that far-off land is of vital importance to our country and the world. Certainly the struggle in Afghanistan is of great strategic military importance. Yet the most important battle involves not guns, but the human spirit—the longing to be free and the duty to help the oppressed. If the free world were to turn its back on Afghanistan, then, in a sense, the free world would become less free and less humane. But

when we support the Afghan people, we become caught up in and ennobled by their struggle for freedom. Isn't that what America is always—what it has always stood for and what we should stand for in 1986 and beyond?

Until next week, thanks for listening. God bless you in the coming new year.

Note: The President spoke at 9:06 a.m. from the Century Plaza Hotel in Los Angeles, CA.

Executive Order 12540—Adjustments of Certain Rates of Pay and Allowances
December 30, 1985

By the authority vested in me as President by the Constitution and laws of the United States of America, it is hereby ordered as follows:

Section 1. In accordance with the Supplemental Appropriations Act, 1985 (Public Law 99–88; 99 Stat. 293, 310), Executive Order No. 12496 of December 28, 1984, is amended by replacing Schedule 7 attached thereto with the corresponding new Schedule 7 attached hereto. The rates of pay so established are effective on the first day of the first applicable pay period beginning on or after January 1, 1985.

Sec. 2. In accordance with section 601 of the Department of Defense Authorization Act, 1986 (Public Law 99–145)—

(a) Section 4 of Executive Order No. 12496 is amended to read as follows:

"*Sec. 4.* Pay and Allowances for Members of the Uniformed Services. Pursuant to the provisions of section 601 of the Department of Defense Authorization Act, 1986, the rates of monthly basic pay (37 U.S.C. 203(a)), the rates of basic allowance for subsistence (37 U.S.C. 402), and the rates of basic allowance for quarters (37 U.S.C. 403(a)) are adjusted as set forth at Schedule 8 attached hereto and made a part hereof, for members of the uniformed services.".

(b) Executive Order No. 12496 is further

amended by replacing Schedule 8 attached thereto with the corresponding new Schedule 8 attached hereto. The rates of pay and allowances so established are effective on October 1, 1985.

Sec. 3. Section 5 of Executive Order No. 12496 is amended to read as follows:

"*Sec. 5.* Effective Dates. The adjustments in rates of pay under sections 1 through 3 of this Order, as set forth at Schedules 1 through 7 attached hereto, are effective on the first day of the first applicable pay period beginning on or after January 1, 1985. The adjustments in rates of monthly basic pay and allowances for subsistence and quarters for members of the uniformed services under section 4 of this Order, as set forth at Schedule 8 attached hereto, are effective on October 1, 1985.".

RONALD REAGAN

The White House,
December 30, 1985.

[Filed with the Office of the Federal Register, 12:04 p.m., January 6, 1986]

Note: The Executive order was released by the Office of the Press Secretary on December 31. The schedules were printed in the Federal Register of January 7, 1986.

Executive Order 12541—Amending Executive Order 11157 as It Relates to a Basic Allowance for Quarters While on Sea Duty
December 30, 1985

By the authority vested in me by Section 403(j)(1) of title 37, United States Code, and in order to define the term "sea duty," it is hereby ordered as follows:

Section 1. Section 401, Part IV, of Executive Order No. 11157 of June 22, 1964, as amended, is further amended:

(a) by adding at the end of subsection (c) of section 401, Part IV, the following sentence:

"Duty for less than three months is not considered to be sea duty. Duty for more than three months under temporary orders which provide for return to the member's same permanent station is not considered sea duty.".

(b) by striking all of subsection (f).

Sec. 2. This Executive Order shall be effective as of January 1, 1986.

RONALD REAGAN

The White House,
December 30, 1985.

[*Filed with the Office of the Federal Register, 12:05 p.m., January 6, 1986*]

Note: *The Executive order was released by the Office of the Press Secretary on December 31.*

Executive Order 12542—President's Blue Ribbon Commission on Defense Management
December 30, 1985

By the authority vested in me as President by the Constitution and laws of the United States of America, including the Federal Advisory Committee Act, as amended, it is hereby ordered that Section 2(c) of Executive Order No. 12526 is amended by deleting "December 31, 1985" as the date for submission of the Commission's conclusions and recommendations on the procurement section of its study and inserting in lieu thereof "February 28, 1986.".

RONALD REAGAN

The White House,
December 30, 1985.

[*Filed with the Office of the Federal Register, 12:06 p.m., January 6, 1986*]

Note: *The Executive order was released by the Office of the Press Secretary on December 31.*

New Year's Message to the People of Japan
December 31, 1985

It is a great pleasure to extend my sincere best wishes for the New Year to the people of Japan. Americans and Japanese alike have much to be thankful for on this first day of the New Year, not least our shared friendship and respect. In both countries, this is an opportunity to be with our families, to look back upon the accomplishments of the past year and ahead to the challenges of the coming year. We are grateful for the bounty that we enjoy and are committed to sharing it with those less fortunate. Most importantly, our families can celebrate this holiday in safety, knowing that we are at peace.

In 1985, we moved a bit closer to the ideal of a lasting, global peace. People around the world began to recognize the value of moving toward a day when we can rely for our security on defensive instead of offensive weapons. And the United States, with the help and advice of our allies, made a serious effort at beginning a dialog with the Soviet Union on issues of concern to all countries, such as arms control and human rights, as well as issues of more regional concern, such as the occupations of Afghanistan and Cambodia, that must be settled in order to achieve global peace and stability. The United States entered into that dialog confident in the support it had at home and abroad. Continued support from our friends and allies in the months ahead will be vital in order to achieve the objective of building a more stable and constructive relationship with the Soviet Union. There is much work to be done, but I promise that the effort will be made.

The strength of the ties between our two countries helped us to put in motion long-needed changes in our trade relations. While these changes will require time to take effect, our shared commitment to preserve the world's free trade system was an essential bulwark against the protectionism that would deprive us of the prosperity for which we and those before us have labored. The cooperative spirit of the relationship gives me great confidence that we will reach our mutual goals. The growing international role of Japan is one of the most welcome trends of the eighties and holds much promise for the last half of the decade. The United States deeply values our consultation and cooperation in dealing with global issues and welcomes a partnership with Japan that threatens no one and holds promise for so many. I look forward to returning to Tokyo for the economic summit in May.

To all the people of Japan: I wish you health and prosperity in the coming year.

Appendix A—Digest of Other White House Announcements

The following list includes the President's public schedule and other items of general interest announced by the Office of the Press Secretary and not included elsewhere in this book.

June 29

Throughout the day, the President met at the White House with his national security advisers and consulted by telephone with other advisers concerning the TWA hijacking situation.

July 1

The President met at the White House with:
—members of the White House staff;
—the Cabinet.

In the afternoon, the President participated in the swearing-in ceremony in the Roosevelt Room for Clayton Yeutter as United States Trade Representative.

July 2

The President met at the White House with:
—members of the White House staff;
—business leaders, to discuss deficit reduction;
—Armando C. Albarron, the 1985 Disabled Veteran of the Year;
—Edward F. Cadman, president of Rotary International.

In the afternoon, the President telephoned the family of Robert D. Stethem, the Navy serviceman killed in Beirut during the hijacking of Trans World Airlines flight 847, to again extend his and Mrs. Reagan's condolences.

July 3

Throughout the day, the President met at the White House with members of the White House staff.

The President transmitted to the Congress the 18th annual report on the operation of the Automotive Products Trade Act of 1965.

July 5

In the morning, the President left the White House for a weekend stay at Camp David, MD.

July 7

The President returned to the White House from Camp David.

July 8

The President met at the White House with:
—members of the White House staff;

—the Vice President and administration officials, for a luncheon meeting to discuss the Vice President's trip to Europe.

July 9

The President met at the White House with:
—members of the White House staff;
—the Republican congressional leadership, to discuss the budget;
—the bipartisan congressional leadership, to discuss the budget.

The President announced his intention to appoint the following individuals to be members of the Advisory Council on Historic Preservation:

James A. Baker III, Secretary of the Treasury; and
Christopher Hicks, Deputy Assistant to the President for Administration.

July 10

The President met at the White House with:
—members of the White House staff;
—members of the Budget Conference Committee.

The President announced his intention to nominate Robert L. Thompson, an Assistant Secretary of Agriculture (Economics), to be a member of the Board of Directors of the National Consumer Cooperative Bank for a term of 3 years. He would succeed William Gene Lesher.

July 11

The President met at the White House with:
—members of the White House staff;
—Senators Strom Thurmond of South Carolina, Orrin Hatch of Utah, and Paul Laxalt of Nevada, to discuss a constitutional amendment for a balanced budget;
—the Domestic Policy Council.

The President transmitted to the Congress a report reviewing preparations for the 1985 Conference to Review and Appraise the Achievements of the United Nations Decade for Women.

July 12

The President met at the White House with members of the White House staff.

In the afternoon, the President went to Bethesda Naval Hospital to have the benign polyp that was discovered during his March 8 physical examination removed. During the procedure, a larger polyp was discovered in his intestines and biopsied. The decision was made to remove it surgically on the following day. Dr. Dale Oller, USN, head of general surgery at the hospital, stated that "The President is in superior condition, and chances for a normal and full recovery are excellent." In the evening, the President underwent preoperative testing and spoke by telephone with Donald T. Regan, Assistant to the President and Chief of Staff, from his room at the hospital, where he remained overnight.

July 13

In the morning, the President met at Bethesda Naval Hospital with Donald T. Regan, Assistant to the President and Chief of Staff; Fred Fielding, Counsel to the President; and Larry M. Speakes, Principal Deputy Press Secretary to the President. Later in the morning, he underwent a right hemicolectomy and an ileo-transverse colostomy. Dr. Dale Oller, USN, stated that the "operation went without incident."

July 14

After spending the night in the recovery room, the President returned to his suite at Bethesda Naval Hospital. Later in the morning, he met with Donald T. Regan, Assistant to the President and Chief of Staff. The White House announced that the President was recovering more quickly than anticipated.

July 15

In the morning, the White House announced that the President continued to recover well from his surgery. In the afternoon, he met at Bethesda Naval Hospital with Donald T. Regan, Assistant to the President and Chief of Staff. Late in the afternoon, Dr. Dale Oller, USN, announced that, based on the results of the biopsy, the tumor was cancerous but that it had not spread, and that no further therapy was indicated.

The President announced his intention to nominate the following individuals to be members of the Board of Directors of the Commodity Credit Corporation:

John William Bode would succeed Mary Claiborne Jarratt. He is an Assistant Secretary of Agriculture-designate (Food and Consumer Services).

Raymond D. Lett would succeed C.W. McMillan. He is an Assistant Secretary of Agriculture-designate (Marketing and Inspection Services).

The President announced his intention to appoint Robert Michael Kimmitt, General Counsel of the Department of the Treasury, to be a member of the Board of Directors of the Federal Financing Bank.

July 16

The White House announced that the President continued to recover well from surgery. He

met in his room at Bethesda Naval Hospital with Donald T. Regan, Assistant to the President and Chief of Staff.

The President announced his intention to appoint the following individuals to serve as ex officio, advisory, nonvoting members of the National Commission on Space:

Orville G. Bentley, Assistant Secretary of Science and Education, Department of Education;

Erich Bloch, Director, National Science Foundation;

Jennifer L. Dorn, Director, Commercial Space Transportation, Department of Transportation;

George A. Keyworth II, Director, Office of Science and Technology Policy; and

Richard H. Shay, Deputy General Counsel, Department of Commerce.

The White House announced that the President received the report of the Blue Ribbon Task Group on Nuclear Weapons Program Management. The report was prepared in compliance with section 1632 of the Department of Defense Authorization Act, 1985 (Public Law 98–525) and Executive Order 12499 of January 18, 1985. The Task Group addressed procedures used by the Departments of Defense and Energy in establishing requirements and providing resources for the research, development, testing, production, surveillance, and retirement of nuclear weapons.

July 17

The White House announced that the President continued to recover well from surgery. He met in his room at Bethesda Naval Hospital with the Vice President; Donald T. Regan, Assistant to the President and Chief of Staff; and Craig L. Fuller, Assistant to the President for Cabinet Affairs. They discussed the budget, the Vice President's and Mr. Regan's meeting with the Senate Finance Committee, and other domestic and foreign issues.

The President requested the Congress to provide the following:

—$3.2 million in transfer authority for fiscal year 1985 for the Department of Housing and Urban Development to handle the increased single-family mortgage insurance workload.

—$3.6 million in fiscal year 1986 for the Department of Justice to enable the Attorney General to participate in a classified project.

—Offsetting budget amendments in fiscal year 1986 to reflect a transfer of functions in the Department of Justice.

—$1.0 million in fiscal year 1986 for the Department of Justice to enable the Presidential Commission on Organized Crime to complete its work.

July 18

The White House announced that the President continued to recover extremely well from surgery. He met in his room at Bethesda Naval Hospital with Donald T. Regan, Assistant to the President and Chief of Staff, who briefed the President on economic issues; and Robert C. McFarlane, Assistant to the President for National Security Affairs, who briefed the President on the conclusion of round two of the U.S.-Soviet nuclear and space arms negotiations and also on terrorism and efforts to combat it.

July 19

The White House announced that the President continued on the road to recovery. He met in his room at Bethesda Naval Hospital with:
—Donald T. Regan, Assistant to the President and Chief of Staff, to review candidates for Director of the Office of Management and Budget and other personnel matters and the budget;
—Robert C. McFarlane, Assistant to the President for National Security Affairs, to discuss Mr. McFarlane's upcoming meeting with Soviet leaders and the final round of the U.S.-Soviet nuclear and space arms negotiations;
—Secretary of State George P. Shultz, to report on his trip to Pacific and Southeast Asian countries.

The President transmitted to the Congress the sixth annual report of the Federal Labor Relations Authority.

The White House announced that the President has declared a major disaster for the State of California as a result of grass, wildlands, and forest fires beginning on or about June 26, which caused extensive property damage.

The White House announced that the President has designated Treasury Secretary James A. Baker III to head the United States Presidential delegation to attend the inauguration of Peruvian President-elect Alan Garcia in Lima, Peru, on July 28. The other two members of the delegation are U.S. Ambassador to Peru David Jordan and Assistant Secretary of State for Inter-American Affairs Elliott Abrams. Secretary Baker will make a brief stop in Guatemala on Monday, July 29, on his return to Washington.

July 20

In the afternoon, the President left Bethesda Naval Hospital and returned to the White House.

July 22

The President met at the White House with members of the White House staff.

July 23

The President met at the White House with Robert C. McFarlane, Assistant to the President for National Security Affairs, Secretary of State George P. Shultz, and other administration officials, who briefed the President on the current status of the proposed China-United States agreement on nuclear energy.

July 24

The President met at the White House with:
—members of the White House staff;
—bipartisan congressional leaders, to discuss the remaining congressional agenda and the budget.

July 25

The President met at the White House with:
—members of the White House staff;
—the Cabinet, to discuss domestic and foreign issues.

The President transmitted to the Congress the 1984 annual report of the Saint Lawrence Seaway Development Corporation and the fiscal year 1984 annual report of the Rehabilitation Services Administration.

July 26

The President met at the White House with:
—members of the White House staff;
—his foreign policy advisers.

The President requested the Congress to provide $2.4 million in transfer authority for fiscal year 1985 for the Small Business Administration to handle the processing of the greater-than-anticipated number of disaster loan applications received during the year.

The President appointed Edward Moore Kennedy, United States Senator from the State of Massachusetts, upon recommendation of the President pro tempore of the Senate and in consultation with the majority leader and minority leader of the Senate, to be a member of the Commission on the Bicentennial of the United States Constitution. This is a new position.

The President requested the Congress to consider amended fiscal year 1986 appropriations requests totaling $1.1 billion. These proposals eliminate the 5 percent pay cut proposed in the President's fiscal year 1986 February budget for Federal civilian employees as endorsed by the administration and are reflected in the Senate budget resolution. The amendments cover all nondefense agencies.

In the afternoon, the President left the White House for a weekend stay at Camp David, MD.

July 28

The President returned to the White House from Camp David.

July 29

The President met at the White House with:
—members of the White House staff;
—Adm. William J. Crowe, Jr., USN, Commander in Chief, Pacific.

July 30

The President met at the White House with:
—members of the White House staff;
—the Republican congressional leadership, to discuss the budget and other issues before the Congress;
—Senator Pete V. Domenici of New Mexico and Representative William H. Gray III of Pennsylvania, chairmen of the Senate and House Budget Committees, respectively, for a luncheon meeting to discuss the budget.

The President announced his intention to appoint Donald P. Hodel, Secretary of the Interior, to be a member and representative of the United States to the Delaware River Basin Commission and the Susquehanna River Basin Commission. He will succeed William P. Clark.

July 31

Throughout the day, the President met at the White House with members of the White House staff.

The President met in the Oval Office at the White House with his daughter Maureen, who reported on her recent trip to Africa, where she participated in the United Nations Conference on Women.

The President telephoned Secretary of Health and Human Services Margaret M. Heckler at Columbia Women's Hospital to wish her well and a speedy recovery from surgery.

The President attended a farewell party for David A. Stockman, Director of the Office of Management and Budget, in the Roosevelt Room at the White House.

August 1

The President met at the White House with:
—members of the White House staff;
—the Economic Policy Council, to receive an update on the farm situation;
—the Vice President, for lunch.

The White House announced that on Tuesday, July 30, a small area of irritated skin on the right side of the President's nose was removed. The irritation had recently been aggravated by the adhesive tape used while the President was in the hospital. It was examined for evidence of infection, and it was determined no further treatment was necessary.

August 2

The President met at the White House with:
—members of the White House staff;

—Secretary of State George P. Shultz, who reported on his recent trip to Helsinki, Finland.

In the afternoon, the President left the White House for a weekend stay at Camp David, MD.

August 4

The President returned to the White House from Camp David.

August 5

Throughout the day, the President met at the White House with members of the White House staff.

August 6

The President met at the White House with:
—members of the White House staff;
—his national security advisers;
—Senator Robert C. Byrd of West Virginia;
—the executive board of the Knights of Columbus, to discuss tax reform;
—Secretary of State George P. Shultz.

In the morning, the President telephoned Gov. Lamar Alexander of Tennessee to congratulate him on his election as Chairman of the National Governors Conference.

August 7

The President met at the White House with:
—members of the White House staff;
—his national security advisers;
—the Economic Policy Council, to review trade policy.

The President declared a major disaster for the State of Wyoming as a result of severe storms, hail, and flooding beginning on August 1, which caused extensive property damage.

August 8

The President met at the White House with:
—members of the White House staff;
—his national security advisers;
—the Cabinet, to review plans for the fiscal year 1987 budget;
—the Vice President, for lunch.

August 9

The President met at the White House with:
—members of the White House staff;
—his national security advisers;
—the Joint Chiefs of Staff;
—Secretary of State George P. Shultz;
—the Economic Policy Council, to review the U.S. International Trade Commission's options concerning shoe imports.

The President announced his intention to recess appoint the following-named persons:

Vance L. Clark, to be Administrator of the Farmers Home Administration. He will succeed Charles Wilson Shuman.

Thomas John Josefiak, to be a member of the Federal Election Commission for a term expiring April 30, 1991. He will succeed Frank P. Reiche.

Raymond D. Lett, to be an Assistant Secretary of Agriculture.

Hugh Montgomery, to be the Alternate Representative of the United States of America for Special Political Affairs in the United Nations with the rank of Ambassador. He will succeed Harvey J. Feldman.

Herbert Stuart Okun, to be Deputy Representative of the United States of America to the United Nations with the rank and status of Ambassador. He will succeed Jose S. Sorzano.

Robert E. Rader, Jr., to be a member of the Occupational Safety and Health Review Commission for the term expiring April 27, 1991. He will succeed Timothy F. Cleary.

John R. Wall, to be a member of the Occupational Safety and Health Review Commission for the remainder of the term expiring April 27, 1987. He will succeed Robert A. Rowland.

August 11

The President left the White House for a trip to California.

August 18

The President spoke by telephone with Senator Paul Laxalt of Nevada, who informed the President of his plans to retire.

August 19

The White House announced that the President has invited Soviet Foreign Minister Eduard A. Shevardnadze to a meeting at the White House on September 27, and the Foreign Minister has accepted. The meeting will review all areas of our relations and will help prepare for the President's meeting with General Secretary Mikhail Gorbachev in November. Among those participating from the U.S. side will be Secretary of State George P. Shultz and Robert C. McFarlane, Assistant to the President for National Security Affairs.

August 28

The White House announced that the President has invited Prime Minister Lee Kuan Yew of the Republic of Singapore to make an official working visit to the United States. Prime Minister Lee has accepted the invitation and will meet with the President at the White House on October 8.

September 2

The President returned to Washington, DC, following his trip to Rancho del Cielo, his ranch near Santa Barbara, CA.

September 3

The President met at the White House with:
—members of the White House staff;
—the Cabinet, to discuss the legislative agenda for the fall and the international situation.

September 4

The President met at the White House with:
—members of the White House staff;
—Secretary of State George P. Shultz.

The White House announced that the President has invited President Samora Moises Machel of the People's Republic of Mozambique to make an official working visit to the United States. President Machel has accepted the invitation and will meet with the President at the White House on September 19.

The President declared a major disaster for the State of Mississippi as a result of Hurricane Elena, beginning on or about September 2, which caused extensive property damage.

September 5

The President met in Room 450 of the Old Executive Office Building with U.S. marshals.

The President met at the White House with his foreign policy advisers to discuss South Africa.

September 6

The President met at the White House with:
—members of the White House staff;
—U.S. Ambassador to the Federal Republic of Germany and Mrs. Richard Burt;
—Martha Seger, member of the Board of Governors of the Federal Reserve System;
—Secretary of State George P. Shultz.

In the afternoon, the President left the White House for a weekend stay at Camp David, MD.

September 7

The President declared a major disaster for the State of Alabama as a result of Hurricane Elena, beginning on or about September 2, which caused extensive property damage.

September 8

The President returned to the White House from Camp David.

September 9

The President met at the White House with:
—members of the White House staff;
—U.S. Ambassador to South Africa Herman W. Nickel, who was returning to his post with a letter from President Reagan to President Pieter Willem Botha;
—the NATO Military Committee and major NATO commanders;
—American Jewish leaders, to discuss Soviet Jews;

—the Economic Policy Council, to discuss trade policy.

The President requested the Congress to provide the following for fiscal year 1986:

—Offsetting amendments that would enable the Department of Health and Human Services to provide an additional $30.8 million for research into the causes of and measures for the prevention of acquired immune deficiency syndrome (AIDS).

—$20.7 million for the Department of the Interior to improve the Minerals Management Services' royalty management program, refinance a loan by the Federal Financing Bank to the Guam Power Authority, and provide for a payment to the Alaska Nature Escrow Account as required by law.

—$8.0 million for the Department of Justice to provide for the consolidation of various offices of the Department in the Washington, DC, area.

The President also proposed amended 1986 budget requests for the Office of Science and Technology Policy, the Department of Housing and Urban Development, the Small Business Administration, and the Navajo and Hopi Relocation Commission.

September 10

The President met at the White House with:
—members of the White House staff;
—members of a coalition for tax reform;
—Senators Robert C. Byrd of West Virginia, Strom Thurmond of South Carolina, Sam Nunn of Georgia, John W. Warner of Virginia, Dennis DeConcini of Arizona, George J. Mitchell of Maine, Claiborne Pell of Rhode Island, and Paul S. Sarbanes of Maryland, who reported on their recent trip to the Soviet Union.

The White House announced that President Reagan sent a message to President José Napoléon Duarte Fuentes of El Salvador expressing his concern regarding the kidnaping of President Duarte's daughter, Inés.

September 11

The President met at the White House with:
—Prince Sultan Bin Salman al-Saud, the Saudi Arabian astronaut who flew on board the space shuttle *Discovery,* and Daniel C. Brandenstein, crew commander of the space shuttle;
—the Republican congressional leadership, to discuss South Africa, trade legislation, tax reform, and the continuing budget resolution;
—Secretary of State George P. Shultz.

September 12

In the evening, the President hosted a reception for the Republican Eagles, major donors to the Republican Party, in the Residence.

The President declared a major disaster for the State of Florida as a result of Hurricane Elena, which caused extensive damage.

September 13

The President met at the White House with:
—members of the White House staff;
—the Intelligence Oversight Board.

In the afternoon, the President left the White House for a weekend stay at Camp David, MD.

September 15

The President returned to the White House from Camp David.

September 16

The President met at the White House with:
—members of the White House staff;
—members of the Republican National Hispanic Assembly.

The President announced his intention to designate Malcolm Forbes, Jr., as Chairman of the Board for International Broadcasting. He has served as a member since September 23, 1983. He will succeed Frank Shakespeare.

The President transmitted to the Congress a report on the recommendations of the Office of Juvenile Justice and Delinquency Prevention and the 1984 annual report of the National Advisory Council on Adult Education.

September 17

The President met at the White House with:
—members of the White House staff;
—the President's Blue Ribbon Commission on Defense Management, to discuss the Commission's activities and plans;
—the Commission on the Bicentennial of the United States Constitution, to receive a report;
—congressional leaders, to discuss agricultural issues.

In an Oval Office ceremony, the President received diplomatic credentials from Ambassadors F. Rawdon Dalrymple of Australia, Eulogio Jose Santarella Ulloa of the Dominican Republic, Edward A. Laing of Belize, Federico Vargas Peralta of Costa Rica, Padraic N. MacKernan of Ireland, and Hector Luisi of Uruguay.

The President announced his intention to nominate Richard N. Holwill, Deputy Assistant Secretary of State for Inter-American Affairs, to be a member of the board of the Panama Canal Commission. He would succeed John Alden Bushnell.

September 18

While en route to address the citizens of Concord, NH, the President called Rev. Benjamin Weir, who had recently been released after being held hostage in Lebanon for 18 months, to express his relief at Reverend Weir's release and his determination to see the remaining hostages freed.

The President met at the White House with Senator Bob Packwood, chairman of the Senate Committee on Finance, to discuss the legislative agenda.

September 19

The President met at the White House with the Domestic Policy Council to discuss a flat-rate per diem, bilingual education, the U.S. Synthetic Fuels Corporation, and aviation safety.

The President declared a major disaster for the State of Michigan as a result of severe storms and flooding beginning on September 5, which caused extensive property damage.

The President announced his intention to appoint the following individuals to be Governors of the Board of Governors of the American National Red Cross for terms of 3 years:

Adm. William J. Crowe, Jr., Chairman of the Joint Chiefs of Staff. He will succeed Gen. John W. Vessey, Jr.; and
George P. Shultz, Secretary of State. This is a reappointment.

The President announced his intention to appoint the following individuals to be members of the National Armed Forces Museum Advisory Board of the Smithsonian Institution for terms expiring April 9, 1990:

John F. Lehman, Jr., of Virginia, Secretary of the Navy; and
John O. Marsh, Jr., of Virginia, Secretary of the Army.

September 20

The President met at the White House with:
—members of the White House staff;
—a group of agricultural leaders.

The President transmitted to the Congress the 1984 annual report of the Federal Prevailing Rate Advisory Committee.

The White House announced that President Reagan sent a letter on September 19 to President Miguel De la Madrid Hurtado of Mexico offering his condolences to the people of Mexico following a serious earthquake on September 19. President Reagan also expressed his willingness to provide any assistance that the Mexican Government or people might require.

In the afternoon, the President left the White House for a weekend stay at Camp David, MD. En route to Camp David, the President stopped at Bethesda Naval Hospital for routine post-operative exams, including a chest x-ray and blood tests.

September 22

The President returned to the White House from Camp David.

September 23

The President met at the White House with:
—members of the White House staff;
—the President's Export Council;
—President Mohammed Hosni Mubarak of Egypt;
—Congressman Jack Kemp of New York and the board of governors of the NFL Alumni Association;
—Congressman Michael Bilirakis of Florida and Scott McQuigg, a high school journalism student;
—Congressmen Norman D. Shumway of California and Howard C. Nielson of Utah;
—Raymond Lansford, president of Kiwanis International;
—Senator Jesse Helms and Congressman Charles O. Whitley of North Carolina and Dr. Norman Wiggins, president of Campbell College;
—Senator John H. Chafee of Rhode Island and a group of Vietnam veterans.

In the evening, the President went to the Washington Hilton to attend the Inner Circle reception.

Later in the evening, the President spoke by telephone with Mrs. Reagan, who had traveled to Mexico to observe conditions after a series of earthquakes struck that country the previous week. While in Mexico City, Mrs. Reagan presented President Miguel De la Madrid Hurtado with a letter from President Reagan conveying the sympathy and support of the American people.

September 25

The President met at the White House with:
—members of the White House staff;
—U.S. Ambassadors Harvey F. Nelson, Jr. (Swaziland), Sheldon J. Krys (Trinidad and Tobago), Owen W. Roberts (Togo), Robert V. Keeley (Greece), Natale H. Bellocchi (Botswana), Michael G. Sotirhos (Jamaica), and Richard W. Bogosian (Niger), prior to their departure for their overseas posts.

September 26

The President met at the White House with:
—members of the White House staff;
—Robert C. McFarlane, Assistant to the President for National Security Affairs, to discuss the September 25 meeting between Secretary of State George P. Shultz and Soviet Foreign Minister Eduard Shevardnadze at the United Nations;
—the Vice President, for lunch;

—U.S. Naval Academy Midshipman Napoleon McCallum, Heisman Trophy candidate;
—a group of new White House fellows;
—the Domestic Policy Council, to discuss synthetic fuel legislation.

September 27
The President met at the White House with:
—Prime Minister Márquez Felipe González of Spain;
—Soviet Foreign Minister Eduard Shevardnadze;
—Secretary of State George P. Shultz.
The President designated J. Fernando Niebla as Chairperson of the National Council on Vocational Education. He has served as a member of the Council since February 12, 1985.
The President transmitted to the Congress amended fiscal year 1986 appropriation requests totaling a net reduction of $207.4 million. These include:

—$54.0 million to assist the armed forces and the law enforcement agencies of El Salvador, Honduras, Costa Rica, Panama, Belize, and Guatemala to combat terrorism in their countries.
—$20.6 million for the Department of Transportation to provide funds to the Federal Aviation Administration for improved civil aviation security and additional safety inspectors. In addition to this amount, $15.0 million would be transferred from unobligated prior year balances in another function to provide for aviation security-related research and development.
—A net reduction of $282.0 million for the Small Business Administration. This reduction is possible because of the lower-than-anticipated need for additional capital for the Business Loan and Investment Fund.

September 30
The President met at the White House with:
—members of the White House staff;
—Secretary of Health and Human Services Margaret M. Heckler.
In the evening, the President hosted a private dinner for the Prince and Princess of Lichtenstein in the Residence.

October 1
The President met at the White House with:
—Republican Senators, for a breakfast meeting;
—the Cabinet, to discuss the continuing resolution, appropriations bills, the status of the 1987 budget process, debt ceiling legislation, recent meetings with foreign leaders, and the upcoming meeting with Soviet General Secretary Mikhail Gorbachev in Geneva;

—the leadership of the Order Sons of Italy in America, the oldest and largest Italian-American organization in the United States.
The President participated in the swearing-in ceremony in the Oval Office for Adm. William J. Crowe, Jr., as Chairman of the Joint Chiefs of Staff.
The President hosted a reception in the State Dining Room for the Justices of the Supreme Court of the United States.

October 2
The President met at the White House with:
—members of the White House staff;
—the Republican congressional leadership.
The President transmitted to the Congress the annual reports for fiscal years 1981 and 1982 by the Secretary of Labor under the Federal Mine Safety and Health Act of 1977.
The President hosted a reception in the Residence for major donors to Citizens for America, a national nonpartisan civic organization that supports the President's economic and national security programs.

October 3
The President announced that upon the confirmation of John Norton Moore, he will be designated as Chairman of the Board of Directors of the United States Institute of Peace for a term of 3 years. Mr. Moore was nominated on September 9.

October 4
The President announced his intention to redesignate Armand Hammer as Chairman of the President's Cancer Panel for a term of 1 year.
In the afternoon, the President went to Parsippany, NJ, to attend a fundraising luncheon for the New Jersey State Republican Party. Following his remarks, he went to Camp David, MD, for a weekend stay.

October 6
The President returned to the White House from Camp David.

October 7
The President met at the White House with:
—members of the White House staff;
—Lord Carrington, Secretary General of NATO, to discuss the President's upcoming meeting with Soviet General Secretary Mikhail Gorbachev and East-West developments;
—Robert C. McFarlane, Assistant to the President for National Security Affairs, to discuss the hijacking of the Italian cruise ship *Achille Lauro*.

October 8

The President met at the White House with:
—members of the White House staff;
—Robert C. McFarlane, Assistant to the President for National Security Affairs, to discuss the hijacking of the Italian cruise ship *Achille Lauro*.

In the morning, the President attended the swearing-in ceremony in the Roosevelt Room for James C. Miller III as Director of the Office of Management and Budget. Mr. Miller was sworn in by the Vice President.

The President declared a major disaster for the Commonwealth of Pennsylvania as a result of severe storms and flooding, beginning on September 27, which caused extensive property damage.

October 9

The President met at the White House with:
—members of the White House staff;
—Robert C. McFarlane, Assistant to the President for National Security Affairs, to discuss the hijacking of the Italian cruise ship *Achille Lauro*.

The White House announced that the President has designated Theodore F. Brophy to be Chairman of the President's National Security Telecommunications Advisory Committee for the term of 1 year. Mr. Brophy has been a member of the Committee since December 16, 1982, and has held the position of Vice Chairman until April 2, 1985. He would succeed Joseph V. Charyk.

October 10

The President declared a major disaster for the Commonwealth of Puerto Rico as a result of severe storms, landslides, mudslides, and flooding, beginning on October 6, which caused extensive property damage.

The President announced his intention to appoint the following individuals to be members of the National Critical Materials Council:

Danny J. Boggs, Deputy Secretary of Energy, to be designated Chairman;

Thomas Gale Moore, a member of the Council of Economic Advisers; and

Robert N. Broadbent, an Assistant Secretary of the Interior.

In the evening, the President called Prime Minister Bettino Craxi of Italy to express his appreciation and praise for Italy's role in the coordinated effort to bring to justice the terrorists involved in the hijacking of the Italian cruise ship *Achille Lauro*.

Throughout the night, the President was kept abreast of the terrorists involved in the hijacking of the Italian cruise ship *Achille Lauro* by Vice

Adm. John M. Poindexter, Deputy Assistant to the President for National Security Affairs.

October 11

The President met at the White House with:
—members of the White House staff;
—Secretary of State George P. Shultz.

The President called the family of Leon Klinghoffer, who was killed during the hijacking of the Italian cruise ship *Achille Lauro*, to express his and Mrs. Reagan's condolences.

The President declared a major disaster for the State of Connecticut as a result of Hurricane Gloria beginning on September 27, which caused extensive property damage.

In the afternoon, the President left the White House for a weekend stay at Camp David, MD.

October 14

The President returned to the White House from Camp David.

October 15

The President declared a major disaster for the State of New Jersey as a result of Hurricane Gloria beginning on September 27, which caused extensive property damage.

The President declared a major disaster for the State of Rhode Island as a result of Hurricane Gloria beginning on September 27, which caused extensive property damage.

October 16

The President met at the White House with:
—members of the White House staff;
—Secretary of State George P. Shultz.

October 17

The President met at the White House with:
—members of the White House staff;
—a group of Republican Governors.

In the evening, the President went to the J.W. Marriott Hotel to attend a fundraising dinner for the Republican Governors Association.

October 18

The President met at the White House with:
—members of the White House staff;
—Secretary of State George P. Shultz.

The President declared a major disaster for the State of New York as a result of Hurricane Gloria beginning on September 27, which caused extensive property damage.

October 21

The President met at the White House with:
—members of the White House staff;
—Congressman G.V. (Sonny) Montgomery of Mississippi and Susan Aiken, Miss America.

October 22

The President met at the White House with:
—members of the White House staff;
—the Republican congressional leadership, to discuss foreign and domestic issues;
—Senator Paul Laxalt of Nevada, to discuss the Senator's meeting with President Ferdinand E. Marcos of the Philippines in Manila;
—Prime Minister Herbert Blaize of Grenada;
—Kamoya Kimeu, of Kenya, recipient of the National Geographic John Oliver La Gorce Medal for his anthropological achievements in Africa;
—the House Appropriations Committee, to discuss the ABM treaty and strategic defense appropriations.

October 23

In the morning, the President went to New York to address the 40th Session of the United Nations General Assembly. Upon arrival, he went to the Waldorf-Astoria Hotel, where he stayed during his visit. In the afternoon, the President went to the United Nations to attend a reception and luncheon for the heads of state and government participating in the session. The luncheon was hosted by United Nations Secretary-General Javier Perez de Cuellar de la Guerra. Following the luncheon, the President returned to his suite at the hotel where he held bilateral meetings with Prime Minister Rajiv Gandhi of India, President Mohammad Zia-ul-Haq of Pakistan, and Prime Minister Margaret Thatcher of the United Kingdom. In the evening, the President hosted a reception for the heads of state and government and their accompanying foreign ministers at the hotel.

October 24

Following his address before the United Nations Assembly, the President went to the United States Mission where he met with Prime Minister Bettino Craxi of Italy and later with allied leaders. The President then returned to his suite at the Waldorf-Astoria Hotel where he met with Prime Minister Brian Mulroney of Canada. In the evening, the President hosted a reception and working dinner for allied leaders at the hotel.

The White House announced that the President has invited President Leon Febres-Cordero of the Republic of Ecuador to make an official working visit to the United States. President Febres-Cordero has accepted the invitation and will meet with President Reagan at the White House on January 8, 1986.

October 25

In the morning, the President held bilateral meetings in his suite at the Waldorf-Astoria Hotel with Prime Minister Yasuhiro Nakasone of Japan

and with Chancellor Helmut Kohl of the Federal Republic of Germany. Later he met with the family of Leon Klinghoffer, who was killed during the hijacking of the Italian cruise ship *Achille Lauro*. The President then returned to Andrews Air Force Base, MD, where he boarded Marine One and left for a weekend stay at Camp David.

October 27

The President returned to the White House from Camp David.

The President spoke by telephone with several members of the Kansas City Royals baseball team, following their winning of the World Series championship in Kansas City, MO.

October 28

The President met at the White House with:
—members of the White House staff;
—the Domestic Policy Council, to receive the final report of the President's Private Sector Survey on Cost Control in the Federal Government;
—family members of hostages abducted in Lebanon.

The President declared a major disaster for the Commonwealth of Massachusetts as a result of Hurricane Gloria beginning on September 27, which caused extensive property damage.

October 29

The President met at the White House with:
—members of the White House staff;
—Senators Mack Mattingly and Sam Nunn and Congressman J. Roy Royland of Georgia and Lucy McTier of Georgia;
—Senator Warren B. Rudman of New Hampshire and Emil Nagy of New Hampshire;
—Congressman Robert H. Michel of Illinois and Christine Green and David Dehymer of Illinois;
—Congressman J. Alex McMillan of North Carolina and Harry Dalton of North Carolina;
—Congressman Michael G. Oxley of Ohio and actor Don Williams, who portrayed the President in a production by Hexagon, a Washington, DC, theater group.

The President attended a reception for Senator James Abdnor of South Dakota at the Sheraton Grand Hotel.

October 30

The President met at the White House with:
—members of the White House staff;
—the Vice President, for lunch;
—a group of new Republicans;
—Secretary of State George P. Shultz.

In the afternoon, the President and Mrs. Reagan went to the National Gallery of Art to view the "Treasure Houses of Britain" exhibit.

October 31

The President met at the White House with:
—members of the White House staff;
—President José Napoleón Duarte Fuentes of El Salvador and his daughter Inés Guadalupe Duarte, who had been kidnaped by terrorists, to express his support for President Duarte's efforts in fighting terrorism;
—Ambassador Robert L. Barry, U.S. Representative to the Conference on Confidence and Security-Building Measures and Disarmament in Europe, who reported on the final round of negotiations in Stockholm.

The President requested the Congress to provide $16.0 million in fiscal year 1986 to the Department of Commerce for the implementation of the National Oceanic and Atmospheric Administration's research and management responsibilities under the United States-Canada pacific salmon treaty.

November 1

The President met at the White House with members of the White House staff.

The President announced the members of the United States delegation to observe the Guatemalan Presidential election in Guatemala on Sunday, November 3.

Senator Richard Lugar and Representative Buddy Roemer of Louisiana will serve as cochairmen of the delegation. The members of the delegation will be:

Senator Mitch McConnell of Kentucky;
Representative William B. Richardson of New Mexico;
Representative Chester Atkins of Massachusetts;
Representative Robert Lagomarsino of California;
Representative John McCain of Arizona;
Alberto Piedra, U.S. Ambassador to Guatemala;
William Walker, Deputy Assistant Secretary of State for Inter-American Affairs;
Louise Hoppe, Deputy Assistant Secretary of State for Legislative and Intergovernmental Affairs;
Raymond F. Burghardt, Senior Director for Latin American Affairs, National Security Council;
Bruce McColm, U.S. Representative to the OAS Commission on Human Rights, Washington, DC;
Dr. Howard Penniman, political scientist, American Enterprise Institute, Washington, DC;
Carl Gershman, president, National Endowment for Democracy, Washington, DC;
Georges Fauriol, author and foreign affairs analyst, Washington, DC;
Bruce Cameron, consultant, formerly with Americans for Democratic Action, Washington, DC;
Jose Sorzano, associate professor of government, Georgetown University, Washington, DC;
Josiah Moore, chairman, Papago Tribe of Arizona;

Richard Ouderkirk, professor of history, Principia College, Elsah, IL;
William Doherty, director, American Federation for Free Labor Development, AFL-CIO, Washington, DC;
Cameron Clark, Jr., president, Production Sharing International, Ltd., Southport, CT;
John Silber, president, Boston University, Boston, MA; and
Charles Bartlett, president, Jefferson Foundation and Pulitzer Prize winner, Washington, DC.

The President declared a major disaster for the State of Louisiana as a result of Hurricane Juan beginning on or about October 27, which caused extensive property damage.

In the afternoon, the President went to Bethesda Naval Hospital, where he underwent a routine post-operative examination. Following the examination, he went to Camp David, MD, for a weekend stay.

November 3

The President returned to the White House from Camp David.

November 4

The President met at the White House with:
—members of the White House staff;
—Wyatt Durrette, Virginia gubernatorial candidate;
—the Economic Policy Council, for an update on the farm credit system.

November 5

The President met at the White House with:
—members of the White House staff;
—James C. Miller III, Director of the Office of Management and Budget.

In an Oval Office ceremony, the President received diplomatic credentials from Ambassadors Stanislas Batchi of the Congo, Leshele A. Thoahlane of Lesotho, Timon S. Mangwazu of Malawi, Salah Ahmed of Sudan, Nalumino Mundia of Zambia, Johannes H.A. Buekes of South Africa, Albert O. Xavier of Grenada, and Edouard Kadigiri of Burundi.

November 6

The President met at the White House with:
—members of the White House staff;
—Secretary of State George P. Shultz, who reported on his recent trip to the Soviet Union.

November 7

The President met at the White House with:
—members of the White House staff;
—private sector supporters of the Strategic Defense Initiative;
—Soviet affairs experts, for lunch.

The President attended the swearing-in ceremony in the Roosevelt Room for Edward V. Hickey, Jr., as Chairman of the Federal Maritime Commission.

November 8

The President met at the White House with:
—members of the White House staff;
—the Republican congressional leadership, to discuss the President's upcoming meeting with Soviet General Secretary Mikhail Gorbachev;
—religious leaders, for lunch;
—Secretary of State George P. Shultz.

The President declared a major disaster for the State of West Virginia as a result of severe storms, landslides, and flooding beginning on or about November 3, which caused extensive property damage.

The President transmitted to the Congress the annual reports for fiscal years 1983 and 1984 under the Federal Mine Safety and Health Act of 1977 as prepared by the Secretary of Labor.

The President transmitted to the Congress the 1984 annual reports on activities under the Occupational Safety and Health Act of 1970 of the Departments of Labor and Health and Human Services and of the Occupational Safety and Health Review Commission.

November 9

In the morning, the President welcomed Prince Charles and Princess Diana of Wales in a ceremony on the South Lawn of the White House.

The President declared major disasters for the Commonwealths of Pennsylvania and Virginia as a result of severe storms, landslides, and flooding, beginning on or about November 3, which caused extensive property damage.

November 12

The President met at the White House with:
—members of the White House staff;
—the congressional leadership, to discuss the President's upcoming meeting with Soviet General Secretary Mikhail Gorbachev and the Gramm-Rudman-Hollings balanced budget legislation.

November 13

The President met at the White House with:
—members of the White House staff;
—the Cabinet, to discuss the President's upcoming meeting with Soviet General Secretary Mikhail Gorbachev;
—George F. Moody, chairman, and Richard F. Schubert, president, of the American National Red Cross, to discuss their disaster relief campaign.

November 14

The President met at the White House with
—members of the White House staff;
—U.S. Ambassador to the Philippines Stephen Warren Bosworth;
—U.S. arms negotiators, to discuss the current status of the nuclear and space arms negotiations in Geneva.

The White House announced that the President has invited Prime Minister Brian Mulroney of Canada to make an official visit to the United States. Prime Minister Mulroney has accepted and will meet with the President at the White House on March 18, 1986.

November 15

The President met at the White House with
—members of the White House staff;
—Secretary of State George P. Shultz;
—Senators Pete Wilson of California and Ernest F. Hollings of South Carolina, who delivered a letter signed by Senators who support the Strategic Defense Initiative.

The President announced the members of the United States delegation to attend ceremonies marking Oman's National Day, November 18–19. Former President Gerald R. Ford will serve as chairman of the delegation. The other members of the delegation are:

Former First Lady Betty Ford, of California;

Joseph D. Ambrose, president, Ambrose Properties, Inc. Fort Worth, TX;

Kathleen A. Warwick, corporate securities counsel, Mobil Corp., New York, NY;

Alexandra Hufty Hayes, of Palm Beach, FL;

Archibald Roosevelt, director of international affairs, Chase Manhattan Bank, New York, NY;

Darius N. Keaton, former chairman of the board and president, Charter Oil Co., and former chairman and owner, Edington Oil Co., San Francisco, CA; and

Robert Barrett, president, Barrett Consultants, of California.

November 16

In the evening, President Reagan arrived at Geneva-Cointrin Airport, where he was greeted by Swiss President Kurt Furgler. He then went to Maison de Saussure, his residence during his stay in Switzerland.

November 17

In the afternoon, the President met with senior advisers at the Pometta residence.

November 18

In the morning, the President met with senior advisers and again later at a working luncheon at the Pometta residence. In the afternoon, the President went to Le Reposoir for a formal welcoming ceremony. Participating in the ceremony were Switzerland's President Kurt Furgler, Foreign Minister Pierre Aubert, and Chief of Protocol Johannes Manz. President Reagan and President Furgler then participated in a bilateral meeting.

November 19

In the morning, the President met with senior advisers at the Pometta residence. Later in the morning, the President began the first day of the Soviet-U.S. summit meeting by conferring at Fleur d'Eau with Soviet General Secretary Mikhail Gorbachev, first in an extended private meeting and then in a plenary session. After a working luncheon with senior advisers at the Pometta residence, the President participated in a plenary session at Fleur d'Eau. After the session, at the suggestion of the President, the two leaders left the residence and walked to a nearby pool house, where they spoke privately. In the evening, the President attended a dinner at the Soviet Mission hosted by General Secretary Gorbachev. The President then returned to Maison de Saussure.

November 20

In the morning, the President met with senior advisers at the Pometta residence. Later in the morning, the President met privately with Soviet General Secretary Mikhail Gorbachev at the Soviet Mission and then participated in a plenary session. After a working luncheon with his senior advisers at the Pometta residence, the President returned to the Soviet Mission for private meetings with General Secretary Gorbachev and a plenary session. The final private meeting of the day was concluded with the two leaders receiving status reports from each of their delegations. In the evening, the President attended a reception for the summit meeting delegations and Swiss community leaders at La Gandole. Later in the evening, the President hosted a dinner for General Secretary Gorbachev at Maison de Saussure.

November 21

In the morning, following their remarks on issuing a joint statement, President Reagan and Soviet General Secretary Mikhail Gorbachev met privately to say goodbye. In the afternoon, the President arrived at Zaventem Airport, Brussels, Belgium, where he was greeted by King Baudouin I and Queen Fabiola. The President went to NATO Headquarters, where he addressed a special meeting of the North Atlantic Council on the Soviet-U.S. summit meeting in Geneva. The President then returned to Washington, DC.

November 22

The President met at the White House with:
—the Vice President, for lunch;

—the Cabinet, to discuss the Soviet-U.S. summit meeting in Geneva.

The President announced his intention to nominate Chester A. Crocker, an Assistant Secretary of State (African Affairs), to be a member of the Board of Directors of the African Development Foundation for a term expiring September 22, 1991. This is a reappointment.

November 25

The President met at the White House with members of the White House staff.

The President presented the Department of Defense Medal for Distinguished Public Service to Verne Orr, Secretary of the Air Force, who is retiring.

In a Rose Garden ceremony, the President was presented with a 60-pound turkey for Thanksgiving by John Holden, president, and Lew Walts, executive vice president, of the National Turkey Federation. The occasion marked the 38th presentation to the Nation's First Family in commemoration of the holiday.

In the afternoon, the President presented the 1985 Sertoma International Service to Mankind Award to John Fling in recognition of his work with the blind and needy of Columbia, SC.

In an Oval Office ceremony, the President received the official 1985 Christmas Seals of the American Lung Association from entertainer Pearl Bailey, the 1985 Christmas Seal chairman.

The White House announced that the Aggregate Report on Personnel was being transmitted to the Speaker of the House and the President of the Senate.

The White House announced that the Consolidated Grain and Barge Co. of St. Louis, MO, has requested an exemption from the requirements of section 7(a)(2) of the Endangered Species Act of 1973, as amended, that would permit establishment of a barge fleeting area on the Ohio River near Mound City, IL. The President has appointed James R. Reilly, chief of staff, Office of the Governor, State of Illinois, and Bruce Williams, administrative assistant, Office of the Governor, State of Kentucky, to represent their respective States on the Endangered Species Committee to consider this application. In addition to the two members from the affected States, the Committee consists of six designated Federal officials, with the Secretary of the Interior serving as Chairman.

November 26

The President left the White House and went to Rancho del Cielo, his ranch near Santa Barbara, CA, for the Thanksgiving holiday weekend.

December 2

The President returned to Washington, DC, after spending the Thanksgiving holiday weekend at Rancho del Cielo, his ranch near Santa Barbara, CA, and traveling to Seattle, WA, to address a fundraising luncheon for Senator Slade Gorton.

December 3

The President met at the White House with:
—members of the White House staff;
—the Republican congressional leadership, to discuss government funding, tax reform, the debt ceiling, and farm legislation;
—Senator Paul Laxalt, of Nevada, to discuss the situation in the Philippines;
—the National Security Council and the Economic Policy Council.

The President declared a major disaster for the State of Florida as a result of Hurricane Kate, which caused extensive damage.

December 4

The President met at the White House with Secretary of State George P. Shultz.

The President transmitted to the Congress the 18th annual report of the U.S.-Japan Cooperative Medical Science Program covering calendar year 1984.

The President transmitted to the Speaker of the House and the President pro tempore of the Senate a report on the Federal agencies implementation of the Privacy Act of 1974.

December 5

The President met at the White House with members of the White House staff.

The President telephoned the Environmental Protection Agency on the 15th anniversary of its existence. His remarks were transmitted to EPA employees over the agency's public address system.

The President met in Room 450 of the Old Executive Office Building with former Members of Congress.

The President appointed Secretary of Defense Caspar W. Weinberger as Chairman of the Interagency Committee for the Purchase of United States Savings Bonds for a term of 2 years.

In the evening, the President attended the 30th anniversary dinner of National Review magazine at the Plaza Hotel in New York City. The President stayed at the hotel overnight. While in New York, the President telephoned Gino Casanova, of Seattle, WA, a veteran who had been fasting since mid-October to promote more active efforts in locating servicemen still missing in Southeast Asia.

December 6

The President met at the White House with:

—the Vice President, for lunch;
—Secretary of State George P. Shultz;
—James C. Miller III, Director of the Office of Management and Budget, to discuss the fiscal year 1987 budget.

The President transmitted to the Congress the eighth annual report on Federal energy conservation programs undertaken during fiscal year 1984.

The President announced the members of the United States delegation to observe the Presidential run-off elections in Guatemala on December 8. Senator Mark O. Hatfield (R–OR) and Representative William B. Richardson (D–NM) will serve as Cochairmen of the delegation. The remaining members of the delegation are:

Senator Claiborne Pell of Rhode Island;

Representative Mickey Edwards of Oklahoma;

Representative Bob McEwen of Ohio;

Georges Fauriol, Center for Strategic and International Studies, Georgetown University, of Washington, DC;

Cameron Clark, Jr., president, Production Sharing International, Ltd., and Central America/Caribbean Investor Advisory Service of Southport, CT;

John Carbaugh, of Washington, DC;

Howard Penniman, political scientist, American Enterprise Institute, of Washington, DC;

Jose Sorzano, professor of history, Georgetown University, and president, Cuban American National Foundation, of Washington, DC;

Carlos Perez, president, Banana Services, Inc., of Miami, FL;

Bruce Cameron, of Washington, DC;

Diego Suarez, president, Inter-American Transport, Inc., of Miami, FL;

Carol Hallett, national field director, Citizens for America, of Sacramento, CA;

Samuel Haddad, deputy director, American Institute for Free Labor Development, of Washington, DC;

Maurice Sonnenberg, investment consultant, of New York, NY;

Luis Acle, Associate Director for Public Liaison, the White House, Washington, DC;

Walt Raymond, Special Assistant to the President for National Security Affairs and Senior Director for International Communications Policy, National Security Council, the White House, Washington, DC;

Alberto Piedra, United States Ambassador to Guatemala; and

Charles Bartlett, of Washington, DC.

December 8

In the evening, the President and Mrs. Reagan attended the annual gala at the John F. Kennedy Center for the Performing Arts honoring the recipients of the Kennedy Center Honors awards for lifetime achievements in the arts.

December 9

The President met at the White House with:
—members of the White House staff;

—Senator Thad Cochran and Congressman G.V. (Sonny) Montgomery of Mississippi and Donna Russell, Mrs. America, 1985;
—Senator James Abdnor of South Dakota and Wallace Wells, chief of the Crow, Creek, and Sioux Tribes;
—Congressman Ronald C. Packard of California and Senator Orrin G. Hatch of Utah;
—Congressman Michael DeWine of Ohio;
—Congressman Bob Stump of Arizona.
Throughout the day, the President telephoned Republican Members of the House of Representatives to discuss pending tax reform legislation.

December 10
The President met at the White House with:
—members of the White House staff;
—the bipartisan congressional leadership, to discuss the continuing resolution, the Gramm-Rudman-Hollings balanced budget legislation, farm legislation, and tax reform;
—U.S. Ambassadors L.W. Lane (Australia and Nauru), Paul M. Cleveland (New Zealand), Joseph A. Ghougassian (Qatar), and Gregory J. Newell (Sweden), prior to departure for their overseas posts.
In an Oval Office ceremony, the President signed H.R. 3327, the Military Construction Appropriations Act, 1986, which was assigned Public Law No. 99–173.
In the evening, the President and Mrs. Reagan hosted a Christmas dance for Members of Congress in the Residence.

December 11
The President met at the White House with:
—members of the White House staff;
—American Friends of Lubavitch;
—the U.S. Savings Bonds Volunteer Committee;
—Republican Members of Congress, to discuss tax reform.
In the morning, the President participated in a review of the budget.
The President telephoned Senator Barry Goldwater of Arizona to convey his sympathy on the death of the Senator's wife.
Throughout the day, the President telephoned Members of Congress to discuss pending tax reform legislation.

December 12
The President met at the White House with:
—members of the White House staff;
—the Vice President, for lunch;
—the Cabinet, to discuss the budget.
In an Oval Office ceremony, the President met with 6-year-old Scott Cunningham, of Eight Mile, AL, the 1986 National Ambassador for the March of Dimes.

Throughout the day, the President telephoned Members of Congress to discuss pending tax reform legislation.

December 13
The President met at the White House with:
—members of the White House staff;
—the leadership of the National Conference of State Legislators;
—Merrett Smith, of the California State Republican Party.

December 16
In the afternoon, the President met with Republican Members of the House of Representatives at the Rayburn House Office Building to discuss tax reform legislation.
Later in the afternoon, the President met with Mother Teresa in the Oval Office.
In the evening, the President spoke by telephone with Speaker of the House of Representatives Thomas P. O'Neill, Jr., discussing pending tax reform legislation.

December 17
The President met at the White House with:
—members of the White House staff;
—Republican Members of Congress, to discuss tax reform legislation.
The White House announced that although there has been no final passage of a continuing resolution, the administration feels there is sufficient assurance of passage to warrant keeping employees on the job through the remainder of the day. If a resolution is not passed by the end of the legislative day, nonessential government employees will be informed through the news media not to come to work tomorrow.
In the afternoon, the President attended a farewell reception for Robert C. McFarlane, Assistant to the President for National Security Affairs, in the Roosevelt Room at the White House.
In the evening, the President went to the John F. Kennedy Center for the Performing Arts to attend a performance of "Aren't We All."
The White House announced that the President has designated Michael H. Armacost, Under Secretary of State for Political Affairs, to represent him at the funeral of former Philippine Foreign Minister Carlos P. Romulo in Manila on December 19.

December 18
The President met at the White House with:
—members of the White House staff;
—leading medical scientists, for lunch;
—Secretary of State George P. Shultz, who reported on his recent 10-day European visit.

December 19

The President met at the White House with:
—members of the White House staff;
—the Vice President, for lunch;
—the Domestic and Economic Policy Councils, in a joint session to discuss possible effects of antitrust laws on U.S. trade abroad and to be briefed on the impact of U.S. programs to combat AIDS.

In the evening, the President attended the White House senior staff Christmas party in the Residence.

December 20

The President met at the White House with:
—members of the White House staff;
—Secretary of State George P. Shultz.

The President attended a reception in the Roosevelt Room for Margaret M. Heckler, the new U.S. Ambassador to Ireland.

The President participated in the swearing-in ceremony in the Roosevelt Room for Otis R. Bowen as Secretary of Health and Human Services.

In the afternoon, the President left the White House for a weekend stay at Camp David, MD. Prior to his departure, the President was presented with a Christmas card signed by the citizens of Westminster, MD.

December 22

The President returned to the White House from Camp David.

December 23

The President met at the White House with:
—members of the White House staff;
—Secretary of Commerce Malcolm Baldrige, who reported on his trip to the Soviet Union.

The President requested the Congress to provide $4.0 billion for fiscal year 1986 for the Department of Agriculture to enable the Commodity Credit Corporation to continue to finance its fiscal year 1986 program obligations under current law.

December 25

The President and Mrs. Reagan spent Christmas at the White House.

December 27

The President and Mrs. Reagan left the White House for a trip to California. In the afternoon, they arrived in Los Angeles and went to the Century Plaza Hotel, where they remained overnight.

The White House announced that by mutual agreement, the President and Soviet General Secretary Mikhail Gorbachev will exchange New Year's greetings. The President will address the people of the Soviet Union and the General Secretary will address the people of the United States on January 1, 1986. Their recorded messages will be broadcast on radio and television.

December 28

While in Los Angeles, CA, the President telephoned Lou Rawls, who was hosting "The Lou Rawls Parade of Stars," an annual nationally broadcast telethon to help raise money for the United Negro College Fund.

December 29

The President and Mrs. Reagan left Los Angeles and traveled to the home of Walter and Leonore Annenberg in Palm Springs, CA, where they stayed through New Year's Day.

December 30

In the morning, the President telephoned Secretary of Labor William E. Brock III to convey his sympathy on the death of the Secretary's wife.

The President appointed the following individuals to be members of the Federal Council on the Aging for terms of 3 years. These are reappointments.

Katie Dusenberry, of Tucson, AZ.
Edna Bonn Russell, of Atherton, CA.

Appendix B—Nominations Submitted to the Senate

The following list does not include promotions of members of the Uniformed Services, nominations to the Service Academies, or nominations of Foreign Service officers.

Submitted July 1

Terrence M. Scanlon,
of the District of Columbia, to be Chairman of the Consumer Product Safety Commission, vice Nancy Harvey Steorts, resigned, to which position he was appointed during the recess of the Senate from October 12, 1984, until January 3, 1985.

Anne Graham,
of Virginia, to be a Commissioner of the Consumer Product Safety Commission for a term of 7 years from October 27, 1984, vice Nancy Harvey Steorts, resigned.

Submitted July 3

Michael E. Baroody,
of Virginia, to be an Assistant Secretary of Labor, vice John F. Cogan.

Richard F. Hohlt,
of Indiana, to be a member of the Board of Directors of the Overseas Private Investment Corporation for a term expiring December 17, 1987, vice William G. Simpson, term expired.

Submitted July 9

Thomas Michael Tolliver Niles,
of the District of Columbia, a career member of the Senior Foreign Service, Class of Minister-Counselor, to be Ambassador Extraordinary and Plenipotentiary of the United States of America to Canada.

Joe M. Rodgers,
of Tennessee, to be Ambassador Extraordinary and Plenipotentiary of the United States of America to France.

Submitted July 11

Robert L. Thompson,
an Assistant Secretary of Agriculture, to be a member of the Board of Directors of the National Consumer Cooperative Bank for a term of 3 years, vice William Gene Lesher.

Submitted July 11—Continued

Curtis E. von Kann,
of the District of Columbia, to be an Associate Judge of the Superior Court of the District of Columbia for a term of 15 years, vice Timothy C. Murphy, retired.

Submitted July 12

Gary L. Matthews,
of Virginia, a career member of the Senior Foreign Service, Class of Minister-Counselor, to be Ambassador Extraordinary and Plenipotentiary of the United States of America to the Republic of Malta.

Harvey Frans Nelson, Jr.,
of California, a career member of the Senior Foreign Service, Class of Minister-Counselor, to be Ambassador Extraordinary and Plenipotentiary of the United States of America to the Kingdom of Swaziland.

Irvin Hicks,
of Maryland, a career member of the Senior Foreign Service, Class of Counselor, to be Ambassador Extraordinary and Plenipotentiary of the United States of America to the Republic of Seychelles.

Submitted July 15

Lydia E. Glover,
of South Carolina, to be United States Marshal for the District of South Carolina for the term of 4 years, vice William C. Whitworth.

Submitted July 17

Douglas H. Ginsburg,
of Massachusetts, to be an Assistant Attorney General, vice J. Paul McGrath, resigned.

Richard Kennon Willard,
of Virginia, to be an Assistant Attorney General, vice William F. Baxter, resigned.

Raymond D. Lett,
of Virginia, to be an Assistant Secretary of Agriculture, vice C.W. McMillan, resigned.

Submitted July 17—Continued

Vance L. Clark,
of California, to be Administrator of the Farmers Home Administration, vice Charles Wilson Shuman, resigned.

The following-named persons to be members of the Board of Directors of the Commodity Credit Corporation:

John William Bode, of Oklahoma, vice Mary Claiborne Jarratt.

Raymond D. Lett, of Virginia, vice C.W. McMillan.

Joyce A. Doyle,
of New York, to be a member of the Federal Mine Safety and Health Review Commission for the remainder of the term expiring August 30, 1986, vice Rosemary M. Collyer, resigned.

Richard S. Nicholson,
of Virginia, to be an Assistant Director of the National Science Foundation, vice Edward A. Knapp.

Anthony J. Calio,
of Maryland, to be Administrator of the National Oceanic and Atmospheric Administration, vice John V. Byrne, resigned.

Submitted July 18

Robert Vossler Keeley,
of Florida, a career member of the Senior Foreign Service, Class of Career Minister, to be Ambassador Extraordinary and Plenipotentiary of the United States of America to Greece.

Francis J. Meehan,
of Virginia, a career member of the Senior Foreign Service, Class of Career Minister, to be Ambassador Extraordinary and Plenipotentiary of the United States of America to the German Democratic Republic.

John Pierce Ferriter,
of Florida, a career member of the Senior Foreign Service, Class of Minister-Counselor, to be Ambassador Extraordinary and Plenipotentiary of the United States of America to the Republic of Djibouti.

Orson G. Swindle III,
of Georgia, to be an Assistant Secretary of Commerce, vice J. Bonnie Newman, resigned.

Submitted July 19

John Gunther Dean,
of New York, a career member of the Senior Foreign Service, Class of Career Minister, to be

Submitted July 19—Continued

Ambassador Extraordinary and Plenipotentiary of the United States of America to India.

James W. Spain,
of California, a career member of the Senior Foreign Service, Class of Career Minister, to be Ambassador Extraordinary and Plenipotentiary of the United States of America to the Democratic Socialist Republic of Sri Lanka, and to serve concurrently and without additional compensation as Ambassador Extraordinary and Plenipotentiary of the United States of America to the Republic of Maldives.

Ferdinand F. Fernandez,
of California, to be United States District Judge for the Central District of California, vice a new position created by P.L. 98–353, approved July 10, 1984.

Brian P. Joffrion,
of Louisiana, to be United States Marshal for the Western District of Louisiana for the term of 4 years (reappointment).

Leo C. McKenna,
of New York, to be a member of the Advisory Board of the Saint Lawrence Seaway Development Corporation, vice Jacob L. Bernheim.

Submitted July 22

John Blane,
of Illinois, a career member of the Senior Foreign Service, Class of Minister-Counselor, to be Ambassador Extraordinary and Plenipotentiary of the United States of America to the Republic of Chad.

Richard Wayne Bogosian,
of Maryland, a career member of the Senior Foreign Service, Class of Counselor, to be Ambassador Extraordinary and Plenipotentiary of the United States of America to the Republic of Niger.

Submitted July 23

Winston Lord,
of New York, to be Ambassador Extraordinary and Plenipotentiary of the United States of America to the People's Republic of China.

Ralph B. Guy, Jr.,
of Michigan, to be United States Circuit Judge for the Sixth Circuit, vice a new position created by P.L. 98–353, approved July 10, 1984.

Submitted July 23—Continued

Stephen H. Anderson,
of Utah, to be United States Circuit Judge for the Tenth Circuit, vice a new position created by P.L. 98–353, approved July 10, 1984.

Glen H. Davidson,
of Mississippi, to be United States District Judge for the Northern District of Mississippi, vice a new position created by P.L. 98–353, approved July 10, 1984.

Robert B. Maloney,
of Texas, to be United States District Judge for the Northern District of Texas, vice a new position created by P.L. 98–353, approved July 10, 1984.

Thomas John Josefiak,
of Virginia, to be a member of the Federal Election Commission for a term expiring April 30, 1991, vice Frank P. Reiche, term expired.

Bill D. Colvin,
of Virginia, to be Inspector General, National Aeronautics and Space Administration, vice June Gibbs Brown, resigned.

Submitted July 24

Frank Shakespeare,
of Connecticut, to be Ambassador Extraordinary and Plenipotentiary of the United States of America to the Republic of Portugal.

Constance Horner,
of the District of Columbia, to be Director of the Office of Personnel Management for a term of 4 years, vice Donald J. Devine, term expired.

Withdrawn July 24

Donald J. Devine,
of Maryland, to be Director of the Office of Personnel Management for a term of 4 years (reappointment), which was sent to the Senate on March 8, 1985.

Submitted July 25

David Bryan Sentelle,
of North Carolina, to be United States District Judge for the Western District of North Carolina, vice Woodrow W. Jones, retired.

Vinton DeVane Lide,
of South Carolina, to be United States Attorney for the District of South Carolina for the term of 4 years, vice Henry Dargan McMaster, resigned.

Submitted July 26

Donald James Quigg,
of Virginia, to be Commissioner of Patents and Trademarks, vice Gerald J. Mossinghoff, resigned.

The following-named persons to be members of the National Advisory Council on Women's Educational Programs for terms expiring May 8, 1988:

> Betty Ann Gault Cordoba, of California (reappointment).
> Irene Renee Robinson, of the District of Columbia (reappointment).
> Judy F. Rolfe, of Montana (reappointment).

Larry L. DeVuyst,
of Michigan, to be a member of the Federal Farm Credit Board, Farm Credit Administration, for a term expiring March 31, 1991, vice Jewell Haaland, term expired.

Submitted July 31

Diana Powers Evans,
of Oregon, to be a member of the National Advisory Council on Women's Educational Programs for a term expiring May 8, 1988, vice Gilda Bojorquez Gjurich, term expired.

Submitted August 1

James C. Miller III,
of the District of Columbia, to be Director of the Office of Management and Budget, vice David A. Stockman, resigned.

Herbert Stuart Okun,
of the District of Columbia, a career member of the Senior Foreign Service, Class of Minister-Counselor, to be the Deputy Representative of the United States of America to the United Nations, with the rank and status of Ambassador Extraordinary and Plenipotentiary.

Hugh Montgomery,
of Virginia, to be the Alternate Representative of the United States of America for Special Political Affairs in the United Nations, with the rank of Ambassador.

George D. Gould,
of New York, to be Under Secretary of the Treasury, vice Norman B. Ture, resigned.

Charles O. Sethness,
of Massachusetts, to be an Assistant Secretary of the Treasury, vice Thomas J. Healey, resigned.

Submitted August 1—Continued

Brian B. Duff,
of Illinois, to be United States District Judge for
the Northern District of Illinois, vice a new position created by P.L. 98–353, approved July 10,
1984.

Donna R. Fitzpatrick,
of the District of Columbia, to be an Assistant
Secretary of Energy (Conservation and Renewable Energy), vice Joseph J. Tribble, resigned.

Anthony G. Sousa,
of Hawaii, to be a member of the Federal Energy
Regulatory Commission for a term expiring October 20, 1988 (reappointment).

J.C. Argetsinger,
of Virginia, to be a Commissioner of the Copyright Royalty Tribunal for the term of 7 years
from September 27, 1984, vice Douglas Coulter,
term expired.

L. William Seidman,
of Arizona, to be a member of the Board of Directors of the Federal Deposit Insurance Corporation for a term of 6 years, vice William M.
Isaac, term expired.

Robert B. Sims,
of Tennessee, to be an Assistant Secretary of Defense, vice Michael Ira Burch, resigned.

Elizabeth Flores Burkhart,
of Texas, to be a member of the National Credit
Union Administration Board for the term of 6
years expiring April 10, 1991 (reappointment).

The following-named persons to be members of
the Board of Directors of the United States
Institute of Peace for the terms indicated:

For terms of 2 years expiring January 19, 1987:

Sidney Lovett, of Connecticut (new position).
Richard John Neuhaus, of New York (new position).
W. Bruce Weinrod, of the District of Columbia
(new position).

For a term of 4 years expiring January 19, 1989:

John Norton Moore, of Virginia (new position).

Submitted September 9

Patricia Mary Byrne,
of Ohio, a career member of the Senior Foreign
Service, Class of Minister-Counselor, to be
Deputy Representative of the United States of
America in the Security Council of the United
Nations, with the rank of Ambassador.

Submitted September 9—Continued

Alan Lee Keyes,
of Maryland, to be an Assistant Secretary of State,
vice Gregory J. Newell.

Natale H. Bellocchi,
of New York, a career member of the Senior
Foreign Service, Class of Minister-Counselor, to
be Ambassador Extraordinary and Plenipotentiary of the United States of America to the Republic of Botswana.

Michael Sotirhos,
of the District of Columbia, to be Ambassador
Extraordinary and Plenipotentiary of the United
States of America to Jamaica.

Jean Broward Shevlin Gerard,
of New York, to be Ambassador Extraordinary
and Plenipotentiary of the United States of
America to Luxembourg.

Clyde D. Taylor,
of Maryland, a career member of the Senior Foreign Service, Class of Minister-Counselor, to be
Ambassador Extraordinary and Plenipotentiary of
the United States of America to the Republic of
Paraguay.

Roger Kirk,
of the District of Columbia, a career member of
the Senior Foreign Service, Class of Career Minister, to be Ambassador Extraordinary and Plenipotentiary of the United States of America to the
Socialist Republic of Romania.

Robert G. Houdek,
of Illinois, a career member of the Senior Foreign
Service, Class of Minister-Counselor, to be Ambassador Extraordinary and Plenipotentiary of
the United States of America to the Republic of
Uganda.

Malcolm Richard Wilkey,
of Texas, to be Ambassador Extraordinary and
Plenipotentiary of the United States of America
to the Oriental Republic of Uruguay.

Elliott Abrams,
of the District of Columbia, to be a member of
the Board of Directors of the Inter-American
Foundation for a term expiring September 20,
1990, vice Langhorne A. Motley.

David A. Nelson,
of Ohio, to be United States Circuit Judge for the
Sixth Circuit, vice a new position created by P.L.
98–353, approved July 10, 1984.

Submitted September 9—Continued

James L. Ryan,
of Michigan, to be United States Circuit Judge for the Sixth Circuit, vice George Clifton Edwards, Jr., retired.

Stephen V. Wilson,
of California, to be United States District Judge for the Central District of California, vice a new position created by P.L. 98–353, approved July 10, 1984.

Alan H. Nevas,
of Connecticut, to be United States District Judge for the District of Connecticut, vice a new position created by P.L. 98–353, approved July 10, 1984.

David Sam,
of Utah, to be United States District Judge for the District of Utah, vice Aldon J. Anderson, retired.

Stephen M. McNamee,
of Arizona, to be United States Attorney for the District of Arizona for the term of 4 years, vice A. Melvin McDonald, resigned.

William A. Maddox,
of Nevada, to be United States Attorney for the District of Nevada for the term of 4 years, vice Lamond Robert Mills, resigned.

Patrick M. McLaughlin,
of Ohio, to be United States Attorney for the Northern District of Ohio for the term of 4 years, vice J. William Petro.

Roger Hilfiger,
of Oklahoma, to be United States Attorney for the Eastern District of Oklahoma for the term of 4 years, vice Gary Loy Richardson, resigned.

Dennis Miles Kass,
of New York, to be an Assistant Secretary of Labor, vice Donald L. Dotson.

Ronald E. Robertson,
of Virginia, to be General Counsel of the Department of Health and Human Services, vice Juan A. del Real, resigned.

Marshall Jordan Breger,
of the District of Columbia, to be Chairman of the Administrative Conference of the United States for the term of 5 years, vice Loren A. Smith.

Carol Gene Dawson,
of Virginia, to be a Commissioner of the Consumer Product Safety Commission for a term of 7 years from October 27, 1985 (reappointment).

Submitted September 9—Continued

Lawrence J. Jensen,
of Virginia, to be an Assistant Administrator of the Environmental Protection Agency, vice Jack E. Ravan.

Jennifer Joy Manson,
of Virginia, to be an Assistant Administrator of the Environmental Protection Agency, vice Josephine S. Cooper, resigned.

M. Alan Woods,
of the District of Columbia, to be a Deputy United States Trade Representative, with the rank of Ambassador, vice Robert Emmet Lighthizer, resigned.

James P. McNeill,
of Maryland, to be an Associate Director of the Federal Emergency Management Agency, vice Fred Joseph Villella.

The following-named persons to be Federal Maritime Commissioners for the terms indicated:

For the remainder of the term expiring June 30, 1986:

Edward V. Hickey, Jr., of Virginia, vice Alan Green, Jr., resigned.

For the remainder of the term expiring June 30, 1987:

Francis J. Ivancie, of Oregon, vice Robert Setrakian, resigned.

William R. Barton,
of Virginia, to be Inspector General, General Services Administration, vice Joseph A. Sickon, resigned.

Craig C. Black,
of California, to be a member of the National Science Board, National Science Foundation, for a term expiring May 10, 1990, vice David V. Ragone, term expired.

Charles L. Hosler,
of Pennsylvania, to be a member of the National Science Board, National Science Foundation, for the remainder of the term expiring May 10, 1988, vice John H. Moore.

Roger A. Yurchuck,
of Ohio, to be a Director of the Securities Investor Protection Corporation for a term expiring December 31, 1987 (reappointment).

The following-named persons to be members of the United States Advisory Commission on Public Diplomacy for the terms indicated:

Submitted September 9—Continued
For a term expiring April 6, 1988:
Herbert Schmertz, of New York (reappointment).

For terms expiring July 1, 1988:
Edwin J. Feulner, Jr., of Virginia (reappointment).
E. Robert Wallach, of California (reappointment).

Anne E. Brunsdale,
of the District of Columbia, to be a member of the United States International Trade Commission for the term expiring June 16, 1993, vice Veronica A. Haggart, resigned.

Richard H. Francis,
of Virginia, to be President of the Solar Energy and Energy Conservation Bank, vice Joseph S. Bracewell.

Raymond D. Lett,
of Virginia, to be an Assistant Secretary of Agriculture, vice C.W. McMillan, resigned.

Raymond D. Lett,
of Virginia, to be a member of the Board of Directors of the Commodity Credit Corporation, vice C.W. McMillan.

Winston Lord,
of New York, to be Ambassador Extraordinary and Plenipotentiary of the United States of America to the People's Republic of China.

Sidney Lovett,
of Connecticut, to be a member of the Board of Directors of the United States Institute of Peace for a term of 2 years expiring January 19, 1987 (new position).

John Norton Moore,
of Virginia, to be a member of the Board of Directors of the United States Institute of Peace for a term of 4 years expiring January 19, 1989 (new position).

Richard John Neuhaus,
of New York, to be a member of the Board of Directors of the United States Institute of Peace for a term of 2 years expiring January 19, 1987 (new position).

James W. Spain,
of California, a career member of the Senior Foreign Service, Class of Career Minister, to be Ambassador Extraordinary and Plenipotentiary of the United States of America to the Democratic Socialist Republic of Sri Lanka, and to serve concurrently and without additional compensation as Ambassador Extraordinary and Plenipotentiary of

Submitted September 9—Continued
the United States of America to the Republic of Maldives.

Helen Marie Taylor,
of Virginia, to be a member of the National Council on the Humanities for a term expiring January 26, 1990, vice Mary Beth Norton, term expired, to which position she was appointed during the recess of the Senate from June 29, 1984, until July 23, 1984.

Charles A. Trabandt,
of Virginia, to be a member of the Federal Energy Regulatory Commission for a term expiring October 20, 1988, vice Georgiana H. Sheldon, term expired.

W. Bruce Weinrod,
of the District of Columbia, to be a member of the Board of Directors of the United States Institute of Peace for a term of 2 years expiring January 19, 1987 (new position).

Submitted September 11

Nicholas Tsoucalas,
of New York, to be a Judge of the United States Court of International Trade, vice Nils A. Boe, retired.

Laurence H. Silberman,
of the District of Columbia, to be United States Circuit Judge for the District of Columbia Circuit, vice a new position created by P.L. 98–353, approved July 10, 1984.

Henry T. Wingate,
of Mississippi, to be United States District Judge for the Southern District of Mississippi, vice a new position created by P.L. 98–353, approved July 10, 1984.

Paul N. Brown,
of Texas, to be United States District Judge for the Eastern District of Texas, vice a new position created by P.L. 98–353, approved July 10, 1984.

Alan A. McDonald,
of Washington, to be United States District Judge for the Eastern District of Washington, vice a new position created by P.L. 98–353, approved July 10, 1984.

Roy C. Hayes, Jr.,
of Michigan, to be United States Attorney for the Eastern District of Michigan for the term of 4 years, vice Leonard R. Gilman, deceased.

Submitted September 12

The following-named persons to be members of the United States Sentencing Commission for the time being and for the terms indicated, subject to the conditions prescribed by Public Law 98–473 of October 12, 1984, as amended (new positions):

For terms of 2 years:
Stephen G. Breyer, of Massachusetts.
Paul H. Robinson, of New Jersey.

For terms of 4 years:
Michael K. Block, of Arizona.
Helen G. Corrothers, of Arkansas.
George E. MacKinnon, of Maryland.

For terms of 6 years:
Ilene H. Nagel, of Indiana.
William W. Wilkins, Jr., of South Carolina.

William W. Wilkins, Jr.,
of South Carolina, to be Chairman of the United States Sentencing Commission (new position).

Esther Kratzer Everett,
of New York, to be a member of the National Advisory Council on Women's Educational Programs for a term expiring May 8, 1987, vice Marie Sheehan Muhler, term expired.

Submitted September 16

William Robert Graham,
of California, to be Deputy Administrator of the National Aeronautics and Space Administration, vice Hans Michael Mark, resigned.

Michael A. McManus, Jr.,
of New York, to be a member of the Board of Directors of the Communications Satellite Corporation until the date of the annual meeting of the Corporation in 1987, vice Robert M. Garrick, term expired.

Submitted September 17

The following-named persons to be members of the Board of Regents of the Uniformed Services University of the Health Sciences for terms expiring June 20, 1991:
Carol Johnson Johns, of Maryland, vice Lauro F. Cavazos, term expired.
Mario Efrain Ramirez, of Texas, vice William R. Roy, term expired.

Paul Freedenberg,
of Maryland, to be an Assistant Secretary of Commerce, vice Lawrence J. Brady, resigned.

Roger Dale Semerad,
of Maryland, to be an Assistant Secretary of Labor, vice Frank C. Casillas, resigned.

Submitted September 17—Continued
Hazel M. Richardson,
of California, to be a member of the National Advisory Council on Women's Educational Programs for a term expiring May 8, 1988, vice Eleanor Thomas Elliott, term expired.

Mark L. Edelman,
an Assistant Administrator of the Agency for International Development, to be a member of the Board of Directors of the African Development Foundation for a term expiring September 22, 1991 (reappointment).

Neal B. Freeman,
of Virginia, to be a member of the Board of Directors of the Communications Satellite Corporation until the date of the annual meeting of the Corporation in 1988 (reappointment).

Jeffrey I. Zuckerman,
of Maryland, to be General Counsel of the Equal Employment Opportunity Commission for a term of 4 years, vice David L. Slate, resigned.

Ford Barney Ford,
of Virginia, to be a member of the Federal Mine Safety and Health Review Commission for a term of 6 years expiring August 30, 1990, vice Frank F. Jestrab, term expired.

Barbara J.H. Taylor,
of Maryland, to be a member of the National Commission on Libraries and Information Science for a term expiring July 19, 1990, vice Gordon M. Ambach, term expired.

Roger William Jepsen,
of Iowa, to be a member of the National Credit Union Administration Board for the remainder of the term expiring August 2, 1987, vice Edgar F. Callahan, resigned.

James M. Stephens,
of Virginia, to be a member of the National Labor Relations Board for the term of 5 years expiring August 27, 1990, vice Robert P. Hunter, term expired.

William J. Merrell, Jr.,
of Texas, to be an Assistant Director of the National Science Foundation, vice Floyd James Rutherford.

Joseph A. Grundfest,
of the District of Columbia, to be a member of the Securities and Exchange Commission for the term expiring June 5, 1990, vice Charles L. Marinaccio, term expired.

Submitted September 17—Continued

To be Representatives and Alternate Representatives of the United States of America to the 40th Session of the General Assembly of the United Nations:

Representatives:

Vernon A. Walters, of Florida.

Herbert Stuart Okun, of the District of Columbia.

Daniel A. Mica, United States Representative from the State of Florida.

Gerald B.H. Solomon, United States Representative from the State of New York.

John David Lodge, of Connecticut.

Alternate Representatives:

Patricia Mary Byrne, of Ohio.

Hugh Montgomery, of Virginia.

Joseph Verner Reed, of New York.

Robinson Risner, of Texas.

Withdrawn September 17

Peter Douglas Keisler,
of Connecticut, to be a member of the National Advisory Council on Women's Educational Programs for a term expiring May 8, 1987, vice Maria Pornaby Shuhi, term expired, to which position he was appointed during the last recess of the Senate, which was sent to the Senate on January 3, 1985.

Submitted September 18

The following-named persons to be members of the Board of Directors of the United States Institute of Peace for terms of 4 years expiring January 19, 1989 (new positions):

Dennis L. Bark, of California.

Evron M. Kirkpatrick, of Maryland.

The following-named persons to the positions indicated, to which positions they were appointed during the last recess of the Senate:

Vance L. Clark,
of California, to be Administrator of the Farmers Home Administration, vice Charles Wilson Shuman, resigned.

Thomas John Josefiak,
of Virginia, to be a member of the Federal Election Commission for a term expiring April 30, 1991, vice Frank P. Reiche, term expired.

Hugh Montgomery,
of Virginia, to be the Alternate Representative of the United States of America for Special Political Affairs in the United Nations, with the rank of Ambassador.

Submitted September 18—Continued

Herbert Stuart Okun,
of the District of Columbia, a career member of the Senior Foreign Service, Class of Minister-Counselor, to be the Deputy Representative of the United States of America to the United Nations, with the rank and status of Ambassador Extraordinary and Plenipotentiary.

Robert E. Rader, Jr.,
of Texas, to be a member of the Occupational Safety and Health Review Commission for the term expiring April 27, 1991, vice Timothy F. Cleary, term expired.

John R. Wall,
of Ohio, to be a member of the Occupational Safety and Health Review Commission for the remainder of the term expiring April 27, 1987, vice Robert A. Rowland.

Submitted September 20

Richard N. Holwill,
of the District of Columbia, to be a member of the board of the Panama Canal Commission, vice John Alden Bushnell.

The following-named persons to be the Representative and Alternate Representatives of the United States of America to the Twenty-ninth Session of the General Conference of the International Atomic Energy Agency:

Representative:

Danny J. Boggs, of Kentucky.

Alternate Representatives:

Richard T. Kennedy, of the District of Columbia.

Nunzio J. Palladino, of Pennsylvania.

Bruce Chapman, of Washington.

Submitted September 23

Mary L. Walker,
of Maryland, to be an Assistant Secretary of Energy (Environment, Safety and Health), vice William Addison Vaughan, resigned.

John A. Gaughan,
of Maryland, to be Administrator of the Maritime Administration, vice Harold E. Shear, resigned.

Kenneth John Hill,
of Virginia, to be a member of the National Transportation Safety Board for the remainder of the term expiring December 31, 1986, vice Donald D. Engen, resigned.

Submitted September 23—Continued

John K. Lauber,
of California, to be a member of the National Transportation Safety Board for the term expiring December 31, 1989, vice George Herbert Patrick Bursley, term expired.

Submitted September 26

Charles J. Cooper,
of Virginia, to be an Assistant Attorney General, vice Theodore B. Olson, resigned.

Stephen J. Markman,
of Virginia, to be an Assistant Attorney General, vice Harold J. Lezar, Jr., resigned.

Charles Fried,
of Massachusetts, to be Solicitor General of the United States, vice Rex E. Lee, resigned.

Donald R. Brookshier,
of Illinois, to be United States Marshal for the Southern District of Illinois for the term of 4 years, vice William J. Nettles, resigned.

Submitted September 27

Joseph Verner Reed,
of Connecticut, to be the Representative of the United States of America on the Economic and Social Council of the United Nations, with the rank of Ambassador.

Fred L. Hartley,
of California, for the rank of Ambassador during the tenure of his service as Commissioner General of the United States Exhibition for the International Exposition, Vancouver, British Columbia, Canada, 1986.

John S. Rhoades, Sr.,
of California, to be United States District Judge for the Southern District of California, vice Leland C. Nielsen, retired.

Lyle E. Strom,
of Nebraska, to be United States District Judge for the District of Nebraska, vice Albert G. Schatz, deceased.

Jose Antonio Fuste,
of Puerto Rico, to be United States District Judge for the District of Puerto Rico, vice Juan R. Torruella Del Valle, elevated.

Richard H. Battey,
of South Dakota, to be United States District Judge for the District of South Dakota, vice Andrew W. Bogue, retired.

Submitted September 27—Continued

Ross O. Swimmer,
of Oklahoma, to be an Assistant Secretary of the Interior, vice Kenneth L. Smith, resigned.

Submitted September 30

Robert L. Barry,
of New Hampshire, a career member of the Senior Foreign Service, Class of Career Minister, for the rank of Ambassador during the tenure of his service as United States Representative to the Conference on Confidence and Security Building Measures and Disarmament in Europe.

Julius W. Becton, Jr.,
of Virginia, to be Director of the Federal Emergency Management Agency, vice Louis O. Giuffrida, resigned.

Francis S.M. Hodsoll,
of Virginia, to be Chairman of the National Endowment for the Arts for a term of 4 years (reappointment).

The following-named persons to be members of the National Commission on Libraries and Information Science for terms expiring July 19, 1990:

Lee Edwards, of Maryland, vice Paulette H. Holahan, term expired.

Frank Gannon, of New York, vice Charles William Benton, term expired.

Submitted October 2

Richard Schifter,
of Maryland, to be Assistant Secretary of State for Human Rights and Humanitarian Affairs, vice Elliott Abrams, resigned.

Edward R. Korman,
of New York, to be United States District Judge for the Eastern District of New York, vice a new position created by P.L. 98–353, approved July 10, 1984.

C. Everett Koop,
of Pennsylvania, to be Surgeon General of the Public Health Service for a term of 4 years (reappointment).

Submitted October 4

Joseph Ghougassian,
of California, to be Ambassador Extraordinary and Plenipotentiary of the United States of America to the State of Qatar.

Submitted October 4—Continued

W. Scott Thompson,
of New Hampshire, to be a member of the Board
of Directors of the United States Institute of
Peace for a term of 4 years expiring January 19,
1989 (new position).

Submitted October 7

David R. Thompson,
of California, to be United States Circuit Judge
for the Ninth Circuit, vice a new position created
by P.L. 98–353, approved July 10, 1984.

Bobby Ray Baldock,
of New Mexico, to be United States Circuit Judge
for the Tenth Circuit, vice Oliver Seth, retired.

Robert E. Cowen,
of New Jersey, to be United States District Judge
for the District of New Jersey, vice a new position created by P.L. 98–353, approved July 10,
1984.

The following-named persons to be members of
the Board of Governors of the United States
Postal Service for the terms indicated:

*For the remainder of the term expiring December
8, 1988:*

   J.H. Tyler McConnell, of Delaware, vice David
   E. Babcock, resigned.

*For the remainder of the term expiring December
8, 1992:*

   Barry D. Schreiber, of Florida, vice Frieda
   Waldman.

For the term expiring December 8, 1993:

   Robert Setrakian, of California, vice William J.
   Sullivan, term expired.

Submitted October 8

Carolyn Miller Parr,
of Maryland, to be a Judge of the United States
Tax Court for a term expiring 15 years after she
takes office, vice William M. Fay.

B. John Williams, Jr.,
of Virginia, to be a Judge of the United States
Tax Court for a term expiring 15 years after he
takes office, vice Howard A. Dawson, Jr.

Submitted October 9

William J. Zloch,
of Florida, to be United States District Judge for
the Southern District of Florida, vice a new position created by P.L. 98–353, approved July 10,
1984.

Submitted October 9—Continued

Dennis Eugene Whitfield,
of Virginia, to be Under Secretary of Labor, vice
Ford Barney Ford.

Submitted October 10

Donald J. Bouchard,
of Maine, to be an Assistant Secretary of State,
vice Robert E. Lamb.

Adele Langston Rogers,
of Maryland, to be an Alternate Representative
of the United States of America to the Fortieth
Session of the General Assembly of the United
Nations.

Ralph W. Tarr,
of Virginia, to be Solicitor of the Department of
the Interior, vice Frank K. Richardson, resigned.

C.M. Naeve,
of Virginia, to be a member of the Federal
Energy Regulatory Commission for a term expiring October 20, 1989, vice Oliver G. Richard III,
resigned.

The following-named persons to be members of
the Board for International Broadcasting for
terms expiring April 28, 1988 (reappointments):

   Edward Noonan Ney, of New York.

   Michael Novak, of the District of Columbia.

Warren J. Baker,
of California, to be a member of the National
Science Board, National Science Foundation, for
a term expiring May 10, 1988, vice Marian E.
Koshland, term expired.

William J. Doyle III,
of Maryland, to be Inspector General, Railroad
Retirement Board (new position).

Submitted October 16

James Curtis Mack II,
of California, to be Deputy Administrator of the
National Oceanic and Atmospheric Administration, vice Anthony J. Calio.

James L. Buckley,
of Connecticut, to be United States Circuit Judge
for the District of Columbia Circuit, vice Edward
Allen Tamm, deceased.

John T. Noonan, Jr.,
of California, to be United States Circuit Judge
for the Ninth Circuit, vice a new position created
by P.L. 98–353, approved July 10, 1984.

Submitted October 16—Continued

Glenn L. Archer, Jr.,
of Virginia, to be United States Circuit Judge for the Federal Circuit, vice Jack R. Miller, retired.

Jane R. Roth,
of Delaware, to be United States District Judge for the District of Delaware, vice Walter K. Stapleton, elevated.

Albert I. Moon, Jr.,
of Hawaii, to be United States District Judge for the District of Hawaii, vice a new position created by P.L. 98–353, approved July 10, 1984.

Patrick A. Conmy,
of North Dakota, to be United States District Judge for the District of North Dakota, vice Bruce M. Van Sickle, retired.

Lynn N. Hughes,
of Texas, to be United States District Judge for the Southern District of Texas, vice Robert O'Conor, Jr., resigned.

Submitted October 17

Gregory J. Newell,
of Virginia, to be Ambassador Extraordinary and Plenipotentiary of the United States of America to Sweden.

Jennifer Lynn Dorn,
of Maryland, to be Associate Deputy Secretary of Transportation (new position).

Bruce M. Carnes,
of Virginia, to be Deputy Under Secretary for Planning, Budget and Evaluation, Department of Education, vice Gary L. Bauer.

Edward H. Fleischman,
of New Jersey, to be a member of the Securities and Exchange Commission for the remainder of the term expiring June 5, 1987, vice James C. Treadway, Jr., resigned.

Allen Weinstein,
of the District of Columbia, to be a member of the Board of Directors of the United States Institute of Peace for a term of 4 years expiring January 19, 1989 (new position).

Submitted October 21

Charles Roger Carlisle,
of Vermont, for the rank of Ambassador during his tenure of service as United States Negotiator on Textile Matters.

Robert Logan Clarke,
of Texas, to be Comptroller of the Currency for a term of 5 years, vice C.T. Conover, resigned.

Submitted October 21—Continued

Gerald Ralph Riso,
of New York, to be an Assistant Secretary of the Interior, vice J. Robinson West, resigned.

Jerry Lee Calhoun,
of Washington, to be a member of the Federal Labor Relations Authority for the remainder of the term expiring July 29, 1987, vice Barbara Jean Mahone, resigned.

William J. McGinnis, Jr.,
of New Jersey, to be a member of the Federal Labor Relations Authority for a term of 5 years expiring July 1, 1989, vice Ronald W. Haughton, term expired, to which position he was appointed during the recess of the Senate from October 12, 1984, until January 3, 1985.

Submitted October 22

Alan B. Johnson,
of Wyoming, to be United States District Judge for the District of Wyoming, vice a new position created by P.L. 98–353, approved July 10, 1984.

Submitted October 23

Frank X. Altimari,
of New York, to be United States Circuit Judge for the Second Circuit, vice Ellsworth A. Van-Graafeiland, retired.

Jefferson B. Sessions III,
of Alabama, to be United States District Judge for the Southern District of Alabama, vice a new position created by P.L. 98–353, approved July 10, 1984.

Morris S. Arnold,
of Arkansas, to be United States District Judge for the Western District of Arkansas, vice a new position created by P.L. 98–353, approved July 10, 1984.

Robert L. Miller, Jr.,
of Indiana, to be United States District Judge for the Northern District of Indiana, vice a new position created by P.L. 98–353, approved July 10, 1984.

Garrett E. Brown, Jr.,
of New Jersey, to be United States District Judge for the District of New Jersey, vice a new position created by P.L. 98–353, approved July 10, 1984.

Stanley A. Twardy, Jr.,
of Connecticut, to be United States Attorney for the District of Connecticut for the term of 4 years, vice Alan H. Nevas.

Submitted October 23—Continued

William C. Carpenter, Jr.,
of Delaware, to be United States Attorney for the District of Delaware for the term of 4 years, vice Joseph J. Farnan, Jr., resigned.

Benjamin L. Burgess, Jr.,
of Kansas, to be United States Attorney for the District of Kansas for the term of 4 years, vice Jim J. Marquez, resigned.

Marvin Collins,
of Texas, to be United States Attorney for the Northern District of Texas for the term of 4 years, vice James A. Rolfe, resigned.

Submitted October 25

John R. Bolton,
of Virginia, to be an Assistant Attorney General, vice Robert A. McConnell, resigned.

Submitted October 28

Laurence William Lane, Jr.,
of California, to be Ambassador Extraordinary and Plenipotentiary of the United States of America to Australia and to serve concurrently and without additional compensation as Ambassador Extraordinary and Plenipotentiary of the United States of America to the Republic of Nauru.

John Edwin Upston,
of Virginia, to be Ambassador Extraordinary and Plenipotentiary of the United States of America to the Republic of Rwanda.

Sam A. Nixon,
of Texas, to be a member of the Board of Regents of the Uniformed Services University of the Health Sciences for a term expiring June 20, 1991, vice Caro Elise Luhrs, term expired.

Alexander Hansen Good,
of the District of Columbia, to be Director General of the United States and Foreign Commercial Service, vice Kenneth S. George.

Helen M. Witt,
of Pennsylvania, to be a member of the National Mediation Board for the term expiring July 1, 1988 (reappointment).

Charles Edward Horner,
of the District of Columbia, to be an Associate Director of the United States Information Agency, vice Charles E. Courtney.

Submitted October 29

Thomas J. McAvoy,
of New York, to be United States District Judge for the Northern District of New York, vice a new position created by P.L. 98–353, approved July 10, 1984.

Sidney A. Fitzwater,
of Texas, to be United States District Judge for the Northern District of Texas, vice Robert M. Hill, elevated.

Submitted October 30

Francis Anthony Keating II,
of Oklahoma, to be an Assistant Secretary of the Treasury, vice John M. Walker, Jr.

Nanette Fabray MacDougall,
of California, to be a member of the National Council on the Handicapped for a term expiring September 17, 1987 (reappointment).

Submitted October 31

Deanell Reece Tacha,
of Kansas, to be United States Circuit Judge for the Tenth Circuit, vice a new position created by P.L. 98–353, approved July 10, 1984.

Submitted November 1

Michael H. Mobbs,
of the District of Columbia, to be an Assistant Director of the United States Arms Control and Disarmament Agency, vice Henry F. Cooper, Jr., resigning.

Wendell L. Willkie II,
of the District of Columbia, to be General Counsel, Department of Education, vice Maureen E. Corcoran.

James J. Carey,
of Illinois, to be a Federal Maritime Commissioner for the term expiring June 30, 1990 (reappointment).

Charles L. Woods,
of California, to be a member of the National Mediation Board for the reminder of the term expiring July 1, 1986, vice Robert Oberndoerfer Harris, resigned.

Walter J. Shea,
of Maryland, to be a member of the Board of the Panama Canal Commission, vice William Sidell.

William R. Kintner,
of Pennsylvania, to be a member of the Board of Directors of the United States Institute of Peace

Submitted November 1—Continued
for a term of 2 years expiring January 19, 1987 (new position).

Submitted November 6

Paul Matthews Cleveland,
of Florida, a career member of the Senior Foreign Service, Class of Minister-Counselor, to be Ambassador Extraordinary and Plenipotentiary of the United States of America to New Zealand.

J. Steven Griles,
of Virginia, to be an Assistant Secretary of the Interior, vice Garrey Edward Carruthers, resigned.

Sylvester R. Foley, Jr.,
of Florida, to be an Assistant Secretary of Energy (Defense Programs), vice William W. Hoover, resigned.

Submitted November 7

J. Spencer Letts,
of California, to be United States District Judge for the Central District of California, vice a new position created by P.L. 98–353, approved July 10, 1984.

Dickran M. Tevrizian, Jr.,
of California, to be United States District Judge for the Central District of California, vice a new position created by P.L. 98–353, approved July 10, 1984.

George H. Revercomb,
of Virginia, to be United States District Judge for the District of Columbia, vice Thomas A. Flannery, retired.

Harry D. Leinenweber,
of Illinois, to be United States District Judge for the Northern District of Illinois, vice a new position created by P.L. 98–353, approved July 10, 1984.

Submitted November 12

Rockwell Anthony Schnabel,
of California, to be Ambassador Extraordinary and Plenipotentiary of the United States of America to the Republic of Finland.

The following-named persons to be members of the Board of Directors of the National Institute of Building Sciences for terms expiring September 7, 1986:

Fred E. Hummel, of California, vice Herbert H. Swinburne, term expired.
Philip D. Winn, of Colorado, vice Rudard A. Jones, term expired.

Submitted November 13

James R. Richards,
of Virginia, to be Inspector General, Department of the Interior, vice Richard Mulberry, resigned.

Harold L. Cushenberry, Jr.,
of the District of Columbia, to be an Associate Judge of the Superior Court of the District of Columbia for a term of 15 years, vice Paul F. McArdle.

Michael L. Rankin,
of the District of Columbia, to be an Associate Judge of the Superior Court of the District of Columbia for a term of 15 years, vice Nicholas S. Nunzio.

Lois Burke Shepard,
of Maryland, to be Director of the Institute of Museum Services, vice Susan E. Phillips.

Submitted November 14

Russell A. Rourke,
of Maryland, to be Secretary of the Air Force, vice Verne Orr.

Duross Fitzpatrick,
of Georgia, to be United States District Judge for the Middle District of Georgia, vice a new position created by P.L. 98–353, approved July 10, 1984.

C. Dale Duvall,
of Washington, to be Commissioner of Reclamation, vice Robert N. Broadbent.

John C. Layton,
of Virginia, to be Inspector General of the Department of Energy, vice James R. Richards.

David M.L. Lindahl,
of Virginia, to be Director of the Office of Alcohol Fuels, vice James G. Stearns, resigned.

Submitted November 15

Arnold I. Burns,
of New York, to be Associate Attorney General, vice D. Lowell Jensen.

Arch L. Madsen,
of Utah, to be a member of the Board for International Broadcasting for a term expiring April 28, 1987 (reappointment).

Truman McGill Hobbs,
of Alabama, to be a member of the Board of Trustees of the Harry S Truman Scholarship Foundation for a term expiring December 10, 1991 (reappointment).

Submitted November 15—Continued

Thomas A. Bolan,
of New York, to be a member of the Board of Directors of the Overseas Private Investment Corporation for a term expiring December 17, 1988 (reappointment).

Submitted November 22

Chapman B. Cox,
of Virginia, to be an Assistant Secretary of Defense, vice Lawrence J. Korb, resigned.

Robert B. Barker,
of California, to be Chairman of the Military Liaison Committee to the Department of Energy, vice Richard L. Wagner, Jr.

Submitted November 25

Frank B. Sollars,
of Ohio, to be a member of the Board of Directors of the National Consumer Cooperative Bank for a term of 3 years (reappointment).

Submitted November 26

Howard V. Adair,
of Alabama, to be United States Marshal for the Southern District of Alabama for the term of 4 years (reappointment).

Robert L. Pavlak, Sr.,
of Minnesota, to be United States Marshal for the District of Minnesota for the term of 4 years (reappointment).

Kernan H. Bagley,
of Oregon, to be United States Marshal for the District of Oregon for the term of 4 years (reappointment).

Submitted December 3

Chester A. Crocker,
an Assistant Secretary of State, to be a member of the Board of Directors of the African Development Foundation for a term expiring September 22, 1991 (reappointment).

Submitted December 4

Otis R. Bowen,
of Indiana, to be Secretary of Health and Human Services.

David R. Hansen,
of Iowa, to be United States District Judge for the Northern District of Iowa, vice Edward J. McManus, retired.

Submitted December 4—Continued

Walter J. Gex III,
of Mississippi, to be United States District Judge for the Southern District of Mississippi, vice a new position created by P.L. 98–353, approved July 10, 1984.

Miriam G. Cedarbaum,
of New York, to be United States District Judge of the Southern District of New York, vice Charles E. Stewart, Jr., retired.

Robert J. Bryan,
of Washington, to be United States District Judge for the Western District of Washington, vice a new position created by P.L. 98–353, approved July 10, 1984.

Submitted December 6

Margaret M. O'Shaughnessy Heckler,
of Massachusetts, to be Ambassador Extraordinary and Plenipotentiary of the United States of America to Ireland.

Submitted December 9

Danny J. Boggs,
of Kentucky, to be United States Circuit Judge for the Sixth Circuit, vice a new position created by P.L. 98–353, approved July 10, 1984.

Joseph M. Whittle,
of Kentucky, to be United States Attorney for the Western District of Kentucky for the term of 4 years, vice Ronald E. Meredith, resigned.

Thomas C. Greene,
of Alabama, to be United States Marshal for the Northern District of Alabama for the term of 4 years (reappointment).

Melvin E. Jones,
of Alabama, to be United States Marshal for the Middle District of Alabama for the term of 4 years (reappointment).

Herman Wirshing Rodriquez,
of Puerto Rico, to be United States Marshal for the District of Puerto Rico for the term of 4 years, vice Jose A. Lopez.

Roger Ray,
of Virginia, to be United States Marshal for the Eastern District of Virginia for the term of 4 years, vice Herbert M. Rutherford III, resigned.

Delaine Roberts,
of Wyoming, to be United States Marshal for the District of Wyoming for the term of 4 years (reappointment).

Submitted December 10

H. Lawrence Garrett III,
of Virginia, to be General Counsel of the Department of Defense, vice Chapman B. Cox.

Jed Dean Christensen,
of Virginia, to be Director of the Office of Surface Mining Reclamation and Enforcement, vice John D. Ward, resigned.

Della M. Newman,
of Washington, to be a member of the National Advisory Council on Women's Educational Programs for the remainder of the term expiring May 8, 1987, vice Peter Douglas Keisler, resigned.

J. Craig Potter,
of Virginia, to be an Assistant Administrator of the Environmental Protection Agency, vice Joseph A. Cannon.

Henry F. Schickling,
of Pennsylvania, to be a member of the Board of Directors of the Overseas Private Investment Corporation for a term expiring December 17, 1988 (reappointment).

Submitted December 11

Wayne D. Angell,
of Kansas, to be a member of the Board of Governors of the Federal Reserve System for the unexpired term of 14 years from February 1, 1980, vice Lyle Elden Gramley, resigned.

Manuel H. Johnson,
of Virginia, to be a member of the Board of Governors of the Federal Reserve System for a term of 14 years from February 1, 1986, vice J. Charles Partee, term expiring.

Submitted December 12

Morton I. Abramowitz,
of Massachusetts, a career member of the Senior Foreign Service, Class of Career Minister, to be an Assistant Secretary of State (new position).

H. Allen Holmes,
of the District of Columbia, a career member of the Senior Foreign Service, Class of Career Minister, to be an Assistant Secretary of State (new position).

Submitted December 12—Continued

Larry K. Mellinger,
of California, to be United States Alternate Executive Director of the Inter-American Development Bank, vice Hugh W. Foster.

Submitted December 13

James L. Malone,
of Virginia, to be Ambassador Extraordinary and Plenipotentiary of the United States of America to Belize.

Michael A. Samuels,
of the District of Columbia, to be a Deputy United States Trade Representative, with the rank of Ambassador, vice Peter Otto Murphy.

Hugh W. Foster,
of California, to be United States Alternate Executive Director of the International Bank for Reconstruction and Development for a term of 2 years (reappointment).

The following-named persons to be members of the National Council on Educational Research for terms expiring September 30, 1988:

Donald Barr, of Connecticut (reappointment).
James Harvey Harrison, Jr., of Virginia (reappointment).
Robert H. Mattson, of Oregon, vice Paul Copperman, term expired.

Submitted December 18

Daniel Oliver,
of Connecticut, to be a Federal Trade Commissioner for the unexpired term of 7 years from September 26, 1981, vice James C. Miller III.

Joan M. Gubbins,
of Indiana, to be a member of the National Council on Educational Research for a term expiring September 30, 1988 (reappointment).

Submitted December 19

Paul H. Lamboley,
of Nevada, to be a member of the Interstate Commerce Commission for a term expiring December 31, 1989 (reappointment).

Submitted December 20

Frances M. Norris,
of Virginia, to be Assistant Secretary for Legislation and Public Affairs, Department of Education, vice Anne Graham.

Appendix C—Checklist of White House Press Releases

The following list contains releases of the Office of the Press Secretary which are not included in this book.

Released June 30

Transcript:
Interview of Assistant to the President for National Security Affairs Robert C. McFarlane by ABC News

Transcript:
Interview of Assistant to the President for National Security Affairs Robert C. McFarlane by CBS News

Transcript:
Interview of Assistant to the President for National Security Affairs Robert C. McFarlane by NBC News

Transcript:
Interview of Assistant to the President for National Security Affairs Robert C. McFarlane by Cable Network News

Transcript:
Interview of Assistant to the President for National Security Affairs Robert C. McFarlane by Independent Network News

Transcript:
Press briefing on the release of American hostages from the Trans World Airlines hijacking incident—by Secretary of State George P. Shultz

Summary of events:
Trans World Airlines hijacking incident

Released July 2

Statement:
Sales of new, single-family homes in May—by Larry M. Speakes, Principal Deputy Press Secretary to the President

Released July 3

Transcript:
Press briefing on the planned summit meeting between the President and Soviet General Secretary Mikhail Gorbachev on November 19–20 in Geneva, Switzerland—by Secretary of State George P. Shultz

Released July 8

Fact sheet:
National Defense Stockpile policy

Released July 9

Transcript:
Press briefing following the President's meeting with the Republican congressional leadership on the budget and deficit reduction—by Senate Majority Leader Robert Dole and House Minority Leader Robert H. Michel

Released July 10

Transcript:
Press briefing following the President's meeting with congressional Budget Committee chairmen—by Senator Pete V. Domenici of New Mexico and Congressman William H. Gray III of Pennsylvania

Released July 11

Announcement:
Nomination of Curtis E. von Kann to be an Associate Judge of the Superior Court of the District of Columbia

Released July 12

Statement:
Producer Price Index figures—by Larry M. Speakes, Principal Deputy Press Secretary to the President

Released July 15

Statement:
On the President's recovery from surgery—by Larry M. Speakes, Principal Deputy Press Secretary to the President

Statement:
President's Blue Ribbon Commission on Defense Management—by Larry M. Speakes, Principal Deputy Press Secretary to the President

Announcement:
Nomination of Lydia E. Glover to be United States Marshal for the District of South Carolina

Released July 16

Statement:
On the President's recovery from surgery—by Larry M. Speakes, Principal Deputy Press Secretary to the President (2 releases)

Announcement:
Receipt of the report of the Blue Ribbon Task Group on Nuclear Weapons Program Management

Released July 17

Statement:
On the President's recovery from surgery—by Larry M. Speakes, Principal Deputy Press Secretary to the President (2 releases)

Statement:
Personal income, disposable income, personal consumption, and housing starts figures for June—by Larry M. Speakes, Principal Deputy Press Secretary to the President

Released July 18

Statement:
On the President's recovery from surgery—by Larry M. Speakes, Principal Deputy Press Secretary to the President (2 releases)

Statement:
Gross national product preliminary estimate figures for the second quarter and the Index of Industrial Production figures for June—by Larry M. Speakes, Principal Deputy Press Secretary to the President

Announcement:
Nomination of Ferdinand F. Fernandez to be United States District Judge for the Central District of California

Announcement:
Nomination of Brian Paul Joffrion to be United States Marshal for the Western District of Louisiana

Released July 19

Statement:
On the President's recovery from surgery—by Larry M. Speakes, Principal Deputy Press Secretary to the President

Transcript:
Press briefing on the conclusion of the second round of the Soviet-U.S. nuclear and space arms negotiations—by Robert C. McFarlane, Assistant to the President for National Security Affairs

Released July 19—Continued
Statement:
On the President's schedule—by Larry M. Speakes, Principal Deputy Press Secretary to the President

Released July 23

Statement:
Consumer Price Index figures for June—by Larry M. Speakes, Principal Deputy Press Secretary to the President

Announcement:
Nomination of Stephen H. Anderson to be United States Circuit Judge for the Tenth Circuit

Announcement:
Nomination of Glen H. Davidson to be United States District Judge for the Northern District of Mississippi

Announcement:
Nomination of Ralph B. Guy, Jr., to be United States Circuit Judge for the Sixth Circuit

Announcement:
Nomination of Robert B. Maloney to be United States District Judge for the Northern District of Texas

Advance text:
Toast at the state dinner for President Li Xiannian of China

Released July 25

Announcement:
Nomination of Vinton DeVane Lide to be United States Attorney for the District of South Carolina

Announcement:
Nomination of David Bryan Sentelle to be United States District Judge for the Western District of North Carolina

Released July 29

Statement:
Administration economic assumptions—by Beryl W. Sprinkel, Chairman of the Council of Economic Advisers (2 releases)

Released July 30

Statement:
Trade with Japan—by Secretary of the Treasury James A. Baker III, Chairman of the Economic Policy Council

Released July 31

Statement:
Index of leading economic indicators for June—by Larry M. Speakes, Principal Deputy Press Secretary to the President

Released August 1

Announcement:
Nomination of Brian B. Duff to be United States District Judge for the Northern District of Illinois

Fact sheet:
Shuttle pricing for foreign and commercial users

Released August 2

Statement:
Unemployment rate figures for July—by Larry M. Speakes, Principal Deputy Press Secretary to the President

Announcement:
Nomination of William A. Maddox to be United States Attorney for the District of Nevada

Announcement:
Nomination of Patrick M. McLaughlin to be United States Attorney for the Northern District of Ohio

Announcement:
Nomination of Roger Hilfiger to be United States Attorney for the Eastern District of Oklahoma

Released August 8

Announcement:
EO 12528, Presidential Board of Advisors on Private Sector Initiatives

Released August 12

Statement:
Producer Price Index figures—by Larry M. Speakes, Principal Deputy Press Secretary to the President

Released August 13

Transcript:
Press briefing on a meeting with members of the White House staff to discuss plans and an agenda for 1985–1986—by Donald T. Regan, Assistant to the President and Chief of Staff, and Robert C. McFarlane, Assistant to the President for National Security Affairs

Released August 14

Statement:
President's meeting with the Vice President to discuss trade issues—by Larry M. Speakes, Principal Deputy Press Secretary to the President

Released August 15

Transcript:
Press briefing on the announcement by President Pieter Willem Botha of South Africa on changes in the system of apartheid—by Robert C. McFarlane, Assistant to the President for National Security Affairs

Released August 20

Statement:
Gross national product estimates for second quarter—by Larry M. Speakes, Principal Deputy Press Secretary to the President

Released August 22

Advance text:
Remarks at a California Republican Party fundraising dinner in Los Angeles

Statement:
Consumer Price Index figures for July—by Larry M. Speakes, Principal Deputy Press Secretary to the President

Released August 27

Fact sheet:
1984 Census Bureau report on family income and poverty

Statement:
Responses to news stories concerning the U.S. investigation of a Soviet tracking agent and on the coup in Nigeria—by Larry M. Speakes, Principal Deputy Press Secretary to the President

Released August 28

Fact sheet:
Nonrubber footwear industry

Transcript:
Press briefing on the nonrubber footwear industry—by Clayton Yeutter, U.S. Trade Representative

Released August 29

Statement:
New homes sales figures—by Larry M. Speakes, Principal Deputy Press Secretary to the President

Released August 30

Statement:
Leading economic indicators for July—by Larry M. Speakes, Principal Deputy Press Secretary to the President

Released September 5

Advance text:
Remarks to students and faculty at North Carolina State University in Releigh

Released September 6

Announcement:
Nomination of David Sam to be United States District Judge for the District of Utah

Announcement:
Nomination of Alan H. Nevas to be United States District Judge for the District of Connecticut

Announcement:
Nomination of Stephen V. Wilson to be United States District Judge for the Central District of California

Announcement:
Nomination of James L. Ryan to be United States Circuit Judge for the Sixth Circuit

Announcement:
Nomination of David A. Nelson to be United States Circuit Judge for the Sixth Circuit

Announcement:
Nomination of Stephen M. McNamee to be United States Attorney for the District of Arizona

Transcript:
Press briefing on recent economic trends—by Beryl W. Sprinkel, Chairman of the Council of Economic Advisers

Fact sheet:
Indicators of real economic activity

Released September 7

Fact sheet:
Section 301 of the Trade Act of 1974

Transcript:
Press briefing on U.S. international trade—by Clayton Yeutter, U.S. Trade Representative

Released September 9

Fact sheet:
Economic sanctions against South Africa

Released September 9—Continued
Statement by the President:
Economic sanctions against South Africa (as read to reporters in the Oval Office)

Transcript:
Press briefing on U.S. actions regarding economic sanctions against South Africa—by Secretary of State George P. Shultz

Released September 10

Announcement:
Nomination of Nicholas Tsoucalas to be a Judge of the United States Court of International Trade

Announcement:
Nomination of Roy C. Hayes, Jr., to be United States Attorney for the Eastern District of Michigan

Announcement:
Nomination of Laurence H. Silberman to be United States Circuit Judge for the District of Columbia Circuit

Announcement:
Nomination of Henry T. Wingate to be United States District Judge for the Southern District of Mississippi

Announcement:
Nomination of Paul N. Brown to be United States District Judge for the Eastern District of Texas

Announcement:
Nomination of Alan A. McDonald to be United States District Judge for the Eastern District of Washington

Released September 11

Transcript:
Press briefing following the President's meeting with the Republican congressional leadership to discuss South Africa, trade legislation, tax reform, and the continuing budget resolution—by House Minority Leader Robert H. Michel

Released September 12

Advance text:
Remarks to senior citizens in Tampa, FL

Released September 13

Transcript:
Press briefing on the Nation's economy—by Beryl W. Sprinkel, Chairman of the Council of Economic Advisers

Released September 17

Announcement:
On the President's meeting with the President's Blue Ribbon Commission on Defense Management

Released September 18

Advance text:
Remarks to citizens in Concord, NH

Released September 20

Statement:
Gross national product for the second quarter—by Larry M. Speakes, Principal Deputy Press Secretary to the President

Released September 23

Advance text:
Remarks to business leaders and members of the President's Export Council and Advisory Committee for Trade Negotiations

Fact sheet:
The President's trade policy action plan

Released September 24

Advance text:
Remarks to citizens in Athens, TN

Statement:
Consumer Price Index figures for August—by Larry M. Speakes, Principal Deputy Press Secretary to the President

Transcript:
Press briefing on tax reform—by Beryl W. Sprinkel, Chairman of the Council of Economic Advisers

Released September 25

Announcement:
Nomination of Donald R. Brookshier to be United States Marshal for the Southern District of Illinois

Released September 26

Announcement:
Submission by Presidential Emergency Board No. 208 of its report to the President concerning a dispute between certain railroads represented by the National Carriers' Conference Committee of the National Railway Labor Conference and their employees represented by the United Transportation Union

Released September 26—Continued
Announcement:
Nomination of Lyle E. Strom to be United States District Judge for the District of Nebraska

Announcement:
Nomination of Richard H. Battey to be United States District Judge for the District of South Dakota

Announcement:
Nomination of John S. Rhoades, Sr., to be United States District Judge for the Southern District of California

Transcript:
Press briefing on the President's meeting with Soviet Foreign Minister Eduard Shevardnadze—by Robert C. McFarlane, Assistant to the President for National Security Affairs

Released September 27

Statement:
The economy and international trade—by Larry M. Speakes, Principal Deputy Press Secretary to the President

Announcement:
Nomination of Jose Antonio Fuste to be United States District Judge for the District of Puerto Rico

Transcript:
Press briefing on the President's meeting with Soviet Foreign Minister Eduard Shevardnadze—by Secretary of State George P. Shultz

Released September 30

Statement:
Leading economic indicators for August—by Larry M. Speakes, Principal Deputy Press Secretary to the President

Advance text:
Remarks at a farewell ceremony for Gen. John W. Vessey, Jr., Chairman of the Joint Chiefs of Staff

Released October 1

Announcement:
Nomination of Edward R. Korman to be United States District Judge for the Eastern District of New York

Released October 2

Transcript:
Press briefing following the President's meeting with the Republican congressional leadership—by

Released October 2—Continued
Senate Majority Leader Robert Dole and House Minority Leader Robert H. Michel

Advance text:
Remarks to the 54th General Assembly of Interpol

Statement:
Sales of single-family homes in August—by Larry M. Speakes, Principal Deputy Press Secretary to the President

Released October 3

Advance text:
Remarks at the Ivorydale Soap Manufacturing Plant in St. Bernard, OH

Advance text:
Remarks to business leaders in Cincinnati, OH

Released October 4

Advance text:
Remarks announcing bipartisan congressional support of proposed balanced budget and emergency deficit control legislation

Fact sheet:
Proposed balanced budget and emergency deficit control legislation

Advance text:
Remarks at a fundraising luncheon for the New Jersey State Republican Party in Parsippany

Statement:
Employment figures for September—by Larry M. Speakes, Principal Deputy Press Secretary to the President

Released October 7

Announcement:
Nomination of Bobby Ray Baldock to be United States Circuit Judge for the Tenth Circuit

Announcement:
Nomination of David R. Thompson to be United States Circuit Judge for the Ninth Circuit

Announcement:
Nomination of Robert E. Cowen to be United States District Judge for the District of New Jersey

Released October 8

Announcement:
Nomination of Carolyn Miller Parr to serve as a Judge on the United States Tax Court

Released October 8—Continued
Announcement:
Nomination of B. John Williams, Jr., to serve as a Judge on the United States Tax Court

Announcement:
Nomination of William J. Zloch to be United States District Judge for the Southern District of Florida

Released October 9

Advance text:
Remarks at a fundraising luncheon for Virginia gubernatorial candidate Wyatt Durrette in Arlington

Released October 10

Advance text:
Remarks at the Kitchens of Sara Lee in Deerfield, IL

Released October 11

Statement:
Retail sales for September—by Larry M. Speakes, Principal Deputy Press Secretary to the President

Transcript:
Press briefing on the hijacking of the Italian cruise ship *Achille Lauro*—by Robert C. McFarlane, Assistant to the President for National Security Affairs

Released October 15

Advance text:
Remarks at a fundraising event for Senator Steven D. Symms in Boise, ID

Advance text:
Remarks at a fundraising dinner for Senator Robert W. Kasten, Jr., in Milwaukee, WI

Released October 16

Fact sheet:
Section 301 of the Trade Act of 1974

Announcement:
Nomination of James L. Buckley to be United States Circuit Judge for the District of Columbia

Announcement:
Nomination of Jane R. Roth to be United States District Judge for the District of Delaware

Announcement:
Nomination of Albert I. Moon, Jr., to be United States District Judge for the District of Hawaii

Released October 16—Continued

Announcement:
Nomination of Patrick A. Conmy to be United States District Judge for the District of North Dakota

Announcement:
Nomination of Lynn N. Hughes to be United States District Judge for the Southern District of Texas

Announcement:
Nomination of Glenn L. Archer, Jr., to be United States Circuit Judge for the Federal Circuit

Announcement:
Nomination of John T. Noonan, Jr., to be United States Circuit Judge for the Ninth Circuit

Released October 17

Statement:
Gross national product for the third quarter—by Larry M. Speakes, Principal Deputy Press Secretary to the President

Released October 18

Statement:
Personal income and personal consumption expenditures for September—by Larry M. Speakes, Principal Deputy Press Secretary to the President

Released October 22

Announcement:
Nomination of Alan B. Johnson to be United States District Judge for the District of Wyoming

Transcript:
Press briefing following the President's meeting with the Republican congressional leadership to discuss foreign and domestic issues—by Senate Majority Leader Robert Dole and House Minority Leader Robert H. Michel

Released October 23

Announcement:
Nomination of Frank X. Altimari to be United States Circuit Judge for the Second Circuit

Announcement:
Nomination of Morris S. Arnold to be United States District Judge for the Western District of Arkansas

Announcement:
Nomination of Garrett E. Brown, Jr., to be United States District Judge for the District of New Jersey

Released October 23—Continued

Announcement:
Nomination of Benjamin L. Burgess, Jr., to be United States Attorney for the District of Kansas

Announcement:
Nomination of William C. Carpenter, Jr., to be United States Attorney for the District of Delaware

Announcement:
Nomination of Marvin Collins to be United States Attorney for the Northern District of Texas

Announcement:
Nomination of Robert L. Miller, Jr., to be United States District Judge for the Northern District of Indiana

Announcement:
Nomination of Jefferson B. Sessions III to be United States District Judge for the Southern District of Alabama

Announcement:
Nomination of Stanley A. Twardy, Jr., to be United States Attorney for the District of Connecticut

Statement:
Consumer Price Index figures for September—by Larry M. Speakes, Principal Deputy Press Secretary to the President

Advance text:
Toast at a luncheon for heads of delegations to the 40th session of the United Nations General Assembly in New York, NY

Released October 24

Advance text:
Address to the 40th Session of the United Nations General Assembly in New York, NY

Fact sheet:
Address to the 40th Session of the United Nations General Assembly in New York, NY

Transcript:
Press briefing on the President's meetings with allied leaders—by Secretary of State George P. Shultz

Transcript:
Interview of Secretary of State George P. Shultz by CBS Morning News

Transcript:
Interview of Robert C. McFarlane, Assistant to the President For National Security Affairs, by NBC News

Released October 24—Continued
Transcript:
Press briefing on the President's meeting with Soviet Foreign Minister Eduard Shevardnadze—by Secretary of State George P. Shultz

Transcript:
Interview of Robert C. McFarlane, Assistant to the President for National Security Affairs, by Cable Network News

Released October 25

Transcript:
Interview of Robert C. McFarlane, Assistant to the President for National Security Affairs, by ABC News "Good Morning America"

Transcript:
Interview of Donald T. Regan, Assistant to the President and Chief of Staff, by NBC News "Today"

Statement:
President's meeting with the family of Leon Klinghoffer, who was killed during the hijacking of the Italian cruise ship *Achille Lauro*—by Larry M. Speakes, Principal Deputy Press Secretary to The President

Released October 28

Statement:
Productivity in the Nation's business sector for the third quarter—by Larry M. Speakes, Principal Deputy Press Secretary to the President

Announcement:
Signing of a proclamation designating the Centennial Year of Liberty in the United States

Released October 29

Announcement:
Nomination of Thomas J. McAvoy to be United States District Judge for the Northern District of New York

Announcement:
Nomination of Sidney A. Fitzwater to be United States District Judge for the Northern District of Texas

Released October 30

Statement:
On the Gramm-Rudman-Hollings balanced budget legislation—by James C. Miller III, Director of the Office of Management and Budget

Transcript:
Press briefing on the Gramm-Rudman-Hollings balanced budget legislation—by James C. Miller

Released October 30—Continued
III, Director of the Office of Management and Budget

Released October 31

Statement:
Leading economic indicators for September—by Larry M. Speakes, Principal Deputy Press Secretary to the President

Announcement:
Nomination of Deanell Reece Tacha to be United States Circuit Judge for the Tenth Circuit

Released November 1

Statement:
Establishment survey of nonfarm business for October—by Larry M. Speakes, Principal Deputy Press Secretary to the President

Released November 7

Announcement:
Nomination of Harry D. Leinenweber to be United States District Judge for the Northern District of Illinois

Announcement:
Nomination of J. Spencer Letts to be United States District Judge for the Central District of California

Announcement:
Nomination of George H. Revercomb to be United States District Judge for the District of Columbia

Announcement:
Nomination of Dickran M. Tevrizian, Jr., to be United States District Judge for the Central District of California

Released November 8

Fact sheet:
Radio address to the Nation and the world on the upcoming Soviet-U.S. summit meeting in Geneva

Released November 9

Fact sheet:
Jamming of Voice of America broadcasts

Advance text:
Radio address to the Nation and the world on the upcoming Soviet-U.S. summit meeting in Geneva

Released November 13

Transcript:
Press briefing on congressional inaction on appropriations and national debt ceiling bills—by James A. Baker III, Secretary, and Robert M. Kimmitt, General Counsel, Treasury Department; and James C. Miller III, Director, and Joseph R. Wright, Deputy Director, Office of Management and Budget

Announcement:
Nomination of Harold L. Cushenberry, Jr., and Michael L. Rankin to be Associate Judges of the Superior Court of the District of Columbia

Released November 14

Announcement:
Nomination of Duross Fitzpatrick to be United States District Judge for the Middle District of Georgia

Transcript:
Press briefing on the upcoming Soviet-U.S. summit meeting in Geneva—by Secretary of State George P. Shultz

Excerpts:
Address to the Nation on the upcoming Soviet-U.S. summit meeting in Geneva

Advance text:
Address to the Nation on the upcoming Soviet-U.S. summit meeting in Geneva

Fact sheet:
Address to the Nation on the upcoming Soviet-U.S. summit meeting in Geneva

Released November 15

Statement:
Producer Price Index figures for October—by Larry M. Speakes, Principal Deputy Press Secretary to the President

Released November 17

Transcript:
Press briefing on the Soviet-U.S. summit meeting in Geneva—by Ambassador Paul H. Nitze, Special Adviser to the President and Secretary of State on arms reduction negotiations

Transcript:
Press briefing on the Soviet-U.S. summit meeting in Geneva—by Robert C. McFarlane, Assistant to the President for National Security Affairs

Released November 17—Continued
Transcript:
Interview of Robert C. McFarlane, Assistant to the President for National Security Affairs, by NBC News "Meet the Press"

Transcript:
Interview of Secretary of State George P. Shultz by ABC News "This Week With David Brinkley"

Transcript:
Interview of Donald T. Regan, Assistant to the President and Chief of Staff, by Lesley Stahl on CBS News "Face the Nation"

Transcript:
Interview of Arthur A. Hartman, U.S. Ambassador to the Soviet Union, by USIA WORLDNET

Released November 18

Transcript:
Interview of Donald T. Regan, Assistant to the President and Chief of Staff, by ABC News "Good Morning America"

Transcript:
Interview of Robert C. McFarlane, Assistant to the President for National Security Affairs, by NBC News "Today"

Transcript:
Interview of Arthur A. Hartman, U.S. Ambassador to the Soviet Union, by Cable News Network

Transcript:
Interview of Arthur A. Hartman, U.S. Ambassador to the Soviet Union, by Independent Network News (2 releases)

Transcript:
Interview of Secretary of State George P. Shultz by CBS "Morning News"

Transcript:
Press briefing on the Soviet-U.S. summit meeting in Geneva—by Robert C. McFarlane, Assistant to the President for National Security Affairs

Transcript:
Interview of Secretary of State George P. Shultz by MacNeil / Lehrer

Transcript:
Interview of Secretary of State George P. Shultz by Cable News Network

Transcript:
Press briefing on the Soviet-U.S. summit meeting in Geneva—by Robert C. McFarlane, Assistant to the President for National Security Affairs

Released November 19

Statement:
Housing starts and building permit figures for October—by Larry M. Speakes, Principal Deputy Press Secretary to the President

Transcript:
Interview of Ambassador Edward L. Rowny, Special Adviser to the President and Secretary of State on arms reduction negotiations, by USIA WORLDNET

Released November 20

List:
Allied participation at a special meeting of the North Atlantic Council in Brussels, Belgium, on the Soviet-U.S. summit meeting in Geneva

Transcript:
Press briefing on the Soviet-U.S. summit meeting in Geneva—by Larry M. Speakes, Principal Deputy Press Secretary to the President

Released November 21

Fact sheet:
Soviet-U.S. general exchanges agreement

Fact sheet:
North Pacific air safety agreement

Fact sheet:
Exchange of consulates in Kiev and New York

Fact sheet:
The President's people-to-people initiatives

Fact sheet:
Magnetic fusion research

Transcript:
Press briefing on the Soviet-U.S. summit meeting in Geneva—by Secretary of State George P. Shultz

Advance text:
Address before a joint session of the Congress on the Soviet-U.S. summit meeting in Geneva

Statement:
Personal income and personal consumption expenditure figures for October—by Larry M. Speakes, Principal Deputy Press Secretary to the President

Released November 22

Statement:
Consumer Price Index figures for October—by Larry M. Speakes, Principal Deputy Press Secretary to the President

Released November 26

Announcement:
Nomination of the following individuals to be United States Marshals: Howard V. Adair, for the Southern District of Alabama; Kernan H. Bagley, for the District of Oregon; and Robert L. Pavlak, Sr., for the District of Minnesota

Released December 2

Advance text:
Remarks at a fundraising luncheon for Senator Slade Gorton in Seattle, WA

Released December 3

Statement:
Leading economic and coincident indicators for October—by Larry M. Speakes, Principal Deputy Press Secretary to the President

Released December 4

Advance text:
Remarks to students and faculty of Fallston High School in Fallston, MD

Announcement:
Nomination of Robert J. Bryan to be United States District Judge for the Western District of Washington

Announcement:
Nomination of Miriam G. Cedarbaum to be United States District Judge for the Southern District of New York

Announcement:
Nomination of Walter J. Gex III to be United States District Judge for the Southern District of Mississippi

Announcement:
Nomination of David R. Hansen to be United States District Judge for the Northern District of Iowa

Released December 9

Announcement:
Nomination of Danny J. Boggs to be United States Circuit Judge for the Sixth Circuit

Announcement:
Nomination of Thomas C. Greene to be United States Marshal for the Northern District of Alabama

Announcement:
Nomination of Melvin E. Jones to be United States Marshal for the Middle District of Alabama

Released December 9—Continued

Announcement:
Nomination of Delaine Roberts to be United States Marshal for the District of Wyoming

Announcement:
Nomination of Joseph M. Whittle to be United States Attorney for the Western District of Kentucky

Announcement:
Nomination of Herman Wirshing Rodriquez to be United States Marshal for the District of Puerto Rico

Announcement:
Nomination of Roger Ray to be United States Marshal for the Eastern District of Virginia

Transcript:
Press briefing on Federal funding and the continuation of the Federal Government's activities—by James C. Miller III, Director of the Office of Management and Budget

Released December 10

Statement:
Economic studies of two House of Representatives tax reform proposals—by Beryl W. Sprinkel, Chairman of the Council of Economic Advisers, and Manuel H. Johnson, Assistant Secretary of the Treasury (Economic Affairs)

Released December 12

Statement:
Retail sales figures for November—by Larry M. Speakes, Principal Deputy Press Secretary to the President

Released December 13

Statement:
Producer Price Index figures for November—by Larry M. Speakes, Principal Deputy Press Secretary to the President

Released December 16

Advance text:
Remarks at a memorial service in Fort Campbell, KY, for victims of the 101st Airborne who died in an airplane crash in Gander, Newfoundland, on December 12

Released December 20

Statement:
Consumer Price Index figures for November—by Larry M. Speakes, Principal Deputy Press Secretary to the President

Transcript:
Press briefing on revisions of the national income and product accounts—by Beryl W. Sprinkel, Chairman of the Council of Economic Advisers

Released December 30

Statement:
Leading economic and coincident indicators for November—by Larry M. Speakes, Principal Deputy Press Secretary to the President

Appendix D—Acts Approved by the President

Approved July 2

H.R. 1699 / Public Law 99–58
Energy Policy and Conservation Amendments Act of 1985

Approved July 3

S. 413 / Public Law 99–59
An act to extend the provisions of title XII of the Merchant Marine Act, 1936, relating to war risk insurance

H.J. Res. 159 / Public Law 99–60
An act commemorating the 75th Anniversary of the Boy Scouts of America

Approved July 9

H.R. 47 / Public Law 99–61
Statue of Liberty-Ellis Island Commemorative Coin Act

Approved July 11

H.R. 2800 / Public Law 99–62
An act to provide authorization of appropriations for activities under the Land Remote-Sensing Commercialization Act of 1984

S. 822 / Public Law 99–63
An act to extend the time for conducting the referendum with respect to the national marketing quota for wheat for the marketing year beginning June 1, 1986

Approved July 12

S. 883 / Public Law 99–64
An act to reauthorize the Export Administration Act of 1979, and for other purposes

S. 1141 / Public Law 99–65
An act relating to certain telephone services for Senators

Approved July 17

H.J. Res. 325 / Public Law 99–66
A joint resolution to designate July 13, 1985, as "Live Aid Day"

Approved July 19

S.J. Res. 154 / Public Law 99–67
A joint resolution to designate July 20, 1985, as "Space Exploration Day"

H.R. 1373 / Public Law 99–68
An act to designate the wilderness in the Point Reyes National Seashore in California as the Phillip Burton Wilderness

Approved July 22

S. 1455 / Public Law 99–69
An act to extend the authority to establish and administer flexible and compressed work schedules for Federal Government employees

H.J. Res. 198 / Public Law 99–70
A joint resolution providing for appointment of Barnabas McHenry as a citizen regent of the Board of Regents of the Smithsonian Institution

Approved July 24

H.J. Res. 342 / Public Law 99–71
A joint resolution making an urgent supplemental appropriation for the fiscal year ending September 30, 1985, for the Department of Agriculture

S.J. Res. 40 / Public Law 99–72
A joint resolution to designate the month of October 1985 as "National Down Syndrome Month"

Approved July 29

H.R. 1617 / Public Law 99–73
National Bureau of Standards Authorization Act for Fiscal Year 1986

S.J. Res. 86 / Public Law 99–74
A joint resolution to designate the week of July 25, 1985, through July 31, 1985, as "National Disability in Entertainment Week"

S.J. Res. 144 / Public Law 99–75
A joint resolution to authorize the printing and binding of a revised edition of Senate Procedure and providing the same shall be subject to copyright by the author

Approved July 31

H.J. Res. 106 / Public Law 99–76
A joint resolution designating August 1985 as "Polish American Heritage Month"

Approved August 2

S.J. Res. 57 / Public Law 99–77
A joint resolution to designate the week of October 20, 1985, through October 26, 1985 as "Lupus Awareness Week"

H.J. Res. 164 / Public Law 99–78
A joint resolution to designate August 4, 1985, as "Freedom of the Press Day"

S.J. Res. 180 / Public Law 99–79
A joint resolution commemorating the tenth anniversary of the signing of the Helsinki Final Act

Approved August 5

H.R. 2378 / Public Law 99–80
An act to amend section 504 of title 5, United States Code, and section 2412 of title 28, United States Code, with respect to awards of expenses of certain agency and court proceedings, and for other purposes

Approved August 6

S.J. Res. 161 / Public Law 99–81
A joint resolution to appeal for the release of Soviet Jewry

Approved August 7

S.J. Res. 168 / Public Law 99–82
A joint resolution designating August 13, 1985, as "National Neighborhood Crime Watch Day"

Approved August 8

S. 960 / Public Law 99–83
International Security and Development Cooperation Act of 1985

S.J. Res. 137 / Public Law 99–84
A joint resolution to designate the week of December 15, 1985, through December 21, 1985, as "National Drunk and Drugged Driving Awareness Week"

S.J. Res. 108 / Public Law 99–85
A joint resolution authorizing the Secretary of Defense to provide to the Soviet Union, on a reimbursable basis, equipment and services necessary for an improved United States/Soviet Direct Communication Link for crisis control

Approved August 9

H.J. Res. 251 / Public Law 99–86
A joint resolution to provide that a special gold medal honoring George Gershwin be presented to his sister, Frances Gershwin Godowsky, and a special gold medal honoring Ira Gershwin be presented to his widow, Lenore Gershwin, and to provide for the production of bronze duplicates of such medals for sale to the public

S. 1195 / Public Law 99–87
An act to amend title 3, United States Code, to authorize the use of penalty and franked mail in efforts relating to the location and recovery of missing children

Approved August 15

H.R. 2577 / Public Law 99–88
Supplemental Appropriations Act, 1985

H.R. 2908 / Public Law 99–89
Indian Education Technical Amendments Act of 1985

S.J. Res. 98 / Public Law 99–90
A joint resolution condemning the passage of Resolution 3379, in the United Nations General Assembly on November 10, 1975, and urging the United States Ambassador and United States delegation to take all appropriate actions necessary to erase this shameful resolution from the record of the United Nations

S. 1147 / Public Law 99–91
Orphan Drug Amendments of 1985

Approved August 16

H.R. 2370 / Public Law 99–92
Nurse Education Amendments of 1985

H.R. 2068 / Public Law 99–93
Foreign Relations Authorization Act, Fiscal Years 1986 and 1987

Approved September 19

S.J. Res. 31 / Public Law 99–94
A joint resolution to designate the week of November 24 through November 30, 1985, and the week of November 23 through November 29, 1986, as "National Family Week"

Approved September 23

H.J. Res. 128 / Public Law 99–95
A joint resolution designating the month of October 1985 as "National High-Tech Month"

Approved September 25

S. 444 / Public Law 99–96
An act to amend the Alaska Native Claims Settlement Act

Approved September 26

S. 818 / Public Law 99–97
An act to authorize appropriations for activities under the Federal Fire Prevention and Control Act of 1974

S.J. Res. 141 / Public Law 99–98
A joint resolution to designate the week beginning on May 18, 1986, as "National Tourism Week"

S.J. Res. 173 / Public Law 99–99
A joint resolution to designate the month of September 1985 as "National Sewing Month"

Approved September 27

S.J. Res. 186 / Public Law 99–100
A joint resolution to designate the week of September 23, 1985, through September 29, 1985, as "National Historically Black Colleges Week"

H.J. Res. 218 / Public Law 99–101
A joint resolution to designate the week beginning September 15, 1985, as "National Dental Hygiene Week"

H.J. Res. 229 / Public Law 99–102
A joint resolution designating the week beginning September 22, 1985, as "National Adult Day Care Center Week"

Approved September 30

H.J. Res. 388 / Public Law 99–103
A joint resolution making continuing appropriations for the fiscal year 1986, and for other purposes

S. 1514 / Public Law 99–104
An act to approve the Interstate Cost Estimate and Interstate Substitute Cost Estimate

S. 817 / Public Law 99–105
An act to authorize appropriations under the Earthquake Hazards Reduction Act of 1977 for fiscal years 1986 and 1987, and for other purposes

S.J. Res. 127 / Public Law 99–106
A joint resolution to grant the consent of Congress to certain additional powers conferred upon the Bi-State Development Agency by the States of Missouri and Illinois

Approved September 30—Continued
H.R. 3452 / Public Law 99–107
"Emergency Extension Act of 1985"

S. 1671 / Public Law 99–108
An act to amend title 38, United States Code, to provide interim extensions of the authority of the Veterans' Administration to operate a regional office in the Republic of the Philippines, to contract for hospital care and outpatient services in Puerto Rico and the Virgin Islands, and to contract for treatment and rehabilitation services for alcohol and drug dependence and abuse disabilities; and to amend the Emergency Veterans' Job Training Act of 1983 to extend the period for entering into training under such Act

H.R. 3414 / Public Law 99–109
An act to provide that the authority to establish and administer flexible and compressed work schedules for Federal Government employees be extended through October 31, 1985

Approved October 1

H.J. Res. 299 / Public Law 99–110
A joint resolution recognizing the accomplishments over the past 50 years resulting from the passage of the Historic Sites Act of 1935, one of this Nation's landmark preservation laws

H.J. Res. 305 / Public Law 99–111
A joint resolution to recognize both Peace Corps volunteers and the Peace Corps on the Agency's twenty-fifth anniversary, 1985–86

S.J. Res. 67 / Public Law 99–112
A joint resolution to designate the week of October 6, 1985, through October 12, 1985, as "Mental Illness Awareness Week"

S.J. Res. 111 / Public Law 99–113
A joint resolution to designate the month of October 1985 as "National Spina Bifida Month"

H.R. 3454 / Public Law 99–114
An act to extend temporarily certain provisions of law

Approved October 4

H.J. Res. 287 / Public Law 99–115
A joint resolution to designate October 1985 as "Learning Disabilities Awareness Month"

H.J. Res. 394 / Public Law 99–116
A joint resolution reaffirming our historic solidarity with the people of Mexico following the devastating earthquake of September 19, 1985

Approved October 7

S. 1689 / Public Law 99–117
An act to amend various provisions of the Public
Health Service Act

S.J. Res. 115 / Public Law 99–118
A joint resolution to designate 1985 as the "Oil
Heat Centennial Year"

H.R. 1042 / Public Law 99–119
An act to grant a Federal charter to the Pearl
Harbor Survivors Association

Approved October 8

H.J. Res. 393 / Public Law 99–120
A joint resolution to provide for the temporary
extension of certain programs relating to housing
and community development, and for other purposes

Approved October 11

H.R. 2475 / Public Law 99–121
An act to amend the Internal Revenue Code of
1954 to simplify the imputed interest rules of
sections 1274 and 483, and for other purposes

Approved October 16

S.J. Res. 72 / Public Law 99–122
A joint resolution to designate October 16, 1985,
as "World Food Day"

S.J. Res. 183 / Public Law 99–123
A joint resolution to provide for the designation
of the week of October 6 through October 12,
1985, as "Myasthenia Gravis Awareness Week"

S.J. Res. 197 / Public Law 99–124
A joint resolution to designate the week of October 6, 1985 through October 13, 1985, as "National Housing Week"

Approved October 18

S.J. Res. 155 / Public Law 99–125
A joint resolution to designate the month of November 1985, as "National Hospice Month"

S.J. Res. 175 / Public Law 99–126
A joint resolution to designate the week of Octo-
ber 20, 1985, as "National CPR Awareness
Week"

S.J. Res. 194 / Public Law 99–127
A joint resolution to designate the week begin-
ning October 1, 1985, as "National Buy American
Week"

Approved October 22

S.J. Res. 158 / Public Law 99–128
A joint resolution designating February 1986 as
"National Community College Month"

H.R. 2410 / Public Law 99–129
Health Professions Training Assistance Act of
1985

Approved October 28

S. 1349 / Public Law 99–130
An act to provide for the use and distribution of
funds awarded in docket 363 to the Mdewakan-
ton and Wahpekute Eastern or Mississippi Sioux
before the United States Court of Claims and
Claims Court

S.J. Res. 92 / Public Law 99–131
A joint resolution to designate October 1985 as
"National Foster Grandparent Month"

S.J. Res. 104 / Public Law 99–132
A joint resolution to proclaim October 23, 1985,
as "A Time of Remembrance" for all victims of
terrorism throughout the world

H.R. 2174 / Public Law 99–133
An act to provide for the transfer to the Colville
Business Council of any undistributed portion of
amounts appropriated in satisfaction of certain
judgments awarded the Confederated Tribes of
the Colville Reservation before the Indian Claims
Commission

H.J. Res. 79 / Public Law 99–134
A joint resolution to designate the week begin-
ning October 6, 1985, as "National Children's
Week"

H.J. Res. 386 / Public Law 99–135
A joint resolution to designate November 24,
1985, as "National Day of Fasting to Raise Funds
to Combat Hunger"

H.J. Res. 407 / Public Law 99–136
A joint resolution designating the twelve-month
period ending on October 28, 1986, as the "Centennial Year of Liberty in the United States"

Approved October 30

H.J. Res. 308 / Public Law 99–137
A joint resolution designating the week begin-
ning on October 20, 1985, as "Benign Essential
Blepharospasm Awareness Week"

H.J. Res. 322 / Public Law 99–138
A joint resolution to provide for the designation
of October 1985, as "National Sudden Infant
Death Syndrome Awareness Month"

Approved October 30—Continued
S. 1726 / Public Law 99–139
An act to amend section 51(b) of the Arms Export Control Act, relating to the funding of the Special Defense Acquisition Fund

Approved October 31

H.R. 3605 / Public Law 99–140
An act to provide that the authority to establish and administer flexible and compressed work schedules for Federal Government employees be extended through December 31, 1985

Approved November 1

H.R. 2959 / Public Law 99–141
An act making appropriations for energy and water development for the fiscal year ending September 30, 1986, and for other purposes

Approved November 5

S.J. Res. 145 / Public Law 99–142
A joint resolution designating November 1985 as "National Diabetes Month"

Approved November 7

H.J. Res. 126 / Public Law 99–143
A joint resolution to designate the week of November 3, 1985, through November 9, 1985, as "National Drug Abuse Education Week"

Approved November 8

S.J. Res. 227 / Public Law 99–144
A joint resolution to commend the people and the sovereign confederation of the neutral nation of Switzerland for their contributions to freedom, international peace, and understanding on the occasion of the meeting between the leaders of the United States and the Soviet Union on November 19–20, 1985, in Geneva, Switzerland

S. 1160 / Public Law 99–145
Department of Defense Authorization Act, 1986

Approved November 11

H.R. 1903 / Public Law 99–146
An act to provide for the use and distribution of funds appropriated in satisfaction of judgments awarded to the Chippewas of Lake Superior in Dockets Numbered 18–S, 18–U, 18–C, and 18–T before the Indian Claims Commission, and for other purposes

Approved November 12

H.J. Res. 282 / Public Law 99–147
A joint resolution designating the week beginning October 27, 1985, as "National Alopecia Areata Awareness Week"

S.J. Res. 29 / Public Law 99–148
A joint resolution designating the week of November 11 through November 17, 1985, as "National Reye's Syndrome Week"

S.J. Res. 130 / Public Law 99–149
A joint resolution designating the week beginning on November 10, 1985, as "National Blood Pressure Awareness Week"

Approved November 13

S. 1570 / Public Law 99–150
Fair Labor Standards Amendments of 1985

H.R. 2942 / Public Law 99–151
Legislative Branch Appropriations Act, 1986

S.J. Res. 47 / Public Law 99–152
A joint resolution designating the week beginning November 10, 1985, as "National Women Veterans Recognition Week"

Approved November 14

S.J. Res. 51 / Public Law 99–153
A joint resolution to designate the week beginning November 24, 1985, as "National Adoption Week"

H.J. Res. 441 / Public Law 99–154
A joint resolution making further continuing appropriations for the fiscal year 1986

H.R. 3721 / Public Law 99–155
An act to temporarily increase the limit on the public debt and to restore the investments of the Social Security Trust Fund and other trust funds

Approved November 15

H.J. Res. 449 / Public Law 99–156
A joint resolution to provide for the temporary extension of certain programs relating to housing and community development, and for other purposes

S. 1851 / Public Law 99–157
An act to extend temporarily the dairy price support program and certain food stamp program provisions, and for other purposes

Passed November 20, over the President's veto

H.R. 2409 / Public Law 99–158
Health Research Extension Act of 1985

Approved November 22

H.R. 1210 / Public Law 99–159
National Science, Engineering, and Mathematics
Authorization Act of 1986

Approved November 25

H.R. 3038 / Public Law 99–160
Department of Housing and Urban Develop-
ment-Independent Agencies Appropriations Act,
1986

H.R. 3447 / Public Law 99–161
Congressional Award Amendments of 1985

S.J. Res. 228 / Public Law 99–162
A joint resolution relating to the proposed sales
of arms to Jordan

S.J. Res. 174 / Public Law 99–163
A joint resolution to designate November 18,
1985, as "Eugene Ormandy Appreciation Day"

Approved November 26

H.J. Res. 259 / Public Law 99–164
A joint resolution to designate November 30,
1985, as "National Mark Twain Day"

Approved December 3

S.J. Res. 139 / Public Law 99–165
A joint resolution to designate the week of De-
cember 1, 1985, through December 7, 1985, as
"National Home Care Week"

H.R. 505 / Public Law 99–166
Veterans' Administration Health-Care Amendments of 1985

S. 1042 / Public Law 99–167
Military Construction Authorization Act, 1986

S.J. Res. 195 / Public Law 99–168
A joint resolution to designate the week of De-
cember 1, 1985, through December 7, 1985, as
"National Temporary Services Week"

Approved December 4

H.R. 2419 / Public Law 99–169
Intelligence Authorization Act for Fiscal Year
1986

Approved December 5

H.R. 1714 / Public Law 99–170
National Aeronautics and Space Administration
Authorization Act of 1986

Approved December 9

H.R. 3235 / Public Law 99–171
An act to authorize the Administrator of the National Aeronautics and Space Administration to
accept title to the Mississippi Technology Transfer Center to be constructed by the State of Mississippi at the National Space Technologies Laboratories in Hancock County, Mississippi

H.R. 1806 / Public Law 99–172
An act to recognize the organization known as
the Daughters of Union Veterans of the Civil
War 1861–1865

Approved December 10

H.R. 3327 / Public Law 99–173
Military Construction Appropriations Act, 1986

Approved December 11

H.J. Res. 459 / Public Law 99–174
A joint resolution reaffirming the friendship of
the people of the United States with the people
of Colombia following the devastating volcanic
eruption of November 13, 1985

S.J. Res. 206 / Public Law 99–175
A joint resolution to authorize and request the
President to designate the month of December
1985, as "Made in America Month"

H.J. Res. 473 / Public Law 99–176
A joint resolution waiving the printing on parchment of the enrollment of H.J. Res. 372

Approved December 12

H.J. Res. 372 / Public Law 99–177
A joint resolution increasing the statutory limit
on the public debt

H.R. 3424 / Public Law 99–178
Departments of Labor, Health and Human Services, and Education and Related Agencies Appropriation Act, 1986

Approved December 13

H.J. Res. 476 / Public Law 99–179
A joint resolution making further continuing appropriations for fiscal year 1986

H.R. 2965 / Public Law 99–180
Departments of Commerce, Justice, and State,
the Judiciary, and Related Agencies Appropriation Act, 1986

H.R. 3918 / Public Law 99–181
An act to extend until December 18, 1985, the
application of certain tobacco excise taxes, trade

Approved December 13—Continued
adjustment assistance, certain medicare reimbursement provisions, and borrowing authority under the railroad unemployment insurance program

H.R. 3919 / Public Law 99–182
An act to extend temporarily the dairy price support program and certain food stamp program provisions, and for other purposes

Approved December 16

S.J. Res. 238 / Public Law 99–183
A joint resolution relating to the approval and implementation of the proposed agreement for nuclear cooperation between the United States and the People's Republic of China

Approved December 17

H.J. Res. 491 / Public Law 99–184
A joint resolution making further continuing appropriations for fiscal year 1986

S. 1639 / Public Law 99–185
Gold Bullion Coin Act of 1985

Approved December 18

S. 727 / Public Law 99–186
An act to clarify the application of the Public Utility Holding Company Act of 1935 to encourage cogeneration activities by gas utility holding company systems

S. 1116 / Public Law 99–187
An act to amend the Act of October 15, 1982, entitled "An Act to designate the Mary McLeod Bethune Council House in Washington, District of Columbia, as a national historic site, and for other purposes"

H.J. Res. 485 / Public Law 99–188
A joint resolution waiving the printing on parchment of enrolled bills and joint resolutions during the remainder of the first session of the Ninety-ninth Congress

H.R. 3981 / Public Law 99–189
An act to extend until December 19, 1985, the application of certain tobacco excise taxes, trade adjustment assistance, certain medicare reimbursement provisions, and borrowing authority under the railroad unemployment insurance program

Approved December 19

H.J. Res. 465 / Public Law 99–190
A joint resolution making further continuing appropriations for the fiscal year 1986, and for other purposes

Approved December 19—Continued
H.R. 1789 / Public Law 99–191
An act relating to the authorization of appropriations for certain components of the National Wildlife Refuge System

H.R. 3735 / Public Law 99–192
An act to designate the pedestrian walkway crossing the Potomac River at Harpers Ferry National Historical Park as the "Goodloe E. Byron Memorial Pedestrian Walkway"

H.J. Res. 424 / Public Law 99–193
A joint resolution to designate the year of 1986 as the "Year of the Flag"

Approved December 20

S. 1264 / Public Law 99–194
Arts, Humanities, and Museums Amendments of 1985

Approved December 23

H.R. 664 / Public Law 99–195
An act to amend the Panama Canal Act of 1979 with respect to the payment of interest on the investment of the United States

H.R. 1534 / Public Law 99–196
An act to convert the temporary authority to allow Federal employees to work on a flexible or compressed schedule under title 5, United States Code, into permanent authority

H.R. 1627 / Public Law 99–197
Kentucky Wilderness Act of 1985

H.R. 2100 / Public Law 99–198
Food Security Act of 1985

H.R. 2976 / Public Law 99–199
An act to direct the Secretary of Agriculture to release the condition requiring that a parcel of land conveyed to New York State be used for public purposes and to convey United States mineral interests in the parcel to New York State

H.R. 3085 / Public Law 99–200
An act to clear title to certain lands along the California-Nevada boundary

H.R. 4006 / Public Law 99–201
An act to extend until March 15, 1986, the application of certain tobacco excise taxes and certain medicare reimbursement provisions

H.J. Res. 436 / Public Law 99–202
A joint resolution to designate 1986 as "Save for the U.S.A. Year", and for other purposes

Approved December 23—Continued

H.J. Res. 450 / Public Law 99–203
A joint resolution to authorize and request the President to issue a proclamation designating April 20 through April 26, 1986 as "National Organ and Tissue Donor Awareness Week"

S. 947 / Public Law 99–204
Overseas Private Investment Corporation Amendments Act of 1985

S. 1884 / Public Law 99–205
Farm Credit Amendments Act of 1985

S.J. Res. 32 / Public Law 99–206
A joint resolution to authorize and request the President to designate September 21, 1986, as "Ethnic American Day"

S.J. Res. 70 / Public Law 99–207
A joint resolution to proclaim March 20, 1986, as "National Agriculture Day"

S.J. Res. 213 / Public Law 99–208
A joint resolution to designate January 19 through January 25, 1986, "National Jaycee Week"

H.R. 729 / Public Law 99–209
An act to amend the Panama Canal Act of 1979 in order that claims for vessels damaged outside-the-locks may be resolved in the same manner as those vessels damaged inside the locks, and for other purposes

H.R. 2694 / Public Law 99–210
An act designating the United States Post Office Building located at 300 Packerland Drive, Green Bay, Wisconsin, as the "John W. Byrnes Post Office and Federal Building"

Approved December 26

H.R. 2391 / Public Law 99–211
An act to authorize the Administrator of General Services to collect additional contributions of money provided to him by private individuals or organizations for the Nancy Hanks Center

H.R. 2542 / Public Law 99–212
An act designating the building located at 125 South State Street, Salt Lake City, Utah, as the "Wallace F. Bennett Federal Building"

H.R. 2698 / Public Law 99–213
An act to designate the United States Courthouse in Tucson, Arizona, as the "James A. Walsh United States Courthouse"

H.R. 2903 / Public Law 99–214
An act to designate the Federal Building and United States Post Office located in Philadelphia,

Approved December 26—Continued
Pennsylvania, as the "Robert N.C. Nix, Sr., Federal Building and United States Post Office"

H.R. 3003 / Public Law 99–215
An act to authorize the Secretary of the Interior to convey certain land located in the State of Maryland to the Maryland-National Capital Park and Planning Commission

H.R. 3718 / Public Law 99–216
District of Columbia Revenue Bond Act of 1985

H.R. 3837 / Public Law 99–217
Sentencing Reform Amendments Act of 1985

H.R. 3914 / Public Law 99–218
An act to preserve the authority of the Supreme Court Police to provide protective services for Justices and Court personnel

H.J. Res. 495 / Public Law 99–219
A joint resolution to provide for the temporary extension of certain programs relating to housing and community development, and for other purposes

S.J. Res. 189 / Public Law 99–220
A joint resolution designating the week beginning January 12, 1986, as "National Fetal Alcohol Syndrome Awareness Week"

S. 1728 / Public Law 99–221
Cherokee Leasing Act

Approved December 28

H.R. 1603 / Public Law 99–222
Shareholder Communications Act of 1985

H.R. 1784 / Public Law 99–223
Panama Canal Commission Authorization Act, Fiscal Year 1986

H.R. 1890 / Public Law 99–224
An act to provide for an equitable waiver in the compromise and collection of Federal claims

H.R. 2962 / Public Law 99–225
An act to remove certain restrictions on the availability of office space for former Speakers of the House

H.R. 3608 / Public Law 99–226
An act to amend the Small Business Investment Act of 1958

H.R. 3974 / Public Law 99–227
An act to provide for temporary family housing or temporary housing allowances for dependents of members of the Armed Forces who die on or after December 12, 1985, and for other purposes

Approved December 28—Continued
S. 1621 / Public Law 99–228
An act to amend title 25, United States Code, relating to Indian education programs, and for other purposes

S. 1706 / Public Law 99–229
An act to authorize the Architect of the Capitol and the Secretary of Transportation, in consultation with the Chief Justice of the United States, to study alternatives for construction of a building adjacent to Union Station in the District of Columbia, and for other purposes

S. 1918 / Public Law 99–230
An act to change the date for transmittal of a report

Approved December 28—Continued
S.J. Res. 198 / Public Law 99–231
A joint resolution to designate the year 1986 as the "Sesquicentennial Year of the National Library of Medicine"

S.J. Res. 235 / Public Law 99–232
A joint resolution to designate the week of January 26, 1986, to February 1, 1986, as "Truck and Bus Safety Week"

S.J. Res. 255 / Public Law 99–233
A joint resolution relative to the convening of the second session of the Ninety-ninth Congress

Subject Index

Administration of Ronald Reagan, 1985

Florida
  Disaster assistance—1075
  President's visit—671, 673, 1075
  Republican Party event—673
  Tampa, mayor—1076
Food and Agricultural Development, Board for International—1095
Food assistance, Africa—6, 248, 249, 305, 377, 409, 481, 554, 806, 820, 1067, 1119, 1289
Food Assistance, President's Task Force on—1161
Food Security Act of 1985—1497, 1498, 1502
Footwear industry—1010, 1015–1017, 1031, 1053, 1128, 1486
Foreign assistance
  See also specific country or region
  Administration—69
Foreign Claims Settlement Commission of the U.S. *See* Justice, Department of
Foreign Commercial Service, U.S. and. *See* Commerce, Department of
Foreign Intelligence Advisory Board, President's. *See* White House Office
Foreign Intelligence Advisory Board, President's—222, 424
Foreign policy
  See also specific country, region, or subject
  Administration policies—55, 57, 71, 134, 228, 971, 998, 1061, 1125, 1333, 1334, 1341
  Bonn Economic Summit policy—551
  Congressional role—66, 202, 421, 442, 453, 454, 467, 497, 536, 719, 730, 737, 753, 971, 982, 1497
  Foreign Relations Authorization Act, fiscal years 1986 and 1987—998
  Security assistance—135, 982, 983
Foreign Scholarships, Board of—1492
Foreign Service. *See* State, Department of
Forest Products Week, National—1250
Forest System, National. *See* Conservation
Fort McHenry—769
Foster Grandparents Month, National—1321
Foundation. *See other part of subject*
France
  Ambassador, U.S.—900
  Arms control negotiations. *See* Nuclear weapons
  Atlantic tuna convention. *See* Maritime affairs
  Defense nuclear cooperation with U.S. *See* Nuclear weapons
  President—456, 537, 550, 555, 1152, 1371
  President Reagan's visit—546, 581, 598, 602, 606
  Relations with U.S.—1154
  Soviet General Secretary's visit—1151, 1152
  Strategic weapons. *See* Nuclear weapons
Franklin Delano Roosevelt Memorial Commission—817, 962
Freedom, Presidential Medal of—413, 656, 802, 1355
Freedom of the Press Day—969
Friends of the Americas—431
Fruit. *See* Agriculture
Fund. *See other part of subject*
Fur seals convention. *See* Conservation
Fusion. *See* Energy
Fusion energy. *See* Energy, nuclear energy
Future Farmers of America—1110

GATT. *See* Commerce, international
GEICO. *See* Government Employees Insurance Co.
GNP. *See* Economy, national, economic indicators
GSP. *See* Commerce, international
Gambia, trade with U.S.—526, 888
General Accounting Office—1471
General Agreement on Tariffs and Trade. *See* Commerce, international
General Pulaski Memorial Day—1176
General Services Administration—65, 88, 90, 321, 530, 541, 655, 814, 832, 924, 1039, 1401
Generalized System of Preferences. *See* Commerce, international
Georgetown University—393
Georgia
  Macon, mayor—721
  President's visit—720, 723
  Republican Party events—720, 723
German Democratic Republic
  Ambassador, U.S.—927
  Berlin. *See* Berlin
  U.S. Army officer, death—344, 347, 380, 483, 523, 586
German Democratic Republic, U.S. Ambassador—927
Germany, Federal Republic of
  Ambassador, U.S.—776
  Berlin. *See* Berlin
  Bonn summit. *See* Bonn Economic Summit
  Chancellor—331, 440, 456, 457, 534, 555, 557, 564, 565, 568, 569
  Internal situation—572
  President—388, 389, 550, 568, 569
  President Reagan's visit—82, 330, 383, 388, 440, 456, 524, 534, 544, 546, 564, 565, 568, 569, 598, 602, 667, 785
  Relations with U.S.—331, 388, 440, 524, 534, 568, 569, 598, 1067
  Strategic defense programs, role—1466
  Terrorist act—800, 807
Girl Scouts of America—292
Globes, imports—196
Goddard Memorial Trophy—366
Gold Bullion Coin Act of 1985—1487
Good Housekeeping—458
Gordon Technical High School—1224, 1226
Government agencies and employees
  See also specific agency
  Administration appointees—15, 19, 20, 26, 29, 48, 70, 81
  Combined Federal Campaign—940
  Litigation, role—977
  Management reform—65, 113, 132, 212, 240, 960, 961, 1296
  Pay and pensions—446, 1018
  Performance Management and Recognition System—1317
  Presidential appointees—1122, 1209, 1400, 1401
  President's views—1097
  Real property management—540
  Regulations. *See* Regulatory reform
  Relocation assistance—216, 814
  Senior Executive Service—648, 1018, 1472
  Social Security. *See* Social Security

Name Index

Administration of Ronald Reagan, 1985